Elements of Language

Third Course
Annotated Teacher's Edition

Lee Odell

Richard Vacca

Renée Hobbs

Grammar, Usage, and Mechanics
Instructional Framework by
John E. Warriner

HOLT, RINEHART AND WINSTON

A Harcourt Education Company

Austin • Orlando • Chicago • New York • Toronto • London • San Diego

STAFF CREDITS

EDITORIAL

Executive Editor
Robert R. Hoyt

Program Editor
Kathryn Rogers

Project Editors
Randy Dickson
Eric Estlund
Ann Michelle Gibson

Copyediting
Michael Neibergall, *Copyediting Manager;*
Mary Malone, *Copyediting Supervisor;*
Elizabeth Dickson, *Senior Copyeditor;*
Christine Altgelt, Emily Force,
Julia Thomas Hu, *Copyeditors*

Project Administration
Marie Price, *Managing Editor;*
Lori De La Garza, *Associate Managing
Editor;* Christine Degollado, Janet
Jenkins, *Editorial Coordinators*

DESIGN

Book Design
Joe Melomo, *Design Director;* Candace
Moore, *Senior Designer;* Rina May
Ouellette, *Design Associate*

Image Acquisitions
Curtis Riker, *Director;* Jeannie Taylor,
Photo Research Supervisor; Rick
Benavides, *Photo Researcher;* Sam
Dudgeon, *Senior Staff Photographer;*
Victoria Smith, *Staff Photographer;*
Lauren Eischen, *Photography Specialist*

Media Design
Richard Metzger, *Design Director*

Cover Design
Bill Smith Studio

EDITORIAL PERMISSIONS

Susan Lowrance

PRODUCTION

Carol Trammel, *Production Manager;*
Belinda Barbosa Lopez, Michael Roche,
Senior Production Coordinators

MANUFACTURING

Shirley Cantrell, *Manufacturing
Supervisor;* Mark McDonald, *Inventory
Analyst;* Amy Borseth, *Manufacturing
Coordinator*

Printed in the United States of America
ISBN 0-03-068687-3
1 2 3 4 5   048   05 04 03 02

LEE ODELL helped establish the pedagogical framework for the composition strand of *Elements of Language*. In addition, he guided the development of the scope and sequence and the pedagogical design of the Writing Workshops. Dr. Odell is Professor of Composition Theory and Research and, since 1996, Director of the Writing Program at Rensselaer Polytechnic Institute. He began his career teaching English in middle and high schools. More recently he has worked with teachers in grades K–12 to establish a program that involves students from all disciplines in writing across the curriculum and for communities outside their classrooms. Dr. Odell's most recent book (with Charles R. Cooper) is *Evaluating Writing: The Role of Teachers' Knowledge about Text, Learning, and Culture* (1999). He is Past Chair of the Conference on College Composition and Communication and of NCTE's Assembly for Research.

RENÉE HOBBS helped develop the theoretical framework for the viewing and representing strand of *Elements of Language*. She guided the development of the scope and sequence; served as the authority on terminology, definitions, and pedagogy; and directed the planning for the video series. Dr. Hobbs is Associate Professor of Communication at Babson College in Wellesley, Massachusetts, and Director of the Media Literacy Project. Active in the field of media education, Dr. Hobbs has served as Director of the Institute on Media Education, Harvard Graduate School of Education; Director of the "Know TV" Project, Discovery Networks and Time Warner Cable; and Board Member, The New York Times Newspaper in Education Program. She works actively in staff development in school districts nationwide. Dr. Hobbs has contributed articles and chapters on media, technology, and education to many publications.

RICHARD VACCA helped establish the conceptual basis for the reading strand of *Elements of Language*. In addition, he guided the development of the pedagogical design and the scope and sequence of skills in the Reading Workshops. Dr. Vacca is Professor of Education at Kent State University. He recently completed a term as the forty-second President of the International Reading Association. Originally a middle school and high school teacher, Dr. Vacca served as the project director of the Cleveland Writing Demonstration Project for several years. He is the co-author of *Content Area Reading; Reading and Learning to Read;* and articles and chapters related to adolescents' literacy development. In 1989, Dr. Vacca received the College Reading Association's A.B. Herr Award for Outstanding Contributions to Reading Education. Currently, he is co-chair of the IRA's Commission on Adolescent Literacy.

JOHN E. WARRINER was a high school English teacher when he developed the original organizational structure for his classic *English Grammar and Composition* series. The approach pioneered by Mr. Warriner was distinctive, and the editorial staff of Holt, Rinehart and Winston have worked diligently to retain the unique qualities of his pedagogy. For the same reason, HRW continues to credit Mr. Warriner as an author of *Elements of Language* in recognition of his groundbreaking work. John Warriner also co-authored the *English Workshop* series and was editor of *Short Stories: Characters in Conflict.* Throughout his long career, however, teaching remained Mr. Warriner's major interest, and he taught for thirty-two years in junior and senior high schools and in college.

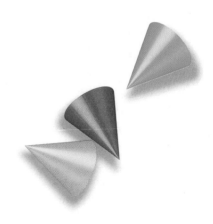

The program consultants reviewed instructional materials to ensure consistency with current research, classroom appropriateness, and alignment with curriculum guidelines.

Ann Bagley
Senior Administrator for Secondary
English
Wake County Public Schools
Raleigh, North Carolina

Vicki R. Brown
Professor of Education, Grambling State
University
Principal, Grambling
Middle School
Grambling, Louisiana

Beth Johnson
Supervisor of Language Arts
Polk District Schools
Bartow, Florida

Kathleen Jongsma
Associate Professor
Department of Education Chair
Texas Lutheran University
Seguin, Texas

Lois King
Dallas Public Schools
Dallas, Texas

Bruce A. Marshall
Secondary Reading/
Dyslexia Teacher
Cypress Falls High School
Houston, Texas

Baird Neville
Principal Teacher
Communications Arts
High School
San Antonio, Texas

Kaye Price-Hawkins
Language Arts Consultant
Abilene, Texas

Olga Samaniego
English Department Chair
Burges High School
El Paso, Texas

The critical reviewers read and evaluated pre-publication materials for this book.

Pupil's Edition
Geralann Barnes
Ozen High School
Beaumont, Texas

Lisa Rehm Bowling
Satellite High School
Satellite Beach, Florida

Janet Burleigh
Broadmoor High School
Baton Rouge, Louisiana

Judy Champney
Science Hill High School
Johnson City, Tennessee

Priscilla Cheney
Troy High School
Fullerton, California

Elizabeth M. Colleran
Washington High School
Sioux Falls, South Dakota

Gail Hayes
South Florence High School
Florence, South Carolina

Marguerite Hickman
Liberty High School
Clarksburg, West Virginia

Dianna Hubbard
South Garland High School
Garland, Texas

Elizabeth Jordan
Valley High School
Sacramento, California

Martha Dixon Kearse
Providence High School
Charlotte, North Carolina

Nancy Levi
Oakland High School
Murfreesboro, Tennessee

Kathleen Marshall
A. A. Stagg High School
Stockton, California

Janet Meeks
Fairmont Junior High School
Boise, Idaho

Andrea Partington
Lake City High School
Coeur d'Alene, Idaho

Vickie H. Smith
William G. Enloe High School
Raleigh, North Carolina

Constance M. Solheim
Corporate Landing Middle School
Virginia Beach, Virginia

Betty Templeton
Riverside High School
Greer, South Carolina

Annotated Teacher's Edition
Lisa Rehm Bowling
Satellite High School
Satellite Beach, Florida

Vincent C. Kimball, Jr.
Patterson High School #405
Baltimore, Maryland

Vickie H. Smith
William G. Enloe High School
Raleigh, North Carolina

Jeannette Spain
Fort Bend Independent School District
Houston, Texas

TEACHER/STUDENT CONTRIBUTORS

The following teachers and students worked with HRW's editorial staff to provide models of student writing for the book.

Teachers

Priscilla Cheney
Troy High School
Fullerton, California

Kay Hannum
Hobbs High School
Hobbs, New Mexico

Steven Heffner
Conrad Weiser High School
Robesonia, Pennsylvania

Dianna Hubbard
South Garland High School
Garland, Texas

Vickie H. Smith
William G. Enloe High School
Raleigh, North Carolina

Students

Mayra Deloa
South Garland High School
Garland, Texas

Cheryl Flugan
Belson High School
Winston, Florida

Amy E. Hofmann
Conrad Weiser High School
Robesonia, Pennsylvania

Anthony King
Morrison Christian Academy
Taichung, Taiwan

Shanessa McClain
Hobbs High School
Hobbs, New Mexico

Amar Patel
Troy High School
Fullerton, California

Matthew Weber
McNeil High School
Round Rock, Texas

Blake Wynia
William G. Enloe High School
Raleigh, North Carolina

FIELD TEST PARTICIPANTS

The following teachers participated in the pre-publication field test or review of prototype materials for the *Elements of Language* series.

Nadene Adams
Robert Gray Middle School
Portland, Oregon

Carol Alves
Apopka High School
Apopka, Florida

Susan Atkinson
O. P. Norman Junior High School
Kaufman, Texas

Sheryl L. Babione
Fremont Ross High School
Fremont, Ohio

Jane Baker
Elkins High School
Missouri City, Texas

Martha Barnard
Scarborough High School
Houston, Texas

Jennifer S. Barr
James Bowie High School
Austin, Texas

Leslie Benefield
Reed Middle School
Duncanville, Texas

Gina Birdsall
Irving High School
Irving, Texas

Sara J. Brennan
Murchison Middle School
Austin, Texas

Janelle Brinck
Leander Middle School
Leander, Texas

Geraldine K. Brooks
William B. Travis High School
Austin, Texas

Peter J. Caron
Cumberland Middle School
Cumberland, Rhode Island

Patty Cave
O. P. Norman Junior High School
Kaufman, Texas

Mary Cathyrne Coe
Pocatello High School
Pocatello, Idaho

Geri-Lee DeGennaro
Tarpon Springs High School
Tarpon Springs, Florida

Karen Dendy
Stephen F. Austin Middle School
Irving, Texas

Dianne Franz
Tarpon Springs Middle School
Tarpon Springs, Florida

Continued on page T6

Doris F. Frazier
East Millbrook Magnet Middle School
Raleigh, North Carolina

Shayne G. Goodrum
C. E. Jordan High School
Durham, North Carolina

Bonnie L. Hall
St. Ann School
Lansing, Illinois

Doris Ann Hall
Forest Meadow Junior High School
Dallas, Texas

James M. Harris
Mayfield High School
Mayfield Village, Ohio

Lynne Hoover
Fremont Ross High School
Fremont, Ohio

Patricia A. Humphreys
James Bowie High School
Austin, Texas

Jennifer L. Jones
Oliver Wendell Holmes Middle School
Dallas, Texas

Kathryn R. Jones
Murchison Middle School
Austin, Texas

Bonnie Just
Narbonne High School
Harbor City, California

Vincent Kimball
Patterson High School #405
Baltimore, Maryland

Nancy C. Long
MacArthur High School
Houston, Texas

Carol M. Mackey
Ft. Lauderdale Christian School
Ft. Lauderdale, Florida

Jan Jennings McCown
Johnston High School
Austin, Texas

Alice Kelly McCurdy
Rusk Middle School
Dallas, Texas

Elizabeth Morris
Northshore High School
Slidell, Louisiana

Victoria Reis
Western High School
Ft. Lauderdale, Florida

Dean Richardson
Scarborough High School
Houston, Texas

Susan M. Rogers
Freedom High School
Morganton, North Carolina

Sammy Rusk
North Mesquite High School
Mesquite, Texas

Carole B. San Miguel
James Bowie High School
Austin, Texas

Jane Saunders
William B. Travis High School
Austin, Texas

Gina Sawyer
Reed Middle School
Duncanville, Texas

Laura R. Schauermann
MacArthur High School
Houston, Texas

Stephen Shearer
MacArthur High School
Houston, Texas

Elizabeth Curry Smith
Tarpon Springs High School
Tarpon Springs, Florida

Jeannette M. Spain
Fort Bend Independent School District
Houston, Texas

Carrie Speer
Northshore High School
Slidell, Louisiana

Trina Steffes
MacArthur High School
Houston, Texas

Andrea G. Freirich Stewart
Freedom High School
Morganton, North Carolina

Diana O. Torres
Johnston High School
Austin, Texas

Jan Voorhees
Whitesboro High School
Marcy, New York

Ann E. Walsh
Bedichek Middle School
Austin, Texas

Mary Jane Warden
Onahan School
Chicago, Illinois

Beth Westbrook
Covington Middle School
Austin, Texas

Char-Lene Wilkins
Morenci Area High School
Morenci, Michigan

CONTENTS IN BRIEF

CONTENTS

CHAPTER 2 — Expressing Your Thoughts 50

Exploring Causes and Effects **122**

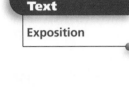

CHAPTER
4

Informational Text

Exposition

Investigating a
Research Question 194

CHAPTER

6

Informational Text

Exposition

Understanding Paragraph Structure

CHAPTER

13

The Parts of a Sentence
Subject, Predicate, Complement...............................**412**

The Phrase

The Clause

Using Verbs Correctly

Using Pronouns Correctly

Using Modifiers Correctly

Comparison and Placement **570**

CHAPTER

19

A Glossary of Usage

Capital Letters

Punctuation
End Marks, Abbreviations, and Commas **636**

The Granger Collection, New York.

Punctuation
Semicolons and Colons

Punctuation
Italics and Quotation Marks

Punctuation
Apostrophes **698**

Punctuation
Hyphens, Dashes, Parentheses, Brackets,
Ellipsis Points **714**

PART 4 | **Quick Reference Handbook** **802**

Features

▷ Grammar Links

▷ Writing Test-Taking Mini-Lessons

▷ Connections to Literature/Life

▷ Designing Your Writing

▷ Viewing and Representing/Speaking and Listening

MODELS

MODELS

- Jack London, **"To Build a Fire"**

- Martina Navratilova with George Vecsey, *Martina*

- Douglas Preston, **"The Granddaddy of the Nation's Trails Began in Mexico"**

- Donald and Lillian Stokes, *The Bird Feeder Book*

- Edwin Way Teale, **"The Death of a Tree"**

STUDENT MODELS

- Mayra Deloa, **"The Use of Symbolism in Dorothy Parker's 'Solace'"**

- Cheryl Flugan, **"What Are the Effects of Running?"**

- Amy E. Hoffman, **"The Call of the Hornet"**

- Anthony King, **"Censored!"**

- Shanessa McClain, **"South Padre Island"**

- Amar Patel, **"The Simpsons: A Real Winner"**

- Matthew Weber, **"CDs and Cassettes, Not So Similar"**

- Blake Wynia, **"Carelessness"**

Elements of Language

Designed for the Information Age

While reading and writing have been traditional topics of instruction for centuries, *what* and *how* students read and write have changed dramatically. Personal computers have become a staple in most homes and classrooms, and the variety of communications coming through television, radio, movies, and the Internet demands that students process information in a number of ways. That's why Holt, Rinehart and Winston has created *Elements of Language.*

Professional Development

To help you make the most of the book and all its parts, Holt offers a comprehensive and systematic training program to complement *Elements of Language,* providing high-quality and accessible professional learning opportunities designed to relate to the unique needs of the educator. For more information on professional development services provided by Holt, email us at **holtinfo@hrw.com**.

Structured for Teacher Flexibility

Elements of Language is comprehensive in scope yet structured to give you flexibility in choosing the most appropriate instruction for each class. Each book opens with a special section on preparing for standardized tests. Parts 1, 2, and 3 develop instructional topics in depth, and Part 4 provides a comprehensive reference tool.

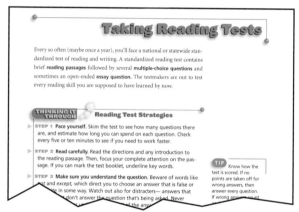

Taking Reading Tests

Every so often (maybe once a year), you'll face a national or statewide standardized test of reading and writing. A standardized reading test contains brief **reading passages** followed by several **multiple-choice questions** and sometimes an open-ended **essay question**. The testmakers are out to test every reading skill you are supposed to have learned by now.

THINKING IT THROUGH   **Reading Test Strategies**

▶ **STEP 1 Pace yourself.** Skim the test to see how many questions there are, and estimate how long you can spend on each question. Check every five or ten minutes to see if you need to work faster.

▶ **STEP 2 Read carefully.** Read the directions and any introduction to the reading passage. Then, focus your complete attention on the passage. If you can mark the test booklet, underline key words.

▶ **STEP 3 Make sure you understand the question.** Beware of words like *not* and *except,* which direct you to choose an answer that is false or opposite in some way. Watch out also for distracters— answers that don't answer the question that's being asked. Never

TIP Know how the test is scored. If no points are taken off for wrong answers, then answer every question. If wrong answers count

Taking Tests: Strategies and Practice

If you are like most teachers, you and your students are concerned about state tests. This chapter helps your students build test-taking skills in reading and writing and provides hands-on practice with the types of tests given in most states.

HOLT Elements of Language

HOLT Elements Lang

HOLT Elements of Language *Second*

Part 1

Communications

Part 1: Communications is dedicated to an intensive study of a variety of literacies—reading, writing, speaking, listening, viewing, and representing—with an emphasis on reading and writing. Each chapter uses nonfiction texts and real-world documents to explore different modes of communication.

Part 2

Sentences and Paragraphs

Part 2: Sentences and Paragraphs gives students focused instruction in how to revise and improve their sentences. After mastering the skills of structuring sentences, students then learn the basics of good paragraphs, including how to achieve unity and coherence and how to use effective transitions between paragraphs in a longer piece of writing.

Part 3

Grammar, Usage, and Mechanics

Part 3: Grammar, Usage, and Mechanics is organized in the classic and effective Warriner's format—rule, followed by example, followed by exercise. Part 3 also contains spelling instruction with spelling rules and an extensive list of words that are often confused.

Part 4

Quick Reference Handbook

Part 4: Quick Reference Handbook gives students an efficient way to access information to help them write, do research, hone speaking and listening skills, learn strategies for studying and taking tests, and develop visual literacy. The **Handbook** also includes "Grammar at a Glance," a concise overview and reference tool.

Part 1 Communications

The Reading Workshop
Connecting Reading and Writing

Holt Connects Reading and Writing

All readers, even the best, sometimes struggle. **Part 1: Communications** offers strategies and skills developed by the experts to help you address the specific reading needs of your students. Reading skills are also strengthened by the connection to **Writing Workshop**, in which students write a piece related to their reading.

Real-World Focus

Each Communications chapter opens with a **Reading Workshop** that focuses on a reading skill students need to become effective communicators. Each **Reading Workshop** features nonfiction texts drawn from real-world sources— such as magazines, newspapers, brochures, or Web sites—to model for students the different ways ideas are communicated through writing.

Reading Skills for Life

The **Reading Workshops** teach students strategies for reading and for understanding different kinds of texts.

> **READING SKILL**

Each **Reading Workshop** targets one essential reading skill, demonstrating the strategies active readers use to maximize comprehension.

> **READING FOCUS**

Each **Reading Workshop** focuses on a unique element characteristic of the informational or persuasive text students are studying.

Expert Advice

Dr. Richard Vacca, past president of the International Reading Association and author of *Reading in the Content Areas*, established the conceptual basis for the reading strand in *Elements of Language.* He was pivotal in shaping both the instructional design and the content of the program, and his classroom experience informs the program's practical, real-world strategies for improving communication.

Reading Workshop

Reading an Informative Web Site

WHAT'S AHEAD?

In this section you will read an informative Web site. You will also learn how to
■ distinguish between fact and opinion
■ analyze the structure of an informative Web site

Aliens invade Earth. A gigantic ship sinks in the middle of the ocean. Huge grasshoppers roam the countryside. When movie directors need to create scenes like these, they often rely on computer animators. The following selections from an informative Web site contain information about animation and *synthespians*. *Synthespians* are characters created digitally, that is, on a computer. As you read, consider whether the information seems well organized, and watch for statements of fact and opinion.

Preparing to Read

Fact and Opinion **Facts** are statements that can be proved true. A fact can always be confirmed by another source. An **opinion** is someone's belief about something. No source can prove an opinion true or false. Informative writing, such as the following Web site, presents many facts and sometimes a few opinions about a subject. As you read the Web site, consider whether each statement you read could be proved by another source.

> **READING SKILL**

> **READING FOCUS**

Informative Web Site Structure A good Web site has a carefully planned **structure,** or organization. Readers navigating a Web site should be able to find the information they need quickly. Web sites help readers find information by providing **links** that allow readers to move from one section of the site to another. Notice how the following Web site is structured to help you find the information you need.

Exposition: Reporting Your Research

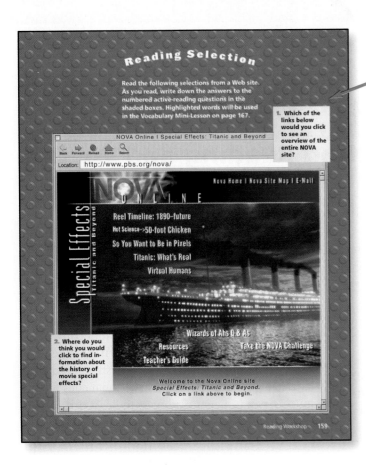

Highlighted words will be used in the Vocabulary Mini-Lesson on page 167.

Active-Reading Questions model the thinking and questioning students need to acquire strong reading skills.

Mini-Lessons demonstrate strategies for acquiring an extensive vocabulary and scoring well on standardized tests.

Thinking It Through walks students through the steps needed to analyze a task and identify the critical path to success.

Expert Advice

Judith L. Irvin helped establish the conceptual basis for the middle school reading strand of *Elements of Language*. Dr. Irvin teaches courses in curriculum, middle school education, and educational leadership at Florida State University. She is also chair of the Research Committee of the National Middle School Association and was the editor of *Research in Middle Level Education* for six years.

The Writing Workshop

Connecting Reading and Writing

Writing by Design

A blank page can be one of the most terrifying things any writer faces. *Elements of Language* recognizes that fear and through its **Writing Workshops** guides students step by step through the writing process with focused exercises for prewriting, writing, revising, and publishing.

Reading/Writing Connection

The *Pupil's Edition* provides clear connections between reading and writing, easing the transition from reading "writing" to writing "reading." In the **Reading Workshop** at the start of each chapter,

students learn how to read a real-world text and identify the techniques authors use. This instruction prepares students to write a similar piece in the **Writing Workshop.**

Visual Delivery of Instruction

The step-by-step instruction is enhanced by its visual presentation. Throughout the **Writing Workshop,** abundant, colorful graphics convey information and key concepts. A writer's model and a student model—both clearly structured and labeled— provide strong instructional cues for putting pen to paper or fingers to keyboard.

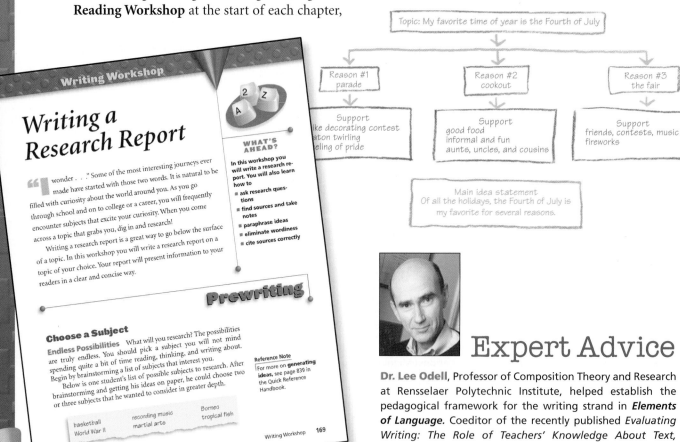

Writing Workshop

Writing a Research Report

WHAT'S AHEAD?

In this workshop you will write a research report. You will also learn how to

- ask research questions
- find sources and take notes
- paraphrase ideas
- eliminate wordiness
- cite sources correctly

"I wonder . . ." Some of the most interesting journeys ever made have started with those two words. It is natural to be filled with curiosity about the world around you. As you go through school and on to college or a career, you will frequently encounter subjects that excite your curiosity. When you come across a topic that grabs you, dig in and research!

Writing a research report is a great way to go below the surface of a topic. In this workshop you will write a research report on a topic of your choice. Your report will present information to your readers in a clear and concise way.

Prewriting

Choose a Subject

Endless Possibilities What will you research? The possibilities are truly endless. You should pick a subject you will not mind spending quite a bit of time reading, thinking, and writing about.

Begin by brainstorming a list of subjects that interest you. Below is one student's list of possible subjects to research. After brainstorming and getting his ideas on paper, he could choose two or three subjects that he wanted to consider in greater depth.

Reference Note
For more on **generating ideas,** see page 839 in the Quick Reference Handbook.

| basketball | recording music | Borneo |
| World War II | martial arts | tropical fish |

Writing Workshop   **169**

Topic: My favorite time of year is the Fourth of July

| Reason #1 parade | Reason #2 cookout | Reason #3 the fair |
| Support ...ike decorating contest ...aton twirling ...eling of pride | Support good food informal and fun aunts, uncles, and cousins | Support friends, contests, music fireworks |

Main idea statement
Of all the holidays, the Fourth of July is my favorite for several reasons.

Expert Advice

Dr. Lee Odell, Professor of Composition Theory and Research at Rensselaer Polytechnic Institute, helped establish the pedagogical framework for the writing strand in *Elements of Language*. Coeditor of the recently published *Evaluating Writing: The Role of Teachers' Knowledge About Text, Learning, and Culture* (1999), Dr. Odell guided the development of both the scope and sequence and the instructional design of the **Writing Workshops.**

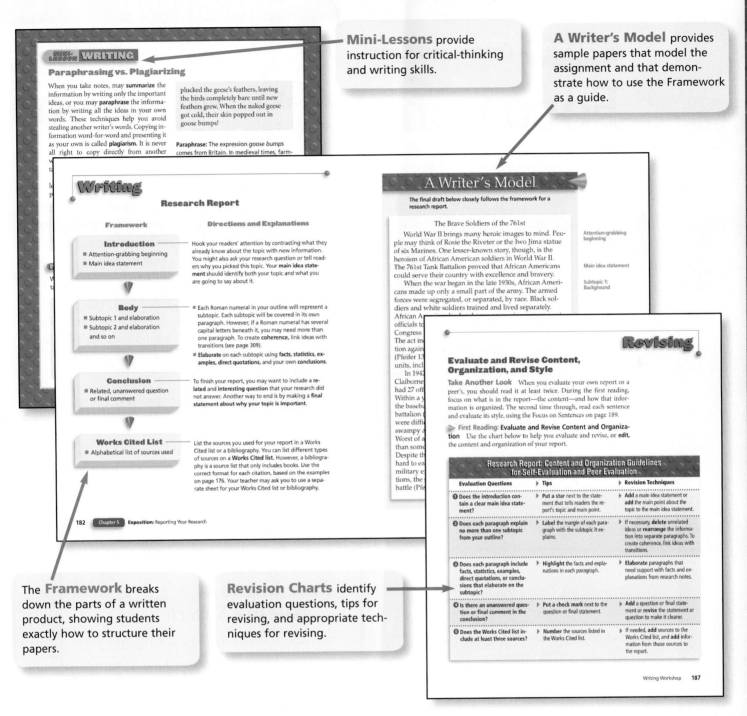

Mini-Lessons provide instruction for critical-thinking and writing skills.

A Writer's Model provides sample papers that model the assignment and that demonstrate how to use the Framework as a guide.

MINI-LESSON WRITING

Paraphrasing vs. Plagiarizing

When you take notes, may **summarize** the information by writing only the important ideas, or you may **paraphrase** the information by writing all the ideas in your own words. These techniques help you avoid stealing another writer's words. Copying information word-for-word and presenting it as your own is called **plagiarism**. It is never all right to copy directly from another

plucked the geese's feathers, leaving the birds completely bare until new feathers grew. When the naked geese got cold, their skin popped out in goose bumps!

Paraphrase: The expression *goose bumps* comes from Britain. In medieval times, farm-

Writing

Research Report

Framework	Directions and Explanations
Introduction ■ Attention-grabbing beginning ■ Main idea statement	Hook your readers' attention by contrasting what they already know about the topic with new information. You might also ask your research question or tell readers why you picked this topic. Your **main idea statement** should identify both your topic and what you are going to say about it.
Body ■ Subtopic 1 and elaboration ■ Subtopic 2 and elaboration and so on	■ Each Roman numeral in your outline will represent a subtopic. Each subtopic will be covered in its own paragraph. However, if a Roman numeral has several capital letters beneath it, you may need more than one paragraph. To create coherence, link ideas with transitions (see page 309). ■ **Elaborate** on each subtopic using **facts, statistics, examples, direct quotations,** and your own **conclusions.**
Conclusion ■ Related, unanswered question or final comment	To finish your report, you may want to include a **related and interesting question** that your research did not answer. Another way to end is by making a **final statement** about why your topic is important.
Works Cited List ■ Alphabetical list of sources used	List the sources you used for your report in a Works Cited list or a bibliography. You can list different types of sources on a **Works Cited list.** However, a bibliography is a source list that only includes books. Use the correct format for each citation, based on the examples on page 176. Your teacher may ask you to use a separate sheet for your Works Cited list or bibliography.

182 Chapter 5 **Exposition:** Reporting Your Research

A Writer's Model

The final draft below closely follows the framework for a research report.

The Brave Soldiers of the 761st

World War II brings many heroic images to mind. People may think of Rosie the Riveter or the Iwo Jima statue of six Marines. One lesser-known story, though, is the heroism of African American soldiers in World War II. The 761st Tank Battalion proved that African Americans could serve their country with excellence and bravery.

When the war began in the late 1930s, African Americans made up only a small part of the army. The armed forces were segregated, or separated, by race. Black soldiers and white soldiers trained and lived separately. African A[merican]...
officials to...
Congress...
The act in...
tion again...
(Pfeifer 13...
units, incl...

In 1942...
Claiborne...
had 27 off...
Within a y...
the baseba...
battalion (...
were diffi...
swampy a...
Worst of a...
than some...
Despite th...
hard to ea...
military e...
tions, the...
battle (Pfe...

Attention-grabbing beginning

Main idea statement

Subtopic 1: Background

Revising

Evaluate and Revise Content, Organization, and Style

Take Another Look When you evaluate your own report or a peer's, you should read it at least twice. During the first reading, focus on what is in the report—the content—and how that information is organized. The second time through, read each sentence and evaluate its style, using the Focus on Sentences on page 189.

First Reading: Evaluate and Revise Content and Organization Use the chart below to help you evaluate and revise, or **edit,** the content and organization of your report.

Research Report: Content and Organization Guidelines for Self-Evaluation and Peer Evaluation

Evaluation Questions	▶ Tips	▶ Revision Techniques
❶ Does the introduction contain a clear main idea statement?	▶ **Put a star** next to the statement that tells readers the report's topic and main point.	▶ **Add** a main idea statement or **add** the main point about the topic to the main idea statement.
❷ Does each paragraph explain no more than one subtopic from your outline?	▶ **Label** the margin of each paragraph with the subtopic it explains.	▶ If necessary, **delete** unrelated ideas or **rearrange** the information into separate paragraphs. To create coherence, link ideas with transitions.
❸ Does each paragraph include facts, statistics, examples, direct quotations, or conclusions that elaborate on the subtopic?	▶ **Highlight** the facts and explanations in each paragraph.	▶ **Elaborate** paragraphs that need support with facts and explanations from research notes.
❹ Is there an unanswered question or final comment in the conclusion?	▶ **Put a check mark** next to the question or final statement.	▶ **Add** a question or final statement or **revise** the statement or question to make it clearer.
❺ Does the Works Cited list include at least three sources?	▶ **Number** the sources listed in the Works Cited list.	▶ If needed, **add** sources to the Works Cited list, and **add** information from those sources to the report.

Writing Workshop **187**

The **Framework** breaks down the parts of a written product, showing students exactly how to structure their papers.

Revision Charts identify evaluation questions, tips for revising, and appropriate techniques for revising.

Features for Developing Style

WORD CHOICE or SENTENCES

Additional instruction and practice help students refine one aspect of their writing style, such as revising wordy sentences or eliminating clichés.

Grammar Link

Instruction and practice show students how to identify and correct common grammatical problems.

Designing Your Writing

This feature teaches students about the visual aspects of writing, helping them choose the most effective design and layout and select the best graphics to convey their message.

Part 1 Communications

Focus on
▶ **Speaking and Listening**
▶ **Viewing and Representing**

Media Literacy and Oral Communication

Today's teenagers are often delighted by the variety and frequency of media. Stimulated from all directions by a multitude of messages, from magazine and television advertising to billboards, movies, and the Internet, students must learn how to understand the power of these messages, how to evaluate them, and how to produce their own messages in a variety of formats. Teaching students to view the media with an analytical eye is a serious responsibility. Students must also learn to receive and interpret verbal messages and to organize ideas and communicate them orally. *Elements of Language* is here to help.

At the end of each Communications chapter, one or more extensive lessons highlight speaking and listening or viewing and representing skills, offering meaningful instruction on ways students can learn to take advantage of the power of the media.

Focus on Viewing and Representing helps students become savvy, critical viewers and creative, responsible media communicators.

Focus on Speaking and Listening encourages students to improve the ways in which they receive and convey oral communications.

Focus on Viewing and Representing

Designing a Web Site

Are you a Web surfer, like millions of other people? The Internet has transformed communication and information deliv-

WHAT'S AHEAD?

In this section you will
design a Web site. You
will also learn how to
use a chart to
[...] ks on your
[...]
boards to
[...]eb pages

Focus on Speaking and Listening

Giving and Listening to a Persuasive Speech

One way to convince others to accept your opinion is to give a persuasive speech. Since you have already written a persuasive essay, you might be tempted to read your essay out loud directly from the page. However, to give an effective persuasive speech, you will need to do much more than read your essay to your audience; you will need to deliver the most important points of your essay in a solid presentation that will keep your audience interested in what you have to say.

WHAT'S AHEAD?

In this section you will
give a speech. You will
also learn how to
■ adapt a persuasive essay for use as a speech
■ use visuals while delivering a speech
■ practice a good speaking voice
■ evaluate a persuasive speech

Adapting Your Persuasive Essay

When giving a persuasive speech, you should be concerned with both the content of your speech and the way you deliver it. As you review your essay to find material for your speech, use these hints to help you.

■ **Get and keep your audience's attention.** Begin your speech by telling a quick anecdote or by asking your audience a question. Then, use a persuasive technique, such as an emotional appeal, to maintain your audience's attention.

■ **Think about your audience.** Try to anticipate and give answers to the main **counterarguments** your audience may have. In other words, tailor your speech to appeal to your listeners. Every story, point, example, and visual you choose should be directed to them.

■ **Adjust the tone of your speech.** Delivering your speech from a simple outline—a list of your main points written on paper or note cards— will help your speech sound more conversational than an essay.

Reference Note

For more on **speaking skills,** see page 794 in the Quick Reference Handbook.

For more information and practice on **identifying persuasive techniques,** see page 254.

For more on **counterarguments,** see the tip on page 217.

Focus on Speaking and Listening **233**

YOUR TURN 13 Delivering a Persuasive Speech

Adapt your persuasive essay for use as a persuasive speech. Then, practice your speech before presenting it to your entire class.

Evaluating a Persuasive Speech

TIP As you listen to a classmate's persuasive speech, evaluate the speaker's **credibility**. Begin by interpreting the speaker's **perspective**, or bias. What is the speaker's relationship to the topic? Does the speaker have personal motives for wanting to persuade you? Listen for the speaker's use of fact and opinion. Credible speakers use facts and other types of evidence to support an opinion. However, speakers who lack credibility fill their speeches with unsupported opinions and let their bias overwhelm the speech.

To evaluate the effectiveness of an essay, you only have to consider the words on the page. However, evaluating a speech is a little more complicated. After all, a speech involves not only words but also a speaker. To help you decide if a classmate's persuasive speech is effective, answer the questions in the chart below as you listen to the speech.

Content	▪ What is the purpose of the presentation?
	▪ What is the topic? What is the speaker's verbal message about the topic? Does the speaker clearly state his or her opinion?
	▪ Does the speaker include convincing reasons and enough strong support for those reasons?
Use of Visuals	▪ Does the speaker use visuals that make important ideas easy to understand?
	▪ Are the visuals easy to see?
	▪ Does the speaker explain the visual thoroughly?
	▪ Overall, do the visuals add to the effectiveness of the presentation?
Delivery	▪ Is the speaker's tone conversational?
	▪ Does the speaker speak loudly and slowly enough?
	▪ Does the speaker make eye contact with the audience?
	▪ Do the speaker's nonverbal messages (such as gestures and facial expressions) match the verbal message?

Reference Note

For more information on **listening to evaluate**, see page 807 in the Quick Reference Handbook. **Note:** For more on **distinguishing fact from opinion**, see page 779 in the Quick Reference Handbook.

YOUR TURN 14 Evaluating a Persuasive Speech

As students in your class deliver their speeches, use the chart above to help you evaluate each speaker's message and delivery. Then, compare your evaluations with the evaluations of one of your classmates. In what ways were your evaluations different or similar?

Your Turn puts students' new knowledge to work in real-world situations with hands-on activities.

Talk / Listen

Expert Advice

Renée Hobbs, one of the nation's leading authorities on media education, guided the development of the Viewing and Representing lessons in *Elements of Language*. As the director of the Media Literacy Project at Clark University in Worcester, Massachusetts, Dr. Hobbs works with school districts to develop programs that build the media literacy of students across the nation.

Features That Connect to Literature and Life

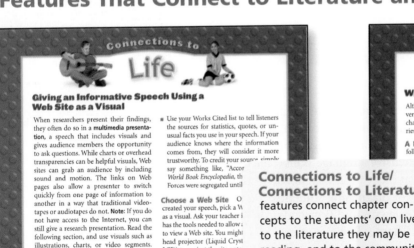

Connections to Life

Giving an Informative Speech Using a Web Site as a Visual

When researchers present their findings, they often do so in a **multimedia presentation**, a speech that includes visuals and gives audience members the opportunity to ask questions. While charts or overhead transparencies can be helpful visuals, Web sites can grab an audience by including sound and motion. The links on Web pages also allow a presenter to switch quickly from one page of information to another in a way that traditional videotapes or audiotapes do not. **Note:** If you do not have access to the Internet, you can still give a research presentation. Read the following section, and use visuals such as illustrations, charts, or video segments. (For more on **creating visuals**, see pages 77–80.)

Adapt Your Report Even though your report is about an interesting topic, simply reading it aloud will not keep your audience interested. You will need to adapt your report in order to use it as a short speech (under ten minutes). Follow these steps.

▪ Make notes about the most important points of your report. One way to organize your speech is by making one note card per category of information. Make sure you include evidence, examples, and elaboration to support and clarify your main points.

▪ Use your Works Cited list to tell listeners the sources for statistics, quotes, or unusual facts you use in your speech. If your audience knows where the information comes from, they will consider it more trustworthy. To credit your source, simply say something like, "Accor[...] *World Book Encyclopedia*, th[...] Forces were segregated until [...]

Choose a Web Site O[...] created your speech, pick a W[...] as a visual. Ask your teacher i[...] has the tools needed to allow [...] to view a Web site. You might [...] head projector (Liquid Cryst[...] LCD) to project the site onto [...] could also print and photoco[...] for your class.

Choose a Web site with a s[...] connection to your topic. For example, look for pictures of important people, places, or things you will mention in your speech, or for charts that show data supporting the ideas in your speech. You can use one page that addresses a key point, or several pages that illustrate ideas in your speech. If the pages you choose are only weakly connected to your ideas, though, they will confuse your audience.

Connections to Life/ Connections to Literature features connect chapter concepts to the students' own lives, to the literature they may be reading, and to the communities in which they live.

Connections to Literature

Writing a Short Story That Persuades

Although pigs cannot write, they can be very persuasive—at least when they are characters in a *fable*. Fables are short stories that teach lessons about life.

A Fabulous Recipe Fables generally follow a formula. Using this formula helps [...] e a persuasive point in just a [...]. The main ingredients of a [...] below.

	finition	Example
	usually animals	an ant who
	at talk and	saves food all
	ct like humans	summer and a grasshopper who relaxes all summer
	he problem the	In winter, the
	characters face	ant has food because he prepared, but the grasshopper has none.
Moral	the lesson	Be prepared.

A Lesson for Us All The most important part of a fable is its *moral*. The **moral**, or lesson, is like the opinion statement of a persuasive essay. It expresses what the writer wants readers to do or believe.

Read the following fable by Aesop, retold by Anne Terry White.

The Dog and His Shadow
by Aesop

Curly the Dog was happily trotting home. It wasn't every day that the butcher gave him a juicy bone with meat on it! The Dog was carrying it very carefully in his mouth.

On the way he had to cross a little stream. He looked down from the footbridge into the clear water. And, to his surprise, he saw another dog under the water. Yes, and that other dog also had a bone in his mouth! It seemed to Curly that it was a bigger bone than his own.

With a growl he dropped his bone in order to grab the other dog's bone too. But he had no sooner done that than the dog under the water also dropped his bone.

For a moment Curly stood looking angrily down at his shadow. He couldn't understand it. All he knew was that he had lost his bone and must now trot home without it.

MORAL: Grasp for all and lose all.

Aesop's is a dog named Curly. The conflict is that Curly wants more than what he has. The moral is that greed will only cause unhappiness.

The steps on the next page will show you how to write a fable of your own.

Foundations for Writing

Part 2

Sentences and Paragraphs

In **Part 2: Sentences and Paragraphs,** *Elements of Language* focuses on the nuts-and-bolts knowledge students need to become successful writers.

The *Pupil's Edition* presents easy-to-follow instruction on writing complete and effective sentences, combining sentences, and correcting common errors such as fragments, wordiness, and lack of parallel structure.

Students also learn to develop strong paragraphs, focusing on unity and coherence. In grades 10, 11, and 12, students focus on composition structure.

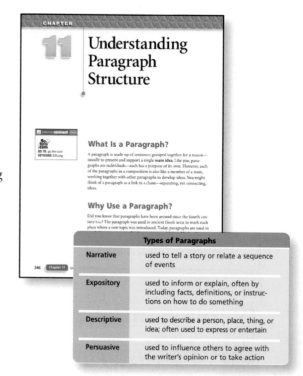

CHAPTER

11 Understanding Paragraph Structure

What Is a Paragraph?

A paragraph is made up of sentences grouped together for a reason—usually to present and support a single **main idea.** Like you, paragraphs are individuals—each has a purpose of its own. However, each of the paragraphs in a composition is also like a member of a team, working together with other paragraphs to develop ideas. You might think of a paragraph as a link in a chain—separating, yet connecting ideas.

Why Use a Paragraph?

Did you know that paragraphs have been around since the fourth century B.C.? The paragraph was used in ancient Greek texts to mark each place where a new topic was introduced. Today, paragraphs are used in

346   Chapter 11

Types of Paragraphs	
Narrative	used to tell a story or relate a sequence of events
Expository	used to inform or explain, often by including facts, definitions, or instructions on how to do something
Descriptive	used to describe a person, place, thing, or idea; often used to express or entertain
Persuasive	used to influence others to agree with the writer's opinion or to take action

Grammar, Usage, and Mechanics

A confident control of grammar, usage, and mechanics helps to ensure clear and effective communication. In **Part 3: Grammar, Usage, and Mechanics,** *Elements of Language* delivers a comprehensive language skills curriculum that's accessible and effective. Diagnostic Previews give opportunities for diagnosing students' strengths and weaknesses. Reviews A and B provide cumulative assessment, and Chapter Reviews offer additional exercises for ongoing assessments.

Time-Tested Model

Part 3 of *Elements of Language* is based on John Warriner's logical model of instruction—teach students the rule, show examples of the rule in action, and provide immediate practice to reinforce the skill or concept. This time-honored approach has been the authoritative standard for teaching grammar, usage, and mechanics skills for over fifty years.

Common Conjunctive Adverbs		
also	incidentally	next
anyway	indeed	nonetheless
besides	instead	otherwise
consequently	likewise	still
finally	meanwhile	then
furthermore	moreover	therefore
however	nevertheless	thus

Common Transitional Expressions		
after all	even so	in fact
as a result	for example	in other words
at any rate	for instance	on the contrary
by the way	in addition	on the other hand

Warriner's Model for Instruction

"Practice makes perfect," and a multitude of exercises, both written and oral, offer students ample opportunities to practice each rule and learn one concept at a time.

Rule
Clearly stated rules are always presented in red.

Examples
A variety of examples illustrate the language skill or concept.

Exercise
Exercises provide immediate practice for every rule.

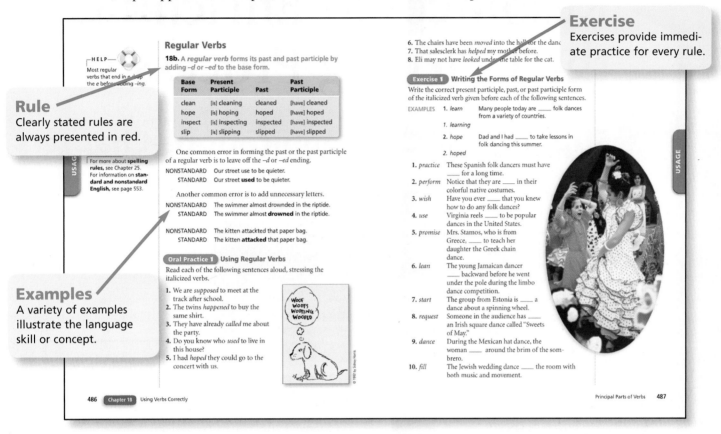

Grammar Expert

John E. Warriner, English teacher for thirty years in junior and senior high schools and college, developed the original organizational structure that serves as the basis for the Grammar, Usage, and Mechanics instruction in *Elements of Language*. His well-known and respected pedagogical concept, a clearly stated rule followed by examples and then immediate practice, continues to stand as the ideal model for authoritative grammar, usage, and mechanics instruction.

 Quick Reference Handbook

Designed to give students quick and convenient access to key communication concepts, this handbook covers the following topics:

▶ **The Dictionary**

▶ **Document Design**

▶ **The History of English: Origins and Uses**

▶ **The Library/Media Center**

▶ **Reading and Vocabulary**

▶ **Speaking and Listening**

▶ **Studying and Test Taking**

▶ **Viewing and Representing**

▶ **Writing**

▶ **Grammar at a Glance**

Resources to Enrich the Learning Process

Support for Communications Chapters

The wide array of print, visual, and technological resources included with *Elements of Language* gives you the visual and academic support needed to make learning come alive for students.

The *Communications* booklet provides support and practice for the Reading and Writing Workshops with graphic organizers, teaching transparencies, and student worksheets. It includes

- writing prompts
- journal warm-ups
- revising charts
- proofreading practice
- fine art transparencies
- guidelines for peer evaluation and self-evaluation
- additional practice

Designing Your Writing transparencies and worksheets model effective techniques for presenting writing. They teach and demonstrate how the choice of formatting, graphics, and other design elements can affect the intended message.

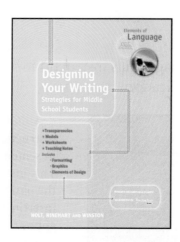

Media Literacy and Communication Skills provides chapter-by-chapter support for speaking, listening, viewing, and representing skills. The package includes videocassettes, *A How-to Handbook,* a set of *Support and Practice* transparencies and worksheets, and *A Teacher's Guide* that pulls these materials together. For more information, see **Technology Resources** on page T49.

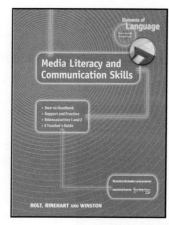

Alternative Readings booklet benefits struggling readers by offering an easier **MiniRead®,** including active-reading questions, for each **Reading Workshop.** Additional reading strategy options target struggling readers and provide tools they can apply to a range of texts.

Language Skills

Elements of Language is a comprehensive program of language skills instruction that gives students a solid foundation for effective communication.

Grammar, Usage, and Mechanics: Language Skills Practice provides additional practice for all grammar, usage, and mechanics rules in **Part 3** of the *Pupil's Edition*. Based on Warriner's rule-example-practice model, this invaluable workbook features exercises, proofreading applications, writing applications, and literary-model activities.

Spelling Lessons and Activities (Grades 6–8) focuses on both sound patterns and word analysis strategies. Analysis and additional practice are included for each word list.
Holt Interactive Spelling CD-ROM engages students with lively animation. (See T49.)

Developmental Language Skills and **Developmental Language Skills Answer Key** includes remedial worksheets for guided instruction, practice, and reinforcement of lessons in **Part 3**. It targets those students who have not yet mastered specific grammar, usage, and mechanics concepts.

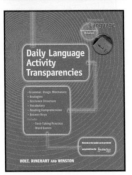

Daily Language Activity Transparencies binder includes test-taking practice in analogies, sentence completion, and reading comprehension. Practice is also included for proofreading in grammar, usage, and mechanics; sentence combining; vocabulary building; and word games.

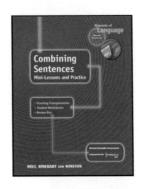

Combining Sentences provides instruction, models, and practice in sentence-combining strategies. This instruction addresses all the basic techniques, such as inserting prepositional or appositive phrases and using compound subjects and verbs.

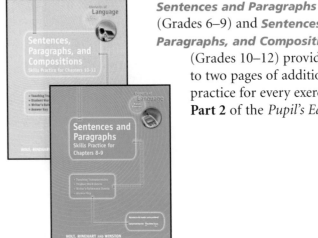

Sentences and Paragraphs (Grades 6–9) and **Sentences, Paragraphs, and Compositions** (Grades 10–12) provide up to two pages of additional practice for every exercise in **Part 2** of the *Pupil's Edition*.

Additional Resource

Vocabulary Workshop helps students build their vocabularies and simultaneously prepare for standardized tests. Concepts and skills include analogies, context clues, prefixes, suffixes, roots, synonyms, antonyms, and etymologies.

Vocabulary Workshop Tests assess knowledge of the words and concepts taught in the **Vocabulary Workshop** and provide practice in standardized test formats.

Planning and Assessment

Elements of Language provides several options for planning and assessment, giving you more flexibility for today's diverse classroom.

One-Stop Planner® CD-ROM with ExamView® Test Generator for Macintosh® and Windows®

Planning and managing lessons has never been easier than with the ***One-Stop Planner CD-ROM.*** This convenient, all-in-one planning software program includes all the teaching resources for *Elements of Language,* plus valuable planning and assessment tools. The ***One-Stop Planner*** provides

• editable lesson plans
• previews of teaching resources
• an easy-to-use test generator

To preview a video segment or transparency or to print out tests and worksheets for your students, simply select and click.

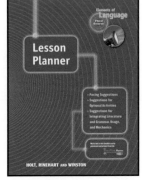

The ***Lesson Planner*** focuses on both classroom time and the independent working time needed for the reading, writing, speaking, listening, viewing, and representing lessons in the *Pupil's Edition.* ***Teaching Strategies for English-Language Learners*** provides suggestions for using lessons with students who are not native speakers of English.

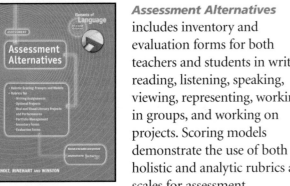

Assessment Alternatives includes inventory and evaluation forms for both teachers and students in writing, reading, listening, speaking, viewing, representing, working in groups, and working on projects. Scoring models demonstrate the use of both holistic and analytic rubrics and scales for assessment.

Chapter Tests provides short-answer questions in traditional formats for each chapter in the *Pupil's Edition.* The tests include assessment for the **Reading and Writing Workshops** in **Part 1**; for the sentences, paragraphs, and compositions instruction in **Part 2**; and for the grammar, usage, and mechanics skills in **Part 3**.

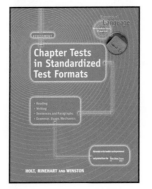

Chapter Tests in Standardized Test Formats offers an additional test for each chapter in the *Pupil's Edition.* Using a range of formats from the most commonly used standardized assessments, these tests include all of the content listed under ***Chapter Tests.***

Technology
The Key to Learning in the Information Age

The wide range of dynamic and interactive resources available with *Elements of Language* gives students the opportunity to learn and retain more.

Elements of Language Online Textbook

The *Online Edition* of *Elements of Language* sets your students free to pursue language learning any time, anywhere.

Elements of Language *Online Edition* provides so many convenient options, including online versions of the textbook pages, an instant grading feature, and interactive versions of textbook activities, exercises, and tests. Of course, the *Online Edition* includes the Warriner's grammar model, the authoritative standard for teaching grammar, usage, and mechanics skills, leading students logically through lessons—from rule to example to exercise.

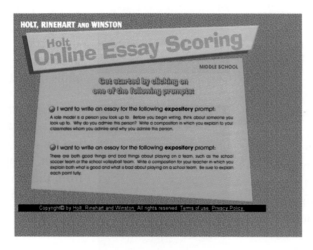

Holt Online Essay Scoring

Looking for more time to enjoy the parts of teaching that you love the most? **Holt Online Essay Scoring** can help carry the paper load. With prompts and rubrics like those found on state assessments, our computer scoring system uses the latest technology to analyze and provide a holistic score for your students' writing.

Additional links connect the student to more specific **Analytic Feedback,** a **Model Essay,** and **Writing Activities** based on the prompt and the student's score.

Holt Interactive Spelling

This exciting computer program can help students improve spelling and vocabulary skills. The interactive CD-ROM allows students to work at their own pace and is adaptable to a wide range of classroom settings. It begins with a diagnostic pretest to determine which areas need work and provides clear, instructive feedback and printable progress reports. Lively animation encourages students' interest in learning.
Levels 1, 2, and 3.
(Recommended for grades 6, 7, 8.)

go.hrw.com

Internet references throughout the *Student Edition* direct students to a Web site for users of *Elements of Language.* This site links students to activities and projects for each **Communications** chapter and allows them to put their reading, writing, speaking, and listening skills into action in real-world situations.

Media Literacy and Communication Skills

Designed to support the speaking, listening, viewing, and representing lessons in *Elements of Language,* this package contains videocassettes, a *How-To Handbook, Support and Practice,* and a *Teacher's Guide.*

Language Workshop Interactive Multimedia CD-ROM Software

This award-winning CD-ROM gives your students a complete course of study in grammar, usage, and mechanics.

Writer's Workshop Interactive Multimedia CD-ROM Software

This award-winning interactive CD-ROM program guides students through the eight most common writing assignments, such as writing a personal narrative, preparing an informative report, or composing a persuasive essay.

All CD-ROMs are available for both Macintosh® and Windows®.

STUDENT'S OVERVIEW

Elements of Language is divided into four major parts.

PART 1 Communications

This section ties together the essential skills and strategies you use in all types of communication—reading, writing, listening, speaking, viewing, and representing.

Reading Workshops In these workshops, you read an article, a story, an editorial—a real-life example of a type of writing you will later compose on your own. In addition, these workshops help you practice the reading process through

- a Reading Skill and Reading Focus specific to each type of writing,
- Vocabulary Mini-Lessons to help you understand unfamiliar words, and
- Test-Taking Mini-Lessons targeting common reading objectives

Writing Workshops In these workshops, you brainstorm ideas and use the writing process to produce your own article, story, editorial—and more. These workshops also include

- Writing and Critical-Thinking Mini-Lessons to help you master important aspects of each type of writing
- an organizational framework and models to guide your writing
- evaluation charts with concrete steps for revising
- Connections to Literature and Connections to Life, activities that extend writing workshop skills and concepts to other areas of your life
- Test-Taking Mini-Lessons to help you respond to writing prompts for tests

Focus on Speaking and Listening
Focus on Viewing and Representing

This is your chance to sharpen your skills in presenting your ideas visually and orally and to learn how to take a more critical view of what you hear and see.

PART 2 Sentences and Paragraphs

Learn to construct clear and effective sentences and paragraphs—what parts to include, how to organize ideas, and how to write these essential parts of compositions with style.

PART 3 Grammar, Usage, and Mechanics

These are the basics that will help you make your writing correct and polished.

Grammar Discover the structure of language—the words, phrases, and clauses that are the building blocks of sentences.

Usage Learn the rules that govern how language is used in various social situations, including standard versus nonstandard and formal versus informal English.

Mechanics Master the nuts and bolts of correct written English, including capitalization, punctuation, and spelling.

PART 4 Quick Reference Handbook

Use this handy guide any time you need concise tips to help you communicate more effectively—whether you need to find information in a variety of media, make sense of what you read, prepare for tests, or present your ideas in a published document, a speech, or a visual.

Elements of Language on the Internet

Put the communication strategies in *Elements of Language* to work by logging on to the Internet. At the *Elements of Language* Internet site, you can dissect the prose of professional writers, crack the codes of the advertising industry, and find out how your communication skills can help you in the real world.

As you move through *Elements of Language*, you will find the best online resources at **go.hrw.com.**

The Reading and Writing Processes

D o these situations sound familiar? While reading, you suddenly realize you have read the same sentences several times without gaining any meaning from them. While writing, you stare at the single sentence you have written, unable to think of anything else to write. When you find yourself stuck, step back and look at the processes of reading and writing.

Reading

The reading you do in school requires you to think critically about information and ideas. In order to get the most from a text, prepare your mind for the task before you read, use effective strategies while you read, and take time to process the information after you read.

- **Before Reading** Get your mind in gear by considering your purpose for reading a particular piece of writing and by thinking about what you already know about the topic. Preview the text by skimming a bit and considering headings, graphics, and other features. Use this information to predict what the text will discuss and how challenging it will be to read.

- **While Reading** As you read, figure out the writer's point about the topic. Notice how the text is organized (by cause and effect or in order of importance, for example) to help you find support for that point. Connect the ideas to your own experiences when you can. If you get confused, slow down, re-read, or jot ideas in a graphic organizer.

- **After Reading** Confirm and extend your understanding of the text. Draw conclusions about the writer's point of view, and evaluate how well the writer communicated the message. Use ideas in the text to create a piece of art, to read more on a related topic, or to solve a problem.

Writing

A perfect text seldom springs fully formed from your mind; instead, you must plan your text before you write and work to improve it after drafting.

TIP Reading and writing are both recursive processes—that is, you can return to earlier steps when needed. For example, you might make new predictions while you are reading a text or you might develop additional support for ideas when you are revising a piece of writing.

- **Before Writing** First, choose a topic and a form of writing, such as a poem or an editorial. Decide who your readers will be and what you want the text to accomplish. Develop ideas based on your knowledge and on research. Organize the ideas, and jot down your main point.

- **While Writing** Grab attention and provide background information in an introduction. Elaborate your ideas to support your point, and organize them clearly. Then, wrap things up with a conclusion.

- **After Writing** To improve a draft, evaluate how clearly you expressed your ideas. Ask a peer to suggest areas that need work. Then, revise. Proofread to correct any mistakes. Share your finished work with others, and reflect on what you learned.

You may have noticed that the reading and writing processes involve similar strategies. The chart below summarizes these similarities.

The Reading and Writing Processes

Reading		Writing
Determine your purpose for reading. Consider what you already know about the topic. Preview the text to make predictions about what it will include.	– **Before** –	Identify your writing purpose and your audience. Draw upon what you know about the topic, and do research to find out more. Make notes or an outline to plan what the text will include.
Figure out the writer's main ideas. Look for support for the main ideas. Notice how the ideas in the text are organized.	– **While** –	Express your main ideas clearly. Support them with details, facts, examples, or anecdotes. Follow prewriting notes or an outline to organize your text so readers can easily follow your ideas.
Evaluate the text to decide how accurate it is and its overall quality. Relate what you have read to the world around you by creating something, reading further, or applying ideas. Reflect on what you have read.	– **After** –	Evaluate and revise your text. Use peer editors' comments to help improve your work. Relate your writing to the world around you by publishing it. Reflect on what you have written.

The Reading and Writing Workshops in this book provide valuable practice for strategies that will help you effectively use these related processes.

PART

1

Communications

Communications   1

Taking Tests: Strategies and Practice

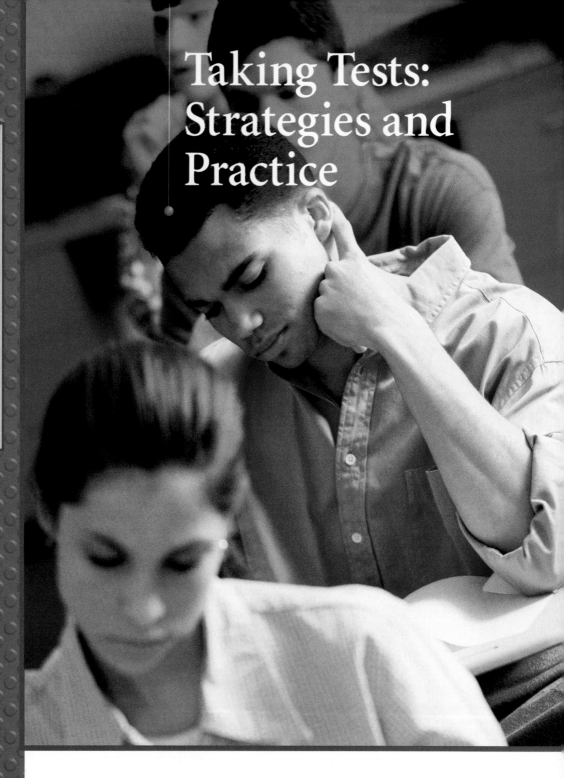

PREVIEWING THE CHAPTER

■ As standardized tests become increasingly important for promotion and graduation, students must become more comfortable with the types of test items they will most often see. In this section students will learn and practice strategies for effectively taking standardized tests of reading and writing skills, both in multiple-choice and essay format. You may want to use this chapter periodically during the school year, first having students use the reading selections, questions, and writing prompts here and later having them apply the strategies to other passages and prompts.

Taking Reading Tests

Every so often (maybe once a year), you'll face a national or statewide standardized test of reading and writing. A standardized reading test contains brief **reading passages** followed by several **multiple-choice questions** and sometimes an open-ended **essay question.** The testmakers are out to test every reading skill you are supposed to have learned by now.

Reading Test Strategies

STEP 1 Pace yourself. Skim the test to see how many questions there are, and estimate how long you can spend on each question. Check every five or ten minutes to see if you need to work faster.

STEP 2 Read carefully. Read the directions and any introduction to the reading passage. Then, focus your complete attention on the passage. If you can mark the test booklet, underline key words.

STEP 3 Make sure you understand the question. Beware of words like *not* and *except,* which direct you to choose an answer that is false or opposite in some way. Watch out also for distracters— answers that are true but don't answer the question that's being asked. Never choose an answer until you've read *all* of the answers.

STEP 4 Make educated guesses. Eliminate answers you know are wrong. Then, make an inference, not a random guess. Remember that your answer must depend entirely on information in the reading passage—not on any prior knowledge you may have about the topic.

STEP 5 Keep on going. Don't get stuck on a difficult question. Skip questions that baffle you and return to them later if you have time.

STEP 6 Watch your bubbles. Make sure you neatly fill in the answer you intend. If you skip a question, don't lose your place.

STEP 7 Check your work. When you finish, try answering questions you skipped. Check your answers carefully, and erase any stray marks.

TIP Know how the test is scored. If no points are taken off for wrong answers, then answer every question. If wrong answers count against you, answer only the questions you know and those you can answer with an educated guess.

Read the following passages carefully. Then, choose the **best** answer to each question.

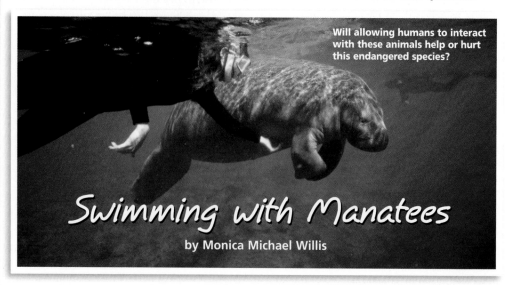

Will allowing humans to interact with these animals help or hurt this endangered species?

Swimming with Manatees
by Monica Michael Willis

My first encounter with a manatee came during a school trip to a science-education center in Jupiter, Florida, when I was about 11 years old. After a lesson on marine biology, my classmates and I were allowed to take a dip in Jupiter Inlet, a narrow swatch of brackish[1] water that connects the Intracoastal Waterway with the Atlantic.

While I was swimming, something massive and scruffy suddenly brushed up against my leg. Thinking I was about to be attacked by a shark—the fear of all ocean-loving Florida kids who had seen the movie *Jaws*—I looked to my side and laid eyes on a huge, unfamiliar, gray creature. The next thing I knew, I was on the beach in a hysterical heap.

After my teacher assessed the situation, she informed me that I had come face-to-face with a manatee, possibly the least-ferocious animal on the planet—a blubbery behemoth[2] that would much rather nibble on sea grass than on my ankle.

Last winter, decades after that chance meeting, I had the opportunity to once again swim with manatees when I visited Florida's Citrus County, home to the biggest winter population of manatees in the world. According to Dr. Bruce Ackerman, a marine scientist who performs aerial surveys for the Florida Department of Environmental Protection, there are about 2,600 manatees in existence, of which he estimates approximately 15 percent winter in and around the Crystal River, a seven-mile waterway

---

1. brackish: a mixture of salt water and fresh water.

From "Swimming with Manatees" by Monica Michael Willis from *Country Living*, vol. 20, November 1, 1997. Copyright ©1997 by **The Hearst Corporation**. Reprinted by permission of the publisher.

---

2. behemoth (bə•hē′məth): an enormous, powerful animal.

that lies about 60 miles north of Tampa on the state's Gulf side.

In hopes of catching a glimpse of this endangered marine mammal, tourists from as far away as Asia and Europe now visit this largely rural area of central Florida, where swimming with manatees has become big business. Cameron Shaw, refuge manager at the Crystal River National Wildlife Refuge, a 45-acre preserve that encompasses Kings Bay (which is the headwaters of the Crystal River) and Kings Spring, one of the most popular spots among freshwater scuba divers, estimates that 60,000 visitors swam with these rare creatures in 1996. Since so many manatees congregate in the springs in the Crystal River and Kings Bay, guides and dive shops can virtually guarantee prospective clients that they'll encounter one or more of the animals while diving there. In Crystal River, Florida, the hub of much of the diving action, a half dozen or so dive shops operate excursions to spots along the shallow, spring-fed Crystal River and Kings Bay during the winter migration season, which runs from about December 1 to March 30.

The official marine mammal of the state of Florida, manatees are nearsighted, slow-moving herbivores that average about 10 feet in length and weigh in at roughly 1,200 pounds. Amazingly, considering their size, manatees are remarkably gentle. They are not territorial and they have no natural enemies and no known agenda—they pretty much just sleep and eat. (In Kings Bay and the Crystal River area, hungry manatees help to control hydrilla, an invasive—and prolific—aquatic plant that is clogging many Southern waterways.)

Taking the Plunge

On the two days I went diving, I left my hotel at 6:00 A.M. to increase my chances of viewing the manatees as they congregate near the warm springs in the early morning. . . .

After we collected our snorkels, masks, and fins, we took a short boat ride to Three Sisters' Spring. Before we disembarked,[3] our guide reminded us that the exceptionally clear spring was not a petting zoo. A sign spelled out other rules: Divers should not pursue, ride, poke, or in any way harass the animals. In the event that we were approached by a manatee, we were told we could extend one open hand to it (placing two hands on an animal is considered riding and is against the law).

Moments after I entered the water, two massive manatees swam toward me. It was exhilarating as well as a little frightening to be in proximity to these enormous marine mammals. They appeared curious and sweet natured and perfectly content to be the center of my—and several other divers'—attention. One of the manatees even seemed to want its belly scratched.

"It's a unique experience for people to see a large aquatic mammal up close," says the Crystal River National Wildlife Refuge's Cameron Shaw. "Most people take away a memory of a lifetime."

Manatee Mania?

Not everyone, however, is thrilled with the number of tourists coming to the area to swim with the manatees. . . .

Members of the Save the Manatee Club—cofounded in 1981 by musician Jimmy Buffett and former Florida governor Bob Graham—worry that the sheer number of people diving in the area will alter the endangered animals' natural behavior.

Patti Thompson, a biologist with the Maitland, Florida–based environmental group, refers to the animals that approached me near the spring as "ambassadors," manatees that she believes have become unnaturally accustomed

---

3. **disembarked:** left, got off.

1. B

2. H

3. A

4. F

5. D

6. J

7. B

8. K

9. This written-response question should take fifteen to twenty minutes to complete. Answers should be one hundred to two hundred words long.

Strategies for Answering the Question Students should begin by identifying the types of articles typically found in general entertainment magazines for teenagers, such as *Teen People,* and by noting the style and content of "Swimming with Manatees." Have students list reasons for their editorial decision before they begin writing.

Description of a Top-Score Response A top-score response will use relevant information from the passage and personal experience to support the student's position. It may include some of the following points.

For Publishing the Article

- The article's first-person point of view and relatively easy diction make it accessible to teenagers.
- The writer first encountered manatees when she was eleven years old, so young readers will relate to her experience.
- Publishing the article might encourage teens to become more involved in conservation issues.

to the presence of divers and that may have possibly been fed by humans in the past. "It's not natural behavior for a wild animal to swim up to you and roll over to have its belly scratched," she said. "Only a few exhibit this behavior." Although the Save the Manatee club wishes tourists would go to a marine park or one of the state's manatee viewing areas to observe the animals from the surface, they acknowledge that many people would much rather swim with them. As a result, the club has begun promoting "passive observation," whereby divers watch manatees from the water but are instructed to refrain from touching the animals or interacting with them.

"Of all the endangered species the Fish and Wildlife Service is supposed to protect, the manatee is the only one they encourage people to interact with," says Thompson. "There is no other endangered species that they would condone such interaction with. It's because manatees are gentle and they know no one will be hurt. When the Fish and Wildlife Service extends the open-hand policy to grizzly bears, then I'll accept it for manatees."

Fostering Advocacy

This apparent disparity[4] of policy may send a conflicting message to the public about endangered species, but many believe that divers who spend time with the manatees will be inclined to support programs that will safeguard this rare mammal and preserve its dwindling habitat. "We've found that swimming with manatees fosters a great advocacy for the species as well as for the whole ecosystem," says Shaw. . . .

---

4. **disparity:** inequality.

1. The article's main idea is that
   A. swimming with manatees is exciting
   B. experts have different opinions about swimming with manatees
   C. manatees naturally interact with humans
   D. tourism involving manatees is a big business in Florida
   E. manatees are an endangered species

2. The author's main purpose is to
   F. entertain the reader
   G. present new scientific research
   H. present both sides of a controversy
   J. describe the manatee's life cycle
   K. narrate a personal experience

3. When the author first swam with a manatee as an adult, she felt
   A. exhilarated
   B. terrified
   C. annoyed
   D. curious
   E. peaceful

4. *Condone* (second to last paragraph) means
   F. approve
   G. forbid
   H. question
   J. protect
   K. disapprove

5. In the last sentence, *advocacy* means
   A. interest in a controversial topic or issue
   B. love of the outdoors
   C. respect for the natural world
   D. support for a cause
   E. opposition to a proposal or idea

6. Biologist Patti Thompson compares manatees to grizzly bears because

   F. the Fish and Wildlife Service allows people to feed both animals

   G. both animals have severely injured people

   H. people should be allowed more contact with grizzly bears

   J. manatees are not protected as well as other endangered species

   K. both animals' habitats are in popular tourist areas

7. The writer describes her personal experiences with manatees in order to

   A. show how much she has changed

   B. add interest and information

   C. state her own opinion on the issue

   D. prove that she is an expert on manatees

   E. encourage readers to swim with manatees

8. Which of the following does *not* appear in the article?

   F. facts about manatees

   G. a personal anecdote

   H. a plan to protect manatees

   J. quotations from scientists

   K. quotations from politicians

Write several paragraphs in response to *one* of the following questions:

9. You are the editor of a general entertainment magazine for teenagers. Would you publish this article in your magazine or reject it? Give two or more reasons for your decision, and refer to the article to support your points.

10. If you had the chance, would you swim with manatees? Explain why or why not. Use details from the article to explain your decision.

MAKING SENSE OF MANATEES

by Doug Stewart

Among the habits of Florida manatees, one is particularly convenient for the biologists who try to keep tabs on these rare animals. "When the water temperature drops to about 68 degrees Fahrenheit, manatees start to move," says Jessica Koelsch, a biologist at Sarasota's Mote Marine Laboratory. "But they don't necessarily head south. Some actually go north to congregate in artificially warm water, such as the water around power plants." These winter-time reunions offer manatee-monitoring scientists a field day.

The hard part may be figuring out which way the animals will meander[1] once spring comes. "Because manatees disperse so widely, the nonwinter months are when it's most difficult to protect them," says Koelsch. In the summer of 1994, a headstrong Florida manatee dubbed Chessie was found swimming in the Chesapeake Bay and was airlifted home. The

From *"Making Sense of Manatees"* by Doug Stewart from *National Wildlife*, vol. 37, issue 3, April/May 1999. Copyright © 1999 by *Doug Stewart*. Reprinted by permission of the author.

1. meander: wander.

Against Publishing the Article

• The topic is too focused or too scientific for a general-interest magazine.

• The article is longer than a typical teen magazine article.

• Some of the vocabulary is difficult enough to require footnotes, which teen magazines rarely, if ever, use.

10. This written-response question should take fifteen to twenty minutes to complete. Answers should be one hundred to two hundred words long.

   Strategies for Answering the Question Students should take a position on the issue and then refer to the passage and their own experiences for relevant details to support their position.

   Description of a Top-Score Response A top-score response will use relevant information from the passage and personal experience to support the student's position on the issue. It may include some of the following details.

   Would Swim with Manatees

   • It is safe to swim with manatees.

   • Swimming with manatees is a once-in-a-lifetime experience.

   • Manatees seem to enjoy the attention and may like being touched.

   Would Not Swim with Manatees

   • Manatees are large, wild animals.

   • It is not natural for manatees to interact with humans. Interacting with a manatee may keep it from behaving naturally, interfering with reproduction or migration.

   • Some people who arrange for tourists to swim with manatees may be more concerned with making money than with protecting the species from harm.

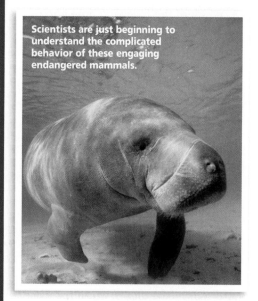

Scientists are just beginning to understand the complicated behavior of these engaging endangered mammals.

following summer, Chessie was spotted off Rhode Island. "We don't know what he is doing up here," confessed U.S. Geological Survey biologist Jim Reid at the time.

Figuring out why manatees do things like this is crucial to ensuring their long-term survival. Fewer than 3,000 of the creatures remain in and around Florida today, and their future is uncertain. Manatee behavior has been studied in depth only in recent years, as the plight of this small but charismatic[2] population—under pressure from habitat loss and frequent boat collisions—has garnered[3] widespread public attention. . . .

"Manatees are an endangered species," says Koelsch. "To protect them, we have to understand their behavior." Knowledge of what they eat when, which waters they prefer, and where they mate can help pinpoint, for example, where aquatic preserves might best be set up

for the animals. But before they can lobby for manatee-friendly sacrifices like new sanctuaries and slower boating speed limits, wildlife managers need to arm themselves with convincing data. . . .

A puzzling feature of sirenian[4] physiology[5] is a surprisingly small brain. In an adult manatee, it's about the size of a grapefruit—comparatively less than a quarter as big as the brain of most other large mammals, aquatic or terrestrial. If its brain is puny,[6] does that mean the manatee is less intelligent than other mammals? Roger Reep, a biologist at the University of Florida's College of Veterinary Medicine who, with Tom O'Shea, has studied the matter, suggests that is not the right question.

"Instead of saying manatees have small brains, you can look at them as having very large bodies," Reep says. The pressures of natural selection have probably made large, bulky bodies advantageous to manatees over time. "First, they're not chasing down prey," he adds, "and they aren't preyed upon to any degree, so they don't need elaborate behavioral repertoires[7] for pursuit or escape."

That does not mean a manatee leads a dull-witted life, just a relatively uncomplicated one. Second, the animal has a low metabolism.[8] Though this helps it avoid overheating in very warm surroundings, the creature still must burn enough energy to stay warm when conditions are cool. And living in water, it loses heat more easily to its surroundings than do, say, cows. "So you need a large body," Reep says. "If you're bigger, you have less surface area in proportion to your weight, so you lose heat less readily."

---

2. **charismatic** (kar´iz•mat´ik): charming, alluring.

3. **garnered:** gathered.

4. **sirenian** (sī•rē´nē•ən): of the order of mammals that includes manatees and dugongs.

5. **physiology:** the biological processes that account for the life functions of an organism.

6. **puny:** small.

7. **repertoires** (rep´ər•twärz´): techniques, special skills.

8. **metabolism:** the sum of all of the chemical and physical processes in an organism.

The manatee's unhurried lifestyle suits its low metabolic rate. Its normal cruising speed is a sedate two to six miles per hour. . . .

The manatee's lumbering pace is often blamed for its high mortality from boat collisions. The conventional wisdom is that the animal is too sluggish to get out of the way. Ed Gerstein, director of marine mammal research at Florida Atlantic University, is unconvinced. "A manatee is not all that slow," he says. "If frightened or excited, it can explode, moving 21 feet per second." . . .

A number of marine sanctuaries have been set aside on the Florida coasts to serve as manatee refuges. This gives agencies like the U.S. Fish and Wildlife Service and the Florida Department of Environmental Protection a chance to educate visitors about the manatee's plight. Federal guidelines allow divers and snorkelers to touch a manatee as long as the animal comes to them first and the swimmers touch it only with one open hand—an intimacy prohibited with other endangered species.

At least one researcher disapproves, however. "Manatees don't have claws and they don't have big teeth, which is unfortunate," says Patti Thompson, a biologist with Save the Manatee Club, a Florida advocacy group.

Manatees that solicit[9] handouts or that seem to pose for photos are behaving unnaturally, says Thompson, pointing out that nonhabituated[10] manatees are spooked by people standing on a beach. Gauntlets[11] of underwater tourists in some areas, she argues, could interfere with natural behavior such as reproduction and nursing.

"People say, 'Oh, manatees are so sweet and gentle,' but that's anthropomorphizing,"[12] observes Thompson. "Manatees' lack of predators has allowed them to evolve without the kinds of defenses that other animals have. They're not being sweet and gentle. They're being manatees."

---

9. **solicit:** seek.
10. **nonhabituated:** not accustomed to (people).
11. **gauntlets:** used here to mean a lot of people.
12. **anthropomorphizing** (an′thrə•pō′môr′fīz′iŋ): giving an animal human qualities.

---

11. Scientists believe that manatees are gentle because manatees
   A. have a small brain and slow metabolism
   B. are large and slow-moving
   C. have no natural predators
   D. enjoy being petted and photographed
   E. live in warm tropical waters

12. What is the main reason scientists are studying manatee behavior?
   F. to teach people how to interact with them
   G. to learn why they have such small brains
   H. to find out where they go in the winter
   J. to compare them with other marine mammals
   K. to help an endangered species survive and recover

13. Unlike many people, Ed Gerstein believes that manatees
   A. can only swim very slowly
   B. can sometimes move quickly
   C. will be hurt by human contact
   D. should not be placed in sanctuaries
   E. are highly intelligent animals

ANSWERS

11. C

12. K

13. B

14. J

15. D

16. F

17. B

18. F

19. This written-response question should take fifteen to twenty minutes to complete. Answers should be one hundred to two hundred words long.
   Strategies for Answering the Question Have students define the task in their own words. Then, have them skim the passages for details that indicate each author's point of view on the subject.
   Description of a Top-Score Response A top-score response will use information and details from the passages to note that the second author quotes only a scientist opposed to swimming with manatees to support the author's opinion that this activity is wrong. On the other hand, the first author presents both sides of the issue, indicating that she may have a more balanced point of view. A top-score response may point out that the first author's description of swimming with manatees herself and her order of details indicate that she may support swimming with them.

20. This written-response question should take fifteen to twenty minutes to complete. Answers should be one hundred to two hundred words long.

Strategies for Answering the Question Students should begin by taking a position on the issue and then skim the passages for relevant information and details to support their side. Encourage students to list support for their chosen side before they begin writing.

Description of a Top-Score Response A top-score response will use relevant information and details from the passage to support the student's position on the issue. It should include some of the following details.

For Swimming with Manatees
- Manatees will not harm humans.
- Tourists who swim with manatees bring money that could be used for conservation efforts.
- Because people must follow the rules, no harm will be done to the animals.
- According to Cameron Shaw, swimming with manatees makes people greater advocates for the species.

Against Swimming with Manatees
- Manatees are endangered animals that should be treated like all other endangered species.
- Manatees are gentle because they lack predators. There is no evidence that it is in their interest to be around humans.
- Large numbers of tourists interacting with manatees may interfere with their natural behavior, such as reproduction and nursing habits.

14. During the summer months, manatees
  F. head south to warmer waters
  G. head north to colder waters
  H. stay in the warm water near power plants
  J. disperse widely
  K. search for tourists

15. In the sentence "The conventional wisdom is that the manatee is too <u>sluggish</u> to get out of the way," *sluggish* means
  A. stubborn
  B. ready to fight
  C. overweight
  D. slow-moving
  E. endangered

16. We can infer from this article that the greatest danger to manatees is
  F. collisions with boats
  G. severe storms
  H. diseases of marine mammals
  J. larger marine animals
  K. aquatic preserves

17. Patti Thompson suggests that as a result of not having any natural predators, manatees
  A. are slow-moving and fierce
  B. lack defenses most animals have

  C. live only in warm waters
  D. have multiplied in great numbers
  E. eat only marine plants

Comparing the Passages

18. The second passage presents only facts about manatees, while the first one
  F. includes a first-person account of an experience with a manatee
  G. poses questions about manatees and then answers them
  H. presents problems and offers solutions
  J. tells the reader what to do to save manatees
  K. strongly encourages interaction with manatees

Write several paragraphs in response to *one* of the following questions:

19. What is each author's opinion of swimming with manatees, and how can you tell? Contrast the authors' points of view, using details and information from the passages to support your response.

20. Write a letter to the editor, arguing for or against allowing people to swim with manatees. Support your opinion with details and information from both passages.

Taking Writing Tests

Writing tests come in two different formats:

- **On-demand writing prompts** ask you to write a narrative, expository, or persuasive essay in a limited time.
- **Multiple-choice questions** test your knowledge of sentence construction and revision, paragraph content and organization, and the conventions of standard English.

There you are, facing a writing prompt you've never seen before, perhaps with less than a hour to produce a coherent, well-written essay. Not to worry. Use the following strategies for writing all types of essays.

THINKING IT THROUGH Writing Test Strategies

▷ **STEP 1 Analyze the writing prompt.** Read it carefully, and analyze what you're being asked to do. Look for key verbs (such as *analyze, argue, explain, summarize*) that define your task. (Before the test, review the chart of **key verbs that appear in essay questions,** page 866.) Consider all parts of the prompt. You'll lose points unless you cover the entire writing task. Identify your audience.

▷ **STEP 2 Plan what you'll say.** If you have forty-five minutes to write the essay, take about ten minutes for prewriting. On scratch paper, brainstorm ideas, make a rough outline or graphic organizer, and think about organization. Before you start writing, decide on your main idea statement and how you'll support it.

TIP Don't skip this prewriting step. Using prewriting strategies will result in a stronger, more interesting essay.

▷ **STEP 3 Draft your essay.** Allow about two thirds of your time to draft your essay, making sure you address all parts of the writing prompt. Include a strong opening paragraph and a definite closing. Strive to express your ideas as clearly as you can, and add relevant details to support and elaborate your main points.

▷ **STEP 4 Edit and revise as you write, but leave some time to re-read your draft.** See if you can add transitions or combine sentences. If you add a word or sentence, insert it clearly and neatly.

▷ **STEP 5 Proofread your essay.** Focus on correcting errors in grammar, usage, mechanics, and spelling. Your score depends in part on how well you follow the conventions of standard English.

Quickly zero in on an incident—you do not have very much time to think. If you draw a blank with "courage," try thinking about a time when you felt frightened.

Narrative Writing

Sample Writing Prompt *Think of an incident in your life that tested your courage. Describe the incident, and tell how you felt at the time. Then, looking back at your experience, tell how you feel and what you think about it now.*

What does the prompt ask you to cover in your autobiographical incident? Use a story map to plan your essay.

Setting: Very cold winter day, sunny; snow and ice on the ground; hill in the playground during recess

Characters: Me as a fourth-grade girl; girls and boys in the playground

Conflict: A group of fifth-grade boys start teasing my little sister Sarah and throwing snowballs at her. I yell at them to leave her alone. Then I get two of my friends to help make a circle around Sarah and lead her away from the bullies.

How I felt then: Very frightened; close to tears but determined, fierce

How I feel now: Amazed that I did it; glad my friends helped me

Reference Note

See **punctuating dialogue,** pages 686–690.

Give your autobiographical incident an interest-catching beginning and a definite end. Add some dialogue to make readers feel as if they're standing at your side, listening.

Expository Writing

Sample Writing Prompt *Describe a change that you have observed in your school or neighborhood. It can be a small change or a big change. Discuss what you think are the causes or effects of that change.*

Find the two key verbs in this writing prompt. What are you being asked to do? Do you have to discuss both causes and effects? Choose a topic and brainstorm main points, specific details, and examples. Before you start drafting, express your main idea in a single sentence. Then, choose your strongest supporting points and arrange them in a logical order. In general, devote a paragraph to each main point, elaborating with specific details and examples. Create a strong introduction that includes your main idea statement and a conclusion that brings your essay to a definite end.

Main Idea: In the last two years, Carver Middle School has grown by several hundred students.	
Causes	**Effects**
New housing developments; young families moving in	Larger classes; portable classrooms in athletic field
Became a magnet school for computer sciences	Better football team—more talent to choose from
Increase in city's population	I no longer know everyone in my class

Persuasive Writing

Sample Writing Prompt *The school board is considering requiring high school students to do 50 hours of community service during each school year. To graduate, a student must complete 200 hours. Consider the effects of such a policy, and decide whether you support it. In an essay, express your opinion and give at least three reasons supporting that point of view.*

Consider both sides of the issue—the pros and cons—to make up your mind. Here's a cluster diagram by a student who supports the policy and is trying to think of three good reasons.

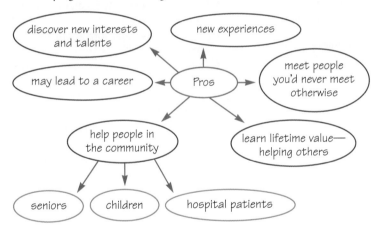

Draft an attention-getting introduction that ends with a clear opinion statement. Give each of your three best reasons, arranged in order of importance, a separate paragraph. You can use your own knowledge and experience to elaborate each reason with facts, examples, anecdotes, and other kinds of evidence. End with a strong concluding paragraph.

Multiple-Choice Writing Questions

You may find a separate section of multiple-choice questions designed to test your understanding of sentences, paragraphs, and the conventions of standard English (grammar, usage, punctuation, capitalization, and spelling). Examples of some common types of multiple-choice writing questions are shown below.

TIP Review the strategies on page 3. They will also help you with multiple-choice writing questions.

Read the following paragraph. Then, choose the best answer for each question.

(1) This week's unexpected heat wave across much of the Northeast and Midwest, coupled with recent reports about the surprisingly fast collapse of an Antarctic ice shelf the size of Rhode Island, has heightened fears of a long-term rise in temperatures brought about by global warming. **(2)** But this fear may be misguided. **(3)** In fact, paradoxically, global warming could actually bring colder temperatures to some highly populated areas like eastern North America and Western Europe.

From "The Heat Before the Cold" by Terrence Joyce from *The New York Times*, April 18, 2002. Copyright © 2002 by **The New York Times Company**. Reprinted by permission of the publisher.

1. To improve this paragraph, where would you place the sentence below?
   Rhode Island, the smallest state in the United States, is one of the thirteen original colonies.
   A. before sentence 1
   B. after sentence 1
   C. after sentence 2
   D. after sentence 3
   E. nowhere; it destroys unity

2. This paragraph suggests that the rest of the article will follow which type of organization?
   F. cause and effect
   G. spatial order
   H. comparison and contrast
   J. chronological order
   K. pros and cons

3. What is the **best** way to elaborate the idea in sentence 3?
   A. a first-person anecdote about the heat wave
   B. a detailed description of the Antarctic ice shelf
   C. information about the size of Rhode Island
   D. details about how melting ice affects world temperatures
   E. the writer's opinion about global warming

4. In sentence 3, the word *temperatures* is the
   F. subject of the sentence
   G. direct object
   H. indirect object
   J. object of a preposition
   K. predicate nominative

5. Which transition can replace "In fact" in sentence 3 without changing the meaning?
   A. For example
   B. As a result
   C. However
   D. For instance
   E. None of the above

6. *Misguided* in sentence 2 means
   F. right
   G. wrong
   H. surprising
   J. serious
   K. essential

7. The word *paradoxically* in sentence 3 is
   A. a noun
   B. a pronoun
   C. an adverb
   D. an adjective
   E. a verb

8. How should the following sentence be corrected?
   Several factors is thought to contribute to global warming.

   F. change *factors* to *factor*
   G. add a comma after *factors*
   H. change *is* to *are*
   J. change *contribute* to *contributes*
   K. no change is needed

9. Maria is doing Internet research about the collapse of the Antarctic ice shelf. When she uses a search engine, which of the following keywords is likely to yield the **best** results?
   A. ice
   B. global warming
   C. heat wave
   D. Rhode Island
   E. melting Antarctic ice

10. Which is the **best** supporting sentence for the topic sentence below?
    The Gulf Stream current in the Atlantic Ocean warms winters in the northeastern U.S.

    F. In 1513, Ponce de León wrote about the Gulf Stream waters.
    G. Its warm waters raise air temperatures close to the eastern seaboard.
    H. Then it turns and heads toward the coasts of Spain and northwest Africa.
    J. It travels at a speed of four miles per hour.
    K. It flows from south to north and then turns east.

ANSWERS

1. E
2. F
3. D
4. G
5. E
6. G
7. C
8. H
9. E
10. G

Reference Note

For more on preparing for reading and writing tests, see the **Test-taking Mini-Lessons** in each Part 1 chapter and **Studying and Test Taking** on pages 862–875.

Creating a Word-Picture

Use this guide to create an instructional plan that suits the individual needs of your students. Assignments marked by an asterisk (*) may be completed out of class. Times given for pacing lessons are estimated. See pp. 16–17 for chapter-wide resources. Resources listed in this guide are point-of-use resources only.

Curriculum Connections

Choices *p. 49*
- Literature
- Viewing and Representing
- Crossing the Curriculum: World Languages

GO TO: go.hrw.com
KEYWORD: EOLang 9-1

All resources for this chapter are available for preview on the *One-Stop Planner CD-ROM with Test Generator*. All worksheets and tests may be printed from the CD-ROM.

		Chapter Opener pp. 16–17	Reading Workshop: Reading a Description of a Place pp. 18–28
DEVELOPMENTAL PROGRAM		⏱ **20 minutes** • Creating a Word-Picture *p. 17* • Your Turn 1 *p. 17*	⏱ **120 minutes** • Preparing to Read *p. 18* • Reading Selection *pp. 19–20* • First Thoughts 1–3 *p. 21* • Implied Main Idea and Supporting Details *pp. 21–23* • Your Turn 2 *p. 23* • Descriptive Details *pp. 24–26* • Your Turn 3 *p. 26* • Vocabulary Mini-Lesson *p. 27*
CORE PROGRAM		⏱ **15 minutes** • Creating a Word-Picture *p. 17* • Your Turn 1 *p. 17*	⏱ **100 minutes** • Preparing to Read *p. 18* • Reading Selection *pp. 19–20* • First Thoughts 1–3 *p. 21* • Implied Main Idea and Supporting Details *pp. 21–23* • Your Turn 2 *p. 23* • Descriptive Details *pp. 24–26* • Your Turn 3 *p. 26* • Vocabulary Mini-Lesson *p. 27* • Test Taking Mini-Lesson *p. 28*
ADVANCED PROGRAM		⏱ **15 minutes** • Creating a Word-Picture *p. 17* • Your Turn 1 *p. 17*	⏱ **45 minutes** • Preparing to Read *p. 18* • Reading Selection * *pp. 19–20* • First Thoughts 1–3 *p. 21* • Implied Main Idea and Supporting Details *pp. 21–23* • Your Turn 2 *p. 23* • Descriptive Details *pp. 24–26* • Your Turn 3* *p. 26* • Vocabulary Mini-Lesson *p. 27*
RESOURCES	**PRINT**	• *Communications,* TP. 10, WS. p. 6	• *Alternative Readings,* Ch. 1 • *Communications,* TPs. 11, 12, WS. pp. 7–15
	MEDIA	• *One-Stop Planner CD-ROM*	• *One-Stop Planner CD-ROM*

TP.=Transparency WS.=Worksheet

Writing Workshop: **Writing a Description of a Place** *pp. 29–45*	**Focus on Viewing and Representing: Creating a Video Postcard** *pp. 46–48*
🕐 **80 minutes** • Prewriting *pp. 29–35* • Critical-Thinking Mini-Lesson *p. 34* • Your Turn 4 *p. 35* • Framework and Your Turn 5* *p. 36* • Writer's Model and Student's Model *pp. 37–38* 🕐 **120 minutes** • Evaluate and Revise Your Draft *pp. 39–40* • Your Turn 6 *p. 40* • Focus on Word Choice and Your Turn 7 *pp. 41–42* • Proofread, Publish, and Reflect on Your Essay *pp. 43–44* • Grammar Link *p. 43* • Your Turn 8 *p. 44*	🕐 **40 minutes** • Why Make a Video Postcard? *p. 46* • Choosing a Place to Tape *pp. 46–47* • Planning and Taping *p. 47* • Your Turn 10* *p. 48*
🕐 **120 minutes** • Prewriting, *pp. 29–35* • Critical-Thinking Mini-Lesson *p. 34* • Your Turn 4 *p. 35* • Framework and Your Turn 5* *p. 36* • Writer's Model and Student's Model *pp. 37–38* • Evaluate and Revise Your Draft *pp. 39–40* • Your Turn 6 *p. 40* • Focus on Word Choice and Your Turn 7 *pp. 41–42* • Proofread, Publish, and Reflect on Your Essay *pp. 43–44* • Grammar Link *p. 43* • Your Turn 8 *p. 44* • Connections to Life* *p. 45* • Your Turn 9* *p. 45*	🕐 **30 minutes** • Why Make a Video Postcard? *p. 46* • Choosing a Place to Tape *pp. 46–47* • Planning and Taping* *p. 47* • Visual Techniques *p. 48* • Your Turn 10* *p. 48*
🕐 **90 minutes** • Prewriting *pp. 29–35* • Critical-Thinking Mini-Lesson* *p. 34* • Framework and Your Turn 5* *p. 36* • Writer's Model and Student's Model *pp. 37–38* • Evaluate and Revise Your Draft* *pp. 39–40* • Your Turn 6* *p. 40* • Focus on Word Choice and Your Turn 7* *pp. 41–42* • Proofread, Publish, and Reflect on Your Essay *pp. 43–44* • Your Turn 8 *p. 44* • Connections to Life* *p. 45* • Your Turn 9* *p. 45*	🕐 **40 minutes** • Why Make a Video Postcard? *p. 46* • Choosing a Place to Tape *pp. 46–47* • Planning and Taping* *p. 47* • Visual Techniques *p. 48* • Your Turn 10* *p. 48*
• *Communications,* TPs. 13–16 WS. pp. 16–23 • *Designing Your Writing*	• *Media Literacy and Communication Skills* —*Support and Practice*, Ch. 1 —*A How-to Handbook* —*A Teacher's Guide*, Ch. 1
• *One-Stop Planner CD-ROM*	• *Media Literacy and Communication Skills* —Videocassette 1, Segment A • *One-Stop Planner CD-ROM*

1

Creating a Word-Picture

CHAPTER OBJECTIVES

- To read a description of a place and analyze how specific details support the main idea
- To write a description of a place
- To use visual techniques to plan and tape a video postcard

Chapter Overview

This chapter is designed to help students understand the importance of using vivid supporting details when they read, write, observe, create a video, and take tests. In the Reading Workshop students read a news article in which they will identify the implied main idea and the supporting details and then analyze how the details support the main idea. The Writing Workshop provides steps for writing a vivid description of a place. Focus on Viewing and Representing provides steps to create a video postcard. While the sections of this chapter may be taught independently, when taught together they provide students with a well-rounded knowledge of how to use details to create a picture for the reader.

Why Study Description?

Making careful observations and writing descriptive details will help students understand and communicate their thoughts and feelings. Students will see how comparison-contrast can be used in descriptive writing to create background narration for video. Students should understand that whatever their purpose may be for writing description, their writing should help the reader mentally see, hear, touch, taste, and smell what is being described.

Teaching the Chapter

Option 1: Begin with Literature

If your classroom focus is literature, you could introduce this chapter after studying poetry and short stories. Emphasize how the use of vivid description interests the reader and helps the reader to "experience" what is happening. Then, have students read the newspaper article in this chapter to illustrate how strong supporting details can be used in nonfiction to create a mental picture and sensory impressions. Once students understand the importance of supporting details in description, they will be ready to write their own descriptive essay.

Option 2: Begin with Nonfiction and Writing

Use the materials in this chapter to show students the importance of using strong supporting details to create verbal pictures. The article in the Reading Workshop and the accompanying instruction (pp. 18–28) describe how supporting details develop a main idea. As students plan and write their essays in the Writing Workshop (pp. 29–45), guide them in observing their surroundings and in creating their own description of a place. When students return to literature, they will have a more complete understanding of why authors choose to include certain details and how these details strengthen a literature selection. Students will also be prepared to write about an author's choice of details and how it supports the main idea.

Making Connections

■ To the Literature Curriculum

Description provides readers with a sense of time and place as well as with characters and actions. Through detailed description writers can transport their readers to the distant past or to the imagined future. For example, by reading "The Round Walls of Home" by Diane Ackerman, students can consider what they would think and see if they were looking at earth while cruising in outer space. In "The Scarlet Ibis," students can experience a beautiful, peaceful American South through author James Hurst's colorful descriptions. Writers can use vivid, tightly written description to create imagery in poetry, background for a story, and compelling characters who make us want to read more about them.

Lesson Idea: Description in "The Scarlet Ibis" by James Hurst

1. Have students examine the opening paragraphs of the short story, listing the specific details that create a picture.

2. Have them label the details as factual, sensory, or figurative, and discuss how each type of detail helps create a mental picture.

3. Encourage students to consider what types of details reveal Doodle's personality and physical characteristics. Ask them why the author included those details and how they support the main idea (which is centered on the narrator's relationship with his brother and his feelings of guilt). Ask students how the selection of details might change if another family member or an outsider had told the story.

4. Following this discussion, introduce students to the newspaper article in this chapter (pp. 19–20). Point out the use of sensory details that help create the sounds of the city and support the main idea of the article.

■ To Careers

Students will better understand the value of writing well-supported description when they explore a career area that interests them. Have students research a career area of their choice. Encourage them to use print media (newspapers, magazines, books), the Internet, or personal interview to learn about specific career areas. Have students examine the role of strong, accurate description within that career area. The class may then wish to create a wall chart listing each job explored and the importance of strong description in carrying out the required duties of that career. See also **Connections to Life** on p. 45.

■ To the Community

The newspaper article in this chapter shows how a place can be characterized by its sounds. To heighten students' sensitivity to sounds, have students close their eyes and listen in the classroom, at home, or at other places, such as sporting events, concerts, and the library, for sounds that blend into the background and those that stand out. Discuss how these noise differences affect people and their views of that location. This activity helps link the classroom activities to the community outside the classroom. If you are sending the students to a location outside of the school, you will need to obtain permission from parents or guardians before beginning this assignment.

■ To the Social Studies Curriculum

Have interested students check local ordinances to see if your community has any regulations concerning noise pollution. Ask them to present this information to the class in an oral or video presentation. Remind students to use descriptive detail to explain what specific sounds or sound levels are prohibited. They may also investigate why these ordinances were enacted.

Creating a Word-Picture

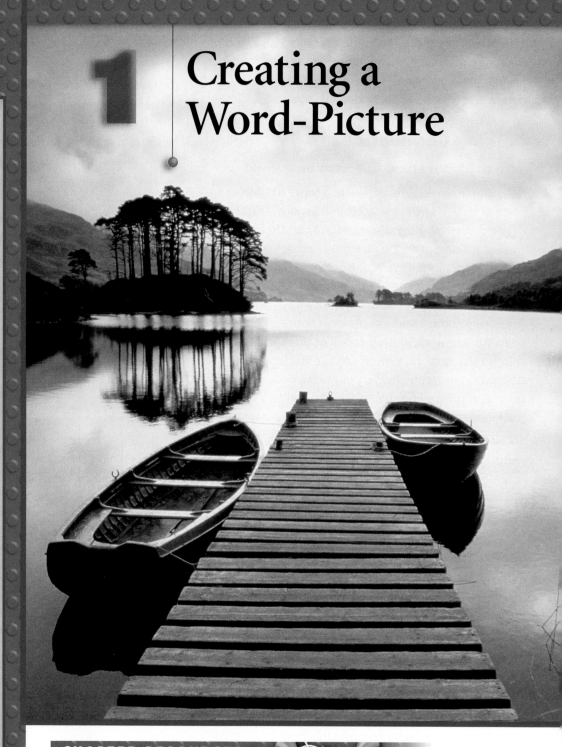

PREVIEWING THE CHAPTER

■ The three workshops in this chapter explore description. Each workshop can be taught separately, but taught together, they help students understand how description and supporting details create a picture for readers, writers, and viewers. Reading a descriptive article filled with strong supporting details prepares students to write effective descriptive essays. After reading and writing descriptive pieces, students should better understand the need for strong images when representing their ideas visually. For help in integrating this chapter with grammar, usage, and mechanics chapters, see the chart on pp. T371A–T371B.

INTRODUCING THE CHAPTER

■ To introduce the chapter, use the Journal Warm-up, Transparency 10, in *Communications*.

VIEWING THE PHOTOGRAPH

■ Ask students how they think the colors in this photograph contribute to its mood. [They create a thoughtful or sad mood.] Finally, challenge students to create a word-picture by brainstorming adjectives that describe the objects or scene in the photo.

Representing. Invite students to find a photograph of a scene that is meaningful to them. Ask them for one word that describes the scene.

CHAPTER RESOURCES

Planning
■ *Lesson Planner, ELL Strategies,* Ch. 1
■ Block Scheduling, p. T15A (this book)
■ *One-Stop Planner CD-ROM*

Practice
■ *Communications,* Ch. 1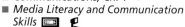
■ *Media Literacy and Communication Skills*

Extension
■ *Designing Your Writing*

Reinforcement
■ *Communications,* Ch. 1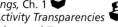
■ *Alternative Readings,* Ch. 1
■ *Daily Language Activity Transparencies*
■ *Vocabulary Workshop* and *Tests*

Reading Workshop

Reading a Description of a Place

Writing Workshop

Writing a Description of a Place

Viewing and Representing

Creating a Video Postcard

Description

- An archaeologist writes about his discovery of the ruins of an ancient city. As he describes what life in the city might have been like, you imagine the city as it once was—filled with people and activity.

- A sportscaster describes a record-breaking home run over the radio. Baseball fans around the world listen and picture the moment.

One reason that descriptions like these are so vivid and powerful is that they come from **direct observations**. You feel as if you are seeing through the eyes of the writers, observing just what they observed.

Of course, vivid descriptions do not have to come only from direct observations. A writer might describe an imaginary world so well that it *seems* genuine to her readers. However, she might base parts of that world on places she has observed. The true power of any vivid written description—whether it is based more on direct observation or more on imagination—is that it makes the thing described become forever real in the mind of a reader.

Informational Text

Narration/Description

YOUR TURN 1 Observing and Describing

When you take time to observe carefully the places you see every day, you will quickly become aware that they are filled with things to describe. Take a careful look around the room you are in now, and then freewrite a short description of something that someone visiting the room for the first time might notice. After you have written your description, share it with a classmate.

internet connect

GO TO: go.hrw.com
KEYWORD: EOLang 9-1

Connecting Reading and Writing **17**

Evaluation and Assessment

- *Test Generator* (One-Stop Planner CD-ROM)
- *Assessment Package*
  — *Chapter Tests,* Ch. 1
  — *Chapter Tests in Standardized Test Formats,* Ch. 1
  — *Assessment Alternatives,* Ch. 1

Internet

- go.hrw.com (keyword: EOLang 9–1)

Preview **17**

Motivate

To help students see how they use descriptive details in their daily lives, divide the class into groups of three or four. Then, write on the chalkboard a sentence that lacks descriptive details (such as "The plane landed.") and have each group provide details to clarify or support the original statement. Point out how the inclusion of descriptive details helps the reader or listener understand better.

ELEMENTS OF *Literature*

Description in Literature.
In *Elements of Literature*, Third Course, see "The Most Dangerous Game," by Richard Connell, pp. 12–28, for examples of descriptions of place that have a strong bearing on a story.

YOUR TURN 1

Here is a sample answer:
The big desk in the room is light wood and is about 30 inches tall. On the top of the desk, metal bookends hold five books upright, including a dictionary and a thesaurus. Across the top lies a large desk pad and a stack of essays.

Reading Workshop

OBJECTIVES

Reading and Writing Connection

- To read a newspaper article in preparation for writing a description of a place

Reading Skills

- To identify an implied main idea and supporting details
- To find and classify descriptive details
- To use context clues to infer the meanings of unfamiliar words in figures of speech

Quotation for the Day

"You can write about *anything,* and if you write well enough, even the reader with no intrinsic interest in the subject will become involved."

(Tracy Kidder, 1945–   , American writer)

Have groups of three or four students discuss Kidder's quotation by restating it in their own words and sharing a time when they have enjoyed reading something outside their usual range of interest. The groups may then share their observations with the class.

TEACHING TIP

Preparing to Read
Implied main idea and *supporting details* are the focuses of the Reading Workshop. **Preparing to Read** introduces the concepts, and **"The Sounds of the City"** is an example of how a main idea is developed using strong supporting details. The rest of the chapter will reinforce students' understanding through analysis of the article.

RESOURCES

Reading Workshop Reinforcement

- *Alternative Readings,* Ch.1

WHAT'S AHEAD?

In this section, you will read an article and learn how to

- **identify an implied main idea and supporting details**
- **find and classify descriptive details**

| READING SKILL |

| READING FOCUS |

Reading a Description of a Place

Try this: the next time you are at a school assembly or other gathering, observe with your eyes closed. Does that seem like a crazy idea? If it does, think about it a little more. Remember that you can observe with more than just your eyes. You can, for example, observe with your ears—using your sense of hearing. In fact, the following article, "The Sounds of the City," is a description based largely on the sense of hearing.

Preparing to Read

Implied Main Idea and Supporting Details In descriptive writing, **main idea** refers to a quality or impression that a writer tries to convey. Sometimes, however, writers do not directly state that quality or feeling. Instead, they build a main idea by carefully selecting details that fit together like the pieces of a mosaic (a picture made of many small, colored pieces). The pieces may be beautiful by themselves, but they join with each other to form an even more beautiful, larger image. As you read "The Sounds of the City," pay careful attention to the writer's details and see if you can figure out the main idea.

Descriptive Details Writers build a main idea in a description through the careful choice of specific details, including

- **sensory details**—details that appeal to the five senses: sight, hearing, smell, taste, and touch
- **figurative details**—details that use **figures of speech** (imaginative comparisons such as **metaphors** and **similes** or examples of **personification**)
- **factual details**—details that involve things like names, dates, and numbers

While reading "The Sounds of the City," see if you can recognize the different types of descriptive details the writer uses.

18   Chapter 1   **Narration/Description:** Creating a Word-Picture

READING PROCESS

PREREADING
Set a Purpose for Reading the Selection.
Explain that **Preparing to Read** sets two purposes for reading **"The Sounds of the City"** on pp. 19–20: to recognize the different types of descriptive details and to see how these descriptive details build a main idea. Remind students that if they read with these purposes in mind, they will quickly detect the writer's details and understand what the main idea is.

Explain to students that they may also set their own purposes for reading. Ask them

The following article offers some interesting observations of city life. As you read this article, write down your responses to the numbered active-reading questions.

from The New York Times

THE SOUNDS OF THE CITY

BY JAMES TUITE

New York is a city of sounds: muted sounds and shrill sounds; shattering sounds and soothing sounds; urgent sounds and aimless sounds. The cliff dwellers of Manhattan—who would be racked by the silence of the lonely woods—do not hear these sounds because they are constant and eternally urban.

The visitor to the city can hear them, though, just as some animals can hear a high-pitched whistle inaudible to humans. To the casual caller to Manhattan, lying restive and sleepless in a hotel twenty or thirty floors above the street, they tell a story as fascinating as life itself. And back of the sounds broods the silence . . .

IMAGINATION TAKES FLIGHT

There are few sounds so exciting in Manhattan as those of fire apparatus dashing through the night. At the outset there is the tentative hint of the first-due company bullying its way through midtown traffic. Now a fire whistle from the opposite direction affirms that trouble is, indeed, afoot. In seconds, other sirens converging from other streets help the skytop listener focus on the scene of excitement.

But he can only hear and not see, and imagination takes flight. Are the flames and smoke gushing from windows not far away? Are victims trapped there, crying out for help? Is it a conflagration, or only a trash-basket fire? Or, perhaps, it is merely a false alarm.

The questions go unanswered and the urgency of the moment dissolves. Now the mind and the ear detect the snarling, arrogant bickering of automobile horns. People in a hurry. Taxicabs blaring, insisting on their checkered priority.

SOUNDS OF THE NEW DAY

Even the taxi horns dwindle down to a precocious few

1. What do you predict the author will describe in the rest of the article?

2. What effect do the words *dashing* and *excitement* create?

3. Which words in this paragraph might be clues to the article's main idea?

TEACHING TIP

Have students buy spiral notebooks to use as learning logs. As they read the Reading Selection, they can write their answers to the active-reading questions in their learning logs.

Active-Reading Questions

The active-reading questions will encourage students to think about the main idea and how the descriptive details support it in the Reading Selection. Student answers will indicate whether they understand the use of descriptive detail to determine the implied main idea of an article.

ANSWERS

1. The author is likely to explain how sounds tell what is going on in New York City.

2. These two words indicate a fast pace and a fascination with a city where something is constantly happening.

3. Possible answers include "urgency," "horns," "hurry," and "blaring."

what purposes they might set for themselves if they were to see this article in the newspaper, based on the title of the selection. Also, ask students how their purposes might affect what they would expect to learn from the article.

4. The jaws of the trucks are compared to predatory animals eating. The gears of the trucks are compared to predatory animals digesting their food.

5. Details in the last three paragraphs that might contribute to the main idea include policemen and doormen making sounds like noisy birds, daytime sounds continuing through the night, and New Yorkers being oblivious to the city sounds because they are so common.

Connecting Reading and Writing

When students are writing descriptions of locations, they can easily start using *you* instead of first or third person. As they read "The Sounds of the City," have them pay particular attention to the author's use of third person. Students should notice his use of synonyms for *the visitor:* "the casual caller," "the mind and the ear," and "beautiful dreamers." They should also notice how these terms avoid the repetition of *the visitor* throughout the article.

in the gray and pink moments of dawn. Suddenly there is another sound, a morning sound that taunts the memory for recognition. The growl of a predatory monster? No, just garbage trucks that have begun a day of scavenging.

Trash cans rattle outside restaurants. Metallic jaws on sanitation trucks gulp and masticate the residue of daily living, then digest it with a satisfied groan of gears.

The sounds of the new day are businesslike. The growl of buses, so scattered and distant at night, becomes a demanding part of the traffic bedlam. An occasional jet or helicopter injects an exclamation point from an unexpected quarter. When the wind is right, the vibrant bellow of an ocean liner can be heard.

The sounds of the day are as jarring as the glare of a sun that outlines the canyons of midtown in drab relief. A pneumatic[1] drill frays countless nerves with its rat-a-tat-tat, for dig they must to perpetuate the city's dizzy motion. After each screech of brakes there is a moment of suspension, of waiting for the thud or crash that never seems to follow.

The whistles of traffic policemen and hotel doormen chirp from all sides, like birds calling for their mates across a frenzied aviary. And all of these sounds are adult sounds, for childish laughter has no place in these canyons.

FAREWELL TO THE DAY

Night falls again, the cycle is complete, but there is no surcease from sound. For the beautiful dreamers, perhaps, the "sounds of the rude world heard in the day, lulled by the moonlight have all passed away,"[2] but this is not so in the city.

Too many New Yorkers accept the sounds about them as bland parts of everyday existence. They seldom stop to listen to the sounds, to think about them, to be appalled or enchanted by them. In the big city, sounds are life.

> **4.** What are two imaginative comparisons about the truck in this paragraph?

> **5.** What details in the last three paragraphs might contribute to the article's main idea?

1. **pneumatic** (noo•mat´ik) air-powered.

2. A line from the song "Beautiful Dreamer" by Stephen Foster (1826–1864)

READING PROCESS

READING

Make Personal Connections. Explain to students that reading makes more sense if it relates to something in their lives. Ask them if they have ever stayed in a place where the sounds kept them awake at night or startled them during the day, or what sounds have changed in their own homes, such as those due to having a new baby in the house or new neighbors next door. Ask a few students to share how these different sounds represent the location.

First Thoughts on Your Reading

The following questions will help you to think about what you have learned by reading "The Sounds of the City." Write your answers on your own paper.

1. How close to the actual contents of the article were your predictions based on the first two paragraphs?

2. Which details in the article do you think are the most memorable? Why do you think so?

3. Based on your first reading of the article, what do you think its main idea might be?

Implied Main Idea and Supporting Details

`READING SKILL`

Piecing It Together The writer of "The Sounds of the City" did not randomly select the details that make up his description. He chose the details very carefully to create the main idea he wanted to convey. A **main idea** is the most important point the writer wants to make. Like many writers of description, though, he never directly states this main idea—he expects his readers to piece it together from the details he provides in his article.

In some types of writing—especially in expository or persuasive writing—it is common for a writer to state the main idea in a **thesis statement** near the beginning. The writer then follows this **explicit** (directly stated) **main idea** with a number of supporting details. If you were to depict this thesis statement/supporting details pattern visually, it would look like the following diagram.

Explicit Main Idea Structure

First Thoughts on Your Reading

ANSWERS
Possible answers are suggested below.

1. The author sets readers up to expect to read about how city sounds are annoying, but readers may be pleasantly surprised that the author ends by hinting that New Yorkers ought to stop to listen to those sounds.

2. Memorable details might include garbage trucks as predatory animals, buses growling and ocean liners bellowing, and the expected crash following the screech of brakes. The details that a student can relate to are likely to be the most memorable.

3. The sounds of the city reflect the fast pace of life there.

Reading Workshop   21

However, there are many pieces of writing—including most narrative and descriptive pieces—that do not follow this pattern. These pieces are said to have an **implied main idea** because they lack a thesis statement. The reader is left to determine the main idea by using the details of the piece to figure out the writer's focus. In a diagram showing the pattern for pieces like these, the main idea/supporting details structure is turned upside down. (The dotted line around the words *Main Idea* indicates that the main idea is implied by the supporting details instead of being directly stated.)

Implied Main Idea Structure

How exactly do you find a main idea when it is implied? The answer is that you need to look at each of the supporting details, because all of the supporting details in a text will often point to a single main idea. For example, look at the following diagram, which summarizes a description of a small country town. Then, read the Thinking It Through steps that follow to see how one student **inferred,** or figured out, the main idea of the description.

Description of a Small Country Town

Finding an Implied Main Idea

To find an implied main idea of a piece of writing, use the following set of steps.

▶ **STEP 1** **Read the whole piece carefully.** Ask yourself what the piece covers. That is its topic.

▶ **STEP 2** **Write a summary of each major section of the piece.** To summarize, condense the information in each section into the smallest number of words that still give a complete picture of the section. For examples, see the three section summaries in the diagram on the previous page.

▶ **STEP 3** **Look at your section summaries, and infer a main idea by writing an "umbrella" sentence that brings them all together.** This sentence will be the implied main idea. You can write this as an equation:

topic + main point = implied main idea.

Life in the town is calm, quiet, and relaxing—especially in contrast to life in the big city.

TIP Sometimes a passage or piece of writing begins with a question. The unwritten answer to that question is often the implied main idea.

YOUR TURN 2 — Identifying an Implied Main Idea

First, look back at "The Sounds of the City" and use a graphic organizer like the one below to summarize the supporting details in each section of the article. Then, based on your summaries, write an umbrella sentence that reflects the main idea the writer is trying to convey. Write the main idea in the oval at the bottom of your graphic organizer.

Section 1 Introduction

Section 2 Imagination Takes Flight

Section 3 Sounds of the New Day

Section 4 Farewell to the Day

YOUR TURN 2

ANSWERS
Here are some possible answers.

1. New York City residents no longer hear the sounds that are a part of life there, but visitors do.

2. At night, people can only imagine excitement from the sirens and whistles coming from emergency fire vehicles.

3. Daytime sounds are the everyday sounds of adults at work.

4. The sounds of the city continue into the night and reflect life.

Umbrella sentence: The sounds of New York City reflect the life of the city and its population.

Reading Workshop   **23**

RESOURCES

Your Turn 2
Practice
■ *Communications,* WS. p. 7
Reinforcement
■ *Communications,* TP. 11, WS. p. 8

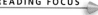

Descriptive Details

Focusing In As you read the first paragraphs of "The Sounds of the City," you probably realized that most of the article's **sensory details** were based on just one sense: the sense of hearing. (For example, look back at the first sentence of the third paragraph: "There are few sounds so exciting in Manhattan as those of fire apparatus dashing through the night.")

The writer planned the article this way, of course. He didn't simply forget about the other four types of sensory details—details based on sight, smell, touch, and taste. He chose to focus on sound details to give his description greater **coherence** and **unity**—a clear connection between details so that the piece as a whole supports one main idea.

Sensory details are just one of three types of descriptive details that you will normally find in descriptive writing. The other two types—**figurative details** and **factual details**—may not be used as heavily, but they can also play a very important part in a well-written description.

Making Comparisons **Figurative details** use **figures of speech** to make imaginative comparisons—"special effects" language not meant to be taken literally. The most commonly used figures of speech in descriptive writing—or in almost any other kind of writing—are *similes, metaphors,* and *personification.*

■ **Similes** are the easiest to spot, because they are comparisons that always use the words *like* or *as.*

   Example:
   The **sounds of the day** are *as* jarring *as* **the glare of a sun** that outlines the canyons of midtown in drab relief.

   As you can see, this simile clearly compares the sounds of the day to the glare of the sun, using the word *as.*

■ **Metaphors** are a little harder to spot because they make imaginative comparisons without using the words *like* or *as.*

   Example:
   The **cliff dwellers of Manhattan**—who would be racked by the silence of the lonely woods—do not hear these sounds because they are constant and eternally urban.

   To recognize that this example is a metaphor, you first have to realize that there are not really any cliffs in Manhattan on which anyone could dwell. Instead, the writer is imaginatively comparing people who live in high-rise hotels and apartment buildings to people who live in cliff dwellings.

Reference Note

For more on **unity** and **coherence,** see pages 355 and 359.

Meeting INDIVIDUAL NEEDS

ADVANCED LEARNERS

Allow students to work with descriptive words and phrases and the meanings they convey. To help with coherence and unity, encourage students to find a focus and select details that reinforce that focus. As practice, ask students to rewrite the following paragraph, adding more specific description, such as accurate and colorful details and feelings toward the subject:

> My school is an interesting place. There are many classes and activities to which students can belong. I have one favorite.

Have students write their responses on the chalkboard and discuss the changes.

LEARNERS HAVING DIFFICULTY

To give students more practice with descriptive details, have them work with partners. One partner gets thirty seconds to give descriptive details about an everyday item, such as an article of clothing or a piece of sports equipment, and the other partner tries to guess what the item is. Then the partners switch roles.

Cooperative Learning

Creative Figures of Speech. Remind students to strive for fresh, original description. To help students avoid clichés, have them work in groups of two or three to brainstorm creative examples of similes, metaphors, and personification. Let each group share their favorites with the rest of the class. If time allows, students could create visuals to accompany their best ideas.

- **Personification,** though not quite as common as similes and metaphors, can also be used to create vivid images. Personification gives human qualities (or sometimes animal qualities) to nonhuman or inanimate things.

Example:
People in a hurry. **Taxicabs** blaring, **insisting** on their checkered priority.

Taxicabs are not really alive, of course. They cannot actually "insist" on anything, as people can. However, it is fun to imagine that the taxicabs' blaring horns are a sign that the cabs, like the hurrying people, are impatient with the city traffic.

Facts and Figures   Good descriptive writing may also include **factual details:** details that describe using names, dates, numbers, and other information that can be tested or checked for accuracy. Factual details are important in creating a precise image that no reader can misunderstand. To describe a certain neighborhood, a writer might provide factual details that tell his readers how many years old the neighborhood is or the number of city blocks the neighborhood covers, or he might list the names of some well-known people who grew up there.

Connecting Details   Did you notice that the simile from "The Sounds of the City" on the previous page—the one about the "glare of a sun," used as an example of a figurative detail—is actually a sensory detail also? As you read more descriptions, you will find that the categories of details often overlap. Some factual details, for example, may also be sensory details. This connection between the three categories of descriptive details can be illustrated by the following diagram. (The numbers in the diagram correspond to the example sentences on the following page.)

The overlapping parts of the diagram represent descriptive details that fit into more than one category.

Sensory Details

1 3
4
Figurative Details   2   Factual Details

TIP   Although "The Sounds of the City" does not contain any factual details, do not let its lack of them lead you to think that they are not used in descriptive writing. Many descriptive writers actually depend quite heavily on factual details.

TEACHING **TIP**

Connecting Details
Have students work with the concept of overlapping details. In randomly selected small groups, have students brainstorm examples of overlapping figurative, factual, and sensory details, and then categorize them. Suggest a location they can describe using a combination of details, such as a shopping mall, a burning building, or a fair. For example:

The red flames licked the sky [figurative] as the fire department poured ten thousand gallons of water on the five-story building. [factual]

1. Sensory/Figurative	The naturalist did not know the bird's name, but he said that its song was "like the sound of an Irish pennywhistle played by a dizzy hyena."
2. Factual/Figurative	The great horned owl (*Bubo virginianus*), which ranges throughout North America, is a common symbol of wisdom—a kind of "philosopher bird."
3. Factual/Sensory	Bobolinks (*Dolichonyx oryzivorus*) like to feed on rice, so rice fields are among the best places to hear the bird's bubbling, exuberant song.
4. Sensory/Factual/ Figurative	Emily Dickinson loved the jarring, whistling song of the orchard oriole (*Icterus spurius*); she once called the oriole "the Meteor of Birds."

ANSWERS

Here are some possible answers.

3. "first-due company bullying its way"—figurative

4. "imagination takes flight"—figurative

5. "snarling, arrogant bickering of automobile horns"—figurative/sensory

6. "growl of predatory monster"—figurative/sensory

7. "trash cans rattle"— sensory

8. "growl of buses"—figurative/sensory

9. "screech of brakes"—sensory

10. "in these canyons"—figurative

11. "beautiful dreamers"—figurative

12. "sounds are life"—figurative

Ask students to answer these questions.

1. What are the three types of supporting details? [sensory, factual, and figurative]

2. When are factual details most important? [when an author is relating objective description that must be understood clearly]

3. State one way to locate an implied main idea. [see what impression the supporting details create]

YOUR TURN 3 Finding and Classifying Descriptive Details

To find and classify the descriptive details in "The Sounds of the City," first create a chart like the one below. Starting with the third paragraph of the article, fill in the chart by copying, from every paragraph, one phrase containing descriptive details. Then, label the type of detail (either *sensory, figurative,* or *sensory and figurative*) the phrase contains. Be careful to look for other figures of speech that relate to the "cliff dwellers" metaphor begun in the first paragraph.

Descriptive Detail Log: "The Sounds of the City"

Paragraph	Example of a Descriptive Detail	Type of Detail
1	"cliff dwellers of Manhattan"	figurative
2	"high-pitched whistle"	sensory
3		
4		
5		
6		
7		

READING PROCESS

EXTENDING

Connect to the World. To help students understand the use of metaphor, simile, and personification as supporting details for an implied main idea, have them look for and record examples of figurative language in advertising. Then, have each student report one example to the class (orally or on paper), and explain how the figurative language supports the advertisement's main idea.

MINI-LESSON VOCABULARY

Figurative Language Context Clues

As you read "The Sounds of the City," you may have found unfamiliar words in a few of the **figures of speech.** You can predict the meanings of some unfamiliar words by looking for **context clues** in the figures of speech. These *figurative language context clues* can often help you infer, or make an educated guess about, the meaning of an unfamiliar word.

THINKING IT THROUGH · Using Figurative Language Context Clues

When you find an unfamiliar word in a figure of speech, try using the steps below to infer the word's meaning. When you can, check your prediction in a dictionary.

Example:
"Metallic jaws on sanitation trucks gulp and *masticate* the residue of daily living, then digest it with a satisfied groan of gears."

▶ **STEP 1** List the words in the figure of speech that seem to be related in meaning.

Jaws, gulp, and *digest* seem to be related.

▶ **STEP 2** Look for a pattern of meaning that connects the related words.

Jaws, gulp, and *digest* all have to do with eating.

▶ **STEP 3** Predict the meaning of the unfamiliar word based on how it might relate to the pattern you found.

Masticate may be similar in meaning to *chew* because *masticate* seems to be done with jaws before digesting.

PRACTICE

Use the steps above to infer the meanings of the following italicized words. Write your answers on your own paper.

1. "The whistles of traffic policemen and hotel doormen chirp from all sides, like birds calling for their mates across a frenzied *aviary*."

2. The *vehement* whine of the fire trucks and police cars wailed through the night like war cries of attacking warriors.

3. Completely covering the streets in an over- whelming blanket of shadows, the *prodigious* buildings rose up from the sidewalks like large beings.

4. The calm of the morning was shattered by the *discordant* noise of empty trashcans angrily banging against one another in the back of a truck.

5. The first rays of the sunrise seemed to signal a rest for the *languid* stars, weary from a night spent lighting the darkness.

MINI-LESSON · VOCABULARY

Figurative Language Context Clues

ANSWERS
Here are some possible answers.

1. *Chirp, birds,* and *mates* seem to be related as they are all words that have to do with birds. *Aviary* must have something to do with where birds live, because birds call their mates from all sides, indicating an enclosure.

2. *Whine, wailed,* and *war cries* seem to be related. These words are all penetrating sounds filled with feeling. *Vehement* may be similar in meaning to "full of emotion."

3. *Overwhelming* and *large* are related—they both have to do with size. *Prodigious* may be similar in meaning to *enormous* because the shadows completely cover the street.

4. *Angrily banging* and *shattered* seem to be related because they have to do with unpleasant sounds. *Discordant* may indicate a disagreeable sound; if trash cans banged so loudly they shattered the calm morning, that would be considered a disagreeable noise.

5. *Rest* and *weary* seem related. The pattern suggests that *languid stars* are weary and need a rest. *Languid* may be related in meaning to "tired."

RESOURCES

Your Turn 3
Practice
■ *Communications,* WS. p. 9
Reinforcement
■ *Communications,* TP. 12, WS. p. 10

Vocabulary
Practice
■ *Communications,* WS. p. 11

Advise students to approach a multiple-choice reading test by reading the questions and possible answers *before* reading the passage. This will activate students' prior knowledge and help focus their reading.

Looking Ahead to Writing

Students will each write a description of a place in the Writing Workshop on pp. 29–45. They will see that descriptive details are vital to support an implied main idea, and will use figurative, sensory, and factual details in their descriptions. Before they begin, you may tell them to review the Implied Main Idea Structure graphic on pg. 22.

MINI-LESSON TEST TAKING

Main Idea and Supporting Details

Reading tests often test your ability to find the main idea of a reading passage and to distinguish it from its supporting details.

Read the example reading passage that follows. Then, using the Thinking It Through steps below, find the best multiple-choice answer to the question that appears after the passage.

> Noise pollution in cities results from a density of noise sources. For example, cities have many trucks, each capable of making ninety decibels of noise from fifty feet away. (One decibel is the smallest amount of sound an average human can hear.) One cross-town train can produce seventy-five decibels from fifty feet, and the outdoor part of one office air conditioner can create sixty decibels from twenty feet. The commonness of such noise sources adds up to a heavy total amount of noise.

1. Which sentence is the best restatement of the main idea of the passage above?

   A. Heavy delivery trucks cause noise pollution in the city.

   B. One decibel is the smallest amount of sound an average human can hear.

   C. Because cities have many noise sources, they also have high levels of noise pollution.

   D. Cities would be much better without trucks, trains, and air conditioners.

THINKING IT THROUGH   Finding a Main Idea and Supporting Details

Use the following steps to find the main idea of a reading passage and to distinguish the main idea from its supporting details.

1. **Don't just choose the first answer that seems good.** It may be correct for only a part of the paragraph. Choice **A** above may look right, but it does not state the main idea of the *whole* paragraph.

2. **Don't choose an answer that states a supporting detail instead of the main idea.** Choice **B**, taken word-for-word from the passage, is a *detail* that supports the main idea—it is *not* the main idea.

3. **Look at the first and last sentences of the passage.** Either might be a topic sentence that **directly states** the main idea. In the example passage, both the first *and* the last sentence seem to state the main idea.

4. **If you cannot find a topic sentence, try summarizing the passage.** Even without the first and last sentence, you could write: *City noise sources such as trucks, trains, and air conditioners make a large amount of noise.* That summary may *seem* like **D** at first, but it actually is much closer to **C**. The passage never suggests that cities would be "better" without noise sources—it simply states that the noise sources exist.

5. **Review the previous steps; then choose an answer.** The answer is **C**.

RESOURCES

Test Taking

Practice

■ *Communications,* WS. pp. 12–14

Writing a Description of a Place

Painters use oils and watercolors to create vivid pictures. Writers use descriptive words—words that make a scene seem to jump right off a page. A novelist, for example, might write a description that conveys the sights, sounds, and sensations of a baseball game where a big event in her novel occurs. A travel writer might write a description that helps you see, hear, and feel the raging surf of the North Shore of Oahu as he experienced it on a visit to the island. Each of these descriptions comes alive through the writer's word-pictures.

In this Writing Workshop, you will write a special kind of description: a description of a place. As you progress through the workshop, keep in mind that your goal is to make the place you describe seem as real to your readers as it does to you.

WHAT'S AHEAD?

In this workshop, you will write a description of a place. You will also learn how to

■ gather, evaluate, and organize details

■ decide on a dominant impression

■ evaluate details for your description

■ eliminate "dead-wood" adjectives

■ select the correct case forms of personal pronouns

OBJECTIVES

■ To write a description of a place

■ To consider purpose, audience, and tone

■ To gather, evaluate, and organize details

■ To convey a dominant impression

■ To evaluate descriptive details

■ To eliminate "deadwood" adjectives

■ To select the correct case forms of personal pronouns

Quotation for the Day

"[The writer] is careful of what he reads, for that is what he will write. He is careful of what he learns, because that is what he will know."

(Annie Dillard, 1945– , American essayist who won the 1975 Pulitzer Prize for her book of essays *Pilgrim at Tinker Creek*)

You may wish to write Dillard's quotation on the chalkboard or on an overhead transparency. Have students discuss why and how writers use other writers' work as models for their own writing. Have them share ideas about the value of using models for their writing assignments. Then, explain that professional and student writing are often used as models for writing assignments in this textbook.

Prewriting

Choose a Place

Snapshots Most great photographers start out by taking snapshots of familiar subjects. As a developing writer, you should start by thinking about everyday subjects that you can describe within a few pages.

■ **Look close to home.** Try sticking to places that you know well. There are probably many wonderful sights to describe right in your own neighborhood—or even right in your own backyard.

■ **See the place with your own eyes.** It is easier to collect details when you observe a place as you write about it. Take a walk with a **learning log** in hand, and jot down notes about interesting sights along the way.

Writing Workshop **29**

KEY CONCEPT

- **Start small.** For example, instead of trying to describe a whole town, or even a single house, focus in on a single important room.

After you have made a list of a few places you could describe well, choose one place from the list that seems to stand out from the rest—the one you feel will be most interesting for you to write about and for others to read about.

Consider Your Purpose, Audience, and Tone

Facts or Feelings?   In this workshop, you will be writing a subjective description. This means that **your purpose** (your reason for writing) **will be not only to describe a place, but also to share your thoughts and feelings about it with your audience.** (Sources that commonly contain subjective descriptions include journal entries, autobiographies, and personal letters.) Subjective descriptions are usually written from a *first-person point of view*, using such pronouns as *I, me, we,* and *us*.

When you are preparing any kind of description, you should always choose an **audience** *before* you write and keep that audience in mind at all times as you write. Once you have selected an audience, it should drive your choice of descriptive details. For example, if your intended audience is already familiar with the place you will be describing, you do not need to include the same kind of descriptive details that you would for an audience unfamiliar with the place.

Your purpose, occasion, and audience all help to determine your **tone**—the attitude with which you address your readers. If you are writing a subjective description for an audience that will expect more than just the facts, your tone should be friendly, informal, and conversational. Your **voice**—the unique style with which you express your ideas in writing—should also come through clearly in a subjective description.

> **TIP** A concept similar to purpose is **occasion,** which is the motivating force behind your writing.

> **TIP** If you write for an audience that wants you to stick to the facts, you should use **objective** description only. (Sources that contain objective descriptions include textbooks, science reports, and encyclopedia articles.)
>
> Purely objective descriptions, which never include writers' personal feelings about the things they are describing, have very definite characteristics.
>
> - They are usually written from a *third-person point of view*, using such pronouns as *he, she,* and *they*.
> - Their tone is neutral, businesslike, and somewhat formal.
> - They emphasize the subject rather than the writer.

T E A C H I N G (TIP)

Consider Your Purpose, Audience, and Tone

To give students a clearer understanding of tone, ask them to re-read the opening paragraph of **"The Sounds of the City,"** paying close attention to the author's tone. Which words or phrases help students identify Tuite's tone? ["[C]liff dwellers" suggests a lighthearted tone, for example.] Invite students to change a key word or phrase that affects the tone. [Replacing "cliff dwellers" with "residents" makes the tone less colorful, more serious.]

Think about Details

A Palette of Colors   While creating a picture, painters work from a set of colors called a *palette*. As a descriptive writer, you also have a palette available—a palette that includes *sensory details*, *factual details*, and *figurative details*.

- **Sensory details** are words and phrases that appeal to the five senses—sight, hearing, touch, smell, and taste. In your writing, you should try to include details from all the senses—not just sight details.

- **Factual details** are things like names, dates, numbers, and quotations, as well as true statements. For example, in a description of a public park, a writer might say: "About a dozen seniors meet every morning to exercise near the fountain." That statement combines a number and a fact the writer has learned. Factual details are very important to objective descriptions, but they can also serve a purpose in a subjective description.

- **Figurative details** include similes, metaphors, or examples of personification. They lose their effectiveness if they are overused. Think of them as spice to be sprinkled lightly on your description.

PEANUTS reprinted by permission of United Feature Syndicate, Inc.

Gather Details

Raw Material   Where can you find details for your description? The raw material is all around you—just observe, recall, and research.

- **Observe the place directly.** Go to the place you plan to describe, and spend at least five minutes observing. Then, take notes in a learning log. Use all of your senses. Consider how the place makes you feel.

- **Recall details.** To describe a place from memory, first shut your eyes and concentrate. Create a complete mental picture—try to recall sounds, smells, tastes, and sensations along with images.

Writing Workshop   **31**

ADVANCED LEARNERS

To show students how description is used for many purposes, have them create advertisements for their favorite cars. The ads should include factual and sensory details. For example, students might want to describe the cars' gas-mileage records and how comfortable and fashionable the cars are. Artwork is optional.

INCLUSION

You may need to clarify the terms *observe, recall,* and *research.* Create three columns on the chalkboard and ask students to work with a helper to suggest examples of each word. For example: *observe* [combing one's hair in front of the mirror, window shopping in the mall], *recall* [taking a test, trying to remember someone's name], *research* [reading a bus schedule to decide which bus to take, looking up a number in the telephone book]

Cooperative Learning

Word Bank. Assign students to work together in randomly selected groups of four to develop word banks containing sensory details. Each member of the group will give at least three details for each sense—for example, *taste: tangy, sharp, bitter.* For variety, students should not duplicate words within a group.

TIP To make your description seem real to your readers, you need to give them the same sensory information they would notice if they were at this place.

■ **Do research.** You can even describe a place where you have never been. By reading about the place or by doing interviews with people who have been there, you can collect secondhand details.

As you observe, recall, and research, your goal should be to collect details that answer questions like the following ones.

■ What **sensory details** will make it real to a reader?

■ If I include **factual details**, what kinds should I use?

■ Which **figures of speech** will spice up a description of the place?

■ What are the place's **unique features?**

■ What **thoughts and feelings** does the place bring to mind?

A writer planning to write a description of her family kitchen used her answers to the questions above to create the following chart. Notice the writer's use of first-person pronouns in her list of details.

	Descriptive Detail Log
Sensory details	• Unique feature: butcher-block table, its edges worn smooth, at the center of the room • filled with the sounds of talking and laughter • taste of fresh, warm bread • heat from the oven radiating out into the room
Factual details	• There are 5 of us living in the house—my mother, father, grandmother, brother, and me. • We have lived in the house for 10 years.
Figurative details	• Our kitchen is the heart of the house. • Thought/feeling: It warms me like a big blanket on a cold morning.

You can gather information about the place you have chosen to describe by making a chart like the one above and then filling it with descriptive details. Whenever possible, use details that *show* rather than *tell.* For example, you could tell your readers that a favorite quilt is old, or you could show its age by describing its mended tears, its frayed edges, its shiny smoothness from repeated washings, and its smell of cedar from years of storage. You will use the list of details in your chart to decide on the dominant impression to convey in your description.

State Your Dominant Impression

Centerpiece   Instead of directly stating their most important point, or **main idea,** in a thesis statement, writers of description often choose details that convey an **implied main idea** to the reader. **In descriptive writing, this implied main idea is known as a dominant impression**—a kind of center-piece or central observation to which all of the descriptive details point. Just like a thesis statement, the dominant impression keeps the writer on track. (The word *dominant* means "controlling" or "ruling.") See the dia-gram below for a visual representation of the relationship between the details and the dominant impression.

Reference Note
For more on **implied main idea,** see page 356.

KEY CONCEPT

TECHNOLOGY **TIP**

You might want to suggest that students input their details on a word processor before they state their dominant impression. Most word-processing software has a fairly simple cut-and-paste procedure. Show students how to move phrases and fragments, using cut-and-paste, from place to place within a document, or from one document to another. Explain to students that they already have typed a major portion of their final work. Have them discuss how they think inputting their "notes" will make the writing process easier.

To decide on a dominant impression to convey in your description, follow the steps below. The student responses are based on the notes on page 32.

THINKING IT THROUGH

Deciding on a Dominant Impression

▶ **STEP 1** **Look at each of the details** you have collected, and ask yourself, "How is this detail related to other details on my list?"

▶ **STEP 2** **Use your answers to the questions in STEP 1 to identify at least one descriptive thread** that runs through your list of details. I included *several related details that all have to do with warmth: warm bread, heat from the oven, a big blanket on a cold morning.*

▶ **STEP 3** **Write down a sentence that clearly states a dominant impression** in terms of one or more of the descriptive threads you have identified. *If I had to describe what the kitchen means to me in one word, it would be the word* <u>warmth</u>*.*

MINI-LESSON CRITICAL THINKING

Evaluating Details

ANSWERS

Here are some sample answers.

1. a comfortable place where I can have fun with my friends [important because it sets the reason for writing]

4. located halfway between my school and my family's apartment [indicates easy access so the writer can use it often]

5. two out of the six goals are missing nets, but no one minds too much—it's still fun [shows that although the court is not perfect, the writer still enjoys it]

8. always alive with shouts: "I'm open—pass the ball!...Good game.... Look out!" [this shows what a good time the players are having]

10. the court is well known in our city because an NBA player played pickup games here when he was in high school [gives a wider focus to the location and shows that good players have used it]

MINI-LESSON CRITICAL THINKING

Evaluating Details

Now that you have a list of details, you need to look at the list carefully, and then (with your **dominant impression** in mind) choose only the details you really want to include. To be able to choose the correct details, you need to practice the skill of **evaluating details**—judging which details will be most important to include in your description and which ones you can do without. Below are some standards, or criteria, that you can use to make your choices.

Evaluating Details for a Description of a Place	
Criteria	Example Sentence with Details
Are details included that will create a clear image of the place in the mind of a reader?	The house looked like a fortress, with wrought-iron grillwork on the windows.
Are details included that describe the location and size of the place?	My neighborhood is on the south side and covers four square blocks.
Are details included to show ways in which the place is unusual?	The huge oak tree in my front yard is more than two hundred years old.

PRACTICE

Below is a list of details a writer made about his neighborhood basketball court. Using the criteria above, evaluate the details and cut the list down to a short list of the five most important details. (Remember that the details as a whole should support a **dominant impression**.) After you have made your short list, get together with two or three classmates and compare your results. You may not all agree on which details to include, so be prepared to explain your choices.

1. a comfortable place where I can have fun with my friends

2. sometimes gets repainted

3. maintained by the parks department

4. located halfway between my school and my family's apartment

5. two out of the six goals are missing nets, but no one minds too much—it's still fun

6. doesn't have a fence around it

7. asphalt is so hot in the summer that you could probably fry an egg on it

8. always alive with shouts: "I'm open—pass the ball! . . . Good game . . . . Look out!"

9. some people don't like to play basketball

10. the court is well-known in our city because an NBA player played pickup games here when he was in high school

11. sometimes used for volleyball

Organize Your Details

Space or Importance?   Arrange your details in an order that makes sense to your audience—an order that supports the dominant impression you plan to convey and shows a **logical progression** of your ideas. For a description of a place, there are two common ways to arrange details.

- **Spatial order** (ordering details according to how they are arranged in space) is used mostly with sight details. One way to use spatial order is to begin by describing how a place looks from a distance, and then to zoom in to describe how it looks up close. You can plan a spatial ordering of your details by first drawing a map of the place you want to describe. Then, draw arrows at the places on the map where you plan to start and end your description.

- **Order of importance** works best when you have some details that are clearly more important than others. To arrange details by order of importance, you can start with your least important details first and then build up to your most important details. The opposite order (from most- to least-important) is sometimes used also. The "family kitchen" writer chose to use order of importance for her description, so she created the following chart to show her arrangement.

Least Important Details	Body Paragraph 1: How the kitchen looks
More Important Details	Body Paragraph 2: How the kitchen looks to our family
Most Important Details	Body Paragraph 3: Why the kitchen is important to me

YOUR TURN 4   Planning Your Description

Before you begin writing your description, make sure that you have completed all of these prewriting steps:

- choose a place to describe
- consider your purpose, audience, and tone
- gather details, including details about your thoughts and feelings
- state the dominant impression you plan to convey
- arrange your details using either spatial order or order of importance

TEACHING TIP

Organize Your Details
If students draw a map of their location to plan a spatial ordering of their details, encourage them to revisit the location mentally. They should see if they can recall any sights, sounds, odors, or tactile experiences (the temperature, a breeze). This activity may help bring their descriptions to life or remind them of how they felt at that location.

Timesaver

Have students write down in a list their plan for **Your Turn 4**. This action will not only give you a way to quickly check that they have all the steps, but will also give students a brief guide to use when writing and revising.

YOUR TURN 4

Briefly check each student's work to make certain that all the steps are completed before he or she begins the drafting stage.

RESOURCES

Critical Thinking
Practice
- *Communications*, WS. p. 15

Your Turn 4
Practice
- *Communications*, WS. p. 16

"A professional writer is an amateur who didn't quit."

(Richard Bach, American writer of the novel *Jonathan Livingston Seagull*)

Ask students to discuss how this quotation might apply to their essays as they begin to draft them. Explain that professional writers often need to keep working even when they have trouble capturing an idea. This knowledge will help students understand that persistence is a vital part of good writing.

TEACHING TIP

Pile on the Details

Because the concept of "showing" versus "telling" is often difficult for students to understand, you might use the statement "It is a nice day" to show that "nice day" means different things to different readers. However, writing "The blue sky was dotted with puffy clouds and the temperature rose to seventy-five degrees" shows exactly what the writer means.

YOUR TURN 5

Check to see that students are following the framework, making sure they are using enough descriptive details to support the main idea. If details are lacking, ask the following questions to help them think of more details:

- How did you engage the reader in the introduction?

- Which details are most effective in helping the reader sense what you are describing?

Writing

Description of a Place

Framework

Directions and Explanations

Introduction
- Clearly identify the place you are describing.
- Include a statement that hints at a dominant impression.

Prepare Your Readers   Avoid opening with a dull introductory statement like "The place I will describe is . . ." Instead, get readers interested in learning more about the place by opening with a catchy sentence.

Present a Dominant Impression   Focusing on a dominant impression keeps your paper from being just a random collection of details. Help your readers get the picture by providing a statement that sets them up for the details that will follow.

Body
- Use a variety of details (sensory, factual, and figurative).
- Include thoughts and feelings.
- Use either spatial order or order of importance.

Pile on the Details   Use a mix of sensory details, not just sight details. Also, remember *show,* don't tell. Instead of just saying that a room is old and run-down, show the room by describing its squeaky floorboards and the cobwebs in its corners.

Reflect   Because this is a subjective description, you also need to reflect on your place by sharing your thoughts and feelings about it with your readers.

Move Your Readers Along   Guide your readers through the place you are describing. Provide your details in a clear spatial order or present them in a logically arranged order of importance.

Conclusion
- End with a statement that wraps up your description.

Close with a Flourish   Restating your dominant impression is a good way to sum up your thoughts about the place you have described.

YOUR TURN 5 Writing a First Draft

Read through the annotated Writer's Model on the next page to see how one writer used the framework to create a description of a place. Then, write the first draft of your paper, using the framework as a guide.

RESOURCES

Writing
Writing Prompts
- *Communications,* TP. 13, WS p. 17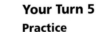

Your Turn 5
Practice
- *Communications,* TP. 14, WS p. 18

A Writer's Model

The following description of a place closely follows the framework on the previous page.

The Kitchen

Good food, sharing, and laughter are three things that come to mind right away when I think of my family's kitchen. It may seem strange to think of the kitchen as a special place, but for my family it is. We say goodbye there before school, and we say hello there when we get home. It is a place for food, of course, but it's also a place for sharing and for laughing. If I had to describe what the kitchen means to me in one word, it would be the word warmth.

A visitor seeing the kitchen for the first time might wonder why I chose that word. The kitchen looks quite ordinary, with the usual assortment of fixtures and appliances. It has wood-grain cabinets, a two-sided stainless-steel sink, a refrigerator/family bulletin board, and an old but sturdy stove. At the center of the room sits a butcher-block table, scuffed from years of use. That's where our family eats most meals. In short, almost any visitor would probably say it seemed like a plain, ordinary kitchen.

However, the five of us in my family see that room in a different way. We have lived in the house for ten years, and for us, the kitchen is a place that holds ten years of special sounds, smells, and memories. We enjoy the sound of my grandmother humming songs from her childhood as she cooks, and the smell of the fresh bread she bakes each week. We often sit in the kitchen talking while we wait for the bread to be ready. If it is cold outside, we might pull up our chairs around the stove, basking in its friendly heat as we talk.

Most importantly, though, our kitchen is the heart of our home. It may not seem like a special place to someone else, but when I am lonely or tired, it warms me—like a big blanket on a winter morning. It is just as important to everyone in my family. It is our place to come together and share our lives.

Most people probably would not think of a kitchen as an extraordinary place. However, for me and my family, our kitchen will always be a warm, wonderful place.

TIP Note that because a subjective description is less formal, the use of contractions is acceptable.

INTRODUCTION
Attention-getting statement

Hint of a dominant impression

BODY

Sensory details—sight

Factual detail

Sensory details—sound, smell, and touch

Word signaling order of importance

Figurative detail

Thoughts and feelings
CONCLUSION

Restatement of dominant impression

Timesaver

As they prepare their own descriptive essays, refer students to **A Writer's Model.** Have students note in the margins of their drafts the elements of description (attention-getting statement, hint of a dominant impression, and types of descriptive details) like those noted alongside the model. The notations allow you to scan drafts to make sure that students have included appropriate details and that they recognize the concepts the chapter has introduced.

Connecting Reading and Writing

Tell students that it will help them in their own writing if they pay attention to descriptive language as they read **A Student's Model.** Divide the chalkboard into three columns. Label the first column "Sensory Details," the second "Factual Details," and the third "Figurative Details." Then, read the model to the class and ask volunteers to write examples from the narrative of each element of description in the appropriate column. Direct students to the chart on p. 26 of the Reading Workshop if they need help identifying descriptive elements.

A Student's Model

Shanessa McClain, a student at Hobbs High School in Hobbs, New Mexico, wrote the following excerpt. It is a description of the beach activity at South Padre Island.

South Padre Island

Attention-getting statement

The sound of the waves crashing against the shore, the sight of the sea gulls swooping overhead, and the smell of sunscreen create an engaging place called South Padre Island. Located where one can relax and experience good times on the beach, South Padre Island offers an island-getaway adventure not soon to be forgotten. The sun, sand, and endless ocean make South Padre unlike any other place I have ever been. When I am on the beach at South Padre Island, I know I am in paradise.

Hint of a dominant impression

Figurative detail—personification

Sensory detail—touch

Perhaps the simplest delight of South Padre is the beach itself. This sparkling retreat embraces unbounded miles of sand. During the day the warmth of the sun beats down upon this sand, making beach goers spring as their feet hit the blistering sand. However, closer to the Gulf of Mexico, where the water moistens and cools the beach, children giggle as their sand castles are overtaken by a massive wave. Towels are no stranger to this sand. Sun worshippers spend hours lying upon them in an attempt to soak up even more blistering rays. The sand provides a soft cover as a teenager dives after the ball in the annual summer volleyball tournament, and it cushions two old men who swap stories as they wait for the hungry game fish that swim the waters of Padre Island. Looking across the beach, I see a rainbow of umbrellas and seashells of exquisite design and enchanting colors: a vision of paradise.

Sensory detail—sight

Thoughts and feelings

Sensory details

Another attraction of South Padre is the Gulf. The rushing waves both calm and provide amusement for many tourists. I could never truly understand complete tranquillity until I stood on the shoreline of Padre Island at night. The feel of the breeze, the smell of the saltwater, and the sight of the boat lights in the distance soothed my senses in a way that nothing else could. . . .

Revising

Evaluate and Revise Your Draft

Two Passes   When you revise your writing, always make at least two reading passes: one for content and organization, and one for style. At each pass, **self-evaluate** your writing and consider **collaborating** or having a **writing conference** with a classmate.

➤ First Reading: **Content and Organization**   Start your evaluation by answering (or having a peer answer) the questions in the left-hand column below. For help with the questions, see the tips in the middle column. To revise, make the changes in the right-hand column.

Description of a Place: Content and Organization Guidelines for Peer and Self-Evaluation

Evaluation Questions	▶ Tips	▶ Revision Techniques
❶ Does the introduction include a statement that hints at a dominant impression?	▶ **Underline** the sentence in the introduction that seems to sum up the details in the paper. If you cannot find a sentence to underline, revise.	▶ **Add** a sentence that hints at the dominant impression conveyed in the paper.
❷ Does the description include a variety of details (sensory, factual, and figurative)?	▶ **Put an S** above sensory words, an **N** above numbers, names, and dates, and an **F** above sentences that make imaginative comparisons—especially those that contain the words *like* or *as*. Revise if you do not see plenty of **S**'s with scattered **N**'s and **F**'s.	▶ **Add** sensory details that appeal to several senses. **Add** significant dates, names, or numbers. **Add** figures of speech that support the dominant impression. **Replace** less-descriptive language with specific descriptive details.
❸ Does the description include details about the writer's thoughts and feelings?	▶ **Put an asterisk** next to every first-person pronoun (*I, me, we, us,* etc.). If you do not see at least one asterisk per paragraph, revise.	▶ **Elaborate** by including first-person thoughts or feelings about the sensory, factual, and figurative details in the paper.
❹ Is the paper clearly organized using either spatial order or order of importance?	▶ **Number** the details. Then, draw a simple map of the place described and place the numbers on it. Revise if you cannot see a clear pattern to the numbers.	▶ **Rearrange** details so that they fall into either a clear spatial order (far to near, top to bottom, and so on) or a clear order of importance (most to least or least to most).
❺ Does the conclusion include a statement that wraps up your description?	▶ **Bracket** the sentence that sums up your thoughts. If you cannot find a sentence to bracket, revise.	▶ **Add** a sentence that summarizes your description or that restates your dominant impression.

RESOURCES

Revising
Practice
■ *Communications*, TPS. 15, 16, WS pp. 19, 20, 21

Quotation for the Day

"The difference between the right word and the almost right word is the difference between lightning and the lightning bug."

(Mark Twain, 1835–1910, American writer and humorist)

Invite students to interpret or respond to Twain's comment in a short freewriting session. Ask them if they can recall a time when they found a word with the meaning they intended but with a connotation that was wrong for their use. Using the responses, stress the importance of selecting the most suitable word for the meaning intended.

TEACHING TIP

▶ **Elaboration**

Students can use an analogy strategy to add details to their essays. Have them look for appropriate places in their papers to draw a comparison to whatever it is they are describing. For example, if their essay describes a favorite hiking trail, they might include a sentence such as:

When I hike along the trail behind my house, I feel like an eagle soaring above the treetops. I become carefree and my problems seem to shrink and drift away.

Analyzing the Revision Process

ANSWERS

1. This metaphor adds emotion and makes the description more personal.

2. The writer adds subjective/figurative details.

   The phrase "when I am lonely and tired" explains why the place is so special. The simile provides a tactile and emotional description of her home.

YOUR TURN 6

Before students actually make the revisions they plan, you might have them show you their underlined statements hinting at the dominant impression, the details marked by type, the asterisked first-person pronouns, and the numbered details to make certain they have a solid list of suggestions for revisions.

Critical Thinking

Synthesis. After students have analyzed the two sentences in **One Writer's Revisions,** pair students and have them revise the sentences in a different way. This activity will reinforce that there are many ways to revise and improve writing. Ask them to share their editing and revising ideas with the class.

Here is a possible alternate revision.

Most importantly, our kitchen comforts me like a heartfelt hug. It may not seem like a special place to someone else, but to me, it is the soul of our house.

ONE WRITER'S REVISIONS   Here is how one writer used the content and organization guidelines to revise part of the description on page 37. Study the revisions, and then answer the questions that follow.

replace

add

replace

> Most importantly, though, our kitchen is ~~central to our lives.~~ *the heart of our home*
>
> It may not seem like a special place to someone else, but ~~it really~~ *when I am lonely or tired,* ~~is to me.~~ *warms me*—like a big blanket on a winter morning.

Analyzing the Revision Process

1. How does the writer's revision of the first sentence improve the paragraph?

2. What kinds of details does the writer add to the second sentence? Why do you think she added them?

YOUR TURN 6 Revising Content and Organization

Study the revisions shown above. Then, use the guidelines in the chart on the previous page to revise your paper's content and organization.

▶ **Second Reading: Style**   On your second pass through your paper, your goal is to improve your style. You have probably used a number of good descriptive adjectives—but have you also used unnecessarily repetitive adjectives like the ones in boldface type in the sentence below?

Example:
The **different, varied** colors of the grasses caught my eye.

Different and *varied* have almost the same meaning. Using both words adds length without adding any new ideas. The guidelines that follow will help you to get rid of these kinds of adjectives in your writing.

Style Guidelines

Evaluation Question	▶ Tip	▶ Revision Technique
Do some sentences contain unnecessarily repetitive adjectives?	▶ **Circle** all pairs of adjectives (adjectives joined by a comma or by *and* or *but*). Revise any circled pair having almost the same meaning.	▶ **Cut** one of the adjectives from a pair, or **replace** one with a contrasting adjective and change the connecting word *and* to *but*.

PEER REVIEW

Ask a classmate to read your paper and answer the following questions.

1. Which details in the paper did you like best? Why?

2. What do you think this paper reveals about the writer who created it?

40   Chapter 1   Narration/Description: Creating a Word-Picture

Deadwood Adjectives

Adjectives often work well in teams. In fact, carefully used pairs of adjectives can leave a powerful impression on readers. However, using two or more adjectives that pointlessly repeat the same meaning just adds useless deadwood to your writing. Like dead limbs on a tree, these words weigh your writing down and sap it of its strength. It is your job to cut out deadwood adjectives so that your writing stays strong. If you are unsure how similar your paired adjectives are, check their meanings in a dictionary or in a thesaurus.

Focus on Word Choice

ONE WRITER'S REVISIONS   Here is another example of some revisions made by the writer of the description on page 37. This time, the writer used the style guidelines on the previous page to evaluate and revise her paper.

> **BEFORE**
>
> It has wood-grain cabinets, a two-sided stainless-steel sink, a
>
> refrigerator/family bulletin board, and an ⟨old, ancient⟩ stove.
>
> At the center of the room sits a butcher-block table, ⟨scraped⟩
>
> ⟨and scuffed⟩ from years of use.

The circled words are pairs of adjectives having almost the same meaning.

> **AFTER**
>
> It has wood-grain cabinets, a two-sided stainless-steel sink, a refrigerator/family bulletin board, and an old but sturdy stove. At the center of the room sits a butcher-block table, scuffed from years of use.

changed to contrasting adjective

deleted repetitive adjective

Analyzing the Revision Process

1. What change in meaning does the writer achieve by replacing the word *ancient* with *sturdy*?
2. If you wanted to describe the table using an adjective that contrasts with the word *scuffed*, what adjective would you add?

Analyzing the Revision Process
ANSWERS

1. The words *old* and *ancient* are synonyms, so having both is redundant. The word *sturdy* shows a more precise and varied detail.

2. Possible answers include *spotless, smooth,* or *polished.*

YOUR TURN 7 Focusing on Style

After studying the revisions on the previous page, revise the style of your paper using the directions in the Style Guidelines chart.

COMPUTER TIP

These are just a few of many considerations to keep in mind when you create Web pages. For more tips, do a search in a Web directory using the keywords *Web style* or *Web page creation.*

Designing Your Writing

Creating Usable Web Pages   At some point, you may want to publish on the World Wide Web your description of a place. When you create a Web page, let the following tips guide some of the choices you make. All of these tips have to do with the concept of *usability*—the idea of designing something (in this case, a Web page) so that it works in the best possible way for the people (your readers) who will actually use it.

- **Loading time.** If your page uses graphics (including background images or scanned photographs), consider how long the graphics will take to load before readers can see them. If your graphics load too slowly, you run the risk of frustrating and annoying your readers.

- **Flipping pages *vs.* scrolling.** Printed documents have real pages that you can turn. Web pages have no page breaks. You read them by scrolling through them, in much the same way that readers did in ancient times with real scrolls. Design your pages in a way that will make scrolling through them easier for your readers. For example, avoid cluttered pages, summarize periodically, and use short blocks of text whenever possible.

- **Tall or wide.** Printed pages are usually taller than they are wide (think of an 8-1/2- x 11-inch page of typing paper). However, readers usually look at Web pages on computer monitors that are wider than they are tall (like an 8-1/2- x 11-inch page turned on its side). Therefore, it makes sense to design Web pages from side to side, rather than from top to bottom. This means that wide images usually work better in Web pages than tall images do.

- **Organization.** Put your most important information, such as the title and your main idea, near the top of the Web page so your readers know what to expect. Organize your information for quick scanning by using headlines that summarize and by using numbered or bulleted lists. Create a standard footer for the bottom of each page with such information as the date of the last update, an e-mail address for feedback, and links to other pages.

- **Free of errors.** You do not want your readers to be distracted by misspelled words or grammatical errors. Therefore, proofread carefully and make any necessary corrections.

Publishing

Proofread Your Essay

A Case for Correctness Your paper should be as error free as you can make it before you prepare a final copy. Check it thoroughly for grammar, usage, and mechanics errors, and fix them as you find them. Because it is common to have first-person pronouns in a subjective description, you will want to be especially careful to check that you have used correct pronoun forms throughout your paper.

Reference Note

For more on **proofreading guidelines,** see page 13.

Grammar Link

The Case Forms of Personal Pronouns

Case is the form that a noun or pronoun takes to show its relationship to other words in a sentence.

- The subject of a verb should be in the nominative case. (*I, he, she, we, they*)

Example:
She wanted to describe a treehouse.

- The direct object of a verb should be in the objective case. (*me, him, her, us, them*)

Example:
Mr. Lopez asked **me** to revise this essay.

- When a sentence uses pronouns in a compound subject or a compound direct object, *all* the parts of the compound must still be in the correct case. For example, it would never be correct to write or say "she and me" or "her and I." To help you know whether the pronoun is correct, try each pronoun separately.

Example:
The **boys and** (*they, them*) helped **him and** (*I, me*) with the pamphlet. [*They helped* or *them helped*? *They* is correct. *The boys and they helped I* or *helped me*? *The boys and they helped me* is correct.]

The boys and **they** helped him and **me** with the pamphlet.

PRACTICE

Revise each incorrect pronoun in the sentences below. If a sentence is already correct, write *C.* Write your answers on your own paper.

Example:
1. Alberto and me made notes about our observations.

1. Alberto and I made notes about our observations.

1. This guidebook from our teacher, Mr. Halas, really helped Steve and I.

2. Marika found us later that same afternoon.

3. Rose and her discovered that this place is difficult to describe.

4. Our teacher took them to a library to get a few reference books.

5. The first group called Marika and they to help load the cameras.

For more information and practice on **pronoun case,** see page 549.

Publish Your Essay

Rewards   You have worked hard to write and polish your description of a place. Now, you can reap the rewards of your hard work by sharing your description with readers. Try one or more of these publishing ideas.

- If your description is of a place in your community, send a copy of the description to your local newspaper. Local newspapers often set aside space for community-related writing from their readers.

- Self-publish your description as a Web page. Scan photographs of the place you described, and include them on the page. If your paper includes descriptions of sounds, record some of the sounds and create hyperlinks to sound files of the recordings. (Look back at the Designing Your Writing section on page 42 for more tips on turning your description of a place into a Web page.)

- If any of your classmates have written descriptions that are related in some way to your description, bind all of your descriptions together as a booklet, give the booklet a title that summarizes the connection between the descriptions, and distribute copies of the booklet.

 PORTFOLIO

Reflect on Your Essay

Decisions   Look back at some of the decisions you made while writing this paper. You will see that in this workshop, you have practiced skills you can carry over into other writing assignments. To reflect on some of your decisions, write responses to the following questions.

- What process did you go through to decide on a place to describe? How well did the process work?

- From revising your description, what insights did you gain into your personal writing style?

    Make sure to attach your responses to your description of a place. Then, decide whether you want to include the paper in your portfolio.

YOUR TURN 8   Proofreading, Publishing, and Reflecting

Make sure that you have completed all of the steps on this page and on the previous page. Remember to

- proofread your work thoroughly before you prepare a final copy and publish it

- reflect on the decisions you made while writing your paper, and think about the skills you have practiced

---

Quotation for the Day

"If you do not write for publication there is little point in writing at all."

(Bernard Shaw, 1856–1950, playwright, critic, and social reformer)

Write the quotation on the chalkboard and ask students in small groups to discuss ways in the past that they have published their writing. Ask them also to talk about which methods of publishing worked best for them.

YOUR TURN 8

As students proofread, remind them to check for omitted words and for typographical errors. While they reflect on their decisions and skills, you might ask them how these decisions and skills can be used in other writing.

Wrap It Up

Metacognition. Ask students to reflect on their choice of details and allow them ten minutes to respond to the following questions.

1. What type of details, factual, sensory, or figurative, worked best in your essay?

2. What part of the writing process was most difficult for you? Why?

Connections to Life

Field Notes

You just wrote a *subjective* description of a place. Now is your chance to try an *objective* form of descriptive writing: *field notes*. **Field notes** are written records of firsthand observations made in the field (instead of in a lab or office, for example). Archaeologists, geologists, and naturalists all use field notes.

Guidelines for Creating Field Notes

In different courses, such as science or social studies, you might be required to go outside of school and make precise observations of something. To record your observations, you will need to keep detailed field notes. Here are some guidelines to help you create field notes.

- **Start with a small, sturdy, bound notebook.** Don't use loose-leaf pages that can fall out and get lost. Choose something easy to carry—a notebook that fits into a pocket is best.

- **Write with a pencil, not a pen.** You may be making notes outdoors—not always in dry conditions. Unlike ink, pencil marks will not run or smear if they get wet.

- **Write down your first impressions quickly.** You can hold details in your short-term memory only very briefly. Don't count on remembering something long enough to write it down later. If you wait too long, you risk adding inaccurate or imagined details that don't reflect what you really observed.

- **Mark the date and location of your observations on each page.** You may need to look back later and check exactly when and where you made an observation.

- **Don't crowd notes onto your notebook pages.** You don't need to fill a page before you start a new one. Later, you may want to be able to find the specific details in your notes quickly—so don't bury all your details on overcrowded pages.

- **Never tear out pages, and avoid erasing anything.** Later, you may wish that you still had the page you tore out, or that you could still read the words you erased and wrote over. Instead, simply draw a line or an *X* through anything you are tempted to erase.

YOUR TURN 9 Taking Field Notes

To practice taking field notes, carefully observe something in the natural world, and make detailed notes describing it. Your subject might be a bird, an insect, a plant, a certain weather phenomenon, or anything else natural which you can observe firsthand.

OBJECTIVES

- To plan and tape a video postcard
- To use visual techniques

Quotation for the Day

"Poetry is fact given over to imagery."

(Rod McKuen, 1933–   , American poet and composer)

Have students write briefly about how this quotation may apply to their video postcard. Then, discuss with them what McKuen means and how in the video postcards they will take facts and use them to create visual images.

Meeting
INDIVIDUAL
NEEDS

MULTIPLE INTELLIGENCES

Linguistic Intelligence. Students who are having difficulty planning their video postcard with a storyboard might find their planning easier if they first describe the dominant impression (implied main idea) they are trying to create, and then write a description of what each location should include (supporting details). This may help students to visualize the video postcards before they create their storyboards.

WHAT'S AHEAD?

In this section, you will create a video postcard and learn how to

- **plan and tape a video**
- **use visual techniques to add interest to a video**

Creating a Video Postcard

To make a word-picture come to life, a writer uses many descriptive devices, such as sensory and figurative details. Imagine creating a description using a videocamera instead of words. A **video postcard** is a special kind of description: a short (one minute or less) series of images, presented without sound, that are chosen to give a viewer a sense of what a place is like. Get ready for a filmmaking adventure: read the steps in this section carefully, arm yourself with a videocamera, give in to your imagination, and create your own video postcard.

Why Make a Video Postcard?

A printed postcard is a visual souvenir from a place. People send postcards to one another as a way of saying, "I wish you were here with me to see this place, but since you are not, I am sending you this postcard to show you how it looks." A video postcard should have the same basic purpose: *It should be a visual memento of a visit to a certain place.* There are two good reasons for creating this kind of a visual memento.

- You can plan and film it so that it represents your personal view of a place—it will be as individual as you are.
- You can make use of a variety of visual techniques to make it a creative, unusual view of a place.

Choosing a Place to Tape

The first step in creating a video postcard is to decide on a place to tape. Below are some points you should keep in mind as you consider places.

- **You do not have to travel.** The place you choose does not have to be a far-away, exotic place. It can be an interesting place close to home—a place you already know well.

46   Chapter 1   **Narration/Description:** Creating a Word-Picture

---

RESOURCES

Focus on Viewing and Representing
Practice

- *Media Literacy and Communication Skills*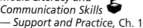
  — *Support and Practice*, Ch. 1
  — *A How-to-Handbook*

Teaching Notes
Practice

- *Media Literacy and Communication Skills*
  — *A Teacher's Guide*, Ch. 1

- **Your focus can be small.** If you are creating a video postcard of a lake near your home, do not try to tape the entire lake—focus on the part of it that interests you the most.

- **You should observe before taping.** Before you decide on a place, observe it carefully and consider how you could make it look interesting on tape. Gather information by using all of your senses—by seeing, touching, tasting, smelling, and hearing. Think about the impression you want to make on your viewers. Some places will work better than others.

Of course, if you know that you will be traveling somewhere soon, you do not need to restrict yourself to filming a local place. You can bring a camera along and tape a place during your trip.

Planning and Taping

The next step in creating a video postcard, creating a *storyboard*, is also an essential step whenever you are planning to tape or film anything. A **storyboard** is simply a set of rough sketches that you make before you begin taping or filming something. The storyboard shows the **sequence**, or order, of the scenes or shots you plan to use. In the case of a video postcard, a storyboard should show each of the major views of a place that you plan to include.

With your sequence of scenes decided and your storyboard in hand, you are ready to begin taping. Most professional directors don't actually film scenes in exactly the same sequence that they will be shown. However, to simplify your taping, you should tape in exactly the same sequence in which you plan for the tape to be shown, a technique called **in-camera editing.** It actually means that you don't do any editing at all after you have finished taping—you just show the original tape.

Critical Thinking

Metacognition. Have students compare the process used to create the video postcard with the process used to create the descriptive essay. They can use the following questions to guide their comparisons.

1. How were the processes similar? How were they different?

2. Which was easier for you? Why?

3. Which techniques from the easier process could you apply to simplify the more difficult process?

Visual Techniques

While videotaping a place, try to use a variety of visual techniques to add interest and meaning to your final video postcard. Some of the visual techniques available to you will depend on the sophistication of the video-camera you use. However, you will want to cover the basics:

- **Use a combination of *close-ups* and *panoramic* (wide) shots.** Use wide shots to give viewers an impression of the grandness of a place; use close-ups to show small but important details.
- **Consider using some form of *time-lapse taping.*** You could set a video-camera on a tripod and tape just a few seconds of each hour—from dawn to dusk—and you would end up with a view of a complete day at that place, compressed into thirty seconds or so.
- **Vary the camera angles you use.** Don't film everything at eye level—try to get up above the place a little, and then shoot down to give a bird's-eye view. Also, think about getting down on the ground and filming up to portray a child's view of the place. Remember that shooting from a high angle makes the subject appear small, while shooting from a low angle makes the subject appear large and dominating.

Certainly, you will want to do a few practice runs *before* your actual taping session. Become comfortable with your camera; learn its parts and their specific functions. If necessary, study the instruction manual. The following terms should help you get started.

- The **iris ring** adjusts the brightness of the image.
- The **zoom ring** magnifies the image and can create a "zoom-in" effect.
- The **focus ring** makes your images sharper.

YOUR TURN 10 — Creating a Video Postcard

Get together with two or three classmates, and create a plan for making a one-minute silent video postcard. Remember to

- choose a place to tape
- create a storyboard showing the sequence of shots you will use
- tape the postcard using in-camera editing to save time and trouble
- use a variety of visual techniques to add interest and meaning

(If you do not have access to a videocamera, you may be able to do only the first two steps.) When you have finished your video postcard, screen it for the class and ask your classmates for feedback.

YOUR TURN 10

Students' video postcards need to hold the viewers' interest and create a feel for the location. For example, if students choose to depict their area as cultural, they may focus on museums, the library, theaters, and bookstores.

Wrap It Up

Metacognition. Ask students the following questions.

1. Do you think your video postcard represented your views? How? [Yes. Because I taped the lake from my grandfather's dock, the film captured what I see whenever I go there with my family.]

2. What are two visual techniques mentioned in the chapter? [a combination of close-up and panoramic shots, time-lapse taping, and varying the camera angle]

3. Which visual technique is the most interesting to you? Why?

RESOURCES

Your Turn 10

Practice and Reinforcement

- *Media Literacy and Communication Skills*

—*Support and Practice,* Ch. 1, transparencies and worksheets

—Videocassette 1, Segment A

Choices

Choose one of the following activities to complete.

▶ CAREERS

1. Describing with Data
Professionals in science careers often create written descriptions from data collected firsthand—measurements, for example. To practice describing with data, first find an object with characteristics you can measure, such as volume, temperature, dimensions, weight, age, and speed. Determine whether any special equipment is necessary for measuring. Then, make your measurements and use them to create a brief **written description** of the object.

▶ LITERATURE

2. Imagined Places Find a vivid description of a place in a novel or short story you have read recently, and analyze the writer's style. For example, does the writer use vivid verbs, series of adjectives, or a particular type of sentence structure? Then, create an **imagined description** of your own, using the short-story or novel description as a model. Be sure to choose a place you really want to describe. It might be a space station in the distant future or a city in the ancient past—just let your imagination guide you.

▶ VIEWING AND REPRESENTING

3. Selling a Place Create a **print ad** based on the description of a place you created in the Writing Workshop. Consider the information you should present to make this destination desirable. For example, explain the ease of traveling there, list its many activities, and praise its unique features. Keep in mind the **dominant impression** of the description, and use graphics and visual techniques to emphasize it.

▶ CROSSING THE CURRICULUM: WORLD LANGUAGES

4. Translating Description
To compare descriptive terms across languages, make a list of ten key descriptive words from the description of a place you wrote for this chapter. Then, use a bilingual dictionary to find the equivalents of the words in another language—a language you have studied or are now studying, or any other language in which you are interested. After you have made your list, create an **illustrated poster** showing the words and their equivalents.

PORTFOLIO

▶ CAREERS

As students collect data, you might wish to have a math book or formulas available to help students determine volume or speed.

▶ VIEWING AND REPRESENTING

To help students create their ads, share the following guidelines with them:

- **Consider your audience.** Explain that ads always have an audience, which is called a target market. Guide students through determining the target market for their ads.

- **Describe your location completely.** Tell students not only to give basic information, but also to explain what makes their place special and unique. They should use words with impact and avoid language that is confusing or muddled. Finally, they should give reasons why people should visit.

- **Use pictures in your ad.** Illustrations are often the most persuasive elements of a print advertisement. Tell students they may draw their own art, create pictures on a computer, take a photograph, cut out magazine photographs, or trace other illustrations and adjust them for the advertisement.

▶ CROSSING THE CURRICULUM: WORLD LANGUAGES

If students are currently studying a language, you might suggest that when they finish translating their lists, they check with their language instructor to see if their translations require idioms or figurative language to create the same meaning as the original.

RESOURCES

Creating a Word-Picture

Assessment
- *Assessment Package*
  —*Chapter Tests*, Ch. 1
  —*Chapter Tests in Standardized Test Formats*, Ch. 1
  —*Assessment Alternatives*, Ch. 1

- *Test Generator (One-Stop Planner CD-ROM)*

Choices

Rubrics
- *Assessment Package*
  —*Assessment Alternatives*, Ch. 1

Expressing Your Thoughts

Use this guide to create an instructional plan that suits the individual needs of your students. Assignments marked by an asterisk (*) may be completed out of class. Times given for pacing lessons are estimated. See pp. 50–51 for chapter-wide resources. Resources listed in this guide are point-of-use resources only.

Curriculum Connections

Connections to Literature *pp. 78–80*
- Writing a Short Story

Choices *p. 85*
- Crossing the Curriculum: History
- Crossing the Curriculum: Music
- Literature
- Speaking and Listening

GO TO: go.hrw.com
KEYWORD: EOLang 9-2

All resources for this chapter are available for preview on the *One-Stop Planner CD-ROM with Test Generator.* All worksheets and tests may be printed from the CD-ROM.

	Chapter Opener pp. 50–51	Reading Workshop: Reading a Personal Narrative pp. 52–61
DEVELOPMENTAL PROGRAM	**20 minutes** • Expressing Your Thoughts p. 51 • Your Turn 1 p. 51	**100 minutes** • Preparing to Read p. 52 • Reading Selection pp. 53–55 • First Thoughts 1–3 p. 56 • Predicting Outcomes pp. 56–58 • Your Turn 2 p. 58 • Expressive Style pp. 58–59 • Your Turn 3 p. 59 • Vocabulary Mini-Lesson p. 60 • Test Taking Mini-Lesson p. 61
CORE PROGRAM	**15 minutes** • Expressing Your Thoughts p. 51 • Your Turn 1 p. 51	**100 minutes** • Preparing to Read p. 52 • Reading Selection pp. 53–55 • First Thoughts 1–3 p. 56 • Predicting Outcomes pp. 56–58 • Your Turn 2 p. 58 • Expressive Style pp. 58–59 • Your Turn 3 p. 59 • Vocabulary Mini-Lesson p. 60 • Test Taking Mini-Lesson p. 61
ADVANCED PROGRAM	**5 minutes** • Expressing Your Thoughts p. 51 • Your Turn 1 p. 51	**60 minutes** • Preparing to Read p. 52 • Reading Selection pp. 53–55 • First Thoughts 1–3 p. 56 • Predicting Outcomes pp. 56–58 • Your Turn 2 p. 58 • Expressive Style pp. 58–59 • Your Turn 3* p. 59 • Vocabulary Mini-Lesson* p. 60
RESOURCES — PRINT	• *Communications,* TP. 17, WS. p. 24	• *Alternative Readings,* Ch. 2 • *Communications,* TPs. 18, 19, WS. pp. 25–32
RESOURCES — MEDIA	• *One-Stop Planner CD-ROM*	• *One-Stop Planner CD-ROM*

TP.=Transparency   WS.=Worksheet

Writing Workshop: Writing a Personal Narrative
pp. 62–80

🕐 120 minutes
- Prewriting *pp. 62–67*
- Your Turn 4 *p. 64*
- Your Turn 5 *p. 66*
- Writing Mini-Lesson *p. 67*
- Framework and Your Turn 6* *p. 68*
- Writer's Model and Student's Model *pp. 69–71*

🕐 100 minutes
- Evaluate and Revise Your Draft *pp. 72–73*
- Your Turn 7 *p. 73*
- Focus on Word Choice and Your Turn 8 *pp. 74–75*
- Proofread, Publish, and Reflect *pp. 76–77*
- Grammar Link *p. 76*
- Your Turn 9 *p. 77*

🕐 180 minutes
- Prewriting *pp. 62–67*
- Your Turn 4* *p. 64*
- Your Turn 5* *p. 66*
- Writing Mini-Lesson *p. 67*
- Framework and Your Turn 6* *p. 68*
- Writer's Model and Student's Model *pp. 69–71*
- Evaluate and Revise Your Draft *pp. 72–73*
- Your Turn 7 *p. 73*
- Focus on Word Choice and Your Turn 8* *pp. 74–75*
- Proofread, Publish, and Reflect *pp. 76–77*
- Grammar Link *p. 76*
- Your Turn 9* *p. 77*
- Connections to Literature* *pp. 78–80*
- Your Turn 10* *p. 80*

🕐 120 minutes
- Prewriting *pp. 62–67*
- Your Turn 4* *p. 64*
- Your Turn 5* *p. 66*
- Writing Mini-Lesson* *p. 67*
- Framework and Your Turn 6* *p. 68*
- Writer's Model and Student's Model *pp. 69–71*
- Evaluate and Revise Your Draft *pp. 72–73*
- Your Turn 7* *p. 73*
- Proofread, Publish and Reflect *pp. 76–77*
- Your Turn 9* *p. 77*
- Connections to Literature* *pp. 78–80*
- Your Turn 10* *p. 80*

- *Communications,* 📖
  TPs. 20–23
  WS. pp. 33–42
- *Designing Your Writing*

- *One-Stop Planner CD-ROM* 💿

Focus on Speaking and Listening: Presenting and Evaluating Oral Narratives *pp. 81–84*

🕐 120 minutes
- Remember Story Essentials *p. 81*
- Use Gestures to Tell Your Story *p. 82*
- Use Vocal Techniques to Tell Your Story *pp. 82–83*
- Practice, Practice, Practice *p. 83*
- Listening *pp. 83–84*
- Your Turn 11 *p. 84*

🕐 100 minutes
- Remember Story Essentials *p. 81*
- Use Gestures to Tell Your Story *p. 82*
- Use Vocal Techniques to Tell Your Story *pp. 82–83*
- Practice, Practice, Practice *p. 83*
- Listening *pp. 83–84*
- Evaluating Oral Narratives *p. 84*
- Your Turn 11* *p. 84*

🕐 100 minutes
- Remember Story Essentials* *p. 81*
- Use Gestures to Tell Your Story *p. 82*
- Use Vocal Techniques to Tell Your Story *pp. 82–83*
- Practice, Practice, Practice* *p. 83*
- Listening *pp. 83–84*
- Evaluating Oral Narratives *p. 84*
- Your Turn 11* *p. 84*

- *Media Literacy and Communication* 📖
  Skills
  —*Support and Practice,* Ch. 2
  —*A How-to Handbook*
  —*A Teacher's Guide,* Ch. 2

- *Media Literacy and Communication Skills* 📼
  —Videocassette 1, Segment B
- *One-Stop Planner CD-ROM* 💿

2

Expressing Your Thoughts

CHAPTER OBJECTIVES

- To read a personal narrative to predict outcomes and recognize elements of expressive style

- To select a significant experience and write a personal narrative that includes vivid details and precise verbs

- To tell a story with appropriate vocal and physical techniques and to listen to and evaluate storytelling

Chapter Overview

This chapter focuses on the concept of personal narrative. The Reading Workshop teaches students how to predict outcomes in a narrative and to analyze the elements of a successful personal narrative. The Writing Workshop offers practice in selecting an appropriate topic and in composing a personal narrative. Extending these skills, the Focus on Speaking and Listening section presents techniques for relating stories orally as well as suggestions for active listening and evaluating storytelling. The three sections in this chapter can be taught separately, but they can also work together to teach a comprehensive understanding of personal narrative.

Why Study Personal Narrative?

A personal narrative demonstrates a direct link between personal experience and writing. In addition to creating historical or cultural records, personal narratives can preserve family tradition, providing insight for future generations. Studying examples of personal narrative can generate students' interest in writing about their own lives. Composing a personal narrative is also an important life skill. When applying for a job or for school admission, students are often required to write a personal narrative to include with their applications.

Teaching the Chapter

Option 1: Begin with Literature

This is a good time to help students distinguish between fiction and nonfiction. Although fiction can be written from a first-person point of view, it should not be mistaken for personal narrative. For example, Edgar Allan Poe uses first-person point of view in "The Cask of Amontillado," but the story is clearly not a personal narrative. Discuss the different kinds of personal narrative with students, focusing especially on autobiography, memoir, or personal essay. You might illustrate the distinctions using the work of N. Scott Momaday, a writer who uses a number of different genres.

Option 2: Begin with Nonfiction and Writing

Students can become acquainted with the personal narrative form by reading the short autobiographical piece on pp. 53–55. The annotations and instruction surrounding the selection provide a guide to help them when they encounter personal narrative in their assigned reading or on their own. After students have written a personal narrative by following the process in the Writing Workshop (pp. 62–80), they will be more aware of the premises and techniques writers of memoirs or autobiographies use. Students will be well prepared to examine nonfictional, personal essay selections in their literature textbooks. See also **Connections to Literature** on pp. 78–80.

Making Connections

■ To the Literature Curriculum

Many stories are based on personal narrative. For example, "When I Lay My Burden Down" (from *I Know Why the Caged Bird Sings* by Maya Angelou) centers on one of Angelou's experiences with her grandmother. Although Angelou never states the exact lesson she learned from her experience, readers can sense the purpose behind her poignant tale about how some children tried to humiliate Angelou's grandmother in front of her. The sensory details and first-person emotions Angelou shares are hallmarks of personal narrative.

> **Lesson Idea:** Elements of personal narrative in "When I Lay My Burden Down," by Maya Angelou
>
> 1. Ask students to analyze the expressive details Angelou includes in "When I Lay My Burden Down." [Some examples include descriptions of minutes as slow as cold molasses; an apron so stiff with starch that it could have stood by itself; children with hair greasy and colorless.] After listing the details they find most curious or impressive, have students write why they think Angelou included each detail and how each furthers the theme of the story.
>
> 2. Invite students to reconsider the story's point of view. How would the tale be different if it were told in third person? from the grandmother's point of view? How would the story change if one of the taunting girls told the tale?

■ To the Community

Invite students to interview members of their community with the goal of collecting a book of stories about their community. Students might interview business owners, professionals, and members of local organizations. Encourage them to visit the local senior center. Request that students prepare their questions in advance of their interviews. Challenge students to sniff out local tales of years gone by or stories about town politics or other interesting tidbits. The students' resulting anthology should give its readers a feel for the community. Make sure that students have permission from their parents or guardians and from the parties they plan to contact before they begin their interviews.

■ To Careers

Encourage students to think of times when personal narrative might be useful in the workplace. For example, travel agents or travel writers might use personal narrative to relate their experiences to promote a particular location as a travel destination. Someone working for an advertising agency might give a personal testimonial about the value of a particular product. A job applicant might express a personal narrative that reveals qualities an employer might want to see. Allow students to try their hand at writing one of these job-related personal narratives.

■ To the Art Curriculum

Encourage students to create a mural depicting a personal narrative studied in class. If possible, collaborate with an art teacher to oversee the project and materials. Students should decide on their own, however, which details and emotions are most important to include in the artwork and how to best convey the events of the narrative.

Expressing Your Thoughts

PREVIEWING THE CHAPTER

- The three workshops in this chapter may be taught independently. Taught as a unit, though, they reinforce the nature of personal narrative. The Reading Workshop introduces a personal narrative and teaches students to analyze it. Next, in the Writing Workshop students will write their own personal narratives. Finally, in Focus on Speaking and Listening students learn storytelling techniques and active-listening skills. To integrate this chapter with grammar, usage, and mechanics chapters, see pp. T371A–T371B.

INTRODUCING THE CHAPTER

- To introduce the chapter, use the Journal Warm-up, Transparency 17, in *Communications*.

VIEWING THE ILLUSTRATION

- The abstract illustration shows objects emerging like a branch from a human head. Have students identify and discuss the meaning of these objects that represent thoughts. Point out that writers generate many images/details as they write in order to create pictures in the reader's mind. Ask students to comment on the artist's use of line. [The straight and wavy lines going into and coming out of the head suggest the brain's power to take in, process, and produce ideas.]

Representing. Encourage students to illustrate their own processes of generating ideas. Then, ask them to write a statement about how they created their artwork.

CHAPTER RESOURCES

Planning
- *Lesson Planner, ELL Strategies*, Ch. 2
- Block Scheduling, p. T49A (this book)
- *One-Stop Planner CD-ROM*

Practice
- *Communications*, Ch. 2
- *Writer's Workshop 2 CD-ROM*

- *Media Literacy and Communication Skills*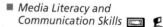

Extension
- *Designing Your Writing*

Reinforcement
- *Communications*, Ch. 2
- *Alternative Readings*, Ch. 2

Reading Workshop

Reading a Personal Narrative

Writing Workshop

Writing a Personal Narrative

Speaking and Listening

Presenting and Evaluating Oral Narratives

Narration/ Description

Michael Jordan's diary . . . Rita Dove's autobiography . . . your fifth-grade "My Last Vacation" essay. People writing about their own lives are creating personal narratives.

"Write about what you know," someone wise once said. People write about what happens in their lives because they want to express themselves and their ideas about the world. People read to learn about the journeys others take to discover those ideas. Think of the possibilities: you may recount a moment of personal triumph when you first jumped off a rope swing, or you may read about the moment when a writer decided to become an astronaut. In any case, personal narratives offer a great opportunity to learn through your experiences or through the experiences of others.

YOUR TURN 1 Keeping Personal Narratives in Mind

With a classmate or two, make a two-column chart. In the first column, make a list of people whose personal narratives you would like to read. In the second column, write what you would like to learn about the people from their personal narratives.

People	What I would like to learn
Maya Angelou	What working for Dr. Martin Luther King, Jr., was like

internet connect

GO TO: go.hrw.com
KEYWORD: EOLang 9-2

Connecting Reading and Writing   **51**

Motivate

To focus on the concept of personal narrative, ask students to think of someone in their lives who has told them about "the good old days"—a grandparent, an older neighbor, or even a favorite writer. Invite students to talk about how those memories have influenced their perceptions of history. [Historical events might seem more vivid if family members were affected.] Suggest that students think about sharing memories with their children or grandchildren: What might students choose to tell future generations? Why?

ELEMENTS OF

Personal Narrative in Literature. In *Elements of Literature*, Third Course, see "A Christmas Memory" by Truman Capote, pp. 145–154, and "New Directions" by Maya Angelou, pp. 328–330, for examples of personal narratives.

YOUR TURN 1

Remind students that they may list famous people. You might model the second column by suggesting that students may wish to learn how the famous people earned success.

- *Daily Language Activity Transparencies*
- *Vocabulary Workshop* and *Tests*

Evaluation and Assessment

- *Test Generator (One-Stop Planner CD-ROM)*

- *Assessment Package*
  —*Chapter Tests*, Ch. 2
  —*Chapter Tests in Standardized Test Formats*, Ch. 2
  —*Assessment Alternatives*, Ch. 2

Internet

- go.hrw.com (keyword: EOLang 9-2)

Quotation for the Day

"It is one thing to remember, another to know. Remembering is merely safeguarding something entrusted to memory; knowing means making everything your own."

(Seneca, 4 B.C.–A.D. 65, Roman statesman, author, and philosopher)

Discuss with the class what this quotation might mean. After students have read **"Paper Airplanes,"** ask them if the meaning of the quotation is any clearer. How do they think it applies to the narrator of the reading selection? [Students may see the change in the narrator once she knows what has happened to the other diaries.]

TEACHING TIP

Preparing to Read
The material on this page is reinforced in the questions and activities that follow **"Paper Airplanes."** This selection offers students a chance to practice making predictions and to analyze elements of expressive style. These concepts will be taught in depth on pp. 56–59.

RESOURCES

Reading Workshop Reinforcement

- *Alternative Readings,* Ch.2

WHAT'S AHEAD?

In this section, you will read a personal narrative and learn how to

- predict outcomes

- recognize elements of expressive style

| READING SKILL |

| READING FOCUS |

Reading a Personal Narrative

What do you remember from your childhood? Remember the time your brother told you to watch your little sister and so you did—while your sister ate dirt? Writers use their memories and powers of description to re-create moments from their lives. We call this kind of re-creation **personal narrative,** which is a form of expressive writing. The selection you will read next is a personal narrative in which the author expresses feelings about memories both lost and found.

Preparing to Read

Predicting Outcomes Do you have friends who always want to tell you what will happen next in a TV show? They like to make predictions. Before a game, do you ever talk about how many points your team will score? You are **predicting an outcome.** You take what you already know and apply it to something you are reading, listening to, watching, or experiencing. Then, you decide what you think will happen. As you read "Paper Airplanes" on the next page, try to make some predictions about what will happen next in the narrative or how a person will react.

Expressive Style Style is the way writers express what they want to say. There are many different ways to write about an event or series of events. In **expressive forms** of writing, such as the personal narrative, writers use an **expressive style** to bring the reader into the writer's personal experience. Two easily recognizable elements of an expressive style are

- **first-person pronouns,** such as *I, me, we,* and *us,* used in order to connect more directly with the reader

- **personal thoughts and emotions** that would be out of place in other kinds of writing

When you read "Paper Airplanes," notice that the writer is neither objective nor removed from the subject: She tells us her unique, personal story.

READING PROCESS

PREREADING
Ask Questions. Explain that asking questions will help students better understand and remember content. Ask open-ended questions to help students activate their prior knowledge before they read **"Paper Airplanes":** What does the title suggest about the story? [Students might imagine a story about school pranks or a piece that teaches the reader how to fold fancy paper

Kyoko Mori was born in Japan and lived there the first twenty years of her life. She has spent another twenty years living, working, and writing in the United States. As you read Mori's personal narrative, write down your answers to the numbered active-reading questions.

from Polite Lies: On Being a Woman Caught Between Cultures

Paper Airplanes
by Kyoko Mori

What I miss most from not having a family close by is a sense that the past is an open and growing manuscript, expansive and forgiving. When we talk about the past with family, we often find that each of us remembers different aspects of the same experience. Though the difference in memory can sometimes lead to bickering, it's a relief to know that none of us has the sole responsibility for remembering—what we forget will be recalled by someone else. We occasionally learn details we didn't know because we were too young at the time or lived too far away. Family stories can shed a new light on the events we think we know. After the conversation, we add the new pieces to our memory. In this way, the past can expand rather than shrink. I look forward to seeing my mother's family on my short visits to Japan because that's one of the few times I can experience memory expanding.

The last time I saw my uncle, Kenichi, he had just finished reading my first novel, *Shizuko's Daughter*, in the Japanese translation. Many of the details in the novel's setting come from my grandparents' house in the country—the house where Kenichi had grown up. He was glad that I had included the child's wooden slide my grandfather built when my mother was born, the purple lantern flowers my grandmother used to grow, the cicadas that were always buzzing in the trees in the yard.

1. What do you think may happen in this personal narrative?

2. How do you know the writer has fond memories of her grandparents' house?

Active-Reading Questions

ANSWERS

The purpose of the active-reading questions is to encourage students to predict outcomes and to recognize elements of expressive style in the Reading Selection. Use students' answers as an informal assessment of their understanding of the personal narrative elements.

1. From the mention of family and different perspectives, it seems Mori may write about an experience that another family member remembers differently.

2. Mori hints at her fondness for her grandparents' home by mentioning specifics like the slide and flowers.

TEACHING TIP

Active-Reading Questions

One way of using the active-reading questions is to have each student read silently to the first question and then determine the answer to the question. Then, lead a brief class discussion in which students share and discuss their answers to the first question before you have them go on to the next question.

---

airplanes.] What clues does the brief biographical information about the author give you as to what the story line might be? [She might compare her upbringing in Japan to her experiences in the U.S.]

3. She appears to feel close to her uncle. Their conversation seems casual.

4. Kenichi may have taken Mori's mother's notebooks.

5. It is possible she would be angry. However, Mori may not be upset about the diaries because she had assumed they were simply misplaced.

"I was amazed by how much you could remember," he said.

"Of course I remember a lot," I reassured him. His own kids, fifteen years younger than I, do not recall our grandparents in the same way—they were just babies when our grandfather died; by the time they were growing up, our grandmother was in her eighties and no longer able to take long walks with them or grow as many flowers in her garden as she used to. Kenichi was happy to have me remember and write about what his kids could not, so that the memories are kept alive.

> **3.** How do you think Mori feels about her uncle? Why?

"There's one thing I felt really bad about," Kenichi confessed. "I thought about it the whole time I was reading your novel."

"What was that?" I asked him, leaning forward over the table where we were having dinner.

"Remember those diaries your mother kept when she was in high school?" he asked. "There were many of them, in those glossy, yellow notebooks."

"Yes," I said. "I have them." Shortly after I left for college, my grandmother had found them in the attic of her house and sent them to me.

"But you don't have all the volumes," Kenichi said. "Do you know why?"

I shook my head. There were a few months missing here and there, but I always assumed that one or two notebooks must have gotten misplaced.

> **4.** Can you make a prediction about what has happened to the notebooks?

"When your mother finished high school and was in Kobe, working as a secretary, I was living in that house in the country with your grandparents and your Aunt Keiko. We were just kids." Kenichi paused.

I nodded, encouraging him to go on. Kenichi is sixteen years younger than my mother, who was the oldest of six children.

"Those diaries were already in the attic then. When I was in grade school, I found them there. The notebooks had such beautiful white paper—thick and glossy. I was only eight or nine, you have to remember. I

> **5.** Do you think the writer will be angry about the loss of the diaries? Why?

tore the pages out and made paper airplanes. Every day, I would sit on top of the stairs, tear out page after page of your mother's diary, and fold paper airplanes. I watched them flying down the stairs. I got pretty good at folding planes. Some of them went quite a long way. That's how a couple of those notebooks got lost. When I read your novel, I remembered that and

---

READING PROCESS

READING

Make Personal Connections. Relating the story to something familiar makes the reading more meaningful and will help students' comprehension. After they have read the selection, ask students to list specific details describing a place that has happy memories. Point out that the wooden slide, the lantern flowers, and the cicadas convey Mori's sentiments more vividly than if she had simply stated that she liked her grandparents' home.

felt so bad." Kenichi made a face. "I can't believe how stupid I was as a kid," he concluded.

"Don't worry about it," I said, feeling suddenly so happy that I was laughing. I was imagining hundreds of white paper airplanes flying. "Your telling me about it now makes up for everything."

I'm not sure if Kenichi was convinced. I couldn't explain my feelings to him very well. But maybe it doesn't matter. In the book of my past, there is now an image of my uncle as a boy sitting on a stairway and flying paper airplanes, made of beautiful paper, with my mother's words in their precise creases. Kenichi might think that each plane deprived me of a page of my mother's writing, a page of memory, but the opposite is true. I see those planes floating down the stairway toward me, passed on from Kenichi to me because we share a past and we both loved my mother—because we belong to the same family. I cannot ask for more, except the impossible: that I had the eloquence[1] to tell my uncle, in his language, what I can only write in mine.

> **6. How does Mori feel about the paper airplanes?**

---
1. **eloquence:** speech or writing that is vivid, forceful, fluent, and graceful.

6. She is delighted by the image of her uncle as a youth sailing the paper airplanes made from her mother's lovely paper and words.

Cooperative Learning
Culture to Culture. After students have finished reading **"Paper Airplanes,"** have them take a moment to reflect upon ways cultural beliefs may have influenced their responses to and understanding of the text. For example, students may consider how views about family differ from culture to culture. How are students' views about family similar to or different from those expressed by Mori in **"Paper Airplanes"**? After students have reflected individually, have them discuss their reactions in groups of three or four.

First Thoughts on Your Reading

ANSWERS

The following are possible answers.

1. From the first paragraph, it is possible to predict correctly that the story involves two people's different perspectives of a memory.

2. The two seem to be on friendly terms. The words and phrases "reassured," "confessed," "leaning forward," and "encouraging" are descriptive of a respectful, friendly relationship.

3. Mori expresses affection for her memories, her uncle, and her mother. She seems to cherish all three even more after learning of the delightful way in which some of the diaries were destroyed. She also expresses amusement at the image of her uncle flying the paper airplanes.

First Thoughts on Your Reading

1. When you predicted an outcome for Mori's narrative, how close did you come to guessing correctly what would happen?

2. Describe the relationship between the writer and her uncle. What words or phrases in the narrative lead you to this description?

3. What emotions did the writer express in her narrative? Did she express anger? joy? affection? Explain your answer.

READING SKILL

TIP The beauty of prediction is, you don't always have to be right—the importance of predicting is to be involved and active as you read.

Predicting Outcomes

Seeing into the Future   You are reading a personal narrative about a week-long camping trip in the wilderness. The author says that he has never been camping before and has rarely left the big city where he was born. You think, "This kid is in for a shock. He'll be miserable and homesick before the second day!" You keep reading to find out whether your prediction is accurate—or whether the author loves the adventure of the outdoors. When you read any well-written personal narrative, it is very likely that you are frequently asking yourself, "What will happen next?" Whenever you try to answer that question, you are **predicting outcomes**. If you are not predicting, then you may be missing what's going on in the personal narrative. Predicting outcomes helps you follow the narrative and keep from getting lost.

You already may be predicting outcomes—without even knowing it. You make predictions every time you

- read a sentence—and predict what will happen in the next sentence

- read the first paragraph—and think about what will happen at the end of the narrative

To predict, you take information and clues from what you are reading and combine them with what you already know to make an educated guess about what will happen next. Written as an equation, predicting outcomes might look like this:

The Prediction Equation

Information and clues in the reading + What you already know = Prediction

Predicting Outcomes

How do you solve the prediction equation? First, you need to sharpen your curiosity. Then, think through the mental steps below. (Here the steps are applied to an example sentence from "Paper Airplanes.")

Example:
"The last time I saw my uncle, Kenichi, he had just finished reading my first novel. . . ."

▶ **STEP 1** Compare what you have read with the catalog of events, behaviors, reactions, and people already in your mind.

He has read her novel. When I read a novel through, it means I really liked it. Maybe he liked the novel.

▶ **STEP 2** Ask yourself a question or two about the characters or events in the section you have read.

Will Kenichi say something about the novel? What will he say?

▶ **STEP 3** Answer your questions from Step 2. As you do, consider the clues in your reading.

The first paragraph is about family sharing memories. Maybe the novel had something to do with the writer's memories of her family in Japan, and Kenichi will have something to say about that.

- **Important events** and **ideas** might cause other events.

- The **sequence** in which things have happened could be a clue to what might happen next.

▶ **STEP 4** Predict an outcome by applying your experience to the clues from the text.

Kenichi probably liked the novel, and it's likely that he will tell her that he did. The writer and Kenichi will share a family memory.

As you continue reading and predicting, your comprehension of the narrative will become more complete and detailed. Better comprehension will help you make more accurate predictions. You will find that your predictions follow a spiral pattern like the one shown to the right. First, you predict. Then, you confirm or correct your predictions by comparing them with what you know. You then start the process all over again by making more predictions. This **prediction spiral** starts at the beginning of the narrative with general predictions and narrows to more specific and accurate predictions at the end.

Critical Thinking

Metacognition. Ask students to think of other stories they have read. Can they think of one in which they were able to predict the outcome before it happened? Have them explain what clues tipped them off.

YOUR TURN 2

ANSWERS

Here are possible responses:

1. Some people might feel anger toward Kenichi for destroying something that cannot be replaced. However, most people would probably forgive Kenichi because of his young age and because he seems so regretful about the whole experience.

2. Will the writer be upset to learn of the missing diaries? Will the writer forgive her uncle?

3. I would be upset, but after I heard my uncle's explanation and apology, I would forgive him.

4. The writer may be upset because she didn't have the diaries when she wrote her book, but she will probably forgive her uncle.

Expressive Style
Have students brainstorm different forms of writing that use expression—journals, diaries, autobiographies, letters—and explain why the expressive style elements are so powerful for those forms. [They show emotions; they make readers feel as if they know the writer.]

YOUR TURN 2 Making Predictions

Although you have already read "Paper Airplanes" and know what happens, by practicing the steps in the Thinking It Through, you will be better able to apply them later to new material. Re-read the thirteenth paragraph in "Paper Airplanes," the one that begins with "Those diaries were already in the attic . . ." Then, work through the Thinking It Through steps to predict how the writer would react to Kenichi's confession about the diaries. On your own paper, copy the chart below and fill in the blanks.

Steps	Responses
1. Write down how you think people in your experience would have reacted to Kenichi's tearing up the notebooks as a child.	
2. Write down questions about the writer's possible reactions to Kenichi's confession.	
3. Write down your answers to the questions you created in Step 2.	
4. Predict how the writer will respond to Kenichi.	

READING FOCUS

Expressive Style

Reading Between the Lines   In a personal narrative, writers use an expressive style to create a personal connection with their readers and to convey their thoughts and feelings. Writers of some forms of nonfiction use formal or neutral language in order to keep their feelings from showing through in their writing. In a personal narrative, however, emotion is an important part of the self-expression the writer is trying to achieve.

When writing personal narratives, writers generally use **first-person pronouns** such as *I*, *me*, *we*, and *us* to bring their readers into their world. In "Paper Airplanes," Kyoko Mori uses first person to tell you a story from her life. She wants her readers to know what she is thinking and feeling; her own thoughts and feelings are what make the story meaningful. For

---

READING PROCESS

EXTENDING
Connect to the World. Have the class research other subjects or contexts that require people to use predictions, such as scientists using predictions to set up experiments that will prove or disprove their theories or mathematicians and engineers using predictions to design and plan space travel. After students have read about various subjects or contexts, have them sketch a rough prediction spiral for one of the areas that interests them.

example, Mori writes about what she thought happened to her mother's missing diaries:

> I shook my head. There were a few months missing here and there, but I always assumed that one or two notebooks must have gotten misplaced.

Writers may insert **personal thoughts and feelings** into a personal narrative by using words such as *anxious*, *beloved*, or *triumphant* that **tell** directly how the writer or another person in a narrative feels. By carefully selecting words with certain shades of meaning, writers also use word choice to communicate thoughts and feelings in a less obvious way—to **show** you indirectly how they or other people in their narratives feel.

The two short passages below are about the same event. Notice, however, how the underlined parts of the second passage make it more personal by communicating thoughts and feelings.

> **Informative:** As a boy, Kenichi flew paper planes down a stairway. He shared the memory with his niece.
>
> **Expressive:** I see those planes <u>floating down</u> the stairway toward me, passed on from Kenichi to me because we share a past and <u>we both loved my mother</u>—because we belong to the same family.

While the first sentence contains information, it does not express any particular feeling. The second sentence **shows** and **tells** the thoughts and feelings the writer experienced. Notice how the writer's word choices give you clues about her feelings. By describing the planes with the gentle word *floating*, Mori **shows** that Kenichi's use of the diaries did not anger her. To **tell** her readers about a feeling she and her uncle shared, she uses the expressive word *loved*.

YOUR TURN 3 Analyzing for Expressive Style

After reading the first and final paragraphs of "Paper Airplanes," complete the following steps.

1. Find and jot down several of the pronouns used. How would the narrative be different if Mori had used "she" instead of "I"?

2. Find and make a list of at least four key words that reveal the expressive style. Describe in your own words the thoughts and feelings you think those words express.

ADVANCED LEARNERS

Allow students to see for themselves the differences in first person and third-person limited. Invite students to rewrite Mori's story in third person and to read their rewritten versions aloud. Ask listeners to determine how the shift affects their feelings about the story. [Most will agree that the emotional impact is lessened in the third-person versions. The third-person versions also may distance the reader and the writer from the subject.]

Wrap It Up

Metacognition. Ask students to reflect on their own reading processes by answering the following question.

1. What part of the prediction spiral is most difficult for you? Why?

Then, ask students to answer this question.

2. Why is making predictions an important part of reading? [It helps readers keep up with their understanding of what is going on in the narrative. It also activates the interest and thoughts of readers.]

YOUR TURN 3

ANSWERS

1. *I, my, me, our, we,* and *us* are all first-person pronouns used in the story. Using third person would make the point seem more distant; first person makes the writing seem personal and inclusive of the reader.

2. "happy"—pleased, lighthearted
   "encouraging"—urging helpfully
   "beautiful"—lovely, precious
   "eloquence"—using perfect words

RESOURCES

Your Turn 2

Practice
- *Communications,* WS. p. 25

Reinforcement
- *Communications,* TP. 18, WS. p. 26

Your Turn 3

Practice
- *Communications,* WS. p. 27

Reinforcement
- *Communications,* TP. 19, WS. p. 28

VOCABULARY

Recognizing Prefixes

ANSWERS

1. c

2. b

3. d

4. c

5. d

VOCABULARY

Prefixes

Kyoko Mori's writing shows that she has mastered her second language. Her vocabulary is varied and includes words with prefixes that can help you determine their meanings. Studying these prefixes will help you to understand and use a wider variety of words. Here is a list of some words with common prefixes that appear in "Paper Airplanes."

sample word	prefix	meaning
misplaced	*mis-*	wrong(ly), not
translation	*trans-*	across, through
expansive	*ex-*	out, from
remember	*re-*	back(ward), again
impossible	*in-*	not

(Note: *In-* changes to *im-* before *m* and *p*.)

THINKING IT THROUGH — Recognizing Prefixes

Here is one way to become familiar with prefixes so that you can identify them and use them to understand new words.

1. Fold a sheet of paper in half. On the left-hand side, make a list of prefixes you want to learn. On the right-hand side, write the meanings of the prefixes.

2. Work to commit the prefixes and their meanings to memory. Quiz yourself on the prefixes by folding your paper to hide one of the two sides.

3. After memorizing the prefixes, find some words in your everyday reading that use them. Write down what you think each word means, given the meaning of the prefix. In these notes, underline the prefix and its meaning. For example,

misplaced   placed wrongly

4. Check your answers in a dictionary.

PRACTICE

Use what you have learned about prefixes to choose the word that corresponds to each of the following definitions.

1. so fine in texture that one can see **through** to the other side
   (a) apparent   (c) transparent
   (b) impart   (d) obscure

2. **not** able to express oneself
   (a) transcendent (c) substantial
   (b) inarticulate (d) retroactive

3. to make someone sure **again**
   (a) ensure   (c) assure
   (b) insure   (d) reassure

4. to put away **wrongly**
   (a) delay   (c) mislay
   (b) relay   (d) inlay

5. to ship materials **out** of a place
   (a) purport   (c) report
   (b) import   (d) export

RESOURCES

Vocabulary

Practice
■ *Communications,* WS. p. 29

Test Taking

Practice
■ *Communications,* WS. pp. 30–32

■ **Think about the first time** you did something—for example, the first time you rode a bike fast down a hill or went alone to the skating rink. Often in these "firsts" you can find a moment in which you learned about yourself or your world.

When you have thought of some memories that might make good topics, write a one-sentence description of each memory. Read over the sentences and choose two or three possibilities.

Evaluate Your Potential Topics

Do the Write Thing   You must judge your topics to decide which one you want to pursue. To select one memory to write about, ask yourself the questions in the following chart. One writer used this chart to help her decide between two topics.

Questions to Consider	Topic 1: I learn to build campfires.	Topic 2: I buy bread by myself for the first time.
Is the experience important to me? Why?	1. I trace my love of camping and the outdoors to this experience. 2. It shows my relationship with my dad.	1. It was the first time I did such a grown-up thing. 2. It shows my mother's trust in me.
How well do I remember the experience? List details.	1. We gathered sticks in the park and arranged them in the shapes of different campfires. 2. We were in New York City.	1. I went to the corner market. I don't remember too many specifics. 2. Walking all alone felt strange.
Am I willing to share the experience?	Yes, it is not too private.	Yes, it is not embarrassing.
Will my experience be interesting to others? Why?	Yes, it is unusual to learn to build campfires in New York City.	Probably not. This experience might seem ordinary, not very lively.

Meeting
INDIVIDUAL
NEEDS

INCLUSION
Students sometimes find it difficult to access their feelings. Allowing students to work through the writing assignments with an encouraging helper may help them recall events that they may use for their personal narratives.

As students create charts comparing their two topics, oversee their progress and steer them toward appropriate subjects.

TECHNOLOGY TIP

Students can use a word processor to create a list of evaluation questions similar to those in the book, leaving space below each question. For each potential topic, they can duplicate their chart and fill it in. Remind them to save each filled-in chart with a new file name.

Meeting INDIVIDUAL NEEDS

MULTIPLE INTELLIGENCES

Interpersonal Intelligence. Some students may find it easier to define an audience, purpose, and tone after talking in small groups about their topic. Once they return to writing, remind students that they can imagine sharing their memories with their group (their audience), a practice that may help them achieve a personal tone and include pertinent details.

With this information, the writer can judge which topic would be the best to pursue. The writer of the chart on the previous page decided that although she would be willing to share either one, the campfire topic would be more interesting. The second one is a more common experience, and the details of it are less vivid in her mind.

YOUR TURN 4 · Choosing and Evaluating Topics

- Brainstorm a list of memories.
- Write a one-sentence description of each memory.
- Choose at least two topics to compare in a chart like the one on the previous page.
- Based on your chart, decide which topic is most appropriate.

Define Your Purpose, Audience, and Tone

Your Side of the Story In a personal narrative, your **purpose** is already decided: You will write to express yourself and to share your experience with your audience. Is the writer of the campfire narrative trying to tell her audience how to build campfires? No. She is writing about the love she has for her father, using campfires to show the bond between them.

Your **audience** is all the people who are going to read your personal narrative. It could be classmates, teachers, friends, or parents—any or all of them. Ask yourself some questions to get a feel for your audience.

Reference Note
For more on **expressive style,** see page 58.

- **Who is my intended audience?** If your audience only includes people who shared your experience, you might write differently than if you are writing for those who were not there.

- **What will the audience need to know to help them understand my experience?** Not everyone knows about campfires, so the writer may have to provide some background information.

- **How will I get my audience's attention?** You can ask a question or make a statement that makes people curious or creates suspense.

KEY CONCEPT

The **tone** of a personal narrative will always be—you guessed it—personal. You are telling your own true story. **Because you will write in your own voice, use first-person pronouns—***I, me,* and perhaps, *we, us,* and *our.* Speak directly to your audience, creating an informal, even friendly, tone in your narrative. Use words that sound friendly. For example, you might use *say* or *show* instead of *express.*

RESOURCES

Your Turn 4
Practice
- *Communications,* WS. p. 33

Gather Details

Let Your Memory Be Your Guide   Your memory will be your chief instrument for gathering details that will bring your readers into your experience. To search your memory for the little things that will make your story live, turn your attention to details about events, people, places, thoughts, and feelings. Remember to think of all five senses when you are gathering details. Often people use their visual memory. However, you must also ask yourself how a place smelled, how a person sounded, how a surface felt, or how a food tasted. You can chart your details, using questions to prompt specifics for your narrative. Below is a chart one writer created.

Who or What	Trigger Questions	Details
Events	What is the main event in the experience? What happened exactly? What are some other events?	walking in the park, practicing building campfires, collecting twigs, laying them in patterns, camp contest, camping in the mountains
People	Who was in my experience? What did they look like? What did they say?	me—age five, tidy, wearing dress; dad—a young man, glasses, dressed for work, inventive
Places	Where did the experience happen? How did the place look, sound, and smell?	a city park, summer, cool, early morning, big trees with full leaves, shady
Thoughts and Feelings	What did I think and feel as the events unfolded?	I loved time alone with my dad, felt happy skipping beside him, felt a bond we shared when camping

Organize Details

Ducks in a Row   Next, order your details. **Chronological order is most frequently used in narrative writing**—the event that happened first is at

MODALITY
Visual Learners. When developing and organizing details for their narratives, some students may benefit from sketching storyboards before they begin to write.

TIP   Using **dialogue,** people's own words, will help your narrative come alive. Think about what the people in your experience said. Also, remember that not everyone sounds alike— your eight-year-old sister and your older neighbor use very different words and sentence structures. Try to make dialogue sound as natural and as real as possible.

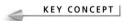 **KEY CONCEPT**

Writing Workshop   **65**

Reference Note
For more on **time lines,**
see page 818.

TIP Personal narratives often do not have a thesis in the first paragraph. The writer will hint at the meaning of an experience but not reveal the meaning entirely until the final paragraph.

the beginning of the narrative, followed by the event that happened next, and so on. Guide readers through the sequence of events by including transitions such as *at first, to begin, then, later, after that, at last,* and *finally*. You might make a time line to organize the events in your narrative. Placing the events into a time line will help you accomplish three things: (1) to see which details connect to which events, (2) to order your details, and (3) to see which details are essential to your narrative.

Reflect on Your Experience

And So It Ends You chose a particular experience to write about because it was important to you in some way. You will want to convey this meaning to your readers, too. To reflect on the meaning of your personal narrative, ask yourself questions like these:

- How did I change from the beginning to the end of the experience?
- What did I learn about myself or the world or other people from the experience?
- What were my feelings at the beginning of, during, and at the end of the experience?

    Write a simple sentence telling what the experience meant to you. Just remember that this meaning can change during the process of writing, as you reflect upon the experience. For the campfire topic, the writer developed this statement about its meaning:

> A simple lesson in building campfires shows the love my dad and I share.

When you read the Writer's Model (page 69), notice how this statement is expressed indirectly throughout the personal narrative.

YOUR TURN 5 **Plotting Details**

Use the prewriting instruction to plan your personal narrative.

- decide on your audience, tone, and purpose
- create a graphic organizer to help you search your memory for details
- arrange your details in chronological order
- reflect on the meaning of your experience

Cooperative Learning
Plotting Details in Different Styles.
Organize students into groups of varied learning styles. Have groups brainstorm details for each of their narratives, allowing each student to contribute in the style most comfortable to him or her. To help group members come up with details, have them ask themselves questions like the following: How can I describe what [name of student] just acted out? How can I write what [name of student] just drew? How can I act out what [name of student] just wrote?

YOUR TURN 5

Advise and guide students through the various prewriting activities suggested in this section. Assess comprehension by discussing with students which activity was most useful to them and why.

RESOURCES

Your Turn 5
Practice
- *Communications,* WS. p. 34

Writing
Practice
- *Communications,* WS. p. 35

Using Figurative Language

How can you help your readers to experience your personal story? Your language, as well as your subject matter, must draw your readers in. The details you include should show your readers something they have not seen before or make a familiar experience become more meaningful. One way to add this kind of life and power to your writing is to use **figurative language**—language that compares two unlike things. Figurative language takes readers by surprise and shows them a new way of seeing something. For example, in the sentence, "Damon looked up at the dishwater sky," the sky is compared to dishwater. The comparison makes you think about what the sky and dishwater have in common. You can probably remember days when the sky was dull and dirty looking, just like dishwater.

Examples of figurative language include **similes, metaphors,** and **personification.**

A **simile** compares two seemingly unlike things using the words *like, as, than,* or *resembles.*	**Original:**	The clouds were heavy.
	Simile:	The clouds felt like an alien spaceship hovering ominously overhead.
A **metaphor** compares two seemingly unlike things without using *like, as, than,* or *resembles.* A metaphor says that something *is* something else.	**Original:**	My dress blew around in the wind.
	Metaphor:	My dress was a sail billowing in a wind, making me feel as if I were about to keel over.
Personification gives human qualities to something that is not human, such as an animal, an object, or an idea.	**Original:**	The spring rain fell.
	Personification:	Spring wept its bitter tears of rain.

PRACTICE

On a piece of paper, rewrite the following sentences using a metaphor, simile, or personification.

Example:

1. The mountain range rose out of the valley.

1. *The mountain range, like a man's craggy profile, rose out of the valley.*

1. The trees made shadows.
2. The building looked sleek and new.
3. I felt sad.
4. There were some scary noises.
5. The carpet was soft.
6. The dog was very smart.
7. The boat moved through the water.
8. She hit the tennis ball.
9. I hurried down the sidewalk.
10. The stream flowed quickly.

Using Figurative Language
Students may find it helpful to read literature to see examples of fresh metaphors and similes. You might use "Marigolds" by Eugenia W. Collier or "I Wandered Lonely as a Cloud" by William Wordsworth. Bring a few passages to class and circulate them. Let students nominate and vote on favorite similes and metaphors or personification found in the passages.

MINI-LESSON WRITING

Using Figurative Language

ANSWERS
You might have students label answers as *metaphor, simile,* or *personification.* Here are some possible answers:

1. The trees, sprouting bare branches like fingers and arms, made spooky shadows. [simile]
2. The building was a sleek, new rocket parked downtown. [metaphor]
3. My mood was as low as the belly of a lizard. [simile]
4. The thunder and wind of the storm were scary monsters rattling at the windows. [metaphor]
5. Under my bare feet, the carpet was velvet. [metaphor]
6. The dog was a genius at sniffing out squirrels. [metaphor]
7. The boat sliced the calm water like a blade. [simile]
8. Her strong tennis serve seemed to leap past opponents. [personification]
9. In my hurry, I was a giddy student skipping down the sidewalk on Friday afternoon. [metaphor]
10. The stream tripped over rocks in its rush to the pond. [personification]

"A word fitly spoken is like apples of gold in pictures of silver."

(Proverbs 25:11)

Ask students to define what "apples of gold in pictures of silver" might mean. How does the quotation apply to the writing process? [Choosing the right words can make images vivid for the reader.]

TEACHING (TIP)

Personal Narrative

For more information on using chronological order in paragraphs, see pp. 359–360.

YOUR TURN 6

Use the elements in the framework to gauge the progress and completeness of student compositions. If students have trouble applying the framework to their narratives, reinforce the lesson by reviewing in class **A Writer's Model** and notes on pp. 69–70. You may also find it helpful to model drafting as students begin their drafts.

Writing

Personal Narrative

Framework

Introduction
- Use an engaging opening.
- Supply background information.
- Hint at the meaning of the experience.

Body
- Discuss first, second, third events and so on, including details.
- Use chronological order.

Conclusion
- Express the meaning of the experience.

Directions and Explanations

Get Your Readers' Attention Draw your readers into your narrative by using a quotation, making an unusual statement, or posing a striking question.

Build Background Give your readers some details they might need before reading your narrative.

Hint at Your Meaning Though you will probably not want to reveal the meaning of the experience at the beginning, you should lay the groundwork for it in your introduction. Think of it as giving your readers clues about where you are going with the narrative.

Work in the Details As the body of your narrative takes shape, think of the events as the skeleton and the details as the muscles that define the body and give it movement and life. When you add details, remember to include people, places, thoughts, and feelings, as well as dialogue, similes, and metaphors. Ordering your events chronologically is the simplest way to start.

Reflect on Your Experience Referring to the groundwork you laid in your introduction, finish your narrative by reflecting on what you learned or how you changed. Show your readers the meaning you discovered in the experience.

YOUR TURN 6 Writing a First Draft

Use the framework above to write a first draft of your personal narrative. The Writer's Model on the next page shows how one writer used the framework.

RESOURCES

Writing
Writing Prompts
- *Communications*, TP. 20, WS. p. 36

Your Turn 6
Practice
- *Communications*, TP. 21, WS. p. 37

A Writer's Model

This personal narrative follows the framework on the previous page. The notes in the margin highlight the elements in the framework that appear in this narrative.

A Campfire Girl

Do people make campfires anymore? I suppose they do, but building campfires is prohibited in many places now. If campfires are not banned by rangers, there is still a common ecological agreement that picking the ground bare of wood and scarring the land with fire rings is a bad idea. Still, I am a campfire girl at heart. Even though I dutifully use camp stoves in the mountains and in the car camps, I still love a small blaze to warm my hands, to dry soggy socks, and to stare into on nights darkened by the distance from a city's glow.

It all began with a walk in a park in New York City. When I was a tidy little skirt-wearing five-year-old, my family lived in New York for a summer. My father and I would go out early, when it was still cool, to walk the dog. Dad would be dressed for work, his shoes treading the asphalt path as I happily did a quickstep along beside him.

One morning, as my father threw sticks for the dog, I started picking up sticks of my own. Always ready to play and teach, my dad crouched down to show me how to build a campfire. He took my sticks and helped me gather others, graduated in size from tiny twigs to hefty branches. Gently propping the twigs together, he started with a tepee shape. I watched his careful hands place sticks of the next size on top of the others. He warned me not to pack the sticks too tightly together, so the air could flow and feed the fire. (This was the theory at least; we did not light our fires there in the middle of the city.) While I worked on the tepee and other structures—the log cabin, the "A"—the sounds of the city faded away.

Several years later, at summer camp, we had a contest: who could make a campfire the fastest using just one match? I have no doubt that my lessons in the park in New York City laid the foundation for my championship fire building at camp. I used the "A" structure. I blew gently on my kindling, giving the flame just enough air to grow and light the larger sticks.

(continued)

INTRODUCTION
Engaging opening
Background

Hint at meaning

BODY
First event

Details about people and places

Feeling
Second event

Details about event and people

Thought

Third event

Details about events and people

(continued)

Fourth event
Feelings

Later, when I was no longer a tidy little girl, but a rugged teenager in jeans and work boots, I took special pleasure in collecting wood, placing each size in a separate pile. Then I would set the kindling and get it burning, making a small cook fire. Dad and I never built great big bonfires in rings with three- to four-foot diameters. We made campfires just big enough for the skillet we packed into the wilderness despite its weight. (It cooked so much better than the aluminum camp pans that came in mess kits.) We ate many meals over our fires—potatoes and onions and just-caught trout.

Details about people, places

CONCLUSION

That day in the park, my dad could not have known of the backpacking trips he and I would share ten years later. Still, I see those little piles of sticks as my introduction to life outdoors. The thickly leafed trees of the park gave way to pines and aspen overhead, but the kinship I experienced with my dad stayed the same. I was his campfire girl, sharing in his love of the outdoors, sharing his skill with a fire. We were building something to warm us then and now.

Meaning of the experience

A Student's Model

This is an excerpt from a personal narrative written by Blake Wynia, a student at William G. Enloe High School in Raleigh, North Carolina. The narrative recounts an incident that happened while the writer was clowning around at band camp and the lesson it taught him about carelessness.

Carelessness

. . . In a moment of carelessness, I started running towards the door with my hands stretched out in front of me. At this time I noticed the door had a three-by-four-foot rectangle of glass (with wires in it, of course) near the bottom of it, glaring at me villainously, almost mischievously. In front of the door, there was a black rubber mat, . . . slick with rain. I ran towards the door, the Mission: Impossible music blaring from my lungs. I was a speeding train off its tracks, about to crash. I stepped on the black mat, and my feet slid out from under me. I was sliding forward with my knees out, headed towards the ground. My knees hit the glass rectangle, and went through, shattering the glass like a hot air balloon bursting from intense air pressure. I immediately got up and saw the look on my friends' faces. They were all stunned, and they were all laughing, immaturely. I saw my own face in the reflection in the window, and it was sheer terror. My first thought was that I was going to get kicked out of the clinic for misbehavior . . . At this time, I felt a slight trickle down my leg. I looked down, and my right knee was bleeding from an inch wide gash. Later, . . . I was taken to the emergency room, where I got three stitches in my knee. Thankfully, I was not kicked out of the camp.

This experience taught me much on how to behave properly. The fear I had had of getting in trouble, combined with the disappointment of my mother in me, changed my attitude greatly. I now had learned how to restrain myself. I no longer do crazy things just to make my friends laugh. I am smart enough to think of safer ways to accomplish this feat.

BODY

Event

Simile

Writer's thought
Sensory detail

CONCLUSION

Meaning of the experience

Critical Thinking

Analysis. Begin a class discussion about **A Student's Model,** using questions such as the ones below:

- How does the writer engage the reader in the introduction?

- Which details are most effective in making the reader understand the writer's feelings?

- How does the writer convey what he learned from the experience?

"My diaries were written primarily, I think, not to preserve the experience but to savor it, to make it even more real, more visible and palpable, than in actual life."

(Anne Morrow Lindbergh, 1906–   , poet, essayist, novelist, and wife of famous aviator Charles A. Lindbergh)

Invite students to relate this comment to the revision process: Revision offers the chance to find stronger phrasing or details that will make the experience more real or lively for readers.

TEACHING TIP

Evaluate and Revise Your Draft

You may approach each question on the chart individually, choosing to focus on the particular needs of the class. Discuss the related tips and revision techniques, and have students check their work until they are satisfied that they can answer yes to the related question.

TEACHING TIP

▶ Elaboration

To help students elaborate on events in their personal narratives, encourage them to include sensory images in their stories. After students have written down events they want to recall, ask them to use clustering to brainstorm details that relate to at least one particular sense.

Recalling the sensation of touching a soft puppy or smelling the smoke from a campfire may help students jog their memories and recall more details for their personal narratives.

Revising

Evaluate and Revise Your Draft

Do Look Back   To improve your draft, you must read it and read it again. Work collaboratively to concentrate first on content and organization and second on style. Looking twice will give you the necessary time to correct mistakes and also to make your writing more accurate and more powerful. Stronger writing will help you create an experience that will affect your readers.

▷ **First Reading: Content and Organization**   With a peer or on your own, use the guidelines below to evaluate your narrative and make improvements. The tips in the second column will help you locate any trouble spots.

Personal Narrative: Content and Organization Guidelines for Peer and Self-Evaluation

Evaluation Questions	▶ Tips	▶ Revision Techniques
❶ Does the introduction include an attention grabber, some background information, and a hint at the meaning of the experience?	**Bracket** the attention grabber and background information. **Underline** the hint about the meaning of the experience. If there are no brackets or underlined sentences, revise.	**Add** background information or attention grabber. **Add** a sentence that suggests the meaning of the experience.
❷ Do details of events, people, and places seem real?	**Circle** details. If you have fewer than three circles in each paragraph, revise.	**Add** details that answer *5W-How?* questions about people, places, or events in the paragraph. **Add** dialogue or draw on the five senses for additional details.
❸ Are there details about thoughts and feelings?	**Highlight** sentences that contain thoughts or feelings. If the paper runs an entire paragraph without a highlighted sentence, revise.	**Elaborate** on details by answering the questions, "What did I think?" or "How did I feel?"
❹ Is the order of events clear?	**Number** the events in chronological order. Revise if the numbers are not in sequence.	**Rearrange** events to show chronological order, or **add** transitional words and phrases to show how events are ordered.
❺ Does the conclusion discuss the meaning of the experience?	**Underline** sentences in the conclusion that explain the meaning of the experience. If no sentences are underlined, revise.	**Add** a statement that shows what your experience means to you.

RESOURCES

Revising
Practice
■ *Communications,* TPs. 22, 23, WS. pp. 38, 39, 40

Extension
■ *Designing Your Writing*

ONE WRITER'S REVISIONS After looking at how one writer changed part of the personal narrative from page 69, answer the questions that follow.

> It all began with a walk in a park in New York City. When
> *a tidy little skirt-wearing five-year-old,*
> I was ~~five~~, my family lived in New York for a summer. My   add and elaborate
>
> father and I would go out early, when it was still cool, to walk
> *his shoes treading*
> the dog. Dad would be dressed for work. ~~He treaded~~ the asphalt   add and elaborate
> *happily*
> path as I did a quickstep along beside him.   add

Analyzing the Revision Process

1. How did adding details improve the paragraph?
2. What does the word "happily" add to the last sentence?

PEER REVIEW

Ask a classmate to answer the following questions after he or she has read your paper.

1. What details helped you to imagine the writer's experience?
2. What details could the writer have included to make things more clear?

YOUR TURN 7 **Focusing on Content and Organization**

Using the guidelines on the previous page, evaluate your personal narrative. Then, revise your paper so that it is clearer, more personal, and more interesting.

Second Reading: Style The first time you went over your paper, you revised your content and organization. Now, you need to refine style to suit your audience and your purpose. One way to shape your style is to use **precise verbs** to express what you mean. This allows your readers to live through the experience with you. In your second reading, use the following style guidelines to help you focus on making your verbs more precise.

Style Guidelines

Evaluation Question	▶ Tip	▶ Revision Technique
Are your verbs precise?	▶ Pick four sentences in each paragraph. **Circle** only the verbs in them. Do the verbs hint at *how* or *in what way* something is done? If not, revise.	▶ **Replace** at least two weak verbs per paragraph with precise ones. (Brainstorm for synonyms or use a thesaurus to find more precise verbs.)

Analyzing the Revision Process

ANSWERS

1. The added details flesh out the scene and make it more vivid.

2. It shows how the narrator felt about these excursions with her father.

YOUR TURN 7

Evaluate papers for their strengths in the five areas of the **Content and Organization Guidelines** on p. 72.

Evaluating Student Writing

The ancillary *Assessment Alternatives* contains a variety of assessment forms, including Inventories and Evaluation Forms and rubrics: Six-Point Scales, Four-Point Scales, and Six Trait Scales.

Precise Verbs

As students comb their narratives for common or vague verbs, suggest that they list their verbs on a separate piece of paper. Then, have students use a thesaurus to equate each listed verb with a more vivid or precise choice. This list should be useful in completing the revision exercise. Remind students that words in a thesaurus do not always have exactly the same meaning or usage as the word being replaced; students may wish to consult a dictionary if they are unsure of a word's usage.

Analyzing the Revision Process

ANSWERS

1. *Watched* implies more careful observation than *saw* does.

2. *Warned* is more direct and implies that there may be consequences, whereas *told* is weaker and bossier. Other words to use could be *cautioned, counseled,* or *advised.*

Meeting INDIVIDUAL NEEDS

ENGLISH-LANGUAGE LEARNERS
General Strategies. When students write about personal experiences, they often use the four most common emotive adjectives: *happy, sad, surprised,* and *scared.* Most students limit the number of words that represent feelings in their vocabularies. Encourage students to use more vivid words by helping them brainstorm for synonyms.

Focus on

Word Choice

Precise Verbs

Precise verbs often tell more than *what* was done. They tell *how* something was done—it's like having a built-in adverb. For example, if you have the word *run* in your narrative, think about more precise words that show **how** people run, such as *hurry, rush, dash,* or *flee.* In your quest for the right verb, choose the one that gives life to your writing. For example, if someone in your narrative is moving slowly in a carefree way, the verb *saunter* is a better choice than the verb *walk.* Writing with precision takes time: time to check the dictionary or thesaurus, and time to think about just the right word.

ONE WRITER'S REVISIONS Using the style guidelines on page 73, the writer of the model on page 69 revised for precise verbs in the following way. Study the revisions and answer the questions that follow.

BEFORE REVISION

I saw his careful hands place sticks of the next size on top of the others. He told me not to pack the sticks too tightly together. . . .

Saw is not very descriptive—how?
Told is fairly common— in what way?

AFTER REVISION

I watched his careful hands place sticks of the next size on top of the others. He warned me not to pack the sticks too tightly together. . . .

Watched better describes what she was doing.
Warned tells how he spoke.

Analyzing the Revision Process

1. How does *watched* better describe what the girl is doing?

2. Why is the verb *warned* better than *told*? What other verbs could the writer use?

TIP Try using your word-processing program's thesaurus to find more precise replacements for imprecise verbs. Enter a tired, boring verb into the thesaurus, and explore the lists of possible replacements that the thesaurus gives. For example, for the word *make,* you will find *create, construct,* and *build.*

RESOURCES

Focus on Word Choice
Practice
■ *Communications,* WS. p. 41

YOUR TURN 8 — Using Precise Verbs

Fine-tune the verbs in your narrative. Use the information on the previous pages to identify common or overused verbs and to replace them with precise ones.

Designing Your Writing

Using Illustrations   Make your paper inviting by illustrating it with a photograph or drawing. Choose an illustration that works well with the narrative. Whether you scan a photograph in on the computer or paste a drawing in manually, consider the following guidelines.

- The eye is drawn to images. Remember that readers will look at your illustration before they read your paper. Therefore, the illustration must truly complement your paper rather than distract from it. For the campfire story, a picture of a forest fire, a tent, or some wildlife—none of which are mentioned—might confuse the readers. A picture of a frying pan on a campfire would work better.

- Because you have written a personal narrative, you may wish to choose a photograph or drawing of yourself. You may even have a photograph of yourself taken at the time the events you have written about took place. For example, the campfire story could be illustrated with a photograph of the writer at five, or with one of her and her father around a campfire.

- You have used a lot of details to make your narrative vivid. Choose an illustration that will draw your readers in—one that gives them clues about key details in your narrative. A snapshot of the campfire girl among her friends or of her at her current age would give the wrong clues to her readers and would mislead them about the content of the paper.

- The placement of your illustration is important. If your illustration complements your paper as a whole, you may choose to place it at the beginning or the end. If your illustration relates to a particular detail, place the illustration near where that detail is mentioned in the text.

TIP   If you are scanning a photograph onto the computer, you will need to decide on the resolution of the image. Resolution refers to the number of dpi (dots per inch) that will form the image. Generally, the higher the resolution (the more dots per inch), the sharper and more detailed the image will be. Keep in mind that your decisions about resolution affect the size of the file needed to store your image.

Writing Workshop   **75**

YOUR TURN 8

Challenge students to change at least two verbs per paragraph. You may compare the new verb choices to the original verbs to see if students understand the concept of precise verbs.

TECHNOLOGY TIP

You may want to remind students that some word-processing applications allow the import of clip art, pictures, and other graphics. If students have access to a digital scanner, they can use it to convert their illustrations into computer graphics.

Publishing

Quotation for the Day

" . . . and for the first time I learned another lesson which every young writer has got to learn. And that lesson is the naked, blazing power of print. "

(Thomas Wolfe, 1900–1938, American author)

Ask students which source seems most reliable: news from a friend, news announced at school, or news printed in the newspaper. Why? [Most will say the newspaper is most reliable because the paper has a professional responsibility to print facts.] Point out that the influential reputation of print is the "power" Wolfe speaks of, and that this power is a strong reason for being sure to publish the most accurate writing possible.

Grammar Link

Subject-Verb Agreement: Interrupting Prepositional Phrases

ANSWERS

1. comes
2. brings
3. are
4. lack
5. note

Proofread Your Personal Narrative

Reference Note

For **proofreading guidelines,** see page 13.

Error-Free Zone Proofread your paper before you prepare a clean copy for publishing. At this stage, you must rely on the **conventions of written English** to eliminate all grammar, punctuation, and spelling errors. One thing to pay special attention to is subject-verb agreement. While writing and revising, you may have added phrases between some of your subjects and verbs. If so, you might be confused about which form of a verb you need. Be sure your verbs agree with their subjects.

Grammar Link

Subject-Verb Agreement: Interrupting Prepostional Phrases

If you want your sentences to make sense to readers, it is important that your verbs agree in number with their subjects.

■ **A singular subject should have a singular verb.**

Example:
That **cat climbs.**

■ **A plural subject should have a plural verb.**

Example:
Those **cats climb.**

The number of a verb does not change even when a phrase comes between it and its subject. If a prepositional phrase following the subject contains a plural noun, you could be tempted to make the verb plural also. However, the verb should remain singular.

Example:
The **cat** as well as the dogs **wants** to chase birds and squirrels.

Example:
Those **cats** at the window **want** to chase birds and squirrels.

Reference Note

For more on **subject-verb agreement,** see page 493.

PRACTICE

From each pair of verbs in parentheses, choose the form that agrees in number with the subject of each sentence.

Example:
1. The passengers on the crowded dock (*hurries, hurry*) to board.
1. The passengers on the crowded dock hurry to board.

1. The ship, along with four tugboats, (*come, comes*) slowly toward the dock.
2. The captain, on the lookout for dangers in the waters, (*bring, brings*) the ship to shore.
3. The passengers in the hold (*is, are*) seasick.
4. Their faces, by the porthole, (*lack, lacks*) any sign of hope or pleasure.
5. Observers of the scene (*note, notes*) that the ship has been at sea for just three hours.

RESOURCES

Grammar Link

Practice

■ *Communications,* WS. p. 42

Publish Your Personal Narrative

Writer Seeks Readers You have written your personal story. It is something to be proud of and to share with other people. Try some of the following ways to reach some readers besides your teacher and classmates.

■ Send your paper in the mail or by e-mail to interested relatives or friends. If your narrative is about an event in their lives or about someone your readers know, they might be especially interested to read it. You might even consider giving your paper as a gift to someone for whom it would mean a lot.

■ Check with your teacher or look for some magazines that have contests for this kind of personal essay. Well-written, authentic stories from students' lives are often welcomed in magazines for young people.

■ Create a class book of personal narratives, dividing them thematically. For example, the themes for memories could be young childhood, school, jobs, and travel.

■ If your personal narrative is about school life, you might consider submitting it to your school's yearbook committee.

Reflect on Your Personal Narrative

PORTFOLIO

Count the Ways Use the following questions to look back at writing your personal narrative and to make a quick account of what you've learned. If you put this paper into your portfolio, include your responses with it.

■ How did your writing this paper help you to understand this experience better or in a new way?

■ Are you satisfied with how you conveyed the meaning of your experience? Why or why not? What would you do differently if you wrote another personal narrative?

YOUR TURN 9 Proofreading, Publishing, and Reflecting

Using the suggestions and questions in the three previous sections of the workshop, take time to proofread your paper, publish it, and reflect on the steps you took to write it.

Metacognition. Have students use the following question to reflect on their writing processes.

1. What tips and suggestions helped you most when revising your narrative? Why?

Then, ask students the following question.

2. What are the most important elements of a personal narrative? [The narrative should include both an account of the writer's experience and some reflections about the meaning of that experience.]

YOUR TURN 9

To help you assess students' reflection processes, you might have them create a sheet for their portfolio titled "I Have Learned These Grammar Concepts." On this sheet, students could list proofreading errors they found in their papers along with their corrections. Have students date their entries.

Writing a Short Story

Many of the techniques that you used in writing your personal narrative can be applied to writing a short story. Like personal narratives, short stories thrive on details, put events in chronological order, and—often—involve more than one character.

When you write a short story, you can use first-person pronouns just as you used them in your personal narrative. However, if you decide to use first-person pronouns in a short story, remember that the narrator (the "I" in the story) does not necessarily have to be you—it can be any fictional character that you create.

Stretch the Imagination In your personal narrative, the events actually happened to you. It is a true story—nonfiction. However, a short story is **fiction**; it comes from your imagination. You can write a short story about almost anything.

- Are you interested in things past or in worlds of the future? Think of something you and your friends would like to read. Create a tale of seventeenth-century piracy or of life in a geodesic dome in the 2050s.

- Even though a story comes from your imagination, you can still write about things you know. Is there something you know about that would serve as the basis for an exciting story? One student's quest to make the basketball team? A person's experience in a new town? Make a list of your ideas and then choose a few to explore when you begin to write.

How to Begin There are four basic building blocks for any story: **plot, characters, point of view,** and **setting.** You will need to use all of them, but you can *start* by considering any one of them.

- **Start with a plot.** What will happen in your story? Most stories have a **conflict**, or problem, that is the center of the action. Events lead up to the conflict and then, after a turning point, events unwind toward a **resolution** of the conflict. The conflict involves the main character and can be either internal (if a character is struggling with himself or herself) or **external** (if a character is struggling with outside forces). To begin, you can make a list of events that will unfold in your story.

- **Start with a character.** Maybe you have a great idea for a character. Jot down what you know about your character, using lots of descriptive words—you know just what this character will look like and sound like, what the character will do, say, and think. Once you have your first character sketched out, you can create any others you will need.

- **Start with a point of view.** Decide who will tell your story. Will one character be the narrator, telling the story from his or her point of view (**first-person point of view**)? Will the narrator be outside the story and able to recount everything that goes on in the mind of each character (**third-person omniscient point of view**)? Whatever point of view you choose, use it consistently throughout the story. Read the examples below to see the difference a choice between first-person point of view and third-person point of view can make.

First Person: I noticed Juana talking to Mark after school. I thought he looked nervous.

Third-Person Omniscient: When Juana spoke to Mark after school, he flushed with nervous excitement. Maybe, he thought to himself, she would go with him to the dance.

■ **Start with a setting.** Where and when does your story take place? What time of year is it? Setting can be as important to the story as character. In stories that show how a character struggles with natural elements, for example, setting is particularly important. Give your story atmosphere, a general mood or feeling to the place where everything happens.

Setting an Example We do not know which of the elements Gwendolyn Brooks began with when she wrote the story below. Still, it is easy to see that she made good use of all the building blocks—plot, character, point of view, and setting. By reading the story and annotations, you may get some ideas about how you could tell your own story.

Maud Martha Spares the Mouse
from *Maud Martha* by Gwendolyn Brooks

There. She had it at last. The weeks it had devoted to eluding her, the tricks, the clever hide-and-go-seeks, the routes it had in all sobriety[1] devised, together with the delicious moments it had, undoubtedly, laughed up its sleeve—all to no ultimate avail.[2] She had that mouse.

It shook its little self, as best it could, in the trap. Its bright black eyes contained no appeal—the little creature seemed to understand that there was no hope of mercy from the eternal enemy, no hope of reprieve[3] or postponement—but a fine small dignity. It waited. It looked at Maud Martha.

She wondered what else it was thinking. Perhaps that there was not enough food in its larder. Perhaps that little Betty, a puny child from the start, would not, now, be getting fed. Perhaps that, now, the family's

Plot—The story starts with the capture of the mouse and flashes back to events and details of past weeks.

Character—The mouse is a character.

Setting—The author imagines how the mouse might perceive the world and elaborates, providing details that reveal setting.

---

1. **sobriety:** seriousness.
2. **avail:** help.
3. **reprieve:** temporary relief or escape from trouble or pain.

(continued)

Timesaver

Rather than having students brainstorm completely new story ideas, you can save class time by asking them to "fictionalize" their personal narratives. Suggest they do this by writing in the third person or using a first-person narrator other than themselves, changing setting and characters, and adding details that didn't really happen.

Meeting INDIVIDUAL NEEDS

MULTIPLE INTELLIGENCES

Musical Intelligence. To introduce the concept of theme, play a piece of music that has a recurrent theme (compositions by Bach lend themselves well to this exercise). Encourage students to listen for the repeating melody, and point out that although it may not be identical each time, it leaves an overall impression. Similarly, in a story, an author often uses details and actions to hint at the theme rather than directly stating the insight—the meaning or idea.

YOUR TURN 10

To evaluate students' writing, use the building blocks mentioned in the text (plot, character, setting, point of view, and theme) as the basis of a rubric. You might also include clear chronology, supporting details, and precise verbs in the rubric.

Point of View—Readers see not only Maud Martha's point of view but the mouse's point of view through Martha's eyes and imagination.

Conflict and Resolution—Maud Martha must decide whether or not to set the mouse free. The resolution of the conflict comes when she imagines how the mouse might think and feel.

(continued)

seasonal house-cleaning, for lack of expert direction, would be left undone. It might be regretting that young Bobby's education was now at an end. It might be nursing personal regrets. No more the mysterious shadows of the kitchenette, the uncharted twists, the unguessed halls. No more the sweet delights of the chase, the charms of being unsuccessfully hounded, thrown at.

Maud Martha could not bear the little look.

"Go home to your children," she urged. "To your wife or husband." She opened the trap. The mouse vanished.

Suddenly, she was conscious of a new cleanness in her. A wide air walked in her. A life had blundered its way into her power and it had been hers to preserve or destroy. She had not destroyed. In the center of that simple restraint was—creation. She had created a piece of life. It was wonderful.

"Why," she thought, as her height doubled, "why, I'm good! I am *good.*"

She ironed her aprons. Her back was straight. Her eyes were mild, and soft with a godlike loving-kindness.

The Heart of the Matter In your personal narrative, you wrote about the meaning of your experience. In fiction, writers also convey a meaning, called **theme.** Gwendolyn Brooks has given her story a theme, or insight about life: By simply letting the mouse go, Maud Martha creates life. The meaning of the story is that creation can come from the most basic of acts—deciding not to do harm. Consider how you could use characters, plot, setting, and point of view to convey the theme, or meaning, of your own story.

YOUR TURN 10 Writing Your Short Story

Now, write your own short story. Use the building blocks—plot, character, setting, point of view—and be sure to choose a theme for your story. Fill your story with details, make sure the order of events is clear, and try to use precise verbs. After you have written a draft of your story, remember to revise, proofread, and publish it.

Presenting and Evaluating Oral Narratives

Talk   Listen

Yℴu have probably already told many personal narratives aloud— what happened when the family car broke down on vacation, what the new kitten did when you first brought it home, or how your team won the championship. When you tell a story aloud, you are giving an **oral narrative.** In this section you will learn how to tell a story aloud to your class or to an unfamiliar audience. You will plan, practice, and present this story, so the experience will be different from your everyday storytelling. Your story does not need to be true; it can be based on fact or imagination. You might tell a story you have heard from friends or relatives, or you might present the personal narrative you wrote for the Writer's Workshop. Just be sure to choose an interesting story that you can tell in a lively way.

WHAT'S AHEAD?

In this section you will learn how to

■ **tell a story, using vocal and physical techniques**

■ **listen to and evaluate storytelling**

OBJECTIVES

■ To tell a story using vocal and physical techniques

■ To listen to and evaluate storytelling

Quotation for the Day

"A poem, a sentence, causes us to see ourselves. I be, and I see my being, at the same time."

(Ralph Waldo Emerson, 1803–1882, American poet, essayist, and philosopher)

Ask students to think of stories in which they recognize themselves. Stories that make students feel such a connection may be good stories for them to tell aloud, as they will sympathize with the characters. This connection to the character will help them use appropriate gestures and emotions in their performance.

Remember Story Essentials

You are probably already familiar with the makings of a good narrative. As you are deciding on a narrative to tell, remember that a good story should

■ describe where and when the narrative took place

■ establish a point of view (let listeners know through whose eyes the events are being viewed)

■ include an interesting series of events and memorable personalities

■ provide details about events, places, people, thoughts, and feelings, including vivid images and sensory descriptions

■ have a meaning or theme

■ appeal to its intended audience (in this case, your listeners)

Focus on Speaking and Listening   **81**

RESOURCES

Focus on Speaking and Listening Practice

■ *Media Literacy and Communication Skills*
—*Support and Practice,* Ch. 2
—*A How-to Handbook*

Teaching Notes

■ *Media Literacy and Communication Skills*
—*A Teacher's Guide,* Ch. 2

Use Gestures to Tell Your Story

"Once upon a time . . ." Even the oldest stories can be made new and exciting with the right storytelling techniques. When you tell a story, you have the opportunity to enhance a narrative using **nonverbal** communication. To convey the meaning of your words, you must use your body, hands, and facial expressions in a **nonverbal** way. A gesture such as flapping your hand in one direction can signify a bird's flight or the escape of your hero. If someone in your narrative is surprised, then show an expression of surprise on your face to emphasize your words.

Use Vocal Techniques to Tell Your Story

Perhaps even more important than gesture is your voice. In storytelling, you must use your voice like a musical instrument so that your listeners will eagerly follow your words. There are three principal ways you can use your voice to make your story more interesting.

- **Change the pitch of your voice** when different characters are speaking. Storytellers will often use a high pitch to represent a small character. Pitch can also create a mood or express feelings. A low, solemn voice, for example, might be appropriate at the beginning of a scary story.

- **Speak more loudly or softly,** depending on the number of people in your audience, and on what is happening in your story. A quieter voice, for example, would probably work better for a suspenseful story. Making your voice thunder can indicate not only a certain mood, but also a change in character.

- **Speak more quickly or more slowly.** To show excitement, speed up the pace of your speech. To show weariness, slow it down. These are just two ways to change your rate of speech to enliven your storytelling. Remember not to talk so fast that your audience cannot understand you or so slowly that your story drags.

Practice, Practice, Practice

You may be able to tell a good story without rehearsing, but you probably cannot tell a great one without it. Take the time to practice in one of these ways.

- **Tell your story to a friend or relative,** and ask for feedback. Have your trial audience tell you whether you were expressive enough with both your voice and your gestures.

- **Use a tape recorder.** Although you may never get completely used to the sound of your own voice when it is played back to you, you still should be able to hear your **inflections,** the changes in the pitch or tone of your voice. If you do not hear many inflections, you should decide where you could vary your pitch, alter the pace, or change the volume of your voice.

- **Try your story out on video.** This is the best way to see and hear yourself as your audience will see and hear you. You can turn the sound off to see better what you are doing with your hands or your facial expressions. Make sure your gestures match the suspense or conflict in the story. You can also dim the picture and just listen to your voice. Evaluate both together to decide whether you are performing your story in the best possible way.

Listening: Focus Your Body

If you are the storyteller, you must make a clear effort to interest and entertain your listeners. However, if you are the listener, you must take an active part in receiving the story so that you will understand and enjoy it. An active listener focuses attention on the story and becomes involved with what is being said. To be an active listener, here is what you should do *physically*.

- **Face the storyteller.** Use your body and the angle of your head to bring yourself to full attention. For example, your shoulders should be parallel to the storyteller's.

- **Look at the storyteller.** You will notice the nonverbal clues the storyteller gives you only if you see them. Keep your eyes on the speaker.

- **Make eye contact.** The storyteller is looking at you. To receive this communication and understand it better, look into the speaker's eyes.

- **Keep quiet.** This one is obvious. It is much harder to pay attention to a storyteller when you are talking as well.

TIP You can use the feedback you get from your audience to evaluate the effectiveness of your presentation and to **set goals for future presentations.**

TIP As you listen, try to monitor the speaker's message for clarity. At the end of the story, ask relevant questions to clarify your understanding.

Evaluating Oral Narratives
An additional activity that you may use to reinforce the evaluation of oral narratives is to ask students to listen to a professional oral narrative given by someone in the community. Have students use the criteria on this page to analyze and evaluate the professional oral narrative. You may have students report their findings to the class.

Wrap It Up

Metacognition. To help students reflect on their speaking and listening processes, ask them the following questions.

1. What part of storytelling is most difficult for you? What part is the easiest? Why?

2. When listening to a story, what aspect of being an active and interested listener is most difficult? Why?

Then, ask students the following question.

3. List three things listeners can do physically to help them listen more actively. [face and look at the speaker, make eye contact, keep quiet, and respond to the storyteller]

YOUR TURN 11

Evaluate whether students have used the guidelines suggested in this chapter to engage their listeners.

TIP As you listen to narratives, try to identify and analyze the effect of **artistic elements** such as imagery, language, character development, and point of view.

■ **Respond to the storyteller.** You can use nonverbal communication as you follow the story. Nod your head; smile at what you think is clever or funny.

Listening: Focus Your Mind

Being an active listener involves more than what you do physically. Here is what you should do *mentally*.

■ **Predict outcomes.** Just as you do when you are reading, ask yourself what will happen next in the story, and as you listen, confirm or correct your prediction.

■ **Create images in your mind.** If you can picture what is going on in the story, you will enjoy it more. Listen for descriptions and flesh out your images of the story.

■ **Remember your own experiences or stories.** Making connections with your own life and the things you know will make the story more clear and more enjoyable to you.

Evaluating Oral Narratives

Whether you are listening to a classmate, a comedian on TV, or an actor in a one-person play, you will **evaluate,** or judge, the performance as you listen. To help you to evaluate, here are some questions you can ask yourself as you listen.

■ Is the storyteller speaking loudly and clearly enough for you to understand?

■ Do the storyteller's gestures highlight the narrative or do they distract listeners? In what way?

■ Does the storyteller vary his or her pitch and pace?

■ Does the storyteller use vivid details about events, places, and people? Does he or she include thoughts and feelings?

YOUR TURN 11 Storytelling Hour

Choose a story to tell. Think about how you will present it: the gestures you will make, how you will use your voice to emphasize and bring meaning to the words. Practice your story and then present it to your class. When you are listening to your classmates' stories, use the guidelines above to help you to be an active and interested listener.

Choices

Choose one of the following activities to complete.

▶ **CROSSING THE CURRICULUM: HISTORY**

1. Be Somebody Pretend you are a historical figure and write a **"personal" narrative** as that figure. You do not necessarily have to choose someone famous. You may wish to be anyone from an Anasazi artist or a nineteenth-century millworker, to a fighter pilot taking part in the Battle of Britain. Do some research to give historical accuracy to your personal narrative.

▶ **CROSSING THE CURRICULUM: MUSIC**

2. Say It with Music Tell a story with music. Write **music** using the framework of a personal narrative (see page 68). Your musical piece should have an introduction with a melody (or theme). It should have events in the form of movements or sections, and a conclusion which sums up the whole musical narrative.

▶ **CAREERS**

3. Job Story Visit someone at his or her place of work and write a **narrative** about your time there.

Use the framework on page 68 so that you are sure to have all the essential elements of a personal narrative. Ask yourself what you learned during your visit and use your answer as a reflection at the end of your narrative.

▶ **LITERATURE**

4. Change Your Point of View Write a **short-story** version of your personal narrative. While in a personal narrative you must recount what really happened, in fiction you can use your imagination. You can fictionalize your personal narrative, inventing other events, characters, or details to make it a short story.

▶ **SPEAKING AND LISTENING**

5. Personal History Learn, practice, and deliver a story from another generation. Does your father tell you about walking ten miles through the snow to get to school? Perhaps you have a relative or a neighbor who could share a good story from the time when he or she was your age. Give an **oral presentation** of the story using first-person point of view.

PORTFOLIO

▶ **CROSSING THE CURRICULUM: MUSIC**

Invite the school band or choir director to talk with students about composing music, emphasizing the concepts required for this assignment. The music director may be able to suggest several examples. Ask a librarian to keep them available for reference.

▶ **CAREERS**

Be sure to get permission from the people students choose to interview and from the students' parents or guardians. Encourage students to write out their questions for this assignment before going to their interviews.

▶ **LITERATURE**

Briefly review the use of third-person point of view. As students change their personal narratives into short stories written in third person, they should distance themselves from the events. Encourage students to feel free to improvise the events, characters, and details. Remind students to re-read their stories carefully to ensure that the stories no longer lapse into first person.

▶ **SPEAKING AND LISTENING**

To gather enough details to be able to retell a story effectively, students may want to think of questions to prompt the original storyteller. Students might ask about the types of clothes, games, hairstyles, slang, politics, and music that were popular at the time.

RESOURCES

Expressing Your Thoughts

Assessment

■ *Assessment Package*
—*Chapter Tests,* Ch. 2
—*Chapter Tests in Standardized Test Formats,* Ch. 2
—*Assessment Alternatives,* Ch. 2

■ *Test Generator (One-Stop Planner CD-ROM)*

Choices

Rubrics

■ *Assessment Package*
—*Assessment Alternatives,* Ch. 2

CHAPTER 3

Exploring Similarities and Differences

Use this guide to create an instructional plan that suits the individual needs of your students. Assignments marked by an asterisk (*) may be completed out of class. Times given for pacing lessons are estimated. See pp. 86–87 for chapter-wide resources. Resources listed in this guide are point-of-use resources only.

Curriculum Connections

Choices *p. 121*
- Crossing the Curriculum: History
- Literature
- Speaking and Listening

internet connect

 GO TO: go.hrw.com
KEYWORD: EOLang 9-3

All resources for this chapter are available for preview on the *One-Stop Planner CD-ROM with Test Generator*. All worksheets and tests may be printed from the CD-ROM.

	Chapter Opener *pp. 86–87*	Reading Workshop: Reading a Comparison-Contrast Article *pp. 88–97*
DEVELOPMENTAL PROGRAM	🕐 **30 minutes** • Comparing and Contrasting *p. 87* • Your Turn 1 *p. 87*	🕐 **120 minutes** • Preparing to Read *p. 88* • Reading Selection *pp. 89–90* • First Thoughts 1–3 *p. 91* • Explicit Main Idea and Supporting Details *pp. 91–93* • Your Turn 2 *p. 93* • Comparison-Contrast Structure *pp. 93–95* • Your Turn 3 *p. 95* • Vocabulary Mini-Lesson *p. 96* • Test Taking Mini-Lesson *p. 97*
CORE PROGRAM	🕐 **30 minutes** • Comparing and Contrasting *p. 87* • Your Turn 1 *p. 87*	🕐 **120 minutes** • Preparing to Read *p. 88* • Reading Selection *pp. 89–90* • First Thoughts 1–3 *p. 91* • Explicit Main Idea and Supporting Details *pp. 91–93* • Your Turn 2 *p. 93* • Comparison-Contrast Structure *pp. 93–95* • Your Turn 3 *p. 95* • Vocabulary Mini-Lesson *p. 96* • Test Taking Mini-Lesson *p. 97*
ADVANCED PROGRAM	🕐 **20 minutes** • Comparing and Contrasting *p. 87* • Your Turn 1 *p. 87*	🕐 **70 minutes** • Preparing to Read *p. 88* • Reading Selection* *pp. 89–90* • First Thoughts 2–3 *p. 91* • Explicit Main Idea and Supporting Details *pp. 91–93* • Your Turn 2 *p. 93* • Comparison-Contrast Structure *pp. 93–95* • Your Turn 3* *p. 95* • Test Taking Mini-Lesson* *p. 97*
RESOURCES — PRINT	• *Communications,* 🔖 TP. 24, WS. p. 43 🖎	• *Alternative Readings,* 🔖 Ch. 3 • *Communications,* 🔖 TPs. 25, 26, WS. pp. 44–51
RESOURCES — MEDIA	• *One-Stop Planner CD-ROM* 💿	• *One-Stop Planner CD-ROM* 💿

CHAPTER PLANNING GUIDE

RESOURCES

TP.=Transparency   WS.=Worksheet

Writing Workshop: Writing a Comparison-Contrast Essay pp. 98–117	Focus on Viewing and Representing: Comparing and Contrasting Media Coverage pp. 118–120
🕐 100 minutes • Prewriting *pp. 98–105* • Critical-Thinking Mini-Lesson *p. 103* • Arrange Your Information *pp. 104–105* • Your Turn 4 *p. 105* • Framework and Your Turn 5 *p. 106* • Writer's Model and Student's Model *pp. 107–108* **🕐 80 minutes** • Evaluate and Revise Your Draft *pp. 109–110* • Your Turn 6 *p. 110* • Focus on Sentences and Your Turn 7 *p. 111* • Proofread, Publish, and Reflect on Your Essay *pp. 112–114* • Grammar Link *p. 112* • Your Turn 8 *p. 114*	**🕐 90 minutes** • Examine Different Accounts of an Event *pp. 118–119* • Looking at the News *pp. 119–120* • Your Turn 10 *p. 120*
🕐 120 minutes • Prewriting *pp. 98–105* • Critical-Thinking Mini-Lesson* *p. 103* • Arrange Your Information *pp. 104–105* • Your Turn 4 *p. 105* • Framework and Your Turn 5* *p. 106* • Writer's Model and Student's Model *pp. 107–108* • Evaluate and Revise Your Draft *pp. 109–110* • Your Turn 6 *p. 110* • Focus on Sentences and Your Turn 7* *p. 111* • Proofread, Publish, and Reflect on Your Essay *pp. 112–114* • Grammar Link *p. 112* • Your Turn 8* *p. 114* • Connections to Life *pp. 115–117* • Your Turn 9 *p. 117*	**🕐 80 minutes** • Examine Different Accounts of an Event *pp. 118–119* • Looking at the News *pp. 119–120* • Your Turn 10 *p. 120*
🕐 120 minutes • Prewriting *pp. 98–105* • Your Turn 4* *p. 105* • Framework and Your Turn 5* *p. 106* • Writer's Model and Student's Model *pp. 107–108* • Evaluate and Revise Your Draft* *pp. 109–110* • Your Turn 6* *p. 110* • Proofread, Publish, and Reflect on Your Essay *pp. 112–114* • Your Turn 8* *p. 114* • Connections to Life* *pp. 115–117* • Your Turn 9* *p. 117*	**🕐 60 minutes** • Examine Different Accounts of an Event *pp. 118–119* • Looking at the News *pp. 119–120* • Your Turn 10 *p. 120*
• *Communications,* TPs. 27–30, WS. pp. 52–60 • *Designing Your Writing*	• *Media Literacy and Communication Skills* —*Support and Practice,* Ch. 3 —*A How-to Handbook* —*A Teacher's Guide,* Ch. 3
• *One-Stop Planner CD-ROM* 🎵	• *Media Literacy and Communication Skills* 📺 —Videocassette 1, Segment C • *One-Stop Planner CD-ROM* 🎵

Exploring Similarities and Differences

CHAPTER OBJECTIVES

■ To read a comparison-contrast article and analyze its organizational structure

■ To write a comparison-contrast essay

■ To compare and contrast media coverage of an event

Chapter Overview

Most good decision-making involves comparing and contrasting. This chapter is designed to teach students how to make effective comparisons when they are reading, writing, and viewing. In the Reading Workshop, students read a comparison-contrast article and analyze its organizational method. The Writing Workshop gives students a chance to follow the steps in the writing process so that they can organize and write their own comparison-contrast essays. Finally, the Focus on Viewing and Representing teaches students how to identify similarities and differences in news coverage among different news media. The three sections of the chapter can be taught as independent units, but taught together, they reinforce a comprehensive understanding of comparisons and contrasts.

Why Study Similarities and Differences?

Students who can recognize similarities and differences will be better able to make sense of their worlds. Analyzing similarities and differences teaches students to break down subjects into their constituent elements. Then, students can understand the various parts of a subject and relate them to other subjects. This process of classifying or grouping items gives students a way to relate new information to old or familiar situations. The process also allows students to give explanations and make more informed decisions and judgments.

Teaching the Chapter

Option 1: Begin with Literature

You could begin by asking students to identify similarities and differences in two literary selections. For example, students could compare and contrast themes, tone, characters, or plot development in novels or short stories. As students analyze the selections, show them how to use Venn diagrams to keep track of the similarities and differences. Then, after students have read the comparison-contrast article in this chapter (pp. 89–90), discuss with them its organizational structure. After reading and analyzing comparison-contrast structures in exposition, students will be ready to write about similarities and differences in both literary and nonliterary subjects.

Option 2: Begin with Nonfiction and Writing

Introduce students to comparison-contrast structures in expository writing by beginning with the material in this chapter. First, teach them to recognize the organizational patterns and techniques of comparison-contrast writing by reading the article in the Reading Workshop and completing its accompanying instruction (p. 88–97). Then, have students apply what they learned as they write their own comparison-contrast essays in the Writing Workshop (pp. 98–117). Once students have learned to identify comparison-contrast structures, they will be better prepared to examine and write about similarities and differences they discover in literary fiction and nonfiction and to generate comparison-contrast writing on their own.

Making Connections

■ To the Literature Curriculum

Comparison and contrast can be a powerful technique in poetry. For example, in "Fire and Ice" Robert Frost juxtaposes fire and ice as well as desire and hate to point out how these different natural and emotional forces can be equally destructive. Essex Hemphill, in the poem "American Hero," includes two contrasting reactions to a sports hero's actions to reveal how people's values change depending on the circumstances.

Lesson Idea: Comparison and contrast in "Fire and Ice" by Robert Frost

1. Work with students to create a Venn diagram illustrating the similarities and differences between the characteristics of fire and ice and the characteristics of desire and hate.

2. Have students identify which emotions fire and ice might represent and why these are effective comparisons. Then, ask students to identify the implied main idea of the poem.

3. When the groups are ready to share their answers, discuss with students the poem's main idea. Take this opportunity to talk to students about how figurative language allows Frost to share with his readers complicated thoughts about human emotions and the end of the world in only a few words.

4. After this discussion, introduce students to the article in this chapter (pp. 89–90). Explain to them that com-parison-contrast writing in exposition, while not generally as dramatic as in poetry, gives readers valuable information about its subjects in an interesting format. Finally, prepare students to write about similarities and differences in literary works and in their own lives by instructing them through the sections on comparison-contrast structures in the Reading Workshop and the Writing Workshop.

■ To Careers

As students compare and contrast news coverage by different news media in the Focus on Viewing and Representing workshop in this chapter, they will discover that journalists and other news professionals make decisions every day about what to include and what to leave out of news stories. Work with students to write letters to local newspaper writers, TV producers, or Web designers asking them to explain how they use comparisons and contrasts to make editorial decisions. Students should type their letters and send them via regular mail or e-mail. Ask students to share with the class any replies they receive. This activity will help students realize that what they are learning applies not only to the classroom, but also to the world of work.

■ To the Community

Ask students to investigate community service positions and compare them. This exercise will show students how identifying similarities and differences helps them to categorize new information and to emphasize the larger applications of what they are learning as well. For example, students could compare the position of a city council member to the position of a school board member, or the position of a park director to the position of a camp director. Remind students to choose subjects that are similar enough for comparison but different enough to make interesting investigations. You may want to obtain permission from parents or guardians and from the parties students will contact before they begin work on this assignment.

■ To the Art History Curriculum

Invite an art teacher to come to your class to talk about the similarities and differences in two styles of painting. If possible, have the teacher use prints or slides in the presentation. You might also want to ask your speaker to discuss how art historians classify works of art into styles. What common stylistic features must paintings share to be grouped into the same category?

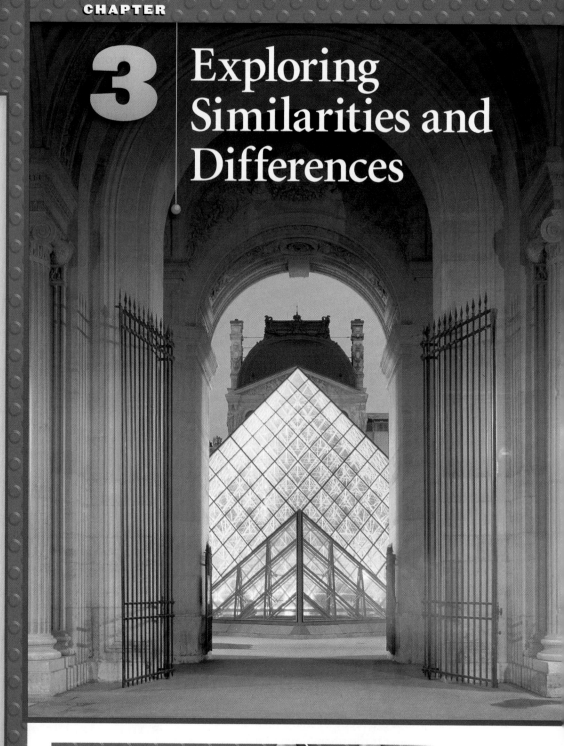

Exploring
Similarities and
Differences

PREVIEWING
THE CHAPTER

■ The workshops in this chapter focus on comparing and contrasting. Although the workshops can be taught separately, taught together they build on one another to give students an understanding of comparison-contrast structures in exposition. Reading the article in the Reading Workshop prepares students for the writing assignment in the Writing Workshop. Once students have practiced reading and writing comparison-contrast essays, they will be better able to report on similarities and contrasts in media coverage in the Focus on Viewing and Representing. To integrate this chapter with grammar, usage, and mechanics chapters, see pp. T371A–T371B.

INTRODUCING
THE CHAPTER

■ To introduce the chapter, use the Journal Warm-up, Transparency 24, in *Communications*.

VIEWING
THE PHOTOGRAPH

■ This photograph shows the Louvre Museum in Paris, France. Framed in the curve of an archway in an old section of the building is the pyramid entranceway designed by architect I. M. Pei in the 1980s. Pei deliberately used shapes and materials to contrast with the original building. Ask students to comment on the contrasts in line, shape, and texture that they see. [The new section appears to be made of glass and metal and is geometrical. The older section is stone, with ornate carvings above the archway.]

86

CHAPTER RESOURCES

Planning
■ *Lesson Planner,* Ch. 3
■ *ELL Strategies,* Ch. 3
■ *Block Scheduling,* p. T85A (this book)
■ *One-Stop Planner CD-ROM*

Practice
■ *Communications,* Ch. 3

■ *Media Literacy and Communication Skills*

Extension
■ *Designing Your Writing*

Reinforcement
■ *Communications,* Ch. 3
■ *Alternative Readings,* Ch. 3

Reading Workshop

Reading a Comparison-Contrast Article

Writing Workshop

Writing a Comparison-Contrast Essay

Viewing and Representing

Comparing and Contrasting Media Coverage

Comparing and Contrasting

- Two candidates are in the runoff for student-government elections. How will you decide which one gets your vote?

- After years of roller-skating, you decide to try ice-skating. Will your experience as a roller skater prepare you to ice-skate?

- How can you explain to a middle school friend what high school is like?

To respond to each of these questions, you would need to ask yourself two simple questions: *How are these things alike?* and *How are they different?* This type of questioning is called **comparison and contrast**. When you compare and contrast, you *classify* items by putting them into groups—a procedure that is particularly useful when you want to explain something new (like high school) by showing how it is similar to and different from something old and familiar (like middle school).

Although you might not be aware of it, you use comparison and contrast every time you make a decision or judgment and every time you weigh your options or compare products.

YOUR TURN 1 **Recognizing Comparison and Contrast**

Brainstorm about times you have used or might use comparison and contrast. Think about when you have asked yourself how two things were alike or how they were different. Create a list of these times and be prepared to share it with a small group of your classmates.

Informational Text

Exposition

internet connect

GO TO: go.hrw.com
KEYWORD: EOLang 9-3

Motivate

Focus students' thinking on comparison and contrast by bringing two objects to class, such as two different brands of fruit juice or two different styles of backpacks, and asking students to list similarities and differences in the products. Discuss with students how classifying items helps them make decisions and judgments.

ELEMENTS OF *Literature*

Personal Narrative in Literature. In *Elements of Literature,* Third Course, see "The Princess and the Tin Box," by James Thurber, pp. 244–246, and "The Struggle to Be an All-American Girl," by Elizabeth Wong, pp. 344–346, for examples of comparison-contrast structures.

YOUR TURN 1

Guide students to list situations or choices that lend themselves to comparison and contrast. Students might include circumstances such as deciding between two class electives.

Connecting Reading and Writing **87**

- *Daily Language Activity Transparencies*
- *Vocabulary Workshop* and *Tests*

Evaluation and Assessment

- *Test Generator (One-Stop Planner CD-ROM)*

- Assessment Package
  —*Chapter Tests,* Ch. 3
  —*Chapter Tests in Standardized Test Formats,* Ch. 3
  —*Assessment Alternatives,* Ch. 3

Internet
- go.hrw.com (keyword: EOLang 9–3)

Reading Workshop

OBJECTIVES

Reading and Writing Connection

- To read an article in preparation for writing a comparison-contrast essay

Reading Skills

- To identify explicit main idea and supporting details

- To analyze point-by-point and block structures

- To use comparison-contrast context clues with unfamiliar vocabulary

TEACHING (TIP)

Preparing to Read

The material in **Preparing to Read** on p. 88 introduces two concepts—explicit main idea and comparison-contrast structure. These concepts will be the instructional focus of the Reading Workshop and will be explained in more detail on pp. 91–95. The reading selection, **"Time Out! Is Baseball Finnished?,"** illustrates both of these concepts.

Quotation for the Day

"Nothing is good or bad but by comparison."

(Thomas Fuller, M.D., 1654–1734, English physician and writer)

Write this quotation on the board or on an overhead transparency, and initiate a discussion about its meaning. Ask students to consider how they decide whether something is good or bad.

RESOURCES

Reading Workshop Reinforcement

- *Alternative Readings,* Ch. 3

WHAT'S AHEAD?

In this section you will read an article and learn how to

- identify explicit main ideas and supporting details

- analyze point-by-point and block structure

| READING SKILL

| READING FOCUS

Reading a Comparison-Contrast Article

Did you know Finland's national pastime is based on our national pastime? That's right, American baseball inspired the creation of a Finnish sport called *pesapallo*. Although the two sports are somewhat similar, the article on the next page, "Time Out! Is Baseball Finnished?" shows that the sports have many differences, too. Reading this article will help you think about the similarities and the differences between sports in the United States and sports in other countries.

Preparing to Read

Identifying an Explicit Main Idea and Supporting Details
All comparison-contrast articles have a **main idea**—a controlling idea for the piece that shows the writer's focus on differences or similarities. If the writer directly announces this idea, it is an **explicit** main idea. In this case, you will find a sentence that states the main idea near the beginning of the article. The **details,** then, are all the information and evidence that support and explain the main idea. As you read the following article, look for the main idea and the details that support it.

Comparison-Contrast Structure   To compare and contrast two subjects, writers organize their writing using the **block method** or the **point-by-point method.** For block, one block of text, usually a paragraph, gives *all* the points the writer wants to make about one subject. Then, a second block of text gives all of the comparable or contrasting points about a second subject. For point-by-point, each section presents a point about the first subject (A) *and* the same point about the second subject (B). Then, the writer uses *another* section to deal with a second point about both subjects, and so on. As you read the following article, look for ways the writer organizes his ideas.

READING PROCESS

PREREADING
Set a Purpose for Reading the Selection.
The **Preparing to Read** section lets students know that their purpose for reading **"Time Out! Is Baseball Finnished?"** on pp. 89–90 is to identify the explicit main idea and recog-

nize comparison-contrast structure. Explain to students that reading with a set purpose in mind improves reading comprehension, allowing them to read faster and retain what they read longer.

Students should understand that in their

How is baseball similar to or different from *pesapallo*? As you read the article below, write down answers to the numbered active-reading questions.

from THE MIAMI HERALD

TIME OUT!

Is Baseball Finnished?

BY BOB SECTER

Hancock, Mich.— There were lots of reasons why Jimmy Piersall was known as a flake back when he played major-league baseball; but one of the best came the day he hit a home run as a New York Met and ran the bases backward.

All of which has little to do with the subject of this story, except to illustrate the maxim that what may seem like buffoonery in one setting could make perfect sense in another. Had Piersall been playing in, say, Helsinki rather than New York, he might have fit right in.

Yes. Baseball has been Finlandized. The Finns call the game *pesapallo* and are so crazy about it that it is considered their national pastime. Of course they do it a little differently.

They don't actually back-pedal their way from base to base à la Piersall, but, looking at it from a chauvinist American perspective, they do take a backward route around the base paths. First base is where third base ought to be, second is sort of around where first should be and third is somewhere out in left field. . . .

The main selling point of *pesapallo*, devotees say, is action. There are no long pauses between pitches, the ball is almost constantly in play, and both fielders and

1. How does the writer grab your attention?

2. What is the main point the writer makes in this paragraph?

Active-Reading Questions

The purpose of the active-reading questions is to point out to students the techniques writers use in comparison-contrast articles.

ANSWERS

1. The writer grabs the reader's attention by telling an amusing anecdote about a baseball player named Jimmy Piersall.

2. In *pesapallo,* the bases are set up in a different order from baseball.

independent reading they will have to identify their own purposes for reading. One way students can discover a purpose is by previewing the questions that accompany a text. Have students read the active-reading questions before they read the selection. This practice will help them figure out what they need to learn from reading the article and will assist them in setting their own purposes for reading.

3. Runners in *pesapallo* take a clockwise route around the bases; in contrast to runners in baseball, runners in *pesapallo* are constantly running from base to base.

4. The originator of *pesapallo* is compared to Abner Doubleday. He combined baseball and native ball-playing sports to create *pesapallo*. This information serves as the background for the comparison and contrast that follows.

5. The word *instead* indicates a difference between the sports.

6. The writer concludes the article on a humorous note by pointing out what baseball and *pesapallo* players do differently at the end of the game: Baseball players hit the showers, while *pesapallo* players go off to the sauna.

> **3.** According to the writer, what do runners do differently in *pesapallo* and baseball?

> **5.** Does the word *instead* indicate a similarity or a difference between the two sports?

runners are forever scampering all over the place.

"In American baseball, a runner on second is in scoring position but in our game, he's just tired," winked Jari Lemonen, who plays for the Repais. "Usually when we get out there, we pack a lunch."

The Abner Doubleday of Finland was Lauri Pihkala, a professor who apparently was mesmerized by baseball during early twentieth-century study tours in the United States. He combined the American game with some native ball-playing sports and *pesapallo* was born.

Both baseball and *pesapallo* feature four bases, three outs an inning, nine innings, nine players on a side, a hard ball, mitts, and a bat—although the Louisville Slugger of Finland is called a *Jarvinen Kanuuna*.

That's where the similarities end. The *pesapallo* pitcher, for instance, stands next to the plate and tosses

> **4.** This paragraph does not have much of a comparison. What other information is included? Why?

the ball up in the air, varying his delivery not with curves or sliders but with the height the ball goes.

Instead of waiting in a dugout, teammates of the batter stand around what is roughly equivalent to the batter's box and scream out advice whether to swing or not at a pitch. The batter can hit as many as three fair balls before he has to run. And the route around the basepaths sort of zigzags first to the left, then to the right, then to the left again.

Confused? Try this. A three-base hit is a *kunnari*, or home run. The batter scores, even though he is allowed to stay on third and score again if somebody knocks him in. But getting a *kunnari* is not easy because a ball that's knocked out of the park—about 300 feet from home to the farthest point of the *pesapallo* outfield—is considered a *laiton* (foul).

When an outfielder catches a fly ball, that doesn't necessarily mean the batter is

out. He might just be *haava* (wounded), a sort of purgatory state for sluggers that requires them to forfeit the turn at bat but doesn't exactly count toward ending the inning. And when someone does make an out, he's not just out, he's *pallo* (killed). This is no game for wimps; that's for sure.

There's one other important difference. At the end of the game, American ballplayers hit the showers. "When we're done," said Thunder Bay shortstop Pavli Kaki, "we go off to the sauna."

> **6.** How does the writer use humor to conclude the article?

90   Chapter 3   **Exposition:** Exploring Similarities and Differences

---

READING PROCESS

READING

Ask Questions. Inform students that asking the *5-W How?* questions of the text when they get stuck in their reading will help them determine meaning. For example, students might ask "How do you run the bases in *pesapallo?*" or "Who invented *pesapallo?*" or "What is a *kunnari?*" Students should jot down answers to their questions as they read.

Explicit Main Idea and Supporting Details

READING SKILL

Primary Importance   "Time Out! Is Baseball Finnished?" contains an **explicit**, or stated, **main idea** and the details that support this main idea. In an article or essay, an explicit main idea, or **thesis statement**, is usually made up of a subject plus the point the author wants to make about that subject. This thesis drives the structure and focus of the piece. For example, an author's subject for an article might be *dogs*, but the author's main idea or thesis statement would be *Dogs make better pets than cats*. While the thesis statement usually appears in the introductory paragraph of an article, the remaining paragraphs develop and support the main idea or thesis. These paragraphs have their own stated main ideas called **topic sentences** and supporting details. Good types of supporting details are facts, statistics, or examples. A graphic depiction of main idea and supporting details might look like this.

TIP The explicit main idea for a single paragraph is called a topic sentence. The stated main idea for an *entire article* or *essay* is called the thesis statement.

Meeting INDIVIDUAL NEEDS

MULTIPLE INTELLIGENCES
Musical Intelligence. Musical concepts might help students as they work to discover the explicit main idea in writing. Play in class a piece that has a clear refrain or melody around which the entire piece revolves. Point out that such a main idea is what also holds writing together coherently. Then, students can return to the reading selection and find the sentence or sentences that correspond to this musical concept.

How can you find a main idea? In many nonfiction pieces, the main idea is stated outright, neatly contained near the beginning of the writing. The main idea in a nonfiction piece might also be found, or alluded to, in the title of the piece. The example paragraph below is an introduction to an essay. It contains a main idea and supporting details for that main idea. Read the paragraph and use the Thinking It Through steps following it to practice identifying the main idea and supporting details.

Two Famous Artists

The European Renaissance of the fourteenth, fifteenth, and sixteenth centuries produced many different artists and writers. However, some of the period's greatest artists were actually not all that different from each other. Leonardo da Vinci and Michelangelo were famous artists with a great deal in common. They were both extremely dedicated to art and often went days without sleeping or eating. Both artists were also masters of perspective and have continued to be famous throughout history.

THINKING IT THROUGH

Finding Explicit Main Idea and Supporting Details

Use the following steps to find a main idea and supporting details.

▶ **STEP 1** Read and determine the subject of the piece. Look at the title, and scan the piece for key words or phrases that repeat. Ask yourself who or what the piece is addressing.

Leonardo da Vinci and Michelangelo are the subjects.

▶ **STEP 2** Look for the **main idea**—one or more sentences that state the point the writer wants to make about the subject or subjects. It is often found in the introduction.

Leonardo da Vinci and Michelangelo were famous artists with a great deal in common.

▶ **STEP 3** Confirm the main idea by looking to see that other details in the piece support it.

These details support the main idea: Both were extremely dedicated to art, both went days without sleeping or eating, both were masters of perspective, and both have continued to be famous throughout history.

YOUR TURN 2 **Finding Main Idea and Details**

Using the Thinking It Through steps on pages 92–93, find the main idea in "Time Out! Is Baseball Finnished?" (You may have to combine several directly stated ideas to figure out the explicit main idea.) Check your answer by making sure the details in the article support the main idea you find. On your own paper, write a sentence stating the main idea and three details that support it.

TIP If you have difficulty finding the main idea, you may want to start by drawing a graphic organizer like the one on page 91.

Comparison-Contrast Structure

The Order of Your Points Writers usually organize comparison-contrast essays so that readers can easily identify the points the writers are comparing about two or more subjects. Figuring out the structure of a comparison-contrast essay will make it easier for you to understand what the piece is about. Once you have determined the structure of a piece, you will be able to make predictions about the information to come. There are two main ways to structure comparison-contrast essays: the block method and the point-by-point method.

Block method Writers use the block method to address each subject in separate paragraphs—in different "blocks" of text. In one paragraph, the writer discusses all the relevant points about one subject; then, in a second paragraph, the writer discusses all the corresponding points about the second subject. In longer essays, a "block" may be several paragraphs.

Point-by-point method Writers use the point-by-point method when they want to focus on the points instead of the subjects. The point-by-point method allows writers to deal with both subjects in the same paragraph or section. The writer presents one point in each paragraph or section, discussing the point for the *first* subject and then for the *second* subject.

◀ **READING FOCUS**

TIP To try out unusual ways of presenting their ideas, professional writers often vary the two common comparison-contrast methods of organization. When you read a professional piece, be on the lookout for hybrid, or mixed, forms of the block and point-by-point methods.

YOUR TURN 2

ANSWER

Main Idea: Baseball has been Finlandized. The Finns call the game *pesapallo* and are so crazy about it that it is considered their national pastime. Of course, they do it a little differently.

(Three sentences are identified as the main idea because the pronoun "they" in the last sentence wouldn't be understood without the sentence before it.)

Details: Fans enjoy *pesapallo* because it is full of action. The bases are run in a clockwise route. Runners are constantly running from base to base.

TEACHING **TIP**

Comparison-Contrast Structure

Help students see that each organizational method seems to suit slightly different situations. The block method may work best when the audience is familiar with one of the two subjects being discussed. In this case, the more familiar subject can be dealt with first, and the relevant points of comparison or contrast can be mentioned without a great deal of explanation. When both subjects are relatively unfamiliar to the audience, the point-by-point method may be easier for readers to follow.

Reading Workshop   **93**

RESOURCES

Your Turn 2
Practice
■ *Communications,* WS. p. 44
Reinforcement
■ *Communications,* TP. 25, WS. p. 45

With either the block or the point-by-point method, writers try to present the information in a consistent order so their readers do not get confused. The chart below shows both methods of organization. The left-hand column shows how a writer would use the block method to compare and contrast ice-skating with roller-skating. The right-hand column shows how a writer would reorganize the same information using the point-by-point method.

Block Method	Point-by-Point Method

Subject 1: Roller-Skating
  Point 1: Wooden rink
  Point 2: Boots with wheels
  Point 3: Jumps and spins
	Point 1: Type of arena (contrast)
	  Subject 1: Wooden rink for roller-skating
	  Subject 2: Ice rink for ice-skating

Subject 2: Ice-Skating
  Point 1: Ice rink
  Point 2: Boots with blades
  Point 3: Jumps and spins
	Point 2: Footwear (contrast)
	  Subject 1: Boots with wheels for roller-skating
	  Subject 2: Boots with blades for ice-skating

	Point 3: Athletic moves (comparison)
	  Subject 1: Jumps and spins in roller-skating
	  Subject 2: Jumps and spins also in ice-skating

TIP Writers often use clue words to signal a transition from one subject to another. Contrast clue words include *however, still, yet, but, on the other hand,* and *although.* Comparison clue words include *similarly, like, as,* and *in the same way.* For example, *Roller-skating boots have wheels,* **but** *ice-skating boots have blades.* If you have trouble identifying the structure of a comparison-contrast article, try highlighting all the comparison and contrast clue words. Then, look for a pattern to the highlighting. Point-by-point structure should use more clue words because the writer has to switch subjects more often.

ARLO AND JANIS reprinted by permission of Newspaper Enterprise Association, Inc.

94   Chapter 3   **Exposition:** Exploring Similarities and Differences

READING PROCESS

EXTENDING

Connect to the World. To show that students have learned to recognize comparison-contrast organizational structures (see the ATE feature, **Prereading,** p. 88), copy a comparison-contrast article from a magazine or newspaper and ask students to identify its organizational method.

The organizational structure of "Time Out! Is Baseball Finnished?" is unusual. The writer examines two subjects, baseball and *pesapallo*. However, through most of the piece, he does not directly state his points about baseball. He assumes that his readers already know them. For example, in one paragraph, he gives the rules only about *pesapallo*. He expects his readers to fill in the rules of baseball for themselves.

 Analyzing Comparison-Contrast Structure

To analyze the structure of "Time Out! Is Baseball Finnished?" fill in the content chart below with the missing points and the missing details about *pesapallo* and baseball. The items 1–8 below correspond to the main points of comparison between *pesapallo* and baseball in the order they appear in the article. Put your answers on your own paper.

Points	Subjects A. *Pesapallo* B. Baseball (implied)
1. direction to run bases	A. runners move clockwise B. (runners move counterclockwise)
2. pace of the game	A. B.
3. number of bases, outs, innings, and players on a side	A. B.
4.	A. B. (on the pitcher's mound)
5.	A. B.
6. rules for a home run	A. B. (a ball hit out of the park)
7.	A. B. the batter is out
8.	A. B.

Reading Workshop   95

ANSWERS
Points
4. rules for pitching; **5.** rules for batting and running the bases; **7.** rules for outs; **8.** post-game practices
Details
2A. fast; **2B.** (slow); **3A.** 4 bases, 3 outs, 9 innings, 9 players; **3B.** the same; **4A.** next to the plate; **5A.** players wait next to the batter's box, run a zigzag route; **5B.** players wait in the dugout, run counterclockwise; **6A.** a three-base hit in the park; **7A.** the batter is wounded (*haava*) or killed (*pallo*); **8A.** hit the sauna; **8B.** hit the showers

Wrap It Up

Metacognition. Ask students to reflect on their reading process and answer the following:

1. Were the differences between baseball and *pesapallo* clear to you from the article? Why or why not? [Students may say that the differences were clear because the writer clearly stated the contrasts.]

Then ask students the following questions:

2. For what reason would you use the point-by-point method to structure a comparison-contrast essay? [to focus on the points rather than the subject of an essay]

3. Why might you use the block method? [to focus on the subject; to address each subject separately]

MINI-LESSON · VOCABULARY

Comparison-Contrast Context Clues

ANSWERS

Possible answers are given below.

1. The word *like* signals that a synonym may follow. The clause *any claim that many different people are alike* may explain the word *stereotype*. A *stereotype* is probably a claim that different people have the same characteristics.

2. The word *but* signals an antonym nearby. The word *open-minded* is an antonym for the word *prejudice*. *Prejudice* probably means "close-minded."

3. The phrase *as diverse as* signals a comparison nearby. The word *multicultural* is a synonym for *diverse*. *Diverse* probably means "various kinds."

4. The word *although* signals an antonym may follow. The word *neutral* is an antonym for *biased*. *Biased* probably means "favoring one side or another."

5. The phrase *in the same way* signals a synonym nearby. The phrase *unreasoning devotion* is synonymous with *chauvinistic*. *Chauvinistic* probably means "excessive attachment to something without thinking through reasons."

Taking a Second Look

Using Comparison-Contrast Clues. You might talk to students about how word histories can help them figure out the meaning of unfamiliar words. Have students look up the etymologies of the vocabulary words *prejudice* and *diverse* and see if they can figure out their meanings from their word origins.

MINI-LESSON · VOCABULARY

Comparison-Contrast Context Clues

Sometimes you can find the meaning of an unfamiliar word by examining **comparison-contrast context clues** near the unfamiliar word. A **comparison context clue** indicates that a synonym, or word with a similar meaning, is nearby. (It may also signal a nearby phrase with a similar meaning.) If you know the meaning of the synonym, then you are fairly close to knowing what the unfamiliar word (or phrase) means. Comparison context clue words include *like, as, in the same way,* and *similar to.* A **contrast clue word** indicates that an antonym, or word with the opposite meaning, is nearby. (It may also signal a nearby phrase with the opposite meaning.) If you know what the antonym means, then you can guess that the unfamiliar word (or phrase) has the opposite meaning. Contrast context clue words include *however, but, although, on the contrary,* and *on the other hand.*

THINKING IT THROUGH — Using Comparison-Contrast Context Clues

Take a look at the example below and the steps following it.

Example:
Louisa's comments about other cultures are *ethnocentric*; Ray's comments, on the other hand, show that he is not convinced that his culture is better than all other cultures.

1. **Look for a comparison or contrast context clue.** The phrase *on the other hand* signals that an antonym or a phrase with the opposite meaning may be nearby.

2. **Look for a synonym (for comparison clues) or an antonym (for contrast clues) of the unfamiliar word.** The phrase *is not convinced that his culture is better than all other cultures* may have the opposite meaning of *ethnocentric.*

3. **Make an informed guess about the meaning of the unfamiliar word.** *Ethnocentric* means something like "convinced that one's own culture is better than all other cultures."

PRACTICE

Use the steps above to find the meaning of the following italicized words. Put your answers on your own paper.

1. A *stereotype*, like any claim that many different people are alike, can be dangerous.

2. Joe did not think he could write without *prejudice*, but his article was open-minded.

3. Few cities are as *diverse* as New York. New York is a very multicultural city.

4. Some say the news story is *biased*, although others say the news story is neutral.

5. Ryan had *chauvinistic* views about his music. In the same way, Mia had an unreasoning devotion to her sports.

RESOURCES

Vocabulary
Practice
- *Communications,* WS. p. 48

Test Taking
Practice
- *Communications,* WS. pp. 49–51

MINI-LESSON TEST TAKING

Answering Analogy Questions

An **analogy** is a special kind of comparison—it points out how the relationship of two sets of words is similar. For example, *moon* and *earth* have the same relationship as *Saturn* and *sun*. In both cases, one orbits the other. **Analogy questions** measure your knowledge of individual words as well as your ability to identify relationships *between* words.

Look at the analogy question to the right. In analogy questions, the symbol : means *is to* and the symbol :: means *as*. For example, the question to the right would read *Scales is to fish as ____ is to ____.*

Examine the five answer choices to the right to determine which pair of words has the same relationship as that between *scales* and

fish. Follow the steps below to see how one student figured out the answer.

SCALES : FISH ::

A. perch : bass

B. eraser : pencil

C. tadpole : frog

D. sea gull : seashore

E. fur : mammal

TIP Don't be fooled by answers that are thematically related to the question. With analogy questions you should match *only the relationship* between the pairs of words. For example, perch and bass are kinds of fish, but **A** may not be the correct answer.

THINKING IT THROUGH Answering Analogy Questions

The following steps will help you answer analogy questions.

1. **Identify the relationship between the first pair of words.** Scales are a part of the larger whole of a fish.

2. **Express the relationship between the first pair of words in the form of a sentence.** The first word, scales, is part of the second word, fish. Scales cover a fish.

3. **Ask if each multiple-choice answer fits the order and relationship of the first pair.**

   A. Is a perch part of a bass? No, they are both kinds of fish.

   B. Is an eraser part of a pencil? Yes, it is.

   C. Is a tadpole part of a frog? No, it is an

   immature form of a frog.

   D. Is a sea gull part of a seashore? No, it lives at the seashore.

   E. Is fur part of a mammal? Yes, it is.

4. **Choose the answer that best completes the analogy.** Both **B** and **E** are examples of part-to-whole relationships. Which of these is even closer to the relationship of *scales* and *fish*? An eraser does not completely cover a pencil, but fur covers a mammal as scales cover fish. **E** is the *best* answer because it more closely matches the relationship between *scales* and *fish*.

Reading Workshop   **97**

TEACHING TIP

Answering Analogy Questions

Some students may have difficulty learning about analogies because they may not recognize them in their everyday life. You may want to stress to students that recognizing analogies present in literature will help them understand the concept of relationships between words. Explain that in an analogy two objects or ideas are not compared; instead, their relationship is. To get them started, offer students these examples from literature and work with them to label the relationships.

1. *Romeo and Juliet* is to *Shakespeare* as the *Odyssey* is to ____. [Homer]

2. *Helen Keller* is to *student* as *Annie Sullivan* is to ____. [teacher]

3. *The Gift of the Magi* is to *love* as *The Cask of Amontillado* is to ____. [horror, suspense]

4. *O. Henry* is to *short story* as *Robert Frost* is to ____. [poem]

Looking Ahead to Writing

In the **Writing Workshop** on pp. 98–117 of this chapter, students will be asked to write their own comparison-contrast essays. Encourage students to use a graphic organizer like the one on p. 91 of the **Reading Workshop** to help them develop the explicit main idea and focus the supporting details in their essays.

Writing Workshop

Writing Workshop

OBJECTIVES

- To write and revise a comparison-contrast essay
- To focus on similarities and differences
- To eliminate irrelevant details
- To gather and organize support
- To combine sentences using phrases
- To correct misplaced modifiers

Quotation for the Day

"You don't write because you want to say something; you write because you've got something to say."

(F. Scott Fitzgerald, 1896–1940, American novelist and short-story writer)

Write this quotation on the chalkboard, and ask students to respond to it orally or in their journals. Guide them to realize that a writer's genuine interest in the subject makes the writing stronger and more interesting and the writer will have more fun doing it.

Meeting INDIVIDUAL NEEDS

ENGLISH-LANGUAGE LEARNERS

General Strategies. English-language learners may enjoy brainstorming about subjects with other students who share similar language and cultural experiences. When subject matter is relevant to personal interests and experiences, and when students are given the autonomy to explore information that has immediate application to their lives, they are more likely to perform successfully.

WHAT'S AHEAD?

In this workshop you will write a comparison-contrast essay. You will also learn how to

- focus on similarities or differences
- eliminate irrelevant details
- organize support
- combine sentences using phrases
- correct misplaced modifiers

Writing a Comparison-Contrast Essay

Picture this: While you are away for the summer, you learn a great new game called fun ball. You are so excited that you write a letter to your friends back home about this new sport. The problem is they have never even heard of fun ball. How can you explain it to them in writing?

One way is to compare and contrast it with a sport they already know, like soccer. By writing about the *similarities* between the two sports, you help your friends make sense of the *differences*. In the following Writing Workshop you will have the opportunity to write an organized, informative essay that compares or contrasts any two subjects you choose.

Prewriting

Find Two Subjects

KEY CONCEPT

"You Can't Compare Apples to Oranges." *Comparison* points out the similarities between people, ideas, or things, while *contrast* points out the differences. However, the word *comparison* is often used to mean both comparing and contrasting. If your teacher assigns a comparison essay, make sure you understand the assignment. For this comparison-contrast essay, you will focus on either similarities or differences between two subjects, but not both.

The two subjects you write about should be similar enough to compare. Sure, apples and oranges are both kinds of fruit, but you will have a hard time finding other features they have in common. They may just be too different to compare.

98   Chapter 3   **Exposition:** Exploring Similarities and Differences

Remember the following when choosing your subjects.

- **Good subjects have plenty of similar features.** Try comparing two types of apples, like Granny Smith apples and Golden Delicious apples. Some features you might choose to compare include their color, taste, texture, and size.

- **Good subjects are different enough to be interesting.** There is no point in comparing two identical apples. A good topic gives your readers new information.

With these guidelines in mind, brainstorm to find a topic to write about. Look around you for places that people make comparisons in everyday life. Here are a couple of suggestions to help you get started:

- **Do a little comparison shopping** before you buy. When you buy a pair of jeans, chances are you don't just pick the first pair off the rack—you compare several different brands or styles first.

- **Try something new.** Go for a walk down a different street. If you watch the news on TV, try reading the newspaper instead. Jot down a list of the differences you notice. In order to explain something that is new, you may want to compare it to something that is older or more familiar. For example, you might compare a movie and its sequel.

After brainstorming a list of topics, circle the one you find most interesting.

Narrow Your Subjects

Whittle It Down   Examine your subjects. Are the subjects you want to compare too huge for one short essay? For example, comparing all of France to all of the United States may be too large a topic for one essay. It would be much more reasonable to compare one aspect of the two countries, such as their school systems, tourist attractions, or climate.

Think About Purpose, Audience, and Tone

For Their Eyes Only   The primary **purpose** of a comparison-contrast essay is to inform readers. A formal **tone** and voice work best for this purpose. When you provide readers with information about the subjects you are comparing or contrasting, you help them see the similarities or differences between people, places, objects, or ideas. For this reason, it is important to evaluate who your **audience** is and what your audience already knows about your subjects. Asking yourself the questions on the next page will help you direct your essay. Notice how the writer of an essay on body language in France and the United States answered each question.

TIP   Try to make your comparison or contrast one that will bring a new subject to light or shed light on a familiar one.

- **Who are my readers?** My readers are American tourists traveling to France.

- **What do my readers already know about the subjects I am comparing or contrasting?** They know a lot about how Americans use body language to communicate.

- **What information might help my readers better understand the similarities or differences between my subjects?** They might need more information about how the French use body language to communicate.

Gather Information About Your Subjects

Collecting Data Before you write your comparison-contrast essay, you will need to gather plenty of information about your subjects to see whether you want to focus on similarities or on differences. Remember, though, that **for a comparison-contrast essay, you are not looking for just any kind of information—you are looking for _similarities and differences_.** One very good way to keep track of similarities and differences between your subjects is to create a Venn diagram like the one below.

KEY CONCEPT

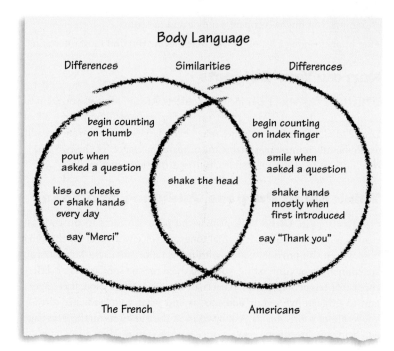

Body Language

Differences   Similarities   Differences

begin counting
on thumb

begin counting
on index finger

pout when
asked a question

smile when
asked a question

shake the head

kiss on cheeks
or shake hands
every day

shake hands
mostly when
first introduced

say "Merci"

say "Thank you"

The French   Americans

The writer who created the Venn diagram on the previous page wanted to inform her audience about the body language used by people in France and the body language used by people in the United States. Notice how she used the middle part—where the two circles of the Venn diagram overlap—to list the similarities she found. In the outer parts of the diagram, she listed differences.

When you create your Venn diagram, place the similarities you find in the middle part of the diagram, and place the differences in the outer parts. Label each circle with the names of the subjects you will be comparing or contrasting. If you are not familiar with your subjects, you may need to do some research—in the library, on the Internet, or through interviews or observation—before you create the diagram.

Write Your Thesis

What's the Big Idea?   A thesis statement tells your audience what your essay will be about. It should identify what people, things, or ideas you are comparing or contrasting. Your **thesis statement** should also clearly state the main idea—whether you want to focus on the similarities or the differences between your subjects.

You can decide whether you want to focus your essay on similarities or on differences by looking at your Venn diagram. If, for example, you find that you have listed many similarities, but only a few differences, you will probably want to focus on similarities. After you have analyzed your information, write a thesis statement that states your subjects plus your focus on either similarities or differences.

For example, the writer who created the Venn diagram about French and American body language might decide that she wants to focus her essay on differences, because she listed more differences than similarities in the diagram. She might then write the following thesis statement.

> Most people know that residents of France and the United States speak different languages. However, few people know that body language in the two countries can be just as different.

TIP   Most thesis statements are one sentence long. Sometimes, however, a particularly complex thesis statement will be two sentences long. One way to get readers' attention in a comparison-contrast essay is to connect two opposite ideas in your thesis statement using a transitional word like *however, yet,* or *still.* For example, *Tamara and Lu came from opposite sides of the globe. Still, they had many of the same ideas, tastes, and friends in common.*

TIP   If you have listed many differences, but only a few similarities, you will probably want to focus on differences.

Writing Workshop   **101**

TIP Classifying ideas into categories takes time. Allow yourself the time to dwell on this important step. The features you come up with now will ultimately help you structure your final essay.

| KEY CONCEPT →

Find Relevant Features

To the Point   When you choose subjects to compare and contrast, you must understand (1) *if* they have any features in common, and (2) *what* features they have in common. When you do this, you are actually using the critical thinking skill of **classifying:** grouping objects or ideas into categories that show their similarities.

When the writer of the Venn diagram on page 100 asked herself what the information in each circle had in common, she came up with the categories or features listed in the right-hand column below.

The French	Americans	Feature
Begin counting on thumb	Begin counting on index finger	Hand signals
Pout when asked a question	Smile when asked a question	Facial expressions
Kiss on cheeks or shake hands every day	Shake hands mostly when first introduced	Greetings
~~Say merci~~	~~Say thank you~~	~~Words to express thanks~~

To come up with names for these categories or features, the writer had to find similar pieces of information in each of the circles of the Venn diagram. Then she had to think of a word or phrase that described both pieces of information.

After classifying the information that you gather in your Venn diagram into categories or **features,** you should pick two to four **relevant features** to support your thesis. **Relevant features are the categories of support that relate to and develop your thesis statement.** For example, the writer who created the Venn diagram chose three relevant features of body language: hand signals, facial expressions, and greetings. All three features support the main idea in her thesis statement that body language in France can be quite different from body language in the United States. She eliminated the fourth feature she found, words to express thanks, because verbal expressions are not relevant to her topic of body language. When you write your essay, you may also need to eliminate irrelevant details or features that do not support your thesis statement.

102   Chapter 3   **Exposition:** Exploring Similarities and Differences

MINI-LESSON CRITICAL THINKING

Evaluating to Eliminate Irrelevant Details

When you write a comparison-contrast essay, you must make sure that all the supporting details you use are related to your main idea. Any irrelevant details will throw your reader off and weaken your essay. For example, a paper that compares or contrasts body language in France and the United States should use supporting details about body language in both countries. Different words, different foods, and different money in both countries would be interesting details to examine, but they are not **relevant** to the subject of body language. Instead, the writer should compare or contrast aspects of body language such as hand signals, greetings, and facial expressions.

If you were playing a game that required you to eliminate irrelevant details from a category, the questioner might ask you, "Which of these things do not belong together: algebra, history, stars, or physics?" The answer is *stars* because the other three items—*algebra*, *history*, and *physics*—are all school courses. *Stars* does not belong in the category of school courses.

PRACTICE

Work with a partner to figure out which of the items in each list below does not belong. Write your answers on your own paper.

Example
1. red, orange, thirteen, green, purple
   1. Thirteen does not belong because it is not a color.

1. Classical period, Middle Ages, Italy, Renaissance, Industrial Age, The Reformation
2. newspapers, videos, photographs, TV shows, movies, paintings, drawings, music
3. mumps, chickenpox, German measles, thermometer, pneumonia, flu, strep throat, tetanus
4. softball, bat, soccer, hockey, volleyball, football, basketball, baseball, lacrosse, tennis
5. balloon, oxygen, hydrogen, nitrogen, helium, neon, fluorine
6. Washington, D.C.; Mexico City, Mexico; Jupiter; Tokyo, Japan; London, England; Warsaw, Poland
7. Colorado, Himalayas, Alps, Rockies, Adirondacks, Cascades, Andes, Appalachians, Sierras
8. a poem, a painting, an opera, a canvas
9. democracy, monarchy, queen, dictatorship
10. a speech, a newspaper, a magazine, a radio program, a television show, a Web site
11. Manet, Monet, Renoir, Degas, Mozart, Gauguin, van Gogh, Matisse
12. Bolivia, South America, Asia, Africa, Australia, North America
13. sonnet, villanelle, sestina, meter, blank verse, free verse
14. Carnegie, Lincoln, Coolidge, Monroe, Washington, Eisenhower, Taft
15. jazz, rock, soul, country, blues, folk, swing, guitar, bluegrass

MINI-LESSON CRITICAL THINKING

Evaluating to Eliminate Irrelevant Details

ANSWERS

1. *Italy*—not a historical era
2. *music*—not primarily a visual medium
3. *thermometer*—not a disease
4. *bat*—not a sport
5. *balloon*—not a gas
6. *Jupiter*—not a world capital
7. *Colorado*—not a mountain range
8. *canvas*—not a type of art
9. *queen*—not a form of government
10. *speech*—not a type of media
11. *Mozart*—not a painter
12. *Bolivia*—not a continent
13. *meter*—not a poetic form
14. *Carnegie*—not a U.S. president
15. *guitar*—not a kind of music

RESOURCES

Critical Thinking
Practice
■ *Communications,* WS. p. 52

Critical Thinking

Evaluation. Ask students to answer the following question.

Why does the point-by-point method work better for longer papers with more comparisons, and the block method work better for shorter papers with fewer comparisons? [Students should point out that if a writer uses the block method of organization in a paper with a lot of comparisons, readers may have difficulty remembering "Main Point 1" about *A* by the time they reach "Main Point 1" about *B.* Too many other comparisons would have intervened.]

Arrange Your Information

Creating Order How will you organize your comparison-contrast essay? After you have chosen two to four relevant features, use a chart like the one below to help you organize your information. You can use either the point-by-point method or the block method to organize and arrange your information.

■ In the **block method,** you discuss all the features about your first subject. Then you discuss all the features about your second subject. The block method works best for shorter pieces with fewer comparisons.

■ In the **point-by-point method,** you present the first feature for *both* subjects. Then you use another sentence or group of sentences to present the second feature for both subjects, and so on. The point-by-point method works best for longer papers with more comparisons.

Block Method	Point-by-Point Method
Subject 1: The French	Feature 1: Hand signals
Feature 1: Hand signals—count on their fingers starting with the thumb	Subject 1: The French—count on their fingers starting with the thumb
Feature 2: Facial expressions—pout when asked a question	Subject 2: Americans—count on their fingers starting with the index finger
Feature 3: Greetings—greet each other by kissing on the cheeks or shaking hands every day	
Subject 2: Americans	Feature 2: Facial expressions
Feature 1: Hand signals—count on their fingers starting with the index finger	Subject 1: The French—pout when asked a question
Feature 2: Facial expressions—smile when asked a question	Subject 2: Americans—smile when asked a question
Feature 3: Greetings—shake hands when first introduced	
	Feature 3: Greetings
	Subject 1: The French—kiss on the cheeks or shake hands every day
	Subject 2: Americans—shake hands when first introduced

Remember to treat the relevant features in the same order for both subjects. The order of features is often most to least important, or least to most important. To figure out which features are the most important, start by examining how much information you have gathered about each feature. The feature you know the most about may very well be the one you want to discuss first. Another way to determine order of importance is to think about your audience's needs. Look back at the information you gathered about your audience on pages 99–100. Ask yourself what information your audience would like most to know about. If you first write about the feature that is most important to your audience, you are likely to grab your audience's attention and to convince your audience to keep reading the rest of your paper.

YOUR TURN 4 · Organizing Ideas

Go over each of the prewriting steps. Before you start writing your essay, remember to

- find two items that are similar enough to compare, but different enough to be interesting
- choose an appropriate audience and tone
- gather information that will support your comparisons or contrasts
- write a thesis statement that indicates whether you will be looking at similarities or differences
- select two to four relevant features to support your thesis statement
- organize your relevant features using the point-by-point method or the block method

COMPUTER TIP

You can create tables within your word-processing program, and use them to organize your prewriting notes.

YOUR TURN 4

You can check to make sure students have chosen features that support their thesis statements and have organized their features using the block method or the point-by-point method by having them turn in their thesis statements along with an ordered list of their features.

HI & LOIS reprinted with special permission of King Features Syndicate, Inc.

RESOURCES

Your Turn 4
Practice
- *Communications,* WS. p. 53

Writing

Comparison-Contrast Essay

Framework

Introduction
- Capture your readers' attention.
- Provide background information.
- State your thesis.

Body
- Organize your information using either the block or point-by-point method.

Conclusion
- Summarize how your support leads to your thesis.
- Bring your essay to a close.

Directions and Explanations

Hook Your Readers   Begin with several details that are contrary to your thesis. Then, include your thesis statement, beginning with a transition to signal the switch to an opposite idea—like *however, yet,* or *still.* For example, begin with statements showing contrasts about the two things you plan to compare, or begin with statements showing similarities between the two things you plan to contrast. This will make your readers want to read more.

Explain the Context   Provide relevant background information to help your readers understand the two subjects you will compare or contrast.

State Your Thesis   Tell your readers what to expect with a thesis that states what two items you will discuss and whether you will compare or contrast them.

Organize Your Support   To deal with each subject separately, use the block method. To deal with both subjects together, use the point-by-point method. Explain each of your subjects and provide supporting details for each feature you are comparing or contrasting.

Sum It Up   Restate your support and your thesis. You may also want to end with an evaluation—a final comment that judges the relative worth of the two subjects. For example, *Although brand A has a sleeker design, brand B really is more efficient.*

 Writing a First Draft

Write the first draft of your essay using the framework and the directions and explanations above as a guide. The Writer's Model on the next page is a sample essay that closely matches the framework.

A Writer's Model

The following short essay uses the point-by-point method to contrast two cultures. Notice how it follows the framework.

Differences in Body Language

A pull on an eyelid, a pat on the wrist—either of these gestures could lead to confusion for an American in Paris. In fact, years of French language classes practicing *je, tu, il,* and *bonjour* may not be enough preparation for an American to communicate with a French person. Most people know that residents of France and the United States speak different languages. However, few people know that body language in the two countries can be just as different.

The difference in hand signals could lead to cultural misunderstandings between Americans and the French. For example, an American visiting France may be surprised when a waiter brings him three cups of coffee even though he thought he only ordered two. His problem? He held up his index finger and his middle finger to indicate the number *two.* Since the French start counting on the thumb, however, the waiter understood that hand gesture to mean *three.*

Hand signals are not the only difference in body language between Americans and the French. Facial expressions can also be different in the two countries. An American who asks a French person for her opinion may be surprised when she reacts by frowning. Americans tend to smile a lot, especially when responding to questions. The French, on the other hand, sometimes react by pouting the lips. This facial gesture shows that a French person is thinking.

The French also greet each other in a different way than Americans do. Every time they meet or say goodbye, French friends and family members kiss on the cheeks or shake hands. Americans, on the other hand, do not touch nearly as often when they greet each other.

A frustrated American with an extra cup of coffee and a pouting companion will probably find the unexpected surprise of a kiss or a handshake quite refreshing. However, an American visiting France may still need more than a dictionary to communicate with the French.

TIP Notice the highlighted contrast clue words signaling differences.

Attention-getting
INTRODUCTION

Thesis statement (focuses on differences)

BODY
Feature 1: Hand signals

Americans

The French

Feature 2: Facial expressions

Americans

The French

Feature 3: Greetings
The French

Americans

CONCLUSION that sums up

Connecting Reading and Writing

Point out to students that **A Writer's Model** emphasizes the differences between two subjects. As students read the model on this page, ask them to identify the elements the writer uses to focus the essay on differences. Students may notice the following:

- the thesis statement focuses on differences

- the essay includes only features that are different

- the writer uses contrast clue words

It may help your students in their own writing if you follow up this discussion by talking about elements writers might use to emphasize similarities instead of differences.

Connecting Reading and Writing

Encourage students to analyze **A Student's Model,** identifying the thesis statement and conclusion and determining whether the body paragraphs are organized point-by-point or in the block method. Ask students to consider the model's effectiveness and decide if they would have written or organized this paper differently.

A Student's Model

The following excerpt from a comparison-contrast essay was written by Matthew Weber, a student at McNeil High School in Round Rock, Texas.

CDs and Cassettes, Not So Similar

INTRODUCTION

From rap to rock and from country to classical, music is one of America's favorite pastimes. I have yet to find someone who has not heard a song from a cassette or CD. I have never been in a car that has not had either a cassette or CD player that was installed in it. When it comes to listening to music, CDs and cassettes are always right up there at the top of the list. Despite the many similarities of these two, though, there are many differences between cassettes and CDs.

Thesis statement

BODY
Feature 1: Price

The first difference comes in the price. As most people know, the price varies in that cassettes are cheaper than CDs. The prices seem to depend upon things like how many tracks there are and if the songs are popular hits or are songs that have never been heard of. However, in the end, the results are the same. CDs are about five dollars more expensive than cassettes. Why then do people buy CDs when cassettes are cheaper? The reason is simple. Americans don't mind paying an extra buck for something that might be a little easier to run.

Feature 2: Mechanics

Another difference between the two is the way CD players and cassette recorders are run. For example, to skip tracks on a CD, people have to press one button, but they have to fast-forward the track on a cassette recorder, a process that usually means stopping every now and then just to see where they are in the song. It is a fairly tedious job just to get past one song.

Feature 3:
Sound quality

Finally, there is a difference in sound quality between CDs and cassettes. CDs are made digitally by computers so that all the extra noise and unwanted sound can be taken out. Cassettes are not made digitally like the CD, so there still can be a static sound. For this reason, CDs are much better in sound quality compared to cassettes. . . .

108   Chapter 3   **Exposition:** Exploring Similarities and Differences

Evaluate and Revise Your Draft

Smoothing Out the Bumps You should carefully read through your entire paper at least twice. During the first reading, work collaboratively to evaluate and to revise for **content** and **organization** using the guidelines below. When you do the second reading, use the guidelines on page 110 to evaluate and revise for **sentence style**.

First Reading: Content and Organization The chart below will help you evaluate and revise your writing. Working with a peer or on your own, start by answering the questions in the left-hand column. Then, if you need help, move on to the middle column of tips. If you need to revise, make the changes suggested in the right-hand column.

Comparison-Contrast Essay: Content and Organization Guidelines for Peer and Self-Evaluation

Evaluation Questions	▶ Tips	▶ Revision Techniques
❶ Do the first one or two sentences grab the audience's attention?	**Put a check** above the interesting parts of the first two sentences. If you see no check marks, revise.	**Add** an interesting statement or example, or **replace** existing sentences with interesting statements or examples.
❷ Does the introduction clearly identify both subjects and the thesis of the essay?	**Underline** the thesis statement and **draw a squiggly line** under each subject. Revise if you cannot identify a thesis and two subjects.	**Add** a sentence that clearly identifies both subjects. **Add** a sentence that states the main idea of the essay.
❸ Is the body organized by the block method or the point-by-point method?	**Put a letter A** above each point about the first subject. **Use a letter B** for each point about the second subject. Block: The A's should be in one block of text, and the letter B's in another. Point-by-point: Each A should be closely followed by a B.	To fix the organization, **rearrange** sentences into either block order or point-by-point order.
❹ Does the conclusion bring the essay to a definite close by summarizing or evaluating the subjects?	**Underline** sentences that summarize and evaluate. If there aren't any, revise.	**Delete** ineffective sentences. **Add** effective statements that summarize or evaluate. **Elaborate** on existing statements that summarize or evaluate.

Quotation for the Day

"You write the first draft really to see how it's going to come out."

(James Michener, 1907–1997, American novelist and Pulitzer Prize winner)

Use this quotation to remind students that all writers, even professional ones, evaluate and revise their work.

TECHNOLOGY TIP

Many word-processing programs have functions that show overprint markings and revisions in a different color than the original text. If students have access to these programs, they can make suggested revisions without deleting their original text. This will allow them to see clearly how the evaluation questions, tips, and revision techniques affected their papers.

TEACHING TIP

▶ **Elaboration**
Students can use a questioning strategy to help them include sufficient detail in their papers. Have them look for places in their papers that lead them to ask these questions: *How?, Why?, For example?, When?*

When a question arises, students should check whether the rest of the sentence or a following sentence answers it. If not, students should add a sentence or sentences to answer the question.

ONE WRITER'S REVISIONS Here is how one writer used the content and organization guidelines to revise part of the comparison-contrast essay on page 107. Look over the revisions and answer the questions following the sentences.

add

replace/add/replace

add

> Most people know that residents of France ^and the United States speak ^a language ^different s. However, few people know ~~about~~ ^that body language in the two countries ^can be just as different.

Analyzing the Revision Process

1. What type of information did the writer add?
2. How do these additions improve the thesis statement?

PEER REVIEW

Ask a few classmates to read your paper and to answer the following questions.

1. Which part of the essay confused you? How could it be made clearer?
2. What did you like best about the essay? Why?

YOUR TURN 6   **Revising for Content and Organization**

Using the sample revisions as a model, revise the content and organization of your essay. Be sure to refer to the content and organization guidelines on the previous page.

> **Second Reading: Style** When you wrote the first draft of your comparison-contrast essay, you may have found yourself using a series of short, choppy sentences. Using a few short sentences sprinkled throughout your paper can be an effective technique. If you use too many, however, your writing will sound very unnatural. To **vary sentence length** in your essay, use the following sentence-style guidelines.

Style Guidelines

Evaluation Question	▶ Tip	▶ Revision Technique
Are sentence lengths varied in the essay?	▶ **Highlight** each sentence with a colored marker so that you can compare sentence lengths. (Alternate between two different colors of marker to help your comparison.) If most sentences are the same length, revise.	▶ **Combine** sentences by reducing some sentences to phrases and inserting them into other sentences.

Varying Sentence Length

When writing about how things are alike or different, as with all writing, it is important that your sentences have a smooth rhythm. To attain rhythm, you need to balance short sentences with longer, more detailed ones. **Sentence combining** helps you create this balance. You can combine closely related sentences by reducing one sentence to a phrase and inserting it into the other sentence. When inserted, the phrase gives additional information about an idea expressed in the sentence.

Focus on
Sentences

ONE WRITER'S REVISIONS Here is how the writer of the model comparison-contrast essay on page 107 used the Style Guidelines to combine some sentences by using phrases.

TIP To decide which sentences to combine, look for repeated words or phrases. They often signal the sentences that need to be reduced to phrases.

BEFORE REVISION

Americans tend to smile a lot. Americans especially respond like this to questions. The French, on the other hand, react another way. The French sometimes pout their lips.

All four sentences are about the same length.

AFTER REVISION

Americans tend to smile a lot, especially when responding to questions. The French, on the other hand, sometimes react by pouting the lips.

Reduce some sentences to phrases
Insert these phrases into other sentences

Analyzing the Revision Process

1. What repetitive information did the writer delete? Why?
2. Why is the revised version better writing?

YOUR TURN 7 Varying Sentence Length in Your Own Paper

Use the guidelines on the previous page to evaluate your sentence length and to combine sentences if necessary.

Reference Note

For more on **varying sentence length,** see page 330.

Meeting INDIVIDUAL NEEDS

ADVANCED LEARNERS

Explain to students that children's stories are often written in short sentences. To reinforce sentence-combining skills, show on an overhead projector several sentences from a children's book. Then, have students combine closely related sentences to create a balance between short sentences and longer ones. After reading the revised version of the story, discuss with students how combining sentences affects the tone and readability of the story and why children's book writers might *not* want to vary sentence lengths.

Analyzing the Revision Process
ANSWERS

1. The writer deleted the word "Americans" from the second sentence and the words "The French" from the last sentence. The writer deleted these words to avoid beginning two sentences in a row with the same words and to combine short sentences into longer, more efficient ones.

2. The revised version is less repetitive and has a smoother rhythm.

YOUR TURN 7

Make sure students use the tips provided on p. 110 to evaluate their sentence lengths. You may want to allow students to work in pairs as they combine sentences.

Publishing

Proofread Your Essay

Reference Note
For **proofreading guide-lines,** see page 13.

Checking It Twice Read your essay at least two more times to make sure it is free of grammar, spelling, and punctuation errors. Be sure to correct any misplaced modifiers, words that modify the wrong word or word group. Just one misplaced modifier can confuse readers about the two items you are comparing. Once you have fixed the misplaced modifiers and any other errors, you will be ready to prepare a final copy of your essay.

Grammar Link

Correcting Misplaced Modifiers: Participial Phrases

When you are comparing and contrasting points about two drastically different subjects, a **misplaced modifier** can throw off your whole essay and confuse your audience. A misplaced modifier is a word, phrase, or clause that is confusing because it modifies the wrong word or group of words. Here, you will focus on misplaced modifiers that are participial phrases.

A participial phrase consists of a participle and its modifiers and complements. *Running through the sand, playing on the beach,* and *catching the beach ball* are examples of participial phrases. A participial phrase acts as an adjective, modifying either a noun or a pronoun. You have to be careful to place the phrase close to the word or words it modifies, or the sentence can take on an unintended meaning. A participial phrase that is in the wrong place is called a misplaced modifier.

Misplaced **Eating bamboo,** the woman photographed the panda. [Was the woman eating bamboo or was the panda eating bamboo?]

Improved The woman photographed the panda **eating bamboo.**

Reference Note
For more about **misplaced modifiers,** see page 587. For more on **using commas with introductory participial phrases,** see page 652.

PRACTICE

Revise each of the following sentences, correcting any misplaced modifiers. Note: You may have to add a comma if you move a participial phrase to the beginning of a sentence. Put your answers on your own paper.

1. Catalina saw a seashell diving into the water.

2. Pablo dreamed about beautiful sunsets sleeping on the blanket.

3. Hiding under a rock, Yumiko found a blue crab with four pairs of legs and two pincers.

4. Kareem hoped to prevent a sunburn adjusting the umbrella.

5. Biting his toes, he felt a little fish.

RESOURCES

Publishing
Extension
■ *Designing Your Writing*

Grammar Link
Practice
■ *Communications,* WS. p. 60

Designing Your Writing

Using Initial Letters One way you can keep readers interested in your comparison-contrast essay is to break up straight text by using **initial letters** and **dropped initial letters**. An initial letter, sometimes called an initial cap, is a large, raised first letter of an essay. The dropped initial letter, sometimes called a drop cap, is just like an initial letter, except that it is dropped into the body of the text. You can draw your initial letter or dropped initial letter by hand, or you can enlarge the size of a letter using a computer word-processing program. A point is a unit of measurement that is used to measure the height of printed letters.

Example: Initial Letter

A pull on an eyelid, a pat on the wrist—either of these gestures could lead to confusion for an American in Paris. In fact, years of French language classes practicing *je, tu, il,* and *bonjour* may not be enough preparation for an American to communicate. . . .

Example: Dropped Initial Letter

A pull on an eyelid, a pat on the wrist—either of these gestures could lead to confusion for an American in Paris. In fact, years of French language classes practicing *je, tu, il,* and *bonjour* may not be enough preparation for an American to communicate. . . .

Initial letters serve as a focal point, drawing the reader into the text. Consequently, your first initial letter should be for the first word of your essay. You can use one or two more initial letters at key points in your essay. For example, if you use the block method, you could use an initial letter to signal the beginning of each block. To avoid clutter, however, limit yourself to two or three initial letters in an essay. If you use the point-by-point method, do not add any extra initial letters.

If your teacher allows, experiment with different fonts for your initial letter until you find a font to fit the mood of your paper. (If you draw your initial letter, try experimenting with stencils or calligraphy pens.) To avoid confusing your reader, use only two fonts—one font and point size for your initial letters and a second, **legible** font for the rest of your paper. Examples of legible fonts include Times, Palatino, Garamond, and Helvetica.

Reference Note

For more on **document design,** see page 806 in the Quick Reference Handbook.

Wrap It Up

Metacognition. After students have
turned in their essays, have them jot
down and share aloud a sentence or
two about the most useful thing they
learned from working through the
comparison-contrast writing process.

YOUR TURN 8

Student responses to the reflective
questions will vary. You can lead
students in a reflective discussion
by asking volunteers to share their
responses with the class.

Publish Your Essay

Time to Shine   You have worked hard revising, editing, and proofreading your comparison-contrast essay. Your finished paper is something
to be proud of, so now is the time to share it. Here are some ways to share
your comparison-contrast essay with an audience.

- If your essay compares consumer items, you could print a shoppers'
  guide and distribute it to friends in your class.
- If your essay compares middle school with high school, you could publish it in a guide for new high school students.
- You could make a Web page with links to information about each item
  you are comparing.
- If your essay compares two movies or books, you could submit the essay
  to the entertainment section of your school newspaper.

PORTFOLIO

Reflect on Your Essay

Learning from Experience   One way to become a better writer is by
reflecting on your writing. Write short responses to the following questions to see how this workshop has helped you improve your writing skills.

- Why did you use the method you chose to organize your essay? Do you
  think you made the most effective choice? Why or why not?
- What do you think is the best part of your essay? Why?
- What would you change about your essay? What might you do differently the next time you write a comparison-contrast essay?
- What did you learn by writing this paper that will come in handy with
  other types of papers?

   If you put your essay in your portfolio, be sure to include your
responses to these questions.

YOUR TURN 8   Proofreading, Publishing, and Reflecting on Your Essay

Review each of the above steps. Before you hand in your comparison-
contrast essay, remember to

- proofread it carefully, remembering to check closely for misplaced
  modifiers
- consider ways to design your writing effectively
- think through your publishing options
- answer the reflective questions about your writing process

Connections to Life

Vocabulary of the Mass Media

Did you know you spend half of your waking hours reading, viewing, and listening to mass media messages? From television to newspapers to the Internet, you are bombarded with hundreds of media messages each day. What do these messages have in common? How are they different? How does something like the news vary from medium to medium? You can use your comparison-contrast skills to answer these questions.

What are the similarities and differences among various news media? One aspect they all have in common is that they report the news every day. News happens constantly. Every day, journalists go out into the world, collect information, and craft it into news reports. They create complex media products such as newspaper articles, TV broadcasts, radio reports, or Web pages in a very short amount of time.

Have you ever wondered how journalists are able to pull off this feat? One answer is that news stories follow set formulas or patterns. Journalists save time by putting new information into old formulas. Another answer is that each medium, whether newspapers, TV, or the World Wide Web, also has its own set of unique features that are repeated over and over again. For example, every newspaper article has a **headline,** a title at the top of the page.

If you are going to be a savvy news consumer, you need to know the similarities and differences among the unique features and news formulas of each mass medium. To get you started, here are some media vocabulary terms for newspapers, television, and the Internet.

Newspapers: On the Page   You probably already know that a newspaper is a print product made up of articles, illustrations, and photographs. A newspaper article is made up of

- **the headline**—the title of the piece
- **the deck**—a subhead, or a smaller headline below the main headline
- **the byline**—a line that lists the author's name
- **the copy**—the text of the news story in column format

Headline

Deck

Newspaper articles may follow the **inverted pyramid pattern,** where the most important and interesting facts of the article are listed at the beginning, and the least important facts are at the very end. The beginning of an article is called the **lead.** It usually answers the questions *who, what, where, why, when,* and *how.* The reason for the inverted pyramid pattern is that if an article must be shortened for space, the last paragraphs can be deleted without losing any important information.

Inverted Pyramid Pattern

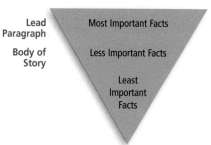

Lead Paragraph — Most Important Facts

Body of Story — Less Important Facts

Least Important Facts

An editor decides the **layout** or placement of articles, photographs, and **information graphics**—charts, graphs, maps, or other illustrations of data—in the newspaper. If a news article is important, it may have a **sidebar**—a second article on a closely related topic—next to it. Important articles are given a lot of **play,** or exposure, by being placed on the front page with large headlines and large photographs. Most photographs have **cutlines**—a few lines of explanatory text—directly underneath them.

TV News: Coming to You Live   Among other things, a TV news report is different from a newspaper article because it contains video and audio pieces that are broadcast to you live. An **anchor,** the newscaster in the studio, usually does a **lead-in**—an introduction to a report from a reporter in the field. Then the camera **cuts**—makes a transition—to either a live segment with the reporter, or a report that was taped earlier in the day.

News reports begin with a **setup**—a few words to grab listeners' attention, and a **cover shot**—a long piece of video used to establish the location of the report. A news report uses a variety of **shots**—segments of video, including

- **close-up**—the camera shows just a person's face
- **medium shot**—the camera shows a person from the waist up
- **long shot**—the camera shows an entire person and the environment surrounding him or her

While these video shots play on your TV screen, audio segments play through your TV speakers. The main types of sound used in news reports are

- **sound bites**—short audio pieces of interviews
- **voice-overs**—the reporter's voice narrating the story over the video
- **natural sound**—birds chirping, cars rushing by, crowds roaring, or any other sounds that are part of the environment of the news report

At the end of a news report, the reporter usually does a **stand-up:** the reporter speaks directly into the camera and offers some finishing commentary to the report.

In contrast to a newspaper article, a TV news report is extremely brief. A typical TV news story is shorter than twenty sentences and runs for less than two minutes. Because of these time constraints, only a few important facts can be presented in a TV news story.

Unlike the Inverted Pyramid Pattern, every fact in a TV news report must be important or interesting

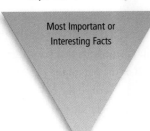

Most Important or Interesting Facts

The Internet: Computer Connections

The Internet is different from newspapers and TV because it is a network of thousands of computers with which you interact. You can log on to this network any time to read the news. You can sign up for **listservs**—news-clipping services that send articles on specific subjects to your personal e-mail address. You can also become part of a **Usenet newsgroup** to read items posted on a bulletin board. **Bulletin boards** are public places where you can read messages that others have posted, or even post your own message. The **World Wide Web** is a system that uses hyperlinks to deliver the news. A **hyperlink** is an image or highlighted section of text that takes you to another Web page when you click on it. A **home page** is the first page of information in a Web document.

The Internet is evolving as a medium. It does not have any set news formulas, but two techniques communicators use to save time when creating news for the Internet are **threading** and **linking**. On bulletin boards, **threaded messages** are messages that are grouped together because they all contain the same subject line. This enables writers to follow and respond to postings on their topics and ignore irrelevant postings. On the Web, reporters do not always have to provide key items such as definitions of terms, or historical context for their news stories. Instead, they provide **links** to other people's Web sites that already contain the definitions or historical context.

YOUR TURN 9 — Practicing Your Mass-Media Vocabulary

With a small group, look for examples of the inverted pyramid pattern, a headline, a byline, a deck, an informational graphic, a close-up shot, a medium shot, a sound bite, a voice-over, natural sound, a bulletin board, a home page, and a hyperlink. Have one person investigate newspapers, one person investigate TV news, and one person investigate the Web. When you have finished collecting your examples, prepare a formal, **workplace report** of your findings.

Timesaver

Rather than have each student log on to the Internet individually, you can save time by guiding the entire class through a single logon, and then asking students to help you find a news site and some threaded messages. Print the appropriate screens, make copies, and distribute them to the students.

TEACHING TIP

Practicing Your Mass-Media Vocabulary

As students prepare their findings for **Your Turn 9,** have them keep in mind the following guidelines:

- State the facts. Give the group a brief description of your findings.

- Be clear and concise. Omit the unnecessary details.

- Ask for help. If necessary, specify areas in which you need advice or assistance.

- Read aloud or distribute. So that the group can better understand your findings, read your report aloud or distribute copies.

YOUR TURN 9

You may need to provide students who do not have access to television or the Internet with class time in your school's computer lab or media center. *Be aware that Internet resources are sometimes public forums and their content can be unpredictable.*

For assessment, make sure students find examples for all the vocabulary terms listed in bold print in **Connections to Life.**

Focus on Viewing and Representing

OBJECTIVES

■ To analyze and critique the way that news stories are put together

■ To compare and contrast different media coverage of the same event

Quotation for the Day

"Facts are stubborn things."

(John Adams, 1735–1826, second president of the United States)

Use this quotation to introduce the idea that news stories must contain the same basic facts even if their accounts of the events differ.

Critical Thinking

Analysis. Remind students that journalists and media professionals are not the only people who have to make editorial decisions. For example, historians have to make decisions about what to include and what to leave out of history books. Ask students to name other professions in which people make editorial decisions. [Possible answers include writing, directing, law, publishing, and marketing.]

WHAT'S AHEAD?

In this section you will learn how to

■ analyze and critique the way news stories are put together

■ compare and contrast different media coverage of the same event

TIP Both stories represent accurate accounts of the game. However, they are different because each newspaper focuses on different details.

Comparing and Contrasting Media Coverage

Have you ever asked two friends to tell you about an event you did not attend, like a school play? Did they tell you exactly the same story, or did their stories vary a bit? Chances are that your friends' stories contained the same basic **facts** (such as the plot of the play) but focused on different **details**. Maybe one friend described the costumes, while the other friend focused on the acting. You might say that each friend put together his or her own *account*, or retelling, of the play.

Examine Different Accounts of an Event

The Way They See It Just as your friends create their own retellings of the same play, media sources put together different accounts of the same news event. For example, an account of a football game in your school's newspaper will look different from an account in the other team's newspaper. The newspaper writers will start with the same basic facts (who won and how many points were scored), but they will put together their own accounts of the game by focusing on different details. Use the chart below to compare and contrast the key features of two different accounts of a football game.

	Winning School's Article	**Losing School's Article**
Headline	*Victory!*	*Disappointing Loss*
Photograph	Team members jumping for joy	Star quarterback holding his head

118 Chapter 3 **Exposition:** Exploring Similarities and Differences

RESOURCES

Focus on Viewing and Representing Practice

■ *Media Literacy and Communication Skills*
—*Support and Practice,* Ch. 3
—*A How-to Handbook*

Teaching Notes

■ *Media Literacy and Communication Skills*
—*A Teacher's Guide,* Ch. 3

None of what you see and hear on TV and radio, in magazines and newspapers, or on the Internet comes to you "pure" or "unfiltered." This is because someone has to decide what will be included and what will be left out of a news story. Examples of these **editorial decisions** include what headlines, titles, sound bites, video clips, photographs, and informational graphics to use to retell news stories. You can compare and contrast the **editorial decisions** journalists and other media professionals make by examining the following aspects of news stories.

KEY CONCEPT

Reference Note
For more on **media terms,** see page 876.

- **The attention-getting techniques in news stories** How are the images, words, and sounds arranged to get readers' and viewers' attention?

- **The point of view in each news story** How is the main subject portrayed—negatively or positively?

- **The complexity of the news stories** Does the story provide background information and multiple points of view or have these items been omitted?

- **The sequence of information in the news stories** In what order does the story present information about its subject?

- **The emotional impact of the news stories** What feeling or impression does the story create in readers or viewers?

Looking at the News

Two Sources/Two Views Think of all the news that comes out every day: political events, natural disasters, accidents, sporting events, community happenings. Important news stories are usually covered in a variety of media: on TV, in newsmagazines, in news sites on the Web, and in newspapers. However, all these media do not cover the same story in exactly the same way. For example, a TV report includes moving images and quick summaries of the story, while a newspaper article includes still photographs and in-depth details. By comparing how different media sources present the same story, you can see how different kinds of editorial decisions finally come across to readers or viewers. You can see how these editorial choices shape your view of the event.

TIP As you look at the news, try to examine the effect of media on your own perception of reality.

One of the most important editorial choices news reporters make is about how to have an **emotional impact** upon the audience. A news story has emotional impact if it arouses the audience's feelings. High emotional impact can have powerful **effects** on audience members, causing them to act on feelings they get from a news story, rather than the accuracy of information in a news story.

Wrap It Up

Ask students to explain why news coverage of the same event may be different in different news media. [TV stories contain moving images and quick summaries, while newspaper articles include still photographs and in-depth details. In addition, journalists and media professionals decide what details of an event to include and what details to leave out, depending on what emotional impact they want to have upon the audience.]

YOUR TURN 10

Be aware that Internet resources are sometimes public forums and their content can be unpredictable.

Consider asking students who may not have access to a television or the Internet to compare the coverage of the same event by two different newspapers. Have students answer the questions in **Your Turn 10** to compare the two versions. Help students express their answers in the terms covered in this section.

News stories try to create an emotional impact by using anecdotes or examples from any of the following five categories:

- Love and Relationships
- Children
- The Unknown
- Death
- Animals

To compare and contrast the emotional impact of a story in a newspaper and on a TV news broadcast, count the number of times love, death, children, animals, or the unknown appear in the text, images, and sounds of each story. How are these categories used differently in each story? Look at the example below.

News Story on a Major Flood		
	TV News Report	**Newspaper Article**
Love and Relationships	Video footage of a man holding a photo of his wife	Photo of a man with a photo of his wife
Death	Sound bite from the man saying his wife died	Quotation from an official saying that 25 people died
Children	Sounds of children crying	Sentence describing the sound of a child crying
Animals	Video footage of a horse struggling in deep water	Sentence saying many livestock died
The Unknown	Video footage of a flooded car whose owners are missing	Description of search for missing owners of car

YOUR TURN 10 — Comparing and Contrasting Media Coverage of an Event

With a small group, look for news coverage of an event in at least two different news media—the Internet, the newspaper, or TV. Make a chart like the one above to organize your relevant features. Then, present a brief oral report to your class, comparing and contrasting the emotional impact of each news story. In your report, answer these questions:

1. If you had seen only one of these stories, how would your impression of the event be different? Use evidence to support your answer, by examining each story separately.

2. How did each news story arouse the audience's emotions?

3. Did one story do a better job of covering your event, or was the coverage similar in both stories? Why do you think so?

RESOURCES

Your Turn 10
Practice and Reinforcement

- *Media Literacy and Communication Skills*
  —*Support and Practice,* Ch. 3, transparencies and worksheets
  —Videocassette 1, Segment C

3 Choices

Choose one of the following activities to complete.

▶ **CROSSING THE CURRICULUM: HISTORY**

1. The More Things Change . . . Famous leaders have often copied the leadership style of earlier leaders. After all, if it works, why change it? Work with a partner to find two major historical leaders from different time periods who have something in common. If you are stuck, ask a history teacher for clues about where to look. Do some research in the library to investigate the leaders. Then, prepare a **report** that compares the two.

▶ **LITERATURE**

2. They've Got Style Over a lifetime an author can create many different works of literature. On close examination, however, you may discover that different works of literature by the same author actually have many aspects in common. Write a **literary essay** comparing two novels, poems, or short stories by your favorite author. Show how the author's unique thumbprint is present in each work. What distinctive features of the author's style can you find in both works?

▶ **CAREERS**

3. Tough Decisions Bosses often have to make decisions, but they do not always have the time to do their own research. That's where you come in. Assume your boss is about to make a purchase. Choose two office items to compare, such as two different pens, computers, or notebooks. Create a two-column chart that compares the advantages and disadvantages of each product. Then, write a **memo** to your boss that briefly summarizes your findings.

▶ **SPEAKING AND LISTENING**

4. On the Other Hand Choose an important issue that divides student opinion in your school. Think about issues like school uniforms, open lunch, or the student-government elections. You might even ask someone on the debate team what topics they are hashing out. Once you have found a topic, interview one student on each side of the issue. Then, prepare a brief **oral report** for your classmates that compares and contrasts both sides of the issue.

PORTFOLIO

▶ **CROSSING THE CURRICULUM: HISTORY**
To help students get started, offer the example of Franklin D. Roosevelt and his fireside chats. To find another president who also used mass media to communicate with the public, students might search encyclopedias for biographies of FDR and of a more recent president such as Jimmy Carter, who often spoke with people on telephone call-in programs.

▶ **LITERATURE**
Explain to students that style refers to the way a writer uses language. For example, a writer's style can be plain, ornate, descriptive, and so on. Students should look at the following elements to determine a writer's style: sentence length and complexity, use of figurative language and imagery, and diction.

▶ **CAREERS**
If available, bring in some office supply catalogs so that students can look at different office items and compare prices. You may need to show students the proper format for a business memo.

▶ **SPEAKING AND LISTENING**
Inform students that oral reports, like written ones, should be organized so that the listener can follow the speaker's ideas easily. Tell students to structure their reports according to either the block method or the point-by-point method.

CHAPTER 4

Exploring Causes and Effects

Use this guide to create an instructional plan that suits the individual needs of your students. Assignments marked by an asterisk (*) may be completed out of class. Times given for pacing lessons are estimated. See pp. 122–123 for chapter-wide resources. Resources listed in this guide are point-of-use resources only.

Curriculum Connections

Connections to Literature *pp. 149–150*
■ Causes and Effects in Fiction

Choices *p. 155*
■ Crossing the Curriculum: Science
■ Speaking and Listening
■ Viewing and Representing

---

 internetconnect

go. hrw .com GO TO: go.hrw.com
KEYWORD: EOLang 9-4

 All resources for this chapter are available for preview on the *One-Stop Planner CD-ROM with Test Generator.* All worksheets and tests may be printed from the CD-ROM.

T121A

	Chapter Opener *pp. 122–123*	**Reading Workshop: Reading a Cause-and-Effect Article** *pp. 124–133*
DEVELOPMENTAL PROGRAM	🕐 **20 minutes** • Cause and Effect *p. 123* • Your Turn 1 *p. 123*	🕐 **90 minutes** • Preparing to Read *p. 124* • Reading Selection *pp. 125–126* • First Thoughts 1–2 in groups *p. 127* • Implied Cause and Effect *pp. 127–128* • Your Turn 2 *p. 128* • Organizational Patterns *pp. 129–131* • Your Turn 3 *p. 131* • Test Taking Mini–Lesson *p. 133*
CORE PROGRAM	🕐 **15 minutes** • Cause and Effect *p. 123* • Your Turn *p. 123*	🕐 **90 minutes** • Preparing to Read *p. 124* • Reading Selection *pp. 125–126* • First Thoughts 1–3 *p. 127* • Implied Cause and Effect *pp. 127–128* • Your Turn 2 *p. 128* • Organizational Patterns *pp. 129–131* • Your Turn 3 *p. 131* • Vocabulary Mini-Lesson *p. 132* • Test Taking Mini-Lesson *p. 133*
ADVANCED PROGRAM	🕐 **20 minutes** • Cause and Effect *p. 123* • Your Turn *p. 123*	🕐 **75 minutes** • Preparing to Read *p. 124* • Reading Selection *pp. 125–126* • First Thoughts on Your Reading 3 *p. 127* • Implied Cause and Effect *pp. 127–128* • Your Turn 2 *p. 128* • Your Turn 3 *p. 131* • Vocabulary Mini-Lesson *p. 132*
RESOURCES **PRINT**	• *Communications,* 🗐 TP. 31, WS. p. 61 🗐	• *Alternative Readings,* 🗐 Ch. 4 • *Communications,* 🗐 TPs. 32, 33, WS. pp. 62–69
RESOURCES **MEDIA**	• *One-Stop Planner CD-ROM* 🎧	• *One-Stop Planner CD-ROM* 🎧

TP.=Transparency   WS.=Worksheet

Writing Workshop: Writing a Cause-and-Effect Explanation *pp. 134–150*	Focus on Speaking and Listening *pp. 151–152;* Focus on Viewing and Representing *pp. 153–154*
🕐 **100 minutes** • Choose a Situation or Event *pp. 134–135* • Narrow Your Topic *p. 135* • Consider Your Audience *pp. 135–136* • Write Your Thesis *pp. 136–137* • Gather Support and Your Turn 4 *pp. 137–138* • Framework and Your Turn 5* *p. 140* • Writer's Model and Student's Model *pp. 141–142* 🕐 **180 minutes** • Evaluate and Revise Your Draft *pp. 143–144* • Your Turn 6 *p. 144* • Focus on Sentences and Your Turn 7 in groups *pp. 145–146* • Proofread, Publish, Reflect on Your Essay *pp. 147–148* • Grammar Link *p. 147* • Your Turn 8 *p. 148*	🕐 **45 minutes** • Carefully Prepare the Speech *pp. 151–152* • Rehearse the Speech* *p. 152* • Deliver the Speech and Solicit Feedback *p. 152* • Your Turn 10 *p. 152* 🕐 **45 minutes** • TV Representations of Real Life *p. 153* • Analyze Media Representations *p. 153* • Investigate and Draw Conclusions* *p. 154* • Your Turn 11* *p. 154*
🕐 **160 minutes** • Choose a Situation or Event *pp. 134–135* • Narrow Your Topic *p. 135* • Consider Your Audience *pp. 135–136* • Write Your Thesis *pp. 136–137* • Gather Support and Your Turn 4 *pp. 137–138* • Critical-Thinking Mini-Lesson in groups *p. 139* • Framework and Your Turn 5* *p. 140* • Writer's Model and Student's Model *pp. 141–142* • Evaluate and Revise Your Draft *pp. 143–144* • Your Turn 6 *p. 144* • Focus on Sentences and Your Turn 7 *pp. 145–146* • Proofread, Publish, and Reflect on Your Essay *pp. 147–148* • Grammar Link *p. 147* • Your Turn 8 *p. 148* • Connections to Literature and Your Turn 9* *pp. 149–150*	🕐 **90 minutes** • Carefully Prepare the Speech *pp. 151–152* • Rehearse the Speech* *p. 152* • Deliver the Speech and Solicit Feedback *p. 152* • Your Turn 10 *p. 152* 🕐 **40 minutes** • TV Representations of Real Life *p. 153* • Analyze Media Representations *p. 153* • Investigate and Draw Conclusions* *p. 154* • Your Turn 11* *p. 154*
🕐 **100 minutes** • Choose a Situation or Event *pp. 134–135* • Write Your Thesis *pp. 136–137* • Gather Support and Your Turn 4 *pp. 137–138* • Critical-Thinking Mini-Lesson *p. 139* • Framework and Your Turn 5* *p. 140* • Writer's Model and Student's Model *pp. 141–142* • Evaluate and Revise Your Draft *pp. 143–144* • Your Turn 6* *p. 144* • Proofread, Publish, Reflect on Your Essay *pp. 147–148* • Your Turn 8 *p. 148* • Connections to Literature and Your Turn 9* *pp. 149–150*	🕐 **75 minutes** • Carefully Prepare the Speech *pp. 151–152* • Rehearse the Speech* *p. 152* • Deliver the Speech and Solicit Feedback *p. 152* • Your Turn 10 *p. 152* 🕐 **30 minutes** • TV Representations of Real Life *p. 153* • Analyze Media Representations *p. 153* • Investigate and Draw Conclusions* *p. 154* • Your Turn 11* *p. 154*

• *Communications,* 🔌
  TPs. 34–37
  WS. pp. 70–78
• *Designing Your Writing*
	• *Media Literacy and Communication Skills* 🔌
	  —*Support and Practice,* Ch. 4
	  —*A How-to Handbook*
	  —*A Teacher's Guide,* Ch. 4

• *One-Stop Planner CD-ROM* 💿	• *Media Literacy and Communication Skills* 📺 —Videocassette 1, Segment D • *One-Stop Planner CD-ROM* 💿

Exploring Causes and Effects

CHAPTER OBJECTIVES

■ To read a news article and analyze cause-and-effect structure

■ To write a cause-and-effect essay

■ To create, present, and evaluate an informative speech

■ To analyze television representations and compare them to real-world experience

Chapter Overview

Causes and effects are part of most good explanations. This chapter is designed to help students use and recognize cause-and-effect organizational patterns when they read, when they write, when they listen, and when they take tests. The Reading Workshop gives students a news article in which they will identify causes and effects. The Writing Workshop provides all the steps students need to write a cause-and-effect explanation.

The Focus on Speaking and Listening offers instruction on how to give an informative speech that explains causes and effects, and the Focus on Viewing and Representing offers students the opportunity to compare TV to real life. While the sections of the chapter can be taught independently, they also work together to give your students a well-rounded working knowledge of cause-and-effect structures in exposition.

Why Study Cause and Effect?

Understanding cause-and-effect relationships in reading and writing will help students understand their worlds. For example, it is good for students to realize that their actions have consequences—that the things they do affect others and the world around them. Students should also understand that events are not just random but have causes, some very specific, some not clear at all. If nothing else, thinking about cause-and-effect relationships should remind students that no one acts or exists in isolation.

Teaching the Chapter

Option 1: Begin with Literature

If literature is the departure point of instruction in your classroom, you could introduce the chapter after studying the use of causes and effects in drama, epics, or short stories. Whatever the genre, the emphasis would be on cause-and-effect relationships, either through how characters affect one another, how events cause changes in characters, or how characters affect plot. Afterwards, have students read the article in this chapter (pp. 125–126), and illustrate how cause-and-effect relationships function in nonfiction as well as in literature. Equipped with a reading knowledge of cause-and-effect explanations, students will be ready to write their own cause-and-effect essays.

Option 2: Begin with Nonfiction and Writing

Familiarize students with cause-and-effect relationships by beginning with the material in this chapter. The short, annotated article in the Reading Workshop and its accompanying instruction (pp. 124–133) provide a simple groundwork on which to base students' understanding of implied and explicit cause and effect. Next, guide students to a direct experience of cause-and-effect explanation as they write the essay in the Writing Workshop (pp. 134–150). When it is time to return to literature, students will have a more complete understanding of cause-and-effect relationships and will be better prepared to examine and write about the causes and effects they discover in fiction. See also **Connections to Literature** on pp. 149–150.

Making Connections

■ To the Literature Curriculum

Literature is filled with cause-and-effect relationships. For example, by reading *Romeo and Juliet,* the *Odyssey,* or "The Necklace," students can see the events that Romeo's rash actions set in motion, or the changes Odysseus' character undergoes as he travels home to Ithaca, or the effect losing a necklace has on a young woman's life. Cause-and-effect relationships shape the stories we read and the stories we tell.

Lesson Idea: Cause and Effect in "The Necklace" by Guy de Maupassant

1. Work with students to create a cause-and-effect chain based on the plot in the short story. You can use the example of a cause-and-effect chain on p. 129 in this chapter.

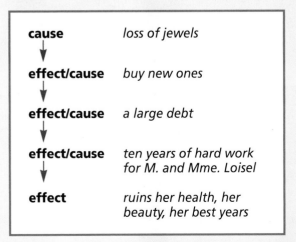

cause	*loss of jewels*
↓	
effect/cause	*buy new ones*
↓	
effect/cause	*a large debt*
↓	
effect/cause	*ten years of hard work for M. and Mme. Loisel*
↓	
effect	*ruins her health, her beauty, her best years*

2. Have students label the events on the chain as a cause, an effect, or both. A sample response is given at the bottom of the first column.

3. Beyond events, encourage students to think about causes and effects in terms of character. Ask students what else besides losing the necklace might be the cause of Mathilde's demise. If her desire to "please, be envied, be fascinating" led her to ten years of deprivation and ruinous work, then what might have caused that desire in her?

4. After this discussion, introduce students to the magazine article in this chapter (pp. 125–126). Point out that the article has a series of causes and effects just as "The Necklace" does. Use the instruction on cause-and-effect organizational patterns on pp. 129–131, which will help prepare students to write about cause and effect in their own lives.

■ To Careers

The chapter is designed to complement your literature book by bringing cause and effect into students' everyday lives. By asking students to think about cause and effect in the world of work, you will help them put their intellectual skills to use outside of school. Invite a speaker to class, such as a chemist, a lawyer, or a business owner, to discuss causes and effects in his or her work. You could prepare your speaker by giving him or her the organizational patterns on pp. 129–131. Ask the speaker to use the patterns in discussing elements of his or her job. Students will have an opportunity to see that what they are learning has applications not only in books or articles, but in contexts all around them.

■ To the Community

Through the chapter's contemporary magazine article, your students will be exposed to an issue beyond their school world but related to their larger community. Before they read the article on surgery and operating rooms (pp. 125–126), students may need some background. Ask your local hospital if it can provide an instructional video intended for patients facing surgery that you can show to students. You will probably want to preview the video and inform parents of the material you will be presenting in the video. Again, this activity emphasizes the relationship between what students are learning and their world.

CHAPTER 4 Exploring Causes and Effects

PREVIEWING THE CHAPTER

■ The four workshops in this chapter explore cause and effect. They can be taught separately, but, taught together, they help students develop a complete conception of cause-and-effect relationships. Reading a cause-and-effect article prepares students to write more effective cause-and-effect essays of their own. After practicing reading and writing about cause-and-effect relationships, students will also be better able to prepare a cause-and-effect informative speech. To integrate this chapter with grammar, usage, and mechanics chapters, see pp. T371A–T371B.

INTRODUCING THE CHAPTER

■ To introduce the chapter, use the Journal Warm-up, Transparency 31, in *Communications*.

VIEWING THE ILLUSTRATION

■ This collage of cartoon drawings and real objects shows a series of causes and effects. Ask students to identify the "real" objects [bells, pulleys, string, cage, hook, red coil, and house frame] and to explain how they recognized them. [The "real" objects are shiny and are not outlined in black, as the drawn objects are.] Point out how the arrows and dotted lines indicate movement and direction. As a class, narrate the chain of events from A to I.

Representing. Challenge students to sketch a contraption of their own that relies on a series of causes and effects.

CHAPTER RESOURCES

Planning
■ *Lesson Planner*, Ch. 4
■ *ELL Strategies*, Ch. 4
■ Block Scheduling, p. T121A (this book)
■ *One-Stop Planner CD-ROM*

Practice
■ *Communications*, Ch. 4
■ *Writer's Workshop 2 CD-ROM*

■ *Media Literacy and Communication Skills*

Extension
■ *Designing Your Writing*

Reinforcement
■ *Communications*, Ch. 4
■ *Vocabulary Workshop* and *Tests*

Reading Workshop

Reading a Cause-and-Effect Article

Writing Workshop

Writing a Cause-and-Effect Explanation

Speaking and Listening

Giving an Informative Speech

Viewing and Representing

Analyzing Stereotypes

Cause and Effect

- The school board has decided to close your school campus at lunch.

- Your mother's promotion will require your family to move.

- The state legislature has instituted a requirement that all high school students complete at least twenty hours of volunteer service each school year.

Any of these scenarios would probably prompt you to ask the question *Why?* or *What are the effects?* In asking and answering these questions, you are examining causes and effects.

Of course you aren't the only one who wonders about causes and effects. Doctors and researchers look for the causes of diseases and the effects of exercise. Historians argue about the causes of the Civil War and the effects of space exploration on world politics. Scientists develop theories to explain the formation of the continents and the possible effects of a hurricane on a coastal city.

Informational Text

Exposition

YOUR TURN 1   Brainstorming About Causes and Effects

With two or three classmates, brainstorm instances where you have observed cause-and-effect relationships and areas in which people work to understand the causes and/or the effects of something. To get started, think about historians, detectives, and astronauts. Be prepared to share your responses with the class.

internet connect

go.hrw.com

GO TO: go.hrw.com
KEYWORD: EOLang 9-4

Motivate

Activate thinking about cause and effect by having students create orally a cause-and-effect chain. Start with a sentence such as "Because I didn't have lunch money, I skipped lunch." Then, ask students to continue the chain with "Because I skipped lunch, . . . " See how many links they can add to the chain.

ELEMENTS OF
Literature
....

Cause and Effect in Literature. In *Elements of Literature,* Third Course, see "The Necklace," by Guy de Maupassant, pp. 221–228, and "The Most Dangerous Game," by Richard Connell, pp. 13–28, for examples of characters who consider the causes and effects of their actions.

YOUR TURN 1

Possible answers include instances such as practicing a musical instrument and studying layers of rock, and areas such as medicine, the law, and advertising.

- *Alternative Readings,* Ch. 4
- *Daily Language Activity Transparencies*

Evaluation and Assessment

- Test Generator (One-Stop Planner CD-ROM)

- *Assessment Package*
  —*Chapter Tests,* Ch. 4
  —*Chapter Tests in Standardized Test Formats,* Ch. 4
  —*Assessment Alternatives,* Ch. 4

Internet

- go.hrw.com (keyword: EOLang 9–4)

Preview   **123**

Reading Workshop

OBJECTIVES

Reading and Writing Connection

- To read a cause-and-effect article in preparation for writing a cause-and-effect essay

Reading Skills

- To identify implied causes and effects

- To analyze cause-and-effect patterns

- To use cause-and-effect context clues with unfamiliar vocabulary

TEACHING TIP

Preparing to Read
The material on p. 124 introduces concepts that will be taught in depth on pp. 127–131. Implied cause and effect and cause-and-effect organizational patterns are the instructional focus of the Reading Workshop. The reading selection, **"Hot Times in the Operating Room,"** illustrates both of these concepts.

Quotation for the Day

" Every why hath a wherefore. "

(*The Comedy of Errors*, William Shakespeare, 1564–1616, English playwright and poet)

You may want to explain that *wherefore* in this instance means "a reason, a cause." Ask pairs of students to list several causes and effects. Start them off with an example such as "Mothers Against Drunk Driving was formed as a result of . . ."

RESOURCES

Reading Workshop Reinforcement

- *Alternative Readings*, Ch. 4

WHAT'S AHEAD?

In this section, you will read a magazine article and learn how to

- identify implied causes and effects
- analyze cause-and-effect patterns

Reading a Cause-and-Effect Article

" **Y**ou can't go to school without your coat. You'll get sick!" Is this expression just something adults say, or is it true that there is a connection between cold temperatures and getting sick? The article on the next page, "Hot Times in the Operating Room," can help you answer this question. In this article, the writer examines the cause-and-effect relationship between patient infection and the cold temperatures usually found in operating rooms.

Preparing to Read

READING SKILL

Implied Cause and Effect The writer of the following article explores the cause-and-effect relationship between patient infection and cold temperatures in operating rooms. When you read about these causes and effects, you will learn how one event causes a later event. The first event is the **cause** of the next event, the **effect**. As you read, see if you can recognize the causes and the effects. Just remember that writers do not always signal causes and effects with clue words such as *if . . . then, because,* or *reasons why*. When signal words are missing, you will have to figure out the **implied** (suggested) **causes and effects.**

READING FOCUS

Cause-and-Effect Organizational Patterns When explaining causes and their effects, writers can organize their ideas in several ways; they can focus on the causes, on the effects, or on both in a causal chain. If you represented these patterns visually, they would look something like this.

As you read the following article, see if you can determine what organizational pattern the writer has chosen to use.

READING PROCESS

PREREADING
Set a Purpose for Reading the Selection.
The **Preparing to Read** section discusses students' purposes for reading **"Hot Times in the Operating Room"** on pp. 125–126: to

recognize implied cause and effect and cause-and-effect patterns. Tell students that when they read with a purpose, they will get more out of what they read and remember what they learn longer.

See if you can find out if cold temperatures have a connection with sickness. As you read, jot down answers to the numbered active-reading questions.

from **DISCOVER**

HOT Times in the Operating Room

Working under bright lights and wearing heavy gowns can make surgery uncomfortably hot for doctors and nurses. Operating rooms, therefore, are traditionally kept quite cold. That makes the surgery patient quite cold, too—even slightly hypothermic. Body temperatures can drop by 4 degrees. Doctors used to think mild hypothermia was actually good for the patient because cold retards the growth of bacteria in the air. But according to a new study, the cold temperatures in operating rooms actually triple the risk of infection.

"What causes wound infection is not really bacteria floating around in the air but the patient's decreased resistance to bacteria on the skin or inside the body," says Daniel Sessler, an anesthesiologist at the University of California at San Francisco and the University of Vienna. To find out how operating-room temperatures affect that resistance, Sessler and his colleagues studied 200 patients undergoing surgery. In 104 patients, warmed intravenous fluid and forced-air blankets (which are like quilts with warm air blown through them) kept body temperature normal. The other 96 patients were not warmed during

> **1. How does the writer immediately get your attention?**

> **2. What is the writer saying here about hypothermia and risk of infection?**

> **3. Why does the writer tell us this story about Sessler's experiment?**

Also, tell students that in their independent reading, they will need to prepare by identifying their own purposes. They can set their own purposes by skimming the reading selection and jotting down predictions about its content. As they read, verifying the accuracy of their predictions will help students engage with the text. Then, they can reflect on whether they achieved their purposes for reading.

4. Low body temperature causes low blood flow and low oxygen.

5. This part mentions that hypothermia interferes with the workings of the immune system.

6. The writer argues that in the future, doctors should warm patients during surgery to lower the risk of infection because doing so is inexpensive and effective.

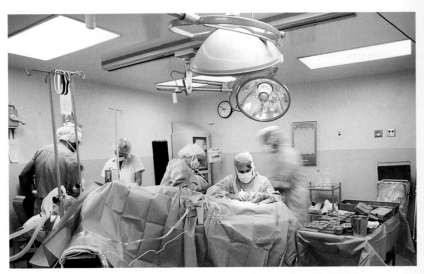

surgery, and their body temperatures dropped to an average of 94.5 degrees. Wound infections, Sessler found, occurred in 19 percent of the patients allowed to become hypothermic but in only 6 percent of the warmed patients. Unwarmed patients also stayed in the hospital nearly three days longer.

Hypothermia probably lowers the body's resistance in two ways, says Sessler. First, low body temperature reduces the flow of blood—and its oxygen cargo—to the wound. "Oxygen is essential to fighting infections," he says. The body's immune system breaks down molecular oxygen into highly reactive atomic oxygen. Immune cells release this oxygen near bacteria. "This is what kills them," says Sessler. Hypothermia also directly inhibits any functions of the immune system. "The cells and enzymes responsible for immunity simply don't work well when the body is cold."

"I think warming will become the standard of care in no time," says Sessler. "None of this is difficult, and none of it is expensive. Keeping people warm costs less than thirty dollars, which is nothing in the scheme of the operation. But it makes a big difference in terms of the outcome, is essentially risk free, and reduces costs. So it's sort of a no-brainer that you should keep people warm."

> **4. What causes low blood flow and low oxygen?**

> **5. What effect of hypothermia is mentioned here?**

> **6. In the conclusion, how does the writer bring the article to a close?**

126   Chapter 4   **Exposition:** Exploring Causes and Effects

READING PROCESS

READING

Make Personal Connections. Tell students that making personal connections will help them relate what they are reading to something they already know so that they can better interpret their reading. Ask students to jot down one or two ways the Reading Selection on pp. 125–126 connects to their lives. You might ask students to write about a time when they felt really cold. Did the coldness make them feel weak?

First Thoughts on Your Reading

Work with a partner to answer the following questions about "Hot Times in the Operating Room." Put your answers on your own paper.

1. Using your answer to active-reading question 2, explain in your own words what the writer presents as the main idea, or thesis, of this article.

2. The second paragraph of this article provides the support for the writer's cause-and-effect explanation. What details in this paragraph support the writer's claim that room temperature affects the risk of infection?

3. Is this statement true or false? "The last paragraph of this article echoes the first paragraph." Explain your answer.

Implied Cause and Effect

◀ READING SKILL

Hidden Identity "Hot Times in the Operating Room," like all cause-and-effect articles, explains how one action or series of actions (the **cause**) causes something to happen (the **effect**). In many cause-and-effect articles, writers use **clue words** to help signal causes and effects for readers. These identity tags include words such as

affect	because	determines	leads to
as a result	consequently	therefore	so that
reasons	if. . . then	in order	since
so	effect	why	thus

Example:

cause   clue word   effect

The use of iodine on the wound   affects   the recovery speed.

As you read about cause-and-effect relationships, however, you will see that whether something is a cause or an effect is not always obvious. After all, causes and effects don't always wear identity tags. So how can you determine causes and effects if there are no signal words? You have to infer the relationship—that is, use known facts and personal experience to determine whether it is a cause or effect. When causes and effects are not openly identified by the writer, they are known as **implied causes and effects.**

First Thoughts on Your Reading

ANSWERS
Possible answers are suggested below.

1. The author's main idea is that doctors now know that hypothermia causes an increase in a patient's risk of infection.

2. Three details support the writer's claim that room temperature has an effect on the risk of infection: 19 percent of hypothermic patients had wound infections; only 6 percent of warmed patients had wound infections; and patients who were not kept warm had longer hospital stays.

3. False. The last paragraph of the article is a logical progression from the first paragraph, but the two paragraphs do not say exactly the same thing. The first paragraph explains that operating rooms have been traditionally kept cold, but that cold temperatures increase the risk of infection. The last paragraph explains that doctors should use warmer temperatures in the operating room.

Reading Workshop   **127**

TIP A cause actually occurs before an effect, but writers may discuss the effect before the cause, as in this example sentence.

In the following sentence, there is a cause-and-effect relationship between low body temperature and slow blood circulation, even though the writer does not signal the cause or the effect with a clue word.

Example:

effect   cause
A person's blood circulation is slowed   by low body temperature.

THINKING IT THROUGH   **Implied Cause and Effect**

Read the sentence below. Then, to figure out the cause or effect in this sentence, use these steps listed below.

A person's blood circulation is slowed by low body temperature.

▶ **STEP 1** Ask yourself, "What happened?"(What is the effect?)   *Blood circulation is slowed down.*

▶ **STEP 2** Ask yourself, "Why?" (What is the cause?)   *Low body temperature.*

▶ **STEP 3** What can you infer?   *Low body temperature is the cause; slowed blood circulation is the effect.*

YOUR TURN 2

ANSWERS

1. Cold temperatures are the cause; higher risk of infection is the effect.

2. Decreased resistance is the cause; wound infection is the effect.

3. Hypothermia is the cause; lowered resistance is the effect.

4. Low body temperature is the cause; a reduction in the flow of blood and oxygen is the effect.

5. Hypothermia is the cause; an inhibited immune system is the effect.

TIP If you have trouble distinguishing between causes and effects as you read, try to represent the relationship visually; sometimes a graphic representation of how ideas relate makes the connections clearer. See the examples on page 124.

YOUR TURN 2   **Recognizing Causes and Effects**

Using the three steps above, identify the causes and the effects in each of the following sentences from "Hot Times in the Operating Room." Put your answers on your own paper.

1. But according to a new study, the cold temperatures in operating rooms actually triple the risk of infection.

2. What causes wound infection is not really bacteria floating around in the air but the patient's decreased resistance to bacteria on the skin or inside the body.

3. Hypothermia probably lowers the body's resistance in two ways, says Sessler.

4. First, low body temperature reduces the flow of blood—and its oxygen cargo—to the wound.

5. Hypothermia also directly inhibits any functions of the immune system.

RESOURCES

Your Turn 2

Practice

■ *Communications,* WS. p. 62

Reinforcement

■ *Communications,* TP. 32, WS. p. 63

Cause-and-Effect Organizational Patterns

READING FOCUS

The Chicken or the Egg? Generally, every writer of a causal article tries to explain how causes and effects are related. However, not all cause-and-effect relationships are simple and straightforward. One cause can have several effects; one effect can result from several causes, and so forth. There are so many different kinds of relationships that the **organization,** or **pattern,** of cause-and-effect writing can vary considerably. Each writer must choose a particular focus on causes, effects, or both. Then the writer can determine the most effective organization for the writing.

Knowing the organizational pattern, or structure, of a text can help you comprehend what you are reading. Specifically, cause-and-effect text structures can help you understand the causal relationship between ideas. Cause-and-effect text patterns, like any organizational pattern, are a kind of road map; they help you navigate unfamiliar text. When you learn these patterns, you will have a better idea of where to look to find the main idea and details in any cause-and-effect article. Examples of three common cause-and-effect text patterns follow.

Three Types of Patterns Depending upon the focus of the writing—causes only, effects only, or both causes and effects—the organizational pattern may vary a great deal. As a reader, it is your task to figure out how the article is organized so that you can more easily identify causes and effects. Does this sound like a difficult task? It is not. In fact, most articles use one or more of three basic cause-and-effect patterns. Master these patterns, and you will have the key to understanding most cause-and-effect articles. The following examples are maps of the three common cause-and-effect patterns: a causal chain, focus on causes, and focus on effects.

Pattern 1: Causal Chain In a causal chain, an initial cause brings about an effect. Then that effect becomes a cause for another effect, and so on, until the final effect is reached.

cause ⟶ effect/cause ⟶ effect/cause ⟶ effect

Example:

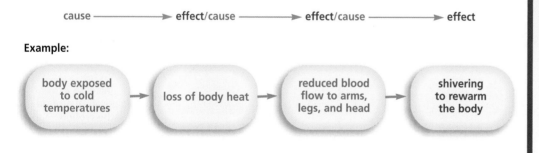

TEACHING TIP

Cause-and-Effect Organizational Patterns

Explain to students that another useful way to show the pattern of causes and an effect is to use a fishbone diagram like the one below.

Meeting INDIVIDUAL NEEDS

LEARNERS HAVING DIFFICULTY

Take a moment to acquaint students with the use of the arrow symbol in the graphic representations of cause and effect that will appear throughout Chapter 4. Explain to students that the arrow could be substituted with the verb "cause(s)," and that the cause will always appear at the tail of the arrow and the effect will appear at its point.

> **Pattern 2: Focus on Causes**   In this pattern, the effect is stated in the thesis; then the causes are explained in the body paragraphs.

Example:

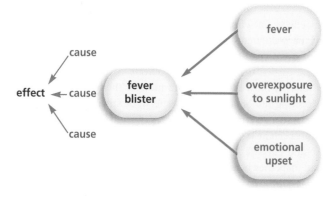

TIP   Notice that in Pattern 2, the writer starts by describing an effect and then jumps backward in time to describe the causes that brought about the effect. Writers tend to use this pattern when they want to emphasize *Why?* questions such as the question *Why do people get fever blisters?*

> **Pattern 3: Focus on Effects**   In this pattern, the cause is stated in the thesis; then the effects are explained in the body paragraphs.

Example:

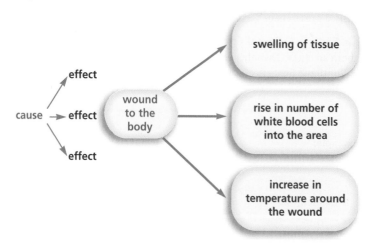

READING PROCESS

EXTENDING
Apply What You Read. Explain to students that they can practice their understanding of cause-and-effect patterns by applying what they have learned to a recounting of a recent school event. Ask them to create and fill in an organizational pattern about an article they read covering last week's sports victory or academic contest results.

TIP Don't be surprised to find that a writer's organization does not exactly fit one of the three cause-and-effect patterns; most professional authors experiment with unusual ways to present their ideas.

For example, "Hot Times in the Operating Room" actually combines all three patterns. Also, the cause-and-effect chain for this article doesn't begin until the third paragraph; however, "decreased resistance" is mentioned in the second paragraph.

YOUR TURN 3 **Analyzing a Cause-and-Effect Pattern**

To analyze the cause-and-effect pattern in "Hot Times in the Operating Room," complete the content map below. Put your answers on your own paper. (Remember, your answers to the active-reading questions and First Thoughts questions can help you analyze this pattern.)

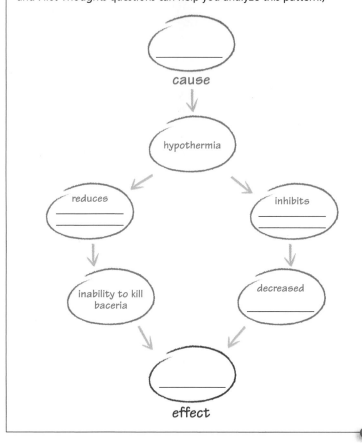

cause

↓

hypothermia

↓ ↓

reduces   inhibits

↓   ↓

inability to kill bacteria   decreased

↓   ↓

effect

Reading Workshop   **131**

YOUR TURN 3

ANSWERS
Suggested answers appear in italics.

cause: *cold operating rooms*

reduces: *the patient's blood flow, and therefore, oxygen*

inhibits: *the ability of the immune system to function*

decreased: *resistance to bacteria*

effect: *infection*

Wrap It Up

Metacognition. Ask students to reflect on their own reading processes. Give students ten minutes to jot down answers to the following questions:

1. What was the most important thing you learned from **"Hot Times in the Operating Room"?**

2. Rate the reading difficulty of the article. Was it hard or easy? Why?

Then, ask students to answer the following question:

3. Why might a writer state an effect first and then move backward in time to describe the causes of that effect? [Writers might state the effect first and then the causes when they want to emphasize *why* something happens.]

RESOURCES

Your Turn 3
Practice
■ *Communications,* WS. p. 64
Reinforcement
■ *Communications,* TP. 33, WS. p. 65

MINI-LESSON   VOCABULARY

Cause-and-Effect Context Clues

ANSWERS
Possible responses are given below.

1. The word *because* tells you why (cause) the patients shivered. What condition would make people shiver? People shiver when their bodies are cold. An informed guess is that *hypothermic* means "very cold."

2. The words *so that* are cause-and-effect context clues. What would cause the heart to pump extra oxygen into the bloodstream to cause the brain to be more alert in an emergency? Hormones might cause the heart to pump extra oxygen. An informed guess is that *induce* means "to bring about or cause."

3. The words *results in* are cause-and-effect clue words. What condition would result in a protective blood clot at the wound site? Platelets might stick together in the rough surfaces of the cut. An informed guess is that *cleave* means "to cling."

4. The words *as a result* give you the clue that a cause precedes them and an effect follows them. What is the result of the white blood cells killing pathogens? Small-scale infections are stopped when white blood cells kill pathogens. So, a *pathogen* must be something that causes infections.

5. The words *due to* tell you why (cause) bacteria and viruses are stopped from penetrating vital organs. What might stop bacteria and viruses from penetrating vital organs? A wall might stop them. An informed guess is that *impermeable* means "not permitting passage."

MINI-LESSON VOCABULARY

Cause-and-Effect Context Clues

Sometimes you can figure out the meaning of an unfamiliar word by examining its **context**: the words that surround the unfamiliar word and the way in which the word is used. One type of context clue, a **cause-and-effect clue,** indicates that something happens because of another event. If you know the likely cause or result of the action in the relationship, you can often use this information to determine the meaning of the unfamiliar word. Whenever possible, it is a good idea to check your guess in a dictionary.

THINKING IT THROUGH   **Using Cause-and-Effect Context Clues**

Take a look at the example below and the steps following it.

Example:
Because four patients had a natural **immunity** to the disease, the doctor did not give them medicine.

1. **Look for cause-and-effect clue words.** The word *because* tells why (cause) the doctor did not give the patients medicine.

2. **Ask a cause-and-effect question about the unfamiliar word.** *Why would an* **immunity** *cause the doctor not to give the patients medicine?*

3. **Answer your question.** *Patients who had a natural protection within their bodies against the disease would not need medicine. Therefore,* **immunity** *could mean "a natural protection against a disease."*

PRACTICE

Use the steps above to find the meaning of the italicized words in the following sentences. Put your answers on your own paper.

1. Because of *hypothermic* conditions, patients shivered during the operations, and many developed infections.

2. So that the brain is more alert in an emergency, hormones from the adrenal glands *induce* the heart to pump extra oxygen into the bloodstream.

3. Platelets *cleave* to the rough surfaces of a cut, a process that results in a protective blood clot at the wound site.

4. When viruses or bacteria enter your body, your immune system activates white blood cells that kill the *pathogens*. As a result, small-scale infections are usually repelled.

5. Partly due to an *impermeable* membrane, bacteria and viruses that bypass the protection of the skin do not penetrate vital internal organs.

RESOURCES

Vocabulary
Practice
■ *Communications,* WS. p. 66

Test Taking
Practice
■ *Communications,* WS. pp. 67–69

Implied Causes and Effects

Local, state, and national reading tests usually check your understanding of causes or effects that are implied, not directly stated. Since the reading passages often don't include any **clue words** like *because* or *since* to point out causes or effects, you have to figure out the answer.

Here is a typical **reading passage** and its cause-and-effect test question:

Solar-heating devices called *flat-plate collectors* have one or more covers made of clear plastic or glass. Beneath the covers is a black plate made of metal or plastic. The black plate gives off heat as it is warmed by sunlight, and this heat is contained by the clear covers.

A flat-plate collector can be very useful for heating household water. Air, water, or some other fluid is pumped through

tubes attached to the black plate of the flat-plate collector. Fluid inside the tubes passes through the collector and absorbs heat from the black plate. Another device called a *heat exchanger* is then used to transfer the heat from the fluid to a household hot-water system.

Heat can be trapped within a flat-plate collector because

A. tubes are attached to the black plate within the collector

B. the clear glass or plastic covers contain the heat inside the collector

C. all of the heat stays inside the black plate; the plate gives off no heat

D. heat energy is added to the collector by the fluid that flows over the black plate

---

THINKING IT THROUGH — **Answering Cause-and-Effect Questions**

Keep the following steps in mind as you work through the question:

1. Don't just skim the passage; read it carefully. Most of the time, these tests evaluate reading comprehension, not speed in answering the questions.

2. Look for important words in the test question that are the same as, or similar to, words in the passage. The test question above contains the words *heat* and *trapped*. The end of the last sentence of the first paragraph (*. . . and this heat is contained by the clear covers*) also includes the word *heat*, along with a word

similar to *trapped*: the word *contained*.

3. Now try asking yourself the cause-and-effect questions about the sentence:

   ■ What happened? (What is the effect?) *Heat was trapped within the collector.*

   ■ Why? (What is the cause?) *The glass covers contained (trapped) the heat.*

4. Select the answer choice that most closely matches your answers to the cause-and-effect questions. The answer is **B**.

Looking Ahead to Writing

In the Writing Workshop for this chapter (pp. 134–150), students will be asked to write their own cause-and-effect explanations. Students, as they prepare their explanations, will realize that focusing on causes or effects will determine the organizational pattern of their papers. Have students refer again to the organizational maps on pp. 129–130 as they plan their papers.

Writing Workshop

OBJECTIVES

- To use the writing process to write and revise a cause-and-effect essay
- To focus on causes or effects
- To gather support for causes or effects
- To recognize false cause and effect
- To vary sentence beginnings
- To correct inexact pronoun reference

Quotation for the Day

"Finally, one just has to shut up, sit down, and write."

(Natalie Goldberg, American writer, poet, and teacher)

Remind students that as part of their prewriting, they may often feel over-whelmed by the task at hand. Tell them that it does not matter what they write as long as their pencil is moving and the ideas are flowing.

TEACHING TIP

Choose a Situation or Event
Cause-and-effect explanations (which tell why) are closely related to process explanations (which tell how). Both are narrative—they explain a sequence of events. As an alternative to the cause-and-effect essay, you could give your students the option of writing an explanation of a process.

Remind students to consider the audience's degree of knowledge and understanding of the process and to provide accurate and complete information. Students could also use layout and design elements to create visuals or use other forms of media that illustrate the process.

WHAT'S AHEAD?

In this workshop, you will write a cause-and-effect essay. You will also learn how to

- focus on causes or effects
- gather support for causes or effects
- recognize false cause and effect
- vary sentence beginnings
- correct inexact pronoun references

Writing a Cause-and-Effect Explanation

Imagine this situation: The editor of your school newspaper wants you to write an article about the passage of a new rule requiring every student at your school to complete twenty hours of community service each year. Your first job as a reporter will be to decide what questions you want the article to answer. Many questions will come up, but two important ones might spring to mind right away: *Why did this happen?* and *What results will it have?*

If you wrote an article that answered those two questions, you would be writing about causes and effects—the same kind of writing you will be undertaking in this Writing Workshop. By completing the steps in the workshop, you can create an interesting, well-supported essay that explains any specific cause-and-effect topic that you choose.

Prewriting

Choose a Situation or Event

A Wonder-full Topic A good topic for a cause-and-effect explanation is a situation or event that makes you wonder "Why?" or "What now?" To find such a situation or event, try a couple of these topic-generating ideas:

- **Keep a "wonder" journal** for a day. Make a note in it every time you find yourself asking "I wonder why . . . ?" or "What might happen if . . . ?" The things you wonder about during the day might make good topics for a cause-and-effect essay.

- **Read through a science magazine** for details on a scientific phenomenon with intriguing causes or effects. Look for interesting topics—the effects of tornadoes, for example, or the causes of black holes.

- **Browse the World Wide Web,** read a newspaper, or watch a TV news broadcast to find facts about an important current event. Look for an event with interesting causes—one with a fascinating "story behind the story"—or one with equally interesting effects.

When you have found a few situations or events that seem promising, list them and circle the one you really want to investigate.

Narrow Your Topic

Limit the Field   Stop and take a second look at your topic; does it seem like too much to cover in a short essay? For example, if you try to write a two-page essay on the causes and effects of the American Revolution, you are bound to run into problems—that topic is just too large and complex for such a short paper. However, if you narrow the topic to two causes of the Boston Tea Party, you will have a much more manageable topic on your hands.

> **TIP**   You may need to think about focusing on either the causes or the effects of your topic, not both.

If you are looking for a topic that is more closely related to your own life, you could narrow your options by writing about the unexpected effects of getting a driver's license. With this specific focus on effects, you could discuss the topic in detail within a short composition.

Consider Your Purpose and Audience

Who's Reading?   Your **purpose** in this essay is to inform your audience about causes and effects. However, do your readers know anything about the situation or event you are planning to write about? Do they care about your topic? **You need to line up your thinking with the needs of your audience.** Begin by analyzing your audience and its knowledge about your topic.

◁— **KEY CONCEPT**

SOMETIMES I LIE IN BED AT NIGHT, AND I ASK MYSELF, "WHY?"

THEN A VOICE COMES TO ME THAT SAYS, "WHY, WHAT?"

3-15

SCHULZ

PEANUTS reprinted by permission of United Feature Syndicate, Inc.

Narrow Your Topic
Students may need help focusing on topics that incorporate cause-and-effect relationships. Encourage them to consider content areas or subjects, such as history, current events, or science, that have obvious connections between causes and effects.

Consider Your Purpose and Audience
Students may have difficulty with the concept of audience. Help students consider audience by asking them to brainstorm television programs or films that might appeal to different kinds of audiences. (You may want to make suggestions, such as *Sesame Street, Monday Night Football, Titanic,* or *Star Wars.*) Then, ask students to identify the audiences that would enjoy the programs or films. Finally, have students work in groups to identify the qualities or levels of knowledge each audience might have. (For example, children like *Sesame Street.* As an audience, children like funny characters and have a limited knowledge of many subjects. Children may also be easily frightened or bored.) Take time to talk to students about the audience for their own writing.

Analyzing Audience

To analyze the audience for your cause-and-effect essay, answer the questions below.

▶ **What do my readers already know about this situation or event?** If you were writing about the effects of getting a driver's license and you had students in mind as readers, you might decide that they already knew about one effect: the sense of freedom that comes with being allowed to drive. That does not mean you can't write about this effect—it just should not be the only one you discuss.

▶ **What might my readers want to know more about?** Your readers may not have thought about the greater responsibilities and lower grades that can sometimes result from being allowed to drive; those are two effects your readers will probably want to know about.

▶ **How can I get my readers to share my interest in the situation or event I am writing about?** When you have an audience in mind, think of a question or other "hook" that will draw them in—and plan to start your essay with this attention-grabber. If your writing is interesting, your audience will want to read on. For example, you might begin an essay on teenagers' getting a driver's license with the question "What privilege does the average teenager most want to have?"

TIP Another aspect to consider as you make stylistic choices is the **occasion** for your writing. Your occasion is what prompts you to write on your particular topic.

Write Your Thesis

Bring It into Focus   The focus that you choose for your essay determines what your thesis, or **main idea,** will be. Here is an example thesis for an essay that focuses on the **causes** of crash dieting. To support this thesis, each of the paragraphs in the body would discuss a different *cause*.

Focus on Causes

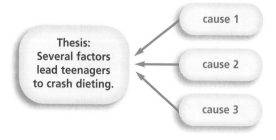

Thesis: Several factors lead teenagers to crash dieting.

cause 1

cause 2

cause 3

TEACHING TIP

Write Your Thesis
Remind students that their thesis statements may change as they gather support. For example, they may be interested in the causes of homelessness in their community, but after researching, they may find that focus too overwhelming and may choose to consider the effects instead.

Students might then change a thesis statement such as "Reductions in government spending on welfare, education, and other social services have resulted in large numbers of homeless families" to "Although all members of a homeless family feel stress, the youngest members are the best able to adjust."

The following example thesis clearly signals that the essay will focus on the **effects** of crash dieting. Each of the body paragraphs would present a different *effect*.

Focus on Effects

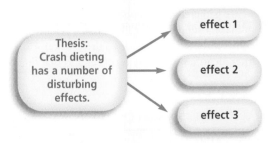

After you have thought about how you want to focus your essay, you will need to write a thesis that expresses the main idea you want to convey. Don't worry about making the thesis perfect right away; you can always refine it when you write, evaluate, and revise your first draft.

> **TIP** In **persuasive writing,** cause-and-effect relationships are often used to explain and support an opinion.

Gather Support

Support Yourself!   **To make your explanation of causes and effects convincing, you need to include your support—examples, facts, and statistics.** Otherwise, your readers might question your entire explanation. For example, an essay on the effects of crash dieting might include statistics on the percentage of dieters who become ill. As you look for sources from which to gather support, keep the following ideas in mind.

KEY CONCEPT

■ **Kinds of Sources**   Choose the right kinds of sources. For example, if your topic deals with the effects of a current world event, choose timely, up-to-date sources such as current newspapers or magazines—not sources that are months or years out of date.

■ **Specialized Sources**   Find specialized sources that relate specifically to your topic. For example, if you are preparing an essay about the effects of a particular battle during the Civil War, look for a book, magazine, or specialized encyclopedia devoted specifically to Civil War history.

Gather Support
The purpose of a cause-and-effect essay need not be expository. Explore with students how cause-and-effect relationships can support an opinion in a persuasive essay. For example, a school board wishes to convince students that closing campuses at lunch time is a good decision. Showing the effects of the decision (e.g., after-lunch classes start on time, attendance in these classes rises sharply) can be a strong source of support.

Critical Thinking
Evaluation. Students may find as they gather support that there are differences of opinion among their sources about the causes or effects of a significant historical or current event. Encourage students to present the differing opinions in their essays and to draw their own conclusions based on their overall research.

TEACHING TIP

Web Searches
The World Wide Web and the Internet are good places for students to start their research, but students should be aware of the reliability or authenticity of a Web site or Web page. Take time to remind students to use only reliable sources on the Web, such as sites produced and maintained by major news organizations, and to be aware that Web pages created by individuals can be biased or contain incorrect information. *You should also be aware that Internet resources are sometimes public forums, and their content can be unpredictable.*

TECHNOLOGY TIP

Remind students that the success of their Web research depends on their ability to refine their topics. They should limit their searches by using key word phrases and adding the words "AND" or "NOT" to their inquiries. Also, because they already know their topics, they may find Web directories more precise than search engines.

YOUR TURN 4

Help students to choose a situation or event for which they already have information or can readily find resources. For example, they could examine school-related topics such as the effects of waking up fifteen minutes earlier than they already do, or the effects of starting a paper the night before it is due. Also, assist students in narrowing their topics as necessary.

■ **Web Searches** If you look for information on your topic by using a World Wide Web search engine, you can narrow your list of search results by adding **cause-and-effect clue words** such as *causes, effects, reasons,* or *results* to your key word searches. For example, you could add the word *effects* to the search key words *Battle of Gettysburg*.

Once you have gathered your support, one of the best ways to keep track of it is to make a support chart like the one below. In the first column the writer lists three effects of getting a driver's license. In the second column the writer identifies specific types of support that she could use to back up each effect.

SUPPORT CHART	
Effects of getting a driver's license	**Support**
A driver's license brings greater independence.	**Example:** My brother doesn't have to count on my parents or his friends for rides to school or events anymore.
A driver's license brings more responsibility.	**Fact:** State law requires drivers to maintain car insurance, to register cars, and to renew licenses yearly.
A driver's license can cause grades to drop.	**Statistic:** According to a survey at my school, fifty percent of students have a drop in grades after getting a driver's license.

 Choosing a Topic and Organizing Ideas

Review each of the prewriting steps. Before you begin writing your essay, make sure to

■ choose a situation or event to write about, and narrow it down to a specific topic

■ think about what your audience will need to know

■ write a thesis that states your main idea

■ gather support for your cause-and-effect explanation

138   Chapter 4   **Exposition:** Exploring Causes and Effects

RESOURCES

Your Turn 4
Practice
■ *Communications,* WS. p. 70

Critical Thinking
Practice
■ *Communications,* WS. p. 71

False Cause and Effect

When you write about causes and effects, you need to avoid an error called **false cause and effect**—a mistake in logic that can make your cause-and-effect explanations less convincing. If your readers decide that some of your reasoning is faulty, they might be suspicious about the soundness of your entire essay.

Never ask your readers to assume that one event caused a second event just because the second event followed the first; you must show a real or logical connection between the two events. For instance, if you wash the family car and it rains the next day, you know that washing the car did not cause it to rain. The two events are not related.

False cause and effect often results from failing to consider more than one cause. For example, say that your school's football team plays a game in another town and loses. If you conclude that the team lost because they played away from home, you are ignoring several other possible causes: that the team had been playing too many games and was tired, that the other team played better, or that two of your school's key players were out with the flu. Look at these further examples of false cause and effect.

False Cause and Effect:
I ate a mango for breakfast.
The next day, I felt ill.
The mango made me sick.

In this example, only coincidence relates the two events. The writer just assumes that eating the mango caused the sickness. Compare the example to the logical reasoning in the example below.

Valid Cause and Effect:
I felt ill, so I went to see a doctor.
She said I had the symptoms of a virus.
A virus may have caused me to feel ill.

PRACTICE

On a piece of paper, write an *F* for each of the following passages that contains a false cause-and-effect relationship. Write *OK* for any relationship that is valid. Be prepared to explain your choices.

1. After my brother installed a radio in his car, the car developed several engine problems. Of course, the radio caused all the problems.

2. In her chemistry class, my sister failed to get two solutions to react at room temperature. After she heated them, though, they reacted. She decided that heat is needed for them to react.

3. One day I saw my friend Tori having a serious conversation with her brother Luis. When I met her later in the day, she was in a bad mood. Something Luis said must have upset her.

4. The final game of the World Series had to be delayed because of rain. My favorite team ended up losing the game. The team is good, so they must have lost because of the rain delay.

5. I came to school with a cold yesterday and talked to my friend Andre in class. The next day, he was absent. He must have caught my cold and stayed home from school.

MULTIPLE INTELLIGENCES
Musical Intelligence. Use this musical example to explain how false cause and effect can often involve assumptions. Bring in two musical instruments of a similar type, for example, brass or woodwind instruments. Standing where the class cannot see you, play a single note. Then, present yourself holding the instrument that did *not* make the sound and ask, "Did you hear the sound I just made on this instrument?" Students will probably say they did. Show students the other instrument. Discuss how the assumption that there was just one instrument led students to the false conclusion that it was the one you had played. Demonstrate the note on the correct instrument.

MINI-LESSON CRITICAL THINKING

False Cause and Effect

A N S W E R S

1. F

2. OK

3. F

4. F

5. F

Quotation for the Day

"The spine of every nonfiction work is the vertebrae of facts which the writer must place together in sensible order to get the story to move."

(Rita Mae Brown, 1944 –   , American novelist)

Explain to students how the ordering of their causes and effects is the backbone of their essay.

Meeting INDIVIDUAL NEEDS

LEARNERS HAVING DIFFICULTY
Students having difficulty preparing a first draft may benefit from adapting the framework on this page to an outline form. Have students prepare their first drafts by writing the outline in sections, based on the framework and its suggestions. After completing all three sections, students would have a brief but complete first draft.

YOUR TURN 5

For assessment, make sure students are following the steps in the framework. If they are having difficulty, refer them to the margin notes next to **A Writer's Model** on p. 141.

Cause-and-Effect Explanation

Framework	Directions and Explanations
Introduction ■ Get your readers interested right away. ■ Give background information. ■ Include a clear thesis.	**Grab Your Readers' Attention** To draw in your readers, begin with an attention-getting statement or question that will make them want to read on. **Provide Needed Background Information** If your essay focuses on effects, you may need to give brief background details on causes. If your essay focuses on causes, you need to give background details on effects. **State Your Thesis** To prepare your readers for the explanations that will follow, clearly state the focus of your essay.

Body ■ Discuss first cause or effect and give support. ■ Discuss second cause or effect and give support. ■ Discuss further causes or effects and give support.	**Present Your Ideas** You can organize your causes, effects, and support in two ways: ■ chronologically (time order) ■ by order of importance As you write, you may discover that you have a cause-and-effect chain—a series of effects that become causes for other effects. Here is an example of a cause-and-effect chain taken from the Writer's Model on the next page: car expenses ➤ more hours of work ➤ less study time ➤ drop in grades

Conclusion ■ Remind your readers about your thesis.	**Wrap It Up** Restate the thesis—your main idea. If you think that your restatement may not be interesting enough, leave your readers with something further to think about by closing with an opinion statement or with a question.

YOUR TURN 5   Writing a First Draft

Using the framework above, write the first draft of your essay. The Writer's Model on the next page follows this framework.

RESOURCES

Writing
Writing Prompts
■ *Communications,* TP. 34, WS. p. 72

Your Turn 5
Practice
■ *Communications,* TP. 35, WS. p. 73

A Writer's Model

The following short essay, which is a final draft, closely follows the framework on the previous page. Notice the highlighted cause-and-effect clue words the writer uses as linking devices.

Getting a Driver's License: The Effects

What one privilege does the average teenager most want? Many would probably say "the right to drive." To a teenager, a driver's license seems like a ticket to freedom: Teen drivers can go where they want when they want—up to a point. However, teenagers who put themselves in the driver's seat often end up facing effects and responsibilities that they may not have anticipated.

For a teenager, a driver's license is a big step toward independence. Teen drivers do not have to count on parents, friends, bus schedules, or good weather. They are not always asking favors, making last-minute arrangements, or following other people's schedules. They can accept jobs on the other side of town, and they will not miss parties because they are stranded at home without a ride.

However, a teen who no longer needs a chauffeur may unexpectedly become one. Many teen drivers find that they are now the ones asked to drive a sister to school or to go to the store for milk. Another effect is that carless friends—including some who never help with expenses—ask for rides.

Owning a car also costs money—in ways a passenger cannot appreciate. Gasoline is not free, insurance for teenagers is expensive, and maintenance (not to mention repairs) drains finances. To meet car expenses, teenagers often have to work more hours and thus have less free time. Unfortunately, some teenagers respond to that situation by studying less, which causes their grades to drop, which in turn may cause their parents to take away their car keys for several weeks.

The ultimate effect of getting a driver's license, then, is that it may help teenagers to grow up. Teen drivers find that they have to balance freedom with responsibility and learn how to afford their dream of driving without losing other things. Car keys can be the keys to a lot of fun and independence, but teenagers need to realize that a driver's license, like most things in life, comes at a price.

INTRODUCTION:
Attention-grabbing question

Thesis (focuses on effects)

BODY: Effect 1

Support for effect 1

Effect 2
Support for effect 2

Effect 3
Support for effect 3

CONCLUSION:
Restatement of thesis

Connecting Reading and Writing

It will help students in their own writing if they read **A Writer's Model** with an awareness of text structure. Before students read the model, refer them to the Reading Workshop (pp. 129–130) to review the common organizational patterns for a cause-and-effect essay. Students should notice that the model on this page emphasizes effects, and that each effect mentioned is immediately followed by support.

Connecting Reading and Writing

Point out to students that **A Student's Model** differs from the cause-and-effect essay on the previous page. Students may notice the following:

- the essay uses the first-person "I"

- the attention-grabbing device is an anecdote that is longer than one paragraph

- the essay includes dialogue

- the thesis statement does not appear until the end of the second paragraph

Students should also see similarities between **A Writer's Model** on p. 141 and **A Student's Model,** including the focus on effects and the way support statements immediately follow each statement of effect.

A Student's Model

The following passages are from a cause-and-effect essay by Cheryl Flugan of Belson High School in Winston, Florida. Cause-and-effect clue words are highlighted.

What Are the Effects of Running?

Attention-grabber

I hovered in the doorway, waiting. Mari was crazy, I was sure. It was the end of our eighth-grade year, and Mari had decided to join the cross-country team. She asked me to do the same, but I said no. Me run three miles? Absurd. Now she was sealing her fate by speaking to the cross-country coach. Impatient to leave, I peered into the classroom. A piercing gaze captured my own.

"You running?" he inquired in a booming voice, his tone making the question seem more akin to a command. He pressed me for my answer while Mari looked on, amused. I squeaked out an "Um, yeah," being too afraid to answer no. The man looked satisfied. Mari looked shocked. I was certain I had signed myself up for five months of torture. Only recently have I realized that that day was a turning point for me, marking not only the birth of my athletic career, but also a major landmark in my growth as a person. I have benefited from the positive effects of running.

Thesis (focus on effects)

Effect 1
Support for effect 1

Effect 2
Support for effect 2

Effect 3

Support for effect 3

I was shy and unassertive coming out of the eighth grade, but running improved my self-confidence. Being part of a team forced me to meet new people. Through cross country I have formed many precious friendships. Running has also given me the confidence to be a leader and mentor for younger runners. Never before had I considered myself a role model, but now I am finding myself in that position. More than anything else, however, I think my improvement in self-confidence has resulted from learning to have the courage to succeed. Often I see girls who are reluctant to display their talents for fear of intimidating, and possibly losing, friends. A runner cannot think like that. I have learned not to apologize for being successful in running or in any other aspect of life.

Revising

Evaluate and Revise Your Draft

Fine-Tuning or Overhauling? To refine your writing, you need to read through your whole paper carefully at least twice. The first time, you should evaluate and revise for content and organization, using the guidelines below. When you read through your paper a second time, you can use the guidelines on page 145 to evaluate and revise for sentence style.

➤ **First Reading: Content and Organization** Work collaboratively with another student in your class to revise the content and organization of your essay. You can use the following chart to guide your revisions. Respond to the questions in the first column. If you need help answering the questions, use the tips in the middle column and make the changes suggested in the last column.

Cause-and-Effect Explanation: Content and Organization Guidelines for Peer and Self-Evaluation

Evaluation Questions	▶ Tips	▶ Revision Techniques
❶ Will the introduction quickly interest readers in the event or situation?	▶ **Circle** the sentences in the introduction that you think will interest your readers. If you don't see any circles, revise.	▶ **Add** information and details about the event or situation. **Delete or replace** repetitive words or phrases.
❷ Can the readers identify a thesis that shows the focus of the essay—either causes or effects?	▶ **Underline** the thesis statement twice. If you don't see a thesis statement, revise.	▶ **Add** a thesis statement near the beginning of the paper. Be sure it focuses on either causes or effects.
❸ Is the explanation of causes or effects supported with evidence? (Beware of false cause and effect.)	▶ **Circle** each sentence that offers support. Revise if you don't see at least one circled sentence per cause or effect.	▶ **Add** examples, facts, and statistics to support each cause and effect you have identified. **Elaborate** on existing support.
❹ Is the information for each cause or effect organized in a clear, easy-to-follow way?	▶ For chronological order, **number** causes and effects in sequence to see jumps. For order of importance, **underline** your most important cause or effect to be sure it is presented last.	▶ **Rearrange** a chronological presentation to show the correct order. For order of importance, **rearrange** causes or effects to put the least important first and the most important at the end.
❺ Does the conclusion include a sentence that restates the focus of the explanation?	▶ **Circle** the sentence in the conclusion that restates the focus of your essay. Revise if the main idea is not restated.	▶ **Add** a sentence that restates the focus of your explanation—either causes or effects.

Writing Workshop **143**

Quotation for the Day

❝Nothing has more lives than an error you refuse to correct.❞

(O. A. Battista, 1917–   , American business executive and chemist)

Critical Thinking

Metacognition. After students revise for content and organization, ask them to jot down a sentence or two explaining how the evaluation questions, tips, and revision techniques affected their papers.

TEACHING TIP

▶ **Elaboration**

So that students can discover areas in their work in need of elaboration, have them read their papers and ask questions such as the following: "Why is this so?" "How do I know this?" "What do I mean by this?" and "Can I give an example or anecdote that shows this?" Asking these questions will help students see areas that need further explanation, support, or development.

Students can elaborate on details in their paragraphs by trying this technique: If a paragraph contains a statistic for support, have students add one detail or comment about the source. If the paragraph still seems underdeveloped, students can always add another detail and gradually build up their paragraph.

RESOURCES

Revising

Practice
- *Communications*, TPs. 36, 37, WS. pp. 74, 75, 76

Extension
- *Designing Your Writing*

Cooperative Learning

Peer Revision. Consider pairing competent writers with writers who are having difficulty or placing students in peer-revision groups to review each other's papers and make suggestions.

Before students begin the peer-revision process, remind them to give only constructive criticism and to respond graciously to peer review of their own work. Tell students that one way to respond productively is to ask questions, such as "Would the meaning be clearer if I reworded this sentence?"

Analyzing the Revision Process

ANSWERS

1. The writer added an additional example. It improves the sentence by adding information and support for the thesis.

2. The writer edited the last sentence because it was an incomplete sentence. She moved it up to put the ideas in logical order: teenagers study less; their grades drop; their keys are taken.

YOUR TURN 6

Make sure that students follow the content and organization guidelines on the previous page.

Evaluating Student Writing

The ancillary *Assessment Alternatives* contains a variety of assessment forms, including Inventories and Evaluation Forms and rubrics: Six-Point Scales, Four-Point Scales, and Six Trait Scales.

ONE WRITER'S REVISIONS   Here's how one writer used the content-and-organization guidelines to revise some sentences from the cause-and-effect essay on page 141. Study the revisions and answer the questions following the paragraph.

> add
>
>   Owning a car also costs money—in ways a passenger can-
> not appreciate. Gasoline is not free, *insurance for teenagers is expensive,* and maintenance (not to
> mention repairs) drains finances. To meet car expenses,
> teenagers often have to work more hours and thus have less free
> time. Unfortunately, some teenagers respond to that situation by
>
> rearrange
>
> add
>
> studying less, which *in turn* may cause their parents to take away their
> car keys for several weeks. *which causes   to* If their grades drop.

PEER REVIEW

Ask a classmate to read your paper and to answer the following questions. Use this feedback to prompt your revisions.

1. What did you like about the writer's paper?
2. Was the explanation of causes or effects clear? Why or why not?

Analyzing the Revision Process

1. What kind of information did the writer add to the second sentence? How does this information improve the sentence?

2. Why did the writer edit and move the last sentence?

YOUR TURN 6   Focusing on Content and Organization

Revise the content and organization of your essay using the guidelines on the previous page; use the example revisions shown above as a model.

➤ **Second Reading: Style**   In this reading, you need to look at the manner in which you have expressed your ideas—your sentence style. As you wrote your cause-and-effect explanation, you might have been tempted to begin each sentence the same way—with the cause or effect you are focusing on. However, this monotonous way of beginning sentences might cause your audience to stop reading altogether. So you won't fall into this rut, use the following sentence-style guidelines to help you **vary sentence beginnings.**

Evaluation Question	▶ Tip	▶ Revision Technique
Do many of the sentences begin the same way? Are some structures overused?	**Put parentheses** around the first five words of each sentence. Do most subjects and verbs fall within the parentheses? If most do, revise.	**Reword** or **reorder** parts of some sentences for more variety. **Combine** sentences. **Add** transitions.

Varied Beginnings

Have you ever read something that sounded monotonous? Sometimes writing seems boring because the writer begins each sentence the same way: a subject followed by a verb. Bored readers will be tempted not to finish reading your essay; varying your sentence beginnings is one way to keep your writing interesting and your readers interested.

Focus on Sentences

ONE WRITER'S REVISIONS Here is how the writer of the model cause-and-effect essay on page 141 used the guidelines above to revise some of her sentence beginnings.

BEFORE REVISION

(There is an unexpected part) of not needing a chauffeur. (It is that you can) become one. (Many teen drivers find that) they are the ones asked to drive a sister to school. (They're asked to go to) the store for milk. (They have carless friends who) ask for rides. (Some friends never help with) expenses.

In every sentence, the subject and verb fall within the parentheses.

AFTER REVISION

However, a teen who no longer needs a chauffeur may unexpectedly become one. Many teen drivers find that they are now the ones asked to drive a sister to school or to go to the store for milk. Another effect is that carless friends—including some who never help with expenses—ask for rides.

reword and combine

combine
reword and combine

Writing Workshop **145**

RESOURCES

Focus on Sentences
Practice
■ *Communications*, WS. p. 77

TEACHING TIP

Varied Beginnings
Students may have trouble varying their sentence beginnings even after consulting pages 342–343. Make available to students examples of writing that use varied sentence beginnings, such as clippings from newspaper and magazine articles. If you have time, conduct a mini-lesson in which you ask students to skim the articles for varied sentence beginnings. Write on the chalkboard the examples they find.

Analyzing the Revision Process

ANSWERS

1. The writer combined the first two sentences to add variety to the sentence beginnings in the paragraph.

2. The writer's revision of the last two sentences makes the cause-and-effect chain seem clearer.

YOUR TURN 7

Have students work in pairs to revise each other's papers. Make sure that they have followed the tip provided in the guidelines on p. 145, marking their papers appropriately.

Timesaver

If you are grading or checking the revision process at each step, ask peer reviewers to highlight the places in the essay they believe need work. Their highlighting will allow you to find trouble spots quickly. Also, your quick check of the highlighted version will assure you that the peer editor has pinpointed the areas that you think need the most work.

Analyzing the Revision Process

1. Why did the writer combine the first two sentences into one sentence?

2. How did the writer's revision of the last two sentences improve the paragraph?

YOUR TURN 7 **Focusing on Sentence Beginnings**

Revise the style of your essay using the guidelines on the previous page. Use the example revisions shown on page 145 as a model.

Designing Your Writing

Cause-and-Effect Graphics   You might want to strengthen your paper by including graphics to focus your explanations. In the example below, a writer has reinforced his explanation of the effects of pollution on the earth's ecosystems through the use of a chart. If you have graphics software at home or at school, use the software to create or edit diagrams, charts, photographs, or images that will support the cause-and-effect explanations in your essay. If not, create your own graphic as a way to summarize and clarify your work.

Remember that a graphic must be made a part of the text, not an ornament to it. Readers must be explicitly told what the graphic accomplishes, what they are to see in it, and why it is there.

Example:
Too much pollution has affected ecosystems all over the world. As the following chart shows, in some European countries, water wells have been polluted, soil has been contaminated, and many forests are either damaged or dying. In the Czech Republic and Slovakia, many rivers no longer support fish or other aquatic life.

Country	Effects of Pollution
Poland	80% of water wells polluted 1/4 of soil contaminated
Bulgaria	1/3 of forest damaged or dying
Czech Republic and Slovakia	1/4 of rivers polluted

RESOURCES

Grammar Link
Practice
■ *Communications*, WS. p. 78

Publishing

Proofread Your Essay

Make No Mistake About It Before you prepare a final copy of your essay, make sure that it follows the **conventions of written language** and that it is free of grammar, spelling, and punctuation errors. You need to be especially careful to correct any inexact pronoun references your essay may contain; a perfectly good explanation of causes and effects can be weakened by one inexact pronoun.

Reference Note

For more information and practice on **clear pronoun reference**, see page 565.

Grammar Link

Inexact Pronoun Reference

The job of a **pronoun** is to stand in for a noun or phrase called the antecedent. *Antecedent* means "that which comes before." In other words, the pronoun refers to the noun or phrase that comes before it. What if two nouns or phrases come before a pronoun? Then your reader may be unsure which noun or phrase is the pronoun's antecedent. This problem is called **inexact pronoun reference.** Your pronoun references should be exact—each pronoun should clearly refer to one noun or phrase. Compare the *Inexact* and *Exact* sentences below to see one way an inexact reference can be fixed—by revising a sentence to completely eliminate the problem pronoun.

Inexact My mother called my sister before she left for work. [Who left for work, the mother or the sister?]

Exact Before leaving for work, my mother called my sister.

Other sentences can be fixed by keeping the problem pronoun, but revising so that it clearly refers to only one antecedent.

Inexact Angel arrived before Cory, so he got a better seat. [Who got a better seat, Angel or Cory?]

Exact Because he arrived before Cory, Angel got a better seat.

PRACTICE

Revise each of the following sentences to correct any inexact pronoun references.

1. School clubs can give students valuable experiences if they are well organized.

2. After seeing my brother's latest painting and my friend's newest sketch at the art club's show, the judges gave him the grand prize.

3. When the drama club members performed a play for the new students, they were nervous and excited.

4. Joe asked his friend to join our writing club, so we asked to see his portfolio.

5. Clubs can make students more enthusiastic about school; they feel a part of the school community.

Quotation for the Day

❝When you have duly arrayed your 'facts' in logical order, lo, it is like an oil-lamp that you have made, filled and trimmed, but which sheds no light unless first you light it.❞

(Antoine de Saint-Exupéry, 1900–1944, French novelist, essayist, and aviator)

Suggest to students that their published essays are like the lit oil-lamp: they shed light when they are read by others.

Meeting INDIVIDUAL NEEDS

ENGLISH–LANGUAGE LEARNERS
General Strategies. Explain to students that inexact pronoun references occur all the time in spoken language. Usually, the listener can tell from the speaker's gestures or expression what the speaker means. If not, the listener can ask for clarification. Since a reader cannot question the writer, it is important for the writer to be clear when using pronoun references.

Grammar Link

Inexact Pronoun Reference

ANSWERS
Student responses will vary.

1. Well-organized school clubs can give students valuable experiences.

2. After seeing my brother's latest painting and my friend's newest sketch at the art club's show, the judges gave my brother the grand prize.

3. When the drama club members performed a play for the new students, club members were nervous and excited.

4. Joe asked his friend to join our writing club, so we asked to see the friend's portfolio.

5. Clubs can make students more enthusiastic about school; students feel a part of the school community.

Wrap It Up

Metacognition. After students hand in their final drafts, ask them to write a couple of sentences about what they learned from writing their cause-and-effect papers.

Then, ask students to answer the following questions:

1. What are three types of support you can use to make a cause-and-effect explanation more convincing? [examples, statistics, and other kinds of facts]

2. Why is it important to avoid false cause-and-effect statements? [Readers may become suspicious about the soundness of your whole essay if some of your reasoning is faulty.]

PORTFOLIO

YOUR TURN 8

As students answer the reflecting questions, ask them to think about how the process they went through to write a cause-and-effect essay might help them on other types of essays in the future.

Publish Your Essay

Taking a Bow   Here are some ways you might share your cause-and-effect explanation with your audience.

- If your topic is about the causes or effects of a current event, try submitting your essay to your school newspaper, which might publish the essay as a feature article.

- Find an Internet newsgroup related to your topic; then, post your essay to the group and ask for responses.

- If your topic deals with a scientific phenomenon and its causes or effects, share your essay with your science teacher and ask him or her to comment on it.

- If your topic is of interest to your peers, make a poster with a graphic showing the cause-and-effect relationships you discussed in your essay. Ask permission to display the poster at your school.

Reflect on Your Essay

Looking in the Mirror   Writing short responses to the following questions will help you to reflect and to build on what you have learned from this workshop.

- How did you select the particular cause-and-effect topic about which you chose to write?

- How did you order the causes and effects in the body of your essay? What made you choose that order instead of the other types you might have used?

- Why did your revisions make your explanations more convincing?

    Use your responses to these questions to **set goals for future writing.** If you decide to include this essay in your portfolio, attach your responses to the essay.

YOUR TURN 8   Proofreading, Publishing, and Reflecting

Review each of the steps discussed on this and the previous page. Before you turn in your essay, make sure to

- proofread it carefully
- consider publishing options
- reflect on your essay by answering specific questions about the steps you went through to create it

Connections to
Literature

Causes and Effects in Fiction

As you have seen, you can write an essay on cause-and-effect relationships in the real world—why something happened, what effects an event had. However, you will also find cause-and-effect relationships in the fiction you read, especially in works that show characters involved in conflicts—for example, short stories, novels, and dramas.

Which Literary Work? A cause-and-effect essay about a literary character should answer questions such as *What causes this character to change?* or *What effects do this character's actions have on the lives of other characters?* You could analyze the causes and effects of the actions of Doodle's brother in "The Scarlet Ibis" by James Hurst or those of Pip or Magwitch from Charles Dickens's *Great Expectations*. Romeo or Tybalt from *The Tragedy of Romeo and Juliet* by William Shakespeare would also make a good subject for a literary cause-and-effect essay.

Causes and Effects with Characters

To help you find a focus for your cause-and-effect essay, use the following questions as a trigger for brainstorming:

■ What is the central conflict?

■ What events cause each of the major characters to change?

■ What actions on the part of the characters affect the lives of other characters? How?

Get It Together! Remember that all the support for your essay will come from the details in the literary work you select. The graphic organizers on the next page show how students gathered support for essays that focus on the effects of Romeo's rash actions in *The Tragedy of Romeo and Juliet* and on the effects of Pip's actions in *Great Expectations*. Your teacher may also want you to quote lines from the literary work you are writing about.

Share and Share Alike After you have written your essay, follow the Revising and Publishing steps given in the Writing Workshop. You may want to save your work in your portfolio.

TEACHING (TIP)

Causes and Effects in Fiction
To help students organize the support for their essays, have them use their knowledge of cause-and-effect structures to make graphic representations of the chains of events in their literature selections. Examples of graphic organizers they may use appear on pp. 136–137.

Meeting
INDIVIDUAL
NEEDS

LEARNERS HAVING DIFFICULTY
It may help students if you select a literary work that the class has read and work with the class as a whole to brainstorm possible essay topics. Students can then work individually or in groups to come up with details from the literary selection to support their essays. As they work to gather supporting details, have them use the notes on p. 150 as models.

Causes and Effects in <u>The Tragedy of Romeo and Juliet</u>

Thesis: Romeo's rash actions have a tragic effect on three other characters in the play.

Character One: Mercutio
Mercutio does not know about Romeo's secret marriage to Juliet, so he fights Tybalt for Romeo's honor. This fight eventually leads to Mercutio's death.

Character Two: Tybalt
Romeo feels responsible for Mercutio's death and, without thinking of the consequences of his actions, kills Tybalt to avenge Mercutio.

Character Three: Juliet
Romeo, thinking that his beloved Juliet is dead, reacts by buying poison and then returning to Verona to see her in the tomb. When he sees her, he drinks the poison, killing himself. She then awakens to find Romeo dead and kills herself.

Causes and Effects in <u>Great Expectations</u>

Thesis: The effects of Pip's growth into adulthood are reflected in his treatment of Joe Gargery.

Beginning of the Novel
Pip appreciates Joe's good nature, tenderness, and simplicity.

Middle of the Novel
After being in Miss Havisham's employ, Pip begins to see deficiencies in Joe. To Pip, Joe is ignorant, awkward, and common.

End of the Novel
At the end of the novel, Pip is reborn. Pip's ingratitude and false pride are gone. He is repentant and asks Joe's forgiveness for deserting him.

You may want to look at students' thesis statements before they begin writing. That way you can be sure that students are focusing on either causes or effects, and not both. For assessment, check that students include supporting details from the literary work and that they follow the revision guidelines in the Writing Workshop.

YOUR TURN 9 **Writing a Literary Cause-and-Effect Essay**

Choose a literary work that interests you and write a cause-and-effect essay based on one of its characters. Remember that your thesis should focus on either causes or effects, not both.

Giving an Informative Speech

Talk   Liste

OBJECTIVES

- To plan and create an informative speech
- To deliver an informative speech and use feedback
- To evaluate an informative speech

Your school is considering extending the passing period between classes. You have been chosen to present information to the faculty committee about the effects of extending the period. Are you up to the job? Giving **informative speeches** is a skill that you will need throughout your life. In this section you will learn how to plan and present an informative speech.

WHAT'S AHEAD?

In this section, you will learn to

- **plan and create an informative speech**
- **deliver your speech and use feedback**
- **evaluate an informative speech**

Quotation for the Day

❝The ability to speak may have come much as did walking and breathing, but speaking well to groups is another matter.❞

(Thomas Leech, executive speech coach and presentations consultant)

Use this quotation to initiate a discussion about why public speaking is usually regarded as more difficult than casual conversation. For example, students may say that the speaker is in the spotlight during a presentation, while conversation allows a more informal interaction with others. Tell students that this workshop will provide instruction to help them make effective informative presentations.

Carefully Prepare the Speech

In an informative speech, your **purpose** is to give your **audience** facts and information. You will need to tailor the language and content of your speech so your audience will understand the facts and information you present. For example, for a general audience, you should use standard language and avoid using technical language. Your **task** and **occasion,** the context and reason behind the speech, are often assigned to you or are decided by circumstances. These two elements also drive your choice of details and the delivery of your speech.

When you have considered your purpose, audience, task, and occasion, you are ready to gather information. Use relevant information from books, periodicals, the Internet, CD-ROMs, and radio or television programs, as well as information you gather through interviews and surveys.

Turn your research results into a speech by organizing the information. Here are four ways to organize an informative speech.

TIP To make organizing easier, you may want to use note cards or an outline created on a word-processing program.

- **Topical order** breaks a topic down into its parts and arranges the parts in an order determined by the speaker.
- **Chronological order** arranges details or events according to the order in which they occurred in time.
- **Order of importance** arranges details from most important to least important or from least important to most important.

RESOURCES

Focus on Speaking and Listening Practice
- *Media Literacy and Communication Skills*
  —*Support and Practice,* Ch. 4
  —*A How-to Handbook*

Teaching Notes
- *Media Literacy and Communication Skills*
  —*A Teacher's Guide,* Ch. 4

Cooperative Learning

Rehearsal Pairs. Pair students with a partner, and have one student practice delivering his or her speech while the other listens and evaluates. Students can answer the evaluation questions on this page as they listen. Remind students that when they listen they should focus their attention on the speaker's message, ask relevant questions for clarification, and provide nonverbal feedback, such as maintaining eye contact with the speaker.

Wrap It Up

Metacognition. Ask students to reflect on their speaking processes by answering the following question:

1. What do you think was most effective about your speech?

Then, ask students to answer the following question:

2. What are four ways to organize an informative speech? [topical order, chronological order, order of importance, and cause-and-effect order]

YOUR TURN 10

For assessment, you may want to use the evaluation questions listed above. You may also wish to have students turn in their peer evaluations so you can check students' understanding of speaking processes.

TIP As you rehearse your speech, practice effectively using the **conventions of oral language,** such as word choice, grammar, and diction. For example, choose words that most clearly and accurately convey information to your audience.

TIP Write down words the speaker uses that you do not understand. Look up the words later so you can interpret the speaker's message accurately.

- **Cause-and-effect order** arranges information to show causes or conditions and the effects or results of those causes or conditions.

Rehearse the Speech

The more thoroughly you rehearse your speech, the less nervous you will be. Try some of the following ideas to practice your delivery.

- Record yourself as you deliver the speech. Then, play the tape back and make notes about what you might want to change.
- Deliver your speech to friends or family, and ask for feedback.
- Deliver your speech in front of a mirror to judge the effects of your facial expressions and body language.

Deliver the Speech and Solicit Feedback

Now it is time to deliver your speech. Remember to be enthusiastic, make eye contact with members of your audience, and speak clearly and audibly. After your speech, conduct a question-and-answer session to make sure your audience has understood your topic. To help you set **future goals as a speaker,** you might ask the audience to complete evaluation forms. See the evaluation questions below. These criteria can be adapted and used for evaluating informative presentations by speakers in your community or informative speeches on television or radio.

Evaluate Informative Speeches

Use the following questions to make oral or written evaluations of informative speeches.

- Was the speaker's message clear? Was the speaker well-informed? (If possible, ask questions to clarify your understanding.)
- Was the information in the speech organized effectively?
- Did the speaker use effective verbal and nonverbal strategies such as pitch and tone of voice, posture, and eye contact?

YOUR TURN 10   Presenting an Informative Speech

Use the steps described in this section to create, rehearse, deliver, and solicit feedback on an informative speech. Use the questions above to evaluate your classmates' speeches.

RESOURCES

Your Turn 10
Practice and Reinforcement

- *Media Literacy and Communication Skills* —*Support and Practice,* Ch. 4, transparencies and worksheets

Analyzing Stereotypes

Do the images and words we see and hear on TV cause us to change the way we think; or does the media just *reflect* current trends in society? The answer to each of these questions is yes. Our view of the world is shaped by the media, and, in turn, the media mirrors the world around us. In this workshop, you will examine how television portrays people over the age of sixty-five, investigate whether this portrayal is accurate, and present your findings.

TV Representations of Real Life

Each day TV brings you comedies about big-city life and dramas set in courtrooms and emergency rooms. Although these **representations** of real-life situations seem realistic, they are not always accurate portrayals of real life. For one thing, television's reality is often more structured and predictable than real life. Think about your favorite half-hour situation comedy. Every week, a conflict is introduced and resolved during a thirty-minute episode. Real life doesn't have that kind of regularity.

Television also creates and reinforces **stereotypes**—oversimplified ideas about groups of people. Stereotyped characters do not represent the complexity that real people have. Although stereotypical characters are more quickly understood than complex ones, they can be harmful. Unconsciously, we may begin to assume that real people are as simple as the ones on television and judge them based on their physical characteristics, occupation, race, or membership in a group, rather than on their individuality.

Analyze Media Representations

Think about how older people are represented on television dramas or sitcoms. Could TV's representations of older people affect how you view real people over the age of sixty-five and how you relate to them? Write down a description of one or two older characters you have seen on TV. To get started, look on the next page at the chart that one student created.

WHAT'S AHEAD?

In this section, you will learn how to
■ analyze television representations
■ compare television representations to real-world experience

TIP The predictability of stereotypes makes them appealing to writers, who expect the viewer to recognize easily stereotypes such as the dumb jock, the ditzy blond, and the computer nerd.

OBJECTIVES

■ To analyze television representations

■ To compare television representations to real-world experience

Quotation for the Day

"Television is not merely one of a number of important influences upon today's child. Through the changes it has made in family life, television emerges as *the* important influence in children's lives today."

(Marie Winn, 1937– , Czech-born American writer)

Write this quotation on the chalkboard, and ask students whether they agree or disagree with the quotation and the reasons for their opinions. Then, tell students that because television does have some impact on their lives, it is important for them to examine closely media representations of real-world experience.

TEACHING TIP

Analyze Media Representations
Some students may not have access to television at home or may not be familiar with a particular television character. Direct those students to write a description of an older character from a movie they have seen or from a novel or short story they have read.

RESOURCES

Focus on Viewing and Representing Practice
■ *Media Literacy and Communication Skills*
  —*Support and Practice*, Ch. 4
  —*A How-to Handbook*

Teaching Notes
■ *Media Literacy and Communication Skills*
  —*A Teacher's Guide*, Ch. 4

Critical Thinking

Analysis. You might also have students analyze how culture is revealed through various media. Place students in groups and ask them to view television programs and to look through magazines and newspapers to find representations of cultures of the Americas, including Canada, Mexico, and Central and South America. Students can look at aspects such as dress, music, traditions, and social customs. Ask students to note any stereotypes that they find.

Metacognition. Have students answer the following question as they conclude the section.

1. What did you learn about television representations that you did not know before?

Then, ask students the following question:

2. What are stereotypes? [Stereotypes are oversimplified ideas about people. They are usually based on physical characteristics, race, or membership in a group rather than on a person's individuality.]

YOUR TURN 11

After students have discussed their findings, ask them to think about the practical applications of what they have learned. You might ask them to consider whether their findings will affect how they view television representations in the future or if what they found will change their perceptions of older people.

*Name	Theodora Wilson
Television program name	"Hearts of Lafayette"
*Age and occupation	around sixty-five, retired
*Marital status	widow
Interactions with other characters	mostly calm, some arguments when children are unreasonable
*Role in family	gives advice and connection to history of family and community
*Where does he or she live?	her own house across the street from one of her daughters
Physical or mental disabilities/ troubles	seems fairly healthy, sometimes complains about "achy bones"
	sometimes she gets short-winded and dizzy (she says it's just part of "getting old")
*Clothing	casual, often she is out gardening in her jeans and T-shirt
*Hobbies	gardening, quilting, part of a seniors' bird-watching group

Investigate and Draw Conclusions

After examining how television portrays older people, find out for yourself what some older people are like. Using the starred questions from the chart above as a starting point, ask seniors about their attitudes, activities, and wants and needs in life. Try to interview at least four people over age sixty-five. You might talk to relatives, neighbors, and friends' relatives. Then, examine your findings and think about the ways television affects your perceptions of reality. Do you think your findings reinforce or challenge the representations of older people presented on television? Present your findings to the class.

TIP Include visual images as you report your findings. You might present a collage of photos, a collection of videoclips, or a chart illustrating statistics about older people.

YOUR TURN 11 Analyzing Television

Follow the directions above to analyze and compare TV's portrayal of people over the age of sixty-five with your own experiences. After all reports have been given, use the following questions to discuss in small groups how television stereotypes might affect your perceptions of older people.

- What generalizations do you make about older people? Are any of these generalizations similar to the stereotypes you see on TV?

- If your findings challenged the representations of older people presented on television, were you surprised by these findings? If so, why?

154   **Chapter 4**   **Exposition:** Exploring Causes and Effects

RESOURCES

Your Turn 11
Practice and Reinforcement
- *Media Literacy and Communication Skills*
  —*Support and Practice*, Ch. 4, transparencies and worksheets
  —Videocassette 1, Segment D

CHAPTER

4 *Choices*

Choose one of the following activities to complete.

▶ CROSSING THE CURRICULUM: SCIENCE

1. A Case from the "Y" Files
Science careers often involve investigations of causes and effects. For example, if you were a working scientist, you might investigate the effects of acid rain or the possible causes of the extinction of the dinosaurs. To practice your investigative skills now, use library and community resources to research the causes and/or effects of a scientific phenomenon. Then, create a **multi-media presentation** explaining the phenomenon and summarizing its causes, its effects, or both.

▶ CAREERS

2. Hypersolutions Some Web designers create pages that use hypertext to explain complex issues. You, too, can exploit the potential of hypertext to "reveal" hidden causes and effects. Choose a social issue like teen smoking or dieting that has many causes and effects. Create a **Web page,** and use hyperlinks to connect causes and effects and text or images that explain or illustrate them.

▶ SPEAKING AND LISTENING

3. The Way It Was Apply your listening skills to a radio or TV program explaining a historical event. Make notes on the discussion of why something happened or what resulted from it; then, create a **visual summary** of the main points of the program to share with the class. Your summary might look something like the following.

▶ VIEWING AND REPRESENTING

4. Rebel with a Cause
Choose a movie or television miniseries in which causes or effects play a central role, and write a brief **analysis** of the cause-and-effect relationships. You might look at works that show character changes and their causes or that focus on the effects of some event on several characters.

PORTFOLIO

▶ CROSSING THE CURRICULUM: SCIENCE
Suggest that students brainstorm a list of science topics. Once they have chosen their topics, you may wish to limit students to three main causes or effects to keep their presentations from becoming too complicated.

▶ CAREERS
To plan, have students draw maps of their Web pages. They can use highlighters to indicate the words that will lead to hypertext explanations. Ask students to consider the elements of good maps, such as flow, focus, appropriateness, and balance of written content and visual material.

▶ SPEAKING AND LISTENING
As students listen, have them pay attention to clue words that signal cause and effect. Right after students hear a statement containing cause-and-effect clue words they can make an arrow diagram in their notes to indicate causes and effects. You might also focus students' listening by listing questions they might hear the answers to during the program.

▶ VIEWING AND REPRESENTING
Tell students to return to the graphic organizers of the various cause-and-effect patterns in the Reading Workshop (pp. 129–130). These may help students determine how causes and effects are related in their stories.

RESOURCES

Exploring Causes and Effects
Assessment
- *Assessment Package*
  —*Chapter Tests,* Ch. 4
  —*Chapter Tests in Standardized Test Formats,* Ch. 4
  —*Assessment Alternatives,* Ch. 4

- *Test Generator (One-Stop Planner CD-ROM)* 🎵

Choices
Rubrics
- *Assessment Package*
  —*Assessment Alternatives,* Ch. 4

CHAPTER 5

Analyzing a Poem

Use this guide to create an instructional plan that suits the individual needs of your students. Assignments marked by an asterisk (*) may be completed out of class. Times given for pacing lessons are estimated. See pp. 156–157 for chapter-wide resources. Resources listed in this guide are point-of-use resources only.

Curriculum Connections

Connections to Literature
pp. 188–189
■ Writing a Poem

Choices p. 193
■ Media and Technology
■ Speaking and Listening
■ Viewing and Representing
■ Crossing the Curriculum: Art

internetconnect

go.hrw.com GO TO: go.hrw.com
KEYWORD: EOLang 9-5

All resources for this chapter are available for preview on the *One-Stop Planner CD-ROM with Test Generator*. All worksheets and tests may be printed from the CD-ROM.

		Chapter Opener pp. 156–157	Reading Workshop: Reading an Analysis of a Poem pp. 158–167
DEVELOPMENTAL PROGRAM		⏰ **30 minutes** ● Analyzing a Poem p. 157 ● Your Turn 1 p. 157	⏰ **100 minutes** ● Preparing to Read p. 158 ● Reading Selection pp. 159–161 ● First Thoughts 1–3 in groups p. 162 ● Making Inferences pp. 162–164 ● Your Turn 2 p. 164 ● Text as Support pp. 164–165 ● Your Turn 3 p. 165 ● Vocabulary Mini-Lesson p. 166 ● Test Taking Mini-Lesson p. 167
CORE PROGRAM		⏰ **20 minutes** ● Analyzing a Poem p. 157 ● Your Turn 1 p. 157	⏰ **90 minutes** ● Preparing to Read p. 158 ● Reading Selection pp. 159–161 ● First Thoughts 1–3 p. 162 ● Making Inferences pp. 162–164 ● Your Turn 2 p. 164 ● Text as Support pp. 164–165 ● Your Turn 3 p. 165 ● Vocabulary Mini-Lesson p. 166 ● Test Taking Mini-Lesson p. 167
ADVANCED PROGRAM		⏰ **15 minutes** ● Analyzing a Poem p. 157 ● Your Turn 1 p. 157	⏰ **80 minutes** ● Preparing to Read p. 158 ● Reading Selection pp. 159–161 ● First Thoughts 1–3 p. 162 ● Making Inferences pp. 162–164 ● Text as Support pp. 164–165 ● Your Turn 3 p. 165 ● Vocabulary Mini-Lesson p. 166
RESOURCES	**PRINT**	● *Communications,* TP. 38, WS. p. 79	● *Alternative Readings,* Ch. 5 ● *Communications,* TPs. 39, 40, WS. pp. 80–87
	MEDIA	● *One-Stop Planner CD-ROM*	● *One-Stop Planner CD-ROM*

TP.=Transparency   WS.=Worksheet

Writing Workshop: Writing an Analysis of a Poem
pp. 168–189

Focus on Speaking and Listening: Presenting and Responding to a Poetry Reading *pp. 190–192*

🕐 100 minutes
- Prewriting *pp. 168–177*
- Your Turn 4 *p. 172*
- Your Turn 5 *p. 177*
- Framework and Your Turn 6* *p. 178*
- Writer's Model and Student's Model *pp. 179–181*

🕐 120 minutes
- Prepare for a Poetry Reading *pp. 190–191*
- Practicing for a Poetry Reading *p. 191*
- Listening to a Poetry Reading *p. 191*
- Evaluating a Poetry Reading *p. 192*
- Your Turn 11* *p. 192*

🕐 100 minutes
- Evaluate and Revise Your Draft *pp. 182–183*
- Your Turn 7 *p. 183*
- Revising Wordy Sentences and Your Turn 8 *p. 184*
- Proofread, Publish, and Reflect on Your Essay *pp. 185–186*
- Grammar Link *p. 185*
- Your Turn 9 *p. 186*
- Test Taking Mini-Lesson *p. 187*

🕐 180 minutes
- Prewriting *pp. 168–177*
- Your Turn 4* *p. 172*
- Writing Mini-Lesson *p. 173*
- Your Turn 5* *p. 177*
- Framework and Your Turn 6* *p. 178*
- Writer's Model and Student's Model, *pp. 179–181*
- Evaluate and Revise Your Draft *pp. 182–183*
- Your Turn 7* *p. 183*
- Revising Wordy Sentences and Your Turn 8* *p. 184*
- Proofread, Publish, and Reflect on Your Essay *pp. 185–186*
- Grammar Link *p. 185*
- Your Turn 9* *p. 186*
- Test Taking Mini-Lesson *p. 187*
- Connections to Literature* *pp. 188–189*

🕐 90 minutes
- Prepare for a Poetry Reading *pp. 190–191*
- Practicing for a Poetry Reading *p. 191*
- Listening to a Poetry Reading *p. 191*
- Evaluating a Poetry Reading* *p. 192*
- Your Turn 11* *p. 192*

🕐 120 minutes
- Prewriting *pp. 168–177*
- Writing Mini-Lesson *p. 173*
- Your Turn 5* *p. 177*
- Framework and Your Turn 6* *p. 178*
- Writer's Model and Student's Model *pp. 179–181*
- Evaluate and Revise Your Draft* *pp. 182–183*
- Your Turn 7* *p. 183*
- Revising Wordy Sentences *p. 184*
- Proofread, Publish, and Reflect on Your Essay *pp. 185–186*
- Your Turn 9 *p. 186*
- Connections to Literature* *pp. 188–189*
- Your Turn 10* *p. 189*

🕐 50 minutes
- Prepare for a Poetry Reading *pp. 190–191*
- Practicing for a Poetry Reading *p. 191*
- Listening to a Poetry Reading *p. 191*
- Evaluating a Poetry Reading* *p. 192*
- Your Turn 11* *p. 192*

- *Communications,* 📖
  TPs. 41–44,
  WS. pp. 88–98
- *Designing Your Writing*

- *Media Literacy and Communication* 📖
  Skills
  —*Support and Practice,* Ch. 5
  —*A How-to Handbook*
  —*A Teacher's Guide,* Ch. 5

- *One-Stop Planner CD-ROM* 💿

- *Media Literacy and Communication Skills* 📼
  —*Videocassette 2, Segment E*
- *One-Stop Planner CD-ROM* 💿

CHAPTER 5

Analyzing a Poem

CHAPTER OBJECTIVES

- To read a literary analysis of a poem
- To write a literary analysis of a poem
- To present and respond to a poetry reading

Chapter Overview

This chapter allows students to explore the style, meaning, and presentation of poetry. In the Reading Workshop, students read a literary analysis and examine the author's use of textual references to support a main idea. Students will also make inferences to interpret a critical text. The Writing Workshop teaches students to write their own literary analyses by studying the major elements they might analyze in a poem and learning to organize and present textual support for a critical thesis. Students then apply what they have learned through analysis to write their own poems. In the Focus on Speaking and Listening section, students prepare, present, and respond to poetry readings. Although the three sections can be taught independently, together they give students a solid grasp of analyzing style and meaning in poetry.

Why Study Analysis of Poetry?

Refining the ability to think analytically about poetry will help students create and interpret meaning in other areas. They can apply the analytical process—breaking apart a whole to examine each individual piece—to everyday experiences such as watching a movie or having lunch with a friend. The ability to identify different aspects of a subject or experience will sharpen students' awareness of not only how the parts are related to the whole, but also how the parts (and the whole) are related to other facts and ideas.

Teaching the Chapter

Option 1: Begin with Literature

Introduce the chapter by discussing ways that your class has already applied analytical techniques to literature. Since this chapter focuses on analyzing poetry, begin by discussing the literary elements students would examine in another genre, such as the short story. Ask them to identify and describe the individual elements of a short story they have read. Students may mention plot, setting, characters, and point of view. Discuss how examining these individual elements helps unlock the story's theme. Then have your class read the literary analysis on pp. 159–161.

Option 2: Begin with Nonfiction and Writing

The Reading Workshop presents an engaging scholarly analysis of an excerpt from William Shakespeare's *The Tempest*. The essay will help students appreciate analysis as a method for discovering meaning in a poem. The reading-skills instruction introduces students to key poetic elements and specific support techniques. The completion of the Writing Workshop will further develop students' ability to understand important elements of poetry as they produce their own analyses. When they return to literature study, they will be better prepared to think about poetry and other genres from the viewpoint of author's craft. See also **Connections to Literature** on pp. 188–189.

Making Connections

To the Literature Curriculum

Students apply basic analytical skills every time they question the meaning of a literary text. Poetry is a particularly effective genre to use when exploring analytical techniques because students can observe how the distilled language of a poem unfolds under their scrutiny. As students examine the elements of poetic language and structure, they can see the poem in a new light as a result of their analysis.

Lesson Idea: Analyzing "in Just-" by E. E. Cummings

1. Read the poem aloud; then ask students to write down memorable words and phrases or to describe any images that the poem brings to mind.

2. Instruct students to read the poem silently and write down three questions. For example: "Why are the names of the children blended? What does 'puddle-wonderful' mean? Why does Cummings repeat the phrase 'far and wee'?"

3. Tell students they could use their three questions as the beginning of a literary analysis. Ask volunteers to read their questions aloud, then work as a class to find answers in the poem. Explain that each element in the poem is related to the work's overall meaning. Ask students to

   a. Write a brief answer to one of their own questions
   b. Find a supporting detail for the answer in the poem
   c. Explain how that part of the poem relates to the overall meaning or effect

   Point out that different readers often have different interpretations of the same poem. Explain that readers support the validity of their analyses by citing supporting details from the text.

4. After this discussion, have the class listen again as you re-read the poem. Ask students to compare their second listening experience to the first. Discuss how analyzing part of the poem affected their perceptions. Then introduce students to the literary analysis on pp. 159–161. Use the instruction on literary analysis to help students understand and evaluate the author's critical interpretation as they read.

To Careers

Reinforce the idea that analysis is an important skill in most career fields. Explain to students that there are certain sub-skills or tools that help workers with analysis tasks. These include listing, planning, questioning, surveying, reporting, graphing, charting, and outlining. Ask students to use an organizer like the one shown to identify how each subskill might be used in a career field that interests them. When individuals have completed their charts, provide time for the class to compare and contrast their responses.

Career field that interests you: Real estate agent

Subskills for analytic thinking	Example of how this skill might be used in the career field
Listing	Listing the positive features of a house to be sold
Planning	
Questioning	
Reporting	
Graphing	
Charting	
Outlining	

To the Community

Students learn from analyzing literature to look at individual elements to understand and respond to a text. Students can apply the analytical process to explore a community issue as well. For example, they might analyze a dispute about the construction of a potentially hazardous facility. Students can gather facts from newspapers, public records, and field research. Have them present the results of their analyses in video documentaries, letters to city council persons, letters to editors of newspapers, or public service reports.

To the Music Curriculum

As students learn more about the analysis of poetry, they may note that poetry and music share many characteristics. For example, musicians use instruments and vocalization to create rhythm and tone; poets use words, line breaks, and punctuation to achieve similar artistic goals. Encourage students to find recordings that blend music and poetry. For example, a student might find a recording of a poet reading his or her work that is enhanced by musical accompaniment. Students who play instruments may want to write their own music to accompany poems they discover as they work through the chapter.

Analyzing
a Poem

PREVIEWING THE CHAPTER

■ The three sections in this chapter teach techniques for analyzing poetry. First, the Reading Workshop presents a literary analysis of a poem to demonstrate the value of making inferences and the importance of using direct textual references to support them. Students will apply these skills in the Writing Workshop as they select poems and write literary analyses. Finally, students will extend what they have learned by presenting and responding to a poetry reading. To integrate this chapter with grammar, usage, and mechanics chapters, see the chart on pp. T371A–T371B.

INTRODUCING THE CHAPTER

■ To introduce the chapter, use the Journal Warm-up, Transparency 38, in *Communications.*

VIEWING THE ILLUSTRATION

■ As students look at the collage, explain that the words in cursive script and the various images are from William Wordsworth's poem "I Wandered Lonely as a Cloud." Explain that *theme, tone,* and *imagery* are key terms for analyzing poetry. Point out that although the poem is traditional, the illustration is not. The mixture of typefaces and type sizes, the irregular blocks of color, and the overlapping of images and text are modern.

Representing. Invite students to illustrate a favorite poem with words and images.

THEME

TONE

imagery

Continuous as th
And twinkle o
th...tched in never-ending...
...the margin of a bay;
Ten thou...and saw...at a glance,
Tossing their heads in sprightly
For oft when on m...
In vacant or in...
...her flash upon...
...hich is the bl...
And then my he...
And dances with the daffod...

CHAPTER RESOURCES

Planning
■ *Lesson Planner,* Ch. 5
■ *ELL Strategies,* Ch. 5
■ Block Scheduling, p. T155A (this book)
■ *One-Stop Planner CD-ROM* 🎵

Practice
■ *Communications,* Ch. 5

■ *Media Literacy and Communication Skills* 🖥

Extension
■ *Designing Your Writing*

Reinforcement
■ *Communications,* Ch. 5

Reading Workshop

Reading an Analysis of a Poem

Writing Workshop

Writing an Analysis of a Poem

Speaking and Listening

Presenting and Responding to a Poetry Reading

"D id you see the movie on channel five last night?" a friend asks. "Yes, I thought it was great," you answer. "Great? It was terrible," your friend responds. Then the debate begins. You point out which elements of the movie you think make it great. Your friend points out which elements she thinks make the movie terrible. Together, you dissect the movie: plot, characters, sequence of events, and special effects.

What are you and your friend really doing as you pick apart the elements of the movie? You are conducting an **analysis:** an examination of the parts, or elements, of the movie to figure out how they fit together as a whole. When you watch a movie, or when you read a story or a poem, you will react to it. When you begin to ask yourself why you respond to a particular work— whether a movie, a poem, or a play—you have taken the first step toward analyzing that work. The more you dissect the pieces of the work and examine your reactions to each piece, the more you gain an understanding of the work as a whole and the reasons for your response to it.

> **Informational Text**
>
> Exposition

 Thinking About Analysis

With a couple of classmates, think of four people whose professions involve analysis. Jot down a brief description of the way each professional uses analysis in his or her job. For example, a biologist analyzes when she dissects a specimen under a microscope. Be prepared to share your answers with the class.

> **internet connect**
>
> **go.hrw.com**
> **GO TO:** go.hrw.com
> **KEYWORD:** EOLang 9-5

Motivate

Read aloud a short poem to the class. Ask students to complete the following framed sentences: Listening to this poem made me feel _____ because _____. I think a point the poet was trying to make is _____ because _____.

Permit volunteers to share their responses. Point out that students have informally analyzed the poem and explain that in this chapter they will learn a more formal approach to analysis.

ELEMENTS OF Literature

Analysis of Poetry. In *Elements of Literature,* Third Course, see "Fog" by Carl Sandburg, p. 503, and "Fire and Ice" by Robert Frost, p. 541, for additional poems that students may analyze.

YOUR TURN 1

Possible answers include auto mechanics, who analyze a car's parts to find a malfunction; lawyers, who analyze testimony to prove a point; doctors, who analyze symptoms and lab results to reach a diagnosis; and store managers, who analyze merchandise and customers to create appealing displays.

OBJECTIVES

Reading and Writing Connection

- To read and study an analysis of a poem
- To analyze the use of literary text as support for main ideas

Reading Skills

- To identify and make inferences
- To determine connotations and denotations of words

TEACHING TIP

Preparing to Read
This page alerts students to focus on making inferences as they read the analysis of a poem. It also encourages them to note how the author of the piece uses information and examples from the poem as support.

Quotation for the Day
"A good critic is the sorcerer who makes some hidden spring gush forth unexpectedly beneath our feet."
(Francois Mauriac, 1885–1970, French novelist, playwright, essayist)

Explain that *critic* here refers to a person who analyzes a literary text. Lead students to see that the "spring" might be a new way of viewing something. Ask students to think of a time when someone's comment caused them to see an issue or situation differently. [Students might mention a teacher who explained a math concept in a new way that suddenly made it clear.]

RESOURCES

Reading Workshop Reinforcement
- *Alternative Readings,* Ch. 5

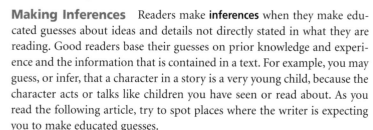

Reading an Analysis of a Poem

WHAT'S AHEAD?

In this section you will read an analysis of a poem and learn how to
- identify and make inferences
- analyze the use of literary text as support for main ideas

Your English teacher tells your class to read a certain poem on a certain page and to be prepared to discuss it. You read the poem, but it is absolutely meaningless to you. Then, your teacher discusses the poem with the class, point by point, and suddenly, it all starts to make sense. Why? Your teacher has led you and your classmates through an **analysis** of a poem, an understanding of its parts. The article on the next page is both a memoir and a literary analysis of a poem about change. In the first half of the article the writer recalls the changes that were happening in her life at the time the poem became her favorite; in the second half of the article she analyzes the elements of the poem that made it one of her favorites.

Preparing to Read

READING SKILL

Making Inferences   Readers make **inferences** when they make educated guesses about ideas and details not directly stated in what they are reading. Good readers base their guesses on prior knowledge and experience and the information that is contained in a text. For example, you may guess, or infer, that a character in a story is a very young child, because the character acts or talks like children you have seen or read about. As you read the following article, try to spot places where the writer is expecting you to make educated guesses.

READING FOCUS

Text as Support   The subject of an **analysis** is usually a single work of literature—a single poem, for example. The most important support for the main idea in an analysis comes from the poem itself. In order to provide support for their main ideas, writers refer to characters, actions, or events, and quote the words, phrases, and lines of the work they are analyzing. As you read the article on the next page, notice how often the writer uses quotations from a poem and specific references to it.

READING PROCESS

PREREADING
Set a Purpose for Reading the Selection.
Point out that the teacher-assigned purpose for reading Willard's essay is to learn how to analyze poetry by making inferences based upon textual details. Remind students that

reading with a purpose helps them focus as they read a text.

Also, explain to students that setting their own purpose for reading will add to their comprehension and enjoyment of the analysis. In order to establish purposes for reading,

The poem below is from Shakespeare's play *The Tempest*. The poem is actually a song that the character Ferdinand hears the spirit Ariel singing. In the analysis that follows, a writer examines the changes described in the poem and some changes in her own life. See if the writer clarifies the poem's meaning for you. As you read, jot down answers to the active-reading questions.

Ding-Dong Bell: "Ariel's Song" from *The Tempest*

by NANCY WILLARD

Ariel's Song
by William Shakespeare

Full fathom five thy father lies,
    Of his bones are coral made:
Those are pearls that were his eyes:
    Nothing of him that doth fade,
But doth suffer a sea-change
Into something rich and strange.
Sea-nymphs hourly ring his knell:
    Burden [*within*]. Ding-dong.[1]
Hark, now I hear them—ding-dong bell.

I grew up near the thumb of a lost mitten floating on the big waters of Lake Michigan and Lake Erie—lost, because only a single mitten remained, the left one. Until I was fifteen I lived my entire life between these two lakes. . . . When my father took a job in Los Alamos,[2] New Mexico, I felt as if we were moving to Mars. I had never seen the desert; the very word tasted like a dead planet. After school let out, my father

> 1. Based on the details in this paragraph, what do you think is the writer's attitude toward moving?

1. *Burden* [*within*]. **Ding-dong:** *Within* is a stage direction. The line means that the word *ding-dong* is sung as a *burden* (an obsolete word meaning *refrain*) by actors who are offstage.

2. **Los Alamos:** sometimes called the "atomic city," the site where the atomic bomb was developed.

Active-Reading Questions

These active-reading questions are designed to help students think about textual analysis in the Reading Selection. Use students' answers as an informal assessment of their ability to make inferences and interpret textual support. Possible answers are suggested below.

ANSWERS

1. By describing New Mexico as a "dead planet," the author conveys her negative attitude toward moving from Michigan to Los Alamos. Further, the phrase "moving to Mars" implies that she considers the New Mexico landscape desolate and forsaken and the move alien to her experiences and desires.

ask students to read the poem reproduced at the beginning of the analysis. Tell them to jot down their questions about individual words or the poem's overall meaning. Guide students to look for the answers to their questions as they read the analysis. Remind them that the answers may be directly stated in the text or may have to be inferred from textual details and prior knowledge. Be sure students understand that having a purpose for reading helps them get more from an analysis.

packed the maps. My mother packed our clothes, sheets, blankets, pots and pans, and the radio. I packed my *Selected Poems of Emily Dickinson* and my *Poems and Songs from the Plays of William Shakespeare.* On the three-day drive from Ann Arbor to Los Alamos, I watched the familiar landscape of trees and cornfields disappear. The roads were so straight and the countryside so bare you could see to the naked rim of the earth.

We unpacked and settled in; my father went off to work every day—he worked in a high security area protected by an impressive fence—and I set myself the task of memorizing three poems a week from the books I'd brought. The first poet on my list was Shakespeare, and the first poem was a song from *The Tempest,* "Full fathom five thy father lies." I went over the poem before I left for my job teaching art to first graders in a summer Bible school. The regular teacher had read them the story of Noah's ark, and my assignment was to help the children produce an illustration for the story. On a long piece of shelf paper I painted the ark . . . and the children painted the water and the animals. Purple tigers roamed the sky, dinosaurs gamboled[3] in the bushes, butterflies as big as cows soared over Noah and his family. The teacher was not pleased; she reminded me that the animals had come in two by two, as if she'd personally witnessed the departure.

There were no drowned people, no flooded homes, no deaths.

After supper I took out my Shakespeare and found that I had effortlessly memorized every word, as if the song had also been memorizing me. Now, many years later, I still marvel that it has stayed with me, perhaps for the very reason that it is a song, in which shape, sound, and image strike us deeper than the sense.

Sound is the very subject of the last lines:

Sea-nymphs hourly ring his knell

A knell, of course, is the sound of a bell rung slowly to announce a death. Though the word "ding-dong" is given only twice in "the burden" (or refrain), the nymphs must have gone on singing it during the remark that follows: "Hark, now I hear them." If the word "ding-dong" were not written out, the effect might be ominous;[4] the word *burden* derives from an old French word, *bourdon,* which can describe both a humming and the drone of a bagpipe.

---

3. **gamboled:** jumped, frolicked.

4. **ominous:** threatening, sinister.

> 2. Why do you think the teacher was not pleased with the children's illustration?

> 3. What purpose do you think this line from the poem serves?

Active-Reading Questions

ANSWERS continued

2. From the children's colorful, fanciful illustrations, it is reasonable to infer that they took a light-hearted view of the event.

3. The quotation supports Willard's statement that sound is the subject of the poem's last lines. It also illustrates her point that sound strikes readers deeper than sense.

READING PROCESS

READING

Make Personal Connections. Explain to students that thinking about ways a text relates to their own lives can help them discover new levels of meaning and increase their reading enjoyment. After students have finished the Reading Selection, invite volunteers to discuss situations in their own lives that were similar to the one the author explains. Ask students to identify how recalling their own experiences helps them understand the feelings the author describes. For

This bell is not rung by human hands, however; it is a sound that seems to come from the waves themselves. And the sea-nymphs ringing it do not feel the fear and sympathy that weigh on the minds of earthly mourners; as creatures of magic, they live outside of human mortality. The singer, Ariel, is a spirit of the air and a trickster. In *The Tempest*, Ferdinand, the son who hears the song, believes his father has drowned in the shipwreck that cast them both upon an enchanted island. Ariel knows that Ferdinand's father is not drowned. Does this make the song a lie? No. Father and son have lost something of their civilized selves and have indeed been changed by their encounter with the sea into "something rich and strange."

Because the sound of the bell is spelled out in syllables that echo Mother Goose ("Ding, dong, bell, / Kitty's in the well"), the listener knows this drowning is not the stuff of tragedy but of fairy tales, in which a transformation so often brings about the happy ending. Though the refrain is a death knell, the drowned man is as exquisite[5] as a temple god, newly wrought[6] in coral and set with pearls. He has crossed over into the kingdom of the spirits of air and water, who sing of human tragedies without participating in them.

I loved that song because it reminded me of water in a place where water was precious and of change in a time when I did not yet know what time would make of me. I have forgotten who I was at fifteen, but I have not forgotten the song. It still holds something of who I was, living in the atomic city where I first learned those words. Hark, now I hear them. Ding-dong, bell.

> **4. Why do you think the writer provides this background information about *The Tempest*?**

> **5. Why do you think the writer ends with the words *Ding-dong, bell*?**

Sir John Everett Millais, *Ferdinand Lured by Ariel* (1849). Oil on panel (60.8 × 50.8 cm). The Makins Collection/Bridgeman Art Library, London/New York

5. **exquisite:** beautiful.
6. **wrought:** fashioned, made of.

Active-Reading Questions
ANSWERS continued

4. The background information gives readers a better understanding of "Ariel's Song." It also prepares readers for the author's conclusions about the poem's link to the events of her life.

5. The words bring the reader's attention back to the text of "Ariel's Song." The author has now established that these words signal change. By ending with them, she concludes her essay on a powerful, meaningful note.

example, Willard's feelings about moving might be compared to a student's emotions when leaving the seashore after a summer vacation. This connection may help the student identify with the author's feelings about the poem.

ANSWERS

Possible answers are suggested below.

1. Ferdinand thinks his father has drowned in the shipwreck. He is wrong.

2. The writer moved with her family from a home surrounded by water to a strange, new home in the desert. Ferdinand and his father were shipwrecked on a strange island. Ferdinand and his father are changed forever by their journey over water to dry land; similarly, the author's journey away from water to desert changes her forever.

3. Students may note that the writer shows optimism about change, as she states that it often leads to a happy ending. On the other hand, her references to the nuclear bomb and the death knell create a sad tone that undercuts her positive declarations.

TEACHING TIP

Making Inferences

As students learn the process of making inferences, suggest they brainstorm a range of interpretations for a particular part of a poem. Then, using evidence from the rest of the poem, have them evaluate each possible inference to see which is most logical and defensible. For example, you might direct their attention to the last two lines of Robert Frost's "The Road Not Taken," asking students to brainstorm what these lines mean. Students might suggest that the lines refer to how the poet's decision to strike out on his own changed his life. Point out that the poet's prediction that he would be telling about his choice in times to come seems to support this idea.

First Thoughts on Your Reading

Work with a classmate to answer the following questions about "Ding-Dong, Bell." Put your answers on your own paper.

1. When Ferdinand hears "Ariel's Song," what does he believe has happened to his father? Is Ferdinand right or wrong?

2. Describe a change the writer says she went through at the time she first read "Ariel's Song." How is this change similar to or different from the "sea-change" that Ferdinand and his father went through? Hint: What role does water play in both changes?

3. What is the writer's attitude toward change? Is it happy like a fairy tale, or sad like a tragedy? Why do you think so?

READING SKILL

Making Inferences

Between the Lines To understand fully "Ding-Dong, Bell" you have to make **inferences**—educated guesses based on information a writer implies but does not directly state. For example, the writer never directly gives the reasons for her family's move. To figure out why they moved, you have to use evidence from the piece and your prior knowledge to make an educated guess.

Think of making inferences as the process of putting pieces of a puzzle together. Some of the pieces represent information, ideas, or other clues provided by the writer, and some represent what you, the reader, already know from your prior knowledge and experience. You make inferences by putting these pieces together until a picture that makes sense emerges.

Question: Why did the writer's family move to Los Alamos?

Inference: The writer's father moved his family to Los Alamos because he got a job working with nuclear weapons.

Stated: Writer says her family moved to Los Alamos when she was fifteen.

Prior Knowledge: Los Alamos was where a lot of secret and important work was done on nuclear weapons.

Stated: Writer's father worked in a "high security area."

Prior Knowledge: High security work is usually secret and important.

The following Thinking It Through provides steps that you can use to make inferences. Specifically, it shows how you can make an inference that answers the question "Why did the writer's family move to Los Alamos?"

THINKING IT THROUGH · *Making Correct Inferences*

Follow the steps below to make inferences when you are reading.

▷ **STEP 1** Read and take note of relevant pieces of information in the text. These are the puzzle pieces the writer provides.

The writer moved to Los Alamos when she was fifteen.
Her father "worked in a high security area protected by an impressive fence."

▷ **STEP 2** Ask as many *5W-How?* questions—*Who? What? When? Where? Why? How?*—as you can about what the writer states.

What is significant or unusual about Los Alamos? **Why** was the writer's family moving there? **Why** was such high security necessary? **What** was her father's job?

▷ **STEP 3** Use your prior knowledge to answer as many of the *5W-How?* questions as you can. Your answers are the puzzle pieces you provide.

Los Alamos is famous for being the site where secret, important work was done on nuclear weapons. High security work, like the work the writer's father did, is usually secret and important.

▷ **STEP 4** To make an inference, put together the information the writer states and the answers you provide.

The family moved to Los Alamos for a high security (secret, important) job **+** Los Alamos is famous for secret, important work on nuclear weapons **=** **Inference:** The father moved his family to Los Alamos because he got a job working with nuclear weapons.

TIP Making inferences is a general skill that can be applied in many different instances while reading. For example, you make inferences when you identify the implied main idea of a reading and when you draw conclusions or make generalizations about what you have read.

Critical Thinking

Analysis. Remind students that the first **Thinking It Through** step is the recording of key details from the text. Have students suggest questions that are not answered explicitly in the text. For example, "Was the writer a rebellious teenager?" [Possible answer: She was likely not rebellious, as shown by her work at a Bible school and her habit of memorizing poems in her spare time.] Then have each student write one unanswered question in the center of a main-idea map. As they re-read the article, students can record details in the radial spaces and refer to the map as they follow the remaining steps to infer answers.

She spent her spare time reading poetry.

She understood the poem when she was just fifteen.

Do you think the writer is an intelligent teenager?

The poetry she picked to read was challenging.

She easily memorized the poem.

YOUR TURN 2

1. The correct answer is C. A sample step-by-step solution follows:

Step 1 The teacher disliked the fanciful imaginary animals in the student picture. She also objected to the lack of destructive images.

Step 2 What are the effects of a real flood? **Why** might the teacher have gotten upset?

Step 3 A real flood causes destruction and death. The teacher's vision of events was obviously different than that of the children.

Step 4 The teacher didn't like the drawing + the drawing didn't stick to the biblical facts + it left out the deadly effects of the flood = **Inference:** The teacher would have liked a more serious illustration of the story of Noah's ark.

2. The correct answer is B. A sample step-by-step solution follows:

Step 1 The writer loved the song because it reminded her of water. She was living in a place where water was precious.

Step 2 Why might water be precious? **Where** might water be precious?

Step 3 Water would be precious in a place where water is scarce. Water is scarce in a desert.

Step 4 Water is scarce in the desert = **Inference:** The writer is living in the desert, a dry place.

Critical Thinking

Analysis. Ask students to revisit the part of the essay that tells about Willard's experiences with her summer job. Challenge students to analyze what this event reveals about the author and how the anecdote relates to the rest of the essay.

YOUR TURN 2 Making Inferences

Read each of the following passages from "Ding-Dong, Bell." Then, using the Thinking It Through steps on page 163, work collaboratively to choose the best inference from the list that follows each passage. Be prepared to explain how you made each inference.

1. "Purple tigers roamed the sky, dinosaurs gamboled in the bushes, butterflies as big as cows soared over Noah and his family. The teacher was not pleased; she reminded me that the animals had come in two by two, as if she'd personally witnessed the departure.
   There were no drowned people, no flooded homes, no deaths."

   It can be inferred from this passage that the teacher

   A. is afraid of tigers

   B. does not like purple paint

   C. thinks the story of Noah's ark should be depicted as it was described in the original text

   D. wants to see more butterflies in the illustration

   I inferred this from _____ .

2. "I loved that song because it reminded me of water in a place where water was precious. . . ."

   It can be inferred from this sentence that the location of the writer's new home is

   A. cold   C. wet

   B. dry   D. humid

   I inferred this from _____ .

READING FOCUS

Text as Support

The Text and Nothing But   As a critical reader, how can you judge Nancy Willard's analysis of "Ariel's Song"? Start by evaluating her use of **textual support—direct quotations** and **paraphrases** of the poem.

Direct Quotations and Paraphrases   Unlike other types of writing, a literary analysis goes straight to a **primary source**—the text of the poem itself—for support of main ideas. The strongest form of textual support in a literary analysis is a **direct quotation** from the text being analyzed.

As a reader, you can spot **direct quotations** fairly easily because they are set off in italics or quotation marks to indicate that the words are someone else's.

Example:
In her poem "the thirty eighth year," author Lucille Clifton says "the thirty eighth year / of my life, / plain as bread."

A **paraphrase** is a form of textual support that does not use the author's exact words. A paraphrase restates or rewords the author's words.

Example:
In her poem "the thirty eighth year," author Lucille Clifton explains that at age thirty-eight she feels like an ordinary woman.

Elaboration Textual support alone should not convince you of a writer's main idea. You also need to examine the writer's **elaboration,** or expanded commentary, on the textual support. In other words, in a poetry analysis you should expect to see solid elaboration that explains how the example from the work supports the writer's main idea.

The paragraph below is from a poetry analysis of "the thirty eighth year." Notice how the writer states the main idea about the poem, supports that main idea with quotations from the poem, and elaborates on that support.

> Poet Lucille Clifton carefully chooses figures of speech that support the image of a plain woman in her poem "the thirty eighth year." For example, the speaker uses two similes to compare herself to common foods. She says that she is "plain as bread" and "round as a cake" (lines 3 and 4). She also uses metaphors, saying she has "built" daughters who "blossom and promise fruit / like Afrikan trees" (lines 34 and 35). These metaphors show that the woman has also given the gift of life that promises to grow and develop.

Main idea

Direct quotations
Direct quotations

Elaboration

 Analyzing Textual Evidence as Support

With a partner, find three examples of textual support from "Ding-Dong, Bell." Answer the following questions about each example:

1. Is the textual support a direct quotation or a paraphrase?
2. What idea does the quotation or paraphrase support?
3. Does the writer's elaboration make the support clear? Why or why not?

Meeting INDIVIDUAL NEEDS

LEARNERS HAVING DIFFICULTY
Some students may have trouble understanding the meaning of textual support. Explain that a writer's ideas about the meaning of a poem come from the poem itself. A writer can try to prove his or her ideas by citing details from the text to support an argument. The writer can include a part of the poem exactly as it is written or can paraphrase a part in his or her own words. To give students practice, write on the chalkboard a comment about a poem you provide. Then, ask students to paraphrase parts of the poem that support your comment.

Wrap It Up

Metacognition. Ask students to reflect on their own reading processes by answering these questions:

1. What did you find most challenging about reading the analysis? What strategy did you use to deal with that?

2. What is one thing you learned about the components of an effective analysis from reading Willard's piece?

YOUR TURN 3

ANSWERS
A sample response follows: "Though the refrain is a death knell, the drowned man is as exquisite as a temple god, newly wrought in coral and set with pearls."

1. It is a paraphrase.

2. It supports the idea that change is positive.

3. The elaboration clarifies the idea by pointing out that a drowned man is now beyond human suffering.

READING PROCESS

EXPLORING
Evaluate Text as Support. After students have written their responses, point out that the active-reading questions required them to use two kinds of information in their answers. Some information was explicitly stated in the text; other ideas had to be inferred by putting together what they read with their own ideas and experiences. Ask students to circle any information in their responses that is taken directly from the essay and underline any information that they had to infer.

MINI-LESSON VOCABULARY

Denotation and Connotation

ANSWERS

Possible responses are given below.

1. Here, "Mars" connotes the most foreign and out-of-the-way place imaginable.

2. Here, "civilized" connotes people being overly educated and out of touch with their true nature.

3. Here, "earthly" connotes flesh-and-blood beings, which are burdened by mortality, as opposed to divine spirits, which are spared such suffering.

4. Here, "drone" connotes a monotonous humming sound.

Taking a Second Look

Denotation and Connotation. Have pairs of students look up each of the underlined words in a thesaurus. Then ask them to discuss the denotation and connotation of each synonym and come to a consensus on which, if any, could be used to replace the underlined word in the sentence from the essay.

MINI-LESSON VOCABULARY

Denotation and Connotation

Poets often use the *connotations* of words to suggest meaning. The **denotations** of a word are its primary dictionary definitions. The **connotations** of a word are all the undertones—the ideas or emotional meanings—associated with the word. For example, *proud* and *arrogant* have similar denotations—"having a sense of self-importance"—but different connotations. "Proud" can mean having self-respect, but "arrogant" often means snobbish.

THINKING IT THROUGH — Understanding Connotations

Use the steps below to determine how a word's denotations and connotations contribute to its meaning in a text.

> Whenever Richard Cory went down town,
> We people on the pavement looked at him:
> He was a gentleman from sole to <u>crown</u>,
> Clean favored, and imperially slim.

▶ **STEP 1** Write down the word's denotation and any alternate definitions you find in the dictionary. It is possible one of these definitions could be a connotation.

"Crown" means "a garland or wreath worn on the head as a sign of honor." "Crown" also means "the position of monarch."

▶ **STEP 2** Describe the undertones of the word. Look at the *context*—the other words surrounding the word—for clues.

"Crown" seems to have positive undertones. "Imperially" suggests Richard Cory has power. "Gentleman" suggests that Richard Cory is of high social standing. "Crown" in this context suggests power and nobility.

▶ **STEP 3** Now re-read the poem, keeping these meanings in mind to determine what the connotations add to the lines.

The author said "sole to crown," instead of "head to toe." The lines seem to mean that Richard Cory is a man of high stature.

PRACTICE

Using the steps above, describe the connotation of each underlined word below.

1. "I felt as if we were moving to <u>Mars</u>."

2. "Father and son have lost something of their <u>civilized</u> selves. . ."

3. "And the sea-nymphs ringing it do not feel the fear and sympathy that weigh on the minds of <u>earthly</u> mourners. . . ."

4. ". . . which can describe both a humming and the <u>drone</u> of a bagpipe."

RESOURCES

Vocabulary
Practice
■ *Communications,* WS. p. 84

Test Taking
Practice
■ *Communications,* WS. pp. 85–87

Inference Questions

To test your ability to infer, many reading tests include **inference questions**. These questions ask you to make inferences based on information provided in a reading passage. When you answer an inference question about a reading passage, you should be able to point to evidence in the passage that led you to your answer.

Below is a typical reading passage and an inference test question about it.

The young man was as dressed up as he had ever been—blue blazer, gray slacks, maroon tie, freshly polished shoes. He waited calmly offstage for his turn to make the first speech of his young life. Hearing his name announced, he marched onto the stage. Reaching the podium, he spread his note cards out carefully and adjusted the height of the microphone. Then he made direct eye contact with as many people as he could. As he gazed into the faces in the auditorium, the giggling and whispering faded into silence. He smiled and began to speak in a voice that reached the entire auditorium. He never glanced at the note cards.

1. A reasonable inference you can make from this passage is that the speaker is
   A. timid about speaking to people
   B. arrogant about his own importance
   C. nervous about how people view him
   D. confident about his public-speaking abilities

THINKING IT THROUGH **Answering Inference Questions**

Use the following steps to answer inference questions.

1. Read the passage slowly and carefully.

2. Pick out key words and phrases in the passage on which you might base your inferences.

   "Waited calmly," "marched," and "direct eye contact" are key words.

3. Consider every answer. You can usually eliminate one or two right away. Using the steps, you can make the following determinations about the multiple-choice answers provided for the example test question above.

   Answer **A** cannot be correct: a person who is timid would not look directly into the eyes of the people in an audience. The way the speaker "marched" onto the stage might show a touch of arrogance—but there is nothing else in the passage to support answer **B**. There are no indications of nervousness in the passage that would support answer **C**. Answer **D** is clearly the most reasonable inference; it is well supported by details in the passage: the speaker "waited calmly," he "marched" onto the stage, he made eye contact with the audience, he spoke in a loud, clear voice, and he never looked at his notes.

Looking Ahead to Writing

In the **Writing Workshop** for this chapter (pp.168–189), students will be asked to write their own analyses of poems. In preparation for this task, they will have to analyze sound elements in poetry and gather support for their analyses. Have the class review "Text as Support" on pp. 164–165 as they gather details and examples to use as elaboration.

Writing Workshop

OBJECTIVES

- To write an analysis of a poem
- To analyze the elements of a poem, including sound elements
- To gather support for a literary analysis
- To remove or reduce unnecessary words and phrases
- To use quotation marks correctly

Quotation for the Day

"A poet is, before anything else, a person who is passionately in love with language."

(W. H. Auden, 1907-1973, English-born poet and essayist)

Have each student write down three words he or she finds intriguing in some way. Ask students to analyze why these words appeal to them. Discuss the different ways a word can be appreciated (for example: for its sound, its denotation, and its connotations). Finally, point out that analyzing a poem entails looking carefully at words that the poet has put together deliberately and, perhaps, even passionately.

Meeting INDIVIDUAL NEEDS

INCLUSION

Since analysis is a challenging task, some students may need assistance in selecting poetry that is at an appropriate level. Have a helper work with these students as they search for poems. When a student has found a piece that he or she is considering for analysis, the helper should ask the student to read the poem and retell its main idea and some supporting details to ensure that the student understands the piece well enough to analyze it.

WHAT'S AHEAD?

In this workshop, you will write an analysis of a poem. You will also learn how to

- analyze the elements of a poem, including sound elements
- gather support for a literary analysis
- remove or reduce unnecessary words and phrases
- use quotation marks

Writing an Analysis of a Poem

Imagine that you are sitting in class just before the bell rings. A friend walks by your desk, opens your notebook, and slips a piece of paper inside. You pull the paper out and begin to read a poem—about *you*. The vivid images and the humorous language describe all the things your friend thinks about you.

How might reading that poem make you feel? Would it make you laugh, or would it make you blush? Would it make you frown, or would it make you want to run and hide? One thing is certain: it would trigger some kind of response from you right away. Then, if you started to think about *why* you reacted to the poem as you did, you would be taking the first step in **analyzing** the poem.

This Writing Workshop will lead you through the process for writing an analysis of a poem. You will learn to analyze and respond to the different elements in a poem. Working through all the steps will allow you to create an essay in which you offer an interesting and authoritative insight into a poem.

Prewriting

Choose a Poem

So Many Options When you begin your search for the right poem to analyze, you need to keep two things in mind. First, the poem cannot be so short and simple that it contains nothing worthwhile to analyze. Second, the poem should not be so long you cannot deal with it in detail in a short essay. A good rule of thumb for a paper of this type is to choose a ten- to fifteen-line poem. To find a good poem, try some of the following ideas.

168   Chapter 5   **Exposition:** Analyzing a Poem

- **Think of poems you have read before.** If you remember a few that you liked, find copies and re-read them.

- **Ask your teacher or librarian to help you** find a collection of poems that share a common theme—such as *conformity and rebellion* or *loss and acceptance*—that interests you.

- **Ask family members and friends** to recommend poems that they found especially memorable or moving.

  After you have found a few poems, look through them and choose the one you like best.

Write Down Your First Thoughts

From a Personal Point of View   What does the poem you have chosen mean to you? Sometimes you know what a poem means to you, but you cannot easily express that knowledge in words. Here are some ideas that will help you turn your first thoughts and feelings about a poem into words on a page.

- **Write a response in your journal.** Start by writing a response to the **title** of the poem or to the line or **image** that you reacted to most strongly. Follow where your thoughts and feelings lead you.

- **Freewrite** about ideas that the poem brings to mind.

- **Copy words or lines** from the poem that you find especially meaningful, and jot down short comments next to them.

Analyze Your Poem

Reaching Deeper   Your personal response to a poem is only the first step toward analyzing that poem. During the process of analyzing your poem, you will need to read and re-read it several times. The process of discovering what a poem means and how the poet communicates its meaning can take time. If you run into parts of your poem that do not make much sense to you right away, do not give up—try some of the following techniques to gain a better understanding of the poem.

- **Read by following the punctuation marks,** not the line breaks. Pause at the end of a line only if the line ends with a punctuation mark. Knowing when to pause and when not to pause will give you a much better understanding of the flow of meaning in the poem.

- **Copy down the entire poem** so that you can underline, circle, and annotate (make notes about) parts of it.

Group Discussions. Before students get into groups to discuss their poems, tell them that effective speakers and listeners show the following behaviors.

Speakers

- make relevant contributions by staying on the topic

- make useful suggestions

- respond respectfully to others and give attention to what has been said

- ask questions to clarify and expand on each other's ideas

Listeners

- focus on the speaker's message by being prepared to listen and by being attentive

- interpret the speaker's message by using their knowledge of language, such as clue words that signal the organization of the speaker's ideas

- monitor their understanding by asking relevant questions

- provide effective verbal and non-verbal feedback, such as asking questions or making eye contact

---

- **Break the poem into sections that express complete thoughts.** Keep in mind that periods, exclamation points, question marks, and semicolons usually mark the end of a complete thought—just as they do in other types of writing.

- **Seek out a second opinion.** Discuss your poem with other students in a response group. Your purpose is to share interpretations. Since this is a group discussion with your peers, choice of language and words will be informal but should still be appropriate for school. Be sure to pay attention to each speaker, to ask appropriate questions, and to respond appropriately to the group's questions.

TIP Some **titles** of poems simply repeat all or part of the first line of the poem. Some titles, however, provide great hints about what a poem means.

ARLO AND JANIS, Newspaper Enterprise Association, Inc.

Find Examples of the Elements of Poetry

Nuts and Bolts Remember that when you analyze something, you examine each of its parts in order to understand how they work together as a whole. **In order to analyze a poem, you need to know the definitions of the elements, or parts, of a poem.** The chart on the next page contains the definitions of some important elements of poetry. To gain a better understanding of how the elements are used in the poem you have chosen, try answering the questions in the **Questions** column. For help, look at the information in the **Tips and Explanations** column. Take notes as you go. Keep in mind that not every element is important in every poem. If you cannot find a particular element or if an element does not seem to be important, do not worry about it. Go on with your analysis.

| KEY CONCEPT |

The Elements of Poetry		
Element	**Questions**	**Tips and Explanations**
Speaker: the voice talking in a poem—the narrator of the poem (not necessarily the poet)	Who is speaking in the poem? Is the speaker the poet or a character created by the poet?	If the poem uses the pronouns *I* or *we*, the speaker (not necessarily the poet) is talking about himself or herself. If the poem uses *he, she,* or *they,* the speaker is talking about someone else.
Diction: the poet's word choice	What key words does the poet use? How does the poet use them? Look up all the definitions of key words from the poem in the dictionary.	If, for example, the word *wall* appears in the poem, ask yourself whether the poet means an ordinary wall in a house or a barrier keeping people apart.
Figures of speech: words or phrases that are not meant to be taken literally	Does the poet use metaphors or similes to make imaginative comparisons?	A **metaphor** is a comparison that equates two unlike things. *Adults are giddy children when they run* compares adults and children. A **simile** is a comparison using *like* or *as.* For example, *The cameras flashed like bursts of lightning.*
Imagery: words or phrases that appeal to the senses	What images are contained in the poem? How do they affect the poem's meaning?	Poets create **images** when they use language that appeals to your sense of sight, hearing, smell, taste, or touch. For example, the poet describes a *prickly* cactus.
Rhyme: the repetition of sounds in accented parts of words in a poem—especially in words that come at the ends of lines	Does the poem contain rhyme? If so, what is the pattern, and how does it affect the theme and tone of the poem?	A pattern of rhyming syllables with a long e sound, like *deep, sleep, creep, keep,* might have a mournful tone that goes with a sad theme.
Rhythm: the repetition of sound patterns organized as meter or as free verse	What sound pattern does the poet use to organize the poem?	Poetry written in **meter** has a regular pattern of stressed and unstressed syllables in each line. For example, the name Eleănŏr Roósĕveĺt has a regular metric beat. Poetry written in **free verse** is free from strict patterns of stressed syllables and unstressed syllables. Free verse sounds very close to prose and to everyday spoken language. (See page 173 for more sound elements of poetry.)
Theme: the meaning, or main idea, that the poem reveals or suggests	Does the poem examine some common life experience or problem? Does it suggest solutions or answers?	A poem might comment on universal topics such as life, death, birth, love, or change.
Tone: the attitude the writer takes toward the audience, a subject, or a character	What is the speaker's attitude toward the subject of the poem?	A poem's speaker might, for example, seem angry or calm, sincere or sarcastic, or proud or ashamed.

Writing Workshop **171**

Meeting

INDIVIDUAL NEEDS

ENGLISH-LANGUAGE LEARNERS
General Strategies. Students who are learning English may find it challenging to analyze poetic language. To facilitate the task, have these students work with a poem that has been published in both English and their native language. Many books print the original poem and the English translation side by side. Encourage students to focus on the poem's overall meaning and how the poet uses the speaker, imagery, theme, and tone to convey that meaning.

Critical Thinking

Analysis. Langston Hughes published this poem at two different times under two different titles: "Dream Deferred" and "Harlem." This fact might provide a good opportunity for a class discussion on the importance of a poem's title. After students have read the poem, tell them about the alternate title and ask them to read the poem again. Then ask them which title they like better and why. Discuss whether or not the meaning of the poem changes when the title changes.

TECHNOLOGY TIP

Students who work on word processors may want to use the table-making application to create their analysis logs. This strategy will help students make revisions while keeping their documents neat and readable. Students may create and print tables with columns and rows labeled as shown, then handwrite the poem and the notes, or they may input the entire log.

YOUR TURN 4

Check that students have chosen poems that are suitable as the subjects of their literary analyses. As you assess students' work, look for appropriate interpretations of the elements reviewed on pages 170–171.

Below you will find the poem "Dream Deferred" by Langston Hughes and an analysis log that shows how one writer used the list of questions in the chart on the previous page to make notes about the poem. Notice how the writer made several guesses about the poem's theme as he filled out the analysis log.

ANALYSIS LOG

Poem: "Dream Deferred" by Langston Hughes	Notes
What happens to a dream deferred? Does it dry up like a raisin in the sun? Or fester like a sore— And then run? Does it stink like rotten meat? Or crust and sugar over— like a syrupy sweet? Maybe it just sags like a heavy load. Or does it explode?	**Line 1** DICTION: "dream" = hope, aspiration for the future. "deferred" = delayed temporarily, to accept politely someone else's wishes. Possible THEME: This is a question about the topic in the title. **Line 3** SIMILE and THEME: Deferred dream shrivels. **Line 4** SIMILE: Deferred dream becomes diseased, infected. **Line 6** SIMILE: Deferred dream stinks of decay. **Line 8** SIMILE: Deferred dream is sickeningly sweet. RHYME: Meat and sweet. **Line 9** Possible THEME: A guess about the topic, not the poet's question. SIMILE: Deferred dream is a burden; it makes the dreamer sag. **Line 11** METAPHOR: Deferred dream is a bomb that explodes and destroys. Possible THEME: A dream deferred explodes. This is the answer to the poet's question.

YOUR TURN 4 — Choosing, Responding to, and Analyzing a Poem

Review each of the prewriting steps on the previous pages. Choose a poem and write down your first thoughts about it. Then, make an analysis log like the one above to collect your notes about the literary elements used in the poem. Copy down the poem in the left-hand column and write your analysis in the right-hand column.

RESOURCES

Your Turn 4
Practice
- *Communications,* WS. p. 88

Writing
Practice
- *Communications,* WS. p. 89

Sound Elements in Poetry

Poets often rely not just on the *meanings* of words, but on the *sounds* of words to reinforce a poem's mood or tone. For example, short *b* and *d* sounds—which interrupt the flow of text when you say them out loud—can show that someone or something in a poem is interrupting or annoying. On the other hand, a long *e* sound can indicate a slow, relaxed mood. Read a poem out loud and listen to its sounds to think about how the sounds contribute to the overall meaning of the poem.

Here are definitions and examples of three sound elements often used in poetry:

- **Alliteration** is the repetition of beginning consonant sounds. For example: *Samuel sang silly songs.*
- **Assonance** is the repetition of vowel sounds. For example: *Don't sit on the kitten or he'll nip your middle.*
- **Onomatopoeia** is the association of the sound of a word to the meaning of the word. For example: *Cling-clang went the bell.*

PRACTICE

For each item below, identify (a) each word that contains any of the sound elements described above, (b) the type of sound elements, and (c) how you think the sound element adds to the meaning of the passage. Since you only have a few lines of each poem, also examine *the title* of each poem for hints about meaning. Put your answers on your own paper.

1. Not answering the telephone is a way of
      rejecting life,
   That it is our business to be bothered, is
      our business
   To cherish bores or boredom, be polite
   To lies and love and many-faceted fuzziness.
   　　　—Gwendolyn Brooks, "The *Chicago Defender*
   　　　Sends a Man to Little Rock"

2. Acceleration is their need:
   A mania keeps them on the move
   Until the toughest nerves are frayed.
   They are the prisoners of speed
   Who flee in what their hands have made.
   　　　—Theodore Roethke, "Highway: Michigan"

3. . . . Winter, you
   old clothes hamper, what mildew
   still molders inside you before March
   dribbles a bit, dries up, and is done for?
   　　　—Kathleen Spivack, "March 1st"

4. He gives his harness bells a shake
   To ask if there is some mistake.
   The only other sound's the sweep
   Of easy wind and downy flake.
   　　　—Robert Frost, "Stopping by Woods
   　　　on a Snowy Evening"

5. The buzz saw snarled and rattled in the
      yard
   And made dust and dropped stove-length
      sticks of wood,
   Sweet-scented stuff when the breeze drew
      across it.
   　　　—Robert Frost, "Out, Out—"

Reference Note

For more on **elements of poetry,** see page 171.

Sound Elements in Poetry

ANSWERS
Possible answers follow.

1. (a) *business, bothered, bores, boredom, be* (b) alliteration (c) The repeated *b* suggests an annoying phone ringing.

2. (a) *need, keeps, speed, flee; mania, frayed, they, made* (b) assonance (c) The long vowels suggest fast cars on the "Highway."

3. (a) *mildew, molders, March; dribbles, dries, done* (b) alliteration (c) The *m* suggests the dampness of "March 1st"; the *d* suggests crispness and drying.

4. (a) *sweep* and *easy* (b) assonance (c) The long *e* suggests the sound of the wind ". . . on a Snowy Evening."

5. (a) *buzz, snarled, rattled* (b) onomatopoeia (c) The words imitate the sound of a saw. (Note also the repeated *s* and *z* sounds throughout, even within words like *dust* and *breeze*, which may be identified as alliteration to suggest the sound of the saw.)

Find the Focus of Your Analysis

In Your Elements   How will you choose the elements you want to focus on in your analysis? Look over your analysis log to find the literary elements emphasized in the poem you have chosen. Choose the one or two most important elements, and plan to make them the basis of your analysis. Remember that you cannot cover every literary element the poem contains and that different literary elements are more important in different poems. For example, imagery and figures of speech may be the most important elements in one poem, while diction and tone might be all-important in another. The writer who created the analysis log for "Dream Deferred" would probably want to focus on diction and figures of speech, since these are the elements that seem to be emphasized in the poem.

Consider Your Purpose, Audience, and Tone

Why, Who, How   Do you have an **occasion** for writing an analysis of a poem? Perhaps your school's literary journal is focusing on analyses of poetry in the next issue, or perhaps your class will read aloud their analyses in a literary circle. **Your occasion will help to define your audience and the tone, the attitude or feeling, you use in your analysis.**

KEY CONCEPT →

At the very least, you have two **audiences** for your essay—your classmates and your teacher. Your **purpose** is to provide your audience with some insights on how the poet created meaning in the poem. To achieve this purpose, relate the poem's meaning to a common, human experience. Your **tone** should be somewhat formal and academic, so you should use formal, standard language.

Write Your Thesis

The Key Point   The thesis statement is the most important sentence in your essay—for both you and your audience—because it makes your task clear to you and your focus clear to your audience. To help you get started you can think of a thesis as a pattern. The pattern of a typical thesis for a poetry analysis can be written like this:

> In *title of poem*, *name of author* uses *key literary elements* to show (illustrate, make the point about) <u>the poem's theme</u>.

When you write your thesis statement, use the notes you made on your poem and follow the Thinking It Through steps on the next page. Keep in mind that you may need to revise your thesis statement as you write your analysis.

TEACHING TIP

Write Your Thesis
Clarify that **Thinking It Through** (on page 175) provides a formula for including all the key parts of a thesis statement. Explain, however, that there are many ways a central idea can be expressed. Provide guided practice by asking pairs to brainstorm ways they could restate the sample thesis in **Thinking It Through.** For instance:

> Keeping people from achieving their dreams can have destructive consequences. In "Dream Deferred," Langston Hughes uses diction and figures of speech to prove this point.

Encourage students to experiment with different variations of their thesis statement and select the strongest.

THINKING IT THROUGH ● Writing a Thesis

Use the following steps to develop your thesis statement.

▷ **STEP 1** Write the title of the poem.

"Dream Deferred"

▷ **STEP 2** Write the name of the poet.

Langston Hughes

▷ **STEP 3** Name the poetic element or elements on which your essay will focus.

diction and figures of speech

▷ **STEP 4** Write a statement of the poem's meaning or theme.

Keeping people from achieving their dreams can have destructive consequences.

▷ **STEP 5** Combine the results of steps 1 through 4 into your thesis statement.

In "Dream Deferred" Langston Hughes uses diction and figures of speech to make the point that keeping people from achieving their dreams can have destructive consequences.

Gather Supporting Evidence

The Poem as Witness   Now that you have written your thesis statement, you need to gather details from the poem, either in your own words or as quotations, that will support it. Here is a strategy you might use.

- **Review your notes and the poem** again, looking for details and quotations you can use to support or illustrate your thesis.

- **Write down the details or quotations** and the line numbers of each in the order they appear in the poem. When quoting poetry, remember to use slashes to indicate where the lines break. For example, the student analyzing "Dream Deferred" could write "Does it dry up / like a raisin in the sun?" (lines 2–3) is an example of the poet's use of a figure of speech.

- **Elaborate—write explanations** of how the details and quotations you have found support your thesis. For example, the student analyzing "Dream Deferred" could explain that in the quotation above, the image created by the simile suggests that a deferred dream shrivels up as its juices evaporate.

Meeting INDIVIDUAL NEEDS

STUDENTS WITH SPECIAL NEEDS
Students who have trouble concentrating in class will be more likely to succeed if the assignment is broken into small increments. This is especially important with analysis assignments, such as this one, that can require considerable work at home. Establish a schedule that students can follow to complete each step in the writing process.

TEACHING TIP

Gather Supporting Evidence
To help students evaluate their evidence, suggest that they use index cards to keep track of details or quotations, writing only one detail per card. Then students may consider the information on each card against their thesis to evaluate which details offer the strongest support. Encourage students to select the three cards that lend the strongest support to their thesis and plan to use these as main points in their essays.

The following chart shows how the student writing about "Dream Deferred" gathered details and quotations that support his thesis.

Element	Detail or Quotation	Explanation
Diction	"dream", line 1 "deferred", line 1	Two words together are the subject of the whole poem. "Dream" means hope for the future—something really important. "Deferred" means put off or postponed—suggests temporary. It also means that someone defers (gives in to) what someone else wants.
Simile	Four similes are questions: Does a deferred dream "dry up like a raisin" lines 2–3 "fester like a sore" line 4 "stink like rotten meat" line 6 "crust and sugar over like a syrupy sweet" lines 7–8 One simile is a guess: "sags like a heavy load" lines 9–10	The similes seem to say that if a dream is postponed for a long time, it shrivels, gets infected, rots and stinks, or spoils and gets a nasty crust on it. In the last simile it is as if, put off time after time, the dream becomes a heavy burden on the back of the dreamer.
Metaphor	"Or does it explode?" line 11	A deferred dream is like a bomb. Finally, it explodes. The shift in figure of speech and to italics make this phrase look like the right answer to the poet's question. This idea fits the theme of destructive consequences.

Make a chart like the one above, and fill it with details, quotations, and explanations that support your thesis.

Organize Your Analysis

Putting Things in Order   The way you organize your ideas depends on the number of poetic elements you discuss. If, for example, you discuss diction and figures of speech, you might arrange your ideas and support by **order of importance**. If you intend to focus on a single element, you would probably want to stick to the order in which the elements appear in the poem. Regardless of the order you choose, you must make sure that the ideas in your analysis follow a **logical progression**.

176   Exposition: Analyzing a Poem

TEACHING TIP

Organize Your Analysis

To help students look at different ways of organizing their essays, have them work collaboratively in groups of two or three to discuss which order is most effective for their essays. Explain that often hearing other people's views and then explaining their own views helps to clarify their thinking. Be sure students address at least two different orders before deciding on one.

The student analyzing "Dream Deferred" created the following organizational map of his thesis, his main supporting ideas, and some supporting details.

YOUR TURN 5 **Writing a Thesis, Gathering Support, and Organizing**

Now it is your turn to write. Start by following the instructions for choosing a poem on page 168. Then, go over each of the prewriting steps on the previous pages. Make sure to write your thesis, gather and explain your supporting evidence, and organize your essay using a map like the one above.

YOUR TURN 5

Check their drafts to be sure students have established an appropriate working thesis and sufficient support. You may need to offer guidance as students map out the order in which they will present their information.

Writing Workshop **177**

Quotation for the Day

"A writer's problem does not change . . . . It is always how to write truly and, having found what is true, to project it in such a way that it becomes a part of the experience of the person who reads it."

(Ernest Hemingway, 1899–1961, American novelist and winner of the 1954 Nobel Prize in Literature)

Ask students to freewrite about the ways a literary analysis of a poem can [1] get at the work's truth and [2] become a part of the reader's experience. Encourage students to keep these two points in mind as they write their essays.

Cooperative Learning

Writing Groups. Organize students into peer writing groups to help them evaluate their plans and drafts. Have students take turns telling the title and main idea of the poem they will analyze. The other members of the group can ask questions about the writer's intentions, using the Framework as a guide. Encourage students to make revisions to their prewriting plans based on this activity.

YOUR TURN 6

Students can assess their work by creating a checklist that includes the headings and bulleted items in the Framework. Guide students to check off each item against their first drafts. Then go over the lists with students and discuss areas where they are having difficulty.

Analysis of a Poem

Framework	Directions and Explanations

Introduction
- Relate the poem's meaning to a common, human experience.
- Introduce the title and author.
- State your thesis.

Body
- Discuss the first key poetic element. Provide support and elaboration.
- Discuss the second key poetic element, and so on.

Conclusion
- Remind readers of your thesis and summarize.

Seize Your Audience's Interest Relate the meaning of the poem to experiences people have in common. The Writer's Model asks what life would be worth without dreams and hope.

Provide Your Readers with Background If either the poet or the subject of the poem are unfamiliar to readers, you might need to provide more background on the poet or the poem.

Write a Clear Thesis Statement Make sure you tell readers what the rest of the essay will show them by stating a main idea about the poem and listing the key element or elements that relate to that main idea.

Discuss the Poem's Key Elements Start at the beginning of the poem and walk your readers through your analysis. Clearly state which key terms—such as *diction* and *figure of speech*—you are analyzing. Use details or quotations from the poem and expand or elaborate on them to explain their meaning.

Close Your Analysis Restate your thesis and summarize your main points. Leave your readers with something to think about by showing them how the poem relates to broader themes in life.

YOUR TURN 6 Writing a First Draft

Using the framework and directions and explanations above, write the first draft of your analysis of a poem. Also, read the Writer's Model on the next page to see a sample analysis.

RESOURCES

Writing
Writing Prompts
- *Communications,* TP. 41, WS. p. 91

Your Turn 6
Practice
- *Communications,* TP. 42, WS. p. 92

A Writer's Model

The following short essay is a final draft. It closely follows the framework on the previous page.

Diction and Figures of Speech in "Dream Deferred"

What is life worth without dreams and the hope that those dreams can come true someday? What happens when the achievement of a dream is postponed—again and again? Langston Hughes answers these questions in a short poem called "Dream Deferred" by using diction and figures of speech to make the point that keeping people from achieving their dreams can have destructive consequences.

Hughes starts with a question to get his readers thinking about his message: "What happens to a dream deferred?"(line 1). His diction here is important. He uses the word "dream" to mean a hope for or vision of a better future. He chooses the word "defer" for its two meanings. It can mean "to put something off until some time in the future." Since most dreamers would not postpone their own dreams, someone else must have deferred the dream to which the speaker refers. "Defer" can also mean "to give in to what someone else wants." Hughes uses the word in both ways. The dream is postponed by someone else, but the dreamer gives in to the delay. The question then is, how long will the dreamer accept the postponement of his or her dream?

In the next part of the poem, Hughes answers the question about what happens to deferred dreams with a series of similes written as questions. The first of these asks if a deferred dream dries up "like a raisin in the sun" (line 3). The image of the dried and wrinkled raisin contrasts with the fat, sweet, and juicy grape the dream once was, before the dream dried up. The images created by the following three similes are worse. Does the deferred dream "fester like a sore— / And then run?" (lines 4–5) or "stink like rotten meat?" (line 6) or "crust and sugar over— / like a syrupy sweet?" (lines 7–8)? The images in these similes seem to say that if a dream is postponed, it rots or spoils or infects the dreamer. The last simile is not a question but a guess. "Maybe" a deferred dream "just sags / like a heavy load." (lines 9–10). This simile makes the

(continued)

INTRODUCTION

Author
Title
Thesis

BODY

First key poetic
element: diction

Second key poetic
element: similes

Connecting Reading and Writing

Before students read **A Writer's Model**, have them re-read page 165 of the Reading Workshop to review the criteria, given in **Your Turn 3,** for evaluating an author's use of textual support. As students read **A Writer's Model,** they should note the seamless presentation of textual support. Point out how partial quotations are smoothly folded into new, grammatically correct sentences. In addition, discuss how the paraphrases and elaboration often include figurative language that echoes the language in Hughes's poem.

Critical Thinking

Evaluation. Point out that **A Writer's Model** analyzes the poem "Dream Deferred." Ask students if this very same essay would work if the writer were analyzing the poem under its alternate title, "Harlem." Have them explain their reasoning.

(continued)

deferred dream seem like a heavy burden the dreamer carries on his back, making him or her sag. All of these similes make it seem that a deferred dream becomes something terrible.

Third key poetic element: metaphor

In the last line, Hughes uses another figure of speech, a metaphor—"Or does it explode?" (line 11)—to address his message. He emphasizes the metaphor even more by using different print from the rest of the poem. He seems to be saying that this is exactly what happens: A deferred dream is a bomb that finally explodes. He might also mean that it is not the dream, but the dreamer that explodes—in anger.

CONCLUSION

Just what does happen when the achievement of a dream is postponed again and again? Hughes uses diction and figures of speech to tell his readers what might happen to a deferred dream. The word "deferred" hints that the dreamer might not always accept the postponement of his or her dream.

Restatement of thesis

The five similes seem to say that only the dreamer is hurt. In the final metaphor, the deferred dream is a bomb that will eventually explode and hurt a lot of people.

ARLO AND JANIS, Newspaper Enterprise Association, Inc.

A Student's Model

The following passages are excerpted from an analysis of a poem written by Mayra Deloa, a student at South Garland High School in Garland, Texas. Notice how the writer uses details, quotations, and elaboration to support her analysis of symbolism in the poem.

The Use of Symbolism in Dorothy Parker's "Solace"

"Solace," by Dorothy Parker, is a short poem about a person who encounters circumstances of a dreadful nature. This person witnesses three incidents in which a life is shattered, and in each case, is told that the loss is not so terrible because many more of those lives exist. With the author's specific use of diction, structure, parallelism, irony, and symbolism, this poem emerges into a metaphorical tale about the coldness and the negligence, rather than the sympathy and the consolation, that many people display during a great misfortune. . . .

The wilting rose, the dying bird, and the abandoned girl all symbolize something that was once beautiful and full of life that dies in some sense. The poet's point is that fate is not fair, nor is it particular, whether a plant, an animal, or a human being. Another point the author makes with these symbols is that comfort and solace cannot be found in others. When the rose fades, "they" say, "What need to care . . .?" (line 4). After the girl's lover flees, "they" remark, "There's many another lad" (line 12). This is not the kind of compassion that the girl is seeking. When a life is lost or suffering, a person wants someone to offer condolences, not insensitivity. Aside from this, the narrator of the poem even turns an uncaring ear to the teller of the woe, stating "I did not answer them" (line 6). Does the narrator honestly not care about the deaths and the suffering, or does the narrator try to turn off feelings to keep from hurting, as so many people often do? When an event occurs that wounds to the core, people often hide their emotions to look strong and courageous. In this poem, however, the narrator looks away from the insensitivity that dismisses tragedy. . . .

Author and title

Thesis

Explanation of symbolism

Connecting to Reading and Writing

Have students notice how the author of **A Student's Model** handled references to the poem. Remind students that it will be important for them to make clear to readers when they are quoting lines from the poem being analyzed.

Critical Thinking

Synthesis. To help students focus on the salient features of this model, have them work in pairs to come up with three compliments for the author of the analysis. Also, ask them to identify one question they wish they could ask the writer and to brainstorm possible replies.

Revising

Evaluate and Revise Your Draft

Rework and Refine   To make your literary analysis as clear, precise, and effective as it can be, you need to read your paper slowly and thoroughly at least two times. You should work collaboratively with your peers to read first for content and organization. During your second reading, you should be concerned with evaluating and revising style.

▶ First Reading: **Content and Organization**   The following chart will help you evaluate and revise your literary analysis. Answer the questions in the first column. If you do not know how to answer a particular question, look at the tips in the second column. If you need to make changes in your essay, look at the third column for suggestions.

Analysis of a Poem: Content and Organization Guidelines for Peer and Self-Evaluation

Evaluation Questions	Tips	Revision Techniques
❶ Are the author and title named in the introduction?	**Highlight** the title and the author. If the title or author is not introduced, revise.	**Add** a sentence or phrase naming the author and the title.
❷ Does the introduction have a clear thesis? Are key poetic elements introduced?	**Underline** the thesis statement. **Circle** the poetic elements introduced by the thesis. If you cannot find anything to circle, revise.	**Add** a sentence or a phrase introducing the key poetic elements.
❸ Is the main idea of each body paragraph clear and does it support the thesis?	**Bracket** the key poetic element, such as *diction* or *figure of speech*, that is discussed in each body paragraph. If no key terms are present, revise.	**Revise** the body paragraphs so that each discusses a literary element using key terms.
❹ Is the main idea of each body paragraph well supported with evidence and explanations?	**Draw a box** around each supporting quotation or detail and **a wavy line** under elaborations. If you don't find a box and one wavy line in each paragraph, revise.	**Add** details or quotations. **Elaborate** on each detail or quotation with commentary.
❺ Does the conclusion effectively remind readers of the thesis and bring the essay to a close?	**Highlight** the sentence in the conclusion that restates the thesis. If there is none, revise.	**Add** a sentence restating the thesis. **Add** a sentence that relates the poem to human experience.

ONE WRITER'S REVISIONS   After looking at how one writer revised the introductory paragraph of the essay on page 179, answer the questions that follow.

> What happens when the achievement of a dream is post-
> poned—again and again? ~~These questions~~ *Langston Hughes answers* ~~are the subject of~~
> ~~my~~ *in a short* ~~poem.~~ *called "Dream Deferred" by using diction and* ~~The poem makes~~ the point that keeping people from *figures of speech to make*
> achieving their dreams can have destructive consequences.

add/delete

delete/add/delete/add

Analyzing the Revision Process

1. What missing information did the writer add to the third sentence? How does this revision improve the introduction?

2. How did the writer improve the thesis statement?

PEER REVIEW

Ask a classmate to read your paper and answer the following questions.

1. What are the strong points of the essay? Explain why.

2. What is the most important sentence in the essay? Why?

YOUR TURN 7   Focusing on Content and Organization

Revise the content and organization of your essay using the guidelines on the previous page and the example revisions shown above.

▶ **Second Reading: Style**   You first concentrated on content and organization. In your second reading, pay attention to your style and its impact on your message. One style mistake many writers of literary analyses make is that they write sentences with more words than they need. Work collaboratively to use the following guidelines to revise wordy sentences.

Style Guidelines

Evaluation Question	▶ Tip	▶ Revision Technique
Do any of my sentences contain clauses that could be reduced to words or phrases?	**Highlight** clauses that begin with the following words: *which is, which are, that is, that are, who is, who are.*	**Reduce** half of these clauses to a participle or a participial phrase by **deleting** the pronouns *who, which,* or *that* and the *be* verb. If necessary, **rearrange** the remaining words.

Writing Workshop   **183**

Timesaver

Suggest that students include all the revision marks and highlights suggested by the chart on their revised drafts. These marks will allow you to skim students' revisions quickly to see that they followed the content and organization guidelines.

Analyzing the Revision Process
ANSWERS

1. The writer added the title of the poem. The revision clarifies the subject of the analysis.

2. The writer added a direct reference to the literary elements that support the thesis statement. By introducing the main literary elements explored in the analysis, the revised thesis provides a more solid starting point for the reader.

TEACHING TIP

Evaluating and Revising

Some students may benefit from reading their papers aloud before they begin to revise. Doing so will help them locate problems with sentence structure and flow, transitional expressions, and so on.

YOUR TURN 7

Make sure that students identify appropriate places to add necessary details and elaboration. Check also that students add transitions to link related ideas and revise sentences as needed to make the revisions read smoothly.

Revising Wordy Sentences

One means of reducing wordiness is to use gerunds. Using the following examples, demonstrate for students how to revise a sentence by replacing clauses with gerunds and then ask that students write two or three sentences of their own using gerunds.

1. The fact that mother had washed the dishes helped us.
   Rev: Mother's washing the dishes helped us.

2. That she called her sister was important.
   Rev: Calling her sister was important.

3. Would you mind it if I asked you how to make your casserole?
   Rev: Would you mind my asking how to make your casserole?

4. It now seems easy to write a sentence that would use a gerund or two.
   Rev: Writing a sentence using a gerund or two seems easy.

Analyzing the Revision Process

ANSWERS

1. The adjective clause "that are written as questions" can be rewritten more concisely as the participial phrase "written as questions."

2. *Deferred* is now placed directly before the noun it modifies, which makes the sentence tighter.

YOUR TURN 8

Check that students have eliminated unnecessary relative clauses, placed adjectives in front of the words they modify, and cut excess verbiage. You might circle wordy sentences that students have overlooked.

Sentences

Revising Wordy Sentences

Because you want to share your insights with your audience, be sure you are concise and clear. Wordiness can make readers want to quit. Writing that gets directly to the point, however, encourages readers to keep reading.

ONE WRITER'S REVISIONS Here is how the writer of the model on page 179 used the Style Guidelines on page 183 to revise wordy sentences.

BEFORE REVISION

two clauses beginning with *that*

In the next part of the poem, Hughes answers the question about what happens to deferred dreams with a series of similes that are written as questions. The first of these asks if a dream that is deferred dries up "like a raisin in the sun."

AFTER REVISION

delete relative pronouns and *be* verbs

rearrange

In the next part of the poem, Hughes answers the question about what happens to deferred dreams with a series of similes written as questions. The first of these asks if a deferred dream dries up "like a raisin in the sun."

Reference Note

For more on **revising wordy sentences,** see page 341. For more on **participles** and **participial phrases,** see pages 449 and 451.

Analyzing the Revision Process

1. Why do you think the writer cut *that are* from the first sentence?

2. What is the effect of moving the word *deferred*?

YOUR TURN 8 **Revising Wordy Sentences in Your Own Paper**

Use the guidelines above to examine your literary analysis for wordy sentences. Use the example above as a model, and revise any wordy sentences you find.

RESOURCES

Focus on Sentences
Practice
- *Communications,* WS. p. 96

Publishing

Proofread Your Analysis

The Final Touch You need to proofread or **edit** your paper carefully to spot and eliminate any errors in grammar, spelling, and punctuation that will weaken it. A couple of mistakes in punctuating quotations can be especially damaging to a literary analysis.

Reference Note

For **proofreading guidelines,** see page 13. For more on **using quotation marks,** see page 686.

Grammar Link

Using and Punctuating Quotations

Correctly punctuated quotations are an important part of every essay that analyzes a poem. First, remember that you use quotation marks when you quote the *exact words* of the author. Then, consult the following guidelines for using quotation marks with other punctuation marks.

■ **Put quotation marks at the beginning and the end of the quotation.**

Example:
Anne Sexton begins, **"**They sit in a row.**"**

■ **Put periods and commas inside the closing quotation marks.**

Example:
Maya Angelou wrote the line **"**You're all that I can call my own**."**

■ **Put question marks and exclamation marks inside the closing quotation marks** *if they are part of the quotation.* Colons and semicolons go outside the quotation marks.

Examples:
Emily Dickinson asked, **"**You may have met him—did you not**?"**

Have you read Alice Walker's poem that begins **"**They were women then**"?**

■ **When you quote more than one line of poetry, use a slash** (/) **with a space before and after it to show where one line stops and the next starts.**

Example:
Emily Dickinson wrote, **"**There is no frigate like a book / To take us lands away.**"**

PRACTICE

Rewrite each of the following sentences on your own paper. Add quotation marks and other punctuation marks where necessary.

1. He memorized the poem that begins, Shall I compare thee to a summer's day?

2. The first words of Elizabeth Barrett Browning's poem are How do I love thee?

3. Wherefore art thou, Romeo might be one of the most often misunderstood lines in Shakespeare.

4. My favorite two lines of poetry are these by Shakespeare: All the world's a stage, And all the men and women merely players.

5. The speaker in Frost's poem says, I took the one less traveled by, And that has made all the difference.

Quotation for the Day

"Punctuation marks are a part of the vocabulary of a civilization; a misunderstanding can be created or erased by them.**"**

(Karen Elizabeth Gordon, writer)

After students discuss what the quotation means, ask them to describe a misunderstanding that might result from incorrect use of quotation marks. [Possible answer: Readers might not realize where a line cited from the poem begins or ends.]

Grammar Link

Using and Punctuating Quotations

ANSWERS

1. He memorized the poem that begins, "Shall I compare thee to a summer's day?"

2. The first words of Elizabeth Barrett Browning's poem are "How do I love thee?"

3. "Wherefore art thou, Romeo?" might be one of the most often misunderstood lines in Shakespeare.

4. My favorite two lines of poetry are these by Shakespeare: "All the world's a stage, / And all the men and women merely players."

5. The speaker in Frost's poem says, "I took the one less traveled by, / And that has made all the difference."

RESOURCES

Publishing
Extension
■ *Designing Your Writing*
Grammar Link
Practice
■ *Communications,* WS. p. 97

Designing Your Writing

Formatting Your Paper When you write a formal paper, such as an analysis of literature, it is important to choose a design that maximizes legibility. You want to make it easy for your readers to focus on the *ideas* in your paper, not the type. Illegible text will frustrate your readers and perhaps even make them quit reading. Below are some general guidelines to help you. Be sure to find out if your teacher has more specific formatting guidelines for you to follow.

- **Line length and margins.** Text in a long, skinny column that extends to the edges of the paper is difficult to read. To avoid these problems, make sure the margins on your paper are about one inch wide.

- **Type size or letter size.** If you are writing your essay by hand, do not write too small or too large. If you are typing on a computer, choose a standard type size—anywhere from 10 to 12 points—and a legible font such as Times or Palatino.

- **Leading or spacing.** Leading (rhymes with *heading*) is the amount of white space *between* lines of text. The accepted standard for school papers is double-spaced text.

Reference Note

For more on **document design,** see page 806 in the Quick Reference Handbook.

TECHNOLOGY TIP

To help students keep track of successive drafts, suggest they name their files according to the date and time of completion. Encourage students to e-mail their final electronic drafts to peers for feedback and last minute revision tips. *If students choose to submit their work to online literary magazines, you need to be aware that Internet resources are sometimes public forums, and their content can be unpredictable.*

Check students' final papers for errors and ascertain that students have published their work in appropriate venues. Sample answers to the reflective questions follow:

- Some students may observe that writing an analysis of a poem reveals layers of meaning that were not apparent upon first reading.

- Students may say that they learned writing techniques such as reducing wordiness and using quotations correctly.

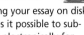

COMPUTER TIP

Storing your essay on disk makes it possible to submit it electronically for publishing.

PORTFOLIO

Publish Your Analysis

Sharing Your Work Here are some suggestions on how you might share your literary analysis with a larger audience.

- Ask a writer to read and critique your essay.
- Submit your essay to your school's literary magazine.

Reflect on Your Analysis

Relive the Experience Write brief responses to the following questions to reflect on what you have learned in this workshop.

- How did writing this paper change your feelings about the poem?
- What new techniques or ideas about writing did you learn?

  If you include your essay in a portfolio, attach your responses.

Wrap It Up

Metacognition. Ask students to think about their own writing processes and to respond to the following questions:

1. What steps did you take to meet your hardest challenge?

2. Will meeting this challenge make it easier for you to write other kinds of essays? Explain.

 Proofreading, Publishing, and Reflecting

Be sure to proofread your essay carefully, think about publishing options, and answer the reflective questions.

Taking the Essay Part of a Writing Test

You have seen it before: the dreaded essay-writing portion of an English test. The reading passage of the test is the story of a boy who goes to great lengths to overcome his paralyzing fear of water. Once you finish reading the selection, you come to this prompt:

A wise person once said *Courage is a mastery of fear—not the absence of fear.* Write an essay explaining what you think this quotation means. You may use examples from the reading selection, real life, books, movies, music, or television to illustrate and support your ideas.

How do you even start your prewriting process? One method you can use to generate ideas for writing is to ask and answer the **5W-How? questions,** as shown in the Thinking It Through steps below.

THINKING IT THROUGH — **Writing an Essay on an English Test**

Here is a prewriting strategy to generate ideas to answer the sample prompt.

▶ **STEP 1** Read and take note of important words in the prompt. Courage, mastery, and fear are important words in the question.

▶ **STEP 2** Restate the prompt in your own words by asking yourself *What am I being asked to explain or show?* I am being asked to explain the relationship between courage and fear.

▶ **STEP 3** Come up with your own interpretation of the quotation you are being asked to explain by asking yourself what you think the quotation means. The quotation means that all people have fears, but courageous people are the ones who face and work through their fears.

▶ **STEP 4** Come up with examples to support your interpretation by asking as many *5W-How?* questions—*Who? What? When? Where? Why? How?*—as you can about the important words in the prompt. Who is a courageous person I know? What are some examples I have seen of courage? When have I seen courage demonstrated? Where have I seen courageous people? Why did the wise person say "Courage is a mastery of fear"? How are courage and fear related?

▶ **STEP 5** Use your answers to the *5W-How?* questions as the first step in your prewriting process and as a springboard to writing your essay. After my sister was thrown off a horse, I watched her climb right back on. I saw a video documentary on people who overcome their fear of airplanes and learn how to fly. I guess courageous people really do have to master their fears.

Cooperative Learning

5W-How? Questions. Divide students into six groups, each group being responsible for answering one of the *5W-How?* questions. Challenge each group to compose as many questions for their group as possible. During class sharing time, engage students in a discussion of which questions might form the best foundation for a response to the prompt.

RESOURCES

Test Taking
Practice
■ *Communications*, WS. p. 98

Critical Thinking

Evaluation. Gather a collection of poems that represent some of the following forms: haiku, sonnet, ode, ballad, free verse, lyric, and limerick. Guide students in looking at several examples of each kind to determine key features and characteristics. Make a chart showing the key features for each type of poem. As students work on the **Connections to Literature** task, invite them to use the examples as models and the charts as self-evaluation tools to be sure they are including the important characteristics of the form of poetry they choose to create.

Writing a Poem

Here are a few guidelines to follow when writing a poem of your own. Keep in mind that poetry is the art of compact or compressed expression; try to pack as much meaning into as few words as possible. Do not simply *describe* a subject to readers; make readers *experience* the subject by using language that stirs their imaginations.

Finding a Subject: Good Verse Hunting   You can choose just about anything as the subject of a poem—a friend, a place, or an experience you remember vividly. The writer of the following poem chose *heat* as her subject.

Title and subject	**Heat** by H. D.
Image of wind	O wind, rend open the heat, cut apart the heat, rend it to tatters.
Image of fruit Image of thick air Alliteration	Fruit cannot drop through this thick air— fruit cannot fall into heat that presses up and blunts the points of pears and rounds the grapes.
Image of wind as plow	Cut the heat— plow through it, turning it on either side of your path.

Making Associations: Put Two and Two Together   Now you need to decide what you want to say about the subject of your poem. One good way to generate ideas is to do some **free association.** Without stopping, freely write down any thoughts that come to mind when you think about your subject. The author of "Heat" associates the concept of heat with wind, fruit, and air.

Creating Imagery: Put It in Sensurround   The next step is to turn your free associations into images you can use in your poem. The images in your poem can be **literal**—*The warm rain soaks my hair.* The images can also be **figurative**—metaphors or similes, for example, as in *Spotted fawn, spring's youngest child.* Your images should connect to the five senses—how things look, taste, smell, feel, or sound.

The poem "Heat" captures the force of heat in images, such as the "thick air" that "presses up and blunts" to suggest the solidity and force of heat.

Reference Note

For more on **imagery** and **figurative language,** see page 171.

Writing Your Poem: Make Like Shakespeare   There are many different forms of poetry. "Heat" is a **free verse** poem—a poem without a regular metrical pattern. Whether or not you choose to write a free verse poem, you should draw on the same elements of poetry you used on page 171 to analyze a poem. You should carefully select elements of poetry which will enhance the subject of your poem. For example, "Heat" relies heavily on imagery.

As you begin to put together ideas, images, and other elements, you should experiment. Try arranging words, phrases, or whole ideas one way, and then try them another way. As you work and rework the elements of your poem, focus on the senses you want readers to use to experience the poem—sight, hearing, taste, touch, and smell.

Polishing Your Poem: Make It Glow
Once you have written a first draft, you should revise your poem to make it more appealing to the imagination. To figure out where you need to revise, try reading your poem aloud to yourself or to friends. If, in reading, you trip across places that do not feel right, think of ways to revise. To the right are a few strategies for revision.

- **Change a descriptive word or phrase to a simile or a metaphor.** An *agonizingly slow pace* could become *like the pace of a slimy snail,* for example.

- **Add or improve images by using vivid words that appeal to the senses.** For example, the *smell of the dump* could become the *sickening stench of the dump.*

- **Change words within a line to create alliteration.** *The crooked road to my aching heart* could become *The winding way to my heavy heart.*

Publishing a Poem: Share It with the World   Since a poem does not mean much without an audience to appreciate it, try sharing your poetry in one of the following ways.

- Post your poem to a poetry magazine on the Internet.

- Publish your poem in a literary journal.

- Organize a poetry swap with fellow poets. Pass around your poems, and read and discuss them as a group.

YOUR TURN 10 Writing a Poem

Now it is your turn to write your very own poem. Remember to
- find a subject about which you have feelings
- make associations
- create imagery
- write a first draft
- revise, polish, and publish your poem

When you finish your poem, you may want to organize a poetry reading with your classmates to share your results.

Meeting INDIVIDUAL NEEDS

MODALITY
Auditory Learners. To help auditory learners articulate their ideas, have them use a tape recorder to record their free associations. They can use the recording to transcribe their spoken words into written form, which they can then shape into poetry. After students have completed drafts, they can record their poems and use the playback function to help them revise and polish.

YOUR TURN 10

In assessing students' work, check that students have used poetic elements such as alliteration, assonance, and metaphors. Also, check that students have supported their theme with imagery and figurative language.

OBJECTIVES

- To prepare and practice delivering a poetry reading
- To respond to and evaluate a poetry reading

Quotation for the Day

"It is a rule in eloquence, that the moment the orator loses command of his audience, the audience commands him."

(Ralph Waldo Emerson, 1803–1882, American lecturer, essayist, and poet)

Have students brainstorm ways that an orator might "command" an audience. Then discuss ways that the speaker might lose command and what might result from such a loss. For example, an orator might speak in a monotone that bores the audience so much they stop listening. Ask students to discuss the speaking styles of commanding orators they have seen in real life, in movies, or on television, or that they have heard on audiocassette or on the radio. (Students might recall speeches by political figures, humorous routines by comics, and dramatic monologues by actors.)

WHAT'S AHEAD?

In this section you will learn to

- prepare and practice delivering a poetry reading
- respond to and evaluate a poetry reading

Presenting and Responding to a Poetry Reading

Most people experience poetry on pages in a book, but poetry was meant to be read aloud to an appreciative audience. Long before writing became a common means of communication, oral recitation was the main way that people shared poems and stories with one another. Today, the tradition of oral poetry continues at poetry readings in places like libraries and bookstores and at oral interpretation contests sponsored by schools. In this workshop you will have the chance to improve skills you would use as a speaker and listener at a poetry reading.

Prepare for a Poetry Reading

Getting Ready To prepare to recite a poem at a poetry reading, start by selecting a poem that you like. Whether the poem is the work of a famous author or one of your own, choose one that gives you the opportunity to be creative with your tone of voice and other presentation techniques. Remember also to pick a poem that fits the time limits you are given. Once you have picked a poem, work on preparing it for a reading by following the steps below.

- **Study the poem for its meaning.** Learn all you can about the **speaker** of the poem and the speaker's attitude toward himself or herself, toward the poem's subject, and toward the audience. Your study of the speaker will tell you what **tone** to take in your reading. Should it be happy or sad? serious or humorous? sincere or sarcastic?

- **Make a copy of the poem to help you prepare.** Mark the parts you need to emphasize, the places you need to pause, and the parts that need to be read slowly or quickly. Remember not to stop at the end of lines of poetry unless a punctuation mark stops you.

RESOURCES

Focus on Speaking and Listening Practice

- *Media Literacy and Communication Skills*
  —*Support and Practice,* Ch. 5
  —*A How-to Handbook*

Teaching Notes

- *Media Literacy and Communication Skills*
  —*A Teacher's Guide,* Ch. 5

- **Decide what impression you want to leave with your audience.** Focus your presentation on the most important aspect of your poem—the one that you think will make the strongest impression.

Practicing for a Poetry Reading

Rehearsal Time   Here are some ways you can make your presentation of a poem more enjoyable for yourself and your audience.

- **Get familiar with your poem.** You do not need to memorize your poem completely. You do, however, need to know it well enough that you can maintain eye contact with your audience while you are speaking. The better you understand your poem, the easier it will be to remember.

- **Practice reading your poem into a tape recorder and to a practice audience.** Play each reading back and critique yourself. At least once before you present your poem, have a dress rehearsal. Read it to one or more family members or friends and ask for ways you might improve your presentation. You can stand relatively still or you can move around, but you should not lose contact with the practice audience. You must make them feel you are speaking directly to them.

Listening to a Poetry Reading

All Ears   When you listen to a poetry reading, your **purpose** is to listen in order to **enjoy** and **appreciate,** just as you listen to music or the dialogue in a movie. The first rule of good listening is, of course, to concentrate and listen carefully. Use the strategies below to listen effectively and appreciatively to poetry.

- **As you listen, try to picture what you are hearing.** Close your eyes if it helps you picture what the words you are hearing describe.

- **Note the rhyme, the rhythm and the sounds of the language.** Notice the rhythm, or motion, you feel when you hear the poem. For example, the rhythm of words in a poem about the ocean may be steady like waves lapping against the shore. Listen also for sounds in the poem. Do bees buzz? Does the snow sweep with repeated *s* sounds? The language of good poetry has both beauty and power. Listen for these qualities just as you do when you listen to music.

- **Pay attention to the reader's style—voice, movement, and contact with the audience.** Every poem has a speaker. The reader should become the speaker of the poem. Is the reader's style right for the poem? For example, if the speaker of the poem is a mouse, the reader might use a high-pitched, hurried tone of voice.

Focus on Speaking and Listening   **191**

TEACHING TIP

Practicing for a Poetry Reading
Suggest that students who have difficulty with public speaking select poems that combine a fixed meter with end rhyme. The repetitive structure will simplify the interpretive aspect of the presentation. Students will also find it easier to learn, and perhaps memorize, poems of this nature.

TEACHING TIP

Listening to a Poetry Reading
As the class listens, students will be asked to evaluate each presentation (see page 192). Before beginning the presentations, remind students that listening is not a passive activity; they must be thinking all the time. Perhaps it would help them to learn how to listen if you lead the class in a discussion of the evaluation criteria listed on page 192. Challenge students to articulate their ideas of a presentation that might earn a perfect score. Then ask them what kinds of presentation flaws might lower that score. Urge presenters to keep these criteria in mind as they recite their poems.

Critical Thinking

Evaluation. To give students practice using their evaluation skills, direct them toward artistic performances such as poetry readings; authors' book readings; or one-person plays at a local library, university, bookshop, or other public venue. Using the criteria on p. 192, ask students to write an evaluation of the event they attend. Students may share their evaluations with the class. Notify parents or guardians prior to this assignment.

YOUR TURN 11

To help assess students' presentation skills, compare the scores they receive with those of other group members. In this way, the relative merit of their presentations should be more obvious. To assess evaluation skills, look for students whose average scores differ significantly from those of their group members for any given presentation. Discuss students' rationales to see if their scoring is reasonable and justifiable.

Wrap It Up

Metacognition. Use the following questions to help students reflect on poetry reading.

1. What new speaking techniques did you learn from presenting your poem?
2. What new oration techniques did you learn by listening to other students present?
3. How might these skills apply to your life?

TIP You can use the scale below to rate each item in the chart and to rate the overall average score.

TIP Use audience feedback to **evaluate** the effectiveness of your poetry reading and to **set goals** for future presentations.

TIP Try to attend a professional poetry reading. Public libraries often offer this type of presentation. As you listen to these professional readings, you can use these criteria to analyze, appreciate, and evaluate the performances.

Evaluating a Poetry Reading

Making the Grade   Giving and receiving feedback to a poetry reading can help you sharpen your listening and presentation skills. Work with other students to evaluate poetry readings by filling out a chart like the one below. After all ratings have been given, add up the numbers and divide the total by six to find the average score.

Scale: 1—poor presentation   4—good
2—improvement needed   5—excellent
3—fair

Criteria	Rating
The reader leaves the audience with an impression of the poem by emphasizing the effects of rhyme, imagery, and language.	
The reader's tone of voice matches the speaker's voice in the poem.	
The reader speaks at a speed that allows the audience to follow the words in the poem.	
The reader stresses appropriate words.	
The reader maintains eye contact with the entire audience.	
The reader is easy to hear and understand.	
TOTAL	
AVERAGE (Divide the TOTAL by six.)	

YOUR TURN 11 Presenting and Responding to a Poetry Reading

With a few classmates, take turns presenting your poems. After you finish your presentation, take notes on the feedback you receive. When you are part of the audience, take notes and fill out a rating chart, and calculate the speaker's average score. Be prepared to share and discuss your evaluation with your classmates.

RESOURCES

Your Turn 11
Practice and Reinforcement
- *Media Literacy and Communication Skills*
  —*Support and Practice,* Ch. 5, transparencies and worksheets
  —*Videocassette 2,* Segment E

Choices

Choose one of the following activities to complete.

▶ MEDIA AND TECHNOLOGY

1. Start a Zine With several classmates, start your own **literary magazine** on the Web. Write, edit, and publish literary analyses, poetry, short stories, and essays. Ask for submissions from students all over the country for future issues of your magazine.

▶ CAREERS

2. Will Write for Pay Do research to find out about careers in writing. Also, write to or interview people who make their living writing—professional poets, for example. Use the results of your research and interviews to compile a **report** on writing as a career. Present the report to your class.

▶ SPEAKING AND LISTENING

3. Critic's Corner Plan and present an **oral response to literature.** Go beyond critical analysis to evaluate a short story, poem, or novel you've read. Tell your listeners whether you think the work is worthwhile, and support that conclusion with accurate and detailed references to the text. If you wish,

use presentation software to summarize important events, details, and ideas in the work.

▶ VIEWING AND REPRESENTING

4. Win a Tony With two or three classmates, find a poem that has two or three characters and tells a story, such as Robert Frost's "The Death of the Hired Man." Transform the poem into a **script** for a play. Then, produce the **play** for the rest of the class, either as a live performance or on videotape.

▶ CROSSING THE CURRICULUM: ART

5. Poetry on the Product Work collaboratively with three classmates to choose a product such as tea or cereal. Next, design a **tea box,** a **cereal box,** or some other label to sell the product. The central selling point should be a few famous lines of poetry which describe the image you want to create for the product. See how many different images you can create simply by varying the lines of poetry you use. Present the three best pieces of poetry you find, and the designs you create with them, to the class.

PORTFOLIO

▶ SPEAKING AND LISTENING

Students can ask an elementary school teacher or librarian to help them choose appropriate poems to present. Suggest that students help each other act out the poems as they recite them.

▶ VIEWING AND REPRESENTING

Tell students that conveying meaning in a short play or scene will require careful attention to word choice and sentence forms. Encourage students to structure their script so that audiences can quickly understand the important circumstances and message of the performance. Provide examples of scripts and point out stage asides, lighting and sound directions, and the way dialogue is presented.

▶ CROSSING THE CURRICULUM: ART

After each group has selected a product to design, have students brainstorm about what kinds of consumers they want to reach and how they can reach them. Suggest that students hunt for lines of poetry that contain vivid imagery. This will help them create strong visual representations of their product. Each group member should write down a few lines of poetry on a sheet of paper and pass it to the member on his or her left. Then, each member should provide an image to go with the poetry given. The group should discuss and refine each suggestion before deciding how image and poetry can work together to convey their product's message. Each member should participate in the final designs.

Choices **193**

RESOURCES

Analyzing a Poem
Assessment

- *Assessment Package*
  —*Chapter Tests,* Ch. 5
  —*Chapter Tests in Standardized Test Formats,* Ch. 5
  —*Assessment Alternatives,* Ch. 5

- *Test Generator (One-Stop Planner CD-ROM)* 🄯

Choices
Rubrics

- *Assessment Package*
  —*Assessment Alternatives,* Ch. 5

CHAPTER 6

Investigating a Research Question

Use this guide to create an instructional plan that suits the individual needs of your students. Assignments marked by an asterisk (*) may be completed out of class. Times given for pacing lessons are estimated. See pp. 194–195 for chapter-wide resources. Resources listed in this guide are point-of-use resources only.

Curriculum Connections

Connections to Literature *p. 237*
- Research for Fiction Writing

Choices *p. 245*
- Literature
- Speaking and Listening
- Viewing and Representing

---

 internet**connect**

GO TO: go.hrw.com
KEYWORD: EOLang 9-6

 All resources for this chapter are available for preview on the *One-Stop Planner CD-ROM with Test Generator.* All worksheets and tests may be printed from the CD-ROM.

	Chapter Opener pp. 194–195	**Reading Workshop: Reading an Investigative Report** pp. 196–206
DEVELOPMENTAL PROGRAM	🕐 **30 minutes** • Research *p. 195* • Your Turn 1 *p. 195*	🕐 **100 minutes** • Preparing to Read *p. 196* • Reading Selection *pp. 197–199* • First Thoughts 1–3 *p. 200* • Summarizing What You Read *pp. 200–202* • Your Turn 2 *p. 202* • Primary and Secondary Sources *pp. 202–204* • Your Turn 3 *p. 204* • Test Taking Mini-Lesson *p. 206*
CORE PROGRAM	🕐 **20 minutes** • Research *p. 195* • Your Turn 1 *p. 195*	🕐 **80 minutes** • Preparing to Read *p. 196* • Reading Selection *pp. 197–199* • First Thoughts 1–3 *p. 200* • Summarizing What You Read *pp. 200–202* • Your Turn 2* *p. 202* • Primary and Secondary Sources *pp. 202–204* • Your Turn 3* *p. 204* • Vocabulary Mini-Lesson *p. 205* • Test Taking Mini-Lesson *p. 206*
ADVANCED PROGRAM	🕐 **5 minutes** • Research *p. 195* • Your Turn 1 *p. 195*	🕐 **55 minutes** • Preparing to Read *p. 196* • Reading Selection * *pp. 197–199* • First Thoughts 1–3 *p. 200* • Summarizing What You Read *pp. 200–202* • Primary and Secondary Sources *pp. 202–204* • Vocabulary Mini-Lesson *p. 205*
RESOURCES — PRINT	• *Communications,* TP. 45, WS. p. 99	• *Alternative Readings,* Ch. 6 • *Communications,* TPs. 46, 47, WS. pp. 100–107
RESOURCES — MEDIA	• *One-Stop Planner CD-ROM*	• *One-Stop Planner CD-ROM*

TP.=Transparency WS.=Worksheet

Writing Workshop: Writing an I-Search Paper pp. 207–237	Focus on Viewing and Representing: Making a Video Documentary pp. 238–244
120 minutes • Prewriting *pp. 207–220* • Your Turn 5* *p. 219* • Critical-Thinking Mini-Lesson *p. 221* • Framework and Your Turn 6* *p. 222* • Writer's Model and Student's Model *pp. 223–230* **100 minutes** • Evaluate and Revise Your Draft *pp. 231–232* • Your Turn 7 *p. 232* • Focus on Sentences and Your Turn 8 *p. 233* • Proofread, Publish, and Reflect on Your Essay *pp. 234–235* • Grammar Link *p. 234* • Your Turn 9 *p. 235*	**100 minutes** • Planning a Video Documentary *pp. 238–243* • Videotape Your Documentary* *pp. 243–244* • Your Turn 11 *p. 244*
180 minutes • Prewriting *pp. 207–220* • Your Turn 4 *p. 211* • Your Turn 5* *p. 219* • Critical-Thinking Mini-Lesson *p. 221* • Framework and Your Turn 6* *p. 222* • Writer's Model and Student's Model *pp. 223–230* • Evaluate and Revise Your Draft *pp. 231–232* • Your Turn 7* *p. 232* • Focus on Sentences and Your Turn 8* *p. 233* • Proofread, Publish, and Reflect on Your Essay *pp. 234–235* • Grammar Link* *p. 234* • Your Turn 9* *p. 235* • Designing Your Writing *p. 236* • Connections to Literature* *p. 237* • Your Turn 10 *p. 237*	**85 minutes** • Planning a Video Documentary *pp. 238–243* • Videotape Your Documentary* *pp. 243–244* • Your Turn 11 *p. 244*
100 minutes • Prewriting *pp. 207–220* • Critical-Thinking Mini-Lesson *p. 221* • Framework and Your Turn 6* *p. 222* • Writer's Model and Student's Model* *pp. 223–230* • Evaluate and Revise Your Draft* *pp. 231–232* • Your Turn 7* *p. 232* • Focus on Sentences and Your Turn 8* *p. 233* • Proofread, Publish, and Reflect on Your Essay *pp. 234–235* • Your Turn 9* *p. 235* • Designing Your Writing* *p. 236* • Connections to Literature* *p. 237*	**60 minutes** • Planning a Video Documentary *pp. 238–243* • Videotape Your Documentary* *pp. 243–244* • Your Turn 11 *p. 244*
• *Communications,* TPs. 48–51, WS. pp. 108–117 • *Designing Your Writing*	• *Media Literacy and Communication Skills* —*Support and Practice,* Ch. 6 —*A How-to Handbook* —*A Teacher's Guide,* Ch. 6
• *One-Stop Planner CD-ROM*	• *Media Literacy and Communication Skills* —*Videocassette 2, Segment F* • *One-Stop Planner CD-ROM*

6

Investigating a Research Question

CHAPTER OBJECTIVES

- To read an investigative report
- To write an I-Search paper
- To create a video documentary

Chapter Overview

This chapter allows students to explore, conduct, and report on the steps of a research investigation. The Reading Workshop gives students the opportunity to read an investigative report. As students study this report, they are encouraged to summarize the author's descriptions and to evaluate his sources and research methods. Students then move on to the Writing Workshop, where they are instructed to ask their own research questions, conduct investigations, and

present their findings in I-Search papers. Students reinterpret these papers as they complete the Focus on Viewing and Representing, which presents the steps for creating informative video documentaries. Each section of the chapter can be completed on its own. Taught together, the workshops provide students with a well-rounded understanding of how the investigative process can inform and contribute to students' knowledge of the world.

Why Investigate a Research Question?

The ability to find answers by asking the right questions of the right sources and the ability to locate, evaluate, and document these sources are skills that can be applied to a variety of real-world situations from buying a car to searching for a job. The critical-thinking tasks that accompany any investigative process, such as distinguishing biased testimony from objective opinion, will help students better understand the information they encounter on a daily basis. Knowing the steps that researchers take to write and present investigative reports, whether a televised news broadcast or a work of historical fiction, will help students analyze and evaluate information they view, hear, and read.

Teaching the Chapter

Option 1: Begin with Literature

Familiarize students with the investigative process by first looking at literature. Ask students to suggest favorite novels, short stories, and dramas they have read. Prompt students to describe how the authors of these works were able to construct believable stories, some of which take place in distant settings and time periods. Point out that in addition to using their imaginations, fiction writers often conduct extensive research to gather realistic details such as the physical description of a setting or of a character's clothing. Students can use what they know about research and fiction as they read and analyze the investigative report on pp. 197–199 in Reading Workshop. Students can keep these different uses of investigative reporting in mind as they write their I-Search papers.

Option 2: Begin with Nonfiction and Writing

The nonfiction essay featured in the Reading Workshop, an investigative report by William Least Heat-Moon, can be used to analyze and explain research techniques. Use the accompanying Reading Workshop instruction to prepare students to evaluate and take notes on research sources. Next, take students through the steps for writing an I-Search paper in the Writing Workshop (pp. 207–237). When it is time to return to literature, students can use what they learn about asking and answering research questions to analyze and evaluate factual information they encounter in fictional works. Students will also be better equipped to interpret research results they encounter when reading biography and autobiography as well as works of historical fiction. Also, see **Connections to Literature** on p. 237.

Making Connections

■ To the Literature Curriculum

Understanding the concept of primary sources will be important to this chapter. Students may not have had much experience with this type of resource. Therefore, provide them with an opportunity to examine a primary source and experience how different interpretations can arise from using this type of information.

Lesson Idea: Examining and interpreting primary sources using the essays and speeches of Abraham Lincoln

1. Explain that research often makes use of primary sources. Tell students they will have a chance to read and interpret a primary source, the words of Abraham Lincoln.

2. Explain that even though they will be reading the same material, individuals in the class may have differing interpretations.

3. Ask them to set up a double-entry journal by drawing a line from top to bottom down the center of a page of notebook paper. Tell them to head the left column *Factual Information* and the right *Reactions.* Assign students to read the piece. Ask them as they read to note under *Factual Information* five of the most important points Lincoln made. Under *Reactions*, have them jot down feelings, thoughts, and associations related to the words of Lincoln.

4. When students have finished the task, provide time for sharing of notes. Point out that there should not be conflicts among class members about the material in the left column. Be sure, however, to note that there will be wide variety in the *Reactions* column and that some of the points may be debatable.

5. Reinforce the idea that the factual information students take from a primary source should not be debatable while interpretations and reactions will vary. Point out that it is important that students keep this distinction clearly in mind as they read and write research reports. Introduce students to the investigative report in this chapter (pp. 197–199). Challenge them to note how the author used primary sources.

■ To Careers

Have students consider the role of research in the world of work. Ask them to search the classified section of a newspaper for jobs listed under the title of "Researcher." (See also Research Assistant and Research Associate.) As a class, discuss information the advertisements provide about the responsibilities, educational requirements, salary range, and subject area of the listed positions.

■ To the Community

The material in this chapter encourages students to form research questions that have practical relevance to their lives and to locate and evaluate sources that provide answers to these questions. Before students begin the chapter, have them work together to create a list of local research facilities and resources. For example, students might compile street and e-mail addresses, phone numbers, and hours of operation of historical societies, community and university libraries, local museums, and town or city records offices.

■ To the Social Studies Curriculum

Students may have attended museum exhibits that displayed historically significant relics and artifacts. Remind students that museums usually provide placards and catalogs which explain the background and meaning of the objects presented in an exhibit. Explain that a curator or historian must conduct a great deal of research in order to create a museum exhibit. Have students work in small groups to curate an exhibit that relates to a historical research question.

Investigating a Research Question

PREVIEWING THE CHAPTER

■ The three workshops in this chapter focus on investigating research questions. In the Reading Workshop, students will read an investigative report and learn to summarize the author's findings and analyze sources. They will apply these skills as they complete the Writing Workshop that introduces techniques for conducting successful research and writing of I-Search papers. In Focus on Viewing and Representing, students will explore the process of creating an informative video documentary. To integrate this chapter with grammar, usage, and mechanics chapters, see pp. T371A–T371B.

INTRODUCING THE CHAPTER

■ To introduce the chapter, use the Journal Warm-up, Transparency 45, in *Communications*.

VIEWING THE ILLUSTRATION

■ Ask students to compare working a maze to investigating a research question. [Both require dedication to follow leads to the end; both often lead to dead ends.] Explore with students the design elements in this drawing: The primary colors of red, blue, and yellow are supplemented by the secondary colors of green and orange; the patches of black within and on the right side of the maze suggest shadows, and the black lines on the walls suggest the texture of bricks.

Representing. Have students work in pairs to design mazes.

CHAPTER RESOURCES

Planning
■ *Lesson Planner, ELL Strategies*, Ch. 6
■ Block Scheduling, p. T193A (this book)
■ *One-Stop Planner CD-ROM* 💿

Practice
■ *Communications*, Ch. 6
■ *Media Literacy and Communication Skills* 📺

Extension
■ *Designing Your Writing*

Reinforcement
■ *Communications*, Ch. 6
■ *Alternative Readings*, Ch. 6

Reading Workshop

Reading an Investigative Report

Writing Workshop

Writing an I-Search Paper

Viewing and Representing

Making a Video Documentary

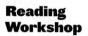

Research

- A detective, unconvinced by a suspect's alibi, investigates the alibi and takes a dangerous criminal off the streets.

- A doctor, puzzled by similar symptoms in several patients, investigates and discovers an outbreak of a rare disease.

- A grandparent, interested in his family's roots, investigates and creates a detailed family tree.

In each of these scenarios, a curious person starts with questions, investigates by conducting research, and discovers answers. This process—investigating through research—requires patience and persistence. Researchers must be willing to ask many questions, to track down sources, and to draw conclusions, even if they do not like what they find. For researchers, investigating a question is much like traveling with an unfinished map. They may know their starting and ending points, but their research will probably take them places they never expected. Researchers write their investigations to share their discoveries with readers.

YOUR TURN 1 From Question to Investigation

Working in small groups, brainstorm a list of at least three famous discoveries. Then, for each discovery, ask what question the discoverer was trying to answer. For example, Columbus's question might have been "Can I find a trade route to the East by sailing west?"

Informational Text

Exposition

internet**connect**

GO TO: go.hrw.com
KEYWORD: EOLang 9-6

Connecting Reading and Writing **195**

Motivate

Present this scenario: "A friend calls you one snowy morning and asks if school is open. You say that you do not know but will find out." Point out that the investigative process is set in motion by a question: Is school open? Discuss the steps students might take to investigate. Use this example to relate the value of conducting research and sharing results to the process of writing an investigative report.

Investigating a Research Question in Literature. In *Elements of Literature,* Third Course, see "Choice: A Tribute to Dr. Martin Luther King, Jr.," pp. 367–370, for examples of source information that could be used in a research report.

YOUR TURN 1

Sample answers follow:

1. Astronaut Neil Armstrong, first man to walk on the moon, answered "Is a lunar landing possible?"

2. Bill Gates answered "Is it possible to create a standard operating system for PC users?"

3. Explorer Matthew Henson answered "What would it take to get to the North Pole?"

- *Daily Language Activity Transparencies*
- *Vocabulary Workshop* and *Tests*

Evaluation and Assessment

- Test Generator (One-Stop Planner CD-ROM)

- Assessment Package
  —*Chapter Tests,* Ch. 6
  —*Chapter Tests in Standardized Test Formats,* Ch. 6
  —*Assessment Alternatives,* Ch. 6

Internet
- go.hrw.com (keyword: EOLang 9–6)

Preview **195**

Reading Workshop

Reading Workshop

OBJECTIVES

Reading and Writing Connection

- To read an investigative report in preparation for writing an I-Search paper

Reading Skills

- To summarize what you read
- To identify and distinguish between primary and secondary sources
- To trace the etymology of given words

TEACHING TIP

Preparing to Read
This page introduces a report that students will read and summarize. It also provides an opportunity for the class to think about the use of primary and secondary sources in investigative reports.

Quotation for the Day

"It is better to ask some of the questions than to know all of the answers."

(James Thurber, 1894–1961, American humorist)

Ask students whether they agree or disagree with Thurber's statement, and have them explain their opinions. Students might agree because people who think they know all the answers are less likely to discover new information. Students may disagree because finding the answer to one key question may be more useful than generating a multitude of unanswered questions. Remind students that asking questions is the first part of the investigative process.

RESOURCES

Reading Workshop Reinforcement
- *Alternative Readings*, Ch. 6

WHAT'S AHEAD?

In this section, you will read an investigative report and learn to

- summarize what you read
- identify and distinguish between primary and secondary sources

READING SKILL

READING FOCUS

Reading an Investigative Report

People are curious, and they like to have their curiosity satisfied—even if some investigative work is necessary to satisfy it. William Least Heat-Moon, the writer of the reading selection on the next page, "Regarding Fokker Niner-Niner-Easy," was curious about Chase County, Kansas, the geographic center of the United States. He wondered about the history and the importance of this core of the country. As you read, you will follow along with Heat-Moon as he recounts the steps in his search and the results of his discoveries.

Preparing to Read

Summarizing What You Read William Least Heat-Moon presents a great deal of information while reporting on his investigation into a plane crash in Chase County, Kansas. As you read, do not let the wealth of details overwhelm you. After you have read about his investigation once, you will have a chance to go back and **summarize** it—use your own words to restate and condense the material to help you see the main ideas and details more clearly.

Primary and Secondary Sources The information that Heat-Moon presents in his investigation comes from many sources. In general, sources consulted in research fall into two categories: primary sources and secondary sources. A **primary source** consists of original, firsthand information—an eyewitness account of a devastating flood, for example. A **secondary source** contains secondhand or indirect information, for example, a magazine article about how government officials hope to prevent another flood. As you read, see if you can begin to recognize the kinds of sources Heat-Moon uses in his investigation.

---

196 Chapter 6 **Exposition:** Investigating a Research Question

---

READING PROCESS

PREREADING
Activate Prior Knowledge. Ask students to read the introduction to the selection and to scan the article. Have them share what they know about plane crashes and how experts find out what caused them. Give

them time to make a Know-Wonder-Learn Chart (K-W-L) as shown on p. 197 and fill out the left and center columns. (Students will fill in the right column when they answer the **Wrap It Up** questions at the end of the workshop.)

TEACHING **TIP**

Reading Selection
Students might not be familiar with the concept of government reports. Explain that committees of government workers and other experts are sometimes responsible for investigating an event or situation. After they finish their work, they write up the results in a formal report so that others may benefit from what they have learned.

Active-Reading Questions
The purpose of the active-reading questions is to reflect on the process and sources the author used in investigating and writing about his topic. Use students' answers to assess informally their understanding of the investigative report.

ANSWERS

1. The Cottonwood historical society, newspapers, and interviews with witnesses and local people

2. Direct quotations from a newspaper article and from people he interviewed

On March 31, 1931, Knute Rockne (Noot RAHK-nee), a famous football coach and former college football star, died in a plane crash between the towns of Cottonwood and Bazaar, Kansas. As Capt. Robert Fry flew the plane in murky weather, co-pilot Jess Mathias received a radio call asking, "Do you think you'll make it? . . . Can you get through?" Mathias's reply, "Don't know yet, don't know yet!" was the last transmission from the plane. In the following excerpt, William Least Heat-Moon reports on his own investigation into the moments just before the plane crashed. As you read, jot down answers to the numbered active-reading questions.

Regarding Fokker Niner-Niner-Easy

from PRAIRYERTH (A DEEP MAP)
BY WILLIAM LEAST HEAT-MOON

I went to the historical society in Cottonwood and looked at the relics: a large piece of the red fabric, a chunk of propeller, the pilot's Indian-head insignia pin, the cockpit nameplate, a piece of seat belt. I read the newspaper accounts; columnist "Peggy of the Flint Hills" wrote a week after the crash: *If Knute Rockne's pockets contained all the articles which local souvenir fans claim to have removed from them, it must have been that extra weight which brought down the plane.* An article four years later carried this headline: GOLD TOOTH IS FOUND ON SITE OF ROCKNE CRASH—VALUE $7. I read a 1942 story: MISSING ROCKNE PLANE TIRE TURNS UP AS SCRAP RUBBER. I talked with a half-dozen people who had been at the scene right after the accident and others who had visited it only years later; I saw in one home a wastebasket made from a piece of the Fokker rudder, and everywhere I heard as many tales as truths: *So-and-so carried off the coach's head in a basket,* and *They tied a rope around Rockne's waist to pull him from the ground with a team of horses,* and *What's-his-name years later found a human jawbone with two teeth out there. . . .*

In all my looking, I couldn't find what actually happened to Fokker 99E while it was struggling above old route 13, what had caused the wing to break off. Then

1. From what kinds of sources did the writer get the information for this paragraph?

2. What do you think the writer's use of italics signifies in this paragraph?

What do you know?	What do you wonder?	What did you learn?
Knute Rockne died in a plane crash.	Was there bad weather?	There might have been a tornado.
	Was the plane badly built?	The wings fluttered in bumpy air.

Guide students to see that using what they already know to ask questions will help them make sense of new information they read.

3. What caused the crash of the Fokker 99E?

4. Because he combined pieces of information from scattered sources and because it is a play on words: He is writing about a plane crash from which only fragments were recovered.

5. Fragment two presents expert opinions that the Fokker 10 model had faulty wings; Fragment four points out that it was difficult for inspectors to judge the condition of these wings. Together, these fragments suggest that the Fokker 99E may have had faulty wing structure.

---

3. What specific question does the writer seem to have set out to answer?

one day I came across something called "Report on the Crash of Fokker F-10A Transport Near Bazaar, Kansas." It contained excerpts from records held at Wright-Patterson Field near Dayton, Ohio. At the top of page one in parentheses this: "Formerly Classified Secret." Within, hidden among all the official words, were things I hadn't heard or read anywhere else, bits and pieces scattered about like debris from the crash itself.

Fragment one: At ten-forty on the morning of the accident, the wife of E. S. Chartier, an Emporia weather observer for the government airmail service, recorded a rapid drop in atmospheric pressure, and she looked out to see in the southwest, toward Bazaar, a dark cloud with a short pendant nearly in a funnel shape; although the sun was shining elsewhere, the cloud appeared to be an isolated weather cell called an *upper-air tornado.*

4. Why do you think the writer refers to the information from different sources in the report as "fragments"?

Fragment two: A week after the disaster, the supervising aeronautical inspector for the Department of Commerce, Leonard Jurden, wrote a confidential letter to the federal director of air regulation, saying he had definite confirmation from pilots (most of whom insisted on anonymity) that the F-10 series planes, *particularly the long-winged job, do set up a decided flutter in the wing when the normal cruising speed is slightly increased and bumpy air encountered.* One pilot told the inspector the flutter was so rapid wing tips would move up and down as much as eight inches and keep increasing if not corrected by pulling the nose up and throttling back; he said all TWA pilots knew about the problem but never discussed it because they were afraid of being fired or blacklisted. After examining the wing of 99E, he said that it had broken at the very center of the flexing; soon afterward the same flier brought in a nonpilot who had also observed the flutter in a Fokker wing, and, on one occasion after a severe jolt from turbulence, saw the plywood skin on the underwing actually open up. Another TWA pilot told Jurden his instructor would never allow an F-10 to exceed the cruising speed, *being afraid of the roof coming off.* Several fliers said they didn't know a Fokker pilot who wasn't afraid of the ship. . . .

Fragment four: A few months before 99E went down, an aircraft inspector complained about the difficulty of periodically examining the internal structure of F-10 wings, sealed up as they were, but Gilbert Budwig, director of air regulation, told him he saw no need for worry as long as the plywood skin stayed glued to the internal trussing. . . .

5. What is the relationship between the details in Fragment two and the information contained in Fragment four?

Fragment seven: Jurden wrote in another letter, *The wing broke off upwards, under compression. Examination of these [wing] parts showed that in the upper*

READING PROCESS

READING
Self-Check. This selection contains aeronautical terminology and references that may be unfamiliar to many students. The author explains some of this information within the body of the article. However, students may need to use active-reading strategies in dealing with other concepts. Ask students to stop after reading each "fragment" to check comprehension. Encourage them to re-read confusing passages and to consult dictionaries or encyclopedias if they are unable to decipher meanings by using context clues and textual definitions.

and lower laminated portions of the box spars, some places the glued joints broke loose very clean, showing no cohesion of the pieces of wood. Other places showed that the glue-joints were satisfactory. Two pieces [revealed] definite compression breaks as well as poor gluing.

And this last fragment: federal inspectors, after stripping off the skin of one F-10 wing, discovered moisture accumulating in the interior had *caused deterioration of the glue, materially decreasing the strength of the wing, since this type construction is to a great extent dependent on glue.*

6. Which details in the last paragraph come from the writer's investigation? Which come from his imagination?

Now: Assembling the shards of what happened after those desperate last words, *Don't know yet, don't know yet!* Following Paul Johnson's mail plane, Captain Fry heads northwest, ninety degrees off course, in search of a way out of the murk and light rain icing the wings and beginning to shut down his instruments and radio, everything happening rapidly; the trimotor catches the tailings of the cyclonic cloud, and the laden plywood wings begin to vibrate, the stress on the spar immense; the cabin fabric shudders terribly, and port-side passengers watch the wing tip flutter ever farther and faster until it appears to be flapping, and their terror—that fear of the novice air traveler of a wing falling off—is unspeakable: and then a loud, shattering report, and half the left wing is gone, severed as squarely as if this black mayhem of a cloud concealed massive shears: the plane turns over violently: cries of the helpless men, engines going silent, the hiss of the wind, the ship turning over again: upside down, the five-hundred-foot plunge begun, Niner-Niner-Easy falls into the prairie snow.

Active-Reading Questions

ANSWERS continued

6. Investigation—statistics about the plane's course, situation of the wing breaking off

Imagination—cries of victims, passengers watching the wings

First Thoughts on Your Reading

ANSWERS

Possible answers are suggested below.

1. The author does not gather much factual information from these sources. He suggests they were unreliable sources that were more likely to repeat gossip and legend than facts.

2. The report includes factual data recorded by an experienced weather observer and several aviation experts, as opposed to stories from less knowledgeable and less objective people who lived in the area. Also, this report contains information the author had not found elsewhere.

3. The author concludes that the plane flew into the tornado and the extreme wind conditions caused the left wing to break.

First Thoughts on Your Reading

Work with a partner to answer the following questions about "Regarding Fokker Niner-Niner-Easy." Write your answers on your own paper.

1. **Explain in your own words what the writer learned from the sources mentioned in the first paragraph of the article. Did the writer seem to find these sources reliable? Why or why not?**

2. **The writer's conclusion about the crash relies on information from a declassified government report. What is the difference between the information contained in this report and the information the writer had obtained from the other sources he mentions?**

3. **In your own words, state the conclusion the writer reached about what caused the plane to crash.**

| READING SKILL →

Summarizing What You Read

The Condensed Version   A **summary** is a restatement of the important ideas in a text in a condensed form. To **summarize** a reading passage, you must analyze the passage to distinguish the most important points and supporting details from the least important. Analyzing a passage in order to make this distinction will help you to better understand the passage; then jotting down a summary based on your analysis will help you remember what you read. Summarizing skills will help you in class discussions, in taking notes for classes and for research, in preparing for tests, and in many other areas.

What's the Difference?   Below is a student's summary of part of the first paragraph of "Regarding Fokker Niner-Niner-Easy." How different is it from the original paragraph?

> In his investigation, William Least Heat-Moon looked at relics, read old newspaper clippings, and interviewed eyewitnesses. He discovered both tales and truths.

- First, the main idea is stated in one short sentence. ("He discovered both tales and truths.")

- **Second, the summary omits most of the supporting details,** such as the items William Least Heat-Moon saw in the historical society exhibit and the direct quotations.
- **Third, the summary condenses all the major supporting details** into one sentence ("In his investigation, William Least Heat-Moon looked at relics, read old newspaper clippings, and interviewed eyewitnesses.")

Keep the following points in mind as you prepare a summary of a reading passage. A summary

- condenses the main idea and important supporting details
- excludes nonessential information
- is much shorter than the original text

As a critical reader, you need to be on the lookout for the main idea and the most important supporting details of passages that you need to understand and remember. Taking the time to jot down a summary of what you read can prevent you from having to re-read an entire passage. Instead, you can re-read your summary to refresh your memory. Jotting down a summary is not a difficult task if you think of summarizing as a formula like the one below.

Main Idea	+	Supporting Details	=	Summary
_____		1. _____		_____
_____		2. _____		_____
		3. _____		

THINKING IT THROUGH — Summarizing What You Read

Remember that a good summary gives you a nutshell version—the absolute essentials—of a passage that you have read. To create a summary of a reading passage, use the steps that follow.

STEP 1 Review the text and identify the main idea. Often the main idea is stated in a topic sentence at the beginning or the end of a paragraph. If there is no topic sentence, the main idea is implied. You have to infer it by considering all of the details in the passage. Then, jot down a main idea statement.

TIP If you need to summarize a passage of several paragraphs, your summary should contain the main idea and most important support for each paragraph in the passage.

▶ **STEP 3** **Use the preceding formula to create a summary.** Check to see that the order of ideas in the summary is the same as in the original. If necessary, include transitions to ensure clarity.

▶ **STEP 4** **Check your summary.** Does it provide a solid understanding of the original so that you will not have to re-read the original?

Here is how one student used the Thinking It Through and the formula to summarize the first paragraph of "Regarding Fokker Niner-Niner-Easy."

Condensed Main Idea	+	Important Supporting Details	=	Summary
William Least Heat-Moon discovered some tales and some truths.		1. He looked at relics. 2. He read old newspaper clippings. 3. He interviewed eyewitnesses.		In his investigation, William Least Heat-Moon looked at relics, read old newspaper clippings, and interviewed eyewitnesses. From these, he discovered both tales and truths.

YOUR TURN 2 **Summarizing What You Read**

Using the Thinking It Through above, summarize the second paragraph of "Regarding Fokker Niner-Niner-Easy," on pages 197–199.

| READING FOCUS

Primary and Secondary Sources

Consider the Sources Writers of articles and investigative reports use research to enhance their knowledge and support their ideas. The information researchers obtain comes from outside sources—sources other than themselves. The two types of sources that these writers consult in their research are **primary sources** and **secondary sources**.

Timesaver

To emphasize the importance of brevity, you might assign a maximum word count for students' summaries. For example, ask them to summarize the second paragraph in twenty-five words or less.

YOUR TURN 2

Sample response:
After an unsuccessful search for information, William Least Heat-Moon finally found pieces of what he was looking for in a declassified airfield report.

TEACHING (TIP)

Consider the Sources
To access prior knowledge before students read the information on pp. 202–204, write the words *primary* and *secondary* on the chalkboard. Ask students how they have heard these words or forms of these words used. Students may be familiar with terms such as *primary colors* and *secondary school*. Then, add the terms *firsthand* and *secondhand* to the chalkboard and have students discuss their prior knowledge of the meanings. Students may be familiar with the phrase *firsthand knowledge* and *secondhand clothes*. After students have read the instruction, add the words *primary source* and *secondary source* to the chalkboard. Ask students to define the terms using their own words.

RESOURCES

Your Turn 2
Practice
■ *Communications,* WS. p. 100
Reinforcement
■ *Communications,* TP. 46, WS. p. 101

Primary Sources   A primary source consists of original, firsthand information or raw data. It is unfiltered and unedited.

Even though William Least Heat-Moon consulted two primary sources—relics from the crash and people who arrived on the scene minutes after the crash—to find out what happened to Fokker Niner-Niner-Easy, neither source provided any useful information. Had Heat-Moon been searching days after the crash instead of more than fifty years later, he probably would have been able to find many useful primary sources.

One of Heat-Moon's sources, the government report on the crash of Fokker Niner-Niner-Easy, relied on information from Leonard Jurden, the supervising aeronautical inspector for the Department of Commerce. One primary source Jurden consulted in seeking the cause of the crash was a pilot experienced in flying the Fokker 10 aircraft. Jurden accepted what this pilot said about the flutter in the wing of the aircraft because other eyewitness accounts confirmed what the pilot told Jurden. In other words, Jurden consulted several primary sources who gave him the same information. As a critical reader, you can accept, as Jurden did, the **firsthand information** his primary sources provided.

Secondary Sources   Secondary sources provide indirect or secondhand information. When Heat-Moon found "Report on the Crash of Fokker F-10A Transport Near Bazaar, Kansas," a declassified government report, he had located an invaluable secondary source. It was invaluable because it was based, among other things, on firsthand information from pilots who had flown the same model Fokker aircraft as Fokker Niner-Niner-Easy. The reason these firsthand accounts were not primary sources for Heat-Moon is that they came to him through the author or authors of the government document.

As a critical reader, you must approach secondary source material with caution. Even well-established and respected secondary sources are guilty of getting their facts wrong or misinterpreting facts from time to time. The best way to check a writer's secondary sources is to check his or her facts against other secondary sources and against your own knowledge. If all the sources present the same set of facts, and these facts do not contradict what you know to be true, you can regard the information as reliable. From your point of view as a critical reader, an investigative report is only as reliable as the sources from which a writer gets his or her material.

The chart on the next page shows common primary sources on the left. On the right is a partial list of secondary sources that could be based on the corresponding primary sources.

TIP   As a critical reader, you should be aware that the conclusions a writer draws from raw data may or may not be valid. For example, to decide which of two completely different interpretations of raw polling data taken a week before an important election was correct, you would have to see the election results.

An interpretation of raw data is not easily and concretely confirmed. You must use prior knowledge and logic to arrive at your own interpretation.

Critical Thinking

Analysis. Illustrate how secondary sources can vary in their interpretations of an event. Select an event that is currently in the news. Ask specific students to collect each of the following: videotaped news stories from different channels, articles from several newspapers, and Internet pieces on the event. *You need to be aware that Internet resources are sometimes public forums and their content can be unpredictable.* Have your class examine these sources to note similarities and differences in main points, details, and tone of these secondary sources.

READING PROCESS

EXPLORING
Evaluate Primary and Secondary Sources. Encourage students to consider and discuss the conclusion of **"Regarding Fokker Niner-Niner-Easy."** Then, have them write paragraphs in which they state whether they agree or disagree with the author's (1) methods of investigation using primary and secondary sources and (2) conclusions about the crash. Challenge students to describe how the author might have used other primary and secondary sources and to identify other possible conclusions that might be reached from the research.

Primary Sources	Secondary Sources
testimonies of eyewitnesses to an event	an article on the event based partly on eyewitness testimony
letters, speeches, personal remembrances	a biography based on a person's letters, speeches, and personal remembrances
autobiographies and diaries	a magazine article profiling a person partly on the basis of that person's autobiography or diary
historical documents	a history book interpreting the meaning or significance of a historical document
interviews	a newspaper or magazine article based on information obtained from interviews
raw data from such sources as scientific experiments, surveys, and polls	a paper or report compiling and interpreting the data from experiments, surveys, polls, and so forth
works of literature	a critical analysis of a work of literature
objects of art	a critical review of an object of art
performances	a critic's article about or review of a performance

ANSWERS

1. Primary; unreliable; reflects the opinion of one person, not an expert
2. Primary; reliable; pilot is an expert who has flown the aircraft in question
3. Primary; reliable; reflects opinion of an expert with no incentive to hide truth
4. Primary; reliable; scientific data
5. Secondary; unreliable; incentive to decrease public fear in order to sell airplanes; experts employed by airplane manufacturer

Wrap It Up

Metacognition. Give students time to reflect on and answer the following question:

1. What strategies did you use to understand unfamiliar terms and phrases as you read **"Regarding Fokker Niner-Niner-Easy"**?

Then, have students answer this question.

2. Identify something you learned from the report and record it in the right column of your K-W-L chart.

YOUR TURN 3 — Evaluating Primary and Secondary Sources

Imagine that you are aeronautical inspector Leonard Jurden, whose letter provided Heat-Moon with his most valuable information. On your own paper, identify each source described below as primary or secondary. Then, label each source as reliable or unreliable, and explain why.

1. A report written by a witness to weather conditions in the area of the crash at the time of the crash.

2. A pilot experienced with the Fokker F-10 who reported a decided flutter in the wings of the Fokker F-10 series at slightly more than normal cruising speed.

3. A report by an aircraft inspector describing the difficulty of examining the internal structure of F-10 wings.

4. Raw data on weather conditions recorded from one hour before until one hour after the crash.

5. A manual written by Fokker designers and engineers describing the F-10's ability to fly in difficult weather conditions.

RESOURCES

Your Turn 3
Practice
- *Communications*, WS. p. 102
Reinforcement
- *Communications*, TP. 47, WS. p. 103

Vocabulary
Practice
- *Communications*, WS. p. 104

Researching the Origins of Words

William Least Heat-Moon tried to research the story behind an airplane crash. Some people, called *etymologists*, research the stories behind words. Every word in the English language has a history; some have a short and simple past, while others have a long and complicated one. When you want to know the **etymology** of a word, you can look it up in a dictionary. By studying etymologies, you can better understand both the current usage of words and your language as a whole.

Here is the entry for a word from the reading selection as it appears in *Webster's New World Dictionary, Third College Edition*. The etymology is enclosed within double brackets—[[. . .]]. You can find a listing of abbreviations and symbols used in the dictionary inside the back cover of most dictionaries.

> **ex•cerpt** (ek surpt´, ik–; *also, and for n., always,* ek´ surpt´) **vt.** [[< L *excerptus,* pp. of *excerpere,* to pick out, choose < *ex–,* out + *carpere,* to pick, pluck < IE * *kerp* < base *(s)ker–,* to cut, scrape > HARVEST]] to select, take out, or quote (passages from a book, etc.); extract—**n.** a passage selected or quoted from a book, article, etc.; extract—**ex•cerption n.**

Below is an explanation of how to decipher the symbols, abbreviations, and other information in the etymology of *excerpt.*

1. *Excerpt* is derived from (<) the Latin (L) word *excerptus,* which is the past participle (pp.) of *excerpere,* which means "to pick out or choose."

2. *Excerpere* is derived from (<) *ex–,* a prefix meaning "out," plus the verb *carpere,* which means "to pick or pluck."

3. *Carpere* is derived from (<) the Indo-European (IE) word * *kerp.*

4. *Kerp* is derived from (<) the base *(s)ker–,* which means "to cut or scrape."

5. The modern English word *harvest* is also derived from (>) the Indo-European base *(s)ker.*

An asterisk (*) is used before Indo-European words because Indo-European is a hypothetical language. Linguists have reconstructed Indo-European—a language spoken long before writing was invented—by studying the many languages derived from it.

PRACTICE

Use the explanations above and a dictionary to trace the etymologies of the following words from "Regarding Fokker Niner-Niner-Easy." Put your answers on your own paper.

1. compression (see *compress*) (page 198)
2. debris (page 198)
3. fabric (page 197)
4. murk (page 199)
5. novice (page 199)
6. pendant (page 198)
7. problem (page 198)
8. relic (page 197)
9. trussing (see *truss*) (page 198)
10. weather (page 198)

Researching the Origins of Words

ANSWERS

1. *compress* [< ME. *compressen* < OF. *compresser* < LL. *compressare* < L. *compressare,* freq. of *comprimere,* to compress <*com–,* with + *premere,* to press.]

2. *debris* [< F. *débris* < OF. *debrisier,* to break to pieces: *de–* + *brisier,* to break < from VL. *brisare,* to press grapes, probably of Celtic origin.]

3. *fabric* [< ME. *fabryke,* something constructed < OF. *fabrique* < L. *fabrica,* craft, workshop < *faber, fabr–* , workman.]

4. *murk* [ME. *mirke* < ON. *myrkr* or OE. *mirce.*]

5. *novice* [ME. < OF. < ML. *novicius* < L., recently entered into a condition < L. *novus,* new.]

6. *pendant* [ME. *pendaunt,* from OF. *pendant* < present participle of *pendre,* to hang < VL. *pendere* < L. *pendere.*]

7. *problem* [ME. *probleme,* OF. *probleme* < L. *problema* < Gr. *proballein,* to throw before, put forward: *pro–,* before + *ballein,* to throw.]

8. *relic* [ME. *relik,* object of religious veneration < OF. *relique* < LL. *reliquiae,* sacred relics < L. *reliquus,* remaining < *reliq–,* to leave behind.]

9. *truss* [< ME. *trusse,* bundle < OF. *trousse,* to truss, possibly from VL. *torsare* < *torsus,* variant of L. *tortus,* past participle of *torquere,* to twist.]

10. *weather* [ME. *weder, wether* < OE. *weder.*]

Looking Ahead to Writing

In the Writing Workshop for this chapter (pp. 207–237), students will be asked to write I-Search papers. Have students set aside a section of a notebook or folder for the Writing Workshop. Suggest they copy the summarizing formula on p. 201 onto the first page as well as the terms *primary source* and *secondary source* and the definitions for each (see p. 196). Students can refer to this page as they conduct research.

MINI-LESSON TEST TAKING

Answering Summary Questions

Standardized reading tests often ask you to identify the best summary of a reading passage. Read the passage and sample test question below. Then, use the steps in Thinking It Through to determine the best answer to the question.

> What happened to aircraft . . . regulations after the plummet of 99E would have happened sooner or later anyway, but the changes came about earlier because of a famous coach [Knute Rockne] going down near Bazaar, Kansas. . . . The government abandoned its policy of secret crash inquiries and records, and it received authority to investigate air accidents, hold formal hearings, subpoena witnesses, and require testimony; the unofficial removal of even the smallest fragment of a wrecked aircraft became a federal crime; and, by the next winter [1932], commercial planes carried a de-icing substance. In fact, a couple of years after the Rock fell, the only defeated proposal to improve airline safety was a law requiring a parachute for every passenger.

Which of the following statements is the best summary of the passage?

A. A law requiring a parachute for every person aboard an airliner was defeated.

B. An airline crash that takes the life of a famous person gets the public's attention very quickly.

C. It became a federal crime to remove fragments of a crashed aircraft.

D. The airplane crash that took the life of Knute Rockne hastened the creation of laws designed to improve airline safety.

THINKING IT THROUGH — Answering Summary Questions

Follow these steps to answer summary questions correctly on standardized tests.

▶ **STEP 1** Look for the main idea and the most important supporting details as you read the passage slowly and carefully.

▶ **STEP 2** Consider every answer choice, eliminating those that restate a single detail from the passage, make a general statement about the passage but include no important details, or have little or nothing to do with the passage.

▶ **STEP 3** Be sure that the answer you choose covers the *entire* passage by including the main idea and major supporting details. A is true, but merely restates a single detail. B is also true, but it is a general statement that excludes details. C is true, but, like A, simply restates a detail. D is the best answer. It summarizes the main idea and the most important details of the entire passage.

RESOURCES

Test Taking
Practice
■ *Communications,* WS. pp. 105–107

Writing an I-Search Paper

Chances are that the last time you were asked to write a research paper, you had a list of topics from which to choose. In this Writing Workshop, you will choose a topic that has immediate relevance to your life—a topic about which you have a genuine need or a real desire to know more. You will write a personal research paper, sometimes called an I-Search paper.

To write an I-Search paper, you pick a subject to which you have a personal connection, and write about it from a personal point of view. Your paper will consist of three major parts:

- **The story of your search** This section tells readers what you knew about your subject before you began your research, what you wanted to know, and the research steps you went through to find out what you wanted to know—including both the steps that led to useful information and the steps that turned out to be dead ends.

- **What you learned** In this section, you give readers the results of your search—both the answers you found and the answers you did not find.

- **Your reflections on the search** You use this final section to tell readers what the experience has taught you about conducting and documenting a search.

Prewriting

Select a Topic

A Need to Know Even though an I-Search paper is usually less formal and more personal than a traditional research paper, its purpose is the

WHAT'S AHEAD?

In this workshop, you will write an I-Search paper. You will also learn how to
- **form a research question**
- **start a search journal**
- **evaluate Web sources**
- **eliminate** *there is* and *there are* sentence beginnings
- **punctuate titles**

Writing Workshop

OBJECTIVES

- To write an I-Search paper
- To form a research question
- To start a search journal
- To evaluate Web sources
- To eliminate *there is/ there are* sentence beginnings
- To punctuate titles

Quotation for the Day

"Knowledge is of two kinds: we know a subject ourselves, or we know where we can find information upon it."

(Samuel Johnson, 1709–1784, English lexicographer, essayist, and poet)

Share the quotation with your class and ask students what they think Johnson could be saying about generating ideas for writing. Then, ask them to think of subjects that interest them but about which they know very little. Where might they look to find information about these topics? Record their responses on the chalkboard.

TEACHING TIP

A Need to Know
Spend a few moments talking with students about topics that are appropriate for school. While acknowledging that all of their questions are valid and worth investigation, help them clarify the parameters of what is acceptable within the context of a school research project.

same—to find information. The difference is that the topic for an I-Search comes from a personal need to know something—that is what the "I" in I-Search represents.

It is very important, then, for you to choose a topic that you truly want to investigate. Here are a few ways to generate ideas for a topic if you do not already have one in mind.

- **Use trigger phrases.** The phrases below are called "trigger" phrases because they prompt you to think about particular subjects. To use these phrases, write them down and fill in the blanks with whatever comes to your mind.

    I always wanted to know how to ____.

    I need help with ____.

- **Take an inventory of places to which you would like to travel.**
- **Make a list of priorities**. Include the factors that have the greatest impact on your life, including family, health, economics, education, law, and so forth.

Remember, your goal is to find a topic you want to know something about—one that is driven by a real desire or need in your life. For example, one student who discovered that he had asthma felt he needed to know everything he could about the disease and its possible effects on his life.

Brainstorm a list of several topics. Then, circle the one you want to research.

TIP When you select a topic, be sure that it is a suitable one. It should be not only interesting and informative, but also lend itself to research. In other words, you should be able to locate adequate information on your topic from a variety of outside sources. If the information on your topic comes only from your knowledge and experience, there is no need for a search.

Form a Research Question

In a Nutshell To avoid gathering information that you cannot use in your I-Search paper, you must focus as tightly as you can on one key aspect of your topic. **The best way to achieve a tight focus is to form a research question**—a question that asks exactly what you want to find out from your research.

KEY CONCEPT →

Keep in mind that you should not be able to answer your research question with a single word. Ideally, it should be a question that gives rise to several more detailed questions. To get started, ask yourself the following questions. One writer's responses are shown as an example.

—**What is my topic?** My topic is asthma.

—**Why am I interested in this topic?** I have asthma, but I want to live an active, full life.

—**What do I hope to learn from my research?** Basically, I want to learn whether I can keep my asthma from interfering with my life. If I can, I need to know how.

—**Research Question:** Can I manage my asthma so that I can lead a full, active life?

Once he had developed a research question, the writer then divided his initial question into several more detailed questions, all having a direct bearing on how he could manage his asthma so that he could live normally.

—What can I do to keep playing sports and doing other physically demanding activities?

—Are there certain foods or plants I should avoid?

—How do different environmental conditions affect my asthma?

—What are the effects of pets on asthma?

—What kinds of medications are available for people suffering from asthma?

—Is there some kind of physical conditioning I could do to lessen the effects of asthma?

After forming his research question and subdividing it, this writer has a specific goal for his research. Focusing his question allows him to gather relevant information and dismiss any information that has nothing to do with his specific topic—managing asthma.

Share Your Research Question

Two (or More) Heads Are Better . . . To get your search off to a good start, spend some time in small groups discussing each other's research questions. Your group can discuss ways to improve your research questions and to find information. One of your group members might know an expert in the very topic you have decided to research. Another might suggest a better way to focus your research question.

TIP Once you begin to search for answers to your research question, step back from the question every so often and ask yourself if you need to revise your question slightly or come up with a completely new one. Such changes are a natural part of the research process.

Cooperative Learning

Research Groups. Once students have defined their research questions, have them form small groups based on disciplines. For example, you might have science, current events, history, and health issues groups. Students can meet periodically to offer each other feedback, ideas, and suggestions for resources throughout the project. Also, encourage group members to share their search journals on a regular basis, offering one another alternative approaches to research procedures.

An easy way to track a student's progress in writing a research paper is to keep a chart showing the steps involved and the dates the student completed each step. This strategy will provide a quick overview of each student's work. A sample chart is shown below.

Student's Name

STEPS	DATE COMPLETED
Select topic and research question	
Find and evaluate sources	
Make source cards	
Finish taking research notes	
Write thesis statement	
Make outline	
Prepare *Works Cited* list	
Write first draft	
Revise first draft	
Prepare final draft	

TIP Remember: **Voice** is the sound and rhythm of a writer's language. You should allow your own **voice** to show through your words.

Identify Your Purpose, Audience, and Tone

Why Write? The **purpose** of your I-Search paper is to demonstrate to your readers that your search has had or will have an impact on your life.

Who Will Read It? Your **audience** consists of your classmates, your teacher, and anyone else with whom you wish to share your experience. Because you want your readers to understand and appreciate your experience, you should ask yourself these questions:

1. Will I need to provide my readers with more information than I knew when I started my search?
2. How can I make my dead-end searches interesting for my readers?
3. How can I be sure that I give my readers complete answers to all aspects of my research question?
4. How can I let my readers know how exciting my search was without sounding insincere?

What Tone of Voice? For an I-Search paper, you adopt a more informal **tone** than you would in some other types of research papers. However, you should not be so informal that you use slang and nonstandard English.

Start a Search Journal

Keeping the Record Straight It is important to keep a daily record of your research process so that you will have this information when you write the story of your search. To record your daily progress, start a **search journal** in a notebook. On the first page, list the following items:

- your research question
- feedback from your group discussion (see "Share Your Research Question," page 209)
- things you already know about your research topic and things you want to learn
- your preliminary research plan—how to tackle your research question

Write in your search journal every day, starting today. Include the day's date, a brief listing of that day's research results and findings (include both successes and setbacks), and a short daily reflection on your progress. Use a chart like the following one to record your information. A record of your research process will be invaluable when you begin to write your paper. A well-kept journal can provide everything you need for the story of your search, the first section of your paper.

Date	Research Results and Findings	Thoughts on my progress
10/18	I found a Web site about asthma and downloaded information about the causes of the illness. I also visited in a chat room with another teen who has asthma.	So far, so good. Getting information has been easy. I'm finding out a lot.
10/23	I wanted to interview Dr. Anders, my asthma specialist, but she is going to be out of town for a few days.	I think I waited too long to call Dr. Anders. Now I'm not sure if I will have time to interview her and still get the paper done. Next time, I'll start the interviews early!
10/24	A packet of information that I requested from one of the online groups came in today's mail. It has a lot of information about athletes who have asthma and still play sports.	This is great information! It answers some of my research questions. Best of all, I got some tips on how to play sports and not get too short of breath.

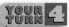 **Planning Your I-Search Paper, Part One**

Review this list of prewriting steps before you start to research for your I-Search paper. Make sure to

- select a topic
- form a research question
- share your research question
- identify your audience, purpose, and tone
- start your search journal

Find Sources

A Wealth of Information   As you conduct your research, you will be looking at two basic sources of information—**primary** and **secondary**. **KEY CONCEPT** **Primary sources include legal documents, letters, diaries, eyewitness accounts, and surveys. Secondary sources are interpretations of primary materials written by other authors.** For example, if a historian studied diaries, letters, official military records, and eyewitness accounts to write a biography of a famous general, he would be using primary sources. If that same historian consulted material from other biographies of the same

Writing Workshop   **211**

YOUR TURN 4

To assess students' readiness to move forward, ask each to sign up for a brief conference with you. At that time, he or she should quickly present the intended topic, research questions, and approach. Ask each student at least one question to help him or her extend or clarify the plan.

RESOURCES

Your Turn 4
Practice
- *Communications,* WS. p. 108

general or from history books that included material about the general, he would be using secondary sources.

The first place to begin your search is your school library, but you should also consider your community library and any college or university libraries in your area. Although your search might start at the library, it certainly should not end there. Check out community resources, including the World Wide Web, and do not forget the various government agencies— local, state, and national—that might be valuable sources. The charts below list resources that may be available in your area libraries and in your community, along with the sources or types of information they provide.

Library Resources	
Resource	**Source or Information**
Card catalog or online catalog	books listed by title, author, and subject; in some libraries this catalog also lists audiovisual materials—videotapes, records, CDs, audiotapes, filmstrips, and films.
Readers' Guide to Periodical Literature	articles in magazines and journals
Microfilm or microfiche or online databases	indexes to major newspapers such as *The New York Times*, back issues of newspapers
General and specialized reference books and CD-ROMs	encyclopedias (electronic or print), biographical references, atlases, almanacs
Videotapes and audiotapes	movies, documentaries, instructional tapes, audiotapes of books
Librarian/media specialist	help in using reference materials and finding sources, including audiovisual materials

Community Resources	
Resource	**Source or Information**
World Wide Web and online services	articles, interviews, bibliographies, pictures, videos, sound recordings; access to the Library of Congress and other libraries
Local government agencies	facts and statistics on various subjects, policies, experts on local government
Local offices of state and federal government officials	voting records, recent or pending legislation, experts on state and federal government
Local newspaper offices	accounts of events of local interest, historical information on city or area
Museums, historical societies, service groups	historical events, scientific achievements, art and artists, special exhibits, and experts on these subjects

Schools and colleges	print and nonprint sources in libraries, experts on various subjects
Video stores	documentary and instructional videotapes and audiotapes
Hospitals, medical offices	brochures, pamphlets, doctors, and other medical experts

Evaluate Your Sources

A Source to Trust?   Just as members of a jury have to decide which witnesses are **credible,** or believable, and which are not, you have to determine the extent to which you can trust your sources of information. Here are some questions you can use to put your sources to the test.

1. **Is the information up-to-date?** Information is generated so quickly now that it is easy to find current material. If information on your topic is constantly changing, be sure that you are as up-to-date as possible. For example, a report on asthma medications from 1975 would not reflect current research and might be incorrect according to today's medical standards.

2. **Does the information seem factual?** Check the information against your own knowledge and against other sources. If you find an inconsistency between two sources, check a third source to determine which information is accurate.

3. **Does the source seem objective and logical?** Some sources may be biased, or slanted, toward one point of view. Others may use poor logic. You would not, for example, expect an objective assessment of one political party's platform from the leader of the opposing political party. However, it is a good idea to investigate all aspects of your topic, including various **points of view** on it.

Prepare Source Cards

Keeping Track of Everything   Since you will use more than one source for your paper, you will need a way to keep track of all of your information. One method is to write each source on a 3- x 5-inch index card (sometimes called a bibliography card) and number the source. If you are keeping your sources on a computer, create a separate file or record for each. Choose the method that works best for you. If you use the guidelines given on the next page to record the information, you will have a head start on your final list of sources.

TIP   You should always consider interviewing experts in the subject area you are researching. Experts can be valuable primary sources, and often they can direct you to other valuable sources. For more on **conducting interviews,** see page 854 in the Quick Reference Handbook.

Reference Note
For more on **punctuating titles,** see page 234.

Guidelines for Recording Source Information

1. **Book with One Author.** Write author's last name, then first name; book title (underlined); place of publication; name of publishing company; year of publication.

   Weinstein, Allan M., M.D. Asthma: The Complete Guide to Self-Management of Asthma and Allergies for Patients and Their Families. New York: McGraw-Hill, 1987.

2. **Book with More Than One Author.** Write first author, last name first. Other authors, first name first. Record other information as for a book with one author. (See source card #1 on page 215.)

3. **Magazine Article.** Write author's last name, then first name; article title; magazine name; day (if given), month, and year of publication; beginning and ending page numbers. If no author, start with the article title. (See source card #5 on page 215.)

4. **Newspaper Article.** Write author's last name, then first name; article title; newspaper name; day, month, and year of publication; section number (if there is one) and page number. If the newspaper has both morning and afternoon editions, write the edition and ed. before the page number. If no author is listed, start with the article title.

   Goode, Erica. "Can an Essay a Day Keep Asthma or Arthritis at Bay?" New York Times 14 April 1999. natl.ed.: A19.

5. **Encyclopedia Article.** Write author's last name, then first name; article title; encyclopedia name; edition number, followed by the abbreviation *ed.*; date of publication. If no author is listed, start with article title.

   Gallagher, Joan S. "Asthma." The World Book Encyclopedia. 1995 ed.

6. **Radio or Television Program.** Write episode or segment title (if any); program name, series title (if any); network name; local station call letters and city (if any); and day, month, and year of broadcast.

   "Stress and Kids' Asthma." Rpt. Michelle Trudeau. All Things Considered. National Public Radio. KUT-FM, Austin, Texas. 30 April 1997.

7. **Film or Video.** Write title; director or producer; medium (for video recordings); distributor; and year of release. (See source card #3 on page 215.)

8. **Personal or Telephone Interview.** Write interviewee's name; interview type (personal or telephone); and day, month, and year of interview. (See source card #4 on page 215.)

9. **Online Sources.** Write author's last name, then first name (if listed); title of document; underscored title of database or site; date of electronic publication; name of sponsoring institution; date information was accessed; <URL> [or] name of online service. (See source card #2 on page 215.)

10. **Portable Databases.** Write author's last name, then first name; title of document, article, or part of work; title of work; database title; edition, release, or version; publication medium (use the term *CD-ROM*, *Diskette*, or *Magnetic tape*); city of electronic publication, electronic publisher, and electronic publication date. (See source card #6 on page 215.)

In the following sample source cards, the writer used standard Modern Language Association (MLA) format. Notice that he gave each source a **source number,** which he wrote on the source card.

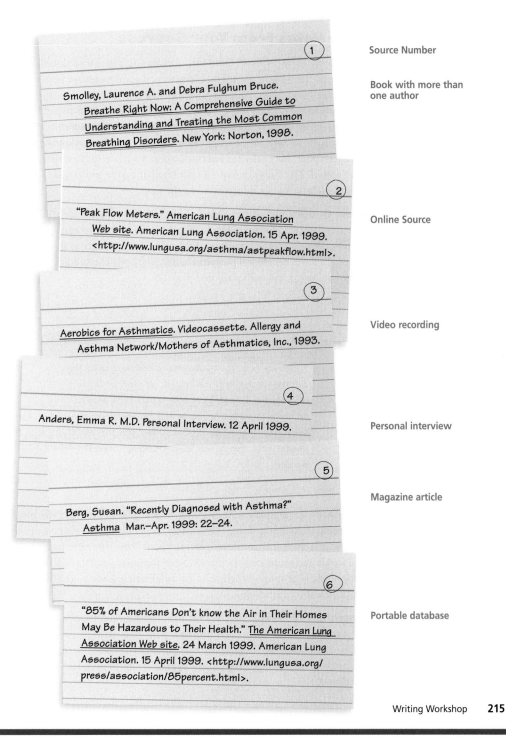

1 — Source Number

Smolley, Laurence A. and Debra Fulghum Bruce. <u>Breathe Right Now: A Comprehensive Guide to Understanding and Treating the Most Common Breathing Disorders</u>. New York: Norton, 1998.

Book with more than one author

2

"Peak Flow Meters." <u>American Lung Association Web site</u>. American Lung Association. 15 Apr. 1999. <http://www.lungusa.org/asthma/astpeakflow.html>.

Online Source

3

<u>Aerobics for Asthmatics</u>. Videocassette. Allergy and Asthma Network/Mothers of Asthmatics, Inc., 1993.

Video recording

4

Anders, Emma R. M.D. Personal Interview. 12 April 1999.

Personal interview

5

Berg, Susan. "Recently Diagnosed with Asthma?" <u>Asthma</u> Mar.–Apr. 1999: 22–24.

Magazine article

6

"85% of Americans Don't know the Air in Their Homes May Be Hazardous to Their Health." <u>The American Lung Association Web site</u>. 24 March 1999. American Lung Association. 15 April 1999. <http://www.lungusa.org/press/association/85percent.html>.

Portable database

Writing Workshop   **215**

Meeting
|INDIVIDUAL|
NEEDS

ENGLISH-LANGUAGE LEARNERS
General Strategies. The punctuation of source titles varies from country to country. Students who have recently come to the United States might punctuate titles as they have done in their native countries. For example, some students might use quotation marks to punctuate book titles. Also, while italics are used for book titles in English, languages such as Chinese and Arabic do not have italics. So that students can punctuate titles correctly in their documentation, use the punctuation shown on the sample source cards to review the rules for punctuating each type of title. You may find that a display listing titles that require underlining (italics) on one side and those that require quotation marks on the other is helpful.

Meeting INDIVIDUAL NEEDS

LEARNERS HAVING DIFFICULTY

Some students may benefit from a review of prereading strategies before starting the task of note taking. Help them recall uses and techniques for scanning ahead, reading the table of contents, and reading introductory paragraphs and lead sentences. Explain that these strategies will help students identify the information they need in an efficient manner.

TIP **Plagiarism** is presenting someone else's words or ideas as your own. Be sure to cite the sources of words and ideas you obtain from any outside sources. Distinguish your own ideas from those of others by using quotation marks if you repeat someone's exact words.

Take Notes from Your Sources

The Researcher's Best Friend   Unless you are one of those fortunate people who has a photographic memory, good notes are invaluable. If you take good notes, you will have a record of the important information you will need when it is time to sit down and draft your paper. When you take notes you can **quote directly, summarize,** or **paraphrase.** Below are examples of each of these methods used to record notes on the same passage. Notice that each card has the number 1 written in the upper right-hand corner. This number matches the number on the source card identifying the source of the information in the note.

Direct Quotation   If the author of a source has a particularly effective or memorable way of saying something, you may want to quote him or her. Be sure to copy the passage you intend to quote exactly as it is in your source. To avoid accidental plagiarism, put clearly visible quotation marks at the beginning and end of quoted passages.

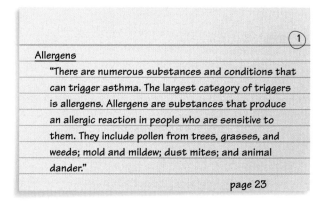

Allergens

"There are numerous substances and conditions that can trigger asthma. The largest category of triggers is allergens. Allergens are substances that produce an allergic reaction in people who are sensitive to them. They include pollen from trees, grasses, and weeds; mold and mildew; dust mites; and animal dander."

page 23

Summary   A **summary note** includes only the main idea and the most important supporting details of a passage. It allows you to save space because it is shorter than the original material. Write the note using your own words and sentence structure. Most of the notes you take will be summary notes. (For more information on summarizing, see page 864 in the Quick Reference Handbook.)

Paraphrase   A **paraphrase note** includes most of the author's ideas, not just the main ones. Like the summary note, it is written in your own words. You paraphrase to simplify the material you have read. (For more information on paraphrasing, see page 834 in the Quick Reference Handbook.)

Allergens

Asthma can be triggered by allergens, the most common of which are pollen from plants; mold and mildew; dust mites; and animal dander.

page 23

Source number

Summary

Allergens

Of the numerous substances that can trigger asthma, allergens are the largest category. These are substances that cause a reaction in people who are allergic to them. Allergens include pollens from plants; mold and mildew; animal dander; and dust mites.

page 23

Source number

Paraphrase

THINKING IT THROUGH — Taking Notes from Sources

To avoid getting lost in the information you gather, follow these steps for taking your notes and keeping them organized.

▶ **STEP 1** **Record your notes on something easy to retrieve.** Use 3- x 5-inch cards, 8-1/2- x 11-inch paper folded in half, or computer files or individual records in a computer database.

▶ **STEP 2** **Use a separate note card, computer file, or database record for each item of information and for each source.** Don't make a note of *every* piece of information. Note only facts or expert opinions that are **relevant** to your search.

▶ **STEP 3** **Put a subject heading consisting of a key word or phrase in the upper left-hand corner above each note.**

▶ **STEP 4** **Write the source number in the upper right-hand corner of each note; write the number of the page on which the information was found at the bottom of the note.**

▶ **STEP 5** **Keep computer printouts in a folder. Highlight key words and make notes in the margin.**

> **TIP** Take two kinds of notes:
>
> **1.** Analyze and synthesize ideas from a variety of print and nonprint sources. Also, note any new questions you have based on what you learn.
>
> **2.** Keep a daily record of your **research progress** in your search journal. Note your reactions and experiences as you do the research, including your failures as well as your successes. This record will be the basis for the story of your search and will also help you reflect on your experience.

Writing Workshop **217**

Write Your Thesis Statement

The Bottom Line Your **thesis** is the main idea of your report. It is the answer to your research question. The writer who began with the research question *Can I manage my asthma so that I can lead a full, active life?* found through research that the answer to his question was "yes." He could lead a full and active life if he carefully managed certain factors that had a direct bearing on his asthma.

KEY CONCEPT

To frame his thesis, he turned his research question into a statement and added the factors he would have to consider in order to manage his asthma. By adding these factors, he developed a short summary of the results of his research.

I can manage my asthma so that I can lead a full, active life by following my doctor's instructions on medication, by avoiding pets, by sticking to an exercise program, and by minimizing the effects of allergens that can trigger asthma episodes.

Develop an Informal Outline

TIP Your teacher may ask you to develop a **formal outline** for your I-Search paper. For more information about formal outlines, see page 895 in the Quick Reference Handbook.

Make a Fluid Plan An outline for a writing project is like a map to a traveler. Good outlines and good maps give guidance and keep people going in the right direction but leave them free to change their plans. Outlines also guide the organization of your ideas. I-Search papers are organized into three basic divisions: the story of the search, the results of the search, and reflections on the search. Your search journal contains the information you need for the story of your search. Your research results—the answers to your research questions—are in the notecards you made from your sources. You can use your search journal and notecards to arrange the information you want in your paper in your informal outline. Here is how one writer organized an informal outline for his I-Search paper.

1. **The story of my search**
   Learning of my condition
   What I knew about asthma
   Questions running through my head
   Research question: *Can I manage my asthma so that I can lead a full, active life?*
   Searching online
   Interviewing my doctor
   Searching the library
   Thesis Statement

2. **The results of my search**

> I can manage my asthma so that I can lead a full, active life if I
> - Follow my doctor's instructions on medications—inhalers and allergy shots
> - Avoid pets
> - Stick to an exercise program for respiratory muscles
> - Minimize environmental factors—dust, pollen, air pollution, weather

3. **In the end: Reflections on my search**

> Made me a better planner and organizer
> Helped me overcome shyness because I had to ask for help
> Improved my writing skills
> Improved my ability to draw conclusions
> Gave me confidence that I can lead a full and active life

YOUR TURN 5 · Planning Your I-Search Paper, Part Two

Review the prewriting steps that follow Your Turn 4 on page 211. Then, find and evaluate sources, prepare source cards, and take notes. Next, write your thesis, and create an informal outline for your paper.

Document Your Sources

Where Credit Is Due   In an I-Search paper, you use information and ideas that you obtained from outside sources. It is very important that you give credit to these sources by citing them in the body of your paper and by listing them at the end of your finished paper.

Citing Sources in the Body   When you are writing the body of your report, you must decide what to give credit for and how to give it.

- **What to Credit**   If the same information can be found in several sources, it is considered common knowledge. You do not have to document it. For example, it is common knowledge that Dr. Martin Luther King, Jr., gave his "I Have a Dream" speech in Washington, D. C. in 1963. However, any information that you obtain from outside sources that is not common knowledge must be documented.

- **How to Credit**   There are several ways to give credit. The two most widely used methods are **footnotes** (see the example footnote on the next page) and **parenthetical citations**. In this chapter you will see examples of the parenthetical citation format recommended by the **Modern Language Association of America (MLA).**

TIP   Your teacher might ask you to use a documentation format other than the MLA. The formats suggested by the **Chicago Manual of Style** and the **American Psychological Association (APA)** are two popular alternatives to MLA. Ask your teacher or librarian where to find them.

Guidelines for Giving Credit Within the Paper

Place the source citation in parentheses at the end of the sentence in which you have used someone else's words or ideas. The following examples follow the **MLA** format.

1. **Source with One Author.** Last name of the author, followed by the page number(s) (if any) of the work being cited: (Berg 23)

2. **Source with No Author Given.** Title, or shortened form of it, followed by page number(s) (if any): ("Peak Flow Meters")

3. **Source with Two or More Authors.** All authors' last names, followed by the page number(s) (if any): (Smolley and Bruce 128)

4. **Author's Name Given in Paragraph.** Page number only. (23)

TIP If your teacher prefers a certain style of documenting sources—**footnotes** or **endnotes,** for example, follow that style exactly. Here is an example of one style of footnote for a magazine article with one author. The number 1 at the beginning of the footnote refers to a number in the report where there is information to document. The footnote gives the author's first and last names (in that order), the book's title, publication information, and a page reference.

1. Susan Berg, "Recently Diagnosed with Asthma?" Asthma March/April 1999:22.

Include a *Works Cited* List At the end of your I-Search paper, you need to include a *Works Cited* list that includes all the sources you have used in your paper. A *Works Cited* list may include both print and non-print sources, such as films or electronic materials. If you are using only print sources in your paper, you can entitle your list of sources *Bibliography*. You provide a *Works Cited* list or a *Bibliography* for readers who are interested in learning more about your topic.

Guidelines for Preparing the List of Works Cited

1. Follow the format you used for your source cards. (See pages 214–215.)

2. List your sources in alphabetical order by the authors' last names (or, if no author is listed, by the title). Ignore *A*, *An*, and *The*, and use the first letter of the next word.

3. Begin each listing at the left margin. If the listing is longer than one line, indent the remaining lines five spaces. Double-space all entries.

4. Put your *Works Cited* list on a separate piece of paper at the end of your final I-Search paper. Center the words *Works Cited* at the top of the page.

Students who are working on their lists of works cited will find it helpful to use word-processing programs that make it easy to create and change indents, tabs, and special formatting. Most word-processing programs also have features for creating footnotes.

Evaluating Web Sources

One of the most important sources you can consult in researching for an I-Search paper is the World Wide Web, perhaps the richest source of information in the world. However, no system exists to ensure that what appears on the Web is accurate, reliable, and objective. You should evaluate every Web site you consider using for your paper, even those maintained by the government and educational institutions. You can evaluate Web sites by using the criteria and related questions explained below.

- **Coverage: How much information on a given topic is provided?** Is the information unique to this site, or is it available from some other source, like the library?

- **Accuracy: Is the information correct?** Remember that anyone can publish anything on the Web. Have you seen the same information in other sources? Do the authors of the Web page support their ideas with evidence?

- **Currency: What are the dates for creation, publication, and revision of the Web site?** These dates should appear at the bottom of the home page. Is the information up-to-date? When was the site last updated? Might the information have changed since then?

- **Authority: What are the qualifications of the creator and publisher of the Web site?** Sometimes authority is difficult to determine. Are the creator's qualifications shown on the Web page? If not, look for the creator's name in print bibliographies of works on the same subject as the Web page.

- **Objectivity: To what extent might the author's feelings about the topic affect the information he or she presents?** Does the Web site try to persuade you to adopt a particular point of view? Do the pages present both sides of an issue? Is the site affiliated with any major institutions or organizations?

PRACTICE

Using the information above as a reference, answer the following questions about a Web site you used in researching for your I-Search paper.

1. Is the information from the Web site available from a more accessible source? If so, name the source. If not, explain why.

2. Could you confirm the accuracy of the information by finding the same information in another source? If so, name the source. If not, explain.

3. Explain why you do or do not believe that the Web site's information is up-to-date.

4. Explain why you do or do not believe the author of the Web site to be qualified to write on the topic.

5. Does the Web site present both sides of an issue? If the Web site does not deal with an issue, what is its purpose?

Evaluating Web Sources

ANSWERS

Here are sample answers based on a Web site about vitamin B_{12} in the diet of vegetarians:

1. The information is available in books about vitamins and vegetarianism. However, I could get what I needed instantly on the Internet rather than having to go to a library or bookstore.
2. I can confirm the information by talking to a nutritionist or looking at a book on vitamins.
3. The site had a recent date showing when it was last modified.
4. The site was provided by a well-known vegetarian association.
5. The Web site is biased in favor of vegetarianism, so I will have to check a reference that provides information about nutrition in general to get a balanced view.

You need to be aware that Internet resources are sometimes public forums and that their content can be unpredictable.

Taking a Second Look

Evaluating Web Sources. Point out that each of the questions in the Practice exercise can also be applied to other sources, such as videos, magazine or newspaper articles, and books. Ask students to answer each of the questions again, substituting one of their other sources for the Web site they evaluated.

RESOURCES

Critical Thinking
Practice
- *Communications,* WS. p. 110

Writing

I-Search Paper

Framework	**Directions and Explanations**

The Search Story

- Hook readers immediately.
- Explain what you already knew about your topic.
- Tell what you wanted to know about your topic.
- Include a thesis statement.
- Retrace your research steps.

Grab Your Readers' Attention   Begin with an attention-getting statement about your topic, and explain why it was important for you to find out more about it.

Tell What You Knew   Briefly mention the most important information and ideas you already knew about your topic.

Tell What You Wanted To Learn and Why   Let readers know what you wanted to find out about your topic and the reasons motivating your search.

State Your Thesis   Turn your research question into a statement and add the factors that complete the statement.

The Search Results

- Describe important results of your research.
- Support your findings.

Retrace Your Steps   Describe the sources you began with and the ones you found later. Discuss successes and setbacks and any changes to your original research question.

Discuss Your Results and Give Support   Devote at least a paragraph to each important research result. Support your findings with direct quotations, paraphrases, and summaries of information from your sources.

Search Reflections

- Describe the significance of your research experience.
- Restate your thesis.

Reflect on Your Search   Describe what you learned from your research experience. Discuss how your experience and your new knowledge might affect your future. Remind readers of your thesis statement.

YOUR TURN 6 Writing a First Draft

Using the Framework above, write the first draft of your I-Search paper.

RESOURCES

Writing
Writing Prompts
- *Communications,* TP. 48, WS. p. 111

Your Turn 6
Practice
- *Communications,* TP. 49, WS. p. 112

A Writer's Model

The I-Search paper below, which is a final draft, closely follows the framework on the previous page.

Living with Asthma

The Story of My Search

"Well, Matt, it looks like you have asthma," the doctor told me. What a shock it was to hear those words. I thought I just had a stubborn cold. As I listened to the doctor explain my condition, questions started going through my head: Wasn't I too old to get asthma now? How could I stay on the basketball team? What about my camping trips?

Attention-grabbing statement

I already knew that asthma is a chronic, or long-lasting, disease which affects the lungs and that certain medications help control the number and severity of asthma episodes (that's when the coughing and wheezing start). I did not know much more than that, though.

Background on known important facts

Since I am on the basketball team and also go on weekend camping trips with my Boy Scout troop, I wanted to find out more about the kinds of things that might trigger an asthma episode. Were there trees and plants I should avoid? Would I be able to keep up with my teammates on the basketball court? Would I still be able to get the dog my parents had finally agreed to let me have?

Brief overview of what the writer wants to learn

I made a list of all of the things I wanted to learn. From that list, I was able to form my research question: *Can I effectively manage my asthma?* Later, I was able to form an answer: I can manage my asthma and live a full, active life by following my doctor's instructions about medications, by avoiding pets, by sticking to an exercise program, and by minimizing the effects of environmental factors that can trigger asthma episodes.

Thesis statement

My search took about three weeks, and it was a new experience for me. I started by doing an online search using the keywords *asthma* and *managing*. I was surprised at the amount of information I found. There were Web sites maintained by doctors, pharmaceutical companies, and support groups. I ordered some free print materials from one of the pharmaceutical companies; unfortunately, I had my first draft finished before they arrived. However, because it turned out to be good information, I went back and reworked part of the draft.

Steps of the research process

(continued)

Critical Thinking

Metacognition. Point out to students that the author used three subheadings to guide readers through the paper. Ask students to explain whether their reading was helped or hindered by the subheadings. Encourage students to suggest other locations and wordings for subheadings and have them explain their thinking. Invite students to consider whether subheadings would be useful as they draft their writing.

Description of narrowing the research topic

First major finding

Direct quotation

Summary

Second major finding

Third major finding

The next thing I did was to call my allergy/asthma specialist, Dr. Anders. I forgot to take her busy schedule into account, and I did not know that she had planned a short vacation during the time I was doing my research. She graciously agreed to meet with me after her office hours one day. I am glad she did, because she gave me some very good advice. She also let me borrow a few videos about asthma.

During that same week I went to my school library. The librarian showed me the reference books and regular books. I went through the latest volumes of the *Readers' Guide to Periodical Literature* and found several magazine articles. By the end of the week, my head was swimming with a huge amount of information.

My original search question remained the same: *Can I manage my asthma?* However, I was able to define exactly what it was that I wanted to manage. I ended up narrowing my topic to four areas I had to deal with in order to manage my asthma: medications, pets, sports/exercise, and environmental factors.

The Results of My Search

The first thing I found out was that certain substances can trigger an asthma attack of "coughing, wheezing, and shortness of breath" (Abramowicz). Allergens constitute the largest category of triggers. According to Susan Berg, "Allergens are substances that produce an allergic reaction in people who are sensitive to them." Common allergens are pollens from plants, animal dander, dust mites, and mold and mildew (23). My doctor said she would test me for allergies right away. If I am allergic to certain things, allergy shots help by desensitizing me to them and make them less likely to trigger an episode (Anders).

If I find that I am allergic to certain pollens, I can reduce the chances of an asthma episode by staying indoors when those pollens are in the air. Indoors, I can reduce the risk of an episode by using the air conditioner to circulate air while keeping windows and doors closed to keep pollens out. Cleaning the air with an air cleaning device can reduce dust mites, mold spores, and other indoor allergens ("85% of Americans").

Several medications and devices help people with asthma. One device is called a peak flow meter. This is a tube about six inches long; its purpose is to measure your ability to push air out of your lungs. When you blow into it, you can find out if your lungs are working at their capacity. If they are not, you know it is time to take some medication ("Peak Flow Meters"). My doctor explained how the different medications work: an inhaler sends medication right into the lungs without a lot of side effects (Anders). She showed me another type of inhaler to use when my peak flow number is low, or if I get short of breath while I am exercising. This inhaler helps me get my breath back right away.

I also found out that certain anti-inflammatory drugs are used to keep air passages open and prevent asthma episodes. One type of these is called corticosteroids. I was glad to find that these are not the same kind of steroids that cause serious side effects in athletes who take them. The risk of side effects with corticosteroids is very small ("Asthma Medicines").

Physical exercise makes an asthmatic's condition worse, or so doctors believed twenty or thirty years ago. At that time doctors believed a quiet, restful life was best. Now new research is showing that "people with breathing disorders who can maintain a regular program of exercise and activity are able to experience maximum cardiovascular fitness along with greater symptom control, or an increased ability to exercise and do the activities of daily living. Exercise trains the respiratory muscles to work more efficiently" (Smolley and Bruce 127–128). I had been worried that I would have to drop off the basketball team and miss the next Boy Scout campout we had planned. These facts, however, make me confident that I can continue to play basketball and go on camping trips.

Nancy Hogshead, a former Olympic athlete, demonstrates some exercises for asthmatics on a video called *Aerobics for Asthmatics*. I tried some of the exercises, and they are great. Nancy is quite a role model. She and other Olympic athletes (including Rob Muzzio, Jim Ryun, Jackie Joyner-Kersee, and Amy Van Dyken) have had to deal with asthma, and many of these athletes still compete (Smolley and Bruce 128).

In fact, a recent study of Olympic athletes revealed that "more than 20 percent of the American athletes who participated in the 1996 Summer Olympic games may have had asthma" ("Olympians"). I am very encouraged by this fact.

(continued)

Fourth major finding

Fifth major finding

TIP I-Search papers and their *Works Cited* lists are normally double-spaced. Because of limited space on these pages, A Writer's Model and A Student's Model are single-spaced. The *Elements of Language* Internet site provides a model of an I-Search paper in the double-spaced format. To see this interactive model, go to **go.hrw.com** and enter the keyword **EOLang 9-6.**

Writing Workshop   225

(continued)

Connecting Reading and Writing

After students read **A Writer's Model,** have them re-read the investigative report featured in the Reading Workshop (pp. 197–199). Ask students to compare and contrast the elements of voice and tone in these two research essays. Guide students to see that while both essays describe a search for information, Least Heat-Moon's tone is more sophisticated and professional, while **A Writer's Model** is quite informal and focuses more on the author. Talk with students about the importance of using the right tone for a specific audience. This discussion will help students establish a comfortable writing voice and tone as they write their I-Search papers.

Olympian Amy Van Dyken

Olympian Jackie Joyner-Kersee

Answer to the research question

After doing the research, I concluded that if I developed a plan for myself, I would be able to manage my asthma. This is my working plan:

1. Medical Treatment: Take allergy shots if it turns out I have allergies. Take my medications and monitor peak flow levels every day. Call the doctor as necessary. Go in for checkups every three months.
2. Environment: Give up going on hikes if the pollen count is very high. Avoid other allergens whenever possible.
3. Pets: Postpone a decision on pets until I find out whether I am allergic to them.
4. Sports/Exercise: Continue with all sports and activities. Use the peak flow meter before and after basketball games. Do warm-up breathing exercises. Keep an inhalator handy for emergency use.

Reflections on My Search

Significance of the research experience

Doing the research took a lot more time than I thought it would. I have learned how to plan my time more efficiently and how to organize my thoughts better. I am getting better at organizing my paperwork, too. Since I am rather shy, it was good for me to be forced to ask the doctor and librarian for assistance. My writing skills also improved. Now I am able to write a paragraph and stick to one topic. I also learned how to evaluate sources of information I find on the World Wide Web. In addition to these

Restatement of thesis

academic benefits, I got a lot of information that will help me lead a full and active life—in spite of my asthma.

Works Cited

Abramowicz, Mark. "Asthma, Bronchial." Microsoft Encarta
    98 Encyclopedia. CD-ROM. Microsoft Corp., 1993–97.

Aerobics for Asthmatics. Videocassette. Allergy and Asthma
    Network/Mothers of Asthmatics, Inc., 1993.

Anders, Emma R., M.D. Personal interview. 12 Apr. 1999.

"Asthma Medicines." American Lung Association Web site.
    American Lung Association. 15 Apr. 1999.
    <http://www.lungusa.org/asthma/astasmeds2.html>.

Berg, Susan. "Recently Diagnosed with Asthma?" Asthma
    Mar.–Apr. 1999: 22–24.

"85% of Americans Don't Know the Air in Their Homes May
    Be Hazardous to Their Health." American Lung
    Association Web site. 24 Mar. 1999. American Lung
    Association. 15 Apr. 1999. <http://www.lungusa.org/
    press/association/85percent.html>.

"Olympians Don't Let Asthma Hold Them Back." Asthma
    Mar.–Apr. 1999: 15.

"Peak Flow Meters." American Lung Association Web site.
    American Lung Association. 15 Apr. 1999.
    <http://www. lungusa.org/asthma/astpeakflow.html>.

Smolley, Laurence A. and Debra Fulghum Bruce. Breathe Right
    Now: A Comprehensive Guide to Understanding and
    Treating the Most Common Breathing Disorders. New
    York: Norton, 1998.

TIP Before you finalize your parenthetical citations or *Works Cited* list, be sure to review **Document Your Sources** on pages 219–220.

CALVIN & HOBBES © 1989 Watterson. Distributed by Universal Press Syndicate. Reprinted with permission. All rights reserved.

Writing Workshop **227**

The following excerpted I-Search paper was written by Amy E. Hofmann, a student at Conrad Weiser High School in Robesonia, Pennsylvania. The *Works Cited* list is not included.

The Call of the Hornet

What I Knew

Interesting opening

    I have always had a fascination with the Sportwagon Hornet, or "Punchbuggy" (whatever you choose to call it). They were cute cars with an odd design that put the engine in the back. I liked their unique shape and style. Hornets seemed to have their own personality and, I thought, would be fun to drive.

Reasons for the search

    I grew up on the lookout for Hornets, straining my eyes out of the school bus window searching for one. "Punchbuggy red (or blue, or black, or green) and no punch backs . . ." was a common phrase heard on the bus. The punches on the arm that followed were common, too. It was a fun way to pass the time.

    I grew to love the Hornets, and last year the idea came to me that I might own one of my very own. This prospect has led to my quest for the Hornet. I hope that in one to two years, I will be able to find a "Punch-buggy" that is perfect for me. For now, though, I must satisfy my curiosity and answer the call of the Hornet.

What I Wanted to Know

Thesis statement

    I decided to base my search on one simple question (though it eventually turned out to be more complex than I thought). I wanted to know where I could find my dream, an affordable vintage Hornet in fairly good condition and fairly close to home. My search begins . . .

How I Searched

The story of the search

    I began with a single Web address: http://www.spwm.com, and a dream. I hardly knew where the combination would take me. Here I learned much about the new Hornet that will come out in the spring of 2004, but that did not help me with what I wanted to know: Where can I find my dream Hornet?

From the Sportwagon Hornet Web site, I decided to try my luck with search engines. I tried only two and was swamped with all kinds of Web sites, ranging from Sportwagon restoration to shrines dedicated to Hornets to (at last!) Hornets for sale! Ha! The joke was on me, though. These Hornets, nice though they were, were all right-hand drive, British models, with their prices listed in pounds. If you are going to Europe, and would like to take a look at a few Hornets, scope it out (Euroauto).

It was really touch and go at times with the search engines. I had to read through many summaries before I came to the word "sale," and even then, I found very little of what I wanted.

The search engines finally led me to the Web site that provided the best information, a site that is basically a directory of advertisements from people all across the United States, with all kinds of cars for sale (Carsite). Being the inexperienced Internet surfer that I am, I began the hard way, searching in the "used cars" section, first by region, then by state, and then by model. If there were no Hornets, I would have to start the process over again. Then, one day, I happened to come across this little finder button, and lo and behold, I could search the entire United States of America for SW Hornets at one time! Here on Carsite, I found six. I printed out the descriptions of each and decided to make my search more personal, so I e-mailed three perfect strangers who shared at least one quality with me—a love for Hornets. . . .

My search for Hornets also led me to my local newspaper, but this, too, was discouraging. Only a small block of the "automobiles for sale" classifieds is dedicated to antique cars. I found this out after days spent poring over the entire classified section before I noticed the "antique" block. In the end, I discovered only one Hornet for sale.

I found the ad in a Friday newspaper. It read: "1966 SW Hornet—67,000 orig. mi., runs great, $1500"

(continued)

Thesis reiterated in the form of a research question

A setback in the search

Citation of online source with neither author nor title

A breakthrough in the search

A modification of the search

Citation of a classified ad in a newspaper

(continued)

("1966 SW Hornet"). On the following Monday I checked the paper again. The advertisement was gone. Needless to say, I was terribly disappointed.

What I Learned

Unless you really know what you are doing or exactly what you are looking for, trying to make your way around the Internet can be difficult. There seemed to be no easy way to find a site advertising only SW's for sale. There were many Web pages that were dedicated as shrines for personal Hornets or sites for restoration. . . .

For the most part, I learned that there are plenty of vintage Hornets around, as vintage Hornets have the highest percentage of vehicles from their era on the road. The catch is that they are already in the hands of restorers and SW fanatics. . . .

What My Search Told Me

What did my search tell me about finding a vintage Hornet that is close to home, affordable, and in good condition? It told me that the Internet is not the only way to search for things, but it is often more helpful than traditional sources. It told me that SW Hornets are hard to find. Even if you do find one, you need to inspect it to make sure it is in good condition.

What did my search tell me? It told me that if I am willing to do a little searching, I have a good chance of finding a Hornet in a year or two, a much better chance than I did before doing this paper. Now I know where to look. I know that all the Hornets will not disappear by then, despite the fact that my closest find was gone within days of discovery. They are out there, and there is a good possibility that mine is out there, just waiting for me to buy it. At least that is what I like to think. . . .

Research results described in separate paragraphs

Reflections on the search

What the search means for future searches

Revising

Evaluate and Revise Your Draft

Touch-Up or Major Overhaul? Did you know that many famous writers revise their works several times? Very few writers get it just right the first time. To refine your writing, read through your paper at least twice. First evaluate the content and organization, using the following guidelines. Then, use the guidelines on page 232 to revise for style.

▶ **First Reading: Content and Organization** If you are one of those writers who has difficulty evaluating and revising your own writing, the following chart should help you. Ask yourself the questions in the first column. If you need help answering the questions, use the tips in the second column. Then, make the changes suggested in the last column. You may want to collaborate with a peer to work through the chart.

I-Search Paper: Content-and-Organization Guidelines for Peer and Self-Evaluation

Evaluation Questions	▶ Tips	▶ Revision Techniques
❶ Does the thesis statement answer the research question completely?	▶ **Underline** the thesis statement. **Box** the research results summarized in the thesis. If one or more results are missing, revise.	▶ **Add** research results to the thesis statement until it is a complete answer to the research question.
❷ Is the story of the search in logical order?	▶ **Number** each step of the search in the order it happened. If the numbers are out of order as you read through the paper, revise.	▶ **Rearrange** the steps of the search so that they are in logical order.
❸ Are the results of the search adequately supported by information from outside sources?	▶ **Circle** the major results of the search. **Underline** sentences containing information from an outside source. If you underline fewer than three sentences, revise.	▶ **Add** information from outside sources. **Elaborate** on each major result with an interesting or surprising detail from an outside source.
❹ Are enough print and nonprint sources of information used? Are they recent, reliable and objective?	▶ **Highlight** information taken from the note cards. Revise if both print and nonprint sources are not used or if some sources seem dated.	▶ Consult a library's card or online catalog and the *Readers' Guide*. **Add** information from these sources to your report.
❺ Does the conclusion describe how the research experience affected the writer?	▶ **Bracket** each sentence that describes the effects of the research experience on the writer.	▶ **Add** statements that explain the effects of the research experience.

Ask students to discuss why an experienced author such as Nabokov would have to erase his words. For example, students may say that in re-reading what he wrote, Nabokov might have realized that he needed to add more background information or that his wording was awkward and needed to be clarified. Remind students that even successful writers have to rework their drafts many times to achieve the clarity and style they wish to have.

T E A C H I N G   TIP

▶ **Elaboration**
Remind students that examples are very helpful in making concepts clear to readers of research papers. Pair students and ask them to read each other's papers with the purpose of looking for places where examples might clarify or extend the reader's understanding of the topic. Direct students to make an "E" in the margin to indicate where these examples could be placed.

If some students are having difficulty adding examples to their papers, you might want to provide additional instruction on elaboration. See pp. 350–353 and pp. 367–369 in Chapter 11.

RESOURCES

Revising
Practice
■ *Communications,* TPs. 50, 51, WS. pp. 113, 114, 115

ONE WRITER'S REVISIONS Here is how one writer used the content-and-organization guidelines to revise some sentences from the I-Search paper on pages 223–227. Study the revisions and answer the questions following the paragraph.

> I made a list of all the things I wanted to learn. From that list,
>
> *rearrange*   I was able to form my research question: Later, I was able to form
>
> an answer: I can manage my asthma and live a full, active life by
>
> *add*   following my doctor's instructions about medications, ~~by avoiding pets,~~ by sticking
>
> to an exercise program, and by minimizing the effects of environ-
>
> *delete*   mental factors that can trigger asthma episodes. ~~The question~~
>
> *Can I effectively manage my asthma?* ~~was answered~~.

Analyzing the Revision Process

1. Why does the writer rearrange the paragraph so that the research question comes in the second sentence?
2. Why is the information added to the paragraph important?

Analyzing the Revision Process

ANSWERS

1. It is more logical to first state the question and then present the answers in the thesis statement.

2. It helps the author answer the research question more completely.

YOUR TURN 7

Use a checklist based on the **Content-and-Organization Guidelines** on p. 231 to assess student work. Provide space beside each evaluation point to provide specific feedback to students.

PEER REVIEW

Ask a classmate to read your paper and answer the following questions.

1. Can you understand the writer's desire to research this topic? Why or why not?

2. About which aspect of the topic would you have liked the writer to tell you more? Why?

YOUR TURN 7   Focusing on Content and Organization

Using the guidelines on the previous page and the example revisions shown above as a model, revise your I-Search paper.

▶ **Second Reading: Style**   In your second reading, look at your sentence style. Avoid beginning sentences with *there is/are* or *there was/were*. The following style guidelines will help you vary your sentence beginnings.

Style Guidelines

Evaluation Question	▶ Tip	▶ Revision Technique
Do sentences begin with the words *there is, there was, there are,* or *there were*?	**Highlight** each sentence that begins this way. Revise highlighted sentences that can be smoothly reworded.	**Rearrange** the sentence so that the subject comes first. Then, reword the sentence using a strong verb.

Eliminating "There is/There are" Sentence Beginnings

Starting sentences with phrases like *there is* makes your writing sound monotonous to readers. You can more effectively present ideas by putting the subject in the place of *there* and using a lively verb. For example, instead of writing *There was the girl (or boy) of my dreams,* write *The girl (or boy) of my dreams suddenly appeared in front of me.*

Focus on Sentences

ONE WRITER'S REVISIONS   The writer of the model I-Search paper on pages 223–227 used the guidelines on the preceding page to revise sentence beginnings.

BEFORE REVISION

There is a video called *Aerobics for Asthmatics*, which features a former Olympic athlete named Nancy Hogshead doing aerobic exercises.

Sentence begins with *there is.*

AFTER REVISION

Nancy Hogshead, a former Olympic athlete, demonstrates some exercises for asthmatics on a video called *Aerobics for Asthmatics*.

Revise by putting subject first and using an active verb.

Analyzing the Revision Process

1. What is better about using the verb *demonstrates*?

2. How does the focus of the sentence change?

 Focusing on Style

Revise the style of your I-Search paper using the guidelines on page 232.

Analyzing the Revision Process

ANSWERS

1. The verb *demonstrates* is a strong, vivid verb; *is* is weaker and less descriptive.

2. The subject in the revised sentence is active. The revision gives the sentence a more powerful, authoritative effect.

YOUR TURN 8

Ask students to show you both the revised paper and the highlighted original to assess their success in locating and rewording sentences that begin with *there is, there are, there was,* or *there were.* Also, assess students' ability to recognize other awkward sentences that can be improved by replacing a verb.

RESOURCES

Focus on Sentences
Practice
■ *Communications,* WS. p. 116

Publishing

Proofread Your Paper

Reference Note

For more information and practice on **punctuating titles,** see page 684 and page 692.

A Fine-Toothed Comb Before you prepare a final copy of your I-Search paper, make sure that it is free of grammar, spelling, and punctuation errors. Punctuating titles correctly is particularly important in an I-Search paper, where you must refer to sources with different types of titles.

Grammar Link

Punctuating Titles

You can use the following guidelines to punctuate any titles you include in your I-Search paper.

- **Use underlining for titles of books, plays, films, periodicals, works of art, and television programs.** (In print, underlining appears as *italic* type. If you are using a computer, you can use an italic font to indicate titles.)

Examples:
The Red Badge of Courage (book)
Newsweek (periodical)
The Lion King (film)
Biography (TV program)

- **Magazine articles, chapter headings, and titles of short poems, short stories, short musical compositions, and individual episodes of TV shows** should be placed in **quotation marks,** not italicized.

Examples:
"What You Need to Know about Vitamins" (magazine article)
"The Caged Bird" (poem)
Chapter 1, "Our Solar System" (book chapter)

- **Underline (or italicize) the title of a poem long enough to be published in a separate volume,** such as *The Rime of the Ancient Mariner.* Also,

italicize the titles of long musical compositions, such as *1812 Overture* by Tchaikovsky.

The words *a, an,* and *the* before a title are italicized when they are part of the title. The article *the* before the title of a newspaper is italicized and capitalized only if it appears in the masthead of the publication.

Examples:
The House on Mango Street
A Separate Peace
the *San Francisco Examiner*

PRACTICE

Copy the following sentences onto your own paper, correctly punctuating the titles in each sentence.

1. Have you read the novel The Dolphins of Pern by Anne McCaffrey?
2. Jane asked to borrow my Time magazine.
3. Yesterday's Philadelphia Inquirer newspaper had an article on asthmatic athletes.
4. The history book chapter titled The Renaissance has some magnificent pictures.
5. How to Make a Piñata was the best article.

Publish Your Paper

Share Your Experience   Here are some ways you might share your I-Search paper with a larger audience.

- **Locate a group or organization that would have a special interest in your research.** For example, the writer of the Writer's Model on pages 223–226 could share his I-Search paper with a support group for people with asthma.

- **Submit your paper to a magazine—online or print—**that publishes either articles on your topic or articles by people your age.

- **Collect other I-Search papers from your class** for a special display at your school or in your classroom.

- **Send a copy of your paper to any professional** you might have interviewed. For example, the writer of the Writer's Model might mail a copy to the doctor he interviewed.

TIP   If you choose to write your paper by hand—either in print or cursive—be sure that your handwriting is **legible;** that is, neat and easy to read. Otherwise, use keyboarding skills to present your ideas in a professional-looking document.

TIP   If you have written your paper for a general audience and now wish to publish it for a more specific audience, you may need to refine it a bit, keeping in mind what that audience knows about your topic. You might also consider presenting your findings in a different format to appeal to a new audience.

 PORTFOLIO

Reflect on Your Paper

Give It Some Thought   Writing short responses to the following questions will help you build on what you have learned in this workshop.

- What difficulties did you encounter while writing this paper? What might you do to avoid them next time?

- What part of the paper was the easiest to write? Why?

- What part of the paper was the hardest to write? Why?

- What discoveries did you make about yourself as a writer while completing this workshop?

YOUR TURN 9   **Proofreading, Publishing, and Reflecting**

Before you turn in your I-Search paper, be sure you

- proofread it carefully
- consider publishing options
- reflect on the effects of the I-Search experience

TEACHING TIP

Proofreading, Publishing, and Reflecting
Tie the proofreading step to grammar instruction by having students look specifically for the problem addressed in the **Grammar Link** as they proofread their papers.

YOUR TURN 9

Before students turn in their final papers, refer them to the discussion of framework on p. 222. Have them pay particular attention to "Discuss Your Results and Give Support." Then, have them ask themselves: Have I included at least three or four findings from my research? To make your assessment easier, you may want to ask students to underline the topic sentences that introduce each major finding. If they find this difficult, ask them to review their note cards and highlight the information they actually used in their papers.

TEACHING TIP

Designing Your Writing

Students who are planning to include illustrations might benefit from a class discussion of captions. Provide magazines and newspapers for students to skim. Ask them to focus on the captions for the illustrations. Encourage students to create a few standards for effective captions. For instance, they might suggest the following:

Effective captions

- are brief

- are directly related to the illustration

- make sense when read alone without reading the rest of the article.

Wrap It Up

Metacognition. Give students time to review the materials they prepared during the Writing Workshop. Then, have them answer the following questions:

1. How did writing an outline help you write your paper?

2. What pleases you most about your final draft? How would you improve it?

Using Graphics Effectively When you read a print document or a Web page, you usually see a combination of words and illustrations. These illustrations—photographs, line drawings, graphs, diagrams, maps, charts, and so on—are meant to increase the effectiveness of the text. Follow these guidelines if you use illustrations in your writing.

- **Think carefully about the information you want to convey to your readers.** Ask yourself which information would have a greater impact if it were presented pictorially. For example, if you are preparing a report on ethnic diversity in the United States, adding a pie chart showing the changes in ethnic distribution over a period of time might be much more effective than presenting such information using text only.

Ethnic Diversity in the United States

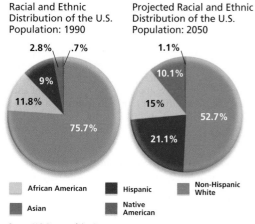

Source: U.S. Bureau of the Census

- **Provide drawings or illustrations of things with which your readers might be unfamiliar.** The writer of "Living with Asthma" describes a device called a peak flow meter. Most of his readers probably have never seen a peak flow meter, so an illustration would have helped his readers understand the use of the device.

- **Be sure the text and the art complement one another.** If your paper describes the great beauty of one of our country's national parks, actual photographs of the park would be much more appropriate than a line drawing or computer clip art. If, on the other hand, your I-Search paper is on the ups and downs of the stock market, a graph showing the actual rise and fall of stock prices would be more appropriate than a photograph of the stock exchange.

236   Chapter 6   **Exposition:** Investigating a Research Question

Connections to Literature

Research for Fiction Writing

Although you might not have thought about it, research plays a part in fiction, especially **historical novels,** fictional works set in particular historical periods. Story characters can participate in historical events and move among actual historical figures, or they can be actual historical figures participating in fictionalized events. To make these fictional works seem real, writers must do the research necessary to lend a feeling of reality to their characters and details of place, time, and action.

Thorough research allows writers to assign their characters the appropriate dress, speech, hobbies, occupations, and so on. For example, a character in a story set in 1880 obviously could not work as a computer engineer—but what engineering work would such a character have been able to do in 1880? Research would answer this question.

Research Tool Time Like other researchers, fiction writers use both primary and secondary sources as tools. For example, to write a historical novel about the Vietnam War, an author might interview veterans of that war and also consult histories about the war.

Keeping It Real Imagine that you decided to write a short story about a famous unsolved crime that took place in your town during the Great Depression of the 1930s. What makes your story fictional is that your fictional hero will solve the crime.

Much of what you will need to research is obvious. You will need to learn all that you can about the people involved in the crime—victim, suspects, investigators—and the facts about the crime itself. However, you will need to research more if you want to make your story seem real. The following list of questions will give you an idea of the kinds of information you would need to make the story realistic.

■ What important events were going on locally, nationally, and internationally at the time of my story which would affect my story and its characters?

■ What did my town look like in the 1930s?

■ How did men and women dress in the 1930s?

■ What did people do for entertainment?

■ What did people do to earn a living?

YOUR TURN 10 Researching for Fiction

Imagine that you and two classmates are collaborating on a story about three fifteen-year-olds growing up in a poor neighborhood in a city in the northeastern United States in 1900. Brainstorm at least five questions you would need to answer to give your story an air of reality. Then, list three or more sources you might consult to answer each question.

Focus on Viewing and Representing

OBJECTIVES

- To create a three-minute video documentary
- To create a script
- To create storyboards
- To videotape, edit, and review your documentary
- To show your documentary and get feedback

Quotation for the Day

"The most interesting development in filmmaking has been the video camera, because, for the first time, you can make a movie all by yourself."

(D. A. Pennebaker, 1925–   , American documentary filmmaker)

Read the quotation aloud and invite students to consider their experiences using video cameras to make home movies. Ask students to describe techniques they have learned that might help them film a documentary. Then, introduce the main objective of this workshop: to create an informative video documentary.

WHAT'S AHEAD?

In this section, you will create a three-minute video documentary. You will also learn how to

- create a script
- create storyboards
- edit and review your documentary
- show your documentary and get feedback

Making a Video Documentary

Most of what you watch on television and in movie theaters— dramas, comedies, and so on—is fictional, or "made-up." Some of what you watch is not fictional. One important type of nonfiction is the **documentary**, a kind of television program or movie that deals with real people and events. Making a documentary requires research, just as writing a research paper does. However, while the research paper uses the printed page to convey its information, a movie or television documentary uses *spoken words*, *images*, *music*, and *action*.

Planning a Video Documentary

First Considerations First   Before you do anything else, you have to make firm decisions about certain basics.

- **Topic**   You can choose a new topic for your documentary, but since you have already done research for your I-Search paper, you might consider using it as your topic and expanding your research as necessary.
- **Purpose**   Exactly what do you want your documentary to accomplish? Is your purpose to instruct, to inform, or to entertain? Is it a combination of all these purposes?
- **Audience**   Who will see your documentary? The content you choose for your documentary and the way you present it should differ according to your intended audience's age, gender, economic status, educational level, and so forth.
- **Length**   How long should your documentary be? In this case, three minutes is predetermined. Obviously, three minutes does not give you enough time to go into great detail in your documentary. The length of your documentary, then, determines the depth with which you can treat your subject.

238   Chapter 6   **Exposition:** Investigating a Research Question

Here are some decisions that one student producer made about the four items listed on the previous page.

Topic	My topic is my search for the answer to an important question: Can I manage my asthma so that I can lead a full, active life?
Purpose	I want to show my audience part of my search for the answers to my question about asthma. I want my documentary to be both informative and engaging.
Audience	My audience will be made up of classmates. They will be male and female ninth-graders who can identify with my need to know how asthma will affect my life.
Length	Since I have only three minutes, I will have to hit the highlights, focusing on only the most important parts of my search.

Delivering the Message   In the second phase of planning, you need to answer questions about three important issues that can make or break your documentary.

- **What is the controlling idea or message you want your documentary to deliver?** What, in other words, do you want your documentary as a whole to say to your audience?

- **How will you capture and hold your audience's attention?** You must engage your audience's emotions by allowing them to share in the emotional highs and lows of your experience. You want your audience to care about your subject.

- **What will you show your audience and what will you tell them?** What visual content and what audio content will you use in your documentary? In general, the best choices for **video content** are **action sequences, interviews, graphs,** and **still photos.** The **audio content**—the voices and music the audience will hear—provides explanations of what the audience is seeing and makes transitions, or bridges, between scenes.

Here is the way the student writing about asthma answered the above questions about his three-minute documentary.

MULTIPLE INTELLIGENCES

Spatial Intelligence. Provide a mini-lesson on graphics for those who wish to include charts, visual organizers, and other illustrations in their documentaries. Video studios usually use computer-generated graphics, and students will probably want to create graphics and take close-up photographs for inclusion in their video presentations. Give students a chance to review one or more documentaries for the purpose of noting the kinds of graphics used. Then, provide support by making books on graphics available, asking an art teacher to provide some tips, or inviting a few students who enjoy art to serve as consultants to others.

Message: The fact that I have asthma does not mean that I cannot live a full and active life. The same is probably true of a lot of people who suffer from asthma if they would just go to the trouble to find out what they can do to keep asthma from ruling their lives.

Audience: I will engage my audience's emotions and make them care about my topic by showing them the fear and disappointment I felt when I first found out that I have asthma. Then, I will take them along on my search for an answer to the question of how much asthma might affect my life.

Content: With the help of a classmate camera operator, I will videotape partial re-enactments of my experience in the doctor's office when I learned that I have asthma and a complete re-enactment of my interview with Dr. Anders. I will have another classmate interview me on the results of my research. I will conclude my documentary with a videotape of me and several classmates demonstrating exercises for people with asthma. My classmate will do voice-over explanations of the exercises' benefits.

Tricks of the Trade   Professional video documentary makers employ many techniques to make their videos interesting and lively. Here are some basic techniques that student documentary makers can use.

Interviews	• Change locations and speakers frequently to avoid losing the attention of the audience. • Divide interviews into short segments of five to ten seconds. • Ask one question at a time and do not interrupt the answer. • Increase interest and pace by showing **B-roll footage**. B-roll is video shown as background for an interview. It can be video of people, events, or objects being spoken of in the **A-roll**, the video of the interview.
Narrator (Voice-over)	• Create transitions between scenes, such as introducing the next scene by relating it to the scene just ending. • Avoid stating the obvious, like explaining something the video makes clear.
Action Sequences	• Alternate long shots of whole scenes with scenes showing people doing something and with close-ups of people's faces. • Hold the camera steady to follow the action.
Transitions	• Use a simple cut (stop taping when a scene is over) most of the time to end a scene and move on to the next. • Use the fade in/out (two- to three-second transition from a full signal to black in video and silence in audio) feature of your video camera for scene changes sparingly. Too much fade-in/out tends to make viewers feel seasick.

Learning the Shorthand   Every profession has its own shorthand—abbreviations and acronyms—to refer to important ideas, concepts, techniques, and so on. Videotaping a documentary (or anything else) has its own special shorthand, too. The following abbreviations are written into scripts so that people who operate the video cameras will know how to shoot (tape) a particular scene.

Abbreviation	Meaning
EXT/INT	exterior or interior shot
SOT	sound on videotape audio track
VO	voice-over: narration heard over a video source and sometimes over music or sound
OSV	off-screen voice; speaker not visible
MIC	microphone other than a video camera's built-in microphone
POV	shot is taken from the point of view of a particular person
OS	over-the-shoulder shot that shows the back of a person's head and possibly one shoulder
SFX or FX	special effects; either *FX audio* or *FX video* for effects that are created during the production to alter reality. Special effects are not used very often in documentaries.

Put It in Writing   Next among planning tasks is to write a script for your documentary. As you go about scripting everything that your audience will see and hear, remember that both a too-slow and a too-fast pace can tire an audience. The norm for a scene is five to ten seconds. **Keep in mind that the most important parts are the beginning—where you want to seize your audience's attention—and the end—where you want to leave your audience with a good impression.** Here are some other guidelines you need to follow in writing your script.

KEY CONCEPT

- **Create a scene-by-scene outline of your documentary.**
- **Use short, concise sentences that get directly to the point.** Use only as many words as you need to make your point.
- **Use punctuation to help speakers correctly phrase their lines.** For example, commas indicate a short pause, dashes a longer pause, and periods a complete stop.

Learning the Shorthand
The shorthand terms presented on this page will be unfamiliar to most students. To help them remember and use the abbreviations, ask volunteers to explain the connection between each abbreviation or acronym and the corresponding longhand film term. If necessary, provide additional explanation. For example:

- **EXT** represents the first three letters of *exterior*, while **INT** represents the first three letters of *interior*. **EXT** refers to a camera shot taken outdoors (exterior), while **INT** refers to a camera shot taken indoors (interior). The distinction is drawn because interiors and exteriors usually require different kinds of lighting.

- **SOT** stands for **S**ound **O**n **T**ape, or the sound on the videotape audio track. **SOT** refers to the sound the camera microphone picks up during shooting.

- **POV** stands for **P**oint **O**f **V**iew and means that the camera is "making believe" it is someone's eyes. The scene shown will be exactly as that person might see it.

TIP Be sure you secure in advance the cooperation of those people you want to appear in your documentary. If at all possible, do a rehearsal of each scene before you film it so that you can make any necessary changes.

- **Make it clear who is speaking before he or she begins to speak.** Use a narrator in voice-overs to introduce the person speaking or have the speaker introduce himself or herself.

- **Do not overwhelm your audience with more information than they can process.** Give your audience time to absorb one point before moving to another.

Outlining the Big Picture   To create an outline of your script before you write it, you have to make several decisions.

- What scenes do I want to include in my documentary?

- In what order do I want to show these scenes?

- How much dialogue do I want to have, and who will say what?

- Do I want to use **voice-over**—dialogue spoken by a narrator who is not shown on camera?

Here is how one documentary maker outlined his script.

My Search for a Way to Manage My Asthma

Scene 1: a re-enactment of my family doctor telling me I have asthma

Scene 2: a re-enactment of my interview with Dr. Anders, allergy and asthma specialist

Scene 3: an interview with me in which I explain the results of my research

Scene 4: videotape of me and several classmates doing exercises recommended for people with asthma, with voice-over explanation of the exercises' benefits

---

Getting Down to Details   Now that you have decided upon the scenes you want in your documentary and the order in which you want to show them, you can concentrate on the way you want to tape the scenes and the words you want the audience to hear. Here is how one student used a word processor to script parts of the first and third scenes of his documentary. Notice that the directions for the scene are in italic print. Special terms and abbreviations are in italic bold. Dialogue is in regular print. If you handwrite your script, use underlining for italics and all capital letters for bold.

Scene 1: *Int.*	*I am sitting in front of the doctor's desk. The camera shows my face over the shoulder (**OS**) of the doctor. [A student plays the part of the doctor.] I look expectantly at the doctor.*	
Doctor:	*Sympathetic and concerned.* "Well, Matt, it looks like you have asthma." *I look surprised, even a little shocked.*	
Scene 3: *Int.*	***Close-up*** *of the interviewer as he introduces me and the subject of the interview.* ***Close-up*** *of me as I smile to acknowledge the introduction. Back to* ***Close-up*** *of interviewer.*	
Interviewer:	What was your mood when you started your research?	
Me:	***Extreme close-up.*** Well, to tell the truth, I was very depressed. Dr. Anders did her best to reassure me, but in the back of my mind I had the awful feeling that my asthma was going to be a lot worse than she told me.	

Only a part of the scene is scripted in the example above. A complete script would include directions for ending each scene.

Now Picture This The next step in the planning stage is to use your script to create a **storyboard**—visual plans of the tape footage you want your documentary to include. A storyboard does not have to be a work of art. All you need to do is sketch out what you want to tape and how you want to tape it. When you are finished, the storyboard will look something like a comic strip. You can arrange and rearrange the scenes until you are certain they are in the order you want them. You can also estimate the time you want each piece of footage to last, so that everything you want to include will fit within your three-minute time limit.

Videotape Your Documentary

Time to Shoot Now that you have completed the planning of your documentary, it is time to videotape it. You will need to do at least two complete dry runs through the script with your cameraman. Then you can proceed to the actual scene-by-scene taping of your documentary.

TECHNOLOGY **TIP**

As an alternative to the format for scripting on this page, show students an example of a two-column script with directions on the left and dialogue on the right. In order to assure clear, easy-to-read scripts, demonstrate, or have a computer-proficient student demonstrate, how to use the column feature on a word-processing program to format this kind of script.

Professional documentary-makers have entire crews of professionals working with them to create their documentaries. One of these professionals is the videotape **editor**, the person who electronically edits tape of scenes until exactly the right effect is achieved. Since you do not have an editor working for you, use **in-camera editing**. In-camera editing means videotaping exactly what you want your audience to see and hear. Tape one scene at a time. Review the tape immediately. Then, if there is a problem, retape the scene before going on to the next one.

A Few Last Words of Wisdom Here are a few hints to keep in mind before you actually begin rolling the tape.

- **Make the bulk of your shots close-ups or medium close-ups** because television's relatively small screens need close-ups.

- **Make sure the people the camera focuses on are not wearing white clothes and are not being filmed against a light background.** Taping this way results in a videotape that has a washed-out look.

- **If possible, use an auxiliary microphone for interviews** instead of the video camera's built-in microphone to make sure that the voices on the tape are clear and steady.

- **If you use music as a background for a narrator's voice, make sure it is instrumental.** The audience cannot follow two voices at once.

A Jury of Your Peers After taping your documentary, it is time to show it to an audience and get their reactions to it. The most efficient way of finding out what you want to know about your audience's reactions is with a questionnaire, or **feedback form**, that you have created in advance. The feedback you receive from your audience might convince you to revise your script and retape your documentary. Here are a few questions you might ask.

- What did you learn from this documentary?

- What was the strongest feature of this documentary? Why?

- What was the greatest weakness of this documentary? Why?

- If you could change one feature of this documentary, what would it be?

Wrap It Up

Metacognition. Allow students time to reflect on the documentary-making process and respond to the following questions:

1. Which part of making a video documentary best suited your talents? Why?

Then, ask the following questions:

2. Did you apply any methods you have seen in movies or on television as you worked on your documentary? Which methods were they?

TIP You can use the feedback you receive from your audience to help you set goals for future projects.

YOUR TURN 11

To assess results of this activity, engage students in deciding upon criteria for an effective documentary. Select a panel of judges to apply the criteria and select several of the documentaries to award certificates of merit.

YOUR TURN 11 **Creating a Video Documentary**

Follow the guidelines provided in this section to plan and to videotape your documentary. Then, show the completed documentary to your classmates. To find out your audience's reactions so that you can revise your documentary, ask them to answer the items in your questionnaire.

RESOURCES

Your Turn 11
Practice and Reinforcement

- *Media Literacy and Communication Skills*
  —*Support and Practice*, Ch. 6, transparencies and worksheets
  —Videocassette 2, Segment F

Choices

Choose one of the following activities to complete.

▶ **CAREERS**

1. Inquiring Minds If you enjoyed researching and writing your I-Search paper, you may want to consider a career as a researcher. Scientists, doctors, historians, and educators conduct research and write about the results. Choose an educator from a technical field (engineering, mathematics, the sciences) or from an academic field (social sciences, languages, arts) and interview him or her. Ask about research and the strategies he or she uses to write about research results. Write a short **report** of the interview and share it with the class.

▶ **LITERATURE**

2. Dear Diary Many famous authors and researchers keep journals or write memoirs. Wouldn't it be interesting to read Thomas Edison's notes about some of the trials, failures, and successes he experienced during his life of research and invention? Choose a famous researcher—inventor, scientist, explorer—who wrote a memoir or kept a journal. Read the memoir or journal. Then, prepare an **oral report** in which you

describe the ups and downs of one of the author's searches.

▶ **SPEAKING AND LISTENING**

3. Hear Ye, Hear Ye One of the best ways to share your I-Search paper is through an informal **panel discussion.** Find other students who wrote on topics similar to yours, and form a panel of three to five students. Then, choose one student to be the moderator. You may want to videotape the discussion and play it for another class.

▶ **VIEWING AND REPRESENTING**

4. Playing the Ad Game Suppose that a major documentary producer decided that your I-Search paper should be made into a documentary for national television. The producer might decide to mount an ad campaign to attract the widest possible audience. You are responsibile for creating the campaign's **print ad**—an ad that will appear as a full page in several national magazines. Create the ad. Select images and words to make the topic of your I-Search paper as appealing as possible to a general audience.

 PORTFOLIO

▶ **CAREERS**

Students may interview educators at your school or at a local college for their reports. To find out about the writing strategies used by professionals in different fields, suggest students pose such questions as the following: What is your purpose for writing? Do you pose questions and then answer them? Do you write chronologically or organize material by subject? Do you write for an audience, for yourself, or both? If both, how do your strategies differ? After the reports have been shared with the class, ask students how analyzing the strategies of writers in different fields can benefit them. They should understand that all writers have some sort of writing process and that each process is different. Analyzing the professionals' processes and comparing them with their own processes will help the students as writers.

▶ **SPEAKING AND LISTENING**

Have students prepare for their panel discussions by summarizing their papers for one another as the moderator notes issues that the topics have in common. Focusing on those common issues, each panel should develop questions to discuss. During the actual panel discussion, the moderator must balance the amount of time each participant has to comment on each issue. If an issue is debatable, the moderator should allow time for speakers to counter each other's points. Suggest that students listen to a panel discussion on a news program to get an idea of the manner in which panelists set forth and argue their points. For more information on informal group discussions, see pp. 855–856.

Choices **245**

RESOURCES

Investigating a Research Question
Assessment

- *Assessment Package*
  —*Chapter Tests,* Ch. 6
  —*Chapter Tests in Standardized Test Formats,* Ch. 6
  —*Assessment Alternatives,* Ch. 6

- *Test Generator*
  (One-Stop Planner CD-ROM)

Choices
Rubrics

- *Assessment Package*
  —*Assessment Alternatives,* Ch. 6

CHAPTER

7

Supporting an Opinion

Use this guide to create an instructional plan that suits the individual needs of your students. Assignments marked by an asterisk (*) may be completed out of class. Times given for pacing lessons are estimated. See pp. 246–247 for chapter-wide resources. Resources listed in this guide are point-of-use resources only.

Curriculum Connections

Choices *p. 281*
- Literature
- Viewing and Representing
- Speaking and Listening

internet**connect**

go.hrw.com **GO TO:** go.hrw.com
KEYWORD: EOLang 9-7

All resources for this chapter are available for preview on the *One-Stop Planner CD-ROM with Test Generator.* All worksheets and tests may be printed from the CD-ROM.

		Chapter Opener *pp. 246–247*	**Reading Workshop: Reading an Opinion Piece** *pp. 248–257*
DEVELOPMENTAL PROGRAM		🕐 **60 minutes** • Persuasion *p. 247* • Your Turn 1 *p. 247*	🕐 **160 minutes** • Preparing to Read *p. 248* • Reading Selection* *pp. 249–250* • First Thoughts 1–3 *p. 251* • Author's Purpose and Point of View *pp. 251–253* • Your Turn 2* *p. 253* • Logical and Emotional Appeals *pp. 253–255* • Your Turn 3 *p. 255* • Vocabulary Mini-Lesson *p. 256* • Test Taking Mini-Lesson *p. 257*
CORE PROGRAM		🕐 **40 minutes** • Persuasion *p. 247* • Your Turn 1 *p. 247*	🕐 **80 minutes** • Preparing to Read *p. 248* • Reading Selection* *pp. 249–250* • First Thoughts 1–3 *p. 251* • Author's Purpose and Point of View *pp. 251–253* • Your Turn 2* *p. 253* • Logical and Emotional Appeals *pp. 253–255* • Your Turn 3* *p. 255* • Vocabulary Mini-Lesson* *p. 256* • Test Taking Mini-Lesson *p. 257*
ADVANCED PROGRAM		🕐 **30 minutes** • Persuasion *p. 247* • Your Turn 1* *p. 247*	🕐 **60 minutes** • Preparing to Read *p. 248* • Reading Selection* *pp. 249–250* • First Thoughts 1–3 *p. 251* • Author's Purpose and Point of View *pp. 251–253* • Your Turn 2* *p. 253* • Logical and Emotional Appeals *pp. 253–255* • Your Turn 3* *p. 255* • Vocabulary Mini-Lesson* *p. 256*
RESOURCES	**PRINT**	• *Communications,* 📖 TP. 52, WS. p. 118	• *Alternative Readings,* 📖 Ch. 7 • *Communications,* 📖 TPs. 53, 54, WS. pp. 119–126
	MEDIA	• *One-Stop Planner CD-ROM* 💿	• *One-Stop Planner CD-ROM* 💿

TP.=Transparency   WS.=Worksheet

Writing Workshop: Writing a Persuasive Paper *pp. 258–278*	Focus on Speaking and Listening: Making a Persuasive Speech *pp. 279–280*
🕐 90 minutes • Prewriting *pp. 258–265* • Your Turn 4 *p. 264* • Framework and Your Turn 5* *p. 266* • Writer's Model and Student's Model *pp. 267–269* **🕐 95 minutes** • Evaluate and Revise Your Paper *pp. 270–271* • Your Turn 6 *p. 271* • Proofread, Publish, and Reflect on Your Essay *pp. 273–275* • Grammar Link *p. 273* • Your Turn 8* *p. 275*	**🕐 90 minutes** • Prepare Your Case *p. 279* • Deliver Your Speech *pp. 279–280* • Rehearse Your Speech* *p. 280* • Your Turn 10 *p. 280*
🕐 180 minutes • Prewriting *pp. 258–265* • Your Turn 4 *p. 264* • Critical-Thinking Mini-Lesson *p. 265* • Framework and Your Turn 5* *p. 266* • Writer's Model and Student's Model *pp. 267–269* • Evaluate and Revise Your Paper *pp. 270–271* • Your Turn 6* *p. 271* • Focus on Word Choice and Your Turn 7* *p. 272* • Proofread, Publish, and Reflect on Your Essay *pp. 273–275* • Grammar Link* *p. 273* • Your Turn 8* *p. 275* • Test Taking Mini-Lesson *p. 276* • Connections to Life* *pp. 277–278* • Your Turn 9 *p. 278*	**🕐 90 minutes** • Prepare Your Case *p. 279* • Deliver Your Speech *pp. 279–280* • Rehearse Your Speech* *p. 280* • Your Turn 10 *p. 280*
🕐 100 minutes • Prewriting *pp. 258–265* • Your Turn 4 *p. 264* • Critical-Thinking Mini-Lesson *p. 265* • Framework and Your Turn 5* *p. 266* • Writer's Model and Student's Model *pp. 267–269* • Evaluate and Revise Your Paper* *pp. 270–271* • Your Turn 6* *p. 271* • Proofread, Publish, and Reflect on Your Essay *pp. 273–275* • Your Turn 8* *p. 275* • Connections to Life* *pp. 277–278* • Your Turn 9 *p. 278*	**🕐 75 minutes** • Prepare Your Case *p. 279* • Deliver Your Speech *pp. 279–280* • Rehearse Your Speech* *p. 280* • Your Turn 10 *p. 280*

• *Communications,* 📖
  TPs. 55–58,
  WS. pp. 127–136
• *Designing Your Writing*
	• *Media Literacy and Communication* 📖
	  Skills
	  —*Support and Practice,* Ch. 7
	  —*A How-to Handbook*
	  —*A Teacher's Guide,* Ch. 7

• *One-Stop Planner CD-ROM* 💿	• *Media Literacy and Communication Skills* 📺 —*Videocassette 2, Segment G* • *One-Stop Planner CD-ROM* 💿

7 Supporting an Opinion

CHAPTER OBJECTIVES

- To read an opinion piece and analyze techniques for persuasive writing
- To write a persuasive paper
- To prepare and present a persuasive speech

Chapter Overview

This chapter is designed to show the importance of identifying opinions, both one's own and those of others, and of understanding the ways those opinions may be expressed persuasively. The Reading Workshop contains an opinion piece that students will analyze for clues to the writer's point of view and use of audience appeal. The Writing Workshop will guide students through the steps for writing a persuasive paper. Students will learn to gather supporting evidence and consider audience and writing style. Students also will take a critical look at persuasion in advertising. The Focus on Speaking and Listening offers instruction in preparing and delivering a persuasive speech. While sections of this chapter may be taught independently, the three workshops are designed to work together to give students a well-rounded understanding of persuasion.

Why Study Persuasive Writing?

Students should understand that they are entitled to express their opinions and that these expressions may inspire healthy debate and positive change. They should also see how they are influenced by the persuasive messages they receive every day. Students should know that stating an opinion is only one part of the persuasive process; other vital steps include gathering supporting evidence and identifying an appropriate audience. A working knowledge of how to express and evaluate opinions will allow students to take more active roles in school, in their communities, and later, in their professions.

Teaching the Chapter

Option 1: Begin with Literature

You may introduce the study of expressing and supporting opinions by having students discuss examples of persuasion in one or more literary works. You could have students read a persuasive monologue, such as "An Indian's Views of Indian Affairs" by Chief Joseph, and discuss the reasons and evidence the speaker offers. Students could also discuss characters who express different opinions on an issue raised by the events in a short story or novel. Lead students to connect the point of view of each character to the opinion he or she expresses. Next, introduce students to the article **"2028 Vision"** (pp. 249–250), a modern opinion piece that appeared in a major newspaper. Students will apply their understanding of persuasion in literature to the study of persuasion in nonfiction writing, and later, to the expression of opinion in their own persuasive papers.

Option 2: Begin with Nonfiction and Writing

Introduce students to the topic of persuasive writing by having them study the article in the Reading Workshop and its accompanying instruction (pp. 248–257). These materials will acquaint students with the basic elements of persuasive writing, including the importance of careful word choice and the effectiveness of logical and emotional appeals. Next, guide students to implement these persuasive strategies by writing their own opinion papers for the Writing Workshop (pp. 258–278). In addition, students will have the opportunity to prepare and deliver persuasive speeches in the Focus on Speaking and Listening (pp. 279–280). When students return to literature they will be more aware of characters who speak persuasively.

Making Connections

■ To the Literature Curriculum

Literature is driven in part by the human need to persuade others to think or act in a particular way. Conflict—the heart of any story, novel, or play—is nearly always resolved by a character who has been persuaded of something. In real life, the persuasive speeches of brave men and women in history continue to impress readers and listeners long after the speeches were delivered.

Lesson Idea: Persuasion in "An Indian's Views of Indian Affairs" by In-mut-too-yah-lat-lat (Chief Joseph).

1. Share the following background with students: Chief Joseph (c. 1840–1904) became the leader of the Wallowa band of Nez Percé around 1871. At that time, the United States government was coercing some American Indian tribes to sign unfavorable treaties. These treaties forced many American Indians to leave their traditional lands and to relocate to distant reservations. Under Chief Joseph's leadership, the Wallowa band of Nez Percé resisted signing such a treaty. In 1877, after months of outmaneuvering U.S. army forces, the Nez Percé were forced to surrender. In 1903 Chief Joseph traveled to Washington, D.C., twice to speak to government leaders on behalf of

the Nez Percé. His goal was to persuade the government to allow the Nez Percé to return to their homeland. Eight years later, the remaining Nez Percés were allowed to return to a reservation in the Northwest— though not to their homeland.

2. After students have read all eight paragraphs of Chief Joseph's speech, have them answer the following questions:
   • What opinion or opinions does Chief Joseph express?
   • What does he want government leaders to do?
   • What is your opinion of the ideas in Chief Joseph's speech?

Discuss students' answers to the questions as a class. Then ask students if they thought Chief Joseph was persuasive in his speech and, if so, why.

3. Finally, introduce students to the opinion piece in the Reading Workshop on pp. 249–250. Point out that the article is persuasive and that it shares certain elements of word choice and audience appeal with Chief Joseph's speech. Ask students to decide which writer was more effective and why. Remind students to use the same elements of persuasion in their own writing.

■ To Careers

Point out that persuasion is not limited to literature or to classroom discussions and assignments. Ask students to compile a list of professions in which persuasion is a key tool. Students may suggest professions such as law, politics, sales, advertising, and film directing. Have students investigate how persuasion functions within these professions.

■ To the Community

The article included in the Reading Workshop (pp. 249–250) addresses an issue that the writer deems worthy of worldwide attention and concern. Ask your students to consider a less global issue that may currently affect their school, neighborhood, town, or city.

■ To the Mathematics or Science Curriculum

Invite a mathematics or science teacher at your school to talk to your class about an unresolved issue or theory in his or her field. The teacher should express and defend his or her opinion on the matter and encourage students to offer their opinions as well.

CHAPTER

7

Supporting an Opinion

Take one teaspoon to
SAVE
natural resources.

Every time a company makes a product, they also use energy and natural resources. Every time you make a purchase, you could save some of that energy and those resources. 'Cause when you buy durable and reusable products, there's less to throw away. And less to replace.

BUY SMART.   **WASTE LESS.**   **SAVE MORE.**   SM

ENVIRONMENTAL DEFENSE FUND EDF

Ad Council

246

CHAPTER RESOURCES

Planning
- *Lesson Planner,* Ch. 7
- *ELL Strategies,* Ch. 7
- Block Scheduling, p. T245A (this book)
- *One-Stop Planner CD-ROM*

Practice
- *Communications,* Ch. 7

- *Media Literacy and Communication Skills*

Extension
- *Designing Your Writing*

Reinforcement
- *Communications,* Ch. 7
- *Alternative Readings,* Ch. 7

Reading Workshop

Reading an Opinion Piece

Writing Workshop

Writing a Persuasive Paper

Speaking and Listening

Making a Persuasive Speech

Persuasion

Sometimes it may seem that everyone is making decisions but you.

■ Your teachers decide how much homework you should have.

■ Your parent decides what your curfew is.

If you had a chance to change these decisions, how would you go about convincing people to accept your ideas? To be successful, you would have to use **persuasion**—the art of convincing others to change their minds or to take a certain action.

Even though you might not realize it, you see persuasion in advertisements, which attempt to convince you to buy certain brands of food, clothing, or other goods. You also hear persuasion in political speeches, in which the speaker tries to convince people to vote a certain way. You even find in many newspapers a section just for persuasion—the opinion page, or *Op-Ed* (*Opinion-Editorial*) section.

Informational Text

Persuasion

  Thinking About Opinions

Locate the opinion page in a newspaper or newsmagazine, and examine one of the letters or editorials. Then, analyze the editorial or letter using the following questions, and share your findings with the class.

■ What is the writer's opinion? How does the writer attempt to convince you? Do you think the piece is convincing? Why or why not?

■ What is your opinion on the subject discussed in the editorial or letter? What are your reasons for this opinion?

GO TO: go.hrw.com
KEYWORD: EOLang 9-7

Connecting Reading and Writing **247**

Motivate

Ask students to recall a time they were persuaded to do something new or different. For example, they might have been persuaded to try a new food. Then, have students respond to the following questions:

• What (or who) persuaded them?

• How were they convinced?

Discuss students' responses. Explain that they will study elements of persuasion in this chapter.

ELEMENTS OF
Literature

Persuasion In Literature. In *Elements of Literature*, Third Course, see "Homeless" by Anna Quindlen, pp. 461–463, and "Misspelling" by Charles Kuralt, pp. 469–470, for examples of authors who express and support their opinions.

YOUR TURN 1

Guide students to articulate their specific reasons for agreeing or disagreeing with the writer. If they disagree, have them cite reasons why the writer failed to convince them.

■ *Daily Language Activity Transparencies*
■ *Vocabulary Workshop* and *Tests*

Evaluation and Assessment

■ *Test Generator (One-Stop Planner CD-ROM)*

■ *Assessment Package*
—*Chapter Tests,* Ch. 7
—*Chapter Tests in Standardized Test Formats,* Ch. 7
—*Assessment Alternatives,* Ch. 7

Internet

■ go.hrw.com (keyword: EOLang 9-7)

Preview **247**

Reading Workshop

OBJECTIVES

Reading and Writing Connection

- To read a newspaper editorial in preparation for writing a persuasive paper

Reading Skills

- To identify an author's purpose and point of view

- To distinguish emotional appeals from logical appeals

- To use context clues to find the meanings of unfamiliar words

---

TEACHING (TIP)

Preparing to Read

The material on this page explains the purpose of an opinion piece or editorial. The influence of point of view on persuasive writing is also introduced. Remind students to be aware of purpose and point of view as they read **"2028 Vision."** Students should also be encouraged to look for emotional and logical appeals. These concepts will be covered in more detail on pp. 251–255.

Quotation for the Day

"Truth persuades by teaching, but does not teach by first persuading."

(Tertullian, A.D. 160–230, Roman theologist)

Suggest to your class that this quote implies that teaching is a vehicle for persuading. Ask students to consider ways of teaching. (For example, explaining reasons, demonstrating, modeling.) Challenge them to give examples of how writers might persuade through teaching.

WHAT'S AHEAD

In this section, you will read a newspaper editorial and learn how to

- **identify an author's purpose and point of view**

- **distinguish emotional appeals from logical appeals**

Reading an Opinion Piece

Newspaper editorials—pieces written by the newspaper's editors about important issues—are the Paul Reveres of persuasion. These pieces urge us to take action or to accept a certain belief. No matter what the issue of the editorial, the writer's first job is to make the reader take the topic seriously. For example, you might laugh at a sensational Web page about asteroids that claims "The sky is falling! The sky is falling!" However, an editorial like the one on the next page might just convince you that you are not completely safe from incoming asteroids.

Preparing to Read

READING SKILL →

Author's Purpose and Point of View   The writer's **purpose** in the following editorial is to persuade his readers of something. Readers can assume an editorial writer's purpose is to persuade. However, if an article is not in an editorial section, readers may have to look for signs that the author is trying to persuade them. Along with a persuasive purpose, a writer of persuasion will have a distinct **point of view** that reflects the writer's opinions, attitudes, and beliefs about the topic of the article or essay. Consequently, readers must be able to determine a writer's point of view so that they can decide if they agree with what the writer is saying.

READING FOCUS →

Logical and Emotional Appeals   Writers of persuasion know that they must appeal to their readers' minds by making **logical appeals—reasons and evidence—to support their opinions.** However, writers also know that readers react as much with their hearts as with their minds. Therefore, along with reasons and evidence, writers include **emotional appeals—words and examples that play upon the readers' feelings.** See if you can tell when the writer of the editorial on the next page is either appealing to your intelligence or tugging at your heartstrings.

RESOURCES

Reading Workshop Reinforcement

- *Alternative Readings,* Ch. 7

In the following editorial, the writer refers to an asteroid that some scientists initially thought might strike the earth on October 26, 2028. The editorial was written after the announcement that the asteroid would not hit the earth, nor even come very close. Try to identify the author's point of view and the appeals used. As you read, write answers to the numbered active-reading questions.

from THE BOSTON GLOBE

2028 VISION

1. What clues does the title give about the article?

BOSTON, MASSACHUSETTS, MARCH 14, 1998

Earth got a scary astronomy lesson this week and shouldn't forget the message: The universe is a rough neighborhood, and scientists must watch it as diligently as municipal authorities keep track of city streets. Maybe more so.

The temptation is for the human race to emit a collective "whew" and dismiss the asteroid-that-could, which, with revised calculations, almost certainly won't hit earth with a 10,000-megaton punch on October 26, 2028.

The mile-wide space rock, called "1997 XF11" and discovered in December, is capable of blowing a 20-mile crater in the planet on a direct hit. So NASA calmed everybody down by announcing that it will probably pass by the earth with a comforting, 600,000-mile margin instead of being the celestial squeaker it would have been at 30,000 miles.

However, the rock has friends—at least an estimated 2,000 others as big or bigger, roaming earth's neighborhood with the potential for doing damage.

The International Astronomical Union has identified only 108 of them, which means that science and government have a lot more to do.

Asteroid XF11

2. What language does the writer use in the first paragraph to appeal to your emotions?

3. What reasons does the writer give to show that the topic is an important one?

Active-Reading Questions

The active-reading questions prompt students to consider the methods and effectiveness of the author's persuasive writing. Use students' answers to informally assess their ability to locate supporting evidence and to gauge their understanding of the author's purpose and point of view.

ANSWERS
The following are sample answers.

1. The title hints that the piece is about the future.

2. The language is informal but alarming. The writer's description of the universe attempts to frighten the reader into paying attention.

3. The writer notes three reasons:

- The asteroid is huge.

- The asteroid is dangerous. If it hits the earth, it could create a huge crater.

- Experts at NASA have become involved.

READING PROCESS *Continued on p. 250*

PREREADING

Ask Questions. Before reading the selection, have students read the introductory paragraph and the title. Explain that to be more alert to the writer's point of view, students should first consider their own points of view by asking themselves questions *before* they read. Guide students to create and complete a table such as the one on p. 250. Encourage them to add information to their charts as they learn new facts or change their opinions.

4. The writer wants to see an international tracking system put into place as well as a plan for deflecting any asteroids that come close to earth.

5. Richard Binzel is an astronomer at a top university; because he takes asteroids seriously, perhaps the public and readers should, too.

6. The writer compares the threat of asteroid collision to a fire drill. The comparison might make readers feel a sense of fear and a desire to take steps to prevent a disaster. The comparison may also make readers feel more familiar with the topic.

---

4. What practical actions is the writer asking people to take?

5. Who is named in this paragraph? Why should the reader care what this person says?

6. To what does the writer compare the threat of an asteroid collision? How does this comparison make you feel?

The close call should inspire an international scientific effort to find, name, and track what's out there and to determine what may be on a collision course with earth. A plan should be in place for deflecting or nudging incoming asteroids out of their orbit. This might be done by firing rockets at them or by detonating nuclear weapons nearby them. Exploding an asteroid with a nuclear bomb would be a bad move, because the rock could splinter into hundreds of lethal pieces.

Richard Binzel, an astronomer at MIT, is also calling for an asteroid rating system, similar to the Richter scale, that would let the public know the danger. He also noted that people should understand that an asteroid must be tracked over time, and that includes "1997 XF11."

This week an asteroid provided the planet with the equivalent of a cosmic fire drill. Now people must make sure that they have enough smoke detectors and hoses—and that they work.

MIKE SHELTON reprinted with special permission of King Features Syndicate, Inc.

READING PROCESS

Topic: Asteroid hitting the earth

Questions	Responses
What do I know about this topic?	
What are my opinions about the topic?	

Author's Purpose and Point of View

READING SKILL

Read the Signs   Writers of persuasive articles are not writing merely to inform their readers about something. They are trying to convince readers to think or act in a certain way. This is their **purpose** in writing. If readers are not conscious of such efforts to persuade them, they could mistake a writer's position on an issue for the truth about that issue. How will you as a reader know if the purpose of an article or essay is persuasive? You can look for clues that writers often leave. The following chart gives explanations and examples of some of these common clues.

Clues	Examples
• words such as *could*, *should*, and *would*	Students *should* be required to complete seventy hours of community service before graduation.
• statements in the future tense, especially when the rest of the article is in the present tense	Installing carpet in all classrooms *will raise* students' attention levels.
• forceful words such as *must* or *need*	The school board *must* approve the purchase of new band uniforms.

First Thoughts on Your Reading

ANSWERS

Possible answers are suggested below.

1. The writer probably wants readers to feel afraid of the possibility of an asteroid collision and yet capable of preparing for such an event.

2. Because readers have not actually experienced a collision, the writer's words may be more effective than the writer's reasons. The language suggests that there is a real and constant threat of asteroids.

3. The writer's ideas include:

   • Creating a worldwide asteroid tracking system

   • Developing ways to deflect asteroids

   • Developing an asteroid rating system to indicate the potential danger of asteroids

   Students might argue that the writer's case is convincing because he makes these ideas sound like simple preventative steps—like practicing for a fire drill. They may also claim that the writer's case is not convincing, because he does not address the costs and time involved in creating such systems, nor does the writer provide evidence that these systems would actually work.

READING PROCESS

READING

Make Predictions. Encourage students to track the writer's persuasive clues. As they read, have students predict where the writer tries to lead the readers. Suggest that students pause after answering each active-reading question to jot down a one- or two-sentence summary of what they have just read. Point out that by tracking the writer's organizational strategy, students can better prepare themselves for the arguments and evidence to come.

What's the Angle?
Point out to students that a title can be expanded into a thesis statement. Indicate that "Spend at Home First" is a condensed thesis statement that functions as a title.

Cooperative Learning

Point of View. Tell students that often a writer's point of view reflects a personal, social, historical, or cultural influence, or bias. Explain the importance of identifying and analyzing the context of a writer's point of view in a persuasive message. Point out that readers may disagree with a writer's point of view even when the facts encourage agreement. To demonstrate the influence of point of view, assign random groups of three or four to discuss an issue that is important to students, for example, class scheduling. Direct each member to spend two minutes expressing an opinion on the topic and a rationale for that point of view. Have one student in the group listen for the context of the point of view or any evidence of bias. Have another student in the group act as a process observer to record signs of persuasion, as described on the chart on p. 251. For example, the observer might note that a group member used the forceful word *ruin* to describe what an altered schedule would do to her chances of getting an after-school job.

What's the Angle?   After deciding that an author's purpose is to persuade, you need to identify that writer's **point of view**—his or her attitude, opinions, or beliefs about the topic. The author's point of view in a persuasive piece can show up in two ways:

- **directly** in a thesis statement
- **indirectly** through the writer's choice of examples and words

Any persuasive message has a point of view. Being *aware* of the point of view will help you follow the reasoning in the message. If you know the point of view, you can determine the position the writer is trying to persuade you to take. Also, knowing the point of view will help you to decide whether or not you agree with the writer's message.

To determine the point of view in the paragraph below, use the steps in the Thinking It Through on the next page.

Spend at Home First

Our government has made the decision to spend millions of our tax dollars on the space program. We foolishly subsidized the space shuttle so that scientists could perform experiments on insects in outer space. We paid so that the Pathfinder could take pictures on Mars. We shelled out money twice for the Hubble Space Telescope—once to put it into orbit, once to fix it. Enough already! We could be spending our money to buy shelter and food for the homeless. Just think how grateful the hungry and cold children would be to have food and a place to live. We could also use those dollars to fund medical research programs. Which is more important: having lovely pictures of the Mars horizon or curing cancer? The choice seems obvious.

252   Chapter 7   **Persuasion:** Supporting an Opinion

READING PROCESS

EXPLORING
Evaluate Purpose and Point of View.
Assess students' comprehension of the role that purpose and point of view play in persuasion. Ask students to rate the article **"2028 Vision"** for overall persuasive power. Students can use a scale of 1 to 10 (10 being most persuasive). Then, ask students to back up their ratings by finding at least one example from the article to show how each of the following elements does or does not support the author's point of view and purpose:
- Facts included
- Word choice
- Tone

Identifying an Author's Point of View

Use the steps below to help you figure out an author's point of view. The right-hand column applies the steps to the passage you have just read.

▶ **STEP 1 Read the introductory paragraph or the title to determine the topic.** Then, check to see if the author reveals his or her point of view in a thesis statement or topic sentence.

There does not seem to be a topic sentence in the paragraph, but the first sentence and the title focus on the topic of spending tax money on the space program.

▶ **STEP 2 Look for words and phrases about the topic that have positive or negative associations** if there is no topic sentence or thesis statement.

Positive: "lovely"—but I don't think the writer used the word to mean "delightful."
Negative: "foolishly," "shelled out," and "Enough already!"

▶ **STEP 3 Determine if the words and phrases create mostly negative or positive associations.** What is the author's tone?

Most of the words are negative; I think "lovely" is used jokingly.

▶ **STEP 4 Determine the author's point of view** by putting what you have found together: topic + word choice = point of view.

The author has a negative point of view toward spending money on the space program.

TIP Remember that **thesis statements** are frequently found in the last one or two sentences of an introductory paragraph. Also, authors of magazine and newspaper articles sometimes use a condensed form of a thesis statement as the title of an article.

Topic sentences are usually the first one or two sentences of paragraphs, although a paragraph can have an implied topic sentence.

YOUR TURN 2 Identifying an Author's Point of View

Using the steps outlined in the Thinking It Through above, determine the author's point of view in "2028 Vision" on page 249.

Logical and Emotional Appeals

Why and Wherefore People write persuasive articles because they want their readers to think or act in a certain way. However, just telling people to do something will not necessarily make them do it. People need convincing. For example, if a writer wants to convince readers that a new law should raise the age requirement for a driver's license, he or she must use **logical appeals** and might choose to include **emotional appeals** as well.

◀ READING FOCUS

Reading Workshop   253

YOUR TURN 2

ANSWERS
Students should number the steps outlined in **Thinking It Through** so that you will be able to see at a glance that they have followed each step of the process.

Sample answers follow.

Step 1: There does not seem to be a clear topic sentence in the first paragraph, but the title and the content of the first paragraph suggest that asteroids pose a threat to earth.

Step 2:

Negative: *punch, lethal*

Positive: *comforting, inspire*

Step 3: Most of the associations are negative. The positive language is usually sarcastic, unless it expresses a wish.

Step 4: The author has a negative point of view toward our planet's preparation for asteroids and thinks we need to be more concerned about them.

Logical Appeals   Writers use the elements of a logical appeal, **reasons** and **evidence**, to target your ability to think. Recognizing reasons and evidence will help you understand a writer's position and decide whether or not you agree with it.

- **Reasons** tell readers why they should accept the writer's opinion.
- **Evidence** supplies support for the reasons. Evidence can be facts, examples, anecdotes, or expert opinions.

The following graphic organizer illustrates how opinions are supported by reasons and, in turn, how reasons are supported by evidence.

TIP   The graphic to the right pictures only one of the writer's reasons. Keep in mind, however, that the writer of an editorial should be expected to include several reasons to support his or her opinion.

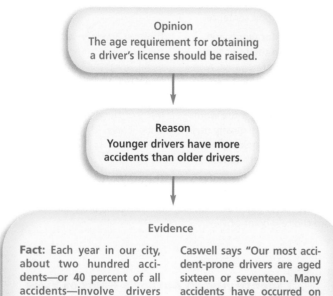

Opinion
The age requirement for obtaining a driver's license should be raised.

Reason
Younger drivers have more accidents than older drivers.

Evidence

Fact: Each year in our city, about two hundred accidents—or 40 percent of all accidents—involve drivers under the age of nineteen. **Expert Opinion:** Police Chief Caswell says "Our most accident-prone drivers are aged sixteen or seventeen. Many accidents have occurred on or near the high school campus."

Emotional Appeals   By using emotional appeals, writers reach their readers' feelings. Think of an emotional appeal as the film footage that accompanies a news story on TV. For example, a reporter giving a story about a Midwest flood might cite statistics of homes lost or natural resources destroyed. However, the picture of one family standing in front of their flooded home is likely to have a greater impact on viewers than the facts alone would. Readers should look for two ways that writers appeal to their emotions: through **anecdotes** (brief stories) and through **word choice.**

■ **Anecdotes** bring situations to life with real people and specific events with which readers can relate.

Example	Explanation
Last week a young woman with two small children was seriously injured when a teenage driver ran a red light. The young mother is still in the hospital.	Many readers will feel strong sympathy for the young mother and for her children, who must live without her while she recuperates.

TIP Often anecdotes appeal to both the reader's logic and emotions. The anecdote to the left, for example, works as evidence—it is a fact. It also carries an emotional appeal.

■ **Word choice** is the palette an author, like an artist, uses to paint a picture for the reader. Writers use words' **connotations,** the associations or feelings that a word suggests, to appeal to the emotions. When words or phrases suggest very strong emotions, we call those words **loaded language.** Because loaded language appeals to strong emotions (for example, disgust or respect), it can bias people for or against something. Words like *victim, home, family,* and *freedom* are just a few of the many words that are loaded with strong connotations.

Example	Explanation
Over ten thousand teenage drivers are **running loose** in our town and are **menacing** other drivers—these teenagers are **an accident waiting to happen.**	Rather than using more neutral terms, the writer uses words that appeal to the readers' fears to make teenage drivers sound uncontrolled and dangerous.

TIP Readers should be suspicious of a writer whose persuasion relies heavily on loaded language. If a writer depends on outrageous terms to provoke strong emotion, the logical appeals could be weak.

YOUR TURN 3 **Recognizing Logical and Emotional Appeals**

On your own paper, make a chart like the one below and fill it in with the logical and emotional appeals used in "2028 Vision" on page 249.

Logical Appeals	Reasons:
	Evidence:
Emotional Appeals	Ancedotes:
	Word Choice:

Reading Workshop **255**

RESOURCES

Your Turn 3
Practice
■ *Communications,* WS. p. 121
Reinforcement
■ *Communications,* TP. 54, WS. p. 122

ENGLISH-LANGUAGE LEARNERS
General Strategies. Some students may not be able to interpret connotations or recognize loaded language in English. Encourage students to look up the "loaded" words presented on this page (*victim, home, family, freedom*) in a dictionary or thesaurus. Then, lead a discussion in English about the emotions that the words elicit.

Wrap It Up

Metacognition. Ask students to answer the following question to reflect on their reading of **"2028 Vision."**

1. How much confidence do you have in the writer's opinion that asteroids pose a real danger? What makes you feel that way?

Then, ask students the following question.

2. What evidence supports a logical appeal? [facts, examples, anecdotes, or expert opinions]

YOUR TURN 3

ANSWERS
Sample answers follow.
Logical Appeals
Reason: Asteroids are dangerous.

Evidence: Fact—An asteroid can create a huge crater in the earth; Expert opinion—astronomer Richard Binzel's warning

Emotional Appeals
Anecdotes: Potential disaster of October 26, 2028; exploding an asteroid with a nuclear bomb
Word Choice: 10,000-megaton punch; roaming earth's neighborhood; close call; collision course; lethal pieces

MINI-LESSON .... **VOCABULARY**

Context Clues: Definition/Restatement

ANSWERS

1. *content.* Clue: comma sets off definition. "We are *content*" makes sense.

2. *pounding.* Clue: *or* signals synonym/restatement. "Imagine the *pounding*" makes sense.

3. *senior member.* Clue: comma sets off definition. "Dr. Tate is the *senior member* of the astronomers" makes sense.

4. *expect the worst.* Clue: semicolon sets off restatement. Substituting this phrase makes sense.

Taking a Second Look

Context Clues: Definition/Restatement. Provide additional practice in understanding definition and restatement context clues by asking each student to locate a one- or two-sentence passage in the reading selection that includes a challenging word and a clue to its meaning.

MINI-LESSON VOCABULARY

Context Clues: Definition/Restatement

Asteroids and their behavior may not be part of your everyday conversation and vocabulary. If an unfamiliar word crops up in your reading, a good strategy to figure out its meaning is to look at the word's **context:** the words surrounding the unfamiliar word. One helpful context clue is a **definition,** which gives the meaning of the word directly or indirectly, usually in the same sentence.

Learning by *rote* involves heavy **reliance on repetition and memorization.**

Another kind of context clue, **restatement,** uses another word or phrase to repeat the meaning of the unfamiliar word.

Voters have grown dissatisfied with the mayor's *vacillation* on spending: **He is unable to make tough decisions.**

Often there are signals that indicate definition and restatement context clues.

- commas that set off or colons that begin the definition or restatement
- words or phrases such as *or, is, who is, which is, that is, in other words*

THINKING IT THROUGH **Using Definition and Restatement Context Clues**

To use definition and restatement context clues, follow these steps. The student responses are based on the italicized word in the sentence from "2028 Vision."

"A plan should be in place for *deflecting* or nudging incoming asteroids out of their orbit."

1. **Look for definition or restatement signals in the words surrounding the unfamiliar word.** *The word "or" might signal that "nudging" is a restatement context clue.*

2. **Try replacing the unfamiliar word** with the word or phrase that you think is the definition or restatement. *"A plan should be in place for nudging incoming asteroids out of their orbit."*

3. **See if your replacement works within the sentence.** *The words "nudging . . . out of their orbit" seem to work.*

PRACTICE

Use definition and restatement context clues to determine the meanings of the italicized words in the following sentences.

1. We are *complacent,* content to believe that asteroids pose no threat.

2. Imagine the *barrage,* or pounding, the earth would take if it passed through an asteroid belt.

3. Dr. Tate, the *doyen* of astronomers, is the senior member of the group.

4. Some people are *pessimistic;* they expect the worst to happen.

RESOURCES

Vocabulary

Practice

- *Communications,* WS. p. 123

Test Taking

Practice

- *Communications,* WS. p. 124–126

Author's Purpose and Point of View

Standardized reading tests often have questions that ask you to identify an author's **purpose** and **point of view.** To answer, you will have to decide whether the author wants to inform, to entertain, or to persuade readers. Here is a typical reading passage and question about the author's purpose.

Now more than ever, it seems that creating news that sells is more important than creating news that is accurate and well analyzed. A prime example is the asteroid story of 1997, which predicted that a mile-wide asteroid would come within 30,000 miles of Earth. We had twenty-four hours of media mayhem, with reports squawking about collision and disaster. Then the story collapsed like a deflating balloon. The story was based on a scientist's initial calculation rather than on conclusive evidence. Using new data, scientists recalculated the asteroid's path and determined it would come no closer than 600,000 miles to Earth.

The author wrote this passage to

A. inform readers of new scientific findings

B. convince readers not to ignore the dangers of asteroids headed for Earth

C. describe how journalists fool people

D. convince people that the media should be more careful about accuracy

THINKING IT THROUGH — **Identifying Purpose and Point of View**

Keep the following steps in mind as you answer a question about an author's purpose and point of view. The student responses are based on the sample passage and question above.

1. **Examine the passage for words with strong connotations.** Such language is a sure indicator of persuasive purpose. The words "mayhem," "squawking," and "irresponsible," are not neutral; therefore, the passage is probably persuasive.

2. **Check to see if the language is positive or negative.** [topic + word choice = point of view] The negative words "squawking," "story collapsed," and "irresponsible news story" indicate the writer's point of view.

3. **Look at the first few sentences to find the topic and to see if a topic sentence states the writer's point of view.** The first sentence suggests that the writer thinks news reporting should be more accurate.

4. **Look for the choice that best matches your analysis.** The answer that best matches is D.

TEACHING TIP

Identifying Purpose and Point of View

For practice in using the strategy described in **Thinking It Through,** ask students to select letters or articles from the editorial page of a newspaper. Have them use the steps to figure out the author's purpose and point of view.

Looking Ahead to Writing

The Writing Workshop will give students a chance to use persuasive techniques in their own persuasive papers. Remind them to revisit the information on logical and emotional appeals (pp. 253–255) as they plan their essays.

Writing Workshop

OBJECTIVES

- To write a persuasive paper
- To analyze audience
- To provide support for reasons
- To avoid circular reasoning
- To eliminate clichés
- To check for pronoun-antecedent agreement

Quotation for the Day

"The world is not run by thought, nor by imagination, but by opinion. . . ."

(Elizabeth Drew, 1887–1965, British writer and literary critic)

Ask students if they agree with this statement. Students could use their opinions about the quotation as the basis for writing a journal entry.

WHAT'S AHEAD

In this workshop, you will write a persuasive paper. You will also learn how to

- analyze your audience
- provide support for your reasons
- avoid circular reasoning
- eliminate clichés from your writing
- check for correct pronoun-antecedent agreement

Writing a Persuasive Paper

Have you ever wanted to change the world? For example, you might care deeply about an endangered species and want to change laws governing its habitat, or you might want to change the laws governing the educational testing in your state. It might seem that writing a persuasive paper has nothing in common with making these important changes, but the written word has been very powerful throughout history. For example, think of Supreme Court judgments, Martin Luther King, Jr.'s "I Have a Dream" speech, or the Declaration of Independence. These writings, all of which include elements of persuasion, have helped to change or create laws that affect the world we live in today.

Writing a persuasive paper is a way to take your own ideas and work to make them a reality. You can write an essay that communicates your own dream and persuades your readers not only to dream with you, but also to take action and help make it come true.

Prewriting

Choose an Issue

Powerful Words from Powerful Beliefs The power of your persuasive writing will come from the strength of your beliefs about an issue. By definition, an **issue** is something about which people have opposing opinions or beliefs. If you do not believe in or feel strongly about one side of an issue, you will probably not convince anyone to agree with you. Therefore, as you search for an issue to write about, let your opinions and beliefs guide you. Choose something that matters to you. If you believe that wildlife protection is more important than urban growth, then you may have arrived at a suitable issue for your persuasive paper.

Use the following methods to find an issue for a persuasive paper:

- **Brainstorm about several issues** on which you have strong opinions. In as many ways as possible, complete the sentence: *If I could change anything in my community, I would _____.*
- **Read a local or national newspaper.** Pay special attention to the opinion and editorial pages. What issues are people concerned about? How do these issues concern you? What issue grabs your attention?
- **Browse high school newspaper Web pages** looking for editorials. Try to choose an issue that affects your own life and that is the subject of debate.
- **Watch television news shows or newsmagazines.** Are any of the issues discussed interesting or relevant to you?
- **Brainstorm collaboratively about issues that affect your school.** With a small group of classmates, discuss these issues, focusing on possible solutions.

When you have listed a number of issues about which you feel strongly, use the following checklist to choose one.

- Eliminate issues about which there cannot be differing opinions.
- Rate each remaining issue from 1 to 5, with 5 being the highest.
- Circle the issue that is most important to you—the one you rated 5.
- Check to be sure the issue you have chosen is an issue about which you feel comfortable sharing your feelings and thoughts.

State Your Opinion

Which Side Are You On?   You have chosen an issue. Now make your **point of view,** your opinion and beliefs about the issue, as clear as possible to the reader. The best way to do this is to write an **opinion statement, one sentence that sums up the issue and your point of view on it**. This statement is the **thesis** of your paper.

◀ KEY CONCEPT

Issue: State senators propose to create legal limits on volume levels for car stereo systems.

Point of view: I think the proposal is a bad idea.

Opinion statement: The state government should not create laws that limit the noise levels coming from car stereos.

Even though your thesis conveys what you believe or think, be careful not to include the words *I think* or *I believe* in your thesis. When you state your opinion your readers already know it is what you think or believe.

 Most word-processing programs have a thesaurus feature. Use this feature to generate word associations and to brainstorm ideas.

TECHNOLOGY TIP

Demonstrate the use of Internet search engines to brainstorm ideas. Enter a word or phrase related to a topic of interest. Have students review the resulting listings for Web sites of organizations or government agencies related to the issue. Such sites will often include newsletters or position papers stating and defending opinions. *You need to be aware that Internet resources are sometimes public forums, and their content can be unpredictable.*

TEACHING TIP

State Your Opinion
Remind students that their opinion (thesis) statements may change. For instance, a student may begin with the thesis: "It is unfair to require all students to put in 100 hours of community service." Further research, however, may convince the student that the benefits outweigh the disadvantages. The revised thesis statement might be "Although the school's community service requirement poses challenges to students, its overall benefits make it a worthwhile policy."

> **TIP** Remember that while a **fact** is a statement that can be proven true, an **opinion** is a belief or judgment that cannot be proven. For example, if a school enrollment report shows that more students take art classes than take music classes, it is a *fact* that more students take art than music classes. However, it is an *opinion* that there should be a new art studio built at the school. When writing a persuasive paper, you can use facts to support the stand you are making, but your stand itself should be an opinion that you are trying to convince your readers to share.

Consider Your Purpose, Audience, and Tone

Rabble-rousing   When you feel strongly about something, you have an **occasion** for writing, and your **purpose** for writing is clear. For example, you might believe it is wrong for the state government to regulate how loudly you can play music in your car. If so, you might feel compelled to write because you want to convince others to share your opinions. You might also want to encourage your readers to take action. However, to do either of these things, you first have to know who your readers are.

THINKING IT THROUGH — Identifying Audience

To identify your **audience**, think of the issue you have chosen and ask yourself the following questions.

▶ **Whom does this issue affect?** For example, if your issue is the closing of your school's campus during lunch, the issue probably does not affect a bachelor who lives across town. Your issue probably does affect, however, your fellow students and their parents, the teachers and administrators of your school, and the residents and business owners near your campus. These are all people who have a natural interest in your topic and will be a natural audience for your paper.

▶ **Whom do I need to convince?** Those who disagree with your opinion are the ones you must convince. For example, if school administrators have made the decision to close the campus during lunch hours, they may be your most important target audience. There may be some parents and students who also fit in this category.

▶ **Whom do I want to take action?** Identify other people who could help further your cause. For example, other students will probably agree with your position; you might call them to action. Also, those who are not sure where they stand on the issue may be swayed by your appeals and could make a difference for your cause.

Part of convincing your audience to accept your opinion or to take action comes with maintaining a respectful, thoughtful tone and voice. **Tone** is the attitude that you take toward your audience and topic. Your **voice** is how you sound as a writer—your unique way of using language. Imagine, for example, that you want to convince an audience that recycling makes a difference. Would you use the words "People who don't recycle are stupid"? Your readers would be much more likely to read on and be convinced if the tone were more formal, serious, and respectful.

The following chart shows notes one writer made about purpose, audience, and tone for a paper on recycling.

Opinion statement: Recycling is so important that it should be required of families in the community.

Purpose	My purpose is to convince people that recycling should be a priority in our community.
Audience	Many people in my community understand the benefits of recycling. I should concentrate on people who still throw away a lot of material that could be recycled.
Tone	Some people might oppose my opinion at first. I need to be respectful toward them and use language that will help them see my point of view.

TIP You can formulate questions about your issue by thinking about how it might affect your audience. Then you can clarify your ideas about your topic by deciding on a purpose for your essay.

Support Your Opinion

Building the Support Pyramid It is not enough to state your opinion. You have to convince your audience that your opinion is logical (that it makes sense) and, perhaps, that action is needed. You do this by including **support** for your opinion. **Support includes reasons that tell *why* your opinion should be accepted and evidence to back up the reasons.** Support can also include stories, examples, details, and words that appeal to readers' hearts rather than their minds.

◄ KEY CONCEPT

You can think of your persuasive paper as a pyramid. The top of the pyramid is your opinion statement. The base of the pyramid is made up of reasons and evidence that support your opinion. Without a base, the pyramid cannot stand. Consequently, if you cannot support your opinion statement with a solid base, then you will have to revise it.

Meeting INDIVIDUAL NEEDS

INCLUSION
For students who need help in understanding the concept of adequate and logical support for an opinion, have a helper guide them in drawing a pyramid graphic and recording their opinion statements at the top. The helper can then ask each student to verbalize several reasons for an opinion and list these below the statement to support it. Finally, for each reason, students can be helped to locate at least two supporting facts or examples.

Critical Thinking

Evaluation. As guided practice in exploring an issue and its support, have each student select an article or letter from the editorial page of a newspaper. Ask students to use the format on p. 261 to chart the purpose, audience, and tone of the piece. Next, have students evaluate how effectively, given the audience and tone used, the author achieved his or her purpose. Have students write rationales for their ratings and present them to the class. The student may have judged a letter to the editor as not very effective in its purpose (for example, trying to convince parents that students should have an extended school year) because the tone was emotional rather than factual.

This Better Be Good Coming up with reasons is probably the toughest part of writing a persuasive paper. Use the following steps to develop strong reasons that support your opinion statement. Each reason can become the topic sentence of a paragraph in your paper.

Reference Note

For more about **generating reasons,** see **T.H.E.M.E.S. Strategy** on page 276.

THINKING IT THROUGH — Generating Reasons

▶ **STEP 1 Add two to three *because* clauses to your opinion statement.**
The state government should not create laws that limit the noise levels coming from car stereos.
1. because there are already laws about disturbing the peace that cover this situation
2. because such a law will only add to the burden of the already over-worked police

▶ **STEP 2 Delete the *because* from each clause and rewrite it as a sentence.** These will be your topic sentences for supporting paragraphs.
Laws already exist about disturbing the peace to cover this situation.

▶ **STEP 3 Add introductory or transitional words (*one important reason, first, secondly, the most important reason*) to each topic sentence, indicating its order in your paper.** One reason for defeating the proposed law is that there are already laws about disturbing the peace that cover this situation.

Building the Foundation Support your reasons with evidence that appeals to both your readers' minds and their hearts—**logical appeals,** also called **logical arguments,** and **emotional appeals.** While you may use both kinds of support, your paper should rely more heavily on logical appeals.

Logical Appeals Logical appeals speak to your readers' minds and are the foundation of your paper. Logical appeals consist of reasons supported by **evidence**—facts, statistics, expert opinions, anecdotes and examples.

- **Facts**—information that can be proven correct by testing or verification by reliable sources—show that there is concrete, reliable support for your opinion. For example, if you are writing about recycling, use **statistics** (facts that present numerical information) on the amount of waste material that could be recycled.

- **Expert opinions**—statements by people who are considered experts on the subject—show that the most knowledgeable people support you. For example, you might quote the city manager's opinion on recycling.

TIP In many school or test situations, persuasive writing must contain only logical appeals. This type of writing is called a **logical argument.**

262　Chapter 7　**Persuasion:** Supporting an Opinion

- **Anecdotes** and **examples** are illustrations of a general idea. While examples show specific instances, anecdotes are brief stories that are usually more personal in nature. To add an example to your evidence about the ease of recycling, you could write about someone who recycles regularly.

Emotional Appeals Anecdotes and **examples** can appeal also to readers' emotions. Another way to appeal to your readers' hearts and complement your logical appeals is through **word choice**.

- **Anecdotes** and **examples** give a specific and often a human element to your paper. For example, when trying to persuade an audience that recycling is not difficult and heighten the emotional appeal, you might use an anecdote about a six-year-old who does the recycling for her family.

- **Word choice** can also enhance the emotional appeal of your paper by suggesting certain feelings that color the readers' understanding. For example, to describe a recycler with the words *avid* and *strong-willed* would give readers one sense of the person. The words *fanatical* and *stubborn* would give readers a less flattering sense of the person. Give clear definitions of any terms the reader might not understand.

TIP Although it may be tempting, you should *never* make up evidence to support your opinion.

TIP Appeals are often logical *and* emotional. For example, both anecdotes and examples are factual and can therefore appeal to logic. However, they are also illustrations that provide human interest and therefore appeal to the emotions. Also, through word choice, facts can be made to appeal to emotions as well as to logic. For example, it is a fact that because some new paper is made of recycled paper, fewer trees are sacrificed to make that paper. Using the word *sacrifice* gives the fact an emotional appeal. As this diagram shows, emotional appeals and logical appeals can blend.

emotional appeals → logical appeals

Pillars and Arches You can find logical appeals for your paper by researching your topic:

- by reading books, newspapers, and magazines at the library
- by searching the World Wide Web
- by interviewing local experts on your topic

You can gather material for emotional appeals from some of the same sources you use for logical appeals, such as articles and interviews. As you review these sources, keep an eye out for touching details and stories rather than just facts and statistics.

TIP Make sure that your evidence has the three R's. It should be

- *relevant*—tied closely to your issue
- *reliable*—from trustworthy sources
- *representative*—not all from one or two sources

Meeting INDIVIDUAL NEEDS

MULTIPLE INTELLIGENCES
Logical-Mathematical Intelligence. Another way to demonstrate how logical and emotional appeals may blend is by drawing a Venn diagram (shown below) on the chalkboard. Label the two circles *Logical Appeal* and *Emotional Appeal,* and fill them in with examples that students suggest for each. Students might suggest facts, examples, and expert opinions for the logical appeal circle. For the emotional appeal circle, students might suggest word choice or personal connections. When students give a response that fits both categories, write it in the intersecting space between the two circles.

Logical Appeal

Emotional Appeal

Making products from recycled materials conserves natural resources. It often takes less energy to make products with recycled materials.

In our town, a recycling system has made a big difference.

Soon, we will have no trees if we keep cutting them down to make paper and other products. We are abusing our planet by not making recycling a higher priority.

TECHNOLOGY TIP

Students are likely to search the World Wide Web for support. Explain that they must use caution when they use information from the Web because it is largely unregulated. Suggest that students use a reliable Web site created exclusively for research by a reliable institution. *You need to be aware that Internet resources are sometimes public forums and their content can be unpredictable.*

Here is a support chart one writer created to make sure he had solid evidence for each reason supporting his position.

Issue: *proposed law to ban large car stereo speakers and set legal volume levels*

Opinion Statement: *Playing a loud car stereo should not be a crime; this legislation must be defeated.*

Reasons	Evidence
1. First, there are already laws about disturbing the peace that cover this situation.	**Expert opinion**—Sheriff Tharpe says that he just uses existing noise-pollution laws. (logical appeal)
2. Another reason such a law should not exist is that it will only add to the burden of the already overworked police.	**Facts, example**—Use information from a newspaper article about overworked police forces. John's father, Deputy Marquez, had to work double shifts. (logical appeals)
3. The most important reason is that singling out noise from car stereos is a form of discrimination.	**Example**—Most people make noise in public or participate in a noisy public event at some time, such as a football game, a concert, or a political rally. "Who would want to go to a quiet football game?" Use word "discrimination" to describe law. (emotional appeals)

YOUR TURN 4

Guide students to choose issues and opinion statements that are appropriate. If necessary, provide blank charts for students from the Reading Workshop, such as the logical and emotional appeal chart used in **Your Turn 3** on p. 255. Check that students are able to build adequate support for their opinions, using strong reasons and a variety of appeals.

YOUR TURN 4 — Choosing an Issue and Developing Support

Use the examples, tips, and suggestions above to

- choose an issue and write an opinion statement
- organize your thoughts about your purpose, audience, and tone
- gather support—logical appeals (reasons and evidence) and emotional appeals

RESOURCES

Your Turn 4
Practice
- *Communications*, WS. p. 127

Critical Thinking
Practice
- *Communications*, WS. p. 128

MINI-LESSON CRITICAL THINKING

Eliminating Circular Reasoning

As you have seen, solid support is important in a persuasive paper. Just stating your opinion in different words is not support; it is **circular reasoning**. Which of the following statements gives a valid reason by answering the question *Why?* instead of repeating itself?

1. Industrial pollution harms the ozone layer because it weakens the atmosphere.

2. Industrial pollution harms the ozone layer by releasing large amounts of carbon dioxide into the atmosphere.

If you decided that the first sentence merely restates the word *harms* as *weakens*, and that the second sentence gives a solid reason (pollution is harmful because it releases carbon dioxide), you were right.

When analyzed, circular reasoning ends up in a repetitive cycle, as shown in the diagram to the right. Valid reasoning, on the other hand, does not go in a circle. Instead, it leads the reader through a progression of thoughts. You can avoid circular reasoning by checking that every statement in your paper is a valid reason and does not merely repeat what you have already stated. Ask the question *Why?* to make sure your statements are valid and progress toward building a reasonable case.

PRACTICE

On a separate piece of paper, write *CR* for each of the following passages that contain circular reasoning. If the reasoning is valid, write *V*. Be prepared to explain your choices.

1. The United States should send its military to stop a foreign civil war because stopping the war would bring peace to the country.

2. Our school should allow restaurants to open food booths on campus because the booths would give students more choices.

3. Cigarettes are harmful to your health because smoking can cause many diseases, such as lung cancer and emphysema.

4. Soccer is more fun to watch than football because soccer is more interesting.

5. Teenagers should be encouraged to hold part-time jobs because jobs teach important lessons such as responsibility and the value of hard work.

Writing

Persuasive Paper

Framework	Directions and Explanations

Introduction

- Grab your readers' attention.
- Describe the issue and give background information.
- State your opinion.

Body

- Present your first reason and give support.
- Present your second reason and give support, and so on.

Conclusion

- Restate your opinion.
- Summarize reasons or include a call to action or both.

Wave a Red Flag Begin with a startling statistic, a powerful quotation, or an anecdote.

Explain the Issue Give brief background information so your readers will understand the issue; remember that you are leading your readers from a general statement in the first sentences to a specific statement of the issue in your thesis.

Present Your Thesis Include a clear **opinion statement** (thesis) so your audience knows your position on the issue.

Support Your Opinion Use the most convincing **logical** and **emotional appeals** from your prewriting notes. You may want to use the following strategy to organize your paper:

- Begin with your **second strongest reason** to make a strong appeal to your audience.
- Place your **least convincing reasons** in the middle.
- Save your **best reason** for last, to leave your audience with an impression of your strong reasoning.

Bring It Home **Restate,** but do not repeat, **your opinion.** You can **summarize your reasons**, give your audience a stirring **call to action,** or do both.

YOUR TURN 5 Writing Your Persuasive Paper

Now it is your turn to draft a persuasive paper. As you write, clearly state your opinion and use the strongest reasons and evidence to provide support; establish your tone and appeal to your specific audience; and use the framework and the Writer's Model as a guide.

266 | Chapter 7 | **Persuasion:** Supporting an Opinion

RESOURCES

Writing

Writing Prompts
- *Communications,* TP. 55, WS. p. 129

Your Turn 5

Practice
- *Communications,* TP. 56, WS. p. 130

A Writer's Model

The following essay closely follows the framework on the previous page. As you read, notice the background details the writer gives. Pay attention also to your responses to this piece. Do you agree with the writer?

Music to Whose Ears?

Warm spring weather has arrived. A person gets in a car, rolls down the windows, pops a CD in the stereo, turns up the volume, and heads out for a lake. This is a recipe for a great feeling and harmless fun, right? Some state senators do not think so. To them, extremely loud car stereos are a public nuisance—even a dangerous one. They have proposed a law that bans car speakers above a certain size and sets legal volume levels. Playing a loud car stereo should not be a crime; this legislation must be defeated.

One reason for defeating the proposed law is that existing state laws already cover the problems the senators mention. According to Richard Tharpe, Hamilton County sheriff, "Right now we can arrest people for disturbing the peace, and state law even sets noise-pollution levels." In addition, if a stereo does cause a traffic accident—which Tharpe notes is uncommon and hard to prove—the driver can be charged. However, in the past five years only one such accident has been reported. To institute the proposed law, then, is just unnecessary repetition. It is obvious that legislators do not need to duplicate laws.

Another reason to stop this proposed legislation is that it will be extremely difficult to enforce. Our police force is already overburdened with enforcing the laws we have. A number of towns and cities in the state have admitted to staffing shortages. In fact, Deputy Marquez, my friend John's father, has had to work double shifts the last six months in order to ensure that all patrols are covered. According to Deputy Marquez, this shortage is due to the fact that officers must spend a large percentage of their time enforcing misdemeanor laws similar to the proposed ban on loud car stereos. Just because serious crime is no longer on the rise, the police should not have to add another misdemeanor to their beats.

(continued)

INTRODUCTION
Attention-grabbing anecdote—emotional appeal

Opinion statement

BODY
First reason
Evidence: Expert opinion and fact

Evidence: Fact

Second reason
Evidence: Fact

Evidence: Anecdote

Evidence: Fact

Connecting Reading and Writing

Students should remember that an anecdote is one of the best ways to hook a reader's interest. By providing an anecdote that describes a moment of fun and relaxation, the author of **A Writer's Model** appeals to readers' emotions and likely has them nodding in agreement—even before they reach the opinion statement. Have students review p. 255 of the Reading Workshop to find another example of an anecdote that elicits logical and emotional responses.

(continued)

Do they really have time to point decibel monitors at passing cars?

Third Reason

Evidence: Fact and examples

The most compelling reason to put a halt to this proposal is that singling out car stereos is a form of discrimination. After all, many other "public noises" are just as loud. Parades and rallies often use high-volume sound trucks. Radio stations broadcast live from stores and parking lots. Loudspeakers, bands, and cheering crowds at football games can be heard for blocks. For example, the cheering during last week's victorious game against the Tigers could be heard as far away as Main Street. Sound from any such event could be seen (or heard) as infringing on the public's right to peace. However, a law to eliminate these noises would be considered unfair and illogical. No one wants to go to a quiet football game. It would spoil the fun. Why should driving to the lake be different?

Emotional appeal

CONCLUSION

Restatement of opinion

Call to action

We all want our streets to be calm and safe, but the senators' approach is misguided. A law restricting the volume of car stereos is unnecessary and unfair, and each of us should write or call our legislators to say so.

ZITS reprinted with special permission of King Features Syndicate, Inc.

268   Chapter 7   **Persuasion:** Supporting an Opinion

268   Persuasion: Supporting an Opinion

A Student's Model

The following is an excerpt of a persuasive paper written by Anthony King, a student at Morrison Christian Academy in Taichung, Taiwan.

Censored!

Is Internet censorship right? That is the question millions of people around the world are asking themselves—people like you and me who freely surf the Web every day reading the latest news or simply checking our e-mail. This freedom that we exercise daily is in danger of becoming another government regulated part of our lives. The Internet is a world of information which may be freely accessed by all; it should stay that way.

There are several arguments for and against the government's proposal for Internet regulations. There are many people who think the Internet should be censored because it gives underage surfers open access to undesirable material. The Internet can be freely accessed by anyone, including minors, and it is a place where people can freely exercise their constitutionally guaranteed freedom of speech. It is no secret that the Internet contains undesirable material, but whether or not an underage "netizen" has access to that type of information can be controlled by that child's parents or guardian. Programs such as NetNanny and Surf-Watch are two of many programs that provide protection against undesirable sites. There is no need for government intervention when the solution is so simple. The argument for Internet censorship based upon open access to this undesirable material is understandable, but since adults are capable of making the right decision to avoid such sites and protection is available for the underage surfer, access to unwanted material can be controlled without government regulations. However, those who do not feel satisfied with home control will be gratified to hear that there is a major Internet movement for private regulation.

INTRODUCTION

Position Statement

BODY

First Reason

Evidence: Facts

Connecting Reading and Writing

As students read **A Student's Model**, direct their attention to the title and the first paragraph. Ask them to consider these questions.

1. How does the exclamation point in the title reveal the author's opinion even before the reader has begun to read the essay?

2. Why does the writer begin with a question?

3. How does the writer use the second sentence to draw the reader into the debate?

Revising

Evaluate and Revise Your Paper

Give Your Paper the Once-Over, Twice As you evaluate and revise your draft, you should work collaboratively to do at least two readings. In the first reading, focus on the content and organization of your draft, using the guidelines below. In your second reading, concentrate on your sentence style, using the style guidelines on the next page.

▶ **First Reading: Content and Organization** In your first reading, look at the paper as a whole and make sure all its elements are working together smoothly. Use the following chart to evaluate and revise your paper so that it is clear and effective.

Persuasive Paper: Content and Organization Guidelines for Peer and Self-Evaluation

Evaluation Questions	▶ Tips	▶ Revision Techniques
❶ Does the introduction have an attention-grabbing opener and a clear opinion statement?	**Bracket** the one or two sentences that capture the reader's interest. **Underline** the opinion statement. Revise if there isn't an attention grabber or an opinion statement.	**Add** or **elaborate** on a sentence that engages the reader. **Add** an opinion statement that clearly states the position you have taken.
❷ Does the paper include at least three valid reasons to support the opinion statement?	**Number** the reasons in the margins. Check each one for circular reasoning. If there is a problem, revise.	**Cut** any reasons that are circular. **Add** valid reasons that support your opinion statement.
❸ Is each reason supported by at least one piece of evidence? If appropriate, are emotional appeals used?	**Circle** each piece of evidence (facts, examples, and so on). **Draw an arrow** from each item to the reason it supports. If you have any reasons without arrows pointing to them, revise.	**Add** facts, expert opinions, examples, or anecdotes to support your reasons. **Elaborate** on existing support by adding details or more evidence.
❹ Are the reasons and evidence arranged in order of importance?	**Put a star** next to the strongest reason. If it is not the last one, revise.	**Reorder** the reasons so that they are in order of importance.
❺ Does the conclusion restate the opinion and include a summary of reasons or a call to action?	**Underline** any sentence that restates the writer's opinion. **Put a check mark** next to any sentence that makes a call to action. If you lack underlining and/or check marks, revise.	**Add** a restatement of your opinion and a summary of reasons or a call to action.

RESOURCES

Revising
Practice
■ *Communications,* TPs. 57, 58, WS. pp. 131, 132, 133

ONE WRITER'S REVISIONS Here is how one writer used the content and organization guidelines to revise some sentences from the persuasive paper on page 267.

> *According to Richard Tharpe, Hamilton County Sheriff, "Right*
> ~~The senators just want to restrict playing car stereos loudly~~
> *now we can arrest people for disturbing the peace, and state*
> ~~because they think rock-and-roll is a lot of extreme noise pollu-~~
> *law even sets noise-pollution levels."* *In addition,*
> ~~tion. Their own law officers do not agree with them.~~ If a stereo
> *Tharpe notes is uncommon and hard to prove*
> does cause an accident—which ~~hardly ever happens anyway~~—
>
> the driver can be charged.

Cut and replace

Add

Cut and replace

Analyzing the Revision Process

1. Why do you think the writer replaced the first and second sentences?

2. Why is the added information important?

YOUR TURN 6 **Revising Content and Organization**

Revise the content and organization of your paper, using the guidelines on the previous page. Use the example revisions above as a model.

▶ **Second Reading: Style** Persuasive writing requires that you use words that have an impact on your readers. After all, you are trying to get them to agree with you. Using **clichés,** or worn-out expressions, may lead your readers to assume that your thoughts are just as boring as your language. Use the following guidelines to find and eliminate clichés, such as *sharp as a tack, safe and sound,* and *rain on your parade,* from your writing.

PEER REVIEW

Ask a few classmates to read your paper and to answer the following questions.

1. Does the paper convince you? Why or why not?

2. Do any reasons need supporting evidence? Why do you think so?

Style Guidelines

Evaluation Question	▶ Tip	▶ Revision Technique
Are there any clichés in the essay?	▶ Put an **X** through clichés—for example, *in a nutshell, rat race,* and *tough as nails.*	▶ **Replace** each Xed-out phrase with a fresh, original expression.

Analyzing the Revision Process

ANSWERS
Some sample answers follow.

1. The new sentence offers a more valid reason to support the opinion statement. Also, the evidence did not support the preceding (topic) sentence.

2. The added information provides expert opinion that supports the topic sentence.

YOUR TURN 6

Make sure students clearly state and support their opinions with paragraphs that include strong topic sentences followed by related evidence and appeals. You might want students to use a peer-revision checklist to provide feedback to each other. The checklist should list the points on the chart on p. 270.

Evaluating Student Writing

The ancillary *Assessment Alternatives* contains a variety of assessment forms, including Inventories and Evaluation Forms and rubrics: Six-Point Scales, Four-Point Scales, and Six Trait Scales.

272

Persuasion: Supporting an Opinion

TEACHING TIP

Eliminating Clichés

Point out that clichés are not only unoriginal, they also create an informal tone that may detract from the authority of a persuasive essay. Review the instruction on audience and tone presented in the Reading Workshop, pp. 260–261. Ask students to discuss how the use of clichés might affect the purpose and alter the tone of a persuasive essay.

Analyzing the Revision Process

ANSWERS
Below are possible answers.

1. The new phrase is more respectful to the senators and is more likely to be taken seriously by readers.

2. The proposed law will be a burden to members of our community.

YOUR TURN 7

Ask students to highlight in their drafts the clichés they cut and the resulting revised sentences so that you may assess quickly whether students are properly eliminating clichés.

Focus on

Word Choice

Eliminating Clichés

Have you ever watched a movie and thought to yourself, "Oh, I've seen this before." We have all seen the action hero who escapes certain death at the last possible second. Like this overused character, there are words and phrases that were once new and fresh but now are just boring and predictable. They are called **clichés** and include phrases like "few and far between," "as strong as an ox," and "last but not least."

ONE WRITER'S REVISIONS Here's how one writer used the evaluation and revision guidelines to eliminate clichés from the persuasive paper on page 267.

BEFORE REVISION

We all want our streets to be calm and safe, but the sena-

cliché   tors are ~~barking up the wrong tree~~. We need this law like we

cliché   need a ~~hole in the head~~.

AFTER REVISION

We all want our streets to be calm and safe, but the sena-

reword   tors' approach is misguided. A law restricting the volume of car stereos is unnecessary. . . .

Analyzing the Revision Process

1. How did replacing "barking up the wrong tree" with another phrase improve the first sentence above?

2. How else could you revise the cliché in the second sentence?

YOUR TURN 7 **Eliminating Clichés**

Revise the style of your persuasive paper; remember to use the guidelines in this section to eliminate clichés.

RESOURCES

Focus on Word Choice
Practice
- *Communications*, WS. p. 134

Publishing

Proofread Your Essay

Once More with Feeling   You do not want to ruin the impact of your well-crafted words by letting little mistakes show up in your final draft. Review your paper to make sure it is free of grammar, spelling, and punctuation errors. If you find it hard to inspect your own paper for these mistakes, trade papers with a partner and examine each other's work closely. One of the things you should look for is correct pronoun-antecedent agreement.

> **Reference Note**
>
> For **proofreading guidelines,** see page 13. For more information and practice on **pronoun-antecedent agreement,** see page 507.

Grammar Link

Pronoun-Antecedent Agreement

When you are writing persuasively about an issue, be sure that your reasoning does not get lost in a pronoun mix-up. Check to see that each **pronoun** agrees with its **antecedent**—the word to which the pronoun refers. There are several rules that govern pronoun-antecedent agreement.

1. **Singular pronouns are used to refer to the following antecedents:** *each, either, neither, one, everyone, everybody, everything, no one, nobody, nothing, anything, anyone, anybody, something, someone,* and *somebody.*

Incorrect	**One** of the horses closed **their** eyes.
Correct	**One** of the horses closed **its** eyes.

Note: In conversation, plural pronouns are often used to refer to singular antecedents that are clearly plural in meaning: **Everyone** raised **their** hands and cheered. However, this usage is considered incorrect in formal writing.

2. **A singular pronoun is used to refer to two or more singular antecedents joined by *or* or *nor.***

Incorrect	**Katy or Val** has **their** grades.
Correct	**Katy or Val** has **her** grades.

3. **Use a plural pronoun to refer to two or more antecedents joined by *and.***

Incorrect	**Dan and Maria** took **his and her** test.
Correct	**Dan and Maria** took **their** tests.

PRACTICE

Revise each of the following sentences, correcting errors in pronoun-antecedent agreement.

1. Each of the students should have to perform community service as part of their normal school curriculum.
2. We cannot assume that the school and the community can take care of itself.
3. Neither our teacher, Mrs. Gomez, nor Mia, the class president, has opposed the idea with their vote.
4. Everyone can create and manage a project of their own.
5. The plan will be implemented unless someone halts it with their veto.

Writing Workshop   **273**

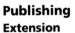

Publish Your Paper

You Better Believe It You cannot persuade anyone if you are the only one who reads your paper. By publishing your paper you take the next step in making your opinion heard and making an impact on an issue. When determining how to publish your paper, think again of the audience you are trying to reach.

- A natural choice for publishing your paper would be the opinion page of your school or local newspaper. You should check the guidelines for letters to the editor in both publications to make sure your paper meets the necessary criteria.

- Send your paper to those who can make a difference on your issue. Whether your audience is the school board or your state representative, offer your opinion to those who can make changes.

- Publish your paper on the World Wide Web and ask other Web page publishers to create links to the paper. For example, if your paper is about an environmental issue, you can ask for a link on a Web page hosted by an organization that shares your views. Look for sites with similar topics, or post your work on your own personal Web page.

- Make a pamphlet from your persuasive paper. Passing out pamphlets at school is one way to get your words out to the public.

Designing Your Writing

Creating Pamphlets Fliers or pamphlets—those sheets of paper that show up clamped under your windshield wiper, tucked in your door, and posted on bulletin boards—have long been an outlet for persuasion. If you choose to create a pamphlet from your paper, you will need to change its format to make it more appealing and accessible to potential readers. Make folds in the paper, and break up the text to fit the folds. Move your text into columns or display your paragraphs in easy-to-read pieces with bold or catchy headings. Here are a few basic guidelines for creating pamphlets.

- **Use typefaces that are easy to read, and limit yourself to no more than two typefaces.** Your text can look too busy with lots of typefaces. Use one main typeface for body text and a second for headings to emphasize them.

- **Rework your paper.** You may have a lot to say, but if you make the print in your pamphlet too small, people will not read it. Rather than making the print tiny, you may need to shorten your paper. For example, you could take out your weakest reason.

- **Use a separate heading for each reason to make your position clear to your readers.** Headings are great tools to guide readers who may just be glancing at the pamphlet you hand to them. *Guide* is the important word here; be careful not to overwhelm your readers with headings that distract them.

- **Avoid using capital letters for emphasis;** they are harder to read than small letters, particularly if they go on for more than one line. If you want to emphasize your words, use italics or boldface.

- **Use drawings, graphs, charts, or tables to deliver your information, if applicable.** Per square inch of space, much more information can be conveyed through graphic presentations than in an explanation in the text. Use drawings to show objects, and include graphs, charts, and tables for presenting numerical data.

- **Be sure to follow these guidelines if you use graphics.**

  1. Create labels to identify important elements.
  2. Include a key if the graphic has shadings, colors, or other details that have special meanings.
  3. Title most graphics.
  4. Position graphics neatly and comfortably within your margins, leaving at least two blank lines above and below each graphic.

Reflect on Your Essay

Take a Deep Breath   Now that the hard work is over, think about your paper and the process you used to create it. Use your answers to the following questions to recognize your achievement and to identify ways you can improve your next effort. Include these answers with your essay if you put it in your portfolio.

1. What was the most convincing and powerful part of your paper? Which part was the weakest? Why do you think so?

2. What methods or techniques did you use that you could use when you write other papers?

 PORTFOLIO

YOUR TURN 8   Proofreading, Publishing, and Reflecting

Use the material on the last several pages to correct grammar, usage, and mechanics errors in your paper, and keep an eye out for pronoun-antecedent agreement; publish your paper to reach your audience; and reflect on your paper.

T.H.E.M.E.S. Strategy

After explaining the T.H.E.M.E.S. strategy and reviewing the student model, have students prepare blank charts as shown below. Provide a thought-provoking issue for students to consider. After a brief class discussion of the subject, give students fifteen minutes to use the T.H.E.M.E.S. chart to organize their responses. Then, allow fifteen more minutes for students to draft letters to the editor. Use students' responses to the exercise to emphasize the importance of time management when taking a writing test.

OPINION:_____	
T.H.E.M.E.S.	Possible Reasons for Opinion
Time	
Health	
Education	
Money	
Environment	
Safety	

MINI-LESSON TEST TAKING

T.H.E.M.E.S. Strategy

Local, state, and national writing tests often ask you to write a persuasive essay in response to a question on an issue. You are given a topic in a writing prompt, but you have to decide your opinion, or position, organize your response, write, and proofread—all in a limited amount of time. Thinking of what to say in support of an opinion can be the most difficult step on a writing test. Use the following strategy to think of supporting ideas quickly.

THINKING IT THROUGH — Using T.H.E.M.E.S. Strategy on a Writing Test

Each letter in T.H.E.M.E.S. stands for a subject category you could use to trigger ideas for reasons supporting your position. You may not be able to use every category, but at least some of them will probably apply.

T = Time	H = Health	E = Education
M = Money	E = Environment	S = Safety

▶ **STEP 1** Memorize each letter and its category.

▶ **STEP 2** Using each letter, ask a question about the effect your opinion will have on time, health, education, and so on. These questions will then trigger ideas about reasons that support your position.

▶ **STEP 3** Answer each question to give you a reason that supports your opinion.

Below is an example of how one student used T.H.E.M.E.S. to generate reasons for a persuasive essay on banning smoking.

Position: The city should ban smoking in all areas.

T = Workers won't have to spend time cleaning ashtrays and picking up cigarette butts.

H = Banning smoking will reduce secondhand smoke inhalation and its health risks.

E = People will be more aware of the health problems associated with smoking.

M = Reduction in smoking might lower healthcare costs.

E = Public areas will have cleaner air, and the litter associated with smoking will be less widespread.

S = Banning smoking will reduce the risk of fire started by discarded cigarettes.

RESOURCES

Test Taking
Practice
■ *Communications,* WS. p. 136

Connections to Life

Critically Viewing Persuasive Messages in the Media

Persuasion does not exist solely on newspaper editorial pages and in magazine articles. You are surrounded by persuasive messages every day, from your parents or teachers urging you to study to your friends telling you why you should listen to a certain new CD. You are also exposed to many different persuasive messages in the form of advertisements: on billboards, on TV, in films—seemingly everywhere. These advertisements try to persuade you to buy products or to adopt a certain point of view through their use of spoken words, music, writing, sound effects, and pictures.

It is important that you be aware of the persuasion used in media messages; otherwise, you might be convinced to do something that could be dangerous or contrary to your own beliefs. Use the following questions to help you analyze and evaluate the messages you receive daily.

- **Who created the message and why?** Think about an ad for a certain brand of pants. The creators of the ad's message are the owners of the brand and their employees. They create the message to convince people to buy this brand of pants.

- **How does the message make me feel?** There could be several reactions to the pants ad, but the advertisers certainly want to create a positive feeling. The people in the ad look happy; do you feel happy, too? If so, the ad's creators have transferred the ad's happy feeling to you.

- **Does the ad attempt to shape my attitudes and perceptions about myself and the world around me?** It is important to be aware that advertisers have **codes** and **conventions** (established techniques or practices) about the portrayal of women and men in ads.

1. **Voice-Over** Because men's voices are lower in pitch than women's, television commercials often have male narrators. Supposedly, a man's voice adds authority to the advertiser's message.

2. **Dismemberment** Another convention is to objectify women and men by showing only certain parts of bodies, such as the slim legs of women or the muscular chests of men.

3. **Foolishness** While men are usually seen as serious and reflective, women often are shown looking foolish.

4. **In Control** Women are often portrayed as subordinate to men, with men being in control of a situation.

5. **Approval** In many ads, women and men are judged as successful only if they are attractive.

The pants ad may subtly communicate attitudes you dislike.

- **What point of view are the creators trying to convince me to accept?** The point of view may be that wearing these pants will make you feel happy and have fun.

- **What techniques do the creators use to persuade me?** You may already know some

Critically Viewing Persuasive Messages in the Media
Talk with students about the need for thinking critically about messages in the media. Encourage students to find and share examples of persuasion in various media—advertisements, articles, or news stories on TV. Have the class evaluate and critique the examples using the information on conventions and techniques given in the text.

Meeting INDIVIDUAL NEEDS

MULTIPLE INTELLIGENCES
Bodily-Kinesthetic Intelligence. Ask students to consider the ways that people use physical gestures in order to persuade. For example, demonstrate how nodding the head while asking a question might persuade a listener to answer in the affirmative. Ask volunteers to act out examples of persuasive body language. Have the other students interpret the gestures and explain their persuasive purposes.

YOUR TURN 9

To help you assess that all the elements are included in their paragraphs, ask students to use a coding system to mark where in their writing each question was addressed.

C – creator of ad

F – feelings generated by message

S – shapes attitudes and perceptions

POV – point of view being promoted

T – techniques used

---

of the techniques advertisers use and may be able to answer this question easily. If not, take a close look at the following chart, which gives definitions and examples of three popular persuasive techniques used in advertising. Recognizing these techniques will help you to analyze, or closely examine the details of, the various persuasive messages you encounter from the media.

Technique	Definition	Examples
Glittering Generality	a word or phrase with positive connotations used to create good feelings about a product or opinion, regardless of any evidence	A brand uses the words *natural* or *organic* to appeal to people who want healthy, ecologically sound products. The word *gold* is often used to imply luxury.
Testimonial	a personal recommendation for a product or idea often offered by an expert or famous person who may not use or like the product or idea	A sports figure who has become a symbol of excellence and success recommends a particular restaurant. A smiling movie star recommends a certain brand of toothpaste.
Transfer	an attempt to connect a product, image, or idea with something respected, pleasing, or admired—even though that connection may not be logical	A TV star who played a trustworthy family man for many years describes a building company. A politician identifies herself with a beloved political figure of the past.

To evaluate persuasive messages, you should also consider how visual techniques add to the meaning. Illustrators, graphic artists, and photographers may use the techniques below to give an ad extra impact.

- **Color** A grape juice ad might use a black-and-white image with bright purple juice to make the product look even more inviting to viewers.

- **Juxtaposition** Placing two images next to each other can create meaning. For example, an image of a person drinking juice followed by an image of a beautiful waterfall points out how refreshing the juice is.

- **Cropping** For images that are not staged by an ad producer, cropping can eliminate a product's negative points. For example, a photo of a taste test might be cropped to show only the face of a person enjoying juice in order to eliminate the giant purple stain the juice made on her shirt.

YOUR TURN 9 Critically Viewing a Persuasive Media Message

Find a printed advertisement or a TV commercial that uses glittering generalities, a testimonial, or transfer, and analyze it in a short paragraph. Use the questions on page 277 as a guide. Present your analysis to a small group of students.

Making a Persuasive Speech

Persuasion is well suited to the spoken word. In fact, most of the persuasive messages you have been exposed to have been spoken ones. Now, you will have the **occasion** to give your own persuasive speech, to speak up—quite literally—for what you believe. You can use your topic from the Writing Workshop, or you can speak on a new topic. Because your purpose is to persuade, be certain that the issue you choose is something about which you feel strongly. You might want to discuss new topic ideas with another student to make sure you choose an appropriate topic for the speaking **task** with which you have been challenged.

Prepare Your Case

After choosing an issue and identifying your position on the issue (or thesis), develop support for your opinion. Back up each reason with facts, statistics, expert opinions, or anecdotes. Use precise language to defend your point of view, and include both logical support (proofs) and emotional appeals. You might want to emphasize emotional appeals more in your speech than you would in a written piece, in order to keep your listeners interested and responsive to your cause. Your **audience** will probably be your classmates unless you have another audience in mind.

Deliver Your Speech

Many speeches are outlined and rehearsed but not memorized. Such preparation is the best method for your persuasive speech. You will be much more persuasive if you make a relaxed presentation rather than giving a word-for-word memorized speech or reading from your paper.

You can adapt your speech from a persuasive essay or start from scratch with a complete outline. One of these options will be the blueprint for your speech, from which you will prepare note cards that list its main

WHAT'S AHEAD?

In this section, you will make a persuasive speech. You will also learn how to

- **present an opinion, or thesis, and reasons and evidence that support it**
- **use verbal and nonverbal cues to present your speech**

TIP In order to win people over to your cause or position, you may be tempted to distort the truth, exaggerate, or attack someone unjustly. Besides being unethical, these methods will cause your audience to lose trust in your words—and perhaps in your cause as well.

Focus on Speaking and Listening **279**

OBJECTIVES

- **To make a persuasive speech**
- **To present an opinion, or thesis, and reasons and evidence that support it**
- **To use verbal and nonverbal cues in the presentation of a speech**

Quotation for the Day

"It takes two to speak the truth—one to speak, and another to hear."

(Henry David Thoreau, 1817–1862, American writer and naturalist)

Invite students to brainstorm techniques speechmakers can use to engage their audiences.

TEACHING TIP

Prepare Your Case

Point out to students that the tone of their speeches will affect the way their audience responds. It is important to have sound, clear reasoning so that the audience will take the speaker's words into consideration. To review the difference between a well-supported opinion and an argumentative attack, have students add examples to the table below.

Persuasive	Argumentative
The widespread fear of wolves is based on misinformation and the influence of fairy tales.	People who fear wolves are silly and misinformed.

Wrap It Up

Metacognition. Have students reflect on the process of preparing and delivering a persuasive speech by answering the following question.

1. Suppose you were asked to deliver your speech again to a different audience. How might you improve your preparation and delivery?

Then, ask students the following question.

2. Name two strategies for effective spoken delivery.

Cooperative Learning

Verbal and Nonverbal Feedback. In small groups, have students consider ways they could respond nonverbally and verbally to peers' speeches. For example, students might nod periodically to let a speaker know that they are listening. In their groups, have each student think of one nonverbal or verbal feedback strategy. The group can then organize these ideas in a chart like the one below and share it with the class. Students should practice giving this feedback as they listen to classmates' persuasive speeches.

FEEDBACK FOR PEERS
Nonverbal Feedback:
• keeping eye contact
• smiling
• nodding the head
• ignoring distracting behavior by the speaker and members of the audience
Verbal Feedback:
• asking questions of the speaker if given the opportunity
• discussing the presentation with others

TIP As you listen to your classmates' speeches, use the bulleted items to the right to help analyze, evaluate, and critique their performances. In addition to these delivery points, you should also listen for clear major ideas and strong supporting evidence.

You can use the same criteria when you evaluate and critique public persuasive speeches and persuasive speeches given on television.

parts: the issue, your opinion statement (thesis), each reason with its support (logical and emotional appeals), and a summary of reasons or a call to action. Make a separate card for each item, and number the cards to help you keep them in order. Practice connecting the material on your note cards by rehearsing your speech with a friend.

A Nod of the Head As you rehearse and deliver your speech, you will need to pay attention to **verbal** and **nonverbal strategies** as well as content.

Here are some essentials for improving your **spoken delivery.**

- **Speak at a reasonable rate and volume.** Practice speaking at a consistent rate, neither too fast nor too slowly, and make sure every member of the audience can hear you clearly.
- **Enunciate.** Do not slur your words or drop word endings. Avoid vocalized pauses such as *uh, um,* and *you know.*
- **Be enthusiastic.** Show that you believe in your material.
- **Use an effective pitch and tone of voice. Pitch** is the highness or lowness of your voice and can be used to convey and emphasize the meaning of your words. **Tone of voice** is the sound of your voice, and it should be appropriate to your subject matter.

Here are some methods for improving your **nonverbal behavior.**

- **Maintain eye contact** with your audience. Give everyone in your audience the feeling you are speaking directly to him or her.
- **Use appropriate gestures and facial expressions.** Try to relax and avoid overdoing gestures and facial expressions.
- **Use good posture.** Do not slouch or speak at the ground.
- **Breathe.** Remembering to breathe can help you feel less nervous.

Rehearse Your Speech

To refine your speech, evaluate yourself in rehearsals or get pointers from others through collaborating or conferring. One rehearsal strategy is to deliver your speech to a friend or to your family, exactly as you plan to deliver it to your real audience. Ask your rehearsal audience for feedback on how to make your speech better, and use the feedback to set goals for future speeches.

YOUR TURN 10 **Making a Persuasive Speech**

Using the information above, prepare, practice, and present your persuasive speech.

YOUR TURN 10

Make sure students express opinions about timely issues and present well-organized reasons and evidence.

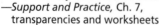

RESOURCES

Your Turn 10
Practice and Reinforcement

- *Media Literacy and Communication Skills*
  —*Support and Practice,* Ch. 7, transparencies and worksheets
  —Videocassette 2, Segment G

Choices

Choose one of the following activities to complete.

▶ **LITERATURE**

1. "The Only Thing We Have to Fear" Great speeches make great literature. Most speeches have an element of persuasion in them. Find a powerful persuasive speech in a book of speeches in the library, and memorize the speech. Locating the logical and emotional appeals in the speech will probably help you to remember it. Once you have committed it to memory, perform a **recitation** of the speech for your class.

▶ **VIEWING AND REPRESENTING**

2. Creatures Great or Small Have you ever noticed that some ads use animals to sell their products? Tigers sell breakfast cereal; koalas sell airlines. Design a **cereal box** or a **billboard,** using any animal you choose. Include text in your design, but focus on making your product visually appealing to a target audience. Then, present your design to a group of classmates as if you were an advertising executive pitching an ad campaign idea to the company whose product you are selling.

▶ **SPEAKING AND LISTENING**

3. Putting Words in Their Mouths Have you ever wondered what it would be like to be a speechwriter for a politician? Now is your chance to find out. Contact the office of a local political leader and ask to talk to his or her speechwriter. If possible, set up an interview. Then, ask the speechwriter about his or her writing strategies. Present your findings in the form of an **oral presentation.**

▶ **CAREERS**

4. Pitching an Idea Imagine that you have just invented or discovered something that will make a huge impact on industry. How can you convince your fellow workers that your discovery will work? Prepare a **media presentation** that introduces your idea and persuades your audience of its importance and benefits. Create visuals to help convince your audience. If you have access to a computer, you may want to take advantage of software designed to help you produce media presentations. Then, deliver your presentation to your fellow employees (that is, your fellow students).

PORTFOLIO

▶ **LITERATURE**

Ask students to consult with you about their selections. You might allow students to use outlines or other memory aids.

▶ **VIEWING AND REPRESENTING**

Have students work in pairs, with one student focusing on copywriting and the other on design. Have them study typical ad copy to define their tone, audience, content, and style. The designer might create original art, use photographs, or use cut-and-paste graphics. For the cereal box, allow students to bring in an empty cereal box and paste each part of the label they design onto the box. To create a billboard, students may work on a large sheet of butcher paper. Have them first create their design and text in a pencil sketch on the paper and then create the final billboard by using ink or paint over the pencil sketch.

▶ **SPEAKING AND LISTENING**

You may also have students analyze the ways people in different fields compose. Ask a media specialist to gather career resources and articles that quote authors discussing how they write. Have students research at least two careers to learn what writing strategies people in these fields use. Then, have students compare these findings with the information learned from the interview. Remind students of the delivery tips included in Focus on Speaking and Listening (pp. 279–280).

Choices **281**

RESOURCES

Supporting an Opinion
Assessment

■ *Assessment Package*
—*Chapter Tests,* Ch. 7
—*Chapter Tests in Standardized Test Formats,* Ch. 7
—*Assessment Alternatives,* Ch. 7

■ *Test Generator (One-Stop Planner CD-ROM)*

Choices
Rubrics

■ *Assessment Package*
—*Assessment Alternatives,* Ch. 7

CHAPTER

8

Reviewing Television

Use this guide to create an instructional plan that suits the individual needs of your students. Assignments marked by an asterisk (*) may be completed out of class. Times given for pacing lessons are estimated. See pp. 282–283 for chapter-wide resources. Resources listed in this guide are point-of-use resources only.

Curriculum Connections

Choices *p. 317*
- Media and Technology
- Viewing and Representing
- Literature

internet connect

GO TO: go.hrw.com
KEYWORD: EOLang 9-8

All resources for this chapter are available for preview on the *One-Stop Planner CD-ROM with Test Generator*. All worksheets and tests may be printed from the CD-ROM.

	Chapter Opener pp. 282–283	Reading Workshop: Reading a Critical Review pp. 284–293
DEVELOPMENTAL PROGRAM	⏱ **30 minutes** • Reviewing Television p. 283 • Your Turn 1 p. 283	⏱ **60 minutes** • Preparing to Read p. 284 • Reading Selection pp. 285–286 • First Thoughts 1–3 p. 287 • Fact and Opinion pp. 287–289 • Your Turn 2 p. 289 • Evaluation Criteria pp. 289–291 • Your Turn 3 p. 291 • Test Taking Mini-Lesson p. 293
CORE PROGRAM	⏱ **20 minutes** • Reviewing Television p. 283 • Your Turn 1 p. 283	⏱ **75 minutes** • Preparing to Read p. 284 • Reading Selection* pp. 285–286 • First Thoughts 1–3 p. 287 • Fact and Opinion pp. 287–289 • Your Turn 2 p. 289 • Evaluation Criteria pp. 289–291 • Your Turn 3 p. 291 • Vocabulary Mini-Lesson p. 292 • Your Turn 4 p. 292 • Test Taking Mini-Lesson p. 293
ADVANCED PROGRAM	⏱ **15 minutes** • Reviewing Television p. 283 • Your Turn 1 p. 283	⏱ **60 minutes** • Preparing to Read p. 284 • Reading Selection * pp. 285–286 • Fact and Opinion pp. 287–289 • Evaluation Criteria pp. 289–291 • Your Turn 3 p. 291 • Vocabulary Mini-Lesson p. 292 • Your Turn 4 p. 292
RESOURCES — PRINT	• *Communications,* TP. 59, WS. p. 137	• *Alternative Readings,* Ch. 8 • *Communications,* TPs. 60, 61, WS. pp. 138–145
RESOURCES — MEDIA	• *One-Stop Planner CD-ROM*	• *One-Stop Planner CD-ROM*

TP.=Transparency   WS.=Worksheet

Writing Workshop: Writing a Critical Review of a TV Sitcom *pp. 294–314*	Focus on Viewing and Representing: Analyzing the Nightly Network News *pp. 315–316*
75 minutes • Prewriting *pp. 294–301* • Your Turn 5 *p. 298* • Critical-Thinking Mini-Lesson *p. 300* • Your Turn 6 *p. 301* • Framework and Your Turn 7* *p. 302* • Writer's Model and Student's Model *pp. 303–305* **100 minutes** • Evaluate and Revise Your Draft *pp. 306–307* • Your Turn 8 *p. 307* • Focus on Sentences and Your Turn 9 *pp. 308–309* • Proofread, Publish, and Reflect on Your Essay *pp. 311–312* • Grammar Link *p. 311* • Your Turn 10* *p. 312*	**75 minutes** • Presentation Techniques *pp. 315–316* • Being a Critical Viewer *p. 316* • Your Turn 12* *p. 316*
120 minutes • Prewriting *pp. 294–301* • Your Turn 5* *p. 298* • Critical-Thinking Mini-Lesson *p. 300* • Your Turn 6* *p. 301* • Framework and Your Turn 7* *p. 302* • Writer's Model and Student's Model *pp. 303–305* • Evaluate and Revise Your Draft *pp. 306–307* • Your Turn 8* *p. 307* • Focus on Sentences and Your Turn 9 *pp. 308–309* • Proofread, Publish, and Reflect on Your Essay *pp. 311–312* • Grammar Link *p. 311* • Your Turn 10* *p. 312* • Connections to Life* *pp. 313–314* • Your Turn 11 *p. 314*	**45 minutes** • Presentation Techniques *pp. 315–316* • Being a Critical Viewer *p. 316* • Your Turn 12* *p. 316*
90 minutes • Prewriting *pp. 294–301* • Your Turn 5* *p. 298* • Critical-Thinking Mini-Lesson *p. 300* • Your Turn 6* *p. 301* • Framework and Your Turn 7* *p. 302* • Writer's Model and Student's Model* *pp. 303–305* • Evaluate and Revise Your Draft *pp. 306–307* • Your Turn 8* *p. 307* • Focus on Sentences and Your Turn 9* *pp. 308–309* • Proofread, Publish, and Reflect on Your Essay *pp. 311–312* • Connections to Life* *pp. 313–314*	**30 minutes** • Presentation Techniques* *pp. 315–316* • Being a Critical Viewer* *p. 316* • Your Turn 12* *p. 316*

• *Communications,*
  TPs. 62–65,
  WS. pp. 146–155
• *Designing Your Writing*
	• *Media Literacy and Communication Skills*
	  —*Support and Practice,* Ch. 8
	  —*A How-to Handbook*
	  —*A Teacher's Guide,* Ch. 8

• *One-Stop Planner CD-ROM*	• *Media Literacy and Communication Skills* —*Videocassette 2, Segment H* • *One-Stop Planner CD-ROM*

8 Reviewing Television

CHAPTER OBJECTIVES

- To read a television sitcom
- To write a television sitcom review
- To analyze the effects of techniques used in television nightly news

Chapter Overview

A successful critical review of a television show depends upon the clear presentation of accurate facts, well-supported opinions, and relevant evaluation criteria. This chapter uses the skills required for reviewing television as the basis for an exploration of critical thinking, reading, writing, and viewing. In the Reading Workshop, students will read and analyze a review of a television sitcom. The Writing Workshop provides all the steps students will need to write their own critical reviews. Focus on Viewing and Representing will help students analyze and evaluate techniques used to present the nightly news. The three sections can be taught independently. Taught together, they give students a foundation for viewing television with a critical eye and offer practice in writing and speaking persuasively.

Why Study Television Reviews?

Many students are avid consumers of television programming. By gaining a deeper understanding of how to read and write television reviews, students will be better prepared to make viewing decisions. They will also be able to apply this knowledge to evaluating books, movies, Web sites, theater performances, and other sources of information and entertainment. As students learn how to write and evaluate critical reviews, they will also be gaining practice in discriminating between fact and opinion and in making judgments based on specific, relevant criteria. This practice will improve their reading, writing, listening, and speaking skills, especially as they relate to persuasive communications.

Teaching the Chapter

Option 1: Begin with Literature

If your program is built on a literature foundation, this chapter can be used following a short story unit focused on literary analysis. After considering the influence of character, plot, theme, mood, and point of view of a short story, ask students to read the review of a sitcom on pp. 285–286 of the Reading Workshop. Lead them to see the connection between analyzing the elements of a short story and evaluating the elements of a television program. Point out the differences as well, directing students' attention to aspects such as casting and acting. Students should be able to apply their knowledge of how to analyze fiction to the process of reading and writing a critical review of a television sitcom.

Option 2: Begin with Nonfiction and Writing

This chapter will furnish students with practice in the skill of selecting effective criteria on which to judge television sitcoms. The activities will also reinforce the essential skill of providing strong support for opinions by using facts and other details to back up statements. Once students have applied these concepts to television programs, they will be ready to adapt and apply what they have learned to the analysis and evaluation of plays, short stories, and chapters from novels.

Making Connections

To the Literature Curriculum

Students can apply the same skills they use to write a critical review of a sitcom to the analysis and evaluation of a short story. For example, a discussion of "The Interlopers," by Saki, can offer students practice with identifying evaluation criteria to support an opinion.

Lesson Idea: Analysis of "The Interlopers" by Saki

1. Begin by having students read the story. Have them write down any thoughts or feelings that the story elicits.

2. Help students create a "Story Evaluation Checklist" in which they establish criteria to judge the elements of a short story. A sample is shown below.

Story Evaluation Checklist	Criteria
plot	• revolves around a central conflict • keeps the reader's interest
characterization	• characters are well developed • characters interact in interesting ways
setting	• is well described through use of detail
theme	• conveys an important message • is relevant to many people
mood	• is established through language

3. Use the student checklists to emphasize the subjectivity inherent to the critical process. Point out that the real challenge of successful critical writing is not just stating opinions, but supporting them with examples and observations from the story.

4. Have the class identify examples and details from "The Interlopers" that meet or fail to measure up to the criteria in the student chart.

5. After this discussion, introduce students to the critical review in this chapter (pp. 285–286). Use the instruction on backing up opinions with evaluation criteria to prepare students to write their own critical reviews of television sitcoms.

■ To Careers

Help students explore career options that make use of the critical skills taught in this chapter. Consider inviting speakers to your class. These may include a journalist who writes reviews of local theater for the community newspaper, a teaching colleague who reviews materials for a professional journal, or a parent who is involved in software review for a computer company. Focus the exploration on identifying skills related to television reviewing that also apply to other occupations. See also **Connections to Life** on pp. 313–314.

■ To the Community

Encourage students to use their reviewing skills for community service. Network with colleagues, friends, and family to find out about local theatrical productions or publications that might profit from publicity. For example, a local organization might be putting on a play as a fundraiser, or a community arts center might be launching a show of local artists' work. Involve students in writing reviews to give to these groups for use in promotional brochures or press releases for local newspapers.

■ To the Social Studies Curriculum

Provide an opportunity to transfer and adapt what students learn about reviewing sitcoms to the critique of a social studies video. Ask one of your colleagues in the social studies department to suggest a video that he or she has used. Involve students in deciding how this type of review would be similar to and different from a sitcom review. Have small groups work together to establish criteria and evaluate the program. During class sharing, encourage students to compare and contrast the criteria they used and the conclusions they drew.

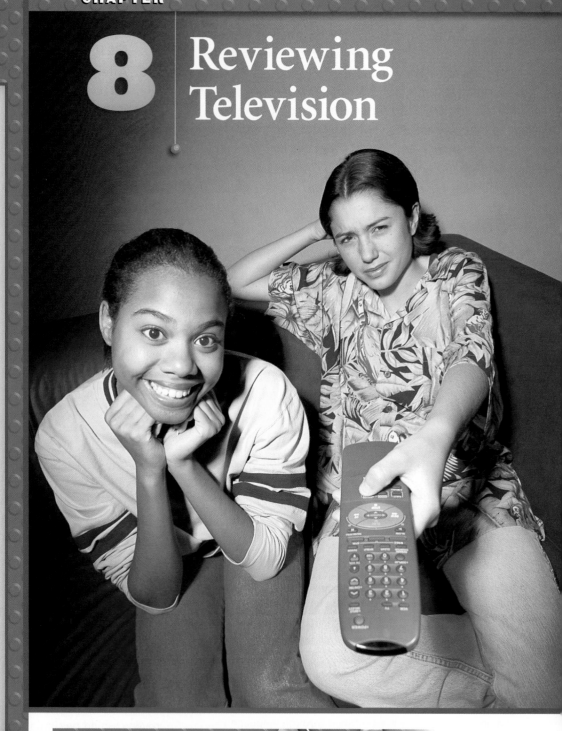

PREVIEWING THE CHAPTER

■ The three workshops in this chapter will help your class respond critically to television programming. In the Reading Workshop, students will read a review distinguishing fact from opinion and evaluating the elements of a sitcom. Students will apply these skills as they write their own reviews during the Writing Workshop. In the Focus on Viewing and Representing section, students will use their critical viewing skills to analyze television news techniques. To integrate this chapter with grammar, usage, and mechanics chapters, see pp. T371A-T371B.

INTRODUCING THE CHAPTER

■ To introduce the chapter, use the Journal Warm-up, Transparency 59, in *Communications.*

VIEWING THE PHOTOGRAPH

■ Ask students to identify what is happening in the photograph. [Two girls are watching television or a video; one seems pleased with what she sees, while the other seems not as pleased. Students can infer the situation from the girls' expressions, from the lighting, and from the props—a sofa and a remote control.] Have students notice how the arrangement of the girls draws viewers' eyes from the face of the pleased girl to the face of the displeased one.
Representing. Have students work in pairs to stage short skits that use facial expressions and body language to show typical reactions of television viewers as they watch TV.

CHAPTER RESOURCES

Planning
■ *Lesson Planner, ELL Strategies,* Ch. 8
■ Block Scheduling, p. T281A (this book)
■ *One-Stop Planner CD-ROM*

Practice
■ *Communications,* Ch. 8
■ *Media Literacy and Communication Skills*

Extension
■ *Designing Your Writing*

Reinforcement
■ *Communications,* Ch. 8
■ *Alternative Readings,* Ch. 8
■ *Daily Language Activity Transparencies*
■ *Vocabulary Workshop* and *Tests*

Reading Workshop

Reading a Critical Review

Writing Workshop

Writing a Critical Review of a TV Sitcom

Viewing and Representing

Analyzing the Nightly Network News

Motivate

Ask a volunteer to name a favorite TV show. Have other students brainstorm words the title brings to mind. Discuss whether the words would elicit positive or negative reactions from someone who had never seen the show. Emphasize the importance of finding the right words to express opinions.

H ow would you like to get paid to watch television, listen to music, or go to the movies? As a professional music, TV, or movie critic, you actually could make money doing these things—but you would also have to write persuasive **critical reviews.** Critical reviews, wherever they appear—in magazines, on the radio, on television—attempt to persuade people that the subject of the review is or is not worth their time and money.

You will find critical reviews almost everywhere you turn. They may be **informal reviews,** such as friends' recommendations of movies, music, and places to meet new people, or they may be **formal reviews** that appear in magazines and newspapers and on TV, radio, and the Internet. Reviews are so abundant because, with so many choices to make, people often find themselves asking questions like *Is that show I've heard about worth watching?* or *What are some good new books I might read?* In their reviews, critics help answer those kinds of questions by providing **informed opinions** on what they think is good or bad, worthwhile or not worthwhile.

Informational Text

Persuasion

ELEMENTS OF *Literature*

Reviewing Television in Literature. In *Elements of Literature,* Third Course, "Thank You, M'am" by Langston Hughes, pp. 120–124, and "A Man Called Horse" by Dorothy M. Johnson, pp. 167–178, can be read and analyzed to help students connect the concept of literary discussion to television review.

YOUR TURN 1

Formal reviews for books, movies, plays, concerts, and restaurants appear in various media. Informal reviews might be a friend's report on a video game or a sibling's discussion of a meal. Students should understand that a reviewer's reasons must include appeals to logic or the emotions; it is not sufficient to say "I like it" or "I hate it."

YOUR TURN 1 Turning Thumbs Up or Down

Working in pairs, brainstorm a list of formal and informal reviews you have seen, read, or heard lately. Try to think of at least four examples of each kind of review. Then, for each item on your list, write down any reasons the reviewer gave for his or her opinion. Be prepared to share your results with the class.

internet connect

go. hrw .com

GO TO: go.hrw.com
KEYWORD: EOLang 9-8

Evaluation and Assessment

- *Assessment Package*
  —*Chapter Tests,* Ch. 8
  —*Chapter Tests in Standardized Test Formats,* Ch. 8
  —*Assessment Alternatives,* Ch. 8

- *Test Generator*
  (One-Stop Planner CD-ROM)

Internet

- go.hrw.com (keyword: EOLang 9–8)

OBJECTIVES

Reading and Writing Connection

- To read a critical review of a television program in preparation for writing a critical review

Reading Skills

- To identify facts and opinions
- To analyze evaluation criteria
- To understand neologisms

TEACHING TIP

Preparing to Read
The material on p. 284 invites students to watch for statements of fact and opinion in the Reading Selection, **"Ray of Hope."** Students are also introduced to the use of evaluation criteria in critical writing.

Quotation for the Day

"Even if your article is basically educational in purpose, you must consider what can be done through language, use of facts, and method of attack to cause that ho-hum-prone reader to perk."

(Peter Jacobi, journalist, professor, and author)

Discuss the meaning of the quotation. Ask students to name qualities of television- or entertainment-related articles that have caused them to "perk." For instance, a student may cite the appeal of a magazine article about the personal life of a familiar actor or a leading statement with which they strongly agree or disagree.

RESOURCES

Reading Workshop
Reinforcement
- *Alternative Readings*, Ch. 8

WHAT'S AHEAD?

In this section, you will read a critical review of a television program. You will also learn how to

- identify facts and opinions
- analyze evaluation criteria

Reading a Critical Review

With so many shows on television, how do you decide what to watch? One way to find out if a certain show is worth watching is to watch it once and then decide if you like it enough to watch a second time. Another way is to read a **critical review** of the program.

The article on the next page, "Ray of Hope," is a critical review of a television sitcom (short for *situation comedy,* the most commonly seen type of comedy program on television). See if the writer is able to convince you that the show is worth thirty minutes of your time.

Preparing to Read

READING SKILL

Fact and Opinion The heart of any review is a critic's, or reviewer's, **opinion,** what he or she thinks of the program. However, **facts**—statements that can be proven true, such as the names of actors, the date and time a show is on, and what the show is about—also play a key role.

As you read "Ray of Hope," be on the lookout for statements of fact and statements of opinion.

READING FOCUS

Evaluation Criteria Television critics and reviewers support their opinions about TV shows by explaining how well the shows measure up against specific **criteria**—standards they think good TV shows should meet. For example, most critics would list "must be funny" as a standard that a sitcom should meet, because a sitcom that is not funny is just not a good sitcom. While people do not always agree on what the criteria should be, or on which criteria are more important than others, there are common standards that most people would use to evaluate any type of TV show. As you read "Ray of Hope," try to determine what criteria the writer is using to evaluate the program.

READING PROCESS

PREREADING
Activate Prior Knowledge. Have students read the introduction at the top of p. 285. Ask if any of them have viewed this program. Explain that students who have seen the show will have a stronger basis upon which to agree or disagree with the opinions of the critic. Prompt students to recall other sitcoms they have seen. Then ask: What qualities do you look for in a sitcom?

The following review by television critic Bruce Fretts originally appeared in *Entertainment Weekly*. *Everybody Loves Raymond* was in its first year at the time of the review. As you read, jot down answers to the numbered active-reading questions.

from Entertainment Weekly

Ray of Hope

by Bruce Fretts

A funny thing happened on the freshman sitcom *Everybody Loves Raymond* (CBS, Mondays, 8:30–9:00 P.M.) this year. It got better. No small feat, considering the fate of this season's other most promising pilots: *Spin City* stumbled badly and took several months to regain its footing, while *Millennium* immediately imploded. . . . Yet Ray Romano's family comedy didn't just grow funnier—it grew deeper.

1. What important information does the writer include in the first sentence?

What started as a likable and witty distillation of Romano's stand-up act—the travails of a dad with three kids under the age of six—transformed itself into a fascinatingly humane portrait of suburban dysfunction.[1] In

2. Judging from the first two paragraphs, what would you say the writer thinks of the quality of the show?

fact, *Raymond* may now be the best sitcom on the air—its only real creative competition being *News Radio*. . . .

The series' setup is simple: Sportswriter Ray Barone (Romano) lives on Long Island with his stay-at-home wife (Patricia Heaton) and their three preschoolers (played by Madylin, Sullivan, and Sawyer Sweeten)—right across the street from his squabbling folks (Peter Boyle and Doris Roberts) and . . . cop brother, Robert (Brad Garrett). At first, this premise lent itself to predictable complications: The elder Barones always barged in unannounced, and Robert was constantly mooching. Yet, as the season progressed, *Raymond* became more about the struggle of a grown man trying to separate from his parents and establish his own family.

Raymond is the rarest of sitcoms—one with a genuinely original point of view. In the show's new and improved opening-

3. Why do you think the writer includes the information given in this paragraph?

---

1. dysfunction (dis•fuŋkˊ shən): used here to denote a family that cannot function normally.

Active-Reading Questions

The active-reading questions are designed to focus attention on facts and opinions that the author presents, as well as to highlight some of the criteria he uses to evaluate the show's quality. Review students' answers to assess their understanding of these elements of critical reviews. Possible answers follow.

ANSWERS

1. title, day, time, and network of the show

2. It has improved—it is now funnier and deeper.

3. to let the viewer know his #1 criteria: originality

Meeting INDIVIDUAL NEEDS

LEARNERS HAVING DIFFICULTY

It may help students to know that this Reading Selection contains three colons on p. 285. Explain to students that a colon can be used instead of other punctuation marks at the end of a sentence or a phrase to show that an illustration, example, or amplification is to follow immediately. When the material after the colon is a complete sentence in itself, it must begin, as all sentences do, with a capital letter.

credits sequence, Ray's family goes by on a conveyor belt, and, as his children pass, he assures viewers the show is "not really about the kids." Refreshingly, it's not. This is life seen through the eyes of one man as he attempts the near-impossible task of simultaneously fulfilling the roles of husband, father, brother, and son.

> **4. What good quality of the show does the writer seem to be discussing here?**

It's a brilliantly realized vision, thanks to *Raymond's* remarkable cast. Like Garry Shandling and Jerry Seinfeld, Romano does such subtle work that it appears as if he's not even acting. His voice—a thick, nasal whine—initially sounds shticky,[2] yet he uses it like a finely tuned instrument, sliding from elation to frustration with only the slightest tonal[3] change.

As wife Debra, Heaton matches Romano beat for beat. She's taken the role's inherent thanklessness—the still center around which Ray's crazy family revolves— and turned it into a virtue. Debra rails[4] against her status as "the normal one," recently launching into a tirade[5] that allowed Heaton to do dead-on impressions of the eccentric

> **5. What quality does he focus on in this paragraph?**

Barones. And old pros Boyle and Roberts have created the most realistically fractious[6] TV marriage since Archie and Edith Bunker's.

Raymond's secret weapon, though, is the towering Garrett. . . . As Ray's eternally unlucky sibling, he has developed a wonderful chemistry with Romano. One charming episode, in which Ray gave his brother a stray bulldog, expertly utilized Garrett's extra-large talents. Underneath that imposing[7] exterior beats the heart of a puppy. . . .

Raymond has skyrocketed in the ratings since CBS moved it to Mondays after Cosby. The network would be wise not only to renew it but to leave it where it is. With his winning mix of heart and humor, Romano seems the natural heir to Cosby's sitcom-dad throne.

> **6. What recommendation comes through in the last two sentences?**

---

2. **shticky** (shtik´ē): like an act intended to be funny.

3. **tonal** (tō´nəl): quality of tone.

4. **rails** (rālz): complains in a bitter way.

5. **tirade** (tī´rād; tī•rād´): a long and passionate speech.

---

6. **fractious** (frak´shəs): irritable; cross.

7. **imposing** (im•pō´ziŋ): impressive because of size or strength.

READING PROCESS

READING

Make Personal Connections. If students have seen the show described in the Reading Selection, encourage them to re-read the review, noting where they agree and disagree with the reviewer. Challenge students who are not familiar with the show to identify a show they have watched that is similar in some ways. Ask them to revisit the review to note how *Everybody Loves Raymond* compares with their show.

Fact and Opinion

READING SKILL

Truths and Views   To be a critical reader of persuasive writing—including critical reviews—you must be able to distinguish between facts and opinions. The writer of "Ray of Hope" provides you with **facts** when he gives you background information about *Everybody Loves Raymond.* For example, here is part of a sentence that provides key facts about the characters on the show and the actors who play them:

> Sportswriter Ray Barone (Romano) lives on Long Island with his stay-at-home wife (Patricia Heaton). . . .

You can confirm the facts in the sentence by watching the opening credits of the show and by observing the show itself.

   "Ray of Hope" also includes a number of the writer's **opinions,** or personal views, about the show. Here is a part of a sentence from the second paragraph of the review that provides a key opinion:

> In fact, *Raymond* may now be the best sitcom on the air. . . .

This is a personal view that the writer has about the program, and it is debatable. If you were to watch *Everybody Loves Raymond,* you might not agree that it "may now be the best sitcom on the air."

   Here is a good rule of thumb that can often help you to distinguish facts from opinions: Any statement, like the example above, that contains words like *best, worst, funniest,* and *saddest* is probably a statement of opinion, not a statement of fact. The chart on the next page lists more of the common signal words and phrases that are often found in opinion statements.

Reading Workshop   **287**

First Thoughts on Your Reading

ANSWERS
Possible answers are suggested below.

1. Paragraph 3 – The situation involves a sportswriter on Long Island who tries to be a good father and husband while dealing with issues related to his parents and brother.

2. the refreshing point of view, the relevant theme, and the cast

3. because the show succeeds at being funny as well as touching

TEACHING TIP

Fact and Opinion
Ask volunteers to use some of the signal words or phrases on p. 288 in sentences. Then, have students tell whether each volunteer's sentence states an opinion or a fact. Have students explain their answers. For example, the sentence, "In my view, black-and-white photos are more interesting than color photos," expresses an opinion because not everyone would agree with that statement, and it cannot be proven.

Opinion Signal Words and Phrases		
• ugly/beautiful	• good/bad	• it is likely that
• funny/boring	• best/worst	• in my opinion
• love/hate	• like/dislike	• it is possible
• happy/sad	• terrible/great	• in my view

Be warned: Some writers will try to make their opinions sound more authoritative by presenting them as if they were facts.

Example:
Everyone knows that today's TV sitcoms are much less entertaining than sitcoms of past years.

The writer of this sentence used the phrase "everyone knows" to make it seem that the statement is not debatable—to make it look like a fact. However, no writer can reasonably claim to speak for everyone, so the statement is clearly *not* a fact. It remains a debatable opinion, despite the writer's attempt to disguise it.

Being able to tell the difference between facts and opinions is a vital reading skill. Without the skill, you run the risk of being persuaded too easily by weak reasoning or by opinions disguised as facts. With the skill, you become a discerning reader, able to see right into a writer's line of thought and recognize it for what it is.

THINKING IT THROUGH   Identifying Facts and Opinions

Read the examples and the following steps to determine whether a statement is a fact or an opinion.

Examples:
A. If you like comedy, you will love *Fishing with John,* one of the funniest shows on television.

B. According to a study conducted by the American Academy of Pediatrics, by age eighteen the average American teenager will have spent more time watching television than in the classroom.

▶ **STEP 1 First, ask yourself, "Can this statement be proven true?"**
The answer for statement **A** is *no,* because it is possible that a person who loves comedy might not like *Fishing with John*—and many people may feel that the show is not funny at all. The answer for statement **B,** however, is *yes.*

► **STEP 2 If your answer in step 1 is *yes*, the statement is probably a fact; consider sources where you might confirm it.** You could put statement **B** to the test by consulting a copy of the document in which the American Academy of Pediatrics reported the results of its study. Keep in mind, however, that most readers commonly accept the accuracy of factual statements that appear in sources they generally consider to be reliable—like established newspapers and magazines that have a history of accurately reporting facts.

► **STEP 3 If the answer in step 1 is *no*, the statement is probably an opinion. One way to confirm this conclusion is to look for *opinion signal words* in the statement.** Statement **A** contains a strong opinion signal word: *funniest*. A statement containing this word will probably not be provable. For example, if you asked a group of your friends what the funniest show on television is, you would probably get several different answers.

 Identifying Facts and Opinions

To practice identifying facts and opinions, look back at "Ray of Hope" and follow the steps below. Write your answers on your own paper.

- Identify two statements of fact and two statements of opinion.
- Label each statement with either the word *fact* or the word *opinion*.
- For a fact, tell how the fact could be proven or confirmed.
- For an opinion, tell how you determined that the statement is an opinion. List any signal words the statement contains.

Evaluation Criteria

 READING FOCUS

Backing Up Opinions Readers of "Ray of Hope" would not find the article very persuasive if the writer had not backed up his opinions about *Everybody Loves Raymond* with some kind of support. Critical readers do not simply accept what critics say. Instead, readers look to see whether the critics support their opinions by explaining how well their subjects measure up to certain standards, or **criteria.** Just as you must meet standards to qualify for your school's volleyball team or to receive an A in a course, a television program should measure up to certain standards to receive a good review from an able critic.

YOUR TURN 2

ANSWERS
Sample responses include:

Facts:

- ". . . The elder Barones always barged in unannounced, and Robert was constantly mooching." (Watch the programs or check the scripts.)

- "Raymond has skyrocketed in the ratings since CBS moved it to Mondays after Cosby." (Check the ratings statistics.)

Opinions:

- ". . . *Raymond* may now be the best sitcom on the air . . ." (Signal word: best)

- "*Raymond* is the rarest of sitcoms —one with a genuinely original point of view." (Signal word: rarest)

Critical Thinking

Metacognition. After students have completed **Your Turn 2,** ask them to write which task was more difficult for them, identifying opinions or facts. Have them describe briefly the techniques they used to find their answers. Note students whose responses reveal a clear ability to discriminate between facts and opinions. Consider asking these individuals to serve as peer tutors for students who are having difficulty with the skill.

RESOURCES

Your Turn 2
Practice
- *Communications,* WS. p. 138
Reinforcement
- *Communications,* TP. 60, WS. p. 139

How do readers know whether critics are using commonly accepted criteria in evaluating a show? First, they have to look at the elements of the show on which the critics base their opinions. The elements critics consider will vary from one type of show to another. However, listed below are some common elements of sitcoms. If reviewers do not base their opinions on these elements, readers should have serious doubts about the quality of the reviews.

- **plot:** the sitcom's "story," including the conflicts and problems the characters experience
- **setting:** the location where the story unfolds
- **characters:** the fictional people in the sitcom
- **acting:** the portrayal of the characters by real people
- **writing:** the script (which includes **dialogue**) that the actors follow
- **theme:** the sitcom's "message"

"Okay," you say, "so a sitcom has these elements. How do critics decide what makes a particular plot or character good or bad?" One way they decide is to think back on good sitcoms of the past, and ask themselves what qualities of plot, character, acting, writing, and theme these shows had. The qualities they identify then become the criteria by which they evaluate current sitcoms.

As a critical reader, you must be aware that not every critic uses exactly the same set of criteria. However, there are common criteria that most of them use. The following checklist shows some of the common criteria that you should look for when you read a review of a sitcom.

Sitcom Evaluation Checklist	
Elements	**Criteria**
Plot	• keeps the viewer's interest • presents entertaining problems or conflicts for the characters to resolve
Setting	• remains the same from week to week • represents a generalized geographic location
Characters	• develop and grow over time • are entertaining people with whom the viewer can sympathize and identify • have interesting points of view • play off each other well
Acting	• makes the characters believable and fun to watch

Writing	▪ creates humorous interactions between characters
	▪ provides natural-sounding dialogue that is funny and appropriate for the characters and plot
Theme	▪ is a message which the audience can recognize—one with which they can easily identify

A reviewer will inform the reader about the evaluation criteria he or she uses to judge a show by the elements discussed in the review. The writer of "Ray of Hope," for example, makes (in the next-to-last paragraph) this statement about the actor who plays Ray's brother: "As Ray's eternally unlucky sibling, he has developed a wonderful chemistry with Romano." This remark tells the careful reader that one of the writer's criteria is that characters should have a "chemistry" with each other—that is, they should play off each other well.

YOUR TURN 3 **Recognizing Evaluation Criteria**

Working with a partner, find five statements that reveal something about the criteria the writer of "Ray of Hope" uses to judge *Everybody Loves Raymond.* Refer to the chart above as often as necessary. Copy each statement onto your paper. Then, explain what each statement reveals about the criteria the writer uses to evaluate the program. Be prepared to share your results with the class.

CALVIN & HOBBES © 1993 Watterson. Distributed by Universal Press Syndicate. Reprinted with permission. All rights reserved.

EXTENDING
Apply What You Read. Provide students with copies of a film review or another review of a television program. Have students read it and mark examples of facts and opinions.

Ask students to list the formal elements the reviewer covers and the criteria he or she uses. Discuss how the review is similar to and different from the review of *Everybody Loves Raymond.*

YOUR TURN 3

In assessing students' work, check that they have matched up appropriate criteria for their found statements. Some students may understand that a statement has valid reasoning, but not be able to classify it under a specific criterion. To help them better apply the **Sitcom Evaluation Checklist** on pp. 290–291, urge them to paraphrase and elaborate on the list of criteria.

Wrap It Up

Metacognition. Ask students to reflect on and answer the following questions:

1. How might you use facts and how might you use opinions in your own reviews?

2. Which criterion for evaluating a sitcom was most challenging for you to apply? Why?

Neologisms

Changes occur so quickly in today's world that language has to change quickly, too. Writers and readers of all kinds of critical reviews—of movies, books, music, automobiles—have to keep up not only with innovations in their subject areas, but also with the new words that come into our language to describe or identify these innovations. These words are called **neologisms** (from *neo–*, meaning "new," and *logo*, meaning "word").

The four most common methods of creating neologisms are explained below.

■ **Combining** Some neologisms are created by putting two existing words together to create a new compound. For example, *free* and *way* were once combined to make *freeway*, a highway free of cross traffic and free of charge, too. A more recent example is *road rage*, a term created to refer to a driver's anger toward other drivers which can result in aggressive driving habits and sometimes violence.

■ **Shortening** Sometimes neologisms are created when an existing word is shortened. At one time, the word *phone* was a neologism created by simply shortening *telephone*. More recently, *nuke*, a shortened and slightly changed version of *nuclear*, was coined as a verb to describe what a person does to food by putting it into a microwave (a relatively new word created by combining the prefix *micro* and *wave*) oven.

■ **Blending** This method of creating new words consists of shortening and combining two existing words. *Emoticon*, for example, is a blend of *emotion* and *icon* that signifies the human expressions—such as :) —created with punctuation marks that often appear in e-mail (another blend). *Sitcom* is a blend created from *situation comedy*, a term describing a type of television program.

■ **Shifting** Sometimes a neologism is created by simply shifting a word's usage or meaning. At some point in the past, for example, the word *host*, a noun meaning "a person who entertains guests," was shifted so that it could also be used as a verb meaning "to entertain guests." A more recent neologism created by shifting is *chill*, a noun used as a verb meaning "to calm down or relax."

YOUR TURN 4 **Creating Neologisms**

Working in groups of three or four, create at least five neologisms, using three of the methods explained above. To generate ideas, think about new technological advances, new fast foods, new courses in your high school curriculum, or new ideas, inventions, attitudes, or practices in any area.

ADVANCED LEARNERS

Challenge students to identify additional examples of neologisms and to make educated guesses about their origins. Ask the class to conduct research using dictionaries and other resources to confirm or revise their guesses. Have students display their results on a chart. Allow time for class discussion of the students' findings. A sample entry follows:

Word: *Telemarketing*

Educated Guess: selling something on television, like on a shopping channel. A blend of *television* and *marketing*.

Dictionary Definition: "using the telephone to market or sell." No origin given.

Revised Guess: A blend of *telephone* and *marketing*.

YOUR TURN 4

Be sure that students use the techniques of combining, shortening, blending, and shifting in creating their words. Students should be able to explain how their group used one of the methods to create each neologism. You might have the groups challenge each other to guess the meanings of the new words. A sample response follows:

Neologism: *e-card:* a greeting card sent out over the Internet as e-mail

Use: My friend Josh sent me an *e-card* on my birthday.

Method: blending

RESOURCES

Vocabulary
Practice
■ *Communications,* WS. p. 142

Test Taking
Practice
■ *Communications,* WS. pp. 143–145

Identifying Facts and Opinions

Telling the difference between fact and opinion is important for more than reading reviews. Standardized reading tests often check your ability to distinguish facts from opinions. Here is a reading passage and a fact/opinion test question about it. A plan for answering the question follows in Thinking It Through.

Inside the Florida Museum of Natural History, an International Shark Attack File keeps track of how many sharks attack humans each year. According to the records in the file, an average of fifty to seventy-five shark attacks occur each year worldwide, with five to ten resulting in death. Statistically, this means that you are less likely to be killed by a shark than to die from a snakebite or a lightning strike.

Studies have proven that on those rare occasions when sharks *do* attack humans, they do so because they mistake the people for seals or other prey. To minimize the risk of attack, scientists advise swimmers to avoid excessive splashing, shiny jewelry, and bright-colored swimsuits, all of which make humans look like prey. Despite the rarity of attacks, sharks are undoubtedly the most terrifying creatures of the sea.

The author of the passage states an opinion when he says that

A. five to ten shark attacks result in death each year

B. sharks sometimes mistake people for prey

C. sharks are the most terrifying sea creatures

D. swimmers should avoid shiny jewelry

Looking Ahead to Writing

In the Writing Workshop, students will write their own reviews of sit-coms. As they express and support their opinions, remind them to consult the steps for distinguishing fact from opinion on pp. 287–288 of the Reading Workshop. Students might also find it helpful to revisit the **Sitcom Evaluation Checklist** on pp. 290–291.

THINKING IT THROUGH **Answering Fact-and-Opinion Questions**

Use the following steps to answer a fact-and-opinion question like the one above.

▶ **STEP 1** Consider all the answer choices before marking your answer sheet.

▶ **STEP 2** Go through each answer choice, asking if the answer could be proven. Those that can be proven are facts. A, B, and D are facts supported by evidence presented in the passage.

▶ **STEP 3** The answers that are left are probably opinions. Look for opinion signal words that might help to confirm that they are opinions. C looks like an opinion. Not everyone would agree with the statement.

▶ **STEP 4** Be on the lookout for opinions disguised as facts. C is the correct answer. It is an opinion even though the word underlined makes it sound like a fact.

OBJECTIVES

- To write a critical review of a television sitcom
- To analyze an audience for a critical review
- To identify and use evaluation criteria
- To evaluate support
- To subordinate ideas to create complex sentences
- To correct run-on sentences

Quotation for the Day

❝The difference between amateur and professional writers is that amateurs write for themselves and professionals write for their readers.❞

(from *The Art of Writing Nonfiction* by André Fontaine, writer and editor, and William A. Glavin, Jr., television news editor)

Write the quotation on the chalkboard or on an overhead transparency. Ask students to brainstorm, in pairs, how writing for an audience might be more demanding than writing for one's self. Responses may include the need to predict the reader's background knowledge and the necessity of careful punctuation to guide the reader.

TEACHING TIP

Strong Opinions, Strong Reviews
Students with little or no access to television or VCRs can be assigned to write reviews of humorous short stories or plays. Offering students an assortment of readings to review will give them more opportunity to find a subject about which they feel strongly.

WHAT'S AHEAD?

In this workshop, you will write a critical review of a television sitcom. You will also learn how to

- analyze the audience for your critical review
- identify and use evaluation criteria
- evaluate support
- subordinate ideas to create complex sentences
- correct run-on sentences

Writing a Critical Review of a TV Sitcom

Imagine that your English class has been assigned a new project—to produce a magazine that reviews popular entertainment. You are given the specific task of writing a **critical review** of a current television program—a situation comedy.

You have no problem with your assigned topic. In fact, having watched a lot of **sitcoms,** you think of yourself as something of an expert on them. You could tell anyone who asks that sitcoms are thirty minutes long, that they feature the same characters in every episode, that these characters face and somehow solve new problems every week, and that the whole point is to make you laugh. You know all of these things about sitcoms, but you need to know more about critical reviews.

To get started, here is what you need to know: a **critical review** is a combination of analysis, evaluation, and persuasion. As a critical reviewer of a sitcom, you will analyze certain elements and evaluate how effectively the sitcom uses them. The purpose of the critical review you write in this Writing Workshop will be to evaluate the show, recommend or not recommend that people watch it, and then convince people to follow your recommendation.

Prewriting

Choose a Sitcom to Review

Strong Opinions, Strong Reviews   When you begin to look for a sitcom to review, keep this in mind: The stronger your opinion of the sitcom, the stronger the review you will be able to write. Here are some suggestions for finding the right sitcom for you.

- **Scan local TV listings** in a newspaper or magazine, or do a World Wide Web search (keywords: *television schedule*) to access listings. Scan the listings, noting titles that look interesting.
- **Read the entertainment or television section** of your newspaper to see which sitcoms seem to have caught the public's attention.
- **Watch one sitcom** recommended by a friend your age and another recommended by an adult, and choose the one that you prefer.
- **Think about reviewing one of your own favorites**—one on which you are an expert.

Make a list of three or four sitcoms, and then choose the sitcom that you would like to review. Unless you choose a sitcom with which you are already familiar, be prepared to watch a few episodes to become familiar with the program.

Consider Your Purpose, Audience, Tone, and Voice

Different Strokes For . . . The **purpose** of any review of a television program is to persuade the audience for whom the review was written that the show is or is not worth watching. The **audiences** for reviews of television shows vary. Some reviews, for example, are written to tell parents how suitable a particular show is for children of various ages. Most reviews, however, are written for a general audience—the readers of newspapers or magazines, for example.

The **tone** of a review is the writer's attitude toward the subject of the review and the intended audience. Your **voice** is the personality you adopt to express the tone. For example, the tone you choose for an audience of peers may be more informal or friendly. (However, it should not be so casual that you lose the authority of your voice.) If, on the other hand, your audience consists of well-educated adults, your tone should be thoughtful and mature.

Considering Your Audience, Tone, and Voice

To analyze your audience and tone, write answers to each of the following questions.

STEP 1 Where do you plan to publish your review? The answer to this question tells you who your readers or audience will be. It might be that you plan to publish your essay in class, or in the school magazine or newspaper, or in an online magazine for teens. In each of these

TIP Be sure to choose a show whose subject matter can be freely discussed in your classroom.

TIP As you consider the audience for your review, keep in mind whether or not those people will all have access to the show you select. For example, some shows can be watched only by viewers with cable television or satellite dishes.

Cooperative Learning

Traits of Writing. Ask students to work together in the prewriting stage to consider the first three of the Six Traits of Writing:

1. **Idea**—the main theme and supporting details of the writing; the writer's message
2. **Organization**—the structure of the piece; how the details are arranged
3. **Voice**—the unique writing style of the writer

You may wish for students to revisit during the revision stage to consider the final three traits:

4. **Word choice**—the appropriate words chosen for best effect
5. **Sentence fluency**—the patterning of words so that language sounds natural and appealing
6. **Conventions**—the standards of grammar and punctuation

Meeting INDIVIDUAL NEEDS

LEARNERS HAVING DIFFICULTY

If students are having trouble grasping the concept of tone, ask them to imagine reading their papers aloud to an appropriate audience. Tell them to envision their body language. For example, if they were presenting to an audience of scholarly adults, they would have a serious look and formal stance. If they were delivering their reviews to friends, they would probably smile and lean casually on the podium. Encourage them to use these mental images as clues to the tone of their writing.

In order to help students avoid the frustration of false starts, review their answers to the **Thinking It Through** questions on pp. 295–296. Be sure students have provided sufficient detail. For instance, they should actually list specific background information their readers would need.

MULTIPLE INTELLIGENCES
Logical-Mathematical Intelligence.
Students may find it helpful to assign numerical values to the criteria they use to review a sitcom. Suggest that they establish a scale and use it to evaluate the extent to which the plot keeps the viewer interested, the ease with which the characters play off each other, and so on. Encourage students to keep the scale simple. For example, they might use a 1–5 scale in which 5 is the most positive rating. Suggest that students use this scale to identify which elements will take top priority in their reviews. For example, if a student rates the acting at 2 and the rest of the elements at 4 or 5, he or she can build a review around the opinion that the actors detract from an otherwise appealing program.

cases, your readers will be your peers. If, on the other hand, you plan to publish your review in the local newspaper, your audience will include adults with a wide variety of interests and levels of education.

▶ **STEP 2 How much will your intended audience know about the sitcom you are reviewing?** This will determine how much background information your audience will need. If the show you choose to review is wildly popular with teenagers and you are writing to an audience of teenagers, you will need to provide little background. If, on the other hand, you are reviewing that show for an audience of adults, you will need to include a lot of background. The reverse will be true if you choose to review a show that is popular among adults.

▶ **STEP 3 What tone is appropriate for your review?** If your audience is composed of peers, you can use a more informal word choice and sentence structure to create a breezy, chatty tone—as if you were speaking to friends. For an audience of adults, you will want to write in a more sophisticated **style,** choosing words and sentence structure to create a mature and thoughtful tone. Remember, you want your readers to agree with you. If readers are turned off by your tone, they might tune out your review.

Understand Evaluation Criteria

| KEY CONCEPT

The Critic's Criteria   Your critical review will give your readers your opinion of a sitcom as a whole. **That opinion, however, is not worth much unless it is based on criteria: standards for evaluating the effectiveness of the individual elements of the sitcom.** For example, the author of the Writer's Model on page 303 bases her high opinion of a sitcom on criteria that address **plot, characters,** and **acting.** After reviewing the sitcom, she concludes that the plot is original, the main character as played by the lead actor is hilarious, and the supporting cast is excellent.

The chart on page 297 lists and defines the five important elements of sitcoms and some of the basic criteria used to evaluate them. The sitcom elements and evaluation criteria in the chart are not arranged by order of importance because the importance of each element is subjective, or based on personal preference. As you study the chart, think about how important the individual elements are for you.

TIP   Critical reviewers rarely discuss all of the sitcom elements in a single review. They might focus on two or three elements important for a particular show. For example, some reviewers put more emphasis on character than on plot. Others are more interested in the quality of the acting than in anything else.

Sitcom Element	Common Evaluation Criteria
Plot: a series of events that occurs as the result of conflicts between and within characters	The plot should be interesting, original, and funny. It should provide believable conflicts that the characters resolve realistically. Conflicts and problems should be creative and entertaining. Plot events may not match the predictions that you make, but they should follow logically from the situation.
Setting: the location where the story unfolds	The setting should be recognizable from week to week. It should give the impression of a general location, such as a newsroom, office building, home, or apartment.
Characters: the fictional people in the show who perform the actions and deliver the dialogue	The characters should be funny, realistic, and sympathetic. They should learn and grow as a result of their experiences. A show's characters should play off each other well.
Acting: the quality of the performances of the actors who play the characters	The acting should be consistent, believable, appealing, and fun to watch.
Writing: the script the actors follow in performing their actions and delivering their dialogue	The writing should provide funny and believable scenes. Dialogue should sound natural and fit the character.
Theme: the underlying message or messages communicated by an episode of a sitcom	The sitcom should develop themes which are relevant to the lives of viewers.

Review Your Sitcom

Attention Focused, Pencil Poised   Before you can write a critical review, you must actually watch your sitcom and evaluate it. If you have chosen to review a show that you don't already watch regularly, you may need to view a few episodes to get a good idea how the program handles the important sitcom elements. Reviewers often watch several weeks' worth of episodes before writing their reviews, although the examples they give to illustrate their ideas may come from a single episode.

Professional reviewers watch and rewatch the shows they review until they develop their opinions and the reasons for their opinions. You must do the same thing. It helps to use a log like the one on the next page, which shows how one writer reviewed a sitcom called *One Cool Million*. The show follows the adventures of a high school student as he tries to do his part-time job—deliver a million dollars from an anonymous benefactor to a different person every week. As she watched the program, this writer took notes by responding (in the right-hand column) to the questions listed in the middle column.

TIP   Another way to generate ideas about your choice of sitcom is to meet and discuss the show with other students who have also chosen this program. Just remember that in informal discussions like this one, you still have responsibilities as a speaker and a listener. For more on **group discussions,** see page 853 in the Quick Reference Handbook.

Cooperative Learning
Evaluation Criteria. Ask students to work in groups to create additional criteria with which to critique sitcoms. Students should then compare the criteria they have created to the criteria presented on this page, providing support for their comparisons. They may wish to use their own criteria instead of, or in addition to, the criteria provided in the Pupil's Edition.

Critical Thinking
Metacognition. Suggest that students use a first viewing to note their initial reactions. Ask them to watch tapes of the episodes they plan to review before using their **Reviewing Logs** on p. 298. Tell them to write down whatever personal reactions they have, including comments that come to mind, responses such as tension or laughter, or questions that occur to them. This exercise will help students tune in to their own reactions and make it easier to use the log during a second viewing. Students may find it interesting to re-read their initial reactions after they have actually studied the show and used the log. Any shifts in their opinions may help students identify a new angle for their reviews.

REVIEWING LOG

Elements of a Sitcom	Questions Based on Evaluation Criteria	Reviewer Responses
Plot	Does the plot hold your attention? Is it entertaining? Is it original? Are conflicts believable?	plot—captivating, original, and funny; real-life conflicts lead to hilarious situations
Characters	Are the characters realistic? Funny? Sympathetic? Do they learn and change? Do they play off each other well?	lead and supporting characters realistic, funny, likable people
Acting	Are the actors believable and consistent? Are they fun to watch?	Lopez, Shoemaker, Crawford, Johnson—always very good
Writing	Are the scenes funny and believable? Is dialogue natural?	scenes are funny but sometimes hard to believe; natural dialogue
Theme	Are the themes relevant to viewers?	themes relevant; viewers easily identify

TECHNOLOGY TIP

Students might wish to use the table function of their word-processing software to create a Reviewing Log. Encourage them to experiment with the format of the table to make the chart easy to use for note taking.

TEACHING TIP

Critic's Checklist
If you judge that students would benefit from guided practice before attempting to write their own reviews, show part of a videotaped program. As a class, work through taking notes on an overhead transparency of the **Reviewing Log**.

YOUR TURN 5

To be sure that each student has created a solid foundation for writing a review, conduct mini-conferences. Have each student spend a few moments giving you an overview of the purpose, audience, tone, and voice. Ask students to refer to their Reviewing Logs in order to justify their overview.

Critic's Checklist

Here is a list of supplies you will need to review the sitcom you have chosen.

- a VCR and a television set
- a videotaped copy of one or more episodes of your show
- pens, pencils, your copy of the reviewing log, and notebook paper
- a quiet place with sufficient light to watch and take notes

YOUR TURN 5 Reviewing Your Sitcom

Review and complete all the prewriting steps covered so far.

- Choose a sitcom to review.
- Consider your purpose, audience, tone, and voice.
- Use a Reviewing Log like the one above to record your evaluation of each of the sitcom elements.

298   Chapter 8   **Persuasion:** Reviewing Television

RESOURCES

Your Turn 5
Practice
- *Communications,* WS. p. 146

Identify Elements and Write Your Thesis

Once you have reviewed the sitcom, you will have formed an initial opinion about whether or not you believe that the show is worth watching. Next, determine which elements most influenced your opinion. These will be the elements you include in your **thesis statement.** Your thesis statement includes your overall opinion of the sitcom and the reasons why the elements you have chosen do or do not measure up to the evaluation criteria. Take a look at the thesis statement from the review of *One Cool Million.*

TIP Your thesis statement may be revised, if necessary, as you develop your essay.

> This show stands out from the pack for three reasons: a winning character played by a consistently hilarious Lopez, a captivating and original storyline, and an excellent supporting cast.

The first part of the sentence delivers the positive opinion of the show, and the second part states three reasons for the positive opinion.

Gather Support

Giving Weight to Opinions Writing a good review involves more than just stating your opinion. **If you want readers to accept your opinion, you must support it by telling them the reasons for your opinion.** Then, you must support your reasons with observations that explain how well or how poorly the elements you have chosen measure up to their evaluation criteria. Take a look at the notes the writer of the review of *One Cool Million* wrote to support her thesis statement.

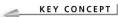
KEY CONCEPT

SUPPORT CHART

Element	Reasons	Support
Main character and actor	good-natured character as played by Lopez	Lopez's gift for comedy as Hooper, his gangly frame and elastic face
Plot	captivating, original, funny; conflicts lead to hilarious situations	Hooper's job; mysterious boss; attitude of recipients of money; obstacles put in Hooper's way
Supporting characters and actors	excellent supporting cast	Shoemaker as sweet and unsuspecting mother; Johnson as loud, bossy best friend; Crawford as voice of Hooper's boss

MINI-LESSON CRITICAL THINKING

Evaluating Support

ANSWERS

1. Weak. It provides no criteria or specific details.

2. Strong. The criteria are clearly stated.

3. Strong. It offers a criterion for judging the team's accomplishments.

4. Strong. It provides two examples of why the book is not good.

5. Weak. It does not specify what is bad.

Taking A Second Look

Evaluating Support. After checking responses, ask students to revise and extend number 5. Have them rewrite this item to include an indication of how the opinion could be supported. Then, have students outline how they would develop their defense. Model by revising item 1 with the class.

Revision: This is the worst car I have ever driven. Both comfort and safety are substandard.

Outline:

Comfort—poor back support, inadequate legroom in back

Safety—poor traction in snow, not enough power when accelerating

---

MINI-LESSON CRITICAL THINKING

Evaluating Support

All critical reviews are based on the reviewer's opinion of how well the thing being reviewed measures up to a set of standards. The most effective reviews are those that back up opinions with convincing support.

You say to a friend, "I'm thinking of buying a new computer."

"Don't even think of buying Brand X," your friend says. "They're terrible."

"Why do you think so?" you ask.

If your friend can give you no logical reason, you are not very likely to take his advice. If, on the other hand, your friend says, "I read a survey that said over half of Brand X owners reported serious problems with their computers," you will probably pay attention, because your friend has support for his opinion. The support you use in your critical review should consist of a reason based on **valid criteria** and backed up by **specific details** and **examples**. Look at the following examples of weak support and strong support.

Weak support:
Whistling in the Graveyard is great. It is much better than the other sitcoms.

In this example, the reviewer's opinion is supported only by a reason that is another opinion. The writer fails to mention any valid criteria and provides no details or examples to back up the idea that the show is better than other sitcoms.

Strong support:
Chasing Cars is a fascinating show. Its unique storyline features a teenager whose secret hobby is hanging out with a couple of car-chasing dogs.

In this example, the opinion is followed by a reason that is based on a valid criterion (plot, or storyline) and is backed by specific details. While other people might disagree with the reviewer's opinion of the show, no one can say that the opinion is not well supported.

PRACTICE

On your own paper, write your own evaluation of the support in each of the following items. Write *strong* if the item contains strong support, and *weak* if it contains weak support. Be prepared to explain your evaluations.

1. That is the worst car I have ever driven. It is so bad that I cringe every time I have to drive it anywhere.

2. Juanita's is a truly fine restaurant. It has great food, wonderful service, and a friendly atmosphere.

3. At the moment, the Rocky Rangers are the best team in the league. They lead in every important statistical category.

4. I do not understand why you recommended that book. The plot consists of one coincidence after another and the characters are colorless stereotypes.

5. The only good thing about the movie is the acting because everything else is terrible.

RESOURCES

Critical Thinking
Practice
- *Communications,* WS. p. 147

Your Turn 6
Practice
- *Communications,* WS. p. 148

Organize Your Paper

Bring Forth Order   Now you need to decide how you will organize your review. Some writers put the most important reason for their overall opinion first and the least important reason last. Take a look at the following map the reviewer of *One Cool Million* created. She started with the most important (1st) reason for her opinion, the main character and the performance of the actor playing him. Then, her second and third most important reasons followed.

TIP   To make your paper coherent, organize your ideas in a logical way. Provide support for each idea. (For more on **logical progression** of ideas, see page 361.)

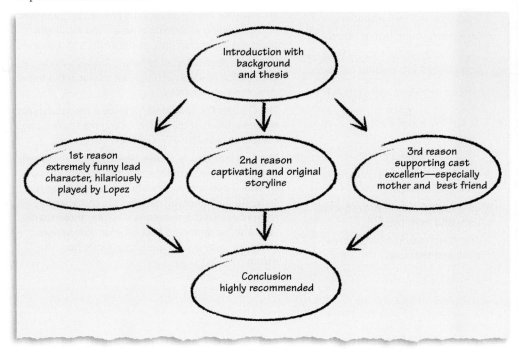

YOUR TURN 6   Getting Ready to Write

Before moving on to the writing stage, be sure you have

- identified the elements that shaped your opinion
- written a thesis that states your opinion and the basic reasons for it
- gathered support for your reasons
- planned the organization of your ideas

Cooperative Learning

Organizing. Working collaboratively can help students with different learning styles to organize their papers. For example, visual learners may respond well to using a chart like the example on p. 301, auditory learners may do better by talking through their papers and creating an outline, and kinesthetic learners may find that using index cards to manipulate their elements will be most helpful. Have students work together, with each student using the strategy he or she is most comfortable with to help one another clarify ideas.

YOUR TURN 6

In preparation for writing, check that students have identified adequate support directly related to the reasons for their opinions. Also, ask them to show you an outline or graphic organizer mapping out their organizational plans.

Writing

Critical Review of a Sitcom

Framework | **Directions and Explanations**

Introduction

- Grab your readers' attention.
- Give background information.
- Include a thesis that states your opinion and lists reasons for it.

Ladies and Gentlemen of the Jury   Draw your readers into your review by asking a provocative question or by providing a fascinating detail. You could also challenge a common idea, as the Writer's Model does.

You Have Been Selected to Hear   Always include the information readers need in order to watch the show: date, time, and channel.

The Charges For or Against   Provide a clear statement of your opinion of the sitcom. Listing the reasons gives readers an overview of your review's structure.

Body

- Give first reason with observations and examples.
- Give second reason with observations and examples.
- Give third reason with observations and examples.

The Evidence Clearly Shows   Present your evaluation of how well the sitcom measured up to your chosen criteria. If possible, you should use at least three criteria. The first time you mention the characters, remember to name the actors who play those characters. Also, remember to back up your observations about the criteria with specific examples from the sitcom.

Conclusion

- Restate your opinion in the form of a recommendation.
- Bring review to a close.

And the Verdict Is   As you bring your review to a close, restate your thesis—your overall opinion of the show—in the form of a recommendation that your audience watch, or not watch, the sitcom.

 YOUR TURN 7   **Writing A First Draft**

Using the framework above and the Writer's Model on the next page as guides, write the first draft of your review.

RESOURCES

Writing
Writing Prompts
- *Communications*, TP. 62, WS. p. 149

Your Turn 7
Practice
- *Communications*, TP. 63, WS. p. 150

A Writer's Model

The following essay closely follows the framework on the previous page. Reviewers offer numerous details to back up their evaluation of a program. As you read this model, notice how many specifics the writer includes in order to convince you.

One Cool Million Is Rich with Laughter

You think it would be easy to give away a million dollars, right? Well, that is what sixteen-year-old Harvey Hooper thought—until he landed the job of giving away a million a week on behalf of a mysterious and anonymous benefactor. As the focus of *One Cool Million* (Fridays at 9 P.M., ET, CBZ-TV), the latest addition to the highly successful "Fridaze" teen comedy lineup, Hooper (Jake Lopez) fills the screen with an active, loose comic energy. This show stands out from the pack for three reasons: a winning character played by a consistently hilarious Lopez, a captivating and original storyline, and an excellent supporting cast.

Those who know Lopez only from his dramatic roles will be utterly surprised by his gift for comedy. His portrayal of Harvey Hooper as a grinning, goofy, good-natured guy is a study in the art of physical comedy. Lopez uses his gangly six-foot frame and rubbery, expressive face to great advantage, often making the teenager he plays seem even younger and more awkward than his age would suggest.

Along with the winning character of Lopez, the unique storyline of *One Cool Million* provides lots of opportunities for laughs. Although much of the action takes place at a fictional high school, the main concern of many of the students, including Hooper, is their minimum-wage, part-time jobs after school. Hooper's job earns him quite a bit more than minimum wage, because his duties are much more challenging. Each week, Hooper is assigned to deliver the sum of one million dollars to a deserving, unsuspecting, and usually suspicious recipient. Hooper must navigate a series of obstacles put in his way by the show's talented writers. The lucky beneficiary's name and location, as well as the money, are supplied by Hooper's boss, a mysterious (and apparently very charitable) oil baroness.

(continued)

INTRODUCTION
Attention-grabbing opening

Background information

Thesis statement

BODY
First reason with support based on observations and examples

Second reason with support based on observations and examples

Point out to students that reviews can be organized in a variety of ways. In **A Writer's Model,** the author identifies three elements in the thesis statement and addresses each in a separate paragraph. For another approach, direct students to examine **"Ray of Hope"** on pp. 285–286. There, the writer provides background information, a paragraph on point of view, and then three paragraphs on various aspects of casting. He uses these paragraphs to prove the single point made in his thesis statement. Tell students they will need to decide what kinds of organization will work best for their reviews.

Meeting INDIVIDUAL NEEDS

ENGLISH-LANGUAGE LEARNERS

General Strategies. Some of the vocabulary in this model might be challenging for students (for example, *benefactor, navigate, baroness*). Invite students to skim the selection, looking for any unfamiliar terms. Students can then check unfamiliar vocabulary with partners before reading the selection. You might also remind students to use dictionaries and thesauruses.

Third reason with support based on observations and examples

Lopez is surrounded by an excellent supporting cast. The two standouts are Sarabeth Shoemaker as his sweetly unsuspecting mother (she still gives him a ten-dollar weekly allowance) and Chris Johnson as his loud, bossy best friend, Tony (the only person who knows what Hooper's job really entails). The presence of '80s film great Sybil Crawford might seem a bit out of place on a show about teenagers, but it works, adding another layer of interest to the proceedings. Though her famous face is never revealed (she is heard only through a speakerphone), her presence as Hooper's boss, "Mrs. B," is felt throughout each episode as she interrupts—predictably—at the most inopportune time. Her distinctive greeting, booming through the speaker phone, produces howls of laughter each time the audience hears her voice because she sets in motion Hooper's attempts to give away the money.

CONCLUSION

Restatement of most of thesis as a recommendation

Despite a few missteps (chalk them up to first-season jitters), *One Cool Million* is a hilarious romp through high school life in the year 2001, with enough uncommon twists to make it stand out from the pack. Crackling with comic dialogue, fast-paced scenes, and well-defined characters, *One Cool Million* is as generous with its laughs as Harvey Hooper's boss is with her dollars.

A Student's Model

The following excerpt is from a review by Amar Patel of Troy High School in Fullerton, California.

The Simpsons: A Real Winner

"Ay Caramba!" Everywhere you turn there are signs of "The Simpsons Fever," which has infected viewers throughout the United States. It is no wonder that The Simpsons, with its huge following and its creative scripts, was named "The Television Show of the [Twentieth] Century." The creation of executive producers James L. Brooks and Matt Groening, The Simpsons is a sitcom about the daily lives of Springfield's most outrageous and hilarious family. Filled with dozens of colorful characters and side-splitting comedic situations, it is one of the most innovative shows on television.

The show's great success is largely due to the charming and interesting identities given to its characters. The show is focused on the characters Bart, Homer, Lisa, Marge, and Maggie. The perennial favorite is Bart, the child who loves mischievous pranks. Bart is the clever, cunning youth who does everything the viewers would like to do, but cannot. Homer, Bart's father, is the town simpleton who always makes the stupid mistakes that are accompanied by his standard phrase of dismay, "DOOOOHHH!!!!" He may be a lazy couch-potato, but he is, nevertheless, a strong-willed, determined man, who is (believe it or not) good at heart. Marge is the cautious, protective parental figure in the show, the wife of Homer, and mother to his children. She is, in fact, the perfect mother: She loves both her children and husband. Although Marge may try to quell the adventure, hers is always the calm voice of reason. Lisa is the odd-one-out in the family, an extremely intelligent child, one who thinks independently and would persuade others to do the same. Despite their differences, though, the Simpsons are held together by love, a hallmark of this remarkable family. Perhaps it is this quality—not their faults—that makes them such a delightful family to watch. . . .

Attention-getting opener

Background information

Thesis statement

First reason: colorful characters

Support based on examples and observations

Connecting Reading and Writing

Ask students to revisit the **Sitcom Evaluation Checklist** on p. 290 of the Reading Workshop. Have them identify which criteria the author of **A Student's Model** used as the basis for the review.

Revising

Evaluate and Revise Your Draft

Refining Your Review   Work collaboratively to make sure that your review is as good as it can be. You need to read your paper closely at least twice—once for the content and organization of your review, and a second time for style.

▷ First Reading: **Content and Organization**   If you have a hard time evaluating and revising your own writing, you will find the following chart very handy. The left column gives you some evaluation questions to ask about your review, the middle column gives tips on how to answer the questions, and the right column suggests ways to make changes.

Critical Review: Content and Organization Guidelines for Peer and Self-Evaluation

Evaluation Questions	Tips	Revision Techniques
❶ Does the introduction contain attention-grabbing sentences?	**Underline** any sentences in the introduction that draw attention. If you cannot underline one, revise.	**Add** a question or statement that will intrigue or challenge readers.
❷ Does the introduction contain a sentence that states an opinion of the show with a brief list of reasons for that opinion?	**Highlight** the sentence that states the writer's opinion and reasons.	**Add** a sentence that clearly expresses the writer's opinion and lists the reasons for it. **Elaborate** on existing sentences.
❸ Does each body paragraph present a reason based on criteria for evaluating sitcoms?	**Circle** key words (*plot, characters, dialogue*) in each paragraph that signal a reason based on criteria.	**Add** sentences that clearly state the reasons for the writer's opinion.
❹ Does each body paragraph provide support for the evaluation in the form of observations and examples?	**Bracket** the supporting observations and examples from the sitcom. There should be at least three in each paragraph.	**Add** sentences containing observations and examples, or **elaborate** on existing sentences by adding observations and examples.
❺ Does the review's organization contribute to its effectiveness?	**Number** the body paragraphs in the order of their importance as support for the thesis.	**Rearrange** the paragraphs so that the review begins or ends with the strongest support for the thesis.
❻ Is the opinion restated as a recommendation in the conclusion?	**Put a checkmark** next to any sentence in the conclusion that restates the reviewer's opinion in the form of a recommendation.	**Add** a sentence that clearly and forcefully reinforces the reviewer's opinion of the sitcom and makes a recommendation.

ONE WRITER'S REVISIONS   Take a look at how the author of the Writer's Model on page 303 used the content and organization guidelines to evaluate and improve the first body paragraph of her critical review. Then, answer the questions following the paragraph.

> Those who know Lopez only from his dramatic roles will be
> utterly surprised by his gift for comedy. His portrayal of Harvey
> *as a grinning, goofy, good-natured guy*
> Hooper is a study in the art of physical comedy. Lopez uses his gangly   **add**
> *and rubbery, expressive face*
> six-foot frame to great advantage, often making the teenager he plays   **elaborate**
> seem even younger and more awkward than his age would suggest.

Analyzing the Revision Process

1. What does the writer achieve by inserting details into the second sentence?
2. What does the writer's elaboration of the third sentence contribute to your image of Lopez?

YOUR TURN 8   Focusing on Content and Organization

Evaluate and revise your review using the content and organization guidelines on the previous page.

> **Second Reading: Style**   Your first reading dealt with content and organization. Now, you need to look at the way you express yourself. Your readers will not consider your opinion very carefully if they have to struggle through repetitive sounding sentences. To write sentences that flow smoothly, use the following sentence-style guidelines.

PEER REVIEW

Choose a partner and read each other's review. Answer these questions and attach your remarks to your partner's review.

1. What did you find most convincing about the writer's opinion of the sitcom?
2. Would you watch the sitcom on the basis of this review? Explain.

Style Guidelines

Evaluation Question	▶ Tip	▶ Revision Technique
Does the review contain several simple sentences in a row?	▶ **Highlight** your sentences with alternating colors. If you see a pattern of simple sentences, revise.	▶ Use adverb clauses to **combine** simple sentences that express closely related ideas.

Analyzing the Revision Process

ANSWERS
Possible responses are given below.

1. Adding concrete details helps explain why the writer admires Hooper's physical comedy.

2. It allows the reader to visualize his amusing facial expressions.

TEACHING TIP

Peer Review
Remind students to use good supporting details to back up their evaluations of their classmates' reviews. A student who is not convinced by a peer's review should be able to specify, using examples, which criteria the review fails to meet. You might have students revisit the **Evaluation Criteria** lesson on pp. 289–291 of the Reading Workshop before conducting peer reviews.

YOUR TURN 8

Check that students marked areas which need improvement and that the revised drafts execute the appropriate revision techniques.

Evaluating Student Writing

The ancillary *Assessment Alternatives* contains a variety of assessment forms, including Inventories and Evaluation Forms and rubrics: Six-Point Scales, Four-Point Scales, and Six Trait Scales.

Critical Thinking

Synthesis. Give students a chance to extend their understanding of combining sentences using adverb clauses by applying the concept to various kinds of reviews. Collect copies of restaurant, music, or other short reviews from a local newspaper. Ask students to work in pairs to highlight examples of adverb clauses in one of the reviews. Challenge students to write two simple sentences that could have been combined to create each of the complex sentences that appear in the reviews.

Focus on Sentences

Combining Sentences Using Adverb Clauses

Sentence patterns that are used over and over can make even an enthusiastic reader tune you out. One way you can make sure that your writing does not sound monotonous is to vary sentence structure.

A good way to vary structure is to use adverb clauses to combine simple sentences that are related in meaning. Adverb clauses begin with subordinating conjunctions, such as *after, although, as if, because, before, if, since, so that, than, unless, until, when, where, while.* You need to choose these conjunctions carefully, though, because besides joining sentences, they also indicate the relationship between the ideas in the adverb clause and the independent clause.

Example 1: Two simple sentences
1. You should see the new television show about photography.
2. The new television show about photography presents some incredible shots of the ocean.

Example 2: One complex sentence with an adverb clause
You should see the new television show about photography <u>because it presents some incredible shots of the ocean.</u>

For more on adverb clauses, see pages 337 and 476.

ONE WRITER'S REVISIONS Here is how the writer of the model review on page 303 used the guidelines to combine simple sentences that express closely related ideas into complex sentences which make the relationships between ideas crystal clear.

BEFORE REVISION

all simple sentences

Much of the action takes place at a fictional high school.

The main concern of many of the students, including Hooper,

is their minimum-wage, part-time jobs after school. Hooper's

job earns him quite a bit more than minimum wage. His

duties are much more challenging.

RESOURCES

Focus on Sentences
Practice
■ *Communications,* WS. p. 154

AFTER REVISION

Although much of the action takes place at a fictional high school, the main concern of many of the students, including Hooper, is their minimum-wage, part-time jobs after school. Hooper's job earns him quite a bit more than minimum wage, because his duties are much more challenging.

Combines using adverb clause

Combines using adverb clause

Analyzing the Revision Process

1. What relationship between the ideas in the adverb clause and the main clause is shown by the conjunction *although*?
2. Why do you think the writer chose *because* to combine the third and fourth sentences?

YOUR TURN 9 Focusing on Adverb Clauses

Using the style guidelines, evaluate the style of the sentences in your review. Then, vary the structure of your sentences by using adverb clauses to combine closely related simple sentences into longer complex sentences.

Designing Your Writing

Titles and Subheads   You can enhance the effectiveness of your review by making it visually appealing to your readers. When readers take their first look at your review, they will see a whole page before they read a single word. Keep in mind that a well-designed page can help to grab your readers' attention. A word of caution—do not overdesign. Well-designed pages can reinforce your ideas, but gaudy, busy pages will only distract readers.

One way to entice readers into reading your review is to create an attention-getting title and then to make it stand out from the text. The title of a critical review should hint at the review's contents and arouse the reader's curiosity. The title of the Writer's Model, "*One Cool Million* Is Rich with Laughter," is a good example. It makes the title of the sitcom the subject of a sentence that delivers—in brief—the writer's opinion of the show. In addition, the word *rich* in the title is a play on words: Every week *One Cool Million* makes a character rich with a gift of one million dollars. A title is always centered on the page, but the writer of the review of *One Cool Million* made her title stand out even

Analyzing the Revision Process

ANSWERS
Possible responses are given below.

1. Using *although* shows that the first clause is less important than the rest of the sentence.

2. The writer used *because* to show a cause-and-effect relationship.

YOUR TURN 9

Have students use the code CS/AC in the margin near any sentence that is a complex sentence with an adverb clause. This technique will allow you to determine at a glance whether students have incorporated the **Focus on Sentences** instruction into their writing.

Meeting INDIVIDUAL NEEDS

MULTIPLE INTELLIGENCES
Spatial Intelligence. Provide the class with colored markers and suggest that students search their papers for sentences that might be combined. Have students circle each pair of closely related simple sentences with the same color. Then, ask them to review the marked sentences to see if they can combine some of the pairs into sentences with adverb clauses. Remind students that sentence variety is important, so they may not want to combine every pair of simple sentences.

more by making the print slightly larger than the print of the text.

In addition, consider providing **subheadings**—attention-getting phrases to hint at the main idea of the paragraph—for each of your main body paragraphs. Subheadings should be aligned with the left margin. You can also make the subheadings darker than the text.

Here is what part of the Writer's Model might have looked like had the writer chosen to use subheads. The subheadings here are like small signposts that help guide the reader through the review.

A Gift for Comedy

Those who know Lopez only from his dramatic roles will be utterly surprised by his gift for comedy. His portrayal of Harvey Hooper as a grinning, goofy, good-natured guy is a study in the art of physical comedy. Lopez uses his gangly six-foot frame and rubbery, expressive face to great advantage, often making the teenager he plays seem even younger and more awkward than his age would suggest.

A Fresh Idea

Along with the winning character of Lopez, the unique storyline of *One Cool Million* provides lots of opportunities for laughs. Although much of the action takes place at a fictional high school, the main concern of many of the students, including Hooper, is their minimum-wage, part-time jobs after school. . . .

COMPUTER TIP

If you create your essay on a computer, stick to two fonts—one for the text and another for titles and subheadings—and make sure that you select fonts that are easy to read.

If you decide to use larger sizes for titles and subheadings, be sure to make them only *slightly* larger. On a computer, titles should be no more than four points larger than the font size you use for the text, and subheads should be no more than two points larger. If, for example, you use 12-point type for the font, use no more than 16-point for your title and 14-point for your subheadings.

Both of these design features—titles and subheads—can be created in a handwritten essay as well as an essay typed into a word-processing program.

TIP Make sure to consult your teacher before doing anything that departs from standard formatting for writing assignments in your class.

Publishing

Proofread Your Review

Increase Magnification Just like professional reviewers, you need to make sure your review is completely error-free. If a serious error like a run-on sentence escapes your eyes, the entire review may be weakened.

Reference Note

For **proofreading guidelines,** see page 13.

Grammar Link

Run-On Sentences

Run-on sentences, which consist of two or more sentences written as one sentence, can confuse a reader because they provide no markers to show where one idea ends and another begins. One type of run-on sentence, a **comma splice,** occurs when a writer separates two or more independent clauses—clauses that should be punctuated as sentences—with a comma and nothing else.

In television, *genre* means type of program, examples of television genres include drama, situation comedy, and nightly news.

Another type of run-on sentence, called a **fused sentence,** has nothing between two or more independent clauses to separate them.

In television, *genre* means type of program examples of television genres include drama, situation comedy, and nightly news.

To revise run-on sentences:

■ Use a period to separate sentences.

In television, *genre* means type of program. Examples of television genres include drama, situation comedy, and nightly news.

■ Separate the clauses with a comma and a coordinating conjunction (*and, but, for, or, nor, so,* or *yet*).

In television, *genre* means type of program, and examples of television genres include drama, situation comedy, and nightly news.

■ Separate the clauses with just a semicolon or with a semicolon and a conjunctive adverb (*for example, then, therefore, however,* and *meanwhile*).

In television, *genre* means type of program; for example, television genres include drama, situation comedy, and nightly news.

PRACTICE

Correct the following run-on sentences. Use each method described above.

1. Lucinda Perez is the star of *Nuevo Latino*, it is the only show broadcast in both Spanish and English on a major network.

2. The network at first provided a very small budget for *Nuevo Latino*, it is considered one of ZBC-TV's successes.

3. *Nuevo Latino* was first shown in Mexico in June of 2000 then, television stations in California and Texas began picking it up.

4. Ms. Perez has said that the key to her success is an ability to listen this is a skill she developed as a child.

Writing Workshop **311**

Wrap It Up

Metacognition. Have students reflect on their writing processes by answering the following questions:

1. What did you find to be the most challenging part of writing a television sitcom review? Why?

2. What is one piece of advice you would give reviewers who want their writing to be convincing?

YOUR TURN 10

Referring to the **Content and Organization Guidelines** chart on p. 306 will help you assess whether or not students have included all important elements covered in this chapter. Check particularly to see that students have included reasons for their opinions and adequate support. Sample answers to the second and fourth **Reflect on Your Review** questions may be similar to the following:

• I focused on character change and the humorous plot because there was so much to say about these elements.

• Peer review helped me realize I needed to provide more background for people who had not seen the show.

Publish Your Review

Reaching Out to a Bigger Audience   To reach a larger audience with your review, try publishing it in one of the following ways.

- Post your review to an Internet discussion group or mailing list. There are many TV-related groups and lists, including some that are devoted to discussions of specific programs.

- Submit your review to your school newspaper or your community newspaper for publication.

- Mail your review to the show's creators. You can find out who they are by watching the show's credits. You can also check to see if the show has a Web site. If it has one, it probably provides an e-mail address to which you can send your review.

- Publish a review magazine that includes all the reviews from your class.

PORTFOLIO

Reflect on Your Review

Reviewing the Reviewing Process   To make what you learned in this workshop an experience you can build on, write responses to the following questions. (You can set goals as a writer based on your responses to the questions.)

- As you went through all the steps leading to your final draft, did your opinion of the sitcom you were reviewing change? If so, why?

- How did you decide which sitcom elements to discuss in your review?

- What other sitcoms would you include in a collection of reviews? Why?

- Which step in the revision process did you find most helpful? Why?

If you intend to put your review in a portfolio, attach your responses to it.

YOUR TURN 10   Proofreading, Publishing, and Reflecting

Before you turn your review in to your teacher, be sure you
- proofread it carefully, looking especially for run-on sentences
- consider ways to let others read your review
- reflect on your review by answering questions about the process you went through in writing it

Connections to Life

Analyzing Your Television Viewing Habits

You are probably used to hearing statements like this one: "Teenagers spend more time watching television than they do studying! It's no wonder that they know more about athletic shoes and chewing gum than they do about math and American history!" Have you ever wondered whether you are one of those teenagers who spend too much time in front of the TV? Keep track of how many hours you spend in front of the television set and what you spend your time watching. You might also ask, *Why am I watching?* and keep track of the many different answers to that question. You might be surprised by your findings.

Diary of a Teenage TV Viewer Before you do anything else, estimate how much time per week you think you spend watching TV. Then, break down this total viewing time into an estimate of the time you think you spend watching different genres of shows. (The word *genre* is a literary term, adapted from French, meaning *type* or *kind.*) Examples of genres in television are **news, documentaries, talk shows, dramas, sitcoms, game shows, soap operas,** and **sports.** Television genres may also be divided into subcategories. For example, the genre of news programs can be divided into national news, local news, and documentaries. Then, subcategories are sometimes referred to as *news genres,* meaning types of news. Later, you can compare your estimates

My Television Viewing Habits	
Day/Date	Mon. 10/5
Time	7–7:30
Program Name	One Cool Million
Channel or Network	24
Genre (Type)	sitcom

to the number of hours you end up actually watching.

To analyze your viewing habits, copy the preceding chart and keep it next to your television set. For a week, record the information required by the chart each time you watch all or most of a program. One entry has been made in the chart as an example.

Totaling the Hours Once you have noted what you spent your time watching during the week, you need to tally the results. Only two rows of your chart—time and genre—need to be tallied. Add up all the time you spent watching shows from each genre. If, for example, the only news programming you watched for seven nights was a thirty-minute nightly news program, you would record three hours, thirty minutes for the genre. If you watched six different sitcoms during the week and each show lasted thirty minutes, you

TEACHING TIP

The "Average" Teenager
If some students do not watch television at all, have them do an alternate study. For instance, they might analyze the time they spend online or the time they spend reading various materials. Have these students work in pairs or small groups to find averages for their adapted data.

YOUR TURN 11

Make sure students identify data-supported responses to the question about popular genres. To reinforce their plans to change viewing habits if they plan to do so, ask students to jot down three concrete steps they will take to change their habits.

---

would record three hours for the genre. The following chart shows how your result totals might look.

> **Sitcoms:** six hours
> **News:** three hours, thirty minutes
> **Dramas:** five hours
> **Documentaries:** one hour
> **Game shows:** five hours
> **Sports:** four hours, thirty minutes
> **Soap operas:** zero hours
> **Talk shows:** four hours, thirty minutes

The "Average" Teenager How do you think your own viewing habits compare with your classmates'? Once you have analyzed your personal viewing habits, get together with your classmates to compare notes. To get a class average, add the total viewing time for each genre,

then divide the total by the number of students in your class. Here are the findings of one class:

average hours per week
5.6 watching sitcoms
students
in class 30 | 168   total hours of sitcoms

Next, add the total viewing time for the week across all genres, then divide by the number of participants in your class to find the average number of *total* hours per week you and your classmates spent watching television. The example class came up with these findings:

average hours per week
28 watching TV
students
in class 30 | 840   total hours of all genres

YOUR TURN 11 Reflecting on Your Viewing Habits

Using your findings, consider your personal viewing habits and the average viewing habits for your class. On your own paper, write answers to the questions in the bulleted list below. Be prepared to share your answers with your class.

- Do you watch more or less TV than your classmates? Are you surprised by your findings?

- Which genres of shows do you like most? Why do you think this is so?

- Which genres of shows are most popular with your classmates? Why do you think these shows are popular with people your age?

- Now that you see how much time you and your peers spend watching television, do you plan to change your viewing habits? Why or why not?

Analyzing the Nightly Network News

Would it surprise you to learn that the people who produce the nightly news want to entertain you? While the primary purpose of a news program is to inform the viewer, it must also be as entertaining and attention-getting as possible to keep you watching. News programs, like other television programs, depend on ratings. Ratings translate into profits for television networks because ratings are based on the size of a program's audience. The bigger the audience, the more money advertisers are willing to spend to sponsor the program, and television networks are in business to make money.

Presentation Techniques

Variety Is the Spice of News One way news programs keep you interested is to vary the way the news is presented. News programs manipulate the news by using four basic presentation techniques. The following chart describes the presentation techniques, provides examples of each, and explains the potential effects they can have on viewers.

Presentation Techniques	Examples	Possible Effects
Personalizing the News: concentrating on the people involved in an event rather than on the event itself	A story emphasizes the personality of a single member of a space shuttle crew while giving only brief mention of the shuttle's unique mission.	Viewers may miss out on information necessary for understanding the story.
Dramatizing the News: making engaging short stories out of news events—producers present the event using the language of drama and storytelling	A reporter says: "Our story begins in this tiny house in a small town." The accompanying video emphasizes the people involved and the events of the "plot."	Producers may omit important information. A viewer might think of a violent event reported on the news and a violent event depicted on a fictional police drama in the same way.

(continued)

OBJECTIVES

- To analyze a network news program
- To identify four techniques used to present the nightly news
- To look behind presentation techniques for the importance of a news story

WHAT'S AHEAD?

In this section, you will analyze a network news program. You will also learn how to

- identify four techniques used to present the nightly news
- look behind presentation techniques for the importance of a news story

Quotation for the Day

"**If you're not doing research at the highest level and delivering information in a compelling and entertaining style, you're not half the expert writer you can and must become.**"

(Hank Nuwer, journalist and author)

Ask students for their opinions about whether the researchers and writers of evening news should be entertaining as well as informative. Have each student write down several points in a pro and con chart. For example:

PRO	CON
More people will watch the news if it is entertaining.	Time should be spent on important news stories—not on entertaining.
News reporters are seen as authoritative. They must "dress the part."	News reporters shouldn't spend too much time on their looks and clothing.

RESOURCES

Focus on Viewing and Representing Practice

- *Media Literacy and Communication Skills* —*Support and Practice,* Ch. 8 —*A How-to Handbook*

Teaching Notes

- *Media Literacy and Communication Skills* —*A Teacher's Guide,* Ch. 8

(continued)

Normalizing the News: reassuring viewers by presenting experts or officials to explain that things are under control and will soon return to normal	When a natural disaster occurs, government officials and experts reassure people that everything possible is being done to lessen the impact of the disaster.	After viewing such normalizing of the news, viewers who are not personally affected by the disaster tend to be left with a distorted view of the serious effects on the victims of the disaster.
Fragmenting the News: presenting bite-sized pieces of information to viewers without explaining why the information is important	You hear on the nightly news that Congress has been unable to agree on a method of saving the Social Security and Medicare systems from financial ruin. Both systems will run out of money by the end of the year.	Viewers who are not dependent on these services might dismiss the story as unimportant because the impact of Congress's failure to agree is not explained.

Being a Critical Viewer

You Be the Critic Viewing the news *critically* does not mean criticizing or finding fault with the news. Instead, it means questioning the news to determine, among other things, whether a news event has been shaped by one of the four techniques listed above. By becoming a critical viewer, you begin to recognize these techniques of manipulating the news and can make better sense of it. In short, the more *you* know about the way networks present news every night, the better you can judge the value of the news.

TIP Another way programmers keep your interest in a news program is by varying the number of personalities who present the news. Anchorpersons do not simply read the news reports as videotaped footage is shown. Instead, correspondents, commentators, and experts interact with them.

YOUR TURN 12 Analyzing the Nightly Network News

Working in groups of four, watch a videotape of a recent nightly network news program. Use a chart like the one below to record the **subject** of each news item, **the length of time** devoted to it, and the **presentation technique** used to present the report. Briefly explain each technique you list. If an item does not conform to any of the four techniques, write *None* in the column. Be prepared to discuss your findings with the rest of the class.

Subject of Report	Length of Report	Presentation Technique
In spite of international aid, hunger is still widespread in Somalia.	2 minutes	Dramatizing the News—Story focuses on people trying to prevent starvation rather than those who are starving

---

YOUR TURN 12

To prepare for students' assignments, you will need to tape or have volunteers tape several news programs. If possible, have students back up their findings by showing the class brief excerpts from the videotapes during the course of their presentations.

Wrap It Up

Metacognition. Ask students to write answers to the following question:

1. What is one new thing you will notice when you watch the nightly news?

Then, ask students the following question:

2. Describe two techniques that news producers often use to keep viewers interested. [personalizing, dramatizing, normalizing, or fragmenting]

RESOURCES

Your Turn 12
Practice and Reinforcement

■ *Media Literacy and Communication Skills*
   —*Support and Practice,* Ch. 8, transparencies and worksheets
   —*Videocassette 2,* Segment H

Choices

Choose one of the following activities to complete.

▶ **CAREERS**

1. Consumer Reporter Apply your analytical skills to plan and present an **oral review** of a real-world product. As part of your review, give a **demonstration** of how the product is used in order to point out its positive or negative qualities. Spell out for listeners what criteria you used and who you think should (or should not) buy and use the product.

▶ **MEDIA AND TECHNOLOGY**

2. The Eyes Have It? To compare how visual information affects the way we remember and learn, use a VCR to record an important news event reported on a nightly network news program. Use a tape recorder to record a radio news version of the same story. Play the television version for three classmates and the radio tape for three different classmates. Be sure neither group sees or hears the other group's tape. Have the members of each group record as much factual information as they can remember and a description of any memorable visual images or sounds from their news report. Write a **report** of the results and share them with the class.

▶ **SPEAKING AND LISTENING**

3. A Voice from the Past Watch a video of a historically significant speech—ask your teacher or librarian for recommendations—and evaluate what makes it memorable. Consider rhetorical devices such as repetition and analogy and other features of the speech's content or delivery. Use your criteria, supported with specific examples from the speech, to write a one- to two-paragraph **analysis.** After summing up your ideas, conclude your analysis by considering what impact you think the speech might have had on listeners at the time.

▶ **LITERATURE**

4. The Rest of the Story Rewrite one of your favorite narratives as a **news story** that will be reported on the nightly news over the course of five nights. Divide the plot of the narrative into segments that could be reported in the same short time most lead news stories are given—about three minutes. The last report should reveal the outcome of the story.

PORTFOLIO

▶ **CAREERS**

Tell students that analyzing the writing strategies of writers can give them ideas on how to approach their own writing and show them that not all writers approach the writing process in the same manner. Students may want to ask the following questions:

• How does the reviewer prepare for creating a review?

• Does the reviewer take notes during the feature?

• How much time does the reviewer set aside for revision? How many times does the reviewer re-read and revise his or her review?

Before assigning this exercise, notify students' parents/guardians and all writers the students wish to interview.

▶ **VIEWING AND REPRESENTING**

Students may want to write their editorials collaboratively. Students in small groups could either view the programming together, so that they can discuss the ratings as they appear, or watch separately and reconvene afterward to compile their findings. As they work together, have students spend time considering their audience. Working to engage a specific audience will help students find a slant that will focus their editorials. Encourage students to generate concerns their specific audience might have about the rating system. For example, an audience of parents might care whether the ratings are clear and helpful. To generate thesis statements, prompt students by asking whether the rating system is working for their audience or whether students can imagine a more effective way to rate programming.

Choices **317**

RESOURCES

Reviewing Television

Assessment

■ *Assessment Package*
—*Chapter Tests,* Ch. 8
—*Chapter Tests in Standardized Test Formats,* Ch. 8
—*Assessment Alternatives,* Ch. 8
■ *Test Generator (One-Stop Planner CD-ROM)*

Choices

Rubrics

■ *Assessment Package*
—*Assessment Alternatives,* Ch. 8

PART 2
Sentences and Paragraphs

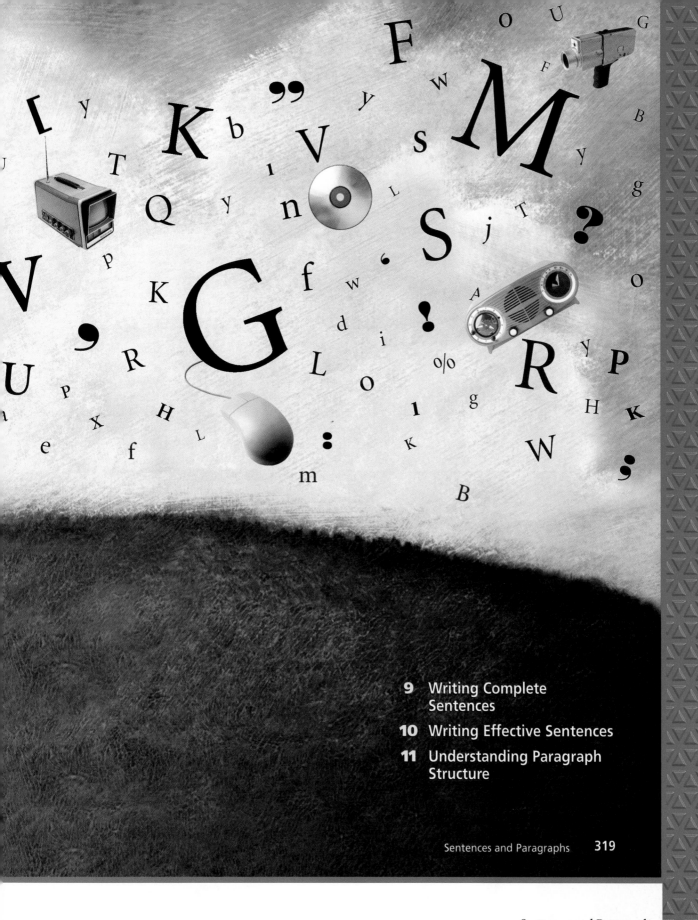

Sentences and Paragraphs   **319**

CHAPTER

Writing Complete Sentences

CHAPTER

9

PREVIEWING THE CHAPTER

■ Complete sentences are the foundation of good writing. In this chapter, students will learn to evaluate sentences for completeness. They will identify and revise sentence fragments, phrase fragments, subordinate clause fragments, and run-on sentences. Use this chapter to teach the concept of complete sentences and also as a reference that students may consult throughout the year as they complete their writing assignments.

internet connect

go.
hrw.
.com
GO TO: go.hrw.com
KEYWORD: EOLang

Sentence Fragments

A *sentence* is a word group that has a subject and a verb and expresses a complete thought. A *sentence fragment,* a word group that does not have all the basic parts of a complete sentence, does not express a complete thought. It is missing some important information.

Sentence fragments usually occur when you write in a hurry or become a little careless. You may leave out a word, or you may chop off part of a sentence by putting in a period too soon.

To find out whether you have a complete sentence or a sentence fragment, you can use a simple three-part test:

1. Does the group of words have a subject?
2. Does it have a verb?
3. Does it express a complete thought?

If you answer *no* to any of these questions, your word group is a fragment. It is missing at least one basic part.

FRAGMENT   Was the best sharpshooter in the United States. [The subject is missing. Who was the best sharpshooter in the United States?]

SENTENCE   Annie Oakley was the best sharpshooter in the United States.

FRAGMENT   Annie Oakley with Buffalo Bill Cody's Wild West show. [The verb is missing. What did she do with the Wild West show?]

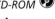

CHAPTER RESOURCES

Planning
■ *One-Stop Planner CD-ROM*

Practice and Extension
■ *Sentences and Paragraphs,* for Ch. 9

Evaluation and Assessment
■ *Assessment Package*
   —*Chapter Tests,* Ch. 9
   —*Chapter Tests in Standardized Test Formats,* Ch. 9

■ *Test Generator (One-Stop Planner CD-ROM)*

SENTENCE   Annie Oakley performed with Buffalo Bill Cody's Wild West show.

FRAGMENT   As it fell through the air ninety feet away. [This group of words has a subject (*it*) and a verb (*fell*), but it does not express a complete thought. What happened as something fell through the air?]

SENTENCE   Annie could shoot a playing card as it fell through the air ninety feet away.

NOTE By itself, a fragment does not express a complete thought. However, fragments can make sense if they are clearly related to the sentences that come before or after them. These sentences give the fragments meaning because they help the reader fill in the missing parts.

The following passage is from an essay that describes the death and the cutting down of a great white oak on the writer's family homestead. The author's grandfather has carefully cut at the dead tree and is about to aim the final blows. See how the author uses fragments to describe the fall of the great tree.

> Then came the great moment. A few last, quick strokes. A slow, deliberate swaying. The crack of parting fibers. Then a long "swoo-sh!" that rose in pitch as the towering trunk arced downward at increasing speed.
>
> Edwin Way Teale, "The Death of a Tree"

Experienced writers like Teale sometimes use sentence fragments to achieve a certain effect. As a developing writer, however, you need to practice and master writing complete sentences before you begin to experiment with writing fragments.

Annie Oakley

Exercise 1 Identifying Sentence Fragments

Some of the following items are sentence fragments. To find out which items are fragments and which are complete sentences, apply the three-part test on page 320. If the item is a complete sentence, write *C*. If a subject is missing, write *S*. If a verb is missing, write *V*. If the item has a subject and verb but does not express a complete thought, write *N*.

EXAMPLE   **1.** After he wrote "A Christmas Memory."

        1. N

Sentence Fragments   **321**

Sentence Fragments

OBJECTIVES

- **To identify and revise sentence, phrase, and subordinate clause fragments**

- **To use subordinate clauses in complete sentences**

Quotation for the Day

❝Writing, the art of communicating thoughts to the mind through the eye, is the greatest invention of the world. Its utility may be conceived by the reflection that to it we owe everything which [helps us become civilized].❞

(Abraham Lincoln, 1809–1865, sixteenth president of the United States)

Discuss with students some of the ways that writing has affected the world as well as students' own lives. Challenge students to explain how writing complete sentences helps people communicate with others.

Internet

- go.hrw.com (keyword: EOLang) go.hrw.com

RESOURCES

Sentence Fragments Practice

- *Sentences and Paragraphs,* WS. pp. 1, 2, 3, 4, 5, 6, 7, 8, 9, 10, 11, 12

Meeting INDIVIDUAL NEEDS

ENGLISH-LANGUAGE LEARNERS
General Strategies. To help students understand the parts of a complete sentence, provide them with a chart like the one below. Let students work in pairs to match subjects, verbs, complements, and modifiers to express complete ideas.

Possible Subjects	People The boys I
Possible Verbs or Verb Phrases	worked play will go
Possible Complements and Modifiers	in the sun baseball to school

Cooperative Learning

Fragments in Advertising. Bring to class or have students find and bring in examples of recent print advertisements. Ask each student to work with a randomly assigned partner to circle sentence fragments or phrase fragments used in the advertisements to capture readers' attention. Direct students to identify the types of fragments or phrases and to rewrite them as complete sentences. Assign one student to act as recorder and the other to present and explain the pair's work to the class. Discuss how the use of complete sentences changes the advertisement.

1. Truman Capote was an American author.   1. C
2. Was born in New Orleans in 1924.   2. S
3. Grew up in Alabama.   3. S
4. Because he hated attending boarding schools.   4. N
5. A movie made from *Breakfast at Tiffany's*, probably his most famous novel.   5. V
6. When he moved to New York City.   6. N
7. Capote's short story "A Christmas Memory" was made into a television movie.   7. C
8. His characters lively and eccentric.   8. V
9. Is one of his most moving stories.   9. S
10. Spent six years researching the nonfiction book that he titled *In Cold Blood*.   10. S

TIPS & TRICKS

To find phrase fragments in your writing, read the sentences in your paragraphs from the last to the first. Reading this way helps you to listen for complete thoughts that make sense.

Reference Note

For more on **verbals** (participles, gerunds, and infinitives), see page 449.

Phrase Fragments

A *phrase* is a group of words that does not have a subject and a verb and that is used as a single part of speech. There are three kinds of phrases that can easily be mistaken for complete sentences: *verbal phrases*, *appositive phrases*, and *prepositional phrases*.

Verbal Phrases

Verbals, forms of verbs that are used as other parts of speech, sometimes fool us into thinking that a group of words has a verb when it really does not. Some verbals end in *–ing, –d,* or *–ed* and do not have helping verbs (such as *is, were,* or *have*) in front of them. Other verbals have the word *to* in front of the base form (*to go, to play*).

A *verbal phrase* is a phrase that contains a verbal. By itself, a verbal phrase is a fragment because it does not express a complete thought.

FRAGMENT   Learning about the Civil War.
SENTENCE   I enjoyed learning about the Civil War.

FRAGMENT   Gaining glory for itself and for all black soldiers.
SENTENCE   Gaining glory for itself and for all black soldiers, the 54th Massachusetts Regiment led the attack on Fort Wagner.

FRAGMENT   To become good soldiers.
SENTENCE   Black volunteers trained hard to become good soldiers.

FRAGMENT   Inspired by the 54th Massachusetts Regiment.
SENTENCE   Inspired by the 54th Massachusetts Regiment, other black soldiers fought bravely.

Learning for Life

Using Fragments. While this chapter will make clear that sentence fragments should not be used in formal writing assignments, students should be aware of fragments in everyday use of language. Ask your class to brainstorm possible situations in which sentence fragments are regularly used to communicate messages. Students may suggest the following situations:

- conversation
- making lists

Appositive Phrases

An *appositive* is a word that identifies or explains the noun or pronoun it follows. An *appositive phrase,* a phrase made up of an appositive and its modifiers, is a fragment. It does not contain the basic parts of a sentence.

FRAGMENT	A twenty-five-year-old soldier.
SENTENCE	The 54th Massachusetts Regiment was commanded by Colonel Shaw, a twenty-five-year-old soldier.

Prepositional Phrases

A *prepositional phrase* is a group of words beginning with a preposition and ending with a noun or pronoun. A prepositional phrase cannot stand alone as a sentence because it does not express a complete thought.

FRAGMENT	With great courage on the battlefield.
SENTENCE	The 54th Massachusetts Regiment acted with great courage on the battlefield.

The 54th Massachusetts Regiment

NOTE Usually a phrase needs to stay as close as possible to the word it modifies in a sentence. However, some phrases, such as the infinitive phrase "to become good soldiers," can make sense at the beginning or the end of a sentence.

Reference Note

For more on **placing phrases in sentences,** see pages 585 and 587.

Exercise 2 Revising Phrase Fragments

Use your imagination to create sentences from the following phrases. You can either (1) attach the fragment to a complete sentence, or (2) develop the phrase into a complete sentence by adding a subject, a verb, or both.

EXAMPLE
1. landing on the planet
1. *Landing on the planet, the astronauts immediately began to explore.*

or

The astronauts were landing on the planet.

1. in a huge spaceship
2. setting foot on the planet
3. to explore the craters

Sentence Fragments **323**

ANSWERS continued

4. Walking around in a spacesuit is not easy.

5. Finding no sign of life, the astronauts returned to their spaceship.

6. The astronauts' spaceship was struck by a meteor.

7. After checking the spaceship for damage, the astronauts prepared to leave.

8. Giganta, the planet's moon, was a beautiful reddish color.

9. The astronauts were anxious to return to Earth.

10. On a successful mission, they gathered valuable information about a planet's surface.

Meeting
INDIVIDUAL NEEDS

MULTIPLE INTELLIGENCES
Spatial Intelligence. As you discuss the terminology used in this section of the chapter, students may benefit from drawing illustrations to explain and provide context for terms such as *independent* and *subordinate*. For example, a student could illustrate how a locomotive, which can operate on its own power, is connected to a boxcar, which lacks its own power. They may do the same with the terms *fused, splice,* and *compound* that appear in later sections of the chapter. Students can display their drawings in the classroom for reference.

4. walking around in a spacesuit
5. finding no sign of life
6. the astronauts' spaceship
7. checking the spaceship for damage
8. the planet's moon
9. to return to Earth
10. on a successful mission

Subordinate Clause Fragments

A *clause* is a group of words that has a subject and a verb. One kind of clause, an *independent clause,* expresses a complete thought and can stand on its own as a sentence. For example, the group of words *I ate my lunch* is an independent clause. However, another kind of clause, a *subordinate clause,* does not express a complete thought and cannot stand by itself as a sentence.

FRAGMENT   When Paris carried off the beautiful Helen of Troy. [What happened when Paris carried off Helen?]

SENTENCE   When Paris carried off the beautiful Helen of Troy, he started the Trojan War.

FRAGMENT   Who was a great hero of the Greeks. [Note that this would be a complete sentence if it ended with a question mark.]

SENTENCE   Odysseus, who was a great hero of the Greeks, took part in the Trojan War.

FRAGMENT   Because the wooden horse concealed Greek soldiers. [What was the result of the concealment?]

SENTENCE   Because the wooden horse concealed Greek soldiers, the Greeks finally won the Trojan War.

NOTE   A subordinate clause telling *why, where, when,* or *how* is called an *adverb clause.* Usually you can place an adverb clause either before or after the independent clause in a sentence.

EXAMPLE   **After he started home from the Trojan War,** Odysseus had many more adventures.

or

Odysseus had many more adventures **after he started home from the Trojan War.**

Using Commas with Adverb Clauses.
Remind students that an adverb clause can be placed at various locations in the sentence. Point out, however, that if an adverb clause is placed at the beginning of a sentence, a comma will need to follow that clause. Ask students to read the following sentences to determine whether a comma is needed. If a comma is needed, have students identify the word it should follow and add the comma. If a sentence is correct, have students write *C.*

If you put the subordinate clause first, use a comma to separate it from the independent clause. The comma makes the sentence easier for the reader to understand.

Reference Note

For more on **punctuating introductory adverb clauses**, see page 653.

Exercise 3 **Revising Subordinate Clause Fragments**

The following paragraph contains some subordinate clause fragments. First, find these clause fragments. Next, revise the paragraph, joining the subordinate clauses with independent clauses. (There may be more than one way to join them.) Change the punctuation and capitalization as necessary. *Here is a possible revision.*

```
     People have been using cosmetics for
thousands of years. In Africa, the ancient
Egyptians used perfumes, hair dyes, and
makeup. That they made from plants and min-
erals. While they often used cosmetics to
be more attractive. They also used them to
protect their skin from the hot sun. Today,
cosmetics are made from over five thousand
different ingredients, including waxes,
oils, and dyes. The cosmetics business is a
huge industry. Advertisers are extremely
successful in selling cosmetics. Because
they appeal to our desire to be attractive.
They often hint. That their products will
make us beautiful, happy, and successful.
Although modern-day cosmetics ads look
different from the ads of eighty years ago.
They still appeal to our emotions.
```

Exercise 4 **Using Subordinate Clauses in Sentences**

Use each of the following subordinate clause fragments as part of a complete sentence. Add whatever words are necessary to make the meaning of the sentence complete. Add capitalization and punctuation as necessary. *Possible sentences appear below.*

1. as we watched the spaceship land   1. , we were terrified.
2. who approached the house in long leaps   2. An alien, /, was ten feet tall.
3. which startled the dog   3. The alien made a strange sound,
4. if we go outside the house   4. , we can get a better look.
5. when they handed me a glowing sphere
           5. , we knew the aliens were friendly.

Relating to Literature

Remind students that in poetry, sentence fragments, phrase fragments, subordinate clause fragments, and series of items are often used for effect. Invite students to look through poetry anthologies for examples, or show students Naomi Shihab Nye's poem "Daily."

Read Nye's poem aloud and ask students what they notice about it. Guide the discussion with the observation that the first six lines of the poem sound like a series of sentence fragments. The sentences are not constructed in the traditional subject-verb-object order, and they do not have end marks. This construction creates the effect of an ongoing series of daily activities.

Critical Thinking

Analysis. Ask students to work with partners to list reasons why sentence fragments are more often used successfully in conversation than in writing. [*Speakers use tone of voice, inflection, pauses, and gestures along with words to convey meaning. The listener can see the speaker and can respond to nonverbal speech as well as verbal messages. In spoken conversation, two-way communication allows a speaker to judge whether meaning is clear to a listener. Writing is, at least in this respect, one-way communication. The reader has to rely solely on the writer's words for understanding.*]

1. Before you leave look at this picture. [*leave,*]
2. I should leave at the sound of the bell. [*C*]
3. Because mother worked all day she is tired tonight. [*day,*]
4. While he was singing at the top of his lungs Lou attracted quite a bit of attention. [*lungs,*]
5. A larger boat is being built next to the kayak. [*C*]

Meeting INDIVIDUAL NEEDS

INCLUSION

Having students remove phrases and subordinate clauses from complete sentences might help them see how these sentence parts function in a complete sentence and why the parts are fragments when left on their own. Write the following sentences on the chalkboard and ask students to work with a helper to identify the indicated sentence parts. You may want to review the types of phrases and clauses first.

Verbal Phrases

1. Emilio wanted to go to law school.

2. He enjoyed researching past cases.

[1. *to go to law school;* 2. *researching past cases*]

Appositive Phrases

3. Marlene moved to New York from Greenville, a small town in Texas.

4. Her aunt, a freelance writer, took her to London.

[3. *a small town in Texas;* 4. *a freelance writer*]

Prepositional Phrases

5. Hasina graduated with honors.

6. She received job offers from many large companies.

[5. *with honors;* 6. *from many large companies*]

Subordinate Clauses

7. Toshio completed his homework as the baseball game began.

8. Because he was a fan, he didn't want to miss the game.

[7. *as the baseball game began;*
8. *Because he was a fan*]

NOTE A **series of items** is another kind of fragment that is easily mistaken for a sentence. Notice that, in the following example, the series of items in dark type is not a complete sentence.

FRAGMENT   I ate several things for lunch. **A sandwich, an apple, four pieces of celery, and some popcorn.**

To correct the fragment, you can

- • make it into a complete sentence

or

- • link it to the previous sentence with a colon

SENTENCE   I ate several things for lunch. I ate a sandwich, an apple, four pieces of celery, and some popcorn.

or

I ate several things for lunch: a sandwich, an apple, four pieces of celery, and some popcorn.

Review A   Identifying and Revising Fragments

Some of the following groups of words are sentence fragments. Identify each fragment, and make it part of a complete sentence, adding commas where necessary. When you find a complete sentence, write *C*.

Reference Note
For more on **punctuating introductory phrases,** see page 653.

EXAMPLE   1. Originally raised to hunt badgers. Dachshunds are now popular as pets.

1. *Originally raised to hunt badgers, dachshunds are now popular as pets.*   Possible revisions follow.

1. Humans have kept dogs as pets and helpers. For perhaps ten thousand years.
2. Herding sheep and cattle and guarding property. Many dogs more than earn their keep.
3. Descended from wolves. Some dogs are still somewhat wolflike.
4. There are over one hundred breeds of dogs now.   4. C
5. If you have a Saint Bernard. You have one of the largest dogs.
6. Because Yorkshire terriers are very tiny and cute. Many people keep them as pets.
7. Since they are all born blind and unable to take care of themselves. Puppies need their mothers.
8. Most dogs are fully grown by the time they are one year old.   8. C

9. Dogs live an average of twelve years⁄Although many live to be nearly twenty.

10. If you like dogs⁄Consider having one for a pet.

Run-on Sentences

A **run-on sentence** is two or more complete sentences run together as one. Because they do not show where one idea ends and another one begins, run-on sentences can confuse your reader. There are two kinds of run-ons. In the first kind, called a **fused sentence,** the sentences have no punctuation at all between them.

RUN-ON   Schools in the Middle Ages were different from ours students usually did not have books.

CORRECT   Schools in the Middle Ages were different from ours. Students usually did not have books.

In the other kind of run-on, the writer has linked together sentences with only a comma to separate them from one another. This kind of run-on is called a **comma splice.**

RUN-ON   Schools today have books for every student, many schools also have televisions and computers.

CORRECT   Schools today have books for every student. Many schools also have televisions and computers.

Revising Run-on Sentences

There are several ways you can revise run-on sentences. As shown in the examples above, you can always make two separate sentences. However, if the two thoughts are equal to one another in importance, you may want to make a **compound sentence.**

RUN-ON   Canada has ten provinces each province has its own government. [fused]

Canada has ten provinces, each province has its own government. [comma splice]

1. You can make a compound sentence by using a comma and a coordinating conjunction (such as *and*, *but*, or *or*).

CORRECTED   Canada has ten provinces, **and** each province has its own government.

Run-on Sentences   **327**

Run-on Sentences

If you have a computer that can be used with a projector screen, open a word-processing program and type some of the sample run-on sentences that appear on pp. 327–329. Then, as students read the instruction and the examples in their textbooks, you or a student may demonstrate on the computer how to revise each sentence. Students may benefit from seeing the actual changes being made for them.

Critical Thinking

Evaluation. Students may have trouble evaluating the importance of ideas in a run-on sentence. Make the process of evaluation visual by writing a run-on sentence on the chalkboard and drawing a box around each of the important ideas. Then, have students evaluate the ideas by asking the following questions:

- Does one idea seem more important than another?
- Does one idea have to happen before the other can? If so, the first idea is more important.
- Does inserting the words *and, or,* or *but* make a difference in the meaning of the sentence? If *and* or *but* makes the sentence seem wrong, then you have a clue about the equality of the ideas.

Model the evaluation process before asking students to try it on their own.

---

2. You can make a compound sentence by using a semicolon.

CORRECTED   Canada has ten provinces**;** each province has its own government.

3. You can make a compound sentence by using a semicolon and a word such as *therefore, instead, meanwhile, still, also, nevertheless,* or *however.* These words are called **conjunctive adverbs.** Follow a conjunctive adverb with a comma.

CORRECTED   Canada has ten provinces**; also,** each province has its own government.

NOTE   Before you join two sentences in a compound sentence, make sure that the ideas in the sentences are closely related to one another. If you link unrelated ideas, you may confuse your reader.

UNRELATED   Canada is almost four million square miles in size, and I hope to visit my relatives there someday.

RELATED   Canada is almost four million square miles in size, but most of its people live on a small strip of land along the southern border.

Reference Note

For more on **compound sentences,** see page 335.

Exercise 5   Revising Run-on Sentences

The following items are confusing because they are run-on sentences. Clear up the confusion by revising the run-ons to form clear, complete sentences. To revise, use the method given in parentheses after each sentence. (The examples on pages 327 and 328 will help you.)

EXAMPLE   **1.** Hollywood is still a center of American moviemaking fine films are made in other places, too. (Use a comma and a coordinating conjunction.)

     1. Hollywood is still a center of American moviemaking, but fine films are made in other places, too.

1. Movies entertain millions of people every day they are popular all over the world. (Make two sentences.)

2. Many films take years to make they require the skills of hundreds of workers. (Use a comma and a coordinating conjunction.)   **2.** , and

George Eastman and Thomas Edison

3. The director of a movie has an important job, the cast and crew all follow the director's instructions. (Use a semicolon.)

4. The director makes many decisions, the producers take care of the business end of moviemaking. (Use a semicolon and a conjunctive adverb.)   **4.** ; however,

5. The first movie theaters opened in the early 1900s they were called nickelodeons. (Make two sentences.)

6. Thomas Edison was a pioneer in early moviemaking, he invented the first commercial motion-picture machine. (Use a semicolon.)

7. The machine was called a kinetoscope, it was a cabinet that showed moving images through a peephole. (Make two sentences.)   **7.** ⊙

8. Early movies were silent, sometimes offscreen actors at movie theaters would fill in the dialogue for the audience. (Use a comma and a coordinating conjunction.)   **8.** , but

9. The first sound films were shown in the late 1920s they marked a milestone in moviemaking history. (Use a semicolon.)

10. Movies are great entertainment, they are also an art form. (Use a semicolon and a conjunctive adverb.)   **10.** ; however,

The following paragraph contains several sentence fragments and run-on sentences. First, identify all fragments or run-ons. Then, revise them, adding words and changing the punctuation and capitalization as necessary to make each sentence clear and complete.

Here is a possible revision.

During the Civil War, Women nurses showed remarkable heroism. They took care of sick and wounded soldiers, they risked and their lives carrying supplies. To military hospitals. Sally L. Tompkins one was such woman. She ran a military hospital in the South she was one of two women , and captains in the Confederate Army. Clara Barton was another heroic Civil War nurse, she worked tirelessly. Caring for ⊙ sick and wounded soldiers in the North. became In 1864, Barton, superintendent of nurses for the Union Army. She later founded the American Red Cross Society, Served as, and its president of the Red Cross. Until 1904.

Clara Barton

Run-on Sentences   **329**

Writing Effective Sentences

internet**connect**

**go.
hrw
.com**

GO TO: go.hrw.com
KEYWORD: EOLang

Combining Sentences

Short sentences are often effective; however, a long, unbroken series of them can sound choppy. For example, notice how dull the following paragraph sounds.

> I have seen a lot of earthling-meets-alien movies. I have seen The Last Starfighter. I have seen all the Star Trek movies. I have noticed something about these movies. I have noticed that there are good humans in these movies. There are bad humans. There are good aliens. There are bad aliens. The humans and aliens are actually not so different from each other.

Notice how much more interesting the paragraph sounds when the short, choppy sentences are combined into longer, smoother sentences.

> I have seen a lot of earthling-meets-alien movies, including The Last Starfighter and all the Star Trek movies. I have noticed that there are good and bad humans in these movies, as well as good and bad aliens. The humans and aliens are actually not so different from each other.

Inserting Words

You can combine short sentences by inserting a key word from one sentence into another. You usually need to eliminate some words in sentences that are combined. You may also need to change the form of the key word.

Using the Same Form	
Original	Edgar Allan Poe led a short life. His life was tragic.
Combined	Edgar Allan Poe led a short, **tragic** life.
Changing the Form	
Original	Edgar Allan Poe wrote strange stories. He wrote horror stories.
Combined	Edgar Allan Poe wrote strange, **horrifying** stories.

NOTE Some verbs and nouns can be made into adjectives by adding
–ed and *–ing,* and some adjectives can be made into adverbs by
adding *–ly.*

Exercise 1 Combining Sentences by Inserting Words

In the following sets of sentences, some words have been italicized. Combine each set of sentences by inserting the italicized word (or words) into the first sentence. The directions in parentheses will tell you how to change the word form if it is necessary to do so.

EXAMPLE
1. Edgar Allan Poe was a writer who wrote stories and poems. Edgar Allan Poe was an *American* writer.

1. *Edgar Allan Poe was an American writer who wrote stories and poems.*

Here are some possible combinations.
1. The mother of Edgar Allan Poe died three years after he was born. She was *young.*
2. Poe was taken in by Mrs. John Allan and her husband. Their taking him in was *fortunate.* (Add *–ly* to *fortunate.*) **2. Fortunately,**
3. Poe created stories. He created *detective* stories.
4. Poe inspired the author of the Sherlock Holmes stories. The author had *talent.* (Add *–ed* to *talent.*) **4. talented**
5. Poe had theories about the writing of fiction. His theories were *original.*

Combining Sentences

OBJECTIVES

- To combine sentences by inserting words and phrases
- To combine sentences by creating compound subjects and verbs
- To combine sentences by creating compound sentences
- To combine sentences by creating complex sentences

Quotation for the Day

"That writer does the most, who gives his reader the most knowledge, and takes from him the least time."

(Charles Caleb Colton, 1780–1832, English writer and clergyman)

Write the quotation above on the chalkboard and ask students to rephrase it in their own words. [Here is a possible response: *The best writers give a lot of information without taking up a lot of my time.*] Guide students in discussing some of the obstacles they meet in reading for information and in writing informative essays. Explain that this chapter will provide them with some strategies for writing clearly and concisely.

Internet
- go.hrw.com (keyword: EOLang)

RESOURCES

Writing Effective Sentences
Practice
- *Sentences and Paragraphs,* WS. pp. 15-28

Extension
- *Combining Sentences,* WS. pp. 1–20

332 Writing Effective Sentences

Meeting
INDIVIDUAL NEEDS

LEARNERS HAVING DIFFICULTY

Students may not understand or retain terms such as *appositive phrase, conjunctive adverb,* and *coordinating conjunction,* and yet they may be able to use sentence-combining techniques correctly. Using simple language, such as "moving a group of words from one sentence to another," instead of "inserting a prepositional phrase," may be more effective.

Relating to Grammar

Students may need a review of participles and their function. Remind students that there are two types of participles, *present participles,* which end in *–ing,* and *past participles,* most of which end in *–d* or *–ed.* Also, participles can be used as adjectives describing a person, place, thing, or idea. Here are a few examples: *paved driveway, estimated cost, moving truck.*

| COMPUTER TIP

You can use a word-processing program's cut and paste commands to find the best placement for a participial phrase within a sentence.

Exercise 2 **Combining Sentences by Inserting Words**

In Exercise 1, the words you needed to insert were italicized. Now, try using your own judgment to combine sentences. There may be more than one way to combine each set; do what seems best to you. Add commas and change the forms of words when needed.

EXAMPLE
1. Luis Valdez is a talented and famous playwright. He is a Mexican American.

1. *Luis Valdez is a talented and famous Mexican American playwright.*

Possible combinations are shown below.

1. Valdez was born in Delano, ~~Delano is in~~ California. **2.** migrant
2. He grew up in a family of farm workers. ~~They were migrant workers.~~
3. As a child, Valdez began to work in the fields. ~~He was six years old.~~
4. He champions the cause of underpaid migrant farm workers. ~~He also champions the cause of migrant farm workers who suffer from overwork.~~ **3.** six-year-old **4.** , overworked
5. He organized the Farm Workers' Theater, a troupe of actors and musicians. ~~The troupe travels.~~ **5.** traveling

Inserting Phrases

You also can combine closely related sentences by taking a phrase from one sentence and inserting it into another sentence.

Prepositional Phrases

A **prepositional phrase,** a preposition with its object and any modifiers of that object, can usually be inserted into another sentence with no changes. Just omit some of the words in one of the sentences.

ORIGINAL   Twelve million immigrants came to the shores of the United States. They came through Ellis Island.

REVISED   Twelve million immigrants came to the shores of the United States **through Ellis Island.**

Participial Phrases

A **participial phrase** contains a verb form that usually ends in *–ing* or *–ed.* The entire phrase acts as an adjective, modifying a noun or a pronoun. Sometimes, you can change the verb from one sentence into a participle by adding *–ing* or *–ed* or by dropping the helping verb if the main verb already ends in *–ing* or *–ed.* Then, you can combine the two

---

MINI-LESSON

Sentence Style. Your students probably already have an intuitive sense of sentence style—when they are looking at someone else's writing. Show them the following sentences and ask the questions that follow.

Lacrosse is a game. Lacrosse is played with sticks with nets on the ends. Lacrosse was first played by the Iroquois. Lacrosse gets its name from the French. Lacrosse comes from the French words for "the hooked stick."

sentences. Place the participial phrase close to the noun or pronoun it will modify to avoid confusing your reader.

ORIGINAL   Many immigrants faced long months of waiting at Ellis Island. They were weakened by their journeys.

REVISED   Many immigrants, **weakened by their journeys,** faced long months of waiting at Ellis Island.

Appositive Phrases

An *appositive phrase* usually follows a noun or pronoun and helps to identify it. Sometimes you can combine sentences that have nouns or pronouns referring to the same thing by changing one of the sentences to an appositive phrase.

ORIGINAL   My grandfather was an immigrant. My grandfather brought with him photographs that are now souvenirs.

REVISED   My grandfather, **an immigrant,** brought with him photographs that are now souvenirs.

Exercise 3   **Combining Sentences by Inserting Phrases**

Revise each of the following sets of sentences to create one sentence. There may be more than one way to combine the sentences. In numbers 1 through 5, the words you need to insert are italicized. In numbers 6 through 10, change the forms of words or omit words as indicated in parentheses, and add commas wherever they are needed.

EXAMPLE   **1.** Auguste Piccard was a Swiss physicist who studied the upper atmosphere. He studied it *by going up in balloons.*

   1. *Auguste Piccard was a Swiss physicist who studied the upper atmosphere by going up in balloons.*

Possible combinations appear below.

1. Auguste Piccard was an inventor, scientist, and explorer. He was *from Switzerland.*

2. Piccard once spent sixteen hours in a balloon. He was *floating across Germany and France.*

Reference Note

For more information on **phrases,** see page 440.

Combining Sentences   **333**

Combining Sentences   **333**

Relating to Usage

Explain to students that when a singular subject and plural subject are joined by *or* or *nor*, the verb should agree with the subject nearer the verb.

EXAMPLES

Neither the roller coaster nor the game *booths were* open.

Neither the game booths nor the *roller coaster was* open.

3. Piccard attended the Swiss Institute of Technology. The institute is *in Zurich, Switzerland*.

4. Piccard was a young man when he became a professor. He became a professor *at the Swiss Institute*.

5. Piccard created an important invention. ~~He invented an airtight gondola.~~ **5.** , an airtight gondola **6.** Attached to a balloon,

6. The gondola took Piccard ten miles into the air. ~~The gondola was attached to a balloon.~~ (Omit *The gondola was*.) **7.** Studying electricity,

7. Piccard then made numerous balloon trips. ~~He studied electricity.~~ (Change *studied* to *studying*.) **8.** Designing a deep-sea diving ship,

8. Piccard turned his interest to the ocean depths. ~~He designed a deep-sea diving ship.~~ (Change *designed* to *designing*.)

9. Piccard and his son Jacques went two miles below the surface of the Adriatic Sea. ~~They went in 1953.~~ (Omit *They went.*) **9.** In 1953,

10. Another deep-sea diving ship went almost ten miles below the surface of the ocean. ~~It set the world's depth record in 1960.~~ (Change *set* to *setting*.) **10.** Setting the world's depth record in 1960,

Using Compound Subjects and Verbs

Another way to combine sentences is to make compound subjects and verbs. First, look for sentences that have the same subject or the same verb. Then, make the subject or verb compound by adding a coordinating conjunction such as *and, but, for, or, nor, so,* or *yet.*

ORIGINAL   The Angles were fierce people. The Saxons were fierce people. [different subjects with same verb]

REVISED   The **Angles and the Saxons** were fierce people. [compound subject with same verb]

ORIGINAL   The Angles and Saxons invaded Britain. The Angles and Saxons conquered Britain. [different verbs with same subject]

REVISED   The Angles and Saxons **invaded and conquered** Britain. [compound verb with same subject]

ORIGINAL   The Angles conquered Britain. The Saxons also conquered Britain. They both pushed back the native Celts. [different subjects and different verbs]

REVISED   The **Angles and the Saxons conquered** Britain and **pushed back** the native Celts. [compound subject and compound verb]

334   Chapter 10   Writing Effective Sentences

Learning for Life

Writing Effective E-mail. Tell students that one advantage of the Internet is that they can communicate their ideas instantly to many people. These people might be friends or relatives, but they might also be politi- cians or business owners. Remind students that effective e-mail is short and informative.

Work with students to create a set of rules for e-mail. Some rules might be:

NOTE When you combine sentences by making compound subjects and compound verbs, make sure that your new subjects and verbs agree in number.

ORIGINAL The dialect of the Angles is an ancestor of Modern English. The dialect of the Saxons is also an ancestor of Modern English.

REVISED The **dialects** of the Angles and the Saxons **are** ancestors of Modern English. [The plural subject *dialects* takes the plural verb *are*.]

Reference Note

For more information on **agreement of subjects and verbs,** see page 493.

Exercise 4 **Creating Compound Subjects and Compound Verbs** Possible combinations appear below.

Here are five sets of short sentences. Combine each set into one sentence that has a compound subject, a compound verb, or a compound subject and a compound verb.

1. Bananas and coconuts are tropical fruits.
1. Bananas are a tropical fruit. Coconuts are also a tropical fruit.
2. Brazil produces bananas. India produces bananas. Both countries export bananas.   2. Brazil and India produce and export bananas.
3. Some bananas are cooked as vegetables are. They are eaten as vegetables are.   3. and
4. By A.D. 600, the Egyptians were eating coconuts. Indians and Koreans were also eating coconuts.
5. Coconuts are not a major crop in the United States. Bananas are not a major crop in the United States, either.
5. Neither coconuts nor bananas are a major crop in the United States.

Creating a Compound Sentence

You can combine two sentences by creating a compound sentence. A *compound sentence* is two or more simple sentences linked by

- a comma and a coordinating conjunction

  or

- a semicolon

  or

- a semicolon and a conjunctive adverb

Before linking two thoughts in a compound sentence, make sure that the thoughts are clearly related and equal in importance. Be sure that you do not link two thoughts in a compound sentence when one thought is clearly more important than the other.

Reference Note

For more information on **compound sentences,** see page 481.

TEACHING (TIP)

Creating a Compound Sentence
You may want to introduce this section by drawing a seesaw on the chalkboard. Explain to students that in creating a compound sentence, both ideas included in the sentence should be equal in importance. Ask students to imagine placing each idea on the seesaw, one on each end. Have them visualize the balance between the two ideas. If one idea were more important, then the seesaw would tip down on that side. In such a case, the ideas probably do not belong in the same sentence.

Combining Sentences **335**

- be brief and to the point
- do not use unnecessary words
- correct any errors before sending

- include the writer's name and e-mail address for a reply

Relating to Literature

To demonstrate how writers use compound sentences, have students read the chase scenes in Richard Connell's short story "The Most Dangerous Game." Then, ask students to consider why Connell uses so many semicolons to combine sentences. Explain that Connell uses semicolons to separate sentences that describe events or thoughts occurring almost simultaneously. Using periods would cause readers to stop fully at the end of each sentence; semicolons allow the reader to continue reading at a quick pace.

Using conjunctive adverbs to join sentences allows you to emphasize the relationship between ideas. Some of the frequently used conjunctive adverbs are *also, besides, consequently, however, meanwhile, moreover, otherwise, then,* and *therefore.*

ORIGINAL	The cat knocked over a lamp. The dog chewed up my shoe.
REVISED	The cat knocked over a lamp**, and** the dog chewed up my shoe. [comma and coordinating conjunction]
	The cat knocked over a lamp**;** the dog chewed up my shoe. [semicolon]
	The cat knocked over a lamp**; meanwhile,** the dog chewed up my shoe. [semicolon and conjunctive adverb]

NOTE You can use the coordinating conjunctions *and, but, nor, for, yet, or,* and *so* to form compound sentences. However, you should avoid overusing them. When you join two sentences with a coordinating conjunction, remember to use a comma before the conjunction.

Exercise 5 Combining Simple Sentences to Create Compound Sentences

The sentences in the following pairs are closely related in meaning. Using the methods you have learned, combine each pair into a compound sentence. Add commas and semicolons where necessary. Possible combinations appear below.

1. Numbers from the United States 2000 census have been released. They show a country becoming more diverse. **1.** , and

2. For the first time, families could choose more than one racial group on the census form. We now have a better picture of the nation's complex ethnic and racial makeup. **2.** ; therefore,

3. Of all ethnic groups, Hispanics are the fastest growing. People of many racial backgrounds consider themselves Hispanic. **3.** , for

4. The number of Asians has also increased over the last ten years. Asians in the United States now number twelve million. **4.** ;

5. The vast majority of the people who live in the United States were born here. Of every ten residents, one is an immigrant. **5.** , but

Creating a Complex Sentence

A *complex sentence* includes one independent clause—a clause that can stand alone as a sentence. It also has one or more *subordinate clauses*—clauses that cannot stand alone as sentences.

Adjective Clauses

You can make a sentence into an *adjective clause* by inserting *who, which,* or *that* in place of the subject. Then you use the adjective clause to provide information about a preceding noun or pronoun.

336 **Chapter 10** Writing Effective Sentences

TEACHING TIP

Creating a Complex Sentence
Some students, despite their proficiency with the meanings of most subordinating conjunctions, struggle with the conjunction *although.* Often, telling students that the word means "even though" does not help. Explain that *although* signals a situation that is the opposite of what the reader expects. Provide straightforward examples based on everyday experiences like the following ones:

1. Although I ate a big breakfast, I am still hungry.

2. Although I ran five miles every day, I still did not lose weight.

ORIGINAL	Many people are afraid of bats. They are usually harmless creatures.
REVISED	Many people are afraid of bats, **which are usually harmless creatures.**

> **NOTE** When you use adjective clauses to combine sentences, remember that *which* is not used to refer to a person, only to places and things. Use *who, whom, whose,* and *that* to refer to people.

Adverb Clauses

You can turn one sentence into an ***adverb clause*** and combine it with another sentence. The adverb clause may modify a verb, an adjective, or another adverb in the sentence (the independent clause) to which it is attached.

Adverb clauses begin with subordinating conjunctions like *after, although, because, if, when,* and *where.* You have to choose these conjunctions carefully. They show the relationship between the ideas in the adverb clause and those in the independent clause. For example, *when* shows how the ideas are related in time, *where* shows how the ideas are related in space, and *although* shows under what conditions the ideas occurred. When you use an adverb clause at the beginning of a sentence, you need to separate it from the independent clause with a comma.

ORIGINAL	Some people think bats are dangerous. They rarely attack humans.
REVISED	**Although some people think bats are dangerous,** they rarely attack humans.

Noun Clauses

You can make a sentence into a ***noun clause*** and insert it into another sentence just as you would an ordinary noun. You create a noun clause by inserting a word like *that, how, what, which,* or *who* at the beginning of the sentence. When you place the noun clause in the other sentence, you may have to change or remove some words.

ORIGINAL	Dracula is such a frightening character. This does not help the bat's reputation.
REVISED	**That Dracula is such a frightening character** does not help the bat's reputation. [The word *that* introduces the noun clause, which becomes the subject of the verb *does help.*]
REVISED	**What does not help the bat's reputation** is that Dracula is such a frightening character. [The word *what* introduces the noun clause, which becomes the subject of the verb *is.*]

⌐ TIPS & TRICKS ⌐

This in the original is an unclear (general) pronoun reference. General references can be corrected by creating a noun clause, as in the revised sentence. For more on **clear pronoun references,** see page 565.

Combining Sentences **337**

For more on **clear pronoun references,** see page 565.

Cooperative Learning

Rule Review. To help students write and punctuate sentences that contain adjective, adverb, and noun clauses, review the related grammar and mechanics rules in small groups. Then, ask each group to write several original sentences using each clause type. You might want to be available for help as students write. Cooperative, mixed-ability group experiences may also help improve writing skills and give more confidence to students.

TECHNOLOGY TIP

If you have the equipment and software for creating Web pages, invite students to create a class Clause Clue Word Web page. On this page, students could list words that are indicators of adjective clauses, noun clauses, or subordinate clauses. Each word on the list could also be a link to another page that explains what the word is (*relative pronoun, subordinating conjunction,* or *introductory word*), what kind of clause it indicates, and an example sentence. Consider assigning students to clause clue word teams, with each team creating its own list. *Students should not need to access external Internet sites to create their Web page. Keep in mind that Internet resources are sometimes public forums and their content can be unpredictable.*

Exercise 6 **Combining Simple Sentences to Create Complex Sentences** Possible combinations are shown below.

Following are five sets of short, choppy sentences that need revision. Use subordinate clauses to combine each set of sentences into a single complex sentence. You may see different ways to combine some of the sets; choose the way that seems best to you. You may need to change or delete some words to make smooth combinations.

1. The shark is a member of a fish family. The family includes the largest and fiercest fish.   **1.** the / that
2. Most sharks have long bodies, wedge-shaped heads, and pointed back fins. The back fins sometimes stick out of the water.   **2.** that
3. Sharks live mostly in warm seas. Some sharks have been found in bodies of cold water.   **3.** Although
4. The whale shark is harmless to people. It feeds on plankton.   **4.** , which feeds on plankton,
5. However, many sharks are ruthless killers. They feed on flesh.   **5.** that

Review A **Revising a Paragraph by Combining Sentences**

Using all of the sentence-combining techniques you have learned, revise and rewrite the following short paragraph. Use your judgment about what sentences to combine and how to combine them. Work for clear, varied sentences that read smoothly; however, do not change the meaning of the original paragraph.   Here is a possible revision.

a series of huge stones

that
It
, and

astronomical

directly

Stonehenge is in southwestern England. It is a series of stones. They are huge stones. They weigh as much as fifty tons each. Stonehenge was built about five thousand years ago. The stones were moved to their present site. They were moved by as many as one thousand people. There are many theories about the purpose of the stones. One popular theory is that the stones served as an observatory. The observatory was astronomical. At one point in the summer, the sun rises over one of the stones. It rises directly over that stone.

Improving Sentence Style

In the first part of this chapter, you learned some techniques for making smooth sentence combinations. Now you will learn how to style your sentences by making them clear, balanced, and varied.

Using Parallel Structure

When you combine several related ideas in one sentence, it is important to make sure that your combinations are balanced. You create balance in a sentence by using the same form or part of speech to express each idea. For example, you balance a noun with a noun, a phrase with a phrase, and a clause with a clause. This balance is called parallelism, or *parallel structure.*

NOT PARALLEL	I am not much of an athlete, but I like softball, soccer, and playing hockey. [two nouns and a phrase]
PARALLEL	I am not much of an athlete, but I like **softball, soccer, and hockey.** [three nouns]
NOT PARALLEL	Dominic does not have enough time to play soccer, join the debating team, and band. [two phrases and a noun]
PARALLEL	Dominic does not have enough time **to play soccer, to join the debating team,** and **to participate in band.** [three phrases]
NOT PARALLEL	He said that he would meet you at the soccer field and not to be late. [clause and phrase]
PARALLEL	He said **that he would meet you at the soccer field** and **that you should not be late.** [two clauses]

Improving Sentence Style **339**

Improving Sentence Style

OBJECTIVES

- To revise sentences to create parallel structure
- To revise stringy and wordy sentences
- To vary sentence beginnings

Quotation for the Day

"Trifles make perfection, and perfection is no trifle."

(Michelangelo Buonarroti, 1475–1564, Italian Renaissance sculptor, painter, and poet as quoted by C. C. Colton in *Lacon*)

After explaining that trifles are things of little importance, ask students to think about Michelangelo's contradiction before putting it into their own words. Students may write their paraphrase or read it aloud. Ask students how the idea applies to their own writing. Guide them toward understanding that in revising, proofreading, and polishing their own writing they are attending to the small things, the trifles, that, once corrected, make for perfection.

Meeting INDIVIDUAL NEEDS

INCLUSION

Some students will learn to identify problems with parallel structure more quickly if sentences are presented graphically. Ask a helper to assist students in seeing the imbalance in non-parallel sentences by identifying and labeling the nouns, phrases, and clauses. Here is an example:

I'm not much of an athlete, but I like softball (noun), soccer (noun), and to play hockey (phrase).

| Exercise 7 | Revising Sentences to Create Parallel Structure |

Bring balance to the following sentences by putting the ideas in parallel form. You may need to add or delete some words. If a sentence is already correct, write *C*. Here are possible answers.

1. Paris, the capital of France, is famous for its history, culture, and ~~eating in~~ excellent restaurants.
2. The Seine River runs through the city and supplies water to all Parisians. 2. C
3. Visiting the Notre Dame Cathedral, walking through the Louvre Museum, and ʌthe Eiffel Tower are all favorite pastimes of tourists.
4. It is interesting that Paris has always attracted artists and ʌrefugees⊙ ~~have always been welcome.~~ 3. seeing   4. welcomed
5. Many famous Americans, including Ernest Hemingway, lived and ʌ ~~were writing~~ in Paris during the 1920s.   5. wrote

Revising Stringy Sentences

Linking together related ideas is a good way to bring variety to your writing. If you overdo it, however, you may end up with a *stringy sentence.*

    A **stringy sentence** just goes on and on. It usually has too many independent clauses strung together with coordinating conjunctions like *and* or *but.* Since all the ideas are treated equally, your reader may have trouble seeing how they are related.

    There are three ways you can fix a stringy sentence. You can

- break the sentence into two or more sentences
- turn some of the independent clauses into subordinate clauses or phrases
- use a combination of the above strategies

STRINGY   The fire alarm bell rang, and everyone started to file out of school, but then our principal came down the hall, and he said the bell had been rung by mistake, and we went back to class.

BETTER   The fire alarm bell rang, and everyone started to file out of school. Then our principal came down the hall to say the bell had been rung by mistake. We went back to class.

BETTER   When the fire alarm bell rang, everyone started to file out of school. Then our principal came down the hall. He said the bell had been rung by mistake, and we went back to class.

Exercise 8 — Revising Stringy Sentences

Decide which of the following sentences are stringy and need revision. Then, revise the stringy sentences by (1) breaking each sentence into two or more sentences, (2) turning some independent clauses into subordinate clauses, or (3) turning some independent clauses into phrases. If you find a sentence that is effective and does not need to be improved, write *C*. Possible revisions are shown below.

EXAMPLE
1. Alexandre Gustave Eiffel was a French engineer, and he designed the Eiffel Tower, and he designed the frame for the Statue of Liberty, but his greatest accomplishment may have been proving that metal was an important building material.

1. *Alexandre Gustave Eiffel was a French engineer who designed the Eiffel Tower and the frame for the Statue of Liberty. His greatest accomplishment may have been proving that metal was an important building material.*

1. Alexandre Gustave Eiffel was a famous Frenchman, and he was born in 1832, and he died in 1923.   **1.** who

2. Eiffel was an engineer, and he designed the Eiffel Tower, and it was built for the World's Fair of 1889.

3. Eiffel's chief interest was bridges, and the Eiffel Tower displays his bridge-designing skills, and so does another historical monument, and it is a monument that you know.   **4.** C

4. In 1885, Eiffel used his engineering knowledge to design part of a great American symbol, the Statue of Liberty in New York Harbor.

5. Toward the end of his life, Eiffel studied the effects of air on airplanes, and then in 1912, he built a wind tunnel and an aerodynamics laboratory, and later he conducted experiments from the Eiffel Tower, which is now a favorite tourist attraction.

Revising Wordy Sentences

If someone says, "It would please me greatly if you would diminish the volume of your verbalizing during the time I am perusing this reading material," you might wonder what language is being spoken. How much easier and clearer to say "Please be quieter while I am reading."

Here are three tips for creating sentences that are not too wordy.

- *Do not use more words than you need.*

- *Do not use fancy words where simple ones will do.*

- *Do not repeat yourself unless it is absolutely necessary.*

Improving Sentence Style   **341**

WORDY   My friend Ken is a talented drummer who plays the drums with great skill.

IMPROVED   My friend Ken is a talented drummer.

WORDY   In the event that we are unable to go to the movie, we can play basketball at Alicia's house.

IMPROVED   If we cannot go to the movie, we can play basketball at Alicia's house.

Exercise 9 **Revising Wordy Sentences**

Exercise 9 **Revising Wordy Sentences**

The writer of the following letter wants to make a complaint, but the wordiness of the letter gets in the way. Revise the letter, making it clearer and more effective. You may add details if you wish.

```
Dear Mr. and Mrs. Wilson,
    At this point in time, it is my unhappy
duty to inform you of the fact that I will
no longer be available to baby-sit Charles.
On the evening of July 13, I was hired by
you to perform the duties of baby sitter
for your three-year-old son. These duties
were performed by me to the best of my
ability. However, I do not feel that any
baby sitter should be in a position of hav-
ing to deal with the threat of harm to the
baby sitter's person. I feel that Charles's
hurling of objects at my person and his
action of locking me in the closet were
threats to my safety. The situation being
what it is, I feel I cannot safely perform
my duties, and I will no longer place
myself in danger by sitting with your son.
                        Sincerely,
                        Miguel Garza
```

ANSWER

Here is a possible revision.

Dear Mr. and Mrs. Wilson,

I am sorry to tell you that I won't be able to baby-sit Charles anymore. You hired me to baby-sit him on July 13, and I did the best job I could; however, Charles behaved very badly. He threw things at me and locked me in a closet. Because he posed a danger to me, I won't baby-sit him again.

Sincerely,

Miguel Garza

Critical Thinking

Synthesis. To help students be more alert to wordiness in their writing, have them create wordy sentences from short sayings or proverbs. Provide students with a book of famous quotations and a thesaurus and ask them to choose a saying or proverb and transform it into a wordy sentence. You may make this activity into a contest by posting the wordy versions and having students guess at the original proverbs. Here is an example:

Currency is many things but it is first and foremost and above all things the radical of all terrible grievances. [*Money is the root of all evil.*]

Varying Sentence Beginnings

Basic English sentences begin with a subject followed by a verb. However, beginning every sentence with a subject makes your writing dull. Notice how boring the following paragraph sounds.

```
    The theater was packed. Jan and I managed
to find our seats. The play began thirty min-
utes late. We were bored. We read the pro-
gram four times. Jan wanted to find out the
```

reason for the delay. She asked an usher.
The usher was amused. The usher said that
the star's costume had been damaged by her
dog. We laughed because the play was <u>Cats</u>.

Now, notice how much more interesting the same paragraph
sounds with varied sentence beginnings. To create the varied beginnings, the writer has combined sentences. Some sentences became
words, some became phrases, and others became subordinate clauses.

Although the theater was packed, Jan and
I managed to find our seats. The play began
thirty minutes late. Bored, we read the program four times. To find out the reason for
the delay, Jan asked an usher. Amused, the
usher said that the star's costume had been
damaged by her dog. We laughed because the
play was <u>Cats</u>.

Varying Sentence Beginnings
Single–Word Modifiers
Excitedly, Marcia opened her presents. [adverb]
Hungry, the family stopped at the restaurant. [adjective]
Phrases
With tears of joy, Carla received her prize. [prepositional phrase]
Smiling happily, Tanya told us the good news. [participial phrase]
To make good grades, you must study. [infinitive phrase]
Subordinate Clauses
Because the coach was angry, the team ran ten laps. [adverb clause]
When Tom found the kitten on his doorstep, he decided to keep it. [adverb clause]

NOTE If you use a prepositional phrase telling *when, where,* or *how* to
vary your sentence beginnings, you can sometimes put the verb of the
sentence before the subject. In the following example sentence, the
subject is underlined once, the verb twice.

EXAMPLE   Down the street <u><u>rumbled</u></u> an old <u>cart</u>.

TIPS & TRICKS

To check your writing for
varied sentence begin-
nings, put parentheses
around the first five words
of each of your sentences.
If most of your subjects and
verbs fall within the parentheses, you need to begin
more of your sentences
with single-word modi-
fiers, phrases, or subordinate clauses.

Crossing the Curriculum

Physical Education. Students may
benefit from a comparison of the
strategy of varying sentence beginnings to strategies players use in different sports in laying up shots,
scoring goals, or throwing pitches.
Ask them to consider why a football
player changes runs for the goal, why
a basketball player uses different
approaches to the net, or why a
pitcher varies pitches. Students will
probably comment on how the different strategies keep the opponents
guessing or how they are a response
to the situation as the player sees it.
Guide students to see how the same
comments apply to writing sentences
with varied beginnings. If possible, use
videotaped examples of different
sports strategies, which your school
coaches should be able to provide.

Meeting INDIVIDUAL NEEDS

ADVANCED LEARNERS
Encourage students who are avid readers to write a five- or six-sentence paragraph about any topic in the style of
their favorite author. Then, have them
display their text next to an excerpt
from a work by the author. Ask students
to write a brief statement about the
author's style (students should consider
how the author used any of the strategies mentioned in this chapter, such as
parallel structure and varied sentence
beginnings) and any problems they
encountered in mimicking the author's
style.

Exercise 10 Varying Sentence Beginnings

ANSWERS
Here are some possible answers.

1. In many different parts of the world, animals are in danger of extinction.

2. A small animal, the aye-aye is related to the monkey, and it is one of the less well-known of the endangered animals.

3. Because the rain forest on its home island is being destroyed, the aye-aye is endangered.

4. To see the desman, a water-dwelling mammal, you must travel to the Pyrenees, Portugal, or the former Soviet Union.

5. By damming mountain streams, people are threatening the desmans' survival.

6. Although the giant otter of South America is protected, poachers continue to threaten its survival.

7. Cautious, mountain lions generally stay away from humans, who hunt them relentlessly.

8. Because its home is being damaged by acid rain, the great peacock moth of Europe is in trouble.

9. Expert hunters, wolves prey on large animals.

10. Sadly, gray wolves are an endangered species.

Exercise 10

ALTERNATIVE LESSON
Ask students to use the facts in the ten sentences of Exercise 10 to write a paragraph about endangered animals. They do not need to use all the sentences, but they should organize the ones they do use into an interesting paragraph, varying sentence beginnings.

Exercise 10 Varying Sentence Beginnings

The following sentences are all good, but they would make a boring paragraph. Here is your chance to practice varying sentence beginnings. The notes in parentheses tell you whether to start your revised sentence with a single-word modifier, a phrase, or a clause. In some cases, you may also want to add or delete a word to make the sentence sound better.

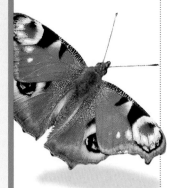

1. Animals are in danger of extinction in many different parts of the world. (phrase)
2. The aye-aye is a small animal related to the monkey, and it is one of the less well-known of the endangered animals. (phrase)
3. The aye-aye is endangered because the rain forest on its home island is being destroyed. (subordinate clause)
4. You must travel to the Pyrenees, Portugal, or the former Soviet Union to see the desman, a water-dwelling mammal. (phrase)
5. People are threatening the desman's survival by damming mountain streams. (phrase)
6. The giant otter of South America is protected, but poachers continue to threaten its survival. (subordinate clause)
7. Mountain lions are cautious and generally stay away from humans, who hunt them relentlessly. (single-word modifier)
8. The great peacock moth of Europe is in trouble because its home is being damaged by acid rain. (subordinate clause)
9. Wolves are expert hunters, and they prey on large animals. (phrase)
10. Gray wolves, sadly, are an endangered species. (single-word modifier)

Exercise 11 Revising Sentences to Create Variety

Use what you have learned about varying sentence beginnings to revise the following paragraph. Reword some sentences so that they begin with single-word modifiers, phrases, or clauses. Some sentences may be reworded in several ways; choose the way that seems best to you. (Consult the chart on page 343 for help.)

> Ocean animals unfortunately are often on endangered-species lists. Penguins are at risk in oceans of the Southern Hemisphere. Many penguin species have problems today because of oil pollution and commercial fishing. Turtles are endangered because they are slaughtered for food and for their

beautiful, highly prized shells. Lobsters become threatened when people overfish. Mediterranean monk seals also are threatened by increased land development and tourism.

Review B Revising a Paragraph

The following paragraphs have many of the problems you have reviewed in this section. Show your writing style by rewriting and revising the paragraphs (1) to correct nonparallel structures, (2) to correct stringy and wordy sentences, and (3) to vary sentence beginnings. You may add or delete details as necessary.

One time in the recent past, we went on a picnic in Big Bend National Park in Texas. It had rained heavily all night north of the park. A friend of ours, Mrs. Brown, went with us. She had lived in that part of Texas for a large number of years. She knew all about what to expect if it rained. She told us that there could be a flash flood in the park and about how the park could be dangerous even if it did not rain there because the water could run across the dry desert sand.

Mrs. Brown made us turn our cars around to face in the other direction because she wanted us to be able to leave the low area quickly if a flood came. The sun was shining with great brightness, and everyone thought Mrs. Brown was crazy, and we started to eat our picnic.

A very high wall of water four feet high came toward us suddenly. We jumped into the cars and getting away just in time. We were glad to be alive, and we thanked Mrs. Brown.

ANSWER
Here is a possible revision.

Unfortunately, ocean animals are often on endangered-species lists. Because of oil pollution and commercial fishing, many penguin species in oceans of the Southern Hemisphere are at risk. Turtles are endangered because they are slaughtered for food and for their beautiful, highly prized shells. When people overfish, lobsters become threatened. Also, Mediterranean monk seals are threatened by increased land development and tourism.

Review B Revising a Paragraph

ANSWER
Here is a possible revision.

Recently, we went on a picnic in Big Bend National Park in Texas with our friend, Mrs. Brown. North of the park, it had rained heavily all night. Having lived in that part of Texas for years, Mrs. Brown knew what to expect. She said that even if it didn't rain in the park, there could be a flash flood because the water could run across the dry desert sand.

She made us turn our cars around so we could leave the low area quickly if a flood came. The sun was shining brightly, and everyone thought Mrs. Brown was crazy, but as we started to eat, suddenly a wall of water four feet high came toward us. We jumped into the cars and got away just in time. We were glad to be alive, and we thanked Mrs. Brown.

RESOURCES

Writing Effective Sentences
Assessment

■ *Assessment Package*
  —*Chapter Tests,* Ch. 10
  —*Chapter Tests in Standardized Test Formats,* Ch. 10

■ *Test Generator (One-Stop Planner CD-ROM)* 🎵

CHAPTER

11

Understanding Paragraph Structure

PREVIEWING THE CHAPTER

■ Paragraphs are important building blocks of writing. In this chapter, students will learn that paragraphs can include a main idea, a topic sentence, supporting details, and a clincher sentence. Students will explore the qualities of good paragraphs: unity, coherence, and elaboration. Finally, students will practice how to divide longer pieces of writing into paragraphs. Students may look back at the paragraph structure explained in this chapter as they complete written assignments throughout the year.

internet**connect**

go. hrw .com

GO TO: go.hrw.com
KEYWORD: EOLang

What Is a Paragraph?

A paragraph is made up of sentences grouped together for a reason—usually to present and support a single **main idea.** Like you, paragraphs are individuals—each has a purpose of its own. However, each of the paragraphs in a composition is also like a member of a team, working together with other paragraphs to develop ideas. You might think of a paragraph as a link in a chain—separating, yet connecting, ideas.

Why Use a Paragraph?

Did you know that paragraphs have been around since the fourth century B.C.? The paragraph was used in ancient Greek texts to mark each place where a new topic was introduced. Today, paragraphs are used in much the same way—to divide an essay or article into blocks of separate thoughts or to divide a story into a series of events. Think for a moment how hard it would be to read a huge block of uninterrupted text. Where would your eyes rest? Wouldn't it be difficult to separate one complete thought from another?

CHAPTER RESOURCES

Planning

■ *One-Stop Planner CD-ROM*

Practice and Extension

■ *Sentences and Paragraphs,* for Ch. 11

Internet

■ go.hrw.com (keyword: EOLang)

go. hrw .com

Evaluation and Assessment

■ *Assessment Package*
  —*Chapter Tests,* Ch. 11
  —*Chapter Tests in Standardized Test Formats,* Ch. 11

■ *Test Generator (One-Stop Planner CD-ROM)*

In fact, even though we do not think much today about why we use paragraphs, they are very important tools. Paragraphs provide a visual sign to the reader that a new thought—or a new speaker—is coming. They also allow readers to take a little pause to digest what they've read so far. When you are writing, you might think of paragraphs as a way to lead your reader by the hand through your essay.

What Are the Parts of a Body Paragraph?

Although some paragraphs—especially in narrative writing—do not have a central focus, most paragraphs do emphasize one **main idea.** Paragraphs like this, often called **body paragraphs,** usually have three major parts: a *topic sentence* (a statement of the paragraph's main idea); additional *supporting sentences* that elaborate on and support the topic sentence; and (often, but not always) a concluding, or *clincher sentence.*

The Main Idea

Together, the sentences in the paragraph make its main idea clear. If the paragraph is part of a longer piece of writing, the surrounding paragraphs help you understand the main idea. Read the following paragraph, and try to determine what its main idea is.

> Those of us who live in the city should be grateful to our language, because the words that have to do with the city are usually flattering. We city-dwellers, at least in ancient days, were supposed to be more *civil* in our manners and more *civilized* in our ways than others, for both of these words, *civil* and *civilized*, are the eventual children of the Latin term *civis* which meant "one who lives in a city." All city folks, you see, were regarded as automatically cultured and well housebroken. And from ancient Latin we have borrowed the word *urbs* which also meant city, and we used it to create the word *urbane* which describes the smooth manners that were presumed to be characteristic of *metropolitan* society. The
> *(continued)*

What Are the Parts of a Body Paragraph?

OBJECTIVES

- To identify main ideas and topic sentences in paragraphs
- To identify and collect different types of supporting details
- To recognize and write clincher sentences

Quotation for the Day

"The house praises the carpenter."

(Ralph Waldo Emerson, 1803–1882, American poet, essayist, and philosopher)

In discussing responses to this quotation, be sure students understand that Emerson is suggesting that a house "appreciates" the good work a carpenter puts into building it. Ask students how this quotation relates to writing. Students should understand that a piece of writing requires well-constructed parts—such as clear and well-supported points—just as a house requires good carpentry to stand. Explain that students will learn how to build effective paragraphs in this chapter.

What Are the Parts of a Body Paragraph?
Practice

- *Sentences and Paragraphs,* WS. pp. 41, 42, 43

INCLUSION

Find a nonfiction paragraph at or slightly below your students' reading level. Have a helper show the following metacognitive questions to students before you read the paragraph to them. After reading, have students work with the helper to answer the questions. This chapter will cover these and other topics related to paragraphs:

1. What do you think the paragraph is about? How do you know?

2. What kinds of details do you notice in the paragraph?

3. Why do you think the author ends the paragraph the way he or she does?

4. After examining this paragraph, what can you conclude about how paragraphs are constructed?

TEACHING TIP

Placement of a Topic Sentence
Provide additional examples of topic sentence placement. Ask each student to bring to class a sample of text from another subject area. Have students work in pairs to find examples of topic sentences at the beginnings of paragraphs and at the ends of paragraphs. Help the class tally their findings to see which placement is more common. Get students to speculate on how authors make decisions about the placement of topic sentences.

STYLE **TIP**

To create surprise or to summarize ideas, you may want to place a topic sentence at or near the end of the paragraph.

COMPUTER TIP

When you are revising a paragraph, try moving the topic sentence to various locations within the paragraph by using your word-processing program's Cut and Paste commands. You can then analyze which placement of the topic sentence is the most effective.

(continued)

Greek parts of the word *metropolitan* are *metro-*, "mother," and *polis*, "city," so a *metropolis* is the "mother city" or the chief or capital city of a country, and he who lives in a metropolis is supposed to inherit the sophisticated ideas and manners that go with such a center. And from the Greek *polis*, "city," we inherited our word *politic*. If you are *politic*, you are expedient, shrewd, discreet, and artful in your address and your procedure which sounds dangerously like a city slicker!

Wilfred Funk, *Word Origins and Their Romantic Stories*

The main idea of Funk's paragraph is stated in its first sentence, the topic sentence. All the other sentences give more specific information to support that idea; they give examples of what the writer calls "flattering" words that have to do with the city.

The Topic Sentence

You will often express the main idea of a paragraph in a single sentence, called the *topic sentence.*

Placement of a Topic Sentence

Although a topic sentence can be placed at any point in the paragraph, it often appears as the first or second sentence. In the passage on page 347, for example, the first sentence is a topic sentence.

A topic sentence at the beginning of a paragraph helps a reader know what to expect in the rest of the paragraph. The diagram below shows the typical three-part structure of a body paragraph that begins with a topic sentence.

Typical Body Paragraph Structure

Beginning - - - - - - - - - Topic Sentence

Middle - - - - Support   Support   Support

End - - - - - - - - - Clincher Sentence

Learning for Life

Considering the Importance of Paragraphs. Most likely, students already recognize the value of paragraphs as the building blocks of novels and of magazine and newspaper articles. Remind students, however, that they often encounter "stand-alone" paragraphs in their everyday lives. Ask students to list contexts in which they encounter stand-alone paragraphs. Responses may include: messages in greeting cards, short

A topic sentence placed at the end of a paragraph can be quite effective. As you read the following paragraph, notice how the writer draws all the details together with a topic sentence at the very end.

> In the summer, hosts of big red-and-yellow grass-hoppers, with heads shaped like horses, will descend and eat holes in all the softer leaves. Walking sticks fly like boomerangs. Shining brown leaf-shaped palmetto bugs scurry like cockroaches. Spiders like tiny crabs hang in stout webs. The birds snap at small moths and butterflies of every kind. A blue racer, the snake that moves across the cleared sand like a whiplash, will with one flick destroy the smooth, careful cup of the ant lion in the hot sand. The whole world of the pines and of the rocks hums and glistens and stings with life.
>
> Marjory Stoneman Douglas, *The Everglades: River of Grass*

Importance of a Topic Sentence

Many paragraphs you read will not have a topic sentence. In fact, some of them, especially those that relate a sequence of events or actions, will not even seem to have a single main idea. However, that does not mean topic sentences are not useful. When you are reading, topic sentences at the beginning of a paragraph provide clues about what to expect in the rest of the paragraph. When you are writing, topic sentences help you focus the ideas in your paragraph. Also, whether you are writing a paragraph or reading one, the topic sentence can suggest the order of details in the paragraph—order by comparison and contrast or by cause and effect, for example.

NOTE If a paragraph is part of a composition, its topic sentence often contains key words or phrases to tie it to the paper's thesis.

Exercise 1 Identifying Main Ideas and Topic Sentences

Each of the paragraphs on the next page develops a main idea. State the main idea of each paragraph and, if there is a topic sentence, identify it. If there is no topic sentence, you may find it a little harder to determine what the main idea is.

| STYLE | TIP |

Although it is possible to omit a topic sentence, you should get into the habit of including it in your own writing. The writing you do for school will benefit from the clarity and focus that a well-written topic sentence provides.

Relating to Literature

Compare paragraphs to stanzas in poetry by providing students with copies of Robert Frost's poem "The Road Not Taken." Explain that stanzas in a poem sometimes function like paragraphs, in that they each can have a main idea that relates to the main idea of the entire poem. Divide the class into groups and assign each group a stanza. Ask each group to identify the main idea of their stanza. [*For example, in the first stanza, the main idea is that the speaker of the poem has to choose which path to follow, and it's not an easy decision.*] After discussing the main idea of each stanza, challenge students to identify the main idea of the entire poem.

---

e-mail notes, directions for health or beauty products, or elaborated captions under pictures. Have students examine a few examples to note how the authors constructed the messages. Students should understand that an effective stand-alone paragraph is a self-contained unit in which an entire message is conveyed clearly and briefly.

1. m.i.—In Navratilova's country, sports have been a safe way to show nationalism.

2. m.i.—Despite popular ideas to the contrary, the jackalope is a hoax.

Fabulous Jackalope

1.   <u>In my country, sports were one way to show national pride, one of the few safe ways.</u> You could cheer for a Czech hockey team or soccer team, even against the Soviet Union. It was a tradition going back to the nineteenth century when people formed sports clubs like Sokol, to compete in gymnastics. It was the only way you could say to the Hapsburgs, "Look, we're still Czechs, even if we now belong to the Austro-Hungarian Empire."

Martina Navratilova with George
Vecsey, Martina

2.   Throughout the Western United States, you can buy postcards with a photograph of the fabulous jackalope. Stuffed specimens of this creature can sometimes be found on display, usually in bars. The jackalope is said to be a rare, nearly extinct antlered species of rabbit. Up close, the jackalope looks like a stuffed rabbit with a pair of horns or antlers stuck onto it. And, of course, that is exactly what it is.

Daniel Cohen, The Encyclopedia
of Monsters

Supporting Sentences: Elaboration

The topic sentence of a paragraph states a general idea. To make that idea clear and interesting to the reader, you have to **elaborate** on it, or develop it in greater detail. Other sentences in the paragraph give specific details or information to support the main idea of the paragraph. Depending on the subject you are writing about, you might support your main idea with sensory details, facts or statistics, or examples.

NOTE With or without a topic sentence, a paragraph always needs specific bits of information to support the main idea. In fact, paragraphs without topic sentences are dependent on their details to reflect their main ideas.

Sensory Details as Support

Sensory details are precise bits of information that you collect using any of your five senses—sight, hearing, smell, touch, taste. You might include a detail about the color of something, how it sounds when it moves, or what it feels like when you touch it.

The writer of the following paragraph uses details of sight, sound, and smell to elaborate on a description of what her childhood home was like in the morning.

In the summer my mother got up just after sunrise, so that when she called Matthew and me for breakfast, the house was filled with sounds and smells of her industrious mornings. Odors of frying scrapple or codfish cakes drifted up the back stairs, mingling sometimes with the sharp scent of mustard greens she was cooking for dinner that night. Up the laundry chute from the cellar floated whiffs of steamy air and the churning sound of the washing machine. From the dining room, where she liked to sit ironing and chatting on the telephone, came the fragrance of hot clean clothes and the sound of her voice: cheerful, resonant, reverberating a little weirdly through the high-ceilinged rooms, as if she were sitting happily at the bottom of a well.	Sight Smell Smell Sight Smell Sound Smell Sound

Andrea Lee, "Mother"

Facts and Statistics as Support

Another way to support a main idea with specific information is to use facts or statistics. A *fact* is a statement that can be proven true, such as the statement "At the end of the Civil War, General Lee surrendered to General Grant in the front parlor of the Wilmer McLean house." A *statistic* is a fact that involves numbers; for example, "During the Civil War, the South lost about 260,000 soldiers, and the North lost about 360,000."

NOTE If you use statistics in your writing, be sure that you choose them from reliable, unbiased sources. When you present statistics, do so in clear language.

Cooperative Learning

Sensory Details. Have students form groups by counting off 1 through 5. Provide each group with a scenario, such as a snowy Saturday, a picnic in a park, or a sunset at a beach. Explain that each group will use a chart like the one below to record sensory details related to their assigned scenario. Determine which student in the group will handle each of the following roles: facilitator (to ensure that each person contributes at least one idea to the chart), recorder (to list responses), and reporter (to share the results with the class).

Scenario: A snowy Saturday

Sense	Sensory Detail
Sight	ground covered with white blanket
Hearing	football game on radio
Smell	cocoa on stove
Touch	scratchy sweaters
Taste	snow tastes like cold metal

As you discuss each group's chart, ask volunteers to verbalize how sensory descriptions help to elaborate on the main idea in a paragraph.

Critical Thinking

Analysis. Select a collection of newspaper articles that are of an appropriate reading level, length, and content for your class. Have students examine the articles to find paragraphs with facts and statistics. Then, have students use highlighters to mark all the facts and statistics in the articles. Ask students to write a sentence or two explaining how facts and statistics function as supporting details in paragraphs.

In the following paragraph about movie theaters, facts and statistics support and prove the main idea that concession sales are big moneymakers. In case you are wondering about the word *Rialto*, it is a name that the writer uses to refer to movie theaters in general.

Statistic	Let's look at how concession sales affect the bottom line of the Rialto. In large cities, about 15–20 percent of all customers will stop at the concession stand (in smaller towns, even more customers eat), and the theater owner figures to gross about 75 cents for every customer who walks through the turnstile, meaning that the average purchase is over $3. The key to making money in the concession area is maintaining a high profit margin, and the items sold do a terrific job. The average profit margin on candy—77 percent; on popcorn—86 percent; on soft drinks—a whopping 90 percent. For every dollar spent at the concession counter, the theater operator nets over 85 cents.

Statistic
Fact
Statistic
Statistic
Statistics

David Feldman, *Imponderables*

Examples as Support

You can also use one or more examples to support a main idea. *Examples* are specific instances, or illustrations, of a general idea. A cow is an example of an animal. Your test score of 67 is an example of what can happen if you do not study. The line "The fog comes/on little cat feet," from Carl Sandburg's poem "Fog," is an example of **personification.** The following paragraph uses specific examples of bird behavior to show how bathing varies among birds.

Main Idea
Example 1

Bathing behavior varies from species to species. Many birds stand in shallow water and, through a complex series of movements—rolling their head and body and fluttering their wings—get water trapped in featherless areas next to their body and then press the water out through their feathers. Some aerial birds, like swallows, may dive into water and immediately fly up. Still others may jump into water and be briefly submerged before getting out. Some birds bathe in rain or drizzle, in dew on grass, or among wet leaves. Take time to watch bathing behavior; it is fascinating.

Example 2
Example 3
Example 4

Donald and Lillian Stokes, *The Bird Feeder Book*

Exercise 2   Collecting Supporting Details

Four general ideas you could write about are listed below. With each idea, a type of support—examples, facts and statistics, or sensory details—is suggested. Think of two details to support each main idea. You may have to do a little research (reading or talking to knowledgeable people) to find support, especially facts or statistics.

EXAMPLE   1. Because the audience loved puns, Shakespeare included several in *Romeo and Juliet*. (examples)

   1. *When Mercutio is dying, he says, "Ask for/me tomorrow and you shall find me a grave/man." The pun is on the word* grave, *which means "serious" as well as "burial place." Romeo creates a pun with* soles *and* soul *in the following lines: "You have dancing shoes/With nimble soles; I have a soul of lead/So stakes me to the ground I cannot move."*

1. Physical education classes develop skills that people use throughout their lives. (examples)
2. Ponce de León, the Spanish explorer, led an expedition to what is now Florida. (facts and statistics)
3. On a rainy, cold afternoon, nothing could be better than going to see a movie. (sensory details)
4. Women's styles have often put appearance before comfort. (examples)

The Clincher Sentence

You may want to end some paragraphs—especially long ones—with a sentence that restates or emphasizes the paragraph's topic sentence or main idea. This concluding sentence is called a *clincher sentence* because it pulls all the details together and signals that the end of the paragraph has come—often using a transitional word or phrase such

⌐HELP⌐

If you have trouble thinking of ideas, use the *5W–How?* questions as trigger words to brainstorm details.

Exercise 2   Collecting Supporting Details

ANSWERS
Here are sample responses:

1. (A) Playing team sports such as basketball and volleyball teaches you how to work toward a common goal. (B) When you practice a sport, you and your teammates develop strategies for winning a game. The same principles apply when you work out strategies for studying, managing a budget, or completing a task.

2. (A) In 1513, Ponce de León obtained a royal grant from Spain to search for the Fountain of Youth. (B) He landed near the site of what is today St. Augustine, Florida.

3. (A) The warm, soft seats feel cozy as you watch scenes of sunshine in Hawaii. (B) Over the voices on the soundtrack, you hear the beating of rain on the roof of the theater.

4. (A) Many fashionable eighteenth-century women, particularly in England and France, wore hoop skirts, or petticoats. These garments had a frame of whalebone or wicker and could be as wide as eighteen feet. Many considered these skirts to be pretty but not very comfortable. (B) Some women today wear high heels even though the shoes can be painful and make walking difficult.

ENGLISH-LANGUAGE LEARNERS
General Strategies. Students may not understand the term *clincher*. Explain that *clincher* comes from the verb *to clinch,* which means "to hold or secure something, like a nail, by flattening it or bending it down." A belt buckle is an excellent example of the concept. The nail of the buckle goes through the leather strap and then is clinched, or pulled down, to hold everything in place. Extend the idea by explaining that a clincher sentence holds together the ideas in a paragraph.

as *therefore, thus, as a result,* and *consequently.* The clincher sentence in the following paragraph is underlined. Notice how the author uses the clincher sentence to emphasize his opinion of Michael Jordan as the "best player in basketball."

> Coming into New Jersey to play the Nets, the Bulls had won five games and lost only two since Jordan's return. Any doubts anyone might have had about his potential to reclaim his standing as the best player in basketball had been effectively removed three days after he hit the winning shot in Atlanta, when the Bulls traveled to New York to play the Knicks in Madison Square Garden. Jordan's performance that night—55 points, 21-for-37 shooting from the field, 10-of-11 free throws, all of this in only 38 minutes on the court—could not have taken place in a better setting for him (the New York and national media were on hand in force), and could not have come at a better time (the game was nationally telecast, to an audience that had been reading the stories about Jordan's struggles, had been seeing the TV coverage of his missed shots and missteps). Since that night he had scored 23 points in a win over the Boston Celtics, then only 12 points on 5-for-19 shooting against the Philadelphia 76ers. But the evening in New York had defined the possibilities inherent in his comeback; now the world was clamoring to watch every shot he took, and tickets to Bulls games, always extremely difficult to get, were just about impossible to buy at any price. <u>No one wanted to miss the next night when Jordan might explode.</u>
>
> Bob Greene, *Rebound*

Exercise 3 **Writing a Clincher Sentence**

ANSWER
Possible response:

Readers won't be able to put down this riveting account of the discovery of the *Titanic.*

Exercise 3 **Writing a Clincher Sentence**

The paragraph on the next page does not have a clincher sentence. Read the paragraph and determine what its main idea is. Then, write a clincher sentence that (1) emphasizes the main idea and (2) signals that the end of the paragraph has come. (Try to include a transitional word or phrase.)

Dr. Robert D. Ballard's book about the discovery of the *Titanic* is fascinating. He begins the book with an interesting account of the search for the ship. A few chapters later, he launches into the thrilling story of the actual discovery. Then comes the climax of the book: the section in which Ballard describes the explorations of the *Titanic* that he conducted using a submarine and an underwater robot.

What Makes a Good Paragraph?

A good paragraph has three major qualities:

- **Unity.** All the parts of the paragraph work together as a unit to express and support one main idea.
- **Coherence.** The ideas in the paragraph are arranged and connected in a way that will make sense to readers.
- **Elaboration.** The paragraph's main idea is developed or expanded using plenty of supporting details.

Unity

A good paragraph has *unity*—all its sentences work together as a unit to express or to support one main idea. Sentences can work as a unit in one of three ways: (1) by supporting a main idea that is stated in a topic sentence, (2) by supporting a main idea that is implied (not directly expressed), or (3) by expressing a related series of actions.

All Sentences Relate to the Topic Sentence

The topic sentence of the following paragraph expresses the paragraph's main idea—that whales are physical wonders. Notice how the supporting sentences all provide specific details about characteristics that make whales physically wonderful or unusual.

Whales not only have fascinating behavior but are physical wonders as well. The Blue Whale is the largest animal that has ever graced our *(continued)*	Topic Sentence Detail

RESOURCES

What Makes a Good Paragraph?
Practice
- *Sentences and Paragraphs,* WS. pp. 44, 45, 46, 47, 48

What Makes a Good Paragraph?
OBJECTIVES

- To choose chronological order, spatial order, logical order, or order of importance for explaining topics
- To identify sentences that destroy unity
- To identify direct references in a paragraph
- To identify and use transitions in a paragraph
- To add elaboration to a paragraph using sensory details, facts and statistics, and examples

Quotation for the Day

"When spider webs unite, they can tie up a lion."

(Ethiopian proverb)

Give pairs of students a few moments to interpret this proverb. Students may suggest that it requires a lot of power to tie up a lion and that the spiders got their power from joining their webs together. Guide students in discussing how this quotation relates to the concept of unity in a paragraph. Students should see that a well-organized paragraph can be a powerful tool: it can describe events or ideas, and it can even persuade a reader to change his or her opinion.

MULTIPLE INTELLIGENCES
Logical-Mathematical Intelligence.
Assist students with the concept of
unity by showing them a deck of cards.
Remind students that in every deck
there are four suits—clubs, spades, diamonds, and hearts, and that each suit
has 9 numbers (2–10), a jack, a queen,
a king, and an ace. Lay out the suits to
show the unity of color and shape
within suits. Then, shuffle the deck
and lay out cards again. The suits'
unity will be destroyed. Challenge students to explain how the demonstration relates to unity in a paragraph.
They should express the basic idea that
unity occurs in a paragraph when all
sentences are of the same "suit," that
is, related to the main idea.

Cooperative Learning

Finding Implied Main Idea. To help
students understand implied main
idea, divide the class into 4–6 groups.
Give each group a subject to write
about, for example, teen fashions.
Have the groups create a topic sentence about their subject. Then, have
groups write two supporting sentences
with elaboration for each support.
Have groups trade paragraphs, leaving
out the topic sentence. Other groups
must figure out the implied main idea,
which should match closely the topic
sentence the group had created
originally.

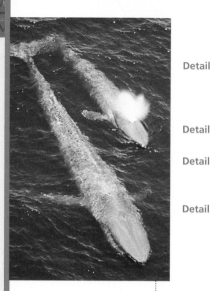

	(continued)
Detail	planet. Such giant herbivorous dinosaurs as the brontosaurus weighed up to fifty tons. A Blue Whale weighs that much long before it reaches puberty; full grown they weigh a hundred and fifty
Detail	tons, as much as three brontosauri! Blue Whales grow to more than a hundred feet—longer than
Detail	any other animals. When such a whale is vertical in the water with its tail at the surface, its nose is deep enough to be subjected to the weight of three
Detail	atmospheres. It is possible that they dive deep enough, more than a mile, to be subjected to more than two hundred times the atmospheric pressure experienced by people on land at sea level.

Paul and Anne Ehrlich, *Extinction*

All Sentences Relate to an Implied Main Idea

The following paragraph does not have a topic sentence. However, each
sentence helps to support the implied main idea that the results of the
battle between Nat and the birds are shocking and horrifying.

> He took the blanket from his head and stared about
> him. The cold gray morning light exposed the room.
> Dawn and the open window had called the living birds;
> the dead lay on the floor. Nat gazed at the little corpses,
> shocked and horrified. They were all small birds, none
> of any size; there must have been fifty of them lying
> there upon the floor. There were robins, finches, spar-
> rows, blue tits, larks, and bramblings, birds that by
> nature's law kept to their own flock and their own terri-
> tory, and now, joining one with another in their urge
> for battle, had destroyed themselves against the bed-
> room walls or in the strife had been destroyed by him.
> Some had lost feathers in the fight; others had blood,
> his blood, upon their beaks.
>
> Daphne du Maurier, "The Birds"

All Sentences Relate to a Sequence of Events

The narrator of the following paragraph is trying to save a man named Harry, who fears that a deadly snake has slithered into his bed. The paragraph does not actually have a main idea. However, each action described in the paragraph is part of a sequence that begins when the narrator leaves the room and that ends as he stands beside the bed wondering what to do.

Like many narrative paragraphs, this paragraph is actually a cause-and-effect paragraph. What one character does (a cause) results in the next action (an effect).

> I went softly out of the room in my stocking feet and fetched a small sharp knife from the kitchen. I put it in my trouser pocket, ready to use instantly in case something went wrong while we were still thinking out a plan. If Harry coughed or moved or did something to frighten the krait and got bitten, I was going to be ready to cut the bitten place and try to suck the venom out. I came back to the bedroom and Harry was still lying there very quiet and sweating all over his face. His eyes followed me as I moved across the room to his bed, and I could see he was wondering what I'd been up to. I stood beside him, trying to think of the best thing to do.
>
> Roald Dahl, "Poison"

NOTE Even though a topic sentence is not usually used in a narrative paragraph, some narrative paragraphs begin with a topic sentence that either presents the writer's impression of the events or states the kind of event being presented.

Exercise 4 **Identifying Sentences That Destroy Unity**

Find the sentences that destroy unity in the paragraphs on the next page. Remember: To have unity, all details in a paragraph must be related to the topic sentence (main idea) or the sequence of actions.

Meeting INDIVIDUAL NEEDS

INCLUSION

If a student needs extra practice in identifying sentences that destroy unity, have a helper use the sample paragraphs on pp. 355–357 as the basis of an informal activity. Ask the helper to read one of the paragraphs to the student after the helper has inserted a sentence that destroys the paragraph's unity. The student needing practice should indicate when he or she hears a sentence that does not fit the topic. Encourage the student to verbalize his or her reason.

1.   A batter who steps up to the plate usually tries to hit the ball as fast and as far as he can. He takes a full swing, putting all of his strength behind the bat. Sometimes, however, he bunts the ball. He tries to tap it lightly so that it will land about halfway between the pitcher and the catcher. To bunt, the batter usually does not swing at the ball. Instead, he just holds out the bat so that the ball strikes it and falls to the ground. <u>Bats are made of single pieces of hardwood or of aluminum.</u> The player who bunts is almost sure to be thrown out at first base. On the other hand, while the opponents are occupied with his play, other runners on his team may be able to move on.

Susan B. Anthony

2.   The women's rights movement began at the Seneca Falls Convention in New York in 1848. At that time, Elizabeth Cady Stanton introduced a resolution demanding suffrage, or the right to vote, for women. In 1869, Stanton and Susan B. Anthony formed a national organization to seek voting rights for women. In 1872, Anthony was arrested for breaking the law by voting in a presidential election, but by 1896, four states had given women the right to vote. In 1912, women's suffrage at last became an issue in a presidential campaign. Two years later, a suffrage petition signed by 404,000 women was presented to Congress. President Woodrow Wilson, responding to pressure by women's groups, endorsed a new amendment. <u>Black males were granted the right to vote after the Civil War by the Fourteenth and Fifteenth Amendments</u>. Finally, in 1919, the Nineteenth Amendment, giving women the right to vote, was passed by Congress.

Coherence

Along with unity, a good paragraph also has *coherence.* If you have ever read a paragraph that did not make any sense to you, it probably did not have coherence. In other words, it was not easy for you to see how all the ideas in the paragraph fit together—how they were arranged and connected. You can create coherence by paying attention to two things: (1) the **order,** or **organizational pattern,** in which you arrange your ideas, and (2) the **connections** you make between ideas.

Order of Ideas

How you arrange, or order, ideas in your paragraph can help your readers to follow those ideas. Often, the subject you are writing about will suggest the order of ideas. Sometimes, however, you will have to pick among several organizational patterns that suit your topic. Here are four useful ways to organize your ideas:

- **chronological order,** used to relate events in the order they happened
- **spatial order,** used to describe things according to where they are located, in relation either to one another or to a viewer
- **order of importance,** used to show importance of details in relation to one another
- **logical order,** used to group related ideas

Chronological Order What happened when Ebenezer Scrooge met the Ghost of Christmas Past? How did the Egyptians build the pyramids? What caused the American Revolution? To answer any of these questions, it makes sense to describe the actions or events as they occurred in time. In other words, you would use chronological order. In fact, the prefix *chrono–* means "time."

Chronological order is used to **explain a process, tell a story,** or **explain a cause-and-effect sequence.** In the following example, the writer explains a process: how to find a honey tree.

> To find a honey tree, first catch a bee. Catch a bee when its legs are heavy with pollen; then it is ready for home. It is simple enough to catch a bee on a flower: hold a cup or glass above the bee, and when it flies up, cap the cup with a piece of cardboard. Carry the bee to a nearby open spot—best an elevated one—release it,
>
> *(continued)*

Reference Note

For more on **telling a story,** see page 62. For more on **explaining cause and effect,** see page 134.

Chronological Order
Students occasionally lose track of chronological order as they read or write paragraphs. Offer them the following questions to help get back on track.

Telling a Story: "What happened next?"
Explaining a Process: "What is done next?"
Explaining a Cause-and-Effect Relationship: "Why did that happen?" or "What happens if I do that?"

Crossing the Curriculum

Art. Explain to students that artists as well as writers use spatial order to indicate depth and dimension in their work. To reinforce this idea, share examples of art and discuss with students the ways an artist can represent placement and depth in a two-dimensional work. You might show René Magritte's *The Human Condition,* or Félix Vallotton's *The Wind,* for example. As you guide viewers' attention around the examples of art, review the concepts of foreground and background, pointing out how size is used to show relative location. If you have time, ask students to write descriptions of the artworks, using spatial order. Post the descriptions next to the art.

Critical Thinking

Metacognition. To reinforce order of importance, encourage students to write in their journals about their decision-making process. As they prepare paragraphs, they should ask themselves questions such as:

- Why do I think this detail is least important?
- Why do I think this detail is most important?
- Is it only important to me or will it be important to others?

(continued)

and watch where it goes. Keep your eyes on it as long as you can see it, and hie you to that last known place. Wait there until you see another bee; catch it, release and watch. Bee after bee will lead toward the honey tree, until you see the final bee enter the tree.

Annie Dillard, *The Writing Life*

Spatial Order   Look at this term closely and you will get a clue to its meaning. Spatial order is used to arrange details according to how they are spaced—nearest to farthest, left to right, or any other reasonable arrangement. Spatial order is especially useful in descriptions because it helps the reader picture how details fit together. In the following example, notice how the writer uses words such as *middle, left, right, east,* and *west* to organize his description into spatial order.

View to the left

View to the right

View ahead (between left and right)

My wife, Christine, and I are standing in the middle of the Jornada del Muerto, or journey of the Dead Man, a vast stretch of desert between Las Cruces and Socorro in south-central New Mexico. We are 40 miles from the nearest paved road, waiting for dawn. The austere Fra Cristóbal Mountains rise to our left, their barren summits flaring pink. To our right, a jagged line of broken basalt against the horizon marks the beginning of the *malpaís,* the badlands, an impassable area of immense lava flows. Between those lava flows in the east and the mountains in the west is a gap of only 500 yards. On geological survey maps it is called Lava Gate, and anyone traveling north or south in the Jornada del Muerto must pass through it.

Douglas Preston, "The Granddaddy of the Nation's Trails Began in Mexico"

Order of Importance   You may find that one detail or piece of supporting information you want to use is more important than another. In this case, you may want to arrange your ideas by order of importance, keeping in mind that readers usually pay more attention to what they read first and to what they read last. The writer of the following paragraph about the effects of a long drought begins with the least serious problem—restrictions on watering lawns and washing cars. The paragraph ends with the most serious problem—the threat of fire.

> The two-year-long drought is causing serious problems in my hometown. For several months we have lived with severe limits on using water. We can water lawns or wash cars only from midnight to 4:00 A.M. Recently, restrictions have become even more severe. Our water use is regulated, so we must monitor how much water we use to wash laundry or dishes and bathe. Water quality has also become a problem. The water now has a sour odor, and most people do not feel safe drinking it. But the worst problem we are facing is the threat of serious fires. Three homes recently burned to the ground when a small grass fire grew out of control. Carelessness with fire, or lightning during a thunderstorm, could set our whole town ablaze.

Logical Order   For something to be logical, it has to make sense. In writing, logical order is created by grouping ideas together in a way that makes sense—that is, in a way that makes the relationships between the ideas clear. Logical order is especially important when you **compare and contrast subjects** or when you **define a subject.**

- **Comparing and Contrasting Subjects**   When you are dealing with two or more subjects, you will often find it useful to compare them (explain how they are alike), contrast them (explain how they are different), or both compare *and* contrast them.

- **Defining a Subject**   To define a subject, you first identify the large class or group to which it belongs. Then, you provide specific examples and details that distinguish the subject from other members of its group. The first sentence in the following paragraph defines the word *mummy,* and the other sentences give examples and details that show more specifically what mummies are and how they are preserved.

Definition	A mummy is the preserved body of a human being or an animal, by any means, either deliberate or accidental. Mummies survive from many ancient cultures, some preserved in a wet state, others dry. The bog bodies of northern Europe, such as the 2,000-year-old Lindow Man, found in Cheshire, England, in 1984, belonged to people who had either fallen, or been thrown, into wet, marshy places. The exclusion of oxygen and acidity in the peat of the bog effectively preserved their bodies. Most mummies, though, were preserved by being dried, or desiccated. Many civilizations, including the Egyptian, Chinese and some South American cultures, tried to achieve this artificially.

Christine El Mahdy, *Mummies, Myth, and Magic*

Exercise 5   **Choosing an Order of Ideas**

Indicate which order (chronological order, spatial order, order of importance, or logical order) would work best for explaining each of the following topics. For some topics, you may indicate that more than one type of order would work well. Be prepared to explain your choices.

1. four characteristics of a good quarterback

2. choosing an after-school job

3. the perfect room for a teenager

4. middle school and high school

5. the right way to study for a test

Review A   **Identifying Order of Ideas**

One of the following paragraphs is not well written; the sentences in it are not arranged in an order that is easy to follow. Read the paragraphs and identify the one that is not well written. Then, rewrite the paragraph, rearranging the sentences into an easy-to-follow order. Also indicate which order (chronological order, spatial order, order of importance, or logical order) is used in the other (well-written) paragraph.

1. The naturalist Paul Rezendes has this advice for seeing nature and the great outdoors: Don't rush. Walk rather than drive a car or take a tour bus. Also try to spend some time alone. You notice new things when you aren't distracted by other people. Most important, he says, is to take your time. Take a pad and draw sketches or keep a journal, but don't take a camera. Rezendes says a camera makes you think you're capturing the place on film, when what you really need to do is to capture it in your mind.

2. On the Fourth of July, we took the train into Boston. The second place we visited was the historic Old North Church. We first visited the *Constitution*, the famous American naval ship. We bought a takeout dinner at a little after five o'clock in the afternoon. We had a quick lunch at noon, and then we took a bus to see the aircraft carrier *John F. Kennedy*. At seven o'clock we ate our takeout dinner as we stretched out on a blanket beside the Charles River, waiting for the concert. By the time we finished our tour of the *John F. Kennedy*, it was almost five o'clock. After enjoying the concert, we made the long trip home.

Connections Between Ideas

Along with putting ideas in an order that makes sense, you gain **coherence** in a paragraph by showing how the ideas are connected. You can show connections in two ways: by using **direct references** and by using **transitions**.

Direct References **Direct references** link ideas by referring to a noun or pronoun that you have used earlier in a paragraph. You can make a direct reference in three ways:

1. Use a noun or pronoun that refers to a noun used earlier.
2. Repeat a word used earlier.
3. Use a word or phrase meaning the same as one used earlier.

STYLE TIP

Direct references and transitional words and phrases can make connections between paragraphs as well as within paragraphs.

Meeting INDIVIDUAL NEEDS

ADVANCED LEARNERS

In the paragraph used to illustrate direct references, Jack London repeatedly uses the pronoun *it*. Challenge students to revise a few of the sentences using other forms of direct reference. For example:

Original: Its instinct told it a truer tale than was to be told to the man by the man's judgment.
Revised: The creature's instinct told it a truer tale than was to be told to the man by man's judgment.

Then, have a student read his or her revised version of the paragraph aloud. Is the paragraph more effective than the original? less effective? Why?

The following paragraph uses several direct references to make connections between ideas. Each reference is coded with the numbers above to show you what type of reference it is.

> At the man's heels trotted a dog, a big native husky,[3] the proper wolf dog,[3] gray-coated and without any visible or temperamental difference from its[1] brother, the wild wolf.[2] The animal[3] was depressed by the tremendous cold. It[1] knew that it was no time for traveling. Its[1] instinct told it[1] a truer tale than was to be told to the man[2] by the man's[2] judgment. In reality, it was not merely colder than fifty below zero; it was colder than sixty below, than seventy below. It was seventy-five below zero.[2] Since the freezing point is thirty-two above zero,[2] it meant that one hundred and seven degrees of frost obtained. The dog[2] did not know anything about thermometers. Possibly in its[1] brain there was no sharp consciousness of a condition of very cold such as was in the man's[2] brain.[2] But the brute[3] had its[1] instinct. It[1] experienced a vague but menacing apprehension that subdued it[1] and made it[1] slink along at the man's[2] heels, and that made it[1] question eagerly every unwonted movement of the man,[2] as if expecting him[1] to go into camp or to seek shelter somewhere and build a fire. The dog[2] had learned fire,[2] and it[1] wanted fire,[2] or else to burrow under the snow and cuddle its[1] warmth away from the air.
>
> Jack London, "To Build a Fire"

Transitional Words and Phrases The prefix *trans–* means "across" or "over." A transition in writing—whether it is a word, a phrase, or even a sentence—reaches *across* or *over* ideas, connecting one idea to another. When you use transitions, you not only connect ideas, but also show *how* they are connected—often by using phrases that include conjunctions and prepositions showing chronological or spatial order. The chart on the next page shows how certain transitions are related to certain types of writing.

364 Chapter 11 Understanding Paragraph Structure

Continued on pp. 365–366

Direct References. Point out to students that the meaning of a pronoun is clear only when the reader knows to which word, or *antecedent,* the pronoun refers. Use the following example to show how unclear pronoun references can confuse readers.

Example: My father and I sent an e-mail to Bob at college. It was his birthday.

Help students discover that the sentence does not make clear who was having the

Transitional Words and Phrases

Comparing Ideas	also	another	similarly
	and	moreover	too
Contrasting Ideas	still	in spite of	on the other hand
	but	instead	although
	yet	however	nevertheless
Showing Cause and Effect	for	so that	as a result
	since	because	therefore
	so	thus	consequently
Showing Chronological Order	after	eventually	at once
	then	finally	at last
	next	first	thereafter
	before	meanwhile	when
Showing Spatial Order	into	above	beyond
	next	across	down
	over	behind	around
	in	before	there
	here	inside	under
Showing Order of Importance	first	mainly	to begin with
	last	then	more important

The following paragraph uses transitional words and phrases, which are underlined, to make connections in time and place.

> With nervous hands he lowered the piece of canvas which served as his door, <u>and</u> pegged it at the bottom. <u>Then</u> quickly <u>and</u> quietly, looking at the piece of canvas frequently, he slipped the records into the case, snapped the lid shut, <u>and</u> carried the phonograph to his couch. <u>There</u>, pausing often to stare at the canvas <u>and</u> listen, he dug earth from the wall and disclosed a piece of board. <u>Behind</u> this there was a deep hole in the wall, <u>into</u> which he put the phonograph. <u>After</u> a moment's consideration, he went <u>over</u> and reached <u>down</u> for his bundle of books and inserted it <u>also</u>. <u>Then</u>, guardedly, he
>
> *(continued)*

STYLE TIP

If you use transitional words and phrases (with the exceptions of *and* and *but*) in every sentence, your writing might sound artificial. Since direct references are more natural, feel free to use them frequently in your writing. Your readers will appreciate it.

Cooperative Learning

Group Paragraph with Transitions. Divide the class into groups of four to six students. Try to include in each group at least one student who is linguistically skilled and one who is logical-mathematically skilled. Provide each student with an index card that has a transition word written on it. Then, offer each group a different prompt, such as: "Explain how to tie your shoes"; "Describe a recent school lunch"; "Explain how to search for a topic on the Internet"; "Describe how to bathe a dog." Ask each group to respond to its prompt by writing a paragraph that includes the group members' transition words. Identify students in each group to serve as scribes, organizers, transition checkers (to make sure all the transitions are used meaningfully), and readers (to read the paragraph to the class). Have each group share its results.

Meeting
INDIVIDUAL
NEEDS

ENGLISH-LANGUAGE LEARNERS

General Strategies. Students may find that the variety of transition words and phrases available in English is confusing. You may find it helpful to pair these students with native English-speakers who can serve as peer readers.

---

birthday. Ask them to brainstorm ways to correct the problem.

Possible revision: My father and I sent an e-mail to Bob at college. It was Dad's birthday.

Ask students to revise the following sentences to make the pronoun references clear.

1. The scientist told the girl not to touch the snake she had found. [*Possible rewrite: The scientist told the girl not to touch the snake the scientist had found.*]

(continued)

once more sealed up the hole with the board <u>and</u> the earth. He <u>also</u> changed his blankets, and the grass-stuffed sack which served as a pillow, <u>so that</u> he could lie facing the entrance. <u>After</u> carefully placing two more blocks of peat on the fire, he stood for a long time watching the stretched canvas, <u>but</u> it seemed to billow naturally with the first gusts of a lowering wind. <u>At last</u> he prayed, <u>and</u> got in <u>under</u> his blankets, <u>and</u> closed his smoke-smarting eyes. On the <u>inside</u> of the bed, <u>next</u> to the wall, he could feel with his hand, the comfortable piece of lead pipe.

Walter Van Tilburg Clark,
"The Portable Phonograph"

Exercise 6 — Identifying Direct References and Transitions

The following paragraph uses both direct references and transitional words and phrases to connect ideas. Make two lists: one list of <u>direct reference words</u> and one list of <u>transitions</u> you find in the paragraph. (Hint: there are at least fourteen direct reference words and six transitions.)

EXAMPLE

My father started high school in Frederick, Maryland. When he was a junior, his family moved, and he finished high school in Baltimore.

Direct References	Transitions
he	in
his	When
he	and
high school	in

Possible answers follow.

At Waterford Crystal <u>in</u> Ireland, each piece of <u>crys-tal</u> is still handmade. <u>First</u>, the glass-blowers dip long pipes <u>into</u> a 1,200-degree furnace. <u>In</u> the <u>furnace</u>, <u>their</u> <u>pipes</u> collect fiery lumps of molten <u>crystal</u>. <u>Then</u> <u>they</u> blow the <u>hot lumps</u> of crystal <u>into</u> "blank" cups, vases, and bowls of various sizes <u>and</u> shapes. <u>Each piece</u> must be thin <u>and</u> clear, <u>yet</u> thick enough to be engraved later. <u>After</u> the <u>blank glass</u> has cooled, the "masters" take over.

MINI-LESSON

2. Teachers were asked to escort their students to the assembly. They liked the presentation very much. [*Possible rewrite: Teachers were asked to escort their students to the assembly. The students liked the presentation very much.*]

Have pairs of students review each other's sentences and suggest ways to improve those revised sentences that still contain unclear antecedents.

They use dime-sized diamond wheels to engrave the glass in one of Waterford's beautiful patterns. A typical Waterford glass takes about eight hours to make. To create a large, expensive piece, experienced engravers may take several weeks and go through a number of blank pieces of glass.

Exercise 7 Using Transitions

The following paragraph is not completely clear. Revise it by adding transitions to make the connections it needs. Feel free to rewrite or combine sentences, too.

```
    Jason decided to hike across Glacier
National Park. He decided this at a young
age. He never actually did much hiking. On
his eighteenth birthday, he and a friend
made plans to explore Glacier National Park
on foot. Jason researched the history and
terrain of the park. He wrote to the park
service. He received a package full of
information and maps. He found out that
much of the park, which is in the northern
Rockies, is very rugged and isolated. He
bought clothing and packed provisions for
wilderness living. He arrived at the park
and talked to the park rangers. They told
Jason the best trails to follow. They gave
him safety tips.
```

Elaboration

Along with unity and coherence, another quality of a good paragraph is **elaboration**. Remember that a good paragraph should contain **supporting sentences** that elaborate on the **main idea** presented in the paragraph's **topic sentence**. However, sometimes writers do not thoroughly develop, or elaborate on, a paragraph's main idea; these writers fail to provide enough supporting sensory details, facts and statistics, or examples. A paragraph with a poorly supported main idea is said to lack elaboration.

If you write a paragraph that lacks elaboration, you run the risk of confusing or misleading your readers—of not giving them enough

TIPS & TRICKS

If you have trouble thinking of details to use for elaboration in a paragraph, try some of the same strategies you use to generate topics, such as the listing strategy: Write your topic on a sheet of paper and list all the details that come to mind.

Exercise 7   Using Transitions

ANSWER

Suggest that students use colored pencils or markers to underline the transitions they add as they rewrite the paragraph. Here is a sample response:

Although Jason was young and had never actually done much hiking, he and a friend made plans to explore Glacier National Park on foot on his eighteenth birthday. Before the trip, Jason researched the history and terrain of the park. He wrote to the park service and received a package full of information and maps. He found out that much of the park, which is in the northern Rockies, is very rugged and isolated. Consequently, he bought clothing and packed provisions for wilderness living. When he arrived at the park and talked to the park rangers, they told Jason the best trails to follow and gave him safety tips.

ALTERNATIVE LESSON

After completing **Exercise 7**, ask students to examine their revised paragraphs for use of the sentence-combining techniques learned in Chapter 10. Have them jot down in the margins of their revised paragraphs the methods they used to eliminate choppy sentences. For example, they may have created a complex sentence with an adverb clause or a compound sentence with a compound verb.

MODALITY

Auditory and Visual Learners. To illustrate the usefulness of elaboration, ask students to close their eyes and listen. Then, tell a bland story, such as "I was sitting by a tree. An animal came up to me. I escaped." Ask students if they liked the story. Point out that they probably couldn't "see" much because you did not include enough details. Have students close their eyes again. Repeat the story, adding probing questions. For example: "I was sitting by a tree. *Where was it? Why was I sitting there?* An animal came up to me. *What kind? What did it do? How did I feel?* I escaped. *How? What happened in the end?*" Next, invite pairs of students to elaborate your story by adding details that answer the questions you posed. Provide time for pairs to listen to each other's stories and identify vivid details.

TIPS & TRICKS

There are several types of elaboration you can use to support the main idea of a paragraph. Use the following mnemonic device to help you remember them. (FACTEES) F = facts, A = anecdotes, C = cause and effect, T = testimonial, E = exaggeration, E = example, and S = statistics.

information to understand the paragraph's main idea. The paragraph below lacks elaboration. Notice how something clearly seems to be missing from it.

    The youngest children in families often
    have a worse situation than their brothers
    or sisters. One reason they have it worse
    is that they are not taken seriously. The
    youngest children also live in the shadow
    of their siblings. Finally, the youngest
    children have parents who often are tired
    of teaching the same things they have
    taught so many times before.

The paragraph above cries out for more details. Do you wonder what the writer means when he writes that the youngest children "are not taken seriously"? What does the writer mean by the phrase "living in the shadow of their siblings"? What are the things the writer thinks that parents have "taught so many times before"? To see how the writer used elaboration to answer these questions, read the paragraph below.

Main Idea	The youngest children in the family often have a worse situation than their siblings. One
Reason 1	reason they have it worse is that they are not
Elaboration	taken seriously. These children often have older brothers and sisters telling them that they are too little or too young or too weak to do something like set the table or program the VCR.
Reason 2	The youngest children also live in the shadow
Elaboration	of their siblings. It is not uncommon, for example, for the youngest child's achievements in school to be compared with the achievements of older brothers and sisters. Finally, the
Reason 3	youngest children have parents who often are tired of teaching the same things over and over.
Elaboration	Mother and Dad wonder how many times they will have to teach a child how to tie shoes and how to tell time. To sum up, with everything they must deal with, maybe the youngest children in the family do not deserve the "spoiled" label they are frequently given.

The expanded details make the paragraph come alive and help the reader to understand more clearly the main idea the writer is trying to communicate.

Exercise 8 Elaborating with Details

The following paragraph lacks elaboration. Add sensory details, facts and statistics, or examples to develop or expand on the ideas already present in the paragraph. To find facts and statistics, you will need to do some research. To find other details, you may want to work with a partner.

```
     Fantasy is often used in television com-
mercials today. Commercials for household
products frequently contain fantastic el-
ements. Fantasy also frequently appears in
fast-food commercials. Finally, commercials
for pet food also sometimes use fantasy.
```

How Are Paragraphs Used in a Longer Piece of Writing?

So far, you have looked at the types of paragraphs that make up the bulk of a composition—body paragraphs. Be aware, though, that the beginning and the end of a composition are usually marked by two other types: an **introductory** paragraph and a **concluding** paragraph. You might think of the body paragraphs in a composition as the road between two destinations. The introductory paragraphs, then, are the points at which you check the map and set off; the concluding paragraphs are the points at which you look back on the journey and summarize it.

Dividing a Piece into Paragraphs

In the introduction to this chapter, you learned that paragraphs are used to mark a movement from one idea to another and to give a reader's eyes time to pause. When you write your own longer pieces, you will usually start a new paragraph for the following reasons:

- to discuss a different part of your subject or to explain another step in a process

- to show a jump forward or back in time

| STYLE   TIP |

Elaboration is vital to writing strong paragraphs. Include at least two elaboration sentences for each of the major points in a paragraph.

Reference Note

For strategies to use when **writing introductions and conclusions,** see page 905 of the Quick Reference Handbook.

Exercise 8 Elaborating with Details

ANSWER

Here is a sample response:

Advertisers know that fantasy gets the viewers' attention. Because of this, many television commercials feature fantastic elements. In an informal survey conducted over the course of half an hour on a Thursday night, twelve examples of fantasy occurred in twenty-three commercials. Three commercials for cleaning products showed well-dressed young women having conversations with their appliances. Among the half-dozen commercials for fast-food products, one included a talking dog, one featured a dancing hamburger, and one starred singing soda cans. In one commercial for pet food, dogs talked to each other, and in another, a dog chased a little wagon driven by tiny people. Clearly, many advertisers will go to fantastic lengths to try to sell their products.

How Are Paragraphs Used in a Longer Piece of Writing?

OBJECTIVE

- **To divide a passage into paragraphs**

RESOURCES

How Are Paragraphs Used in a Longer Piece of Writing?
Practice
- *Sentences and Paragraphs,* WS. p. 49

Quotation for the Day

"Order is the shape upon which beauty depends."

(Pearl S. Buck, 1892–1973, American novelist and humanitarian, from her book *To My Daughters, With Love*)

Challenge students to provide examples of how beauty often depends on order. [*Students may mention that we often think of things that are symmetrical, such as flowers, butterflies, and even people's faces, as more pleasing to look at than things that are not symmetrical.*] Then, ask them to relate this quotation to writing. They may note that well-structured paragraphs help create order in a writing passage.

Exercise 9 **Dividing a Passage into Paragraphs**
ANSWER
Here are suggested paragraph breaks, which create three paragraphs:

- after the third sentence
- after the sixth sentence

- to introduce another point of support for your opinion
- to indicate that the location of the action has changed
- to show (in a section of dialogue in a story) that a different person or character is speaking

Exercise 9 **Dividing a Passage into Paragraphs**

The passage that follows was originally broken into three paragraphs. Discuss with some classmates where you think the paragraph breaks went—or should go. Be prepared to explain your choices.

> Both cattle and sheep ranches demanded hard work from everyone. As one Texan explained, the ranch owners "got right out with the boys on the trail" and did "just as much work." This description also applied to women, who played an integral part in ranch life. On most ranches, women did housework, cooked for all the cowboys, and helped with fence-mending, herding, or other chores. Many women organized their own ranch-related businesses. For example, Ella Bird accumulated her first herd of cattle by trading hand-sewn leather gloves and vests for yearlings. Ranch children often took on adult responsibilities at a young age. In addition to doing chores around the house, some boys and girls broke horses and herded cattle. The cowboy life offered children some interesting experiences, but the work was hard. John Norton, a young cowboy, said that he and his brother "leaped with joy" when the cattle they were herding were finally shipped for slaughter.
>
> from *The American Nation*

Review B **Writing a Paragraph**

Use elaboration to develop one of the skeleton paragraphs given on the next page. Be sure you use transitions and direct references to show how your ideas are connected.

1. Classrooms of the Ideal High School

The classrooms in the ideal high school are a dream come true for students. The desks are unbelievable. The technology is even better. The decorating contributes to a wonderful atmosphere.

2. Three Influential Areas

There are three areas of teenagers' lives that have a large influence on them. Early education and training affects them. Neighborhoods contribute to teens' lives. Friends are probably the most influential.

3. Fashion or Comfort?

People often seem to choose fashion over comfort. One area that reflects this idea is hair styles. Choices of clothing also show that comfort is secondary. Finally, make-up use definitely is not driven by comfort.

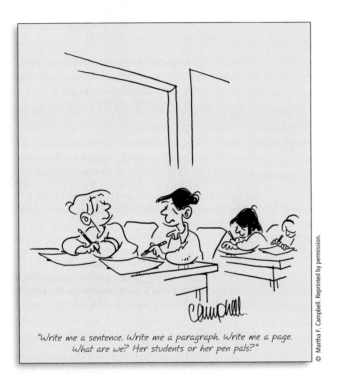

"Write me a sentence. Write me a paragraph. Write me a page. What are we? Her students or her pen pals?"

© Martha F. Campbell. Reprinted by permission.

Classrooms of the Ideal High School

The classrooms of the ideal high school are a dream come true for students. First, the desks are unbelievable. They have more spacious work areas and more storage space than traditional desks. Even more important is the comfort. Seats are slightly padded and adjustable. The technology in the classroom is even better than the seating. Each classroom has a mini-computer lab and all computers are hooked up to the Internet. The most current word-processing software is also available for student use. Finally, the decorating contributes to a wonderful atmosphere. Interesting color schemes and contemporary artwork provide a great learning environment. Good quality carpeting, natural light, and soundproofing add to the positive effect. This learner-friendly atmosphere is what makes the Ideal High School so special.

Teaching Strands

This teaching-strand chart shows you some possibilities for connections between grammar instruction and the writing assignments in Part 1 of this textbook.

The *Elements of Language* grammar handbook is designed to be a flexible teaching tool that accommodates many teaching philosophies and styles. For example, some teachers will prefer to use the handbook as a reference source, having students refer to it only as the need for explicit grammar instruction arises. Others will use the handbook as a teaching text, having their classes work through the instruction, examples, and exercises in a more methodical fashion. Your personal teaching style and the needs of your students will determine the best way for you to teach this material.

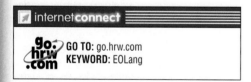

GO TO: go.hrw.com
KEYWORD: EOLang

All resources for this chapter are available for preview on the *One-Stop Planner CD-ROM with Test Generator.* All worksheets and tests may be printed from the CD-ROM.

Writing Assignments	Rationale
DESCRIPTIVE ESSAY (Chapter 1)	Good descriptive writing relies on the precise images created by modifiers, including vivid single-word adjectives, proper adjectives, and adverbs and well-chosen prepositional and verbal phrases. These modifiers are most effective when correctly capitalized and punctuated.
PERSONAL NARRATIVE (Chapter 2)	Personal narratives call for the clear depiction of people and their actions (subjects and verbs). To keep such writing lively, writers often use active-voice verbs. Personal narratives may be less formal than some other types of writing and may involve dialogue; therefore, correctly using contractions, apostrophes, quotation marks, and commas is essential.
COMPARISON/ CONTRAST ESSAY (Chapter 3)	Comparing and contrasting usually involves comparative forms of adjectives and adverbs. Coordinating and correlative conjunctions are used to show how the writer's ideas are related.
CAUSE-EFFECT ESSAY (Chapter 4)	Subordinating conjunctions and conjunctive adverbs are essential to show many cause-effect relationships. Because these relationships often have many elements, writers choose complex and compound-complex sentences to describe them.
LITERARY ANALYSIS OF A POEM (Chapter 5)	Analyzing literature involves understanding point of view, which relates to correct use of pronoun case. Using pronouns requires knowledge of subject-verb and pronoun-antecedent agreement. Precise verb forms and correctly punctuated and capitalized quotations can capture the flavor of the literature.
I-SEARCH PAPER (Chapter 6)	Because the I-Search paper will show relationships among the original questions posed and the answers found, effectively using and punctuating independent and subordinate clauses is a must. Maintaining a reader's interest requires varying sentence structure, using precise, correct language, and correctly citing and punctuating support.
OPINION PIECE (Chapter 7)	Persuasion may require including questions and exclamations. Careful use of pronoun-antecedent agreement and properly punctuated and placed adjectives and adverbs help clarify the author's stance.
REVIEW OF A TV PROGRAM (Chapter 8)	A writer's effective use of action verbs in appropriate tenses helps a reader grasp the intent of the review. Quotations from the program and from other sources require the reviewer to demonstrate appropriate pronoun choice and correct use of quotation marks and apostrophes.

Links to Grammar	Links to Usage	Links to Mechanics
→ adjectives, adverbs (Ch. 12)	→ comparison of modifiers (Ch. 19)	→ capitalization of proper adjectives (Ch. 21); punctuation of items in a series (Ch. 22)
→ phrases (Ch. 14)	→ placement of phrase modifiers (Ch. 19)	→ punctuation of introductory and nonessential phrases (Ch. 22)
→ subjects, predicates (Ch. 13)	→ subject-verb agreement (Ch. 16)	→ apostrophes with contractions (Ch. 25)
→ action verbs, linking verbs (Ch. 12)	→ active voice (Ch. 17)	→ punctuating dialogue (Ch. 24)
→ pronouns (Ch. 12)	→ pronoun-antecedent agreement (Ch. 16)	→ apostrophes with possessives (Ch. 25)
→ adjectives, adverbs (Ch. 12)	→ form and use of modifiers (Ch. 19)	→ spelling with suffixes (Ch. 27)
→ conjunctions (Ch. 12); compound subjects and verbs (Ch. 13); compound sentences (Ch. 15)	→ subject-verb agreement with compound subjects (Ch. 16)	→ punctuating compound sentences (Ch. 22 & Ch. 23)
→ subordinate clauses (Ch. 15)	→ placement of clause modifiers (Ch. 19)	→ punctuation of introductory and nonessential phrases (Ch. 22)
→ subordinating conjunctions (Ch. 15)		→ punctuating sentences with semi-colons and commas (Ch. 22 & Ch. 23)
→ pronouns (Ch. 12)	→ agreement (Ch. 16); case forms of personal pronouns (Ch. 18)	→ quotation marks for titles and direct quotations (Ch. 24); capitalizing titles (Ch. 21)
→ verbs (Ch. 12)	→ active voice, passive voice (Ch. 17)	→ spelling with suffixes –ing, –d, –ed (Ch. 27)
→ independent and subordinate clauses (Ch. 15)	→ uses of verb tenses (Ch. 17)	→ punctuating with commas, semi-colons, colons (Ch. 22 & Ch. 23)
→ sentence structure (Ch. 13 & Ch. 15)	→ common usage errors (Ch. 20)	→ quotation marks (Ch. 24); italics, hyphens, dashes, parentheses, ellipsis points, brackets (Ch. 26)
→ sentences classified by purpose (Ch. 13)	→ pronoun-antecedent agreement (Ch. 16)	→ end marks (Ch. 22)
→ adjectives, adverbs (Ch. 12)	→ placement of modifiers (Ch. 19)	→ punctuating items in a series (Ch. 22)
→ verbs (Ch. 12)	→ verb tense (Ch. 17)	→ quotation marks (Ch. 24)
→ pronouns (Ch. 12)	→ case forms of personal pronouns (Ch. 18)	→ apostrophes (Ch. 25)

PART 5

3 Grammar, Usage, and Mechanics

Grammar, Usage, and Mechanics   **373**

CHAPTER

12

CHAPTER

12 Parts of Speech Overview

Parts of Speech Overview
The Work That Words Do

Diagnostic Preview

─HELP─

Some items in the Diagnostic Preview have more than one italicized word. These words work together as a single part of speech.

1. adj. 2. verb
3. prep. 4. adj.
5. adj. 6. adv.
7. verb 8. noun
9. conj. 10. prep.
11. noun 12. pro.
13. int. 14. adj.
15. pro. 16. conj.
17. adv. 18. noun
19. adj. 20. noun

Identifying Parts of Speech

Write the part of speech (*noun, pronoun, adjective, verb, adverb, preposition, conjunction,* or *interjection*) of the italicized words in the paragraph below.

EXAMPLE Pioneers [1] *learned* how to recognize danger.
1. verb

The [1] *first* pioneers on the Great Plains [2] *encountered* many kinds [3] *of* dangerous animals. Grizzly bears and [4] *huge* herds of bison were menaces to [5] *early* settlers. One of the [6] *most* ferocious beasts of the plains [7] *was* a [8] *grizzly* protecting her cubs. However, [9] *neither* the bison *nor* the grizzly was the most feared animal [10] *on* the frontier. Not even the deadly [11] *rattlesnake*—nor [12] *any* of the other prairie creatures—was dreaded as much as the skunk. You may think, [13] "*Oh,* that is [14] *ridiculous.*" However, it is true. Skunks were not feared because [15] *they* smelled bad [16] *but,* instead, because they [17] *so* often carried [18] *rabies.* Since there was no vaccine for rabies in [19] *those* days, the bite of a rabid skunk spelled certain [20] *doom* for the unlucky victim.

The Noun

12a. A *noun* is a word or word group that is used to name a person, a place, a thing, or an idea.

Persons	Sharon, Major Brown, hairstylist, joggers
Places	Iowa, districts, Mars, Antarctica, library
Things	okra, Great Pyramid, toothpicks, merry-go-round
Ideas	peace, truth, artistry, excellence, beauty

Common and Proper Nouns

A *proper noun* names a particular person, place, thing, or idea and is capitalized. A *common noun* names any one of a group of persons, places, things, or ideas and is generally not capitalized.

Common Nouns	Proper Nouns
scientist	Marie Curie, Charles Drew
woman	Coretta Scott King, Rita Moreno
city	Cairo, St. Louis, Paris
building	World Trade Center, Eiffel Tower
continent	North America, South America, Africa
day	Monday, Thursday, Labor Day

Exercise 1 **Classifying Nouns**

Identify each of the following nouns as a *common noun* or a *proper noun*. If the noun is proper, name a corresponding common noun.

EXAMPLE　　**1.** Zora Neale Hurston
　　　　　　1. proper noun—writer

1. man　1. c.
2. month　2. c.
3. Vietnam　3. p.
4. singer　4. c.
5. Athena　5. p.
6. city　6. c.
7. gumbo　7. c.
8. self-esteem　8. c.
9. Virginia　9. p.
10. ocean　10. c.
11. Mount Hood　11. p.
12. Australia　12. p.
13. Detroit　13. p.
14. street　14. c.
15. Amelia Earhart　15. p.
16. mercy　16. c.
17. cousin　17. c.
18. automobile　18. c.
19. blues　19. c.
20. Christopher Columbus　20. p.

Reference Note

For more information on **capitalizing proper nouns,** see page 620.

Corresponding common nouns may vary.

3. country
5. goddess
9. state
11. mountain
12. continent
13. city
15. pilot
20. explorer

The Noun
Rule 12a *(pp. 375–378)*

OBJECTIVES

- To identify and classify common and proper nouns and give examples of both
- To identify compound nouns used in sentences
- To identify nouns used in sentences

RESOURCES

The Noun
Practice
- *Grammar, Usage, and Mechanics,* pp. 2, 3, 4
- *Language Workshop CD-ROM,* Lesson 1

INCLUSION

Students might better understand the concept of nouns if they associate the various kinds of nouns with familiar words. Have the students fill in the following chart with names of persons, places, things, and ideas that have personal meaning. Students might need help filling in the *Idea* column.

PERSON	PLACE	THING	IDEA

BORN LOSER reprinted by permission of Newspaper Enterprise Association, Inc.

Concrete and Abstract Nouns

A *concrete noun* names a person, place, or thing that can be perceived by one or more of the senses (sight, hearing, taste, touch, and smell). An *abstract noun* names an idea, a feeling, a quality, or a characteristic.

Concrete Nouns	cloud, poison ivy, thunder, silk, yogurt, Sarah
Abstract Nouns	freedom, well-being, beauty, kindness, Buddhism

Exercise 2 **Identifying and Classifying Nouns**

Write all the nouns that you find in each sentence. Then, circle the proper nouns.

EXAMPLE
1. English grows daily with the addition of new words.
1. (English,) addition, words

1. Some words come from other languages, such as (Spanish) and (French.)
2. Books, music, and movies often feature new words that are then added to everyday (English.)
3. Many useful and amusing words came into our language during (World War II.)
4. Now these words are familiar throughout the (United States.)
5. One of these words is *gremlin.*
6. Fliers were often troubled by mysterious mechanical problems.
7. Not knowing what caused these problems, they joked that gremlins—small, mischievous creatures—were in the aircraft.
8. According to (Grandpa Leroy,) these gremlins could be helpful as well as harmful.
9. Many fliers claimed that they had miraculously escaped danger only because the gremlins had come to their rescue.
10. Artists drew the imps as little men with beards and funny hats who played all over the planes.

Compound Nouns

A *compound noun* consists of two or more words used together as a single noun. The parts of a compound noun may be written as one word, as separate words, or as a hyphenated word.

Capitalizing Proper Nouns. While discussing proper nouns, you may also want to discuss capitalization rules with students. Explain that a common noun is not capitalized unless it begins a sentence or is part of a title. Most proper nouns are capitalized. Some proper nouns consist of more than one word. In names, such as *Statue of Liberty,* articles and prepositions of fewer than five letters are generally not capitalized.

One Word	firefighter, Iceland, newspaper
Separate Words	prime minister, Red River Dam, fire drill
Hyphenated Word	sister-in-law, Port-au-Prince, pull-up

NOTE If you are not sure how to write a compound noun, look in a dictionary. Some dictionaries may give more than one correct form for a word. For example, you may find the word vice-president written both with and without the hyphen. As a rule, use the form the dictionary lists first.

Exercise 3 Identifying Compound Nouns

Each of the sentences below contains at least one compound noun. Write the compound noun(s) in each sentence.

EXAMPLE   **1.** My cousin John is a political scientist.

    1. political scientist

1. I use a word processor or a typewriter in class.
2. We went swimming in the Gulf of Mexico.
3. My sister and my brother-in-law live in Council Bluffs, Iowa.
4. My Old English sheepdog is still a puppy.
5. Some almanacs give exact times for sunrises and sunsets.
6. We used to play hide-and-seek in the old barn.
7. Sitting Bull was the war chief who masterminded the Sioux victory at the Battle of the Little Bighorn.
8. Meet me at the bowling alley near the post office.
9. The fountain pen is not as popular as the ballpoint.
10. Luís Valdez is a playwright, actor, and director.

Collective Nouns

A *collective noun* is a word that names a group.

People	audience, chorus, committee, crew
Animals	brood, flock, gaggle, herd
Things	assortment, batch, bundle, cluster

Reference Note

For more on **collective nouns,** see page 501.

Relating to Spelling
Students often have difficulty deciding whether a specific compound noun should be written as one word, as two words, or as a hyphenated word. Point out that the typical pattern is for the hyphen to be used in a compound when it is new, but for it to be dropped after the word becomes familiar. For example, *school-boy* became *schoolboy*.

You may wish to ask students to hunt for new compound words to put on the bulletin board. Suggest that they use several different dictionaries to see if the words are treated differently.

Write on the chalkboard items 1–5 and have students correct the capitalization. For additional help or practice, refer students to **Chapter 21: Capital Letters.**

1. isle of pines
2. ohio state fair
3. mayor gernhardt
4. the wizard of oz
5. webster's new world dictionary

GRAMMAR

Critical Thinking

Analysis. To make students aware of how they figure out the parts of speech, ask them to begin a chart to show what questions to use to determine the part of speech of a word. Students can add to the chart as they study successive parts of speech in this chapter.

EXAMPLE
Noun: Is it the name of a person, place, thing, or idea? Does the word make sense with *the* or *a* in front of it?

The Pronoun

Rule 12b *(pp. 378–381)*

O B J E C T I V E

■ To identify pronouns and their antecedents in sentences

Crossing the Curriculum

Art/Computer Graphics. As students complete their parts of speech charts by including pronouns, ask those who are interested in art or computer graphics to create a chart for the classroom using these media. If several students are interested in this project, ask them to divide the tasks: creating icons for each part of speech; selecting a color to identify each part of speech; working out placement on the chart; editing the text for spelling, parallelism, and other usage and mechanics points.

Exercise 4 **Identifying Nouns**

Identify the twenty-five <u>nouns</u> in the sentences below.

EXAMPLE
1. To enter the wildlife <u>park</u>, we walked through the <u>mouth</u> of a huge fake <u>alligator</u>.

    1. *park, mouth, alligator*

1. <u>Businesses</u> sometimes use gigantic <u>objects</u> to advertise their <u>products</u>.
2. A <u>stand</u> that sells <u>fruit</u> might look like an enormous <u>orange</u>, complete with <u>doors</u> and <u>windows</u>.
3. A <u>restaurant</u> in <u>Austin</u>, <u>Texas</u>, has a delivery <u>van</u> shaped like a <u>dinosaur</u>.
4. Huge <u>dogs</u>, <u>windmills</u>, and <u>figures</u> of <u>Paul Bunyan</u> are formed with <u>cement</u> or <u>fiberglass</u> to help sell <u>chain saws</u>, <u>trucks</u>, and <u>souvenirs</u>.
5. An old <u>hotel</u> in <u>New Jersey</u> was even built to look like an <u>elephant</u>!

The Pronoun

12b. A *pronoun* is a word that is used in place of one or more nouns or pronouns.

EXAMPLES   Stan bought a suit and an overcoat. **He** will wear **them** tomorrow. [The pronoun *He* stands for the noun *Stan*. The pronoun *them* stands for the nouns *suit* and *overcoat*.]

             Several of the horses have gone into the stable because **they** are hungry. [The pronoun *Several* refers to the noun *horses*. The pronoun *they* stands for the pronoun *Several*.]

Reference Note

For more information about **antecedents,** see page 507.

The word that a pronoun stands for or refers to is called the ***antecedent*** of the pronoun. In the following examples, the arrows point from the pronouns to their antecedents.

EXAMPLES   The tour guide showed the **students** where **they** could see Mayan pottery.

             Why did **Oscar** give **his** camera to the film school?

             Darius scored a **field goal. It** was his first of the season.

Notice that a pronoun may appear in the same sentence as its antecedent or in a nearby sentence.

RESOURCES

The Pronoun
Practice

■ *Grammar, Usage, and Mechanics,* pp. 5, 6, 7, 8, 9
■ *Language Workshop CD-ROM,* Lesson 2

Personal Pronouns

A *personal pronoun* refers to the one speaking (first person), the one spoken to (second person), or the one spoken about (third person).

First Person	I, me, my, mine, we, us, our, ours
Second Person	you, your, yours
Third Person	he, him, his, she, her, hers, it, its, they, them, their, theirs

EXAMPLES   **I** hope that **they** can find **your** apartment by following **our** directions.

She said that **we** could call **them** at home.

He asked **us** to help **him** clear away the fallen branches from **his** backyard.

Their dog obeyed **them** immediately and went to **its** bed.

NOTE In this book, the words *my, your, his, her, its* and *their* are called pronouns. Some authorities prefer to call these words adjectives. Follow your teacher's instructions on labeling these words.

Exercise 5   Identifying Antecedents

Give the antecedent for each italicized pronoun in the following paragraph.

EXAMPLE   In about A.D. 1150, a historian wrote down a strange tale English villagers had told **[1]** *him*.

    1. him—historian

Since numerous people told the same story, the historian believed **[1]** *it*. Supposedly, a young boy and girl with bright green skin had been found wandering in the fields. **[2]** *They* spoke a foreign language and wore clothing made of an unknown material. At first, the two children would eat only green beans, but after **[3]** *they* learned to eat bread, **[4]** *their* skin gradually lost **[5]** *its* greenness. After learning English, the girl said **[6]** *she* and **[7]** *her* brother had come from a land called Saint Martin. The story sounds like science fiction, doesn't **[8]** *it*? Perhaps the villagers invented **[9]** *it* to amuse **[10]** *their* friends and fool historians.

Reference Note

For information on **choosing pronouns that agree with their antecedents,** see page 507. For information on **clear pronoun reference,** see page 565.

STYLE   TIP

To keep your readers from getting confused, place pronouns near their antecedents—generally within the same sentence or in the next sentence.

CONFUSING

Please hand me the scissors. I also need some strapping tape. They are in the top drawer on the left. [Does They refer to the scissors or to both the scissors and the strapping tape?]

CLEAR

Please hand me the **scissors. They** are in the top drawer on the left. I also need some strapping tape. [Only the scissors are in the top drawer on the left.]

GRAMMAR

Meeting
INDIVIDUAL NEEDS

ENGLISH-LANGUAGE LEARNERS

General Strategies. Differentiating among the different kinds of pronouns may seem overwhelming to students; therefore, you may wish to concentrate on the personal pronouns with English-language learners in your class. The chart for personal pronouns should be broken down into nominative, objective, and possessive categories with example sentences. Work with students while they write sentences with each of the possessive pronouns. Students may wish to create a chart of these pronoun cases for the classroom.

Exercise 5   Identifying Antecedents

ANSWERS

1. story
2. boy, girl
3. children
4. children
5. skin
6. girl
7. girl
8. story
9. story
10. villagers

ALTERNATIVE LESSON

To reinforce what students have learned about nouns, have them list all the nouns in the second sentence of the exercise. [*boy, girl, skin, fields*]

For students who need more practice, select other sentences and repeat the process.

Meeting
INDIVIDUAL
NEEDS

ENGLISH-LANGUAGE LEARNERS

Spanish. Because Spanish has more verbs that require reflexive pronouns than English does, Spanish-speaking students may overuse reflexive pronouns and may think that certain English verbs take reflexive pronouns because their Spanish counterparts do. For example, the Spanish equivalent of *repent* is *arrepentirse,* which translates literally as "to repent oneself" (the ending *se* makes the verb reflexive).

Spanish. The English pronouns *your, his, her, its,* and *their* can all be translated in formal Spanish as *su* (or *sus* if more than one thing is possessed). *Your* can be expressed as *tu* (singular) or *tus* (plural) familiarly, among family and close friends. *Yourself, himself, herself, itself,* and *themselves* can all be translated as *se.* Watch for any difficulties Spanish-speaking students may have distinguishing among pronouns in their written work.

TIPS & TRICKS

To find out if a pronoun is reflexive or intensive, leave it out of the sentence. If the meaning of the sentence stays the same without the pronoun, the pronoun is intensive.

EXAMPLES

Ron looked at himself in the mirror. [*Ron looked at in the mirror* doesn't mean the same thing. The pronoun is reflexive.]

Jenny painted the room herself. [*Jenny painted the room* means the same thing. The pronoun is intensive.]

Reference Note

For more information on **relative pronouns,** see page 473. For information on **subordinate clauses,** see page 471.

Reflexive and Intensive Pronouns

A *reflexive pronoun* refers to the subject of a sentence and functions as a complement or as an object of a preposition. An *intensive pronoun* emphasizes its antecedent and has no grammatical function.

First Person	myself, ourselves
Second Person	yourself, yourselves
Third Person	himself, herself, itself, themselves

EXAMPLES   Elena treated **herself** to a snack. [reflexive]

Albert **himself** organized the fund-raiser. [intensive]

Demonstrative Pronouns

A *demonstrative pronoun* is used to point out a specific person, place, thing, or idea.

this	that	these	those

EXAMPLES   **That** is Soon-Hee's favorite restaurant in San Francisco.

The tacos I made taste better than **those.**

Interrogative Pronouns

An *interrogative pronoun* introduces a question.

who	whom	which	what	whose

EXAMPLES   **Which** of the songs is your favorite?

What is your parakeet's name?

Relative Pronouns

A *relative pronoun* introduces a subordinate clause.

that	which	who	whom	whose

EXAMPLES   The ship **that** you saw is sailing to Greece.

Isabel is my friend **who** is training for the Boston marathon.

Indefinite Pronouns

An *indefinite pronoun* refers to one or more persons, places, ideas, or things that may or may not be specifically named.

all	each	most	one
another	either	much	other
any	everyone	neither	several
anybody	everything	nobody	some
anyone	few	none	somebody
anything	many	no one	something
both	more	nothing	such

EXAMPLES   Angelo has **everything** he will need to go rock climbing.

Is **anyone** at home?

Most of the birds had already flown south for the winter.

> ┌ **HELP** ─────
> Many of the pronouns you have studied so far may also be used as adjectives.
>
> EXAMPLES
>   **this** street
>   **whose** puppy
>   **many** acorns

Reference Note

For more about using **pronouns,** see Chapter 18.

Exercise 6   Identifying Pronouns

Identify all the pronouns in the sentences below.

EXAMPLE   **[1]** My friend Hideko invited me to a Japanese tea ceremony at her house.

   1. *My, me, her*

[1] The tea ceremony at Hideko's house was more like some I have seen in movies than the traditional one shown in this picture. [2] "What happens during the tea ceremony, Hideko?" I asked as we entered the house. [3] According to Hideko, the purpose of the tea ceremony, a custom that dates back hundreds of years, is to create a peaceful mood. [4] In the ceremony, everyone sits quietly and watches the tea being made. [5] Before entering the room for the ceremony, I reminded myself to take off my shoes. [6] During the ceremony, each of us kneeled on a straw mat. [7] Hideko's mother was our tea hostess, the person who conducts the ceremony and prepares all of the tea. [8] She prepared the tea and served it in bowls that had been in the family for generations. [9] Then she served us sweet cakes called *kashi* (KAH-shee). [10] Afterward, Hideko herself gave me a box of tea leaves to take home with me.

Looking at Language

Students might not realize that English is more closely related to German than to Latin-based languages like French or Spanish. During the Middle Ages, as the sounds of English changed, English nouns lost most of their Germanic case endings. Only possessive nouns and certain pronouns, such as *he, his,* and *him,* still indicate case.

Exercise 6

ALTERNATIVE LESSON
Have students review nouns by finding the following items in the third sentence:

1. two plural nouns [*hundreds, years*]

2. a proper noun [*Hideko*]

The Adjective

Rule 12c *(pp. 382–386)*

OBJECTIVES

- To distinguish between adjectives and nouns
- To add appropriate adjectives to sentences

Meeting
INDIVIDUAL NEEDS

ENGLISH-LANGUAGE LEARNERS
General Strategies. In English, adjectives usually precede the nouns they modify, as in *big house.* However, in many languages, such as Khmer, Portuguese, Spanish, Tigre, and Vietnamese, adjectives usually follow the noun, as in *casa grande* ("house big"). Speakers of these languages may try to identify adjectives in English by their position, so they might think *big* is the noun and *house* is the adjective. You may wish to stress the adjective/noun order in English—perhaps by writing several adjective/noun pairs on the chalkboard and having students correctly label the parts of speech.

TIPS & TRICKS

The phrase *these five interesting books* can help you remember the questions an adjective can answer: Which books? These books. How many books? Five books. What kind of books? Interesting books.

Reference Note

For more information about **demonstrative pronouns,** see page 380.

The Adjective

12c. An *adjective* is a word that is used to modify a noun or a pronoun.

To **modify** a word means to describe the word or to make its meaning more definite. An adjective modifies a noun or a pronoun by telling *what kind, which one,* or *how many.*

What Kind?	**gray** skies	**Irish** lace
	far-fetched tale	**lowest** price
Which One?	**either** way	**those** girls
	next day	**last** chance
How Many?	**five** fingers	**fewer** hours
	one river	**some** problems

Demonstrative Adjectives

This, that, these, and *those* can be used both as adjectives and as pronouns. When they modify nouns or pronouns, they are called *demonstrative adjectives.* When they take the place of nouns or pronouns, they are called *demonstrative pronouns.*

Demonstrative Adjectives	Did Jennifer draw **this** picture or **that** one?
	Let's take **these** sandwiches and **those** apples on our picnic.
Demonstrative Pronouns	**This** is mine and **that** is his.
	These are much more expensive than **those** are.

Pronoun or Adjective?

Some words may be used as either pronouns or adjectives. When used as pronouns, these words take the place of nouns or other pronouns. When used as adjectives, they modify nouns or pronouns.

RESOURCES

The Adjective
Practice

- *Grammar, Usage, and Mechanics,* pp. 10, 11, 12, 13
- *Language Workshop CD-ROM,* Lesson 3

Pronoun	Adjective
I like **that**.	I like **that** shirt.
Either will do.	**Either** car will do.
Which is yours?	**Which** one is yours?
Whose is it?	**Whose** hat is it?

NOTE In this book, demonstrative, interrogative, and indefinite terms, such as those in boldface in the preceding chart, are called pronouns when they function as pronouns, and adjectives when they function as adjectives.

The words *my, your, his, her, its, our,* and *their* are called possessive pronouns throughout this book. Some authorities, however, prefer to call these words adjectives. Follow your teacher's instructions on labeling these words.

Noun or Adjective?

Many words that can stand alone as nouns can also be used as adjectives modifying nouns or pronouns.

Common Nouns	Adjectives
cheese	**cheese** sandwich
snow	**snow** sculpture
winter	**winter** sale
weather	**weather** report
steel	**steel** girder

Adjectives formed from proper nouns are called *proper adjectives.*

Proper Nouns	Proper Adjectives
Choctaw	**Choctaw** tradition
Texas	**Texas** coast
Picasso	**Picasso** painting
Dublin	**Dublin** streets
Roosevelt	**Roosevelt** administration

┌HELP┐
Possessive forms of nouns are also sometimes referred to as adjectives. Follow your teacher's instructions regarding these forms.

Cooperative Learning

Explain to students that overused adjectives, such as *nice* and *great,* can sometimes weaken a description. Have students work in groups of four to fill in the blank in the following sentence with at least five vague or overused adjectives:

Love is _____. [*nice, awesome, terrible, neat, wonderful*]

Then, have each group member suggest one adjective that is more specific [*blissful, troublesome, turbulent, fickle, romantic*].

Have each student make a list of specific adjectives on a specified topic—color, size, beauty, shape, and so on. Then, have the group discuss the lists and add to them. Post completed lists on the bulletin board.

Reference Note

For information about **capitalizing proper adjectives,** see page 620. See page 376 for more on **compound nouns.**

NOTE Sometimes a proper adjective and a noun are used together so frequently that they become a compound noun: *Brazil nut, French bread, Christmas tree, Swiss cheese.*

TEACHING TIP

Exercise 7 Direct students' attention to the **Note** above the exercise. Remind students that a compound noun consists of two or more words used together as a single noun.

Exercise 7 Identifying Nouns and Adjectives

Indicate whether each italicized word in the paragraph below is used as a *noun* or an *adjective.*

EXAMPLE   Do you want to see my new [1] *baseball* card?

　　　　　1. baseball—adjective

1. noun	6. adj.
2. noun	7. noun
3. adj.	8. adj.
4. noun	9. adj.
5. adj.	10. noun

I love anything that has to do with [1] *baseball.* I save the [2] *money* I make mowing the golf course, and then I go to the [3] *card* [4] *store.* The [5] *store* owner sold me a terrific [6] *Don Mattingly* [7] *card* today. It came in its own [8] *plastic* case. I'll display my new card with my other favorites in a special [9] *glass* [10] *case* on the wall in my room.

Articles

The most frequently used adjectives are *a, an,* and *the.* These words are usually called ***articles.***

A and *an* are called ***indefinite articles*** because they refer to any member of a general group. *A* is used before words beginning with a consonant sound. *An* is used before words beginning with a vowel sound.

EXAMPLES   **A** girl won.

They are having **a** one-day sale. [Even though *o* is a vowel, the term *one-day* begins with a consonant sound.]

An elephant escaped.

This is **an** honor. [Even though *h* is a consonant, the word *honor* begins with a vowel sound. The *h* is not pronounced.]

The is called the ***definite article*** because it refers to someone or something in particular.

EXAMPLES   **The** girl won.

The one-day sale is on Saturday.

Where is **the** elephant?

The honor goes to her.

MINI-LESSON

Punctuating Adjectives Before Nouns. Explain to students that a comma is generally used to separate two or more adjectives that come before a noun, as in *I rode a gentle, old horse.*

Sometimes when the final adjective in a series is closely linked to the noun, a comma is not needed before the final adjective: *Maya is a respected broadcast journalist.*

Adjectives in Sentences

An adjective usually comes before the noun or pronoun it modifies.

EXAMPLES   Ms. Farrell tells **all** students that **good** workers will be given **special** privileges.

A **sweating, exhausted** runner crossed the line.

In some cases, adjectives follow the word they modify.

EXAMPLE   A dog, **old** and **overweight,** snored in the sun.

Other words may separate an adjective from the noun or pronoun it modifies.

EXAMPLES   Beverly was **worried.** She felt **nervous** about the play.

Cheered by the crowd, the band played an encore.

> NOTE   An adjective that is in the predicate and that modifies the subject of a clause or sentence is called a *predicate adjective*.

Reference Note

For more information about **predicate adjectives,** see page 573.

Exercise 8   Revising Sentences by Using Appropriate Adjectives

Add adjectives to make two entirely different sentences from each of the sentences below.

EXAMPLE   1. The waiter showed the woman to a table in the corner.

1. *The kindly waiter showed the shy woman to a pleasant table in the sunny corner.*

   The haughty waiter showed the elegant woman to a private table in the shadowy corner.

1. The blossoms on the trees filled the air with a scent.
2. As the clouds gathered in the sky, the captain spoke to the crew.
3. At the end of the hall were stairs that led to a room.
4. The car has a stereo and an air conditioner.
5. The singers and comedians gave a performance for the audience.
6. The birds flew to the birdhouse near the barn.
7. Theresa's interest in science began when she attended the class.
8. The house in the valley was constructed by builders.
9. The curtains on the windows added to the look of the room.
10. As the waves washed onto the shore, the children ran away.

COMPUTER TIP

Using a software program's thesaurus can help you choose appropriate adjectives. To make sure that an adjective has exactly the connotation you intend, look up the word in a dictionary.

The Adjective   **385**

Exercise 8   Revising Sentences by Using Appropriate Adjectives

POSSIBLE ANSWERS

1. The [*delicate; purple*] blossoms on the [*young; enormous*] trees filled the [*misty; humid*] air with a [*sweet; heavy*] scent.

2. As the [*dark; billowy*] clouds gathered in the [*threatening; evening*] sky, the [*confident; enthusiastic*] captain spoke to the [*frightened; inexperienced*] crew.

3. At the end of the [*long; cluttered*] hall were [*steep; narrow*] stairs that led to a [*hidden; storage*] room.

4. The [*sports; flashy*] car has a [*state-of-the-art; cheap*] stereo and a [*high-performance; leaky*] air conditioner.

5. The [*talented; solemn*] singers and [*silly; angry*] comedians gave a [*creative; poor*] performance for the [*appreciative; confused*] audience.

6. The [*tired; mother*] birds flew to the [*tiny; gray*] birdhouse near the [*dilapidated; scarlet*] barn.

7. Theresa's interest in [*biological; physical*] science began when she attended the [*zoology; meteorology*] class.

8. The [*stone; ranch*] house in the [*lush; hidden*] valley was constructed by [*master; amateur*] builders.

9. The [*tattered; lace*] curtains on the [*grimy; sparkling*] windows added to the [*forsaken; gracious*] look of the [*dingy; inviting*] room.

10. As the [*crashing; foamy*] waves washed onto the [*forlorn; sandy*] shore, the [*frightened; giggling*] children ran away.

To test if the final adjective and the noun are closely linked, have students insert the word *and* between the adjectives. If *and* makes sense, they should use a comma.

Ask students to find a piece of their own writing and to check for the proper punctuation of two or more adjectives preceding a noun. For further instruction and practice, refer students to **Chapter 22: Punctuation.**

The Verb

Rule 12d *(pp. 386–393)*

OBJECTIVES

■ To identify transitive and intransitive verbs

■ To identify linking verbs and words they link

■ To add linking verbs to sentences

■ To write sentences with action verbs and linking verbs

■ To identify helping verbs

■ To identify verbs and verb phrases, including all helping verbs

■ To revise dialogue by using precise verbs

| Link to | Literature |

1. adj. / noun
2. noun / adj.
3. adj. / pro.
4. pro. / adj.
5. noun / pro.
6. noun / pro.
7. adj. / adj.
8. noun / pro.
9. adj. / pro.
10. pro. / noun

Reference Note

For more about **objects and their uses in sentences,** see page 431.

Review A **Identifying Nouns, Pronouns, and Adjectives**

Indicate whether each of the italicized words in the following paragraph is used as a *noun*, a *pronoun*, or an *adjective*.

EXAMPLE   [1] Most high school *students* read at least *one* play by William Shakespeare.

1. students—noun; one—adjective

[1] *This* article tells about Shakespeare's *life.* [2] *Shakespeare,* perhaps the most *famous* playwright of all time, was born in Stratford-on-Avon in 1564. [3] He was baptized in the *small* church at Stratford shortly after *his* birth. [4] In 1616, *he* was buried in the *same* church. [5] If you visit his grave, you can find an *inscription* placing a curse on *anyone* who moves his bones. [6] Out of *respect* for his wish or because of fear of his curse, *nobody* has disturbed the grave. [7] As a result, his remains have never been moved to Westminster Abbey, where many *other* famous *English* writers are buried. [8] Visitors to *Stratford* can also see the house in *which* Shakespeare was born. [9] At *one* time tourists could visit the large house that Shakespeare bought for *himself* and his family. [10] *This* was where they lived when he retired from the London *theater.*

The Verb

12d. A *verb* is a word that is used to express action or a state of being.

In this book verbs are classified in two ways—(1) as transitive or intransitive verbs and (2) as action, linking, or helping verbs.

Transitive and Intransitive Verbs

A *transitive verb* is a verb that expresses an action directed toward a person, place, or thing. The action expressed by a transitive verb passes from the doer—the subject—to the receiver of the action. Words that receive the action of a transitive verb are called *objects.*

EXAMPLES   When **will** Neil **ring** the bell? [The action of the verb *will ring* is directed toward the object *bell.*]

Juanita **mailed** the package. [The action of the verb *mailed* is directed toward the object *package.*]

Tell the truth. [The action of the verb *Tell* is directed toward the object *truth.*]

RESOURCES

The Verb

Practice

■ *Grammar, Usage, and Mechanics,* pp. 14, 15, 16, 17, 18

■ *Language Workshop CD-ROM,* Lesson 4

An *intransitive verb* expresses action (or tells something about the subject) without the action passing to a receiver, or object.

EXAMPLES   Last Saturday we **stayed** inside. [The verb *stayed* does not pass the action to an object.]

             After their long walk, the children **ate** quickly. [The verb *ate* does not pass the action to an object.]

             When she told her story, my, how we **laughed**! [The verb *laughed* does not pass the action to an object.]

A verb may be transitive in one sentence and intransitive in another.

EXAMPLES   Marcie **studied** her notes. [transitive]
             Marcie **studied** very late. [intransitive]

             The poet **wrote** a sonnet. [transitive]
             The poet **wrote** carefully. [intransitive]

Exercise 9   Using Transitive and Intransitive Verbs

Choose a verb from the following list for each blank in the paragraph below. Then, identify each verb as *transitive* or *intransitive*.

drifted	landed	watched	experienced
floated	rode	met	admired
climbed	arrived	left	did
awaited	suggest	tried	drove

EXAMPLE   Can you [1] ＿＿＿ an activity for this weekend?

             1. suggest—transitive

    Aunt Pam and I [1] ＿＿＿ something really different last summer. We [2] ＿＿＿ on inner tubes down a river in the wilderness. A guide [3] ＿＿＿ our group with a truckful of giant tubes and picnic lunches and [4] ＿＿＿ us about twenty miles upstream. Then everyone [5] ＿＿＿ into a tube in the water. The guide [6] ＿＿＿ in the truck for a picnic spot downstream, halfway back to the base. All morning, we [7] ＿＿＿ lazily along in the sunshine and [8] ＿＿＿ the wildlife along the shore. When we [9] ＿＿＿ at the picnic spot, a delicious lunch [10] ＿＿＿ us.

Verbs will vary.
1. did—tr.
2. rode—int.
3. met—tr.
4. drove—tr.
5. climbed—int.
6. left—int.
7. floated—int.
8. admired—tr.
9. landed—int.
10. awaited—tr.

Action Verbs

An *action verb* expresses either physical or mental action. Action verbs can be transitive or intransitive.

Relating to Literature

If your literature book contains Emily Dickinson's poem "A Bird Came Down the Walk," read the poem to students. Have them listen for verbs and tell how Dickinson's choice of verbs contributes to the poem.

[*The use of action verbs gives the reader a sense of the bird's quick and definite movements. The poet writes concisely, taking full advantage of each verb to create an effective image.*]

Cooperative Learning

Divide the class into groups of four to play a game with action verbs. Give each group five index cards with one of the following sentences on each card:

1. Mom drove through the traffic.

2. Al walked across the stage.

3. Pedro sang for the audience.

4. The team came onto the field.

5. Maya threw the ball too hard.

The object of the five-minute game is for the groups to replace the verbs on the cards with as many specific verbs as possible. After five minutes, have the groups share their sentences with the rest of the class.

Physical Action	write	sit	arise
	describe	receive	go
Mental Action	remember	think	believe
	consider	understand	know

EXAMPLES   The audience **cheered** the lead actors. [transitive]

                The audience **cheered.** [intransitive]

Exercise 10   Writing Action Verbs

Write twenty action verbs, not including those previously listed. Include and underline at least five verbs that express mental action.

EXAMPLES   **1.** *soar*   **2.** *imagine*

Linking Verbs

A *linking verb* connects the subject to a word or word group that identifies or describes the subject. The most commonly used linking verbs are forms of the verb *be*.

be	shall be	should be
being	will be	would be
am	has been	can be
is	have been	could be
are	had been	should have been
was	shall have been	would have been
were	will have been	could have been

Here are some other frequently used linking verbs.

appear	grow	seem	stay
become	look	smell	taste
feel	remain	sound	turn

Reference Note

For more about **intransitive verbs,** see page 386.

NOTE Because they do not have objects (words that tell who or what receives the action of the verb), linking verbs are considered intransitive.

Exercise 10   Writing Action Verbs

POSSIBLE ANSWERS

1.	catch	11.	listen
2.	throw	12.	strum
3.	eat	13.	display
4.	walk	14.	jog
5.	read	15.	bounce
6.	study	16.	<u>suppose</u>
7.	stay	17.	<u>ponder</u>
8.	dance	18.	<u>analyze</u>
9.	ski	19.	<u>realize</u>
10.	sing	20.	<u>yearn</u>

Relating to Writing

Students often use linking verbs in their writing when action verbs would be more concise. For example, a student might write "I am a fast runner and a high jumper" instead of "I run fast and jump high."

Ask each student to write a one-paragraph character sketch about an admired person. Tell students that when they revise their paragraphs, they should each replace all but two linking verbs. Make sure that students understand that there is nothing wrong with using forms of *be* if necessary but that action verbs often provide more specific images.

TECHNOLOGY TIP

To help students complete the one-paragraph assignment above, have them use online dictionaries linked to the HRW Web site to check the spelling of irregular verb forms.

MINI-LESSON

Subject Complements. Explain to students that a subject complement is a noun, pronoun, or adjective that completes the meaning of a linking verb and identifies or describes the subject. If the complement is a noun or pronoun, it is called a *predicate nominative;* if it is an adjective, it is called a *predicate adjective.* Write sentences 1–3 on the chalkboard. Ask students to label each subject complement *predicate nominative*

The noun, pronoun, or adjective that is connected to the subject by a linking verb completes the meaning of the verb and refers to the verb's subject.

EXAMPLES   **The answer is "three."** [The verb *is* links *answer* and *"three."*]

            The answer is correct. [The verb *is* links *answer* and *correct.*]

            The winners are they. [The verb links *winners* and *they.*]

            The winners are happy. [The verb links *winners* and *happy.*]

Many linking verbs can be used as action verbs as well.

EXAMPLES   **The wet dog smelled horrible.** [The linking verb *smelled* links *dog* and *horrible.*]

            The dog smelled the baked bread. [action verb]

            The motor sounded harsh. [The linking verb *sounded* links *motor* and *harsh.*]

            The engineer sounded the horn. [action verb]

            The chef tasted the casserole. [action verb]

            The casserole tasted strange. [The verb *tasted* links *casserole* and *strange.*]

Even *be* is not always a linking verb. Sometimes *be* expresses a state of being and is followed only by an adverb.

EXAMPLE   **I was there.** [*There* tells *where.* It does not identify or describe the subject *I.*]

To be a linking verb, the verb must be followed by a ***subject complement***—a noun or a pronoun that names the subject or an adjective that describes the subject.

Reference Note
For a discussion of **adverbs,** see page 393.

Reference Note
For more on **subject complements,** see page 429.

> **Exercise 11**   **Identifying Linking Verbs and the Words They Link**

Identify the linking verb in each of the sentences below. Then, give the words that are linked by the verb.

EXAMPLE   **1.** Dixie can be a very obedient dog.

          1. can be—Dixie, dog

1. He felt foolish when his car ran out of gas.
2. Suddenly, it turned very dark, and the wind began to blow fiercely.
3. We had waited so long for dinner that anything would have tasted wonderful.

The Verb   **389**

---

or *predicate adjective.*

1. Mario is a good soccer *player.* [*predicate nominative*]

2. The hyacinths along the path smelled *sweet.* [*predicate adjective*]

3. The one who called this morning was *she.* [*predicate nominative*]

For more information on subject complements, refer students to **Chapter 13: The Parts of a Sentence.**

4. The plot of that fantasy novel seems awfully childish to me now.
5. Kevin and I stayed best friends throughout middle school.
6. I am happy that you won the chess match.
7. If the coach had let me play, this game would have been my first one with the Tigers.
8. My father thinks that you should become a lawyer.
9. After practicing hard, Stef's band sounded great in the concert.
10. For a moment, Dr. Kostas thought the planet's rings appeared smaller.

Exercise 12 **Writing Appropriate Linking Verbs**

Choose a linking verb for each blank. Try to use a different verb for each sentence.   Verbs will vary.

EXAMPLE   **1.** The baby _____ sleepy after he was fed.

   1. *The baby grew sleepy after he was fed.*

1. That building _____ the new public library.   **1.** is
2. The car _____ funny.   **2.** sounds
3. The moose _____ huge.   **3.** was
4. I _____ very nervous about the driving test.   **4.** felt
5. Her garden _____ dried and brown in the drought.   **5.** became
6. Let's hope the evening _____ cool.   **6.** will be
7. We can eat the raspberries when they _____ red.   **7.** turn
8. Burt _____ grouchy early in the morning.   **8.** would be
9. The soup _____ too salty.   **9.** tasted
10. The puppy _____ healthy and playful.   **10.** appears

Exercise 13 **Writing Sentences with Action Verbs and Linking Verbs**

Choose five nouns from the numbered items below. For each noun, write two sentences, using the noun as the subject of each sentence. Use an action verb in one sentence and a linking verb in the other. Indicate which sentence contains the action verb and which contains the linking verb.

EXAMPLE   **1.** fireworks

   1. *The fireworks filled the night sky with bursts of color.—action verb*

   The fireworks grew more colorful toward the end of the program.—linking verb

Exercise 13 **Writing Sentences with Action Verbs and Linking Verbs**

ANSWERS
Sentences will vary, but students should correctly label the action verbs and linking verbs that they use in their sentences.

Learning for Life

Giving Accurate Directions. People are often called upon to give directions to others for getting to a specific place. Ask students to write a set of directions for getting from the classroom to some other location in the school, such as the library, the principal's office, or the cafeteria. Ask them to use nouns, pronouns, adjectives, and verbs that are specific and that describe the landmarks a person will encounter in following the directions.

1. pilot   4. skater   7. foghorn   9. movie
2. locomotive   5. football   8. Mrs. Wu   10. Lincoln
3. taco   6. coins

Verb Phrases

A **verb phrase** consists of at least one main verb and one or more helping verbs. A **helping verb** (also called an **auxiliary verb**) helps the main verb express action or a state of being.

Besides all forms of the verb *be,* the following verbs can be used as helping verbs.

can	do	has	might	should
could	does	have	must	will
did	had	may	shall	would

Notice how helping verbs work together with main verbs to form complete verb phrases.

EXAMPLES   **is** leaving   **may** become   **might have** remained

               had seemed   **should** move   **must have** thought

Sometimes the parts of a verb phrase are interrupted by other parts of speech.

EXAMPLES   She **had** always **been thinking** of her future.

               Has my sister **played** her new CD for you?

NOTE   The word *not* is an adverb. It is never part of a verb phrase, even when it is joined to a verb as the contraction *–n't.*

EXAMPLES   She **should** not **have borrowed** that necklace.

               She **should**n't **have borrowed** that necklace.

Reference Note

For information about **contractions,** see page 707.

Exercise 14   Identifying Helping Verbs

Identify all the helping verbs in each of the following sentences.

EXAMPLE   **1.** How well did your brother recover from his back injury?

            1. did

1. Fortunately, he didn't need surgery.
2. His physical therapist has designed an exercise program for him.

Meeting **INDIVIDUAL** NEEDS

ENGLISH-LANGUAGE LEARNERS
General Strategies. The placement of negative adverbs varies across languages. The following grammatical patterns and examples might help clarify the placement of *not* in English.

1. helping verb + *not* + main verb
   a. I do **not** type.
   b. He may **not** understand.
   c. He has **not** noticed me.

2. linking verb + *not* + predicate nominative or predicate adjective
   a. I am **not** sick.
   b. She was **not** tardy.
   c. We are **not** musicians.

After students have completed their directions, allow them to work in groups of four to test how accurate their directions are. Have each student read his or her directions aloud to the group, and let group members add, delete, or amplify aspects of the directions to make them clearer and easier to follow.

3. Before exercising, he <u>must</u> <u>spend</u> at least five minutes warming up.
4. He <u>will</u> <u>be</u> <u>using</u> a back-extension machine.
5. <u>Does</u> he <u>walk</u> indoors on a treadmill or outdoors on a track?
6. At home, he <u>will</u> <u>be</u> <u>exercising</u> on a treadmill.
7. The doctor <u>is</u> always <u>reminding</u> my brother about proper techniques for lifting.
8. When lifting heavy objects, my brother <u>must</u> <u>wear</u> a back brace.
9. <u>Should</u> he <u>try</u> acupuncture or massage therapy?
10. Without physical therapy, he <u>might</u> not <u>have</u> <u>healed</u> as quickly and as completely.

Exercise 15 Identifying Verbs and Verb Phrases

Identify all the <u>verbs</u> and <u>verb phrases</u> in the sentences below. Include all helping verbs, even if the parts of a verb phrase are separated by other words.

EXAMPLE   1. We will probably go to the movie if we can finish our assignment.
       1. *will go, can finish*

1. Mr. Jensen always <u>sweeps</u> the floor first.
2. Then he <u>washes</u> the chalkboards.
3. He <u>works</u> slowly but steadily.
4. The weather forecaster <u>had</u> not <u>predicted</u> rain.
5. All morning the barometer <u>was</u> <u>dropping</u> rapidly.
6. The storm <u>was</u> slowly <u>moving</u> in.
7. Your dog <u>will</u> <u>become</u> fat if you <u>feed</u> it too much.
8. Dogs <u>will</u> usually <u>eat</u> everything you <u>give</u> them.
9. Generally, cats <u>will</u> <u>stop</u> when they <u>have</u> <u>had</u> enough.
10. After our team <u>has</u> <u>had</u> more practice, we <u>will</u> <u>win</u>.

Exercise 16 Revising Dialogue Using Verbs

Using a variety of verbs can make dialogue more interesting. Rewrite the dialogue below. In six of the ten items, replace *said* with one of the verbs from the following list. In the other four items, choose your own verbs.

wailed	bellowed	gloated	reported
responded	teased	soothed	confessed
exclaimed	replied	whined	accused
snapped	cried	muttered	called
howled	roared	pleaded	snapped

Relating to Literature

Popular novels and magazines often use strong, specific verbs like those listed for **Exercise 16.** Direct students to stories such as Toni Cade Bambara's "Blues Ain't No Mockin Bird" to demonstrate the creative use of such verbs in speaker tags. Ask students to bring to class examples of effective verb usage that they find in their reading. Tell them to be ready to share the examples with the class.

Exercise 16 Revising Dialogue Using Verbs

ANSWERS

Answers will vary, but students should be careful to follow the context clues of the sentences in order to choose appropriate verbs.

EXAMPLE   **1.** "Mom, I'm home!" said Tony, sprinting in the door.

   1. *"Mom, I'm home!" bellowed Tony, sprinting in the door.*

   2. "I've got great news!" he said.

   2. *"I've got great news!" he shouted.*

Verbs will vary.

1. "Guess what? I won the spelling bee," he ~~said~~.

2. "Honey, that's wonderful," ~~said~~ his mother.

3. "I spelled 'expeditious' when no one else could, not even Stephanie Greenblatt," ~~said~~ Tony.

4. "I'm so proud of you," ~~said~~ his mother.

5. "Who cares?" ~~said~~ his sister Amy.

6. "You're just jealous," ~~said~~ Tony.

7. "I am not!" Amy ~~said~~, running out of the kitchen.

8. "Don't let her bother you," ~~said~~ his mother. "You should enjoy your success."

9. "I am enjoying it," ~~said~~ Tony, "but I wish I could share my happiness with Amy."

10. "She'll come around," his mother ~~said~~. "Meanwhile, sit down and tell me all about it."

1. shouted
2. cried
3. reported

4. responded
5. whined
6. accused
7. snapped
8. whispered

9. replied

10. soothed

The Adverb

12e. An *adverb* modifies a verb, an adjective, or another adverb.

An adverb tells *where, when, how,* or *to what extent* (*how long* or *how much*). Just as an adjective makes the meaning of a noun or a pronoun more definite, an adverb makes the meaning of a verb, an adjective, or another adverb more definite.

Adverbs Modifying Verbs

In the following examples, each boldface adverb modifies a verb.

Where?	When?
We lived **there**.	May we go **tomorrow**?
Please step **up**.	Water the plant **weekly**.
I have the ticket **here**.	We'll see you **later**.
Put that **down**.	He arrived **early**.

┌─ TIPS & TRICKS ─┐

To identify a word as an adverb, ask yourself:

Does this word modify a verb, an adjective, or an adverb?

Does it tell *when, where, how,* or *to what extent*?

The Adverb

Rule 12e *(pp. 393–399)*

OBJECTIVES

■ **To complete sentences by adding appropriate adverbs**

■ **To identify adverbs that modify adjectives and to name the adjectives modified**

■ **To revise phrases and sentences by adding adverbs that modify adjectives**

■ **To identify adverbs that modify other adverbs and to identify the words modified**

■ **To revise sentences by using appropriate adverbs**

The Adverb   **393**

┌─ **RESOURCES** ─

The Adverb

Practice

■ *Grammar, Usage, and Mechanics,* pp. 19, 20, 21

■ *Language Workshop CD-ROM,* Lesson 5

Meeting INDIVIDUAL NEEDS

MODALITIES

Auditory Learners. Some students will benefit from hearing and answering the adverb questions *How?, When?, Where?,* or *To what extent?* Start by saying "Jane walked . . ."

Ask students *how* she walked. Have them supply adverbs until they run out of ideas. [*sadly, gladly, happily, slowly, tiredly, sluggishly*] Then, ask *when* she walked. Students should again supply adverbs. [*today, yesterday, Tuesday, then*] Continue with *where* and *to what extent.*

INCLUSION

Adverbs can be especially difficult for inclusion students because an adverb can modify so many parts of speech and can easily be confused with a preposition. You may want to pair inclusion students with advanced students who can answer questions, read the text aloud, and clarify concepts. As inclusion students sometimes have problems with self-confidence, positive statements acknowledging good team effort can be reinforcing.

ENGLISH-LANGUAGE LEARNERS

Spanish. Point out to your Spanish-speaking students that the English –ly suffix is equivalent to the Spanish –mente suffix. Both convert adjectives to adverbs. (In French the suffix is –ment.)

How?	To What Extent?
She **quickly** agreed.	Fill the tank **completely**.
The rain fell **softly**.	He **hardly** moved.
Drive **carefully**.	Did she hesitate **slightly**?
He sang **beautifully**.	They **partly** completed the form.

As you can see in the preceding examples, adverbs may come before or after the verbs they modify. Sometimes adverbs interrupt the parts of a verb phrase.

Adverbs may also introduce questions.

EXAMPLE   **Where** in the world did you ever find that pink-and-purple necktie? [The adverb *Where* introduces the question and modifies the verb phrase *did find*. The adverb *ever* interrupts the verb phrase and also modifies it.]

NOTE   Although many adverbs end in –ly, the –ly ending does not necessarily mean that a word is an adverb. Many adjectives also end in –ly: the *daily* newspaper, an *early* train, an *only* child, a *lonely* person. Also, some words, such as *now, then, far, already, somewhat, not,* and *right,* are often used as adverbs, yet they do not end in –ly.

Exercise 17   Completing Sentences by Supplying Appropriate Adverbs

Complete each of the following sentences by supplying an appropriate adverb. The word or phrase in parentheses tells you what information the adverb should give about the action.   Adverbs will vary.

EXAMPLE   **1.** He moved his hand (*how*).

      1. gracefully

1. The soldiers must travel (*how*).   1. quietly
2. You will probably sleep well (*when*).   2. tonight
3. They whispered (*how*) to Mr. Baldwin.   3. cautiously
4. Tonya took a deep breath and dove (*where*).   4. in
5. Did you study (*to what extent*)?   5. much
6. Handle the ducklings (*how*).   6. carefully
7. My uncle Hans is (*when*) in a bad mood.   7. never
8. Your taxi should be (*where*) soon.   8. here
9. I could (*to what extent*) taste the tangy pizza.   9. almost
10. (*When*), you should paste the pictures on the poster.   10. First

Adverbs Modifying Adjectives

EXAMPLES   Beth did an **exceptionally** fine job. [The adverb *exceptionally* modifies the adjective *fine*, telling *to what extent*.]

Slightly cooler temperatures are forecast. [The adverb *slightly* modifies the adjective *cooler*, telling *to what extent*.]

Mr. Lomazzi is an **especially** talented chef. [The adverb *especially* modifies the adjective *talented*, telling *to what extent*.]

STYLE   TIP

The most frequently used adverbs are *too, so, really,* and *very*. In fact, these words are often overworked. To make your speaking and writing more interesting, replace these general adverbs with more specific ones, such as *completely, especially,* and *quite*.

Exercise 18 Identifying Adverbs That Modify Adjectives

Identify the adverbs that modify adjectives in the sentences below. For each adverb, give the adjective it modifies.

EXAMPLE   1. The compass I bought was incredibly cheap.

    1. *incredibly—cheap*

HELP

In Exercise 18, a sentence may contain more than one adverb modifying an adjective.

1. If you are ever really lost in the woods at night, knowing how to find the North Star may be extremely important.
2. Here is one method that is quite useful.
3. First, find the Big Dipper, which is surprisingly easy to spot.
4. It consists of seven rather bright stars in the northern sky that are arranged in the shape of a large dipper.
5. Do not confuse it with the Little Dipper, which is somewhat smaller.
6. After you have found the Big Dipper, you must be very careful to sight along the two stars that form the front of the dipper bowl.
7. They are two points on an almost straight line to the North Star.
8. This method for getting your bearings is completely reliable—except when the clouds are so dense that you cannot see the stars.
9. It would be especially wise to check the weather forecast before going on a hike.
10. Remember to take a compass, water, and a fully stocked first-aid kit.

The Adverb   **395**

Cooperative Learning

To help students review adverbs before they tackle **Exercise 19**, pair them to play a game that focuses on adverbs and vocabulary development. Because the game is challenging, you may wish to pair learners having difficulty with advanced ones, but be willing to monitor activity to see that all students are making progress.

The object of the game is for each pair to come up with an adverb and a word for it to modify (verb, adjective, or other adverb) beginning with each letter of the alphabet. Some examples are *always active; bashfully brings; carefully cuts; delightfully delicious;* and *exceedingly edgy.*

Give students ten minutes to work on their lists. Encourage them to use a dictionary. When time is up, have pairs exchange lists to check for accuracy.

Reference Note

For information about **compound sentences,** see page 481. For information on **adverb clauses,** see page 476.

Exercise 19 **Revising with Adverb Modifiers**

Make each of the phrases and sentences below more descriptive by adding one adverb that modifies each of the italicized adjectives. Use a different adverb in each item.   Adverbs will vary.

EXAMPLE   1. a *confusing* sentence

1. an *especially confusing sentence*

1. a *sharp* turn   **1.** quite
2. *playful* kittens   **2.** extremely
3. an *easy* question   **3.** unusually
4. a *swept* floor   **4.** cleanly
5. Her little brother has a *bright* smile.   **5.** cheerily
6. Terri felt *satisfied* that she had done her best.   **6.** completely
7. The old mansion was *silent*.   **7.** eerily
8. Robert became *sick* and had to leave early.   **8.** terribly
9. Had Clara been *safe*?   **9.** especially
10. Most of the questions on the test were *difficult*.   **10.** dreadfully

Adverbs Modifying Other Adverbs

EXAMPLES   Calvin was **almost** never there. [The adverb *almost* modifies the adverb *never,* telling *to what extent.*]

We'll meet **shortly** afterward. [The adverb *shortly* modifies the adverb *afterward,* telling *to what extent.*]

She slept **too** late. [The adverb *too* modifies the adverb *late,* telling *to what extent.*]

NOTE   One kind of adverb—the ***conjunctive adverb***—is an adverb used as a connecting word between independent clauses in a compound sentence.

EXAMPLE   We tried to be at the stadium by 6:30 P.M.; **however,** we arrived at the wrong time.

Another kind of adverb—the ***relative adverb***—is often used to introduce adjective clauses.

EXAMPLES   Uncle Lionel told us about the time **when** he drove across the country.

In 1815, Napoleon was sent into exile on the island of St. Helena, **where** he died in 1821.

396   **Chapter 12**   Parts of Speech Overview

MINI-LESSON

Unnecessary Adverbs in Writing.
Unnecessary adverbs can clutter students' writing. Copy the following paragraph on the chalkboard, underlining the adverbs as shown. Have students determine which

adverbs seem necessary, and why.

I would <u>really</u> enjoy taking a vacation to a sunny beach. My idea of paradise is lying <u>quietly</u> and <u>peacefully</u> in the sun

Noun or Adverb?

Some words that can be used as nouns can also be used as adverbs.

EXAMPLES   **Tomorrow** never seems to arrive. [*noun*]

We will leave **tomorrow.** [*Tomorrow* is used as an adverb telling *when*.]

Think of this place as your **home.** [*noun*]

He was eager to come **home.** [*Home* is used as an adverb telling *where*.]

When identifying parts of speech, remember: A word used to modify a verb, an adjective, or another adverb is called an adverb.

"I miss the good old days when all we had to worry about was nouns and verbs."

© 1984 by Sidney Harris–*Punch.*

Exercise 20 Identifying Adverbs That Modify Other Adverbs

Identify all the adverbs that modify other adverbs in the sentences below. After each adverb, give the adverb it modifies.

EXAMPLE   **1.** Brian is so terribly shy that he blushes when people speak to him.

    1. so, terribly

1. The cat leapt to the windowsill quite agilely.
2. The books were stacked rather haphazardly.
3. Corrie knew she'd have to get up incredibly early to watch the eclipse tomorrow.
4. The tornado almost completely destroyed the barn.
5. The famous diamond was more heavily guarded than any other exhibit at the museum.
6. My brother is nearly always finished with his paper route before I am finished with mine.
7. She registered too late to be eligible for the classes she wanted.
8. In the final four minutes of the game, Isiah Thomas shot extremely accurately.
9. Usually it seems that each month goes more rapidly than the month before.
10. They walked onto the stage most calmly, as if they felt completely relaxed.

and watching the clouds drift lazily overhead. Of course, going snorkeling and watching brightly colored fish swim rapidly through the ocean would surely be fun, too. I certainly hope I get to go, because I know it'll be totally great.

[*Students will probably agree that* peacefully, lazily, overhead, brightly, *and* too *enhance the paragraph.*]

Relating to Writing

Before students do **Exercises 21** and **22**, have them practice using adverbs by writing free-verse poems about their favorite holidays. Tell them to use at least seven adverbs.

Poems will vary greatly, but you may want to use the following student poem as an example:

Fourth of July

Rockets scream *angrily* through the sky.

Fireworks explode *brightly.*

Flags wave *proudly.*

Crowds cheer *wildly.*

Trumpets blare *loudly.*

Drums beat *rhythmically.*

Then the parade begins.

Relating to Listening

Students might be unaware of how much the position of an adverb can affect the meaning of a sentence. Read the following sentences to the class. Have volunteers comment on how the position of *only* affects the meaning of each sentence.

1. The teacher *only* looked at me as I prepared to give my speech.

2. The teacher looked *only* at me as I prepared to give my speech.

3. The teacher looked at me *only* as I prepared to give my speech.

[*The first sentence indicates that all the teacher did was look at me. The second indicates that the teacher focused her attention on me. The third tells when the teacher looked at me.*]

Exercise 21 Identifying Adverbs and the Words They Modify

Identify the adverb or adverbs in each of the following sentences. Then, give the word or expression that each adverb modifies. If a sentence does not contain an adverb, write *none.*

EXAMPLE **1.** Have you ever thought about writing a movie script?
1. *ever—have thought*

1. Successful movie scripts, or screenplays, are written according to a very rigid formula.
2. The main character and the action of the story must grab an audience's interest quickly.
3. Almost (exactly) twenty-five minutes into the movie comes a "plot point."
4. A plot point is a surprising event that swings the story around in another direction.
5. Most of the action and conflict occurs in the next hour of the movie.
6. Then comes another plot point, about eighty-five minutes into the movie.
7. Finally, the audience learns what happens to the characters.
8. The last time I went to a movie I really liked, I checked my watch.
9. It was quite interesting to find that the movie's timing matched this formula.
10. Try this test yourself sometime.

3. Exactly is modified by Almost and modifies twenty-five.

5. none

Exercise 22 Revising Sentences by Using Appropriate Adverbs

Revise each of the sentences below by adding at least one appropriate adverb. Try not to use the adverbs *too, so, really,* and *very.*

EXAMPLE **1.** Dana, bring me the fire extinguisher!
1. *Dana, bring me the fire extinguisher now!*

1. Angelo ‸ promised me that he would try to meet the train.
2. My coat was ‸ torn during the long hike, so Barbara lent me her plastic poncho.
3. Engineering degrees are ‸ popular with students because job opportunities in engineering are good.
4. The Wallaces are ‸ settled into a new house, which they built by themselves.

Adverbs will vary.

1. definitely
2. badly
3. particularly
4. comfortably

5. When the baseball season begins, I will be‸attending games every day.   **5. happily**

6. Ronald‸dribbled to his left and threw the ball into a crowd of defenders.   **6. hastily**

7. Visits to national monuments and parks remind us that our country has an‸exciting history.   **7. especially**

8. We returned the book to Marcella, but she‸had planned her report without it.   **8. already**

9. Georgia O'Keeffe displayed her paintings and‸received the admiration of a large audience.   **9. later**

10. The recipe calls for two eggs, but I‸did not have time to buy any at the store.   **10. certainly**

Review B Identifying Nouns, Pronouns, Adjectives, Verbs, and Adverbs

Indicate whether the italicized words in the paragraph below are used as *nouns, pronouns, adjectives, verbs,* or *adverbs.*

EXAMPLE   [1] *You* may know that Brazil is the *largest* country in South America.

    1. *You*—pronoun; *largest*—adjective

[1] My *best* friend's mother just *came* back from visiting her family in Brazil. [2] *She* showed us *some* pictures she took in Brasília, the capital, and told us about it. [3] It was amazing to learn that *this* area had been *jungle* until construction began in the 1950s. [4] At first, few people lived in Brasília because it was so *isolated.* [5] However, over the *years* hundreds of thousands of people *have* moved *there.* [6] Several other Brazilian cities *also* lie within one hundred *miles* of Brasília. [7] *A* number of *good* highways *connect* Brasília with other major cities. [8] Residents enjoy the wide streets and open spaces *that* are *shown* in this picture. [9] *One* of Brasília's *most* striking features is its bold architecture. [10] Aren't the government buildings at the *Plaza* of the Three Powers *fantastic?*

Review B Identifying Nouns, Pronouns, Adjectives, Verbs, and Adverbs

ANSWERS

1. adj./v.
2. pro./adj.
3. adj./n.
4. adj.
5. n./v./adv.
6. adv./n.
7. adj./v.
8. pro./v.
9. pro./adv.
10. n./adj.

The Preposition

GRAMMAR

The Preposition

Rule 12f *(pp. 400–403)*

OBJECTIVES

■ To identify prepositions and their objects in sentences

■ To complete sentences by adding appropriate prepositions

TEACHING TIP

Activity. Some prepositions show direction. To reinforce what students have learned about prepositions, have students play a game called Treasure Hunt.

Divide the class into two groups. Have one group hide something (a poster or a book, for example) somewhere in the classroom and create clues that will eventually lead the other team to the hidden item. Each clue should include a preposition. The clues should cause the hunters to wander in many different directions before reaching the hidden item. [*Sample direction: Go* to *the back* of *the room. Look* inside *the third desk* from *the rear.*]

The Preposition

12f. A *preposition* is a word that shows the relationship of a noun or a pronoun to another word.

By changing the prepositions in the following examples, you can change the relationship of *Saint Bernard* to *bed* and *Everything* to *beach*.

The Saint Bernard slept **near** my bed.	Everything **about** the beach was wonderful.
The Saint Bernard slept **under** my bed.	Everything **except** the beach was wonderful.
The Saint Bernard slept **on** my bed.	Everything **from** the beach was wonderful.
The Saint Bernard slept **beside** by bed.	Everything **on** the beach was wonderful.

The noun or pronoun that a preposition relates another word to is called the *object of the preposition*. In the examples above, *bed* and *beach* are the objects of the prepositions.

Commonly Used Prepositions			
aboard	below	from	since
about	beneath	in	through
above	beside	inside	throughout
across	besides	into	till
after	between	like	to
against	beyond	near	toward
along	but (meaning *except*)	of	under
amid		off	underneath
among	by	on	until
around	concerning	onto	up
as	down	out	upon
at	during	outside	with
before	except	over	within
behind	for	past	without

RESOURCES

The Preposition

Practice

■ *Grammar, Usage, and Mechanics,* p. 22

■ *Language Workshop CD-ROM,* Lesson 6

NOTE Many words in the preceding list can also be used as adverbs. To be sure that a word is used as a preposition, ask whether the word relates a noun or a pronoun to another word. Compare the following sentences:

Welcome **aboard.** [adverb]
Welcome **aboard** our boat. [preposition]

The runner fell **behind.** [adverb]
The paper fell **behind** the cabinet. [preposition]

Prepositions that consist of two or more words are called *compound prepositions*.

Compound Prepositions	
according to	in place of
as of	in spite of
aside from	instead of
because of	next to
by means of	on account of
in addition to	out of
in front of	prior to

STYLE TIP

In casual speech and informal writing, people often end sentences with prepositions. However, in formal speech and writing, it is best to avoid doing so.

NOTE As a rule, the object of the preposition follows the preposition.

EXAMPLE   Add a teaspoon of freshly ground **cinnamon.**
[*Cinnamon* is the object of the preposition *of*.]

Sometimes, however, the object of the preposition comes before the preposition.

EXAMPLE   He is a singer **whom** I've never heard of before.
[*Whom* is the object of the preposition *of*.]

Objects of prepositions may be compound.

EXAMPLES   Kyoko called **to Nancy** and **me.**
[Both *Nancy* and *me* are objects of the preposition *to*.]

The marbles were scattered **under** the **table** and **chairs.**
[Both *table* and *chairs* are objects of the preposition *under*.]

The Preposition   **401**

The preposition, its object, and any modifiers of the object together form a *prepositional phrase.* Notice in the following examples that modifiers of the object of the preposition can come before or after the object.

Reference Note

For more information about **prepositional phrases,** see page 442.

EXAMPLES Joe went **to the nearest store.** [The noun *store* is the object of the preposition *to*. The adjectives *the* and *nearest* modify the noun *store*.]

Is she one **of those trailing behind**? [The pronoun *those* is the object of the preposition *of. Those* is modified by the participial phrase *trailing behind*.]

The kitten hopped **into the big paper bag that Anita brought.** [The noun *bag* is the object of the preposition *into. Bag* is modified by the adjectives *the, big,* and *paper* and by the subordinate clause *that Anita brought*.]

Reference Note

For more information about **infinitives,** see page 457.

NOTE Be careful not to confuse a prepositional phrase that begins with *to* (*to town, to her club*) with an infinitive that begins with *to* (*to run, to be seen*). Remember: A prepositional phrase always has a noun or a pronoun as an object.

Exercise 23 **Identifying Prepositions and Their Objects**

Identify each preposition and its object in the following sentences.

EXAMPLE **1.** I've been studying Spanish in school for three years.
  1. in—school; for—years

HELP

Sentences in Exercise 23 may have a compound object of a preposition.

1. Last week, my Spanish class went on a field trip to Monterrey, Mexico, 140 miles southwest of Laredo, Texas, where we live.
2. Señora Ayala, our teacher, wanted us to practice speaking and reading Spanish outside the classroom.
3. Everyone was supposed to speak only Spanish during the trip.
4. We first went to the *Museo de la Historia Mexicana* and saw colorful displays of art and crafts and many other cultural exhibits.
5. J. D., Leo, Yolanda, and I looked around the museum and read the information about each exhibit.
6. Besides the museum, we visited the *Barrio Antiguo,* a beautiful district that dates from the seventeenth century.
7. Later, we decided to go to a restaurant near the *Gran Plaza,* the big square.
8. As Señora Ayala walked among our tables, she listened to us order our tacos, enchiladas, and frijoles in Spanish.

9. We walked around the *Gran Plaza* and then went into the cathedral, which was completed in the eighteenth century.

10. As we got ready to leave, we chatted in Spanish about all of the interesting things we had seen.

Exercise 24 **Using Appropriate Prepositions**

Use appropriate prepositions to fill the blanks in the following sentences. Prepositions may vary.

EXAMPLE
1. Tasty, fresh lobster is a treat, ____ many diners.

1. Tasty, fresh lobster is a treat, *according to many diners.*

1. Lobsters are large, green or gray, bottom-dwelling shellfish that live ____ the sea. **1.** in

2. The people who fish ____ these creatures are hardy and very determined folk. **2.** for

3. Using small, specially built boats and a number ____ cratelike traps made ____ wood, they go to work. **3.** of / from

4. Lobster fishing ____ the United States has been practiced only ____ the last century; before that time people thought lobster was not good to eat. **4.** throughout / within

5. For centuries, farmers used the plentiful lobsters as fertilizer ____ their gardens. **5.** for

6. To catch lobsters, the fishers first lower traps ____ chunks ____ bait ____ the sea. **6.** with / of / into

7. Then the fishers mark the location ____ colorful floats that identify the owners. **7.** with

8. If the fishers are lucky, the lobster enters the trap ____ the part called the *kitchen,* tries to escape ____ another opening called the *shark's mouth,* and then is trapped ____ the section called the *parlor.*

8. by means of / through / inside

9. Fishers call a lobster ____ only one claw a *cull;* one ____ any claws is called a *pistol* or a *buffalo.* **9.** with / without

10. By law, undersized lobsters must be returned ____ the sea. **10.** to

The Conjunction

12g. A *conjunction* is a word that joins words or word groups.

A *coordinating conjunction* joins words or word groups that are used in the same way.

The Conjunction

Rule 12g *(pp. 403–405)*

O B J E C T I V E

■ **To identify and classify conjunctions**

TIPS & TRICKS

You can remember the coordinating conjunctions as FANBOYS:

For
And
Nor
But
Or
Yet
So

Coordinating Conjunctions

and	but	or	nor
for	yet	so	

EXAMPLES   streets **and** sidewalks [two nouns]

on land **or** at sea [two prepositional phrases]

Judy wrote down the number, **but** she lost it. [two independent clauses]

Correlative conjunctions are pairs of conjunctions that join words or word groups that are used in the same way.

Correlative Conjunctions

both . . . and	not only . . . but also
either . . . or	neither . . . nor
whether . . . or	

Reference Note

A third kind of conjunction—the **subordinating conjunction**—is discussed on page 477.

EXAMPLES   **Both** Jim Thorpe **and** Roberto Clemente were outstanding athletes. [two proper nouns]

We want to go **not only** to Ontario **but also** to Quebec. [two prepositional phrases]

Either we will buy it now, **or** we will wait for the next sale. [two independent clauses]

Neither Mark Twain **nor** James Joyce won the Nobel Prize in literature. [two proper nouns]

We should decide **whether** to stay **or** to go. [two infinitives]

HELP

In the first example for Exercise 25, *and* is a coordinating conjunction, and *both . . . and* is a correlative conjunction. In the second example, *Neither . . . nor* is a correlative conjunction.

Exercise 25   Identifying and Classifying Conjunctions

Identify all the coordinating and correlative conjunctions in the sentences below. Be prepared to tell which ones are *coordinating* conjunctions and which ones are *correlative conjunctions.*

EXAMPLES   1. For my family and me, moving is both an exciting and a dangerous experience.
1. *and, both . . . and*

2. Neither my father nor I have a sense of our limitations.
2. *Neither . . . nor*

1. When we bought our new house, my mother wanted to hire movers, but my father <u>and</u> I said we could do the moving more efficiently by ourselves.
2. We said that doing the job ourselves would be <u>not only</u> much faster <u>and</u> easier <u>but also</u> far less expensive than having movers do it for us.
3. <u>Neither</u> my mom <u>nor</u> my brother was enthusiastic, <u>but</u> at last Dad <u>and</u> I convinced them.
4. Luckily, Uncle Waldo <u>and</u> my cousin Fred volunteered to help, <u>for</u> they thought it was a great idea.
5. <u>Both</u> Uncle Waldo <u>and</u> Fred lift weights, <u>and</u> they love to show off their muscles.
6. The rental truck we had reserved wasn't large enough, <u>so</u> we had to make several trips.
7. At the new house, we could get the sofa through <u>neither</u> the back door <u>nor</u> the front door, <u>and</u> Uncle Waldo strained his back trying to loosen the sofa from the door frame.
8. On the second load, <u>either</u> Fred <u>or</u> my father lost his grip, <u>and</u> the refrigerator fell on Dad's foot.
9. By the end of the day, all of us were tired <u>and</u> sore, <u>but</u> we had moved everything ourselves.
10. <u>Whether</u> we saved money <u>or</u> not after paying <u>both</u> Uncle Waldo's <u>and</u> Dad's medical bills <u>and</u> having the doorway widened is something we still joke about in our family.

The Interjection

12h. An *interjection* is a word that expresses emotion. An interjection has no grammatical relation to the rest of the sentence.

ah	hurrah	uh-oh	wow
aha	oh	well	yahoo
boy-oh-boy	oops	whew	yikes
hey	ouch	whoa	yippee

Since an interjection is not grammatically related to other words in the sentence, it is set off from the rest of the sentence by an exclamation point or by a comma or commas.

The Interjection **405**

The Interjection
Rule 12h *(pp. 405–406)*

OBJECTIVE

- To use interjections in sentences and to select correct punctuation for interjections

STYLE TIP

Interjections are common in casual conversation. In writing, however, they are usually used only in informal notes and letters, in advertisements, and in dialogue. When you use an interjection, make sure the punctuation after it reflects the intensity of emotion you intend. Use an exclamation point to indicate strong emotion and a comma to indicate mild emotion.

EXAMPLES   **Hey!** Be careful of that wire!

There's a skunk somewhere, **ugh!**

Well, I guess that's that.

I like that outfit, but, **wow,** it's really expensive.

Oops! The stoop is slippery.

Our team won the playoff! **Yippee!**

Exercise 26   Using Interjections

In the following dialogue, Jason is telling his friend Michelle about a concert he attended. Use appropriate interjections to fill in the numbered blanks. Be sure you punctuate each interjection that you use.

EXAMPLES   **[1]** "_____ You mean you actually got to go?" Michelle gasped.

     1. *"Wow! You mean you actually got to go?" Michelle gasped.*

     [2] "_____ I wish I could have gone!"

     2. *"Boy-oh-boy! I wish I could have gone!"*

1. Well,

2. Ugh!

3. Come on!

4. Wow!

5. Man,

[1] "_____ how was the concert?" asked Michelle. "Tell me all about what happened."

Jason shook his head. "The opening act was terrible. [2] _____ It seemed as if they played forever!"

"How was the rest of the show, though? [3] _____ Give me some details, Jason!"

"The drummer was fantastic. [4] _____ He acted like a wild man. He was all over the drums! But the best part was Stevie's twenty-minute guitar solo. [5] _____ he really let loose. The crowd went crazy!"

Determining Parts of Speech

Determining Parts of Speech

Rule 12i (pp. 406–408)

12i. The way a word is used in a sentence determines what part of speech it is.

OBJECTIVES

■ To identify the parts of speech of words in sentences

■ To apply knowledge of parts of speech to individual sentences

The same word may be used as different parts of speech. To figure out what part of speech *well* is in each of the sentences on the next page, read the entire sentence. What you are doing is studying the word's ***context***—the way the word is used in the sentence.

RESOURCES

Determining Parts of Speech
Practice

■ *Grammar, Usage, and Mechanics,* p. 25

■ *Language Workshop CD-ROM,* Lesson 9

EXAMPLES   At the bottom of the old **well** were more than five
thousand pennies. [noun]

Whenever the reunion was mentioned, tears of joy
would **well** in her eyes. [verb]

Well, you may be right. [interjection]

Do you really speak four languages **well**? [adverb]

Fortunately, the baby is quite **well** now. [adjective]

Exercise 27 **Identifying Words as Different
Parts of Speech**

Read each of the sentences below. Then, identify the part of speech of
the italicized word. Be ready to justify your answer by telling how the
word is used in the sentence.

EXAMPLE   **1.** Aunt Shirley got a *raise*.

1. noun

1. Did Gander Pond *ice* over last year?   **1.** verb
2. An *ice* storm struck.   **2.** adjective
3. *Many* of these items are on sale.   **3.** pronoun
4. The light flashed *on* and we entered the garage.   **4.** adverb
5. We rode *on* the subway.   **5.** preposition
6. The radio is *on*.   **6.** adjective
7. They went to the *park*.   **7.** noun
8. We can *park* the car here.   **8.** verb
9. We waited, *oh*, about five minutes.   **9.** interjection
10. We are all here *but* Natalya.   **10.** preposition
11. I slipped, *but* I didn't fall, thank goodness.   **11.** conjunction
12. *Off* the road they could see a light.   **12.** preposition
13. The shop was *off* the main street.   **13.** preposition
14. The deal was *off*.   **14.** adjective
15. "Can you climb *up* that tree?" asked Yolanda.   **15.** preposition
16. The sun was already *up* when they left for work.   **16.** adjective
17. Ernesto lives a few miles *up* the coast.   **17.** preposition
18. We had a long wait before the show started, but, *wow*, it was
worth it!   **18.** interjection
19. *Most* cats dislike taking baths.   **19.** adjective
20. Did they go all the way *through* the town?   **20.** preposition

Crossing the Curriculum

History. To help students elaborate
when they answer essay questions,
show them how to use the parts of
speech to build sentences. First, give
the class the name of a historical figure or of an event they have recently
studied in history class. Then, have
students build the sentence by
adding words that answer these
questions:

1. Who did it? [*noun or pronoun*]

2. What did that person do? [*verb*]

3. When did the person do it?
[*adverb or prepositional phrase*]

4. What kind of person was this?
[*adjective or prepositional phrase*]

5. What else did this person do?
[*conjunction*]

[Possible sentence: *In the 1930s, the
determined Franklin Delano
Roosevelt quickly took firm control
over the government and set up
many programs to help people hurt
by the Great Depression.*]

GRAMMAR

Review C — Writing Sentences Using the Same Words as Different Parts of Speech

ANSWERS
Sentences will vary, but students should correctly label the part of speech used in each of their pairs of sentences.

HELP
Each missing word in Exercise 28 is a different part of speech.

Alas (interjection)
and (conjunction)
capture (verb)
beside (preposition)
encampment (noun)
early (adjective)
you (pronoun)
immediately (adverb)

HELP
Some words may be used as more than two parts of speech. You need to give only two uses for each word in Review C.

Exercise 28 — Determining Parts of Speech

A soldier in the American Revolution brings his general this spy message he found in a hollow tree. Unfortunately, termites have eaten holes in the paper. For each hole, supply one word that makes sense, and give its part of speech. Answers may vary.

EXAMPLE   Please _____ this message to General Baxter immediately.
deliver—verb.

The Redcoats are chasing me, I expect them _____ me soon. They are camped _____ the river and they are well rested. They will attack your _____ at dawn's _____ light tomorrow. General, _____ must prepare your troops to leave _____

Yours in haste, John Cadrain

Review C — Writing Sentences Using the Same Words as Different Parts of Speech

Write forty sentences, using each of the words in the list below as two different parts of speech. Underline the word and give its part of speech in parentheses after each sentence.

EXAMPLE   1. up
1. We looked *up*. (adverb)
   We ran *up* the stairs. (preposition)

1. light
2. run
3. over
4. line
5. cook
6. ride
7. in
8. love
9. below
10. picture
11. help
12. drive
13. plant
14. well
15. for
16. that
17. right
18. signal
19. home
20. one

Chapter Review

A. Identifying Parts of Speech

In each of the following sentences, identify the italicized word or word group as a *noun*, *pronoun*, *adjective*, *verb*, *adverb*, *conjunction*, *preposition*, or *interjection*.

Using the Chapter Review

To assess student progress, you may want to compare the types of items missed on the **Diagnostic Preview** to those missed on the **Chapter Review**. You may want to work out specific goals with individual students who are still having difficulty mastering essential information.

1. v.	**1.** Kofi Annan, who *became* secretary-general of the United Nations in 1997, is from Ghana.
2. pro.	**2.** *All* of the episodes of that show have been interesting.
3. pro.	**3.** I made *myself* a pimento cheese sandwich to take along.
4. pro.	**4.** This copy of the magazine is *hers*.
5. adj.	**5.** I wondered *whose* sculptures were on exhibit at the Dallas Museum of Art.
6. pro.	**6.** *That* is the third time Luisa has called me today.
7. int.	**7.** "*Wow*, that was the fastest fly ball I've ever seen!" exclaimed Ernesto.
8. pro.	**8.** Rajiv *himself* was planning to show them around Kashmir.
9. adj.	**9.** Which of the liquids in the *smaller* beakers is clear?
10. n.	**10.** Are those the bonsai trees *Mr. Yamamoto* told you about?
11. n.	**11.** One of the oldest poems in the collection deals with the concept of *honor*.
12. n.	**12.** The *cast* of the film includes many genuine descendants of Napoleon.
13. v.	**13.** Erika and Mike *wrote* the screenplay together.
14. v.	**14.** *Should* the alarm clock *have been set* to go off at 6:00 A.M.?
15. adv.	**15.** Those Italian clothes are well-made and *extremely* stylish.
16. pro.	**16.** *We* had been warned not to be late, yet by the time we arrived the show had already begun.
17. prep.	**17.** Warn Selena and him *about* the fire ants in the backyard before it's too late!
18. conj.	**18.** Marcel was coming down with a cold, *but* he felt obliged to keep his appointments.
19. n.	**19.** Nancy enjoys reading about current affairs because it helps to broaden her general *knowledge*.
20. pro.	**20.** The gorilla admired *itself* in the mirror.

Chapter Review   **409**

B. Identifying Parts of Speech

In each of the following sentences, identify the italicized word or word group as a *noun*, *pronoun*, *adjective*, *verb*, *adverb*, *conjunction*, *preposition*, or *interjection*.

21. verb	**21.** Football's most important contest *is* the annual Super Bowl game.
22. conj.	**22.** Thousands attend the game at the stadium, *and* millions watch it on television.
23. adv.	**23.** Professional football began with no system for *fairly* choosing a championship team.
24. noun	**24.** Later, the *National Football League* was formed.
25. prep.	**25.** The two NFL teams *with* the best records play a championship game.
26. pro.	**26.** In the late 1950s the American Football League was formed, and *it* also held a championship game every year.
27. adv.	**27.** *Eventually,* the AFL and NFL championship teams played each other at the end of the season.
28. adj.	**28.** Ever since the *first* Super Bowl was played in Los Angeles in 1967, the competition has continued to improve.
29. pro.	**29.** Do *you* know any amazing records set by NFL players?
30. int.	**30.** *Amazing!* Fran Tarkenton threw over three hundred touchdown passes in his professional football career.

C. Identifying Parts of Speech

Identify the part of speech of each italicized word or word group in the following paragraph.

31. pro.	41. conj.
32. noun	42. pro.
33. adj.	43. noun
34. adj.	44. verb
35. verb	45. adj.
36. adj.	46. adv.
37. prep.	47. verb
38. noun	48. noun
39. prep.	49. int.
40. verb	50. adv.

For [**31**] *me*, no [**32**] *spot* is [**33**] *better* than the beach. On [**34**] *hot*, sunny days, when the sand [**35**] *burns* my feet, I am always [**36**] *careful* [**37**] *about* putting on [**38**] *sunscreen*. I like to run [**39**] *through* the foaming surf and later relax under a beach umbrella. Most of the time, I [**40**] *enjoy* [**41**] *both* being with friends *and* being by [**42**] *myself*. With only [**43**] *strangers* around me, I [**44**] *feel* free to think my [**45**] *own* thoughts. I wander [**46**] *slowly* along the waterline, looking at all the interesting things that the sea [**47**] *has* washed up. Once I accidentally stepped on a [**48**] *jellyfish* and couldn't help but yell [**49**] "*ouch!*" when it stung my foot. Since then, I've learned to be [**50**] *more* careful about where I step.

RESOURCES

Parts of Speech Overview
Review
- *Grammar, Usage, and Mechanics,* pp. 26, 27, 28

Assessment
- *Assessment Package*
  —*Chapter Tests,* Ch. 12
  —*Chapter Tests in Standardized Test Formats,* Ch. 12
- *Test Generator (One-Stop Planner CD-ROM)*

Writing Application

Writing a Descriptive Paragraph

Using Specific Adjectives   Your class visited a wildlife park, but one of your friends was sick and could not go. Write a paragraph telling your friend about the field trip. Use specific adjectives to help your friend picture what he or she missed.

Prewriting   Make a list of the animals and the scenes that will interest your friend. Beside each item on your list, write one or two specific adjectives.

Writing   You may want to look at pictures of wildlife in magazines or books to help you think of exact descriptions as you write your first draft. Use a thesaurus to find adjectives that will help your reader visualize the animals you are describing.

Revising   Have a friend or classmate read your paragraph to see if you have created clear images. Revise your paragraph by adding specific adjectives if any descriptions are unclear or too general.

Publishing   Check your paragraph for errors in spelling and punctuation. Be sure that you have capitalized any proper adjectives. You and your classmates may want to create a wildlife-park bulletin board or multimedia presentation.

Reference Note

For more about **proper adjectives,** see page 620.

Writing Application
(p. 411)

OBJECTIVE

■ **To write a paragraph using specific adjectives**

Writing Application

Tip. The writing assignment asks students to create a word-picture about a field trip to a wildlife habitat. To spark their imaginations, students might benefit from using resource books with colorful pictures.

Scoring Rubric. While you will want to pay particular attention to students' use of adjectives, you will also want to evaluate overall writing performance. You may want to give a split score to indicate development and clarity of the composition as well as grammar skills.

Critical Thinking

Application. Students might find it difficult to get away from stereotypes in describing animals. Some adjectives seem almost automatic: *ferocious* lion, *long-necked* giraffe, *enormous* elephant, *silly* monkey.

To have students think critically in applying learned material to new situations, tell them to think of other aspects of these animals that they could include to develop the descriptions more fully. For example, a lion might also be *sinewy, massive,* or *regal.* The animals could include a *gangling* giraffe, a *swaying* elephant, and a *screeching* monkey. Emphasize the importance of finding adjectives that convey a sensory impression of the animal described.

RESOURCES

Writing Application

Extension

■ *Grammar, Usage, and Mechanics,* p. 31
■ *Language Workshop CD-ROM,* Lessons 1–9

CHAPTER

13

The Parts of a Sentence
Subject, Predicate, Complement

Diagnostic Preview

A. Identifying the Parts of a Sentence

In the following paragraphs, identify each of the numbered italicized words, using these abbreviations:

s.	subject	***p.a.***	predicate adjective
v.	verb	***d.o.***	direct object
p.n.	predicate nominative	***i.o.***	indirect object

EXAMPLE   Are you a mystery **[1]** *fan*?
        1. *p.n.*

Sir Arthur Conan Doyle certainly gave **[1]** *readers* a wonderful **[2]** *gift* when he **[3]** *created* the character of Sherlock Holmes. **[4]** *Holmes* is a **[5]** *master* of the science of deduction. He **[6]** *observes* seemingly insignificant **[7]** *clues*, applies logical reasoning, and reaches simple yet astounding conclusions. The Hound of the Baskervilles is an excellent **[8]** *example* of how Holmes solves a baffling **[9]** *mystery*. The **[10]** *residents* of a rural area are afraid of a supernatural dog that **[11]** *kills* people at night. Helpless against this beast, they seek the **[12]** *services* of Sherlock Holmes. Using logic, he solves the mystery and relieves the people's **[13]** *fear*. This story is **[14]** *one* of Conan Doyle's best because it is both **[15]** *eerie* and mystifying.

Link to Literature

1. i.o.	**2.** d.o.
3. v.	**4.** s.
5. p.n.	**6.** v.
7. d.o.	**8.** p.n.
9. d.o.	**10.** s.
11. v.	**12.** d.o.
13. d.o.	**14.** p.n.
15. p.a.	

B. Identifying and Punctuating the Kinds of Sentences

Copy the last word of each of the following sentences. Then, punctuate each with the correct end mark. Classify each sentence as *imperative*, *declarative*, *interrogative*, or *exclamatory*.

EXAMPLE   **1.**   Sherlock Holmes has many dedicated fans

   1.   fans. —declarative

16. How clever Sherlock Holmes is!   **16.** exc.

17. Sir Arthur Conan Doyle wrote four novels and fifty-six short stories about Holmes.   **17.** dec.

18. Have you read any of these stories?   **18.** int.

19. I particularly like the stories in which Holmes confronts the evil Professor Moriarty.   **19.** dec.

20. Read just one of these stories, and see why millions of mystery fans love Sherlock Holmes.   **20.** imp.

The Sentence

In casual conversation, people often leave out parts of sentences. In writing, however, it is better to use complete sentences most of the time. They help to make meaning clear to the reader.

13a. A *sentence* is a word or word group that contains a subject and a verb and that expresses a complete thought.

A *sentence fragment* is a word or word group that is capitalized and punctuated as a sentence but that does not contain both a subject and a verb or does not express a complete thought.

FRAGMENT   Was waiting by the door. [no subject]
SENTENCE   The clerk was waiting by the door.

FRAGMENT   The room with the high ceiling. [no verb]
SENTENCE   The room with the high ceiling glowed in the sunset.

FRAGMENT   After you have finished the test. [not a complete thought]
SENTENCE   Exit quietly after you have finished the test.

Some sentences contain an understood subject (*you*).

EXAMPLES   [You] **Stop!**
[You] **Pass the asparagus, please.**

Reference Note

For information on **how to correct sentence fragments,** see Chapter 9. For information on **punctuating sentences,** see page 637.

COMPUTER TIP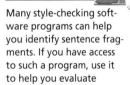

Many style-checking software programs can help you identify sentence fragments. If you have access to such a program, use it to help you evaluate your writing.

Reference Note

For more about **understood subjects,** see page 423.

The Sentence   **413**

The Sentence
Rule 13a *(pp. 413–414)*

OBJECTIVE

- To distinguish between fragments and sentences, revise the fragments to form complete sentences, and use correct capitalization and punctuation

GRAMMAR

Meeting
INDIVIDUAL
NEEDS

LEARNERS HAVING DIFFICULTY

To assist students with **Exercise 1,** help them formulate questions to determine whether a group of words is a sentence.

EXAMPLES

1. Is there a verb? (Is there a word that tells the action or indicates state of being?)

2. Is there a subject? (Is there a word that tells who or what is doing the action?)

3. Does the group of words express a complete idea?

Timesaver

To reinforce students' grasp of the concept of complete sentences, have pairs of students use the three examples above to test each other's sentences for completeness.

Subject and Predicate

Rules 13b–d *(pp. 414–419)*

OBJECTIVES

■ **To identify complete subjects in sentences**

■ **To form complete sentences by adding complete predicates to fragments**

■ **To form complete sentences by adding complete subjects to fragments**

■ **To identify complete predicates and verbs in sentences**

■ **To make sentence fragments into sentences by adding subjects or verbs or both**

Exercise 1 **Identifying Sentences and Revising Fragments**

Decide whether each of the following word groups is a sentence or a sentence fragment. If the word group is a sentence, correct its capitalization and punctuation. If the word group is a sentence fragment, revise it to make a complete sentence. Be sure to use correct capitalization and punctuation.   Revisions will vary.

EXAMPLES   **1.** here are your glasses
   1. Here are your glasses.

   2. before going out
   2. Before going out, I always turn off the lights.

1. on Monday or later this week   **1.** the hunters will return.
2. patiently waiting for the mail carrier.   **2.** Our neighbors are
3. will you be there tomorrow?
4. four people in a small car.   **4.** We saw
5. just yesterday I discovered   **5.** the missing shoes.
6. two strikes and no one on base.   **6.** The team has
7. it runs smoothly.
8. leaning far over the railing   **8.** the guide helped grab the lines.
9. give me a hand.
10. while waiting in line at the theater   **10.** we were drenched with rain.
11. on the way to the science fair.   **11.** Karen struggled with her boxes
12. stand up.   [*or* !]
13. learning English.   **13.** Otto listens carefully because he is
14. when is the marathon?
15. it is time.
16. to the left of the spiral staircase.   **16.** The door is
17. romping along the shore this morning.   **17.** The dogs enjoyed
18. it is theirs.
19. you surprised me, Ellen!
20. how you are.   **20.** Jennifer was asking

Subject and Predicate

Sentences consist of two basic parts: *subjects* and *predicates*.

13b. The *subject* tells whom or what the sentence is about, and the *predicate* says something about the subject.

RESOURCES

Subject and Predicate
Practice

■ *Grammar, Usage, and Mechanics,* pp. 35, 36, 37, 38
■ *Language Workshop CD-ROM,* Lessons 33, 34

In the following examples, the subjects are separated from the predicates by blue vertical lines. Notice that the subject and the predicate may be only one word each, or they may be more than one word.

Coyotes | were howling in the distance.

The telephone in the lobby | rang.

The woman wearing the red blouse | is my aunt.

In these three examples, the words that appear to the left of the vertical line make up the *complete subject*. The words to the right of the vertical line make up the *complete predicate*.

The subject may appear anywhere in the sentence—at the beginning, in the middle, or at the end.

EXAMPLES   In the dim light, **the eager scientist** examined the cave.

Does **Brian's car** have a CD player?

On the table stood **a silver vase.**

Exercise 2   Identifying the Complete Subject

Identify the <u>complete subject</u> of each of the following sentences.

EXAMPLE   1. The art of quilting has been popular in America
                for a long time.
           1. *The art of quilting*

1. Ever since colonial times, <u>Americans</u> have made quilts.
2. <u>Traditional designs, with names like Honeycomb, Tumbling Blocks, and Double Diamond,</u> have been handed down from generation to generation.
3. <u>The designs on this page</u> are quilt blocks from a modern quilt.
4. <u>They</u> certainly don't look like Great-grandmother's quilts!
5. However, <u>quilting techniques</u> have stayed basically the same for well over a hundred years.
6. <u>Small scraps of bright cloth</u> are still painstakingly stitched together to create each block.
7. As in many antique quilts, <u>each quilt block shown here</u> was designed and sewn by a different person.
8. <u>Some of the designs</u> are simple.
9. In others, <u>colorful details</u> bring circus scenes to life.
10. <u>A dark background</u> is sometimes chosen to set off the brilliant colors of a quilt.

Subject and Predicate   **415**

Exercise 3   Writing Complete Predicates

POSSIBLE ANSWERS

1. Justice is one of democracy's ideals.
2. Some commercials use several methods of persuasion.
3. Is the store on the corner closed permanently?
4. The woman next door sells pecans.
5. One way to study is to use memory aids.
6. These guitars are expensive.
7. Is the bicycle on the porch yours?
8. The family reunion will be held late this year.
9. A band marched onto the field.
10. The best route is not always the shortest.

Meeting
INDIVIDUAL
NEEDS

INCLUSION

Give students pictures of people running, playing, swimming, and so on. Have students working in pairs take turns asking one another to state what action is being performed and who is doing the action.

ENGLISH-LANGUAGE LEARNERS

Japanese and Korean. In Japanese, the subject is always followed by the functional word *wa* or *ga*. In Korean, the subject is always followed by *i* (ee) or *ga*. Speakers of these languages should consider which word(s) in English sentences would be followed by one of these functional words in their language.

Reference Note

A compound noun, such as *Gloria Estefan,* is considered one noun. For more about **compound nouns,** see page 376.

Exercise 3   Writing Complete Predicates

Rewrite each of the following items, adding a complete predicate to make a complete sentence. Be sure to use correct capitalization and punctuation.

EXAMPLE   **1.** that famous painting
           1. *That famous painting sold for three million dollars.*

1. justice   6. these guitars
2. some commercials   7. the bicycle on the porch
3. the store on the corner   8. the family reunion
4. the woman next door   9. a band
5. one way to study   10. the best route

The Subject

13c. The main word or word group that tells whom or what the sentence is about is called the *simple subject.*

The *complete subject* consists of the simple subject and any words, phrases, or clauses that modify the simple subject.

EXAMPLES   A triumphant Gloria Estefan stepped up to the microphone.
            complete subject   A triumphant Gloria Estefan
            simple subject   Gloria Estefan

            Out of the beaker rose a foul-smelling foam.
            complete subject   a foul-smelling foam
            simple subject   foam

            Did you make the grits, Travis?
            complete subject   you
            simple subject   you

NOTE   In this book, the term *subject* generally refers to the simple subject unless otherwise indicated.

Exercise 4   Writing Complete Sentences

Make each of the following fragments a sentence by adding a complete subject. Underline each simple subject.   Answers will vary.

EXAMPLE   **1.** Did _____ watch the Super Bowl?
           1. *Did your little <u>brother</u> watch the Super Bowl?*

MINI-LESSON

Placement of Adverbial Modifiers.
Students may expect the complete subject always to begin a sentence. Point out to students sentence 1, **Exercise 2.** Explain that the sentence begins with adverbial modifiers—words that modify the verb and are

therefore not part of the complete subject. Present the following sentence:
After many long years of experimentation, the mad scientist invented a youth-restoring potion.
Explain that the first phrase is an adver-

1. _____ was baying at the moon.   1. A black <u>wolf</u>
2. _____ can make the pizza.   2. The club <u>officers</u>
3. _____ is needed for this recipe.   3. <u>Buttermilk</u>
4. Was _____ the person who won the match?   4. your <u>son</u>
5. _____ rose and soared out over the sea.   5. The wandering <u>albatross</u>
6. _____ stood on the stage singing.   6. The military <u>choir</u>
7. _____ were late for their classes.   7. <u>Sara</u> and <u>James</u>
8. Over in the next town is _____.   8. the county <u>courthouse</u>
9. Buzzing around the room was _____.   9. a large <u>mosquito</u>
10. In the middle of the yard grew _____.   10. some beautiful red <u>roses</u>

The Predicate

13d. The *simple predicate,* or *verb,* is the main word or word group that tells something about the subject.

The *complete predicate* consists of a verb and all the words that describe the verb and complete its meaning.

EXAMPLES   The ambulance raced out of the hospital driveway and down the street.

complete predicate	raced out of the hospital driveway and down the street
simple predicate	raced

Diego may have borrowed my book.

complete predicate	may have borrowed my book
simple predicate	may have borrowed

Are you following Mr. Fayed's advice?

complete predicate	Are following Mr. Fayed's advice
simple predicate	Are following

Notice that the simple predicate may be a single verb or a *verb phrase* (a verb with one or more helping verbs).

Commonly Used Helping Verbs

am	did	has	might	was
are	do	have	must	were
can	does	is	shall	will
could	had	may	should	would

Meeting
INDIVIDUAL
NEEDS

ADVANCED LEARNERS

Advanced students may want to work with higher-level sentence structures. You may want to remind them that good writers are able to vary sentence beginnings, placing different parts of the sentence first for variety's sake.

Direct students to **Exercise 5,** and ask them to write each sentence in as many ways as possible, beginning the sentence in a different way each time. Each version should give the same information, but forms of words may be changed.

Here is an example using the first sentence:

a. Surfing, a warm-weather sport, makes use of the force of incoming waves.

b. Making use of the force of incoming waves, surfing is a warm-weather sport.

INCLUSION

Group students in pairs to work on **Exercise 6.** Work with pairs to brainstorm ideas for item 1. Ask students to tackle item 2 individually and then to compare sentences with their partners to see whether they used the same constructions or took different approaches. Students may prefer tape-recording answers to writing them.

NOTE   In this book, the word *verb* refers to the simple predicate unless otherwise indicated.

Exercise 5 Identifying the Complete Predicate and Verb

For each of the following sentences, write the complete predicate. Then, underline the verb or verb phrase in each complete predicate.

EXAMPLE   1. Surfing and snow skiing are different in many ways.

1. *are different in many ways*

1. The warm-weather sport of surfing uses the force of incoming waves.
2. The wintertime activity of snow skiing relies on gravity.
3. Surfers can pursue their sport with only a surfboard, a flotation vest, a swimsuit, and a safety line.
4. A skier's equipment includes ski boots, skis with bindings, safety cables, ski poles, warm clothing, and goggles.
5. Under their own power, surfers paddle out to their starting places, far from shore.
6. Must a skier buy a ticket for a ski-lift ride to the top of the mountain?
7. Oddly enough, some important similarities exist between surfing and skiing.
8. Both depend on the cooperation of nature for pleasant weather and good waves or good snow.
9. Do both surfing and snow skiing require coordination and balance more than strength?
10. In fact, each of these sports would probably make an excellent cross-training activity during the other's off-season.

Exercise 6 Writing Complete Sentences

Make each of the following sentence fragments a complete sentence by adding a subject, a predicate, or both. Be sure to add correct capitalization and punctuation.   Sentences will vary.

EXAMPLE   1. the barking dog

1. *We were kept awake by the barking dog.*

1. the trouble with my class schedule 1. is that I have no lunch period.
2. the legs of the table 2. were scarred by dogs and children.
3. appeared deserted. 3. The dark school building
4. my billionaire aunt from Detroit 4. bought us all tickets for a cruise.
5. thousands of screaming fans 5. welcomed the team at the airport.

6. my grandparents in Oaxaca. 6. We visited
   ∧
7. thought quickly. 7. Called on to answer the question, Aaron
   ∧
8. after the intermission 8. they returned to their seats.
   =   ∧
9. until sunset. 9. The offer is good only
   ∧
10. the science fair. 10. Jaime's project was a great success at
    ∧

Review A **Distinguishing Between Sentence Fragments and Sentences; Identifying Subjects and Predicates**

Identify each word group as a sentence (*S*) or a sentence fragment (*F*). Then, for each sentence, write the simple subject, underlining it once, and the simple predicate (verb), underlining it twice.

EXAMPLE   **1.** The talented musicians played well together.

1. *S—musicians—played*

1. Jazz music filled the room. **1.** S
2. Supporting the other instruments, the piano carried the melody. **2.** S
3. The saxophonist, with lazy, lingering notes. **3.** F
4. Beside him, the bass player added depth to the band. **4.** S
5. A female vocalist with a deep, rich voice. **5.** F
6. Charmed the audience with her delivery. **6.** F
7. The band's star performer was the drummer. **7.** S
8. For most of the evening, she stayed in the background. **8.** S
9. Until the last half-hour. **9.** F
10. Then she dazzled everyone with her brilliant, high-speed technique. **10.** S

Finding the Subject

To find the subject of a sentence, find the verb first. Then, ask "Who?" or "What?" before the verb.

EXAMPLES   **Here you can swim year-round.** [The verb is *can swim*. Who can swim? *You* can swim. *You* is the subject.]

There is Aunt Ivory's new truck. [What is there? *Truck* is. *Truck* is the subject.]

Into the pond jumped the frog. [What jumped? *Frog* jumped. *Frog* is the subject.]

Please close the window. [Who is to close the window? *You* are—that is, the person spoken to. *You* is the understood subject.]

Reference Note

For information on the **understood subject,** see page 423.

Subject and Predicate   **419**

Finding the Subject

Rule 13e *(pp. 419–423)*

OBJECTIVES

- To identify subjects and verbs in sentences

- To write sentences that are requests or commands

RESOURCES

Finding the Subject

Practice

- *Grammar, Usage, and Mechanics,* pp. 39, 40
- *Language Workshop CD-ROM,* Lesson 33

ENGLISH-LANGUAGE LEARNERS
General Strategies. Help students find the subjects of sentences by first identifying the verbs for them. Suggest they find the subject of each sentence by asking "Who or what does the action?"

Cooperative Learning

Tell students their assignment is to invent a board game for creating sentences with subjects and verbs. Ask the class to consider board games they have played and to figure out what those games have in common—a board, a means of moving around the board, cards to give directions, pieces to move, rules, goals, scoring, and so forth.

Divide students into teams of five. Have each student be responsible for a specific task—writing goals, writing rules, designing the board, developing a scoring system, or creating cards.

Students should review peers' ideas and assemble the game. Then, have students demonstrate their games and take turns playing each game.

Have students compile team reports describing the game, the development process, and what they learned.

Reference Note

For more information about **prepositional phrases,** see page 442.

Exercise 7 **Identifying Subjects and Verbs**

Identify the verb and its subject in each of the following sentences. Be sure to include all parts of a verb phrase.

EXAMPLE 1. Long before the equal rights movement of the 1960s, women in the United States were excelling in their professions.

    1. *were excelling—verb; women—subject*

1. Anne Bissell ran a carpet sweeper business in the late 1800s.
2. For a time, she served as corporation president.
3. Under her direction, the company sold millions of sweepers.
4. In the late nineteenth century, a journalist named Nellie Bly reported on social injustice.
5. On assignments, she would often wear disguises.
6. Ida Wells-Barnett became editor and part owner of the *Memphis Free Speech* in 1892.
7. By the early 1930s, she had been crusading for forty years against racial injustice and for suffrage.
8. At the end of her fourth term as general of the Salvation Army, Evangeline Booth retired in 1939.
9. Booth's efforts helped to make the Salvation Army a financially stable organization.
10. She also improved many Salvation Army services.

13e. The subject of a verb is never in a prepositional phrase.

EXAMPLES **Most** of the women voted. [Who voted? *Most* voted. *Women* is the object in the prepositional phrase *of the women.*]

One of the parakeets in the pet shop looks like ours. [What looks? *One* looks. *Parakeets* and *pet shop* are each part of a prepositional phrase.]

Are **two** of the books missing? [What are missing? *Two* are missing. *Books* is the object in the prepositional phrase *of the books.*]

A *prepositional phrase* includes a preposition, the object of the preposition, and any modifiers of that object.

EXAMPLES   next to Jorge   by the open door   on the floor

                 of a good book   at intermission   after class

                  in the photograph   for all of them   instead of this

Prepositional phrases can be especially misleading when the subject follows the verb.

EXAMPLE   Around the corner from our house is a **store.** [What is? *Store* is. Neither *corner* nor *house* can be the subject because each is part of a prepositional phrase.]

Exercise 8   Identifying Verbs and Subjects

Identify the <u>verb</u> and the <u>subject</u> in each of the following sentences.

EXAMPLE   1. Most of the students in our class have enjoyed discussing our town's folklore.

        1. *have enjoyed—verb; Most—subject*

1. Many <u>regions</u> of the United States <u>have</u> local legends.
2. One pine-forested <u>area</u> in New Jersey <u>is</u> supposedly <u>inhabited</u> by the Jersey Devil.
3. This fearsome <u>monster</u> reportedly <u>chases</u> campers and wayward travelers through the woods.
4. In contrast, <u>Oregon</u> <u>is haunted</u> by numerous legends of the less aggressive Bigfoot.
5. This humanlike <u>creature</u> supposedly <u>hides</u> in heavily forested areas.
6. Its shaggy <u>coat</u> of hair <u>looks</u> like a bear's fur.
7. According to legend, <u>Bigfoot</u> <u>is</u> gentle and shy by nature, avoiding contact with strangers.
8. <u>Stories</u> from the Lake Champlain area <u>tell</u> about a monster resembling a sea serpent in the depths of the lake.
9. Many <u>sightings</u> of this beast <u>have been reported</u> to authorities.
10. No <u>one</u>, however, <u>has</u> ever <u>taken</u> a convincing photograph of the monster.

Sentences That Ask Questions

Questions often begin with a verb, a helping verb, or a word such as *what, when, where, how,* or *why*. The subject of a question usually follows the verb or helping verb.

EXAMPLES   How is the **movie** different from the book?

            Where is the **CD** I gave you?

            Does **she** have a ride home?

In questions that begin with a helping verb, like the third example above, the subject comes between the helping verb and the main verb.

Meeting INDIVIDUAL NEEDS

LEARNERS HAVING DIFFICULTY

Before students begin **Exercise 9,** point out pitfalls in finding the subjects of sentences by listing the following items with examples on the chalkboard:

1. prepositional phrases [*A few of the deer jumped the fence.*]

2. questions [*Are you ready to go to the mall?*]

3. sentences beginning with *there* [*There were many sports fans in the crowded auditorium.*]

4. understood subjects [*Please answer the phone.*]

Encourage students to check for these constructions before deciding on the subject.

MULTIPLE INTELLIGENCES

Spatial/Linguistic Intelligence.
Form groups of three students to make a visual display to help them remember the pitfalls listed above. After students brainstorm what kind of display they wish to make, assign specific students to carry out parts of the plan. For example, students might decide to make posters. One student might design the poster while another draws or paints it and a third writes the text. For example, students might feature a sentence with a prepositional phrase marked out with an international "no" symbol.

You can find the subject by turning the question into a statement and then finding the verb and asking "Who?" or "What?" before it.

EXAMPLES   Was the train late? becomes The train was late. [What was late? The *train* was.]

Has she answered the letter? becomes She has answered the letter. [Who has answered? *She* has.]

Sentences Beginning with *There* or *Here*

The word *there* or *here* is almost never the subject of a sentence. Both *there* and *here* may be used as adverbs telling *where*. To find the subject in a sentence beginning with *there* or *here*, ask "Who?" or "What?" before the verb and the adverb.

EXAMPLES   There are my cousins. [Who are there? *Cousins* are.]

Here is your backpack. [What is here? *Backpack* is.]

NOTE Sometimes *there* starts a sentence but does not tell where. In this use, *there* is not an adverb but an expletive. An **expletive** is a word that fills out a sentence's structure but does not add to its meaning.

                          V   S
EXAMPLES   There is a drawbridge over the river. [*There* adds no information to the sentence, which could be rewritten as *A drawbridge is over the river.*]

                          V   S
There are insects in our garden. [The sentence could be rewritten as *Insects are in our garden.*]

To find the subject in such a sentence, omit *there* and ask "Who?" or "What?" before the verb.

EXAMPLE   There was a clerk at the counter. [Who was? A *clerk* was.]

Exercise 9   Identifying Subjects and Verbs

Identify the subjects and the verbs in the following sentences.

EXAMPLE   1. Will you help me study for my history test?
           1. you—subject; will help—verb

1. There are many questions on American history in my book.
2. Naturally, there are answers, too.
3. Under whose flag did Columbus sail?
4. Here is Plymouth Rock, Anita.
5. How much do you know about the Lost Colony?

Learning for Life

Sample Lesson Plan
Purpose: [*To make children aware of the implications of signs*]
Materials: [*Pictures of outlines of signs, paper, crayons*]
Activities: [*Present child with signs and*

allow child to explain his or her response.]
Sample answer: [*STOP. Stop your car, your bicycle, or yourself when you reach this sign. Don't move until there is no danger from traffic.*]

6. What does *squatter's rights* mean?
7. In what area did most of the early Dutch colonists settle?
8. Was there disagreement among settlers in Massachusetts?
9. What kinds of schools did the colonists' children attend?
10. How did people travel in colonial America?

The Understood Subject

In a request or a command, the subject of a sentence is usually not stated. In such sentences, *you* is the **understood subject.**

REQUEST	Please answer the phone. [Who is to answer? *You* are—that is, the person spoken to.]
COMMAND	Listen carefully to his question. [Who is to listen? *You*—the person spoken to—are.]

Sometimes a request or a command includes a name.

EXAMPLES	Amber, please send us your new address.
	Line up, class.

Amber and *class* are not subjects in the sentences above. These words are called **nouns of direct address.** They identify the person spoken to or addressed. *You* is the understood subject of each sentence.

EXAMPLES	Amber, [you] please send us your new address.
	[You] line up, class.

Exercise 10 **Writing Requests or Commands**

Using the following five situations, write sentences that are requests or commands. In two of your sentences, use a noun of direct address.

EXAMPLES	*Setting*	*Person Speaking*	*Person Addressed*
1.	castle	queen	wizard
2.	kitchen	parent	teenager

1. Wizard, make this straw into gold.
2. Please don't drink out of the carton.

Setting	*Person Speaking*	*Person Addressed*
1. desert oasis	Aladdin	genie
2. courtroom	judge	defense attorney
3. child's room	child	baby sitter
4. spaceship	alien invader	crew member
5. forest	Big Bad Wolf	Little Red Riding Hood

TEACHING TIP

Activity. Before students begin **The Understood Subject** lesson, write the following imperative sentence on the chalkboard:

Take the dog outside, please.

Then, ask for a volunteer to name the subject of the sentence [*you, understood*].

Review understood subjects with the class. Then, ask students to list as many situations as they can in which an understood subject would be used (such as recipes, directions for VCR programming, directions on tests or exercises, or "how-to" books). Ask students to bring examples of these items to class. Allow contributors to create a bulletin board display or a booklet of examples.

Exercise 10   **Writing Requests or Commands**

POSSIBLE ANSWERS

1. Bring me water!
2. Mr. Nye, approach the bench.
3. Please help me clean up.
4. Go into orbit around the planet.
5. Let me escort you through the woods.

Evaluation: [*Have the child draw a picture showing his or her response to each sign. To show sequence of actions, children might create comic strips.*]

If students actually teach the lesson, they should create an oral or written evaluation of their teaching experience to show what they taught and what they learned.

Compound Subjects and Compound Verbs

Rules 13f, g *(pp. 424–427)*

OBJECTIVES

- To identify compound subjects and their verbs in sentences
- To identify compound verbs and their subjects in sentences
- To identify complete subjects and predicates

**Meeting
INDIVIDUAL
NEEDS**

ENGLISH-LANGUAGE LEARNERS
Spanish. Inform students that in English, a comma is commonly used before *and* or *or* when there are three or more parts of a compound subject. In Spanish a comma is not used.

INCLUSION

Have students create their own sentences with compound subjects and compound verbs. Give them patterns to imitate, and then have them work with a helper who can write the sentences down as students say them aloud. The following are some possible patterns:

1. <u>Joe</u> and <u>Elena</u> wiped the tables.

2. The <u>drummer</u>, <u>guitarist</u>, and <u>lead singer</u> joined the band.

3. Two bears <u>slept</u> and <u>ate</u> in their dens.

4. The driver <u>signaled</u> but did not <u>turn</u>.

Encourage students to keep copies of these patterns in their notebooks for future reference.

Reference Note

For more information about **conjunctions,** see page 403. For more about using **commas between words in a series,** see page 644.

Compound Subjects

13f. A *compound subject* consists of two or more subjects that are joined by a conjunction and that have the same verb.

The conjunctions most commonly used to connect the words of a compound subject are *and* and *or*.

EXAMPLE   **Antony** and **Mae** baked the bread. [Who baked the bread? Antony baked it. Mae baked it. *Antony* and *Mae* form the compound subject.]

When more than two words are included in the compound subject, the conjunction is generally used only between the last two words. Also, the words are separated by commas.

EXAMPLE   Antony**,** Mae**, and** Pamela baked the bread. [compound subject: *Antony, Mae, Pamela*]

Correlative conjunctions, such as *neither . . . nor* and *not only . . . but also,* may be used with compound subjects.

EXAMPLE   **Either** Antony **or** Mae baked the bread. [compound subject: *Antony, Mae*]

Exercise 11 **Identifying Compound Subjects and Their Verbs**

Identify the compound subjects and their verbs in the following sentences.

EXAMPLE   1. Roast turkey and cranberry sauce are often served at Thanksgiving.

       1. *turkey, sauce—compound subject; are served—verb*

1. Gerbils and goldfish make good, low-maintenance pets.
2. April, May, and June provide the best opportunity for studying wildflowers in Texas and Oklahoma.
3. Kettles of soup and trays of sandwiches sat on the counter.
4. Both you and I should go downtown or to the movies.
5. Either *Macbeth* or *Othello* features witches in its plot.
6. In that drawer lay her scissors, ruler, and markers.
7. Star-nosed moles and eastern moles live in the United States.
8. There are many good jokes and riddles in that book.
9. Where will you and your family go on vacation this year?
10. There were eggs and milk in the refrigerator.

RESOURCES

Compound Subjects and Compound Verbs
Practice

- *Grammar, Usage, and Mechanics,* pp. 41, 42, 43
- *Language Workshop CD-ROM,* Lessons 11, 33, 34

Compound Verbs

13g. A *compound verb* consists of two or more verbs that are joined by a conjunction and that have the same subject.

EXAMPLES   Jim Thorpe **entered** and **won** several events in the 1912 Olympics.

The committee **met, voted** on the issue, and **adjourned.**

My sister **will buy** or **lease** a car.

Both the subject and the verb may be compound.

EXAMPLES   The **students** and **teachers wrote** the play and **produced** it.

Either **Jan** or **Beverly will write** the story and **send** it to the paper.

> NOTE There are other cases in which a sentence may contain more than one subject and verb.

EXAMPLES   The **defeat** of the Germans at Verdun in 1916 **was** a victory for France, but the **battle cost** each side nearly half a million casualties. [This kind of sentence is called a *compound sentence.*]

Because **crocodiles are** descended from dinosaurs, **they are** the nearest living relatives of birds. [This kind of sentence is called a *complex sentence.*]

Before the **movie started, Siva offered** to buy popcorn; **Melissa said** that **she would save** his seat. [This kind of sentence is called a *compound-complex sentence.*]

Exercise 12 Identifying Subjects and Compound Verbs

Identify the compound verbs and the subjects in the following sentences. Be sure to include helping verbs. If a sentence contains an understood subject, write *(You)*.

EXAMPLE   **1.** Should I buy this pair of jeans now or wait for a sale?

      1. *compound verb—should buy, wait; subject—I*

1. Tony rewound the cassette and then pressed the playback button.
2. Toshiro sings, acts, and dances in the show.
3. At the fair, Dan ran faster than the other boys and won the prize of twenty-five dollars.

STYLE   TIP

The helping verb may or may not be repeated before the second part of a compound verb if the helping verb is the same for both parts of the verb.

EXAMPLES
My sister **will buy** or **will lease** a car.

My sister **will buy** or **lease** a car.

Reference Note

For more about **compound, complex, and compound-complex sentences,** see page 481.

HELP

Sentences in Exercise 12 may contain an understood subject.

Relating to Literature

Explain to students that compound structures, such as compound subjects and verbs, should be parallel. Refer students to **Chapter 10.** Have students look through the poetry section of their literature books to find poetry with compound subjects or verbs. ("I Never Saw a Moor" by Emily Dickinson and "Kidnap Poem" by Nikki Giovanni have examples of compound verbs.) Ask students to share with the class samples of compound verbs and subjects they have found in poems. Have students explain how the compound structures are parallel. Ask students to explain what is being emphasized through the use of compound subjects or verbs. [*This style usually emphasizes the equal importance of the compound components.*]

As students proceed through the chapter, have them return to the poems and look for other compounds, such as compound direct objects, predicate nominatives, and prepositional phrases. Have them read to the class examples they have found and discuss the effectiveness of the usage. Students might want to rewrite the section of poetry, eliminating the compound elements, and discuss the change in the effect of the language.

MODALITIES

Visual Learners. On the chalkboard or overhead projector, create a two-column graphic organizer using the following labels:

Subject	Predicate

Ask students to fill in both columns for **Exercise 13.** You may want to adapt this format to three columns for **Exercise 16** on p. 430.

4. Will you walk home or wait for the four o'clock bus?
5. This kitchen appliance will slice, dice, and chop.
6. Velma will not only bring the salad but also bake bread for the party.
7. Please pick your socks up and put them either in the hamper or downstairs by the washing machine. **7.** (You)
8. The marching band practiced hard and won the state competition.
9. Visit, rest, and relax. **9.** (You)
10. The newborn calf rose to its feet with a wobble and stood.

Exercise 13 **Identifying Subjects and Predicates**

Write each of the following sentences, underlining the complete subject once and the complete predicate twice. Be sure to include all parts of compound subjects and compound verbs.

EXAMPLE **1.** Gary Soto and Amy Tan are my favorite authors.

 1. *Gary Soto and Amy Tan are my favorite authors.*

┌ Link to [ ] Literature ┐

1. Soto's poetry and short stories often are about his life.
2. Will he read from his works and sign books here tonight?
3. Carlos, Ted, and I will find front-row seats.
4. Where is your copy of *Too Many Tamales*?
5. Here is Gary Soto's latest collection of poetry.
6. His realistic way of presenting life appeals to me.
7. This particular poem brings back childhood memories.
8. Something similar happened to me in the first grade.
9. There are Sandra Cisneros and Rudolfo Anaya, other successful Hispanic American authors.
10. Their stories reflect a rich cultural heritage.

Review B **Finding Subjects and Verbs**

Copy each of the sentences in the following paragraph. Then, complete steps A through D to find the subject and the verb in each sentence.

┌HELP┐

Not all steps apply to every sentence in Review B.

A. Cross out all prepositional phrases to help you isolate the verb and the subject.
B. Cross out *Here* or *There* at the beginning of a sentence to eliminate these words as possible subjects.
C. Underline all verbs twice, including all helping verbs and all parts of any compound verbs.

D. Underline all subjects once, including all parts of any compound subjects. If a sentence contains an understood subject, write and underline *you*.

EXAMPLE **[1]** Quicksand can be dangerous to a hiker.

1. *Quicksand* <u>can be</u> *dangerous to a hiker*.

[**1**] In quicksand, <u>you</u> <u>must remain</u> calm. [**2**] Violent <u>movement</u>, such as kicking your legs, <u>will</u> only <u>worsen</u> the situation. [**3**] There <u>are</u> several <u>steps</u> to escaping from quicksand. [**4**] First, <u>discard</u> your backpack or any other burden. [**5**] Next, gently <u>fall</u> onto your back and <u>spread</u> your arms. [**6**] In this position, <u>you</u> <u>will be</u> able to float. [**7**] Only then <u>should</u> <u>you</u> slowly <u>bring</u> your feet to the surface. [**8**] Perhaps a <u>companion</u> or <u>someone</u> else nearby <u>can reach</u> you with a pole or a rope. [**9**] <u>Are</u> <u>you</u> alone? [**10**] Then <u>you</u> <u>should look</u> for the shortest distance to solid ground and <u>paddle</u> slowly toward safety.

4. (you)
5. (you)

Complements

13h. A *complement* is a word or word group that completes the meaning of a verb.

Some groups of words need more than a subject and a verb to express a complete thought. Notice how the following sentences need the boldfaced words to complete their meaning. These boldfaced words are called *complements*.

EXAMPLES   It is a good **car** even though it is **old.**

           Who gave **Mr. Garcia** the **present**?

A complement may be compound.

EXAMPLES   Aunt Edna looks **happy** and **relaxed** today.

           My cats enjoy **eating** and **napping.**

A complement may be a noun, a pronoun, or an adjective.

                S   V   C
EXAMPLES   Marcella might become a **chemist.**

                  S   V   C
           The raccoon watched **us** gardening in the backyard.

                  S   V   C
           The clerks at that store are **helpful.**

Complements   **427**

Complements

Rule 13h *(pp. 427–429)*

OBJECTIVES

- **To identify subjects, verbs, and complements in sentences**

- **To form complete sentences by adding complements to groups of words**

Meeting
INDIVIDUAL
NEEDS

Visual Learners. Give students oral practice adding complements to the sentence base. Make flashcards for students out of 3" x 5" cards. On one side of the cards, put a subject, an action verb, and a blank, or put a subject, a linking verb, and a blank. On the back put possible complements. Here are some sample cards:

1. Dogs chew [bones].

2. Mom gave [me] a hug.

3. A bear is [furry].

4. Robbie is a [Boy Scout].

Have students work in pairs to complete the sentences.

ENGLISH-LANGUAGE LEARNERS

Spanish. Because English has one verb for *to be* while Spanish has both *estar* and *ser*, Spanish-speaking students may have difficulty understanding sentences using forms of *be* such as those in sentences 6 and 8 in **Exercise 14.** Before students can find subject complements in the exercises, you may need to focus on vocabulary with them.

Reference Note

For information on **adverbs,** see page 393.

Reference Note

For information on **prepositional phrases,** see page 442.

Reference Note

For information on **independent and subordinate clauses,** see Chapter 15.

An adverb is not a complement.

EXAMPLES   **Where** did we go **wrong?** [*Wrong* is used as an adverb, not a complement.]

That answer is not **wrong.** [*Wrong*, an adjective, is a complement in this sentence.]

Sentence complements are never in prepositional phrases.

EXAMPLES   She watched the **cardinals.** [*Cardinals* is the complement.]

She watched **all** of the cardinals. [*Cardinals* is part of the prepositional phrase *of the cardinals*.]

NOTE   Both independent and subordinate clauses contain subjects and verbs and may contain complements.

                         S   V   C   S   V   C
EXAMPLES   This **kitten is** the **one that climbed** the **curtains.**

                     S   V   C   S   V   C
Before **Eli rides** his **bicycle, he checks** his **tires.**

Exercise 14 **Identifying Subjects, Verbs, and Complements**

Identify the subject, verb, and [complement] in each of the following sentences.

EXAMPLE   1. Many modern slang expressions sound okay to my great-grandfather.

                1. *expressions—subject; sound—verb; okay—complement*

1. Like every generation, my great-grandfather's generation had its own [slang.]
2. He still uses [it] all the time, particularly in stories about his youth.
3. Great-grandpa played the [trombone] in a jazz band in the 1930s.
4. He and other musicians developed many slang [expressions.]
5. Their language became [jive talk.]
6. Many of Great-grandpa's expressions are [sayings] of the entertainer Cab Calloway.
7. Great-grandpa uses [phrases] such as Calloway's *beat to my socks* (tired) and *out of this world* (perfect).
8. Great-grandpa's speech is [full] of words like *hepcat* (a lover of jazz music) and *hip* (wise) and *groovy* (wonderful).
9. Such language became [popular] all over the United States.
10. My great-grandfather, at least, still uses [it.]

Exercise 15 Writing Sentence Complements

Write ten sentences by adding a complement to each of the following word groups. Be sure to punctuate each sentence correctly.

Sentences will vary.

EXAMPLE **1.** The puppy is

1. *The puppy is playful.*

1. Jesse usually seems∧ 1. confident.
2. Tomorrow the class will hear∧ 2. a speech from the principal.
3. That broiled fish looks∧ 3. hot and delicious.
4. Last week our class visited∧ 4. the art museum.
5. Do you have∧ 5. change for a dollar?
6. Coretta finished the∧ 6. assignment.
7. The winners felt∧ 7. exhausted.
8. Saturday the museum will sell∧ 8. replicas of the statue.
9. Fruits and vegetables filled the∧ 9. plates and trays.
10. How do you like∧ 10. your new apartment?

The Subject Complement

13i. A *subject complement* is a word or word group in the predicate that describes or identifies the subject.

EXAMPLES The surface felt **sticky.** [*Sticky* describes *surface.*]

Mark Twain's real name was **Samuel Clemens.** [*Samuel Clemens* identifies *name.*]

Subject complements may be compound.

EXAMPLES That winter seemed especially **mild** and **sunny.**

The prizewinners are **Jennifer, Marcus,** and **Raul.**

Subject complements sometimes precede the subject of a sentence or a clause.

EXAMPLES How **kind** he is! [*Kind* is a predicate adjective describing *he.*]

I know what a **treat** this is for her. [*Treat* is a predicate nominative identifying *this.*]

NOTE Subject complements always complete the meaning of linking verbs. A word that completes the meaning of an action verb is not a subject complement.

TIPS & TRICKS

To find the subject complement in an interrogative sentence, rearrange the sentence to make a statement.

EXAMPLE
Is Darnell the treasurer?
Darnell is the **treasurer.**

To find the subject complement in an imperative sentence, insert the understood subject *you.*

EXAMPLE
Be good.
(You) Be **good.**

Reference Note
For more about **action and linking verbs,** see page 387.

Complements   **429**

The Subject Complement

Rule 13i *(pp. 429–431)*

OBJECTIVES

■ To identify subject complements as predicate nominatives or predicate adjectives

■ To complete sentences by adding subject complements to groups of words and to identify these complements as predicate nominatives or predicate adjectives

---

Meeting
INDIVIDUAL
NEEDS

LEARNERS HAVING DIFFICULTY

Tell students that a linking verb is like an equal sign (=) because it links the subject to its complement, whereas an action verb shows the relationship between the subject and a direct object through some action.

Ask students to create four sentences of their own using only linking verbs. Two should have predicate nominatives, and two should have predicate adjectives. Students might want to put the sentences on index cards, add illustrations, and keep the cards as study tools.

| STYLE | TIP |

The use of the nominative-case pronoun, as in the last example of the predicate nominative, is uncommon in everyday speech. You will often hear *It is him,* rather than *It is he.* Remember that in formal English you should use the nominative-case pronoun.

Reference Note

For more about the **nominative case**, see page 550.

(1) A *predicate nominative* is a word or word group that is in the predicate and that identifies the subject or refers to it.

EXAMPLES   Has she become a **dentist**?

Friendship is **what I value most.**

The new teacher is **he**—the man in the blazer.

(2) A *predicate adjective* is an adjective that is in the predicate and that modifies the subject.

EXAMPLES   The soup is **hot.** [hot soup]

That soil seems **dry** and **crumbly.** [dry and crumbly soil]

How **expensive** are those shoes? [expensive shoes]

Exercise 16 Identifying Subject Complements

Each of the following sentences has at least one subject complement. For each sentence, give the complement or complements and tell whether each is a *predicate nominative* or a *predicate adjective.*

EXAMPLE   1. Gloria is my favorite character on the show.

        1. character—predicate nominative

1. p.a.
2. p.a.

3. p.a.
4. p.a.
5. p.n.
6. p.a.
7. p.n.
8. p.a.
9. p.n.
10. p.a.

1. Does the lemonade taste too <u>sour</u>?
2. The chirping of the birds became more and more <u>shrill</u> as the cat approached.
3. The window washers on the fifteenth floor appeared <u>tiny</u>.
4. Why does he always look so <u>serious</u>?
5. Our candidate for the city council was the <u>winner</u> in the primaries.
6. You should feel <u>proud</u> of yourself.
7. Will the hall monitors for Wednesday be <u>Charlene</u> and <u>LaReina</u>?
8. <u>Soft</u> and <u>cool</u> was the grass under the catalpa tree.
9. Be a <u>friend</u> to animals.
10. The crowd grew <u>quiet</u> when Governor Markham spoke.

Exercise 17 Writing Subject Complements

Make complete sentences of the following word groups by adding nouns, pronouns, or adjectives as subject complements. Use five compound complements. Identify each subject complement as a *predicate nominative* or a *predicate adjective.*

EXAMPLE   1. The sky turned

        1. The sky turned cloudy and dark. —predicate adjectives

1. The artist frequently was
2. Those are
3. Sara Brown became
4. It could be
5. The house looked
6. Are you
7. The weather remained
8. The test seemed
9. Manuel had always felt
10. That recording sounds

Objects

Objects are complements that do not refer to the subject. Objects follow transitive verbs—verbs that express an action directed toward a person, place, or thing.

EXAMPLE   Lee Trevino sank the **putt.** [The object *putt* does not explain or describe the subject *Lee Trevino. Sank* is a transitive verb, not an intransitive verb.]

NOTE   Transitive verbs may express mental action (for example, *believe, trust, imagine*) as well as physical action (for example, *give, hit, draw*).

EXAMPLE   Now I remember your name. [Remember *what*? Name.]

13j. A *direct object* is a noun, pronoun, or word group that tells who or what receives the action of a verb or shows the result of the action.

A direct object answers the question "Whom?" or "What?" after a transitive verb.

EXAMPLES

    S   **V**   **DO**
Germs cause **illness.** [Germs cause *what*? Germs cause illness. *Illness* shows the result of the action of the verb.]

    S   **V**   **DO**
Peter said *Gesundheit.* [Peter said *what*? Peter said *Gesundheit. Gesundheit* receives the action of the verb.]

   S   **V** **DO**
Lucy visited **me.** [Lucy visited *whom*? Lucy visited me. *Me* receives the action of the verb.]

        DO **S** **V**
What a scary **movie** we saw! [We saw *what*? We saw a movie. *Movie* receives the action of the verb.]

   S   **V**   **DO**
They were taking **whatever was left.** [They were taking *what*? They were taking whatever was left. *Whatever was left* receives the action of the verb.]

Reference Note

For more about **transitive and intransitive verbs,** see page 386.

Complements   431

RESOURCES

Objects
Practice

■ *Grammar, Usage, and Mechanics,* pp. 48, 49, 50, 51

Exercise 17 Writing Subject Complements

POSSIBLE ANSWERS

1. The artist frequently was cold and hungry. p.a.
2. Those are my shoes and John's boots. p.n.
3. Sara Brown became my partner. p.n.
4. It could be a whole new idea. p.n.
5. The house looked lonely and cold. p.a.
6. Are you the substitute teacher? p.n.
7. The weather remained sunny and clear. p.a.
8. The test seemed endless. p.a.
9. Manuel had always felt honored and respected. p.a.
10. That recording sounds ancient. p.a.

Objects

Rules 13j, k (pp. 431–435)

OBJECTIVE

■ To identify direct objects and indirect objects in sentences

Meeting INDIVIDUAL NEEDS

ENGLISH-LANGUAGE LEARNERS
Spanish. In Spanish, the direct object pronoun generally precedes the verb. Ask a student to write a short sentence in Spanish on the board. Tell the student that the sentence should contain a direct object. Ask the student to label the parts and rewrite the sentence in English. Label the parts of the English sentence, emphasizing the difference in the position of the direct object.

Crossing the Curriculum

Social Studies. Students can improve their note-taking skills by using these basic sentence structures: subject/verb/direct object, subject/verb/ predicate nominative, and subject/verb/predicate adjective.

From a social studies teacher, get a time line of the unit students are studying. Have students use the basic sentence structures to write sentences about events during the time period.

Sample sentences about Nelson Mandela in South Africa:

1. Nelson Mandela had been a prisoner for many years. (S-V-PN)

2. He was considered dangerous to the current government. (S-V-PA)

3. After his release, he helped his people greatly. (S-V-DO)

MULTIPLE INTELLIGENCES

Kinesthetic Learners. To introduce indirect objects, give pairs of students slips of paper with sample sentences such as "He gave her a book." Have pairs act out or pantomime the sentence. Ask a volunteer to create a sentence based on the scene. Write the sentence on the board, and label the parts. Follow the same procedure as other students act out or pantomime other sentences that have direct and indirect objects. Students could create labeled stick-figure drawings on index cards to use as study guides.

┌─HELP─────

Indirect objects generally precede direct objects.

Reference Note

For information on **transitive verbs,** see page 386.

Direct objects are generally not found in prepositional phrases.

EXAMPLES Josh was riding on his bicycle. [*Bicycle* is part of the prepositional phrase *on his bicycle*. The sentence has no direct object.]

Josh was riding his **bicycle.** [*Bicycle* is the direct object.]

Exercise 18 Identifying Direct Objects

Identify the direct object in each of the following sentences.

EXAMPLE   1. I enjoy this magazine very much.
          1. *magazine*

1. This article gives interesting facts about libraries.
2. The city of Alexandria, in Egypt, had the most famous library of ancient times.
3. This library contained the largest collection of plays and works of philosophy in the ancient world.
4. The Roman emperor Augustus founded two public libraries.
5. Fire destroyed all of these libraries.
6. Readers could not borrow books from either the library in Alexandria or the Roman libraries.
7. During the Middle Ages, the monastery libraries introduced a circulating library.
8. By the sixth century, Benedictine monks were borrowing books from their libraries for daily reading.
9. In the United States, we now have thousands of libraries.
10. Readers borrow millions of books from them every year.

13k. An *indirect object* is a noun, pronoun, or word group that often appears in sentences containing direct objects. An indirect object tells *to whom* or *to what* (or *for whom* or *for what*) the action of a transitive verb is done.

EXAMPLES

S   V   IO   DO
Natalie knitted her **friend** a sweater. [Natalie knitted a sweater for whom? For her *friend.*]

S   V   IO   DO
My little sister sang **me** a song. [My little sister sang a song to whom? To *me.*]

S   V   IO   DO
Uncle Gene sends **whoever requests it** a pamphlet on earthworms. [Uncle Gene sends a pamphlet to whom? To *whoever requests it.*]

If the word *to* or *for* is used, the noun or pronoun following it is part of a prepositional phrase and not an indirect object.

OBJECTS OF PREPOSITIONS	My teacher showed the bird's nest to the **class.** I left some dessert for **you.**
INDIRECT OBJECTS	The teacher showed the **class** the bird's nest. I left **you** some dessert.

Both direct and indirect objects may be compound.

EXAMPLES   Lydia sold **cookies** and **lemonade.** [compound direct object]

Lydia sold **Geraldo, Freddy,** and **me** lemonade. [compound indirect object]

NOTE   Do not mistake an adverb in the predicate for a complement.

ADVERB   Go **inside,** Skippy. [*Inside* is an adverb telling *where.*]

COMPLEMENT   Tamisha sanded the **inside** of the wooden chest. [*Inside* is a noun used as a direct object.]

Exercise 19   Identifying Direct Objects and Indirect Objects

Identify the direct and indirect objects in the following sentences. Make sure that you give all parts of compound direct and indirect objects.

EXAMPLE   1. Sometimes I read my little brother stories from Greek mythology.

1. *indirect object—brother; direct object—stories*

1. In one myth, the famous artist and inventor Daedalus built the king of Crete a mysterious building known as the Labyrinth.
2. The complicated passageways of this building give us the word *labyrinth,* ("a maze or confusing structure").
3. After the completion of the Labyrinth, the king imprisoned Daedalus and his son, whose name was Icarus.
4. To escape, Daedalus made Icarus and himself wings out of feathers and beeswax.
5. He gave Icarus careful instructions not to fly too near the sun.
6. However, Icarus soon forgot his father's advice.
7. He flew too high, and when the sun melted the wax in the wings, he plunged to his death in the ocean.

Reference Note

For information on **prepositional phrases and objects of prepositions,** see page 442.

Reference Note

For information on **adverbs,** see page 393.

┌ H E L P ┐

Not every sentence in Exercise 19 contains an indirect object.

┌──────────────────────┐
│ Link to [ ] Literature │
└──────────────────────┘

Relating to Writing

Based on the information in the sentences for **Exercise 19** or from the story of Daedalus and Icarus found in a literature book, have the class write an epitaph for Icarus of at least eight lines, using direct objects and indirect objects in at least four lines. Explain that an epitaph is an inscription used to mark a burial place.

Timesaver

For easier checking, have students circle direct objects and underline indirect objects in their epitaphs.

Meeting
INDIVIDUAL
NEEDS

MULTIPLE INTELLIGENCES

Spatial Intelligence. You may want to use diagramming to illustrate the structure of a sentence. Diagramming helps students with strong spatial sense to visualize an abstract concept. For examples of diagramming, see p. 928. Encourage students to break down sentences in **Review D** (p. 434) into simple sentences and to diagram the basic parts of the simple sentences.

SAMPLE DIAGRAMS

1. Before this winter, I couldn't draw a human face well.

2. However, our neighbor, Mr. Teng, is a portrait painter.

3. He has been giving me some instructive tips.

—HELP—

Not every sentence in Review C contains a complement; some sentences contain more than one.

1. i.o./d.o.   2. p.n.
3. d.o.   4. n.c.
5. d.o./d.o.   6. d.o.
7. p.a.   8. d.o.
9. p.a./i.o./   10. p.n.
   d.o.

—HELP—

Remember that subordinate clauses contain subjects and verbs and may also contain complements.

1. d.o.   2. s.
3. p.n.   4. i.o.
5. d.o.

8. Though saddened by the death of his son, Daedalus flew on and reached Sicily in safety.
9. Mythology tells us other stories of his fabulous inventions.
10. Even today, the name Daedalus suggests genius and inventiveness.

Review C Identifying Complements

Identify the complements in the following sentences. Then, tell whether each complement is a *predicate nominative*, a *predicate adjective*, a *direct object*, or an *indirect object*. If a sentence does not contain a complement, write *no complement*.

EXAMPLE   **[1]** My brother Bill gave Mom a birthday surprise.
   1. Mom—indirect object; surprise—direct object

[1] My brother made Mom a birthday cake. [2] However, the project soon became a fiasco. [3] First, Bill cracked three eggs into a bowl. [4] Unfortunately, bits of the shells went in, too. [5] Then he added the flour and other dry ingredients. [6] The electric mixer whirled the batter right onto the ceiling. [7] The batter was so sticky that it stayed there and didn't fall off. [8] Bill did not clean the ceiling immediately, and the sticky substance hardened overnight. [9] Mom was not angry, but she did give Bill a suggestion for a gift. [10] "A clean kitchen would be a great birthday present."

Review D Identifying the Parts of a Sentence

Identify the italicized words in the following passage. Use these abbreviations.

s.	subject	*p.a.*	predicate adjective
v.	verb	*d.o.*	direct object
p.n.	predicate nominative	*i.o.*	indirect object

EXAMPLE   When you draw faces, do they look **[1]** *realistic*?
   1. p.a.

Before this winter, I couldn't draw a human **[1]** *face* well. However, our **[2]** *neighbor*, Mr. Teng, is a portrait **[3]** *painter*, and he has been giving **[4]** *me* some instructive **[5]** *tips*. He says that the most important

[6] *thing* is the correct [7] *placement* of the eyes. Apparently, most [8] *people* draw the [9] *eyes* too high. In fact, [10] *they* should be placed halfway down the head. Many people also [11] *make* the ears too small. The [12] *top* of each ear [13] *should align* with the eyebrow, and the [14] *bottom* should align with the tip of the nose. Getting the width of the face right is also [15] *important*. Mr. Teng says, "Use one eye's [16] *width* as a unit of measure and make the head five eye-widths wide." There are many other [17] *guidelines*, but these tips from Mr. Teng are the most [18] *basic*. By following them, I can now draw a human [19] *face* that [20] *looks* realistic.

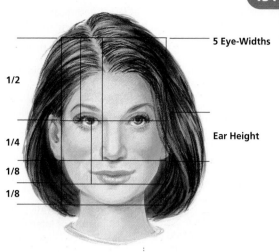

5 Eye-Widths

1/2

1/4   **Ear Height**

1/8

1/8

6. s.	7. p.n.	8. s	9. d.o.	10. s.	11. v.	12. s.
13. v.	14. s.	15. p.a.	16. d.o.	17. s.	18. p.a.	19. d.o.	20. v.

Classifying Sentences by Purpose

13l. A sentence may be classified, depending on its purpose, as *declarative, imperative, interrogative,* or *exclamatory.*

(1) A *declarative sentence* makes a statement and ends with a period.

EXAMPLES   Jody Williams won the Nobel Peace Prize in 1997.

         That one-celled organism is an amoeba.

(2) An *imperative sentence* gives a command or makes a request. Most imperative sentences end with a period. A strong command ends with an exclamation point.

EXAMPLES   Please keep to the right. [request]

         Take care of your little brother, Rick. [command]

         Stop! [strong command]

Notice in these examples that a command or a request has the understood subject *you.*

Classifying Sentences by Purpose
Rule 13l *(pp. 435–436)*

OBJECTIVE

- To choose the correct end punctuation for sentences and to classify them according to type

Reference Note

For more information about **understood subjects,** see page 423.

Classifying Sentences by Purpose   **435**

RESOURCES

**Classifying Sentences by Purpose
Practice**

- *Grammar, Usage, and Mechanics,* p. 52

Meeting
INDIVIDUAL
NEEDS

LEARNERS HAVING DIFFICULTY

Use the following information to help students associate sentence classification terms with more familiar words.

- **Declarative:** form of *declare*, meaning "to make a statement"
- **Interrogative:** form of *interrogate*, meaning "to ask questions"; associated with interrogating criminals or spies
- **Imperative:** think of an emperor giving commands
- **Exclamatory:** form of *exclaim*, meaning "to cry out"

Students can illustrate these terms with cartoons to use as study aids.

Looking at Language

Students might enjoy knowing about other designations for punctuation marks. An *interrobang (‽)* is a combination of a question mark (interrogative) and an exclamation point (called a "bang" in printers' slang). It indicates a sentence that is both a question and an exclamation. (Students might enjoy creating such sentences.) A *screamer* is another slang term for an exclamation point. Challenge students to create their own humorous slang terms for punctuation.

S T Y L E   T I P

Sometimes writers use both a question mark and an exclamation point to express the combined emotions of surprise and disbelief or wonder.

EXAMPLE
Is it really you‽

Such usage is appropriate only in informal situations and in dialogue, to convey the speaker's emotions.

(3) An *interrogative sentence* asks a question and ends with a question mark.

EXAMPLES   Can they finish in time?

How did she find Yoshi and Sarah?

(4) An *exclamatory sentence* shows excitement or expresses strong feeling and ends with an exclamation point.

EXAMPLES   What a good friend you are!

The battery is dead!

I can't believe this is happening!

NOTE In conversation, any sentence may be spoken so that it becomes exclamatory or interrogative. When you are writing dialogue, use periods, exclamation points, and question marks to show how you intend a sentence to be read.

EXAMPLES   They won. [declarative]
They won! [exclamatory]
They won? [interrogative]

Exercise 20 Identifying the Four Kinds of Sentences

Punctuate each of the following sentences with an appropriate end mark. Classify each sentence as *imperative*, *declarative*, *interrogative*, or *exclamatory*.

EXAMPLE   1. There are many delicious foods from India

1. *period—declarative*

1. Do you like spicy food? 1. int.
2. Some Indian food is hot, and some isn't. 2. dec.
3. *Sambar* is a soup made with lentils and vegetables. 3. dec.
4. Save me some of those curried shrimp. 4. imp.
5. What is that wonderful bread called? 5. int.
6. *Palek alu* is a spicy dish of potatoes. 6. dec.
7. Watch out for the hot chilies. [or !] 7. imp.
8. Isn't this yogurt drink called *lassi* good? 8. int.
9. Be sure to add the curry and other spices to the onions. 9. imp.
10. How tasty this rice-and-banana pudding is! 10. exc.

Chapter Review

A. Identifying Types of Sentences and Sentence Fragments

Identify each of the following word groups as a *declarative sentence*, an *interrogative sentence*, an *imperative sentence*, an *exclamatory sentence*, or a *sentence fragment*. Supply the appropriate end mark after the last word of each item that is *not* a sentence fragment.

1. Why don't we go to the wildlife park tomorrow **?**   1. int.
2. What a good time we'll have **!**   2. exc.
3. The big cats especially at feeding time   3. frag.
4. Actually, I enjoy the entire park **.**   4. dec.
5. Meet me at the front gate at ten o' clock **.**   5. imp.
6. We'll first go see the elephants **.**   6. dec.
7. Don't forget the camera **.**   7. imp.
8. My favorite animal is Bonzo the baboon **.**   8. dec.
9. His amazing stunts and antics   9. frag.
10. How graceful the gazelles are **!**   10. exc.

┌─HELP─┐

In Part B of the Chapter Review, the simple subject may be compound.

B. Identifying the Complete Subject and the Simple Subject

Identify the (complete subject) in each of the following sentences. Then, underline the simple subject.

11. (One of the first advocates of medical hygiene and the use of antiseptics) was Ignaz Semmelweis.
12. (This German-Hungarian physician) was born in 1818.
13. In 1844, (he) earned a degree from Vienna University.
14. (His first position) was as an assistant at the obstetric clinic in Vienna.
15. (Semmelweis) was appalled by the high mortality rate among his patients.
16. (He) taught medical staff members always to wash their hands in a chlorine solution and by doing so soon reduced the mortality rate.
17. (Semmelweis, who was a true pioneer,) lobbied the medical establishment to make antiseptic operating conditions a top priority.

Chapter Review   **437**

Using the Chapter Review

The **Chapter Review** requires students to identify sentences by purpose as well as to identify the function of specific words in sentences. The results of this test can be compared to those of the **Diagnostic Preview** (p. 412) to assess student progress.

GRAMMAR

18. (The medical establishment in many countries) remained hostile to Semmelweis for many years.

19. In 1865, the year of Semmelweis's death, (a famous British surgeon named Joseph Lister) performed his first antiseptic operation.

20. (The method introduced by Semmelweis) made medicine safer and more humane.

┌─HELP──
In Part C of the Chapter Review, the simple predicate may be compound.

C. Identifying Complete Predicates and Simple Predicates (Verbs)

Identify the (complete predicate) in each of the following sentences. Then, underline the simple predicate (or verb).

21. (Have) you (met my brother Lewis?

22. (Then listen to this!

23. My brother (often dawdles).

24. He (chooses odd times for some activities).

25. (One day last week), Lewis (gathered all of the pencils in the house and sharpened them).

26. (Today) he (woke early and completely rearranged his room).

27. (Then) my poor little brother (was almost late for the school bus).

28. I (reminded him, however, of his first-period test).

29. (Somehow), Lewis (finishes all his chores and assignments).

30. I (might buy him a book about time management, though).

D. Identifying Sentence Parts

Identify each italicized word in the following paragraphs as a *subject*, a *verb*, a *predicate nominative*, a *predicate adjective*, a *direct object*, or an *indirect object*.

31. s.	32. p.n.
33. v.	34. s.
35. p.a.	36. v.
37. s.	38. i.o.

A [31] *carwash* can be a good [32] *fund-raiser*. The freshman class [33] *planned* a carwash for last Saturday. On Saturday morning, the [34] *sky* did not look [35] *good*. In fact, the weather forecast [36] *predicted* thunderstorms. Did [37] *any* of this send [38] *us* a message? Yes, but we

RESOURCES

The Parts of a Sentence

Practice

■ *Grammar, Usage, and Mechanics,* pp. 53, 54, 55, 56

Assessment

■ *Assessment Package*
    —*Chapter Tests*, Ch. 13
    —*Chapter Tests in Standardized Test Formats*, Ch. 13
■ *Test Generator (One-Stop Planner CD-ROM)* 🎵

had our **[39]** *carwash* anyway. Our first **[40]** *customer*, at 9:00 A.M., was a **[41]** *woman* in a pickup truck. Glancing at the sky, she paid **[42]** *us* a compliment. "You're really **[43]** *brave*," she said. The rain **[44]** *began* as she was speaking, and our disappointment must have been **[45]** *obvious*. "Don't worry," she added "there is **[46]** *nothing* like a rainwater rinse." We **[47]** *charged* her only one **[48]** *dollar* because she had cheered us up so much. The morning was intermittently **[49]** *rainy*. Later, however, the clouds parted and the weather was **[50]** *perfect*.

39. d.o.	40. s.
41. p.n.	42. i.o.
43. p.a.	44. v.
45. p.a.	
46. s.	
47. v.	48. d.o.
49. p.a.	
50. p.a.	

Writing Application
Using Verbs in a Summary

Fresh, Lively Verbs   Your little sister likes you to tell her exciting stories. You have told her so many stories that you have run out of new ones. To get ideas for new stories, you think about events you have read about or seen. Write a summary of an exciting incident from a book, a movie, or a television show. Use action verbs that are fresh and lively. Underline these verbs.

Prewriting   Think about books that you have read recently or movies and television shows that you have seen. Choose an exciting incident from one of these works. Freewrite what you remember about that incident.

Writing   As you write your first draft, think about how you are presenting the information. When telling a story, you usually should use chronological order (the order in which events occurred). This method would be easiest for your young reader to follow, too. Try to use fresh, lively action verbs.

Revising   Imagine that you are a young child hearing the story for the first time. Look over your summary and ask yourself if you could follow this account of the story.

Publishing   Read over your summary again, looking for any errors in grammar, usage, and mechanics. You may want to share your story with a younger sibling or with children at a local preschool or kindergarten.

Chapter Review   **439**

Writing Application
(p. 439)

OBJECTIVE

■ To write a summary of an incident using action verbs

Writing Application

Tip. Linking verbs are also referred to as state-of-being verbs because the words they link to the subject often describe the subject's condition. The words linked to the subject by linking verbs are often adjectives and describe the writer's perspective as well as the subject's physical attributes.

Scoring Rubric. While you will want to pay particular attention to students' use of parts of the sentence, you will want to evaluate the students' overall writing performance. You may want to give a split score to indicate development and clarity of the composition as well as grammar skills.

Critical Thinking

Analysis. Illustrate the difference between a strictly objective description and a description using sensory details. Have students picture a doctor's office; then, ask them how the picture would change from the perspective of a health care professional or a young patient.

[*The scene would change according to the feelings of the person describing it. A health care professional might describe a clean, sterile, efficient clinic, while a child might describe needles and the cries of patients. In other words, sensory details are reflections of the writer's judgment.*]

CHAPTER

14

The Phrase
Prepositional, Verbal, and Appositive Phrases

Diagnostic Preview

A. Identifying and Classifying Prepositional Phrases

Identify each prepositional phrase in the following sentences. After each phrase, write the word(s) it modifies and the type of phrase it is (*adj.* for adjective phrase, *adv.* for adverb phrase).

┌ H E L P ┐

Some sentences in Part A have more than one prepositional phrase.

EXAMPLE   1. The museums of different cities are fascinating to tourists.

   1. of different cities—museums—adj.
      to tourists—fascinating—adv.

1. New York City offers tourists a number of museums.   **1.** adj.
2. Perhaps the best-known museum is the American Museum of Natural History.   **2.** adj.
3. This huge museum has exhibits on human history and culture and also shows animals, even dinosaurs, in natural-looking displays, called dioramas.   **3.** adj./adv.
4. The museum houses the Hayden Planetarium, which teaches visitors about the heavens.   **4.** adv.
5. Exhibits about earth and space interest young and old alike.   **5.** adj.
6. The entire complex of exhibits is popular because it offers something for everyone.   **6.** adj./adj.

7. The city's other museums, which are also fascinating, attract visitors who are <u>interested</u> <u>in specific topics</u>.   **7.** adv.

8. New York is <u>home</u> <u>to the Museum of Broadcasting</u>, which is <u>filled</u> with old films and radio broadcasts.   **8.** adj./adj./adv.

9. <u>One</u> <u>of the city's newest museums</u>, Ellis Island Immigration Museum, <u>opened</u> <u>during 1990</u> and displays many artifacts that <u>had been owned</u> <u>by immigrants</u> who <u>entered</u> the United States <u>through Ellis Island</u>.   **9.** adj./adv./adv./adv.

10. People who enjoy art can visit <u>museums</u> <u>like the Metropolitan Museum of Art</u> and the <u>Museum of Modern Art</u>.   **10.** adj./adj./adj.

B. Identifying Verbals and Appositives

In the following sentences, identify each <u>italicized word or word group</u> as a *participle*, a *gerund*, an *infinitive*, or an *appositive*.

EXAMPLES   **1.** For some reason, *cleaning* a room, that *dreaded project,* always seems *to create* new projects.

   1. cleaning—gerund; dreaded—participle; project—appositive; to create—infinitive

11. John began with every intention of *cleaning* his entire room, the official disaster *area* of his home.   **11.** ger./app.

12. He first tackled the pile of CDs *lying* near his *unused* sound system.   **12.** part./part.

13. *Sorting* through them, he found them mostly *outdated*.   **13.** part./part.

14. John decided that his *broken* stereo system, a *gift* from his parents, was the reason.   **14.** part./app.

15. By *repairing* the stereo, he could give himself a reason *to update* his music collection.   **15.** ger./inf.

16. *Trained* in electronics, John soon saw the problem and began *to work* on it.   **16.** part./inf.

17. Some hours later, John had a *working* stereo system but an *uncleaned* room.   **17.** part./part.

18. He had just started *playing* a CD when his sister announced, "Mom's coming *to see* how your room looks!"   **18.** ger./inf.

19. A tough *taskmaster,* Mom wanted him *to have* it spotless.   **19.** app./inf.

20. She applauded his success in *fixing* his stereo but insisted that he clean the room before *doing* anything else.   **20.** ger./ger.

GRAMMAR

What Is a Phrase?

Rule 14a (p. 442)

OBJECTIVE

■ To identify phrases

Prepositional Phrases

Rules 14b–e (pp. 442–448)

OBJECTIVES

■ To identify adjective phrases and the word or words they modify

■ To identify adverb phrases and the word or words they modify

■ To write an article combining sentences by using adjective and adverb phrases

■ To distinguish between adverb and adjective phrases and to identify what each phrase modifies

Reference Note

For more about **clauses,** see Chapter 15.

Reference Note

For a list of **commonly used prepositions,** see page 400.

What Is a Phrase?

14a. A *phrase* is a group of related words that is used as a single part of speech and that does not contain both a verb and its subject.

EXAMPLES   could have been [no subject]

instead of Debra and him [no subject or verb]

A group of words that has *both* a verb and its subject is not a phrase.

EXAMPLES   **We found** your pen. [*We* is the subject of *found.*]

if **she will go** [*She* is the subject of *will go.*]

NOTE   If a group of words contains both a verb and its subject, it is called a *clause.*

Exercise 1   Identifying Phrases

Identify each of the following groups of words as a *phrase* or *not a phrase.*

EXAMPLES   **1.** with a hammer   **2.** because we agree
          1. phrase   *2. not a phrase*

1. was hoping 1. p.
2. if she really knows 2. n. p.
3. with Abdullah and me 3. p.
4. will be writing 4. p.
5. inside the house 5. p.
6. since Mallory wrote 6. n. p.
7. after they leave 7. n. p.
8. has been cleaned 8. p.
9. on Miriam's desk 9. p.
10. as the plane lands 10. n. p.

Prepositional Phrases

14b. A *prepositional phrase* includes a preposition, the object of the preposition, and any modifiers of that object.

EXAMPLES   **to** the pool   **at** the Jacksons' house   **instead of** them

Notice that one or more modifiers may appear in a prepositional phrase. The first example contains *the;* the second contains *the Jacksons'.*

14c. The noun or pronoun in a prepositional phrase is called the *object of the preposition.*

EXAMPLE   Clarice went to the **ballet.** [The noun *ballet* is the object of the preposition *to.*]

RESOURCES

What Is a Phrase? and Prepositional Phrases
Practice

■ *Grammar, Usage, and Mechanics,* pp. 61, 62, 63, 64, 65

■ *Language Workshop CD-ROM,* Lesson 24

NOTE Do not be misled by a modifier coming after the noun or pronoun in a prepositional phrase. The noun or pronoun is still the object.

EXAMPLE   Heidi and Mrs. Braun worked **at the polls** today. [*Polls* is the object of the preposition *at*. The adverb *today* tells when and modifies the verb *worked*.]

Objects of prepositions may be compound.

EXAMPLES   On the plaza, a guitarist sang for **Victor** and **me.** [The preposition *for* has a compound object: *Victor* and *me*.]

In A.D. 79, the city of Pompeii was buried beneath **lava, rocks,** and **ashes.** [The preposition *beneath* has a compound object: *lava, rocks,* and *ashes.*]

A prepositional phrase can modify the object of another prepositional phrase.

EXAMPLE   Next to the door **of the old barn** stood two horses. [The prepositional phrase *of the old barn* modifies *door,* which is the object of the compound preposition *Next to*.]

A prepositional phrase can contain another prepositional phrase.

EXAMPLE   Meet us **at the Museum of Science and Industry.** [The prepositional phrase *at the Museum of Science and Industry* contains the prepositional phrase *of Science and Industry*.]

NOTE Sometimes a prepositional phrase is combined with a noun to form a compound noun.

EXAMPLES   Strait of Hormuz   hole in one

Stratford-on-Avon   University of Pittsburgh

The Adjective Phrase

14d. A prepositional phrase that modifies a noun or pronoun is called an *adjective phrase.*

EXAMPLE   The members **of the club** want sweatshirts **with the club emblem.** [The prepositional phrase *of the club* is used as an adjective to modify the noun *members. With the club emblem* is used as an adjective to modify the noun *sweatshirts.*]

TIPS & TRICKS

Be careful not to confuse the preposition *to* with the *to* that is the sign of the verb's infinitive form: *to swim, to know, to see.*

Reference Note

For more about **infinitives,** see page 457.

Reference Note

For more about **compound nouns,** see page 376.

Meeting INDIVIDUAL NEEDS

ENGLISH-LANGUAGE LEARNERS

General Strategies. Some English-language learners might have difficulty sorting out the meanings of the various prepositions. To help eliminate this confusion, have students act out the following prepositional phrases.

across the room
on the chair
in her purse
from me
to you
at the pencil sharpener
between the two desks
in front of the chalkboard
behind the door

If you notice that students are confusing one preposition with another in their writing, explain the correct uses of both the preposition they used and the preposition they should have used, providing examples and a simple definition of each one. Then, have students draw simple illustrations to show the distinction between the words that they are confusing.

Unlike a one-word adjective, which usually precedes the word it modifies, an adjective phrase almost always follows the noun or pronoun it modifies.

ADJECTIVE	Amy closed the **cellar** door.
ADJECTIVE PHRASE	Amy closed the door **to the cellar.**

More than one adjective phrase may modify the same word.

EXAMPLE   Here's a letter **for you from Aunt Martha.** [The prepositional phrases *for you* and *from Aunt Martha* both modify the noun *letter.*]

An adjective phrase may also modify the object of another prepositional phrase.

EXAMPLE   The horse **in the trailer with the rusted latch** broke loose. [The phrase *in the trailer* modifies the noun *horse. Trailer* is the object of the preposition *in.* The phrase *with a rusted latch* modifies *trailer.*]

Often you can convert the objects of adjective phrases into adjectives. Doing so makes your writing less wordy.

Adjective Phrases	Nouns Used as Adjectives
The light **in the kitchen** is on.	The **kitchen** light is on.
The airports **in Chicago and New York** are crowded.	The **Chicago** and **New York** airports are crowded.

However, not all adjective phrases can be changed into one-word modifiers that make sense. Sometimes, changing an adjective phrase makes a sentence awkward and ungrammatical.

CLEAR	Please hand me the book on the table.
AWKWARD	Please hand me the table book.

Exercise 2   Identifying Adjective Phrases

Identify the adjective phrases in the following paragraph, and give the word that each modifies.

EXAMPLE   **[1]** A few years ago our family visited South Dakota and saw a famous monument to great American leaders.

1. *to great American leaders—monument*

[1] My mom took the pictures on the next page when we were visiting this scenic spot at Mount Rushmore National Memorial. [2] As

┌HELP─

Some sentences in Exercise 2 contain more than one adjective phrase.

you can see, the mountainside behind us is a lasting tribute to George Washington, Thomas Jefferson, Theodore Roosevelt, and Abraham Lincoln. [3] The figures on the granite cliff were carved under the direction of Gutzon Borglum, an American sculptor. [4] Looking at the sculpture, I can certainly believe that this is one of the world's largest. [5] The faces are sixty feet high and show a great deal of detail and expression. [6] Each president symbolizes a part of United States history. [7] Washington represents the founding of the country, and Jefferson signifies the Declaration of Independence. [8] Lincoln symbolizes an end to slavery, and Roosevelt stands for expansion and resource conservation. [9] Tourists on the viewing terrace must gaze up nearly five hundred feet to see this art. [10] As both symbols for the nation and works of art, these massive faces are an inspiration to all who visit Mount Rushmore.

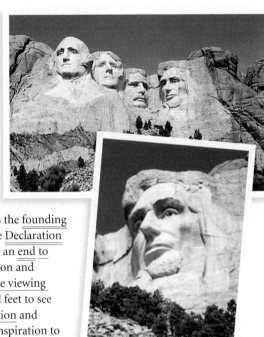

The Adverb Phrase

14e. A prepositional phrase that modifies a verb, an adjective, or an adverb is called an *adverb phrase.*

An adverb phrase tells *how, when, where, why,* or *to what extent.*

EXAMPLES   Britney answered **with a smile.** [The adverb phrase *with a smile* tells *how* Britney answered.]

They sailed **across the lake** yesterday. [The adverb phrase *across the lake* tells *where* they sailed.]

By Wednesday Christopher will be finished. [The adverb phrase *By Wednesday* tells *when* Christopher will be finished.]

The calculations erred **by more than two inches.** [*By more than two inches* is an adverb phrase telling *to what extent* the calculations erred.]

In the examples above, the adverb phrases all modify verbs.

Exercise 2

ALTERNATIVE LESSON
Have students find the following items:

1. a compound proper noun used in a prepositional phrase and referring to a place [*sentence 1: Mount Rushmore National Memorial*]

2. a two-word proper adjective [*sentence 6: United States*]

3. a compound proper noun used as a direct object [*sentence 7: Declaration of Independence; sentence 10: Mount Rushmore*]

Relating to Writing

Divide the class into small groups. Have each group collaborate to write a brief description of Mount Rushmore. Give each student in the group the chance to add one or two prepositional phrases. Then, have each group edit its description collaboratively. Volunteers may read completed descriptions to the class.

Viewing the Art

About the Artist. Gutzon Borglum was born John Gutzon de la Mothe Borglum in 1867 in Idaho. The son of Danish parents, he studied art in both Paris and San Francisco. His sculptures include a head of Abraham Lincoln in the rotunda of the Capitol building in Washington, D.C., the *Mares of Diomedes* at the Metropolitan Museum in New York City, and the carvings of the apostles at the cathedral of St. John the Divine, also in New York City.

An adverb phrase may modify an adjective or an adverb.

EXAMPLES   Melissa is good **at tennis** but better **at volleyball.** [The adverb phrase *at tennis* modifies the adjective *good*. The adverb phrase *at volleyball* modifies the adjective *better*.]

Is the water warm enough **for swimming**? [The adverb phrase *for swimming* modifies the adverb *enough*.]

Adjective phrases almost always follow the words they modify, but an adverb phrase may appear at various places in a sentence.

EXAMPLES   **Before noon** the race started.
The race started **before noon.**

Like adjective phrases, more than one adverb phrase may modify the same word.

EXAMPLE   **During summers,** my older sister works **at the museum.** [The adverb phrases *During summers* and *at the museum* both modify the verb *works*. The first phrase tells *when* my sister works; the second phrase tells *where* she works.]

Exercise 3 Identifying Adverb Phrases

Identify the adverb phrases in the following sentences, and give the word or words each phrase modifies.

EXAMPLE   1. The concept of time has inspired many figures of speech over the years.

1. *over the years—has inspired*

1. We use time expressions in everyday speech.
2. In conversation, you may have heard the expression "time out of mind," which means "long ago."
3. When you fall in love, you may feel that "time stands still."
4. Is twenty minutes too long for a "time-out"?
5. If something happens "in no time," it happens very fast.
6. Have you ever noticed that "time flies" when you are chatting with your friends?
7. However, if you are sitting in a waiting room, "time drags."
8. Are you keeping someone's secret "until the end of time"?
9. Do people stop you on the street to ask if you "have the time"?
10. In the meantime, "time marches on" under the steady gaze of "Father Time."

Crossing the Curriculum

Art. After students complete **Exercise 3,** ask them to select one of the adverb phrases from the exercise and create an artwork that illustrates the meaning of the sentence. Encourage students to be as creative as possible, and remind them that representing the relationship indicated by the adverb phrase is more important than the quality of their drawings. You can point out that even stick figures can communicate the meaning of an adverb phrase.

TECHNOLOGY TIP

Students who are comfortable with computer graphics programs could create their illustrations on computers and could show others how to do so.

STYLE TIP

Be sure to place phrases carefully so that they express the meaning you intend.

EXAMPLES
The conductor complimented Lia's performance after the concert. [Did Lia perform after the concert was over?]

After the concert, the conductor complimented Lia's performance. [The compliment was made after the concert.]

HELP

Some sentences in Exercise 3 contain more than one phrase.

Review A Writing Sentences Using Adjective and Adverb Phrases

You are a reporter for your school newspaper. The Young Business Leaders Club has given you an announcement for its upcoming banquet. Write an article about this event, using the information from the announcement below. Use five adjective phrases and five adverb phrases to help you include the necessary information in your article.

Young Business Leaders Club

What?	Annual Banquet
Where?	Executive Inn Restaurant
	North Highway 53
When?	Friday, May 11, 6:30 to 9:00 P.M.

Tickets are $15.00 per person, available from Alonzo Jackson.

Program

6:30	**Welcome Address**—Anna Wong, *president*
6:45	**Introductory Remarks**—J. Zarr, *club sponsor*
7:00	**Dinner**
8:00	**Speakers' Forum: "Planning Now for Your Future"**—
	Rebecca López, *nutritionist, Memorial Hospital*
	John Perri, *owner, Computer Solutions*
	Susanne Drennan, *financial planner, United Savings Bank*
8:45	**Presentation of Young Business Leader Award**

Review B Identifying Adjective and Adverb Phrases

Identify each italicized prepositional phrase in the following paragraph as an *adjective phrase* or as an *adverb phrase*. Then, identify the word or words each phrase modifies.

EXAMPLE   I enjoy reading all sorts **[1]** *of myths and legends.*

1. *adjective phrase—sorts*

Have you heard the Greek myth **[1]** *about Narcissus and Echo*? It is a story rich **[2]** *in irony.* Narcissus was a handsome young man **[3]** *with many admirers.* However, he rejected everyone who loved him, including the nymph Echo. As punishment **[4]** *for his arrogant behavior*, the gods sentenced Narcissus to stare forever **[5]** *at his own reflection* **[6]** *in a pond.* **[7]** *For days*, Narcissus gazed adoringly **[8]** *at himself.* Echo the nymph stayed **[9]** *with him* until she wasted away. Finally Narcissus, too, wasted away, and when he died he turned **[10]** *into the narcissus flower.*

| Link to | Literature |

1. adj.
2. adv.   3. adj.
4. adj.
5. adv.   6. adj.
7. adv.   8. adv.
9. adv.
10. adv.

Prepositional Phrases   **447**

Meeting
INDIVIDUAL
NEEDS

MODALITIES

Visual Learners. To reinforce the concept that a sentence develops by adding chunks of information, use specific colors to denote parts of the sentence and the prepositional phrases. For example, make the simple subject red, the verb or verb phrase yellow, the complements blue, and prepositional phrases green. As colors will occasionally overlap, you may want to point out that a sentence part can contain a prepositional phrase.

Show sentence 1 from **Review C** written on a transparency, and let students identify the parts of the sentence and prepositional phrases and tell which color to use to highlight them. [*Edwin Hubble:* red; *discovered:* yellow; *the existence:* blue; *About seventy years ago:* green; *of galaxies:* green; *outside the Milky Way:* green.]

You may wish to have students use this color coding to continue **Review C** on their own or in pairs. You may also want to have students use a similar color-coding technique as they work with other types of phrases in the chapter.

┌─ HELP ─

In the example for Review C, *about the universe* modifies *Theories*, and *over the years* modifies *have changed.*

1. adv./adj./adj.
2. adv./adj.

3. adj./adj.

4. adv./adj.

5. adv./adv.

6. adv./adv./adj./adj.

7. adv./adj.

8. adv./adv./adj.

9. adv./adv.

10. adv./adj./adj.
    [*or* would be amazed]

Review C **Identifying and Classifying Prepositional Phrases**

List all the prepositional phrases in each of the following sentences. Write *adj.* if the phrase is used as an adjective; write *adv.* if the phrase is used as an adverb. Be prepared to identify the word each phrase modifies.

EXAMPLE   1. Theories about the universe have changed over the years.

　　　　　 1. *about the universe—adj.; over the years—adv.*

1. In 1929, Edwin Hubble discovered the existence of galaxies outside the Milky Way.
2. Now we know that perhaps a million galaxies exist inside the bowl of the Big Dipper alone.
3. Astronomers believe that our galaxy is only one among billions throughout the universe.
4. Knowledge has expanded since 500 years ago, when most people believed that the earth was the center of the entire universe.
5. By the 1500s, the Polish astronomer Copernicus suggested that the earth and other planets revolved around the sun.
6. In 1633, the Italian scientist Galileo was tried and convicted for the crime of teaching that the sun is the center of the universe.

7. The Catholic Church condemned Galileo because in his teachings earth and humans were not the center of all things.
8. In Galileo's time, people knew of only five planets besides our own—Mercury, Venus, Mars, Jupiter, and Saturn.
9. Since then we have identified the planets Uranus, Neptune, and Pluto, and we have sent probes into our solar system.
10. Galileo, Copernicus, and other early astronomers would be amazed at the extent of our knowledge of space today.

Verbals and Verbal Phrases

Verbals are formed from verbs. Like verbs, they may have modifiers and complements. However, verbals are used as nouns, adjectives, or adverbs, not as verbs. The three kinds of verbals are *participles, gerunds,* and *infinitives.*

The Participle

14f. A *participle* is a verb form that can be used as an adjective.

EXAMPLES   We saw the raccoon **escaping** through the back door. [The participle *escaping,* formed from the verb *escape,* modifies the noun *raccoon.*]

          Waxed floors can be dangerously slippery. [The participle *Waxed,* formed from the verb *wax,* modifies the noun *floors.*]

Two kinds of participles are *present participles* and *past participles.*

(1) Present participles end in *–ing.*

EXAMPLES   We ran inside to get out of the **pouring** rain. [The present participle *pouring* modifies the noun *rain.*]

          Watching the clock, the coach became worried. [The present participle *watching* modifies the noun *coach.*]

Although participles are forms of verbs, they cannot stand alone as verbs. Participles need to be joined to a helping verb to form a verb phrase. When a participle is used in a verb phrase, it is part of the verb and is not an adjective.

VERB PHRASES   The rain **was pouring.**

              The coach **had been watching** the clock.

(2) Past participles usually end in *–d* or *–ed.* Other past participles are formed irregularly.

EXAMPLES   A **peeled** and **sliced** cucumber can be added to a garden salad. [The past participles *peeled* and *sliced* modify the noun *cucumber.*]

          The speaker, **known** for her strong support of recycling, was loudly applauded. [The irregular past participle *known* modifies the noun *speaker.*]

Reference Note

For a discussion of **irregular verbs,** see page 519.

Verbals and Verbal Phrases   **449**

The Participle and the Participial Phrase

Rules 14f, g *(pp. 449–453)*

OBJECTIVES

- To identify participles and the words they modify

- To complete sentences by supplying appropriate participles

- To identify participial phrases and the words they modify

Meeting
INDIVIDUAL
NEEDS

ENGLISH-LANGUAGE LEARNERS
Spanish. Point out to students that the English *–ing* suffix corresponds to *–ando* and *–iendo* in Spanish; the English *–(e)d* suffix corresponds to *–ado* and *–ido* in Spanish.

RESOURCES

The Participle and the Participial Phrase
Practice
- *Grammar, Usage, and Mechanics,* pp. 66, 67, 68
- *Language Workshop CD-ROM,* Lesson 25

LEARNERS HAVING DIFFICULTY

Students may have difficulty with verbals ending in –ing, –ed, and –en because the same endings can be used for main verbs. Because students also may be confused by participial phrases, have them begin by finding one-word participles in sentences 1, 3, 7, and 10 in **Exercise 4.** [1. *prancing*; 3. *swaggering, boasting*; 7. *banging (students may also spot* walking, *which is part of a participial phrase)*; 10. *stirring (students may also spot* marching, *which is part of a participial phrase)*].

Have students approach the exercise by first finding and color-coding the subject and verb for the sentences designated above, as students did for the visual learners activity on p. 448. Then, have students find each participle and the noun or pronoun it modifies.

To help students recognize that participles act as adjectives, have them substitute adjectives for participles (for example, *gray* for *prancing* in sentence 1).

Exercise 4

ALTERNATIVE LESSON

To review verbs, have students list the verbs or verb phrases in sentences 1, 4, 7, 9, and 10 of **Exercise 4.**

1. were applauded

4. was postponed

7. thought, was

9. turned, fled

10. crossed

Reference Note

For more about the **passive voice,** see page 535.

HELP

Some sentences in Exercise 4 contain more than one participle used as an adjective.

Like a present participle, a past participle can also be part of a verb phrase. When a past participle is used in a verb phrase, it is part of the verb and is not an adjective.

VERB PHRASES   I **have peeled** and **sliced** the cucumber.

The speaker **was known** for her strong support of recycling.

NOTE Notice in the second example above that a past participle used with a form of the verb *be* creates a *passive-voice* verb. A verb in the passive voice expresses an action done to its subject.

EXAMPLE   The goal **was made** by Josh. [The action of the verb *was made* is done to the subject *goal.*]

Exercise 4 **Identifying Participles and the Words They Modify**

Identify the participles used as adjectives in each of the following sentences. After each participle, write the noun or pronoun it modifies.

EXAMPLES   **1.** We searched the island for buried treasure.

1. buried—treasure

2. The speeding train raced past the platform.

2. speeding—train

1. The prancing horses were loudly applauded by the audience.
2. Colorful flags, waving in the breeze, brightened the gloomy day.
3. Swaggering and boasting, the new varsity quarterback made us extremely angry.
4. The game scheduled for tonight was postponed because of rain.
5. Leaving the field, the happy player rushed to her parents sitting in the bleachers.
6. Branches tapping on the roof and leaves rustling in the wind made an eerie sound.
7. We thought the banging shutter upstairs was someone walking in the attic.
8. Painfully sunburned, I vowed always to use sunscreen and never to be so careless again.
9. Terrified by our dog, the burglar turned and fled across the yard.
10. The platoon of soldiers, marching in step, crossed the field to the stirring music of the military band.

MINI-LESSON

Punctuating Participial Phrases. Explain to students that commas are used to set off nonessential participial phrases. Then, write the following sentences on the chalkboard, and discuss them with the class.

1. Written by hand, the essay was messy. [*Introductory participial phrases always require a comma.*]

2. Tenth-graders entering the essay contest should go to the auditorium. [*The phrase*

Exercise 5 Using Appropriate Participles

For each blank in the following sentences, provide a participle that fits the meaning of the sentence.

EXAMPLE   1. The _____ tide washed over the beach.
           1. *rising*
           Answers will vary.

1. Mr. Ortiz explained the effects of pollution and drought on plants _____ in a rain forest.   1. growing
2. _____ from the point of view of a firefighter, the story is full of accurate details.   2. Told
3. The tiger, _____ from the hunters, swam across the river to safety.   3. running
4. _____ at the traffic light, the driver put on his sunglasses.   4. Waiting
5. The tourists _____ in the hotel were given a free meal.   5. staying
6. _____ as an excellent place to camp, the park lived up to its reputation.   6. Known
7. _____ by a bee, Steven hurried to the infirmary.   7. Stung
8. The poem describes a spider _____ on a thread.   8. dangling
9. We stumbled off the racecourse, _____.   9. gasping
10. _____, I quickly phoned the hospital.   10. Aching

The Participial Phrase

14g. A *participial phrase* is used as an adjective and consists of a participle and any complements or modifiers the participle has.

EXAMPLES   **Seeing the cat,** the dog barked loudly.

            The cat hissed at the dog **barking in the yard next door.**

            The dog **noisily barking at the cat** had to be brought in.

In each of the following sentences, an arrow points from the participial phrase to the noun or pronoun that the phrase modifies.

EXAMPLES   **Switching its tail,** the mountain lion paced back and forth. [participle with object *tail*]

            She heard me **sighing loudly.** [participle with the adverb *loudly*]

            Living within his budget, Adam never needs to borrow money. [participle with adverb phrase *within his budget*]

            Quickly grabbing the keys, I dashed for the front door. [participle with preceding adverb *Quickly* and object *keys*]

Reference Note

For information on **punctuating participial phrases,** see page 653. The participle as a **dangling modifier** is discussed on page 585. For information on **using participles to combine sentences,** see page 332.

STYLE   TIP

A participial phrase should be placed very close to the word it modifies. Otherwise, the phrase may appear to modify another word, and the sentence may not make sense.

MISPLACED
He saw a moose riding his motorcycle through the woods. [The placement of the modifier *riding his motorcycle* calls up a silly picture. He, not the moose, is riding the motorcycle.]

IMPROVED
Riding his motorcycle through the woods, he saw a moose.

Cooperative Learning

Ask each student to brainstorm a list of five to ten present and past participles. Then, begin a round robin game by calling on a student to use the participle *smiling* as an adjective in a sentence. After presenting the sentence to the class, this student will call upon a classmate to identify the noun modified by the participle. If correct, the second student will select a participle from his or her list and repeat the process you initiated. Alternatively, the first student can challenge a classmate to use *smiling* as part of a verb phrase. Incorrect respondents lose a turn but are still in the game.

Meeting INDIVIDUAL NEEDS

LEARNERS HAVING DIFFICULTY
Before introducing participial phrases, write the following sentence fragments on the chalkboard:

1. The egrets flying low above the grazing cattle.

2. The four-year-old delighted by the clown's funny dance.

3. In the nick of time, the firefighter thrown clear of the blast.

4. The movie classic *Casablanca* showing at the midnight theater.

After students have studied examples on this page, have them add words to turn the fragments into complete sentences.

---

entering the essay contest *is necessary to the meaning of the sentence.*]

3. The Carters' house, built in the early 1950s, has beautiful hardwood floors. [*The phrase* built in the early 1950s *con-*

tains information that is not needed to understand the meaning of the sentence.*]

For more information on punctuating participial phrases, refer students to **Chapter 22: Punctuation.**

Meeting
INDIVIDUAL
NEEDS

LEARNERS HAVING DIFFICULTY
Sometimes students have trouble seeing that a participial phrase functions as an adjective in a sentence. Write the following pairs of sentences on the chalkboard, and have students compare how participles are used in them. Be sure to explain that the participle in each pair modifies the same word.

1. The confused contestant failed to answer in time.

Confused by the tricky question, the contestant failed to answer in time.

2. The damaged boat rocked wildly.

Damaged by the storm, the boat rocked wildly.

Relating to Writing

To give students further practice using verbals, ask them to write descriptive paragraphs about a journey from one place to another. The paragraphs may describe a real event, such as taking the wrong bus home from school or traveling on a family vacation, or an imaginary account of a fictional character's adventure. Instruct students to use participles and participial phrases to add detail and give variety to their sentences.

┌─ **HELP** ─
Some sentences in Review D contain more than one participle or participial phrase.

Exercise 6 **Identifying Participial Phrases**

Identify the participial phrases in the following sentences, and give the word each phrase modifies.

EXAMPLE **1.** The sight of skyscrapers towering against the sky always impresses me.

1. towering against the sky—skyscrapers

1. How are skyscrapers created, and what keeps them standing tall?
2. As the drawing shows, columns of steel, or of concrete reinforced with steel, are sunk into bedrock beneath the building.
3. If a layer of rock isn't present, these columns are sunk into a thick concrete pad spread across the bottom of a deep basement.
4. From this foundation rises a steel skeleton, supporting the walls and floors.
5. This cutaway drawing shows how this skeleton, covered with a "skin" of glass and metal, becomes a safe working and living space for people.
6. This method of building, first developed in the United States, is used now in many other places in the world.
7. Chicago, nearly destroyed by fire in 1871, was later rebuilt with innovative designs.
8. The first skyscraper constructed on a metal frame was built there during this period.
9. Architects, using the latest materials, were glad to design in new ways.
10. Chicago, known as the site of the original 10-story skyscraper, now is home to the 110-story Sears Tower.

Review D **Identifying Participles and Participial Phrases**

Identify the participial phrases and participles that are used as adjectives in the following sentences. Then, give the words they modify.

EXAMPLE **1.** Cats, known for their pride and independence, are supposedly hard to train.

1. known for their pride and independence—Cats

1. One day I was giving Chops, my spoiled cat, treats.
2. Standing on her hind legs, she reached up with her paw.
3. Chops, grabbing for my fingers, tried to bring the tasty morsel closer.

MINI-LESSON

Misplaced Modifiers. Remind students that participles, like adjectives, must be placed near the words they modify. A participle placed by the wrong word is called a **misplaced modifier.**

Have students try to correct the following misplaced modifier: *Rising above the*

horizon, the scientists viewed the full moon. [*The scientists viewed the full moon rising above the horizon.*] A volunteer might draw cartoon-style illustrations of both the sentence with the misplaced modifier and the corrected version.

4. Pulling my hand back a little, I tugged gently on her curved paw, and she stepped forward.

5. Praising my clever cat, I immediately gave her two treats.

6. The next time I held a treat up high, Chops, puzzled but eager, repeated the grab-and-step movement.

7. Soon Chops was taking steps toward treats held out of her reach.

8. I now have an educated cat who can walk on two legs.

9. Grabbing the treats and gobbling them down, she has learned that certain moves always get her a snack.

10. Sometimes after Chops has had her treat, she just sits and looks at me, no doubt thinking that humans are truly a strange bunch!

The Gerund

14h. A *gerund* is a verb form ending in *–ing* that is used as a noun.

Like other nouns, gerunds are used as subjects, predicate nominatives, direct objects, indirect objects, and objects of prepositions.

EXAMPLES   The **dancing** was fun. [subject]

My favorite part of the show was his **juggling.** [predicate nominative]

Shauna tried **climbing** faster. [direct object]

Give **winning** the game your best. [indirect object]

We worked better after **resting.** [object of a preposition]

Like other nouns, gerunds may be modified by adjectives and adjective phrases.

EXAMPLES   We listened to **the beautiful** singing **of the famous soprano.** [The article *the,* the adjective *beautiful,* and the adjective phrase *of the famous soprano* modify the gerund *singing. Singing* is used as the object of the preposition *to.*]

The Mallorys enjoy talking **about their vacation.** [The adjective phrase *about their vacation* modifies the gerund *talking,* which is the direct object of the verb *enjoy.*]

The harsh clacking **of the tappets** alerted us to a serious problem in the car's engine. [The article *The,* the adjective *harsh,* and the adjective phrase *of the tappets* modify the gerund *clacking.*]

Verbals and Verbal Phrases   **453**

The Gerund and the Gerund Phrase
Rules 14h, i *(pp. 453–456)*

OBJECTIVES

■ **To identify and classify gerunds**

■ **To identify and classify gerund phrases**

Meeting
INDIVIDUAL
NEEDS

ENGLISH-LANGUAGE LEARNERS
General Strategies. Before introducing the gerund, you may want to review the basic functions of nouns. Remind students of the following points:

• A subject is the main part of a sentence or a clause and must have a predicate; it is the doer of the action.

• A predicate nominative is usually placed after a linking verb and explains or identifies the subject.

• A direct object answers the question *what* or *whom* after the verb.

T E A C H I N G **(TIP)**

Activity. Divide the class into four teams, and assign each team one of these four categories: subject, predicate nominative, direct object, and object of a preposition.

Write the following gerunds on the chalkboard:

asking	leaping	swinging
diving	marching	tumbling
flying	skipping	twirling

Ask each team to write sentences using these gerunds according to the team's designation (the subject team will use the gerunds only as subjects, and so on). Allow a time limit of fifteen minutes, and then have teams share their sentences with the rest of the class.

T E A C H I N G **(TIP)**

Exercise 7 Challenge students to find present participles used as adjectives in three of the sentences. [5. *Smiling;* 7. *fading;* 10. *crying*]

Like verbs, gerunds may also be modified by adverbs and adverb phrases.

EXAMPLES Reading **widely** is one way to acquire judgment, maturity, and a good education. [The gerund *Reading* is the subject of the verb *is.* The adverb *widely* modifies the gerund *Reading.*]

Floating **lazily in the pool** is my favorite summer pastime. [The gerund *Floating* is used as the subject of the sentence. It is modified by the adverb *lazily* (telling *how*) and also by the adverb phrase *in the pool* (telling *where*).]

Brandywine likes galloping **briskly on a cold morning.** [The gerund *galloping* is the direct object of the verb *likes.* The adverb *briskly* (telling *how*) and the adverb phrase *on a cold morning* (telling *when*) both modify *galloping.*]

Gerunds, like present participles, end in *–ing.* To be a gerund, a verbal must be used as a noun. In the following sentence, three words end in *–ing,* but only one of them is a gerund.

EXAMPLE **Circling** the runway, the pilot was **preparing** for **landing.** [*Circling* is a present participle modifying *pilot. Preparing* is part of the verb phrase *was preparing.* Only *landing,* used as the object of the preposition *for,* is a gerund.]

Exercise 7 **Identifying and Classifying Gerunds**

Identify each gerund in the following sentences. Then, write how each is used: as a *subject,* a *predicate nominative,* a *direct object,* or an *object of a preposition.*

EXAMPLE **1.** Instead of driving, let's walk.

  1. *driving—object of a preposition*

1. subj. **1.** Her laughing attracted my attention.
2. o.p. **2.** By studying, you can improve your grades.
3. d.o. **3.** Why did the birds stop chirping?
4. subj. **4.** Writing in my journal has helped me understand myself better.
5. d.o. **5.** Smiling, Dad said that we would all go to a movie when we had finished the cleaning.
6. p.n. **6.** What Joseph liked best was hiking to the peak.
7. o.p. **7.** Before leaving the beach, we sat and watched the fading light.
8. d.o. **8.** Yesterday, Mrs. Jacobs was discussing having a garage sale.
9. p.n. **9.** One of Alvin's bad habits is boasting.
10. o.p. **10.** Without knocking, the crying child threw open the door.

The Gerund Phrase

14i. A *gerund phrase* consists of a gerund and any modifiers or complements the gerund has. The entire phrase is used as a noun.

EXAMPLES **The gentle pattering of the rain** was a welcome sound. [The gerund phrase is the subject of the sentence. The gerund *pattering* is modified by the article *The,* the adjective *gentle,* and the prepositional phrase *of the rain.* Notice that the modifiers preceding the gerund are included in the gerund phrase.]

I feared **skiing down the mountain alone.** [The gerund phrase is used as the object of the verb *feared.* The gerund *skiing* is modified by the prepositional phrase *down the mountain* and by the adverb *alone.*]

My dog's favorite game is **bringing me the newspaper.** [The gerund phrase is used as a predicate nominative. The gerund *bringing* has a direct object, *newspaper,* and an indirect object, *me.*]

Evelyn Ashford won a gold medal for **running the 100-meter dash.** [The gerund phrase is the object of the preposition *for.* The gerund *running* has a direct object, *dash.*]

Exercise 8 **Identifying and Classifying Gerund Phrases**

Find the gerund phrases in the following sentences. Then, tell how each phrase is used: as a *subject,* a *predicate nominative,* a *direct object,* or an *object of a preposition.*

EXAMPLE **1.** My favorite hunting trophies are the ones I get by photographing wild animals.

  1. *photographing wild animals—object of a preposition*

1. Exciting and challenging, wildlife photography is surprisingly similar to pursuing prey on a hunt.   **1.** o.p.
2. In both activities, knowing the animals' habits and habitats is vital to success.   **2.** subj.
3. Scouting out locations is important to both the hunter and the nature photographer.   **3.** subj.
4. This preparation gives you time for figuring out the best natural light for photography.   **4.** o.p.

STYLE TIP

A noun or a pronoun that comes before a gerund should be in the possessive form.

EXAMPLES

My playing the radio loudly is a bad habit.

Ed's constant TV watching interferes with **our** studying.

HELP

Sentences in Exercise 8 may contain more than one gerund phrase.

Meeting
INDIVIDUAL
NEEDS

MULTIPLE INTELLIGENCES
Visual-Spatial Intelligence.
Provide pieces of construction paper, glue sticks, and strips of brown, red, blue, green, and yellow paper. Tell students they will be using the art materials to color-code sentence parts and prepositional phrases. Tell students to begin by finding the verb in the first sentence of **Exercise 8** and writing it on a strip of brown paper. Then, assign red to subjects, blue to direct objects, yellow to predicate nominatives, and green to prepositional phrases. Ask students to re-create these portions of the sentences by writing the words on appropriate strips, arranging the strips on the construction paper, and gluing them into place. Students may want to write the missing parts of the sentences in the appropriate places using a standard lead pencil.

Timesaver

A quick glance at the students' color-coded answers will inform you which parts of each sentence are giving students difficulty.

ADVANCED LEARNERS
You may give advanced students revision practice by asking them to rewrite a sentence in two ways, once with a present participle and once with a gerund.

Here are two sentences you might use:

1. Dad is preparing tonight's dinner.

   [*Possible revisions: We could hear Dad preparing tonight's dinner. (Part.) Preparing tonight's dinner was Dad's idea. (Ger.)*]

2. His first priority is to prepare for final exams.

   [*Possible revisions: Preparing for final exams, he saw grades as his first priority. (Part.) Preparing for final exams is his first priority. (Ger.)*]

Challenge students to show their flexibility with language by finding and rewriting other sentences.

5. Other important skills are being quiet and keeping your aim very steady.   **5.** p.n./p.n.   **6.** d.o.

6. In photography, you must also consider choosing the correct film.

7. Photographers often like taking pictures of animals feeding near ponds and rivers.   **7.** d.o.

8. Setting up a tripod and camera in underbrush nearby is a way to be ready when the animals come.   **8.** subj.

9. Advance preparation often makes the difference between getting good pictures and getting great ones.   **9.** o.p./o.p.

10. Your patience and skill are rewarded when you "capture" a wild creature without killing it.   **10.** o.p.

Review E **Identifying and Classifying Gerunds and Gerund Phrases**

Identify the gerunds or gerund phrases in the following sentences. Then, tell how each is used: as a *subject*, a *predicate nominative*, a *direct object*, or an *object of a preposition*.

EXAMPLE   **1.** Drawing a good caricature is hard to do.

   1. *Drawing a good caricature—subject*

1. A caricature is a picture, usually of a person, that draws attention to key features by emphasizing them.   **1.** o.p.

2. Usually, caricature artists enjoy poking fun at famous people.   **2.** d.o.

3. Looking at caricatures is an entertaining way to capture the "feel" of a historical period.   **3.** subj.

4. No one looking at this sketch of Teddy Roosevelt can help smiling.   **4.** d.o.

5. The artist began by simplifying the shape of his subject's head.

6. Then he started outlining the temples and round cheeks with bold strokes of his pen.   **6.** d.o.   **5.** o.p.

7. As you probably realize, magnifying reality is very important to good caricature.   **7.** subj.

8. By enlarging Roosevelt's engaging grin and bristly mustache, the artist emphasizes these features and suggests Roosevelt's energetic, outgoing personality.   **8.** o.p.   **9.** o.p.

9. The artist also uses his subject's narrowed eyes and oval glasses for comic effect by drawing them closer together than they really were.

10. Exaggerating Roosevelt's features has resulted in an amusing but unmistakable likeness.   **10.** subj.

The Infinitive

14j. An *infinitive* is a verb form that can be used as a noun, an adjective, or an adverb. Most infinitives begin with *to*.

Infinitives can be used as nouns.

EXAMPLES   **To fly** is glorious. [*To fly* is the subject of the sentence.]

Brandon wanted **to work** on the play. [*To work* is the object of the verb *wanted*.]

Infinitives can be used as adjectives.

EXAMPLES   The place **to visit** is Williamsburg. [*To visit* modifies the noun *place*.]

That record was the one **to beat**. [*To beat* modifies the pronoun *one*.]

Infinitives also can be used as adverbs.

EXAMPLES   Sabina jumped **to shoot**. [*To shoot* modifies the verb *jumped*.]

Ready **to go**, we soon loaded the car. [*To go* modifies the adjective *Ready*.]

NOTE   *To* plus a noun or a pronoun (*to school, to him, to the beach*) is a prepositional phrase, not an infinitive.

Exercise 9   Identifying and Classifying Infinitives

Identify the infinitives in the following sentences. Then, tell how each infinitive is used: as a *noun*, an *adjective*, or an *adverb*.

EXAMPLE   1. I would like to help you.

1. *to help—noun*

1. Tamisha's ambition is to teach.   **1.** n.
2. To persist can sometimes be a sign of stubbornness.   **2.** n.
3. Chen has learned to tap dance.   **3.** n.
4. I am happy to oblige.   **4.** adv.
5. An easy way to win at tennis does not exist.   **5.** adj.
6. We need to weed the garden soon.   **6.** n.
7. The hockey team went to Coach Norton's house to study last night.   **7.** adv.
8. We met at the lake to swim.   **8.** adv.
9. That is not the correct amount of paper to order for this project.   **9.** adj.
10. According to the map, the road to take is the one to the left. **10.** adj.

STYLE   TIP

A *split infinitive* occurs when a word is placed between the sign of the infinitive, *to*, and the base form of a verb. Although split infinitives are common in informal speaking and writing, you should avoid using them in formal situations.

SPLIT
The bear seemed to suddenly appear from the shadows.

REVISED
The bear seemed **to appear** suddenly from the shadows.

Reference Note

For more about **prepositional phrases,** see page 442.

COMPUTER TIP

Some software programs can identify and highlight split infinitives in a document. Using such a feature will help you eliminate split infinitives from your formal writing.

The Infinitive and the Infinitive Phrase

Rules 14j, k *(pp. 457–461)*

OBJECTIVES

■ To identify and classify infinitives

■ To identify and classify infinitive phrases

Meeting
INDIVIDUAL
NEEDS

ENGLISH-LANGUAGE LEARNERS
Spanish and French. Point out to students that in Spanish the infinitive ends in *–ar*, *–er*, or *–ir* (for example, *hablar, vender, partir*); in French, it ends in *–er*, *–ir*, *–oir*, or *–re* (for example, *aimer, finir, recevoir, rompre*).

Relating to Literature

If your literature textbook contains the poem "At Woodward's Gardens" by Robert Frost, have students read it. Ask them to identify the six infinitives that include *to*.

Explain to students that the infinitive form helps sustain the rhythm of the poem, giving it movement and vitality.

Verbals and Verbal Phrases   **457**

RESOURCES

The Infinitive and the Infinitive Phrase
Practice

■ *Grammar, Usage, and Mechanics,* pp. 73, 74, 75, 76, 77
■ *Language Workshop CD-ROM,* Lesson 27

Critical Thinking

Analysis. To help students become familiar with some English-language patterns, have them use the following sentences to fill in a three-column chart like the one below.

I enjoy swimming.
I need to work.

VERB	DIRECT OBJECT	VERBAL
enjoy	swimming	gerund
need	to work	infinitive

Have students add to the chart by writing their own sentences using *enjoy* and *need.* Ask students to try forming a generalization about the types of verbals that will follow these verbs. [*After some practice, students should realize that* enjoy *is followed by a gerund and* need *by an infinitive.*]

Then, tell students that in general, verbs that involve a future action will be followed by an infinitive, while verbs that involve the completion of an action will take a gerund. Some examples of verbs that usually go with infinitives are *want, plan, expect,* and *ask.* Verbs such as *avoid, finish, deny,* and *admit* most often have gerunds following them.

Students might want to make two new charts, one for verbs and infinitives and one for verbs and gerunds, and complete them using combinations of the verbs above and appropriate verbals.

TIPS & TRICKS

To find out if an infinitive phrase is being used as a noun, replace the phrase with *what.*

EXAMPLES

To fix an air conditioner is my next project. [*What is my next project? To fix an air conditioner is my next project.* The infinitive is a noun.]

In New York, we went to see Gramercy Park. [*We went what?* This question makes no sense. The infinitive is not a noun. It is used as an adverb modifying the verb *went.*]

The Infinitive with *to* Omitted

Sometimes the sign of the infinitive, *to,* is omitted in a sentence.

EXAMPLES   She's done all her chores except [to] **feed** the cat.

I'll help you [to] **pack.**

The dogs like **to roam** in the field and [to] **chase** rabbits.

Fuel injection helps cars [to] **run** better and [to] **last** longer.

The Infinitive Phrase

14k. An *infinitive phrase* consists of an infinitive and any modifiers or complements the infinitive has. The entire phrase can be used as a noun, an adjective, or an adverb.

EXAMPLES   **To make tamales quickly** was hard. [The infinitive phrase is used as a noun, as the subject of the sentence. The infinitive has a direct object, *tamales,* and is modified by the adverb *quickly* and by the predicate adjective *hard.*]

Chris is the player **to watch in the next game.** [The infinitive phrase is used as an adjective modifying the predicate nominative *player.* The infinitive is modified by the adverb phrase *in the next game.*]

We are eager **to finish this project.** [The infinitive phrase is used as an adverb modifying the predicate adjective *eager.* The infinitive has a direct object, *project.*]

NOTE   An infinitive may have a subject. An *infinitive clause* consists of an infinitive with a subject and any modifiers and complements of the infinitive. The entire infinitive clause functions as a noun.

EXAMPLES   I wanted **him to help me with my algebra.** [The entire infinitive clause is the direct object of the verb *wanted. Him* is the subject of the infinitive *to help.* The infinitive *to help* has a direct object, *me,* and is modified by the adverb phrase *with my algebra.*]

Would Uncle Jim like **us to clear the brush in the backyard**? [The entire infinitive clause is the direct object of the verb *Would like. Us* is the subject of the infinitive *to clear.* The infinitive *to clear* has a direct object *brush,* which is modified by the adjective phrase *in the backyard.*]

Notice that a pronoun that functions as the subject of an infinitive clause is in the objective case.

458   Chapter 14   The Phrase

Learning for Life

To show students that verbals are a part of their everyday lives, ask them to have a conversation and analyze it. Divide the class into groups of four or five students with like interests so that each group can have a conversation on a topic that interests all

the group members. Each group should choose a topic, such as sports, movies, school activities, or hobbies, on which they can have an informal conversation. Ask students to talk together for five to ten minutes and to tape-record their conversations.

Exercise 10

Exercise 10 **Identifying and Classifying Infinitives and Infinitive Phrases**

Identify the <u>infinitives and infinitive phrases</u> in the following sentences. After each, tell whether it is used as a <u>noun</u>, an <u>adjective</u>, or an <u>adverb</u>.

EXAMPLE   **1.** Scott is the person to elect.

          1. *to elect—adjective*

1. <u>To dance gracefully</u> requires coordination.   **1.** n.
2. Raymond wanted <u>to join the team</u>.   **2.** n.
3. Sandy needs <u>to study</u>.   **3.** n.
4. I'm going to the pond <u>to fish</u>.   **4.** adv.
5. A good way <u>to lose weight</u> is <u>to eat moderately</u>.   **5.** adj./n.
6. After our long vacation, we needed <u>to get back in training</u>.   **6.** n.
7. The best way <u>to get there</u> is <u>to take the bus</u>.   **7.** adj./n.
8. Don't you dare <u>open that present before your birthday</u>.   **8.** n.
9. Juanita and Matt tried <u>to find the perfect gift</u>.   **9.** n.
10. He lives <u>to swim and water-ski</u>.   **10.** adv.

Exercise 11 **Identifying and Classifying Infinitive Phrases**

Identify the <u>infinitive phrases</u> in the following sentences. Then, tell how each phrase is used: as a <u>noun</u>, an <u>adjective</u>, or an <u>adverb</u>.

EXAMPLE   **1.** To create a miracle fabric was the aim of the chemist Joe Shivers.

          1. *To create a miracle fabric—noun*

1. He succeeded with spandex, and athletes of all shapes and sizes have learned <u>to appreciate the qualities of his "power cloth."</u>   **1.** n.
2. This material has the ability <u>to stretch and snap back into shape</u>.   **2.** adj.
3. Its sleek fit lessens friction <u>to give the wearer faster movement through air or water</u>.   **3.** adv.
4. Its slick surface makes an athlete such as a wrestler hard <u>to hold</u>.   **4.** adv.
5. <u>To say that spandex has athletes covered</u> is not stretching the truth.   **5.** n.
6. Spandex is just one of many synthetic fibers <u>to meet today's fashion needs</u>.   **6.** adj.
7. Nylon was the first synthetic; it originally was made <u>to take the place of silk in women's garments</u>.   **7.** adv.
8. <u>To replace silk</u> was also the purpose of rayon, another early, low-priced synthetic.   **8.** n.

—**HELP**—

The sign of the infinitive, *to,* is sometimes omitted. Also, a sentence in Exercise 10 may contain more than one infinitive or infinitive phrase.

—**HELP**—

In Exercise 11 the sign of the infinitive, *to,* is sometimes omitted.

ALTERNATIVE LESSON

Ask students to find the following sentence parts in the designated sentences.

1. complete subject [*To dance gracefully*]
2. direct object [*to join the team*]
5. predicate nominative [*to eat moderately*]

Next, have them play their conversations back slowly, stopping frequently to note the sentences used and to write down all sentences with verbals. Once all the sentences with verbals are listed, ask students to study the verbals in context and identify them as participles, gerunds, or infinitives.

9. Polyester, developed later, often is combined with natural fibers to reduce wrinkling.   **9.** adv.

10. To distinguish synthetic fibers (most made from plastic) from natural fibers is not easy.   **10.** n.

Review F Identifying Infinitives and Infinitive Phrases

Identify the infinitives and infinitive phrases in the following paragraph.

EXAMPLE   **[1]** Laurel and Hardy are a comic team to remember.

1. to remember

[**1**] Together, Stan Laurel and Oliver Hardy have made millions of moviegoers laugh. [**2**] In their day, to be funny in the movies required the use of body language. [**3**] Both of them were geniuses in their ability to keep audiences laughing. [**4**] For his famous head scratch, Stan grew his hair long so that he could scratch and pull it to make a comic mess. [**5**] Stan also developed a hilarious cry that he used to show his character's childish nature. [**6**] He would shut his eyes tightly, pinch up his face, and begin to wail. [**7**] Ollie, too, had an uncanny ability to create his own distinctive mannerisms. [**8**] For example, he was known for the long-suffering look he used to express frustration. [**9**] He would also waggle his tie at a person he and Stan had managed to offend and then start giggling nervously. [**10**] Ollie's intent was to make the person less angry, but his gesture usually had the opposite effect.

Review G Identifying and Classifying Verbals and Verbal Phrases

Identify each verbal or verbal phrase in the following paragraph as a *participle, participial phrase, gerund, gerund phrase, infinitive, infinitive phrase,* or as a part of an *infinitive clause.*

EXAMPLE   **[1]** Building the railroad across the United States in the late 1800s required thousands of workers.

1. Building the railroad across the United States in the late 1800s—gerund phrase

[**1**] The government commissioned two companies to build railway tracks between Omaha, Nebraska, and Sacramento, California. [**2**] Building eastward from Sacramento, the Central Pacific Railroad relied on Chinese workers. [**3**] One-fourth of the Chinese immigrants

---HELP---

In Review F, the sign of the infinitive, *to,* is sometimes omitted.

Review G Identifying and Classifying Verbals and Verbal Phrases

A N S W E R S

1. inf. cl.

2. part. phr.

in the United States in 1868 helped with <u>laying the track</u>. [4] The terrain was difficult <u>to cover</u>, but the laborers rose to the challenge. [5] <u>Known for their dependability</u>, the Chinese were strong workers. [6] <u>Complaining</u> was a problem with some workers, but seldom with Chinese laborers. [7] It was often necessary <u>to blow up parts of mountains</u>, and the Chinese workers became experts at this task. [8] Chinese and Irish workers set a record on April 28, 1869, by <u>spiking ten miles and fifty-six feet of track in twelve hours</u>. [9] The railroad company divided the Chinese immigrants into <u>working</u> groups, or gangs, each with twelve to twenty men. [10] <u>Keeping many of their traditional ways</u>, Chinese workers ate food that was shipped to them from San Francisco's Chinatown.

Appositives and Appositive Phrases

14l. An *appositive* is a noun or a pronoun placed beside another noun or pronoun to identify or describe it.

EXAMPLES   The sculptor **Isamu Noguchi** has designed sculpture gardens. [The appositive *Isamu Noguchi* identifies the noun *sculptor.*]

Eric, a talented **musician,** plans to study in Europe. [The appositive *musician* describes the noun *Eric.*]

Those, the **ones** on the right, are on sale. [The appositive *ones* identifies the pronoun *Those.*]

14m. An *appositive phrase* consists of an appositive and any modifiers it has.

EXAMPLES   Lucy Sánchez, **my longtime friend from my old neighborhood,** has a new Scottish terrier.

Dr. Jackson has a degree in entomology, **the scientific study of insects.**

NOTE Sometimes, an appositive phrase precedes the noun or pronoun to which it refers.

EXAMPLE   **The terror of our block,** little Anthony was on the warpath.

Appositives and Appositive Phrases   **461**

Review G **Identifying and Classifying Verbals and Verbal Phrases**

ANSWERS continued

3. ger. phr.
4. inf.
5. part. phr.
6. ger.
7. inf. phr.
8. ger. phr.
9. part.
10. part. phr.

Appositives and Appositive Phrases

Rules 14l, m *(pp. 461–464)*

OBJECTIVE

- To identify appositives and appositive phrases in sentences

---

RESOURCES box:

RESOURCES

Appositives and Appositive Phrases

Practice

- *Grammar, Usage, and Mechanics*, pp. 78, 79, 80
- *Language Workshop CD-ROM*, Lesson 28

Reference Note

For more about **essential and nonessential phrases,** see page 648.

Appositives and appositive phrases that are not essential to the meaning of the sentence are set off by commas. If the appositive is essential to the meaning, it is generally not set off by commas.

EXAMPLES   My teacher, **Mr. Byrd,** trains parrots. [The writer has only one teacher. The appositive is not necessary to identify the teacher. Because the information is nonessential, it is set off by commas.]

My teacher **Mr. Byrd** trains parrots. [The writer has more than one teacher. The appositive is necessary to tell which teacher is meant. Because this information is essential to the meaning of the sentence, it is not set off by commas.]

NOTE   Commas are generally used with appositives that refer to proper nouns.

EXAMPLE   Linda, **the editor,** assigned the story.

However, a word or phrase that is commonly accepted as part of a person's name or title is not set off by a comma.

EXAMPLE   The Roman Army defeated Attila **the Hun** in A.D. 451.

Exercise 12   Identifying Appositive Phrases

Identify the appositive phrases in the following sentences. Then, give the noun or pronoun that each appositive phrase identifies or describes.

EXAMPLE   1. I usually write haiku, poems in a traditional Japanese form.

          1. *poems in a traditional Japanese form—haiku*

1. Our community has a new organization, a writers' club called Writers, Inc.
2. Marquita Wiley, a college instructor, started the group at the request of former students.
3. A published author, she conducts the meetings as workshops.
4. The writers meet to read their works in progress, fiction or poetry, and to discuss suggestions for improvement.
5. The members, people from all walks of life, have varied interests.
6. A mechanic by trade, J. D. Ellis writes funny poems about his hobby, bird-watching.
7. My friend Lusita just had a short story about her people, the Zuni, published in a national magazine.

┌─HELP─

A sentence in Exercise 12 may contain more than one appositive or appositive phrase.

8. Next week, we'll meet at our regular <u>time</u>, <u>3:30 P.M.</u>

9. Our guest speaker is <u>Pat Mora</u>, <u>a Mexican American poet whose</u> <u>work emphasizes harmony</u> between cultures.

10. Have you read her <u>poem</u> <u>"Bribe"</u>?

Review H **Identifying Verbal Phrases and Appositive Phrases**

Find the <u>verbal phrases and appositive phrases</u> in the following sentences. Identify each phrase as a *participial phrase*, a *gerund phrase*, an *infinitive phrase*, or an *appositive phrase*.

┌─HELP─┐
A sentence in Review H may contain more than one verbal or appositive phrase.

EXAMPLE

1. Automobiles have been partly responsible for drastically changing life in the twentieth century.

1. *drastically changing life in the twentieth century—* *gerund phrase*

1. <u>Developing the automobile</u> was actually the creative work of many people, but Henry Ford deservedly receives much credit. **1.** g.p.

2. Ford's company, <u>using an assembly line and interchangeable parts</u>, first produced the Model T in 1909. **2.** p.p.

3. Many people in the early 1900s wanted <u>to buy cars because of their low prices and novelty</u>. **3.** i.p.

4. By <u>giving people an alternative to mass transit</u>, automobiles did much <u>to change the social and business scene of the United States</u>. **4.** g.p./i.p.

5. No longer dependent on streetcars and trains, the first motorists used automobiles for <u>going on recreational and family trips</u>. **5.** g.p.

6. <u>Clearly overjoyed with their vehicles</u>, many Americans regarded automobiles as necessities by the 1920s. **6.** p.p.

7. One writer, <u>a famous historian</u>, noted that the automobile industry led to such new businesses as gas stations, repair garages, tire companies, and motels. **7.** a.p.

8. <u>To get a clear idea of changes in automobile designs over the years</u>, look at the picture to the right. **8.** i.p.

9. The photo shows Henry Ford, <u>looking contented and proud</u>, in his first car. **9.** p.p.

10. What are some of the main differences between Ford's car, <u>one of the most advanced vehicles of its day</u>, and modern cars? **10.** a.p.

TEACHING **TIP**

Review H   You may wish to use the first five items of **Review H** as guided practice. Then, have students complete the exercise as independent practice.

Meeting
INDIVIDUAL
NEEDS

LEARNERS HAVING DIFFICULTY
First, review the use of commas with appositives, using examples from **Review H**. Then, have students write the following sentences on strips of white paper, and have them write the appositives on strips of yellow paper.

SENTENCES

1. Jose wrote a paper about George Washington.

2. Lasagna was served for dinner.

3. California has over 800 miles of coastline.

4. Toni Morrison has written a new book.

APPOSITIVES
the largest state on the Pacific coast
an Italian food
a general and president
a famous author

Have students cut apart each sentence and insert an appositive where it makes sense, using commas where required.

Review I

Writing Appropriate Phrases

POSSIBLE ANSWERS

1. of the oranges—prep.
2. to the music—prep.
3. my former football coach—appos.
4. to see the Mayan ruins—inf.
5. Forgotten in the rush—part.
6. in the mud—prep.
7. Exercising every day—ger.
8. from the reservation—prep.
9. To win the championship—inf.
10. shown in the catalog—part.
11. hanging at the window—part.
12. in the basket—prep.
13. from the oven—prep.
14. An inline six-cylinder—appos.
15. struggling to keep up—part.
16. a well-known radio personality —appos.
17. waiting to see Dr. Patel—part.
18. To pass the exam—inf.
19. in Ms. Walter's class—prep.
20. Observing a strict diet—ger.

─HELP─

Although several possible answers are given in the example in Review I, you need to write only one sentence for each item.

Review I Writing Appropriate Phrases

Rewrite each of the following sentences, supplying an appropriate prepositional, verbal, or appositive phrase to fill in the blank. Use each type of phrase at least twice. Identify each phrase you use as *prepositional, participial, infinitive, gerund,* or *appositive.*

EXAMPLE 1. We have room for only a single passenger _____.

1. *We have room for only a single passenger weighing less than one-hundred fifty pounds. — participial*

or

We have room for only a single passenger in the boat. — prepositional

or

We have room for only a single passenger, a small one! — appositive

or

We have room for only a single passenger to come aboard. — infinitive

1. Only one _____ was left on the plate.
2. Joyfully, she danced _____.
3. Richard, _____, is moving back to the town!
4. During the whole trip to Mexico, her goal was _____.
5. _____, the new computer still sat in boxes on the floor.
6. At the bottom of the river, a huge old catfish lay _____.
7. _____ made them strong enough for the race.
8. Navajo dancers _____ stepped lightly into the open circle.
9. _____ became their goal for the rest of the year.
10. All the clothes _____ had been made in the United States.
11. The lace curtains _____ were not for sale.
12. Are these puppies _____ all yours?
13. What a marvelous aroma is rising _____!
14. _____, the engine finally started.
15. With a glance at the other runners _____, Gretchen pulled ahead.
16. Bill Briggs, _____, greeted the enthusiastic fans.
17. Everyone _____ should move down one seat.
18. _____ was the thought of each student in the class.
19. The children _____ made mud pies.
20. _____ gave them the endurance they needed.

Chapter Review

A. Identifying Phrases

In each of the following sentences, identify each italicized phrase as *prepositional*, *participial*, *gerund*, *infinitive*, or *appositive*.

1. Now I would like *to tell you about my sister Alexandra*. **1.** inf.

2. She likes *arriving at school early*. **2.** ger.

3. By *doing so*, she can spend extra time preparing for her day. **3.** ger.

4. She will resort to anything to get *to school* early, including waking me up, too. **4.** prep.

5. For example, when *the beeping of my alarm* woke me yesterday, the sky was as dark as night. **5.** ger.

6. I soon realized that Alexandra, *a volunteer crossing guard at school*, had adjusted the alarm. **6.** app.

7. It was, I could see, an occasion for *applying my special technique*. **7.** ger.

8. *Called my slow-motion technique*, it always achieves the result I want. **8.** part.

9. I moved *around the house* as if I were underwater; Alexandra watched until she could stand it no longer. **9.** prep.

10. Then, I moved faster; I certainly did not want *to be late for school*. **10.** inf.

B. Identifying and Classifying Prepositional Phrases

Identify the prepositional phrases in the following sentences. Identify the word or words modified by each phrase. Then, state whether the prepositional phrase is an *adjective phrase* or an *adverb phrase*.

11. A daily newspaper has something for almost everyone. **11.** adj.

12. In addition to news, the paper offers entertainment, classified ads, and much more. **12.** adv.

13. Our entire family reads the newspaper in the morning. **13.** adv.

14. Dad always begins with the sports pages; Mom prefers the general news. **14.** adv.

15. My sister's favorite part of the newspaper is the lifestyle section. **15.** adj.

16. She enjoys features like "How-to Hints." **16.** adj.

17. I find the editorial and opinion pages interesting, especially when a debate between two sides develops. **17.** adj.

18. Sometimes I see the logic behind an argument. **18.** adj.

Chapter Review   **465**

Using the Chapter Review

The **Chapter Review** requires students to identify the different kinds of phrases within sentences. The results of this test can be compared to those of the **Diagnostic Preview** (pp. 440–441) to assess student progress.

TEACHING (TIP)

Chapter Review. Remind students that a compound noun consists of two or more words used together as a single noun. Prepositional phrases need not be identified within compound nouns such as *American Museum of Natural History, lady-in-waiting*, and *Stratford-on-Avon*.

GRAMMAR

19. Other times I wonder why grown people <u>argue</u> about a trivial issue.

20. I also like to read <u>news</u> about local events. 20. adj. 19. adv.

C. Identifying Verbals

Identify each italicized verbal in the following sentences as a *participle*, a *gerund*, or an *infinitive*.

21. inf. **21.** Many amateur athletes want *to earn* medals for their abilities.

22. part. **22.** *Enjoyed* by people throughout history, amateur athletic competitions can be very beneficial.

23. ger. **23.** *Winning* an event is only part of the reason athletes compete.

24. inf. **24.** When talented amateurs compete *to test* their skills, they learn a great deal about their sport.

25. ger. **25.** In addition, the love of a sport, the best reason for *entering* into competition, usually grows as an athlete's performance improves.

26. ger. **26.** Furthermore, *sharing* hard work with teammates leads a person to appreciate cooperative efforts.

27. part. **27.** Competitions *organized* on many levels give amateur athletes a motive for increased practice.

28. ger. **28.** *Participating* in state, national, and international competitions is important to many amateur athletes.

29. part. **29.** *Wanting* to be recognized for their talent, the athletes compete against their peers in such events.

30. inf. **30.** These competitions also provide athletes with opportunities *to put* their abilities to the test.

D. Identifying Verbal Phrases

In each of the following sentences, identify the italicized verbal phrase as a *participial phrase*, an *infinitive phrase*, or a *gerund phrase*.

31. ger. **31.** Maxine gets her exercise by *dancing for at least three hours a week*.

32. inf. **32.** Eddie likes *to make pizza for his friends*.

33. part. **33.** The mother baboon watched her infant *eating a berry*.

34. inf. **34.** Yolanda went *to get her book*.

35. part. **35.** Is the man *pushing the grocery cart* an employee or a customer?

RESOURCES

The Phrase

Review

- *Grammar, Usage, and Mechanics,* pp. 81, 82, 83

Assessment

- *Assessment Package*
  —Chapter Tests, Ch. 14
  —Chapter Tests in Standardized Test Formats, Ch. 14
- *Test Generator (One-Stop Planner CD-ROM)*

36. *Winning the contest* was a thrill for our cheerleaders.
37. I made a tote bag *to hold my gym clothes.*
38. Richard's summer job is *delivering groceries to the hospital.*
39. Enzo Ferrari became famous by *building fast and stylish cars.*
40. *Preparing for that play* took quite a long time.
41. Samantha overheard Tina and Sue *talking about their vacation plans.*
42. Prepare *to run your fastest.*
43. *Excited by the thought of the trip,* we finished packing early.
44. Koalas get most of their nutrition by *eating eucalyptus leaves.*
45. *Tired of the noise outside,* we closed the window.

36. ger.
37. inf.
38. ger.
39. ger.
40. ger.
41. part.
42. inf.
43. part.
44. ger.
45. part.

Writing Application
Using Prepositional Phrases in a Game

Adjective and Adverb Phrases   You are planning a treasure hunt for a group of neighborhood children. The treasure hunt will include six stops for clues. For each clue, write a sentence containing at least one prepositional phrase. Use a combination of adjective and adverb phrases.

Prewriting   First, think about your neighborhood and pick a good place to hide a treasure. Then, think of six places to hide clues.

Writing   Write a sentence giving a clue about each location. The final sentence should lead the children directly to the hidden treasure.

Revising   Ask someone who is familiar with the area of the treasure hunt to look over your clues. Revise any clues that are not clear. Be sure that each clue contains at least one prepositional phrase and that you have used both adjective and adverb phrases in your clues.

Publishing   Check to be sure that your prepositional phrases are properly placed. An adverb phrase may occur at various places in a sentence. Proofread your sentences for correct capitalization and punctuation. You may want to organize a treasure hunt for younger children in your family or for children that you baby-sit.

Writing Application
(p. 467)

OBJECTIVE

■ To write instructions using both adjective and adverb phrases

Writing Application

Tip. Brainstorm with students, and have them write as many hiding places as they can. Then, tell them to choose six of the most appealing spots. Remind them of their youthful audience. Suggest that students write their rough drafts without being concerned about whether all the prepositional phrases are included. Tell them that they can add the required phrases in the revision stage.

Scoring Rubric. While you will want to pay particular attention to students' use of adjective and adverb phrases, you will also want to evaluate overall writing performance. You may want to give a split score to indicate development and clarity of the composition as well as grammar skills.

Critical Thinking

Synthesis. Sometimes a compound preposition has greater impact than a one-word preposition. Students might find some of the following compound prepositions particularly suited to this writing assignment: *in front of, in back of, next to, on top of,* and *up against.* Ask students to think of other compound prepositions to use in their writing.

RESOURCES
Writing Application
Extension
■ *Grammar, Usage, and Mechanics,* p. 86
■ *Language Workshop CD-ROM,* Lessons 24–28

The Clause
Independent and Subordinate Clauses

Diagnostic Preview

A. Identifying and Classifying Subordinate Clauses

Identify the subordinate clause in each of the following sentences. Then, classify each subordinate clause as an adjective clause (*adj.*), an adverb clause (*adv.*), or a noun clause (*n.*). If the clause is used as an adjective or adverb, write the word or phrase it modifies. If the clause is used as a noun, indicate whether it is used as a subject (*subj.*), a direct object (*d.o.*), an indirect object (*i.o.*), a predicate nominative (*p.n.*), or an object of a preposition (*o.p.*).

EXAMPLES
1. After our last class, Elena, Frieda, and I agreed that we would go bicycling in the park.
   1. *that we would go bicycling in the park—n.—d.o.*

2. As we set out for the park, we had no idea of the difficulties ahead.
   2. *As we set out for the park—adv.—had*

1. adv.
2. adj.
3. adv.
4. n.—subj.
5. n.—o.p.
6. n.—d.o.
7. adv.

1. Since none of us own bicycles, we decided to rent them there.
2. The man who rented us the bikes was helpful.
3. After we had bicycled six miles, Frieda's bike got a flat tire.
4. What we found was a nail in the tire.
5. We decided to take the bike to whatever bike shop was the nearest.
6. The woman at the bike shop told us that she could fix the tire.
7. After we had paid for the repair and gotten a receipt, we rode back to the park and bicycled for an hour.

8. Our only worry was that the man at the rental shop might not
pay us back for the repair.

9. When we returned our bikes, we showed the man the receipt.

10. He refunded the money we had spent to fix the tire.

8. n.—p.n.

9. adv.

10. adj.

B. Classifying Sentences According to Structure

Classify each of the following sentences as *simple, compound, complex,*
or *compound-complex.* Be sure that you can identify all subordinate
and independent clauses.

EXAMPLES   **1.** Amanda now plays the violin because of a winter concert
that she heard when she was in the third grade.

     1. complex

    2. The concert featured a talented, young violinist from
Russia and a famous local pianist.

     2. simple

11. Amanda loved the sound of the orchestra at her school's winter
concert, and she decided then to study the violin.

12. Amanda's first violin was not the standard size, for she was still
quite small.

13. When she started the sixth grade, however, Amanda was playing a
full-sized violin.

14. She did not always enjoy the many hours of practice, but they were
necessary because playing the instrument is complicated.

15. Amanda knew that playing the proper notes could be especially
difficult on a violin.

16. On a keyboard instrument, you simply press a key and hear the
note for that key.

17. On a violin, however, the placement of a finger on a string can
affect the pitch of a note.

18. If the pitch of each note is not exact, even a common tune can be
difficult to recognize.

19. Once a student has mastered finger placement to some extent, he
or she still has a great deal to think about; posture, hand position,
and bowing technique all require great concentration.

20. When students can actually create music with this stubborn
instrument, they have reason to be proud.

11. cd.

12. cd.

13. cx.

14. cd.-cx.

15. cx.

16. s.

17. s.

18. cx.

19. cd.-cx.

20. cx.

TEACHING TIP

Motivation. To make students
aware that the sentence structures
presented in this chapter appear frequently in printed material, you may
want to give each student a copy of
a newspaper or magazine story to
use while working on this chapter.
As students study each type of clause
and each sentence classification, ask
them to look for examples in the
story. Ask them to underline and
label each example they find.

You might expand the discovery
approach by asking students to find
and bring to class examples of each
structure from their own outside
reading. You may want to bring personal or library copies of newspapers
and magazines to use as a classroom
resource.

What Is a Clause?

Rules 15a–c *(pp. 470–472)*

OBJECTIVE

- To identify independent and subordinate clauses

Meeting
INDIVIDUAL
NEEDS

LEARNERS HAVING DIFFICULTY

To reinforce the point that independent clauses can be joined in a variety of ways, you could write the following patterns on the chalkboard or on an overhead transparency. Then, ask students to compose three original sentences using the following patterns:

1. Independent clause, comma, coordinating conjunction, independent clause [*Sample response: The night sky is clear, and the moon is full.*]

2. Independent clause, semicolon, independent clause [*Sample response: The stars shine brightly; no city lights are visible.*]

3. Independent clause, semicolon, conjunctive adverb, comma, independent clause [*Sample response: The breeze feels warm; however, the temperature can drop quickly.*]

┌HELP┐

A subordinate clause that is capitalized and punctuated as a sentence is a ***sentence fragment.***

Reference Note

For information about **correcting sentence fragments,** see page 320.

Reference Note

For a list of **coordinating conjunctions,** see page 404. For more about using **semicolons** and **conjunctive adverbs** to join independent clauses, see page 670.

What Is a Clause?

15a. A *clause* is a word group that contains a verb and its subject and that is used as a sentence or as part of a sentence.

Although every clause contains a subject and a verb, not every clause expresses a complete thought. Clauses that do are called ***independent clauses.*** Clauses that do not express a complete thought are called ***subordinate clauses.***

INDEPENDENT CLAUSE	The people left the building
SUBORDINATE CLAUSE	when the fire alarm sounded
SENTENCE	When the fire alarm sounded, the people left the building.

The Independent Clause

15b. An *independent* (or *main*) *clause* expresses a complete thought and can stand by itself as a sentence.

In the following examples, each boldface clause has its own subject and verb and expresses a complete thought.

EXAMPLES **Ms. Santana works in a law office in downtown Concord.**

Ms. Santana works in a law office that has a view of downtown Concord.

Ms. Santana works in a law office in downtown Concord, and **she has a successful practice.**

In the last example, the independent clauses are joined by a comma and the coordinating conjunction *and*. The clauses also could be written with a semicolon between them:

Ms. Santana works in a law office in downtown Concord; she has a successful practice.

or with a semicolon, a conjunctive adverb, and a comma:

Ms. Santana works in a law office in downtown Concord; **indeed,** she has a successful practice.

or as separate sentences:

Ms. Santana works in a law office in downtown Concord. She has a successful practice.

RESOURCES

What Is a Clause?

Practice

- *Grammar, Usage, and Mechanics,* pp. 88, 89, 90, 91
- *Language Workshop CD-ROM,* Lesson 29

The Subordinate Clause

15c. A *subordinate* (or *dependent*) *clause* does not express a complete thought and cannot stand by itself as a sentence.

Words such as *when, whom, because, which, that, if,* and *until* signal that the clauses following them are likely to be subordinate. *Subordinate* means "lesser in rank or importance." To make a complete sentence, a subordinate clause must be joined to an independent clause. Like phrases, subordinate clauses can be used as adjectives, adverbs, or nouns.

SUBORDINATE CLAUSES	when you arrive at the airport in Dallas
	which grow only locally
	that he had granted us an interview

SENTENCES	**When you arrive at the airport in Dallas,** call us.
	These wildflowers, **which grow only locally,** are of interest to scientists.
	Did you know **that he had granted us an interview**?

As the preceding examples show, subordinate clauses may appear at the beginning, in the middle, or at the end of a sentence. The placement of a subordinate clause depends on how the clause is used in the sentence.

NOTE Many subordinate clauses contain complements (such as predicate nominatives, predicate adjectives, direct objects, or indirect objects), modifiers, or both.

EXAMPLES   **what** it is . . . [*What* is a predicate nominative: It is *what*?]

because you look **tired** . . . [*Tired* is a predicate adjective modifying *you*.]

that you chose . . . [*That* is the direct object of *chose*.]

before he gave **us** the **quiz** . . . [*Us* is the indirect object of *gave; quiz* is the direct object of *gave*.]

that I bought **yesterday** . . . [*Yesterday* is an adverb modifying *bought*.]

when the coach was calling **to her** . . . [*To her* is an adverb phrase modifying *was calling*.]

Reference Note

For more about **sentence complements,** see page 427. For more information on **modifiers,** see Chapter 19.

For more about **sentence complements,** see page 427. For more information on **modifiers,** see Chapter 19.

Meeting INDIVIDUAL NEEDS

LEARNERS HAVING DIFFICULTY
Students might find it confusing that although a subordinate clause has a subject and a verb, it cannot stand alone as a sentence. Therefore, you may wish to write subordinate clauses on the chalkboard to help students see that more information is needed to form complete thoughts.

Sample clauses:

After the team competes for the championship

Because the roof was damaged during the storm

What we need for the picnic

That you are reading

Have students suggest ways to make the clauses complete sentences. Point out that they may add independent clauses to the subordinate clauses to form complete thoughts.

The Subordinate Clause   **471**

Meeting
INDIVIDUAL
NEEDS

ENGLISH-LANGUAGE LEARNERS

Spanish. Emphasize to students that in English the subject usually precedes the verb. Because word order in Spanish is often different from that used in English, some Spanish-speaking students might have a tendency to invert subjects and verbs in subordinate clauses. You may wish to have students locate the subject and verb in each subordinate clause in **Exercise 1** to emphasize this structural difference.

MODALITIES

Auditory Learners. You may wish to read aloud the examples in this lesson and the italicized clauses in **Exercise 1**. Students may be better able to hear the difference between complete and incomplete thoughts than to recognize the difference visually.

STYLE TIP

Although short, simple sentences can be effective, a variety of sentence structures is usually more effective. To make choppy sentences into smoother writing, combine shorter sentences by changing some into subordinate clauses. Also, avoid unnecessary repetition of subjects, verbs, and pronouns.

CHOPPY

I enjoy feta cheese. It comes from Greece. It is traditionally made from sheep's or goat's milk.

SMOOTH

I enjoy feta cheese, which comes from Greece and is traditionally made from sheep's or goat's milk.

In the example above, two of the short sentences are combined into a single subordinate clause.

Exercise 1 **Identifying Independent and Subordinate Clauses**

For each of the following sentences, identify the clause in italics as *independent* or *subordinate*.

EXAMPLE 1. *When you think of baseball,* you may think of lightning-fast pitches, bat-splitting home runs, or secret hand signals from coaches and catchers.

1. subordinate

1. *Baseball is a game* that generally depends on good eyesight as well as athletic skill.
2. For this reason, until recently, playing the great American game has been something *that people with visual impairments found virtually impossible.*
3. Only sighted players could participate *until an engineer named Charley Fairbanks invented beep baseball.*
4. *In this version of baseball, the ball beeps and the bases buzz* so that players like the one pictured here can tell when to swing and where to run.
5. Each team has a sighted pitcher and a sighted catcher, *who never get a turn at bat,* and six fielders who wear blindfolds so that they don't have a visual advantage.
6. The pitcher shouts "Ready!" *before the ball is pitched* and "Pitch!" when the ball is released.

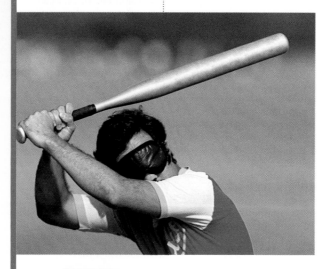

7. When the bat strikes the ball, the umpire activates the buzzer in first base, *to which the batter must then run.*
8. When a team is on defense, the pitcher and catcher cannot field the batted ball themselves; *they can only shout directions to the fielders.*
9. *Beep baseball is fun to play,* and its challenges create a bond between sighted players and players with visual impairments.
10. Sighted players *who put on blindfolds and join in* come away from a game with a new respect for the abilities of their visually impaired teammates.

The Adjective Clause

15d. An *adjective clause* is a subordinate clause that modifies a noun or a pronoun.

An adjective clause usually follows the word or words it modifies and tells *what kind* or *which one*. An *essential* (or *restrictive*) clause is necessary to the basic meaning of the sentence; it is not set off by commas. A *nonessential* (or *nonrestrictive*) clause gives only additional information and is not necessary to the meaning of a sentence; it is set off by commas.

EXAMPLES   This is the new music video **that I like best.** [The clause *that I like best* is necessary to tell which video is being mentioned. Because this information is essential to the meaning of the sentence, it is not set off by commas.]

                Griffins, **which are mythological beasts,** are included on many coats of arms. [The clause *which are mythological beasts* is not necessary to identify *Griffins.* Because this information is nonessential to the meaning of the sentence, it is set off by commas.]

Relative Pronouns

Adjective clauses are often introduced by relative pronouns.

Common Relative Pronouns	who, whom, whose, which, that

These words are called *relative pronouns* because they *relate* an adjective clause to the word that the clause modifies. Besides introducing an adjective clause and relating it to another word in the sentence, the relative pronoun has a grammatical function within the adjective clause.

EXAMPLES   Luís, **who enjoys running,** has decided to enter the marathon. [The relative pronoun *who* relates the adjective clause to *Luís. Who* also functions as the subject of the adjective clause.]

                The students questioned the data **on which the theory was based.** [The relative pronoun *which* relates the adjective clause to *data* and functions as the object of the preposition *on.*]

                We met the singer **whose new CD was released this week.** [The relative pronoun *whose* relates the adjective clause to *singer. Whose* functions as a possessive pronoun in the adjective clause.]

Reference Note

For help in deciding whether a clause is **essential or nonessential,** see page 648.

Reference Note

For more information on **using *who* and *whom*** correctly, see page 559. For more about **using *that* and *which*** correctly, see page 607.

The Subordinate Clause   **473**

The Adjective Clause
Rule 15d *(pp. 473–476)*

OBJECTIVES

- To identify adjective clauses, relative pronouns, and relative adverbs
- To revise sentences by adding adjective clauses

Relating to Writing

You may want to illustrate how using adjective clauses can help students add sentence variety and reduce the number of short, simple sentences in their writing. Have students combine the following sentences, using the relative pronouns in parentheses.

1. Pedro is the candidate. Pedro got the most votes. (who) [*Pedro is the candidate who got the most votes.*]

2. I interviewed a man. His daughter is an astronaut. (whose) [*I interviewed a man whose daughter is an astronaut.*]

3. Do you enjoy the music? The orchestra is playing it. (that) [*Do you enjoy the music that the orchestra is playing?*]

Encourage students to find two sentences in a piece of their writing and combine them using adjective clauses.

Meeting
INDIVIDUAL
NEEDS

ENGLISH-LANGUAGE LEARNERS

General Strategies. You may wish to reinforce that in English a relative pronoun introduces an adjective clause and refers to a noun in the main clause. Because the use of relative pronouns varies with languages, some non-native speakers might place a relative pronoun before an essential clause but after a nonessential clause. Some languages do not even use relative pronouns.

MODALITIES

Visual Learners. Write the following adjective/noun pairs on the chalkboard, and draw arrows from the adjectives to the nouns they modify.

1. the tasty soup

2. the curious child

Then, rephrase the pairs using adjective clauses, as in the following examples. Draw arrows from the clauses to the nouns they modify.

1. the soup that was tasty

2. the child who was curious

Conclude by telling students that, in most cases, an adjective clause immediately follows the word it modifies.

Janice, **whom I have known for years,** is my lab partner this semester. [The relative pronoun *whom* relates the adjective clause to *Janice. Whom* functions as the direct object of the verb phrase *have known* in the adjective clause.]

In many cases, the relative pronoun in the clause may be omitted. The pronoun is understood and still has a function in the clause.

EXAMPLES   Here is the salad **you ordered.** [The relative pronoun *that* is understood. The pronoun relates the adjective clause to *salad* and functions as the direct object of the verb *ordered* in the adjective clause.]

He is the one **I met yesterday.** [The relative pronoun *whom* or *that* is understood. The pronoun relates the adjective clause to *one* and functions as the direct object of the verb *met* in the adjective clause.]

Occasionally an adjective clause is introduced by the word *where* or *when*. When used in such a way, these words are called ***relative adverbs***.

EXAMPLES   They showed us the stadium **where the game would be held.**

Saturday is the day **when I mow the lawn.**

Exercise 2   Identifying Adjective Clauses

Each of the following sentences contains an adjective clause. Write the adjective clause, and underline the relative pronoun or relative adverb that introduces it. If the relative pronoun has been omitted, write it in parentheses and then underline it.

EXAMPLE   **1.** Do you know anyone who is familiar with briffits, swalloops, and waftaroms?

     1. who is familiar with briffits, swalloops, and waftaroms

1. Cartoonists use a variety of unusual names for the symbols that commonly appear in comic strips.
2. For example, a *briffit* is the little puff of dust hanging in the spot where a swiftly departing character was previously standing.
3. For times when cartoonists want to make something appear hot or smelly, they use wavy, rising lines called *waftaroms.*
4. *Agitrons* are the wiggly lines around an object that is supposed to be shaking.

MINI-LESSON

Placement of Adjective Clauses. An adjective clause placed incorrectly can create a confusing sentence.

First, write this sentence on the chalkboard:

There is a picture of a dragon in the

literature book that breathes fire.

Ask students to identify the adjective clause. (*that breathes fire*) Then, ask students to identify which noun or pronoun the clause modifies—[*dragon*]—and underline the word *dragon.* Point out that the adjective

5. The limbs of a character who is moving are usually preceded or trailed by a set of curved lines called *blurgits* or *swalloops.*

6. *Plewds,* which look like flying droplets of sweat, are drawn around the head of a worried character.

7. In fact, there are very few motions or emotions for which cartoonists have not invented a clever, expressive symbol.

8. Almost everyone who likes to doodle and draw has used some of these symbols, probably without knowing the names for them.

9. Look at the example cartoon, where you will find the names of other common symbols from the world of cartooning.

10. Now you know a "language" almost nobody outside the cartooning profession knows! **10.** (that)

dites   agitrons   swalloop   plewds   briffit   blurgits   lucaflect   hites   waftarom

Exercise 3 Revising Sentences by Supplying Adjective Clauses

Revise the following sentences by substituting an adjective clause for each italicized adjective. Add specific details to make your sentences interesting. Underline the adjective clauses in your sentences.

EXAMPLE   **1.** The *angry* citizens gathered in front of City Hall.

          1. *The citizens, who were furious over the recent tax increase, gathered in front of City Hall.*

1. As I entered the building, a *colorful* painting caught my eye.
2. The *patient* photographer sat on a small ledge all day.
3. The two attorneys argued all week over the *important* contract.
4. The team of mountain climbers decided to try to reach the top of the *tallest* peak.
5. At the assembly, Ms. León made two *surprising* announcements.
6. Saburo and his friends cautiously entered the *dark* cave.
7. Edna Jackson easily won her *first* political campaign.

The Subordinate Clause   **475**

Exercise 3 Revising Sentences by Supplying Adjective Clauses

POSSIBLE ANSWERS

1. As I entered the building, a painting that used every color in the spectrum caught my eye.

2. The photographer, whose patience was legendary, sat on a small ledge all day.

3. The two attorneys argued all week over the contract, which was important to both of them.

4. The team of mountain climbers decided to try to reach the top of the peak, which was the tallest on the continent.

5. At the assembly, Ms. León made two announcements that surprised everybody in the room.

6. Saburo and his friend cautiously entered the cave, which was completely dark.

7. Edna Jackson easily won her political campaign, which was the first ever launched by a woman in that district.

Exercise 3

ALTERNATIVE LESSON
Have students find the following constructions in sentences 2, 4, and 9.

2. prepositional phrase [*on a small ledge*]

4. two infinitive phrases [*to try, to reach the top*]

9. participle modified by prepositional phrases [*Dodging to his left, to his right*]

---

clause, as placed, appears to modify *book.* Remind the students that an adjective clause should be placed just after the word that it modifies; in this case, the sentence should read "In the literature book there is

a picture of a dragon that breathes fire." For more information on placement of modifiers, refer students to **Chapter 19: Using Modifiers Correctly.**

Exercise 3 Revising Sentences by Supplying Adjective Clauses

POSSIBLE ANSWERS continued

8. The trainer spoke harshly to the dog, <u>who had been disobedient for the entire session</u>.

9. Dodging to his left and then to his right, Manuel scored the goal <u>that won the game</u>.

10. The veterinarian told Pamela that he was taking good care of her horse, <u>which was lame</u>.

The Adverb Clause

Rule 15e *(pp. 476–478)*

OBJECTIVE

■ To identify and classify adverb clauses

Relating to Writing

You might explain to students that they can often switch the placement of adverb clauses to change the structure of the sentence. To make this point clear, write the following sentences on the chalkboard or an overhead transparency:

1. I feverishly practiced my lines until it was my turn to speak.

2. When my name was called, I looked for a place to hide.

3. Unless a miracle happens, I have no way out!

Have students rewrite each sentence, switching the position of the adverb clause and the main clause. Point out the use of a comma after an introductory adverb clause. Encourage students to check their writing for opportunities to vary the position of adverb clauses.

Reference Note

For more about using **commas** to set off introductory elements, see page 652.

Reference Note

For more about **complete comparisons,** see page 583.

8. The trainer spoke harshly to the *disobedient* dog.

9. Dodging to his left and then to his right, Manuel scored the *winning* goal.

10. The veterinarian told Pamela that he was taking good care of her *lame* horse.

The Adverb Clause

15e. An *adverb clause* is a subordinate clause that modifies a verb, an adjective, or an adverb.

An adverb clause generally tells *how, when, where, why, how much, to what extent,* or *under what condition* the action of a verb takes place.

EXAMPLES **After I had proofread my paper,** I input the corrections. [The adverb clause *After I had proofread my paper* tells *when* I input the corrections.]

Because crêpes are delicious, Joy makes them on special occasions. [*Because crêpes are delicious* tells *why* Joy makes them on special occasions.]

You and your brother may come with us **if you want to.** [*If you want to* tells *under what condition* you and your brother may come with us.]

NOTE As you can see in the first two examples above, introductory adverb clauses are usually set off by commas.

Like adverbs, adverb clauses may also modify adjectives or adverbs.

EXAMPLES Have computers made office work easier **than it was before**? [The adverb clause *than it was before* modifies the adjective *easier,* telling *to what extent* work is easier.]

My cousin Adele reads faster **than I do.** [The adverb clause *than I do* modifies the adverb *faster,* telling *how much* faster my cousin Adele reads.]

NOTE When using adverb clauses to make comparisons, be sure your comparisons are complete.

INCOMPLETE I like dancing better than you. [Do I like dancing better than I like you? Do I like dancing better than you like dancing?]

COMPLETE I like dancing better **than you do.**

Subordinating Conjunctions

Adverb clauses are introduced by **subordinating conjunctions**—words that show the relationship between the adverb clause and the word or words that the clause modifies.

Common Subordinating Conjunctions			
after	because	since	when
although	before	so that	whenever
as	even though	than	where
as if	if	though	wherever
as long as	in order that	unless	whether
as soon as	once	until	while

Some subordinating conjunctions, such as *after*, *before*, *since*, and *until*, may also be used as prepositions.

EXAMPLES   Be sure to hand in your report **before the end** of class today. [prepositional phrase]

Be sure to hand in your report **before class ends today.** [adverb clause]

Exercise 4   Identifying and Classifying Adverb Clauses

Identify each adverb clause in the following sentences. Then, write what the clause tells: *when, where, how, why, to what extent,* or *under what condition.* A sentence may have more than one adverb clause.

EXAMPLE   **1.** When you see the humble man on the next page, can you believe that he is considered one of the twentieth century's greatest leaders?

     1. When you see the humble man on the next page—when

1. If you look through newspapers from the first half of the twentieth century, you will see many pictures of Mohandas K. Gandhi.
2. This man led India to independence from Britain, and he took his spinning wheel wherever he went.
3. He did so because he viewed spinning as a symbol of the peaceful, traditional Indian lifestyle.
4. He also hoped to encourage the Indian people to make their own clothes so that they would not have to depend on British industry.
5. As a form of protest, he led marches or fasted until the government met his requests.

STYLE	TIP

Because an adverb clause does not have a fixed location in a sentence, you must choose where to put the clause. Write different versions of a sentence containing an adverb clause. Then, read aloud each version to see how the placement of the clause affects flow, rhythm, and overall meaning.

EXAMPLES
   After we leave for school, Mom works on her novel.

   Mom works on her novel after we leave for school.

COMPUTER TIP	

If you use a computer to write compositions, you can easily experiment with the placement of adverb clauses in sentences.

GRAMMAR

Meeting INDIVIDUAL NEEDS

ENGLISH-LANGUAGE LEARNERS
General Strategies. Hearing and writing numerous adverb clauses will help students who are accustomed to a different syntax. Students can practice writing adverb clauses by writing a sentence containing an adverb clause for each subordinating conjunction on the list of common subordinating conjunctions. You may want to have students share sentences in small groups.

Crossing the Curriculum

Science. To reinforce that what students learn in one course applies to other subjects, you might work with the students' science teachers to help students write lab reports. You can emphasize that adverb clauses are especially useful to establish the order of events and to show cause and effect.

Exercise 4   Identifying and Classifying Adverb Clauses

POSSIBLE ANSWERS

1. under what condition
2. where
3. why
4. why
5. to what extent

GRAMMAR

Exercise 4 Identifying and Classifying Adverb Clauses

POSSIBLE ANSWERS
continued

6. to what extent
7. under what condition
8. why; when
9. when
10. why

The Noun Clause

Rule 15f *(pp. 478–480)*

OBJECTIVE

■ To identify and classify noun clauses

Critical Thinking

Analysis. Have students work in small groups to create noun clauses, using the introductory words listed on p. 478. Ask students to create sentences using the noun clauses. Then, have them analyze which introductory words work with clauses used as subjects, as predicate nominatives, as direct objects, as indirect objects, and as objects of prepositions. Students could organize their findings in a five-column chart as follows:

SUBJ	DO	IO	PN	OP
that	that		that	

Reference Note

For more information on **subjects, predicate nominatives, direct objects,** and **indirect objects,** see Chapter 13. For more about **objects of prepositions,** see page 442.

6. Gandhi's nonviolent methods were more powerful than anyone could have predicted.
7. As India's Congress and people increasingly supported Gandhi's nonviolent program, the British government was forced to listen.
8. Gandhi was well qualified to represent India as a diplomat since he had studied law in London before he became involved in India's freedom movement.
9. After independence was assured, Gandhi turned his attention to helping India's many poor people.
10. Because he was loved throughout India and the world, Gandhi was called *Mahatma,* meaning "Great Soul."

The Noun Clause

15f. A *noun clause* is a subordinate clause that is used as a noun.

A noun clause may be used as a subject, as a complement (such as a predicate nominative, direct object, or indirect object), or as the object of a preposition.

SUBJECT	**What Mary Anne did to rescue the injured bird** was brave.
PREDICATE NOMINATIVE	The winner of the race will be **whoever runs fastest in the final stretch.**
DIRECT OBJECT	She finally discovered **what the answer to her question was.**
INDIRECT OBJECT	Give **whatever parts need cleaning** a rinse in detergent.
OBJECT OF PREPOSITION	He checks the ID cards of **whoever visits.**

Noun clauses are usually introduced by

that	when	whether	whom
what	whenever	who	whomever
whatever	where	whoever	why

RESOURCES

The Noun Clause

Practice

■ *Grammar, Usage, and Mechanics,* pp. 99–100, 101
■ *Language Workshop CD-ROM,* Lesson 32

Sometimes these words have a grammatical function in the noun clause. Other times they just introduce the clause and have no other function in it.

EXAMPLES   They did not know **who it could be.** [The introductory word *who* is the predicate nominative of the noun clause—*it could be who.* The entire clause is the direct object of the verb *did know.*]

        Show us **what you bought.** [The introductory word *what* is the direct object in the noun clause—*you bought what.* The entire clause is the direct object of the verb *show.*]

        What you learn is your decision. [The introductory word *what* is the direct object in the noun clause—*you learn what.* The entire clause is the subject of the verb *is.*]

        She wished **that she were older.** [The introductory word *that* simply introduces the noun clause and has no function within the noun clause. The entire clause is the direct object of the verb *wished.*]

Sometimes the word that introduces a noun clause is omitted. In such cases, the introductory word is understood.

EXAMPLE   Didn't you know **the party was canceled?** [The introductory word *that* is understood.]

Exercise 5   Identifying and Classifying Noun Clauses

Most of the following sentences contain noun clauses. If a sentence contains a <u>noun clause</u>, identify that clause. Then, tell how the clause is used: as a *subject,* a *predicate nominative,* a *direct object,* an *indirect object,* or an *object of a preposition.* If a sentence does not contain a noun clause, write *no noun clause.*

EXAMPLE   1. We moved to Massachusetts and did not know what we would find there.

          1. *what we would find there—direct object*

1. <u>What surprised me first</u> were the yellowish green fire engines.
2. I had thought <u>fire engines were always red.</u>
3. Our neighbors explained <u>that this color keeps the fire engines from being confused with other large red trucks.</u>
4. My sister Michelle made another discovery at the bowling alley.
5. The small grapefruit-sized bowling balls with no holes were not <u>what she was used to!</u>
6. We learned <u>that this sport is called candlepin bowling.</u>

1. subj.
2. d.o.
3. d.o.

4. no noun clause
5. p.n.

6. d.o.

Meeting INDIVIDUAL NEEDS

ENGLISH-LANGUAGE LEARNERS

Spanish. Some Spanish-speaking students might have difficulty with the omission of the introductory word *that* in noun clauses. You may wish to write the following sentences on the chalkboard and have students read them aloud, omitting *that* in parentheses.

1. I wish (that) I could fly.
2. I understand (that) you will be moving soon.
3. The principal said (that) she would visit our class.

LEARNERS HAVING DIFFICULTY

To teach noun clauses from another perspective, you could write the following clauses on the chalkboard, asking pairs of students to use each noun clause in a sentence and identify how each clause is used.

1. that the train was late
   [*The conductor announced that the train was late.* (direct object)]
2. what we plan to do
   [*What we plan to do will surprise Mother.* (subject)]
3. whatever you need
   [*Ask the counselor for whatever you need.* (object of preposition)]
4. whomever I choose
   [*I will give whomever I choose the gift certificate.* (indirect object)]

The Subordinate Clause   **479**

MULTIPLE INTELLIGENCES
Spatial Intelligence. Some students will understand sentence structure more clearly by marking the clauses. You could ask students to copy the sentences in **Review A** and use a different colored highlighter to mark each type of subordinate clause, leaving the independent clause unmarked.

You may want to demonstrate the first sentence on an overhead transparency.

If you stop to think about it [adverb clause]
why painters had a problem [noun clause]

---

7. subj.

8. o.p.

9. i.o.

10. no noun clause

7. <u>Whoever can knock down the pins with one of those bowling balls</u> must be an expert.

8. Later, I was surprised by <u>how delicious the baked beans were.</u>

9. Someone should give <u>whoever invented Boston baked beans</u> an award for this marvelous creation.

10. Now, after we have lived in New England for a year, both Michelle and I are happy in our new home.

Review A Identifying Subordinate Clauses

For most of the sentences in the following paragraph, identify the <u>subordinate clause or clauses</u>. Then, tell whether each clause is an *adjective clause*, an *adverb clause*, or a *noun clause*. If a sentence has no subordinate clauses, write *none*.

EXAMPLE **[1]** In paintings created before 1880, horses are usually shown in poses that now look quaint and unnatural.

1. *that now look quaint and unnatural—adjective clause*

1. adv./n.
2. adv./n.

3. adv./adj.
4. none

5. n.
6. adj.

7. adj.

8. adv.
9. n.
10. n.

[1] If you stop to think about it, you can see <u>why painters had a problem</u>. **[2]** Stop-action photography had not yet been invented, and <u>when painters looked at rapidly moving horses</u>, they could not possibly see <u>where the legs and hooves were at any one instant.</u> **[3]** <u>Whenever painters wanted to portray a galloping horse</u>, they made up a position <u>they thought suggested speed.</u> **[4]** The horses in some paintings had both front legs extended far to the front and both hind legs stretched far behind. **[5]** Today, we know <u>that this is an impossible position for a horse.</u> **[6]** Stop-action photography was first used in the 1870s by a Californian named Eadweard Muybridge, <u>who took this series of photographs of a galloping horse.</u> **[7]** Along a racetrack, he set up many cameras <u>whose shutters were controlled by threads stretched across the track.</u> **[8]** <u>As the horse ran by</u>, it broke the threads and tripped the cameras' shutters one after the other. **[9]** Painters of the time thought <u>this new technology was truly amazing!</u> **[10]** They were the first artists in history to know <u>what a horse really looked like at each point in its stride.</u>

Sentences Classified According to Structure

Sentences may be classified according to purpose as declarative, imperative, interrogative, or exclamatory. Sentences may also be classified according to structure. The term *structure* refers to the number and types of clauses in a sentence.

15g. Depending on its structure, a sentence can be classified as simple, compound, complex, or compound-complex.

In the following examples, independent clauses are underlined once. Subordinate clauses are underlined twice.

(1) A *simple sentence* contains one independent clause and no subordinate clauses. It may have a compound subject, a compound verb, and any number of phrases.

EXAMPLES	The boys wanted to take a vacation last summer.
	Ray and Joe worked and saved enough for a trip to Ohio.

(2) A *compound sentence* contains two or more independent clauses and no subordinate clauses.

The independent clauses in a compound sentence may be joined by a comma and a coordinating conjunction; by a semicolon; or by a semicolon, a conjunctive adverb, and a comma.

EXAMPLES	Originally, they wanted to ride bikes all the way, **but** they decided to take the train instead.
	Ray looked forward to seeing his cousins; Joe was eager to play with his uncle's band.
	Uncle James played in a country-music band; **however,** Joe preferred rock music.

Reference Note

For more on **classifying sentences by purpose,** see page 435.

STYLE TIP

Paragraphs in which all the sentences have the same structure can be monotonous to read. To keep your readers interested in your ideas, evaluate your writing to see whether you've used a variety of sentence structures. Then, use revising techniques—adding, cutting, replacing, and reordering—to enliven your writing by varying the structure of your sentences.

Sentences Classified According to Structure **481**

Sentences Classified According to Structure
Rule 15g *(pp. 481–486)*

OBJECTIVE

- To classify sentences as simple, compound, complex, or compound-complex

Meeting INDIVIDUAL NEEDS

ENGLISH-LANGUAGE LEARNERS
General Strategies. You may wish to remind students that in English a clause contains both a subject and a verb. (In some languages, such as Spanish, clauses do not always require expressed subjects.) Have students pay particular attention to the subject and verb for each clause in the example sentences on p. 481.

Relating to Literature

If your literature book contains "The Sniper" by Liam O'Flaherty, have students look at the third, fourth, and fifth paragraphs of the story and state what they notice about the sentence structure. [*They should recognize the repetitive use of simple sentences with an occasional compound sentence.*] Then, ask students to discuss the effect produced by such a style. [*The short, choppy sentences add suspense and help quicken the pace of the narrative.*]

Relating to Writing

To illustrate how different types of sentences are constructed, write the following sentences on the chalkboard or on a transparency and have students use the words in parentheses to combine the sentences. Then, ask students to identify the structures of new sentences.

1. Eric read an article about book groups. He started a science fiction club. (after) [*After Eric read an article about book groups, he started a science fiction club.—complex*]

2. The members chose a book. The book appealed to everyone. A local bookstore ordered multiple copies. (that; and) [*The members chose a book that appealed to everyone, and a local bookstore ordered multiple copies.—compound-complex*]

Point out that the revised sentences are less choppy than the originals. Then, you may want to ask students to use these same patterns to create original sentences.

Exercise 6

ALTERNATIVE LESSON
Have students identify the verbs in the independent clauses in sentences 1, 3, and 4.

1. have

3. comes

4. are

TEACHING TIP

Exercises You may wish to use **Exercise 6** as guided practice. Then, have students complete **Exercise 7** as independent practice.

COMPUTER TIP

A word processor can help you check for varied sentence structure in your writing. Make a copy of your document to work on. By inserting a return or a page break after every period, you can view the sentences in a vertical list and compare the structures of each sentence in a particular paragraph. Make any revisions on the properly formatted copy of your document.

NOTE Don't confuse a simple sentence that contains a compound predicate with a compound sentence. Compound sentences always have two or more complete clauses.

	S V V
COMPOUND PREDICATE	**Joe considered** country music corny and **said** so.

	S V S V
COMPOUND SENTENCE	**Joe considered** country music corny, and **he said** so.

(3) A *complex sentence* contains one independent clause and at least one subordinate clause.

EXAMPLES
S V
Because Joe wanted to keep his guitar with him,

S V
they decided against taking a plane.

S V S V
If they took a train, they could see all the sights, too.

(4) A *compound-complex sentence* contains two or more independent clauses and at least one subordinate clause.

EXAMPLES
S V S V
The band played at a dance, and Ray was pulled into a line

S V
dance that was starting.

S V
To his surprise, he was good at line dancing; afterward,

S V S V
he joined in whenever he got the chance.

Exercise 6 Classifying Sentences According to Structure

Classify each of the following sentences as *simple, compound, complex,* or *compound-complex.* Be sure that you can identify all subordinate and independent clauses.

Learning for Life

Continued on pp. 483–485

Writing a Business Letter. Tell students that one's writing can be an ambassador creating a first impression. For example, prospective employers read letters of application, and college admissions officers read essays as part of the selection process.

Creating a good first impression in writing requires clarity of thought. Dependent clauses connect additional information and clarify main and supporting ideas.

To demonstrate, you may want to invite guest speakers to your class to reinforce the

EXAMPLE   **1.** The Iroquois are American Indian peoples originally from New York State.

        1. simple

| Link to 🏛 Literat |

1. Members of the Iroquois—which include the Mohawk, Oneida, Onondaga, Cayuga, Tuscarora, and Seneca—have an ancient history of storytelling.   **1.** cx.
2. In the early days, professional storytellers went from house to house, and they were paid for their storytelling with small gifts.   **2.** cd.
3. Most of what is known today about Iroquois folk tales comes from the Senecas, whose stories have been written down by historians.   **3.** cx.
4. Some of the most popular stories are about a creature who is hairless except for one strip of fur down his back.   **4.** cx.
5. He is so huge that his back can be seen above the trees.   **5.** cx.
6. He eats people; because he cannot be killed in any ordinary way, he is especially frightening.   **6.** cd.-cx.
7. The tales about this creature are even more frightening than are the ones about Stone Coat, who has skin like stone.   **7.** cx.
8. Fortunately, Stone Coat is not very smart, and many of the folk tales tell of ways that the Iroquois outsmart him.   **8.** cd.-cx.
9. There are also tales about the Whirlwinds, who usually appear as bodiless heads with fiery eyes; in some stories, the Whirlwinds eat sticks and rocks when they cannot catch people.   **9.** cd.-cx.
10. Other Iroquois stories tell about the adventures of Elk, Partridge, Skunk, and Rattlesnake.   **10.** s.

Exercise 7 Classifying Sentences According to Structure

Classify each of the following sentences as *simple, compound, complex,* or *compound-complex*.

EXAMPLE   **1.** In all the world, there is only one art museum for children's art, and it is located in Norway.

        1. compound

1. This museum is the International Museum of Children's Art, which occupies a big, old house in Oslo. **1.** cx.
2. The walls are covered from top to bottom with brilliantly colored creations by young artists up to age seventeen. **2.** s.

Sentences Classified According to Structure   **483**

TEACHING TIP

Activity. To provide students with more practice using clauses, you might divide the class into groups of three or six and give each group identical sets of cards with the following subordinate clauses:

1. whom I trust

2. if the concert is canceled

3. who won the race

4. that you bought

5. until the bell rings

6. where the treasure is hidden

Have each team write as many sentences as possible with the clauses in three minutes. Award a point for each correct sentence. You may wish to continue the game by having each team write clauses of their own on cards and give the cards to another team. Again, give the teams a time limit to write sentences with the clauses.

Exercise 7

ALTERNATIVE LESSON
Have students find the simple subject and verb in sentences 2, 4, and 8.

2. walls—are covered

4. few—depict; most—express

8. Mr. Goldin—has hung

---

importance of clear, concise writing. Possible guests could include a college admissions officer, the editor of the local newspaper, or a business executive. Ask them to talk about what impresses them most about a piece of writing.

Then, assign each student to write a letter of application for a job or for school or camp admission. Tell students they must use the development on the following page.

Cooperative Learning

Revising a Children's Story. To emphasize the concept that sentence structure should vary for different audiences, have students work in groups to revise the simple sentences often found in children's books. You may wish to provide a stack of these books for students or ask students in advance to bring the books.

Divide the class into groups of four. Tell the students they will be revising the sentences in a children's book for an older audience. First, have the group read the book and identify sentence types. Then, have them decide what type of audience they want to address—middle school, high school, or adult.

Then, assign each group member specific pages. Remind students to use a combination of simple, compound, complex, and compound-complex sentences. Once each student has a draft of his or her pages, the group should revise it for added variety if necessary. Students may want to number their sentences and use a four-column chart to record the sentence numbers of each type of sentence used.

EXAMPLE

SIMPLE	COMPD	COMPX	CC
1, 7	2, 5	3, 4	6

You may want to ask volunteers from each group to read aloud both versions of their stories and allow the class to make suggestions for further changes.

3. Many of the 100,000 works, which come from 150 countries, deal with objects from nature, but a few, like the bicycle sculpture on the previous page, focus on manufactured objects. **3.** cd.-cx.

4. Of course, a few of the paintings depict troubles or problems, but most of the works express happiness and energy. **4.** cd.

5. Rafael Goldin, the museum's director, says a child's first meeting with exhibited art is very important. **5.** cx.

6. Children visit the museum, and they "see that a museum can mean joy and color." **6.** cd.-cx.

7. "If their first visit is to a boring, dusty museum, children will always associate museums with *dusty* and *boring*." **7.** cx.

8. Mr. Goldin has even hung some of the paintings at toddlers' eye level to encourage each young visitor's own personal relationship with art. **8.** s.

9. Young visitors are very excited when they learn that all the artwork was created by children, and they are often inspired to start painting. **9.** cd.-cx.

10. Wouldn't it be great if there were a museum like that here? **10.** cx.

Review B **Identifying and Classifying Subordinate Clauses**

Identify the subordinate clause or clauses in each of the following sentences. Tell whether each clause is used as an *adjective*, an *adverb*, or a *noun*. If a clause is used as an adjective or an adverb, write the word or words the clause modifies. If a clause is used as a noun, write *subj.* for subject, *d.o.* for direct object, *i.o.* for indirect object, *p.n.* for predicate nominative, or *o.p.* for object of a preposition.

EXAMPLES
1. When our science teacher described insect-eating plants, we listened with amazement.

   1. *When our science teacher described insect-eating plants—adverb—listened*

2. What we heard sounded like science fiction.

   2. *What we heard—noun—subj.*

1. Plants that eat insects usually live in swampy areas. **1.** adj.

2. Because the soil in these regions lacks nutrients, these plants do not get enough nitrogen through their roots. **2.** adv.

3. The nitrogen that these plants need comes from the protein in the bodies of insects. **3.** adj.

4. How these plants catch their food is interesting. **4.** n.—subj.

5. A pitcher plant's sweet scent appeals to whatever insect is nearby. **5.** n.—o.p.

Learning for Life

DEVELOPMENT OF LETTER	
Paragraph 1	Introduce self, giving other background
Paragraph 2	Announce goal and means of achieving it
Paragraphs 3 and 4	Outline and support qualifications
Paragraph 5	Summarize desires and thank recipient

6. The insect thinks that it will find food inside the plant. 6. n.—d.o.
7. What happens instead is that the insect drowns in the plant's digestive juices. 7. n.—subj./n.—p.n.
8. The Venus' flytrap shown here has what looks like small bear traps at the ends of its stalks. 8. n.—d.o.
9. When a trap is open, an insect can wander in and spring the trap. 9. adv.
10. The insect is then digested by the plant in a process that can take several days. 10. adj.

Review C **Classifying Subordinate Clauses**

Classify each of the following italicized clauses as an *adjective*, an *adverb*, or *a noun clause*. Be prepared to explain your answers.

EXAMPLES
[1] *Until our class visited the county courthouse,* we had imagined [2] *that most court cases were like the ones on TV.*

1. adverb

2. noun

[1] *As we left the courtroom,* we thought about the men [2] *who had been on trial.* [3] *Although they had not committed a serious crime,* they had broken the law. The law says [4] *that removing sand from our local beach is illegal.* A police officer caught the men [5] *when they could not move their truck,* [6] *which had become stuck in the sand.* [7] *After the judge had read the law to them,* the men claimed [8] *that they had never heard of that law.* The judge, who reminded them [9] *that ignorance of the law is no excuse,* fined each man one hundred dollars. The men promised [10] *that they would not take any more beach sand.*

─HELP─

In the examples in Review C, the first italicized clause is an adverb clause that modifies the verb phrase *had imagined*. The second italicized clause is a noun clause that acts as a direct object of the verb phrase *had imagined*.

1. adv.
2. adj. 3. adv.
4. n.
5. adv.
6. adj. 7. adv.
8. n.
9. n.

10. n.

Review D **Rewriting a Paragraph to Include a Variety of Sentence Structures**

You and a partner are working together on an essay about life in the 1800s. While researching the topic, the two of you discover a diary written by a young woman named Barbara Sneyd. You and your partner have made copies of Sneyd's paintings and have recorded information about her life. Your job is to rewrite the paragraph on the next page to improve its style. You will need to vary the sentence structure, and you may want to add or delete details to improve the organization. Write at least one sentence with each kind of structure: *simple, compound, complex,* and *compound-complex.* Be prepared to identify the structure of each sentence you write.

Sentences Classified According to Structure **485**

You might want students to work in small groups to brainstorm material for their letters. Once students have created their first drafts, you could allow them to share their drafts with their groups for input.

Students should make revisions, proofread, and present a final draft for publication. They can publish the letters either by sending them to a prospective interviewer or by posting them on the class bulletin board.

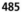

Review D Rewriting a Paragraph to Include a Variety of Sentence Structures

POSSIBLE ANSWERS

Barbara Sneyd lived more than one hundred years ago *(simple)*. Her wealthy family lived in the English countryside, and they loved to ride and hunt *(compound)*. Barbara had a governess, and although the governess kept her very busy studying, Barbara did have time to pursue her greatest passion, which was riding *(compound-complex)*. Barbara's mother encouraged her to keep a diary about her life *(simple)*. When Barbara was fourteen, she started her diary *(complex)*. It took the form of a sketchbook, and in it she recorded her family's life *(compound)*. She painted many small pictures of her family's activities: fishing, visiting, and picnicking *(simple)*. Barbara was also a keen observer of nature; she drew and painted her family's horses and pets and the flowers from the garden, as well as many small landscapes of the countryside around her home *(compound)*. Above all, her diary is full of paintings of horses, which she loved *(complex)*. If you want to see what her paintings look like, some pictures from her diary are shown on this page *(complex)*.

Barbara Sneyd lived more than one hundred years ago. Her home was in the English countryside. She came from a wealthy family. Her family loved to ride and hunt. Barbara had a governess. The governess kept Barbara very busy studying. Barbara did have time to pursue her greatest passion. Her greatest passion was riding. Her mother encouraged her to keep a diary. The diary would be about Barbara's life. Barbara started the diary. She was fourteen. It took the form of a sketchbook. In it she recorded her family's life. She painted many small pictures of her family's activities. They went fishing, visiting, and picnicking. Barbara was also a keen observer of nature. She drew and painted her family's horses and pets and the flowers from the garden. She painted many small landscapes. The landscapes showed the countryside around her home. Above all, her diary is full of paintings of horses. She loved horses. You may want to see what her paintings look like. Some pictures from her diary are shown on this page.

Chapter Review

A. Identifying Clauses

Identify each italicized clause in the following sentences as *independent* or *subordinate*.

1. The fire started *because someone did not smother a campfire*.
2. The family *that bought our house* is moving in next week.
3. Did you know *that Dr. Joel is the new ambassador to Lebanon*?
4. Mr. Kim will buy the store *if the bank lends him the money*.
5. According to Ms. Garza, our math teacher, *the binary system is important to know*.
6. *Wherever Maggie goes*, her poodle Jack follows.
7. *She won the golf match* because she had practiced diligently.
8. *Whatever you decide* is fine with me.
9. *I saw the job advertised in the school paper* and decided to apply for it.
10. We were proud *that you conceded defeat so graciously*.

B. Identifying and Classifying Subordinate Clauses

Identify the subordinate clause in each of the following sentences. Tell whether each clause is used as an *adjective*, an *adverb*, or a *noun*.

11. adj.
11. Emily Dickinson, who was born in 1830 in Amherst, Massachusetts, was a great American poet.

12. adv.
12. She appeared to lead a fairly normal life until she became a recluse in her family's home.

13. adj.
13. There she wrote poems that literary critics now call "great American poetry."

14. adv.
14. Unfortunately, only a few of Dickinson's poems were published while she was alive.

15. adv.
15. After she died in 1886, her other poems were published.

16. n.
16. I think everyone should read at least some of Dickinson's poetry.

17. adj.
17. Dickinson is a poet whose work I now read often.

18. adj.
18. The poems I have just finished reading are "A Narrow Fellow in the Grass" and "Apparently with No Surprise."

Using the Chapter Review

To assess student progress, you may want to compare the types of items missed on the **Diagnostic Preview** to those missed on the **Chapter Review**. You may want to work out specific goals for mastering essential information with individual students who are still having difficulty.

GRAMMAR

19. adv.

19. The rhythms of Dickinson's poems are best appreciated when you read the poems aloud.

20. n.

20. Whatever I read by Emily Dickinson surprises and inspires me.

C. Classifying Sentences According to Structure and Identifying Independent and Subordinate Clauses

Classify each of the following sentences as *simple, compound, complex,* or *compound-complex*. Identify all subordinate and independent clauses.

21. s.

21. After eating and drinking, the elephants galloped through the wheat field.

22. cd.

22. Mr. Chisholm wanted to go bowling, but Mrs. Chisholm preferred the dinner theater.

23. cd.

23. Ten steps up the dark staircase, the twins lost their nerve; dinner at home suddenly seemed much more appealing.

24. cx.

24. Kenzuo insisted that the bullet train was the best way to get to Osaka after midnight.

25. cx.

25. When the travelers arrived at the inn, the innkeeper greeted them.

26. cd.-cx.

26. Dr. Bourgeois knew that singing loudly would only irritate others, so he decided to keep his high spirits to himself.

27. s.

27. While preparing to eat, the dog spotted itself in the mirror.

28. cd.

28. Mom always wanted to live in New Mexico, but Dad was too used to living in North Carolina to move.

29. cd.-cx.

29. Before the concert began, the first violinist leaned forward to tie his shoe; this innocent action set off a whole chain of unlikely events.

30. cd.

30. Tom Bell is Angela's favorite actor, but Sally likes Ricky Blake.

31. s.

31. While washing the car, Benito paused to admire the vintage biplane flying overhead.

32. cd.-cx.

32. Joseph had worked hard for straight A's on his exams, and when the results came in, he discovered that his hard work had paid off.

33. cx.

33. When the crocodile approached, the heron flew away.

34. cd.

34. Arnie carefully lined up the pieces on the chessboard; however, Dario's foot caught the edge of the board, and both board and pieces flew into the air.

35. cd.-cx.

35. We had hoped that being subtle would be enough, and, indeed, for a while this tactic seemed to be working; but as the day wore on, we slowly realized that a bolder approach was needed.

RESOURCES

The Clause
Review
- *Grammar, Usage, and Mechanics,* pp. 104, 105, 106, 107

Assessment
- *Assessment Package*
  —*Chapter Tests,* Ch. 15
  —*Chapter Tests in Standardized Test Formats,* Ch. 15
- *Test Generator (One-Stop Planner CD-ROM)*

36. President Kennedy was assassinated while riding through Dallas on November 22, 1963.

37. Charles argued that a picnic lunch was the best idea.

38. Professor Chan showed his class his slides of the Great Wall of China, and he used the slides later as the basis for a lecture on Genghis Khan.

39. After the cyclists rounded the bend, the Swiss champion Michel Neibergall took the lead.

40. When the crows descended on the barren field, the field mice scurried for shelter.

36. s.

37. cx.

38. cd.

39. cx.

40. cx.

Writing Application
Using Sentence Variety in Postcards

Sentence Structures   You are writing postcards about your summer activities, such as baseball or soccer camp, computer camp, or cheerleading camp. Write a brief note telling your six-year-old cousin about a few experiences that you think he or she would find interesting. Write another note to an adult friend or relative about your experiences. Use sentence structure and language that are appropriate to each reader.

Prewriting   If you have been to a summer camp, make a list of experiences that you could describe. If you haven't been to camp, list activities that you enjoy during the summer.

Writing   As you write your first draft, make sure to include details that would interest your different audiences. Show the relationships between your details by using a variety of subordinate adjective, adverb, and noun clauses.

Revising   Read your notes to a classmate, without telling which note is to your cousin and which is to your adult friend or relative. If your classmate can't tell which note is to which person, you should revise your language, information, and sentence structures.

Publishing   Check to be sure that all your sentences are complete sentences. Pay special attention to the use of commas to separate clauses. You may want to post your notes on a class bulletin board or create a Web page for them.

Reference Note

For more about using **commas,** see page 643.

Chapter Review   **489**

Writing Application
(p. 489)

OBJECTIVE

■ To write a letter using varied sentence structure

Writing Application

Tip. Because students will be writing for two different audiences, you may suggest that they create two separate prewriting lists. Remind them that the experiences that interest a six-year-old sister may not be the experiences they want to share with an adult friend or relative.

Scoring Rubric. While you will want to pay particular attention to students' use of appropriate language and sentence structure, you will also want to evaluate overall writing performance. You may want to give a split score to indicate development and clarity of the composition as well as grammar skills.

Critical Thinking

Analysis. Depending on their familiarity with summer camps, students might create extensive lists in the prewriting stage. Tell them that they must narrow their lists to fit the length of their letters. Limiting a broad topic requires analysis. Remind students that they must keep their audience and purpose in mind when narrowing their topics.

RESOURCES

Writing Application
Extension

■ *Grammar, Usage, and Mechanics,* p. 110
■ *Language Workshop CD-ROM,* Lessons 29–32, 38

CHAPTER
16

PREVIEWING THE CHAPTER

■ This chapter offers a review of subject-verb agreement and pronoun-antecedent agreement, with special emphasis on the compound subject and on agreement problems including *don't* and *doesn't,* collective nouns, titles, amounts, and plural forms with singular meanings.

■ The chapter concludes with a **Chapter Review** including a **Writing Application** feature that asks students to write a description using correct subject-verb agreement.

■ For help in integrating the chapter with writing chapters, use the **Teaching Strands** chart on pp. T371A–T371B.

USING THE DIAGNOSTIC PREVIEW

■ The informal **Diagnostic Preview** requires students to understand and use correct subject-verb and pronoun-antecedent agreement. Item numbers 2, 4, 6, and 10 in Part A and 20, 22, 23, and 25 in Part B have pronoun errors. If students miss all or most of these, you may want to emphasize the **Agreement of Pronoun and Antecedent** section.

490

CHAPTER
16 Agreement
Subject and Verb, Pronoun and Antecedent

Diagnostic Preview

A. Proofreading Sentences for Subject-Verb and Pronoun-Antecedent Agreement

Each of the following sentences contains an error in agreement. Identify each <u>incorrect verb or pronoun</u>, and supply the correct form.

EXAMPLE   1. Rochelle Richardson, one of our city's former mayors, live next door to me.

       1. live—lives

1. was
2. his or her
3. is
4. her
5. has
6. their
7. give
8. are
9. has
10. it

1. When the truck overturned, a herd of cattle were set free on the expressway.
2. The teacher reminded everyone to sharpen their pencil.
3. Not one of our tomato plants are producing any fruit, but the green beans seem to be thriving.
4. Has each of the girls memorized their part?
5. Everybody have been talking about the class picnic ever since you thought of the idea.
6. Both of the finalists played his or her best.
7. Many of their experiments have failed, but neither Dr. Jenkins nor his assistants ever gives up hope.
8. There is a brush, a comb, and a mirror on the dresser top.
9. Many a sailor have perished when his or her ship ran aground on that reef.
10. Read *Little Women* and write a plot summary about them.

CHAPTER RESOURCES

Planning
■ *One-Stop Planner CD-ROM* 🎧

Practice and Extension
■ *Grammar, Usage, and Mechanics,* p. 111
■ *Developmental Language Skills,* pp. 61–68

Internet

■ go.hrw.com (keyword: EOLang)

Evaluation and Assessment
■ *Chapter Tests,* Ch. 16
■ *Chapter Tests in Standardized Test Formats,* Ch. 16
■ *Test Generator (One-Stop Planner)* 🎧

B. Proofreading a Paragraph for Subject-Verb and Pronoun-Antecedent Agreement

Most of the following sentences contain at least one agreement error. For each error, identify the incorrect verb or pronoun and supply the correct form. If the sentence is already correct, write *C*.

EXAMPLE   **1.** Filming an animal in its natural surroundings present many problems.

       1. present—presents

11. One problem is that the filmmaker, in most cases, have to get quite close to the animal.

12. Ten yards often make the difference between a good scene and no scene at all.

13. A zoom lens or a telephoto lens are generally used, but even then, getting good photographs can be very difficult.

14. Before filming, the crew usually take turns watching the animal for weeks to learn its habits and find good vantage points for taking pictures.

15. In addition, the filmmaker and the crew uses every trick of the trade in filming wild animals.

16. For example, *Foxes at Night* were almost certainly not filmed at night!

17. "Nighttime" films are generally made during daylight hours, when there is plenty of natural light.

18. Later, all of the daytime footage are darkened through the use of filters.

19. Also, many of the animals used in a nature film has been trained or partially tamed.

20. For example, if a filmmaker or a member of the crew take care of a bird from the moment it hatches, it will instinctively follow them.

21. The photographer can then easily take close-up pictures of the bird after it matures.

22. In many films, scenes of animals giving birth and raising its young are filmed in a studio, not in the wild.

23. Photographers get good footage by building a den where he or she can film the baby animals through a window beside the nest.

24. This film, along with footage taken in the natural habitat, are then skillfully edited.

25. As a result, few of the viewers ever suspect that the film shown to him or her has been shot indoors.

11. has

12. makes

13. is

14. C

15. use

16. was

17. C

18. is

19. have

20. takes / him or her

21. C

22. their

23. they

24. is

25. them

USAGE

Number

Number
Rule 16a (p. 492)

OBJECTIVE

- To classify nouns and pronouns by number

USAGE

TEACHING TIP

Activity. Remind students that some words, especially names of animals like *deer*, are the same in both their singular and plural forms. Ask students to suggest and keep a list of other words that are the same in both singular and plural forms. [*Possibilities include* moose, reindeer, sheep, *and* squid.]

Once students have completed and discussed their lists, you might want to have them work in pairs or small groups to create humorous poems including the words from their lists.

Exercise 1 Classifying Nouns and Pronouns by Number

ANSWERS

1. pl.
2. pl.
3. pl.
4. sing.
5. sing.
6. sing.
7. pl.
8. sing.
9. sing.
10. pl.

Number is the form a word takes to indicate whether the word is singular or plural.

16a. A word that refers to one person, place, thing, or idea is *singular* in number. A word that refers to more than one is *plural* in number.

Singular	Plural
student	students
princess	princesses
child	children
tooth	teeth
it	they
himself	themselves
berry	berries
deer	deer

Exercise 1 Classifying Nouns and Pronouns by Number

Identify each italicized word as either *singular* or *plural*.

EXAMPLE　　As a child, the girl in the [1] *photograph* was sure she was not very good at anything.

　　　　　1. singular

Link to Literature

She was overshadowed by the other [1] *children* in her family, especially by her older sister Madge, who wrote [2] *stories* and plays. Lonely and full of self-doubt, the girl surrounded herself with imaginary [3] *companions*. [4] *Everything* changed, though, when she caught influenza and became restless during her recovery. Her mother brought her a [5] *notebook* and suggested that, like Madge, she might write a story. After practicing on short stories, she decided to tackle a detective [6] *novel*. [7] "*They* are very difficult to do," said Madge. "I don't think you could write one." Madge was wrong: The young author was Agatha Christie, who became the most successful mystery [8] *writer* in history. Her mystery novels and story collections have sold many millions of copies in [9] *English* and in at least sixty other [10] *languages*.

RESOURCES

Number

Practice

- *Grammar, Usage, and Mechanics*, p. 112
- *Language Workshop CD-ROM*, Lesson 10

Agreement of Subject and Verb

16b. A verb should agree in number with its subject.

(1) Singular subjects take singular verbs.

EXAMPLES   **He washes** the dishes. [The singular verb *washes* agrees with the singular subject *He*.]

A **girl** in my neighborhood **plays** in the band. [The singular subject *girl* takes the singular verb *plays*.]

(2) Plural subjects take plural verbs.

EXAMPLES   **They wash** the dishes.

Several **girls** in my neighborhood **play** in the band.

In the examples above, the verbs agree in number with their subjects. Like the single-word verbs above, verb phrases also agree with their subjects. However, in a verb phrase, only the first helping (auxiliary) verb changes its form to agree with a singular or plural subject.

EXAMPLES   **He has been washing** the dishes.

They have been washing the dishes.

A **girl** in my neighborhood **was playing** in the band.

Several **girls** in my neighborhood **were playing** in the band.

NOTE   Generally, nouns ending in *–s* are plural (*friends, girls*), but verbs ending in *–s* are generally singular (*sees, hears*).

16c. The number of the subject usually is not determined by a word in a phrase or clause following the subject.

EXAMPLES   The apartments **across the street** do not have balconies. [*Do have* agrees with *apartments*, not *street*.]

The planes **pulling up to the gate** were purchased by a movie company. [*Were purchased* agrees with *planes*, not *gate*.]

Eli, **one of my friends,** was late. [*Was* agrees with *Eli*, not *friends*.]

The movie **that I saw two weeks ago** was reviewed in today's paper. [*Was reviewed* agrees with *movie*, not *weeks*.]

Reference Note

For more about **helping verbs,** see page 391.

Reference Note

For guidelines on **forming plurals of nouns,** see page 739.

Reference Note

For more about **phrases,** see Chapter 14. For more about **clauses,** see Chapter 15. For examples of **subjects whose number is determined by a phrase following the subject,** see page 496.

Agreement of Subject and Verb

Rules 16b–f *(pp. 493–498)*

OBJECTIVES

- To identify verbs that agree in number with their subjects
- To identify subjects and choose verbs that agree in number
- To choose verbs with the correct number

USAGE

TEACHING (TIP)

Activity. To demonstrate to students that they may naturally recognize correct subject-verb agreement, you might put the following nonsense sentences on the chalkboard and ask students to select the correct "verb."

1. The shink (grimp, grimps) the vork. [*grimps*]

2. The shinks (grimp, grimps) the vork. [*grimp*]

Then, ask students to explain how they chose their "verbs." [*Students may say that plural nouns and singular third-person verbs commonly end in –s.*]

RESOURCES

Agreement of Subject and Verb

Practice

- *Grammar, Usage, and Mechanics,* pp. 113–114, 115–116
- *Language Workshop CD-ROM,* Lesson 10

Exercise 2

ALTERNATIVE LESSON
For a review of **Chapters 14** and **15**, have students find the following items in sentences 1, 4, 5, 6, and 7.

1. a noun clause [*how noodles are prepared*]

4. an infinitive phrase [*to prevent sticking*]

5. an adverb clause [*After the noodles have dried a little*]

6. a prepositional phrase [*from either wheat flour, called* udon, *or buckwheat flour, called* soba]

7. two past participles [*cooked, mixed*]

Meeting INDIVIDUAL NEEDS

INCLUSION

To reinforce subject-verb agreement, you might have students color-code sentence parts in sentences they copy or write themselves. For example, students might use yellow for subjects and blue for verbs. To help students focus on endings, have them indicate –s endings on nouns and verbs by using red. Remind them that if both the subject and the verb end in –s, something is probably wrong.

Continue the color-coding project by using a felt board with colored rectangles to represent specific sentence parts. Allow students to create sentences and identify sentence parts by placing words written on self-adhesive notes on the squares.

NOTE *As well as, along with, together with,* and *in addition to* are compound prepositions. Words in phrases beginning with compound prepositions do not affect the number of the subject or verb.

EXAMPLE **Anne,** together with her cousins, **is** backpacking in Nevada.

Exercise 2 Identifying Verbs That Agree in Number with Their Subjects

For each of the following sentences, choose the <u>verb</u> in parentheses that agrees with the subject.

EXAMPLE **1.** Did you know that people in Japan frequently (*eat, eats*) noodles?

1. eat

1. These pictures (*show, shows*) how noodles are prepared.
2. First, the noodle maker (*roll, rolls*) out the dough as thin as possible.
3. Then, the cook (*slice, slices*) the folded layers.
4. Next, the strands of noodles (*is, are*) separated and dusted with flour to prevent sticking.
5. After the noodles have dried a little, they (*go, goes*) into boiling water or broth to cook.
6. The Japanese (*enjoy, enjoys*) noodles made from either wheat flour, called *udon,* or buckwheat flour, called *soba.*
7. A dish of cooked noodles mixed with sauce, broth, fish, or vegetables (*makes, make*) a popular lunch.
8. Noodle shops all over Japan (*serves, serve*) a variety of noodle dishes.
9. These shops often (*resemble, resembles*) fast-food restaurants in the United States.
10. For lunch or a snack, customers at a noodle shop (*order, orders*) noodles with their favorite toppings.

MINI-LESSON

Forming Plurals. As a quick review, you may want to remind students of common ways plural nouns are formed in English:

- add –s (car, cars)
- add –es (fox, foxes)
- change letters in the word (woman, women)
- keep the same form (sheep, sheep)

Ask students to write in their journals examples of each type of plural form.

Exercise 3 Identifying Subjects and Verbs That Agree in Number

Identify the subject of each verb in parentheses in the following para-graph. Then, choose the form of the verb that agrees with the subject.

EXAMPLE   Units of measure sometimes [1] (*causes, cause*) confusion.

      1. *Units—cause*

Confusion among shoppers [1] (*is, are*) understandable because the traditional system for indicating quantities [2] (*makes, make*) shopping a guessing game. For example, the quantity printed on yogurt containers [3] (*is, are*) the number of ounces in a container. A shopper on the lookout for bargains [4] (*does, do*) not know whether liquid or solid measure is indicated. In addition, different brands of juice [5] (*shows, show*) the same quantity in different ways. A can labeled "twenty-four ounces" [6] (*contains, contain*) the same quantity as a can labeled "one pint eight ounces." Shoppers' confusion over such labeling, along with rising prices, [7] (*is, are*) a matter of concern to consumer groups. These groups believe that the metric system, in use in European countries, [8] (*clears, clear*) up most of the confusion. The units in the metric system [9] (*has, have*) fixed relationships to one another. As a result, consumer groups in this country [10] (*continues, continue*) to advocate our adopting this system of measurement.

Exercise 4 Choosing Verbs with the Correct Number

Each of the following sentences contains an italicized pair of verbs in parentheses. From each pair, choose the form of the verb that agrees with its subject.

EXAMPLE   1. Of all numbers, the number 12 (*is, are*) one of the most versatile.

      1. *is*

1. The even division of 12 by 1, 2, 3, 4, and 6 (*is, are*) possible.
2. Curiously, the sum of these five divisors (*is, are*) a square, 16; and their product is 144, which is the square of 12 itself.
3. When the Greek philosopher Plato devised his ideal state, the sys-tem of weights and measures (*were, was*) based on the number 12 because it could be evenly divided in so many ways.
4. To this day, many quantities in our lives (*involve, involves*) the number 12.

Agreement of Subject and Verb   **495**

Exercises   You may wish to use Exercise 3 as guided practice. Then, have students complete Exercise 4 as independent practice.

Timesaver

Encourage all students to color-code answers to an exercise when applica-ble. This method will allow them to focus on specific concepts when reviewing and will save you time checking papers.

Meeting INDIVIDUAL NEEDS

ENGLISH-LANGUAGE LEARNERS
Japanese and Korean. In these languages, objects often appear before their verbs. For example, the English sentence "Mary sees the boys" might be ordered "Boys Mary sees" or "Mary boys sees." To help students avoid lapsing into these pat-terns and making the verb agree with the object, you might stress that those just becoming comfortable with English write most sentences in subject-verb-object order.

Looking at Language

Many of the forms that were once used to show number, tense, person, and gender were dropped as Old English evolved into Modern English. In addition to the pronouns that became *I, we,* and *you,* there were once forms used to refer to only two people: *wit* (we two) and *git* (pro-nounced *yit,* "you two").

EXAMPLES
1. alphabet (alphabets)
2. box (boxes)

3. man (men)
4. Chinese (Chinese)

Students may want to use their words in a rhyme or a sentence.

5. The number of months in a year, inches in a foot, and items in a dozen (*is*, *are*) 12.
6. In our courts of law, 12 members of a jury (*decides*, *decide*) a defendant's guilt or innocence.
7. Each player in a game of checkers (*begin*, *begins*) with 12 pieces.
8. In bowling, 12 consecutive strikes (*give*, *gives*) you a perfect game.
9. The number of black pentagons on a soccer ball (*equal*, *equals*) the number of buttons on a push-button telephone—12.
10. Samuel Clemens even used this number as his pen name—the riverboat slang for 2 fathoms, or 12 feet, (*are*, *is*) *mark twain*!

TIPS & TRICKS

The words *one, thing,* and *body* are singular and so are the indefinite pronouns that contain these words.

EXAMPLES
Is [any]**one** late?

[Every]**body was** welcome.

[No]**thing has** been lost.

16d. The following indefinite pronouns are singular: *anybody, anyone, anything, each, either, everybody, everyone, everything, neither, nobody, no one, nothing, one, somebody, someone,* and *something.*

EXAMPLES **Each** of the athletes **runs** effortlessly.

Neither of the women **is** ready to start.

Someone was waving a large flag.

Does everyone who signed up **enjoy** playing tennis?

16e. The following indefinite pronouns are plural: *both, few, many,* and *several.*

EXAMPLES **Were both** of the games **postponed**?

Few that I know of **have qualified.**

Several of the runners **are exercising.**

16f. The indefinite pronouns *all, any, more, most, none,* and *some* may be singular or plural, depending on their meaning in a sentence.

These pronouns are singular when they refer to a singular word and plural when they refer to a plural word.

EXAMPLES **Some** of the test **is** hard. [*Some* refers to the singular noun *test.*]

Some of the questions **are** easy. [*Some* refers to the plural noun *questions.*]

All of the exhibit **is** open to the public.

All of the paintings **are** on display.

Cooperative Learning

To help students learn when the pronouns mentioned in **Rule 16f** are singular and when they are plural, divide the class into groups of three and have each group contribute six prepositional phrases beginning with *of.* Then, have groups trade phrases and make complete sentences by inserting the pronouns *some, all, more, most, any,* and *none* before the *of* phrases and using the pronouns as subjects. Have groups trade sentences to check for correct agreement.

496 Chapter 16   Agreement

MINI-LESSON

Prepositional Phrases. Familiarity with prepositional phrases should help simplify subject-verb agreement for students. Refer students to the list of prepositions on p. 400, and remind them that a prepositional phrase includes a preposition, a noun or pronoun as an object, and any modifiers of that object. Use the following example to illustrate that the verb must agree with the subject—not the object of the preposition.

  subj.   *prep.*   *obj.*   *v.*
This bag [of old clothes] is heavy.

Most of his routine **sounds** familiar.

Most of his jokes **sound** familiar.

Was any of the feedback positive?

Were any of the reviews positive?

The rice was eaten. **None is** left.

The potatoes were eaten. **None are** left.

More of the class **is** going to the archaeological dig.

More of the students **are** going to the archaeological dig.

Reference Note

For more information about **adjectives**, see page 382. For more about **correlative conjunctions**, see page 404.

Exercise 5 **Identifying Subjects and Verbs That Agree in Number**

Identify the subject of each verb in parentheses. Then, choose the form of the verb that agrees with that subject.

EXAMPLE   1. Several of the kittens (*has, have*) been adopted.

1. *Several—have*

1. Each of the comedians (*tries, try*) to outdo the other.
2. Somebody on the bus (*was, were*) whistling.
3. (*Is, Are*) all of the apples spoiled?
4. Neither of these books (*has, have*) an index.
5. (*Do, Does*) everybody in the class have a pencil?
6. Few of these jobs (*sounds, sound*) challenging.
7. (*Is, Are*) more of the vendors in the market?
8. She said that no one in the office (*leaves, leave*) early.
9. Both of her parents (*has, have*) offered us a ride.
10. (*Do, Does*) most of those CDs belong to her?

TIPS & TRICKS

Some of the words listed in **Rule 16d** can also be used as adjectives or as parts of correlative conjunctions: *each, either, neither, one.* Used as these parts of speech, such words cannot function as subjects.

Review A **Proofreading a Paragraph for Subject-Verb Agreement**

Identify the agreement errors in the following paragraph. Then, supply the correct form of each incorrect verb.

EXAMPLE   **[1]** On weekends, I often goes with my mother to antique shops.

1. *goes—go*

[1] Until recently, this hunt for old things were very boring.
[2] Then one day I noticed that a dusty shoe box full of antique postcards were sitting near me on a counter. [3] Soon I was flipping through the cards, and before you knows it, I had decided to start a

Reference Note

For more information about **indefinite pronouns**, see page 381. For information on distinguishing **indefinite pronouns from adjectives**, see page 382.

Meeting
INDIVIDUAL
NEEDS

USAGE

LEARNERS HAVING DIFFICULTY
To help students avoid making the verb agree with the object of a preposition rather than with the subject, you might ask them to use removable adhesive strips to cover prepositional phrases in sentences 1, 2, 4–6, 8, and 9 of **Exercise 5.** Remind them to find the subject by starting with the verb and asking *who* or *what* is doing the action.

Review A **Proofreading a Paragraph for Subject-Verb Agreement**

ANSWERS

1. were—was
2. were—was
3. knows—know

Agreement of Subject and Verb   **497**

Ask students to locate a piece of their own writing and highlight all prepositional phrases to determine whether such phrases have interfered with subject-verb agreement. Have students make any necessary corrections.

For additional information and practice, refer students to **Chapter 12: Parts of Speech Overview** and **Chapter 14: The Phrase.**

Review A Proofreading a Paragraph for Subject-Verb Agreement

ANSWERS continued

4. is—are
5. has—have
6. glows—glow
7. shows—show
8. are—is
9. are—is
10. was—were

The Compound Subject

Rules 16g–i *(pp. 498–500)*

OBJECTIVES

- To read aloud sentences with correct subject-verb agreement
- To choose correct verb forms in sentences with compound subjects

Relating to Literature

If your literature book contains Toni Cade Bambara's short story "My Delicate Heart Condition," have students look at the sixth sentence in the third paragraph. In her list of food vendors she passed, Bambara uses a number of conjunctions in close succession. Ask students to explain why the author might have chosen this construction. [*It makes the sentence sound like conversation, emphasizes the number of food vendors she passed, and creates a rhythmic pace.*] Ask students to read the sentence without the conjunctions, as though the items in the list were joined with commas, and explain how the effect changed. [*The rhythm is slower because the commas call for pauses.*]

Reference Note

For more information about **compound subjects,** see page 424.

postcard collection! [4] The cards in my collection is very precious to me. [5] Because I am interested in American history, I has chosen to specialize in cards showing American Indians. [6] On one of my cards, the flames of a campfire glows in front of several Plains Indian tepees under a colorful sunset. [7] Most of the postcards in my collection shows pictures of Native American leaders and warriors. [8] On my favorite card, a Navajo mother wrapped in beautiful blankets are posing with her baby on her back. [9] Collecting postcards are not an expensive hobby either. [10] Many of my cards was priced at a dollar or less.

The Compound Subject

A *compound subject* consists of two or more subjects that are joined by a conjunction and that have the same verb.

16g. Subjects joined by *and* generally take a plural verb.

The following compound subjects joined by *and* name more than one person, place, thing, or idea and take plural verbs.

EXAMPLES **George Lucas** and **Steven Spielberg make** movies. [Two persons make movies.]

Rhyme, rhythm, and **imagery help** poets express their feelings. [Three things help.]

Compound subjects that name only one person, thing, place, or idea take a singular verb.

EXAMPLES My **pen pal and best friend is** my cousin. [One person is my best friend and pen pal.]

Broccoli and melted cheese makes a tasty dish. [The one combination makes a dish.]

16h. Singular subjects joined by *or* or *nor* take a singular verb. Plural subjects joined by *or* or *nor* take a plural verb.

EXAMPLES After dinner, either **Anne** or **Tony loads** the dishwasher. [Anne loads the dishwasher *or* Tony loads the dishwasher.]

Neither the **coach** nor the **principal is** happy with the team's performance. [Neither *one* is happy.]

Either the **boys** or their **sisters take** the garbage out.

Neither the **dogs** nor the **cats come** when we call them.

RESOURCES

The Compound Subject

Practice

- *Grammar, Usage, and Mechanics,* pp. 117–118
- *Language Workshop CD-ROM,* Lesson 11

16i. When a singular subject and a plural subject are joined by *or* or *nor,* the verb agrees with the subject nearer the verb.

ACCEPTABLE   Neither the children nor their **mother was** ready for the trip.

ACCEPTABLE   Neither the mother nor her **children were** ready for the trip.

Oral Practice 1 **Using Verbs That Agree in Number with Their Subjects**

Read the following sentences aloud, stressing the italicized words.

1. The *books* on that shelf *need* dusting.
2. A *carton* of duck eggs *is* in the refrigerator.
3. *Tina and Betty are* first cousins once removed.
4. *Playing* games *or listening* to old records *is* an enjoyable way to spend a rainy Saturday.
5. *Several* of these insects *eat* through wood.
6. Every *one* of you *has* met my friend Phil.
7. Neither the *twins nor Greg enjoys* listening to that kind of music.
8. Both *Mr. and Mrs. Chen agree* to be chaperons for our spring dance.

Exercise 6 **Choosing Verbs That Agree in Number with Their Subjects**

Choose the correct form of the verb in parentheses in each of the following sentences.

EXAMPLE   **1.** In August, eager players and their fans (*looks, look*) forward to the start of football season.

  1. *look*

1. The coach and the player (*was, were*) surprised by the referee's call.
2. (*Is, Are*) Drew or Virgil going out for the pass?
3. Neither the quarterback nor the wide receiver (*hear, hears*) the referee's whistle.
4. The marching band or the pep squad (*has, have*) already performed.
5. (*Do, Does*) Christopher and Alexander enjoy football as much as Rachel does?
6. Either Albert or Selena (*leads, lead*) the student fight song.
7. The drum major and student council president (*is, are*) my older sister Janet.
8. The principal, the band director, and the gymnastics coach (*was, were*) proud of the half-time show.

STYLE **TIP**

Constructions like those shown with Rule 16i can sound awkward. Try rephrasing sentences to avoid such awkward constructions.

EXAMPLES
The **children were** not ready for the trip, and neither **was** their **mother.**

or

The **mother was** not ready for the trip, and neither **were** her **children.**

Meeting
INDIVIDUAL
NEEDS

USAGE

LEARNERS HAVING DIFFICULTY
Students who have trouble with compound subjects and their verbs should not be introduced to the finer points of compound subject-verb agreement until they have mastered the basics. Have students do **Oral Practice 1** as a group. Ask them whether any of the verbs sounded strange to them as they said them. If so, ask students to read these sentences again, omitting any prepositional phrases.

MODALITIES
Visual Learners. For **Exercise 6,** you might encourage students to make stick-figure diagrams to indicate how many people are mentioned in the subject of each sentence. (If no specific number is indicated, have students draw three figures.) Students should draw the stick figures with conjunctions placed appropriately between them. If the sentence contains a singular and a plural subject joined by *or* or *nor,* have students cross out the stick figure or figures representing the noun farther from the verb. Then, have students choose the correct verb and write it in the appropriate place in the diagram.

EXAMPLE
Either the boys or Jo (is, are) ordering fruit cups.

TEACHING TIP

Activity. For a different review approach, you might have students play Verb Cube. Start by writing the following pattern on a sheet of paper and folding and taping it to form a cube:

Be sure that each of the six sides of the cube shows a different combination of person and number. Ask a volunteer to roll the cube and call out the person and number appearing on the top of the cube. Allow students to call out a subject and verb with the given person and number, such as "I read." If an answer is incorrect, ask for a second response.

Other Problems in Agreement

Rules 16j–r *(pp. 500–506)*

OBJECTIVES

- To use *doesn't* and *don't* correctly in sentences

- To write sentences with collective nouns

- To read aloud sentences with correct subject-verb agreement

- To identify the subjects of sentences and choose verbs that agree in number with their subjects

1. aunts are

2. Has / or
3. Many / plan

4. grandparents / raise

5. salads / are

6. aides / librarian has

7. Macaroni and cheese makes

8. One / takes
9. Neither / was

10. puppies / sister are

9. Neither the coach nor the players (*has, have*) ever won a state championship game.
10. (*Was, Were*) the announcer or the referees prepared for the triumphant fans to rush the field?

Review B **Revising Sentences for Subject-Verb Agreement**

Revise each of the following sentences according to the directions given in parentheses. Change the verb in the sentence to agree with the subject as necessary.

EXAMPLE   1. The teachers have finished grading the tests. (Change *The teachers* to *Each of the teachers.*)
1. *Each of the teachers has finished grading the tests.*

1. My aunt is planning a trip to Nairobi National Park in Kenya. (Change *aunt* to *aunts.*)
2. Have Yoko and Juan already seen that movie? (Change *and* to *or.*)
3. Nobody on the team plans to attend the award ceremonies. (Change *Nobody* to *Many.*)
4. My grandmother, as well as my mother and aunts, raises tropical fish to earn extra money. (Change *grandmother* to *grandparents.*)
5. Most of the food for the party is in the refrigerator. (Change *food* to *salads.*)
6. Neither the librarian nor the aides have found the missing book. (Change *Neither the librarian nor the aides* to *Neither the aides nor the librarian.*)
7. Black bean soup and a tossed salad make an inexpensive meal. (Change *Black bean soup and a tossed salad* to *Macaroni and cheese.*)
8. Some of my friends take the bus to school. (Change *Some* to *One.*)
9. Few of the reporter's questions were answered in detail. (Change *Few* to *Neither.*)
10. The puppy playing with my sisters is two months old. (Change *puppy* to *puppies* and *sisters* to *sister.*)

Other Problems in Agreement

16j. The contractions *don't* and *doesn't* should agree with their subjects.

The word *don't* is the contraction of *do not.* Use *don't* with all plural subjects and with the pronouns *I* and *you.*

RESOURCES

Other Problems in Agreement
Practice

- *Grammar, Usage, and Mechanics,* pp. 119, 120, 121, 122, 123, 124
- *Language Workshop CD-ROM,* Lesson 12

EXAMPLES	I **don't** know.	They **don't** give up.
	You **don't** say.	**Don't** these shrink?
	We **don't** want to.	Apathetic people **don't** care.

The word *doesn't* is the contraction of *does not*. Use *doesn't* with all singular subjects except the pronouns *I* and *you*.

EXAMPLES	He **doesn't** know.	One **doesn't** give up.
	She **doesn't** say.	This **doesn't** shrink.
	It **doesn't** want to.	**Doesn't** Donna care?

Exercise 7 Using *Doesn't* and *Don't* Correctly

Write the correct form (*doesn't* or *don't*) for each of the following sentences.

EXAMPLE 1. _____ that bouquet of roses look great?

1. *Doesn't*

1. This apple _____ taste sweet.   **1.** doesn't
2. _____ he want to see the game?   **2.** Doesn't
3. These _____ impress me.   **3.** don't
4. One of the players _____ plan to go.   **4.** doesn't
5. _____ Jason and Tanya like the new band uniforms?   **5.** Don't
6. You and she _____ have time to play computer games now.   **6.** don't
7. The engine in that old pickup _____ start in winter.   **7.** doesn't
8. Tonio asked why we _____ want to go mountain biking.   **8.** don't
9. _____ several of those in the front window cost more than these in the fruit cart?   **9.** Don't
10. The international children's chorus is so marvelous that their new fans _____ want to leave the theater.   **10.** don't

16k. A collective noun may be either singular or plural, depending on its meaning in a sentence.

The singular form of a *collective noun* names a group of persons or things.

Collective Nouns				
army	class	family	group	public
assembly	club	fleet	herd	swarm
audience	committee	flock	jury	team

Agreement of Subject and Verb   **501**

STYLE TIP

Many people consider contractions informal. Therefore, it is generally best not to use contractions in formal speaking and writing.

Reference Note

For more information about **collective nouns,** see page 377.

Relating to Writing

Since **Rules 16j–r** each address a different aspect of agreement, you may want to discuss each rule individually as it applies to the class's writing or speech activities during the school year. The fact that titles of books, poems, and stories are treated as singular, for instance, may be mentioned when students prepare for their literary-analysis assignments in **Chapter 5** or as they write book reports.

Critical Thinking

Analysis. Students might ask why they need to study subject-verb agreement. In response, ask students how language usage affects perceptions of one's degree of knowledge or education. [*Answers might include the perceptions of ignorance or lack of education; students might also mention that certain usage might make a person identifiable as a member of a certain group.*]

You might organize students' responses on the board or overhead projector using the following chart.

Nonstandard	Perception	Standard
he don't	uneducated	he doesn't

Evaluation. Students might object to some of the negative perceptions associated with nonstandard or error-riddled usage. Ask them about the fairness of impressions based on the ways people use language. Encourage them to discuss ways to improve or overcome the situation.

Learning for Life

Continued on pp. 502–503

Writing a Business Letter. Although informal usage is acceptable in casual conversation, students must be able to write according to the rules of standard, formal usage when they need to make a good impression. Agreement errors are particularly noticeable, so written communication, especially letters of application, must be drafted carefully. To review agreement while building skills for real-life situations, have each student compose a letter for a job application.

Meeting
INDIVIDUAL
NEEDS

INCLUSION

Allow students to choose five nouns from a list like the following one, and have students use the nouns as subjects with both singular and plural verbs in oral sentences. Next, students should write these sentences and re-read them. Then, students can high-light singular verbs in one color and plural verbs in another.

army	committee	herd
assembly	family	jury
audience	fleet	public
class	flock	swarm
club	group	team

Exercise 8 Writing Sentences with Collective Nouns

ANSWERS

Sentences will vary. Here are some possibilities:

1. The club meets every Monday.
   The club are wearing their new T-shirts.

2. The team is ready to play.
   The team are comparing their statistics for the past season.

3. The audience has shown its approval by clapping.
   The audience have read their programs.

4. The flock is making its way south for the winter.
   The flock already have their winter feathers.

5. The modern family has its challenges.
   The family have finished their chores.

Reference Note

See page 511 for more about **pronoun-antecedent agreement** with **collective nouns.**

TIPS & TRICKS

To find the subject in a sentence in which the subject follows the verb, rearrange the sentence.

EXAMPLES

A **list** of addresses **is** here.

My **notebooks are** there.

Heather and **Chris are** where?

Use a plural verb with a collective noun when the noun refers to the individual parts or members of the group. Use a singular verb when the noun refers to the group as a unit.

EXAMPLES   The class **have completed** their projects. [*Class* is thought of as individuals.]

The class **has elected** its officers. [*Class* is thought of as a unit.]

Notice in the examples above that any pronoun referring to a collective noun has the same number as the noun. In the first example, *their* refers to *class*. In the second example, *its* refers to *class*.

Exercise 8 Writing Sentences with Collective Nouns

Select five collective nouns, and write five pairs of sentences that show clearly how the nouns you choose may be singular or plural.

EXAMPLE   1. *The jury is ready.*

The jury are still arguing among themselves.

16l. A verb agrees with its subject, but not necessarily with a predicate nominative.

EXAMPLES
The marching **bands are** the main attraction.
[S above *bands*, PN above *attraction*]

The main **attraction is** the marching bands.
[S above *attraction*, PN above *bands*]

16m. When the subject follows the verb, find the subject and make sure that the verb agrees with it.

The subject generally follows the verb in questions and in sentences that begin with *here* and *there*.

EXAMPLES   Here **is** a **list** of addresses.
Here **are** two **lists** of addresses.

There **is** my **notebook.**
There **are** my **notebooks.**

Where **is Heather**? Where **is Chris**?
Where **are Heather** and **Chris**?

Learning for Life

Enlist the help of guidance counselors for sample job applications. Then, suggest that students brainstorm in small groups about what to include in their letters. [*They might begin by introducing themselves and then outlining the reasons they believe they would be suitable candidates for employment.*]

After students have written their letters, pair them to work on identifying subjects

Contractions such as *here's*, *where's*, *how's*, and *what's* include the singular verb *is*. Use these contractions only with singular subjects.

NONSTANDARD	There's some facts on that topic in a chart.
STANDARD	There **are** some **facts** on that topic in a chart.
STANDARD	There**'s** a **chart** with some facts on that topic.

16n. An expression of an amount (a measurement, a percentage, or a fraction, for example) may be singular or plural, depending on how it is used.

A word or phrase stating an amount is singular when the amount is thought of as a unit.

EXAMPLES **Thirty dollars is** too much for a concert ticket.

Two hours is a long time to wait.

Sometimes, however, the amount is thought of as individual pieces or parts. If so, a plural verb is used.

EXAMPLES **Five dollars were scattered** on the desk.

Two hours—one before school and one after—**are** all I have for practice.

A fraction or a percentage is singular when it refers to a singular word and plural when it refers to a plural word.

EXAMPLES **Three fourths** of the pizza **is** gone.

Of these songs, **three fourths are** new.

16o. Some nouns that are plural in form take singular verbs.

EXAMPLES **Politics is** a controversial topic.

The **news** of the nominee **was** a surprise.

Rickets is a serious health problem in some countries.

NOTE Some nouns that end in –*s* take a plural verb even when they refer to a single item.

EXAMPLES The **scissors need** to be sharpened.

Were these **pants** on sale?

The **Olympics are** on television.

Reference Note

For more on **contractions,** see page 707.

Reference Note

For a discussion of **standard and nonstandard English,** see page 595.

—HELP—

If you do not know whether a noun that is plural in form is singular or plural in meaning, look up the word in a dictionary.

USAGE

Cooperative Learning

Because words that appear to be plural but take singular verbs can be troublesome, you might want to have the class brainstorm a list of such words. [*Examples include* mathematics, economics, physics, measles, genetics, *and* blues.]

Then you might assign small groups of students to create worksheets for the class to practice using these words. Encourage students to study exercises in this book as examples for writing the practice exercises. Students might choose to create a paragraph for revision or a multiple-choice format.

Have students evaluate their material and check for errors, but review the worksheets before groups copy and distribute them.

TEACHING (TIP)

Mnemonics. You might reinforce the note following **Rule 16o** by asking students what the examples *scissors* and *pants* have in common. [*They are pairs.*] In a short brainstorming session, ask students to suggest tricks they could use for remembering these exceptions. [*For example, "Pairs are plural."*] Ask students if they can think of other examples of pairs to test their new memory device(s). Conclude by suggesting that interested students develop their own mnemonic devices for other rules as they appear in the text.

and verbs and editing their letters for correctness and effectiveness. Encourage students to examine their usage, especially of verbs, very carefully; they should strive for variety and clarity.

When students have completed their editing, they should type their final drafts and file them for later use.

16p. Even when plural in form, the title of a creative work (such as a book, song, film, or painting), the name of an organization, or the name of a country or city generally takes a singular verb.

EXAMPLES **The Souls of Black Folk is** often **cited** as a classic of African American literature. [one book]

"Greensleeves" is an old English folk song. [one piece of music]

The United Nations was founded in 1945. [one organization]

White Plains is home to several colleges. [one city]

Review C **Using Titles That Agree with Verbs in Number**

Terence and Janeese are at the video rental store deciding what movies they will rent for the weekend. In the following sentences, wherever *TITLE* appears, supply the name of one of the movies shown here or of a movie of your own choice. Then, choose the <u>correct form of the verb</u> to complete each sentence.

Movie titles will vary.

EXAMPLE   1. Look, Terence. TITLE (*is, are*) supposed to be very funny.

1. Horse Feathers—*is*

1. Terence: According to LaShonda, TITLE and TITLE (*is,* <u>*are*</u>) very exciting.
2. Janeese: Well, TITLE or TITLE (<u>*sounds,*</u> *sound*) more interesting to me. Let's ask the clerk.
3. Terence: Sir, (<u>*is,*</u> *are*) TITLE in stock?
4. Clerk: I'm afraid not, but TITLE (*entertain,* <u>*entertains*</u>) almost everyone, and you might enjoy it.
5. Terence: Janeese, TITLE (<u>*is,*</u> *are*) a fairly recent movie, but TITLE (*are,* <u>*is*</u>) an old-timer.
6. Janeese: Well, I like animated films, and TITLE (*fit,* <u>*fits*</u>) that category.
7. Clerk: If you ask me, TITLE (*beat,* <u>*beats*</u>) every other film we have, but someone just rented my last copy.
8. Janeese: Both TITLE and TITLE (<u>*are,*</u> *is*) good, but I've seen each of them twice.
9. Terence: (*Isn't, <u>Aren't</u>*) TITLE any good? I'm surprised.
10. Janeese: All right, here's my vote. TITLE (<u>*is,*</u> *are*) tonight's movie, and either TITLE or TITLE (<u>*is,*</u> *are*) the movie for Saturday night's party.

USAGE

16q. Subjects preceded by *every* or *many a* take singular verbs.

EXAMPLES   **Every** homeowner and storekeeper **has joined** the cleanup drive sponsored by the town council.

Many a litterbug **was surprised** by the stiff fines.

16r. When the relative pronoun *that, which,* or *who* is the subject of an adjective clause, the verb in the adjective clause agrees with the word to which the relative pronoun refers.

EXAMPLES   This is the store **that has** the discount sale. [*That* refers to the singular noun *store.*]

London, **which is** the capital of England, is the largest city in Europe. [*Which* refers to the singular noun *London.*]

The Garcias, **who live** next door, are going with us to the lake. [*Who* refers to the plural noun *Garcias.*]

Reference Note

For more about **relative pronouns,** see page 380. For more about **adjective clauses,** see page 473.

Oral Practice 2 **Using Subject-Verb Agreement**

Read each of the following sentences aloud, stressing the italicized words.

1. Of the inhabitants, *two thirds are* registered to vote.
2. *Many a* writer and scholar *has* puzzled over that problem.
3. *Is economics* taught at your high school?
4. *Are* there any green *apples* in that basket?
5. *Romeo and Juliet has* been made into a ballet, a Broadway musical, and several movies.
6. *Two weeks is* more than enough time to write a report.
7. My *family is* planning to hold its reunion in October.
8. My *family are* planning their schedules now.

Exercise 9 **Identifying Subjects and Verbs That Agree in Number**

Identify the subject of each verb in parentheses. Then, choose the form of the verb that agrees with the subject.

EXAMPLE   1. (*Do, Does*) Meals on Wheels deliver in your neighborhood?

1. Meals on Wheels—*Does*

1. The class (*has, have*) chosen titles for their original plays.
2. First prize (*was, were*) two tickets to Hawaii.

3. <u>Three quarters</u> of the movie (*was*, *were*) over when we arrived at the theater.

4. <u>Rattlesnakes</u> (*was*, <u>*were*</u>) the topic of last week's meeting of the hiking club.

5. (*Has*, *Have*) every <u>student</u> in the class memorized a poem to present for the oral interpretation contest?

6. *Crime and Punishment* (<u>*is*</u>, *are*) a world-famous novel.

7. <u>Two thirds</u> of the missing books (*was*, <u>*were*</u>) returned to the downtown branch of the library.

8. <u>Mathematics</u> (<u>*is*</u>, *are*) an important part of many everyday activities.

9. Where (*is*, <u>*are*</u>) the <u>paragraphs</u> you wrote?

10. <u>Four weeks</u> (<u>*is*</u>, *are*) enough time to rehearse the play.

Review D Identifying Verbs That Have the Correct Number

Choose the <u>correct form of the verb</u> in parentheses in each of the following sentences.

EXAMPLE   1. Fifty pesos (*was*, *were*) a great price for that carving.
          1. *was*

1. Mumps (<u>*is*</u>, *are*) a common childhood disease that causes swelling in glands in the neck.

2. Politics (<u>*is*</u>, *are*) always a popular subject both to debate and to study at college.

3. Not one of the ushers (*know*, <u>*knows*</u>) where the lounge is.

4. The team (<u>*is*</u>, *are*) on a winning streak.

5. Carol, as well as Inés, (*write*, <u>*writes*</u>) a weekly column for the *East High Record*.

6. "Beauty and the Beast" (<u>*is*</u>, *are*) a folk tale that exists in many different cultures.

7. Ten pounds (<u>*is*</u>, *are*) too much weight for a young child to carry in a backpack.

8. It is difficult to concentrate when there (*is*, <u>*are*</u>) radios and stereos blasting away.

9. (*Has*, *Have*) either of you read the book or seen the movie version of *To Kill a Mockingbird*?

10. In most situation comedies, there (*is*, <u>*are*</u>) a very wise character, a very foolish character, and a very lovable character.

Agreement of Pronoun and Antecedent

A pronoun usually refers to a noun or another pronoun that comes before it. The word that a pronoun refers to is called its *antecedent.*

16s. A pronoun should agree in number and gender with its antecedent.

(1) A pronoun that refers to a singular antecedent is singular in number.

EXAMPLES   **Daniel Defoe** wrote **his** first book at the age of fifty-nine.

The **elephant** is a long-lived animal. **It** grows **its** tusks at maturity.

(2) A pronoun that refers to a plural antecedent is plural in number.

EXAMPLES   Reliable **cars** make **their** owners happy.

We walk **our** dogs daily.

A few singular pronouns have forms that indicate the gender of the antecedent. Masculine pronouns refer to males; feminine pronouns refer to females. Neuter pronouns refer to places, things, ideas, and, often, to animals.

Masculine	Feminine	Neuter
he	she	it
him	her	it
his	hers	its
himself	herself	itself

Often, when the antecedent of a personal pronoun is another kind of pronoun, a word in a phrase following the antecedent will help to determine gender.

EXAMPLES   **One** of the **women** designs **her** own costumes.

Each of the **boys** rode **his** bicycle to school.

Neither of the **kittens** has opened **its** eyes yet.

Reference Note

For a further discussion of **antecedents**, see page 378.

USAGE

Agreement of Pronoun and Antecedent

Rules 16s–z *(pp. 507–512)*

O B J E C T I V E

- To identify antecedents and write pronouns that agree with them

Relating to Literature

If your literature book includes "The Necklace" by Guy de Maupassant, you might use the selection to point out the literary use of masculine and feminine pronouns. This short story, which explores the relationship between a husband and wife, emphasizes the use of personal pronouns over names. Ask students why the author might have chosen to use pronouns so extensively. [*The use of* he *and* she *emphasizes the main characters' viewpoints, presenting a nineteenth-century version of "he said, she said"; eliminating most of the proper names makes the story universal but also personal.*]

Meeting
INDIVIDUAL
NEEDS

LEARNERS HAVING DIFFICULTY

To help students focus on singular indefinite pronouns, write these three lists on the chalkboard and ask students to tell what the words in each list have in common. [*The words in the first list all contain* one; *the words in the second list all contain* body; *and the words in the third list all contain* thing.]

LIST 1	LIST 2	LIST 3
one	everybody	nothing
everyone	somebody	everything
anyone	nobody	anything
someone	anybody	something
no one		

You might want to have students work in pairs to write sentences using each word in the list. Students could draw stick-figure illustrations of these singular pronouns.

Once students have written their sentences, they might want to compose five-sentence worksheets for their classmates to use as practice. Students may want to use a multiple-choice format, giving both singular and plural verb choices.

STYLE   TIP

In many cases you can avoid the awkward *his or her* construction by rephrasing the sentence and using the plural form of the pronoun or by substituting an article (*a, an,* or *the*).

EXAMPLES

The **passengers** will be shown where **they** can check in.

A **person** should choose **a** college carefully.

STYLE   TIP

In informal conversation, plural personal pronouns are often used to refer to singular antecedents that can be either masculine or feminine. Such usage is becoming increasingly common in writing and may someday become acceptable as standard written English. For now, however, avoid such usage in formal writing and speaking.

INFORMAL

Everybody has packed their lunch in an insulated cooler.

FORMAL

Everybody has packed **his or her** lunch in an insulated cooler.

When a singular antecedent may be either masculine or feminine, use both the masculine and the feminine forms, connected by *or*.

EXAMPLES   **Each passenger** will be shown where **he or she** can check in.

A **person** should choose **his or her** college carefully.

If you talk on the phone with **someone** you don't know well, speak clearly to **him or her.**

16t. Some indefinite pronouns are singular, and some are plural. Other indefinite pronouns can be either singular or plural, depending on their meaning in a sentence.

(1) Use a singular pronoun to refer to *anybody, anyone, anything, each, either, everybody, everyone, everything, neither, nobody, no one, nothing, one, somebody, someone,* or *something.*

EXAMPLES   **Either** of the girls can bring **her** CD player.

Neither of the workmen forgot **his** tool belt.

Did **each** of the mares recognize **her** own foal?

Someone left **his or her** hat on the field.

One of the parakeets escaped from **its** cage.

NOTE   Sometimes the meaning of *everyone* or *everybody* is clearly plural. In informal situations, the plural pronoun should be used.

CONFUSING   Everyone laughed when he or she saw the clowns.
INFORMAL   **Everyone** laughed when **they** saw the clowns.

In formal situations, it is best to revise the sentence so that it is both clear and grammatically correct.

FORMAL   The **audience** laughed when **they** saw the clowns.

(2) Use a plural pronoun to refer to *both, few, many,* and *several.*

EXAMPLES   **Both** of the sisters recited **their** lines.

Few of the animals willingly leave **their** natural habitat.

Many of the volunteers shared **their** coats with the flood victims.

Several of the audience were late getting to **their** seats.

(3) The indefinite pronouns *all, any, more, most, none,* and *some* may be singular or plural, depending on their meaning in a sentence.

EXAMPLES **All** of the water has melted; **it** is pooling in the valley.

All of the streams are full; **they** are rushing torrents.

Most of her cooking tastes good. In fact, **it** is delicious.

Most of the dishes she cooks taste good. **They** contain unusual spices.

16u. Use a singular pronoun to refer to two or more singular antecedents joined by *or* or *nor.*

EXAMPLES Neither **Richard nor Bob** distinguished **himself** in the finals.

Paula or Janet will present **her** views on the subject.

16v. Use a plural pronoun to refer to two or more antecedents joined by *and.*

EXAMPLES **Mona and Janet** left early because **they** had to be home before ten o'clock.

Mom and Dad celebrated **their** twentieth wedding anniversary yesterday.

16w. The number of a relative pronoun (such as *who, which,* or *that*) is determined by its antecedent.

EXAMPLES Aretha is one **friend who** always keeps **her** word. [*Who* refers to the singular noun *friend.* Therefore, the singular form *her* is used to agree with *who.*]

Many who volunteer **their** time find **their** experiences rewarding. [*Who* refers to the plural pronoun *Many.* Therefore, the plural form *their* is used to agree with *who.*]

Review E **Identifying Antecedents and Writing Pronouns**

Each of the sentences on the following page contains a blank where a pronoun should be. Complete each sentence by inserting at least one pronoun that agrees with its antecedent. Identify the antecedent.

EXAMPLE 1. Carmen and Tina said that _____ thought my idea was sensible.

1. *they—Carmen and Tina*

| S T Y L E ✏ T I P |

Sentences like those shown under Rule 16u can sound awkward if the antecedents are of different genders. If a sentence sounds awkward, revise it to avoid the problem.

AWKWARD
Ben or Maya will read his or her report.

REVISED
Ben will read **his** report, or **Maya** will read **hers.**

Reference Note

For more information on **relative pronouns in adjective clauses,** see page 473.

Meeting
INDIVIDUAL
NEEDS

ENGLISH-LANGUAGE LEARNERS

General Strategies. You may want to have students relate pronoun-antecedent agreement in English to agreement in their native languages by asking them how pronouns are used in those languages. Ask whether the pronouns indicate gender or number. If someone mentions that in Spanish it is possible to identify the gender of a group (as in *ellos hablan,* "the males speak," or *ellas hablan,* "the females speak"), note that in English the pronoun *they* is used for both males and females in the third-person plural.

Critical Thinking

Analysis. You might ask students to think about how pronoun-antecedent agreement compares to subject-verb agreement. They might consider what factors make a pronoun agree with its antecedent. [*for all personal pronouns: person and number; for third-person singular pronouns: gender*] Then, ask what factors are considered in making a subject agree with its verb. [*person and number*]

Critical Thinking

Metacognition. As a concluding activity and review, ask students to make a chart listing their own most frequent or noticeable agreement errors.

SAMPLE CHART

INCORRECT	CORRECT
There's two buildings.	There are two buildings.

Then, ask them to formulate a plan for eliminating errors. [*For example:* To find the true subject, look after the verb when an introductory *there* is used.]

Meeting
INDIVIDUAL NEEDS

MULTIPLE INTELLIGENCES

Logical-Mathematical and Intrapersonal Intelligences. So that students can keep track of their progress, you might suggest that they count and record the number of times per day or week they make their most frequent mistakes. Then, they can chart their progress for a chosen length of time. Students might use a simple tick chart to tally their errors.

TIME	M	T	W	TH	F	WKLY TOTAL
Errors	////	//	////	///	/	ᵗᴴᴸ ᵗᴴᴸ ////

After students have collected their data, they can plot their progress with a bar or line graph.

TECHNOLOGY TIP

Students could also chart or graph their progress using a computer spreadsheet.

1. him
2. they

3. she

4. their

5. his or her
6. their

7. its
8. her
9. he or she

10. themselves

---HELP---

Some sentences in Review F may contain more than one error in agreement.

1. Please give me Ronald's address so that I can send _____ a letter.
2. The uniform company finally sent Jerome and Ken the shirts that _____ had ordered.
3. Claire or Ida will go to the nursing home early so that _____ can help the residents into the lounge.
4. Several of the volunteers contributed _____ own money to buy the shelter a new van.
5. Did each of the contestants answer _____ questions correctly?
6. Both of the girls packed _____ suitcases carefully for the trip to Canada and Alaska.
7. Every car at the service center had _____ oil changed.
8. Neither of the women withdrew _____ job application.
9. Anyone can belong to the International Students Association if _____ is interested.
10. Neither the coaches nor the players blamed _____ for the loss.

Review F   Proofreading Sentences for Pronoun-Antecedent Agreement

Many of the following sentences contain errors in agreement between pronouns and their antecedents. Identify each of these errors, and give the form of the pronoun that agrees with its antecedent. If a sentence is already correct, write *C*.

EXAMPLE   1. All of us need to choose a topic for his or her reports.
            1. *his or her—our*

1. George has chosen Walt Disney as the subject of his report.   1. C
2. Several others in our class have also submitted his or her topics.   2. their
3. Dominic, one of the Perrone twins, has chosen Alfred Hitchcock as their subject.   3. his
4. Neither George nor Dominic will have difficulty finding material for their report.   4. his
5. Each of these moviemakers has left their mark on the world.   5. his
6. Either Minnie or Sue offered their help with proofreading.   6. her
7. Each of the boys refused politely, saying that they would proofread the report on their own.   7. he / his
8. Does everyone, including George and Dominic, know that they must assemble facts, not opinions?   8. he or she
9. Neither George nor Dominic should forget to include amusing anecdotes about their subject.   9. his
10. Nobody likes to discover that they just read a dull report about an interesting subject.   10. he or she

16x. A collective noun is singular when it refers to the group as a unit and plural when it refers to the individual members of the group.

EXAMPLES   The **pride** of lions is hunting **its** prey on the savanna. [*Pride* is thought of as a unit.]

The **pride** of lions are licking **their** chops in anticipation. [*Pride* is thought of as separate individuals.]

NOTE Sometimes the number of a collective noun depends on the meaning the writer intends.

EXAMPLES   The swim **team** proudly displayed **their** trophies. [The members of the team displayed individual trophies.]

The swim **team** proudly displayed **its** trophy. [The team as a whole displayed a shared trophy.]

Reference Note

For information on **subject-verb agreement** with **collective nouns,** see page 501. For a list of **collective nouns,** see page 377.

16y. An expression of an amount (a measurement, a percentage, or a fraction, for example) may be singular or plural, depending on how it is used.

A word or phrase stating an amount is singular when the amount is thought of as a unit.

EXAMPLES   **Ten minutes** isn't long; **it** will go by quickly.

Here is **five dollars.** Is **it** enough?

Sometimes, however, the amount is thought of as individual pieces or parts. If so, a plural verb is used.

EXAMPLES   **Ten** of the twenty minutes were wasted; we spent **them** arguing.

Five dollars were counterfeit, weren't **they**?

A fraction or a percentage is singular when it refers to a singular word and plural when it refers to a plural word.

EXAMPLES   **One third** of the total is yours. Would you like **it** in ones?

One third of the birds have left. Are **they** migrating?

16z. Singular pronouns are used to refer to some nouns that are plural in form.

EXAMPLES   Aunt Jean rarely watches the **news** because she finds **it** depressing.

USAGE

Agreement of Pronoun and Antecedent   **511**

The **United States** celebrated **its** bicentennial in 1976.

After Chad finished reading **Mules and Men,** he wrote a report on **it.**

Future Farmers of America meets tomorrow to plan **its** convention.

Marble Falls is in Texas; **it** is north of San Antonio and Blanco.

NOTE Plural pronouns are used to refer to some nouns that end in –s but that refer to a single item.

EXAMPLES I'll buy these **pants** because **they** fit better and are a better value than **those.**

If you're looking for the **scissors,** you'll find **them** in the third drawer on the left.

Review G **Agreement of Pronoun and Antecedent**

Some of the following sentences contain errors in pronoun-antecedent agreement. Identify each incorrect pronoun, and give the pronoun that agrees with its antecedent. If a sentence is already correct, write *C.*

EXAMPLE 1. Several people in the neighborhood have expressed his or her views.

1. *his or her—their*

1. they
2. C
3. its
4. it
5. its
6. his or her

7. C

8. his or her
9. they're
10. is

1. The school finally sent Michael and Kathryn the results of the tests he or she had taken.
2. On the Serengeti Plain, a cheetah enjoys its freedom.
3. After World War II, the United States gave most of their foreign aid to help Europe rebuild.
4. Five percent of the profit will be donated, won't they?
5. The U.S. Olympic team won their third gold medal.
6. A person with a health problem should always select the best doctor for their needs.
7. During *ferragosto,* or August holiday, the Italian Parliament takes its recess.
8. Each of the mimes gave their impression of a chimney sweep.
9. I like the way the pants look; also, at that price, it's a great bargain.
10. *War and Peace* are the most famous of Leo Tolstoy's works.

Chapter Review

A. Identifying Verbs that Agree in Number with Their Subjects

For each of the following sentences, choose the correct form of the verb in parentheses.

1. (*Doesn't, Don't*) she know when she'll be back?
2. Most of my jewelry (*was, were*) lost in the fire.
3. For better or for worse, politics (*play, plays*) an important part in all our lives.
4. Many ideas in her book (*requires, require*) a great deal of thought.
5. (*Has, Have*) Lisa and Haruo been paid for their work?
6. (*Is, Are*) everybody finished with the project?
7. Neither the president nor the vice-president (*goes, go*) to every meeting.
8. There (*has, have*) been many accidents at that intersection.
9. Three fourths of the apartments (*was, were*) rented before the building was completed.
10. Our class president, with the help of several others, usually (*sets, set*) the agenda for the meeting.
11. Nobody here (*has, have*) the correct time.
12. A herd of cattle (*is, are*) by the river.
13. Some of Pat's nacho recipes (*contains, contain*) very hot spices.
14. One of the owners (*work, works*) at the store on weekends.
15. Physics (*is, are*) a challenging and fascinating subject.
16. Where (*do, does*) the scissors go?
17. The main attraction in the parade (*is, are*) the student floats.
18. Van Gogh's *The Potato Eaters* (*show, shows*) a Dutch farm family at dinner.
19. If two thirds of the people (*vote, votes*) for the measure, it will become law.
20. Here (*is, are*) a new football and a helmet for your birthday.

B. Proofreading Sentences for Subject-Verb Agreement

Each of the following sentences contains an error in agreement. Identify each incorrect verb, and supply the correct form.

21. was

21. Every man and woman were questioned by the police.

Chapter Review **513**

22. was	**22.** The pile of papers were scattered by the wind.
23. her	**23.** Each of the girls brought their own tennis balls.
24. are	**24.** Some of the sheep from that flock is lost.
25. doesn't	**25.** Your explanation don't really help that much.
26. is	**26.** Most of the poetry are in English.
27. was	**27.** Each of the students were happy the exam was over.
28. has	**28.** Many a student have been grateful for being in Ms. Makowski's history class.
29. his or her	**29.** Someone forgot their umbrella.
30. are	**30.** Either Bill or his uncles is waiting downstairs.

C. Identifying Antecedents and Writing Pronouns

Each of the following sentences contains a blank where a pronoun should be. Complete each sentence by writing a pronoun that agrees with its antecedent. Identify the antecedent.

31. they	**31.** Uncle Harry and Aunt Nell said that _____ would be happy to contribute to the silent auction.
32. him	**32.** Can I have Trevor's phone number, so that I can tell _____ about the ceremony?
33. its	**33.** Every horse in the stable had _____ own bucket of oats.
34. his	**34.** Louis Pasteur, the great French scientist, made _____ first scientific discovery at the age of 26.
35. she	**35.** Teresa or Sandra will go to the airport early so that _____ will be sure to meet Jorge's plane.
36. they	**36.** Patsy and Debbie will be late because _____ forgot the appointment.
37. his	**37.** Neither of the men changed _____ mind on the issue.
38. their	**38.** Because of the strike, several of the drivers had to change _____ own oil.
39. their	**39.** Both Henry James and his brother William became famous through _____ writings.
40. themselves	**40.** Neither the film crew nor the writers blamed _____ for the mistake.

D. Proofreading a Paragraph for Subject-Verb and Pronoun-Antecedent Agreement

For each error in the following paragraph, identify the incorrect verb or pronoun and supply the correct form.

---

[41] CDs of popular music is getting very expensive. [42] The economics of this situation have hit young people right in the wallet! [43] Few has enough money to buy all the best new songs. [44] A teenager will have to use their brains if they want to save money in the music store. [45] Several of my friends buy an audiotape instead of a CD if he or she want to save a little money. [46] Danny, one of my best friends, take another approach. [47] His favorite group are The Avengers, and he tapes every new Avengers song straight off the radio. [48] He don't have to pay for anything but the blank tape. [49] Copying tapes is perfectly legal if all the music you record are just for your own use. [50] Kristi and Selena, two of my friends, save as much as four or five dollars a tape by buying her tapes on sale.

41. are
42. has
43. have
44. his or her / he or she wants
45. they
46. takes
47. is
48. doesn't
49. is
50. their

Writing Application
Using Agreement in a Paragraph

Subject-Verb Agreement   During Career Day, the school counselor asks you to write a paragraph beginning with this statement: "People I know work at a variety of jobs." Using subjects and verbs that agree, describe the jobs of three people you know.

Prewriting   Start by listing at least three people you know who have different kinds of jobs. Think of action verbs that describe what these people do. For example, instead of saying "Mrs. Ruíz is a chemistry teacher," say "Mrs. Ruíz teaches chemistry."

Writing   As you write your first draft, be sure to include some details that clearly show how the jobs differ from one another.

Revising   Check your rough draft to be sure that the examples you have chosen show a variety of jobs. If not, you may want to replace some examples or add new ones. Make sure each job is described vividly.

Publishing   Identify the subjects and verbs in each sentence, and be sure that they agree. Read your paragraph aloud to help you recognize any errors in usage, spelling, and punctuation. Be sure that you have capitalized all proper names. Your class might photocopy and display their paragraphs during career day. With the permission of the people you wrote about, your class could also prepare a job information directory.

Writing Application

(p. 515)

OBJECTIVE

■ **To write a description using correct subject-verb agreement**

Writing Application

Tip. To help students think of details for their paragraphs, have them respond to the following questions for each person they describe.

1. What job does the person do?

2. How does he or she do the job?

3. What kinds of tools does he or she use?

4. Where does he or she work?

Scoring Rubric. While you will want to pay particular attention to students' use of subject-verb agreement, you will also want to evaluate the students' overall writing performance. You may want to give a split score to indicate development and clarity of the composition as well as usage skills.

Critical Thinking

Synthesis. Making a list of differences might be a good way for students to prepare descriptions that clearly define each job. Some possible areas of difference are location, clientele/patrons, finished product, co-workers, amount of travel involved, and amount of time worked.

USAGE

CHAPTER

17

Using Verbs Correctly
Principal Parts, Tense, Voice, Mood

PREVIEWING THE CHAPTER

■ The first part of this chapter covers the principal parts of verbs, concentrating on the correct use of regular and irregular verbs. The second part deals with tense and tense consistency. The third explains active and passive voice, six troublesome verbs, and mood.

■ The chapter concludes with a **Chapter Review** including a **Writing Application** feature that asks students to write instructions using verbs correctly.

■ For help in integrating this chapter with composition chapters, see the **Teaching Strands** chart on pp. T371A–T371B.

USING THE DIAGNOSTIC PREVIEW

■ While many students at this level will know the principal parts of common irregular verbs, some will still have difficulty with troublesome verbs such as *lie* and *lay*. You may want to have students who are unable to demonstrate mastery read the definitions of the troublesome verbs and work the exercises together. Even though students may show mastery on the preview, they may make verb errors in their writing. If students have this problem, encourage them to circle all the verbs in their sentences when proofreading and to check each one for appropriate tense, consistency, and form.

┌HELP┐

Some sentences in the Diagnostic Preview have more than one incorrect verb.

Diagnostic Preview

Proofreading Sentences for Correct Verb Forms

Read the following sentences. If a sentence contains an incorrect or awkward verb form, write the correct form or revise the sentence. If a sentence is already correct, write *C*.

EXAMPLES 1. I have always wanted a pet.

1. C

2. As a child, I use to dream about having a dog or cat.

2. *used*

1. asked/said *or* ask/say

2. sitting/spotted

3. folded/hopped

4. saw

5. lying

6. reached

7. C

8. took

1. Every time I ask my parents, they said, "No, not in an apartment."
2. One day last year, I was setting on the front steps reading the newspaper when I spot an ad for a female ferret.
3. Deciding to investigate, I fold the paper, hop on my bike, and rode to the pet shop that had placed the ad.
4. When I walked into the store, I seen the ferret right away.
5. She was laying in a cardboard box on top of the counter.
6. I told the owner I wanted to hold her, and he reaches into the box.
7. When he withdrew his hand, the ferret was holding on to his finger with what looked like very sharp teeth.
8. I cautiously reached out and taked the ferret's hindquarters in my cupped hands.

Planning
■ *One-Stop Planner CD-ROM* 💿

Practice and Extension
■ *Grammar, Usage, and Mechanics*, p. 137
■ *Developmental Language Skills*, pp. 69–82

Internet
■ go.hrw.com (keyword: EOLang)

Evaluation and Assessment
■ *Chapter Tests*, Ch. 17
■ *Chapter Tests in Standardized Test Formats*, Ch. 17
■ *Test Generator (One-Stop Planner)* 💿

9. The rest of her long body poured slowly into my hands until she was sitting on her haunches.

10. She looked up at me and suddenly clamps her teeth on my thumb.

11. The ferret done it to show me who was boss.

12. I should have knowed then that my troubles had just began.

13. I ran all the way home and persuaded my parents to let me keep the ferret on a trial basis.

14. I had already give her a name—Ferris the Ferret—and I lose no time rushing back to the pet shop.

15. When I come home with Ferris, I sit a dish of cat food in front of her.

16. She stuck her snout into the dish and ate greedily.

17. After she had went into each room in the apartment, she choosed the top of the TV as her special place.

18. When my parents objected, I made a cardboard house with two entry holes and set it in a corner of my bedroom.

19. Ferris sniffed around her new home; then she goes in and laid down for a nap.

20. For the next few days, Ferris spent her time either napping or nipping.

21. She always attackted me when I least expected it.

22. Once, as she lies on my desk while I am studying, she suddenly locked her teeth onto my earlobe.

23. I was so startled that I jump up quickly, and Ferris wound up laying on the floor with a look that makes me feel guilty.

24. The next day the bad news was gave to me by my parents: Ferris had to go back to the pet shop.

25. I no longer want a pet ferret, but I have wrote to the local zoo-keeper to ask about snakes.

9. C
10. clamped
11. did
12. known/begun
13. C
14. given/lost
15. came/set
16. C
17. gone/chose
18. C
19. went / lay
20. C
21. attacked
22. lay/was
23. jumped/lying/made
24. given
25. written

TEACHING **TIP**

Diagnostic Preview. You may wish to accept answers in either the active or passive voice for sentence 24.

The Principal Parts of Verbs

The four basic forms of a verb are called the *principal parts* of the verb.

17a. The four principal parts of a verb are the *base form,* the *present participle,* the *past,* and the *past participle.*

The principal parts of the verb *ring,* for example, are *ring* (base form), *ringing* (present participle), *rang* (past), and *rung* (past participle). These principal parts are used to form all of the different verb tenses.

HELP

Some teachers refer to the base form as the *infinitive.* Follow your teacher's directions when labeling this form.

The Principal Parts of Verbs **517**

Regular Verbs

Rule 17b *(pp. 518–519)*

OBJECTIVE

- To pronounce the past and past participle forms of regular verbs correctly

Meeting
INDIVIDUAL
NEEDS

ENGLISH-LANGUAGE LEARNERS
Spanish. Remind Spanish speakers that the English present participle suffix *–ing* is equivalent to the Spanish *–ando* and *–iendo* (e.g., *hablando,* "speaking," from *hablar* "to speak" and *comiendo,* "eating," from *comer* "to eat") and that the English past participle suffix *–(e)d* is equivalent to the Spanish *–ado* and *–ido* (e.g., *marcado,* "marked," and *adquirido,* "acquired"). In English and in Spanish, the past participle can also be used as an adjective.

General Strategies. Provide an exercise to help students who mistakenly use the present tense form instead of the past tense, especially with an expression of time, as in "Last week I pass my test." First, provide a reading passage and have students underline all the *–ed* forms. Second, read a short passage aloud and have them count the *–ed* forms they hear. Finally, ask them to pick out words that indicate time and are not verbs.

Reference Note

For more about how **participles and helping verbs** work together, see page 449.

Reference Note

See page 735 for more on **spelling words when adding suffixes.**

STYLE TIP

A few regular verbs have an alternate past form ending in *–t.* For example, the past form of *burn* is *burned* or *burnt.* Both forms are correct.

EXAMPLES   The bells **ring** every day.   The bells **rang** at noon.
            The bells **are ringing** now.   The bells **have rung** already.

Notice that the tenses made from the present participle and past participle contain helping verbs, such as *am, is, are, has,* and *have.*

Regular Verbs

17b. A *regular verb* forms its past and past participle by adding *–d* or *–ed* to the base form.

Base Form	Present Participle	Past	Past Participle
ask	[is] asking	asked	[have] asked
use	[is] using	used	[have] used
suppose	[is] supposing	supposed	[have] supposed
risk	[is] risking	risked	[have] risked

The words *is* and *have* are included in the preceding chart because helping verbs are used with the present participle and past participle to form some tenses.

NOTE The present participle of most regular verbs ending in *–e* drops the *–e* before adding *–ing.*

EXAMPLE   smile + ing = smil**ing**

One common error in the use of the past and the past participle forms is to leave off the *–d* or *–ed* ending.

NONSTANDARD   We use to play soccer.
    STANDARD   We **used** to play soccer.

NONSTANDARD   She was suppose to come home early.
    STANDARD   She was **supposed** to come home early.

Another common error is to misspell or mispronounce verbs.

NONSTANDARD   We were attackted by mosquitoes.
    STANDARD   We were **attacked** by mosquitoes.

RESOURCES

The Principal Parts of Verbs and Regular Verbs
Practice
- *Grammar, Usage, and Mechanics,* pp. 138, 139
- *Language Workshop CD-ROM,* Lesson 14

Oral Practice 1 **Pronouncing the Past and Past Participle Forms of Regular Verbs Correctly**

Read each sentence aloud, stressing the italicized verb.

1. Aunt Rosie *used* to do needlepoint.
2. What has *happened* to your bicycle?
3. Several people were *drowned* in the flood.
4. The agents *risked* their lives.
5. Aren't you *supposed* to sing?
6. The game was well *advertised*.
7. The critics *praised* Amy Tan's new book.
8. He *carried* the suitcases to the car.

Irregular Verbs

17c. An *irregular verb* forms its past and past participle in some other way than by adding *–d* or *–ed*.

An irregular verb forms its past and past participle in one of these ways:

- changing consonants
- changing vowels
- changing vowels *and* consonants
- making no change at all

	Base Form	Past	Past Participle
Consonant Change	bend	bent	[have] bent
	send	sent	[have] sent
Vowel Change	sing	sang	[have] sung
	begin	began	[have] begun
Vowel and Consonant Change	catch	caught	[have] caught
	go	went	[have] gone
	fly	flew	[have] flown
No Change	set	set	[have] set
	burst	burst	[have] burst

"When I say 'runned,' you know I mean 'ran.' Let's not quibble."

© 1998 by Sidney Harris.

—HELP—

If you are not sure about the principal parts of a verb, look in a dictionary, which lists the principal parts of irregular verbs. If no principal parts are listed, the verb is regular.

The Principal Parts of Verbs **519**

Irregular Verbs
Rule 17c *(pp. 519–528)*

OBJECTIVES

- To pronounce the past and past participle forms of irregular verbs correctly
- To write the past and past participle forms of irregular verbs
- To identify the correct forms of irregular verbs in sentences

TEACHING **TIP**

Motivation. To show students how irregular verbs can be misused, you might ask students to work in pairs to write a brief conversation between a preschooler and an adult. Have pairs use the verb forms each speaker might be expected to use. Students might use the following format to organize their examples.

BASE FORM	CHILD'S FORM	STANDARD FORM
catch	catched	caught
see	seed	saw
go	goed	went

Ask volunteers to read their conversations aloud.

Critical Thinking

Analysis. To conclude the Teaching Tip activity described on p. 519, ask students why they think young children just learning English regularize irregular verbs. [*Students might say that young children acquire language through listening and form generalizations based in part on the number of times they have heard a particular pattern; some may add that children form conclusions about usage rules but don't understand the exceptions and apply the rules to all situations. Some might even recognize that young learners are testing their use of language by constant practice and feedback from others.*]

Relating to Literature

To show students how a skilled writer uses the present tense effectively, you might refer them to "Salvador Late or Early" by Sandra Cisneros if the selection is included in their literature books. Call on members of the class to read the passage aloud, substituting past-tense verbs. Then, ask students why they think Cisneros chose to use present-tense verbs. [*Present tense gives a sense of immediacy.*]

Reference Note

For more about **standard and nonstandard English,** see page 595.

NOTE Since most English verbs are regular, people sometimes try to make irregular verbs follow the regular pattern. However, such words as *throwed, knowed, shrinked,* or *choosed* are considered nonstandard.

Principal Parts of Common Irregular Verbs

Base Form	Present Participle	Past	Past Participle
become	[is] becoming	became	[have] become
begin	[is] beginning	began	[have] begun
blow	[is] blowing	blew	[have] blown
break	[is] breaking	broke	[have] broken
bring	[is] bringing	brought	[have] brought
build	[is] building	built	[have] built
burst	[is] bursting	burst	[have] burst
buy	[is] buying	bought	[have] bought
choose	[is] choosing	chose	[have] chosen
come	[is] coming	came	[have] come
cost	[is] costing	cost	[have] cost
cut	[is] cutting	cut	[have] cut
do	[is] doing	did	[have] done
draw	[is] drawing	drew	[have] drawn
drink	[is] drinking	drank	[have] drunk
drive	[is] driving	drove	[have] driven
eat	[is] eating	ate	[have] eaten
fall	[is] falling	fell	[have] fallen
feel	[is] feeling	felt	[have] felt
fight	[is] fighting	fought	[have] fought
find	[is] finding	found	[have] found
fly	[is] flying	flew	[have] flown
freeze	[is] freezing	froze	[have] frozen
get	[is] getting	got	[have] gotten *or* got
give	[is] giving	gave	[have] given
go	[is] going	went	[have] gone
grow	[is] growing	grew	[have] grown

USAGE

Principal Parts of Common Irregular Verbs

Base Form	Present Participle	Past	Past Participle
have	[is] having	had	[have] had
hear	[is] hearing	heard	[have] heard
hide	[is] hiding	hid	[have] hidden or hid
hit	[is] hitting	hit	[have] hit
hold	[is] holding	held	[have] held
keep	[is] keeping	kept	[have] kept
know	[is] knowing	knew	[have] known
lead	[is] leading	led	[have] led
leave	[is] leaving	left	[have] left
let	[is] letting	let	[have] let
light	[is] lighting	lighted or lit	[have] lighted or lit
lose	[is] losing	lost	[have] lost
make	[is] making	made	[have] made
put	[is] putting	put	[have] put
read	[is] reading	read	[have] read
ride	[is] riding	rode	[have] ridden
ring	[is] ringing	rang	[have] rung
run	[is] running	ran	[have] run
say	[is] saying	said	[have] said
see	[is] seeing	saw	[have] seen
seek	[is] seeking	sought	[have] sought
shake	[is] shaking	shook	[have] shaken
sing	[is] singing	sang	[have] sung
sink	[is] sinking	sank or sunk	[have] sunk
slide	[is] sliding	slid	[have] slid
speak	[is] speaking	spoke	[have] spoken
spend	[is] spending	spent	[have] spent
stand	[is] standing	stood	[have] stood
steal	[is] stealing	stole	[have] stolen
sting	[is] stinging	stung	[have] stung
strike	[is] striking	struck	[have] struck or stricken

(continued)

STYLE TIP

Some verbs have two correct past or past participle forms. However, these forms are not always interchangeable.

EXAMPLES
I **shone** the flashlight into the woods. [*Shined* would also be correct.]

I **shined** my shoes. [*Shone* would be incorrect in this usage.]

If you are unsure about which past participle form to use, check an up-to-date dictionary.

Crossing the Curriculum

History. Work with a history teacher to coordinate a writing project based on historical research. Assign students to work in pairs to write brief narratives about a particular historical event they have studied. Have one student write a present-tense eyewitness account of the event while the second student writes a past-tense account. Read the samples to the class, and allow students to compare and contrast the effect of the pieces. [*They may suggest that the present-tense account makes them feel as though they are there. They may suggest that the past-tense account distances them from the event but adds the authority time brings to a perspective on history.*]

Meeting INDIVIDUAL NEEDS

ENGLISH-LANGUAGE LEARNERS

General Strategies. Reassure students that many people have trouble conjugating irregular verbs because the past and past participle may often look and sound quite different from their base forms. Reinforce the principal parts of irregular verbs through oral practice. Encourage students to use a dictionary or the **Principal Parts of Common Irregular Verbs** chart when they are unsure of any irregular verb form.

(continued)

| \multicolumn{4}{c}{Principal Parts of Common Irregular Verbs} |
Base Form	Present Participle	Past	Past Participle
swim	[is] swimming	swam	[have] swum
take	[is] taking	took	[have] taken
teach	[is] teaching	taught	[have] taught
tear	[is] tearing	tore	[have] torn
tell	[is] telling	told	[have] told
think	[is] thinking	thought	[have] thought
throw	[is] throwing	threw	[have] thrown
wear	[is] wearing	wore	[have] worn
win	[is] winning	won	[have] won
write	[is] writing	wrote	[have] written

Meeting INDIVIDUAL NEEDS

MODALITIES

Visual-Kinesthetic Learners. A tactile approach might help students remember the principal parts of irregular verbs. Provide each student with four colors of paper. Designate a specific color for each principal part (for example, purple for base form, orange for past). Have each student choose an irregular verb and write four sentences on the correct colored paper, one for each of the four principal parts of the verb. Then, have students make mobiles with the sentence strips. Hang the mobiles around the room as reminders of the correct use of irregular verbs.

USAGE

TIPS & TRICKS

To avoid nonstandard usage, include a form of *be* with the present participle and a form of *have* with the past participle. Say *do, is doing, did, have done,* for example, or *see, is seeing, saw, have seen.*

NONSTANDARD
  We already seen that program.

STANDARD
  We **have** already **seen** that program.

Reference Note

For more about **passive voice**, see page 535.

When the present participle and past participle forms are used as verbs in sentences, they require helping verbs.

Helping Verb	+	Present Participle	=	Verb Phrase
forms of *be*	+	taking	=	am taking
		walking		was walking
		going		have been going

Helping Verb	+	Past Participle	=	Verb Phrase
forms of *have*	+	taken	=	have taken
		walked		has walked
		gone		had gone

NOTE Sometimes a past participle is used with a form of *be: was chosen, are known, is seen.* This use of the verb is called the **passive voice.**

Oral Practice 2 · Using the Past and Past Participle Forms of Irregular Verbs Correctly

Read each of the following sentences aloud, stressing the italicized verbs.

1. *Have* you *begun* the research for your report?
2. Last week we *saw* a video about Alexander the Great.
3. The bell *rang*, and the door *burst* open.
4. I *have known* her since the first grade.
5. He *brought* his rock collection to school.
6. They *fought* to rescue the survivors.
7. Elizabeth *has written* a short article for the school newspaper.
8. She *has given* us her permission.

Exercise 1 · Writing the Past and Past Participle Forms of Irregular Verbs

Change each of the following verb forms. If the base form is given, change it to the past form. If the past form is given, change it to the past participle. Use *have* before the past participle form.

EXAMPLES
1. eat **2.** took
1. ate *2. have taken*

1. do	**5.** went	**9.** blew	**13.** drink	**17.** ran
2. began	**6.** know	**10.** bring	**14.** froze	**18.** ring
3. see	**7.** spoke	**11.** choose	**15.** drove	**19.** fell
4. rode	**8.** stole	**12.** broke	**16.** sang	**20.** swim

Exercise 2 · Identifying Correct Forms of Irregular Verbs

Choose the correct form of the verb in parentheses in each of the following sentences.

EXAMPLE
1. Mai's parents (*telled, told*) her about their journey in a boat from South Vietnam to Malaysia.
1. told

1. They (*rode, rid*) in a crowded boat like the one you see in the picture on the next page.
2. Along with many other people, Mai's parents (*chose, choosed*) to make such a journey rather than stay in South Vietnam after the Vietnam War ended.

The Principal Parts of Verbs   **523**

USAGE

The Principal Parts of Verbs   **523**

Crossing the Curriculum

World Languages. Involve students in the study of irregular verbs by drawing on their prior knowledge; ask them for examples of irregular verbs in other languages. Record their responses in a graphic organizer like the one below.

LANGUAGE	VERB	ENGLISH EQUIVALENT

Social Studies. To encourage further practice and real-world application, work with other teachers to help students find pen pals in other countries. Students and teachers should work out a list of questions to ask pen pals about their cultures. As students begin their correspondence, choose a particular editing focus, such as irregular verb forms, for students to concentrate on each week when writing and editing their letters.

Art. Students might like to paint or draw illustrations for postcards to send to their pen pals; others might use magazine clippings.

3. These refugees (*came, come*) to be called "boat people."
4. Mai's parents abandoned their home after the South Vietnamese capital, Saigon, had (*fell, fallen*) to North Vietnamese forces.
5. The people on the boat (*brang, brought*) few possessions or supplies.
6. After they had (*drank, drunk*) what little water was on board, they went thirsty.
7. Mai's father said the people had (*ate, eaten*) all the food in a few days.
8. When another boat of refugees had (*sank, sunk*), its passengers crowded onto Mai's parents' boat.
9. They spent many days and nights on the ocean before they (*saw, seen*) land again.
10. Then it (*took, taked*) months for Mai's parents to be moved from Malaysian refugee camps to the United States.

Exercise 3 **Identifying Correct Forms of Irregular Verbs**

For each sentence in the following paragraph, choose the correct form of the verb in parentheses.

EXAMPLE   I just **[1]** (wrote, written) to my Russian pen pal!

    1. *wrote*

Joining the Russian-American pen-pal club Druzhba is one of the most interesting things I have ever **[1]** (*did, done*). The founder of the club **[2]** (*chose, chosen*) the name *Druzhba* because it means "friendship" in Russian. This club has **[3]** (*given, gave*) American and Russian students the chance to become friends. I **[4]** (*began, begun*) to write to my pen pal Vanya last September. His reply to my first letter **[5]** (*took, taken*) weeks to get to me. I wish it could have **[6]** (*flew, flown*) here faster from the other side of the globe. In his letters, Vanya has often **[7]** (*written, wrote*) about his daily life, his family, and his thoughts and feelings. We have **[8]** (*become, became*) good friends through our letters even though we have never **[9]** (*spoke, spoken*) to each other. Reading each other's essays in the club newsletter has also **[10]** (*brung, brought*) us closer together.

**Writing the Past and Past Participle
Forms of Verbs**

For each of the following sentences, write the correct past or past
participle form of the verb given.

EXAMPLE   **1.** run   Yesterday we _____ around the track twice.

       1. ran

1. *sing*   Boyz II Men _____ last night.   *1. sang*
2. *burst*   The car suddenly _____ into flames.   *2. burst*
3. *drink*   Yesterday they _____ juice with their tossed salads and
       turkey sandwiches.   *3. drank*
4. *use*   He _____ to camp out every summer.   *4. used*
5. *do*   They _____ their best to repair the damage caused
       by the very large hail.   *5. did*
6. *give*   Grandma has _____ us some old photos.   *6. given*
7. *risk*   The detective _____ her life.   *7. risked*
8. *ring*   My alarm _____ at six o'clock.   *8. rang*
9. *speak*   Toni has not _____ to me since our argument.   *9. spoken*
10. *fall*   A tree has _____ across the highway.   *10. fallen*

**Writing the Past and Past Participle
Forms of Verbs**

Write the correct past or past participle form of each italicized verb
in the following paragraph.

EXAMPLE   All my life I have **[1]** (*know*) that I must make my own
       choices.

       1. known

    I have never **[1]** (*choose*) to be on a sports team because I am
not a very athletic person. Some people are surprised because my
brother and sister have **[2]** (*drive*) themselves very hard and have
[3] (*become*) excellent athletes. For example, my brother, Emilio,
[4] (*break*) three swimming records this year alone. He has
[5] (*swim*) better than anyone else in our school. He also
[6] (*go*) out for tennis and track this year. My sister, Elena, is only
a junior, but she has already **[7]** (*run*) the 100-meter dash faster
than any senior girl. I **[8]** (*use*) to think I wanted to follow in my
brother's and sister's footsteps, but now I have **[9]** (*take*) a different
path in life. My English teacher just **[10]** (*give*) me a chance to lead
the debating team, and I am going to grab it!

I'VE BEEN EXPERIENCING A LOT OF STRESS LATELY, BUT THE FEELING SEEMS TO BE GONE NOW!!

WE HAVE A NAME FOR THAT, YOU KNOW!

WHAT IS IT?

"PAST TENSE"!

BORN LOSER reprinted by permission of Newspaper Enterprise Association, Inc.

Meeting
INDIVIDUAL
        NEEDS

MODALITIES

Auditory Learners. An oral game
of Verb-down will reinforce students'
knowledge of past and past-partici-
ple forms of irregular verbs and give
students practice hearing the correct
forms. Divide the class into two
teams. Use the present-tense form of
a verb in a question, and then have a
player rephrase the question and
answer it by using the past and past-
participle forms correctly in two sentences. [*Teacher: Do you write letters
often? Student: Do I write letters
often? I wrote one last week. I have
written many letters.*]

If a student succeeds, he or she then
poses a question for the other team.
If the student misses, the original
question goes to the other team.

Review B   **Writing the Past
and Past Participle Forms of
Verbs**

ANSWERS

1. chosen
2. driven
3. become
4. broke
5. swum
6. went
7. run
8. used
9. taken
10. gave

Review C Writing the Past and Past Participle Forms of Verbs

Write the correct past or past participle form of the verb given for each of the following sentences.

EXAMPLES **1.** *go* We _____ to the Ozark Mountains.
1. *went*

2. *swim* I have never _____ in an ocean.
2. *swum*

1. thrown   **1.** *throw* Kerry should have _____ the ball to Lee, who could have tagged the runner out.

2. frozen   **2.** *freeze* Has the water _____ yet?

3. written   **3.** *write* Theo has _____ me a long letter.

4. seen   **4.** *see* Have you _____ that actor in person?

5. sung   **5.** *sing* The tenors have _____ in Rome, Paris, and New York.

6. threw   **6.** *throw* I finally _____ my old running shoes away and bought a new pair at the mall.

7. drowned   **7.** *drown* Nobody has ever _____ in this lake.

8. gave   **8.** *give* Taro _____ me a bowl of miso soup.

9. blew   **9.** *blow* The strong wind this afternoon _____ down our tree-house in the backyard.

10. taken   **10.** *take* I have already _____ a picture of you, Molly.

Review D

ALTERNATIVE LESSON
Have students find the following items.

1. an appositive phrase [*the mule (between 6 and 7)*]

2. a reflexive pronoun [*myself (between 9 and 10)*]

Review D Writing the Past and Past Participle Forms of Verbs

Write the correct past or past participle form of each of the ten italicized verbs in the following paragraph.

EXAMPLE Have you ever **[1]** (*take*) a trip to the country?
1. *taken*

1. spent   We have always **[1]** (*spend*) summer vacations at Uncle Dan's farm
2. did   in Vermont. We **[2]** (*do*) the most relaxing things there last year! We
3. swam   **[3]** (*swim*) in the millpond and **[4]** (*eat*) watermelon on the back porch.
4. ate   A few times, we **[5]** (*ride*) our bikes into town to get groceries. We also
5. rode   **[6]** (*take*) turns riding Horace, the mule. I have **[7]** (*fall*) off Horace twice,
6. took   but I have never **[8]** (*break*) any bones. Both times, I **[9]** (*come*) down in a
7. fallen   pile of soft hay. Then I dusted myself off and **[10]** (*climb*) on again.
8. broken
9. came
10. climbed

Review E — Proofreading Sentences for Correct Verb Forms

Some of the following sentences contain an incorrect verb form. If a verb form is wrong, write the correct form. If the sentence is already correct, write *C*.

EXAMPLE   1. Marian Anderson sung her way out of poverty.

   1. *sang*

1. She went on to earn fame and the Medal of Freedom.   **1.** C
2. Can you tell from this picture that she ~~use~~ to sing classical music?   **2.** used
3. In 1955, Marian Anderson ~~become~~ the first African American singer to perform with the Metropolitan Opera in New York City.   **3.** became
4. She performed in concerts and operas all over the world, but she ~~begun~~ her career as a child singing hymns in church.   **4.** began
5. Anderson, who was from a poor Philadelphia family, was awarded a scholarship to study music in Europe.   **5.** C
6. European audiences soon ~~taked~~ notice of her.   **6.** took
7. Audiences admired her determination and courage.   **7.** C
8. In 1939, Anderson was not permitted to sing at a hall in Washington, D.C., so she ~~give~~ a free concert, attended by 75,000 people, at the Lincoln Memorial.   **8.** gave
9. In the 1950s, the U.S. government ~~choosed~~ her to go on a goodwill tour of Asia and to be a United Nations delegate.   **9.** chose
10. Anderson ~~writed~~ of her experiences in her autobiography, *My Lord, What a Morning.*   **10.** wrote

Review F — Proofreading a Paragraph for Correct Verb Forms

The following paragraph contains ten incorrect verb forms. If a verb form is wrong, write the correct form. If a sentence is already correct, write *C*.

EXAMPLE   **[1]** A Confederate search party had went out to get boots for their soldiers and saddles for their horses.

   1. *had gone*

[1] By chance, the search party ~~runned~~ into the Union cavalry.
[2] It is not clear who ~~attackted~~ first, but a battle ~~begun~~ near

1. ran
2. attacked/began

USAGE

TECHNOLOGY TIP

Students who have the skills might choose to plan a Web site about Marian Anderson. They could include text, photographs, sound, and video clips in their proposal for the site.

Meeting INDIVIDUAL NEEDS

MULTIPLE INTELLIGENCES

Musical Intelligence. Add interest to **Review E** by having students find recordings of Anderson's singing to share with the class.

Logical/Mathematical Intelligence. You might ask students to read **Review F,** do a statistical comparison of the impact of the losses on each army, and present the results. Encourage them to use bar or pie graphs of the numbers to show the relative significance of the 45,000 deaths.

The Principal Parts of Verbs   **527**

3. went
4. C
5. burst
6. climbed/flew
7. drove
8. come/fallen

Gettysburg, Pennsylvania, on July 1, 1863. [3] The fighting ~~goed~~ on for three days. [4] First one side and then the other got the upper hand. [5] Shells ~~bursted~~ in the air, and cannonballs whistled in all directions. [6] At one point, some Confederate soldiers ~~clumb~~ to the top of Cemetery Ridge, and their flag ~~flown~~ there a brief time. [7] However, the Union army ~~drived~~ them back. [8] By the time the battle had ~~came~~ to an end, 20,000 Union soldiers and 25,000 Confederate soldiers had ~~fell~~.

Tense

Rules 17d–f *(pp. 528–534)*

O B J E C T I V E S

- To identify and explain the use of tenses in sentences
- To change verbs in sentences from one tense to another
- To proofread a paragraph to make verb tenses consistent

Meeting
INDIVIDUAL
NEEDS

ENGLISH-LANGUAGE LEARNERS

General Strategies. Use the question "Have you ever _____?" to introduce present perfect tense. Have students work in pairs to ask and answer the following questions or others like them.

1. Have you ever studied Chinese? [*I have never studied Chinese.*]

2. Has he ever been to Europe? [*He has been to Europe.*]

3. Have you ever slept outside? [*I have never slept outside.*]

4. Have you ever seen a flamingo? [*I have seen a flamingo at a bird preserve.*]

5. Has she ever had the mumps? [*She has had the mumps.*]

Have students continue the question-answer session using the same format. Rhythmic repetition is a key method of language acquisition and will help English-language learners fix this construction in their minds.

Tense

17d. The *tense* of a verb indicates the time of the action or of the state of being expressed by the verb.

The tenses are formed from the verb's principal parts. Verbs in English have the six tenses shown on the following time line:

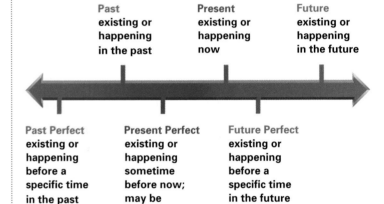

EXAMPLES   Max **has worked** [present perfect] all summer, and now he **has** [present] enough money to buy a bicycle.

The chorus **had practiced** [past perfect] for weeks before they **sang** [past] in public last night.

The surgeon **will have reviewed** [future perfect] the test results by next Friday, and she **will decide** [future] whether or not to operate then.

528   Chapter 17   Using Verbs Correctly

RESOURCES

Tense
Practice
- *Grammar, Usage, and Mechanics,* pp. 145, 146–147
- *Language Workshop CD-ROM,* Lesson 15

Conjugation of the Verb *Give* in the Active Voice

Present Tense

Singular	Plural
I give	we give
you give	you give
he, she, *or* it gives	they give

Past Tense

Singular	Plural
I gave	we gave
you gave	you gave
he, she, *or* it gave	they gave

Future Tense

Singular	Plural
I will (shall) give	we will (shall) give
you will (shall) give	you will (shall) give
he, she, *or* it will (shall) give	they will (shall) give

Present Perfect Tense

Singular	Plural
I have given	we have given
you have given	you have given
he, she, *or* it has given	they have given

Past Perfect Tense

Singular	Plural
I had given	we had given
you had given	you had given
he, she, *or* it had given	they had given

Future Perfect Tense

Singular	Plural
I will (shall) have given	we will (shall) have given
you will (shall) have given	you will (shall) have given
he, she, *or* it will (shall) have given	they will (shall) have given

Reference Note

See page 536 for a **conjugation of *give* in the passive voice.**

S T Y L E   T I P

Traditionally, the helping verbs *shall* and *will* were used differently. Now, however, *shall* can be used almost interchangeably with *will*.

Critical Thinking

Analysis. To help students realize that there are strong similarities and differences among verb forms in various languages, you might ask them to provide textbooks of the languages they speak or are studying. Then, group students according to languages. Ask groups to examine verbs in various languages and to draw conclusions about language and verb tense. [*Students will probably notice that many languages use the same general verb tenses and forms, and some will point out cognates—words that are recognizable to speakers and readers of other, usually related, languages.*]

USAGE

Crossing the Curriculum

World Languages. So that students can draw on prior knowledge of other languages and so that they can see similarities among languages, ask them to work in small groups to create charts showing translations of common English verbs in **progressive** and **emphatic** forms. Students may ask world language teachers for input. Have students post the charts on the bulletin board.

Relating to Literature

If students' literature books include "The Scarlet Ibis," by James Hurst, help make students aware of the use of tenses by reading aloud the first two paragraphs. Have students listen for shifts in verb tense, and then discuss the effect of the shift from past tense in the first paragraph to present tense in the second paragraph. [*The past-tense description creates intrigue, foreboding, and suspense. The switch to present tense in the second paragraph changes the setting and places the reader with the writer in the present.*]

STYLE	TIP

The emphatic form is also used in questions and negative statements. These uses do not place special emphasis on the verb.

QUESTION
Why **do** bears hibernate?

NEGATIVE STATEMENT
If the car **does**n't [does not] start, check the battery.

The Progressive Form

Each of the six tenses has an additional form called the *progressive form,* which expresses continuing action. It consists of a form of the verb *be* plus the present participle of a verb. The progressive is not a separate tense but an additional form of each of the six tenses.

PRESENT PROGRESSIVE	am, are, is giving
PAST PROGRESSIVE	was, were giving
FUTURE PROGRESSIVE	will (shall) be giving
PRESENT PERFECT PROGRESSIVE	has, have been giving
PAST PERFECT PROGRESSIVE	had been giving
FUTURE PERFECT PROGRESSIVE	will (shall) have been giving

NOTE The *emphatic form* of a verb is used to show emphasis. The emphatic form consists of the present or past tense of *do* with the base form of the main verb.

PRESENT EMPHATIC	Although the grass is green, the lawn **does need** watering.
PAST EMPHATIC	The writer endured many setbacks in his career, yet he **did** finally **become** famous.

17e. Each of the six tenses has its own special uses.

(1) The *present tense* is used mainly to express an action or a state of being that is occurring now.

EXAMPLES   The new jet **has** two engines.

Leotie **belongs** to the Latin Club.

They **are decorating** the gym. [progressive form]

The present tense is also used

- to show a customary or habitual action or state of being
- to express a general truth—something that is always true
- to make historical events seem current (such use is called the *historical present*)
- to discuss a literary work (such use is called the *literary present*)
- to express future time

Learning for Life

Continued on pp. 531–533

Eyewitness news. For this activity, tell students they are reporters for the *Good News Gazette,* a local magazine that reports on positive happenings. Their assignment is to write brief eyewitness reports about true or imagined good-news events in their neighborhood or school. Because using proper tense sequence is necessary to relate an event accurately, students should be particularly careful in their choice of verb forms.

You may want to share the following model with students.

EXAMPLES   We **recycle** newspapers, glass, and aluminum cans.
[customary actions]

The sun **sets** in the west. [general truth]

In 1905, Albert Einstein **makes** history when he **proposes** his theory of relativity. [historical present]

In *David Copperfield,* Dickens **shows** us the extremes of Victorian life. [literary present]

Finals **begin** next week. [future time]

(2) The *past tense* is used to express an action or state of being that occurred in the past but that is not occurring now.

EXAMPLES   They **looked** for seashells.

The manatees **were swimming** in the canal.
[progressive form]

NOTE A past action or state of being may also be shown with the past form *used,* plus *to,* plus the base form of the main verb.

EXAMPLE   Chicago **used to be** the second-largest U.S. city.

(3) The *future tense* is used to express an action or a state of being that will occur. It is formed with *will* or *shall* and the main verb's base form.

EXAMPLES   **Shall** we **set** the table?

The new model cars **will arrive** soon.

They **will be selling** them soon. [progressive form]

NOTE A future action or state of being may also be shown in other ways.

EXAMPLES   We **are going to make** our own Mardi Gras costumes.

The president **holds** a press conference **next Monday.**

(4) The *present perfect tense* is used to express an action or a state of being that occurred at some indefinite time in the past. It is formed with the helping verb *have* or *has.*

EXAMPLES   The Mendozas **have invited** us over for a cookout.

The Red Cross **has been delivering** medical supplies.
[progressive form]

Tense   **531**

Rerun Returns

After a frantic hour of searching, Ms. Rachel Bowen of 12345 Tabby Trail was reunited with her five-month-old kitten, Rerun. Ms. Bowen reported that Rerun had disappeared while conducting his daily survey of the butterfly population.

Ms. Bowen combed the area, interviewing children and peering down rabbit holes. Back in her yard, she was relieved to hear Rerun's distant mew, but she could not see him. Ms. Bowen searched in the nearby

Cooperative Learning

To help students practice the use of verb tense forms, divide the class into small groups, providing each group with a tape recorder and a sentence that begins a narrative. [*For example,* As I stumbled down the dark path, I heard footsteps behind me.] Have the first student in each group record the sentence provided, and then have each subsequent student record a sentence to further the story. Once the group has completed the story, have members play the tape back. Have a student list each verb in the story. The others should take turns identifying and justifying the choice of the verb tense. Allow students to rerecord the tape to replace inappropriate verbs with appropriate ones. Have each group play the revised tape for the class.

NOTE Do not use the present perfect tense to express a specific time in the past. Instead, use the past tense.

NONSTANDARD   We have seen that movie last Saturday. [*Last Saturday* indicates a specific time in the past.]

STANDARD   We **saw** that movie last Saturday.

The present perfect tense is also used to express an action or a state of being that began in the past and continues into the present.

EXAMPLES   Li Hua **has taken** violin lessons for eight years.

We **have been living** in Amarillo since early 1998. [progressive form]

(5) The *past perfect tense* is used to express an action or a state of being that was completed in the past before some other past action or event. It is formed with the helping verb *had.*

EXAMPLES   Once the judges **had viewed** the paintings, they announced the winners. [The viewing occurred before the announcing.]

By the time that the Spanish conquistadors arrived, that redwood **had been growing** for three centuries. [progressive form]

(6) The *future perfect tense* is used to express an action or a state of being that will be completed in the future before some other future occurrence. It is formed with the helping verbs *will have* or *shall have.*

EXAMPLES   By the time Mom returns, I **will have done** my chores. [The doing will be completed before the returning.]

In August, Aaron **will have been taking** Hebrew lessons for two years. [progressive form]

┌HELP─

In the examples for Exercise 4, the first sentence expresses customary action and the second sentence expresses action that is happening right now.

Exercise 4 Explaining the Uses of Tenses in Sentences

Each item on the next page contains two correct sentences. Identify the tense or tenses used in each sentence. Be prepared to explain the meanings of the two sentences in each pair.

EXAMPLE   **1. a.** For breakfast she eats a bagel and some cereal.
      b. For breakfast she is eating a bagel and some cereal.

   1. a. *simple present*
      b. *present progressive*

Learning for Life

garage and in the peach tree. Finally, she looked up and discovered Rerun asleep in the rain gutter, his chin resting on the roof's edge, his plume of a tail floating above the oleander bush.

Ms. Bowen retrieved a stepladder for

the rescue. When she returned, she found Rerun happily jumping off the peach tree. On the ground, he arched his back, flexed his claws, and raced at high speed after a grasshopper.

Ms. Bowen said, "The insect population

1. **a.** You will put down your pencils when the bell rings.
   b. You will have put down your pencils when the bell rings.
2. **a.** He worked at the gas station in the summertime.
   b. He has worked at the gas station in the summertime.
3. **a.** What caused the computer to crash?
   b. What has been causing the computer to crash?
4. **a.** When I arrived, Morton left.
   b. When I arrived, Morton had left.
5. **a.** Shelley was working on her bicycle.
   b. Shelley had been working on her bicycle when we arrived.

Exercise 5 **Using the Different Tenses of Verbs in Sentences**

Change the tense of the verb in each of the following sentences to the tense indicated in parentheses.

EXAMPLE
1. Maria always goes home at five o'clock. (*past*)
   1. *went*

1. The quick, graceful otter swam to the edge of the pool. (*present perfect*)
2. Our class will read Shakespeare's *Much Ado About Nothing*. (*future progressive*)
3. Before the concert, the orchestra practices the new pieces. (*past perfect*)
4. The guests will be arriving at the train station. (*present perfect progressive*)
5. By then, I will solve the riddle. (*future perfect*)
6. The three sisters regularly meet for lunch. (*past*)
7. The new computers have been working fine for three weeks. (*past perfect progressive*)
8. Wasps were entering the house through the torn screen. (*present*)
9. The lawn mower has started after all! (*past emphatic*)
10. We reset the clocks for daylight saving time. (*future*)

1. has swum

2. will be reading

3. had practiced

4. have been arriving

5. will have solved
6. met
7. had been working

8. enter
9. did start
10. will reset

Consistency of Tense

17f. Do not change needlessly from one tense to another.

When describing events that occur at the same time, use verbs in the same tense. When describing events that occur at different times, use different tenses to show the order of events clearly.

Tense   **533**

USAGE

will be safe for at least two weeks. Rerun is grounded."
   Students can compile their issue of the *Good News Gazette*, or volunteers could read their features aloud.

Exercise 6 Some students may be confused by the verbals in **Exercise 6** (*to study; fishing; going; fishing; Getting; to be; beginning; to form*). You may want to review the three kinds of verbals—participles, gerunds, and infinitives—and tell students to focus on verbs rather than verbals as they do this exercise.

Exercise 6 Proofreading a Paragraph to Make the Tenses of the Verbs Consistent

ANSWERS

Answers will depend on whether students decide to use present or past tense in their revisions.

	Present Tense	Past Tense
1.	C	was, had planned
2.	is	C
3.	drops	C
4.	C	dashed, ran, called
5.	wants	was
6.	C	had been thinking
7.	C	became, could, was
8.	know	saw, were
9.	C	rained
10.	are	C

┌HELP─
For the paragraph in Exercise 6, either the present tense or the past tense can be used correctly.

NONSTANDARD	Cara fielded the ball and throws the runner out. [*Fielded* is past tense; *throws* is present tense.]
STANDARD	Cara **fielded** the ball and **threw** the runner out. [*Fielded* and *threw* are both past tense.]
STANDARD	Cara **fields** the ball and **throws** the runner out. [*Fields* and *throws* are both present tense.]

NONSTANDARD	She stands on the mound and will stare at the batter. [*Stands* is present tense; *will stare* is future tense.]
STANDARD	She **stands** on the mound and **stares** at the batter. [*Stands* and *stares* are both present tense.]
STANDARD	She **will stand** on the mound and **stare** at the batter. [*Will stand* and *stare* are both future tense.]

NONSTANDARD	The batter wished that he practiced more before the game. [Because the action of practicing was completed before the action of wishing, the verb should be *had practiced*, not *practiced*.]
STANDARD	The batter **wished** that he **had practiced** more before the game.

Exercise 6 **Proofreading a Paragraph to Make the Tenses of the Verbs Consistent**

Proofread the following paragraph, looking for needless changes of verb tense. Choose whether to rewrite the paragraph in the present or past tense. Then, change the verbs to make the tenses consistent.

EXAMPLE [1] It all started as soon as I come home from school.

1. *It all started as soon as I came home from school.*

or

It all starts as soon as I come home from school.

[1] I am in my room, and I have planned to study for two hours. [2] It was about five o'clock in the afternoon. [3] To my surprise, Nancy Chang dropped by. [4] She dashes into the house, runs up the stairs, and calls my name. [5] What she wanted is a fishing companion. [6] All week she has been thinking about going fishing. [7] Getting my fishing gear together, I become excited and can almost see the fish fighting over which one is to be my first catch of the day. [8] On our way out to the lake, we see clouds beginning to form, and we knew we are in for trouble. [9] It rains all right—for the whole weekend. [10] The fish were safe for another week.

Active and Passive Voice

17g. A verb in the *active voice* expresses an action done by its subject. A verb in the *passive voice* expresses an action done to its subject.

ACTIVE VOICE	The coach **instructed** us. [The subject, *coach*, performs the action.]
PASSIVE VOICE	We **were instructed** by the coach. [The subject, *We*, receives the action.]

ACTIVE VOICE	**Did** Brandon **score** the winning touchdown? [The subject, *Brandon*, performs the action.]
PASSIVE VOICE	**Was** the winning touchdown **scored** by Brandon? [The subject, *touchdown*, receives the action.]

Compare the following related sentences:

	S O
ACTIVE	The author **provides** helpful diagrams.

	S
PASSIVE	Helpful diagrams **are provided** by the author.

In these two sentences, the object of the active sentence is the subject of the passive one. The subject of the active sentence is expressed in a prepositional phrase in the passive sentence. Note that this phrase can be omitted.

PASSIVE	Helpful diagrams **are provided.**

In a passive sentence, the verb phrase includes a form of *be* and the past participle of the main verb. Other helping verbs may also be included.

	S O
ACTIVE	The tutor **is helping** Sharon.

	S
PASSIVE	Sharon **is being helped** by the tutor.

	S O
ACTIVE	Someone **has erased** the tapes.

	S
PASSIVE	The tapes **have been erased.**

The chart on the following page shows the conjugation of the verb *give* in the passive voice.

Reference Note

For more information on **helping verbs,** see page 391.

Reference Note

For the **conjugation of the verb *give* in the active voice,** see page 529.

Active and Passive Voice **535**

Active and Passive Voice
Rule 17g (*pp. 535–538*)

OBJECTIVES

- To identify active and passive voice in sentences

- To revise sentences in the passive voice to make them active voice

USAGE

RESOURCES

Active and Passive Voice

Practice

- *Grammar, Usage, and Mechanics,* pp. 148, 149
- *Language Workshop CD-ROM,* Lesson 17

Meeting
INDIVIDUAL NEEDS

ENGLISH-LANGUAGE LEARNERS
General Strategies. Because of the many helping verbs that must be correctly sequenced, some students have difficulty forming the passive voice. Using the conjugation of the verb *give* as a model (p. 536), you might want to have them practice changing active-voice transitive verbs to the passive voice.

In addition, give students newspaper articles and ask them to highlight any passive forms. Then, have them identify the receiver of the action, performer of the action (if any), and verb tense.

Critical Thinking

Evaluating. After students have edited their writing to eliminate the unnecessary use of passive voice, ask them for their conclusions about the effectiveness of changing some verbs to the active voice. [*Sometimes the writer's purpose or message requires the passive voice; the doer of the action may be unknown or unnecessary. Using active voice often makes the writing direct and succinct.*]

Conjugation of the Verb *Give* in the Passive Voice	
Present Tense	
Singular	**Plural**
I am given	we are given
you are given	you are given
he, she, *or* it is given	they are given
Past Tense	
Singular	**Plural**
I was given	we were given
you were given	you were given
he, she, *or* it was given	they were given
Future Tense	
Singular	**Plural**
I will (shall) be given	we will (shall) be given
you will (shall) be given	you will (shall) be given
he, she, *or* it will (shall) be given	they will (shall) be given
Present Perfect Tense	
Singular	**Plural**
I have been given	we have been given
you have been given	you have been given
he, she, *or* it has been given	they have been given
Past Perfect Tense	
Singular	**Plural**
I had been given	we had been given
you had been given	you had been given
he, she, *or* it had been given	they had been given
Future Perfect Tense	
Singular	**Plural**
I will (shall) have been given	we will (shall) have been given
you will (shall) have been given	you will (shall) have been given
he, she, *or* it will (shall) have been given	they will (shall) have been given

536 Chapter 17 Using Verbs Correctly

MINI-LESSON

What Is an Object? Remind students that a **direct object** is a noun or pronoun that receives the action of the verb or shows the result of the action and answers the question "Whom?" or "What?"

An **indirect object** is a noun or pronoun that precedes the direct object and usually indicates *to whom* or *to what* or *for whom* or *for what* the action of the verb is done.

NOTE The progressive forms of the passive voice exist for all six tenses. However, the use of *be* or *been* with *being* is extremely awkward—*give,* for example, in the passive future perfect is *will (shall) have been being given.* Consequently, the progressive form of the passive voice is generally used only in the present and past tenses.

Using the Passive Voice

Although the passive voice is not any less correct than the active voice, it is less direct, less forceful, and less concise. In general, you should avoid using the passive voice. First, it generally requires more words to express a thought than the active voice does. Consequently, the passive voice can result in awkward writing. Second, the performer of the action in a passive voice construction is revealed indirectly or not at all. As a result, a sentence written in the passive voice can sound weak. Compare the following pairs of sentences.

PASSIVE   The ball **was hit** over the outfield fence by Jody.
ACTIVE   Jody **hit** the ball over the outfield fence.

PASSIVE   The totals for the new budget **were** carefully **checked.**
ACTIVE   The club treasurer carefully **checked** the totals for the new budget.

The passive voice is useful, however, in situations such as the following ones:

(1) when you do not know the performer of the action

EXAMPLES   Over three thousand roses **were planted.**

Are the peaches **being harvested** on schedule?

(2) when you do not want to reveal the performer of the action

EXAMPLES   Charges **were brought** against the vandals.

Many large donations to the building fund **have been made.**

(3) when you want to emphasize the receiver of the action

EXAMPLES   Jacques Chirac **was elected** president of France in 1995.

These remarkable fossils **were found** nearby.

COMPUTER TIP

Some software programs can identify and highlight verbs in the passive voice. If you use such a program, keep in mind that it can't tell why you used the passive voice. If you did so for a particular reason, you may want to leave the verb in the passive voice.

Active and Passive Voice   **537**

Provide students with a few sentences containing direct and indirect objects, and ask volunteers to draw illustrations of the sentences on the board using stick figures.

EXAMPLE
Mary saw Darren.   Darren brought her a present.

[See p. 431 for more information.]

Relating to Writing

To have students examine voice in their own writing, ask each of them to find a piece of narrative writing in his or her portfolio. Next, have them label the voice of each verb. Then, as in **Exercise 8,** have them change passive-voice verbs to active-voice verbs if appropriate.

Exercise 8   **Using Verbs in the Active Voice and the Passive Voice**

A N S W E R S

2. Initially, only farm children joined 4-H clubs.

5. Members often exhibit projects at county fairs.

7. Many 4-H members attend summer camps.

8. Our club plans community projects yearly.

10. Participation in 4-H helps many young people.

Exercise 7   **Identifying Active and Passive Voice**

For each of the following sentences, tell whether the verb is in the *active* or *passive* voice.

EXAMPLE   **1.** In the morning, I am awakened by the alarm clock.

　　　　　　　1. passive

1. passive   **1.** The newest CD by my favorite group was not reviewed by most music critics.
2. active   **2.** The student body elects the council president.
3. active   **3.** Angelo's courageous act of putting out the fire in the basement prevented a tragedy.
4. active   **4.** W. C. Handy composed the famous jazz classic "St. Louis Blues."
5. passive   **5.** Your generous contribution to help the homeless is greatly appreciated.
6. passive   **6.** The half-time show at the state championship was performed by the band from Millersville.
7. active   **7.** This afternoon the baby stood up by himself.
8. passive   **8.** Was Mr. Yañez awarded the trophy?
9. active   **9.** I don't understand this math problem.
10. passive **10.** Brian has been appointed captain of the basketball team.

Exercise 8   **Using Verbs in the Active Voice and the Passive Voice**

Identify the verb in each of the following sentences as either *active* or *passive*. Then, revise each sentence that is in the passive voice so that it is in active voice.

EXAMPLE   **1.** My 4-H project was just completed.

　　　　　　　1. passive; I just completed my 4-H project.

1. For my project I grew vegetables in containers. **1.** active
2. Initially, 4-H clubs were joined only by farm children. **2.** passive
3. Their projects focused on crops and livestock. **3.** active
4. Later projects, such as personal safety and career studies, interested young people in the city. **4.** active
5. Projects are often exhibited by members at county fairs. **5.** passive
6. The 4-H club members also learn about good citizenship. **6.** active
7. Summer camps are attended by many 4-H members. **7.** passive
8. Community projects are planned by our club yearly. **8.** passive
9. The city appreciated our tree-planting project. **9.** active
10. Many young people are helped by participation in 4-H. **10.** passive

Six Troublesome Verbs

Lie and *Lay*

17h. The verb *lie* means "to rest," "to recline," or "to remain in a lying position." *Lie* does not take an object. The verb *lay* means "to put" or "to place (something somewhere)." *Lay* generally takes an object.

Reference Note

For more about **objects of verbs,** see page 431.

Principal Parts of *Lie* and *Lay*			
Base Form	Present Participle	Past	Past Participle
lie	[is] lying	lay	[have] lain
lay	[is] laying	laid	[have] laid

EXAMPLES   **Lie** down if you don't feel well.
          Lay those books down.

          Lambert **lay** on the lounge chair.
          Lambert **laid** the towel on the lounge chair.

          He **had lain** on the couch too long.
          He **had laid** the newspaper on the couch.

STYLE TIP

The verb *lie* can also mean "to tell an untruth." Used in this way, *lie* still does not take an object. The past and past participle forms of this meaning of *lie* are *lied* and *[have] lied*.

Exercise 9 **Choosing the Correct Forms of *Lie* and *Lay***

Write the correct form of *lie* or *lay* for the blank in each of the following sentences.

EXAMPLE   **1.** Jennifer _____ the flowers on the table and looked for a vase.
           1. *laid*

1. He _____ the report aside and called for order. **1.** laid
2. Alma will _____ down for a siesta. **2.** lie
3. She has _____ on the couch all morning, watching those silly cartoons and eating cereal. **3.** lain
4. The baby was _____ quietly in the nurse's arms. **4.** lying
5. Is that today's paper _____ in the mud? **5.** lying
6. I have _____ the shoes near the fire to dry, and I hung my wet clothes in the garage. **6.** laid
7. _____ down, Spot. **7.** Lie
8. The lace had _____ in the trunk for years before we explored Grandmother's attic. **8.** lain

---

USAGE

Six Troublesome Verbs

Rules 17h–j *(pp. 539–543)*

OBJECTIVE

- To complete sentences by writing the correct forms of *lie* and *lay, sit* and *set,* and *rise* and *raise*

TEACHING TIP

Activity. To help students remember the difference between *lie* and *lay,* you might have them write five sentences using forms of *lie* and five using forms of *lay* and illustrate the sentences with stick figures. Then, have students label each sentence either "resting" or "putting."

Meeting INDIVIDUAL NEEDS

ENGLISH-LANGUAGE LEARNERS

General Strategies. Some students might have difficulty distinguishing the vowel differences in the troublesome verbs. To focus on these differences, you may want to write numbered verbs on the chalkboard and pronounce them in random order.

    1—lie, **2**—lay, **3**—sit,
    4—set, **5**—rise, **6**—raise

Have students identify by number which verb they hear. Then, pair English-language learners with English-proficient speakers who can give feedback on pronunciation as students read aloud the forms of the troublesome verbs in the exercises in this section.

RESOURCES

Six Troublesome Verbs

Practice

- *Grammar, Usage, and Mechanics,* pp. 150, 151, 152, 153
- *Language Workshop CD-ROM,* Lesson 16 🎧

Critical Thinking

Analysis. Challenge students to examine the sentences in **Exercises 9, 10,** and **11** and determine what *lie, sit,* and *rise* all have in common. [*All three are used as intransitive verbs and therefore do not take direct objects.*]

Then, ask what *lay, set,* and *raise* have in common. [*All three are used as transitive verbs, requiring direct objects to complete a thought.*]

TEACHING (TIP)

Mnemonics. To help students choose the correct forms of *sit* and *set,* suggest that they use the following mnemonic sentence:

I sit with an *i; I set* the book on the *edge* with an *e.*

You may also want to demonstrate the actions as you say the sentences.

STYLE TIP

You may know that the word *set* has more meanings than the two given here. Check in a dictionary to see if the meaning you intend requires an object.

EXAMPLE
We watched silently as the sun **set.** [Here, *set* does not take an object.]

---

9. Our cat _____ in the sun whenever it can.   9. lies
10. After reading for almost three hours, I _____ back and rested my head on the cushions.   10. lay

Sit and Set

17i. The verb *sit* means "to rest in an upright, seated position." *Sit* seldom takes an object. The verb *set* means "to put" or "to place (something somewhere)." *Set* generally takes an object.

Principal Parts of *Sit* and *Set*			
Base Form	**Present Participle**	**Past**	**Past Participle**
sit	[is] sitting	sat	[have] sat
set	[is] setting	set	[have] set

EXAMPLES   **Sit** down.
Set it down.

The cups **sat** on the tray.
I **set** the cups there.

How long **has** it **sat** on the bench?
She **had set** the picnic basket on the bench.

Exercise 10 Writing the Forms of *Sit* and *Set*

Write the correct form of *sit* or *set* for the blank in each of the following sentences.

EXAMPLE   1. Will you _____ with me, Josh?
          1. *sit*

1. Please _____ here, Mrs. Brown.   1. sit
2. Have you _____ the seedlings in the sun?   2. set
3. We were _____ in the park during the Fourth of July fireworks display.   3. sitting
4. Someone has already _____ the kettle on the stove.   4. set
5. Grandpa is busily _____ several varieties of tomato plants in the vegetable garden.   5. setting
6. At the concert, Keith _____ near Isabelle.   6. sat
7. Mrs. Levine _____ the menorah on the mantel and asked Rachel to light the first candle.   7. set

8. They were ____ on the rocks, watching the surfers who were riding the large waves.   8. sitting

9. We had ____ still for almost an hour.   9. sat

10. Have you ever ____ on the beach at sundown and waited for the stars to come out?   10. sat

Rise and *Raise*

17j. The verb *rise* means "to go in an upward direction." *Rise* does not take an object. The verb *raise* means "to move (something) in an upward direction." *Raise* generally takes an object.

Principal Parts of *Rise* and *Raise*			
Base Form	**Present Participle**	**Past**	**Past Participle**
rise	[is] rising	rose	[have] risen
raise	[is] raising	raised	[have] raised

EXAMPLES   She **rises** early.
She **raises** that question.

The price of cereal **rose.**
The store **raised** prices.

The lakes **have risen** since the spring rains.
The rains **have raised** the water level.

Exercise 11   **Writing the Forms of *Rise* and *Raise***

Write the correct form of *rise* or *raise* for the blank in each of the following sentences.

EXAMPLE   **1.** The river has been ____ rapidly since noon.

1. rising

1. Please ____ and face the audience; then, begin your oral interpretation of the poem.   **1.** rise

2. After the speech, the reporters ____ several questions that the senator refused to answer.   **2.** raised

3. Will the governor ____ sales tax again this year, or will he wait until after the election?   **3.** raise

4. The price of fuel has ____ steadily.   **4.** risen

5. Let's get there before the curtain ____.   **5.** rises

STYLE   TIP

The verb *raise* has definitions other than the one given here. Another common definition is "to grow" or "to bring to maturity."

EXAMPLES
They **raise** cotton.
He **raises** cattle.

Notice that both of these uses also take an object.

TEACHING   TIP

Mnemonics. Tell students that one trick for remembering *rise* and *raise* is to memorize the sentence "All *rise* and *raise* the window."

USAGE

MODALITIES

Visual/Kinesthetic Learners. As a review strategy after student papers for **Review G** have been corrected, you might ask students who had trouble distinguishing between any two verbs to pantomime the action of the correct verb.

Crossing the Curriculum

Art. To depict the correct forms of easily confused verbs in **Review G**, you may wish to assign each student to draw images related to the correct and incorrect verb forms in an assigned sentence. For example, for sentence 1 a student would illustrate *mother sat* and *mother set*. After discussing the drawings, display them where students can refer to them or have students create a booklet of the illustrations.

Viewing the Art

Ideas for Writing. For immigrants like the Hungarian family pictured here, coming to Ellis Island must have been a frightening experience. Even though New York Harbor held many dreams for the immigrants, the newcomers were also faced with a new country, language, and culture. You may want to have students imagine being one of the thousands of immigrants shuffled through Ellis Island Station. Have students write diary entries describing their immigration experiences. Remind students to be aware of verb tense as they write their entries.

6. Jerry and Alexander, two of the stagehands, will ____ the curtain for each act.   **6.** raise
7. The bread has ____ beautifully.   **7.** risen
8. The moon ____ and slipped behind a cloud, but there was still plenty of light for us to find our way home.   **8.** rose
9. The candidate ____ to address her supporters.   **9.** rose
10. The children ____ their flag for Cinco de Mayo.   **10.** raised

Review G   **Identifying the Correct Forms of *Lie* and *Lay*, *Sit* and *Set*, and *Rise* and *Raise***

Choose the <u>correct verb</u> in parentheses in each of the following sentences.

EXAMPLE   **1.** The number of immigrants coming to the United States (*rose, raised*) steadily during the late 1800s and early 1900s.

1. rose

1. The Hungarian mother shown below (*sat, set*) with her children for this picture around 1910.
2. They were among thousands of immigrant families who (*sat, set*) their baggage on American soil for the first time at the immigration station on Ellis Island in New York Harbor.
3. (*Lying, Laying*) down was often impossible on the crowded ships that brought these immigrants to the United States.
4. Most immigrants were thankful to be able to (*lie, lay*) their few belongings on the deck and think of the future.

The Granger Collection, New York

5. Their hopes for new lives must have (*risen, raised*) as they drew closer to the United States.
6. The history book (*lying, laying*) on my desk states that eleven million immigrants came to the United States between 1870 and 1899.
7. (*Sit, Set*) down and read more about the immigrants who came from Germany, Ireland, Great Britain, Scandinavia, and the Netherlands in the early 1800s.
8. After 1890, the number of immigrants from Austria-Hungary, Italy, Russia, Poland, and Greece (*rose, raised*).
9. Many United States citizens were (*rising, raising*) concerns that there would not be enough jobs for everyone in the country.

10. However, we know now that immigrant workers helped the country to (*rise*, *raise*) to new industrial heights.

Mood

17k. *Mood* is the form a verb takes to indicate the attitude of the person using the verb.

(1) The *indicative mood* is used to express a fact, an opinion, or a question.

EXAMPLES   Seamus Heaney **is** the Irish poet who **won** the Nobel Prize in literature in 1995.

I **think** he **is** the best of the poets featured in this book.

Have you **read** the poem, Anita?

(2) The *imperative mood* is used to express a direct command or request.

EXAMPLES   **Halt!** [command]

Please **write** your answers on a separate sheet of paper. [request]

(3) The *subjunctive mood* is used to express a suggestion, a necessity, a condition contrary to fact, or a wish.

EXAMPLES   Gerald suggested that we **be** ready to board the train. [suggestion]

It is essential that all of the delegates **be** available for questions. [necessity]

If I **were** you, I would call them immediately. [condition contrary to fact]

Leilani wishes she **were** scuba diving off the Yucatán peninsula. [wish]

Review H   Identifying the Mood of Verbs

For each of the sentences on the following page, identify the mood of the italicized verb as *indicative*, *imperative*, or *subjunctive*.

EXAMPLE   **1.** Ferryboats *sail* frequently between Calais, France, and Dover, England.

     1. indicative

PEANUTS reprinted by permission of United Feature Syndicate, Inc.

Mood   **543**

Mood

Rule 17k *(pp. 543–544)*

O B J E C T I V E

■ **To identify the mood of verbs as indicative, imperative, or subjunctive**

Meeting INDIVIDUAL NEEDS

MULTIPLE INTELLIGENCES

Linguistic. Challenge students to write a dialogue between a coach and a player using the three moods. Before students begin writing, have them brainstorm which situations are suited to each mood. [*Imperative mood is used for commands:* "Joe, replace *Jones at forward.*" *Indicative mood is used for straightforward conversation:* "The game *will begin at 7:30.*" *Subjunctive indicates, among other things, the conditional:* "If the field *were dry, the players wouldn't get so muddy.*"]

USAGE

RESOURCES

Mood

Practice

■ *Grammar, Usage, and Mechanics,* p. 154

1. imp.
2. ind.
3. ind.
4. sub.
5. imp.
6. sub.
7. ind.
8. ind.

9. imp.

10. sub.

1. Please *hold* your applause until after all of the presentations.
2. La Paz, in Bolivia, *is* the world's highest capital city.
3. Female marsupials *carry* their young in pouches.
4. Is it necessary that he *rehearse* tonight?
5. *Take* out the trash immediately, Paul!
6. If I *were* you, I would not swim in that lake.
7. How much interest *does* State Bank *pay* on savings accounts and checking accounts?
8. Angela *intends* to continue her work at the humane society after school.
9. Mr. Guzman, please *consider* postponing the practice until next week.
10. For rust to form, it is essential that four atoms of solid iron and three molecules of oxygen *be* present.

Review I Identifying Correct Uses of Verbs

From each pair of words in parentheses, choose the correct item.

EXAMPLE **[1]** Look at this great old photograph that Grandma has just (*gave, given*) me.

  1. given

Grandma told me that the Pop Corn King **[1]** (*been, was*) her grandfather and, consequently, my great-great-grandfather. This warmhearted man **[2]** (*took, taken*) Grandma and her sister into his home after their parents had **[3]** (*drowned, drownded*) in a flood. He would sometimes let the girls **[4]** (*sit, set*) in the driver's seat with him. The photograph was **[5]** (*maked, made*) in 1914 in the resort town of

Petoskey, Michigan. During the summer, my great-great-granddad **[6]** (*use, used*) to drive through the streets in the late afternoon. He **[7]** (*rang, rung*) a bell, and children **[8]** (*run, ran*) out to buy treats just as kids do today. Look— the popcorn **[9]** (*cost, costed*) only five cents! The last time I **[10]** (*buyed, bought*) popcorn at the movies, I paid $3.75!

USAGE

Chapter Review

A. Identifying Correct Forms of Verbs

If a sentence contains an incorrect verb form, write the correct form. If a sentence is already correct, write *C*.

1. That car ~~breaked~~ the land speed record.
2. Grandfather ~~walks~~ around the park every morning when he lived in Madrid.
3. The crocodile ~~ran~~ across the marsh and ~~slips~~ into the water.
4. Are the bells of Sant' Angelo rung every day at sunset?
5. After Lourdes had ~~drove~~ two hours, she stopped for a break.
6. Grandpa has ~~swam~~ across Santa Rosa Sound.
7. Our dog Pippa likes to ~~set~~ in the doorway and watch the traffic.
8. Will the bread ~~raise~~ faster in the oven or on the table?
9. Uncle Ben ~~brung~~ us a giant jigsaw puzzle of the Mojave Desert.
10. I could have sworn that the Green Bay Packers won the Super Bowl that year.
11. Carmilla's blouse was stained, but she ~~knowed~~ how to get the stain out.
12. Lilly has drunk two glasses of milk and still wants more.
13. Toucans ~~fly~~ by the window and a cool breeze ~~blew~~ from the gulf.
14. Last night, Dr. Madison ~~talks~~ about the new laser operation.
15. The dogs are ~~laying~~ under the porch.
16. The curtains ~~raised~~ at the beginning of the first act.
17. She has apparently ~~choosed~~ the color blue.
18. The heron ~~waits~~ for the fish before it ~~caught~~ it.
19. We laid the tools down and had lunch.
20. It's a good thing that truck hasn't ~~broke~~ down—it was certainly an expensive investment.

B. Identifying Active and Passive Voice

For each of the following sentences, tell whether the verb is in the *active* or *passive* voice.

21. The United States president is elected every four years by a majority of popular and electoral votes.

Answers (margin column)

1. broke
2. walked
3. runs/slips *or* ran/slipped
4. C
5. driven
6. swum
7. sit
8. rise
9. brought
10. C
11. knew
12. C
13. flew/blew *or* fly/blows
14. talked
15. lying
16. rose
17. chosen
18. waited/caught *or* waits/catches
19. C
20. broken

21. passive

Using the Chapter Review

To assess students' progress, you may want to compare the types of items missed on the **Diagnostic Preview** to those missed on the **Chapter Review**. If students have not made significant progress, you could refer them to **Chapter 28: Correcting Common Errors, Exercises 10–13** for additional practice.

USAGE

22. active	**22.** Yesterday the fawn ate its first full meal.
23. passive	**23.** Was Oscar told the news beforehand?
24. passive	**24.** The Veterans of Foreign Wars banquet was well attended.
25. active	**25.** Jenny speaks French and Arabic as well as English.
26. passive	**26.** Was Ruth Lopez appointed goodwill ambassador by the secretary-general?
27. active	**27.** Most early British racing cars had superchargers.
28. passive	**28.** The best songs in the show were performed by a husband-and-wife duet from San Marcos, Texas.
29. active	**29.** Our club sponsors a variety of community projects.
30. passive	**30.** Large numbers of elephants are herded into different areas of the park in order to preserve the foliage.

C. Proofreading a Paragraph for Correct Verb Forms

The following paragraph contains errors in verb usage. If a verb form is wrong, write the correct form. If a sentence is already correct, write *C*.

31. blew	[31] Last night the wind ~~blowed~~ for hours during the snowstorm.
32. fallen	[32] When Libby and I looked outside in the morning, at least a foot of
33. C	snow had fell. [33] Instead of a brown, lifeless yard, we saw a glittering
34. eaten	fantasy world. [34] Never in our lives had we ate our cereal as fast as we
35. C	did that morning! [35] We quickly put on our parkas and ran out the
36. came	door to build a snow fort. [36] Mom, smiling, ~~come~~ outside, too.
37. known	[37] We should have ~~knowed~~ she would start a snowball fight!
38. went	[38] Before we could get our revenge, mom ~~goes~~ back into the house to
39. frozen	warm up. [39] Soon afterward, our feet felt as if they had ~~freezed~~ solid.
40. brought	[40] When we were finally back inside, Mom ~~brung~~ us hot apple cider as a peace offering.

D. Identifying the Correct Forms of Six Troublesome Verbs

Choose the correct verb in parentheses for each of the following sentences.

41. Their hopes (*raised*, *rose*) when the sun broke through and shone on the city below.

RESOURCES

Using Verbs Correctly
Review
■ *Grammar, Usage, and Mechanics*, pp. 155, 156, 157, 158, 159

Assessment
■ *Assessment Package*
—Chapter Tests, Ch. 17
—Chapter Tests in Standardized Test Formats, Ch. 17
■ *Test Generator (One-Stop Planner CD-ROM)*

42. Please (*set, sit*) the orchid next to the rhododendron in the greenhouse.

43. Tim (*sat, set*) in the old armchair and recalled long summer evenings from his childhood.

44. Was that you I saw (*laying, lying*) in the hammock a minute ago?

45. (*Lay, Lie*) that magazine down and listen to what I have to say!

46. The cadets stood at attention as the color sergeant (*rose, raised*) the flag.

47. The mythical phoenix is a bird that (*rises, raises*) from its own ashes.

48. He has a cold, so he has (*laid, lain*) on the couch most of the afternoon.

49. The seals were (*laying, lying*) on the beach.

50. He has (*sat, set*) his tools on the workbench.

Writing Application
Using Verbs in Instructions

Verb Tense   You have been asked to teach your eight-year-old brother to make his own after-school snack. Write instructions for making a nutritious treat. Use correct verb tense so that your directions are easy to follow.

Prewriting   You will need to choose a snack that a child would be able to make and would enjoy. You may want to list all of the steps first and then go back and number them in order.

Writing   As you write your first draft, think about how to define or clarify words that an eight-year-old might not know. Make sure that your verb tenses show the sequence of the steps.

Revising   Ask a friend or young child you know to act out your instructions. Revise any steps that confuse your assistant. Add words that indicate chronological order (such as *first, second, then*, and *next*).

Publishing   Check to be sure your verb tenses are correct. Use your textbook or a dictionary to check the spelling of the verbs in your instructions. Pay special attention to irregular verbs. Your class may decide to make its own snack cookbook to share with elementary school students or your local parent-teacher organization.

Writing Application
(*p. 547*)

OBJECTIVE

- To write instructions using correct verb tense

Writing Application

Tip. The writing assignment helps students understand the importance of using verb tenses consistently. It also gives practice in using transitions to show the sequence of events.

Scoring Rubric. While you will want to pay particular attention to students' correct use of verb tense, you will also want to evaluate overall writing performance. You may want to give a split score to assess development and clarity of the composition as well as usage skills.

Critical Thinking

Analysis. Remind students that as they write instructions, they will have to analyze their audience's knowledge and vocabulary. For instance, if the instructions on a box of cake mix are read to a five-year-old who has never made a cake, the phrase "add one egg" might need explanation. Without the added directions to crack open the egg, the child might lay the egg, shell and all, on top of the mix.

RESOURCES

Writing Application
Extension

- *Grammar, Usage, and Mechanics*, p. 162
- *Language Workshop CD-ROM*, Lessons 14–17

CHAPTER

18

Using Pronouns Correctly

Nominative and Objective Uses; Clear Reference

Diagnostic Preview

A. Correcting Pronoun Forms

Identify each incorrectly used <u>pronoun</u> in the following sentences. Then, write the correct form of that pronoun. If a sentence is already correct, write *C*.

EXAMPLE   **1.** Excuse me, Rhonda, but this arrangement is strictly between Carl and I.

      1. *I—me*

1. us   **1.** The author spoke to <u>we</u> history students about Slavic culture in Eastern Europe.

2. her   **2.** During the Olympic trials every diver except <u>she</u> received a low score from the judges.

3. C   **3.** The instructor, who seemed nervous during the show, was proud of Lani's performance.

4. she   **4.** It couldn't have been <u>her</u>.

5. I   **5.** Van is more energetic than <u>me</u>.

6. me   **6.** Rick couldn't spot Maura and <u>I</u> in the huge crowd at the state fairgrounds.

7. C   **7.** Tyrone and he are playing backgammon at Regina's house this afternoon.

8. Laura gave <u>he</u> and Edwin a beautiful poem that she had written about friendship.

9. Angie's neighbors, Mrs. Brandt and he, helped plant the trees for Arbor Day.

10. <u>Whomever</u> can possibly take her place?

8. him

9. C

10. Whoever

B. Proofreading a Paragraph for Correct Pronoun Forms

Some of the sentences in the following paragraph contain <u>pronouns</u> that have been used incorrectly. Identify each incorrectly used pronoun. Then, write the correct form of that pronoun. If a sentence is already correct, write *C*.

EXAMPLE   **[1]** To Velma and I, Dizzy Dean is one of the greatest baseball players of all time.

       1. *I—me*

[11] We think there never has been another baseball player like him. [12] Fans still talk about <u>he</u> and his teammates. [13] Dean pitched for the St. Louis Cardinals, to <u>who</u> his fastball was a great help, especially in the 1934 World Series. [14] Dean was such a character that his fans never knew what crazy notion might come to <u>he</u> during games. [15] He had a real confidence about him, too. [16] According to one famous story about Dean, <u>whom</u> was also known for his quips, he once said, "Tain't braggin' if you kin really do it!" [17] When Dean became a sportscaster, <u>him</u> and his informal speech appealed to fans. [18] He liked his fans, and they liked him. [19] A big honor for <u>he</u> was being elected to baseball's Hall of Fame. [20] <u>Us</u> fans can go to the Dizzy Dean Museum in Jackson, Mississippi, to find out more about Dean's career.

11. C
12. him
13. whom
14. him
15. C
16. who

17. he
18. C
19. him
20. We

Case

18a. *Case* is the form that a noun or pronoun takes to show its relationship to other words in a sentence.

In English, there are three cases: *nominative, objective,* and *possessive.* Choosing the correct case form for a noun is usually simple because the form remains the same in the nominative and objective cases.

NOMINATIVE   My **dentist** has opened a new practice in the office building next to the mall.

OBJECTIVE   The receptionist who works for my **dentist** recently graduated from junior college.

Meeting INDIVIDUAL NEEDS

ENGLISH-LANGUAGE LEARNERS
Spanish. In Spanish, *su* can mean *your, his, her, its,* or *their,* and *suyo* can mean *yours, his, hers,* or *theirs.* These possessive pronouns, *su* and *suyo,* agree in gender and/or number with the thing possessed, not with the possessor. Therefore, Spanish speakers may be tempted to say "her class" and "hers classes." To help your students distinguish between the possessive pronouns that can be used to modify nouns [*my, our,* and so on] and those that can be used only as pronouns [*mine, ours,* and so on], use template sentences such as "This is ____ apartment." and "This apartment is ____."

The Nominative Case

Rules 18b, c *(pp. 550–552)*

OBJECTIVES

- To read aloud sentences containing pronouns used as subjects

- To identify pronouns used as subjects

- To read aloud sentences containing pronouns used as predicate nominatives

- To identify correct nominative case pronouns and their use as subjects or predicate nominatives in sentences

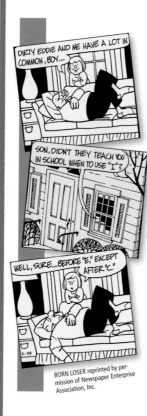

BORN LOSER reprinted by permission of Newspaper Enterprise Association, Inc.

Reference Note
For more about the **subjects of verbs,** see page 416.

Only in the possessive case does a noun change its form, usually by adding an apostrophe and an *s.*

POSSESSIVE   My **dentist's** business is thriving.

Personal pronouns, however, have distinct case forms. In the following example, the pronouns in boldface type all refer to the same person. They have different forms because of their different uses.

EXAMPLE   **I** [nominative] **forgot to bring my** [possessive] **notebook with me** [objective].

The Case Forms of Personal Pronouns

Personal Pronouns		
Nominative Case	**Objective Case**	**Possessive Case**
Singular		
First Person I	me	my, mine
Second Person you	you	your, yours
Third Person he, she, it	him, her, it	his, her, hers, its
Plural		
First Person we	us	our, ours
Second Person you	you	your, yours
Third Person they	them	their, theirs

Notice that *you* and *it* have the same form in the nominative and the objective cases. All other personal pronouns have different nominative and objective forms.

The Nominative Case

Nominative case pronouns—*I, you, he, she, it, we,* and *they*—are used as subjects of verbs and as predicate nominatives.

18b.   The subject of a verb should be in the nominative case.

EXAMPLES   **I** told Phillip that **we** would win. [*I* is the subject of *told; we* is the subject of *would win.*]

Were **Renata** and **he** on time? [*Renata* and *he* are the compound subject of *were.*]

Case and The Nominative Case
Practice
- *Grammar, Usage, and Mechanics,* pp. 164, 165, 166–167
- *Language Workshop CD-ROM,* Lesson 18

Oral Practice 1 Using Pronouns as Subjects

Read the following sentences aloud, stressing the italicized pronouns.

1. *He* and *I* agree that lacrosse is the most exciting game *we*'ve ever played.
2. *They* and their friends enjoyed the field trip.
3. Will Sue Ann and *she* enter the art contest?
4. Our teacher and *we* are glad that *he* and *she* are returning from their vacation soon.
5. *He* and *she* said that *we* were responsible for counting the ballots and posting the results.
6. Where are *they* and my parents?
7. Will *you* and *he* help us with the book sale?
8. When are *you* and *I* going to Arizona?

Exercise 1 Identifying Pronouns Used as Subjects

The following paragraph contains ten pairs of pronouns in parentheses. For each pair, choose the <u>correct pronoun</u> to use as a subject.

EXAMPLE **[1]** (*They, Them*) may be the most famous husband and wife scientist team ever.

    1. They

Although Marie and Pierre Curie were both brilliant physicists, **[1]** (*she, her*) is better known than her husband is today. In fact, **[2]** (*I, me*) was genuinely surprised to learn that **[3]** (*them, they*), along with another scientist, shared the Nobel Prize in physics in 1903. **[4]** (*We, Us*) tend to remember only Marie primarily because **[5]** (*her, she*) was the first woman to win a Nobel Prize. During their life together, Marie Curie always felt that **[6]** (*her, she*) and Pierre were a team. Working in a small laboratory in Paris, **[7]** (*they, them*) didn't have room for independent research. Before his death in 1906, **[8]** (*them, they*) collaborated on almost every project. In 1911, **[9]** (*she, her*) was again honored by the Nobel committee when **[10]** (*she, her*) was awarded the prize in chemistry.

<table>
<tr><td>┌ TIPS & TRICKS ┐</td></tr>
</table>

TIPS & TRICKS

To choose the correct pronoun forms in a compound subject, try each pronoun separately with the verb.

EXAMPLE
(*She, Her*) and (*they, them*) answered the ad. [*She answered* or *Her answered*? *They answered* or *Them answered*?]

She and **they** answered the ad.

Meeting INDIVIDUAL NEEDS

INCLUSION

For further practice with pronouns used as subjects, have students work with a helper to change declarative sentences in **Oral Practice 1** into questions (for example, "Do he and I agree that lacrosse is the most exciting game we've ever played?") and questions into statements (for example, "Sue Ann and she will enter the art contest").

ENGLISH-LANGUAGE LEARNERS

Spanish. In some languages, including Spanish, the meaning of a pronoun used as a subject is contained in the verb ending. The pronoun is stated only for clarification or stress. Emphasize that in English a pronoun used as a subject is stated unless the sentence is a command or request with an understood *you*, such as "Open the window."

Case   **551**

MINI-LESSON

Continued on p. 552

Using You. Students often use the indefinite *you* in writing. Sometimes the *you* is an inexact substitute for the indefinite pronoun *one* or for *a person,* and sometimes it is an avoidance of a first-person pronoun like *I, me, we,* or *us.* Remind students that in formal writing, second-person pronouns are used only when a writer addresses the reader directly, as in commands and directions.

    Use the following examples to illustrate vague uses of *you.*

Relating to Literature

If your textbook includes Abraham Lincoln's speech "With a Task Before Me," you might use the selection to emphasize how personal pronouns in the first person are used. Have students find all the first-person pronouns and classify them by case. Students could use a chart like the following to present their findings:

SENTENCE NUMBER	PRONOUN	CASE
1.	my	possessive

Meeting
INDIVIDUAL NEEDS

LEARNERS HAVING DIFFICULTY

To test for correct case forms in compound constructions, have students use each pronoun alone in the sentence. (For example, in **Exercise 2**, sentence 2, students would say "She will move to San Miguel" and "He will move to San Miguel.") Remind them that when trying this trick, they may need to change the verb form to agree with a singular subject. (For example, in **Exercise 2**, sentence 4, "You and I are . . ." would become "I am . . .")

Looking at Language

Tell students that *nominative*, as in *predicate nominative*, comes from *nomen*, Latin for "name." Predicate nominatives usually appear after the verb in the complete predicate and rename the subject.

Reference Note
For more information about **predicate nominatives**, see page 430.

STYLE TIP

Widespread usage has made such expressions as *It's me, That's him,* or *Could it have been her?* acceptable in informal conversation and writing. Avoid using them in formal speaking and in your written work unless you are writing notes, informal dialogue, or friendly letters.

STYLE TIP

Sometimes pronouns such as *I, he, she, we,* and *they* sound awkward when used as parts of a compound subject. In such cases, it is a good idea to revise the sentence.

AWKWARD
She and we are going to the concert.

BETTER
We are going to the concert with **her.**

7. p.n.

552 | **Chapter 18** | Using Pronouns Correctly

18c. A predicate nominative should be in the nominative case.

A *predicate nominative* is a word or word group in the predicate that identifies the subject or refers to it. A predicate nominative is connected to its subject by a linking verb. A pronoun used as a predicate nominative generally follows a form of the verb *be* or a phrase ending in *be* or *been.*

EXAMPLES　　This is **he.**

Did you know that the pitcher was **she**?

Oral Practice 2 Using Pronouns as Predicate Nominatives

Read the following sentences aloud, stressing the italicized pronouns.

1. Do you know whether it was *he*?
2. I thought it was *they.*
3. The winner of the marathon is *she.*
4. The ones you saw dancing were not *we.*
5. Can the valedictorian be *she*?
6. The first ones to arrive were *he* and *she.*
7. Do you think it may have been *they*?
8. The best speakers are *she* and *I.*

Exercise 2 Identifying Pronouns Used as Subjects and Predicate Nominatives

Identify the correct pronoun in parentheses for each of the following sentences. Then, give its use in the sentence—as a *subject* or *predicate nominative.*

EXAMPLE　　1. If the phone rings, it will probably be (*she, her*).
　　　　　1. she—predicate nominative

1. How did you know the guest speakers were (*they, them*)?　**1.** p.n.
2. (*She, Her*) and (*he, him*) will move to San Miguel.　**2.** sub./sub.
3. Open the door! It is (*I, me*)!　**3.** p.n.
4. You and (*me, I*) are the only candidates left.　**4.** sub.
5. It was wonderful to hear that the winner was (*he, him*).　**5.** p.n.
6. (*Us, We*) and (*them, they*) will meet at five o'clock.　**6.** sub./sub.
7. That man looked a little like Harry, but it was not (*he, him*) after all.
8. Believe it or not, (*she, her*) was on the radio this morning.　**8.** sub.
9. Yes, the one in costume was really (*she, her*)!　**9.** p.n.
10. You and (*we, us*) were the first visitors.　**10.** sub.

MINI-LESSON

1. Sunny weather may make you feel optimistic. [*Revision: Sunny weather may make people feel optimistic.*]

2. My mother always offers you fresh fruit. [*Revision: My mother always offers me fresh fruit.*]

The Objective Case

Objective case pronouns—*me, you, him, her, it, us,* and *them*—are used as direct objects, indirect objects, and objects of prepositions.

18d. A direct object should be in the objective case.

A **direct object** is a noun, pronoun, or word group that tells who or what receives the action of the verb or shows the result of the action.

EXAMPLES Phil called **her** last night. [*Her* tells *whom* Phil called.]

We still don't know what caused **them**. [*Them* shows the results of the action caused.]

Oral Practice 3 **Using Pronouns as Direct Objects**

Read the following sentences aloud, stressing the italicized pronouns.

1. They saw Liang and *me* at the fair.
2. Julia said that she recognized *him* and *me* at once.
3. Has anyone called *her* or *him* lately?
4. They took *us* to the reggae concert.
5. Alicia often visits Charlene and *her.*
6. A dog chased *her* and *me* out of the yard.
7. Within a few hours, the search party found Duane and *him.*
8. Did you ask *them* or *us?*

Exercise 3 **Choosing Pronouns Used as Direct Objects**

For each item below, write an appropriate pronoun in the objective case. Use a variety of pronouns. Do not use *you* or *it.* Answers will vary.

EXAMPLE **1.** Have you told _____ yet?

   1. him

1. I found Nina and _____ in the library.   **1.** her
2. Will you help _____ or _____ with their homework?   **2.** us/them
3. Sylvia Chu drove Candy and _____ to the movies.   **3.** me
4. We all watched Aaron and _____ as they ran the marathon.   **4.** him
5. These gloves fit both Carl and _____.   **5.** me
6. Did you tell _____ about the picnic?   **6.** them
7. If you don't call _____, I will.   **7.** her
8. The realtor showed _____ and _____ the apartment.   **8.** her/me
9. That solution suits _____.   **9.** us
10. The doctor cured _____.   **10.** him

Reference Note

For more about the different types of **objects,** see page 431.

STYLE TIP

When the object is compound, try each pronoun separately with the verb. All parts of the compound must be correct for the sentence to be correct.

EXAMPLE

Phil's call surprised (*she, her*) and (*I, me*). [*Phil's call surprised she* or *Phil's call surprised her? It surprised I* or *It surprised me?*]

Phil's call surprised **her** and **me.**

The Objective Case and the Possessive Case

Rules 18d–g *(pp. 553–559)*

OBJECTIVES

■ To read aloud sentences containing pronouns used as direct and indirect objects

■ To complete sentences by supplying appropriate pronouns as direct and indirect objects

Meeting INDIVIDUAL NEEDS

ENGLISH-LANGUAGE LEARNERS

Spanish. Because use of case is not the same in Spanish and English, Spanish-speaking students may need extra practice with English cases. To personalize the activity, use a sentence with students' names. ("Roberto will ask Candace to take notes for Jorge.") Then, let volunteers substitute pronouns. "_____ will ask _____ to take notes for _____." [*He will ask her to take notes for me.*]

USAGE

Meeting INDIVIDUAL NEEDS

ENGLISH-LANGUAGE LEARNERS

Spanish. Spanish uses three different objective forms for third-person pronouns: one for direct objects, another for indirect objects, and a third for objects of prepositions. Tell students that in English, the objective case pronouns are the same for all kinds of objects. Provide simple cloze activities for practice.

EXAMPLES

1. Mother gave _____ a book.
[*him, her, them*]

2. Mother called _____ to dinner.
[*him, her, them*]

3. Mother gave the book to _____.
[*him, her, them*]

MODALITIES

Auditory Learners. For further oral practice with indirect objects, have students reword the sentences in **Oral Practice 4** to change the indirect objects to objects of prepositions. (For example, sentence 1 becomes "Mrs. Petratos offered delicious moussaka to them.")

TEACHING TIP

Activity. To help students become more familiar with objective case pronouns, divide the class into small groups and have them find examples of objective case pronouns in newspapers, magazines, and books. Provide poster board and markers for students to use to list labeled examples and the source of each example.

TIPS & TRICKS

Generally, the indirect object comes between the verb and the direct object.

EXAMPLES
Grandma knitted **us** sweaters.

We gave **climbing the cliff** our full attention.

18e. An indirect object should be in the objective case.

An *indirect object* is a noun, pronoun, or word group that appears in sentences containing direct objects. An indirect object tells *to whom* or *to what* or *for whom* or *for what* the action of the verb is done.

EXAMPLES   Molly made **me** a tape. [*Me* tells *for whom* the tape was made.]

The puppies were muddy, so we gave **them** a bath. [*Them* tells *to what* we gave a bath.]

NOTE   Indirect objects do not follow prepositions. If a preposition such as *to* or *for* precedes an object, the object is an object of a preposition.

Oral Practice 4 · Using Pronouns as Indirect Objects

Read the following sentences aloud, stressing the italicized pronouns.

1. Mrs. Petratos offered *them* delicious moussaka.
2. Show Yolanda and *her* your snapshots of Chicago.
3. Sara made Dad and *me* mittens and matching scarves.
4. Send Tom and *him* your new address.
5. My parents told *her* and *me* the news.
6. Mrs. Morita gave *him* and *her* applications.
7. Tell Willie and *them* the story that you told Erin and *me*.
8. The judges awarded *us* the trophy.

Exercise 4 · Writing Pronouns Used as Indirect Objects

For each item below, write an appropriate pronoun in the objective case. Use a variety of pronouns. Do not use *you* or *it*. Answers will vary.

EXAMPLE   **1.** The teacher gave _____ their homework assignments.
1. them

1. them
2. her
3. him/me
4. me
5. her/him
6. us
7. them
8. her
9. him
10. him

1. Hassan asked _____ the most difficult question.
2. Alex baked _____ a loaf of banana bread.
3. The teacher handed _____ and _____ the homework assignments.
4. Linda threw _____ the ball.
5. Mr. Young has never told _____ and _____ the real story.
6. Writing stories gives _____ great pleasure.
7. We brought _____ T-shirts from California.
8. Mr. Cruz sent _____ a pen as a graduation gift.
9. My little sister gave _____ an animal carved out of soap.
10. Lee's cousin knitted _____ a sweater.

Identifying Correct Forms of Pronouns

Identify the correct pronoun in parentheses for each of the following sentences. Then, give its use in the sentence—as a *subject*, *predicate nominative*, *direct object*, or *indirect object*.

EXAMPLE   **1.** Brian and (*I, me*) visited the computer fair.

       1. I—subject

  1. A guide showed (*we, us*) the latest in technology.   **1.** i.o.
  2. She told Brian and (*I, me*) some interesting facts about software.   **2.** i.o.
  3. In a short time, we had surprised (*she, her*) and several bystanders with our new computer game.   **3.** d.o.
  4. The new computer aces were (*we, us*)!   **4.** p.n.
  5. Another guide showed Brian and (*I, me*) all kinds of robotic machines.   **5.** i.o.
  6. The guide said that (*he, him*) and his twin sister were going to dance with two robots.   **6.** sub.
  7. The crowd and (*they, them*) seemed to enjoy the performance.   **7.** sub.
  8. One robot reached out and touched (*us, we*) with a metal hand.   **8.** d.o.
  9. Brian and (*I, me*) asked our guides how the machines worked.   **9.** sub.
10. (*They, Them*) patiently explained the control panels.   **10.** sub.

18f. **An object of a preposition should be in the objective case.**

A noun or pronoun that follows a preposition is called the ***object of a preposition.*** Together, a preposition, its object, and any modifiers of that object make up a prepositional phrase.

EXAMPLES   with **me**   before **her**   next to **them**
            for **us**   behind **him**   instead of **me**

NOTE Many people use incorrect pronoun forms with prepositions. You may have heard phrases like *between he and they* and *for you and I.* These phrases are incorrect. The pronouns are objects of a preposition and should be in the objective case: *between him and them, for you and me.*

EXAMPLES   The coaches rode in a bus in front of **us**.

           She is always very polite to **him** and **me**.

           May I play soccer with **you** and **them**?

           Between **you** and **me**, I am worried about **them**.

Reference Note

For a **list of common prepositions,** see page 400.

TIPS & TRICKS

To determine the correct pronoun form when the object of a preposition is compound, try each pronoun separately in the prepositional phrase.

EXAMPLE
The company sent a letter to (*she, her*) and (*I, me*). [*To she* or *to her*? *To I* or *to me*?]

The company sent a letter to **her** and **me**.

ALTERNATIVE LESSON
To review concepts taught earlier, ask students to find examples of the following items and write down the example and the number of the sentence in which the example appears.

1. past perfect tense verb
[3. *had surprised*]

2. two infinitives
[6. *to dance*, 7. *to enjoy*]

3. the object of an infinitive
[7. *performance*]

4. noun clause
[6. *that he and his twin sister were going to dance with two robots*, 9. *how the machines worked*]

Relating to Literature

If your literature book includes Langston Hughes's poem "Dream Deferred," also known as "Harlem," read it to the class and ask students to consider how Hughes uses the pronoun *it* in the poem. [*The pronoun clearly refers to the dream in the first line of the poem. Repetition of* dream *in lines 2, 6, 9, and 11 would lessen that word's impact. It* is *not only concise but also unstressed, allowing the stress to fall on the important words that follow the pronoun:* "dry up," "stink," "sags," *and* "explode."]

USAGE

MINI-LESSON

What Is a Preposition? You might need to remind students that a preposition is a word used to show the relationship of a noun or a pronoun to some other word in the sentence. Have students refer to **Chapter 12: Parts of Speech Overview,** for examples of commonly used prepositions. Then, ask students to use the following prepositions in phrases.

    1. beyond [*beyond the horizon*]
    2. before [*before Sunday*]
    3. until [*until bedtime*]

Review B Proofreading a Paragraph for Correct Pronoun Forms

ANSWERS

1. me—I; us—C

2. You—C; us—we

3. we—us

4. Her—She; we—us

5. her—she

6. they—them; they—C

Review B Proofreading a Paragraph for Correct Pronoun Forms

Identify the ten personal pronouns in the following paragraph. If a pronoun is incorrect, write the correct form. If a pronoun is already correct, write *C.*

EXAMPLE **[1]** She thinks all of we should have the experience of working at a store checkout counter.

   1. She—C; we—us

[1] Mrs. Jenkins, the home economics teacher that Tricia and me admire, told us all about the Universal Product Code (UPC) yesterday. [2] You and us have seen the black-striped UPC symbols on nearly everything that is for sale. [3] Mrs. Jenkins patiently showed the other classes and we how to interpret the twelve-digit number on the UPC. [4] Her explained to we that the first digit identifies the product, the next five digits stand for the manufacturer, the next five digits tell things about the product (such as color and size), and the last digit is a check number that tells the computer if another digit is incorrect. [5] Tricia said that Gregory and her found the lesson especially interesting. [6] The two of they had used the code when they worked as clerks in a store last summer.

The Possessive Case

18g. The personal pronouns in the possessive case—*my, mine, your, yours, his, her, hers, its, our, ours, their, theirs*—are used to show ownership or possession.

(1) The possessive pronouns *mine, yours, his, hers, its, ours,* and *theirs* are used as parts of a sentence in the same ways in which the pronouns in the nominative and the objective cases are used.

SUBJECT	Your car and **mine** need tune-ups.
PREDICATE NOMINATIVE	This backpack is **hers.**
DIRECT OBJECT	We finished **ours** yesterday.
INDIRECT OBJECT	Ms. Kwan gave **theirs** a quick review.
OBJECT OF PREPOSITION	Next to **yours,** my Siamese cat looks puny.

(2) The possessive pronouns *my, your, his, her, its, our,* and *their* are used as adjectives before nouns.

EXAMPLES **My** alarm clock is broken.

Do you know **their** address?

NOTE Some authorities prefer to call these possessive forms adjectives. Follow your teacher's instructions regarding these words.

Generally, a noun or pronoun preceding a gerund should be in the possessive case.

Reference Note
For more about **gerunds,** see page 453.

EXAMPLES We were all thrilled by **Ken's** scoring in the top 5 percent. [*Ken's* modifies the gerund *scoring.* Whose scoring? *Ken's* scoring.]

We were all thrilled by **his** scoring in the top 5 percent. [Whose scoring? *His* scoring.]

Review C **Identifying Correct Forms of Pronouns**

Choose the <u>correct pronoun</u> from each pair given in parentheses in the following paragraph.

EXAMPLE My cousin Felicia showed **[1]** (*I, me*) some photographs of buildings designed by I. M. Pei.

    1. me

Felicia, who is studying architecture, told **[1]** (*I, me*) a little about Pei. **[2]** (*He, Him*) is a famous American architect who was born in China. In 1935, **[3]** (*him, he*) came to the United States to study, and in 1954, **[4]** the government granted (*he, him*) citizenship. Pei's reputation grew quickly, and by the 1960s many people easily recognized the structures **[5]** (*he, him*) designed. His buildings, such as the East

Activity. To review case forms, you could create a cube with the following words written on each of the six sides: *first-person nominative, first-person objective, first-person possessive, third-person nominative, third-person objective,* and *third-person possessive.*

Tell students they will compose a story based on a beginning you will give them. Each person will have a chance to roll the cube and to add a sentence using the form required in either singular or plural form.

You may want to use one of the following beginnings:

- As the swirling whirlpool threatened to suck the child into its inky depths, . . .

- Eyes squinting, cameras focused, the group saw the first lion. . . .

You may want to record students' stories for future use.

USAGE

MINI-LESSON

Point of View. Point out that pronoun forms indicate point of view in writing. A piece written in the first-person point of view uses *I, we, me,* or *us,* whereas third person uses *he, she, they, him, her,* or *them.*

Tell students that they should choose the point of view they find most comfortable and appropriate in their writing, but that they must be careful to use point of view correctly.

Building of the National Gallery of Art in Washington, D.C., are quite distinctive; consequently, many people greatly admire [6] (*they, them*). [7] (*Him, His*) being in charge of numerous projects in the United States, Europe, and Canada earned Pei an international reputation. Did you know that the architect of the glass pyramids at the Louvre is [8] (*him, he*)? Felicia doesn't like the pyramids because [9] (*they, them*) look so different from the buildings that surround them. However, I think that design of [10] (*him, his*) is a work of art.

DRABBLE reprinted by permission of United Feature Syndicate, Inc.

Review D **Identifying Correct Pronoun Forms**

For each of the following sentences, choose the correct pronoun in parentheses. Then, give its use in the sentence—as a *subject*, *predicate nominative*, *direct object*, *indirect object*, or *object of the preposition*.

EXAMPLE 1. Did Alva or (*she, her*) leave a message?

    1. *she—subject*

1. The pranksters were (*they, them*). **1.** p.n. **2.** sub./sub.
2. (*He, Him*) and (*I, me*) are working on a special science project.
3. Is that package for Mom or (*I, me*)? **3.** o.p.
4. No one saw Otis or (*I, me*) behind the door. **4.** d.o.
5. I hope that you and (*she, her*) will be on time. **5.** sub.
6. The teacher gave Rosa and (*I, me*) extra math homework. **6.** i.o.
7. That's (*he, him*) on the red bicycle. **7.** p.n.
8. Between you and (*I, me*), I like your plan better. **8.** o.p.
9. When are your parents and (*they, them*) coming home? **9.** sub.
10. Everyone in the class except (*she, her*) and (*I, me*) had read the selection from the *Mahabharata.* **10.** o.p./o.p.

Review E **Identifying Correct Pronoun Forms**

For each sentence in the following paragraph, choose the correct pronoun in parentheses. Then, give its use in the sentence—as a *subject*, *predicate nominative*, *direct object*, *indirect object*, or *object of the preposition*.

EXAMPLE You may not know [1] (*they, them*) by name, but you may remember the actors Ossie Davis and Ruby Dee from movies or television shows.

    1. *them—direct object*

For many years, the actors Ossie Davis and Ruby Dee have entertained [1] (*we*, *us*) fans of movies and television with their talented performances. My friend Elvin and [2] (*me*, *I*) really admire both of [3] (*they*, *them*). Did you know that [4] (*they*, *them*) have been married since 1948? When Davis worked on Broadway, [5] (*he*, *him*) wrote and starred in *Purlie Victorious*, and critics gave [6] (*he*, *him*) great reviews. In addition, [7] (*him*, *he*) has appeared on the TV show *Evening Shade*. One of the stars of the movie *The Jackie Robinson Story* was [8] (*she*, *her*). What Elvin and [9] (*me*, *I*) admire most about Davis and Dee is that [10] (*them*, *they*) are fine performers who actively support civil rights and other humanitarian causes.

1. d.o.
2. sub.
3. o.p.
4. sub.
5. sub.
6. i.o.
7. sub.
8. p.n.
9. sub.
10. sub.

Special Pronoun Problems

Who and *Whom*

Nominative Case		Objective Case	
who	whoever	whom	whomever

18h. The use of *who* or *whom* in a subordinate clause depends on how the pronoun functions in the clause.

When you are choosing between *who* or *whom* in a subordinate clause, follow these steps:

STEP 1   Find the subordinate clause.

STEP 2   Decide how the pronoun is used in the clause—as a subject, a predicate nominative, a direct or indirect object, or an object of a preposition.

STEP 3   Determine the case of the pronoun according to the rules of formal standard English.

STEP 4   Select the correct form of the pronoun.

EXAMPLE   Do you know (*who*, *whom*) she is?

STEP 1   The subordinate clause is (*who*, *whom*) she is.

STEP 2   The pronoun (*who*, *whom*) is the predicate nominative: *she is who.*

STEP 3   As a predicate nominative, the pronoun is in the nominative case.

STEP 4   The nominative form is *who.*

ANSWER   Do you know **who** she is?

STYLE   TIP

In informal English, the use of *whom* is becoming less common. In fact, when you are in informal situations, you may correctly begin any question with *who* regardless of the grammar of the sentence. In formal English, however, you should distinguish between *who* and *whom.*

Reference Note

For information on **subordinate clauses,** see page 471.

STYLE   TIP

Frequently, *whom* in subordinate clauses is omitted, but its use is understood.

EXAMPLE
The people (whom) you imitate are your role models.

Leaving out *whom* tends to make writing sound informal. In formal situations, it is generally better to include *whom.*

USAGE

Special Pronoun Problems

Rules 18h–k (*pp. 559–566*)

OBJECTIVES

- To read aloud sentences containing *who* and *whom*

- To choose correct usage of *who* and *whom* in clauses and to identify their functions within the clauses

- To identify the correct forms of pronouns used as appositives

- To complete incomplete clauses using the correct pronoun forms and to tell how pronouns are used in clauses

- To correct inexact pronoun references

Special Pronoun Problems   **559**

RESOURCES

Special Pronoun Problems
Practice

- *Grammar, Usage, and Mechanics,* pp. 174, 175, 176, 177, 178–180

- *Language Workshop CD-ROM,* Lesson 20

Meeting
INDIVIDUAL
NEEDS

MULTIPLE INTELLIGENCES
Logical-Mathematical Intelligence. After stressing that words outside the clause do not affect the case of the pronoun in the clause, you might point out that this rule is similar to that of math expressions in which the operation inside the parentheses is not affected by operations outside it until the operation in parentheses has been completed. Write the following simple equation on the chalkboard to demonstrate your point: $2(10 \times 2)$.

Remind students that they would do the operation in parentheses first and then multiply that number by 2.

LEARNERS HAVING DIFFICULTY
If students have trouble distinguishing between *who* and *whom*, suggest that they reword clauses like those in **Oral Practice 5** to make statements using *he* or *she* in place of *who*, and *him* or *her* in place of *whom*. (For example, in sentence 1, students would say, "You met him yesterday." For sentence 2, they would say, "He lives next door to us.")

ENGLISH-LANGUAGE LEARNERS
General Strategies. Because many languages do not distinguish between *who* and *whom*, English-language learners may not have a context for this concept. You may want to have students practice with *who/whom* using the method explained above.

TIPS & TRICKS

If you are not sure whether to use *who* or *whom* in a sentence, try the following test. Omit everything but the subordinate clause; then, substitute a nominative case pronoun such as *he, she,* or *they* for *who* or substitute an objective case pronoun such as *him, her,* or *them* for *whom*. If the nominative case pronoun is correct, use *who*. If the objective case pronoun is correct, use *whom*.

EXAMPLE
The coach will help anyone (*who, whom*) tries hard. [*He tries hard* or *Him tries hard*? *He tries hard* is correct.]

The coach will help anyone **who** tries hard.

In the example on the previous page, the entire clause *who she is* is used as a direct object of the verb *do know*. However, the way the pronoun is used within the clause—as a predicate nominative—is what determines the correct case form.

EXAMPLE	Susan B. Anthony, about (*who, whom*) Sam reported, championed women's right to vote.
STEP 1	The subordinate clause is *about (who, whom) Sam reported.*
STEP 2	The subject is *Sam,* and the verb is *reported.* The pronoun is the object of the preposition *about: Sam reported about (who, whom).*
STEP 3	The objective of a preposition is in the objective case.
STEP 4	The objective form is *whom.*
ANSWER	Susan B. Anthony, about **whom** Sam reported, championed women's right to vote.

Oral Practice 5 — Using the Pronouns *Who* and *Whom* in Subordinate Clauses

Read each of the following sentences aloud, stressing the italicized pronouns.

1. Take this book to Eric, *whom* you met yesterday.
2. Mr. Cohen is the man *who* lives next door to us.
3. Can you tell me *who* they are?
4. Toni Morrison is an author *whom* many readers admire.
5. *Whom* Mona finally voted for is a secret.
6. The coach will penalize anyone *who* misses the bus.
7. *Whoever* wins the race will get a prize.
8. The woman to *whom* I was speaking is conducting a survey of people who ride the bus.

Exercise 5 — Classifying Pronouns Used in Subordinate Clauses and Identifying Correct Forms

For each of the following sentences, choose the correct pronoun in parentheses. Then, give its use in the sentence—as a *subject, predicate nominative, direct object, indirect object,* or *object of a preposition.*

EXAMPLE
1. I know (*who, whom*) you are.
   1. *who—predicate nominative*

1. Mrs. James, (*who, whom*) I work for, owns a pet shop in the mall and a feed store in our town. **1. o.p.**

2. Is there anyone here (*who, whom*) needs a bus pass? **2.** sub.

3. She is the only one (*who, whom*) everybody trusts. **3.** d.o.

4. Both of the women (*who, whom*) ran for seats on the city council were elected. **4.** sub.

5. I helped Mr. Thompson, (*who, whom*) was painting his garage and shingling his porch roof. **5.** sub.

6. Eileen couldn't guess (*who, whom*) the secret agent was. **6.** p.n.

7. It was Octavio Paz (*who, whom*) won the Nobel Prize in literature in 1990. **7.** sub.

8. Her grandmother, to (*who, whom*) she sent the flowers, won the over-fifty division of the marathon. **8.** o.p.

9. The person (*who, whom*) you gave the daisies is none other than my long-lost twin! **9.** i.o.

10. Shirley Chisholm, (*who, whom*) we are studying in history class, was the first African American woman elected to Congress. **10.** d.o.

Appositives

18i. A pronoun used as an appositive is in the same case as the word to which it refers.

An *appositive* is a noun or pronoun placed next to another noun or pronoun to identify or describe it.

EXAMPLES The winners—**he, she,** and **I**—thanked the committee. [The pronouns are in the nominative case because they are used as appositives of the subject, *winners*.]

The teacher introduced the speakers, Laura and **me.** [The pronoun is in the objective case because it is used as an appositive of the direct object, *speakers*.]

NOTE Sometimes a pronoun is followed by an appositive that indentifies or describes the pronoun. The case of the pronoun is not affected by the appositive.

EXAMPLES **We** soloists will rehearse next week. [The pronoun is in the nominative case because it is the subject of the sentence. The appositive *soloists* identifies *We*.]

Give **us** girls a turn to bat. [The pronoun is in the objective case because it is the indirect object of the verb *Give*. The appositive *girls* identifies *us*.]

Reference Note
For more about **appositives,** see page 461.

TIPS & TRICKS

To determine the correct form for a pronoun used with an appositive or as an appositive, read the sentence with only the pronoun.

EXAMPLE
(*We, Us*) scouts offered to help. [*We offered to help* or *Us offered to help*? *We offered to help* is correct.]

We scouts offered to help.

Looking at Language

Appose, the verb form of *apposition,* means "to put one thing near another" or "to place side by side," "to juxtapose." *Apposition* is defined as a relation between consecutive expressions in which one expression identifies or explains the other.

Crossing the Curriculum

Art/Science. To connect apposition to other curriculums, have interested students inform the class about apposition in art and architecture and provide examples (for example, the juxtaposition of visual elements, as in a stained-glass window or a facade). Students might also investigate apposition in connection to biology (for example, the accumulation of layers next to each other, as in the case of cell walls). Encourage students to check the *Oxford English Dictionary* (*OED*) to find more cross-curricular links to *appositive.*

TECHNOLOGY TIP

The *OED* is available on CD-ROM and online, as are other dictionaries.

USAGE

ALTERNATIVE LESSON
To review pronoun functions, have students name the sentence parts the appositive pronouns identify or describe in sentences 2, 3, 6, and 8.

2. subject

3. object of preposition

6. direct object

8. predicate nominative

USAGE

Exercise 6 **Identifying Correct Pronoun Forms as Appositives and with Appositives**

For each of the following sentences, give the correct form of the pronoun in parentheses.

EXAMPLE **1.** The principal named the winners, Julia and (*I, me*).

   1. *me*

1. The coach showed (*we, us*) girls the new uniforms.
2. Our friends, (*she, her*) and Lucas, made the refreshments.
3. All of the class saw it except three people—Floyd, Ada, and (*I, me*).
4. Mrs. López hired (*we, us*) boys for the summer.
5. (*We, Us*) girls are excellent chess players.
6. Kiole listed her three favorite actors: Leonardo DiCaprio, Cuba Gooding, Jr., and (*he, him*).
7. Come to the game with (*we, us*) hometown fans, and you'll have a better time.
8. The best singers in school may be the quartet, Ellen and (*they, them*).
9. I want to go to the concert with two friends, Iola and (*he, him*).
10. The librarian gave the best readers, Craig and (*I, me*), two books by our favorite authors.

Review F **Identifying Correct Pronoun Forms**

For each of the following sentences, choose the correct pronoun in parentheses. Then, give its use in the sentence—as a *subject, predicate nominative, direct object, indirect object, object of a preposition* or an *appositive.*

EXAMPLE **1.** The cyclist gave (*we, us*) a smile as she rode past.

   1. *us—indirect object*

1. sub.   **1.** Students (*who, whom*) want to help organize the Kamehameha Day celebration should speak to Kai or me.
2. sub.   **2.** Give these magazines to (*whoever, whomever*) wants them.
3. sub./sub.   **3.** Don't (*they, them*) know that (*we, us*) students do our best?
4. app.   **4.** The candidates, Ralph and (*he, him*), will speak at the rally tomorrow.
5. p.n.   **5.** The Earth Day planners from our community are (*they, them*).
6. sub.   **6.** Len and (*I, me*) had planned to watch the laser light show together.
7. i.o.   **7.** Will you pass (*I, me*) the dictionary, please?
8. d.o./sub.   **8.** Céline Dion, (*who, whom*) I saw in concert, sings many songs that (*I, me*) like.

Learning for Life   *Continued on pp. 563–564*

Speaking on the Telephone. Remind students that it is important to make a good impression when answering the phone, particularly in a professional situation. Emphasize that one way to create a good telephone impression is to use correct pronoun forms.

Copy onto the chalkboard the following beginnings of phone conversations, and ask pairs of volunteers to read them aloud.

1. #1 Hello.
#2 Is Leah there?
#1 This is she.

9. It would be a great help to (*we*, *us*) beginners if (*they*, *them*) would give us more time.

9. o.p./sub.

10. Visiting Australia is an exciting opportunity for Clay and (*she*, *her*).

10. o.p.

Review G **Identifying Correct Pronoun Forms**

Choose the correct pronoun from each pair in parentheses in the following paragraph.

EXAMPLE   **[1]** My sister Angela is one of many women in our society (*who*, *whom*) use makeup.

1. *who*

The use of makeup to enhance beauty has a longer history than most of **[1]** (*we*, *us*) might imagine. In fact, **[2]** (*we*, *us*) cosmetic historians must look back to ancient times for the origins of makeup. For example, heavy, black eye makeup was worn by the ancient Egyptians, **[3]** (*who*, *whom*) originally used it as protection from reflected sunlight. It was they **[4]** (*who*, *whom*) first lined their eyes with a dark liquid called *kohl*, which **[5]** (*they*, *them*) applied with a small wooden or ivory stick. During the reign of Queen Nefertiti, **[6]** (*she*, *her*) and her noblewomen used not only *kohl* but other cosmetics as well. To **[7]** (*they*, *them*), dark, heavily made-up eyes and red lips were the marks of beauty. European nobles in the Middle Ages and the Renaissance wanted to emphasize their pale skin, so **[8]** (*them*, *they*) dusted their faces with chalk-white powder. It was Queen Elizabeth I, an English monarch, **[9]** (*who*, *whom*) set this style in her court. Although we might think that **[10]** (*them*, *they*) look strange today, both Nefertiti and Queen Elizabeth I were fashionable in their times.

---

2. #1 Hello.
#2 May I please speak with Paul?
#1 Who is speaking, please?

3. #1 Hello.
#2 Is Mrs. Tays there?
#1 Yes, she is. May I say who is calling?

Then, have students incorporate lines like the ones listed into a conversation about one of the following situations.

• You are a volunteer answering phones at a care facility for senior citizens.

The Pronoun in an Incomplete Construction

18j. After *than* and *as* introducing an incomplete construction, use the form of the pronoun that would be correct if the construction were completed.

Notice how pronouns change the meaning of sentences with incomplete constructions.

EXAMPLES   Everyone knows that you like Jolene much better than **I** [like Jolene].

Everyone knows that you like Jolene much better than [you like] **me.**

Did you help Ira as well as **they** [helped Ira]?

Did you help Ira as well as [you helped] **them**?

Exercise 7   Students' answers may include the following possibilities, which are grammatical but illogical.

1. Justin throws a football better than he throws me.

2. The story mystified him as much as we did.

14. Do you like cantaloupe as much as you like her?

16. When you serve dessert, don't serve yourself more than he serves you.

—HELP—
Some items in Exercise 7 may have more than one correct answer.

1. than I do—sub.
2. as it mystified us—obj.
3. than he is—sub.
4. as we have—sub.
5. than she has—sub. *or* than we have known her—obj.
6. than he is—sub.
7. as I did—sub.
8. than they do—sub. *or* than I like them—obj.
9. than we are—sub.
10. as she is—sub.
11. than they were—sub.
12. than I am—sub.
13. than he has—sub.

Exercise 7   **Completing Incomplete Constructions and Classifying Pronoun Forms**

Beginning with *than* or *as,* write the understood clause for each sentence, using the correct form of the pronoun. Then, tell whether the pronoun in the completed clause is a *subject* or an *object.*

EXAMPLE   **1.** Did the noise bother you as much as (*she, her*).

1. *as the noise bothered her—object*

or   Answers may vary slightly.

as she bothered you—subject

1. Justin throws a football better than (*I, me*).
2. The story mystified him as much as (*we, us*).
3. Is your sister older than (*he, him*)?
4. Have they studied as long as (*we, us*)?
5. We have known him longer than (*she, her*).
6. Are you more creative than (*he, him*)?
7. Did you read as much as (*I, me*)?
8. I like René better than (*they, them*).
9. Many people are less fortunate than (*we, us*).
10. Are you as optimistic as (*she, her*)?
11. After winning the city championship, there were no girls happier than (*they, them*).
12. When did you become taller than (*I, me*)?
13. Mary has collected more coins than (*he, him*).

Learning for Life

- You are taking phone orders at a restaurant.

- You are acting as an office receptionist.

Record conversations, and allow peers to review the use of pronouns.

14. Do you like cantaloupe as much as (*she, her*)?
15. This label says the toy is not safe for a child as young as (*he, him*).
16. When you serve dessert, don't serve yourself more than (*he, him*).
17. Can he really play saxophone as well as (*I, me*)?
18. To win the contest, you must do as many sit-ups as (*she, her*).
19. I'm shocked that you gave her a nicer card than (*I, me*)!
20. Daniel doesn't visit his relatives as often as (*she, her*).

14. as she does—sub.
15. as he is—sub.
16. than you serve him—obj.
17. as I can—sub.
18. as she does—sub.
19. than I did—sub. *or* than you gave me—obj.
20. as she does—sub. *or* as he visits her—obj.

Clear Pronoun Reference

18k. A pronoun should refer clearly to its antecedent.

(1) An *ambiguous reference* occurs when any one of two or more words can be a pronoun's antecedent.

AMBIGUOUS   My uncle called my brother after he won the marathon.
            [Who won the marathon, my uncle or my brother?]
   CLEAR   After my brother won the marathon, my uncle called him.
   CLEAR   After my uncle won the marathon, he called my brother.

(2) A *general reference* is the use of a pronoun that refers to a general idea rather than to a specific antecedent.

The pronouns commonly found in general-reference errors are *it, that, this, such,* and *which.*

GENERAL   The ski jumper faces tough competition and a grueling schedule, but she says that doesn't worry her.
  CLEAR   The ski jumper faces tough competition and a grueling schedule, but she says these problems don't worry her.

(3) A *weak reference* occurs when a pronoun refers to an antecedent that has been suggested but not expressed.

WEAK   Paul likes many of the photographs I have taken; he thinks I should choose this as my profession.
CLEAR   Paul likes many of the photographs I have taken; he thinks I should choose photography as my profession.

(4) An *indefinite reference* is the use of a pronoun that refers to no particular person or thing and that is unnecessary to the meaning of the sentence.

INDEFINITE   In the book it explains how cells divide.
   CLEAR   The book explains how cells divide.

Cooperative Learning

Have students work in small groups to prepare and present a lesson on clear pronoun reference. Have them brainstorm how to present the material. Then, have each person choose a specific role to play in the teaching process. Possible roles include *administrative,* such as arranging for a student or group of students to tutor, setting up a time and place to teach the lesson, and getting permissions needed; *creative,* such as preparing materials, which might include pantomimes, worksheets, charts, or cartoons for the lesson; *instructional,* such as giving and evaluating the lesson; *media,* such as making a video or audiotape of the lesson or material to be used in instruction; and *reporting,* such as preparing and delivering an oral report on the experience or preparing a written report for a school or classroom newspaper.

Exercise 8 Correcting Inexact Pronoun References

ANSWERS

Possible answers are given.

1. Meals on Wheels can help when older persons, people with disabilities, and people who are ill cannot prepare meals for themselves.

2. Meals on Wheels is an organization that arranges to have meals delivered to people's homes.

3. Because the nonprofit organization Meals on Wheels has a limited budget, it relies on volunteers.

4. Many businesses, churches, clubs, and organizations supply volunteers and contribute money.

5. People who receive services provided by Meals on Wheels usually help to pay for these services, but contributions are voluntary and based on a person's ability to pay.

6. In addition to delivering meals, some Meals on Wheels organizations offer clients a variety of other services.

7. Grocery shopping is a service provided to clients by volunteers who purchase and then deliver groceries.

8. When some clients have appointments and errands to run, they depend on volunteers for rides.

9. To lift clients' spirits, some volunteers regularly call clients on the phone; other volunteers help clients by performing minor home safety repairs.

10. Since volunteers not only provide needed services but also often form personal bonds with their clients, you may want to volunteer at a local Meals on Wheels.

STYLE / TIP

Familiar expressions such as *it is raining, it seems as though . . .,* and *it's early* are correct even though they contain inexact pronoun references.

Exercise 8 Correcting Inexact Pronoun References

Revise each of the following sentences, correcting each inexact pronoun reference.

EXAMPLE 1. Have you ever been physically unable to prepare a meal for yourself? That can be a serious problem.

1. *Being physically unable to prepare a meal for yourself can be a serious problem.*

1. Older persons, people with disabilities, and people who are ill sometimes cannot prepare meals for themselves, which is when Meals on Wheels can help.

2. Meals on Wheels is an organization in which they arrange to have meals delivered to people's homes.

3. Because it is a nonprofit organization, Meals on Wheels has a limited budget, which is why it relies on volunteers.

4. Many businesses, churches, clubs, and organizations supply volunteers, and they contribute money.

5. People who receive services provided by Meals on Wheels usually help to pay for these services, but it's voluntary and based on a person's ability to pay.

6. In some Meals on Wheels organizations, they offer clients a variety of other services in addition to delivering meals.

7. Grocery shopping is a service provided to clients by volunteers who purchase and then deliver them.

8. Some clients depend on volunteers for rides when they have appointments and errands to run.

9. To lift their spirits, some volunteers regularly call clients on the phone; other volunteers help clients by performing minor home safety repairs.

10. Volunteers not only provide needed services but also often form personal bonds with their clients; that is why you may want to volunteer at a local Meals on Wheels.

Chapter Review

A. Identifying Correct Forms of Pronouns

For each of the following sentences, choose the <u>correct form</u> of the pronoun or pronouns in parentheses.

1. Janell and (*I, me*) painted the room together.
2. Alan, for (*who, <u>whom</u>*) I did the typing, said that he would pay me on Friday.
3. The young Amish couple drove us and (*they, <u>them</u>*) into town in a horse-drawn buggy.
4. Carolyn has been playing the guitar longer than (*she, her*).
5. The last two people to arrive, Tranh and (*me, <u>I</u>*), had trouble finding the skating rink.
6. Hector wrote this song for you and (*I, <u>me</u>*).
7. The winner is (*<u>whoever</u>, whomever*) finishes first.
8. Ellis was worried about his project, but Ms. Atkinson gave (*he, <u>him</u>*) an A.
9. Was the winner of the race (*<u>he</u>, him*) or Aaron?
10. The pictures of the Grand Canyon made a greater impression on the Rileys than on (*we, <u>us</u>*).
11. To (*who, <u>whom</u>*) did you speak?
12. Schuyler and (*<u>she</u>, her*) will lead the group sing-along.
13. Imagine my surprise when I saw Todd Franklin sitting behind Kenan and (*I, <u>me</u>*) in the theater.
14. The most productive employees at the plant were (*<u>they</u>, them*).
15. He was going to have dinner with (*<u>her and me</u>, she and I*), but fog delayed his departure from New York.
16. The prince knew precisely (*who, <u>whom</u>*) to appoint as his chamberlain.
17. Stanislas and Tina were at a Pulaski Day parade in Chicago, and I saw (*they, <u>them</u>*) there on the television news.
18. The ferret, annoyed at being woken up, bit (*she, <u>her</u>*) on the arm.
19. Why don't you come to the play with Carrie and (*I, <u>me</u>*)?
20. The first one to arrive was (*<u>she</u>, her*).

USING the Chapter Review

To assess student progress, you may want to compare the types of items missed on the **Diagnostic Preview** to those missed on the **Chapter Review**. If students have not made significant progress, you may want to refer them to **Chapter 28: Correcting Common Errors, Exercises 14, 15,** and **16** for additional practice.

USAGE

Chapter Review

B. Proofreading a Paragraph for Correct Pronoun Forms

ANSWERS

21. me—I
22. C
23. me—I
24. me—I
25. Us—We
26. me—I
27. whom—who
28. C
29. whom—who
30. I—me

USAGE

B. Proofreading a Paragraph for Correct Pronoun Forms

Some of the sentences in the following paragraph contain a pronoun that has been used incorrectly. If a pronoun is incorrect, write the correct form. If the sentence is already correct, write *C*.

[**21**] Do you grow as many plants as me? [**22**] Nowadays, scientists are hard at work trying to develop blue roses for us plant enthusiasts. [**23**] My science teacher, Ms. Phillips, and me wonder whether they can do so. [**24**] She doubts even more than me that breeding a blue rose is possible. [**25**] Us modern rose-lovers have never seen a blue rose. [**26**] However, Ms. Phillips and me learned that an Arab agriculturist in the thirteenth century once grew one. [**27**] For centuries, rose breeders whom have tried to produce the legendary blue rose have failed. [**28**] Some genetic engineers that I read about are working on this project now. [**29**] Scientists aren't sure whom would buy a blue rose. [**30**] Still, like you and I, they can't resist a challenge.

C. Identifying Pronouns Used as Subjects and Objects

For each of the following sentences, give the correct form of the pronoun or pronouns in parentheses. Then, tell whether each pronoun is in *nominative* case or *objective* case.

31. obj.   **31.** Dr. Schultz sang to the birthday brothers, Otto and (*I*, *me*).

32. obj.   **32.** Ms. Vlatkin showed (*we*, *us*) how to dance a *pas de deux*.

33. nom.   **33.** (*Him and her*, *He and she*), the brother-and-sister team, were the first archaeologists present at the opening of the royal tomb.

34. obj.   **34.** They went on the trip with their cousins, Jin-Hua and (*he*, *him*).

35. nom.   **35.** The last remaining contestants—(*she and they*, *her and them*)—walked in silence to the podium.

36. nom.   **36.** (*We*, *Us*) students at King High are very proud of our football team.

37. obj.   **37.** The teacher gave the best students, (*her and him*, *she and he*), a commendation.

38. obj.   **38.** I thought they should give (*we*, *us*) junior actors a chance to shine.

39. obj.   **39.** Rosa mentioned her favorite Tejano musicians, Emilio, David Lee Garza, and (*he*, *him*).

40. obj.   **40.** With regard to the Garcia twins, Blair said the best way to tell (*they*, *them*) apart was to make them laugh.

RESOURCES

Using Pronouns Correctly

Review

- *Grammar, Usage, and Mechanics,* pp. 181, 182, 183–184, 185

Assessment

- *Assessment Package*
  —*Chapter Tests,* Ch. 18
  —*Chapter Tests in Standardized Test Formats,* Ch. 18
- *Test Generator (One-Stop Planner CD-ROM)*

D. Correcting Unclear Pronoun Reference

Revise each of the following sentences, correcting each unclear pronoun reference.

41. Sally called Carla while she was doing her homework.

42. The ship's captain explained to the passenger the meaning of the announcement he had just made.

43. Police Sergeant Molloy's daily assignments involve hard work and a certain amount of risk, but he claims that it doesn't bother him.

44. Jill is impressed by Jeff's track-and-field records. She thinks he should do it professionally.

45. On the radio it said that afternoon thunderstorms were likely.

Writing Application
Using Pronouns in a Magazine Article

Using Correct Case Forms You and three of your friends are planetary explorers. Write a magazine article about your exploration of Mars. Use a variety of pronouns as subjects, predicate nominatives, direct objects, indirect objects, and objects of prepositions.

Prewriting To get started, jot down what you know about space travel and astronomy. You could get additional ideas from books and magazine articles about Mars. Think of things that a person might see or do while exploring that planet.

Writing As you write your first draft, be sure to include details that draw your reader into the story.

Revising Ask a classmate to read your story. Should you add or delete any details? Using your classmate's suggestions, revise your story to make it clearer and more entertaining.

Publishing Do your pronouns clearly show who did what? As you check over the grammar, spelling, and punctuation of your story, make sure that all of your pronouns are in the correct case. With your teacher's permission, you may want to post the story on your class bulletin board or create a Web page for it on the Internet.

Chapter Review   **569**

RESOURCES

Writing Application
Extension

■ *Grammar, Usage, and Mechanics*, p. 188

■ *Language Workshop CD-ROM*, Lessons 18–20, 51

Chapter Review
D. Correcting Unclear Pronoun Reference

POSSIBLE ANSWERS

41. While Carla was doing her homework, Sally called her.

42. After the ship's captain made an announcement, he explained its meaning to the passenger.

43. Police Sergeant Molloy claims that the hard work and certain amount of risk involved in his daily assignments don't bother him.

44. Jill is impressed by Jeff's track-and-field records and thinks he should become a professional athlete.

45. The radio announcer said that afternoon thunderstorms were likely.

USAGE

Writing Application
(p. 569)

OBJECTIVE

■ **To write a magazine article containing a variety of pronouns used in the correct case as subjects, predicate nominatives, direct objects, indirect objects, and objects of prepositions**

Writing Application

Tip. To help students get a feeling for the writing style used in travel magazines, you might want to have students look at such publications before they begin writing.

Scoring Rubric. While you will want to pay particular attention to students' use of pronouns, you will also want to evaluate the students' overall writing performance. You may want to give a split score to indicate development and clarity of the composition as well as usage skills.

CHAPTER

19

Using Modifiers Correctly

Comparison and Placement

Diagnostic Preview

A. Correcting Modifiers

The following sentences contain dangling modifiers, misplaced modifiers, and mistakes in comparisons. Revise each sentence so that it is clear and correct.

┌ HELP ┐

A sentence in the Diagnostic Preview may contain more than one error.

EXAMPLE   1. When traveling through Scotland, I discovered that stories about monsters were more popular than any kind of story.

1. *When traveling through Scotland, I discovered that stories about monsters were more popular than any other kind of story.*

1. Having received a great deal of publicity, I had already read several articles about the so-called Loch Ness monster.
2. One article described how a young veterinary student spotted the monster who was named Arthur Grant.
3. While cycling on a road near the shore of Loch Ness one day, Grant came upon the most strangest creature he had ever seen.
4. Cycling closer, the monster took a leap and plunged into the lake.
5. Numerous theories have been discussed about the origin and identity of the monster in the local newspapers.

6. Of all the proposed theories, the better and more fascinating one was that the monster must be a freshwater species of sea serpent.

7. Having found a huge, dead creature on the shore of the lake in 1942, the mystery of the monster was thought to be solved finally.

8. One famous photograph of the monster has recently been revealed to be a hoax that seemed to confirm the creature's existence.

9. Skeptical, stories about the Loch Ness monster have always struck some people as unbelievable.

10. However, reported sightings of the monster have continued, perhaps more than of any mysterious creature.

B. Using Modifiers Correctly in Sentences

Most of the following sentences have mistakes in the use of modifiers. Revise each incorrect sentence to correct these errors. If a sentence is already correct, write *C*.

EXAMPLE   1. In the United States, is the use of solar energy more commoner than the use of geothermal energy?

     1. *In the United States, is the use of solar energy more common than the use of geothermal energy?*

11. Kay has a better understanding of both solar and geothermal energy than anyone I know.

12. Yoko isn't sure she agrees with me, but I have talked with Kay more than Yoko.

13. Kay thinks that, of the two, solar energy is the best method for generating power.

14. She claims that the energy from the sun will soon be easier to harness than geothermal energy.

15. Arguing that the sun's energy could also be less expensive to use, Kay says that more research into solar energy is needed.

16. Yoko disagrees and thinks that geothermal energy would provide more cheaper power than solar energy.

17. She told me that for centuries people in other countries have been using geothermal energy, such as Iceland and Japan.

18. However, she added that geothermal energy is less well known than any source of power in our country.

19. Although infrequently used in the United States, Yoko feels that geothermal energy has already proven itself to be safe and efficient.

20. Unconvinced, both points of view seem to me to offer promising new sources of energy.

┌─HELP─
Although some sentences in Part B of the Diagnostic Preview can be correctly revised in more than one way, you need to give only one revision.

Diagnostic Preview   571

Diagnostic Preview: Part A
POSSIBLE ANSWERS
continued

6. Of all the proposed theories, the best and most fascinating one . . .

7. When a huge, dead creature was found on the shore of the lake in 1942, . . .

8. One famous photograph that seemed to confirm the creature's existence has recently been revealed to be a hoax.

9. Stories about the Loch Ness monster have always struck some skeptical people as unbelievable.

10. However, reported sightings of the monster have continued, perhaps more than of any other mysterious creature.

Diagnostic Preview: Part B
POSSIBLE ANSWERS

11. . . . than anyone else I know.

12. Yoko may not agree with Kay, but I have talked with Kay more than Yoko has.

13. Kay thinks that, of the two, solar energy is a better method for generating power.

14. C

15. C

16. Yoko disagrees and thinks that geothermal energy would provide cheaper power than solar energy.

17. She told me that for centuries people in other countries, such as Iceland and Japan, . . .

18. However, she added that geothermal energy is less well known than any other . . .

19. Yoko feels that geothermal energy, although infrequently used in the United States, has already proven . . .

20. Although I am unconvinced of which plan is better, . . .

USAGE

What Is a Modifier?

Rules 19a–c *(pp. 572–575)*

OBJECTIVE

■ To determine whether words, phrases, and clauses are modifiers

TEACHING (TIP)

Activity. Ask students to generate a list of words that have both adjective and adverb forms. [*nice, nicely; cold, coldly; calm, calmly*] Then, write a two-column list of these words on the chalkboard or an overhead transparency. Ask students to work in pairs to write on individual slips of paper three sentences using adverbs and three using adjectives. Distribute the sentences randomly to other pairs, and ask them to write on the back of each slip an explanation of why the adjective or adverb forms are used correctly. Encourage students to refer to the explanation in the textbook as they complete this task. If some sentences are incorrect, ask the second pair of students to make corrections and explain why they made the changes. (For more information about adjectives and adverbs, see **Chapter 12: Parts of Speech Overview.**)

USAGE

Reference Note
For more about **adjectives,** see page 382. For more about **adverbs,** see page 393.

What Is a Modifier?

A *modifier* is a word or word group that makes the meaning of another word or word group more specific. The two kinds of modifiers are *adjectives* and *adverbs*.

One-Word Modifiers

Adjectives

19a. An adjective makes the meaning of a noun or pronoun more specific.

EXAMPLES   Samia gave a **broad** smile. [The adjective *broad* makes the meaning of the noun *smile* more specific.]

Only she knows the answer. [The adjective *only* makes the meaning of the pronoun *she* more specific.]

The sweater is **soft** and **warm.** [The adjectives *soft* and *warm* make the meaning of the noun *sweater* more specific.]

Isn't he a **well-mannered** boy? [The compound adjective *well-mannered* makes the meaning of the noun *boy* more specific.]

Adverbs

19b. An adverb makes the meaning of a verb, an adjective, or another adverb more specific.

EXAMPLES   Samia grinned **broadly.** [The adverb *broadly* makes the meaning of the verb *grinned* more specific.]

Sometimes I wonder about the future. [The adverb *sometimes* makes the meaning of the verb *wonder* more specific.]

The dog is **very** hungry. [The adverb *very* makes the meaning of the adjective *hungry* more specific.]

The alarm rang **surprisingly** loudly. [The adverb *surprisingly* makes the meaning of the adverb *loudly* more specific.]

Adjective or Adverb?

While many adverbs end in *–ly*, others do not. Furthermore, not all words with the *–ly* ending are adverbs. Some adjectives also end in *–ly*.

572   Chapter 19   Using Modifiers Correctly

RESOURCES

What Is a Modifier?
Practice
■ *Grammar, Usage, and Mechanics,*
pp. 190, 191, 192, 193, 194, 195, 196, 197, 198
■ *Language Workshop CD-ROM,* Lesson 21

Therefore, you can't tell whether a word is an adjective or an adverb simply by looking for the *–ly* ending. To decide whether a word is an adjective or an adverb, determine how the word is used in the sentence.

Adverbs Not Ending in *–ly*		
broadcast **soon**	return **home**	run **loose**
not sleepy	stand **here**	**very** happy

Adjectives Ending in *–ly*		
elderly people	**only** child	**silly** behavior
curly hair	**holy** building	**lonely** person

Some words can be used as either adjectives or adverbs.

Adjectives	Adverbs
She is an **only** child.	She has **only** one brother.
Tina has a **fast** car.	The car goes **fast**.
We caught the **last** train.	We left **last**.

19c. If a word in the predicate modifies the subject of the verb, use the adjective form. If it modifies the verb, use the adverb form.

ADJECTIVE The gazelles were **graceful.** [*Graceful* modifies *gazelles*.]
ADVERB The gazelles moved **gracefully.** [*Gracefully* modifies *moved*.]

ADJECTIVE The boy grew **tall.** [*Tall* modifies *boy*.]
ADVERB The boy grew **quickly.** [*Quickly* modifies *grew*.]

Phrases Used as Modifiers

Like one-word modifiers, phrases can also be used as adjectives and adverbs.

EXAMPLES It was time **for celebration.** [The prepositional phrase *for celebration* acts as an adjective that modifies the noun *time*.]

Uprooting trees and bushes, the tornado swept across the Panhandle. [The participial phrase *Uprooting trees and bushes* acts as an adjective that modifies the noun *tornado*.]

USAGE

Meeting INDIVIDUAL NEEDS

LEARNERS HAVING DIFFICULTY
To help students visualize phrases and clauses used as modifiers, have them create captions using these forms. Provide students with magazines from which to cut pictures, and have them work in pairs to find and mount on construction paper pictures that illustrate adjective or adverb phrases or clauses. Then, have them add appropriate captions labeling the adjective or adverb phrases and clauses. ["Sitting in the car, *she made herself comfortable.*" (participial phrase) or "By the door, *she paused and smiled.*" (adverbial prepositional phrase)] Post the labeled pictures on the bulletin board.

Reference Note
For more about **subjects** and **predicates,** see page 414.

Reference Note
For more about different **kinds of phrases,** see page 442.

Crossing the Curriculum

Math. Point out to your students that modifiers have algebraic equivalents. For example, in *3x, 3* is equivalent to the modifier and *x* is equivalent to the word modified.

Professor Martinez is the one **to ask.** [The infinitive phrase *to ask* acts as an adjective that modifies the pronoun *one*.]

Ray is becoming quite good **at soccer.** [The prepositional phrase *at soccer* acts as an adverb that modifies the adjective *good.*]

Walk **with care on icy pavements.** [The prepositional phrases *with care* and *on icy pavements* act as adverbs that modify the verb *Walk*.]

The guide spoke slowly enough **to be understood.** [The infinitive phrase *to be understood* acts as an adverb that modifies the adverb *enough*.]

Clauses Used as Modifiers

Like words and phrases, clauses can also be used as adjectives and adverbs.

Reference Note

For more about **clauses,** see Chapter 15.

EXAMPLES
Vermeer is the painter **that I like best.** [The adjective clause *that I like best* modifies the noun *painter*.]

Before Toni left for work, she took the dog for a walk. [The adverb clause *Before Toni left for work* modifies the verb *took*.]

Exercise 1 Identifying Modifiers

Identify the italicized word or word group in each of the following sentences as a *modifier* or *not a modifier*. M or Not M

EXAMPLES
1. Rudyard Kipling, *who was born in India,* wrote a wonderful story about a brave mongoose.
   1. *modifier*

2. The mongoose's *name* was Rikki-tikki-tavi.
   2. *not a modifier*

Link to Literature

1. Rikki-tikki was adopted by a *very* kind family. **1.** M
2. The family fed him meat and bananas and *boiled* eggs. **2.** M
3. *Like all mongooses,* Rikki-tikki was always curious. **3.** M
4. While exploring the garden, he *heard* Darzee and his wife, the tailorbirds, crying in their nest. **4.** Not M
5. One of their babies had fallen out *of the nest* and been eaten by a cobra. **5.** M
6. Rikki-tikki had to protect his family and friends *against the snakes.* **6.** M

MINI-LESSON Continued on pp. 575–576

What Is a Clause? Quickly review the following definitions:

• A **clause** is a group of words that contains a subject and a verb and that is used as a sentence or as part of a sentence.

• An **independent clause** expresses a complete thought and can stand alone as a sentence.

• A **subordinate clause** does not communicate a complete thought even though it has a subject and a verb; it cannot stand

7. Mongooses and snakes are *natural* enemies.   **7.** M
8. Rikki-tikki overheard *two* cobras planning to kill the family.   **8.** M
9. He attacked the first cobra *while it was waiting for the father to come into the room.*   **9.** M
10. The second *cobra* dragged Rikki-tikki down a hole in the ground, but Rikki-tikki killed the snake and came out alive.   **10.** Not M

Eight Troublesome Modifiers

Bad and *Badly*

Bad is an adjective. In most uses, *badly* is an adverb.

ADJECTIVE   The dog was **bad.**
ADVERB   The dog behaved **badly.**

Remember that a word that modifies the subject of a verb should be in adjective form.

NONSTANDARD   The stew tasted badly.
STANDARD   The stew tasted **bad.**

> **NOTE** In informal situations, *bad* or *badly* is acceptable after *feel.*
>
> INFORMAL   He feels **badly** about the incident.
> FORMAL   He feels **bad** about the incident.

Good and *Well*

Good is an adjective. It should not be used to modify a verb.

NONSTANDARD   He speaks Italian good.
STANDARD   He speaks Italian **well.**
STANDARD   His Italian sounds **good.** [*Good* is an adjective that modifies the noun *Italian.*]

Well may be used either as an adjective or as an adverb. As an adjective, *well* has two meanings: "in good health" and "satisfactory."

EXAMPLES   John is **well.** [John is in good health.]

All is **well.** [All is satisfactory.]

As an adverb, *well* means "capably."

EXAMPLE   They did **well** in the tryouts.

ENGLISH-LANGUAGE LEARNERS
Romance Languages. Point out that the English *–ly* suffix is equivalent to the Spanish and Portuguese *–mente* suffix and the French *–ment.* All of these endings convert adjectives to adverbs.

MODALITIES
Visual Learners. You may want to place students in pairs to create illustrations of adjectives and adverbs. Assign one student to illustrate the four troublesome adjectives and the other to illustrate the four troublesome adverbs. Then, have students label their illustrations with the appropriate word and part of speech. When they have finished, have them compare their drawings and discuss whether or not the same illustrations could be used for adjectives as for adverbs.

---

alone as a sentence.

- An **adjective clause** is a subordinate clause used to modify a noun or pronoun; it tells *what kind* or *which one* and starts with a relative pronoun like *who, whom, whose,* *which,* or *that* or occasionally the relative adverbs *where* or *when.*

- An **adverb clause** is a subordinate clause used to modify a verb, adjective, or adverb; it tells *why, where, when, how*

Slow and *Slowly*

Slow is used as both an adjective and an adverb.

EXAMPLES   We took a **slow** drive through the countryside. [*Slow* is an adjective modifying the noun *drive*.]

    Go **slow**. [*Slow* is an adverb modifying the verb *Go*.]

Slowly is an adverb. In most adverb uses, it is better to use *slowly* than to use *slow*.

EXAMPLES   The train **slowly** came to a stop.

    Drive **slowly** on slippery roads.

Real and *Really*

Real is an adjective meaning "actual" or "genuine." *Really* is an adverb meaning "actually" or "truly." Although *real* is commonly used as an adverb meaning "very" in everyday situations, avoid using it as an adverb in formal speaking and writing.

INFORMAL   He batted real well in the game.

FORMAL   He batted **really** well in the game.

┌HELP┐

A sentence in Exercise 2 may contain more than one error.

Exercise 2 Revising Sentences with Modifier Errors

Most of the following sentences contain at least one error in modifier usage. If a sentence contains an error, revise the sentence with the correct modifier. If a sentence is already correct, write *C*.

EXAMPLE   1. The ball was thrown so bad it went over the fence.

    1. *The ball was thrown so badly it went over the fence.*

1. You have done very ~~good~~ today, Marcia. **1.** well
2. The nurse shark was moving very ~~slow~~ over the seabed. **2.** slowly
3. The fireworks exploded with a ~~real~~ loud bang. **3.** really
4. The team did not play badly, but they lost anyway. **4.** C
5. James thinks that Jakob Dylan is a ~~well~~ singer. **5.** good
6. The box was not damaged too ~~bad~~ when it fell. **6.** badly **7.** slow
7. The turtle is very ~~slowly~~ on land, but it is much faster underwater.
8. Is that really Sammy Sosa's autograph? **8.** C   **9.** badly
9. Even if your day is going ~~bad~~, getting angry at me will not help.
10. Slowly but surely, the fawn improved until it could run ~~real good~~.

    10. really well

MINI-LESSON

much, or *to what extent* and begins with a subordinating conjunction like *after*, *although*, *because*, *if*, *when*, and *where* (for more examples, see the **Common**

Subordinating Conjunctions chart on p. 477). For more information and examples, see p. 471.

Comparison of Modifiers

19d. Modifiers change form to show comparison.

There are three degrees of comparison: *positive, comparative,* and *superlative.*

Positive	Comparative	Superlative
young	younger	youngest
fearful	more fearful	most fearful
rapidly	more rapidly	most rapidly
good	better	best

Regular Comparison

(1) Most one-syllable modifiers form the comparative degree by adding *–er* and the superlative degree by adding *–est.*

Positive	Comparative	Superlative
large	larger	largest
deep	deeper	deepest

(2) Two-syllable modifiers may form the comparative degree by adding *–er* or by using *more.* They may form the superlative degree by adding *–est* or by using *most.*

Positive	Comparative	Superlative
wealthy	wealthier	wealthiest
lovely	lovelier	loveliest
rapid	more rapid	most rapid
softly	more softly	most softly
common	commoner	commonest
	or	*or*
	more common	most common

Reference Note

For guidelines on **how to spell comparative and superlative forms** correctly, see page 735.

STYLE	TIP

Most two-syllable modifiers can form their comparative and superlative forms either way. If adding *–er* or *–est* makes a word sound awkward, use *more* or *most* instead.

AWKWARD   frugaler
   BETTER   more frugal

AWKWARD   rapidest
   BETTER   most rapid

Comparison of Modifiers
Rule 19d *(pp. 577–580)*

OBJECTIVES

- To form and write comparative and superlative forms of given words
- To use the correct comparative and superlative forms of words
- To proofread sentences for correct comparative and superlative forms of modifiers

USAGE

Relating to Literature

The poem "The Girl Who Loved the Sky" by Anita Endrezze will give students extra practice with comparative and superlative forms. Go through the poem line by line, asking students to identify the modifiers and record the appropriate forms using a three-column organizer similar to the following one.

POSITIVE	COMPARATIVE	SUPERLATIVE
yellowed	more yellowed	most yellowed
big	bigger	biggest

RESOURCES

Comparison of Modifiers

Practice

- *Grammar, Usage, and Mechanics,* pp. 199, 200, 201, 202
- *Language Workshop CD-ROM,* Lessons 21, 22

USAGE

Exercise 3 Writing Comparative and Superlative Forms

POSSIBLE ANSWERS

1. faster, fastest
2. sooner, soonest
3. happier, happiest
4. more careful, most careful
5. simpler, simplest
6. hazier, haziest
7. safer, safest
8. more wisely, most wisely
9. calmer, calmest
10. prettier, prettiest

Relating to Speaking

To make students aware of the common use of comparative and superlative modifiers, involve them in a sports commentary. Provide or have students bring to class pictures of sports events such as swim team competitions, track meets, or basketball games. Have students work in pairs to prepare an oral presentation for the class; one student can hold up a picture while the other plays the role of a sports announcer, providing a brief commentary using comparative- and superlative-degree words to describe the sports event. Then, have partners reverse roles.

Crossing the Curriculum

World Languages. Ask your students for equivalents in other languages of each of the words in the table under **Irregular Comparison.** Have students write responses on the chalkboard using the table as a guide; ask the students who offer the examples if the forms are regular or irregular.

STYLE TIP

The word *little* also has regular comparative and superlative forms: *littler, littlest.* These forms are used to describe physical size (the **littlest** puppy). The forms *less* and *least* are used to describe an amount (**less** homework).

Exercise 3 Writing Comparative and Superlative Forms

Write the comparative and superlative forms of the following words.

EXAMPLE   1. bright
           1. *brighter, brightest*

1. fast	3. happy	5. simple	7. safe	9. calm
2. soon	4. careful	6. hazy	8. wisely	10. pretty

(3) Modifiers that have three or more syllables form the comparative degree by using *more* and the superlative degree by using *most.*

Positive	Comparative	Superlative
energetic	more energetic	most energetic
significantly	more significantly	most significantly

(4) To show a decrease in the qualities they express, modifiers form the comparative degree by using *less* and the superlative degree by using *least.*

Positive	Comparative	Superlative
helpful	less helpful	least helpful
frequently	less frequently	least frequently

Irregular Comparison

The comparative and superlative degrees of some modifiers are irregular in form.

Positive	Comparative	Superlative
bad	worse	worst
good/well	better	best
many/much	more	most
far	further/farther	furthest/farthest
little	less	least

NOTE Do not add *–er / –est* or *more / most* to irregularly compared forms. For example, use *worse,* not *worser* or *more worse.*

Exercise 4 Using Comparative and Superlative Forms

In the blank in each of the following sentences, write the correct form of the modifier in italics.

EXAMPLE   *little*   **1.** Both pairs of jeans are on sale, but I will buy the _____ expensive pair.

              1. less

1. *well*   I can skate _____ now than I could last year.
2. *many*   She caught the _____ fish of anyone in our group that day.
3. *bad*   That is the _____ movie I have ever seen.
4. *much*   We have _____ homework today than we had all last week.
5. *good*   Felicia has the _____ attendance record of anyone.
6. *many*   Are there _____ plays than poems in your literature book?
7. *good*   Tyrone is the _____ pitcher on our baseball team this year.
8. *much*   Of the three groups of volunteers, our group cleaned up the _____ litter.
9. *bad*   My notebook looks _____ than Joshua's.
10. *little*   I have _____ time to finish than he does.

Review A Writing Comparative and Superlative Forms

Write the comparative and superlative forms of the following modifiers. Do not include decreasing comparisons.

EXAMPLE   **1.** meaningful

    1. more meaningful, most meaningful

1. bad   **6.** loose   **11.** far   **16.** much
2. good   **7.** well   **12.** special   **17.** unlikely
3. early   **8.** noisy   **13.** happily   **18.** elaborate
4. many   **9.** patiently   **14.** eager   **19.** quiet
5. fuzzy   **10.** graceful   **15.** sleepy   **20.** rich

Exercise 5 Proofreading Sentences for Correct Comparative and Superlative Forms

Identify the comparative and superlative modifiers in the following sentences. If the form of a modifier is incorrect or awkward, write the correct form. If the form is already correct, write *C*.

┌─ HELP ─
A dictionary will tell you when a word forms its comparative or superlative form in some way other than by adding –*er* / –*est* or *more* / *most*. Look in a dictionary if you are not sure whether a word has irregular comparative or superlative forms or whether you need to change the spelling of a word before adding –*er* or –*est*.

Exercise 4 Using Comparative and Superlative Forms

POSSIBLE ANSWERS

1. better   **6.** more
2. most   **7.** best
3. worst   **8.** most
4. more   **9.** worse
5. best   **10.** less

Review A Writing Comparative and Superlative Forms

POSSIBLE ANSWERS

1. worse, worst
2. better, best
3. earlier, earliest
4. more, most
5. fuzzier, fuzziest
6. looser, loosest
7. better, best
8. noisier, noisiest
9. more patiently, most patiently
10. more graceful, most graceful
11. farther, farthest; further, furthest
12. more special, most special
13. more happily, most happily
14. more eager, most eager
15. sleepier, sleepiest
16. more, most
17. more unlikely, most unlikely
18. more elaborate, most elaborate
19. quieter, quietest
20. richer, richest

USAGE

Use of Comparative and Superlative Forms

Rules 19e–h *(pp. 580–584)*

OBJECTIVES

- To identify and correct comparative and superlative forms of modifiers in sentences

- To revise faulty comparisons for logic and clarity

- To revise sentences to eliminate double comparisons

- To rewrite sentences to correct unclear comparisons

| STYLE | TIP |

In informal situations and in standard expressions, people sometimes use the superlative degree in comparing two things: *Put your best foot forward.* Generally, however, you should use the comparative degree in formal situations when you are comparing two things.

EXAMPLE 1. The Romany make up one of Europe's interestingest cultures.

   1. *interestingest—most interesting*

1. The Romany, also known as Gypsies, are commonlier found in Eastern Europe than anywhere else in the world.   **1.** more commonly

2. Although most Romany live in Romania, Hungary, and other European countries, the culture of the Romany suggests that they migrated to Europe from other lands.   **2.** C

3. The bestest theory about the origin of the Romany is that they came from India.   **3.** best

4. As this photograph shows, the Romany wear some of their colorfulest traditional clothing for their celebrations.   **4.** most colorful

5. They also brighten their lives with the most wild violin music they can play.   **5.** wildest

6. On the move frequentlier than most other Europeans, they used to travel in brightly painted wagons.   **6.** more frequently

7. The Romany usually live in groups, with the largest groups consisting of several hundred families.   **7.** C

8. The most high law in Romany society is the *kris,* a system of rules based on the religious beliefs of the Romany.   **8.** highest

9. The Romany generally earn their living as migrant agricultural workers and, less frequently, as entertainers.   **9.** C

10. Although change has come slowlier to these wanderers than to most other ethnic groups in Europe, some Romany now are living in settled communities.   **10.** more slowly

Use of Comparative and Superlative Forms

19e. Use the comparative degree when comparing two things. Use the superlative degree when comparing more than two.

COMPARATIVE   Writing mysteries seems **more challenging** than writing nonfiction.

In my opinion, Dorothy L. Sayers is a **better** writer than Agatha Christie.

RESOURCES

Use of Comparative and Superlative Forms
Practice

- *Grammar, Usage, and Mechanics,* pp. 203–205
- *Language Workshop CD-ROM,* Lesson 21

SUPERLATIVE   Writing a mystery story is the **most challenging** assignment I've had so far.

This is the **best** Sherlock Holmes story that I have ever
read.

Exercise 6 **Identifying Correct Comparative and
Superlative Forms**

Identify the comparative and superlative modifiers in the following
sentences. If the form of a modifier is incorrect, write the correct form.
If the form is correct for the number of items compared, write *C.*

EXAMPLE   **1.** Nina's report on American Indian star legends was the
more interesting report in the class.

1. most interesting

1. Although Nina and I both researched our reports carefully, her
report was the ~~most thorough~~ one of the two.
2. The American Indian stories about the stars and the sky are more
diverse than the Norse myths, in my opinion.
3. Nina told several stories; I found the myth that she told about the
cluster of stars known as the Pleiades to be the ~~more fascinating~~.
4. The ~~stranger~~ tale, which is from the Monache Indian people of
central California, tells how a little girl and six women who
wouldn't give up eating onions became the Pleiades.
5. The scariest of the tales is the Skidi Pawnee myth about six
brothers and an adopted sister who fight the Rolling Skull.
6. That story was the ~~longer~~ legend that Nina told, and Frank
said it was the ~~more interesting~~.
7. Of all the earthly creatures in the stories Nina told, Coyote is
perhaps the ~~more important~~.
8. In fact, in some stories people often play a ~~least important~~ role
than Coyote plays.
9. I told Nina that, compared with my report, hers was ~~the best~~.
10. She said that telling the stories was easier than finding them.

19f. Include the word *other* or *else* when comparing one
member of a group with the rest of the group.

NONSTANDARD   Juan is more considerate than any boy in his school.
[Juan is a boy in his school, and he cannot be more considerate than himself. The word *other* should be added.]

STANDARD   Juan is more considerate than any **other** boy in his
school.

Link to   Literature

1. more thorough

2. C

3. most fascinating

4. strangest

5. C

6. longest
    most interesting

7. most important

8. less important

9. better

10. C

Reference Note

For a discussion of
**standard and non-
standard English,**
see page 595.

Comparison of Modifiers   **581**

Exercise 6

ALTERNATIVE LESSON
Have students find the following
items in sentences 1, 2, and 5 in
Exercise 6.

1. an adverb clause [*Although Nina
and I both researched our reports
carefully*]

2. compound objects of a preposition
[*stars, sky*]

5. a subordinate clause [*who fight the
Rolling Skull*]

Meeting
INDIVIDUAL
NEEDS

ENGLISH-LANGUAGE LEARNERS
General Strategies. Because many
languages use only one form to show
comparisons, you may need to
explain to English-language learners
that English may differ from their
first languages by having a special
form for comparing more than two
items.

LEARNERS HAVING DIFFICULTY
So students can understand the
thought process involved in choosing
between the comparative and
superlative forms, discuss **Exercise 6**
sentence by sentence, asking students to point out the number of
people or things compared in each
sentence. Remind students that the
number of people or things being
compared determines whether the
comparative (two) or the superlative
(more than two) form is used.

USAGE

Meeting
INDIVIDUAL
NEEDS

MODALITIES
Auditory Learners. Have students work in small groups to complete **Exercise 7** orally. Tell them to read each sentence aloud as it is written and then to read it again, making the necessary corrections.

NONSTANDARD	Dana arrived earlier than anyone. [*Anyone* includes all people, and Dana is a person. Since she cannot arrive earlier than herself, *else* should be added.]
STANDARD	Dana arrived earlier than anyone **else.**

Exercise 7 **Revising Faulty Comparisons**

Revise each of the following sentences to make the comparisons logical and clear.

EXAMPLE 1. Rodney spells better than anyone in his class.
          1. *Rodney spells better than anyone else in his class.*

1. other
2. else
3. other
4. other
5. else
6. other
7. other
8. else
9. other
10. other

1. Today has been colder than any day this year.
2. Kumiko eats more slowly than anybody in this cafeteria.
3. Flying is faster than any type of travel.
4. My sunflowers grew taller than any flowers I planted this year.
5. Luís enjoys swimming more than anyone in his family.
6. Dad bought that sedan because it gets better mileage than any car.
7. This hot-and-sour soup is spicier than any soup I've ever tasted.
8. Does Renee study harder than anyone?
9. Whales are bigger than any animals.
10. In my opinion, cycling is more fun than any type of exercise.

19g. Avoid using double comparisons.

A *double comparison* is incorrect because it contains both *–er* and *more* (*less*) or *–est* and *most* (*least*).

NONSTANDARD	She is more funnier than he.
STANDARD	She is **funnier** than he.

NONSTANDARD	It was the least cloudiest night of the year.
STANDARD	It was the **least cloudy** night of the year.

Exercise 8 **Revising Modifiers to Correct Double Comparisons**

Write each underlined incorrect modifier in the following sentences. Then, correct the double comparison by crossing out the unnecessary part.

EXAMPLE 1. Today is more colder than yesterday.
          1. ~~more~~ colder

1. That is the ~~most~~ softest sweater I have ever had.
2. You seem to be trying ~~more~~ harder in school this year.

582 Chapter 19 Using Modifiers Correctly

Learning for Life

Continued on pp. 583–584

Personal Marketing. Tell students that one life skill they must learn is to market themselves. They will need to "sell" themselves to employers, colleges, organizations, and even friends.

Explain to students that during an application process they may be asked to answer questions in a way that they might consider to be bragging. Encourage them to see that those interviewing them are trying to get

3. Is she the least tiredest runner on the team?
4. Illustrations help make the explanations more clearer to the readers.
5. Georgia is more larger in area than any other state east of the Mississippi.
6. We had the most best basketball team in our division.
7. The first day of winter is the most shortest day of the year.
8. Parrots are more smarter than other birds.
9. Cynthia's room is much less cleaner than John's.
10. Did you know that Rome is one of the most oldest capitals in the world?

19h. Be sure your comparisons are clear.

UNCLEAR   Weeds in the lawn are harder to get rid of than the garden.
           [This sentence incorrectly compares weeds to a garden.]
CLEAR   Weeds in the lawn are harder to get rid of than **weeds in** the garden.

UNCLEAR   Is the skin of the rhinoceros harder than the alligator?
CLEAR   Is the skin of the rhinoceros harder than **the skin of** the alligator?
                                   or
           Is the skin of the rhinoceros harder than the **alligator's?**

Both parts of an incomplete comparison should be stated if there is any chance of misunderstanding.

UNCLEAR   Theresa called Greg more than Maria.
CLEAR   Theresa called Greg more than Maria **did.**
CLEAR   Theresa called Greg more than **she called** Maria.

Exercise 9 Correcting Unclear Comparisons

Rewrite the following sentences to correct unclear comparisons.

EXAMPLE   1. The annual rainfall in Seattle is higher than London.
           1. *The annual rainfall in Seattle is higher than that in London.*

1. A kangaroo's jump is higher than a rabbit.
2. The power of that truck's engine is greater than a sports car.
3. In those days, the Pottstown Panthers' winning streak was longer than the Lindale Lions.
4. Is a baboon's grip stronger than a human?

┌─HELP─
Although some sentences in Exercise 9 may be correctly revised in more than one way, you need to give only one revision for each sentence.

Comparison of Modifiers   **583**

Exercise 9 Correcting
Unclear Comparisons

**POSSIBLE ANSWERS
continued**

5. . . . as Juan's.

6. . . . than those in Venice,
California.

7. . . . than Houston's.

8. . . . than those in the Costellos'
house.

9. . . . than those of the ibex.

10. . . . Jessica's.

Review B Correcting
Modifiers in a Paragraph

POSSIBLE ANSWERS

1. . . . as one of their strongest
symbols . . .

2. C

3. . . . some of the better-known
countries . . .

4. . . . a better symbol . . .

5. . . . the more practical choice . . .

6. . . . the better choice of the two.

7. While eagles are not larger than
all other . . . [*More effective* can
also be *most effective.*]

8. . . . than the turkey's.

9. The eagle's wings are also
stronger and very wide.

10. . . . the eagle is more beautiful,
too.

5. Tony's bike is as new and gleaming as Juan.

6. The canals in Venice, Italy, are wider than Venice, California.

7. Rome's climate is milder than Houston.

8. Our new windows are bigger than the Costellos' house.

9. The kudu's horns are longer than the ibex.

10. Pat's assignments are usually better written than Jessica.

Review B Correcting Modifiers in a Paragraph

Identify and correct the incorrect comparative and superlative forms
in each sentence in the following paragraph. Some sentences contain
more than one incorrect or unclear comparison. If a sentence is
already correct, write *C*.

EXAMPLE [1] Eagles are widely regarded as more majestic than any
bird in the world.

1. *Eagles are widely regarded as more majestic than any
other bird in the world.*

[1] Many cultures have revered the eagle as one of their most
strongest symbols of bravery and power. [2] In fact, the eagle
seems to be the most popular bird used as a national symbol.
[3] Mexico, Austria, and Egypt are some of the more best-
known countries with eagles on their national flags. [4] In the
United States, early colonial leaders thought that the bald eagle
would be a more better symbol for their new country than the
turkey. [5] Benjamin Franklin had argued that the turkey was
the most practical choice of the two birds, but he was outvoted.

[6] I think most people would
agree that the eagle is the best
choice of the two. [7] While
eagles are not more larger than
all birds, they are among the
more effective hunters and
fliers. [8] As you can see from
these pictures, the eagle's sharp
beak and long claws are more
powerful than the turkey.
[9] The eagle's wings are also
more strong and very wide.
[10] I think the eagle is beauti-
fuller, too.

584 Chapter 19 Using Modifiers Correctly

Learning for Life

degrees. A student might write, "My typing
skills have improved greatly over the last
year since I have spent more hours than ever
using my computer, both to write better
school compositions and to research material
for personal and academic reasons."

Next, assign students to write answers
and present them in a peer-editing session.
Then they may type a formal copy or prepare an audiotape or videotape of their
response.

Dangling Modifiers

19i. Avoid using dangling modifiers.

A modifying word, phrase, or clause that does not clearly and sensibly modify a word or a word group in a sentence is a ***dangling modifier.***

DANGLING	Together, the litter along the highway was picked up, bagged, and hauled away. [Was the litter together?]
CORRECT	Together, we picked up, bagged, and hauled away the litter along the highway.
DANGLING	Time seemed to stand still, watching the sunset and listening to the cicadas. [Was time watching and listening?]
CORRECT	Time seemed to stand still as we watched the sunset and listened to the cicadas.

When a modifying participial or infinitive phrase comes at the beginning of a sentence, the phrase is followed by a comma. Immediately after that comma should come the word or word group that the phrase modifies.

DANGLING	Jogging in the park, a rabbit peered at me from the underbrush. [Was the rabbit jogging?]
CORRECT	Jogging in the park, **I** saw a rabbit peering at me from the underbrush.
DANGLING	Listening closely, distant thunder could be detected. [Was the thunder listening?]
CORRECT	Listening closely, **she** could detect distant thunder.
DANGLING	To master a musical instrument, practice or natural talent is usually needed. [Is practice or talent mastering an instrument?]
CORRECT	To master a musical instrument, **a musician** usually needs practice or natural talent.
DANGLING	Even when equipped with the best gear, the rock cliff was difficult to climb. [Was the rock cliff equipped?]
CORRECT	Even when equipped with the best gear, **the mountaineers** had difficulty climbing the rock cliff.

A sentence may appear to have a dangling modifier when *you* is the understood subject. In such cases, the modifier is not dangling; instead, it is modifying the understood subject.

EXAMPLE   To find the correct spelling, (you) look up the word.

Reference Note

For more information on **participial phrases,** see page 451. For more information on **infinitive phrases,** see page 458.

Reference Note

For more about the **understood subject,** see page 423.

Dangling Modifiers   **585**

Dangling Modifiers
Rule 19i *(pp. 585–587)*

O B J E C T I V E S

■ **To write sentences with introductory modifiers**

■ **To revise sentences by correcting dangling modifiers**

Relating to Writing and Listening

You may wish to have students work in groups of three to write and evaluate sentences for the correct use of modifiers. Each student should write two sentences—one with a dangling modifier and one without—and choose one of them to read aloud. Listeners should determine whether or not the sentence has a dangling modifier and should offer corrections.

USAGE

Exercise 10 **Writing Sentences with Introductory Modifiers**

POSSIBLE ANSWERS

1. Leaping from branch to branch, the squirrel entertained us.
2. Yawning, JoAnn stretched.
3. While eating our lunch, we watched a fashion show.
4. Surrounded by the cheering crowd, the athlete waved.
5. To make sure he wouldn't be late, Lance set three alarms.
6. Alone, Melanie walked through the storm.
7. Following Leila's example, Jason searched the Internet for information.
8. Not wanting to wake them up, Jon tiptoed past the kittens.
9. Having filled out the forms, Mother mailed the family's tax return.
10. To solve this riddle, the children thought and thought.

Timesaver

To lessen labor-intensive marking of **Exercise 10** and to help students analyze sentences, work with students to create models for the first half of the exercise. Write sample sentences on the board, drawing arrows to the words modified. Assign students to small groups so that they can analyze and revise each other's sentences by following your process. Have volunteers read sample sentences to the class.

Exercise 10 **Writing Sentences with Introductory Modifiers**

Write complete sentences that begin with the following introductory modifiers.

EXAMPLE   1. Having solved one problem,

               1. *Having solved one problem, Joe Harris found that another awaited him.*

1. Leaping from branch to branch,
2. Yawning,
3. While eating our lunch,
4. Surrounded by the cheering crowd,
5. To make sure he wouldn't be late,
6. Alone,
7. Following Leila's example,
8. Not wanting to wake them up,
9. Having filled out the forms,
10. To solve this riddle,

Correcting Dangling Modifiers

To correct a dangling modifier, rearrange the words in the sentence and add or change words to make the meaning logical and clear.

DANGLING   While lighting the birthday candles, the cake started to crumble.

CORRECT   While **I was** lighting the birthday candles, the cake started to crumble.

or

While lighting the birthday candles, **I noticed** the cake **starting** to crumble.

DANGLING   To become a physicist, years of study and research are required.

CORRECT   To become a physicist, **you** must spend years studying and doing research.

or

If you want to become a physicist, **you** must spend years studying and doing research.

or

If a person wants to become a physicist, **he or she** must spend years studying and doing research.

USAGE

Exercise 11 Correcting Dangling Modifiers

Most of the following sentences contain dangling modifiers. If a sentence has a dangling modifier, revise the sentence to correct it. If a sentence is already correct, write *C*.   Answers may vary.

EXAMPLE
1. While mopping the kitchen, my baby brother woke up from his nap.

1. *While I was mopping the kitchen, my baby brother woke up from his nap.*

1. Walking through the gate, the swimming pool is on the right.
2. Lost, the small village was a welcome sight.
3. To earn money, Mom suggested shoveling snow for our neighbors.
4. After studying hard, a long walk can be refreshing.
5. Walking in the woods, listening to the singing birds is enjoyable.
6. To understand a sentence, even little words can be important.
7. To become a great athlete, you need dedication and self-discipline.
8. Standing on the beach, a school of dolphins suddenly appeared.
9. After winning the last game of the season, the celebration lasted nearly all night.
10. Tired and sore, the job was finally finished.

1. As you walk
2. I welcomed the sight of
3. that I earn money by
4. he finds that
5. I enjoy
6. remember that
7. C
8. As we were
9. players celebrated
10. we finally finished

Misplaced Modifiers

19j. Avoid using misplaced modifiers.

A word, phrase, or clause that seems to modify the wrong word or word group in a sentence is a *misplaced modifier.* Place modifying words, phrases, and clauses as near as possible to the words they modify.

MISPLACED	My cousin's dog was chasing the geese, yapping and barking.
CORRECT	**Yapping and barking,** my cousin's dog was chasing the geese.
MISPLACED	I read about the bank robbers who were captured in this morning's paper.
CORRECT	I read **in this morning's paper** about the bank robbers who were captured.
MISPLACED	Blackened beyond recognition, even the birds refused to eat the toast.
CORRECT	Even the birds refused to eat the toast **blackened beyond recognition.**

S T Y L E   T I P

Be sure to place modifiers correctly to show clearly the meaning you intend.

EXAMPLES

Only Uncle Jim sells bikes. [Uncle Jim, not anybody else, sells bikes.]

Uncle Jim **only** sells bikes. [Uncle Jim sells bikes; he does not repair them.]

Uncle Jim sells **only** bikes. [Uncle Jim does not sell cars or motorcycles.]

Meeting INDIVIDUAL NEEDS

LEARNERS HAVING DIFFICULTY
Before students begin **Exercise 12,** remind them that unlike dangling modifiers, misplaced modifiers do modify a word in the sentence. It might be helpful for students to ask themselves what the phrase or clause modifies or to sketch the image created by both the properly placed and the misplaced modifiers.

Review C Correcting **Dangling and Misplaced Modifiers**

POSSIBLE ANSWERS

1. Seeing the tremendous force of Niagara Falls was awe inspiring.
2. When reading about the falls, I was impressed by many facts.
3. We discovered that Goat Island separates the two principal parts of the falls.
4. Most visitors admire both sets of falls, the Horseshoe Falls and the American Falls, which form the border between Canada and the United States.
5. While we were climbing the tower, Niagara Falls, shown on the next page, looked magnificent.
6. Because we were trying to see and do everything around Niagara Falls, the days passed quickly.

Answers may vary.
1. with Uncle Saburo
2. With my binoculars
3. When I was
4. roses

5. From my sister,
6. in the attic
7. patiently
8. in a tank at the aquarium
9. Watching TV,
10. children

Exercise 12 Correcting Misplaced Modifiers

Revise the following sentences to correct misplaced modifiers. In revising a sentence, be sure not to misplace another modifier.

EXAMPLE   1. The security guard was watching for the arrival of the armored car through the window.

1. *The security guard was watching through the window for the arrival of the armored car.*

1. Michiko went outside to trim the bonsai trees with Uncle Saburo.
2. I could see the scouts marching over the hill with my binoculars.
3. As a child, my grandfather taught me how to make tortillas.
4. One advertiser handed out roses to customers with dollar bills pinned to them.
5. I borrowed a radio from my sister with a weather band.
6. Did you find any of the hats your mother used to wear in the attic?
7. Our cat waited on the porch for us to come home patiently.
8. In a tank at the aquarium, we watched the seals play.
9. She ate two peaches and a plate of strawberries watching TV.
10. We gave the boxes of cereal to the children with prizes inside.

Review C Correcting Dangling and Misplaced Modifiers

Most of the following sentences contain dangling or misplaced modifiers. If a sentence is incorrect, revise it. If a sentence is already correct, write *C*.

EXAMPLE   1. Only the American Falls are slightly higher than the Horseshoe Falls.

1. *The American Falls are only slightly higher than the Horseshoe Falls.*

1. Arriving at Niagara Falls, the sight of nature's tremendous force was awe inspiring.
2. When reading about the falls, many facts impressed me.
3. Separated by Goat Island, we discovered that the falls are in two principal parts.
4. Forming the border between Canada and the United States, most visitors admire both the Horseshoe Falls and the American Falls.
5. While climbing the tower, Niagara Falls, shown on the next page, looked magnificent to us.
6. Trying to see and do everything around Niagara Falls, the days passed quickly.

7. While riding in a tour boat called the *Maid of the Mist*, the spray from the base of the falls drenched us.
8. Roaring constantly, an awesome amount of power is generated.
9. After walking through Queen Victoria Park, a hearty lunch at the restaurant was refreshing.
10. To see the waterfalls at their most beautiful, a visit at night—when they are illuminated—was recommended by the tour guide.

Misplaced Clause Modifiers

Adjective clauses should be placed near the words they modify.

| MISPLACED | There is a car in the garage that has no windshield. |
| CORRECT | In the garage, there is a car **that has no windshield.** |

| MISPLACED | The money and tickets are still in my wallet that I meant to return to you. |
| CORRECT | The money and tickets **that I meant to return to you** are still in my wallet. |

Reference Note

For more information on **adjective clauses,** see page 472.

Exercise 13 Correcting Misplaced Clauses

Revise each of the following sentences by placing the misplaced clause near the word it modifies.

EXAMPLE
1. Alejandro searched the sand dunes for shells, which were deserted.
1. *Alejandro searched the sand dunes, which were deserted, for shells.*

1. Birds are kept away by scarecrows, ~~many of which eat seeds~~.
2. The disabled truck is now blocking the overpass ~~that suddenly went out of control~~.
3. There was a bird ~~in the tree~~ that had a strange-looking beak.
4. A huge dog ~~chased me as I rode my bicycle~~ that was growling and barking loudly.
5. An old log ~~sat in the fireplace~~ that was covered with moss.

1. , many of which eat seeds,
2. that suddenly went out of control
3. In the tree
4. chased me as I rode my bicycle
5. sat in the fireplace

USAGE

Review C **Correcting Dangling and Misplaced Modifiers**

POSSIBLE ANSWERS continued

7. While riding in a tour boat called the *Maid of the Mist,* we were drenched by the spray from the base of the falls.
8. Roaring constantly, the falls generate an awesome amount of power.
9. After walking through Queen Victoria Park, we enjoyed a hearty lunch at the restaurant.
10. A guide recommended that we visit the waterfalls at night to see them when they are illuminated and at their most beautiful.

TEACHING **TIP**

Activity. To offer an alternative to using logical thought processes and memorization, you might suggest that students use their imaginations. For each sentence in **Exercise 13** and **Review D,** ask students what images are evoked by the mistakes in modification. [*For example, Exercise 13, sentence 1, might inspire the image of scarecrows eating seeds; sentence 2 might suggest thoughts of overpasses out of control.*]

Exercises You may wish to use **Exercise 13** as guided practice. Then, have students complete **Review D** as independent practice.

6. At the post office

7. On our shelves

8. was standing at the bus stop

9. , on a ferry
10. Behind the shed

6. We thanked the clerk ~~at the post office~~ that had helped us with our overseas packages.
7. There are several books ~~on our shelves~~ that were written by Rolando Hinojosa-Smith.
8. A boy ~~was standing at the bus stop~~ that looked remarkably like my cousin.
9. She crossed the river ~~on a ferry~~, which was more than a mile wide.
10. There is a flower garden ~~behind the shed~~ that is planted with prize-winning dahlias.

Review D Correcting Dangling and Misplaced Modifiers

POSSIBLE ANSWERS

1. Awakening from a nap, I saw the island of Puerto Rico through my airplane window.
2. Our guide was waiting inside the baggage-claim area to take us to our hotel.
3. To understand the guide's presentation, we found some knowledge of both Spanish and English helpful.
4. Driving along the Panoramic Route, we saw breathtaking scenery!
5. We stopped for lunch at a roadside stall made from palm branches.
6. To hungry people, the spicy rice and beans was delicious.
7. From a young boy, we bought a souvenir rock decorated with island scenes.
8. Look at that strange fish that is puffing up in the water!
9. Anxious to shower and unpack, we stopped next at our hotel room.
10. To fully appreciate all the island had to offer, we needed more time.

Review D Correcting Dangling and Misplaced Modifiers

Revise each of the following sentences by correcting the placement of a modifier or by rephrasing the sentence.

EXAMPLE   1. Feeling nervous about flying, the twin-engine plane looked small but dependable.

1. *Feeling nervous about flying, we thought the twin-engine plane looked small but dependable.*

1. Awakening from a nap, the island of Puerto Rico came into view through my airplane window.
2. Our guide was waiting to take us to our hotel inside the baggage-claim area.
3. To understand the guide's presentation, some knowledge of both Spanish and English proved to be helpful.
4. Driving along the Panoramic Route, the scenery was breathtaking!
5. We stopped for lunch at a stall along the road that was made from palm branches.
6. Hungry, the spicy rice and beans was delicious.
7. We bought a souvenir rock from a young boy that was decorated with island scenes.
8. Look at that strange fish in the water that is puffing up!
9. Anxious to shower and unpack, our hotel room was the next stop.
10. To fully appreciate all the island had to offer, more time was needed.

Chapter Review

A. Identifying Modifiers

Identify the italicized word or word group in each of the following sentences as a *modifier* or *not a modifier*. M or Not M

1. Sammy Sosa is a *natural* baseball talent. **1. M**
2. The elephant ambled *out of the trees* into the clearing. **2. M**
3. Two well-known Mexican *authors* are Carlos Fuentes and Octavio Paz. **3. Not M**
4. Austin, Texas, is a *pleasant* place to live. **4. M**
5. As Stan *entered* the house, the cat dashed under the bed. **5. Not M**
6. Amrit the waiter is a *very* helpful person, don't you think? **6. M**
7. Jean-Marc joined the resistance to fight *against the enemy*. **7. M**
8. The group Los Lobos is *well established* as a major force in the Latino music world. **8. M**
9. Chi *fed* the three horses in the stables. **9. Not M**
10. Gustav Mahler was a *gifted* Austrian composer and conductor. **10. M**

B. Correcting Dangling and Misplaced Modifiers

For each of the following sentences, identify the dangling or misplaced modifier and revise the sentence to correct the error.

11. Growing up in a big family, that family movie rings true to me.
12. To paint landscapes, patience and a steady hand are helpful.
13. Almost hidden under the pile of old books, Janelle saw the letter.
14. In different parts of the world I read about unusual customs.
15. A tree was almost destroyed by a bulldozer that was two hundred years old.
16. Jogging in the park, it was a sunny day.
17. The convicts were caught by the police trying to escape from jail.
18. Rushing out the door, Ben's homework was left on the table.
19. When told of the potential threat, nothing was done.
20. The mayor pledged she would build more roads at the political rally.

Chapter Review **591**

Using the Chapter Review

To assess student progress, you may want to compare the types of items missed on the **Diagnostic Preview** to those missed on the **Chapter Review**. If students have not made significant progress, you may want to refer them to **Chapter 28: Correcting Common Errors, Exercises 17–19** and **21–23** for additional practice.

USAGE

Chapter Review

B. Correcting Dangling and Misplaced Modifiers

POSSIBLE ANSWERS

11. Because I grew up in a big family, I find that family movie rings true.
12. To paint landscapes, one needs patience and a steady hand.
13. Janelle saw the letter that was almost hidden under the pile of old books.
14. I read about unusual customs from different parts of the world.
15. A two-hundred-year-old tree was almost destroyed by a bulldozer.
16. The team jogged in the park on a sunny day.
17. The police caught the convicts trying to escape from jail.
18. Rushing out the door, Ben left his homework on the table.
19. Although the potential threat was reported, nothing was done.
20. At the political rally, the mayor pledged she would build more roads.

C. Identifying Correct Comparative and Superlative Forms and Revising Faulty Comparisons

Identify the comparative and superlative modifiers in the following sentences. If the form of the modifier is incorrect, write the correct form. If the form is already correct, write *C*. Add words to sentences in which a faulty or unclear comparison is made.

21. easier
22. C
23. other
24. worse
25. more
26. most

27. C
28. C
29. best
30. else
31. deeper
32. less
33. better
34. longer

35. more

36. C
37. else
38. C

39. worse

40. the tree in / yard

21. Which plan is more easier to follow, his or hers?
22. My bowling was worse than usual last night.
23. This paella is more delicious than any dish I've ever eaten.
24. His problem is more worse than yours.
25. I like both shirts, but I think I like this one the most.
26. That was one of the interestingest movies he's seen.
27. The tomatoes from our garden taste sweeter than those from the store.
28. This is the nicest surprise I've ever had!
29. Which route is better—upstream, downstream, or overland?
30. The sun is brighter than anything in our solar system.
31. The water in the pond was more deep than Nicky expected.
32. Arnie is the least helpful of the two brothers.
33. Doesn't Granddad feel more better now that he's rested?
34. Did you know that the Nile is more longer than any other river in the world?
35. When Marcos was five, he was carefuller than he is now.
36. Which do you like better—Theseus Flatow's older or more recent music?
37. Ken completed the exercise faster than anyone.
38. The last problem is the most complicated one in the entire exercise.
39. Jesse is feeling more badly about the accident today than he did yesterday.
40. The tree in our yard is bigger than our neighbors.

D. Correcting Misplaced Clause Modifiers

Revise each of the following sentences by placing the misplaced clause near the word it modifies.

41. There is a magazine on the table that has no cover.

Chapter Review

D. Correcting Misplaced Clause Modifiers

POSSIBLE ANSWERS

41. On the table is a magazine that has no cover.
42. The test papers that I want to hand in to Mr. Saenz are still in my locker.
43. In that display case is a vase that was made during the Ming dynasty.
44. In the street was a Dalmatian that had a silver collar.
45. The young chestnut mare that just won the steeplechase is drinking water.
46. We called the helpful lady at the nursing home.
47. Tom looked for dents on the cars on the dealer's lot.
48. A trailer covered with rust sat in the empty field.
49. There is a five-thousand-year-old mummy in the museum.
50. A woman that I thought was my friend Fran was running along the lake.

RESOURCES

Using Modifiers Correctly
Review
■ *Grammar, Usage, and Mechanics,* pp. 210, 211, 212, 213, 214

Assessment
■ *Assessment Package*
—*Chapter Tests,* Ch. 19
—*Chapter Tests in Standardized Test Formats,* Ch. 19
■ *Test Generator (One-Stop Planner CD-ROM)*

42. The test papers are still in my locker that I want to hand in to Mr. Saenz.

43. There is a vase in that display case that was made during the Ming dynasty.

44. There was a Dalmatian in the street that had a silver collar.

45. The young chestnut mare is drinking water that just won the steeplechase.

46. We called the lady at the nursing home that had been so helpful.

47. Tom inspected the cars for dents, which were on the dealer's lot.

48. A trailer sat in the empty field that was covered with rust.

49. There is a mummy in the museum that is five thousand years old.

50. A woman was running along the lake that I thought was my friend Fran.

Writing Application

Using Modifiers in a Restaurant Review

Comparative and Superlative Forms   As the restaurant critic for *Good Food* magazine, you always give a year-end summary of the best restaurants and their foods. Discuss your choices in a paragraph in which you use five comparative and five superlative forms of both adjectives and adverbs.

Prewriting   Using either real or imaginary restaurants, make a list of several places and their best dishes. Think of some ways to compare the restaurants (food, atmosphere, service, price).

Writing   As you write your first draft, use your list to help you make accurate comparisons.

Revising   Read your paragraph to a classmate to see if your comparisons are clearly stated. Revise any comparisons that are confusing.

Publishing   As you correct any mistakes in spelling, grammar, and punctuation, pay special attention to the spelling of comparative and superlative forms made by adding *–er* and *–est*. You and your classmates could prepare a *Good Food* newcomer's guide to local restaurants. Decide how you want the guide to look. Then, type the guide and make photocopies or input the guide on a computer and print it out.

Reference Note

For information about **spelling words with suffixes,** see page 735.

Writing Application

Tip. You may wish to bring in newspaper and magazine reviews of local restaurants for students to study and use as resources.

Scoring Rubric. While you will want to pay particular attention to students' use of comparative and superlative modifiers, you will also want to evaluate the students' overall writing performance. You may want to give a split score to indicate development and clarity of the composition as well as usage skills.

CHAPTER

20

A Glossary of Usage
Common Usage Problems

Diagnostic Preview

Correcting Errors in Standard Usage

Each of the sentences in the following passage contains at least one error in formal standard usage. Revise the passage, correcting all such errors.

EXAMPLE   [1] Everyone accept him joined this here club.

    1. *Everyone except him joined this club.*
       Some answers may vary.

1. teaches
2. have
3. anywhere
4. take
5. fewer
6. Besides
7. who
8. affects/than

10. anything/ unless
11. can
12. these
13. burst

[1] Our school has a hiking club that ~~learns~~ us how to appreciate nature. [2] Our club usually goes to parks that we might not ~~of~~ discovered by ourselves. [3] We go hiking ~~anywheres~~ that can be reached by bus in a few hours. [4] Before we go, we decide what to ~~bring~~ with us. [5] The ~~less~~ things that we have to carry, the better off we are. [6] ~~Beside~~ water, a hat, and a jacket, little else is needed. [7] Those ~~which~~ pack too much soon wish they hadn't ~~of~~. [8] After all, a ten-mile hike ~~effects~~ you differently when you are weighted down ~~then~~ when you are not.

[9] Our adviser, Mr. Graham, ~~he~~ knows where all the best hiking areas are ~~at~~. [10] He always tells us that we won't see ~~nothing~~ interesting ~~without~~ we're willing to exert ourselves. [11] We ~~can't~~ hardly keep up with him once he starts walking.

[12] We go on ~~this~~ sorts of walks because we enjoy them. [13] Although we sometimes think our lungs will ~~bust~~, everyone wants

to keep up with the others. [14] The real reward is ~~when we see~~ an unusual sight, like a fawn, a family of otters, a panoramic view, ~~and~~ etc. [15] ~~Than~~ we're sure that all of our hiking and time spent outdoors ~~ain't~~ been wasted. [16] We also ~~except~~ nature ~~like~~ it is and do not try to change it ~~none~~. [17] When we find bottles or cans in the woods, we get upset with people who can't seem to go ~~anywheres~~ without leaving some mark.

[18] Everyone in the club feels the same way, so we're going to start ~~an~~ cleanup campaign. [19] People ought to enjoy being inside ~~of~~ a park without ~~busting~~ or changing anything there. [20] We'd rather have more hikers enjoying the wilderness and ~~less~~ people destroying nature.

14. seeing

15. Then/haven't
16. accept/as/any
17. anywhere

18. a
19. breaking
20. fewer

About the Glossary

This chapter provides a compact glossary of common problems in English usage. A *glossary* is an alphabetical list of special terms or expressions with definitions, explanations, and examples. You will notice that some examples in this glossary are labeled *nonstandard*, *standard*, *formal*, or *informal*.

The label *nonstandard* identifies usage that is suitable only in the most casual speaking situations and in writing that attempts to re-create casual speech. *Standard* English is language that is grammatically correct and appropriate in formal and informal situations. *Formal* identifies usage that is appropriate in serious speaking and writing situations (such as in speeches and in compositions for school). The label *informal* indicates standard usage common in conversation and in everyday writing such as personal letters. In doing the exercises in this chapter, be sure to use only standard English.

The following are examples of formal and informal English.

Formal	Informal
angry	steamed
unpleasant	yucky
agreeable	cool
very impressive	totally awesome
accelerate	step on it

Reference Note

For a list of **words often confused,** see page 746. Use the **index** at the back of the book to find discussions of other usage problems.

TEACHING TIP

Motivation. Start the chapter by having each student complete the sentence "The usage mistake I make the most is . . ." Refer students who need ideas to the glossary entries in boldface type.

Have students work in small groups, creating mnemonics to help eliminate their errors. [*Example: I can* accept *help with* anything *except* prepositions.] Finally, have each person write his or her most common mistake and mnemonic on a classroom chart.

Crossing the Curriculum

Art. You may want to have students draw and compile cartoons of the most common mistakes and create a scrapbook or a Web site.

Usage: *A, An—Good, Well*

(pp. 596–602)

OBJECTIVES

■ To choose the correct word from given pairs in sentences

■ To proofread sentences to correct common usage problems

Meeting INDIVIDUAL NEEDS

MODALITIES

Auditory Learners. To help students distinguish between homonyms, like *accept/except,* have them use language laboratory equipment. Prepare a master tape using exaggerated distinctions like /aksept/ and /eksept/. Allow space on the tape between models for students to record their pronunciations. As students listen and record, have them respond to the questions below using the following answer choices.

NEVER   SOMETIMES   ALWAYS

- Can you hear the differences in pronunciation between these words by listening to the model?
- Can you tell the difference in these words by listening to the recording?

Relating to Literature

If your literature book includes "Ain't I a Woman?" by Sojourner Truth, refer students to the selection for a literary example of the use of *ain't.* After students have heard an interpretive reading of the selection, ask them how nonstandard usage, especially of the word *ain't,* affected the message. [*Students will probably defend the author's usage as a reflection of her speech patterns and as appropriate for her audience and for her purpose of communicating her outrage.*]

Reference Note

For more about **articles,** see page 384.

STYLE   TIP

The expression *a lot* is overused. Try replacing *a lot* with a more descriptive, specific word or phrase.

EXAMPLES
mountains of homework

four subjects' worth of homework

a, an These *indefinite articles* refer to one of a general group. Use *a* before words beginning with a consonant sound; use *an* before words beginning with a vowel sound.

EXAMPLES   We saw **a** blue jay and **an** owl.

A hawk flew over us **an** hour ago. [*An* is used before *hour* because *hour* begins with a vowel sound.]

This is **a** one-way street. [*A* is used before *one-way* because *one-way* begins with a consonant sound.]

accept, except *Accept* is a verb that means "to receive." *Except* may be either a verb or a preposition. As a verb, *except* means "to leave out" or "to omit." As a preposition, it means "excluding."

EXAMPLES   I couldn't **accept** such a valuable gift!

Why should they be **excepted** from the test?

No one in my class **except** me has been to Moscow.

affect, effect *Affect* is a verb meaning "to influence." *Effect* used as a verb means "to bring about" or "to accomplish." Used as a noun, *effect* means "the result of some action."

EXAMPLES   The bright colors **affect** how the patients feel.

The treatment will **effect** a cure for the disease.

The bright colors have a beneficial **effect** on the patients.

ain't Avoid using this word in speaking or in writing; it is nonstandard English.

all the farther, all the faster This expression is used in some parts of the country to mean "as far as" or "as fast as."

NONSTANDARD   This is all the faster I can go.
STANDARD   This is **as fast as** I can go.

all right See page 747.

a lot Do not write the expression *a lot* as one word. It should be written as two words.

EXAMPLE   I have **a lot** of homework tonight.

among See **between, among.**

RESOURCES

Usage: *A, An—Good, Well*
Practice

■ *Grammar, Usage, and Mechanics,* pp. 219, 220
■ *Language Workshop CD-ROM,* Lesson 63

USAGE

and etc. *Etc.* is an abbreviation of the Latin phrase *et cetera*, meaning "and other things." Thus, *and etc.* means "and and other things." Do not use *and* with *etc.*

EXAMPLE   We'll need paint, brushes, thinner, some rags, **etc.**
[not *and etc.*]

anyways, anywheres, everywheres, nowheres, somewheres Use these words without a final *s.*

EXAMPLE   That bird is described **somewhere** [not *somewheres*] in this book.

as See **like, as.**

as if See **like, as if.**

at Do not use *at* after *where.*

NONSTANDARD   This is where I live at.
STANDARD   This is **where** I live.

bad, badly See page 575.

because See **reason ... because.**

beside, besides *Beside* is a preposition that means "by the side of" someone or something. *Besides* as a preposition means "in addition to." As an adverb, *besides* means "moreover."

EXAMPLES   Sit **beside** me on the couch.

Besides songs and dances, the show featured several comedy sketches.

It's too late to rent a movie. **Besides,** I'm sleepy.

between, among Use *between* when you are referring to two things at a time, even if they are part of a group consisting of more than two. Use *among* when you are thinking of a group rather than of separate individuals.

EXAMPLES   Take the seat **between** Alicia and Noreen in the third row.

On the map, the boundaries **between** all seven counties are drawn in red. [Although there are more than two counties, each boundary lies between only two.]

Among our graduates are several prominent authors.

There was some confusion **among** the jurors about the defendant's testimony. [The jurors are thought of as a group.]

COMPUTER TIP

The spellchecker on a computer will usually catch misspelled words such as *anywheres* and *nowheres.* The grammar checker may catch errors such as double negatives. However, in the case of words often confused, such as *than* and *then* and *between* and *among,* a computer program may not be able to help. You will have to check your work yourself for correct usage.

USAGE

Meeting
INDIVIDUAL
NEEDS

INCLUSION
Students may benefit from visualizing the difference between words like *beside* and *besides, between* and *among.* Discuss the meanings with students, and have them draw stick-figure sketches for these words, or have a helper draw sketches based on student directions. You may want to continue this technique throughout the chapter.

ENGLISH-LANGUAGE LEARNERS
Spanish. Students who speak Spanish may need further explanation of the difference between *between* and *among* because one word (*entre*) is used for both prepositions in Spanish.

MINI-LESSON

The Parts of Speech. Because the glossary entries refer to parts of speech without explanation, you may want to review each part of speech as it appears in the glossary. (See **Chapter 12: Parts of Speech Overview.**)

For practice, have students identify the parts of speech of often-confused pairs such as *accept* (verb), *except* (verb; preposition); and *affect* (verb), *effect* (noun; verb).

Mnemonics. Tell students to use the following memory aids to determine the correct use of *bring* and *take*: *bring it **to*** and ***take it away*** or ***to bring*** something when you ***come*** and ***take*** it when you ***go.***

Meeting
INDIVIDUAL
NEEDS

LEARNERS HAVING DIFFICULTY
To personalize the glossary entries, place students in groups of four and have each student create an exercise item based on one glossary entry. (You may wish to have students use the items in **Exercise 1** on pp. 598–599 as models.) Then, have the group members work together to find the correct answers. Have students repeat this process several times. Then, have them compile their items into a practice test to share with other groups.

Exercise 1

ALTERNATIVE LESSON
To reinforce what students have learned about the parts of speech, ask them to identify the part of speech of the correct answers in sentences 3, 9, and 10.

3. noun

9. preposition

10. verb

borrow, lend, loan *Borrow* means "To take [something] temporarily." *Lend* means "to give [something] temporarily." *Loan*, a noun in formal language, is sometimes used in place of *lend* in informal speech.

EXAMPLES Tadzio **borrowed** a copy of *O Pioneers!* from the library.

I try not to forget to return things people **lend** me.

Could you **loan** me a dollar? [informal]

bring, take *Bring* means "to come carrying something." *Take* means "to go carrying something." Think of *bring* as related to *come*, *take* as related to *go*.

EXAMPLES **Bring** that box over here.

Now **take** it down to the basement.

bust, busted Avoid using these words as verbs. Use a form of either *burst* or *break* or *catch* or *arrest*.

EXAMPLES Even the hard freeze didn't **burst** [not *bust*] the pipes.

When aircraft **break** [not *bust*] the sound barrier, a sonic boom results.

Molly **caught** [not *busted*] Mr. Whiskers nibbling her tuna sandwich.

Did the police **arrest** [not *bust*] a suspect in the burglary?

Exercise 1 Solving Common Usage Problems

For each sentence, choose the correct word or words in parentheses, according to standard usage.

EXAMPLE **1.** Everyone seemed greatly (*affected, effected*) by her speech on animal rights.

1. affected

1. There was complete agreement (*between, among*) the members of the council.
2. Is that (*all the farther, as far as*) you were able to hike?
3. The (*affects, effects*) of lasers on surgical procedures have been remarkable.
4. My schedule includes English, math, science, (*etc., and etc.*)
5. The boiler (*busted, burst*) and flooded the cellar.

6. Liza promised to (*bring, take*) me the new cassette when she comes to visit.

7. I don't know where it (*is, is at*).

8. Please (*bring, take*) this note to the manager's office when you go.

9. (*Beside, Besides*) my aunts and uncles, all my cousins are coming to our family reunion.

10. Ms. Yu (*accepted, excepted*) my excuse for being late.

Exercise 2 Proofreading Sentences for Standard Usage

The following sentences contain errors in standard English usage. Identify the error or errors you find in each sentence. Then, write the correct usage. If a sentence is already correct, write *C*.

EXAMPLE   1. It isn't pretty, but the fossilized skull in the picture below has caused alot of talk in the scientific world.

   1. *alot—a lot*

1. Discussions between various groups of scholars focus on what killed the dinosaurs.
2. Some scientists believe an asteroid hit earth and wiped out the dinosaurs, but others think there was a severe climate change where the dinosaurs lived at.
3. Even if we don't know why the dinosaurs disappeared, most of us enjoy looking at dinosaur fossils in museums, in exhibitions, on TV, and etc.
4. The San Juan, Argentina, area is one of the best places anywheres to find dinosaur fossils.
5. In 1988, the biologist Paul Sereno's discovery there busted the old record for the most ancient dinosaur remains.
6. On a expedition with some of his students from the University of Chicago, Sereno found the oldest dinosaur fossils unearthed up to that time.
7. Besides being in good shape, Sereno's herrerasaurus fossil doesn't even look its age.
8. In fact, the 230-million-year-old skeleton was amazingly complete accept for the hind limbs.

A Glossary of Usage   **599**

Timesaver

When using **Exercise 2,** you may want to discuss and analyze with students only the even-numbered sentences. Have students check the odd-numbered sentences in small groups.

Exercise 2 Proofreading Sentences for Standard Usage
ANSWERS

1. between—among
2. lived at—lived
3. and etc.—etc.
4. anywheres—anywhere
5. busted—broke
6. a—an
7. C
8. accept—except

USAGE

Exercise 2 **Proofreading**
Sentences for Standard Usage
A N S W E R S c o n t i n u e d

9. ain't—isn't

10. effected—affected

Meeting INDIVIDUAL NEEDS

ENGLISH-LANGUAGE LEARNERS

Spanish. You may want to point out to your Spanish-speaking students that *good* and *well* are the English equivalents of *bueno* and *bien,* respectively.

Also, when discussing the problems writers have with *had of* and *would of,* you may need to give more attention to Spanish speakers because Spanish does not have as many helping verbs as English does.

TEACHING TIP

Mnemonics. Show students the following examples to distinguish between the uses of *good* and *well.*

They didn't feel **well** digging the well. (adj.)

They dug a **good** well. (adj.)

They dug the well **well.** (adv.)

They did a **good** job on the well. (adj.)

---

9. That quality of find certainly ain't ordinary.

10. Sereno and his herrerasaurus have effected the work of biologists and dinosaur-lovers everywhere.

can, may Use *can* to express ability. Use *may* to express possibility or permission.

EXAMPLES
Can you speak German? [ability]

Pedro **may** join us at the restaurant. [possibility]

May I be excused? [permission]

could of Do not write *of* with the helping verb *could.* Write *could have.* Also avoid *had of, ought to of, should of, would of, might of,* and *must of.*

EXAMPLE
Diane **could have** [not *could of*] telephoned us.

discover, invent *Discover* means "to be the first to find, see, or learn about something that already exists." *Invent* means "to be the first to do or make something."

EXAMPLES
Who **discovered** those fossil dinosaur eggs?

Robert Wilhelm Bunsen, for whom the Bunsen burner is named, **invented** the spectroscope.

don't, doesn't *Don't* is the contraction of *do not. Doesn't* is the contraction of *does not.* Use *doesn't,* not *don't,* with *he, she, it, this,* and singular nouns.

EXAMPLES
It **doesn't** [not *don't*] matter.

The trains **don't** [not *doesn't*] stop at this station.

effect See **affect, effect.**

everywheres See **anyways,** etc.

fewer, less *Fewer* is used with plural words. *Less* is used with singular words. *Fewer* tells "how many"; *less* tells "how much."

EXAMPLES
Fewer students have enrolled this semester.

Therefore, there will be **less** competition.

good, well *Good* is an adjective. Do not use *good* to modify a verb; use *well,* an adverb.

NONSTANDARD   Tiger Woods played good.

STANDARD   Tiger Woods played **well.**

| STYLE | TIP |

Many people consider contractions informal. Therefore, it is usually best to avoid using them in formal writing and speech.

MINI-LESSON

Definitions. You may want to review with students the following definitions.

• **contraction:** shortened form of a word or group of words

• **apostrophe:** symbol indicating where letters have been omitted or where possessive form has been added (see p. 699)

While *well* is usually an adverb, it is also used as an adjective to mean "healthy."

EXAMPLE   She does not feel **well.**

NOTE *Feel good* and *feel well* mean different things. *Feel good* means "to feel happy or pleased." *Feel well* simply means "to feel healthy."

EXAMPLES   Compliments make you feel **good.**

Do dogs and cats really eat grass when they don't feel **well**?

Reference Note

For more information about **formal** and **informal English,** see page 595.

Exercise 3   Solving Common Usage Problems

For each sentence, choose the correct word in parentheses, according to standard usage.

EXAMPLE   **1.** Today people are using (*fewer, less*) salt than they did years ago.
          1. less

1. You should (*of, have*) written sooner.
2. Who (*discovered, invented*) what makes fireflies glow?
3. (*Don't, Doesn't*) Otis know that we're planning to leave in five minutes?
4. I usually do (*good, well*) on that kind of test.
5. Our doctor advised my uncle to eat (*fewer, less*) eggs.
6. He (*don't, doesn't*) look angry to me.
7. If I had known, I might (*of, have*) helped you with your project.
8. We had (*fewer, less*) snowstorms this year than last.
9. (*Can, May*) I please be excused now?
10. Whoever (*discovered, invented*) the escalator must have been ingenious.

Review A   Solving Common Usage Problems

Most of the following sentences contain errors in standard usage. If a sentence contains an error in standard usage, write the correct form. If a sentence is already correct, write *C.*

EXAMPLE   **1.** Don't anyone know when this game will start?
          1. Doesn't

1. Perhaps I should of called before visiting you.
2. Who discovered the cellular phone system?

1. have
2. invented

A Glossary of Usage   **601**

- **helping verb:** verb form that precedes the main verb in a verb phrase and that may indicate tense—all forms of *be* plus *do, has, have, had, shall, will, can,* etc. (see p. 391)

TEACHING TIP

Activity. As preparation for **Reviews A** and **B,** have students play Usage Baseball. Divide the class into two teams. Set up four chairs in a diamond formation, each chair representing a base. As each batter sits at home plate, ask him or her to compose a sentence using one of the chapter's problem words, chosen from a list on the chalkboard. Have the other team judge each sentence by reading the entry that applies to it. A student whose sentence is correct moves to first base; students proceed from base to base with each correct answer given. If the sentence is incorrect, the student is out. After the first team has three outs, send the second team to bat. As a word is used, put a check by it. Students will not be allowed to reuse a word until all other words have been used.

3. affecting   3. The beautiful weather is ~~effecting~~ my powers of concentration.

4. C   4. We can't decide between this movie and that one.

5. fewer   5. That box contains ~~less~~ cookies than this one.

6. C   6. We felt good because practice went so well.

7. effect   7. What ~~affect~~ did the quiz have on your grade?

8. accept   8. Why won't you ~~except~~ my help?

9. C   9. We stood beside the lake and watched the swans.

10. take   10. Did you ~~bring~~ flowers to your aunt when you went to visit her in her new home?

Review B   **Solving Common Usage Problems**

Choose the word or expression in parentheses that is correct according to standard usage.

EXAMPLE   Alvin Ailey significantly **[1]** (*affected, effected*) modern dance in America.

     1. *affected*

Alvin Ailey **[1]** (*could of, could have*) just dreamed of being a famous choreographer; instead, he formed **[2]** (*a, an*) interracial dance company that is known all over the world. Ailey started his dance company with **[3]** (*less, fewer*) than ten dancers in New York City in 1958. Today, the Alvin Ailey American Dance Theater has a very **[4]** (*good, well*) reputation **[5]** (*between, among*) modern-dance lovers **[6]** (*everywhere, everywheres*). Ailey also ran a dance

school and **[7]** (*discovered, invented*) many fine young dancers there. **[8]** (*Beside, Besides*) teaching, he choreographed operas, television specials, and numerous ballets. The scene shown to the left is from Ailey's ballet *Revelations*, an energetic and emotional celebration of the cultural heritage of African Americans. During his lifetime, Ailey **[9]** (*accepted, excepted*) much praise, countless compliments, numerous rave reviews, **[10]** (*and etc., etc.*), for his creativity.

Viewing the Art

Exploring the Subject. Alvin Ailey (1931–1989) is noted for having composed many of his modern dances to African American folk music and jazz. One of his most famous compositions is *Revelations* (1960), a powerful work set to African American spirituals. Ailey formed his own company, composed primarily of African Americans, in 1958. In 1965, he quit performing to concentrate on choreography. Ailey composed dances for ballet, television, and opera, as well as for his own company.

had of See **could of.**

had ought, hadn't ought Unlike other verbs, *ought* is not used with *had.*

NONSTANDARD	Lee had ought to plan better; he hadn't ought to leave his packing until the last minute.
STANDARD	Lee **ought** to plan better; he **ought not** to leave his packing until the last minute.
STANDARD	Lee **should** plan better; he **shouldn't** leave his packing until the last minute.

hardly, scarcely See **The Double Negative** (page 609).

he, she, they Do not use an unnecessary pronoun after the subject of a clause or a sentence. This error is called a **double subject.**

NONSTANDARD	My mother she grows organic vegetables.
STANDARD	My mother grows organic vegetables.

hisself, theirself, theirselves Avoid using these nonstandard forms.

EXAMPLE   He bought **himself** [not *hisself*] a new notebook.

invent See **discover, invent.**

its, it's See page 751.

kind, sort, type The words *this, that, these,* and *those* should always agree in number with the words *kind, sort,* and *type.*

EXAMPLE   **This kind** of wrench is more versatile than **those** other **kinds.**

kind of, sort of In formal situations, avoid using *kind of* for the adverb *somewhat* or *rather.*

INFORMAL	We are kind of anxious to know our grades.
FORMAL	We are **somewhat** [or **rather**] anxious to know our grades.

learn, teach *Learn* means "to acquire knowledge." *Teach* means "to instruct" or "to show how."

EXAMPLE   Some of our coaches **teach** classes in gymnastics, where young gymnasts can **learn** many techniques.

leave, let *Leave* means "to go away" or "to depart from." *Let* means "to allow" or "to permit."

Usage: *Had of—Ought to of*

(pp. 603–605)

OBJECTIVE

■ To choose the correct word from given pairs in sentences

Relating to Literature

Explain to students that informal and nonstandard English can be used as valuable writing tools to create vivid characters. The short story "Blues Ain't No Mockin Bird" by Toni Cade Bambara exemplifies the craft of writing dialect. If your literature text includes this selection, ask students to identify at least five examples of dialect and to show how its use characterizes the speaker.

Relating to Writing

Suggest to your students that just as a person's appearance makes an impression on others, so does one's language. Whether written or spoken, language affects the image an individual projects.

Ask your students to work in pairs to write paragraphs describing the appearance of a real or fictitious character. Have them write their descriptions in a dialect that is indicative of the character's background. Remind students that dialect involves differences in both usage and pronunciation.

RESOURCES

Usage: *Had of—Ought to of*

Practice

■ *Grammar, Usage, and Mechanics,* p. 221
■ *Language Workshop CD-ROM,* Lesson 64

Cooperative Learning

Reinforce correct usage with a game of Sentence Sense. Compose twelve short sentences of four words each, using *good, well, affect, effect, bring, take, discover, invent, fewer, less, among,* or *between* in each sentence. Write each word of the sentences on a separate note card, and shuffle the cards.

Form groups of three or four students, and give each group an equal number of cards. Tell students that they are to use their cards to form four-word sentences. They can trade cards with other groups. The game ends when each group has composed three sentences.

Reference Note

For more information about **prepositional phrases,** see Chapter 14. For more about **subordinate clauses,** see Chapter 15.

NONSTANDARD	Just leave him walk in the rain if he wants.
STANDARD	Just **let** him walk in the rain if he wants.
STANDARD	**Leave** the dishes for tomorrow, and we'll take a walk.

lend, loan See **borrow, lend, loan.**

less See **fewer, less.**

lie, lay See page 539.

like, as In informal English, the preposition *like* is often used as a conjunction meaning "as." In formal English, use *like* to introduce a prepositional phrase, and use *as* to introduce a subordinate clause.

EXAMPLES   She looks **like** her sister. [The preposition *like* introduces the phrase *like her sister.*]

We should do **as** our coach recommends. [The clause *our coach recommends* is introduced by the conjunction *as.*]

like, as if, as though In formal written English, *like* should not be used for the compound conjunctions *as if* or *as though.*

INFORMAL   Scamp looks like he's been in the swamp again.

FORMAL   Scamp looks **as though** he has been in the swamp again.

may See **can, may.**

might of, must of See **could of.**

no, none, nothing See **The Double Negative** (page 609).

nowheres See **anyways,** etc.

of Do not use *of* with prepositions such as *inside, off,* or *outside.*

EXAMPLES   He fell **off** [not *off of*] the ladder **outside** [not *outside of*] the garage.

What's **inside** [not *inside of*] that box?

ought to of See **could of.**

Exercise 4   Solving Common Usage Problems

For each sentence, choose the correct word or words in parentheses, according to formal, standard usage.

EXAMPLE   **1.** I (*had ought, ought*) to write my report on the Chinese inventions of paper and printing.

1. *ought*

MINI-LESSON

Terminology. Subordinating conjunctions that introduce adverb clauses sometimes have two words (*as if, as though*). Have students use *as, if,* and *though* in sentences alone and then use *as if* and *as though* as subordinating conjunctions in sentences. Ask students to explain the difference between the words as they have used them. [As *is used in comparisons,* if *is used in conditional statements, and* though *is used to show contrast.* As if *and* as though *are used to compare things with possible or imaginary situations.*]

1. The report must be on ancient Chinese history, (*like, as*) my teacher directed.
2. For (*this, these*) kind of report, I should start with the information that the Chinese invented paper as we know it early in the second century A.D.
3. If I (*had of, had*) seen them make paper by soaking, drying, and flattening mulberry bark, I would have been amazed.
4. (*The Chinese they, The Chinese*) didn't have the technology to mass-produce paper for another four hundred years.
5. By A.D. 200, the Chinese were using paper for writing and painting (*like, as if*) they always had done so.
6. I (*hadn't ought, ought not*) to forget that the Chinese also used paper for making umbrellas, fans, and lanterns.
7. In addition to (*this, these*) sorts of uses, the Chinese were using paper money by the seventh century.
8. You could have knocked me (*off of, off*) my chair when I learned that the Chinese were printing by A.D. 600—some eight hundred years before the invention of modern printing in Germany.
9. (*Leave, Let*) me tell you about how they used wooden blocks with characters carved on them for printing.
10. By the tenth century, the Chinese had (*learned, taught*) themselves how to print entire books with wooden blocks and had invented movable type.

reason . . . because In formal situations, do not use the construction *reason . . . because*. Instead, use *reason . . . that*.

INFORMAL   The reason for his victory is because he knew what the voters wanted.

FORMAL   The **reason** for his victory is **that** he knew what the voters wanted.

rise, raise See page 541.

sit, set See page 540.

some, somewhat In formal situations, do not use *some* for the adverb *somewhat*.

INFORMAL   I've neglected the garden some.

FORMAL   I've neglected the garden **somewhat.**

sort See **kind,** etc.

A Glossary of Usage   **605**

Exercise 4

ALTERNATIVE LESSON
Have students find the items indicated for the following sentences in **Exercise 4.**

1. adverb clause [*as . . . directed*]

3. gerunds used as the objects of a preposition [*soaking, drying,* and *flattening*]

 noun used as the direct object of gerunds [*bark*]

4. infinitive phrase including a direct object [*to mass-produce paper*]

5. adverb clause [*as if . . . so*]

7. prepositional phrase with a compound preposition [*In addition to these sorts of uses*]

USAGE

Usage: *Reason . . . because—Your, You're*

(pp. 605–609)

OBJECTIVE

■ **To choose the correct word from given pairs in sentences**

RESOURCES

Usage: *Reason...because—Your, You're*
Practice
■ *Grammar, Usage, and Mechanics,* pp. 222, 223

TEACHING TIP

Mnemonics. To help students distinguish between *than* and *then*, suggest the following "equation": *then* = *when*.

TECHNOLOGY TIP

Remind students that a spellchecker will not help them distinguish between words like *than* and *then*. As long as the word is spelled correctly, the program will accept it, even if it is not used correctly.

supposed to, suppose to Do not leave off the *d* when you write *supposed to.*

EXAMPLE   I am **supposed to** [not *suppose to*] clean my room.

take See **bring, take.**

teach See **learn, teach.**

than, then Do not confuse these words. *Than* is a subordinating conjunction used in comparisons; *then* is an adverb meaning *next* or *at that time.*

EXAMPLES   Algebra is easier **than** I thought it would be.

Read the directions; **then,** follow each step.

their, there, they're See page 754.

them *Them* should not be used as an adjective. Use *those.*

EXAMPLE   I like **those** [not *them*] jeans, don't you?

this here, that there The words *here* and *there* are unnecessary after *this* and *that.*

EXAMPLE   I'm buying **this** [not *this here*] cassette instead of **that** [not *that there*] one.

this kind, sort, type See **kind,** etc.

try and, try to Use *try to,* not *try and.*

EXAMPLE   We will **try to** [not *try and*] be on time.

type See **kind,** etc.

used to, use to Do not leave off the *d* when you write *used to.*

EXAMPLE   I **used to** [not *use to*] play badminton, but now I don't have time.

way, ways Use *way,* not *ways,* in referring to a distance.

EXAMPLE   We hiked a long **way** [not *ways*].

well See **good, well.**

what Do not use *what* for *that* to introduce an adjective clause.

EXAMPLE   The part of the car **that** [not *what*] lets the wheels turn at different speeds is called the differential gear.

Learning for Life

Continued on pp. 607–608

Formal and Informal English. Because students must be able to use English in ways ranging from formal business communications to the slang of their peers, they must be flexible.

Lead students to realize that word choice, expressions, and structure are all part of varying styles. You might start with a discussion on the following types of English students hear or read.

when, where In formal situations, do not use *when* or *where* to begin a definition.

INFORMAL	In botany, a "sport" is when a plant is abnormal or has mutated in some way.
FORMAL	In botany, a "sport" is a plant **that is** abnormal or **that has** mutated in some way.

where Do not use *where* for *that* to introduce a noun clause.

EXAMPLE   I read in this magazine **that** [not *where*] Carol Clay is a champion parachutist.

which, that, who The relative pronoun *who* refers to people only; *which* refers to things only; *that* refers to either people or things.

EXAMPLES   Here is the man **who** will install the new carpet. [person]

We decided to replace our old carpet, **which** we have had for nearly ten years. [thing]

The dealer is a person **that** stands behind all of her products. [person]

It is the kind of carpet **that** will wear well. [thing]

without, unless Do not use the preposition *without* in place of the conjunction *unless*.

EXAMPLE   A rattlesnake won't strike you **unless** [not *without*] you surprise or threaten it.

would of See **could of.**

your, you're *Your* is a possessive form of you. *You're* is the contraction of *you are.*

EXAMPLES   Is that **your** bike?

I hope **you're** going to the party.

Exercise 5 Solving Common Usage Problems

For each sentence, choose the correct word or words in parentheses, according to formal, standard usage.

EXAMPLE   **1.** (*That, That there*) motorcycle belongs to my cousin.

    1. That

1. Don't use more paper (*than*, *then*) you need.
2. (*Them*, *Those*) dogs have impressive pedigrees.

Critical Thinking

Metacognition. As a form of self-evaluation, have students record the following statements in their grammar logs and evaluate each statement as *rarely, sometimes,* or *often.*

- I know when and how to use formal English.

- I recognize my own usage errors and work to correct them.

- I use language to communicate with others rather than to distinguish myself from them.

- I find myself being misunderstood by my elders.

After students have completed their logs, ask them to write one rubric to help them develop their language usage. [*Possible answers: Is my language appropriate to my audience? Does my language aid or inhibit communication?*]

Timesaver

To save grading time and to check students' understanding of the material, have students do **Exercise 5** orally, giving explanations for their choices.

- **Formal English:** used in formal business letters, reports, and documents

- **Informal English:** used in conversation and personal letters and e-mails

- **Slang:** special words used by a group or subculture

After the discussion, have students form groups of three, one student for each category: formal, informal, and slang.

3. Manuel prefers (*this, these*) kind of skateboard.
4. It is only a short (*way, ways*) to the video store.
5. Tricia relaxed (*some, somewhat*) after she began to speak.
6. On the news, I heard (*where, that*) the game was called off because of rain.
7. Please set the books on (*your, you're*) desk.
8. Is she the player (*who, which*) is favored by most to win at Wimbledon this year?
9. He would not have released the report (*without, unless*) he had first verified his sources.
10. The reason we've requested your help is (*that, because*) you know the grounds better than we do.

─HELP─

Some sentences in Review C contain more than one error.

Review C **Correcting Usage Errors**

Identify each usage problem that you find in the sentences in the following paragraph. Then, write the usage that is correct according to formal, standard usage. If a sentence is already correct, write *C.*

EXAMPLE   **[1]** The legendary statue, the Sphinx at Giza in Egypt, would of weathered away completely if it had not been rescued by modern technology.

1. *would of—would have*

[1] Some famous monuments, such as the Eiffel Tower, don't look like they need any restoration. [2] However, monuments older than the Eiffel Tower, like Egypt's Sphinx, often need alot of care. [3] The Sphinx, who has the head of a human and the body of a lion, was built around 4500 B.C. [4] Some historians think the Sphinx, shown below, might of been built at the same time as the pyramid of King Khafre, which stands beside it. [5] Those historians they believe the Sphinx's face is a portrait of Khafre. [6] The Sphinx was suffering some from old age, exposure, and bad restoration attempts, so Egyptian museum officials began a major renewal project in 1990. [7] Scientists knew that the world eventually would lose that famous statue without restoration was begun immediately. [8] Workers

dismantled many stones, set new ones in their places, and than added natural mortar to let them stones breathe. [9] Workers also stabilized the water table under the mammoth Sphinx, which towers sixty-six feet above the desert sands. [10] These kind of restorations will help to preserve the Sphinx against the harmful affects of wind, rain, and sand for many years to come.

Review C Correcting
Usage Errors
A N S W E R S continued

8. than—then; them—those

9. C

10. These kind—These kinds; affects—effects

USAGE

Review D Correcting Usage Errors

Revise each of the following sentences, correcting the error or errors in usage.   Answers may vary.

EXAMPLE   **1.** I saw on the news where the mayor doesn't plan to run for re-election.

        1. I saw on the news that the mayor doesn't plan to run for re-election.

1. Optimism is ~~when a person~~ look on the bright side.
2. Luanne was ~~suppose~~ to buy a birthday card for Jo.
3. Take this rake and ~~them~~ seedlings to Mae ~~like~~ I asked.
4. I would ~~of~~ begun my report sooner ~~then~~ I did if I had known it would need this much research.
5. I heard ~~where~~ people will not be allowed back in the concert hall after intermission ~~without~~ they show their tickets.
6. The tire came off ~~of~~ the truck and rolled a long ~~ways~~ away.
7. Heather Ruiz has promised to ~~learn~~ us karate.
8. The people ~~which~~ witnessed the crime ~~hadn't ought~~ to have left before the police arrived.
9. Did Thomas Edison ~~discover~~ the lightbulb?
10. Is it safe to ~~leave~~ the dog to run around the park without a leash?

1. a tendency to
2. supposed
3. those/as
4. have/than
5. that/unless
6. way
7. teach
8. who/ought not
9. invent
10. let

The Double Negative

In a ***double negative,*** two or more negative words are used when one is sufficient. Do not use double negatives in formal writing and speaking.

hardly, scarcely The words *hardly* and *scarcely* convey a negative meaning. They should not be used with another negative word.

EXAMPLES   I **can** [not *can't*] **hardly** turn the key in the lock.

        We **have** [not *haven't*] **scarcely** enough time.

WET PAINT

"Dropping out of school never done me no harm."

© Jim Unger; distributed by United Media, 1998.

The Double Negative   **609**

The Double Negative

(pp. 609–610)

O B J E C T I V E

■ To revise sentences by correcting errors in double negatives

RESOURCES

The Double Negative
Practice

■ *Grammar, Usage, and Mechanics*, p. 224
■ *Language Workshop CD-ROM*, Lesson 64

Crossing the Curriculum

Math. Have students consider the use of double negatives in mathematical terms. Ask a volunteer to determine the value of x in the following problem:

$$x = 6 - (-4)$$

[*The answer is x = 10. When a double negative appears in such an equation, the numbers are added rather than subtracted.*] Explain that the effect in English is the same as in mathematics: The redundancy of the two negatives creates a positive.

Meeting
INDIVIDUAL
NEEDS

ENGLISH-LANGUAGE LEARNERS
General Strategies. Tell students that some languages, such as French and Spanish, use two or more words to express the negative. Because the use of double and sometimes triple negatives to indicate one negative idea is common in these languages, you will need to work closely with French- or Spanish-speaking students to help them avoid double negatives in their English usage.

Nonsexist Language

(pp. 610–612)

OBJECTIVE

■ To rewrite sentences to avoid gender-specific and awkward expressions

---

no, nothing, none Do not use these words with another negative word.

NONSTANDARD	That answer doesn't make no sense.
STANDARD	That answer **doesn't make any** sense.
STANDARD	That answer **makes no** sense.

NONSTANDARD	The field trip won't cost us nothing.
STANDARD	The field trip **won't cost** us **anything.**
STANDARD	The field trip **will cost** us **nothing.**

NONSTANDARD	We wanted grapes, but there weren't none.
STANDARD	We wanted grapes, but there **weren't any.**
STANDARD	We wanted grapes, but there **were none.**

Exercise 6 Correcting Double Negatives

Revise each of the following sentences, correcting the usage errors.
Answers may vary.

EXAMPLE   1. It doesn't make no difference to me.

   1. It makes no difference to me.
                     or
   It doesn't make any difference to me.

1. Rachel didn't say ~~nothing~~ to him.   1. anything
2. There ~~isn't~~ hardly anything left to eat.   2. is
3. I haven't borrowed ~~no~~ books from the library this week.   3. any
4. Laura ~~couldn't~~ hardly make herself heard.   4. could
5. What you're saying doesn't make ~~no~~ sense to me.   5. any
6. By the time we wrote for tickets, there weren't ~~none~~ available. 6. any
7. Hasn't ~~no one~~ in the class read *And Now Miguel*?   7. anyone
8. There ~~wasn't~~ scarcely enough water to keep the fish alive.   8. was
9. Didn't you ~~never~~ say ~~nothing~~ about the noise?   9. ever/anything
10. I haven't ~~never~~ told ~~no one~~ about our discovery.   10. ever/anyone

Nonsexist Language

Nonsexist language is language that applies to people in general, both male and female. For example, the nonsexist terms *humanity, human beings,* and *people* can substitute for the gender-specific term *mankind.*

In the past, many skills and occupations were generally closed to either men or women. Expressions like *seamstress, stewardess,* and

┌HELP──
Although two revisions are shown for the example in Exercise 6, you need to give only one for each sentence.

RESOURCES

Nonsexist Language
Practice
■ *Grammar, Usage, and Mechanics,* p. 225

mailman reflect those limitations. Since most jobs can now be held by both men and women, language is adjusting to reflect this change.

When you are referring generally to people, it is best to use nonsexist expressions rather than gender-specific ones. Below are some widely used nonsexist terms that you can use to replace the gender-specific ones.

Gender-specific	Nonsexist
businessman	executive, businessperson
chairman	chairperson, chair
deliveryman	delivery person
fireman	firefighter
foreman	supervisor
housewife	homemaker
mailman	mail carrier
man-made	synthetic, manufactured
manpower	workers, human resources
May the best man win!	May the best person win!
policeman	police officer
salesman	salesperson, salesclerk
seamstress	needleworker
steward, stewardess	flight attendant
watchman	security guard

If the antecedent of a pronoun may be either masculine or feminine, use both masculine and feminine pronouns to refer to it.

EXAMPLES   **Anyone** who wants to enter the poster contest should bring **his or her** entry to Room 21 by Friday.

Any student may bring a poster with **him or her** to Room 21.

You can often avoid the awkward *his or her* construction (or the alternative *his/her*) by substituting an article (*a, an,* or *the*) for the construction. You can also rephrase the sentence, using the plural forms of both the pronoun and its antecedent.

EXAMPLES   Any interested **student** may submit **a** poster.

All interested **students** may submit **their** posters.

| STYLE   TIP |
You can make similar revisions to avoid using the awkward expressions *s/he* and *wo/man.*

Looking at Language

History of English. Remind students that until recent years, masculine nouns and pronouns were used in English to indicate both male and female. For example, students might recognize the quotation "All men are created equal" from the Declaration of Independence.

Cooperative Learning

Assign students to work in small groups to investigate nonsexist language. Provide students with recent magazines, newspapers, catalogues, or brochures. Have each student skim one of the samples, looking for examples of both gender-specific and nonsexist language. Have students share their examples with the class. If possible, have students investigate thirty-year-old copies of similar publications and pool their findings to compile charts showing examples of changes in language usage. Students could also compare language in a current sitcom with that from a 1950s or 1960s sitcom like *The Andy Griffith Show, I Love Lucy,* or *Father Knows Best.*

Exercise 7 **Using Nonsexist Language**

Rewrite each of the following sentences to avoid using gender-specific terms and awkward expressions. Answers may vary.

EXAMPLE   1. An airline stewardess works hard to keep her passengers comfortable.

1. *Flight attendants work hard to keep their passengers comfortable.*

1. workers

2. firefighters

3. salespeople get/ they are

4. person

5. person/mail carrier

6. police officer

7. chairperson

8. supervisor

9. homemaker

10. synthetic

1. The project was short of manpower, so the management hired more staff.
2. A three-alarm fire broke out in the factory, and the firemen were soon on the scene.
3. Whether or not s/he gets a commission depends on how persuasive each salesman is.
4. May the best wo/man win!
5. Our dog growls when it sees a delivery man and barks loudly at every mailman.
6. Being a policeman is a demanding job.
7. Did you hear that Susan was elected chairman of the board?
8. The foreman of the crew will distribute the helmets.
9. When Aunt Tina and Uncle Lewis had a baby, Aunt Tina decided to become a housewife.
10. Some man-made medicines are considerably cheaper than natural medicines.

USAGE

Chapter Review

A. Correcting Errors in Standard Usage

For each of the following sentences, identify and correct the error or errors in usage. If a sentence is already correct, write *C*.

1. doesn't
2. let
3. outside
4. well
5. C
6. fewer
7. C
8. that
9. as though
10. have

1. Why ~~don't~~ Guadalupe try out for the team?
2. Please ~~leave~~ Mike solve the problem by himself.
3. The ball can't go ~~outside of~~ the boundary lines.
4. You are playing ~~good~~ now that you practice every day.
5. We sat beside the lake and fished.
6. Every spring we see ~~less~~ bluebirds than the year before.
7. Tyrone doesn't like this kind of frosting.
8. I read ~~where~~ another royal wedding is taking place.
9. Terry looked ~~like~~ she needed a rest after the relay.
10. They wouldn't ~~of~~ missed going to the mountains.

B. Proofreading a Paragraph for Standard Usage

For each sentence in the following paragraph, identify and correct the error in standard English usage. If a sentence is already correct, write *C*.

HELP

Each sentence in Part B of the Chapter Review may contain more than one error.

[11] Please bring me a dictionary so that I can look up what *left-handed* means, like I started to do earlier. [12] Left-handedness is where the person uses the left hand more than the right hand. [13] It don't matter which hand a person mainly uses because a left-hander functions just as good as a right-hander does. [14] Being left-handed couldn't hardly be a handicap; alot of clever people have been left-handed. [15] For example, artists like Leonardo da Vinci and Michelangelo Buonarroti were left-handed. [16] Of course, less people are left-handed than right-handed. [17] Many scientists learn their students the theory that left-handedness is determined by which side of the brain is dominant. [18] Some scientists they say that the left side of the brain is more dominant in a right-handed person. [19] They also say that the right side of the brain is more dominant in a left-handed person, but there isn't nobody who knows for sure. [20] Discussions on this subject between various groups of scientists will probably continue into the distant future.

Chapter Review **613**

Using the Chapter Review

To assess student progress, you may want to compare the types of items missed on the **Diagnostic Preview** to those missed on the **Chapter Review**. If students have not made significant progress, you may want to refer them to **Chapter 28: Correcting Common Errors, Exercises 20, 24, 25, 38,** and **39** for additional practice.

Chapter Review
B. Proofreading a Paragraph for Standard Usage
ANSWERS

11. like—as
12. is where—occurs when [answers will vary]
13. don't—doesn't; good—well
14. couldn't hardly—could hardly [*or* couldn't]; alot—a lot
15. C
16. less—fewer
17. learn—teach
18. scientists they—scientists
19. isn't nobody—isn't anybody [*or* is nobody]
20. between—among

C. Solving Common Usage Problems

For each sentence, choose the correct word in parentheses, according to formal, standard usage.

21. I looked for the library book all over the house, but I couldn't find it (*anywheres, anywhere*).

22. The deer searched the ground for food, but there wasn't (*none, any*).

23. When the temperature dropped to zero, we worried that the pipes might (*bust, burst*).

24. In the 1820s and 30s, the French scientists Louis Daguerre and Nicéphore Niépce (*discovered, invented*) photography.

25. That airline's slogan is "We fly (*everywhere, everywheres*)."

26. Dr. Mendez advised me to eat (*less, fewer*) sweets.

27. What (*affect, effect*) did the good news have on her?

28. However much you try to outrun a tornado, it doesn't make (*no, any*) difference; the best idea is to seek shelter immediately.

29. Who (*discovered, invented*) what a comet's tail is made of, Kai?

30. Nick admitted that he (*should of, should have*) told his family what time he was planning to come home.

31. "If you study hard now, you will be more confident later, and you will do (*good, well*) on the final," declared Ms. Echevarria.

32. Although it has (*fewer, less*) options than the car advertised, that car on the lot is a better deal, overall.

33. From New Orleans to Los Angeles is quite a long (*ways, way*).

34. That orchestra has a top-notch reputation (*between, among*) music lovers worldwide.

35. The author (*accepted, excepted*) the award with the grace that had long been characteristic of her.

36. Mother asked Simon to (*leave, let*) her read her book in peace.

37. I heard (*where, that*) today's discounts are the best ever.

38. Is Belle the singer (*which, that*) had that TV special last week?

39. It's hard to imagine how ice got onto the moon (*without, unless*) there had once been water there.

40. (*Their, They're*) comments didn't make sense, but they were funny.

D. Using Nonsexist Language

Rewrite each of the following sentences to avoid gender-specific terms and awkward expressions. Answers may vary.

RESOURCES

A Glossary of Usage
Review
■ *Grammar, Usage, and Mechanics,* pp. 226, 227, 228, 229

Assessment
■ *Assessment Package*
—*Chapter Tests,* Ch. 20
—*Chapter Tests in Standardized Test Formats,* Ch. 20
■ *Test Generator (One-Stop Planner CD-ROM)*

41. The ~~foreman~~ issued her first work order of the day.

42. May the best ~~man~~ win!

43. Caroline's friend was an ~~airline stewardess~~.

44. Only the very courageous need apply to be ~~firemen~~.

45. Three of the ~~salesmen~~ were under twenty-five.

46. The space shuttle is the most useful ~~man-made~~ device ever.

47. The ~~deliverymen~~ for that company wear brown shorts.

48. My next-door neighbor was a first-rate ~~seamstress~~.

49. Fewer women become ~~housewives~~ these days than in the past.

50. The computer plant is advertising for a ~~watchman~~, I hear.

Writing Application
Writing a Business Letter

Using Formal Standard English   After reading studies showing the benefits of school uniforms, the school board in your district has proposed requiring students to wear uniforms. One study found that schools that require uniforms experience less violence. Another study concluded that students who wore uniforms made better grades. Write a letter to the school board, telling why your district should or should not require students to wear uniforms.

Prewriting   If you already have an opinion about school uniforms, jot down some reasons to support your view. If you are undecided, you may want to make two lists—one pro and one con. Give several reasons to support each position. Then, choose the more persuasive side.

Writing   As you write your first draft, keep focused on your topic. Choose only the best reasons from your list and expand on these.

Revising   Add, delete, or rearrange details to support your argument. Also, see that the tone and word choice of your letter conform to the standards of a polite business letter.

Publishing   Proofread your paper for any errors in spelling and punctuation. Then, use the glossary entries in this chapter to correct common usage errors. You and your classmates may wish to have a debate on the school uniform issue. You might also like to post your letter on the class bulletin board or Web page.

41. supervisor
42. person
43. flight attendant
44. firefighters
45. salespeople
46. manufactured
47. delivery people
48. needleworker
49. homemakers
50. security guard

Reference Note

For more about **writing business letters,** see "Writing" in the Quick Reference Handbook.

PREVIEWING THE CHAPTER

- This chapter presents the basic rules of capitalization. Some of the material is in the form of notes and examples that are given after the rules. While students are studying the examples in the textbook, they may wish to develop their own examples.

- The chapter closes with a **Chapter Review** including a **Writing Application** feature that asks students to write a paragraph about a foreign city and its attractions. Students should use correct capitalization.

- You may want to refer students to this chapter throughout the year, especially when they are in the proofreading stage of a writing assignment.

- For help in integrating this chapter with composition chapters, use the **Teaching Strands** chart on pp. T371A–T371B.

USING THE DIAGNOSTIC PREVIEW

- The **Diagnostic Preview** contains two parts. **Part A** asks students to correct capitalization errors in sentences. **Part B** checks the students' ability to proofread a paragraph for correct capitalization. After identifying problem areas, have students make lists of their particular problems to use as checklists when they revise their writing assignments.

Capital Letters
The Rules for Capitalization

Diagnostic Preview

A. Correcting Sentences That Contain Errors in Capitalization

Correct the errors in capitalization in the following sentences by capitalizing or lowercasing letters as needed. If a sentence contains no errors, write *C*.

EXAMPLE   1. My Aunt and I visited the White house in Washington, D.C.

         1. *aunt, House*

1. Val's new schwinn bike had a flat tire.
2. My father is taking a course in public speaking.   **2.** C
3. The atmosphere on venus is one hundred times denser than the atmosphere on earth.
4. Has your favorite team ever won the rose bowl?
5. The opossum can be found as far south as Argentina and as far north as Canada.   **5.** C
6. For our spring project, our club raised money for the American heart association.
7. The maya of the Yucatán peninsula worshiped nature gods such as chac, a god of rain, and Itzamná, a sky god.
8. My uncle Scott works at Apex hardware store.
9. In drama 2, we staged a production of Denise Chávez's *The flying tortilla Man*.

CHAPTER RESOURCES

Planning
- *One-Stop Planner CD-ROM*

Practice and Extension
- *Grammar, Usage, and Mechanics*, p. 233
- *Developmental Language Skills*, pp. 105–118

Internet
- go.hrw.com (keyword: EOLang)

Evaluation and Assessment
- *Chapter Tests*, Ch. 21
- *Chapter Tests in Standardized Test Formats*, Ch. 21
- *Test Generator (One-Stop Planner)*

616

10. The U.S. senate and the house of representatives may pass a bill into law, but the president can veto it.   **10.** (*or* President)

11. Mr. Williams is a Reporter for United Press international.

12. We went to Sea World over easter vacation.

13. Both rabbi Frankel and reverend Stone organized aid for the many victims of the fire.

14. The Winter Games of the 1998 olympics were held in Nagano, Japan.

15. Michelangelo's *The creation of the World* and *The Last Judgment* are paintings that depict scenes from the bible.

B. Correcting Capitalization Errors in a Paragraph

Correct the errors in capitalization in the following paragraph by capitalizing or lowercasing letters as needed. If a sentence contains no errors, write *C*.

EXAMPLE   **[1]** A gentle elephant named jumbo was once the largest, most popular captive animal in the World.

    1. *Jumbo, world*

[16] When p. t. barnum bought Jumbo in 1882, the elephant had already become a star with the London royal circus. [17] All of england protested the sale when the unhappy elephant refused to board the ship for New York city. [18] however, even queen Victoria and the Prince of wales could not prevent Jumbo's going, since the sale had been completed. [19] Jumbo's Trainer, Matthew Scott, kept the elephant content on the journey across the atlantic ocean. [20] In april, the new addition to the show arrived in New York, and the 13,500-pound star marched up broadway to the cheers of a huge crowd. [21] Soon Jumbo-mania swept across the United States.   **21.** C

[22] The elephant was so popular that his name became a common word in the english language—*jumbo,* meaning "extra large." [23] He died tragically on September 15, 1885, in the canadian town of St. Thomas, Ontario. [24] The big-hearted giant, seeing a train bearing down on a baby elephant, pushed the youngster to safety but could   **24.** C
not save himself. [25] To keep Jumbo's memory alive, Barnum donated the skeleton of his beloved elephant to the American Museum of natural history.

BORN LOSER reprinted by permission of Newspaper Enterprise Association, Inc.

MECHANICS

Capitalizing First Words, *I*, and *O*

Rules 21a–e *(pp. 618–619)*

OBJECTIVES

- To capitalize the first words of sentences in a paragraph and to add appropriate end marks
- To correct capitalization errors in sentences

TEACHING TIP

Motivation. To illustrate that the placement of capital letters is vital to effective communication, write the following pairs of sentences on the chalkboard for volunteers to explain.

1. Won't we need that heavy-duty jack at Cecil's Garage to lift my father's Bronco? [*Won't we need the equipment at Cecil's auto repair shop to lift my father's car?*]

   Won't we need that heavy-duty Jack at Cecil's garage to lift my father's bronco? [*Won't we need the strong person named Jack at a garage owned by Cecil to lift my father's horse?*]

2. Some Friends in south Dakota are getting together to watch the orange bowl. [*Some Quakers in the southern part of a place named Dakota are congregating to watch a bowl with oranges in it (or to watch an orange bowling or an orange-colored bowl).*]

   Some friends in South Dakota are getting together to watch the Orange Bowl. [*Some friends in the state of South Dakota are congregating to watch a football game.*]

STYLE TIP

Some professional writers do not follow the rules shown in this chapter. When you are quoting a person, use capital letters as they are used in the source of the quotation.

Reference Note

For more information on using **capital letters in quotations,** see page 687.

Using Capital Letters Correctly

A capital letter at the beginning of a word is an important signal to the reader. A capital letter may indicate the beginning of a sentence and also may mark a significant difference in meaning, such as the difference between *may* (as in *you may*) and *May* (as in *May 3, 1996*).

21a. Capitalize the first word in every sentence.

EXAMPLES **T**he world of computers has its own vocabulary. **C**omputer equipment is called *hardware,* and the programs are called *software.*

Exercise 1 Capitalizing Sentences in a Paragraph

Rewrite the following paragraph. Capitalize the ten words that should begin with a capital letter. Add the appropriate punctuation mark to the end of each sentence.

EXAMPLE 1. what are some new developments in science
        1. *What are some new developments in science?*

work has begun on a new kind of laser radar this instrument would be especially useful for people with visual impairments how does the radar work a laser device that is small enough to fit onto an eyeglass frame emits invisible infrared light beams when the light strikes an object, it bounces back to a receiver placed in the wearer's ear the receiver, in turn, sounds a small tone with this sort of device, the person can "hear" any object nearby the device is very promising in fact, it may one day replace the cane or the guide dog as an aid for people who are blind there are few better examples of how beneficial laser research can be

21b. Traditionally, the first word of a line of poetry is capitalized.

EXAMPLES **A** bird came down the walk:

        He did not know I saw;

        He bit an angleworm in halves

        And ate the fellow, raw.

                Emily Dickinson, "A Bird Came Down the Walk"

21c. Capitalize the first word of a directly quoted sentence.

EXAMPLE Eduardo wondered, "**W**here did I put my backpack?"

RESOURCES

Capitalizing First Words, *I*, and *O*

Practice

- *Grammar, Usage, and Mechanics,* p. 234
- *Language Workshop CD-ROM,* Lesson 57

21d. Capitalize the first word in both the salutation and the closing of a letter.

EXAMPLES   **D**ear Service Manager: **S**incerely,

                   Dear Amy,   **Y**ours truly,

21e. Capitalize the pronoun *I* and the interjection *O*.

Although it is rarely used, *O* is always capitalized. Generally, it is reserved for invocations and is followed by the name of the person or thing being addressed. You will more often use the interjection *oh*, which is generally not capitalized unless it is the first word in a sentence.

EXAMPLES   "Exult **O** shores! and ring **O** bells!" is a line from Walt Whitman's poem "**O** Captain! My Captain!"

                The play was a hit, but **o**h, how nervous I was!

                Oh, I forgot my book.

Exercise 2   Correcting Capitalization Errors in Sentences

Correct the errors in capitalization in the following sentences. If a sentence contains no errors, write *C*.

EXAMPLE   **1.** in "Jazz Fantasia," the speaker tells the Musicians, "Go to it, o jazzmen."

          1. *In, musicians, O*

1. yesterday i learned two psalms that begin, "Bless the Lord, o my soul."
2. Ms. Jones asked, "can anyone name the author of that poem?"
3. I haven't decided, but Øh, how I'd like to be an astronaut!
4. "you must be careful of the coral snake," said the guide, "because it is the most poisonous snake in our region."
5. In the poem "The Fool's Prayer," the jester pleads, "O Lord, be merciful to me, a fool!"   **5.** C
6. do you know that the fifth of May is a Mexican American holiday?
7. most trucks have rear-wheel drive.
8. Two days ago—oh, such a short time!—I left without a care.   **8.** C
9. The car stopped suddenly, and Øh, was i glad for my seat belt!
10. My favorite verses from that scene are
     see how she leans her cheek upon her hand!
     oh, that i were a glove upon that hand,
     that i might touch that cheek!

MECHANICS

Proper Nouns and Proper Adjectives

Rules 21f–g *(pp. 620–629)*

OBJECTIVES

- To recognize the correct use of capital letters in sentences

- To write sentences using correct capitalization

- To correct the capitalization of words and phrases

Meeting
INDIVIDUAL NEEDS

ENGLISH-LANGUAGE LEARNERS

Spanish. Because names of nationalities, races and peoples, days of the week, and months of the year are not capitalized in Spanish, you may wish to give Spanish-speaking students extra practice in these areas.

MECHANICS

Reference Note

For more about **common** and **proper nouns,** see page 375. For a discussion of **proper adjectives,** see page 383.

STYLE TIP

Proper nouns and proper adjectives sometimes lose their capitals through frequent usage.

EXAMPLES

watt   **t**itanic   **s**andwich

To find out whether a noun should be capitalized, check in a dictionary. The dictionary will tell you whether a word should always be capitalized or whether it should be capitalized only in certain uses.

COMPUTER TIP

The spellings of personal names can challenge even the best spellchecking software. However, you may be able to customize your spellchecker. If your software allows, add to it any names that you use frequently but have difficulty spelling or capitalizing.

21f. Capitalize proper nouns and proper adjectives.

A *common noun* names any one of a group of persons, places, things, or ideas. A *proper noun* names a particular person, place, thing, or idea. A *proper adjective* is an adjective formed from a proper noun.

Proper nouns are capitalized. Common nouns are generally not capitalized unless they

- begin a sentence
  - *or*
- begin a direct quotation
  - *or*
- are part of a title

Common Nouns	Proper Nouns	Proper Adjectives
a **p**atriot	**T**homas **J**efferson	**J**effersonian ideals
a **c**ountry	**T**urkey	**T**urkish border
a **q**ueen	**Q**ueen **E**lizabeth	**E**lizabethan drama
a **r**eligion	**I**slam	**I**slamic beliefs
a **r**egion	the **S**outhwest	**S**outhwestern cooking

In proper nouns of more than one word, do not capitalize

- short prepositions (generally, ones with fewer than five letters, such as *in*, *on*, and *with*)
- articles (*a, an, the*)
- coordinating conjunctions (*and, but, for, nor, or, so, yet*)
- the sign of the infinitive (*to*)

EXAMPLES   Mary, Queen **o**f Scots

           Eric **t**he Red

           *Romeo **a**nd Juliet*

           "Writing **t**o Persuade"

(1) Capitalize the names of persons and animals.

Given Names	Alana	Mark	LaVerne
Surnames	**D**iaz	**C**ollins	**W**illiams
Animals	**T**rigger	**S**ocks	**R**over

RESOURCES

Proper Nouns and Proper Adjectives

Practice

- *Grammar, Usage, and Mechanics,* pp. 235, 236, 237, 238, 239, 240, 241, 242, 243
- *Language Workshop CD-ROM,* Lesson 58

NOTE For names having more than one part, capitalization may vary.

EXAMPLES **De V**ere   **d**e l**a G**arza

                 Mc**G**regor   **O'L**eary

                 Ibn-**K**haldun   **v**on **B**raun

Always check the spelling of such a name with the person who has that name, or look in a reference source.

(2) Capitalize initials in names and abbreviations that come before or after names.

EXAMPLES **A. E.** Roosevelt   Lewis **F.** Powell, **Jr.**   **Sr.** Gomez

                 Ms. Sonstein   Sabra Santos, **M.D.**   **Dr.** Alan Berg

(3) Capitalize geographical names.

Type of Name	Examples	
Towns and Cities	**P**ortland	**M**exico **C**ity
	Detroit	**R**io de **J**aneiro
Counties, Townships, and Provinces	**K**ane **C**ounty	**E**ast **B**aton **R**ouge **P**arish
	Hayes **T**ownship	**Q**uebec **P**rovince
	Plum **B**orough	**W**illiamson **C**ounty
States	**I**owa	**A**laska
	Missouri	**N**orth **C**arolina
Countries	**E**l **S**alvador	**U**nited **A**rab **E**mirates
	New **Z**ealand	**S**witzerland
Continents	**A**sia	**S**outh **A**merica
Islands	**W**ake **I**sland	the **I**sle of **P**alms
	the **W**est **I**ndies	the **F**lorida **K**eys
Mountains	**M**ount **A**rarat	the **A**lps
	Himalayas	the **M**ount of **O**lives
Bodies of Water	**I**ndian **O**cean	**R**ed **R**iver
	Adriatic **S**ea	**L**ake of the **W**oods

(continued)

Reference Note

For more about **capitalizing titles used with names,** see Rule 21h(1). For information on **punctuating abbreviations** that come before or after names, see page 639.

Reference Note

Abbreviations of the names of states are capitalized. See page 640 for more about **using and punctuating such abbreviations.**

| S T Y L E | | T I P |

Words such as *north, west,* and *southeast* are not capitalized when they indicate direction.

EXAMPLES
  farther **n**orth
  traveling **s**outheast

However, these words are capitalized when they name a particular region.

EXAMPLES
  states in the **N**orthwest
  driving in the **S**outh

Meeting INDIVIDUAL NEEDS

ENGLISH-LANGUAGE LEARNERS
General Strategies. Students might not realize that certain words in English are proper nouns. Select names that are well known to the students for practice. Include the names of classmates, school personnel, local parks, teams, and malls, as well as major global geographical names.

Spanish. Students may need practice capitalizing street and highway names since these names are not capitalized in Spanish, except at the beginning of a line.

Crossing the Curriculum

Geography/Art. Have students plan a cruise to a location they have studied. Suggest that students draw ornamental maps including geographic names that are correctly capitalized.

MINI-LESSON

Punctuation and Abbreviations. Remind students that abbreviations usually end with periods. Ask students to volunteer examples of each of the following:

Titles: [*Mr. Brown*]
Personal Names: [*A. J. Foyt*]
Times of Day: [*7:00 A.M.*]
Years: [*A.D. 1776*]
Addresses: [*500 Tamerine Tr.*]

Type of Name	Examples	
Parks and Forests	**C**leburne **S**tate **P**ark the **E**verglades **N**ational **P**ark	**P**almetto **S**tate **P**ark **O**uachita **N**ational **F**orest
Regions	the **W**est the **S**outheast	**G**reat **P**lains **C**orn **B**elt
Other Geographical Names	**S**inai **P**eninsula **C**arlsbad **C**averns	**H**arding **I**cefield **B**ryce **C**anyon
Roads, Streets, and Highways	**S**tate **R**oad 17 Interstate 787	**M**o-**P**ac **E**xpressway **W**est **F**irst **S**treet

MECHANICS

Meeting
INDIVIDUAL
NEEDS

MULTIPLE INTELLIGENCES

Interpersonal Intelligence. Have students interview speakers of other languages to find out how capitalization rules differ from language to language. Ask students to report their findings to the class. Students might post their findings on the school's Web site.

Reference Note

In addresses, abbreviations such as St., Blvd., Ave., Dr., and Ln. are capitalized. For information about **punctuating abbreviations,** see page 639.

STYLE TIP

Since *rio* is Spanish for "river," *Rio de la Plata River* is redundant. Use only *Rio de la Plata.*

Other terms to watch for are

- *sierra*, Spanish for "mountain range" [Use only *Sierra Nevada*, not *Sierra Nevada Mountains*.]

- *yama*, Japanese for "mountain" [Use only *Fujiyama* or *Mount Fuji*, not *Mount Fujiyama*.]

- *sahara*, Arabic for "desert" [Use only *Sahara*, not *Sahara Desert*.]

- *gobi*, Mongolian for "desert" [Use only *Gobi*, not *Gobi Desert*.]

Exercise 3

ALTERNATIVE LESSON

To review phrases and sentence parts, have students find the following items: two-word prepositional phrases [3. *in Oregon*, 8. *of Mexico*, 9. *of California*]; a three-word predicate nominative [4. *1614 Robin Street*].

NOTE In a street name that is a hyphenated number, the second word begins with a lowercase letter.

EXAMPLE Twenty-**s**econd Street

Words like *city, island, river, street,* and *park* are capitalized when they are part of a name. When words like these are not part of a proper name, they are common nouns and are not capitalized.

Common Nouns	Proper Nouns
life in a big **c**ity	life in **N**ew **Y**ork **C**ity
the **r**iver	the **S**pokane **R**iver
a small **i**sland	**L**iberty **I**sland
on a narrow **s**treet	on **S**tate **S**treet

Exercise 3 **Recognizing the Correct Use of Capital Letters**

Write the of the correctly capitalized sentence in each of the following pairs.

EXAMPLE 1. **a.** Drive Northeast until you get to New Haven.
              b. Drive northeast until you get to New Haven.

    1. **b**

Learning for Life

Finding a Pen Pal. Have students practice capitalization by writing personal ads for pen pals. The following template offers a possible wording:

Are you looking for a pen pal from _____ who belongs to the _____? Do you like listening to _____ and _____? Do you want to travel to _____ to see the _____? If so, then we should be pen pals! Write _____ at _____.

1. **a.** We went canoeing on the Ohio river.
   (b.) We went canoeing on the Ohio River.
2. **a.** I read the article on south America.
   (b.) I read the article on South America.
3. **(a.)** Farewell Bend State Park is in Oregon.
   b. Farewell Bend State park is in Oregon.
4. **(a.)** Her address is 1614 Robin Street.
   b. Her address is 1614 Robin street.
5. **a.** I will be at Forty-Second Street and Park Avenue.
   (b.) I will be at Forty-second Street and Park Avenue.
6. **(a.)** The North Sea is east of Great Britain.
   b. The North sea is East of great Britain.
7. **a.** Atlanta is a fast-growing City in the south.
   (b.) Atlanta is a fast-growing city in the South.
8. **a.** Pensacola is on the gulf of Mexico.
   (b.) Pensacola is on the Gulf of Mexico.
9. **(a.)** The Hawaiian Islands are southwest of California.
   b. The Hawaiian islands are Southwest of California.
10. **a.** Laredo is on the Mexican Border in Webb county.
    (b.) Laredo is on the Mexican border in Webb County.

(4) Capitalize the names of organizations, teams, government bodies, and institutions.

Type of Name	Examples	
Organizations	**U**nited **N**ations	**B**oy **S**couts of **A**merica
	National **W**eather **S**ervice	**M**illersville **O**rchid **S**ociety
Teams	**G**reen **B**ay **P**ackers	**R**iver **C**ity **A**llstars
	Golden **S**tate **W**arriors	**L**ady **L**obos
		Pitt **P**anthers
Government Bodies	**C**ongress	**P**eace **C**orps
	Federal **T**rade **C**ommission	**S**tate **D**epartment
		Austin **C**ity **C**ouncil
Institutions	**S**mithsonian **I**nstitution	**N**ew **C**ollege
	Stanford **U**niversity	**N**orth **H**igh **S**chool
		Bellevue **H**ospital

Exercise 4 Writing Sentences Using Lowercase and Capital Letters

POSSIBLE ANSWERS

1. During flood season, we can see the raging **river** from the cabin window.

2. The scouts went canoeing on the **Ohio River**.

3. Art club members will stay in a **hotel** when they visit Fort Worth to see the Picasso exhibit.

4. My grandparents once visited the **Ritz Hotel** in London.

5. On which **street** do the Deans live now?

6. My brother plays baseball at the field on **First Street**.

7. The band will play a **march** before Friday's football game.

8. Grandfather's favorite composer is John Philip Sousa, the "**March** King."

9. Because the baseball field faces **west,** fans sometimes see the sun set during the game.

10. When we studied the **West** in geography, we learned that California is known not only for the gold rush, but also for agricultural products.

NOTE Do not capitalize words such as *democratic, republican,* or *socialist* when they refer to principles or forms of government. Capitalize these words when they refer to specific political parties.

EXAMPLES The new regime promises to institute **d**emocratic reforms.

The **D**emocratic candidate will debate the **R**epublican candidate tonight.

The word *party* in the name of a political party may be capitalized or not; either way is correct. Be consistent in the use of the word throughout a particular piece of writing.

EXAMPLES Libertarian **p**arty *or* **P**arty

Federalist **p**arty *or* **P**arty

(5) Capitalize the names of historical events and periods, special events, holidays, and other calendar items.

Type of Name	Examples	
Historical Events and Periods	**F**rench **R**evolution	**W**orld **W**ar II
	Age of **R**eason	**B**attle of **B**ritain
Special Events	**S**pecial **O**lympics	**G**ulf **C**oast **T**rack-and-**F**ield **C**hampionship
	Parents' **D**ay	
Holidays and Other Calendar Items	**T**hursday	**V**alentine's **D**ay
	December	**L**abor **D**ay
	New **Y**ear's **D**ay	**A**ugust

NOTE Do not capitalize the name of a season unless it is personified ("Here is **S**pring in her green dress!") or used in the name of a special event (**F**all **F**estival, **S**pring **J**ubilee).

Exercise 4 Writing Sentences Using Lowercase and Capital Letters

Correctly use each of the following words in a sentence.

EXAMPLE 1. river
1. *The river is rising.*

1. river	3. hotel	5. street	7. march	9. west
2. River	4. Hotel	6. Street	8. March	10. West

(6) Capitalize the names of nationalities, races, and peoples.

EXAMPLES   **C**anadian, **K**orean, **C**aucasian, **A**sian, **K**urds, **Z**ulu, **S**eminole

(7) Capitalize the names of religions and their followers, holy days and celebrations, sacred writings, and specific deities.

Type of Name	Examples		
Religions and Followers	**J**udaism **B**uddhism	**M**uslim **T**aoist	**B**aptist **Q**uaker
Holy Days and Celebrations	**L**ent **D**iwali	**P**assover **E**piphany	**R**amadan **R**osh **H**ashanah
Sacred Writings	**B**ible **T**almud	**U**panishads **D**euteronomy	**K**oran **D**ead **S**ea **S**crolls
Specific Deities	**A**llah	**B**rahma	**G**od

NOTE The words *god* and *goddess* are not capitalized when they refer to the deities of ancient mythology. However, the names of specific mythological gods and goddesses are capitalized.

EXAMPLE   The Greek poet paid tribute to the **g**od **Z**eus.

(8) Capitalize the names of businesses and the brand names of business products.

BUSINESSES   **M**otorola, **I**nc., **B**ank of **A**merica, **S**am's **S**hoes

BRAND NAMES   **F**ormica, **C**hevrolet, **A**ce, **K**leenex, **W**hirlpool

NOTE Do not capitalize a common noun that follows a brand name: **F**ormica **c**ounter **t**op, **C**hevrolet **v**an, **A**ce **b**andage.

(9) Capitalize the names of planets, stars, constellations, and other heavenly bodies.

Type of Name	Examples		
Planets and Other Heavenly Bodies	**S**aturn the **M**ilky **W**ay	**O**rion **V**ega	**J**upiter **P**roxima **C**entauri

STYLE   TIP

The words *black* and *white* may or may not be capitalized when they refer to races. However, within a particular piece of writing, be consistent in the way you capitalize these words.

STYLE   TIP

In some writings, you may notice that pronouns referring to deities are always capitalized as a sign of respect. In other cases, writers capitalize such pronouns only to prevent confusion.

EXAMPLE
The Lord called upon Moses to lead **H**is people out of Egypt. [*His* is capitalized to show that it refers to *the Lord*, not *Moses*.]

STYLE   TIP

The word *earth* is not capitalized unless it is used along with the names of other heavenly bodies that are capitalized. The words *sun* and *moon* generally are not capitalized.

Cooperative Learning

Tell students they will work in groups to create stories using proper nouns and proper adjectives. Have each student prepare three slips of paper, each slip indicating a type of name from one of the twelve numbered subrules of **Rule 21f**. (For example, a slip might read *a dog's name, a street name,* or *a state.*)

Place students in groups of five. Have each student draw one of the prepared slips of paper and write for the story a sentence using the type of word indicated on the slip. (For example, for the word type *state,* the sentence might be *When I lived in Rhode Island, I joined a club.*) Have students add to the story until all of the slips have been drawn. Groups should record their narratives on audiotape to play for the class.

MECHANICS

Using Capital Letters Correctly   **625**

┌─HELP─
The proper
names of vehicles such as
boats or cars generally are
capitalized: **B**lue **B**ird
[boat], **M**ustang [car].

(10) Capitalize the names of ships, trains, aircraft, and spacecraft.

Type of Name	Examples		
Ships, Trains, Aircraft, and Spacecraft	**A**rgo **S**putnik	**Y**ankee **C**lipper **F**lying **S**cotsman	**C**olumbia **T**hunder **B**ird

(11) Capitalize the names of awards, memorials, and monuments.

Type of Name	Examples	
Awards, Memorials, and Monuments	**N**obel **P**rize **S**ilver **S**tar	**L**incoln **M**emorial **T**omb of the **U**nknown **S**oldier

(12) Capitalize the names of particular buildings and other structures.

Type of Name	Examples		
Buildings and Other Structures	**T**ower of **L**ondon **G**olden **G**ate **B**ridge	**P**laza **H**otel the **A**lamo **F**ort **K**nox	**S**hasta **D**am **G**reat **W**all of **C**hina

NOTE Generally, do not capitalize words like *hotel, theater, college, high school,* and *courthouse* unless they are part of a proper name.

EXAMPLES
Jackson **H**igh **S**chool	a **h**igh **s**chool principal
Copley Square **H**otel	a **h**otel in Boston
Fox **T**heater	a **t**heater in Dallas
Victoria County **C**ourthouse	a **c**ourthouse hallway

Exercise 5 **Correcting the Capitalization of Words and Phrases**

Correct the following words and phrases, using capital letters as needed.

EXAMPLE 1. a methodist minister
1. *a Methodist minister*

1. somewhere between mars and jupiter

2. a shopping center on twenty-third street

TEACHING **TIP**

Exercise 5 You may want to use the first ten items as guided practice and the second ten as independent practice.

3. lafayette park in tallahassee, florida
4. some wheaties cereal
5. jefferson racquet club
6. harvard university
7. at the new jewish synagogue
8. on memorial day
9. an african american
10. the sinking of the *lusitania*
11. making easter baskets for the children
12. a visit to the washington monument
13. seeing venus through a telescope
14. reading a passage from the koran
15. flying in the *spruce goose*
16. to the ritz hotel
17. stories about the Egyptian god ra
18. a hammer from Ridgeway hardware store
19. passed by a dodge minivan
20. taking pictures of the eiffel tower

Review A Identifying and Correcting Errors in Capitalization

| Link to Literature |

Correct the capitalization errors in each of the following sentences by capitalizing and lowercasing letters as needed.

EXAMPLE   1. The earliest African American Folk tales have their roots in africa.
           1. folk, Africa

1. Africans who first came to the americas enjoyed folk tales that blended their own african songs with stories they heard here.
2. Before the civil war, African Americans created new tales that reflected their experiences as Slaves and their desire for Freedom.
3. Many of these tales are about Animals, especially the small but clever character named brer rabbit.
4. Zora neale hurston collected a number of these animal stories and published them in *Mules and Men.*
5. Brer rabbit, a character that was especially popular in the south in the 1800s, constantly plays tricks on brer fox and brer wolf.
6. In some later tales, the main Character isn't a rabbit but a slave, john, who outsmarts the slave owner.

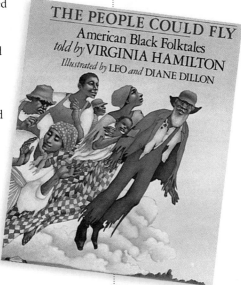

THE PEOPLE COULD FLY
American Black Folktales
told by VIRGINIA HAMILTON
Illustrated by LEO *and* DIANE DILLON

INCLUSION
Because it contains so many errors, **Review A** may be overwhelming to students. Set specific tasks such as "Find and correct errors in place names." Have students work on the exercise with a helper—one error at a time—until all the rules that apply have been covered.

Using Capital Letters Correctly   **627**

7. The author virginia hamilton, winner of the newbery medal and the national book award, tells other tales in *The People Could Fly: American Black Folktales.*

8. Both the title of that Book and the Painting on its cover refer to another popular kind of black folk tale that developed during the years of slavery.

9. Can you tell that the People on the book's cover are flying above the Earth?

10. "The People Could Fly" is one of many fantasy tales about enslaved people who use Magic Powers to fly away from their troubles.

21g. Do not capitalize the names of school subjects, except the names of language classes or course names that contain a number.

EXAMPLES This year I am taking **g**eometry, **E**nglish, **c**ivics, **D**rafting **I**, and a **f**oreign **l**anguage. Next year I plan to take **A**merican **g**overnment, **E**nglish, **t**rigonometry, **B**iology **I**, and **S**panish.

Review B **Correcting Capitalization Errors in Sentences**

Correct the following sentences by changing lowercase letters to capital letters as needed.

EXAMPLE 1. mi kyung's mother told us that buddhism and confucianism have a long history in korea.

1. *Mi Kyung's mother told us that Buddhism and Confucianism have a long history in Korea.*

1. in tuesday's class, mrs. garcía explained that the diameter of earth is only 405 miles greater than that of venus.

2. this year's freshmen will be required to take more courses in english, science, and math than prior freshmen at briarwood county high school were.

3. in chicago we visited soldier field and the museum of science and industry, which are known all over the world.

4. Aboard the space shuttle *columbia* in january 1986, franklin Chang-Díaz became the first astronaut to send a message in spanish back to earth.

5. are latin and biology the most helpful courses for someone planning to go into medicine?

6. after i went to the mall and the hardware store, i stopped at quik mart on twenty-second street.

┌HELP───

Do not capitalize the class names *freshman, sophomore, junior,* or *senior* unless they are part of a proper noun.

EXAMPLES

All **f**reshmen should meet after school to discuss the **F**reshman-**S**ophomore **B**anquet.

Meeting
INDIVIDUAL
NEEDS

ENGLISH-LANGUAGE LEARNERS

General Strategies. For an exercise such as **Review B**, students might benefit from knowing the number of errors in each sentence. They can use the process of elimination to find the proper nouns more easily.

Spanish. In Spanish, proper adjectives are not capitalized. Names of languages are not capitalized except as part of a course title.

Timesaver

Assign pairs of students to be authorities on particular rules. Have each pair check **Review B** for their specialty, noting the sentences to which their rule applies. Then, have a monitor read the correct answers aloud so that class members can check their own papers. Students should call on authorities to give rules to explain any problems they may have with capitalization.

7. we vacationed in the west, stopping to see pikes peak and to go camping and fishing in colorado.

8. in kentucky, one of the border states between the north and the south, you can visit mammoth cave, churchill downs, and the lincoln birthplace national historic site.

9. after labor day last fall, the columbus youth fellowship sponsored a softball tournament at maxwell field.

10. augustus saint-gaudens, a great sculptor who came to the united states from ireland as a child, portrayed abraham lincoln as a tall, serious man standing with his head bowed.

21h. Capitalize titles.

(1) Capitalize a person's title when the title comes before the person's name.

EXAMPLES   **P**resident Kennedy   **M**r. Nakamura

               Dr. Dooley   **F**riar Tuck

               Professor Simmons   **P**rincipal Phillips

               Mrs. Robinson   **L**ady Jane Grey

Generally, a title that is used alone or following a person's name is not capitalized, especially if the title is preceded by *a* or *the.*

EXAMPLES   We saw the **m**ayor at the park.

               Daniel Inouye was first elected **s**enator in 1962.

               Who was the **q**ueen of England during the Victorian Age?

Titles used alone in direct address, however, generally are capitalized.

EXAMPLES   Well, **D**octor, what is your diagnosis?

               There's a message for you, **A**dmiral.

               Good morning, **M**a'am [or *ma'am*].

(2) Capitalize a word showing a family relationship when the word is used before or in place of a person's name, unless the word follows a possessive noun or pronoun.

EXAMPLES   **U**ncle Jack, **C**ousin Joshua, **G**randfather,

               my **u**ncle Jack, your **c**ousin Joshua, Kim's **g**randfather

Reference Note

For information about **capitalizing** and **punctuating abbreviations,** see pages 621 and 639.

S T Y L E   T I P

For special emphasis or clarity, writers sometimes capitalize a title used alone or following a person's name.

EXAMPLES

Many young people admire the **M**ayor.

How did the **S**enator vote on this issue?

At the ceremony, the **Q**ueen knighted Paul McCartney.

Titles

Rule 21h *(pp. 629–632)*

O B J E C T I V E

- **To correct capitalization errors, including errors in titles**

Meeting
INDIVIDUAL
NEEDS

ENGLISH-LANGUAGE LEARNERS
General Strategies. You may need to explain the term *title* to students. Before you begin your explanation, be sure students understand that this word is used for both people and documents. Drawing a stick figure, a book, and a painting on the chalkboard may help students see how each has a title. (For example, you may write *Dr. Rodriguez* under the stick figure, *Great Expectations* under the book, and *Mona Lisa* under the painting.)

Spanish. The titles of persons are not capitalized before a name in Spanish unless the title is abbreviated. Words showing family relationships also are not capitalized, even when they are used before or in place of a person's name.

With the exception of names and other words normally capitalized, only the first word of a title is capitalized in Spanish (for example, *Cien años de soledad,* or *One Hundred Years of Solitude*, by Gabriel García Márquez).

MECHANICS

Using Capital Letters Correctly   **629**

RESOURCES

Titles
Practice

- *Grammar, Usage, and Mechanics,* pp. 244, 245, 246
- *Language Workshop CD-ROM,* Lessons 57, 58

Relating to Writing

Have students imagine that they have created works like the ones listed on the chart on pp. 630 and 631. Have each student name his or her imagined work, correctly punctuate the title, and write a brief synopsis or description of the work. [*comic strip: "Dogwood"—canine hero is noted for his eating habits and his adventures in space; song: "Cloudy Weekend"—a hip-hop lament about Saturday plans threatened by storms; computer game: "Space Angel"—the object is for angels to reach heaven without being grounded during an intergalactic war.*]

Reference Note

For information on using **italics with titles,** see page 684. For information on using **quotation marks with titles,** see page 692.

┌HELP─

The official title of a book is found on the title page. The official title of a newspaper or other periodical is found on the masthead, which usually appears on the editorial page or the table of contents.

(3) Capitalize the first and last words and all important words in titles and subtitles.

Unimportant words in a title include

- articles: *a, an, the*
- short prepositions (fewer than five letters): *of, to, for, from, in, over*
- coordinating conjunctions: *and, but, for, nor, or, so, yet*
- the sign of the infinitive: *to*

NOTE   Capitalize an article (*a, an,* or *the*) at the beginning of a title or subtitle only if it is the first word of the official title or subtitle.

EXAMPLES   "**A**n Ancient Gesture"   **t**he *Saturday Review*

The Miami Herald   **t**he *Houston Chronicle*

A Christmas Carol   **t**he *Odyssey*

Type of Name	Examples	
Books	*The Sea Around Us*	*Nisei Daughter*
	Ultimate Visual Dictionary	*Island of the Blue Dolphins*
Chapters and Other Parts of Books	"The Circulatory System"	Chapter 11
	"Lesson 5: Manifest Destiny"	"Unit 3: Poetry"
Periodicals	*The New York Times*	the *Hispanic Review*
Poems	"Woman Work"	*The Song of Hiawatha*
	"Mending Wall"	
Stories	"The Pit and the Pendulum"	"Raymond's Run"
		"The Eclipse"
Historical Documents	Treaty of Paris	Magna Carta
	The Declaration of Independence	The Emancipation Proclamation
Movies and Videos	*It's a Wonderful Life*	*Fly Away Home*
	Willy Wonka and the Chocolate Factory	*Yoga: Beginners' Level*

MINI-LESSON

Prepositions. Before students attempt to capitalize titles that include prepositions, you may wish to review prepositions. Then, give students a list of prepositions. For each preposition, have students write a title including that preposition and using correct capitalization. Students may use actual titles or make up their own.

Type of Name	Examples	
Television and Radio Programs	*Ancient Mysteries* *Meet the Press* *Law and Order*	*60 Minutes* *All Things Considered* *Sesame Street*
Plays	*The Three Sisters*	*A Doll's House*
Works of Art	*The Rebel Slave*	*La Primavera*
Musical Works	"The Flight of the Bumblebee"	*Liverpool Oratorio* *Sweeney Todd*
Audiotapes and CDs	*Romantic Adagio* *Left of the Middle* *Dos Mundos*	*Blue* *This Fire* *Ray of Light*
Computer Games and Video Games	*Sonic the Hedgehog* *Logical Journey* *Legend of Zelda*	*Sim City* *Frogger* *X-Men*
Cartoons and Comic Strips	*Jump Start* *For Better or Worse* *Scooby Doo*	*Dilbert* *Daria* *Peanuts*

Review C Correcting Capitalization Errors

If the capitalization in a word group below is incorrect, rewrite it correctly. If a word group contains no errors, write *C*.

EXAMPLE   1. watched the classic movie *casablanca*
            1. *watched the classic movie* Casablanca

1. mayor Cartwright
2. "Home on The Range"
3. the *Reader's Digest*   3. C
4. visiting Yosemite national park
5. the president of the United States   5. C (*or* President)
6. was a hindu priest
7. saying hello to grandma higgins
8. my Cousin's parents
9. N. Scott Momaday won the Pulitzer Prize.   9. C
10. *the Mystery of Edwin Drood*

Review D **Correcting Capitalization Errors in Paragraphs**

Correct the sentences in the following paragraphs by capitalizing or lowercasing letters as needed. If a sentence is already correct, write *C*.

EXAMPLE   **[1]** Louis armstrong was one of america's most gifted Jazz Vocalists and Performers.

    1. Louis Armstrong was one of America's most gifted jazz vocalists and performers.

1. C

[1] In social studies last week, we learned all about Louis Armstrong. **[2]** Nicknamed "satchmo," Armstrong was born in poverty in new Orleans in august, 1901. **[3]** He learned to play the Cornet, a kind of small trumpet, while serving a sentence for delinquency. **[4]** While growing up, he also played the trumpet on the paddleboats that sailed on the Mississippi river.

[5] In 1922, his favorite bandleader, king Oliver, asked him to play second trumpet in a band in chicago. **[6]** King Oliver's band was called the creole jazz band. **[7]** While performing with the Creole Jazz band, Armstrong was coached by the band's classically trained pianist, Lil hardin, who became mrs. Armstrong in 1924. **[8]** Armstrong soon left Oliver and joined the Fletcher henderson band in New York city.

[9] Louis Armstrong soon established himself as a great Trumpeter and Vocalist. **[10]** One of his innovations was scat, a vocal technique in which a Musician's rhythmic, wordless voice imitates the sound of instruments. **[11]** This technique first appeared in recordings such as "Heebie jeebies," issued under the band name hot Five. **[12]** The scat technique was later imitated by other famous african american singers such as ella Fitzgerald and Al jarreau.

[13] As a Composer, Armstrong was known for such classic jazz songs as "dippermouth blues" and "Wild Man Blues." **[14]** Armstrong's outgoing personality and Style attracted new audiences to jazz. **[15]** By the Mid-1930's, Armstrong had become a popular entertainer.

16. C

[16] He retained his brilliance as a jazz trumpeter, however. **[17]** After world war II, he formed a series of small bands. **[18]** When the U.S. state department made Armstrong a goodwill ambassador, it honored his worldwide reputation as a generous and well-liked personality. **[19]** In his capacity as Ambassador, he traveled widely around the world. **[20]** Louis Armstrong died at his home in queens, New York, in July 1971.

Chapter Review

A. Correcting Sentences That Contain Errors in Capitalization

Most of the following sentences contain at least one error in capitalization. Write each sentence, capitalizing or lowercasing letters where necessary. If a sentence is already correct, write *C*.

1. The only U.S. President who was never elected was Gerald Ford.
2. The program was titled *Animals of the serengeti plain.*
3. Would you say that the South and the Northeast are the regions of the United States with the most distinctive accents?   3. C
4. Although the wheel was unknown to the inca people, their Empire contained many miles of roads.
5. Students at a yeshiva, or Jewish Seminary, study the torah.
6. The highest peak in the alps is Mont Blanc, on the French-italian border, or so I'm told.
7. I later learned that uncle Steve had been taking three courses in night school.
8. Henri Matisse's early paintings include *A glimpse of Notre Dame in the late afternoon* and *Green stripe.*
9. My aunt Terry is an Editor at a large textbook Publishing Company in Texas.
10. The united nations building is on the east River in New York city.
11. The letter was mistakenly delivered to 1408 West Twenty-third Street instead of 1408 east Twenty-third Street.
12. Uncle Matt served in the Vietnam war before he studied medicine at Iowa state university.
13. While recovering from surgery, Mr. Gomez watched *Good morning, America* every day on television.
14. What is the date of easter Sunday this year?
15. The woman from the U.S. department of labor was sent to our community hospital when she became sick.
16. The *Queen Elizabeth 2* was delayed by serious storms while crossing the Atlantic ocean.
17. Last Thursday, July 4, we Americans celebrated Independence Day. 17. C

Chapter Review   **633**

Using the Chapter Review

To assess student progress, you may want to compare the types of items missed on the **Diagnostic Preview** to those missed on the **Chapter Review**. If students have not made significant progress, you may want to refer them to **Chapter 28: Correcting Common Errors, Exercises 26, 27,** and **28** for additional practice.

MECHANICS

18. The tenor sang "America the beautiful" at the dedication of the new monument.

19. Did you know, professor, that the *Mona Lisa* will be shown this year at the Metropolitan Museum of Art?

20. On Thanksgiving day, my family thanks god for many blessings.

B. Correcting Errors in Capitalization

Correct the errors in capitalization in the following paragraph by capitalizing or lowercasing words as needed.

[21] almost everybody has heard of pasteurization, but how many people know what it is, or who originated it? [22] The French Chemist Louis Pasteur developed the process, which involves destroying disease-causing microorganisms by applying heat. [23] That was only one of many accomplishments of this Scientific Genius. [24] Born in 1822 in a small town in Eastern France, he made his first scientific discovery at the age of 26. [25] As his reputation grew, he was elected to the academy of Scientists in Paris and named Director of Scientific studies at one of the Capital City's most prestigious schools. [26] Pasteur's discovery that Microorganisms can cause disease led to recognition of the importance of vaccination. [27] The Great Scientist developed vaccines for rabies, anthrax, and a form of Cholera found in farmyard fowl. [28] Thanks to the support of emperor Napoleon III, a special laboratory was created for Pasteur. [29] In 1874, the French parliament granted him a lifetime stipend, and the Pasteur institute was inaugurated in Paris a few years before he died. [30] His discoveries were crucial, but perhaps Pasteur's greatest contribution to Science was his new way of looking at things.

C. Proofreading for Correct Capitalization

Correct the following word groups, using capital letters as needed.

31. the cities of san miguel and cuernavaca
32. an irish american
33. the great ship *titanic*
34. at the hotel bristol
35. on christmas day

RESOURCES

Capital Letters
Review
■ *Grammar, Usage, and Mechanics,* pp. 247, 248, 249, 250

Assessment
■ *Assessment Package*
  —*Chapter Tests,* Ch. 21
  —*Chapter Tests in Standardized Test Formats,* Ch. 21
■ *Test Generator (One-Stop Planner CD-ROM)*

MECHANICS

36. a call from uncle Ernesto
37. smith and garcia, inc.
38. gulf of mexico
39. southwest texas state university
40. whoever won the nobel prize
41. driving a dodge colt
42. zilker park in austin, texas
43. sarge's deli on third avenue
44. on labor day
45. the greek god apollo

Writing Application
Using Capital Letters Correctly in a Paragraph

Proper Nouns   Your school's language club plans to publish a booklet about foreign cities that most interest students. Write a paragraph telling about one city and its major attractions.

Prewriting   Choose a foreign city that interests you, and jot down the reasons you find it interesting. You may want to gather some information about it from encyclopedias, travel books or brochures, and magazine or newspaper articles. Make a list of the city's major attractions.

Writing   As you write your first draft, be sure to include information about the city's location and historical or cultural importance.

Revising   Ask a friend who is unfamiliar with the city to read your paragraph. Does the information you have presented make your friend want to visit the city? Add or delete details to make your writing more interesting and informative.

Publishing   Be sure that you have correctly capitalized geographical names and the names of businesses, institutions, places, and events. Pay particular attention to the spelling of foreign words. With your teacher's permission, post your paragraph on the class bulletin board or Web page.

Writing Application
(p. 635)

OBJECTIVE

- To write a paragraph about a foreign city, using correct capitalization

Writing Application

Tip. You may wish to have students brainstorm for cities about which they would like to write. Some students might want to make up cities or places to visit. Encourage students to use their imaginations and to include details to describe each place fully to give the reader a clear picture of what the city is like.

Scoring Rubric. While you will want to pay particular attention to students' use of capitalization, you will also want to evaluate overall writing performance. You may want to give a split score to indicate development and clarity of the composition as well as skill in capitalization.

Critical Thinking

Analysis. To help students decide which city to choose, have them analyze and evaluate other students' traveling interests. The booklet should contain information about cities that have attractions of interest to other teenagers. You may want to suggest to students that they poll their peers outside class to decide which cities would be appropriate to include in the booklet.

RESOURCES
Writing Application
Extension
- *Grammar, Usage, and Mechanics,* p. 253
- *Language Workshop CD-ROM,* Lessons 57, 58

Punctuation

End Marks, Abbreviations, and Commas

PREVIEWING THE CHAPTER

- This chapter discusses the rules for punctuating sentences with end marks and commas. The first two sections present the use of end marks in sentences classified according to purpose and the use of periods with abbreviations.

- The third section explains the use of commas in series, independent clauses, and with introductory and interrupting elements. It also explains conventional uses of commas.

- The chapter concludes with a **Chapter Review** including a **Writing Application** feature that asks students to write directions using commas correctly.

- For help in integrating the chapter with writing chapters, use the **Teaching Strands** chart on pp. T371A–T371B.

USING THE DIAGNOSTIC PREVIEW

- Although your ninth-graders may not have trouble with end marks, the results of the **Diagnostic Preview** may indicate a need to review the comma rules in this chapter. You may want to have each student make a chart including the rules he or she has not mastered. Students may refer to their charts as guides to areas for additional study and for problem areas to target when proofreading writing assignments.

Diagnostic Preview

Correcting Sentences by Adding Periods, Question Marks, Exclamation Points, and Commas

Write the following paragraphs, adding periods, question marks, exclamation points, and commas where necessary.
Optional commas are underscored.

EXAMPLE [1] Computers therefore are not my cup of tea

1. Computers, therefore, are not my cup of tea.

[1] Although TV commercials tell you otherwise computers are not for everyone.[2] One day in the showroom of a computer store I stared at a personal computer for more than half an hour but I was still unable to locate the on-off switch.[3] The demonstrator Pearl Rangely PhD tried her best to be helpful.[4] A computer consultant she quickly explained the functions of various switches buttons and boxes.[5] She pressed keys she flashed words on the screen and she pushed around the mouse very quickly.[6] I was confused and puzzled and frustrated yet I was also fascinated.

[7] Dr Rangely who had often encountered confused consumers before told me that I had a "terminal" phobia.[8] With a frown I asked her what that meant.[9] She replied grinning broadly that it was the fear that bits and bytes can actually bite.[10] What a comedian she was! [11] Totally disenchanted I left the store.

[12] I headed straight for the library to check out everything that I could find about computers: books magazines catalogs and pamphlets.

3. Ph.D. *or* PhD

10. ! *or* .

CHAPTER RESOURCES

Planning
- *One-Stop Planner CD-ROM* 🎵

Practice and Extension
- *Grammar, Usage, and Mechanics*, p. 254
- *Developmental Language Skills*, pp. 119–128

Internet
- go.hrw.com (keyword: EOLang)

Evaluation and Assessment
- *Chapter Tests*, Ch. 22
- *Chapter Tests in Standardized Test Formats*, Ch. 22
- *Test Generator (One-Stop Planner)* 🎵

[13] For example, I read *The Soul of a New Machine*, a fascinating book written by Tracy Kidder. [14] When I had finished the book, I knew about input, output, high-level languages, and debugging. [15] Armed with this knowledge, I confidently returned to the store on Friday, March 13. [16] Well, the same demonstrator was there smiling like a Cheshire cat. [17] I rattled off several technical questions that I think must have surprised her. [18] By the end of a single afternoon, Dr. Rangely had taught me something about every computer in the store. [19] I left, however, without asking one simple, embarrassing question. [20] Could you please tell me where the on-off switch is?

End Marks

Sentences

End marks—periods, question marks, and exclamation points—are used to indicate the purpose of a sentence.

22a. **A statement (or declarative sentence) is followed by a period.**

EXAMPLES   Nancy López won the golf tournament.

What Balboa saw below was the Pacific Ocean.

Flora wondered who had already gone.

NOTE   Notice in the third example that a declarative sentence containing an indirect question is followed by a period. (An **indirect question** is one that does not use the speaker's exact words.) Be sure to distinguish between a declarative sentence that contains an indirect question and an interrogative sentence, which asks a direct question.

INDIRECT QUESTION   I wondered what makes that sound. [declarative]
DIRECT QUESTION   What makes that sound? [interrogative]

22b. **A question (or interrogative sentence) is followed by a question mark.**

EXAMPLES   Do you know American Sign Language?

Why don't you ask Eileen?

Who wrote this note? Did you?

| STYLE   TIP |

As you speak, the tone and pitch of your voice, the pauses in your speech, and the gestures and expressions you use all help make your meaning clear. In writing, marks of punctuation, such as end marks and commas, show readers where these verbal and nonverbal cues occur.

Punctuation alone won't clarify the meaning of a confusing sentence, however. If you have trouble punctuating a sentence, check to see whether rewording it would help express your meaning more clearly.

Reference Note

For information about how **sentences** are **classified according to purpose,** see Chapter 13.

End Marks
Rules 22a–d (pp. 637–639)

O B J E C T I V E

- **To correct sentences by adding end marks and to identify kinds of sentences**

T E A C H I N G TIP

Activity. Divide students into small groups, and ask each group to compose a statement, a question, an exclamation, and a command, punctuating each sentence correctly. Have students write their sentences on a transparency or on the chalkboard, and have a group spokesperson explain to the class the reasons why each punctuation mark is used.

MECHANICS

End Marks   **637**

Meeting INDIVIDUAL NEEDS

ENGLISH-LANGUAGE LEARNERS

General Strategies. Because the question mark takes different forms in languages other than English, students may make punctuation errors when writing in English. For example, Spanish uses an inverted question mark at the beginning of a question (¿Where is Bill?); Greek uses a semicolon to indicate a question (Where is Bill;).

You may want to ask students to give all of their writing assignments one proofreading pass just to check the punctuation of questions.

Critical Thinking

Analysis. Students may be aware that publications sometimes customize punctuation rules. Have students use periodicals, particularly advertisements, to find sentences ending in exclamation points. Students should contribute their samples to a class list. Ask the class to use **Rules 22c** and **22d** to analyze sentences and to form generalizations about the current commercial use of exclamations and imperative sentences.

 S T Y L E   T I P

Sometimes declarative and interrogative sentences show such strong feeling that they are more like exclamations than like statements or questions. In such cases, an exclamation point should be used instead of a period or a question mark.

EXAMPLES
Here comes the bus!
Can't you speak up!

 S T Y L E   T I P

An interjection is generally set off from the rest of the sentence by a comma or an exclamation point.

EXAMPLES
Well, I guess so.
Ouch! That hurt.

Reference Note

For more about **interjections,** see page 405.

 S T Y L E   T I P

Sometimes a command or request is expressed as if it were a question. The meaning, however, may be imperative, in which case a period or exclamation point is used.

EXAMPLES
May I say a few words now.

Will you leave me alone!

A direct question may have the same word order as a declarative sentence. Since it is a question, it is followed by a question mark.

EXAMPLES   You know American Sign Language?

You're not asking Eileen?

22c. An exclamation (or exclamatory sentence) is followed by an exclamation point.

EXAMPLES   Hurrah! The rain stopped!

Ouch!

Look out!

22d. A command or request (or imperative sentence) is followed by either a period or an exclamation point.

When an imperative sentence makes a request, it is generally followed by a period. When an imperative sentence expresses a strong command, an exclamation point is generally used.

EXAMPLES   Please answer my question. [request]

Turn off your radio. [command]

Answer me right now! [strong command]

Exercise 1   **Using Periods, Question Marks, and Exclamation Points**

Write the following sentences, adding periods, question marks, and exclamation points where they are needed. Identify each sentence as *declarative, imperative, interrogative,* or *exclamatory.*

EXAMPLE   1. Are you familiar with lacrosse, a field game

1. *Are you familiar with lacrosse, a field game?—interrogative*

1. Do you know how to play lacrosse?   1. int.
2. On TV last night there was a segment on teams playing lacrosse.   2. dec.
3. What a rough sport lacrosse must be!   3. exc.
4. Did you know that North American Indians developed this game?   4. int.
5. Before Columbus came to the Americas in A.D. 1492, the Iroquois were playing lacrosse in what is now upper New York State and Canada.   5. dec.
6. Do you realize that this makes lacrosse the oldest organized sport in America?   6. int.

MINI-LESSON

Punctuating with Quotation Marks. Tell students that question marks and exclamation points may be placed either inside or outside quotation marks depending on whether the entire sentence or just the quotation is a question or exclamation.

Have students analyze sentences from their writing and tell whether the question marks and exclamation points should be placed inside or outside the quotation marks. See **Chapter 24: Punctuation.**

7. Lacrosse is played by two opposing teams. 7. dec.
8. Use a stick to catch, carry, and throw the ball. 8. imp.
9. The name of the game comes from *la crosse*, French for a bishop's staff, which the lacrosse stick resembles. 9. dec.
10. Lacrosse is especially popular in Canada, the British Isles, and Australia, and it is played in the United States, too. 10. dec.

Abbreviations

22e. Use a period after certain abbreviations.

An *abbreviation* is a shortened form of a word or word group. Notice how periods are used with abbreviations in the examples in this part of the chapter.

Personal Names

Abbreviate given names only if the person is most commonly known by the abbreviated form of the name.

EXAMPLES   Ida **B.** Wells   **T. H.** White   **M.F.K.** Fisher

Titles

(1) Abbreviate social titles whether used before the full name or before the last name alone.

EXAMPLES   **Mr.** Tom Evans   **Ms.** Jody Aiello   **Mrs.** Dupont

                Sr. (Señor) Cadenas   **Sra.** (Señora) Garza   **Dr.** O'Nolan

(2) You may abbreviate civil and military titles used before full names or before initials and last names. Spell such titles out before last names used alone.

EXAMPLES   **Sen.** Kay Bailey Hutchison   **Senator** Hutchison

                Prof. E. M. Makowski   **Professor** Makowski

                Brig. Gen. Norman Schwarzkopf   **Brigadier General** Schwarzkopf

(3) Abbreviate titles and academic degrees that follow proper names.

EXAMPLES   Hank Williams, **Jr.**   Peter Garcia, **M.D.**

STYLE   TIP

Only a few abbreviations are appropriate in the text of a formal paper written for a general audience. In tables, notes, and bibliographies, abbreviations are used more freely in order to save space.

STYLE   TIP

Leave a space between two initials, but not between three or more.

HELP

If a statement ends with an abbreviation, do not use an additional period as an end mark. However, do use a question mark or an exclamation point if one is needed.

EXAMPLES
Mrs. Tavares just received her Ph.D.

When did she receive her Ph.D.?

Abbreviations   **639**

Abbreviations

Rule 22e *(pp. 639–643)*

OBJECTIVE

■ **To correct errors in the use of abbreviations in sentences**

TEACHING TIP

Activity. To give students practice in using end marks and abbreviations, try a team game. Divide the class into five teams. Specify a sentence type and a specific abbreviation to be used in that sentence. You could combine the following types:

Sentence Type	Abbreviation
statement	personal name
question	title with name
exclamation	state
request	address
command	organization/ company
	time
	unit of measure

Team members may confer for thirty seconds; then, each team must send a member to the chalkboard to write the sentence. Give a point each for the correct sentence type, end mark, and abbreviation. Continue the game by having every student take a turn at the chalkboard.

RESOURCES

Abbreviations

Practice

■ *Grammar, Usage, and Mechanics,* pp. 256, 257, 258, 259

Cooperative Learning

Tell students they will be creating an abbreviation game based on a television game show. Assign small groups of writers to investigate an assigned category, such as military titles or sports abbreviations.

Writing groups will each develop ten questions, such as "What is the abbreviation for *General*?" or "What does the acronym *scuba* stand for?" (For help developing questions and answers, refer students to a dictionary of acronyms and abbreviations, if available.)

Once questions have been created, assign values of 10, 20, 30, 40, or 50 points, depending on difficulty. Then, choose three contestants, a moderator to read the questions, and a judge with the answers. Allow a set of contestants to play the game for ten minutes; then, introduce a new set of contestants. Allow the game to continue until all students have had a chance to play and all questions have been asked.

Critical Thinking

Metacognition. After students have completed the **Cooperative Learning** activity above, ask them to consider the following questions:

Which abbreviation seemed most difficult? Why?

What did I learn through the process of forming questions?

NOTE Do not include the titles *Mr., Mrs., Ms.,* or *Dr.* when you use a professional title or degree after a name.

EXAMPLE   **Dr.** Joan West *or* Joan West, **M.D.** [*not* Dr. Joan West, M.D.]

Agencies and Organizations

An *acronym* is a word formed from the first (or first few) letters of a series of words. Acronyms are written without periods. After spelling out the first use of the names of agencies and organizations, abbreviate these names and other things commonly known by their acronyms.

EXAMPLE   My older sister works for the **National Institute of Mental Health (NIMH).** She is compiling data for one of **NIMH**'s behavioral studies.

AMA American Medical Association	**USAF** United States Air Force
HUD (Department of) Housing and Urban Development	**UN** United Nations
CPU Central Processing Unit	**NEA** National Endowment for the Arts
RAM random-access memory	**FM** Frequency Modulation

NOTE A few acronyms, such as *radar, laser,* and *sonar,* are now considered common nouns. They do not need to be spelled out on first use and are no longer capitalized. When you're not sure whether an acronym should be capitalized, look it up in a recent dictionary.

Geographical Terms

In text, spell out names of states and other political units whether they stand alone or follow other geographical terms. Abbreviate such names in tables, notes, and bibliographies.

TEXT   On our vacation to Canada, we visited Victoria, the capital of British Columbia.

CHART
London, U.K.	Tucson, Ariz.
Victoria, B.C.	Fresno, Calif.

FOOTNOTE	[3]The Public Library in Annaville, Mich., has an entire collection of Smyth's folios.
BIBLIOGRAPHY ENTRY	"The Last Hurrah." Editorial. *Star-Ledger* [Newark, N.J.] 29 Aug. 1991: 30.

NOTE Include the traditional abbreviation for the District of Columbia, *D.C.,* with the city name *Washington* to distinguish it from the state of Washington.

In text, spell out every word in an address. Such words may be abbreviated in letter and envelope addresses and in tables and notes.

TEXT	We live at 413 West Maple Street.
ENVELOPE	413 W. Maple St.

NOTE Two-letter state abbreviations without periods are used only when the ZIP Code is included.

EXAMPLE	Cincinnati, **OH** 45233

Time

Abbreviate the frequently used era designations *A.D.* and *B.C.* The abbreviation *A.D.* stands for the Latin phrase *anno Domini,* meaning "in the year of the Lord." It is used with dates in the Christian era. When used with a specific year number, *A.D.* precedes the number. When used with the name of a century, it follows the name.

EXAMPLES	In **A.D.** 476, the last Western Roman emperor, Romulus Augustulus, was overthrown by Germanic tribes.
	The legends of King Arthur may be based on the life of a real British leader of the sixth century **A.D.**

The abbreviation *B.C.,* which stands for "before Christ," is used for dates before the Christian era. It follows either a specific year number or the name of a century.

EXAMPLES	Homer's epic poem the *Iliad* was probably composed between 800 and 700 **B.C.**
	The poem describes battles that probably occurred around the twelfth century **B.C.**

S T Y L E   T I P

In your reading, you may come across the abbreviations *C.E.* and *B.C.E.* These abbreviations stand for *Common Era* and *Before Common Era.* These terms are sometimes used in place of *A.D.* and *B.C.,* respectively, and are written after the date.

EXAMPLES
752 **C.E.**

1550 **B.C.E.**

MECHANICS

STYLE TIP

Do not use the words *morning, afternoon,* or *evening* with numerals followed by *A.M.* or *P.M.*

INCORRECT
The next bus for Roanoke leaves at 1:30 P.M. in the afternoon.

CORRECT
The next bus for Roanoke leaves at **1:30 P.M.** (or **one-thirty in the afternoon**).

In regular text, spell out the names of months and days whether they appear alone or in dates. Both types of names may be abbreviated in tables, notes, and bibliographies.

TEXT   Please join us on Thursday, March 21, to celebrate Grandma and Grandpa's anniversary.

NOTE   Thurs., Mar. 21

Abbreviate the designations for the two halves of the day measured by clock time. The abbreviation *A.M.* stands for the Latin phrase *ante meridiem,* meaning "before noon." The abbreviation *P.M.* stands for *post meridiem,* meaning "after noon." Both abbreviations follow the numerals designating the specific time.

EXAMPLE   My mom works four days a week, from 8:00 **A.M.** until 6:00 **P.M.**

Units of Measurement

Abbreviations for units of measurement are usually written without periods. However, do use a period with the abbreviation for inch (*in.*) to prevent confusing it with the word *in.*

EXAMPLES   mm, kg, ml, tsp, doz, yd, ft, lb

In regular text, spell out the names of units of measurement whether they stand alone or follow a spelled-out number or a numeral. Such names may be abbreviated in tables and notes when they follow a numeral.

TEXT   The speed limit here is fifty-five **miles per hour** [not *mph*].

The cubicle measured ten **feet** [not *ft*] by twelve.

TABLE

| 1 **tsp** pepper | 97° **F** |
| 12 **ft** 6 **in.** | 2 **oz** flour |

Exercise 2   **Using Abbreviations**

Rewrite the following sentences, correcting errors in the use of abbreviations.   Answers may vary.

EXAMPLE   1. Hillary Clinton was born in Chicago, IL.

1. *Hillary Clinton was born in Chicago, Illinois.*

1. The flight for Montevideo departs at 11:15 A.M. <del>in the morning.</del>

2. Julius Caesar was assassinated in the Roman Forum in B.C. 44.

3. Harun ar-Rashid, whose reign is associated with the Arabian
   Nights, ruled as caliph of Baghdad from 786 to 809 A.D.

4. The Mississippi River flows from Lake Itasca, MN, all the way
   to the Gulf of Mexico at Port Eads, LA.   **4.** Minnesota/Louisiana

5. I will be leaving soon to visit Mr. Nugent on Elm St. in New
   Paltz, NY.   **5.** Street/New York

6. The Fbi. is the chief investigative branch of the U.S. Department
   of Justice.   **6.** FBI

7. The keynote speaker was Dr. Matthew Villareal, Ph.D.

8. We will meet at 4:00 P.M..

9. I wrote "56 in." in the blank labeled "height."

10. G. Washington was the first president of the United States.   **10.** George

Review A   **Correcting Sentences by Adding Periods,**
Question Marks, and Exclamation Points

Write the following sentences, adding periods, question marks,
and exclamation points as needed.

EXAMPLE   **1.** Does Josh come from Chicago

   1. Does Josh come from Chicago?

1. What a great car that is!
2. Whose car is that?
3. We asked who owned that car.
4. Roman troops invaded Britain in 54 BC.   **4.** [or BC]
5. By AD. 809, Baghdad was already an important city.   **5.** [or AD]
6. Dr. Edward Jenner gave the first vaccination against smallpox in 1796.
7. Why do so many children enjoy using computers?
8. Please explain why so many children enjoy using computers.
9. When did Alan Keyes run for president?
10. Terrific! Here's another coin for my collection.   **10.** [or !]

Commas

If you fail to use necessary commas, you may confuse your reader.

CONFUSING   The friends I have invited are Ruth Ann Jerry Lee Derrick
            Martha and Julie. [How many friends?]

   CLEAR   The friends I have invited are Ruth Ann, Jerry Lee, Derrick,
           Martha, and Julie. [five friends]

Commas   **643**

Timesaver

Ask students to write the answers to
Review A and to cite rules for each
answer. Have a monitor write
answers and rule numbers on the
chalkboard or on a transparency so
that students may check each other's
papers.

MECHANICS

Commas

Rules 22f–l *(pp. 643–662)*

OBJECTIVES

- To correct sentences by using commas in series
- To answer questions by writing sentences that include commas in series
- To correct sentences by adding commas between independent clauses
- To use commas correctly in sentences with nonessential and essential clauses
- To use commas correctly in sentences with participial phrases
- To use commas correctly in sentences with introductory elements
- To use commas correctly in sentences with appositives and appositive phrases
- To use commas correctly in sentences with words used in direct address
- To use commas correctly in sentences with parenthetical expressions

MECHANICS

| STYLE   TIP |

Because using the final comma is never wrong, some writers prefer always to use the comma before the *and* in a series. Follow your teacher's instructions on this point.

Items in a Series

22f. Use commas to separate items in a series.

Notice in the following examples that the number of commas in a series is one fewer than the number of items in the series.

EXAMPLES
All my cousins, aunts, and uncles came to our family reunion. [words in a series]

The children played in the yard, at the playground, and by the pond. [phrases in a series]

Those who had flown to the reunion, who had driven many miles, or who had even taken time off from their jobs were glad that they had made the effort to be there. [subordinate clauses in a series]

When the last two items in a series are joined by *and*, the comma before the *and* is sometimes omitted if the comma is not necessary to make the meaning clear.

CLEAR WITH
COMMA OMITTED
The salad contained lettuce, tomatoes, onions, cucumbers, carrots and radishes.

NOT CLEAR WITH
COMMA OMITTED
Our school newspaper has editors for news, sports, humor, features and art. [How many editors are there, four or five? Does one person serve as a features and art editor, or is an editor needed for each job?]

CLEAR WITH
COMMA INCLUDED
Our school newspaper has editors for news, sports, humor, features, and art. [five editors]

NOTE Some words—such as *bread and butter, rod and reel, table and chairs*—are used in pairs and may be considered one item in a series.

EXAMPLE
Our collection includes pop, reggae, mariachi, **rhythm and blues,** and hip-hop music.

(1) If all items in a series are joined by *and, or,* or *nor,* do not use commas to separate them.

EXAMPLES
I need tacks **and** nails **and** a hammer.

Sam **or** Carlos **or** Yolanda will be able to baby-sit tomorrow.

Neither horses **nor** elephants **nor** giraffes are carnivorous.

644 Chapter 22 Punctuation

RESOURCES

Commas
Practice
- *Grammar, Usage, and Mechanics,* pp. 260, 261, 262, 263, 264, 265, 266, 267, 268
- *Language Workshop CD-ROM,* Lessons 46–50, 55

(2) Short independent clauses may be separated by commas.

EXAMPLE   The engine roared, the wheels spun, and a cloud of dust
           swirled behind the sports car.

> NOTE Sentences that contain more than one independent clause are
> *compound* or *compound-complex sentences.*
>
> COMPOUND   The Wilsons grow organic vegetables, and they sell them
>   at the farmers' market.
>
> COMPOUND-   When the weather is bad, the dog hides under the bed,
> COMPLEX   and the cat retreats to my closet.

(3) Use commas to separate two or more adjectives preceding a noun.

EXAMPLE   Are you going to that hot, crowded, noisy mall?

When the last adjective in a series is thought of as part of the
noun, the comma before the adjective is omitted.

EXAMPLES   I study in our small **dining room.**

            Let's have our picnic under that lovely, shady **fruit tree.**

Compound nouns like *dining room* and *fruit tree* are considered single
units—the two words act as one part of speech.

> NOTE If one of the words modifies another modifier, do not separate
> those two words with a comma.
>
> EXAMPLE   Do you like this **dark blue** sweater?

Exercise 3   Correcting Sentences by Adding Commas

Write each series in the following sentences, adding commas where
needed.   Optional commas are underscored.

EXAMPLE   1. Rita plays soccer volleyball and softball.
           1. *soccer, volleyball, and softball*

1. Dr. Charles Drew worked as a surgeon developed new ways of
   storing blood and was the first director of the Red Cross blood
   bank program.
2. I am going to take English science social studies and algebra.
3. The loud insistent smoke alarm woke us just before dawn.

Reference Note

Independent clauses in a
series can be separated by
semicolons. For more
about this use of **semi-colons,** see page 470.

Reference Note

For more information
about **compound** and
**compound-complex
sentences,** see page 481.

Reference Note

For more information on
compound nouns, see
page 376.

Meeting INDIVIDUAL NEEDS

LEARNERS HAVING DIFFICULTY

Students will probably be familiar
with the use of commas to separate
single-word items in a series, but
they may not be familiar with com-mas
used to separate phrases or
clauses in a series. You may want to
review **Chapter 14: The Phrase** and
Chapter 15: The Clause and to
give additional examples of phrases
and clauses in series.

INCLUSION

Students with processing problems
may have difficulty if many new con-cepts
are introduced at one time.
Be prepared to spend ample time
on each rule before proceeding to
the next one.

ENGLISH-LANGUAGE LEARNERS

Spanish. A comma is not used in
Spanish after the penultimate item
in a series.

MECHANICS

Meeting INDIVIDUAL NEEDS

MULTIPLE INTELLIGENCES

Interpersonal Intelligence. Hold a team race to help reinforce the use of commas in a series of words or phrases. Give teams of four students five minutes to write sentences with commas in series. To help them begin, list the following examples on the chalkboard.

Word Series

• Red, gold, and blue were her colors.

• She was tall, gentle, and graceful.

Phrase Series

• The water flowed over the tub, onto the floor, and under the door.

• Counting the money, writing checks, and making deposits took four hours.

Award a point for each correct use of a comma in a series.

Exercise 4 Using Commas Correctly in Series

ANSWERS

Individual sentences will vary, but answers must follow the style requested.

Timesaver

Assign students to work in pairs to evaluate each other's work for **Exercise 4.** Remind students that items in a series entirely joined by *and*s, *or*s, or *nor*s are not separated by commas.

TIPS & TRICKS

When two or more adjectives precede a noun, you can use two tests to determine whether the last adjective and the noun form a unit.

TEST 1

Insert the word *and* between the adjectives. If *and* fits sensibly between the adjectives, use a comma.

EXAMPLE

A juicy, tangy apple makes a good snack. [*Juicy and tangy* makes sense, so the comma is correct.]

TEST 2

Change the order of the adjectives. If the order of the adjectives can be reversed sensibly, use a comma.

EXAMPLE

The quiet, polite girl sat next to her mother. [*Polite, quiet girl* makes sense, so the comma is correct.]

---

4. Please pass those delicious blueberry pancakes, the margarine, and the syrup.

5. My twin sister can run faster, jump higher, and do more push-ups than I can.

6. Where is the nearest store that sells newspapers, magazines, and paperbacks?

7. Horns tooted, tires screeched, a whistle blew, and sirens wailed.

8. Steel is made from iron, other metals, and small amounts of carbon.

9. The clown wore a long, blue raincoat; big, red plastic gloves; and floppy, yellow tennis shoes.

10. Robert Browning says that youth is good, that middle age is better, and that old age is best.

Exercise 4 Using Commas Correctly in Series

Your school's new counselor wants to get to know the students better. He has developed the following personality questionnaire, and today he has given a copy to all the students in your class. Answer each question by writing a sentence that includes a series of words, phrases, or clauses. Use commas where needed in each series.

EXAMPLE   1. What do you consider your most outstanding traits?

          1. I am considerate, thoughtful, and loyal.

Personality Questionnaire

1. What do you consider your most outstanding traits?

2. What qualities do you admire most in a person?

3. Who are the people who have influenced you most?

4. What are your favorite hobbies?

5. What famous people would you like to meet?

6. What countries would you most like to visit?

7. For what reasons do you attend school?

8. What are your favorite subjects in school?

9. What things about the world would you most like to change?

10. What goals do you hope to achieve during the next ten years?

Independent Clauses

22g. Use a comma before *and, but, for, nor, or, so,* or *yet* when it joins independent clauses.

EXAMPLES   Hector pressed the button**, and** the engine started up.

She would never argue**, nor** would she complain to anyone.

Are you going to the football game**, or** do you have other plans for Saturday?

He is an accomplished actor**, yet** he's very modest.

Do not be misled by compound verbs, which can make a sentence look like a compound sentence.

SIMPLE SENTENCE   Mara **cleared** the table and **did** the dishes. [one subject with a compound verb]

COMPOUND SENTENCE   **Mara cleared the table,** and **Roland did the dishes.** [two independent clauses]

NOTE The comma joining two independent clauses is sometimes omitted before *and, but, or,* or *nor* when the independent clauses are very short and when there is no possibility of misunderstanding.

CLEAR   The dog barked and the cat meowed.

AWKWARD   Bill bathed the dog and the cat hid under the bed. [confusing without comma]

CLEAR   Bill bathed the dog**,** and the cat hid under the bed.

Exercise 5 Correcting Sentences by Adding Commas Between Independent Clauses

Where a comma should be used, write the word preceding the comma, the comma, and the conjunction following it. If a sentence is already correct, write *C*.

EXAMPLE   **1.** Accident-related injuries are common and many of these injuries can be prevented.

    1. common, and

1. It is important to know first aid for an accident can happen at almost any time.

2. More than 83,000 people in the United States die in accidents each year and many millions are injured.

Reference Note

For more about **compound sentences,** see page 481. For information on **compound subjects** and **compound verbs,** see page 424.

STYLE   TIP

For clarity, some writers prefer always to use the comma before a conjunction joining independent clauses. Follow your teacher's instructions on this point.

MECHANICS

TECHNOLOGY **TIP**

Point out to students that because word-processing software is not able to identify punctuation errors, even sophisticated spellchecking and grammar checking programs cannot replace a thorough knowledge of punctuation rules.

Meeting
INDIVIDUAL
NEEDS

MULTIPLE INTELLIGENCES

Linguistic Intelligence. To give students more practice analyzing subordinate clauses, write the following sentence on the chalkboard and ask students to determine whether or not the underlined clause should be set off with commas. Tell students to be prepared to explain their answers.

Washington <u>which is the only state named after a president</u> shares a border with Canada. [commas; the clause is nonessential]

Next, have students write similar sentences, using essential and nonessential clauses without commas. Have pairs of students exchange papers, adding required punctuation. Ask students to write some examples on the chalkboard and to explain why the clause is essential or nonessential.

Reference Note

For more information about **subordinate clauses,** see page 471. For more about **participial phrases,** see page 451.

3. Many household products can cause illness or even death but are often stored where small children can reach them.   3. C

4. Biking accidents are common wherever cars and bicycles use the same road₎so many communities have provided bicycle lanes.

5. Car accidents are the leading cause of childhood fatalities₎but seat belts have saved many lives.

6. Everyone should know what to do in case of fire₎and different escape routes should be tested.

7. If you need to escape a fire, you should stay close to the floor and be very cautious about opening doors.   7. C

8. Holding your breath, keep low and protected behind a door when opening it₎for a blast of superheated air can be fatal.

9. An injured person should not get up₎nor should liquid be given to someone who is unconscious.

10. Always have someone with you when you swim₎or you may find yourself without help when you need it.

Nonessential Clauses and Phrases

22h. Use commas to set off nonessential subordinate clauses and nonessential participial phrases.

A *nonessential* (or *nonrestrictive*) clause or participial phrase adds information that is not necessary to the main idea in the sentence.

| NONESSENTIAL CLAUSES | Eileen Murray₎ **who is at the top of her class,** wants to go to medical school. |
| | Texas₎ **which has the most farms of any state in this country,** produces one fourth of our oil. |

| NONESSENTIAL PHRASES | Tim Ricardo₎ **hoping to make the swim team,** practiced every day. |
| | *The Lord of the Rings*₎ **written by J.R.R. Tolkien,** has been translated into many languages. |

Omitting each boldface clause or phrase in the preceding examples does not change the main idea of the sentence.

EXAMPLES	Eileen Murray wants to go to medical school.
	Texas produces one fourth of our oil.
	Tim Ricardo practiced every day.
	The Lord of the Rings has been translated into many languages.

When a clause or phrase is necessary to the meaning of a sentence—that is, when it tells *which one(s)*—the clause or phrase is **essential** (or **restrictive**), and commas are not used.

Notice how the meaning of each of the following sentences changes when the essential clause or phrase is omitted.

ESSENTIAL CLAUSE	All students **whose names are on that list** must report to Ms. Washington this afternoon. [All students must report to Ms. Washington this afternoon.]
ESSENTIAL PHRASE	A Ming vase **displayed in the museum** was once owned by Chiang Kai-shek. [A Ming vase was once owned by Chiang Kai-shek.]

Depending on the writer's meaning, a participial phrase or clause may be either essential or non-essential. Including or omitting commas tells the reader how the clause or phrase relates to the main idea of the sentence.

NONESSENTIAL CLAUSE	LaWanda's brother, who is a senior, works part time at the mall. [LaWanda has only one brother. He works at the mall.]
ESSENTIAL CLAUSE	LaWanda's brother who is a senior works part time at the mall. [LaWanda has more than one brother. The one who is a senior works at the mall.]

NOTE An adjective clause beginning with *that* is usually essential.

EXAMPLE Was Hank Aaron the first major league baseball player **that** broke Babe Ruth's home run record?

Exercise 6 **Correcting Sentences with Essential and Nonessential Clauses by Adding or Deleting Commas**

The following sentences contain essential and nonessential clauses. Add or delete commas as necessary to punctuate each of these clauses correctly. If a sentence is already correct, write *C*.

EXAMPLE **1.** My mother who is a Celtics fan has season tickets.
  1. My mother, who is a Celtics fan, has season tickets.

"SURE I GOT ALL THE PUNCTUATION: COMMA, COMMA, PERIOD, PERIOD, QUESTION MARK, COMMA, SEMI-COLON, COMMA, EXCLAMATION POINT, PERIOD..."

© 1998 by Sidney Harris.

Crossing the Curriculum

Math. This exercise will give students practice working with percentages while also reviewing comma **Rules 22f–i.** Assign students to choose a ten-sentence-long passage from a short story or novel to analyze comma usage. Next, have students track how each comma in the passage is used. For example, students might list the rules simply by their number and place a mark next to each rule every time it is used, as in the following example:

22f	22g	22h	22i
////	///	/	///

Then, students can divide the number of times a specific rule is used by the total number of commas to determine the percentage of times a specific comma rule is illustrated in the passage. After students complete their calculations, ask volunteers to share their findings. Ask if anyone can propose a generalization about comma usage based on this exercise.

Commas **649**

1. *Jump Start*, which is my favorite comic strip, makes me think as well as laugh.

2. Ms. Lopez, who teaches social studies and gym, will leave at the end of the year.

3. The amusement rides that are the most exciting may be the most dangerous.   **3.** C

4. Many of the first Spanish settlements in California were founded by Father Junípero Serra, who liked to take long walks between them.

5. People, who carry credit cards, should keep a record of their account numbers at home.

6. Amy Kwan, who is our class president, plans to go to Yale after she graduates from high school.

7. A town like Cottonwood, which has a population of five thousand, seems ideal to me.

8. All dogs that pass the obedience test get a reward; those that don't pass get to take the test again later.   **8.** C

9. Have you tried this pemmican, which my mother made from an old Cree recipe?

10. "The Gift of the Magi" is a story, in which the two main characters, who are deeply in love, make sacrifices in order to buy gifts for each other.

Exercise 7 **Correcting Sentences with Participial Phrases by Adding or Deleting Commas**

Add or delete commas as necessary to punctuate the following sentences correctly. If a sentence is already correctly punctuated, write *C*.

EXAMPLE   **1.** Our dog startled by the noise began to bark.

    1. Our dog, startled by the noise, began to bark.

1. People, visiting the reservation, will be barred from burial sites, which are considered holy by American Indians.

2. Players breaking training will be dismissed from the team.   **2.** C

3. Students, planning to go on the field trip, should bring their lunches.

4. When Tony, holding up a parsnip, asked whether parsnips are related to carrots, I said, "Well, they certainly look alike."

5. Joe told me that kudzu, introduced into the United States in the 1800s, now grows in much of the South.

6. Elizabeth Blackwell, completing her medical studies in 1849, became the first female doctor in the United States.

7. Pressure and heat acting on the remains of plants and animals turn those remains into gas or oil or coal.   **7. C**

8. Every child, registering for school for the first time, must present evidence of certain vaccinations.

9. The astronauts living in the space station studied the effects of weightlessness.   **9. C**

10. Windsor Castle, built during the reigns of Henry III and Edward III, stands twenty-one miles west of London.

Review B **Correcting Sentences with Nonessential Clauses and Participial Phrases by Adding Commas**

Some of the following sentences contain clauses and phrases that need to be set off by commas. If a sentence is incorrect, add the necessary comma or commas. If a sentence is already correctly punctuated, write *C*.

EXAMPLE   **1.** Hanukkah which is also called the Feast of Lights is a major Jewish celebration.

   1. Hanukkah, which is also called the Feast of Lights, is a major Jewish celebration.

1. The picture on this page shows a part of the Hanukkah celebration that is very beautiful.   **1. C**

2. The girl, following an ancient custom, is lighting the menorah.

3. The menorah, which is an eight-branched candlestick, symbolizes the original festival.

4. Hanukkah, which means "dedication," celebrates the rededication of the Temple of Jerusalem in 165 B.C.

5. This event followed the Jewish people's victory over Syria, which was led by a pagan king.   **5. C**

6. During the first Hanukkah, according to traditional lore, the Jews had a one-day supply of lamp oil that lasted for eight days.   **6. C**

7. Today, celebrating the memory of this miraculous event, modern Jews light one candle on the menorah each day of the eight-day festival.

8. Hanukkah starts on the twenty-fifth day of the Hebrew month of Kislev, which is usually in December on the Gregorian calendar.

Commas   **651**

Meeting
INDIVIDUAL NEEDS

MODALITIES

Auditory Learners. Have students work in groups of three on **Review B.** Students should rotate to a new position with each sentence. Have one student read each sentence aloud while another student writes it, adding commas where necessary. The third student then checks the sentences against the rules to see if each comma is in the right place.

ENGLISH-LANGUAGE LEARNERS

Russian. In Russian, almost all subordinate clauses are set off by commas, even if the clauses are essential. For example, "I wonder, who is playing that trombone. Maybe it's the radio, that I am hearing." Tell students to avoid putting commas around essential clauses.

9. The festival‚celebrated all over the world‚is a time of feasting, gift giving, and happiness.
10. During Hanukkah, children play a game with a dreidel‚which is a four-sided toy that is like a top.

Review C **Correcting Sentences by Adding Commas**

Add commas where they are needed in the following sentences. If a sentence does not require any commas, write *C*.

Optional commas are underscored.

EXAMPLE 1. The emu is a large flightless bird from Australia.

1. *The emu is a large, flightless bird from Australia.*

1. The students sold crafts‚used books‚and baked goods at the bazaar.
2. John Wayne‚whose real name was Marion Morrison‚won an Academy Award for *True Grit*.
3. Add flour‚mix the ingredients‚and stir the batter.
4. People who come to the game early will be allowed to take pictures of the players. **4. C**
5. *Exiles*‚written by James Joyce‚will be performed by the Grantville Community Players and will run for three weeks.
6. The float in the homecoming parade was covered with large‚pink rose petals and small‚silvery spangles.
7. Members of the committee met for three hours‚but they still have not chosen a theme for the dance.
8. Helium‚which is used by balloonists‚deep-sea divers‚and welders‚is an inert gas.
9. An eclipse that occurs when the earth prevents the sun's light from reflecting off the moon is called a lunar eclipse. **9. C**
10. In one month our little town was hit by a tornado and a flood and a fire‚yet we managed to survive.

Introductory Elements

22i. Use commas after certain introductory elements.

(1) Use a comma to set off a mild exclamation such as *well, oh,* or *why* at the beginning of a sentence. Other introductory words such as *yes* and *no* are also set off with commas.

EXAMPLES **Why,** you're Andy's brother, aren't you?

Yes, she's going to the cafeteria.

(2) Use a comma after an introductory participial phrase.

EXAMPLES   **Switching on a flashlight,** the ranger led the way down the path to the caves.

Disappointed by the high prices, we made up a new gift list.

Given a choice, I would rather work in the yard early in the morning.

(3) Use a comma after two or more introductory prepositional phrases or after a long one.

EXAMPLES   **Near the door to the garage,** you will find hooks for the car keys.

Inside the fence at the far end of her property, she built a potting shed.

By the time they had finished, the boys were exhausted.

NOTE One short introductory prepositional phrase does not require a comma unless the comma is necessary to make the meaning clear.

EXAMPLES   **At our house** we share all the work.

At our house, plants grow best in the sunny, bright kitchen. [The comma is necessary to avoid reading *house plants.*]

(4) Use a comma after an introductory adverb clause.

EXAMPLES   **After Andrés Segovia had played his last guitar concert,** the audience applauded for more than fifteen minutes.

If you see smoke, you know there is a fire.

NOTE An adverb clause in the middle or at the end of a sentence is generally not set off by a comma.

EXAMPLES   Miranda, please remember to phone me **when you get home this evening.** [No comma is necessary between *me* and *when.*]

We stayed a long time **because we were having fun.** [No comma is necessary between *time* and *because.*]

Reference Note
For information on **participial phrases,** see page 451. For information on **prepositional phrases,** see page 442.

Reference Note
For information on **adverb clauses,** see page 475.

Relating to Speaking and Listening

Assign students to small groups, and tell group members to have a conversation using sentences that start with an introductory element. Tell them they will naturally have slight pauses in their spoken sentences where commas would be if the sentences were written. You might encourage the conversation by offering pictures or topics such as "A Day at a Theme Park," "An Aquarium Tour," or "My Most Exciting or Enlightening Experience." Have students speak in the order in which they are seated so that all of them speak an equal number of times. You might want to tape-record the conversations and play the tape for the class to analyze where the pauses occur that signify places where commas would be in written sentences.

MECHANICS

Commas   **653**

Viewing the Art

Exploring the Subject. Chinese art has a lengthy history that predates Western civilization. Although art styles changed with the dynasties, one characteristic of Chinese art that has remained constant throughout its history is the depiction of nature as the main subject of artwork. There are many examples of nature found in Chinese art. One bronze container from the Shang dynasty incorporates animal features into parts of the vessel. In the Chou dynasty, animals became more ornamental, as with a dragon adjoined to a plate.

Meeting
INDIVIDUAL
NEEDS

MODALITIES

Visual Learners. To help students visualize specific comma usage rules, show examples in three columns on the chalkboard. Label the columns "Nonessential Clause," "Introductory Element," and "Interrupter." Then, help students write their own examples. Ask volunteers to put their sentences in the proper columns. For example:

NONESSENTIAL CLAUSE	INTRODUCTORY ELEMENT	INTERRUPTER
Nico, who passed the test, was exempt from the course.	Before he could get to the gym, the rainstorm began.	Charlie, my neighbor, will soon be moving.

Exercise 8 **Correcting Sentences with Introductory Elements by Adding Commas**

Add commas where they are needed after introductory elements in the following sentences. If a sentence is already correct, write *C*.

EXAMPLE   1. When Marco Polo visited China in the thirteenth century he found an advanced civilization.

1. *When Marco Polo visited China in the thirteenth century, he found an advanced civilization.*

1. Although there was a great deal of poverty in China the ruling classes lived in splendor.
2. Valuing cleanliness, Chinese rulers took baths every day.   2. C
3. Instead of using coins as currency the Chinese used paper money.
4. After marrying a Chinese woman usually lived in her mother-in-law's home.
5. After one Chinese emperor had died he was buried with more than eight thousand statues of servants and horses.
6. Respected by their descendants elderly people were highly honored.
7. Built around 200 B.C. the main part of the Great Wall of China is about four thousand miles long.
8. Why until modern freeways were built, the Great Wall was the world's longest construction.
9. In the painting on this page you can see that Chinese landscapes look different from those created by Western artists.
10. In Chinese art people are very small and are usually shown in harmony with nature.   10. [*or C*]

Interrupters

22j. Use commas to set off elements that interrupt the sentence.

Two commas are used around an interrupting element—one before and one after.

EXAMPLES   His guitar, **according to him,** once belonged to Bo Diddley.

Mr. Gonzales, **my civics teacher,** encouraged me to enter my essay in the contest.

Sometimes an "interrupter" comes at the beginning or at the end of a sentence. In such cases, only one comma is needed.

EXAMPLES   **Nevertheless,** you must go with me.

I need the money, **Josh.**

(1) Nonessential appositives and nonessential appositive phrases should be set off with commas.

A *nonessential* (or *nonrestrictive*) *appositive* or *appositive phrase* provides information that is unnecessary to the basic meaning of the sentence.

EXAMPLES   Their new parrot, **Mina,** is very gentle. [The sentence means the same thing without the appositive.]

Elizabeth Peña, **my favorite actress,** stars in the movie I rented. [The sentence means the same thing without the appositive phrase.]

An *essential* (or *restrictive*) *appositive* or *appositive phrase* adds information that makes the noun or pronoun it identifies more specific.

EXAMPLES   My friend **Tamisha** lost her wallet. [The writer has more than one friend. *Tamisha* identifies which friend. The meaning of the sentence changes without the appositive.]

He recited the second stanza of "Childhood" by the poet **Margaret Walker.** [The appositive *Margaret Walker* identifies which poet.]

We **art club members** made the decorations. [The appositive phrase *art club members* explains who is meant by *We.*]

Reference Note

For more information on **appositives** and **appositive phrases,** see page 461.

> **Exercise 9** **Correcting Sentences with Appositives and Appositive Phrases by Adding Commas**

Correctly use commas to punctuate the appositives in the following sentences. If a sentence needs no commas, write *C.*

EXAMPLE   **1.** My cousin consulted Dr. Moniz an allergy specialist about the harmful effects of pollution.

1. *My cousin consulted Dr. Moniz, an allergy specialist, about the harmful effects of pollution.*

1. *Ecology,* an obscure word forty years ago, is now a popular term.
2. The word *ecology* comes from *oikos,* the Greek word meaning "house."   **2.** C

Commas   **655**

MECHANICS

> **Exercise 9**

ALTERNATIVE LESSON
To help students see the relationship between appositives and adjective clauses, have them rewrite sentences 1, 7, and 10, changing the appositives into adjective clauses.

1. *Ecology,* which was an obscure word forty years ago, is now a popular term.

7. She and many of her friends attended Earth Day, which is a festival devoted to ecology.

10. The mayor, who was a member of the audience, promised to appoint a committee to study the problem.

3. Ecology is the study of an enormous "house," the world of all living things.
4. Ecologists study the bond of a living organism to its environment, the place in which it lives.
5. Humans, one kind of living organism, affect their environment in both beneficial and harmful ways.
6. My twin sister, Margaret Anne, is worried about the future of the environment.
7. She and many of her friends attended Earth Day, a festival devoted to ecology.
8. An amateur photographer, my cousin prepared a slide show on soil erosion in Grant Park.
9. One of many displays at the Earth Day Festival, my cousin's presentation attracted wide attention and won a prize.
10. The mayor, a member of the audience, promised to appoint a committee to study the problem.

(2) Words used in direct address are set off by commas.

EXAMPLES   **Linda,** you know the rules.

I did that exercise last night, **Ms. Ryan.**

Sir, are these your keys?

Your room, **Bernice,** needs cleaning.

Exercise 10   **Correcting Sentences with Words in Direct Address by Adding Commas**

Correct the following sentences by adding commas where they are needed.

EXAMPLE   1. Annabella when will you be at the station?

         1. Annabella, when will you be at the station?

1. Dad, why can't I go to the movies tonight?
2. As soon as you're ready, Virginia, we'll leave; the car is all packed, and the gas tank is full.
3. Yes, Mom, I washed the dishes.
4. What we need, Mayor Wilson, are more playgrounds.
5. Will you answer the last question, Jim?
6. Rex, fetch the ball!
7. I think, ma'am, that my piano playing has improved this year.

Meeting INDIVIDUAL NEEDS

INCLUSION

Have students work with helpers to use the sentences in **Exercise 10** as a pattern for their own sentences. Have the helper create a sentence modeled on sentence 1. [*Mom, may I go to the homecoming game tomorrow?*] Then, have students create their own versions of sentence 1 and state them orally to their helpers. Students should also tell what punctuation is needed. After students have created several sentences based on sentence 1, have them write or dictate their own versions of three more of the sentences in **Exercise 10.**

8. We left some for you, Bella.
9. José, how far from here is the teen recreation center that has the heated swimming pool?
10. May I help you with the gardening, Grandma?

(3) Parenthetical expressions are set off by commas.

Parenthetical expressions are side remarks that add information or relate ideas.

Reference Note

For information on using **parentheses** and **dashes** to set off parenthetical expressions, see Chapter 26.

Commonly Used Parenthetical Expressions		
after all	generally speaking	nevertheless
at any rate	however	of course
consequently	I believe	on the contrary
for example	in the first place	on the other hand
for instance	moreover	therefore

EXAMPLES **Of course,** I am glad that he called me about the extra movie tickets.

She is, **in fact,** a dentist.

You should try out for quarterback, **in my opinion.**

Some expressions may be used either parenthetically or not parenthetically. Do not set them off with commas unless they're truly parenthetical.

EXAMPLES Sandra will, **I think,** enjoy the program. [parenthetical]
I think Sandra will enjoy the program. [not parenthetical]

However, Phuong Vu finished her report on time. [parenthetical]
However did Phuong Vu finish her report on time? [not parenthetical—similar to "How did she finish?"]

To tell the truth, he tries. [parenthetical]
He tries **to tell the truth.** [not parenthetical]

After all, we've been through this situation before. [parenthetical]
After all we've been through, we need a vacation. [not parenthetical]

Commas **657**

MECHANICS

MINI-LESSON

Parenthetical Expressions. To help students use commas with parenthetical expressions, have them choose favorite pieces of writing from their portfolios and exchange papers with partners. Next, have each student choose a parenthetical expression from the list on p. 657 and rewrite a sentence from his or her partner's paper, including the expression and proper punctuation. Finally, ask students to return the sample sentences to the original authors and to explain why they chose particular parenthetical expressions.

Critical Thinking

Metacognition. To help students analyze the processes they use in working **Exercise 11,** first have them complete the exercise. Then, randomly assign two sentences from the exercise to each student. Have students explain in their Language Logs how they selected the punctuation they used. After students have written their analyses, ask for volunteers to read explanations of their processes, and allow others to offer alternative processes.

NOTE A contrasting expression introduced by *not* is parenthetical and should be set off by commas.

EXAMPLES The divisor, **not the dividend,** is the bottom number of a fraction.

The coach and I believe the winner of the long jump will be Rachel, **not her.**

Exercise 11 **Correcting Sentences with Parenthetical Expressions by Adding Commas**

Correctly punctuate the parenthetical expressions in the following sentences.

EXAMPLE 1. In my opinion my little sister Iona has great taste in music.

1. *In my opinion, my little sister Iona has great taste in music.*

1. For instance, her favorite collection of songs is called *Gift of the Tortoise.*
2. Performed, I believe, by Ladysmith Black Mambazo, the lyrics of the songs are a blend of English and Zulu words and phrases.
3. The South African performers, in fact, sing a cappella (without musical instruments accompanying them).
4. Not surprisingly, their powerful style of music is known by millions of people worldwide.
5. Fudugazi, by the way, is the storytelling tortoise who explains the meaning of the songs.
6. By listening to the song "Finger Dance," Iona has learned, believe it or not, to count to five in Zulu.
7. She has not yet learned to sing any of her favorite songs in Zulu, however.
8. Of course, our whole family enjoys listening to these lovely South African songs.
9. The spirited music and moving sound effects, moreover, seem to transport us to a faraway land and culture.
10. Everyone should, I think, follow Fudugazi's advice: "There is magic in these songs; close your eyes and listen, and you will feel the magic, too!"

Learning for Life

Continued on pp. 659–660

Writing Letters to Public Figures. To give students practice with the comma rules covered in this chapter, ask them to write letters about issues important to them. Allow the class to brainstorm possible important issues [*pollution, curfews, summer jobs, teenage* *smoking, and so forth*] and possible public figures who could address these issues.

Then, assign students to small groups that share a common issue, and have members discuss specifically what they want to achieve or request. Students may discover

Conventional Uses of Commas

22k. Use commas in certain conventional situations.

(1) Use commas to separate items in dates and addresses.

EXAMPLES After Tuesday, November 23, 2001, address all orders to
Emeryville, CA 94608.

Please send your cards by November 23, 2000, to 7856
Hidalgo Way, Emeryville, CA 94608.

Notice that no comma divides the month and day (November 23) or
the house number and the street name (7856 Hidalgo Way) because
each is considered one item. Also, the ZIP Code is not separated from
the abbreviation of the state by a comma (Emeryville, CA 94608).

> NOTE Commas are not needed if the day precedes the month or if only
> the month and year are given.
>
> EXAMPLES President Bill Clinton took office on **20 January 1993.**
>
> Hurricane Andrew hit southern Florida in **August 1992.**

(2) Use a comma after the salutation of a personal letter and after
the closing of any letter.

EXAMPLES Dear Mr. Arpajian,   Sincerely yours,

My dear Anna,   Yours very truly,

(3) Use commas to set off abbreviations such as *Jr., Sr.,* or *M.D.*
when they follow persons' names.

EXAMPLES Please welcome Allen Davis, Sr.

Carol Ferrara, M.D., is our family physician.

Review D Correcting Sentences by Adding Commas

Add commas where they are needed in the following sentences. If a
sentence is already correct, write *C.*

EXAMPLE   **1.** On July 14 1789 the people of Paris stormed the Bastille.
            1. On July 14, 1789, the people of Paris stormed the Bastille.

1. Please address the envelope to Ms. Marybeth Correio, 1255 S.E.
   56th Street, Bellevue, WA 98006.

┌─ **HELP** ─
Use a colon
after the salutation of
a business letter.

EXAMPLE
  Dear Service Manager:

Reference Note
For more about using
colons, see page 675.
For more about writing
business letters, see
"Writing" in the Quick
Reference Handbook.

Meeting
INDIVIDUAL
NEEDS

MODALITIES

Visual Learners. To illustrate two
common uses of commas, write the
following sentence on the chalkboard:

> Halley's comet could be seen in the
> night sky on November 30 1835 in
> the town of Florida Missouri the
> birthplace of Samuel Clemens.

After students have read the sentence, ask them whether they spotted any mistakes. Have volunteers
use colored chalk to insert commas in
the proper places. Then, ask other
students to explain why these commas were included in the text.

*[Halley's comet could be seen in the
night sky on November 30, 1835, in
the town of Florida, Missouri, the
birthplace of Samuel Clemens.]*

MECHANICS

---

that there are several aspects of the problem
they would like to deal with and that a variety of people might be able to help them. If
so, have the group divide the topic and the
people to be addressed so that each student

has a topic and a person to address.
Otherwise, more than one student could
write a letter to the same public figure.

Next, have each student write and share
with the group a rough draft of his or her

Relating to Literature

As a review of punctuation usage, have students select a poem with commas—like "American Hero," "Lucinda Matlock," or "The Road Not Taken"—from their literature anthology. Assign students to work in small groups based on their choice of poem, and have them analyze the poem's punctuation. Students should suggest a punctuation rule to apply to each comma used in the poem. (You may want to tell students that since writing poetry is a highly creative activity, poets may sometimes ignore standard comma use.) Have groups share their poems and their analyses with the class.

TEACHING TIP

Review E You may wish to use the first ten items in **Review E** as guided practice. Then, have students complete the review as independent practice.

2. Sources claim that on April 6, 1909, Matthew Henson, assistant to Commander Robert E. Peary, reached the North Pole.
3. I glanced quickly at the end of the letter, which read, "Very sincerely yours, Alice Ems, Ph.D."
4. The Constitution of the United States was signed on September 17, 1787, eleven years after the adoption of the Declaration of Independence on July 4, 1776.
   5. C
5. Did you go on a field trip to the desert in March or April of 1999?
6. We used to live in Monterrey, but now we live at 100 Robin Road, Austin, Texas.
7. Tony, watch out for that spider.
8. My grandmother, a Russian, learned English late in life.
9. That man is the governor, by the way.
10. The gauchos crossed the hot, windy, vast expanse of the pampas.

Unnecessary Commas

22l. Do not use unnecessary commas.

Have a reason for every comma and other mark of punctuation that you use. When there is no rule requiring punctuation and when the meaning of the sentence is clear without it, do not insert any punctuation mark.

INCORRECT   My friend, Jessica, said she would feed my cat, and my dog while I'm away, but now, she tells me, she will be too busy.

CORRECT   My friend Jessica said she would feed my cat and my dog while I'm away, but now she tells me she will be too busy.

Review E   Correcting Sentences by Adding Commas

For each of the following sentences, write all the words that should be followed by a comma. Place a comma after each of these words.

EXAMPLE   1. Yes Phyllis I know that you want to transfer to Bayside the high school that has the best volleyball team in the city.

   1. *Yes, Phyllis, Bayside,*

Optional commas are underscored.

1. Scuttling across the dirt road, the large, hairy spider, a tarantula, terrified Steve, Ellen, and me.
2. Whitney, not Don, won first prize.
3. German shepherds are often trained as guide dogs; other breeds that have also been trained include Labrador retrievers, golden retrievers, and Doberman pinschers.

Learning for Life

letter. Once the content of each letter has been evaluated and revised, ask students to create double-spaced copies and to write beneath the commas the numbers of the rules that apply to each comma they used.

Then, have students get input from other group members. After you have reviewed their work and students have written their final drafts, have them send their letters.

4. According to her official birth certificate, Mary Elizabeth was born September 7, 1976, in Juneau, Alaska, but she does not remember much of the city.

5. Angela and Jennifer, are you both planning to write poems to enter in the contest?

6. All entries for the essay-writing competition should be submitted no later than Friday to Essay Contest, 716 North Cliff Drive, Salt Lake City, UT 84103.

7. The best time to plant flower seeds, of course, is just before a rainy season, not in the middle of a hot, dry summer.

8. Our next-door neighbor, Ms. Allen, manages two large apartment buildings downtown.

9. As a matter of fact, most horses can run four miles without having to stop.

10. The Comanches, like some other nomadic American Indians, once traveled throughout the states of Kansas, New Mexico, Texas, and Oklahoma.

11. My favorite story, "The Most Dangerous Game," was written back in 1924.

12. Even though I ran quickly around the base of the tree, the squirrel always stayed on the opposite side of the tree from me.

13. We planted irises because they are perennials, flowers that bloom year after year.

14. One of Cleopatra's Needles, famous stone pillars from ancient Egypt, stands in Central Park in New York City, New York.

15. In April 1976, a fifth-grader in Newburgh, New York, released a helium balloon; it was found in Strathaven, Scotland, on the other side of the Atlantic Ocean two days later.

16. Danny's father just bought a 1967 Ford Mustang with green, white, and red stripes on the sides.

17. Before we begin reading *The Odyssey*, we will see a movie about ancient Greece.

18. Mount Waialeale, Hawaii, receives an average of 460 inches of rain each year, making it the rainiest place in the world.

19. A light frost was on the ground, the leaves were falling, the air was cool, and the wind was blowing stronger; autumn had arrived overnight.

20. The performance of our school's spring musical has been sold out for weeks, but those of us who helped build the set will get free tickets.

TECHNOLOGY TIP

Let the Web help you create a practical punctuation-editing review. When people visit chat rooms at various Web sites on the Internet, they often type conversations very hastily and make many errors in punctuation. Print out a page or two of conversation from an appropriate site. Have students correct any errors in end-mark usage and comma usage. Then, you can have students discuss their changes in class. *Preview any Internet activity that you suggest to students. Because these resources are public forums, their content can be unpredictable.*

Review **F** Adding End Marks and Commas

Add end marks and commas where they are needed in each sentence in the following paragraph.

EXAMPLE **[1]** As you can see from the map below Cabeza de Vaca explored areas in North America and South America

1. *As you can see from the map below, Cabeza de Vaca explored areas in North America and South America.*

[1] Did you know that Álvar Núñez Cabeza de Vaca a Spanish explorer participated in two trips to this region [2] To tell the truth neither trip ended successfully [3] In the summer of 1527 he was treasurer of an expedition that was sent to conquer and colonize Florida. [4] However the invasion didn't work out as planned and he was one of a handful of survivors [5] These men intended to sail to Mexico but their ship wrecked off the coast of Texas. [6] What an unlucky expedition that was [7] Cabeza de Vaca was captured by a native people but he later escaped and wandered through Texas and Mexico for eight years [8] He tells about his Florida expedition in the book *Naufragios* which has the Spanish word for "shipwrecks" as its title. [9] In 1541 this adventurer led an expedition to South America and he became governor of Paraguay [10] When the colonists revolted Cabeza de Vaca returned to Spain under arrest but he was later pardoned.

Chapter Review

A. Correcting Sentences by Adding End Marks and Commas

Most of the following sentences contain errors in the use of end marks and commas. Write each sentence, adding end marks and commas where needed. If no additional punctuation is needed, write *C*.

1. She says tae kwon do, a Korean martial art, improves concentration.
2. Well, that's the last time that I'll ever ride in one of those taxis.
3. Is the card addressed to Robert Danieli, Jr., or to Robert Danieli?
4. The batter, hoping to advance the runners, laid down a perfect bunt.
5. Use light colors, by the way, to make a small room seem larger.
6. We used to live in Lansing, but now we live at 457 Cleveland Road, Huntsville, Alabama.
7. Did you ask Joe to bring the forks, plates, and cups to the picnic?
8. What an interesting, enjoyable book that is!
9. When we complained to Mrs. Finch about the remark, she apologized to us.
10. Reva, look out for that pothole in the road.   **10.** [*or . . .* road!]
11. If the worn tire had not been replaced, it could have caused an accident.
12. The green flag, the signal to begin the race, was seen by thousands.
13. Send your application to Box 36, New York, NY, before June 30, 2003.
14. Your homework, of course, must be finished before you go hiking.
15. Sitting on their front porch, my grandparents talk to the children who pass.
16. We looked after our neighbors' dog while they toured Canada for two weeks, and they offered to feed our cat next Thanksgiving.
17. Wow, this movie is exciting.   **17.** [*or . . .* exciting!]
18. People watching the parade were sitting on curbs and standing on sidewalks.   **18.** C
19. At the convenience store on the corner, my sister bought juice.
20. Désirée, I would like to know your secret for a beautiful complexion.

Using the Chapter Review

To assess student progress, you may want to compare the types of items missed on the **Diagnostic Preview** to those missed on the **Chapter Review**. If students have not made significant progress, you may want to refer them to **Chapter 28: Correcting Common Errors, Exercises 29** and **30**, for additional practice.

MECHANICS

B. Using Periods, Question Marks, and Exclamation Points

Add commas, periods, question marks, and exclamation points where needed in the following sentences. Identify each sentence as *declarative*, *imperative*, *interrogative*, or *exclamatory*.
Optional commas are underscored.

21. Did the author Willa Cather write about life on the prairie? **21. int.**
22. Angelo had cereal, a muffin, a boiled egg, and toast for breakfast. **22. dec.**
23. How long did that project take? **23. int.**
24. Well, wouldn't hearing Domingo sing be worth the trip? **24. int.**
25. Oh boy, what a great idea! **25. exc.**
26. Students, sign up in the office if you are going on the field trip. **26. imp.**
27. You will find the test on my desk, which is near the bookcase. **27. dec.**
28. Rita wants to invite Ingrid, Ingrid's cousin, and their friend Jamila. **28. dec.**
29. My younger sister, who will be twelve, wants to have a birthday party. **29. dec.**
30. Turn down the radio. **30.** [*or* radio!] **imp.**

C. Using Abbreviations

Rewrite the following sentences, correcting errors in the use of abbreviations. Answers may vary.

31. The guest of honor was Dr. Steve Welch, ~~M. D.~~
32. ~~Maj. Gen.~~ McCambridge, the base commander, was on TV. **32. Major General**
33. This statue was probably sculpted between ⟨B.C.⟩ 500 and 400.
34. At 9:35 A.M. ~~in the morning,~~ the race started.
35. Following family custom, Samuel Brandt, ~~Junior,~~ named his first-born son Samuel Brandt III. **35. Jr.**
36. The interns working in the ~~ER~~ enjoyed the challenges and the unpredictability of life in an ~~emergency room.~~ **36. emergency room / ER⊙**
37. In ⟨1271⟩ A.D., the Italian adventurer Marco Polo left Venice on his long voyage to China.
38. My parents spent their early years in Wilmington, ~~DE~~, and Miami, ~~FL.~~ **38. Delaware / Florida**
39. The explorers set up camp in what would later become Seattle, ~~Wash.~~ **39. Washington**
40. The speeding car was clocked at seventy-five ~~m.p.h.~~ **40. miles per hour**

D. Proofreading a Paragraph for End Marks and Commas

In the following paragraph, insert end marks and commas as needed.

[41] As I took photos last Saturday with an instant camera, I became increasingly curious about the origin of this type of camera. [42] Being the persistent seeker after knowledge that I am, how could I not spend time the next day researching the topic? [43] The results of my research, needless to say, were quite interesting. [44] Apparently, Edwin Land's daughter once asked him why a camera couldn't immediately produce pictures. [45] Land, who had taught himself physics, quickly worked out the basic principles and design of an instant camera. [46] What a tremendous achievement that was! [47] He became head of Polaroid Corp. and that company produced the first Polaroid Land camera in 1948. [48] Did you know that Land later made important contributions to the study of lasers and color vision? [49] Land died on March 1, 1991. [50] Among his honors were the Presidential Medal of Freedom and, of course, the National Medal of Science.

47. [or Corporation]

Writing Application

Writing Clear Directions

Using Commas   A friend asks you for directions from your school to a particular destination. In your instructions, use commas to separate items in a series, to join independent clauses, to set off an introductory adverb clause, to set off a noun of direct address, and to separate items in an address.

Prewriting   Choose a destination (real or imagined), and then outline on paper the way to get there.

Writing   As you write your first draft, concentrate on making the directions clear and easy to follow.

Revising   Read your directions to be sure they are arranged in a logical order. Check to see that you have used commas in the five ways specified in the instructions for this writing activity.

Publishing   Proofread your directions for correct grammar and punctuation. You and your classmates may want to collect your directions into a newcomers' guide for new students at your school.

Writing Application

(p. 665)

OBJECTIVE

■ **To write directions using commas correctly**

Writing Application

Tip. This activity involves many concepts. Students will have to use what they know about writing imperative sentences. Also, organization is important because students will have to specify actual steps that follow a prescribed order.

Scoring Rubric. While you will want to pay particular attention to students' use of commas, you will also want to evaluate overall writing performance. You may want to give a split score to assess development and clarity of the composition as well as mechanics skills.

CHAPTER
23 Punctuation
Semicolons and Colons

Diagnostic Preview

A. Correcting Sentences by Adding Semicolons and Colons

For the following sentences, write each word or numeral that should be followed by a semicolon or colon, and then insert the missing semicolon or colon. If a sentence is already correct, write *C*.

EXAMPLE 1. Someday, robots may do many simple household chores, wash windows, answer the telephone, make repairs, and serve dinner.

1. *chores:*

1. I didn't go to the game last night, instead, I took care of my baby brother, Carl.   **1. night;**
2. The band members will perform at the civic center on Tuesday, January 15, at the Kiwanis Club on Saturday, January 19, and at the Oak Nursing Home on Friday, January 25.   **2. 15;/19;**
3. For the lesson on figures of speech, we had to find examples of similes, metaphors, personification, and hyperbole.   **3. C**
4. Dr. Enríquez has traveled to rain forests in many parts of the world, Borneo, Brazil, Costa Rica, and Sri Lanka.   **4. world:**
5. The first Spaniards who settled in America built forts, missions, and pueblos, evidence of Spanish influence on American architecture can be found throughout the Southwest.   **5. pueblos;**

666

6. The Tower of Babel, as described in Genesis 11 1–9, resembled a ziggurat, or terraced pyramid.   **6. 11:1–9**

7. Erica seldom misses a football playoff on TV, last Saturday, for example, she watched the NFC championship game from noon to 3 00 P.M.   **7. TV; / 3:00**

8. I invited Peggy, Josefina, and Sonya, and Beth, Errol, and Randy are coming too.   **8. Sonya;**

9. My brother doesn't like many TV shows; instead of watching TV, he prefers to read books.   **9. C**

10. follows:

10. The events for the annual Ironman Triathlon, which is held in Hawaii and is open to men and to women, are as follows, swimming in the ocean 2.4 miles, bicycling 112 miles, and running 26.2 miles.

B. Proofreading a Letter for Correct Use of Semicolons and Colons

Find the ten places where a semicolon or a colon should be used in the following letter. Write each word or number that should be followed by a semicolon or a colon; then, add the necessary punctuation mark.

EXAMPLE   **[1]** Last summer we stayed home during summer vacation, this summer we took a trip in the car.

   1. vacation;

290 Eureka Street
Dallas, TX 76013

August 15, 2001

Director
California Department of Parks and Recreation
Box 2390
Sacramento, CA 95811

[11] Dear Sir or Madam,

   [12] While on vacation this summer, my family and I visited the following states Washington, Oregon, and California. **[13]** We wanted you to know that we especially enjoyed our stay in California, we learned a lot and are planning to return soon.

   [14] What we liked best was visiting the Spanish missions in the Los Angeles area they gave us a real sense of history. **[15]** My favorite places were Mission San Fernando Rey de España, located in Mission Hills, Mission San Gabriel Arcangel, located in San Gabriel, and El Pueblo de Los Angeles. **[16]** The Old Plaza Church, Nuestra Señora la

11. Madam:

12. states:
13. California;

14. area:

15. Hills; / Gabriel;

Looking at Language

History of Printing. Imagine a situation in which a writer could decide that a semicolon looked attractive between a subject and its predicate or a word processor ran out of commas. Centuries ago there were no standardized punctuation rules: Writers or scribes used punctuation at will, and typesetters punctuated sentences based on the type they had available in their typecases.

Regularization of printing and punctuation began in Italy in the 1400s and 1500s. The consistent use of specific symbols by an Italian printer, Aldus Manutius, was one origin of the systematic punctuation used in many languages today.

16. wonderful**;**
    / 5**:**00

17. great**;**

18. Francisco**;**

Reina de Los Angeles, which dates from 1822, was especially <u>wonder-</u><u>ful</u>, we stayed there from noon to <u>500</u> P.M., when the mission closed.
   [17] Our stay in California was <u>great</u>, we hope to return next summer when we will have more time. **[18]** I would like to visit some of the missions around San <u>Francisco</u> therefore, I would appreciate it if you could send me some information on that area. Thank you very much.

Yours truly,

Angie Barnes

Angie Barnes

Semicolons

Rules 23a–d *(pp. 668–675)*

OBJECTIVE

- **To correct sentences by adding semicolons between independent clauses**

STYLE TIP

Use a semicolon to join independent clauses only if the ideas in the clauses are closely related.

INCORRECT
   Josh wants to go to Venezuela; Elaine wants to swim.

CORRECT
   Josh wants to go to Venezuela**;** Elaine wants to go to Paraguay.

Reference Note
For information on **simple and compound sentences,** see page 481.

Semicolons

23a. Use a semicolon between independent clauses that are closely related in meaning if they are not joined by *and, but, for, nor, or, so,* or *yet.*

Notice in the following pairs of examples that the semicolon takes the place of the comma and the conjunction joining the independent clauses.

EXAMPLES First, I had a sandwich and a glass of milk**,** **and** then I called you for the homework assignment.
   First, I had a sandwich and a glass of milk**;** then I called you for the homework assignment.

   Patty likes to act**,** **but** her sister gets stage fright.
   Patty likes to act**;** her sister gets stage fright.

Similarly, a semicolon can take the place of a period to join two or more clauses that are closely related.

EXAMPLES Manuel looked out at the downpour**.** **T**hen he put on his raincoat and boots. [two simple sentences]
   Manuel looked out at the downpour**;** then he put on his raincoat and boots. [one compound sentence]

   Rain soaked the earth**.** **P**lants became green**.** **F**ragrant flowers bloomed. [three simple sentences]
   Rain soaked the earth**;** plants became green**;** fragrant flowers bloomed. [one compound sentence]

MECHANICS

Exercise 1 Correcting Sentences by Adding
Semicolons Between Independent Clauses

Indicate where a semicolon should be placed in each of the following
sentences. In some instances, you may prefer to use a period. Be
prepared to explain your choice.   Answers may vary.

┌HELP─
In the example
for Exercise 1, a semicolon
is used because the two
independent clauses are
closely related.

EXAMPLE   1. Great earthquakes usually begin gently only one or two
               slight shocks move the earth.

           1. *Great earthquakes usually begin gently; only one or two
               slight shocks move the earth.*

1. Pressure builds along faults, or cracks, in the earth's crust the weight
   of this pressure causes earthquakes.
2. The San Andreas fault, shown here, extends nearly the entire
   length of California earthquakes often occur all along this fault.
3. During an earthquake, huge chunks of the earth's crust begin to
   move. The San Francisco earthquake of 1906, pictured here, was
   one of the most destructive earthquakes recorded in history.
4. Energy released during an earthquake is tremendous it
   can equal the explosive force of 180 metric tons of TNT.
5. Scientists study the force of earthquakes they measure
   this force on a scale of numbers called the Richter scale.
6. An earthquake measuring less than 5 on the Richter scale
   is not serious more than 1,000 earthquakes measuring
   2 or less occur daily.
7. In 1906, one of the most powerful earthquakes in history
   occurred in the Pacific Ocean near Ecuador it measured 8.9
   on the Richter scale.
8. Tidal waves are a dangerous result of
   earthquakes geologists use the Japanese
   word *tsunami* for these destructive
   ocean waves.
9. Predicting when earthquakes will occur
   is not yet possible predicting where they
   will occur is somewhat more certain.
10. Earthquakes seem to strike in a regular
    time sequence in California, for example,
    a major earthquake usually occurs every
    fifty to one hundred years.

ENGLISH-LANGUAGE LEARNERS
Spanish. Spanish punctuation rules
do not require that the independent
clauses joined by a semicolon be
closely related. You may want to
define what is meant by "closely
related" in **Rule 23a** on p. 668 and
use the sentences in **Exercise 1** as
examples. (In *1, 2, 4, 5, 7, 8,* and *9,*
the second clause gives additional or
more specific information; in *3, 6,*
and *10,* the second clause provides
examples; and in *4* and *7,* it adds
more specific information.)

Relating to Research
and Speaking

Divide the class into groups of three
to search for semicolons in professional writing. Assign each member
of the group to find semicolons in
one specified source: a novel, a magazine article, or a technical manual.

When students have completed their
searches, have them give brief oral
reports describing where semicolons
are found, how they are used, and
what effect is created by using the
semicolons.

MECHANICS

Crossing the Curriculum

Music. When printers first began to standardize punctuation, one authority compared punctuation marks to musical symbols, equating a period with a whole rest, a colon with a dotted half rest, a semicolon with a half rest, and a comma with a quarter rest.

Critical Thinking

Metacognition. As students become more comfortable with the use of semicolons, ask them to record in their writing logs how they distinguish between the use of commas and semicolons. [*Some students may say they go by the rules; others may say they consider what types of things are being joined and what the relationships are between the things being linked.*]

Meeting

INDIVIDUAL NEEDS

MODALITIES

Visual Learners. Have students create a bulletin board display or poster as an aid to remembering semicolon rules. Students may want to work in small groups to develop sentences as examples for each rule, using oversized and brightly colored semicolons and drawing illustrations for the sentences.

STYLE TIP

Use a semicolon between clauses joined by a coordinating conjunction only when a semicolon is needed to prevent misreading, as in the examples of confusing sentences given for Rule 23c. If a sentence is clear without a semicolon, don't add one just because the clauses contain commas.

EXAMPLE
Lana, you are the best musician I know, and you're a great dancer, too. [clear without semicolon]

23b. Use a semicolon between independent clauses joined by a conjunctive adverb or transitional expression.

EXAMPLES   Emma felt shy; **however,** she soon made some new friends.

My bird does unusual tricks; **for example,** he rings a bell and says "Wow."

Commonly Used Conjunctive Adverbs

accordingly	furthermore	meanwhile	otherwise
also	however	moreover	still
besides	indeed	nevertheless	then
consequently	instead	next	therefore

Commonly Used Transitional Expressions

as a result	for instance	in fact	on the other hand
for example	in addition	that is	in other words

Notice in the examples under Rule 23b that the conjunctive adverb and the transitional expression are preceded by semicolons and followed by commas.

NOTE When a conjunctive adverb or transitional expression appears within one of the clauses and not between clauses, it is usually punctuated as an interrupter (set off by commas). The two clauses are still separated by a semicolon.

EXAMPLES   Our student council voted to have a Crazy Clothes Day; the principal, **however,** vetoed the idea.

That quilt is quite old; it is, **in fact,** filled with cotton, not polyester, batting.

23c. A semicolon (rather than a comma) may be needed to separate independent clauses joined by a coordinating conjunction when the clauses contain commas.

CONFUSING   Alana, Eric, and Kim voted for her, and Scott, Roland, and Vanessa voted for Jason.

CLEAR   Alana, Eric, and Kim voted for her; and Scott, Roland, and Vanessa voted for Jason.

MINI-LESSON

Identifying Independent Clauses.
Students may need a review of independent clauses in order to see clearly where these clauses should be punctuated. Remind students that an independent clause includes a subject and a verb and expresses a complete thought. Refer students to **Chapter 13: Parts of a Sentence** and **Chapter 15: The Clause.**

Ask students to identify independent clauses in each of the following sentences and to add a semicolon between the clauses.

CONFUSING Scanning the horizon for the source of the whirring sound, Pedro saw a huge, green cloud traveling in his direction, and, suddenly recognizing what it was, he knew that the crops soon would be eaten by a horde of grasshoppers.

CLEAR Scanning the horizon for the source of the whirring sound, Pedro saw a huge, green cloud traveling in his direction**;** and, suddenly recognizing what it was, he knew that the crops soon would be eaten by a horde of grasshoppers.

Exercise 2 **Correcting Sentences by Adding Semicolons Between Independent Clauses**

Write each word that should be followed by a semicolon in the following sentences and add the semicolon. In some cases, you may prefer to use a period. Be prepared to explain your choice.   Answers may vary.

EXAMPLE   1. Cape Cod is only one of many attractions in Massachusetts, Boston and the Berkshires are also worth visiting.

1. *Massachusetts;*

1. My mother and I sometimes go to Massachusetts in late summer**;** however, last year we went in July.

2. We visit Cape Cod once a year**;** my grandparents live there, so we always have a place to stay.

3. I miss my friends and sometimes find the yearly trip to Cape Cod boring**.** Besides, my cousins in Massachusetts are all older than I am.

4. To my great surprise, we had a very good time last year**;** we even did some sightseeing in Boston, Plymouth, and Marblehead.

5. One hot day my mother, my grandparents, and I went to the beach**;** and my grandfather, the most active man I know, immediately went down to the water for a swim.

6. My grandfather loves the water and is a strong swimmer**;** nevertheless, because the currents are strong and tricky, we worried when we saw that he was swimming out farther and farther.

7. Grandpa, to our great relief, finally turned around and swam back to shore**;** he was astonished that we had been worried about him.

8. While he was in the water, Mom had gathered driftwood, dug a shallow pit in the sand, and built a fire in it**;** and Grandma had put lobster, corn, and potatoes on the coals.

9. By the time we had finished eating, it was quite late**;** consequently, everyone else on the beach had gone home.

10. We didn't leave for home right away**;** instead, we spent the evening watching the darkening ocean, listening to the whispering waves, and watching the stars come out.

┌─HELP─┐
In the example for Exercise 2, a semicolon is used because the independent clauses are closely related.

Semicolons   **671**

Exercise 2

ALTERNATIVE LESSON
Have students identify by sentence number the following constructions: a sentence with three independent clauses [2]; a compound-complex sentence including a *that* clause used as a direct object [6]; a compound-complex sentence beginning with an adverb clause [8]; a compound sentence including a series of participial phrases [10]; five sentences with independent clauses joined by conjunctive adverbs [1, 3, 6, 9, 10].

MECHANICS

1. I recently visited Savannah, Georgia, it was the first city established in the original thirteen colony. [*I . . . Georgia; it . . . colony.*]

2. Georgia was originally a debtors' colony, it gave people who could never hope to get out of debt in their homeland a second chance. [*Georgia . . . colony; it . . . chance.*]

Semicolons   **671**

23d. Use a semicolon between items in a series if the items contain commas.

EXAMPLES   I would like to introduce Mrs. Boyce, our mayor; Mr. Bell, her secretary; Ms. Lincoln, the editor of our newspaper; and Mr. Quinn, our guest of honor.

The Photography Club will meet on Wednesday, September 12; Wednesday, September 19; and Tuesday, September 25.

Review A Correcting Sentences by Adding Semicolons

Write each word or numeral that should be followed by a semicolon in the following sentences and add the semicolon. If a sentence needs no semicolons, write *C*.

EXAMPLE   1. Tina likes playing basketball, I prefer hockey.
             1. *basketball;*

1. The first passenger jet was Britain's *Comet*, first flown in 1949; it had some problems at first but later became a quite popular plane.
2. On our trip to Paris, my sister wanted to visit the Louvre, but I was more interested in the Eiffel Tower.
3. Africa's kingdoms included Mali, on the Niger River; Benin, in what is now Nigeria; and Mwanamutapa, in southern Africa.
4. Formerly, most cars had carburetors; the newer models have fuel injectors.
5. Many words in modern Japanese come from English; for instance, the word *doonatsu* comes from *doughnut*.
6. The Incas planted crops, such as corn; they domesticated animals, such as the llama; and they developed crafts, such as weaving.
7. Many scientists believe that one of the elephant's closest living relatives is not a large animal at all; surprisingly, it is a small rodentlike creature called the hyrax.
8. Mrs. Gillis said that we could write about Dekanawidah, the Huron founder of the Iroquois League; Mansa Musa, the Muslim emperor of Mali; or Tamerlane, the Mongol conqueror of the Ottoman Turks.
9. Most of Grandmother's belongings were packed away in the attic; however, Mother discovered another suitcase in the cellar, and there were things locked up in the safe-deposit box, too.
10. In the fifteenth century, the kings of France, England, and Spain grew stronger as they unified their lands.

2. C

10. C

Meeting INDIVIDUAL NEEDS

LEARNERS HAVING DIFFICULTY
You may wish to pair students to work on **Review A.** To give students help on where to place semicolons, instruct pairs to identify the subjects and verbs of all independent clauses before they think about where to place the semicolons. Then, have students use the list on p. 670 to identify conjunctive adverbs. Also, have students identify any series of items in which the items contain commas.

MECHANICS

Correcting Sentences by Adding Semicolons

Most of the following sentences contain at least one error in the use of semicolons. Write <u>the word preceding and following each error</u>, and add the semicolon. If a sentence is already correct, write *C*.

EXAMPLE
1. The largest animal in the world today is the blue whale the largest blue whale ever caught measured slightly more than 113.5 feet and weighed about 170 tons.

    1. *whale; the*

1. Each of the more than seventy-five species of whales is <u>different</u> <u>however</u>, all whales migrate with the seasons.
2. Whales, which are warmblooded marine mammals, are divided into two main <u>families</u> <u>these</u> families are the toothed whales (the larger family) and the toothless whales.
3. The biggest toothed whale, the sperm whale, hunts giant squid along the bottom of the <u>ocean</u> <u>like</u> all toothed whales, it uses its teeth for catching food, not chewing it.
4. The sperm whale is a record holder in the animal kingdom; it has the largest brain and the thickest skin. **4.** C
5. Other species of whales include the gray whale, which is probably the best-known toothless <u>whale</u> <u>the</u> Baird's beaked whale, which is also called the giant bottlenose <u>whale</u> <u>the</u> bowhead whale, which is also known as the arctic <u>whale</u> <u>and</u> the killer whale, which is also called *orca*.

Meeting

INDIVIDUAL
NEEDS

MULTIPLE INTELLIGENCES
Spatial Intelligence. You may want to try the following activity to give students additional practice using semicolons. First, assign students to small groups and distribute to each group slips of paper containing words or phrases from one sentence in **Review B**. Next, have groups rearrange the words to form a sentence and add the proper punctuation. Ask students to explain why they arranged the sentence parts and used the punctuation as they did. Repeat the process with other sentences until students are comfortable with using semicolons.

MECHANICS

Semicolons   **673**

6. Whales take very full, deep breaths;consequently, they can dive almost a mile below the surface of the ocean and remain underwater for more than an hour at a time.

7. Some whale species exhibit remarkable social behavior; for example, members of a group may stay with a wounded animal or even support it in the water.   7. C

8. During the past 250 years, whalers have nearly wiped out many species of whales; the whaling industry continues to threaten those species that have managed to survive.

9. Several countries, including the United States, have banned the killing of certain whale species; but the blue whale, which is close to extinction, remains an endangered species.   9. C

10. Whale-watching cruises originated with the public's growing concern over the survival of whales;today whalewatching attracts as many as 350,000 people a year.

Review C **Correcting Sentences by Adding Semicolons**

Most of the following sentences need at least one semicolon. For each incorrectly punctuated sentence, write the word preceding each missing semicolon, the semicolon, and the word following the semicolon. If a sentence needs no semicolon, write *C*.

EXAMPLE   1. American Indian pottery fascinates me, whenever I can, I watch potters like this woman at the Tigua (pronounced TEE-wah) Indian Reservation and Pueblo in El Paso, Texas.

1. *me; whenever*

1. I could have watched for hours as this artist painted designs on the vases; however, I knew that the rest of my family was eager to see more of the reservation.

2. C   2. There is much to see there, and they were determined to see it all!

3. [*or* C]   3. The Tiguas have a large adobe visitors center, where they display their arts and crafts and have dance demonstrations; and my younger brothers, Jaime and Lucas, ran all around it.

4. Of course, we had to sample the Tigua specialties at the restaurant; otherwise, we would have missed a unique experience.

5. I've eaten American Indian dishes in Phoenix, Arizona; Muskogee, Oklahoma; and Taos, New Mexico; but the food at the Tigua Reservation was my favorite.

6. I especially enjoyed the *gorditas,* which are a little like tacos; the bread, which was fresh out of the oven; and the chili, which was very spicy.

Timesaver

Choose a small group of volunteers who have done well on the previous review exercises in this chapter to be roving tutors to help other students with **Review C.** Be sure tutors know the rules and know what questions to ask to help students decide on the correct punctuation. (Example: Does the sentence contain two complete thoughts? What are they? Does the sentence contain a conjunctive adverb or transitional expression? Does it contain a series of items that include commas?)

MECHANICS

7. After lunch, a guide told us that the community was established in 1682 by Tiguas who were displaced from northern New Mexico; he said the reservation is the oldest inhabited community in Texas today.

7. C

8. The Tiguas are especially proud of their mission;they certainly should be.

9. Now known as the Ysleta Mission, it is a beautiful restored building;we enjoyed seeing it.

10. It is the oldest mission in Texas;moreover, it is one of the oldest in all of North America.

Colons

23e. Use a colon to mean "note what follows."

(1) Use a colon before a list of items, especially after expressions like *the following* and *as follows.*

EXAMPLES You will need to bring **the following equipment:** a sleeping bag, a warm sweater, and extra socks.

Additional supplies are **as follows:** a toothbrush, toothpaste, a change of clothes, and a pillow.

Sometimes the items that follow a colon are used as appositives. If a word is followed by a list of appositives, the colon makes the sentence clear.

EXAMPLES At the air base we saw three signs: To Norway, To Paris, and To Lisbon.

You need to shop for several items: brown shoelaces, a quart of milk, and five or six carrots.

Reference Note

For more on **appositives** and **appositive phrases,** see page 461.

Colons **675**

RESOURCES

Colons
Practice
- *Grammar, Usage, and Mechanics,* pp. 280, 281, 282
- *Language Workshop CD-ROM,* Lessons 47, 55

MECHANICS

Colons
Rules 23e, f *(pp. 675–678)*

O B J E C T I V E

- To correct sentences by adding colons

Crossing the Curriculum
Math. Remind students that colons are often used with numbers. A colon is used to separate hours and minutes [2:30 P.M.] and to indicate a ratio [2:3].

Cooperative Learning

Introduce colon usage by offering students a list of activities such as making chili, shopping for groceries, preparing for a camping trip, and so forth. Have each student choose an activity, and form groups based on their choices. Each group should complete the model statement below, adding the proper punctuation.

To _____ , we will need the following items _____.

Be sure students add a colon after the *following items*.

Reference Note

For more about using **long quotations,** see page 690.

---HELP---

Use a comma after the salutation of a personal letter.

EXAMPLES
Dear Kim,

Dear Uncle Remy,

Reference Note

For more about **writing letters,** see "Writing" in the Quick Reference Handbook.

NOTE Do not use a colon between a verb and its complements or between a preposition and its objects.

| INCORRECT | Additional supplies are: a toothbrush and toothpaste, a change of clothes, a towel, a pillow, and an air mattress. |
| CORRECT | Additional supplies are a toothbrush and toothpaste, a change of clothes, a towel, a pillow, and an air mattress. |

| INCORRECT | You need to shop for: brown shoelaces, a quart of milk, and five or six carrots. |
| CORRECT | You need to shop for brown shoelaces, a quart of milk, and five or six carrots. |

(2) Use a colon before a long, formal statement or a long quotation.

EXAMPLE   Horace Mann had this to say: "Do not think of knocking out another person's brains because he differs in opinion from you. It would be as rational to knock yourself on the head because you differ from yourself ten years ago."

(3) Use a colon between independent clauses when the second clause explains or restates the idea of the first.

EXAMPLE   Thomas Jefferson had many talents: He was a writer, a politician, an architect, and an inventor.

NOTE The first word of a sentence following a colon is capitalized.

EXAMPLE   Lois felt that she had done something worthwhile: She had designed and sewn her first quilt.

23f. Use a colon in certain conventional situations.

(1) Use a colon between the hour and the minute.

EXAMPLES   10:30 A.M.   6:30 P.M.

(2) Use a colon between the chapter and the verse in Biblical references and between titles and subtitles.

EXAMPLES   Exodus 1:6–14   *Whales: Giants of the Sea*

(3) Use a colon after the salutation of a business letter.

EXAMPLES   Dear Ms. González: Dear Dr. Fenton:

Dear Sir or Madam: To Whom It May Concern:

TECHNOLOGY TIP

Encourage students to use computers to create their book covers for the **Learning for Life** activity. Students can write the text, set up measurements, lay out the material, and select appropriate type sizes and styles. They can use graphics programs to create designs and pictures and use the spellchecking and grammar-checking features on a word-processing program when proofreading their text.

Learning for Life Continued on pp. 677–678

Correct Colon Usage. Many schools require that students use book covers for their textbooks, and many businesses pay for these covers by placing advertisements on them. Make arrangements with local businesses to have students work with them to write and design these ads. You might want students to work in pairs with one member responsible for the final wording of the ad and the other in charge of generating artwork. Emphasize that students must brainstorm and work out their ideas together.

MECHANICS

Exercise 3 Correcting Sentences by Adding Colons

Correct the following sentences by adding necessary colons. If a sentence does not need a colon, write *C*.

EXAMPLE

1. When I came into class at 9 15 A.M., everyone was writing an essay based on this West African proverb "To know nothing is bad; to learn nothing is worse."

1. *When I came into class at 9:15 A.M., everyone was writing an essay based on this West African proverb: "To know nothing is bad; to learn nothing is worse."*

1. Last summer I read "Choices:A Tribute to Dr. Martin Luther King, Jr.," by Alice Walker.
2. Mrs. Hughes named the three students who had completed extra projects:Marshall, Helena, and Regina.
3. At the festival we bought tacos and refried beans.   **3. C**
4. The qualities she likes most in a person are as follows:reliability, a good sense of humor, and willingness to work.
5. Learn to spell the following new words:*aneurysm, fluoroscope, peregrination,* and *serendipity.*
6. An enduring statement of loyalty, found in Ruth 1:16, begins as follows:"Entreat me not to leave thee or to return from following after thee, for whither thou goest, I will go."
7. The desk was littered with papers, pencils, paperback books, food wrappers, and dirty socks.   **7. C**
8. From 8:00 A.M. until 6:00 P.M., Mr. Brooks sells brushes, brooms, and cleaning products.
9. Alone in the house at night, I heard some scary sounds:the creaking of a board, the scratching of tree branches against a window, and the hissing of steam in the radiator.
10. Tomorrow's test will include the punctuation marks that we have studied so far:commas, semicolons, and colons.

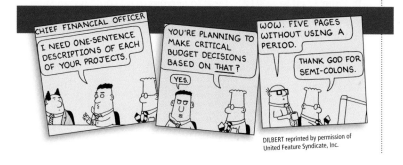

DILBERT reprinted by permission of United Feature Syndicate, Inc.

COMPUTER TIP

Some software programs can evaluate your writing for common errors in the use of end marks, commas, semicolons, and colons. Such grammar-checking programs can help you proofread your drafts.

MECHANICS

Colons   **677**

Review D **Correcting Sentences by Adding Semicolons and Colons**

Correct the following sentences, using semicolons and colons where they are needed.

EXAMPLE 1. We didn't have time to go to Michigan, instead we went to New Mexico.

1. *We didn't have time to go to Michigan; instead, we went to New Mexico.*

1. A small, windowless log cabin stood against the rail fence directly behind it ran a muddy stream.
2. Because the club has run out of funds, the following supplies must be brought from home pencils, erasers, paper, and envelopes.
3. Other jobs take too much time for example, if I worked in a store, I probably would have to work most nights.
4. I enjoy the following hobbies fly-fishing, reading, and riding my bike.
5. American cowhands used the ten-gallon hat as protection from the sun and as a dipper for water the leather chaps they wore served as protection from thorny bushes.
6. A rabbi, a Lutheran minister, and a Catholic priest discussed their interpretations of Isaiah 2 2 and 5 26.
7. In his speech Dr. Fujikawa quoted from several poets Rudyard Kipling, David McCord, and Nikki Giovanni.
8. Sojourner Truth, a former slave, could neither read nor write however, this accomplished woman spoke eloquently against slavery and for women's rights.
9. From 1853 to 1865, the United States had three presidents Franklin Pierce, a Democrat from New Hampshire James Buchanan, a Democrat from Pennsylvania and Abraham Lincoln, a Republican from Illinois.
10. From 12 30 to 1 00 P.M., I was so nervous that I could not sit still I paced up and down, swinging my arms and taking deep breaths, while I rehearsed my lines in my mind.

Learning for Life

advertiser for input and approval. When the advertiser and students have reached an agreement, students should create the final book cover.

Chapter Review

A. Correcting Sentences by Adding Semicolons Between Independent Clauses

The following sentences are missing semicolons. Write each sentence, adding semicolons where needed.

┌─ H E L P ─┐
In Part A of the Chapter Review, you may need to delete some commas and replace them with semicolons.

1. Irma likes cats; her sister is allergic to them.

2. First I cleaned my room; then I called the movie theater to find out the time of the next show.

3. Two of the world's longest railway tunnels are in Italy; moreover, one of the longest motor-traffic tunnels is also located there.

4. My brother Manuel enjoys cooking; I prefer eating.

5. Marty decided to invite Adam, Oliver, and Dorian; and Don, Guy, and Sarah would be there, too.

6. On our first trip to Houston, I wanted to see the Astrodome; my little brother wanted to visit the Johnson Space Center.

7. Tim and Maria often spend Christmas at home; however, this year they are going to visit Maria's family in Guanajuato.

8. The popular names of certain animals are misleading; for example, the koala bear is not really a bear.

9. French and Spanish were Charlotte's most difficult subjects; accordingly, she gave them more time than any of her other subjects at school.

10. The teacher settled the argument; he told us we each had to give a presentation.

B. Correcting Sentences by Adding Colons

Correct the following sentences by adding necessary colons. If a sentence is already correct, write *C*.

11. You will need to bring the following equipment: a hammer, a screwdriver, and safety goggles.

12. At the crossroads we saw three signs: To Quebec, To Montreal, and To Ottawa.

13. We need to shop for several items: salad greens, milk, and a loaf of bread.

Chapter Review   **679**

Using the Chapter Review

To assess student progress, you may want to compare the types of items missed on the **Diagnostic Preview** to those missed on the **Chapter Review**. If students have not made significant progress, you may want to refer them to **Chapter 28: Correcting Common Errors, Exercises 31** and **32,** for additional practice.

MECHANICS

14. Exodus 1:6–14 is my favorite passage in the Old Testament.

15. The corner store is open from 6:00 A.M. until 11:00 P.M.

16. Last year I read the following novels: *David Copperfield,* by Charles Dickens; *The Joy Luck Club,* by Amy Tan; and *Bel-Ami,* by Guy de Maupassant.

17. The desert floor was strewn with rocks, pebbles, tumbleweed, and mineral shards.   17. C

18. This evening's program will focus on what we have discussed so far: the changes in the West over the last two centuries.

19. Especially challenging were the following spelling words: *fluorescent, dissuade, annotate,* and *fortuitous.*

20. At 11:45 A.M. the flight to Mexico City, Bogotá, Brasilia, and Buenos Aires will depart from Gate 2.

C. Proofreading for Correct Use of Semicolons and Colons

The following advertisement contains errors in the use of semicolons and colons. Write the word or number preceding the error, and add the needed punctuation mark.

┌─HELP─┐
In Part C of the Chapter Review, you may need to delete some commas and replace them with semicolons and colons.

[21] Your pet probably loves to watch TV; therefore, it should have the best in quality entertainment. [22] Forcing your dog or cat to watch only what humans watch is not only boring for the pet; it is somewhat inconsiderate on your part. [23] Buy your faithful friend the new *Rockin' and Rollin' Pets* video; it will change your pet's life. [24] No dog or cat will be bored with this movie; on the contrary, Fidos and Tabbies everywhere have been sitting up and taking notice. [25] With this video, your pet will get the exciting, up-to-date entertainment it has been craving; as a concerned owner, you will feel good about what your pet is watching. [26] Science has proven that dogs and cats like the movement and music on television; moreover, they like human contact while watching TV. [27] Ask yourself this question: Are you thinking about your pet's happiness when you turn on the set at 7:00 or 8:00 in the evening? [28] Do you think your pet really likes to watch situation comedies, which are about families it doesn't know; movies, which are too long; and news programs, which are too serious? [29] You already know the answer: order your pet a *Rockin' and Rollin' Pets* video today! [30] To place your order, call the following toll-free number: 1-000-PET-ROCK.

RESOURCES

Punctuation
Review
- *Grammar, Usage, and Mechanics,* pp. 283, 284, 285, 286

Assessment
- *Assessment Package*
  —*Chapter Tests,* Ch. 23
  —*Chapter Tests in Standardized Test Formats,* Ch. 23
- *Test Generator (One-Stop Planner CD-ROM)*

Writing Application
Punctuating a Business Letter

Semicolons and Colons   You have volunteered to order the items that the members of your school band will sell to raise money for road trips. Write a short letter to order these items.

Prewriting   First, decide what kinds of items to sell (for example, ballpoint pens, dried fruit, candles, or book covers) and how many to order. Also, decide on each item's price and make up a name and address for the company from which you will purchase the items.

Writing   As you write your first draft, try to keep the body of your letter short and to the point.

Revising   Be sure that you have followed the correct form for a business letter. Make sure that you have included all the information necessary for the order.

Publishing   Check that you have used a colon after the salutation and before the list of items that you are ordering. Slowly read your letter, focusing on spelling and punctuation. Have you capitalized all proper names, company names, addresses, and brand names? You may want to put your letter-writing abilities to use for your school band or for another school or community organization that holds fund-raisers.

Reference Note

For more about the proper form for **business letters,** see "Writing" in the Quick Reference Handbook.

Writing Application
(p. 681)

OBJECTIVE

- To write a short letter ordering items for a school band trip fund-raiser, using proper business-letter style

Writing Application

Tip. You may wish to brainstorm with students what constitutes a formal tone. [*Students may mention a formal vocabulary, excluding slang and contractions, as well a serious, businesslike approach.*] This writing application offers students the chance to apply their knowledge of colon usage as well as any fund-raising experience they might have had for school and community clubs and activities.

Scoring Rubric. While you will want to pay particular attention to students' use of colons, you will also want to evaluate overall writing performance. You may want to give a split score to indicate development and clarity of the composition as well as mechanics skills.

RESOURCES

Writing Application
Extension

- *Grammar, Usage, and Mechanics,* p. 289
- *Language Workshop CD-ROM,* Lessons 47, 49, 55

CHAPTER

24

Punctuation
Italics and Quotation Marks

PREVIEWING THE CHAPTER

- The first part of the chapter explains the use of italics for titles, names of vehicles, words and letters referred to as such, and foreign words. The second part explains the use of quotation marks for dialogue, quoted material, and titles.

- The material in this chapter will be of use to students as they write literary analyses, reviews of TV programs, personal narratives, and stories.

- The chapter closes with a **Chapter Review** including a **Writing Application** feature that asks students to write a dialogue in which characters tell a story, either fact or fiction, through a conversation. Students must use quotation marks correctly.

- For help in integrating this chapter with composition chapters, use the **Teaching Strands** chart on pp. T371A–T371B.

USING THE DIAGNOSTIC PREVIEW

- Since the concepts in this chapter pertain specifically to writing, you may want to use this preview to assess students' knowledge of punctuating direct and indirect quotations and titles before students are given writing assignments requiring these skills. You may want to have students chart the areas they need to concentrate on, work through appropriate exercises, and pay particular attention to these areas of punctuation when proofreading personal narratives, literary analyses, I–Search essays, and analyses of TV programs.

Diagnostic Preview

A. Correcting Sentences by Adding Underlining (Italics) and Quotation Marks

Add underlining (italics) and quotation marks where they are needed in each of the following sentences.

EXAMPLE
1. Don't forget your umbrella, said Jody. I read in the Sun Times that it's going to rain today.

1. *"Don't forget your umbrella," said Jody. "I read in the Sun Times that it's going to rain today."*

1. "My grandmother asked me which one I wanted for my birthday," Laura said, "a subscription to Time or one to Popular Mechanics."
2. "Welcome aboard the Elissa," said the skipper. "It was built in the 1800s, but it has been restored and is still a seaworthy ship."
3. Emerson once said, "The only way to have a friend is to be one; I think he's right.
4. In the book The Complete Essays of Mark Twain, you'll find an essay titled "Taming the Bicycle."
5. Jennifer said, "I never can remember how many c's and s's the word necessary has."
6. Beth finally figured out that when Tranh used the Vietnamese phrase không biết, he was telling her that he didn't understand.

CHAPTER RESOURCES

Planning
- *One-Stop Planner CD-ROM*

Practice and Extension
- *Grammar, Usage, and Mechanics*, p. 290
- *Developmental Language Skills*, pp. 133–138

Internet
- go.hrw.com (keyword: EOLang)

Evaluation and Assessment
- *Chapter Tests*, Ch. 24
- *Chapter Tests in Standardized Test Formats*, Ch. 24
- *Test Generator (One-Stop Planner)*

682

7. "The <u>18</u> on her uniform looks like a <u>13</u>," Earl said.

8. Alexandra replied, "I'm surprised you watched <u>Gone with the Wind.</u> Two days ago you said, 'I don't want to see the movie until I've read the book.' "

9. Every week the whole family gathered in front of the television to watch <u>7th Heaven.</u>

10. The Beatles' song "Yesterday" has been a favorite of several generations.

B. Correcting Paragraphs of Dialogue by Adding Underlining (Italics) and Quotation Marks

The following dialogue contains errors in the use of underlining (italics) and quotation marks. Correct these errors by adding appropriate marks of punctuation. If a sentence is already correct, write *C*.

EXAMPLES   **[1]** I thought the poetry unit in English class would be dull, Ella said, but it's not. **[2]** We're studying Langston Hughes, and he's great!

    1. *"I thought the poetry unit in English class would be dull,"* Ella said, *"but it's not.* 2. *We're studying Langston Hughes, and he's great!"*

[11] "Oh, I've heard of him," Chet said. [12] "Didn't he write a poem called <u>The Dream Keeper?</u>"

[13] "Yes, that's one of my favorites," Ella said. [14] "An entire book of his poems is called <u>The Dream Keeper,</u> too. [15] Another one of his best-known poems is called 'Dreams.' "

[16] "I guess he dreamed a lot," Chet replied.

[17] Ella said, "He did much more than that! [18] Mrs. Berry told us that Langston Hughes traveled extensively. [19] For a time, he was on the crew of a steamer that sailed around Africa and Europe. [20] In fact, one of his autobiographies is called <u>The Big Sea.</u>"

18. C
19. C

—HELP—

In Part B of the Diagnostic Preview, each error in the use of quotation marks involves a pair of single or double quotation marks.

Italics

Italic letters slant to the right, *like this.* When writing or typing, indicate italics by underlining. If your composition were to be printed, the typesetter would set the underlined words in italics. For example, if you typed the sentence

    `Helen Keller wrote `<u>`The Story of My Life`</u>`.`

it would be printed like this:

    Helen Keller wrote *The Story of My Life.*

Italics   **683**

Timesaver

To save time evaluating the results of the **Diagnostic Preview,** give students a chart like the one below to keep a tally of their strengths and weaknesses.

TOPICS	CORRECT	INCORRECT
italics for titles		
italics for ship, train, and aircraft and spacecraft names		
italics for words, letters, symbols, and numerals referred to as such, and foreign words		
punctuation of direct quotations		
punctuation of divided quotations		
single quotation marks		

Italics

Rules 24a–c *(pp. 683–686)*

OBJECTIVE

- **To correct sentences by adding underlining (italics)**

Meeting INDIVIDUAL NEEDS

ENGLISH-LANGUAGE LEARNERS
General Strategies. You may need to clarify the difference between the terms *underlining* and *italics.* Explain that italics are used in publishing and can now be easily produced on word processors, and underlining is used to indicate italics when writing by hand or on a typewriter. Direct students to examples of italics in the text and reproduce some sample titles on the chalkboard using underlining.

TEACHING TIP

Activity. Newspapers and magazines may have their own house styles regarding punctuation of titles. For example, some publications use quotation marks rather than italics for movie titles.

Have students research the use of italics in various newspapers and magazines from your school library. Suggest that students look at art, music, and film reviews to find examples of the use of italics. Ask volunteers to share their findings with the class.

COMPUTER TIP

If you use a personal computer, you can probably set words in italics yourself. Most word-processing software and many printers are capable of producing italic type.

Reference Note
For information on **capitalizing titles,** see page 630.

STYLE TIP

Chapter headings and titles of magazine articles, short poems, short stories, short musical compositions, and individual episodes of TV shows should be placed in quotation marks, not italicized.

TIPS & TRICKS

Generally, the title of an entire work (book, magazine, TV series) is italicized, while the title of a part (chapter, article, episode) is enclosed in quotation marks.

Reference Note
See page 686 for more about using **quotation marks.**

24a. Use italics (underlining) for titles and subtitles of books, periodicals, long poems, plays, films, television series, long musical works and recordings, and works of art.

Type of Title	Examples
Books	*Vanity Fair: A Novel Without a Hero*
Periodicals	*Seventeen, The New York Times*
Long Poems	*Evangeline, Beowulf*
Plays	*The Piano Lesson, King Lear*
Films	*Casablanca, Harvey*
Television Series	*60 Minutes, Home Improvement*
Long Musical Works and Recordings	*The Magic Flute, Sinfonia Antarctica, The Three Tenors, Dos Mundos*
Works of Art	*The Thinker, Birth of Venus*

The words *a, an,* and *the* written before a title are italicized only when they are part of the title. The official title of a book appears on the title page. The official title of a newspaper or other periodical appears on the masthead, which is usually found on the editorial page or the table of contents.

EXAMPLES   I am reading John Knowles's ***A** Separate Peace.*

An *Incomplete Education* is a book that tries to summarize everything you should have learned in college.

My parents subscribe to ***The** Wall Street Journal* and ***the** Atlantic.*

NOTE   A long poem is one that is long enough to be published as a separate volume. Such poems are usually divided into titled or numbered sections, such as cantos, parts, or books. Long musical compositions include operas, symphonies, ballets, oratorios, and concertos.

EXAMPLES   In my report on Coleridge, I plan to quote from the seventh stanza of ***The Rime of the Ancient Mariner.***

At her recital, she will play a selection from ***Swan Lake.***

24b. Use underlining (italics) for the names of ships, trains, aircraft, and spacecraft.

Type of Name	Examples
Ships	*Titanic, Queen Elizabeth 2*
Trains	*Orient Express, City of New Orleans*
Aircraft and Spacecraft	*Spirit of Saint Louis, Apollo 1*

24c. Use italics (underlining) for words, letters, symbols and numerals referred to as such and for foreign words that are not yet a part of the English vocabulary.

EXAMPLES   The word ***Mississippi*** has four ***s***'s and four ***i***'s.

The ***8*** on that license plate looks like an ***&.***

The ***corrido,*** a fast-paced ballad, evolved from a musical form brought to the Americas by early Spanish explorers and settlers.

NOTE English has borrowed many words from other languages. Once such words are considered a part of the English vocabulary, they are no longer italicized.

EXAMPLES
amoeba (Greek)
boss (Dutch)
canyon (Spanish)
chimpanzee (Bantu)
chipmunk (Algonquian)

judo (Japanese)
kibbutz (Modern Hebrew)
okra (West African)
résumé (French)
vermicelli (Italian)

HELP

If you are not sure whether to italicize a word of foreign origin, look in a recently published dictionary to see if the word is italicized there.

Italics **685**

MECHANICS

MINI-LESSON

Using Italics. To help students remember to italicize words, letters, and numerals referred to as such, encourage them to look for phrases like *the word, the letter,* or *the numeral* before a word, letter, or numeral.

If one of these expressions is present, or could be added without changing the meaning of the sentence, then the word, letter, or numerals should be italicized or underlined.

Italics **685**

Exercise 1

ALTERNATIVE LESSON
Have students identify sentences 1, 3, 9, and 10 as simple, compound, complex, or compound-complex. [1. *complex*, 3. *simple*, 9. *compound*, 10. *compound-complex*]

TECHNOLOGY TIP

Encourage students to write answers to **Exercise 1** on word processors so they can italicize as needed.

MECHANICS

Quotation Marks
Rules 24d–l *(pp. 686–694)*

OBJECTIVES

■ To rewrite sentences, using direct and indirect quotations correctly

■ To correct sentences by adding quotation marks for titles

Exercise 1 **Correcting Sentences by Adding Underlining (Italics)**

Rewrite the following sentences. Then, underline all the words and word groups that should be italicized.

EXAMPLE   1. We gave Mom a subscription to Working Woman.
            1. *We gave Mom a subscription to Working Woman.*

1. Jason named his ship Argo because Argos had built it.
2. The motto of the United States Marine Corps is Semper Fidelis, which means "always faithful."
3. Have you read the novel Great Expectations by Charles Dickens?
4. When I spelled occurrence with one r, I was eliminated from the spelling contest.
5. The Gilbert and Sullivan comic opera The Mikado and the Puccini opera Madama Butterfly are both set in Japan.
6. Shari asked if she could borrow my copy of Sports Illustrated.
7. Mrs. Hopkins said that if she had to describe me in one word, the word would be loquacious.
8. My grandmother, who grew up in Chicago, still subscribes to the Chicago Tribune.
9. My favorite painting is Georgia O'Keeffe's Black Iris; my favorite sculpture is Constantin Brancusi's Bird in Space.
10. My parents own a set of the Encyclopaedia Britannica; and my aunt, who lives within walking distance of us, just bought a set of The World Book Encyclopedia.

Quotation Marks

24d. Use quotation marks to enclose a *direct quotation*—a person's exact words.

EXAMPLES   Melanie said, "This car is making a very strange noise."
            "Maybe we should pull over," suggested Amy.

Always be sure to place quotation marks at both the beginning and the end of a direct quotation.

INCORRECT   She shouted, "We can win, team!
CORRECT   She shouted, "We can win, team!"

Do not use quotation marks for an *indirect quotation*—a rewording of a direct quotation.

RESOURCES

Quotation Marks
Practice

■ *Grammar, Usage, and Mechanics,* pp. 294, 295–296, 297, 298–299

■ *Language Workshop CD-ROM,* Lessons 53–54

DIRECT	Stephanie said, "I'm going to wash the car."
QUOTATION	[the speaker's exact words]
INDIRECT	Stephanie said that she was going to wash the car.
QUOTATION	[not the speaker's exact words]

An interrupting expression is not a part of a quotation and therefore should not be inside quotation marks.

INCORRECT	"Let's sit here, Ann whispered, not way down there."
CORRECT	"Let's sit here," Ann whispered, "not way down there."

When two or more sentences by the same speaker are quoted together, use only one set of quotation marks.

INCORRECT	Brennan said, "I like to sit close to the screen." "The sound is better there."
CORRECT	Brennan said, "I like to sit close to the screen. The sound is better there."

24e. A direct quotation generally begins with a capital letter.

EXAMPLES   Explaining the lever, Archimedes said, "**G**ive me a place to stand, and I can move the world."

Miss Pérez answered, "**T**he rest of the chapter, of course." [Although this quotation is not a sentence, it is Miss Pérez's complete remark.]

NOTE   If the direct quotation is obviously a fragment of the original quotation, it may begin with a lowercase letter.

EXAMPLE   Are our ideals, as Scott says, mere "**s**tatues of snow" that soon melt? [The quotation is obviously only a part of Scott's remark.]

24f. When an interrupting expression divides a quoted sentence into two parts, the second part begins with a lowercase letter.

EXAMPLES   "I wish," she said, "**t**hat we went to the same school."

"I know," I answered, "**b**ut at least we are friends."

If the second part of a quotation is a new sentence, a period (not a comma) follows the interrupting expression, and the second part begins with a capital letter.

EXAMPLE   "I requested an interview," the reporter said. "**S**he told me she was too busy."

Reference Note

For more about **capitalizing quotations**, see page 618.

Meeting INDIVIDUAL NEEDS

ENGLISH-LANGUAGE LEARNERS

Spanish. Quotation marks in Spanish look like this: « ». However, dashes rather than quotation marks are often used to indicate dialogue in Spanish. The style would look like the following:

—No —he said—, I don't believe it.

—¿Why not? —she asked.

Periods and commas are placed outside the closing quotation marks or dashes.

Crossing the Curriculum

History. Have students choose two historical figures from a period they have studied and compose a dialogue between them using direct quotations. Students might use figures from different periods. For example, Joan of Arc could talk to Eleanor Roosevelt, or Napoleon could converse with Richard Nixon.

Cooperative Learning

Divide the class into groups of three or four. Have each group role-play real or imaginary situations in which they have been displeased consumers. Then, have group members collaborate on writing a complaint letter to a consumer protection agency or a newspaper consumer column, using both direct and indirect quotations in describing the transaction.

MECHANICS

MODALITIES

Visual Learners. You may wish to hand out some cartoon strips, explaining that the speech bubble and accompanying pointer take the place of direct quotations and dialogue tags (speaker identification). Have each student rewrite the words from one cartoon strip as a conversation using quotation marks and dialogue tags.

Looking at Language

Unconventional Punctuation. Ways of indicating a person's exact words have varied over the years. Currently, some writers, such as Cormac McCarthy, have dropped both quotation marks and dialogue tags in their novels. You might want to provide students with a few passages from a novel like McCarthy's *All the Pretty Horses* and have them consider what they must do to follow the conversation in the book without the help of standard punctuation.

24g. A direct quotation can be set off from the rest of a sentence by a comma, a question mark, or an exclamation point, but not by a period.

EXAMPLES   Delores explained, "You know how much I like chicken," as she passed her plate for more.

"When will we be leaving?" asked Tony.

The plumber shouted, "Turn off that faucet!" when the water started gushing out of the pipe.

24h. When used with quotation marks, other marks of punctuation are placed according to the following rules:

(1) Commas and periods are placed inside closing quotation marks.

EXAMPLES   "I haven't seen the movie," remarked Jeannette, "but I understand that it's excellent."

(2) Semicolons and colons are placed outside closing quotation marks.

EXAMPLES   Socrates once said, "As for me, all I know is that I know nothing"; I wonder why everyone thinks he was such a wise man.

The following actresses were nominated for the award for "best performance in a leading role": Helen Hunt, Meryl Streep, Cher, and Jodie Foster.

(3) Question marks and exclamation points are placed inside the closing quotation marks if the quotation itself is a question or an exclamation; otherwise, they are placed outside.

EXAMPLES   "Is it too cold in here?" the manager asked as I shivered.

"Yes!" I answered. "Please turn down the air conditioner!"

Can you explain the saying "Penny wise, pound foolish"?

It's not an insult to be called a "bookworm"!

NOTE   When both a sentence and the quotation at the end of that sentence are questions or exclamations, only one question mark or exclamation point is used. It goes inside the closing quotation marks.

EXAMPLE   Did Elizabeth Barrett Browning write the poem that begins with "How do I love thee?"

Exercise 2 Writing Sentences with Direct and Indirect Quotations

If a sentence contains a direct quotation, change it to an indirect quotation. If a sentence contains an indirect quotation, change it to a direct quotation. Make sure your answers are correctly punctuated.

EXAMPLES
1. "Where should we go for vacation?" asked my mother.
1. *My mother asked where we should go for vacation.*

2. My little brother Jason said that he wanted to see castles like the ones in the brochures.
2. *My little brother Jason said, "I want to see castles like the ones in the brochures."*

1. When we planned our trip to England, Mom said, "Our stops should include some castles."
2. Our tour book says that Colchester Castle, begun in 1076, is a good place to start.
3. Jason asked whether the castles were haunted.
4. "No," said Mom, "and, besides, we'll stay close together."
5. In England, Jason told Mom that he wanted to swim in a moat.
6. "Warwick Castle," said our guide, "is one of the most beautiful."
7. "One of its towers," he went on to say, "was built in 1066."
8. The guide said that the castle contains many works of art.
9. "I like the collection of suits of armor best," said Jason.
10. "Is it still the home of the Earls of Warwick?" I asked.

24i. When you write dialogue (a conversation), begin a new paragraph every time the speaker changes.

EXAMPLE
"What's that?" Sally demanded impatiently.

Luisa seemed surprised. "What's what?"

"That thing, what you got in your hand."

"Oh this . . ." and she held it up for Sally to inspect. "A present."

"A what?"

"A present I picked up."

"Oh." Sally moved her eyes to the house. "Looks like his place burned down. What d'you find inside?"

"Just this," Luisa said, gazing blankly at the house.

"What d'you want that for?"

Ron Arias, "El Mago"

| STYLE | TIP |

In dialogue, a paragraph may be only one line long and may consist of one or more sentence fragments.

Exercise 2 Writing Sentences with Direct and Indirect Quotations

POSSIBLE ANSWERS

1. When we planned our trip to England, Mom said that our stops should include some castles.
2. Our tour book says, "Colchester Castle, begun in 1076, is a good place to start."
3. Jason asked, "Are the castles haunted?"
4. Mom said that they weren't but that we would stay close together.
5. In England, Jason told Mom, "I want to swim in a moat."
6. Our guide said that Warwick Castle is one of the most beautiful.
7. He went on to say that one of its towers had been built in 1066.
8. The guide said, "The castle contains many works of art."
9. Jason said that he liked the collection of suits of armor best.
10. I asked whether it was still the home of the Earls of Warwick.

MECHANICS

24j. When a quoted passage consists of more than one paragraph, put quotation marks at the beginning of each paragraph
and at the end of the entire passage. Do not put quotation marks
after any paragraph but the last.

EXAMPLE   "At nine o'clock this morning someone entered the Mill
Bank by the back entrance, broke through two thick steel
doors guarding the bank's vault, and escaped with sixteen
bars of gold.

"No arrests have been made, but state police are
confident the case will be solved within a few days."

NOTE   A long passage (not dialogue) quoted from a book or another
printed source is usually set off from the rest of the text. The entire passage is usually indented and double-spaced. When a quoted passage has
been set off in one of these ways, no quotation marks are necessary.

EXAMPLE   In his autobiography The Interesting
Narrative of the Life of Olaudah Equiano, or
Gustavus Vassa, the African, Olaudah Equiano
describes encountering African languages
other than his own:

From the time I left my own nation
I always found somebody that understood me till I came to the sea coast.
The languages of different nations
did not totally differ, nor were they
so copious as those of the Europeans,
particularly the English. They were
therefore easily learned; and while
I was journeying thus through Africa,
I acquired two or three different
tongues.

24k. Use single quotation marks to enclose a quotation within a
quotation.

EXAMPLES   Annoyed, Becky snapped, "Don't tell me, 'That's not the way
to do it.'"

My uncle said, "Remember the words of Chief Joseph: 'I
have heard talk and talk, but nothing is done. Good words
do not last long unless they amount to something.' This is
good advice."

Tiffany exclaimed, "How dare you say, 'Yuck!'"

Review A **Correcting Sentences by Adding Quotation Marks for Dialogue**

Correct each of the following passages, adding quotation marks where necessary. Remember to begin a new paragraph each time the speaker changes.   Carets indicate paragraph breaks.

EXAMPLE   **1.** Is Rio de Janeiro the capital of Brazil, asked Linda, or is Brasília?

   1. *"Is Rio de Janeiro the capital of Brazil," asked Linda, "or is Brasília?"*

1. "Race-car driver Janet Guthrie," said Chet, reading from his notes, "is a trained physicist who has spent many years working at an aircraft corporation."

2. "Who shot that ball?" Coach Larsen wanted to know. "I did," came the reply from the small, frail-looking player. "Good shot," said the coach, "but always remember to follow your shot to the basket." "I tried, but I was screened," the player explained.

3. "The *Brownsville Beacon*," the editorial began, "will never support a candidate who tells the taxpayers, 'Vote for me, and I will cut taxes.' The reason is simple. Taxes, just like everything else in this inflationary society, must increase. Any candidate who thinks otherwise is either a fool or a liar."

4. In the interview, the candidate said, "I am a very hospitable person." "Yes," her husband agreed, "Ralph Waldo Emerson must have been thinking of you when he said, 'Happy is the house that shelters a friend.'"

"WOULD YOU STOP PUTTING QUOTES AROUND EVERYTHING I SAY?!"

© Leo Cullum 1998; reprinted by permission.

Quotation Marks   **691**

Meeting **INDIVIDUAL** **NEEDS**

INCLUSION

For **Review A,** provide students with strips of paper, each containing a word or phrase from sentence 1, and with self-adhesive squares containing marks of punctuation. Have students physically arrange the parts of the sentence and the punctuation. Then, have them work with a helper to continue this process for the rest of the exercise.

MECHANICS

Learning for Life **Continued on pp. 692–693**

Lead students in a brief discussion of popular music or current television programs. Point out that commenting on artistic work is something they will continue to do throughout life, whether in newspaper columns, in letters to the editor, in e-mail correspondence, or in lunch table conversation.

Allow students to work in small groups to create a four-point rating scale for

Activity. To help students review, have a helper prepare an index card for each type of item listed in **Rules 24a–c** and **24l.** For example, one card might say *name of a submarine,* while another might read *television show episode.* Divide the class into two teams, designating one team as *X* and the other as *O,* and draw a tic-tac-toe grid on the chalkboard. Have each team in turn draw a card and identify the correct punctuation for the item (italics or quotation marks). The correct answer earns the team a mark on the tic-tac-toe grid. When the stack has been completed, shuffle the cards and repeat the process. Play continues until one team has made three of its marks in a row.

Reference Note

Remember that the **titles of long poems and long musical works are italicized,** not enclosed in quotation marks. See the examples on page 684.

24l. Use quotation marks to enclose titles and subtitles of articles, essays, short stories, poems, songs, individual episodes of TV series, and chapters and other parts of books and periodicals.

Type of Title	Examples
Articles	"What Teenagers Need to Know About Diets" "Satellites That Serve Us"
Essays	"Charley in Yellowstone" "An Apartment in Moscow"
Short Stories	"The Man to Send Rain Clouds" "The Pit and the Pendulum"
Poems	"Fog" "Incident" "The End of My Journey"
Songs	"The Ballad of Gregorio Cortez" "Peace Train"
Episodes of TV Series	"The Sure Thing" "Monarch in Waiting"
Chapters and Other Parts of Books and Periodicals	"Life in the First Settlements" "The Talk of the Town"

NOTE For short titles within quotations, use single quotation marks.

EXAMPLE "Did Thomas Hardy write 'The Dynasts'?" asked Terri.

Exercise 3 Correcting Sentences by Adding Quotation Marks for Titles

Correct the following sentences by adding quotation marks as needed. If a sentence is already correctly punctuated, write *C.*

EXAMPLE 1. Did O. Henry write the story The Last Leaf?

  1. Did O. Henry write the story *"The Last Leaf"?*

1. That address to the United Nations can be found in our literature book, in the chapter titled "Essays and Speeches."
2. One popular Old English riddle song is "Scarborough Fair."

Learning for Life

evaluating a television series or a musical work. Groups should come up with at least three or four valid criteria on which to rate the work.

Then, have students choose a favorite TV series or CD to review for a friend. Tell students their work will be evaluated based on clear support of the criteria they have chosen and on the correct use of quotation marks and italics. For review, students should also

3. Have you read the story "Split Cherry Tree" by Jesse Stuart?

4. Which Eve Merriam poem is that, "Cheers" or "How to Eat a Poem"?

5. Have you read Fran Lebowitz's essay "Tips for Teens"?

6. One of Pat Mora's poems about being bilingual and bicultural is titled "Legal Alien."

7. I read Kurt Vonnegut's short story "Harrison Bergeron" last week.

7. C

8. In his essay "Misspelling," Charles Kuralt examines some of the difficulties people have with spelling.

9. Fiona said, "My favorite Irish ballad is 'Cliffs of Dooneen.'"

10. The whole class enjoyed reading Naomi Shihab Nye's poem "Daily."

Review B **Correcting Sentences by Adding Underlining (Italics) and Quotation Marks**

Write the following sentences, adding underlining (italics) and quotation marks where needed.

EXAMPLE
   1. Please turn to the chapter titled A Walk in the Highlands.

   1. Please turn to the chapter titled "A Walk in the Highlands."

1. The Bay Area Youth Theater is presenting Bernard Shaw's play Major Barbara.

2. Tyrone announced that he is going to sing "Some Enchanted Evening" from the musical South Pacific.

3. "I have tickets to the opera Carmen," said Karen, "and I would like you to be my guest."

4. Does the Swahili word kwa heri mean the same thing that the Spanish word adiós does?

5. My favorite story by Sir Arthur Conan Doyle is "The Adventure of the Dying Detective," which is included in the anthology The Complete Sherlock Holmes.

6. Ms. Loudon said, "I enjoyed your report on Ernest Hemingway. Remember, however, that the name Ernest is spelled without an a."

7. In her review of The King and I, the drama critic for the Los Angeles Times commented, "This production is an excellent revival of a play that never seems to wear thin."

8. In my paper, which I titled "The Hispanic Soldier in Vietnam," I cited several passages from Luis Valdez's play The Buck Private.

9. Mrs. Howard asked, "In the play Julius Caesar, who said, 'This was the noblest Roman of them all'? Which Roman was being described?"

10. Have you read "Hannah Armstrong," one of the poems in the Spoon River Anthology by Edgar Lee Masters?

Quotation Marks   **693**

check for the correct use of capital letters and commas.

Have students offer their reviews for publication in a classroom or school newspaper or for posting on a classroom or all-school Web page.

MECHANICS

Relating to Literature

If your literature textbook contains the selection "The Fifty-First Dragon" by Heywood Broun, have students read it as a review of dialogue. This story can be used to demonstrate several points, including how tone can be achieved by placement of dialogue tags. Have students refer to the conversation between the dragon and Gawaine. Ask them to note the differences in how the quotations are attributed to the dragon and to Gawaine. [*The dragon's comments are attributed with interrupting expressions. Gawaine's are attributed at the ends of his speeches.*] Then, ask what effects the use of interrupting expressions has. [*It gives the effect of the dragon toying with Gawaine. It makes the reader wait a little longer for the full development of the dragon's thoughts, thereby increasing suspense.*] Suggest that students consider the effects of their dialogue tags as they write their dialogues.

Review C **Correcting Paragraphs by Adding Underlining (Italics) and Quotation Marks**

Correct the following paragraphs by adding underlining (italics) and quotation marks where necessary.

EXAMPLE   **[1]** Are all of these books by or about Benjamin Franklin? asked Bonnie Lou.

    1. *"Are all of these books by or about Benjamin Franklin?" asked Bonnie Lou.*

[1] "Yes, Bonnie Lou," Mr. Reyes answered. [2] "There's even one, Ben and Me by Robert Lawson, that's a biography written from the point of view of Amos, Franklin's pet mouse."

[3] "This one, The Many Lives of Benjamin Franklin by Mary Pope Osborne, sounds really interesting," said Jasmine.

[4] "It is," Mr. Reyes said. [5] "That's exactly what we're going to talk about today—the many lives of this early American genius. [6] Who can tell me about one of them?"

[7] "He invented electricity, didn't he?" asked Liam.

[8] "Well, he didn't invent electricity," corrected Mr. Reyes, "but his experiments proved that lightning is a form of electricity."

[9] "Franklin," he continued, "also helped draft some of our important historical documents, and he was a diplomat, a printer, and a publisher. [10] Franklin's writings, especially his Autobiography and Poor Richard's Almanack, have given us many well-known sayings."

Chapter Review

A. Correcting Sentences by Adding Underlining (Italics) and Quotation Marks

The following sentences contain errors in the use of underlining (italics) and quotation marks. Write each sentence, adding underlining and quotation marks where needed.

1. The concert ended with a stirring rendition of "The Stars and Stripes Forever."

2. "There's Still Gold in Them Thar Hills," an article in Discover, describes attempts to mine low-grade gold deposits on Quartz Mountain in California.

3. Mozart's opera The Magic Flute is being performed tonight.

4. The fifth episode in the TV series The African Americans is titled "The Harlem Renaissance."

5. I Am Joaquín is an epic poem about Mexican American culture.

6. As a baby sitter I have read the children's book The Pokey Little Puppy at least a dozen times.

7. The journalist Horace Greeley founded the New York Tribune, an influential newspaper.

8. Although the poem "When You Are Old" has three stanzas, it contains only one sentence.

9. The word recommended has two m's but only one c.

10. Robert Fulton's steamboat, Claremont, was the first one that could be operated without losing money.

11. My father always swore by Newsweek, but Mother preferred U.S. News & World Report.

12. In his novel David Copperfield, Dickens draws a vivid picture of Victorian life.

13. In Spanish, sí means yes; in French, si is also used to mean yes, but only in answer to a negative statement. 13. [or "yes"]

14. Tim asked, "What time did they say they would be here?"

15. Usually, they read the Daily News on Sundays.

16. Those b's look like 6's.

17. "I didn't think I would be able to sit through an opera," said Brittany, "but I really enjoyed Hansel and Gretel."

Chapter Review **695**

Using the Chapter Review

To assess student progress, you may want to compare the types of items missed on the **Diagnostic Preview** to those missed on the **Chapter Review**. If students have not made significant progress, you may want to refer them to **Chapter 28: Correcting Common Errors, Exercises 33** and **34**, for additional practice.

18. On Mondays during football season, the entire family watches Monday Night Football on television.

19. "How many m's and t's does the word committee have?" asked Betty.

20. One of Kathryn's favorite novels is Martin Chuzzlewit by Charles Dickens.

B. Punctuating Dialogue by Adding Quotation Marks

The following dialogue contains errors in the use of quotation marks. Write each sentence, adding quotation marks where needed.

[**21**] "Before our field trip begins," continued Mrs. Garcia, "be sure that you have a notebook and a collection kit."

[**22**] "Will we need binoculars?" asked Melvin.

[**23**] "Leave your binoculars at home," answered Mrs. Garcia. "Your ears will be more helpful than your eyes on this trip."

[**24**] "What will we be able to hear out there?" asked Arnold.

[**25**] "What a question!" exclaimed Felicia. "This time of year, you can hear all sorts of sounds."

[**26**] "I hope that we hear and see some birds," said Koko. "Didn't someone once say, 'The birds warble sweet in the springtime?'"

[**27**] "When," asked James, "do we eat lunch? My mom packed my favorite kinds of sandwiches."

[**28**] "Don't worry," said Mrs. Garcia. "Most birds are quiet at midday. We can have our lunch then."

[**29**] Ruth Ann said, "Mrs. Garcia, would you believe that I don't know one birdcall from another?"

[**30**] "That's all right, Ruth Ann," laughed Mrs. Garcia. "Some birds call out their own names. For example, the bobolink repeats its name: 'Bob-o-link! Bob-o-link!'"

C. Correcting Paragraphs by Adding Underlining (Italics) and Quotation Marks

The following paragraph contains errors in the use of underlining (italics) and quotation marks. Write each sentence, adding underlining and quotation marks where necessary. Be sure to start a new paragraph each time the speaker changes.   Carets indicate paragraph breaks.

[**31**] "As most of you probably know," said Mr. Sundaresan, our geography teacher, "Everest, on the border of Tibet and Nepal, is the

RESOURCES

Punctuation
Review

■ *Grammar, Usage, and Mechanics,* pp. 300, 301, 302, 303

Assessment

■ *Assessment Package*
  — *Chapter Tests,* Ch. 24
  — *Chapter Tests in Standardized Test Formats,* Ch. 24
■ *Test Generator (One-Stop Planner CD-ROM)*

world's highest mountain; does anyone know the name of the world's second-highest peak? Yes, Elaine?"[32]"It's K2."[33]"Yes," said Mr. Sundaresan, impressed. "How did you know?"[34]"Well," said Elaine, "for Christmas my parents gave me a book called K2: Challenging the Sky by Roberto Mantovani. I just finished reading it last night."[35]"Very good," said Mr. Sundaresan. "Now can anyone tell me the name of the highest mountain in Europe? I'll give you a hint: It's not in Switzerland." Elaine's hand shot up again. [36]"Isn't it Mont Blanc, on the border of France and Italy?" she asked. [37]"Quite right," said Mr. Sundaresan. "May I ask how you knew that?"[38]"For my birthday I got a copy of The Alps and Their People by Susan Bullen. It's a really interesting book."[39]"Well, have you read any books on the Rockies, Elaine?" asked Mr. Sundaresan. [40]"As a matter of fact, I just started reading The Rockies by David Muench, and before you ask, I can tell you that Mount Elbert is the highest peak in the Rockies!"

Writing Application
Writing a Dialogue

Using Quotation Marks   Write a page of dialogue in which characters tell a story, either fact or fiction, through a conversation.

Prewriting   Decide on a story and a few characters to tell it. You could retell a favorite anecdote, report the exact words of an amusing conversation, or write an imaginary interview with a famous person.

Writing   As you write your first draft, think about making the characters sound different from one another.

Revising   First, ask a classmate to read your dialogue. Revise any parts that are unclear or uninteresting to your reader. Be sure that you have begun a new paragraph every time the speaker changes. Also, check that you have followed the rules for punctuating direct quotations and quotations with interrupting expressions.

Publishing   Read through your dialogue again, this time concentrating on correcting errors in grammar, spelling, and punctuation. You and your classmates may want to work in small groups to present your dialogues to the class.

OBJECTIVE

- To write a dialogue in which characters tell a story, either fact or fiction, through a conversation

Writing Application

Tip. This activity encourages students to try out some of the many variations possible in constructing dialogue. Students may have to refer to the rules repeatedly, so you may want to hand out a summary sheet of rules from the textbook.

Scoring Rubric. While you will want to pay particular attention to students' use of italics and quotation marks, you will also want to evaluate overall writing performance. You may want to give a split score to indicate development and clarity of the composition as well as mechanics skills.

Critical Thinking

Analysis. Characterization—making characters sound different from one another—requires the use of a variety of elements. Choose a few lines of dialogue from a short story in which the characterization is clear, such as Truman Capote's "A Christmas Memory" or Toni Cade Bambara's "Blues Ain't No Mockin Bird." Have students analyze the dialogue. They might point out that the use of formal or informal speech, slang, or dialect can create a distinct style; sentence length can convey information about mood or personality; and the length and placement of dialogue tags can contribute to the emotional tone of the situations and characters.

MECHANICS

PREVIEWING THE CHAPTER

- The first part of this chapter explains the use of apostrophes to form the possessive case of nouns and covers the absence of apostrophes in possessive personal pronouns. The second part of the chapter discusses the use of apostrophes to form contractions and plurals.

- The chapter closes with a **Chapter Review** including a **Writing Application** feature that asks students to write a paragraph using possessive nouns, plural nouns, indefinite pronouns, and the possessive case correctly.

- You may want to direct students' attention to the information in this chapter as they proofread writing assignments, particularly descriptive essays and personal narratives. After reviewing correct apostrophe usage, have students proofread their papers for apostrophe errors only.

- For help in integrating this chapter with composition chapters, use the **Teaching Strands** chart on pp. T371A–T371B.

USING THE DIAGNOSTIC PREVIEW

- You may wish to use the **Diagnostic Preview** to determine the problems students might have using apostrophes. Give this test when students are assigned to write descriptive essays or personal narratives using contractions in dialogue or possessives in descriptions such as *sister's hair* or *brothers' favorite activities*.

Punctuation
Apostrophes

Diagnostic Preview

Revising Sentences in a Journal Entry by Using Apostrophes Correctly

In the following journal entry, Josh often incorrectly uses contractions and possessive forms. Write the correct form of each incorrect word or expression used.

EXAMPLE   [1] Im still working on todays assignment.

    1. *I'm; today's*

1. I've/tonight's
2. hours'/I'm
3. I'll/handwriting's
4. *d's/t's/o's*
5. *and's/so's*
6. there's/I'll
7. That's/isn't
8. composition's
9. Mom's/Who's
10. family's/friends
11. we're

12. Pepper's/I'm
13. owners'
14. council's/owners/their

[1] Ive just finished tonights homework. [2] Writing a composition is usually two hours hard work for me, but Im pleased with this one. [3] Ill read it over in the morning to make sure that my handwritings legible. [4] My teacher has trouble reading my ds, ts, and os. [5] He also objects to my overuse of ands and sos. [6] If theres an error, Ill have to revise my composition. [7] Thats one good reason for being careful, isnt it?

[8] My compositions title is "The Reign of Animals." [9] Moms friend suggested that I call it "Whose in Charge Here?" [10] My familys love for animals is well known in the neighborhood and among our friends'. [11] At the moment were owned by two inside cats; three outside cats; our resident dog, Pepper; and a visiting dog we call Hugo.

[12] During Peppers walks, Im usually followed by at least one other dog. [13] Some owners care of their dogs never seems to go beyond feeding them. [14] The city councils decision to fine owners'

CHAPTER RESOURCES

Planning
- *One-Stop Planner CD-ROM*

Practice and Extension
- *Grammar, Usage, and Mechanics,* p. 307
- *Developmental Language Skills,* pp. 139–140

Internet
- go.hrw.com (keyword: EOLang)

Evaluation and Assessment
- *Chapter Tests,* Ch. 25
- *Chapter Tests in Standardized Test Formats,* Ch. 25
- *Test Generator (One-Stop Planner)*

who let they're dogs run loose makes sense. [15] Hugos a huge dog who's always wandering loose in my neighborhood. [16] We took him in several times after hed narrowly escaped being hit by a car. [17] In fact, Hugos and Peppers feeding dishes sit side by side in our kitchen.

[18] Peter, our senior cat, who was once one of our neighborhoods strays, isnt about to run from anyones dog. [19] At times weve seen him safeguarding other cats of ours' by running in front of them and staring down an approaching dog and it's owner. [20] Our dogs and cats different personalities never cease to fascinate me.

15. Hugo's

16. he'd

17. Hugo's/Pepper's

18. neighborhood's/
    isn't/anyone's

19. we've/ours/its

20. dogs'/cats'

Possessive Case

The *possessive case* of a noun or pronoun shows ownership or possession.

EXAMPLES **Larry's** friend Dana uses a wheelchair.

You need a good **night's** sleep.

Can I count on **their** votes?

I appreciate **your** waiting so long.

25a. To form the possessive case of most singular nouns, add an apostrophe and an *s*.

EXAMPLES Yuki**'s** problem   a bus**'s** wheel

the mayor**'s** desk   this evening**'s** paper

Mrs. Ross**'s** job   a dollar**'s** worth

NOTE For a proper name ending in *s,* add only an apostrophe if the name has two or more syllables and if the addition of *'s* would make the name awkward to pronounce.

EXAMPLES **Ulysses'** plan   **West Indies'** export

Mrs. Rawlings' car   **Texas'** governor

For a singular common noun ending in *s*, add both an apostrophe and an *s* if the added *s* is pronounced as a separate syllable.

EXAMPLES the actress**'s** costumes   the dress**'s** sleeves

the class**'s** teacher   a platypus**'s** tail

Possessive Case

Rules 25a–f *(pp. 699–707)*

OBJECTIVES

- To form the possessive case of singular and plural nouns

- To revise phrases by forming the possessive case of nouns

- To identify correct forms of pronouns

- To revise phrases by using the possessive case

TEACHING TIP

Activity. Prepare a list of singular and plural nouns and pronouns (for example, *student, seniors, it, our, Paula and Li*) and a list of possible possessions (for example, *diamonds, video collection, best-selling novel*). Cut each list into strips that each contain one noun, pronoun, or possession, and form one stack of noun and pronoun strips and a second stack of the possible possessions strips. Then, have each student draw one strip from each of the two stacks and create a possessive phrase by adding an apostrophe or apostrophe and an *s* where needed. (*Possible answers: student's diamonds, seniors' video collection.*) You may wish to have volunteers write their combinations on the chalkboard and have the class check for accurate apostrophe placement.

MECHANICS

Possessive Case **699**

TEACHING **TIP**

Exercise 1 You may wish to use the first ten items in **Exercise 1** as guided practice. Then, have students complete the exercise as independent practice.

Exercise 1 Using Apostrophes to Form the Possessive Case of Singular Nouns

POSSIBLE ANSWERS

1. baby's bottle
2. uncle's house
3. year's events
4. cent's worth
5. class's problem
6. Terry's friend
7. Ellen's plans
8. mouse's cheese
9. Mr. Chan's daughter
10. Miss Reynolds' car
11. plane's wings
12. boss's secretary
13. child's game
14. Ms. Sanchez's son
15. horse's mane
16. Paris's cafés
17. system's problem
18. judge's robe
19. Mr. Jones's car
20. synagogue's location

Exercise 1 Using Apostrophes to Form the Possessive Case of Singular Nouns

Form the possessive case of each of the following nouns. After each possessive word, give an appropriate noun.

EXAMPLE   **1.** Teresa

1. Teresa's pencil

1. baby	**8.** mouse	**15.** horse
2. uncle	**9.** Mr. Chan	**16.** Paris
3. year	**10.** Miss Reynolds	**17.** system
4. cent	**11.** plane	**18.** judge
5. class	**12.** boss	**19.** Mr. Jones
6. Terry	**13.** child	**20.** synagogue
7. Ellen	**14.** Ms. Sanchez	

25b. To form the possessive case of a plural noun ending in *s*, add only the apostrophe.

EXAMPLES   two bird**s'** feathers   all three cousin**s'** vacation

the Garza**s'** patio   the Girl Scout**s'** uniforms

Although most plural nouns end in *s*, some are irregular. To form the possessive case of a plural noun that does not end in *s*, add an apostrophe and *s*.

EXAMPLES   children**'s** shoes   those deer**'s** food

Reference Note

For more examples of **irregular plurals,** see page 740.

1. men's
2. cats'
3. teachers'
4. enemies'
5. princesses'
6. dollars'
7. elves'
8. cattle's
9. mice's
10. parents'
11. the Smiths'
12. sheep's
13. wives'
14. O'Gradys'
15. runners'
16. attorneys'
17. allies'

Exercise 2 Forming the Possessive Case of Plural Nouns

Form the possessive case of each of the following plural nouns.

EXAMPLE   **1.** knives

1. knives'

1. men	**8.** cattle	**15.** runners
2. cats	**9.** mice	**16.** attorneys
3. teachers	**10.** parents	**17.** allies
4. enemies	**11.** the Smiths	**18.** friends
5. princesses	**12.** sheep	**19.** women
6. dollars	**13.** wives	**20.** bats
7. elves	**14.** O'Gradys	

18. friends'   19. women's   20. bats'

MINI-LESSON

Plurals. Before students create plural possessive forms, you may want to review with them how to form plurals. Provide a list of words like the following, and ask students to give the plural form of each word.

watch   [*watches*]   tax   [*taxes*]

potato   [*potatoes*]   woman   [*women*]

Refer students to **Chapter 27: Spelling,** for rules and examples for forming plurals.

Exercise 3 Revising Phrases by Forming the Possessive Case of Nouns

Revise the following phrases by using the possessive case.

EXAMPLE   **1.** the parties for seniors
                1. the seniors' parties

1. prizes for winners
2. manners for teenagers
3. yokes of oxen
4. duties of nurses
5. names of players
6. suits for women
7. ideas of inventors
8. medals for veterans
9. routines for dancers
10. roles for actresses

NOTE In general, you should not use an apostrophe to form the plural of a noun.

INCORRECT	Two player's left their gym suits on the locker room floor.
CORRECT	Two **players** left their gym suits on the locker room floor. [plural]
CORRECT	Two **players'** gym suits were left on the locker room floor. [The apostrophe shows that the gym suits belong to the two players.]

© 1993 by Sidney Harris.

Review A Recognizing Correct Forms of Nouns

Choose the correct form of each noun in parentheses in the following paragraph.

EXAMPLES   Several **[1]** (*photographs, photograph's*) taken by *Voyagers 1* and *2* were combined into the illustration on the next page to show a few of **[2]** (*Saturns, Saturn's*) many satellites.

                1. photographs
                2. Saturn's

At least eighteen natural satellites, or celestial **[1]** (*bodies, body's*), revolve around the planet Saturn. Seven of our solar **[2]** (*systems, system's*) nine planets have satellites, but Saturn and Jupiter have the most. **[3]** (*Scientists, Scientists'*) figures on the true number of **[4]** (*satellites, satellite's*) vary, and new space **[5]** (*probes, probe's*) sometimes reveal more satellites. Two **[6]** (*planets, planets'*), Earth and Pluto, have only one satellite each. Of course, you are already familiar with our

Possessive Case   **701**

Exercise 3 Revising Phrases by Forming the Possessive Case of Nouns

ANSWERS

1. winners' prizes
2. teenagers' manners
3. oxen's yokes
4. nurses' duties
5. players' names
6. women's suits
7. inventors' ideas
8. veterans' medals
9. dancers' routines
10. actresses' roles

Meeting INDIVIDUAL NEEDS

LEARNERS HAVING DIFFICULTY

To personalize the use of possessive case, have students use possessive case nouns and pronouns to describe objects in their immediate surroundings. To begin, have each student write three items that belong to other students in the classroom and three things that are shared by two people. Then, have students write the name of the owner or owners in front of each object listed, using apostrophes correctly. You may want to offer models like the following:

Maija's backpack
winner's prize
his sweater
Tina and Jed's teacher

MECHANICS

Possessive Case   **701**

own [7] (*planets, planet's*) satellite, the moon. As you can see from this illustration, [8] (*satellite's, satellites'*) sizes and features vary greatly. Titan, a satellite of Saturn, is the largest of that [9] (*planets, planet's*) satellites. Another of [10] (*Saturns, Saturn's*) satellites, Mimas, has a crater that covers about one third of its diameter.

Reference Note

For more about **using pronouns correctly,** see Chapter 18.

Reference Note

For more about **whose, its,** and **their,** see pages 756, 603, and 606.

Meeting INDIVIDUAL NEEDS

ENGLISH-LANGUAGE LEARNERS

Spanish. Spanish has a possessive form for pronouns but not for nouns; therefore, students may be confused about the use of apostrophes. For example, in Spanish, "his book" would be translated as *su libro,* but "Javier's book" would be translated as *el libro de Javier* ("the book of Javier"). You may want to give students a series of statements to change by using the possessive form of the noun. An example is "This book belongs to José. It is _____ book." (*José's*)

Relating to Writing

You may wish to have students write short poems using possessive case/contraction homonyms such as *their/they're, whose/who's,* and *your/you're.* Students may wish to keep copies of their poems in their writing logs for quick reference. You may want to write the following example on the chalkboard.

> You're too smart to give up
> Your dreams.
> They're there to give you
> Their guidance.
> Who's going to reach your dreams
> If not you?
> Whose dreams will you reach
> If not your own?

MECHANICS

25c. Possessive personal pronouns do not require an apostrophe.

Possessive Personal Pronouns	
Singular	**Plural**
my, mine	our, ours
your, yours	your, yours
his, her, hers, its	their, theirs

My, your, her, its, our, and *their* are used before nouns or pronouns. *Mine, yours, hers, ours,* and *theirs,* on the other hand, are not used before a noun or pronoun; they are used as subjects, subject complements, or objects in sentences. *His* may be used in either way.

EXAMPLES

Lee has **your** sweater.   Lee has a sweater of **yours.**

That is **your** watch.   That watch is **yours.**

Her idea was wonderful.   **Hers** was the best idea.

This is **our** plant.   This plant is **ours.**

There is **his** CD.   There is a CD of **his.**

NOTE The possessive form of *who* is *whose,* not *who's.* Similarly, do not write *it's* for *its,* or *they're* for *their.*

EXAMPLES **Whose** [not *Who's*] book is this?

Its [not *It's*] cover is torn.

Is that **their** [not *they're*] copy?

Exercise 4 Choosing Correct Forms of Possessive Personal Pronouns

Choose the <u>correct pronoun in parentheses</u> in each of the following sentences.

EXAMPLE   **1.** Ralph Ellison, (*who's, whose*) book *Invisible Man* won a National Book Award, studied music at Tuskegee Institute.

    1. *whose*

1. Did you know, Sumi, that two poems of (*yours, yours'*) have been chosen for the literary magazine?
2. When I first read that book, I was surprised by the high quality of (*its, it's*) artwork.
3. (*Hers, Her's*) is the bicycle with the reflectors on (*its, it's*) fenders.
4. Eudora Welty, (*who's, whose*) short stories often involve eccentric characters, is my favorite writer.
5. "The trophy is (*ours, our's*)!" shouted the captain as the *Flying S* crossed the finish line.
6. (*Theirs, Theirs'*) is the only house with blue shutters.
7. Penny and Carla worked as gardeners this summer and saved (*their, they're*) money for a ski trip.
8. The students (*who's, whose*) names are called should report backstage.
9. (*Their, They're*) schedule calls for a test on Tuesday.
10. (*Who's, Whose*) signature is this?

25d. Indefinite pronouns in the possessive case require an apostrophe and *s*.

EXAMPLES   nobody's wishes   another's viewpoint

              someone's license   neither's school

Exercise 5 Choosing Correct Forms of Possessive Pronouns

Choose the <u>correct pronoun in parentheses</u> in each of the following sentences.

EXAMPLE   **1.** That Mozart CD is (*hers, her's*).

    1. *hers*

1. (*No ones, No one's*) guess was correct.
2. (*Ours, Our's*) works better than (*theirs, their's*).
3. (*Who's, Whose*) game is that?

Reference Note

For a list of **indefinite pronouns,** see page 381.

HELP

For the expressions *everyone else* and *nobody else,* the correct possessives are *everyone else's* and *nobody else's.*

Exercise 4

ALTERNATIVE LESSON

Have students find the following constructions in the designated sentences: sentence 1—a direct address [*Sumi*]; sentence 4—a predicate nominative [*writer*]; sentence 7—a compound verb [*worked, saved*]

Cooperative Learning

You may want to use the following activity to reinforce the correct use of apostrophes. Ask the class to develop a list of possible errors in plural and possessive forms. Divide the class into small groups, and ask each group to write a paragraph including three errors in the use of plurals and three in the use of possessives, as well as correctly used plural and possessive forms. Ask each group to write an answer key listing corrections for the errors.

Then, distribute the paragraphs to other groups to revise. You may wish to allow time for the groups to share their work.

MECHANICS

Possessive Case   **703**

Review B **Writing the Singular, Plural, and Possessive Forms of Nouns**

POSSIBLE ANSWERS

1. friend, friend's house, friends, friends' houses

2. typist, typist's desk, typists, typists' desks

3. bicycle, bicycle's tire, bicycles, bicycles' tires

4. referee, referee's whistle, referees, referees' whistles

5. sheep, sheep's nose, sheep, sheep's noses

6. woman, woman's dress, women, women's dresses

7. penny, penny's date, pennies, pennies' dates

8. dress, dress's collar, dresses, dresses' collars

9. musician, musician's fee, musicians, musicians' fees

10. lioness, lioness's cub, lionesses, lionesses' cubs

11. actor, actor's part, actors, actors' parts

12. mechanic, mechanic's car, mechanics, mechanics' cars

13. deer, deer's tail, deer, deer's tails, *or* deers, deers' tails

14. artist, artist's easel, artists, artists' easels

15. purse, purse's strap, purses, purses' straps

16. man, man's shirt, men, men's shirts

17. truck, truck's headlights, trucks, trucks' headlights

18. dish, dish's pattern, dishes, dishes' patterns

19. window, window's shape, windows, windows' shapes

20. mouse, mouse's ear, mice, mice's ears

Reference Note

For information on **forming the plurals of nouns,** see Chapter 27.

1. women's
2. village's
3. their
4. Shakers'/its
5. Everyone's
6. children's

---

4. (*Theirs, Their's*) is the best frozen yogurt in town.
5. Your car needs to have (*its, it's*) oil changed.
6. It wasn't (*anyone's, anyones'*) fault that we missed the bus.
7. (*Her's, Hers*) is the best project in the Science Fair.
8. (*Someones, Someone's, Someones'*) choir robe was left on the bus.
9. (*Everybodys, Everybody's, Everybodys'*) morale suffered.
10. That dog of (*their's, theirs*) should be on a leash.

Review B **Writing the Singular, Plural, and Possessive Forms of Nouns**

On a piece of paper, make four columns headed *Singular, Singular Possessive, Plural,* and *Plural Possessive*. Write each of those forms of the following nouns. Add a suitable noun to follow each word in the possessive case. If you do not know how to spell a plural form, use a dictionary.

EXAMPLE

	Singular	Singular Possessive	Plural	Plural Possessive
1.	dog	dog's owner	dogs	dogs' owners

1. friend
2. typist
3. bicycle
4. referee
5. sheep
6. woman
7. penny
8. dress
9. musician
10. lioness
11. actor
12. mechanic
13. deer
14. artist
15. purse
16. man
17. truck
18. dish
19. window
20. mouse

Review C **Correcting the Forms of Nouns and Pronouns**

Identify and correct the ten incorrect possessive forms in the following paragraph.

EXAMPLE [1] The women shown in these photographs welcomed us to the Shaker village of Pleasant Hill, Kentucky, during our history class' field trip last spring.

1. *class's*

[1] As you can see, the style of the ~~womens~~ dresses is quite old. [2] In fact, the ~~villages~~ history goes back to 1806. [3] That was the year that the religious group known as the Shakers founded ~~they're~~ own community. [4] We learned that the ~~Shaker's~~ lively way of dancing gave the group ~~it's~~ name. [5] ~~Everyones~~ life in the Shaker village was supposed to be orderly, simple, and productive. [6] This basic harmony was true of even the ~~childrens'~~ routines. [7] During the ~~days~~ tour of the village, we saw several people practicing Shaker crafts. [8] One guide of ~~our's~~

told us that the Shakers invented the common clothespin and the flat broom and designed useful furniture and boxes. **[9]** I enjoyed visiting the gardens and the Centre Family House and imagining what a Shakers' life must have been like.

25e. Generally, in compound words, names of organizations and businesses, and words showing joint possession, only the last word is possessive in form.

COMPOUND WORDS	community **board's** meeting
	vice-president's contract
	her brother-in-**law's** gifts
ORGANIZATIONS	the Museum of **Art's** budget
	United **Fund's** drive
BUSINESSES	Berkeley Milk **Company's** trucks
JOINT POSSESSION	Peggy and **Lisa's** tent [The tent belongs to both Peggy and Lisa.]
	children and **parents'** concerns [The children and the parents have the same concerns.]

When one of the words showing joint possession is a pronoun, both words should be possessive in form.

EXAMPLE   **Peggy's** and **my** tent [not *Peggy and my tent*]

│ STYLE   TIP │

Use a phrase beginning with *of* or *for* to avoid awkward possessive forms.

AWKWARD
the Society for the Prevention of Cruelty to Animals' advertisement

BETTER
the advertisement **for** the Society for the Prevention of Cruelty to Animals

Crossing the Curriculum

Science. As a short research project that will give students a chance to practice using the possessive case while also learning about important achievements, challenge students to research and create short reports on mathematic or scientific concepts that bear their discoverers' names in the possessive case. One example is Bernoulli's principle, which explains how the speed of a fluid affects its pressure. Students should create short written versions of their research, and volunteers may want to explain their findings to the class.

MECHANICS

Possessive Case   **705**

TECHNOLOGY TIP

Tell students who use word processors to take advantage of the search function when they are proofreading. By searching for apostrophes and contractions, students can check each usage for correctness.

Exercise 6 Using the Possessive Case

ANSWERS

1. Sylvia's and Eric's tickets
2. the FBI's investigation
3. Gwen and Carlos's duet
4. the master sergeant's uniform
5. the Grand Canyon's history
6. Isabel's and my job
7. the Acme Life Insurance Company's agent
8. my uncle's and our tractors
9. the Sales Department's award
10. her mother-in-law's and her cousin's businesses

Crossing the Curriculum

Social Studies. Refer students to any social studies report they have written about a person, and ask them to check for the correct use of apostrophes. If students do not have an essay to check, ask them to write two paragraphs about the accomplishments of their favorite role model and then check for the correct use of apostrophes.

Reference Note
For more about **acronyms** see page 640.

NOTE The possessive of an acronym (NASA, DOS, CIA, CBS) is formed by adding an apostrophe and *s*.

EXAMPLES NASA**'s** latest space probe

CBS**'s** hit television series

25f. When two or more persons possess something individually, each of their names is possessive in form.

EXAMPLES **Mrs. Martin's** and **Mrs. Blair's** cars [the cars of two different women]

Asha's and **Daniella's** tennis rackets [individual, not joint, possession]

Exercise 6 Using the Possessive Case

Use the possessive case to rewrite the following word groups.

EXAMPLE 1. the book owned by Natalie and Stan
1. *Natalie and Stan's book*

1. the ticket of Sylvia and the ticket of Eric
2. an investigation by the FBI
3. the duet of Gwen and Carlos
4. a uniform belonging to the master sergeant
5. the history of the Grand Canyon
6. the job shared by Isabel and me
7. an agent for the Acme Life Insurance Company
8. one tractor belonging to my uncle and one to us
9. the award received by the Sales Department
10. the business of her mother-in-law and the business of her cousin

Review D Identifying Words That Require Apostrophes

Identify the ten words requiring apostrophes in the following paragraph. Then, write the words, inserting the apostrophes.

EXAMPLE [1] Have you ever heard of the U.S. Patent Offices Hall of Fame for inventors?
1. *Offices—Office's*

1. Fame's

[1] The Hall of Fames members, who are both American and foreign, include many people that you've probably heard of as well as some you haven't. [2] Vladimir Kosma Zworykin's picture tube helped

lead to televisions development. [3] Charles Richard Drew changed peoples lives all over the world with his work on blood plasma in transfusions. [4] Luther Burbanks accomplishment was the development of more than eight hundred new plant varieties. [5] Heart patients pacemakers were invented by Wilson Greatbatch. [6] You'll probably recognize such famous inventors as the Ford Motor Companys founder, Henry Ford. [7] Of course, Thomas Edisons and Alexander Graham Bells achievements assured their enduring fame. [8] No ones pleasure is greater than mine that Orville and Wilbur Wrights invention of the airplane landed them in such good company, too.

2. television's
3. people's
4. Burbank's
5. patients'

6. Company's
7. Edison's/Bell's
8. one's/Wright's

Contractions

25g. Use an apostrophe to show where letters, numerals, or words have been omitted in a contraction.

A ***contraction*** is a shortened form of a word, a group of words, or a numeral. The apostrophes in contractions indicate where letters, numerals, or words have been left out.

EXAMPLES

who is . . . who**'s**   I am . . . I**'m**

1991 . . . **'91**   you are . . . you**'re**

of the clock . . . **o'**clock   we had . . . we**'d**

let us . . . let**'s**   she has . . . she**'s**

she will . . . she**'ll**   I had . . . I**'d**

Bill is . . . Bill**'s**   we have . . . we**'ve**

Ordinarily, the word *not* is shortened to *n't* and added to a verb without any change in the spelling of the verb.

EXAMPLES

is not . . . is**n't**   were not . . . were**n't**

are not . . . are**n't**   has not . . . has**n't**

does not . . . does**n't**   have not . . . have**n't**

do not . . . do**n't**   had not . . . had**n't**

did not . . . did**n't**   would not . . . would**n't**

EXCEPTIONS   will not . . . wo**n't**   cannot . . . ca**n't**

STYLE   TIP

Many people consider contractions informal. Therefore, it is usually best to avoid using them in formal writing and speech.

INFORMAL
The Founding Fathers couldn't foresee the mobility of modern life.

FORMAL
The Founding Fathers **could not** foresee the mobility of modern life.

Contractions

Rule 25g *(pp. 707–709)*

O B J E C T I V E

- To correct sentences by using apostrophes for contractions

T E A C H I N G (TIP)

Activity. Tell students that they are going to work as a class to create a conversation. Begin the conversation with an opener like "I can't believe that . . . ," and call on students at random to build the conversation by each adding a sentence that includes a contraction.

MECHANICS

Contractions   **707**

RESOURCES

Contractions

Practice

- *Grammar, Usage, and Mechanics*, p. 312

Relating to Literature

You may want to assign parts to students and have them read aloud dialogue from a short story such as Daphne du Maurier's "The Birds." Ask students why the author used contractions. [*Contractions make dialogue sound natural because they are informal and conversational.*]

Then, have students re-read the dialogue, replacing all contractions with complete words. Discuss with students what effect removing the contractions has on the dialogue. [*Removing contractions may cause the language to sound stilted and unnatural.*]

Meeting

INDIVIDUAL
NEEDS

ENGLISH-LANGUAGE LEARNERS

Spanish. Because Spanish has no written contracted verb forms, you may wish to use a visual aid to show students how contractions are formed. Write the following groups of words on the chalkboard.

    is not   she will   let us

Then, cross out the *o* in *not* and cover the *o* with an index card on which you have written a large apostrophe. Do the same for the *wi* in *will* and for the *u* in *us.* Emphasize that when the apostrophe is added, the pronunciation of the words changes: *isn't, she'll,* and *let's.* Have students work in small groups to practice forming and pronouncing other contractions.

Do not confuse contractions with possessive pronouns.

Contractions	Possessive Pronouns
Who's at bat? [Who is]	**Whose** bat is that?
It's roaring. [It is]	Listen to **its** roar.
You're too busy. [You are]	**Your** friend is busy.
There's a kite. [There is]	That kite is **theirs.**
They're tall trees. [They are]	**Their** trees are tall.

Exercise 7 Correcting Sentences by Using Apostrophes for Contractions

Write each incorrect contraction in the following sentences, adding an apostrophe as necessary. If a sentence is already correct, write *C.*

EXAMPLE   1. Hes pleased by his promotion.

     1. He's

1. You've
2. '45
3. Who's
4. store's
5. C
6. We'll
7. C
8. o'clock
9. I'm
10. C

1. "Youve changed," she said.
2. World War II ended in 45.
3. Whos coming to the party?
4. "The stores about to close," said the clerk.
5. Several stores were closed because of the storm.
6. Well have to try to make it there on time.
7. Whose telescope is that, Richard?
8. She gets up at 6 oclock.
9. Im very glad to meet you.
10. Don't you play chess?

Review E Recognizing the Correct Use of Apostrophes

Choose the correct word in parentheses in each sentence in the following paragraph.

EXAMPLE   [1] (*Your, You're*) likely to see fiesta scenes like the one on the next page in Mexican American communities across the United States each year on September 16.

     1. You're

[1] (*It's, Its*) a day of celebration that includes parades, speeches, music, and, as you can see, even colorful folk dances. Of course, [2] (*theirs, there's*) plenty of food, including stacks of tortillas and bowls of beans and soup. [3] (*Who's, Whose*) to say how late the merry-making will last? [4] (*It's, Its*) a joyful holiday of fun, but everyone remembers [5] (*it's, its*) importance, too. Mexican Americans know that

---

Learning for Life

Meeting Minutes. Writing the minutes for a meeting should allow students to use possessives and contractions. Ask students to take minutes for a real or imagined student organization using a specified number of possessives and contractions. Students should post or distribute minutes for input from classmates.

[6] (*they're*, *their*) celebrating the beginning of Mexico's rebellion to gain independence from Spain. On September 16, 1810, Father Miguel Hidalgo y Costilla gathered his forces for the rebellion and uttered [7] (*it's*, *its*) first battle cry. Father Hidalgo, [8] (*who's*, *whose*) parish was in west central Mexico, led an army across the country. If [9] (*your*, *you're*) in Mexico City on the eve of September 16, you can hear the president of Mexico ring what is believed to be the bell that Hidalgo rang to summon his people for [10] (*they're*, *their*) historic march.

Plurals

25h. To prevent confusion, use an apostrophe and an *s* to form the plurals of lowercase letters, some capital letters, numerals, symbols, and some words that are referred to as words.

EXAMPLES   Grandma always tells me to mind my *p*'s and *q*'s.

I got A's on both tests I took last week. [An apostrophe is used because without one the plural spells the word *As*.]

The *1*'s in this exercise look like *l*'s.

Two different Web site addresses began with ##'s and ended with *.com*'s.

His *hi*'s are always cheerful. [An apostrophe is used because without one the plural spells the word *his*.]

Exercise 8 Forming Plurals by Using Apostrophes

Use an apostrophe to form the plural of each of the italicized items in the following word groups.

EXAMPLE   **1.** margins filled with *?*
        1. ?'s

1. *s* that look like *f*
2. to put *U* at the end
3. two *r* and two *s*
4. adding columns of *$* and *%*

STYLE   TIP

Many writers add only *s* when forming the kinds of plurals listed in Rule 25h. However, using both an apostrophe and *s* is not wrong and may be necessary to make your meaning clear. Therefore, it is a good idea always to include the apostrophe.

Reference Note

For more information on **forming these kinds of plurals,** see page 743.

1. *s*'s/*f*'s   **3.** *r*'s/*s*'s
2. *U*'s   **4.** *$*'s/*%*'s

Plurals

Rule 25h (*pp. 709–710*)

OBJECTIVE

■ To form the plurals of letters used as letters and words used as words

Meeting INDIVIDUAL NEEDS

LEARNERS HAVING DIFFICULTY

You may wish to simplify **Exercise 8** by giving students options from which to choose. For example, write the following choices on the chalkboard:

    a. *s*'s that look like *f*'s

    b. *ss* that look like *fs*

Do the same for the remainder of the exercise, and then have students discuss the correct answers.

Meeting

INDIVIDUAL NEEDS

MODALITIES

Visual Learners. The eight categories of rules in this chapter for the use of apostrophes might be displayed on the border of an octagon as a review for students or as a memory device to include in their notebooks. In the following example, the rule categories are written on the inside of the border; students should add examples on the outside of the border.

Students might work in pairs to come up with appropriate examples for each rule.

MECHANICS

---

5. *q's/g's* 8. *her's/*
6. *C's/B's*   *their's*
7. *his's/* 9. *i's/t's* 10. *I's*
   its's

┌─ H E L P ─
You may need
to change the spelling of
some words in Review F.

1. Don't/their

2. isn't/mats/windows

3. artists/engineers/
   history's

4. systems

5. techniques/weren't

6. Buffalo's/
   citizens/whose

7. technology's

8. Wasn't /o'clock

5. these *q* or *g*   8. too many *her* and *their*
6. all *C* and *B*   9. your *i* and your *t*
7. replace all the *his* with *its*   10. two *I* in the sentence

Review F **Using Apostrophes Correctly**

Add or delete apostrophes as needed in the following sentences.

EXAMPLE   1. Summers here, but because of air conditioning its more
             bearable than it used to be.

          1. *Summer's; it's*

1. Dont you wonder when people started cooling they're homes
   with air conditioning?
2. Air cooling isnt a new practice; in fact, in ancient Rome, wet grass
   mat's were hung over window's to cool incoming air by evaporation.
3. In the early sixteenth century, one of the greatest Italian artist's
   and engineer's, Leonardo da Vinci, built historys first
   mechanical fan.
4. The British scientist David B. Reid's air-ventilation system's were
   installed in the British House of Commons in 1838.
5. However, modern technique's of air conditioning werent
   invented until the early twentieth century in Buffalo, New York.
6. One of Buffalos most famous citizen's, Willis Carrier, who's name
   is still on many air conditioners, invented the first air-condition-
   ing unit in 1902.
7. By 1928, the technologys' rapid development had produced the
   first fully air-conditioned office building, the Milam Building in
   San Antonio, Texas.
8. Wasnt Texas—where in summer the temperature can reach
   90 degrees by eleven oclock in the morning—a logical place to
   have the first air-conditioned office building?
9. By the late 1950's, more and more homes' had
   window air conditioner's, and smaller unit's
   for motor vehicle's were becoming increasingly
   common. 9. homes/conditioners/units/vehicles
10. Arent you glad air conditioning is so common
    nowaday's? 10. Aren't/nowadays

25

Chapter Review

A. Correcting Sentences by Using Apostrophes Correctly

In the following sentences, apostrophes are either missing or incorrectly used. Write the correct form of each incorrect word. In some cases, an apostrophe must be added or deleted; in others, the spelling of the word also must be changed.

1. its

2. elders/tribe's

3. We're/centuries

4. There's/their

5. Spain's/years

6. Peruvians'

7. Someone's/ weren't

8. one's/characters

9. Store's/systems

10. whose/Hardwick's/ store's

1. Ancient peoples felt that writing had a magic power of it's own.

2. Writing was practiced by the elders' of a tribe to preserve the tribes lore as well as its laws.

3. Were not sure when or how writing began, but we do know that it existed several century's before 3000 B.C.

4. Theres plenty of evidence that people communicated through they're drawings long before they had a system of writing.

5. Spain and France's wonderful cave drawings were painted more than thirty thousand year's ago.

6. The ancient Peruvians message system was a complicated arrangement of knots.

7. Someones research has shown that *W*'s and *J*'s werent used in English writing until the late Middle Ages.

8. In China, ones mastery of basic reading depends on learning one thousand character's.

9. Hardwick Book Stores window display features early system's of writing, such as cuneiform.

10. Bess and Robert, who's reports were on the history of writing, asked one of Mr. Hardwicks clerks for permission to examine the stores display.

B. Proofreading a Paragraph for Correct Use of Apostrophes

The following paragraph contains errors in the use of apostrophes. For each sentence, write the correct form of each incorrect word.

11. years'

12. Napoleon's

[11] Despite many years work, scholars were not able to decipher hieroglyphics until the early nineteenth century. [12] In 1799, one of Napoleons soldiers serving in Egypt discovered a stone tablet. [13] The

To assess student progress, you may want to compare the types of items missed on the **Diagnostic Preview** to those missed on the **Chapter Review.** If students have not made significant progress, you may want to refer them to **Chapter 28: Correcting Common Errors, Exercise 35,** for additional practice.

MECHANICS

13. Europeans
14. tablet's/languages

15. experts'

16. Their/names

17. wasn't

18. scholar's

19. stone's

20. doors

tablet came to be known as the Rosetta Stone after the town in which it was found: Rashid, which ~~European's~~ called Rosetta. **[14]** The ~~tablets~~ surface was inscribed in three ancient ~~language's~~: Greek, Egyptian hieroglyphics, and Coptic, a language derived from ancient Egyptian. **[15]** The ~~experts~~ translations of the Greek text revealed that the same information had been written in all three languages in 196 B.C. **[16]** ~~They're~~ next step was to use their knowledge of Greek and Coptic to identify how ~~names'~~ of specific people and places were written in hieroglyphics. **[17]** It ~~wasnt~~ until 1822, however, that a Frenchman named Jean-François Champollion deciphered the ancient Egyptians' writing. **[18]** Following another ~~scholars'~~ theory that hieroglyphic symbols represent sounds, Champollion figured out which symbols represent which sounds. **[19]** He also established that the ~~stones'~~ hieroglyphics were a translation from the Greek—not, as had been thought, the other way around. **[20]** Though many ~~door's~~ remained to be opened, a key to ancient Egyptian history had been found.

C. Using Apostrophes to Form Possessive Nouns

Write the possessive form for each of the following nouns. After each possessive word, give an appropriate noun.

21. Humble Oil Company	**26.** Massachusetts
22. buffalo	**27.** Northern Ireland
23. anything	**28.** bishops
24. geese	**29.** NBC
25. Lori	**30.** mosque

D. Using Apostrophes Correctly

The following sentences contain errors in the use of apostrophes. Write each incorrect word or expression, adding or deleting apostrophes where needed. You may need to change the spelling as well.

31. Haven't/refrigerators
32. Romans'

33. cellars/pits

34. Didn't/India's/Egypt's

31. ~~Havent~~ you ever wondered when the first ~~refrigerator's~~ were used?

32. Wealthy ~~Romans~~ main method of refrigeration was to cool food in snow cellars.

33. Snow ~~cellar's~~ were ~~pit's~~ dug in the ground, insulated with straw, and filled with snow and ice.

34. ~~Didnt~~ ancient ~~India~~ and ~~Egypts'~~ cooling techniques include using evaporative cooling to freeze perishable products?

Chapter Review

C. Using Apostrophes to Form Possessive Nouns

POSSIBLE ANSWERS

21. Humble Oil Company's profits
22. buffalo's horns
23. anything's effect
24. geese's feathers
25. Lori's backpack
26. Massachusetts' capital
27. Northern Ireland's linen mills
28. bishops' robes
29. NBC's programs
30. mosque's ceiling

RESOURCES

Punctuation

Review

■ *Grammar, Usage, and Mechanics*, pp. 314–315, 316, 317, 318, 319

Assessment

■ *Assessment Package*
 —*Chapter Tests*, Ch. 25
 —*Chapter Tests in Standardized Test Formats*, Ch. 25
■ *Test Generator (One-Stop Planner CD-ROM)*

35. Evaporative cooling means placing water in shallow ~~tray's~~ and using the ice ~~thats~~ formed during rapid evaporation.

36. In the sixteenth century, ~~Italians'~~ discovered that a mixture of water and potassium nitrate could be used to cool bottled liquids.

37. During the 1850's, Ferdinand Carré, a French inventor, developed the ~~worlds'~~ first absorption system using ammonia.

38. Absorption ~~system's~~ use the direct application of heat to initiate the refrigeration cycle by changing ~~refrigerant's~~ from liquid to gas and back again.

39. Another system that produces refrigeration is compression, in which ~~compressor's~~ are used to bring about refrigeration cycles.

40. In 1876, the scientific world learned the name of Carl von Linde, a German engineer ~~who's~~ compression system using ammonia was the foundation of modern refrigeration.

35. trays/that's

36. Italians

37. world's

38. systems/refrigerants

39. compressors

40. whose

Writing Application
Using Apostrophes in a Paragraph

Possessive Case   Write a paragraph about the musical preferences of one or more family members or friends. Use at least two singular possessive nouns, two plural possessive nouns, and one indefinite pronoun in the possessive case.

Prewriting   First, make a list of family members or friends, and beside each name write what you know about that person's musical tastes. If you are not sure about someone's preferences, ask him or her.

Writing   As you write your first draft, think about ways of organizing your information by type of music, age of listener, and so on.

Revising   Ask a family member or friend to read your paragraph. Is it clear whose preferences are discussed? Are the preferences accurately expressed?

Publishing   Check your placement of apostrophes. As you read through your paragraph, correct errors in spelling, grammar, and punctuation. With the permission of the person or persons whose musical tastes you have discussed in your paragraph, post your piece on a class bulletin board, or use it as a basis for a class discussion.

Writing Application
(p. 713)

OBJECTIVE

■ **To write a paragraph correctly using possessive nouns, plural nouns, and indefinite pronouns in the possessive case**

Writing Application

Tip. This writing assignment gives students practice using singular possessive nouns, plural nouns, and indefinite pronouns in the possessive case. You may want to write **Rules 25a, 25b, 25c,** and **25d** on the chalkboard for students to refer to as they develop and proofread their paragraphs.

Scoring Rubric. While you will want to pay particular attention to students' punctuation of possessive nouns and indefinite pronouns, you will also want to evaluate overall writing performance. You may want to give a split score to indicate development and clarity of the composition as well as mechanics skills.

Critical Thinking

Application. Remind students to apply their knowledge of correct possessive forms to their writing. If they want to describe their friend Juan's taste in music, then they must use the singular possessive. If they are describing several friends' CD collections, then they must use plural nouns.

RESOURCES

Writing Application
Extension
■ *Grammar, Usage, and Mechanics,* p. 322
■ *Language Workshop CD-ROM,* Lessons 51, 52

PREVIEWING THE CHAPTER

- The punctuation marks taught in this chapter—hyphens, dashes, parentheses, brackets, and ellipsis points—differ from one another in the frequency with which they are used, even by professional writers. Ninth-graders are probably familiar with parentheses and the use of hyphens to divide words into syllables, but the other marks may be new to them. Students may need to be reminded of the rules for brackets, ellipsis points, and parentheses when they proofread research papers.

- The chapter closes with a **Chapter Review** including a **Writing Application** feature that asks students to write a three-paragraph report using hyphens, dashes, parentheses, brackets, and ellipsis points.

- For help integrating this chapter with writing chapters, see the **Teaching Strands** chart on pp. T371A–T371B.

USING THE DIAGNOSTIC PREVIEW

- You may want to use the **Diagnostic Preview** to assess students' knowledge of the use of hyphens, dashes, brackets, and parentheses. Students could tally the number of errors in each of the four categories to determine which rules and exercises need attention.

Punctuation
Hyphens, Dashes, Parentheses, Brackets, Ellipsis Points

Diagnostic Preview

A. Using Hyphens, Dashes, and Parentheses

Use hyphens, dashes, and parentheses to punctuate the following sentences. Do not add commas to these sentences. Answers may vary.

EXAMPLE   1. Henry Viscardi he founded the National Center for Disability Services dedicated his life to creating opportunities for people who have disabilities.

1. *Henry Viscardi—he founded the National Center for Disability Services—dedicated his life to creating opportunities for people who have disabilities.*

┌─HELP─┐

There may be more than one way to correct a sentence in the Diagnostic Preview, but you need to give only one.

1. hyp. / hyp.
2. hyp. / par. / par. / hyp.

3. par. / par.

4. hyp. / dash / hyp. / dash

5. dash / dash / hyp.
6. dash / dash

7. hyp. / dash

8. dash

1. The soup was three fourths water and one fourth vegetables.
2. Twenty six students most of them from the advanced math class represented our school at the all state chess match.
3. The Battle of Bunker Hill June 17, 1775 damaged the confidence of the British.
4. The ex treasurer of our club he's an extremely self confident person is now running for class president.
5. My sister she lives in Boston now is studying pre Columbian art.
6. If you have ever dreamed of finding buried treasure and who hasn't? your search could begin on Padre Island.
7. George Grinnell was a self taught expert on the American West and helped negotiate treaties with three American Indian peoples the Blackfoot, the Cheyenne, and the Pawnee.
8. Aunt Jo murmured, "Please turn out the" and then fell asleep.

CHAPTER RESOURCES

Planning
- *One-Stop Planner CD-ROM*

Practice and Extension
- *Grammar, Usage, and Mechanics*, p. 323
- *Developmental Language Skills*, pp. 141–144

Internet
- go.hrw.com (keyword: EOLang)

Evaluation and Assessment
- *Chapter Tests*, Ch. 26
- *Chapter Tests in Standardized Test Formats*, Ch. 26
- *Test Generator (One-Stop Planner)*

9. Rachel Carson was working for the U.S. Fish and Wildlife Service∧ created in 1940∧when she first recognized the threat of pesticides.
10. Her book *Silent Spring*∧copyright 1962∧alerted the public to the dangers of environmental pollution.

B. Using Hyphens, Dashes, Brackets, and Parentheses

Use <u>hyphens</u>, <u>dashes</u>, <u>brackets</u>, and <u>parentheses</u> to punctutate the following sentences. If a sentence is already correct, write *C*. Do not add commas.

EXAMPLE   **1.** There are several countries Senegal, Gambia, Guinea, Guinea-Bissau, Sierra Leone, and Liberia along the west-central coast of Africa.

         1. *There are several countries—Senegal, Gambia, Guinea, Guinea-Bissau, Sierra Leone, and Liberia—along the west-central coast of Africa.*

11. Liberia's history∧its founding, that is∧is unique.
12. Liberia was settled in pre∧Civil War days by freed slaves from the United States.
13. An antislavery group known as the American Colonization Society∧ it was officially chartered by the U.S. Congress∧started sending freed slaves to a colony in Africa in 1822.
14. Twenty∧five years later, the colonists∧how proud they must have been!∧declared Liberia independent.
15. They named their capital Monrovia in honor of President James Monroe∧in office 1817–1825∧.
16. They also modeled their country's constitution and government∧ not surprisingly∧on those of the United States.
17. The first president of Liberia, Joseph Jenkins Roberts (he originally served for eight years∧1848–1856∧and again during an economic crisis∧1872–1876∧), was born in Virginia.
18. Roberts began his political career as an aide to the colonial governor, Thomas H. Buchanan∧a white member of the American Colonization Society∧.
19. During Liberia's early years, the United States provided aid.
20. However, the U.S. government didn't officially recognize Liberia until President Lincoln's administration∧1862∧.

9. par. / par.

10. par. / par.

11. dash / dash
12. hyp.

13. dash / dash

14. hyp. / dash / dash

15. par. / par.

16. dash / dash

17. br. / br. / br. / br.

18. par. / par.

19. C
20. par. / par.

TEACHING (TIP)

Motivation. Explain to students that although the punctuation marks covered in this chapter are not the most common, they are needed to communicate effectively in some writing situations. To illustrate the confusion caused by missing punctuation and to introduce hyphens, dashes, parentheses, brackets, and ellipses, copy the following sentences on the chalkboard, omitting the new marks of punctuation. Ask volunteers to try to clarify the following sentences by indicating where a punctuation mark should occur. Then, insert hyphens, dashes, parentheses, brackets, and ellipses for the class.

1. "Well, I think . . . no, I really don't know," he admitted.

2. An area paper, the *Times-Journal*, reported on commencement ceremonies:

 "On Friday evening Tamara Larken, a local valedictorian, addressed the audience: 'I am pleased to speak on behalf of my classmates [the Ratcliffe High School Class of 2001]. We are proud to take our place in a new century armed with what we have learned in the old.'"

3. Lana Kelly, my neighbor, just celebrated her twenty-first birthday.

4. They will meet us at the movie (the one about a sinking ship).

5. I think I'll stop—oh, excuse me, Mary—right here.

Hyphens

Rules 26a–d *(pp. 716–719)*

OBJECTIVES

- To use hyphens to divide words at the ends of lines
- To hyphenate words correctly in sentences

Relating to Literature

The poet E. E. Cummings uses hyphens to create images in his poem "in Just-." If the poem is available, ask students to read it and to notice the ways Cummings uses hyphens to link words and, therefore, images. Ask them what the images "Just-spring," "mud-luscious," and "puddle-wonderful" bring to mind. [*Students may visualize "Just-spring" as a miniseason at the very beginning of spring when winter is still hanging on, creating mud puddles from melting snow and allowing children a place to splash and squish and celebrate the wonder of spring.*]

MECHANICS

┌HELP─
If you need to divide a word and are not sure about its syllables, look it up in a dictionary.

Hyphens

Word Division

26a. Use a hyphen to divide a word at the end of a line.

EXAMPLE   The new governor's victory celebration will be organ‑ized by her campaign committee.

When you divide a word at the end of a line, keep in mind the following rules:

(1) Do not divide a one-syllable word.

INCORRECT   The line of people waiting to buy tickets stret‑ched halfway down the block.

CORRECT   The line of people waiting to buy tickets stretched halfway down the block.

CORRECT   The line of people waiting to buy tickets stretched halfway down the block.

(2) Divide a word only between syllables.

INCORRECT   The stars Betelgeuse and Rigel are in the conste‑llation known as Orion.

CORRECT   The stars Betelgeuse and Rigel are in the constel‑lation known as Orion.

CORRECT   The stars Betelgeuse and Rigel are in the constella‑tion known as Orion.

(3) A word containing double consonants usually may be divided between those two consonants.

EXAMPLES   con‑nect   drum‑mer

(4) Divide a word with a prefix or a suffix between the prefix and the base word (or root) or between the base word and the suffix.

EXAMPLES   pre‑judge   post‑pone   half‑back

　　　　　　　 fall‑ing   frag‑ment   con‑fusion

(5) Divide an already hyphenated word only at a hyphen.

INCORRECT   The speaker this morning is my moth‑er-in-law.

CORRECT   The speaker this morning is my mother‑in-law.

RESOURCES

Hyphens
Practice
- *Grammar, Usage, and Mechanics,* pp. 324, 325, 326
- *Language Workshop CD-ROM,* Lesson 56

(6) Do not divide a word so that one letter stands alone.

INCORRECT   The utility company built a new turbine to generate e-
lectricity.

CORRECT   The utility company built a new turbine to generate electricity.

Exercise 1 Using Hyphens to Divide Words at the Ends of Lines

Write each of the following words, using hyphens to indicate where the word may be divided at the end of a line. If a word should not be divided, write _one-syllable word._ Carets indicate where hyphens could be placed to divide each

EXAMPLES **1.** thoroughly   **2.** cooked   word correctly.

              1. thor-ough-ly   *2. one-syllable word*

1. Olympics
2. library
3. fourth 3. o.s.w.
4. unchanged
5. impolite

6. tomorrow
7. breathe 7. o.s.w.
8. corporation
9. through 9. o.s.w.
10. merry-go-round

┌HELP┐

If necessary,
check a dictionary for the
proper syllabication of the
words in Exercise 1.

Word breaks are
based on *Webster's
New World College
Dictionary, Third
Edition.*

Compound Words

Some compound words are hyphenated (*red-hot*); some are written as one word (*redhead*); and some are written as two or more words (*red tape*). Whenever you need to know whether a word is hyphenated, look it up in a current dictionary.

26b. Use a hyphen with compound numbers from *twenty-one* to *ninety-nine* and with fractions used as modifiers.

EXAMPLES **seventy-six** trombones

                 three-quarters cup [but *three quarters* of a cup]

26c. Use a hyphen with the prefixes *ex–, self–, all–,* and *great–;* with the suffixes *–elect* and *–free;* and with all prefixes before a proper noun or proper adjective.

EXAMPLES

ex-coach	**great-**aunt	**mid-**July
self-made	president**-elect**	**pro-**American
all-star	fat**-free**	**pre-**Columbian

Reference Note

For more information
on **using a dictionary,**
see "The Dictionary" in
the Quick Reference
Handbook.

STYLE   TIP

The prefix *half–* often
requires a hyphen, as in
half-life, half-moon, and
half-truth. However, sometimes *half* is used without a
hyphen, either as a part of
a single word (*halftone,
halfway, halfback*) or as a
separate word (*half shell,
half pint, half note*). If you
are not sure how to spell a
word containing *half,* look
up the word in a dictionary.

Exercise 1 Answers may vary according to the dictionaries used. Some dictionaries recommend, for the sake of style, that words not be broken at the end of a line between certain syllables. For example, the vertical lines in the first, second, fifth, and tenth words indicate places where the words should not be divided at the ends of lines, according to *Webster's New World College Dictionary,* Third Edition.

Critical Thinking

Metacognition. Write the following words on the chalkboard, and ask students to divide them with hyphens as if the words were at the end of a written line.

1. apple [*ap-ple*]

2. doctor [*doc-tor*]

3. strength [*not divided*]

Then, ask students to explain how they knew where to place the hyphens correctly. [*Some possible explanations include experience or knowledge of rules.*]

MECHANICS

26d. Hyphenate a compound adjective when it precedes the noun it modifies.

EXAMPLES   a **well-written** book [but *a book that is well written*]

a **small-town** boy [but *a boy from a small town*]

Do not use a hyphen if one of the modifiers is an adverb that ends in –*ly.*

EXAMPLE   a **bitterly cold** day

NOTE   Some compound adjectives are always hyphenated, whether they precede or follow the nouns they modify.

EXAMPLES   a **brand-new** shirt
a shirt that is **brand-new**

a **down-to-earth** person
a person who is **down-to-earth**

─HELP─

If you are unsure about whether a compound adjective is hyphenated, look up the word in a current dictionary.

Exercise 2   **Hyphenating Words Correctly**

Insert hyphens in the words that should be hyphenated in the following sentences. If a sentence is already correct, write *C.*

EXAMPLE   1. The world famous speaker was very well informed.

1. *The world-famous speaker was very well informed.*
    Carets indicate where hyphens should be inserted.

1. The exgovernor presented the all American trophy at the competition.
2. Until 1959, the United States flag had forty eight stars.
3. In twenty five days my great grandparents will celebrate their seventy fifth wedding anniversary; about three fourths of the family will attend the celebration.
4. The exambassador's lecture focused on the post Napoleonic era.
5. He added one half teaspoon of sugar free vanilla extract to the mixture and set the timer for thirty five minutes.
6. A documentary called "The Self Improvement Culture" was on TV last night.
7. Herman's new mountain bike was very up to date.
8. Well designed buildings have clearly marked fire escapes.
9. Sally has always been very down-to-earth. 9. C
10. The President elect gathered his Cabinet to discuss future policy.

Identifying the Correct Use of Hyphens

You have just received the following e-mail message from your friend Eduardo. His computer is acting up again, and it's putting in hyphens that are not supposed to be there. Make a list of words containing incorrectly used hyphens and another list of words containing correctly used ones.   Hyphens used incorrectly are circled.

EXAMPLES   Incorrect   Correct
            early-bird   *brother-in-law*

Hey there!

[1] So, how have you⊖been? [2] I can't believe it's mid-April. [3] I've really been running myself ragged with home⊖work, club⊖ meetings, sports, and ninety-nine other things. [4] You wouldn'⊖ t believe how busy I've been!

[5] I've got a role in our spring⊖play. [6] It's not a big role, but I'm part of an all-star cast. [7] We're doing *Our Town*. [8] I am managing the props, too.

[9] Enclosed is a good recipe that I used last week to make pop-corn topping. [10] I'm president-elect of the foreign language⊖club, and it was once again my turn to host the monthly meeting. [11] Thirty-three members came to my house on Friday (we have a total of fifty-one members). [12] Of course, I served refreshments, and every⊖one loved this topping.

[13] Recipe for Mexican Popcorn Topping: In a small bowl, mix one-fourth cup of chili⊖powder and one-half teaspoon of salt. Then, add one⊖teaspoon each of garlic powder, cilantro, and cumin. [14] (Those last two are herbs.) [15] Sprinkle mixture over plain⊖popcorn.

Take care, and write soon.

Eduardo

YOU CORRECT MY GRAMMAR, MY SPELLING, MY PUNCTUATION! I CAN'T STAND THE PRESSURE OF LIVING WITH A PERFECTIONIST!'

Hyphens   **719**

ALTERNATIVE LESSON
Have students find examples of the following items and give the sentence number in which each was found.

- a reflexive pronoun [3. *myself*]

- an adjective clause [9. *that I used last week to make popcorn topping*]

- two infinitive phrases [9. *to make popcorn topping;* 10. *to host the monthly meeting*]

Timesaver

Direct students to the rules on hyphens on p. 716. Have a group of volunteers create a chart of numbered hyphen rules and examples. Then, have students, working in small groups, use the chart to mark each other's papers for **Review A,** citing the rule numbers for wrong answers.

MECHANICS

Parentheses

Rule 26e (pp. 720–721)

OBJECTIVE

■ To use parentheses to set off parenthetical elements in sentences

Meeting INDIVIDUAL NEEDS

ENGLISH-LANGUAGE LEARNERS

General Strategies. In their native languages, some students may use a feature called the topic-comment subject, or double subject. For example, the construction "My mother, she. . ." includes a topic (*mother*) and a comment (*she*. . .). Students who use this feature may have trouble telling the difference between the topic-comment subject and a parenthetical element. These students may need individual help in editing their papers to eliminate the topic-comment feature. Point out that students may choose to use either the topic or the subject of the comment to write a clear, complete sentence.

Cooperative Learning

Have students work in small groups to write sentences with parentheses. Have groups exchange sentences to evaluate each other's use of parenthetical information. The groups that wrote the sentences should rewrite overloaded sentences to make them smooth without losing any of the information in the parentheses.

STYLE TIP

Commas, parentheses, and dashes are all used to set off parenthetical information, but they affect meaning differently. Commas separate elements, usually without emphasizing them. Parentheses indicate that the information they contain is of minor importance. Dashes set off parenthetical information abruptly, emphasizing it. Choose your punctuation according to the meaning you intend.

STYLE TIP

Too many parenthetical expressions in a piece of writing can distract the reader from the main idea. Keep your meaning clear by limiting the number of parenthetical expressions you use.

Parentheses

26e. Use parentheses to enclose material that is added to a sentence but is not considered to be of major importance.

Notice in the following examples that parenthetical material may be omitted without changing the basic meaning and construction of the sentence.

EXAMPLES During the Middle Ages (from about A.D. 500 to A.D. 1500), both Moors and Vikings invaded parts of Europe.

The music of Liszt (always a favorite of mine) was quite popular in the nineteenth century.

Material enclosed in parentheses may range from a single word to a short sentence. A short sentence in parentheses may stand by itself or be contained within another sentence.

Use punctuation marks within the parentheses when the punctuation belongs to the parenthetical matter. Do not use punctuation within the parentheses if such punctuation belongs to the sentence as a whole.

EXAMPLES Fill in the application carefully. (Use a pen.)

That old house (it was built at the turn of the century) may soon become a landmark.

After we ate dinner (we had leftovers again), we went to the mall.

Exercise 3 Using Parentheses Correctly

Use parentheses to set off the parenthetical elements in the following sentences. Carets indicate where parentheses should be inserted.

EXAMPLE 1. A fly-specked calendar it was five years out-of-date hung on the kitchen wall.

1. *A fly-specked calendar (it was five years out-of-date) hung on the kitchen wall.*

1. I have read all the *Oz* books that I own˄a considerable number˄.
2. Edna St. Vincent Millay˄1892–1950˄began writing poetry as a child.
3. In 1850, California entered the Union as a free state˄read more about free states in Chapter 5˄.
4. Gwendolyn Brooks˄her first book was *A Street in Bronzeville*˄has received high praise from critics.

RESOURCES

Parentheses

Practice

■ *Grammar, Usage, and Mechanics*, p. 327
■ *Language Workshop CD-ROM*, Lessons 48, 56

MECHANICS

5. Killer whales‸they're the ones with the black-and-white markings‸ often migrate more than one thousand miles annually.

6. We arrived in Poland through the port city of Gdańsk‸called Danzig in German‸.

7. The black rat‸scientific name *Rattus rattus*‸is found on every continent.

8. During the French Revolution and the Terror‸1789–1793‸ France underwent dramatic changes.

9. Paulo Coelho‸born 1947‸is a bestselling Brazilian author.

10. The cooking of New Mexico‸my home state‸is rich and varied.

Dashes

Sometimes words, phrases, and sentences are used *parenthetically;* that is, they break into the main thought of a sentence.

EXAMPLES   The penguin, **however,** has swum away.

                Her worry **(how could she explain the mix-up?)** kept her up all night.

Most parenthetical elements are set off by commas or parentheses. Sometimes, however, parenthetical elements are such an interruption that a stronger mark is needed. In such cases, a dash is used.

26f. Use a dash to indicate an abrupt break in thought or speech or an unfinished statement or question.

EXAMPLES   There are a thousand reasons—well, not a thousand, but many—that we should go.

                Our dog—he's a long-haired dachshund—is too affectionate to be a good watchdog.

                "Why—why can't I come, too?" Janet asked hesitatingly.

                "You're being—" Tina began and then stopped.

26g. Use a dash to indicate *namely, that is,* or *in other words* or to otherwise introduce an explanation.

EXAMPLES   I know what we could get Mom for her birthday—a new photo album. [namely]

                She could put all those loose pictures—the ones she's taken since Christmas—in it. [that is]

NOTE   Either a dash or a colon is acceptable in the first example above.

| STYLE | | TIP |

Do not overuse dashes. When you evaluate your writing, check to see that you have not used dashes carelessly for commas, semicolons, and end marks. Saving dashes for instances in which they are most appropriate will make them more effective.

| COMPUTER TIP |

When you use a word processor, you can type two hyphens to make a dash. Do not leave a space before, between, or after the hyphens. When you write by hand, use an unbroken line about as long as two hyphens.

Reference Note
For information on using **colons,** see page 675.

Dashes, Ellipsis Points, and Brackets
Rules 26f–i *(pp. 721–726)*

O B J E C T I V E

■ To insert dashes, ellipsis points, and brackets into the appropriate places in sentences

Relating to Listening and Speaking

Explain to students that interrupting a train of thought with a parenthetical element may be more common in casual conversation than in formal writing. To make students aware of oral pauses indicating abrupt breaks or unfinished thoughts, have students read the examples in this section aloud. Then, have pairs of students create a conversation including breaks in the train of thought.

Suggested topics:

• talking while watching a basketball game

• talking to a friend on the phone in the presence of a parent who wants the line cleared

• talking to a supermarket checker while soothing an impatient child

MECHANICS

RESOURCES

Dashes, Ellipsis Points, and Brackets
Practice
■ *Grammar, Usage, and Mechanics,* pp. 328, 329, 330, 331
■ *Language Workshop CD-ROM,* Lessons 48, 56

TECHNOLOGY TIP

Standard keyboards for computers and typewriters do not have a key for dashes. On a typewriter, dashes are keyed by using two hyphens without any spacing before, between, or after them. Word-processing programs may use a combination of the shift key and another key in addition to the hyphen key to create a dash. (Users should check manuals for exact keys for particular software.) Remind students to proofread for the correct use of hyphens and dashes in their writing.

Exercise 4 Inserting Dashes in Sentences

Insert dashes where they are appropriate in the following sentences. Carets indicate where dashes should be inserted.

EXAMPLE
1. The winner is but I don't want to give it away yet.
1. *The winner is—but I don't want to give it away yet.*

2. It was an exciting game Brazil had taken the lead, but Italy scored in overtime.
2. *It was an exciting game—Brazil had taken the lead, but Italy scored in overtime.*

1. Tom said, "I'd like to thank" and then blushed and sat down.
2. We were surprised in fact, amazed to learn that the game had been called off.
3. The valedictorian that is, the student with the highest average will be given a scholarship.
4. She remembered what she wanted to tell them the plane was leaving at seven, not eight.
5. My brother's engagement it's been kept a secret till now will be announced Sunday.
6. The ancient Mediterranean seafaring cultures the Phoenician, the Greek, and the Roman all used versions of the trireme, a ship driven by three rows of oars.
7. The truth is and I'm sure you realize this we have no way of getting to the airport.
8. The manager of the restaurant I can't remember his name said he would reserve a table for us.
9. Because Maria she's the one who accompanies us will be away next week, choral practice will be postponed until the following week.
10. Very few carmakers three, to be precise offer models exclusively with full-time all-wheel drive.

─HELP─

Although some sentences in Review B can be corrected in more than one way, you need to give only one revision for each.

Review B Using Hyphens, Dashes, and Parentheses Correctly

Rewrite each of the following sentences, inserting hyphens, dashes, and parentheses where they are needed. If a sentence is already correct, write *C*.   Answers may vary.

EXAMPLE
1. State flags you can tell by looking at those shown on the next page are as different as the states themselves.
1. *State flags—you can tell by looking at those shown on the next page—are as different as the states themselves.*

MINI-LESSON

Parenthetical Expressions. Remind students that parenthetical expressions as they have studied them in relationship to commas are usually restricted to a set list of words or phrases that provide emphasis or transition (see p. 657).

To review this concept, ask students to add commas to the following sentences:

Karen is in fact already on her way to Chicago. [*Karen is, in fact, already on her way to Chicago.*]

1. I think the shield on the Oklahoma flag reflects that state's pre͜statehood years as the territorial home of the Osage, the Cherokee, and other American Indian peoples. **1.** hyp.

2. "What kind of tree is in the center of the South Carolina flag?" Emilio asked. "Is it͜oh, it's a palmetto." **2.** dash

3. Two goddesses͜Ceres, or the goddess of agriculture, and Liberty͜are in the center of New Jersey's flag. **3.** par. / par.

4. On the Colorado flag, one third of the background is white and the rest is blue. **4.** C

5. Arkansas͜by the way, a major diamond-producing state͜has a large diamond on its flag. **5.** par. / par.

6. An ancient Pueblo symbol of the all͜important sun is on New Mexico's flag. **6.** hyp.

7. The Union Jack of the United Kingdom͜look closely͜is on a corner of the Hawaiian flag. **7.** dash / dash

8. "The Texas flag is red, white, and blue and contains one lone star because͜" Megan said before she was interrupted. **8.** dash

9. Blue is a dominant color in forty͜one state flags. **9.** hyp.

10. Only one state flag͜Washington's͜has a green background.

10. dash / dash

Review C Using Hyphens, Dashes, and Parentheses Correctly

Insert <u>hyphens</u>, <u>dashes</u>, and <u>parentheses</u> where they are needed in the following sentences. Do not add commas. If a sentence is already correct, write *C.* Answers may vary.

EXAMPLE **1.** You might be able to tell from the photograph on the next page that the Comanche chief Quanah Parker 1845–1911 was a man of strong character.

1. You might be able to tell from the photograph on the next page that the Comanche chief Quanah Parker (1845–1911) was a man of strong character.

Dashes **723**

MECHANICS

Rich Williams deserved the raise in my opinion. [*Rich Williams deserved the raise, in my opinion.*]

To tell the truth I do not know. [*To tell the truth, I do not know.*]

TEACHING (TIP)

Review C Either parentheses or dashes may be used in answers 1, 2, 4, 5, 8, 9, and 10.

1. Parker͜can you tell this from the photograph?͜was both a great war chief and a great peace chief. **1.** dash / dash
2. He was the son of a Comanche tribal leader and a young woman ͜Cynthia Ann Parker͜who was captured during a raid on a Texas homestead. **2.** par. / par.
3. In the 1870s, Parker himself led a band of Comanche warriors in the Texas Panhandle. **3.** C
4. Parker surrendered with his band͜the Quahadi͜in 1875; they were the last Comanches on the southern plains to surrender. **4.** par. / par.
5. After surrendering, Parker became a prosperous rancher͜quite a change of lifestyle͜and even owned railroad stock. **5.** dash / dash
6. In fact, he embodied the ideal of the self͜made man. **6.** hyp.
7. Parker encouraged his people to learn modern ways and to farm.͜ **7.** C
8. Parker guided the Comanches͜his title was principal chief͜dur͜ing difficult times after the war ended. **8.** par. / par. / hyp.
9. In later years, he went to Washington, D.C., and͜this fact may surprise you͜became a friend of President Theodore Roosevelt. **9.** dash / dash
10. The Texas city called Quanah͜a Comanche word meaning "sweet smelling"͜was named after this chief. **10.** par. / par.

Ellipsis Points

26h. **Use ellipsis points (. . .) to mark omissions from quoted materials and pauses in a written passage.**

ORIGINAL   The streetlights along Toole Street, which meandered down-hill from the Language Academy to the town, were already lit and twinkled mistily through the trees. Standing at the gates were small groups of students, clustered together according to nationality. As Myles passed by, he could not help overhearing intense conversation in Spanish, German, and Japanese; all of his students had momentarily abandoned English in the urgency of deciding where to go for the weekend and how to get there.

(1) **When you omit words from the middle of a sentence, use three spaced ellipsis points.**

EXAMPLE   The streetlights along Toole Street **. . .** were already lit and twinkled mistily through the trees.

NOTE Be sure to include a space before the first ellipsis point and after the last one.

Relating to Writing

Because ellipsis points are often used in connection with quoted material in research papers, you may want to teach this section while students are working on **Chapter 6**, the I-search essay, or any other writing assignment in which they would use portions of quoted material. If students have completed research assignments, ask them to work in small groups to examine quoted passages in each other's papers. Assign the group to rewrite passages, eliminating unnecessary parts of the quotations by using ellipsis points.

Learning for Life   **Continued on pp. 725–726**

Newsletter. Tell students they will be responsible for creating a classroom newsletter in which they will use the types of punctuation they have learned in this chapter, as well as reviewing marks studied in previous chapters.

To prepare students, provide samples of newsletters or ask a newsletter editor to speak to the class about the process involved. Suggest that the expert relate an

(2) When you omit words at the beginning of a sentence within a quoted passage, keep the previous sentence's end punctuation and follow it with the ellipsis points.

EXAMPLE   Standing at the gates were small groups of students, clustered together according to nationality. . . . [A]ll of his students had momentarily abandoned English in the urgency of deciding where to go for the weekend and how to get there.

NOTE Be sure not to begin a quoted passage with ellipsis points.

(3) When you omit words at the end of a sentence within a quoted passage, keep the sentence's end punctuation and follow it with the ellipsis points.

EXAMPLE   Standing at the gates were small groups of students. . . . As Myles passed by, he could not help overhearing intense conversation in Spanish, German, and Japanese; all of his students had momentarily abandoned English in the urgency of deciding where to go for the weekend and how to get there.

(4) When you omit one or more complete sentences from a quoted passage, keep the previous sentence's end punctuation and follow it with the ellipsis points.

EXAMPLE   The streetlights along Toole Street, which meandered downhill from the Language Academy to the town, were already lit and twinkled mistily through the trees. . . . As Myles passed by, he could not help overhearing intense conversation in Spanish, German, and Japanese; all of his students had momentarily abandoned English in the urgency of deciding where to go for the weekend and how to get there.

(5) To show that a full line or more of poetry has been omitted, use an entire line of spaced periods.

ORIGINAL   Half a league, half a league,
Half a league onward,
All in the valley of Death
Rode the six hundred.
"Forward the Light Brigade!
Charge for the guns!" he said.
Into the valley of Death
Rode the six hundred.

Alfred, Lord Tennyson,
"The Charge of the Light Brigade"

⌐HELP⌐

Notice in the example to the left that the *a* beginning *all* has been capitalized because it begins the sentence following the ellipsis points. Brackets are used around the *A* to show that it was not capitalized in the original passage.

Meeting
INDIVIDUAL
NEEDS

MULTIPLE INTELLIGENCES
Musical Intelligence. Have small groups of students brainstorm ways punctuation marks and musical notations are similar. To get them started, ask what punctuation mark might correspond to a musical rest. [*Students might suggest either a comma or a period.*]

---

anecdote about a misunderstanding created by incorrect punctuation.

Then, brainstorm with students what topics they might include in the newsletter and what punctuation is required for specific needs. (For example, ellipsis points might be used in a long quotation from the principal praising the class for a service project, while brackets or parentheses might be used in schedules.)

Crossing the Curriculum

All Subjects. Assign students to groups of four or five based on their choice of a preferred area of study, such as math or social studies. Then, explain that they will look through textbooks or reference books on their chosen subject to find uses of parentheses, dashes, ellipses, and brackets. Before students look for examples, have them brainstorm possible uses of these punctuation marks. Assign groups to prepare their examples for a bulletin board display. [*Hints: Students may find that brackets and parentheses are used in algebraic equations and scientific formulas and in literature or social studies books for biographical information or for dates of historical periods. Ellipses are used generally in any text to indicate material that is left out of a quotation.*]

WITH OMISSION

Half a league, half a league,
Half a league onward,
. . . .
Into the valley of Death
Rode the six hundred.

Notice that the line of periods is as long as the line above it.

(6) To indicate a pause in dialogue, use three spaced ellipsis points with a space before the first point and a space after the last point.

EXAMPLE   "Well, I could . . . I can't honestly say," he hedged.

Brackets

26i. Use brackets to enclose an explanation within quoted or parenthetical material.

EXAMPLES   In her acceptance speech, the star said: "I am honored by this award [the Oscar], and I want to thank my parents and everybody who worked with me." [The words are enclosed in brackets to show that they have been inserted into the quotation and are not the exact words of the speaker.]

The growth of the Irish economy in recent years is a great success story. (See page 15 [Graph 1A] for a time line.)

Exercise 5   **Using Ellipsis Points and Brackets Correctly**

Revise the following sentences, using ellipsis points and brackets correctly.

EXAMPLE   1. Franklin said, "That cat just . . . . . flew up to the top of the refrigerator!"

1. *Franklin said, "That cat just . . . flew up to the top of the refrigerator!"*

1. br. / br.
2. ell. . . .
3. br. / br.
4. br. / br.
5. ell. . . .

1. At the committee meeting, Judy said, "We have to make this (the Homecoming Dance) the most memorable event of the year."
2. "I . . I can't believe she would have said that!" Aaron exclaimed.
3. The levels of photosynthesis activity varied drastically with the different cycles of light and darkness. (See page 347 (Chart 17D) for details.)
4. "Do you really believe they have a chance to win the (Stanley) Cup this year?" asked Martin skeptically.
5. "But . . . . . then how can we be sure it's true?" Carla asked.

Learning for Life

After students have worked individually to write an article, place them in small groups to proofread each other's work. Finally, groups may staple individual articles together to make a class newsletter or produce the newsletter, complete with graphics and illustrations, by using a desktop-publishing program. Students may decide that they want to continue publishing a newsletter for a group or club.

Chapter Review

A. Using Hyphens to Divide Words at the Ends of Lines

Write each of the following words, using a hyphen to indicate where the word may be divided at the end of a line. If a word should not be divided, write *do not divide*.

Carets indicate where a hyphen should be used.

1. baked 1. d.n.d.
2. complete
3. input
4. unexpected
5. yo-yo
6. bagel
7. thorough
8. divide
9. away 9. d.n.d.
10. whale 10. d.n.d.

┌─HELP─┐
Some sentences in Part B may be correctly punctuated in more than one way, but you need to give only one answer per item.

11. hyp.
12. dash
13. hyp. / hyp.

14. dash / dash
15. dash / dash

16. par. / par.
17. hyp. / hyp. /

18. hyp.

19. par. / par.

20. dash / dash

B. Using Hyphens, Dashes, and Parentheses Correctly

Use hyphens, dashes, and parentheses to punctuate the following sentences. Do not add commas to these sentences.

Answers may vary.

11. Yuri, our Russian exchange student, will be twenty one on the first of September this year.
12. "That sounds like" gasped Jeff as he dashed for the window.
13. A former all state quarterback, our coach insists that there is no such thing as a self made star.
14. A dog I think it was a poodle jumped into the lake.
15. The Historical Society the local members, that is will conduct a tour of the harbor.
16. My sister Patricia she is in college now wants to be a marine biologist.
17. This recipe for savory bread calls for one and one half cups of whole wheat flour.
18. At the auction someone bid one thousand dollars for a pre Revolutionary desk.
19. The Inca empire flourished during the reign of the emperor Pachacuti 1438–1471.
20. Next month of course, I'll write you before then we're going on an overnight trip.

Chapter Review **727**

Using the Chapter Review

To assess student progress, you may want to compare the types of items missed on the **Diagnostic Preview** to those missed on the **Chapter Review**. You may want to work out specific goals for mastering essential information with individual students who are still having difficulty.

21. par. / par.

21. John F. Kennedy‸1917–1963‸was the first Roman Catholic president of the United States.

22. dash / dash

22. Four of our former classmates‸yes, Beth was among them‸traveled to Australia with the U.S. athletes.

23. hyp.

23. My grandparents will celebrate their fiftieth wedding anni‸versary on the third of October.

24. dash / dash

24. My friend Juan‸he went back to Puerto Rico‸has always wanted to be a veterinarian.

25. par. / hyp. / par.

25. Linda Wing‸she is the ex‸champion‸will award the trophies.

26. hyp.

26. Doing homework and seeing their improvement raised their self‸esteem.

27. hyp.

27. Add exactly one half‸tablespoon of sugar to that recipe.

28. par. / par.

28. Napoleon's reign as emperor of France‸1804–1815‸was marked by great achievements and great setbacks.

29. dash

29. "You don't mean to‸" exclaimed Renata.

30. dash / dash

30. The Friends of Silesia‸the Midwestern chapter, of course‸will have their annual dinner in Chicago this year.

31. hyp.

31. Four players have been chosen for the state's all‸star team.

32. par. / par.

32. Beth‸I don't know her last name‸plays the lead role in the play.

33. dash / dash

33. She said wearily‸she often sounded weary‸"I'll go tomorrow."

34. hyp. / hyp.

34. By mid‸January twenty‸four inches of snow had fallen.

35. par. / par.

35. Mr. Brandt‸our neighbor of twelve years‸moved back to Germany after that country's reunification.

36. par. / par. / hyp.

36. Franklin D. Roosevelt‸1882–1945‸was the thirty‸second president.

37. hyp.

37. The ex‸governor of Kansas will speak at the reception.

38. dash / dash

38. Blake‸Ricky Blake, I mean‸was waiting for me downstairs.

39. par. / par.

39. Reggae music‸I heard it in the West Indies‸is popular here.

40. dash

40. We all grew up in the same town‸Boise, Idaho.

┌HELP┐

Some sentences in Part C may be correctly punctutated in more than one way, but you need to give only one answer for each item.

C. Using Hyphens, Dashes, Parentheses, Ellipsis Points, and Brackets Correctly

Correctly use <u>h</u>yphens, <u>d</u>ashes, <u>p</u>arentheses, <u>e</u>llipsis points, and <u>b</u>rackets where needed in the following sentences. If a sentence is already correct, write *C*. Answers may vary.

41. The Italian flag‸red, white, and green‸is similar in design to the French tricolor flag‸red, white, and blue.   **41.** dash / dash / dash

42. "Well, I'll try‸.....or maybe not," she stammered.   **42.** ell. . . .

RESOURCES

Punctuation

Review

■ *Grammar, Usage, and Mechanics,* pp. 332, 333, 334, 335

Assessment

■ *Assessment Package*
 —*Chapter Tests,* Ch. 26
 —*Chapter Tests in Standardized Test Formats,* Ch. 26
■ *Test Generator (One-Stop Planner CD-ROM)* 🄯

43. The large building on the corner of Elm Street is the headquarters of the organization.

44. The Battle of Verdun, February–July 1916, was a crucial French victory over the Germans in World War I.

45. In Mexico, San Miguel de Allende, population approximately 80,000, is a popular destination for American artists and retirees.

46. [See page 100 (Map 2) for a more detailed look at the developing military situation.]

47. "My goodness!" exclaimed Grandpa. "Isn't that the?" and he hurriedly consulted his program.

48. The museum's preColumbian artifacts are well worth seeing.

49. I can think of dozens of people, well, maybe not dozens, but quite a few, who would agree with me.

50. Lorenzo Da Ponte was the man who wrote the libretto for Mozart's opera *Don Giovanni* and later, and this came as a surprise to me, taught Italian in New York City.

43. C

44. par. / par.

45. par. / par.

46. par. / br. / br. / par.

47. dash

48. hyp.

49. dash / dash

50. dash / dash

Writing Application
Writing a Report

Using Punctuation   Write a short report of no more than three paragraphs on your favorite author. Use at least three of the five elements of punctuation (hyphens, dashes, parentheses, ellipsis points, and brackets) discussed in this chapter.

Prewriting   First, gather biographical information on your chosen author. Include any details you find interesting or unusual.

Writing   As you write your first draft, think about how you plan to organize your information: by type of writing (fiction, nonfiction, poetry) or chronologically; or you could focus on a particular story, novel, or poem. Compare your draft to other short treatments of the author.

Revising   Read through your draft. Is the organization clear? If not, add, cut, or rearrange information to make it clearer.

Publishing   Proofread your essay for errors in grammar, spelling, and punctuation. You and your classmates may want to post the finished report on the class bulletin board or on a school Web page.

Reference Note

For more about **writing reports and research papers,** see Chapter 6: Investigating a Research Question.

Writing Application
(p. 729)

OBJECTIVE

■ To write a three-paragraph report on an author by using at least three of the five elements of punctuation discussed in this chapter

Writing Application

Tip. Before students begin their prewriting, you may want to have them brainstorm a list of authors to consider.

Scoring Rubric. While you will want to pay particular attention to students' use of punctuation marks, you will also want to evaluate the students' overall writing performance. You may want to give a split score to indicate development and clarity of the composition as well as mechanics skills.

Critical Thinking

Synthesis. Before students can begin writing their reports, they must synthesize the information they have gathered into an orderly format. For example, students must decide what to use from their research. Remind students that the main idea must go in the first paragraph and the other material they use should support the main idea.

RESOURCES

Writing Application
Extension

■ *Grammar, Usage, and Mechanics,* p. 338
■ *Language Workshop CD-ROM,* Lessons 48, 56

27 Spelling
Improving Your Spelling

Diagnostic Preview

A. Choosing Correct Spelling

Choose the correct word from the pair in parentheses.

EXAMPLE **1.** I was very careful not to (*brake*, *break*) the vase.

    1. break

1. After the Paris-Lyon high-speed train (*past*, *passed*) the waving onlookers and raced (*threw*, *through*) the tunnel, it reached a maximum speed of more than 180 miles per hour.
2. When the new (*principle*, *principal*) talked to her staff, she tried to get (*there*, *their*, *they're*) honest opinions.
3. The auctioneer (*led*, *lead*) the bidding on the original White House (*stationary*, *stationery*) on which was written President Roosevelt's actual signature.
4. Cuenca, near Madrid, is a lovely old town that is known for its (*piece*, *peace*) and (*quite*, *quiet*).
5. My aunt (*who's*, *whose*) picture appeared in yesterday's paper was (*formerly*, *formally*) a vice-president at First State Bank.
6. (*Altogether*, *All together*), the guitar music, the songs, and the aroma of *pan dulce* were a wonderful (*compliment*, *complement*) to the relaxed atmosphere.
7. Of (*course*, *coarse*), I found it nearly impossible to (*choose*, *chose*) between those two movies.

8. I took a (*plain*, *plane*) to Houston, and I visited family members who live (*there*, *their*, *they're*).

9. Although (*its*, *it's*) smaller than both Geneva and Zurich, Bern is the (*capital*, *capitol*) of Switzerland.

10. The new British (*council*, *consul*, *counsel*) and her husband returned to the embassy after having coffee and (*desert*, *dessert*) with the emir.

B. Proofreading a Paragraph for Spelling Errors

Identify any ~~misspelled or misused words~~ in the following paragraph, and then write the words correctly. If all the words in a sentence are already correct, write *C*.

EXAMPLE　　**[1]** I have read about Santa Fe, but I have never been their.

　　　　　　1.　*their—there*

[1] Santa Fe, New Mexico, is an ~~all together~~ charming and unusual city. [2] It is not only the ~~capitol~~ of the state but also a major tourist center. [3] The city lies in the north-central part of New Mexico at a ~~hieght~~ of about 7,000 feet and enjoys outstanding ~~whether~~ year-round. [4] The altitude sometimes has a bad ~~affect~~ on first-time visitors. [5] They are ~~adviced~~ not to exert themselves for the first day or so. [6] Santa Fe is one of the oldest ~~citys~~ in the United States. [7] It was founded in 1610 as the seat of government of the Spanish colony of New Mexico. [8] In 1912, New Mexico joined the United States as the ~~47th~~ state. [9] I think the food in Santa Fe is ~~awsome~~. [10] I suggest ~~sampleing~~ Southwestern cuisine, some of which is very spicy.

1. altogether
2. capital
3. height/weather
4. effect
5. advised
6. cities
7. C
8. forty-seventh
9. awesome
10. sampling

Good Spelling Habits

27a. To learn the spelling of a word, pronounce it, study it, and write it.

(1) Pronounce words carefully.

Mispronunciation can lead to misspelling. For instance, if you say *mis • chē • vē • əs* instead of *mis • chə • vəs,* you will be more likely to spell the word incorrectly.

- First, make sure that you know how to pronounce the word correctly, and then practice saying it.

HELP

If you are not sure how to pronounce a word, look in a dictionary. In the dictionary, you will usually find the pronunciation given in parentheses after the word. The information in parentheses will show you the sounds used, the syllable breaks, and any accented syllables. A guide to the pronunciation symbols is usually found at the front of the dictionary.

Good Spelling Habits　　**731**

Good Spelling Habits
Rule 27a (*pp. 731–733*)

OBJECTIVES

- **To pronounce spelling words correctly**

- **To spell by syllables using a dictionary**

- **To correctly spell commonly misspelled words containing silent letters**

Internet
- go.hrw.com (keyword: EOLang)

RESOURCES

Good Spelling Habits
Practice

- *Grammar, Usage, and Mechanics,* p. 340

- *Language Workshop CD-ROM,* Lesson 59

Meeting INDIVIDUAL NEEDS

INCLUSION

You may wish to motivate students with a spelling-bee round robin. Set up teams of three or four students, and have a helper dictate a word to students in the group. The first student names the first letter, the second student names the second letter, and so on. As the team names letters, the helper should record the letters on the chalkboard or on a transparency. The helper may want to prompt students with phonics clues.

Timesaver

Because students' spelling skills may vary widely, you may wish to give individual assignments for **Exercises 1–13,** providing a key for students to use to check their answers independently. Have students add any misspelled words to their spelling notebooks. You can then use **Reviews A–C** for assessment purposes.

STYLE TIP

Different dictionaries show variations in spelling in different ways. To understand a dictionary's arrangement of such variations, check the guide (usually found in the front) that explains how to use the book.

When you look up the spelling of a word, make sure that its use isn't limited by a label such as *British* or *chiefly British* (*honour* for *honor*), *obsolete* (*vail* for *veil*), or *archaic* (*innocency* for *innocence*). In general, optional spellings that are not labeled, such as *jeweler* and *jeweller,* are equally correct.

Reference Note

For information on using a **dictionary** to determine the **pronunciation** of a word, see "The Dictionary" in the **Quick Reference Handbook.**

- Second, study the word. Notice especially any parts that might be hard to remember.
- Third, write the word from memory. Check your spelling.
- If you misspelled the word, repeat the three steps of this process.

(2) Use a dictionary.

Whenever you find that you have misspelled a word, look it up in a dictionary. Don't guess about correct spelling.

(3) Spell by syllables.

A *syllable* is a word part that is pronounced as one uninterrupted sound.

EXAMPLES   thor • ough [two syllables]

sep • a • rate [three syllables]

Instead of trying to learn how to pronounce a whole word, break it up into its syllables whenever possible. It's easier to learn a few letters at a time than to learn all of them at once.

Oral Practice   **Pronouncing Spelling Words Correctly**

Study the correct pronunciations in parentheses after each of the following words. Then, pronounce each word correctly three times.

1. athlete (ath′ • lēt′)
2. children (chil′ • drən)
3. drowned (droʊnd)
4. escape (e • skāp′)
5. library (lī′ • brer • ē)
6. lightning (līt′ • ning)
7. perhaps (pər • haps′)
8. probably (prŏb′ • ə • blē)

Exercise 1   **Spelling by Syllables**

Look up the following words in a dictionary, and divide each one into syllables. Pronounce each syllable correctly, and learn to spell the word by syllables.

EXAMPLE   1. possibility
                  1. *pos′ • si • bil′ • i • ty*

1. representative
2. awkward
3. candidate
4. temperature
5. apparent
6. similar
7. definition
8. benefit
9. acquaintance
10. fascinate

1. [*or* representative]
9. [*or* acquaintance]

---

(4) Proofread for careless spelling errors.

Re-read your writing carefully, and correct any mistakes and unclear letters. For example, make sure that your *i*'s are dotted, your *t*'s are crossed, and your *g*'s don't look like *q*'s.

(5) Keep a spelling notebook.

Divide each page into four columns:

COLUMN 1   Correctly spell the word you missed. (Never enter a misspelled word.)

COLUMN 2   Write the word again, dividing it into syllables and marking its accents.

COLUMN 3   Write the word once more, circling the letters that give you trouble.

COLUMN 4   Jot down any comments that might help you remember the correct spelling.

Here is an example of how you might make entries for two words that are often misspelled.

Correct Spelling	Syllables and Accents	Trouble Spot	Comments
probably	prob′•a•bly	prob(ab)ly	Pronounce both b's.
usually	u′•su•al•ly	usua(ll)y	usual+ly (Study rule 27f.)

Exercise 2   **Spelling Commonly Misspelled Words**

Copy each of the following words or expressions, paying special attention to the italicized letters. Then, without looking at this page or the copy you made of the correctly spelled words, write the words as a friend dictates them to you.

1. answer	6. *knowle*d*ge*	11. *rhythm*	16. toni*gh*t
2. a*w*kward	7. *written*	12. use*d* to	17. sure*ly*
3. *whole*	8. often	13. inste*ad*	18. thou*gh*
4. toward	9. condem*n*	14. me*a*nt	19. thro*ugh*
5. *know*	10. colum*n*	15. *a*isle	20. nine*t*y

COMPUTER TIP

Spellcheckers can help you proofread your writing. Even the best spellcheckers aren't foolproof, however. Many accept British spellings, obsolete words, archaic spellings, and words that are spelled correctly but used incorrectly (such as *affect* for *effect*). Always double-check your writing to make sure that your spelling is error-free.

Meeting INDIVIDUAL NEEDS

MODALITIES

Auditory Learners. Encourage students to spell and pronounce new or problematic words aloud as they practice writing the words. You might suggest that students pronounce words and give exaggerated stress to troublesome letters. For example, students might pronounce any silent consonants, such as the *w* in *answer*.

Crossing the Curriculum

All Disciplines. Encourage students to use their spelling notebooks for all subjects, not just for language arts. Ask students to record in their notebooks any words they misspell and any difficult words they encounter in other subjects. Then students can check this chapter for the rules that apply to the words in their lists.

TEACHING TIP

Exercise 2   Have students circle the italicized letters as they copy the words for the first part of this exercise. This reinforcement should help students with the dictation part of the exercise. You may want to have students continue to circle silent letters while they work on exercises throughout the chapter.

MECHANICS

Spelling Rules

Rules 27b–p *(pp. 734–746)*

OBJECTIVES

- To proofread sentences to correct spelling errors

- To spell correctly words with pre-fixes and suffixes

- To form the plurals of regular and irregular nouns, compound nouns, Latin and Greek loan words, numerals, letters, symbols, and words used as words

- To determine whether numbers in sentences should be spelled out

MECHANICS

TEACHING TIP

Activity. To make students aware of how to spell words they hear, you might tape-record and play a segment from a familiar television show. Stop the tape when there is a word you want students to spell. After they have created a list, provide the correct spellings. Have students read **Rules 27b–p** and write the appropriate rule by any troublesome words.

Exercise 3 **Proofreading Sentences to Correct Spelling Errors**

ANSWERS

1. freind—friend
2. sheild—shield

TIPS & TRICKS

Remember this rhyme:
I before *e* except after *c*
or when sounded like *a*
as in *neighbor* and
weigh.

Spelling Rules

ie and *ei*

27b. Write *ie* when the sound is long *e*, except after *c*.

EXAMPLES	ach**ie**ve	ch**ie**f	n**ie**ce	sh**ie**ld	c**ei**ling
	bel**ie**ve	f**ie**ld	p**ie**ce	th**ie**f	dec**ei**t
	br**ie**f	gr**ie**f	rel**ie**f	y**ie**ld	rec**ei**ve

EXCEPTIONS   **ei**ther, l**ei**sure, n**ei**ther, s**ei**ze, prot**ei**n

27c. Write *ei* when the sound is not long *e*.

| EXAMPLES | counterf**ei**t | h**ei**ght | r**ei**gn | forf**ei**t |
| | for**ei**gn | h**ei**r | v**ei**l | w**ei**gh |

EXCEPTIONS   fr**ie**nd, misch**ie**f, kerch**ie**f

> **NOTE** Rules 27b and 27c apply only when the *i* and the *e* are in the same syllable.
>
> EXAMPLES   de • i • ty   sci • ence

–cede, –ceed, and *–sede*

27d. Only one English word ends in *–sede: supersede.* Only three words end in *–ceed: exceed, proceed,* and *succeed.* Almost all other words with this sound end in *–cede.*

| EXAMPLES | ac**cede** | inter**cede** | re**cede** |
| | con**cede** | pre**cede** | se**cede** |

Exercise 3 **Proofreading Sentences to Correct Spelling Errors**

The following sentences contain errors involving the use of *ie, ei, –ceed, –cede,* and *–sede.* For each sentence, identify the misspelled word or words and then write them correctly. If a sentence has no spelling errors, write *C.*

EXAMPLE   **1.** On my birthday I recieved a wonderful gift.
         1. recieved—received

1. My neighbor, who is a good freind of mine, went on a trip out West.
2. He sent me a Dream Catcher like those used by the Sioux to sheild themselves from bad dreams.

RESOURCES

Spelling Rules

Practice

- *Grammar, Usage, and Mechanics*, pp. 341, 342, 343, 344, 345, 346, 347, 348, 349, 350, 351, 352, 353, 354, 355, 356

- *Language Workshop CD-ROM*, Lessons 59, 60

3. Charms like this once hung in each tepee, and mine hangs from the cieling near my bed.

4. According to legend, bad dreams get caught in the web and only good ones succede in reaching the sleeper.

5. I do not really believe that my Dream Catcher can interceed on my behalf, but I have not had one bad dream since my birthday!

6. The Plains Indians moved their homes often, so their possessions could be niether bulky nor heavy.

7. Consequently, the Sioux who made the Dream Catcher used common, lightweight materials.

8. The twig bent into a ring is willow wood, and tiny glass beads represent nightmares siezed by the web.

9. Gracefully hanging from either side is a beautiful feather or a horsehair tassel.

10. Wonderful peices of workmanship like this help ensure that the culture of the Sioux will never resede into the past.

Adding Prefixes

27e. When a prefix is added to a word, the spelling of the original word itself remains the same.

EXAMPLES   im + mobile = im**mobile**   mis + spell = mis**spell**

un + certain = un**certain**   over + rule = over**rule**

Adding Suffixes

27f. When the suffix –*ness* or –*ly* is added to a word, the spelling of the original word itself remains the same.

EXAMPLES   time + ly = **time**ly   even + ness = **even**ness

real + ly = **real**ly   late + ness = **late**ness

EXCEPTIONS   1. Words ending in *y* usually change the *y* to *i* before –*ness* and –*ly:* empty—empt**i**ness; easy—eas**i**ly

2. However, most one-syllable adjectives ending in *y* follow Rule 27f: shy—**shy**ly; dry—**dry**ness

3. *True, due,* and *whole* drop the final *e* before –*ly:* truly, duly, wholly.

Spelling Rules   **735**

Meeting
INDIVIDUAL
NEEDS

LEARNERS HAVING DIFFICULTY
To make the number of rules less intimidating to students, help them personalize applying rules. You might suggest that students add spelling rules one at a time to their notebooks, adding a sample word that they know how to spell. Encourage students to think of this word when applying the rule to other words. For example, when adding *ing* to a word with a silent *e*, they can use a sample word like *living* as a clue.

Exercise 4 **Spelling Words with Prefixes and Suffixes**

Spell each of the following words, including the prefix or suffix that is given.

EXAMPLE 1. un + common
1. *uncommon*

1. unnecessary
2. illegal
3. occasionally
4. cleanliness
5. meanness

1. un + necessary	6. im + moral	6. immoral
2. il + legal	7. sly + ly	7. slyly
3. occasional + ly	8. speedy + ly	8. speedily
4. cleanly + ness	9. same + ness	9. sameness
5. mean + ness	10. un + usual	10. unusual

27g. Drop the final silent *e* before adding a suffix that begins with a vowel.

EXAMPLES   tame + ing = **tam**ing   loose + est = **loos**est
noble + er = **nobl**er   admire + ation = **admir**ation
tickle + ish = **tickl**ish   move + able = **mov**able

EXCEPTIONS   1. Keep the final silent *e* in most words ending in *ce* or *ge* before a suffix that begins with *a* or *o*:

*knowledg**e**able, courag**e**ous.*

Sometimes the e becomes *i*, as in *graci**o**us* and *spaci**o**us.*

2. To avoid confusion with other words, keep the final silent *e* in some words:

*dy**e**ing* and *dying, sing**e**ing* and *singing*

3. mile + age = mil**e**age

Exercise 5 **Spelling Words with Suffixes**

Spell each of the following words, including the suffix that is given.

EXAMPLE 1. write + ing
1. *writing*

1. becoming
2. guidance
3. continuous
4. surprised
5. determination

1. become + ing	6. sense + ible	6. sensible
2. guide + ance	7. save + ing	7. saving
3. continue + ous	8. advantage + ous	8. advantageous
4. surprise + ed	9. dine + ing	9. dining
5. determine + ation	10. hope + ed	10. hoped

736 **Chapter 27** Spelling

MINI-LESSON

Suffixes and Parts of Speech. You may want to point out to students that adding or changing a suffix will often change the part of speech of the original word. Write the following examples on the chalkboard or on a transparency.

1. *nice* (adj.) + –*ly* = *nicely* (adv.)

2. *kind* (adj.) + –*ness* = *kindness* (n.)

3. *sense* (n.) + –*ible* = *sensible* (adj.)

27h. Keep the final silent *e* when adding a suffix that begins with a consonant.

EXAMPLES   safe + ty = saf**e**ty   large + ly = larg**e**ly

              hope + ful = hop**e**ful   awe + some = aw**e**some

              care + less = car**e**less   pave + ment = pav**e**ment

EXCEPTIONS   awe + ful = **aw**ful   true + ly = **tru**ly

                nine + th = **nin**th   argue + ment = **argu**ment

Review A   **Spelling Words with Suffixes**

Spell each of the following words, including the suffix that is given.

EXAMPLE   **1.** use + less

          1. useless

1. announce + ment   **1.** announcement
2. use + age   **2.** usage
3. imagine + ary   **3.** imaginary
4. care + ful   **4.** careful
5. write + ing   **5.** writing

6. station + ary   **6.** stationary
7. hope + less   **7.** hopeless
8. type + ing   **8.** typing
9. advertise + ment   **9.** advertisement
10. use + ful   **10.** useful

27i. When a word ends in *y* preceded by a consonant, change the *y* to *i* before any suffix except one beginning with *i*.

EXAMPLES   tidy + er = tid**i**er   glory + ous = glor**i**ous

              worry + ed = worr**i**ed   terrify + ing = terrif**y**ing

EXCEPTIONS   **1.** Some one-syllable words:

                  shy + ness = sh**y**ness   sky + ward = sk**y**ward

            2. *lady* and *baby* with most suffixes:

                  lad**y**like   lad**y**ship   bab**y**hood

27j. When a word ends in *y* preceded by a vowel, simply add the suffix.

EXAMPLES   play + ful = **play**ful   boy + hood = **boy**hood

              array + ed = **array**ed   gray + est = **gray**est

              pray + ing = **pray**ing   pay + ment = **pay**ment

EXCEPTIONS   day + ly = **dai**ly   pay + ed = **pai**d

              say + ed = **sai**d   lay + ed = **lai**d

INCLUSION

Spelling may present problems for students with visual-processing deficiencies. To help students, offer a multisensory approach. Have the students or a helper print in large letters on flashcards the correct spellings of words they are studying. Students can then study the words by simultaneously tracing the letters with their fingers and pronouncing the word on the card. For an added sensory dimension, letters can be written in puff paint so that students can actually feel the letters once the paint has dried.

MECHANICS

---

4. *use* (v. or n.) + *–ful* = *useful* (adj.)

5. *argue* (v.) + *–ment* = *argument* (n.)

Ask volunteers to use both words from each example in a sentence. Conclude by explaining that being familiar with how suffixes change a word's part of speech can help students expand their vocabularies.

LEARNERS HAVING DIFFICULTY
You may want to initiate a discussion about the necessity of rules. On the chalkboard, write *stop sign, referee,* and *lifeguard.* Ask students what these words have in common. [*They are associated with rules.*]

Stress that rules make life safer and easier. Just as understanding and obeying traffic rules may prevent accidents, understanding and following spelling rules may prevent unclear communication.

Have students suggest other words to add to the list on the chalkboard, and then discuss what might happen if the rules associated with the words did not exist.

Exercise 7

ALTERNATIVE LESSON
Ask students to identify all the possible parts of speech for the following words.

1. swim [*noun, verb*], swimmer [*noun*]

2. accept [*verb*], acceptance [*noun*]

5. riot [*noun, verb*], riotous [*adjective*]

Exercise 6 **Spelling Words with Suffixes**

Spell each of the following words, including the suffix that is given.

EXAMPLE **1.** ply + able

　　　　　 1. pliable

1. extraordinarily
2. trying
3. denial
4. satisfied
5. reliable

1. extraordinary + ly	**6.** baby + ish	6. babyish
2. try + ing	**7.** say + ing	7. saying
3. deny + al	**8.** joy + ful	8. joyful
4. satisfy + ed	**9.** bray + ing	9. braying
5. rely + able	**10.** fly + ing	10. flying

Doubling Final Consonants

27k. When a word ends in a consonant, double the final consonant before a suffix that begins with a vowel only if the word:

- has only one syllable or is accented on the last syllable

　　　　　　　　　and

- ends in a *single* consonant preceded by a *single* vowel

EXAMPLES   dim + est = di**mm**est   red + ish = re**dd**ish

　　　　　　 plan + ed = pla**nn**ed   propel + er = prope**ll**er

　　　　　　 sit + ing = si**tt**ing   refer + ed = refe**rr**ed

Otherwise, simply add the suffix.

EXAMPLES   jump + ed = **jump**ed   tunnel + ing = **tunnel**ing

　　　　　　 sprint + er = **sprint**er   appear + ance = **appear**ance

---

┌ H E L P ─
The final consonant in some words may or may not be doubled. In such cases, both spellings are equally correct.

EXAMPLES
travel + er = trave**ler** *or* trave**ller**

shovel + ed = shove**led** *or* shove**lled**

Exercise 7 **Spelling Words with Suffixes**

Spell each of the following words, including the suffix that is given.

EXAMPLE **1.** rebel + ed

　　　　　 1. rebelled

1. swimmer
2. acceptance
3. numbering
4. excelled
5. riotous

1. swim + er	**6.** prepare + ing	6. preparing
2. accept + ance	**7.** control + ed	7. controlled
3. number + ing	**8.** slim + er	8. slimmer
4. excel + ed	**9.** prefer + ing	9. preferring
5. riot + ous	**10.** glamor + ous	10. glamorous

The following paragraph contains spelling errors involving the use of prefixes and suffixes. For each sentence, write the misspelled word or words correctly. If a sentence is already correct, write *C*.

┌HELP┐
No proper
nouns in Review B
are misspelled.

EXAMPLE [1] Few people know that a teenage boy helped create the awsome Mount Rushmore monument.

1. *awesome*

[1] Begining when he was fifteen, Lincoln Borglum helped his famous father, Gutzon Borglum, who planed and made this gigantic sculpture. [2] First, Gutzon Borglum built a plaster model one-twelfth as large as the complleted sculpture would be. [3] On top of this model Borglum attached the equipment from which he controlled a plumb line. [4] The plumb line could be dangled in front of each president's likness to record carefuly each feature. [5] Lincoln Borglum helped in making these measurments. [6] Then, on top of the cliff, they fastenned an identical machine twelve times as large. [7] Lincoln Borglum was one of the workers who operatted this machine. [8] Using it, he copyed the movements of the smaller machine and marked exactly where to cut away the rock. [9] The closer the workers got to finishing the faces, the more carefully the Borglums studied the heads. [10] There were numerous problems, but the monument was finally inaugurated in 1941.

Forming Plurals of Nouns

27l. To form the plurals of most English nouns, simply add *s*.

SINGULAR	boat	care	storm	radio	Jim
PLURAL	boat**s**	care**s**	storm**s**	radio**s**	Jim**s**

Review B Spelling Words with Prefixes and Suffixes

ANSWERS
1. Beginning; planned
2. completed
3. C
4. likeness; carefully
5. measurements
6. fastened
7. operated
8. copied
9. studied
10. C

Critical Thinking

Metacognition. Write on the chalkboard a list of correctly and incorrectly spelled words that apply to **Rules 27l** and **27m.** Ask students if the words are spelled correctly. Next, have students think about how they came to their conclusions. You might have volunteers share their responses or suggest that all students record their processes in their spelling logs.

Synthesis and Evaluation. Tell each student to choose five rules from **27b** to **27m** and to write a brief narrative paragraph including five words that exemplify those rules but that are intentionally misspelled. Students will also want to include correctly spelled words using the same rules.

Have students trade papers with each other and underline any misspelled words in their classmates' paragraphs. Then, they should correct the spelling and give the number of the rule that applies to each misspelled word.

27m. To form the plurals of other nouns, follow these rules.

(1) If the noun ends in *s, x, z, ch,* or *sh,* add *es.*

SINGULAR	moss	fox	Sanchez	clutch	dish
PLURAL	moss**es**	fox**es**	Sanchez**es**	clutch**es**	dish**es**

NOTE Some one-syllable words ending in *z* double the final consonant when forming plurals.

EXAMPLES	quiz	fez
	qui**zz**es	fe**zz**es

Exercise 8 Spelling the Plurals of Nouns

Spell the plural of each of the following nouns.

EXAMPLE   **1.** Evans
            1. Evanses

1. guess   1. guesses   **6.** boss   6. bosses
2. ax   2. axes   **7.** student 7. students
3. tongue   3. tongues   **8.** Owens   8. Owenses
4. cafeteria 4. cafeterias **9.** box   9. boxes
5. wash   5. washes   **10.** ditch   10. ditches

(2) If the noun ends in *y* preceded by a consonant, change the *y* to *i* and add *es.*

SINGULAR	fly	pony	cry	story
PLURAL	fl**ies**	pon**ies**	cr**ies**	stor**ies**

EXCEPTION   plurals of proper nouns: the Hard**ys,** the Car**ys**

(3) For some nouns ending in *f* or *fe,* add *s.* For other nouns ending in *f* or *fe,* change the *f* to *v* and add *s* or *es.*

EXAMPLES	giraffe	roof	self	life	elf	thief	wolf
	giraffe**s**	roof**s**	sel**ves**	li**ves**	el**ves**	thie**ves**	wol**ves**

NOTE Some nouns can correctly form their plurals either way.

EXAMPLES	hoof	scarf
	hoo**ves**	scar**ves**
	or	*or*
	hoof**s**	scarf**s**

⌈ TIPS & TRICKS ⌉

Noticing how the plural is pronounced will help you remember whether to change the *f* to *v.*

Exercise 9 — Spelling the Plurals of Nouns

Spell the plural of each of the following nouns.

EXAMPLES   **1.** shelf
1. *shelves*

      2. poppy
2. *poppies*

1. thief	1. thieves	6. wife	6. wives	
2. chef	2. chefs	7. loaf	7. loaves	
3. theory	3. theories	8. comedy	8. comedies	
4. gulf	4. gulfs	9. trophy	9. trophies	
5. ally	5. allies	10. self	10. selves	

┌HELP┐

To correctly complete Exercise 9, you may wish to refer to a recent dictionary.

(4) If the noun ends in *o* preceded by a vowel, add *s*.

SINGULAR	radio	cameo	kangaroo	Julio
PLURAL	radio**s**	cameo**s**	kangaroo**s**	Julio**s**

(5) If the noun ends in *o* preceded by a consonant, add *es*.

SINGULAR	echo	hero	tomato	veto
PLURAL	echo**es**	hero**es**	tomato**es**	veto**es**

EXCEPTIONS   Some common nouns ending in *o* preceded by a consonant (especially musical terms) and proper nouns form the plural by adding only *s*.

SINGULAR	peso	sombrero	photo	alto
	piano	solo	Sotho	Sakamoto
PLURAL	peso**s**	sombrero**s**	photo**s**	alto**s**
	piano**s**	solo**s**	Sotho**s**	Sakamoto**s**

NOTE   A number of nouns that end in *o* preceded by a consonant have two correct plural forms.

SINGULAR	cargo	grotto	mosquito
PLURAL	cargo**s**	grotto**s**	mosquito**s**
	or	*or*	*or*
	cargo**es**	grotto**es**	mosquito**es**

The best way to determine the plurals of words ending in *o* preceded by a consonant is to check their spellings in a dictionary.

Crossing the Curriculum

Science. Words from students' science textbooks can provide extra spelling practice. Ask students to find in their science textbooks examples of words that fit the rules covered in this chapter and to add the words to their spelling notebooks.

To correctly complete Exercise 10, you may wish to refer to a recent dictionary.

Exercise 10 Spelling the Plurals of Nouns

Spell the plural of each of the following nouns.

EXAMPLE **1.** stereo

1. stereos

1. igloo	**1.** igloos	**6.** banjo	**6.** banjos [*or* banjoes]
2. soprano	**2.** sopranos	**7.** taco	**7.** tacos
3. patio	**3.** patios	**8.** cello	**8.** cellos
4. veto	**4.** vetoes	**9.** Romeo	**9.** Romeos
5. torpedo	**5.** torpedoes	**10.** studio	**10.** studios

(6) The plurals of some nouns are formed in irregular ways.

SINGULAR	child	foot	goose	man	tooth
PLURAL	child**ren**	**fee**t	g**ee**se	m**e**n	t**ee**th

(7) Some nouns have the same form in both the singular and the plural.

SINGULAR and PLURAL	Japanese	spacecraft	sheep

Compound Nouns

(8) For most compound nouns, form the plural of only the last word in the compound.

SINGULAR	spoonbill	smashup	icebox	six-year-old
PLURAL	spoonbill**s**	smashup**s**	icebox**es**	six-year-old**s**

(9) For compound nouns in which one of the words is modified by the other word or words, form the plural of the word modified.

SINGULAR	sister-in-law	notary public	attorney at law
PLURAL	sister**s**-in-law	notar**ies** public	attorney**s** at law

NOTE Whenever you are not sure about how to spell the plural form of a compound noun, check a recent dictionary.

Exercise 11 Spelling the Plurals of Nouns

Spell the plural form of each of the following nouns.

EXAMPLE **1.** ox

1. oxen

1. Vietnamese	1. Vietnamese	6. brother-in-law	6. brothers-in-law
2. earmuff	2. earmuffs	7. aircraft	7. aircraft
3. mouse	3. mice	8. woman	8. women
4. cross-reference		9. runner-up	9. runners-up
5. goose	4. cross-references	10. twenty-year-old	
	5. geese		10. twenty-year-olds

Latin and Greek Loan Words

(10) Some nouns borrowed from Latin and Greek form the plural as in the original language.

SINGULAR	PLURAL
alumnus [male]	alumn**i**
alumna [female]	alumn**ae**
analysis	analys**es**
crisis	cris**es**
datum	dat**a**
phenomenon	phenomen**a**

NOTE   A few Latin and Greek loan words have two correct plural forms.

SINGULAR	appendix	formula
PLURAL	appendi**ces** *or* appendi**xes**	formula**s** *or* formula**e**

Check a dictionary to find the preferred spelling of a plural loan word. The preferred spelling is generally the one listed first.

Numerals, Letters, Symbols, and Words Used as Words

(11) To form the plurals of numerals, most capital letters, symbols, and words used as words, add either an *s* or an apostrophe and an *s*.

EXAMPLES   Put the **4°s** (*or* **4s**) and the **T°s** (*or* **Ts**) in the second column.

Change the **&°s** (*or* **&s**) to **and°s** (*or* **and**s).

My parents were teenagers during the **'60°s** (*or* **'60s**).

Many immigrants came to this country during the **1800°s** (*or* **1800s**).

BORN LOSER reprinted by permission of Newspaper Enterprise Association, Inc.

MECHANICS

Exercise 12 Spelling the Plurals of Nouns, Numerals, Letters, Symbols, and Words Used as Words

ANSWERS

1. +'s *or* +s
2. parentheses
3. *so's*
4. *9's or 9s*
5. fulcrums *or* fulcra
6. *C's or Cs*
7. 1840's *or* 1840s
8. indexes *or* indices
9. *!'s or !s*
10. *ho-ho-ho's*

TEACHING TIP

Review C You may wish to use the first five sentences as guided practice and the last five as independent practice.

Review C Spelling the Plurals of Nouns

ANSWERS

1. oxen; geese; calves
2. butterflies; mice; burros; giraffes *or* giraffe
3. Armies; jalopies
4. wives; sons-in-law; children
5. ponies; sheep; C [*or* deers]
6. heroes
7. mosquitoes *or* mosquitos; kangaroos
8. *p's; q's*
9. leaves
10. C

To prevent confusion, always use an apostrophe and an *s* to form the plurals of lowercase letters, certain capital letters, and some words used as words.

EXAMPLES   What do these **a**'s in the margins mean?

Ramon got **A**'s last semester.

Her muffled **tee-hee**'s did not interrupt the speaker.

Exercise 12 Spelling the Plurals of Nouns, Numerals, Letters, Symbols, and Words Used as Words

Give the plural form of each of the following words, numerals, symbols, and words used as words.

EXAMPLE   **1.** *o*

1. *o's*

1. +
2. parenthesis
3. *so*
4. *9*
5. fulcrum
6. *C*
7. 1840
8. index
9. *!*
10. *ho-ho-ho*

Review C Spelling the Plurals of Nouns

Most lines in the following silly poem contain misspelled words. Correct each misspelled word. If a line contains no misspellings, write *C*.

EXAMPLES   **1.** A group of mans and womens started up a local zoo.

1. *men; women*

   2. They bought a lot of animales and put them all on view.

2. *animals*

1. They caged the oxes with the gooses, the lion with the calfs,
2. The butterflys and mouses with the burroes and giraffs.
3. Armys of people soon arrived. In jalopys they were piled,
4. With wifes and husbands, son-in-laws, and lots of little childs.
5. The boys and girls rode poneys, and they fed the sheeps and deer,
6. And thought their folks were heros to bring them all right here.
7. The mosquitoses had a fine time feasting on the kangarooes;
8. Most of the other animals minded their *p*s and *q*s.
9. The moon shone brightly through the leafs as night began to fall.
10. Why do you think the lion had the nicest day of all?

Spelling Numbers

27n. Spell out a number that begins a sentence.

EXAMPLE   **One thousand five hundred** band members attended this year's State Marching Band Festival.

27o. Within a sentence, spell out numbers that can be written in one or two words; use numerals for other numbers.

EXAMPLES   I have only **one** week in which to write **four** reports.

We picked **twenty-one** quarts of peaches.

Agnes has sold **116** magazine subscriptions.

EXCEPTION 1   If you use some numbers that have one or two words and some that have more than two words, use numerals for all of them.

EXAMPLE   Our school had **563** freshmen, **327** sophomores, **143** juniors, and **90** seniors.

EXCEPTION 2   Use numerals for dates when you include the name of the month. Always use numerals for years.

EXAMPLES   School closes on June **6.** [This example could also be correctly written as *the sixth of June,* but not *June 6th.*]

Egypt fell to the Romans in **30** B.C.

27p. Spell out numbers used to indicate order.

EXAMPLE   My brother graduated **second** [not *2nd*] in his class.

Reference Note

For more about **writing dates,** see page 659.

Spelling Rules   **745**

Exercise 13 Spelling Numbers

POSSIBLE ANSWERS

1. Ninety people applied for the job.

2. Of the candidates, fifty-two seem qualified, but only one can be hired.

3. The contest jar held 231 red jelly beans, 83 green ones, and only 15 yellow ones.

4. Jim finished fourth in the Memorial Day Marathon.

5. My birthday is December 23.

Words Often Confused

(pp. 746–757)

OBJECTIVES

- To distinguish between words that are often confused

- To proofread sentences for correct use of words that are often confused

---

Exercise 13 Spelling Numbers

Write five original sentences, following the directions given below.

EXAMPLE 1. Write a sentence giving the year in which your best friend was born.

  1. *Rudy Garza was born in 1986.*

1. Write a sentence beginning with a number.

2. Write a sentence containing two numbers, both of which can be written in one or two words.

3. Write a sentence containing three numbers, two of them with one or two words and one of them with more than two words.

4. Write a sentence using a number to indicate the order in which a person placed in a race.

5. Write a sentence giving the month and date of your birthday.

Words Often Confused

You can prevent many spelling errors by learning the difference between the words grouped together in this section. Some of them are confusing because they are **homonyms**—that is, they are pronounced alike. Others are confusing because they are spelled the same or nearly the same.

advice	[noun] *counsel* Why don't you ask your father for *advice*?
advise	[verb] *to give advice* The weather service *advises* boaters.
affect	[verb] *to influence* Do sunspots *affect* the weather?
effect	[verb] *to bring about, to accomplish*; [noun] *result, consequence* Our new boss *effected* some startling changes in our use of technology. Name three *effects* of the Industrial Revolution on family life.
all ready	[adjective] *everyone or everything prepared* We were *all ready* to go.
already	[adverb] *previously* Sharon has *already* gone.

RESOURCES

Words Often Confused

Practice

- *Grammar, Usage, and Mechanics,* pp. 357, 358, 359, 360, 361

- *Language Workshop CD-ROM,* Lessons 61, 62

all right	[This is the only acceptable spelling. Although the spelling *alright* is in some dictionaries, it has not become standard usage.]
all together	[adjective or adverb] *everyone or everything in the same place* *All together* at last, the travelers relaxed. The band simply must play *all together*.
altogether	[adverb] *entirely* You're *altogether* mistaken, I fear.
altar	[noun] *a table used for a religious ceremony* The *altar* was draped with a white cloth.
alter	[verb] *to change* This actor can *alter* his appearance.
brake	[noun] *a stopping device*; [verb] *to stop* The *brakes* on our car are good. I *brake* for deer.
break	[verb] *to shatter, sever* A high-pitched sound can *break* glass.
capital	[noun] *center of government; money or property used in business*; [adjective] *punishable by death; of major importance; excellent; uppercase* Raleigh is the *capital* of North Carolina. We need more *capital* to buy the factory. Is killing a police officer a *capital* crime? I made a *capital* error in judgment. This is a *capital* detective story. You need a *capital* letter here.
capitol	[noun] *building, statehouse* The *capitol* is on East Edenton Street.
choose	[verb, used for present and future tense] *select* You may *choose* your own partner.
chose	[verb, past tense, rhymes with *nose*] *selected* They *chose* to postpone the meeting.

(continued)

Reference Note

In the Glossary of Usage, Chapter 20, you can find many other words that are often confused or misused. You can also look them up in a dictionary.

TIPS & TRICKS

To remember the correct spelling of *capitol,* use this memory aid: There is a d**o**me on the capit**o**l.

MULTIPLE INTELLIGENCES
Spatial Intelligence. Divide the **Words Often Confused** list among students, and have each student create a large chart for his or her assigned group of words. Students might want to vary the materials used for each chart. (For example, students with tactile orientation might write the words with puff paint or cut the words out of a fabric like velour to trace with their fingers while learning the words.) Then, as the class studies each group of words, hang the corresponding chart in the classroom.

MECHANICS

coarse	[adjective] *rough, crude*
	This *coarse* fabric is very durable.
	He never uses *coarse* language.
course	[noun] *path of action or progress; unit of study; track or way; part of a meal;* [also used with *of* to mean *naturally* or *certainly*]
	The airplane strayed off its *course* in the storm.
	I'm taking an algebra *course*.
	She's at the golf *course*.
	The main *course* at the banquet was roasted turkey with dressing.
	Cats, of *course*, are predators.

TEACHING TIP

Activity. You may want to introduce students to several pairs of words that are spelled the same but that are different parts of speech and are pronounced differently. For example, when *address* is used as a noun, the stress is on the first syllable. When it is used as a verb, the stress falls on the second syllable. Other examples include *con*flict—con*flict, per*mit—per*mit, pre*sent—pre*sent,* and *pro*duce—pro*duce.* Have students repeat these words as you model the correct pronunciations. Have students work with partners to create sentences using the word pairs—for example, "My father won't per*mit* me to get a driving *per*mit until next year."

MECHANICS

Exercise 14 Distinguishing Between Words Often Confused

Choose the correct word or expression from the pair in parentheses.

EXAMPLE
1. I was proud to (*accept, except*) the award.

    1. *accept*

1. Betty has (*all ready, already*) handed in her paper.
2. (*All right, Alright*), I'll wrap the package now.
3. The mechanic adjusted the (*brakes, breaks*).
4. Do you know which city is the (*capital, capitol*) of your state?
5. They were (*all together, altogether*) at dinner.
6. The rule goes into (*affect, effect*) today.
7. His (*coarse, course*) manners offended everyone.
8. A fragile piece of china (*brakes, breaks*) easily.
9. Our state (*capital, capitol*) is built of limestone and marble.
10. When will they (*choose, chose*) the winners?

Exercise 15 Proofreading for Words Often Confused

Correct the ~~errors~~ in word choice in the following sentences.

─HELP─

Some sentences in Exercise 15 contain more than one error.

EXAMPLE
1. After taking that class, we were already to shoot our own videos.

    1. *all ready*

1. advice

1. The best movie-making ~~advise~~ I ever received came from Ms. Herrera.

MINI-LESSON

Confusing Words. Give students the following dictation to test their ability to distinguish between words often confused.

Counselors advise that correct spelling is important. You may fear that *it's already too* late, that your skills are *too weak* to be improved. However, if *you're* willing *to* learn a few basic *principles,* you can *break* the pattern of failure and *effect quite* a change in *your* life.

Next, have each student exchange papers with a classmate and use a colored pen to

2. She taught the video ~~coarse~~ that I ~~choose~~ as an elective last semester.

3. Once we would-be movie makers were ~~altogether~~, she said simply, "Rule number one: Take the lens cap off."

4. Everyone laughed, but she said, "It's no joke—in every class at least one person ~~brakes~~ this one basic rule."

5. "Of ~~coarse~~," she added, "forgetting to put a videocassette in the camera has much the same ~~affect~~."

6. If you ~~chose~~ to make your own home videos, I'd ~~advice~~ you to remember Ms. Herrera's words.

7. They will seriously ~~effect~~ you.

8. I remembered her advice when I went to the steps of the ~~capital~~ for my first shoot.

9. I checked the lighting and angle and chose a subject that was ~~all together~~ satisfactory.

10. When I started to shoot, I realized I had made a ~~capitol~~ error—I had forgotten to take the lens cap off!

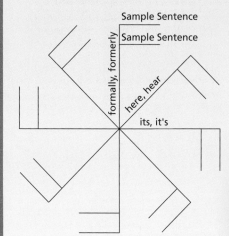

2. course/chose
3. all together
4. breaks
5. course/effect
6. choose/advise
7. affect
8. capitol
9. altogether
10. capital

complement	[noun] *something that completes or makes perfect;* [verb] *to complete or make perfect*
	The office now has a full *complement* of personnel.
	The rug *complemented* the cozy room.
compliment	[noun] *a remark that expresses approval, praise, or admiration;* [verb] *to pay a compliment*
	Ms. Garcia paid me a *compliment*.
	The review *complimented* Rosemary on her performance.
consul	[noun] *the representative of a foreign country*
	Did you meet the Greek *consul* at the reception?
council	[noun] *a group called together to accomplish a job*
	Our town *council* meets next Tuesday.
counsel	[noun] *advice;* [verb] *to give advice*
	Her *counsel* is invaluable to the president.
	The engineers *counsel* them to use additional support for the crossbeams.

(continued)

MODALITIES

Visual Learners. Students may find the following design helpful in learning the frequently confused words presented in this section.

Each shorter line contains a sentence using both of the words being studied, while each longer line lists the pair of words. Suggest that students develop this diagram for the words that are frequently confused and put the diagram in their notebooks. Ask volunteers to share a few sample sentences they have written.

TIPS & TRICKS

To remember the correct spelling of *complement*, use this memory aid: A compl**e**ment compl**e**tes.

MECHANICS

circle any incorrect words. Explain to students that these are words that a spellchecker in a word-processing program would not correct and that they usually require extra practice or memorization to learn. Suggest that students make flash-cards for the words in this section, or, if time permits, you could give students a different word pair from this section each day and have them write example sentences in their notebooks.

Looking at Language

Word Origins. Many of the word pairs in this section (for example, *moral* and *morale*) have similar origins. You might want to assign each student a pair of words, and have him or her research whether the two words have similar roots (for example, *brake* and *break*, *plane* and *plain*, *quiet* and *quite*, and *stationary* and *stationery*). Then, have students present their findings to the class.

(continued)

councilor	[noun] *a member of a council* At the council meeting, my mother plans to introduce Dr. Watkins, the new *councilor*.
counselor	[noun] *one who gives advice* I don't think I'm qualified to act as your *counselor*.
desert	[noun, pronounced des′•ert] *a dry region* The Sahara is the world's largest *desert*.
desert	[verb, pronounced de•sert′] *to leave* She would never *desert* her comrades.
dessert	[noun, pronounced des•sert′] *a sweet, final course of a meal* What would you like for dessert tonight?

Exercise 16 Distinguishing Between Words Often Confused

Choose the correct word from the choices in parentheses.

EXAMPLE   1. The town (*counselor*, *councilor*) voted on the bill.

   1. *councilor*

1. The funds are for a (*desert*, *dessert*) irrigation project.
2. The Security (*Consul*, *Council*, *Counsel*) of the United Nations consists of fifteen members.
3. The new tie will (*complement*, *compliment*) my suit.
4. Miss Jee is my guidance (*councilor*, *counselor*).
5. The house looks (*deserted*, *desserted*).
6. Listen to your parents' (*consul*, *council*, *counsel*).
7. I passed on your charming (*complement*, *compliment*) to Isabel.
8. All the members of the city (*council*, *counsel*) agreed.
9. Frozen yogurt is my favorite (*desert*, *dessert*).
10. The American (*consul*, *counsel*) in Bahrain announced the recent trade agreement.

formally	[adverb] *properly, according to strict rules* Should he be *formally* introduced?
formerly	[adverb] *previously, in the past* The new consul was *formerly* a professor.

hear	[verb] *to receive sounds through the ears* Did you *hear* the president's speech?
here	[adverb] *at this place* The bus will be *here* soon.
its	[possessive of *it*] *belonging to it* The lion stopped in *its* tracks.
it's	[contraction of *it is* or *it has*] *It's* snowing! *It's* started snowing!
lead	[verb, present tense, rhymes with *deed*] *to go first* I'll *lead* the way.
led	[verb, past tense of *lead*] *went first* Last week she *led* us to victory.
lead	[noun, rhymes with *red*] *a heavy metal; graphite in a pencil* We made fishing sinkers out of *lead*. Use a sharp *lead* to draw fine lines.
loose	[adjective, rhymes with *noose*] *not tight, not securely fastened; not close together* The string on the package is too *loose*.
lose	[verb, rhymes with *choose*] *to suffer loss* Don't *lose* your ticket.
moral	[adjective] *having to do with good or right;* [noun] *a lesson in conduct* It's a *moral* question. These fables all have a *moral*.
morale	[noun] *mental condition, spirit* Letters from home raised our *morale*.
passed	[verb, past tense of *pass*] *went by* He *passed* us in the corridor.
past	[noun] *history, what has gone by;* [adjective] *former;* [preposition] *farther than; after* I didn't ask him about his *past*. Her *past* employer recommended her. I went *past* the house. It's ten minutes *past* noon.

(continued)

MECHANICS

(continued)

peace	[noun] *absence of conflict*
	Only after war is *peace* truly appreciated.
piece	[noun] *a part of something;* [verb] *to assemble slowly*
	Have a *piece* of my homemade bread.
	We *pieced* together the puzzle.

TIPS & TRICKS

To remember the correct spelling of *piece,* use the following memory aid: a **pie**ce of **pie**.

Exercise 17 Distinguishing Between Words Often Confused

Choose the correct word of the pair in parentheses.

EXAMPLE   1. The two countries settled their dispute and now live in (*piece, peace*).

1. *peace*

1. The coach's praise after the game raised the team's (*morale, moral*).
2. It's already (*passed, past*) nine o'clock.
3. The searchers hoped that the search dog would (*lead, led*) them to the missing skier.
4. The two forwards (*led, lead*) the team to victory.
5. I'm more interested in math than I (*formally, formerly*) was.
6. Several children asked what the (*moral, morale*) of the story was.
7. I need a pencil with soft (*led, lead*).
8. Everyone at the dance was dressed (*formally, formerly*).
9. Molly (*past, passed*) the open doorway.
10. Is the bank offering good interest rates on (*it's, its*) savings accounts and loans?

Exercise 18 Proofreading for Words Often Confused

Correct the errors in word choice in the following sentences.

EXAMPLE   1. My dad's promotion lead to a move for our family.

1. *led*

1. Sometimes relocating can feel like abandoning everything and everyone you formally cared about.   1. formerly
2. However, before my family and I moved, one of my friends gave me very good council.   2. counsel
3. "Moving away," she said, "doesn't mean that you are desserting your old friends."   3. deserting

4. After my family moved across the country, I remembered that ~~peace~~ of advice.   **4.** piece

5. For the first few months after we moved ~~hear~~, I felt as though I'd been cut ~~lose~~ from everything I loved.   **5.** here/loose

6. To boost my morale, my parents told me something that I needed to ~~here~~.   **6.** hear

7. If you dwell on the ~~passed~~, you will ~~loose~~ out on the present.   **7.** past/lose

8. They both moved often when they were young, so I guess they know what ~~its~~ like.   **8.** it's

9. Now that a year has ~~past~~, I understand that every place has ~~it's~~ good points.   **9.** passed/its

10. I've made quite a few new friends, and I'm finally at ~~piece~~ with myself—and with my parents.   **10.** peace

plain	[adjective] *clear, not fancy;* [noun] *a flat area of land* She made her point of view *plain*. Steven wears very *plain* clothes. The storm lashed the open *plain*.
plane	[noun] *a flat surface; a level; a tool; an airplane* Each *plane* of the granite block was smooth. The debate was conducted on a high *plane*. Chris smoothed the wood with a *plane*. The *plane* arrived on time.
principal	[noun] *head of a school;* [adjective] *main, most important* Our new *principal* addressed the assembly. Product design is my *principal* responsibility.
principle	[noun] *a rule of conduct; a law* His *principles* do not allow compromise. Please explain the *principle* of gravity.
quiet	[adjective] *silent, still* The library is usually fairly *quiet*.
quite	[adverb] *to a great extent or degree, completely* My little brother is *quite* clever for his age. I'm not *quite* finished.

(continued)

TIPS & TRICKS

To remember the correct spelling of *principal*, use the following memory aid: The princi**pal** is your **pal**.

Relating to Vocabulary Skills

Vocabulary and spelling problems are closely linked in the words covered in this segment. Ask students to choose five words from the **Words Often Confused** list that are not part of their usual vocabularies and to record the definitions in their spelling logs. Then, have students write several original sentences using each word on their lists correctly. Finally, have students revise the sentences to create a fill-in-the-blank or a multiple-choice exercise. Assign the exercises to class members needing extra practice.

TECHNOLOGY TIP

Remind students that computer spellcheckers do not identify words that have been confused with other words, because the program finds only misspellings, not incorrect usage. For example, a spellchecker will not point out that *affect* has been confused with *effect* since *affect* is a correctly spelled word in other contexts.

MECHANICS

Crossing the Curriculum

Art/Home Economics. Have each student involved in art or home economics design a quilt square illustrating a pair of words often confused. (For example, a student might illustrate *peace* and *piece* by drawing a large *peace* sign and a *piece* of pie.) Encourage students to use various methods (needlework, batik, collages, computer graphics, and so forth) they have learned in art or home economics classes to create their squares. Then, have students stitch or tape their squares together to make a spelling quilt to display in the classroom.

Exercises You may wish to use **Exercise 19** as guided practice and **Review D** as independent practice.

TIPS & TRICKS

To remember the correct spelling of *stationery*, use the following memory aid: "You write a lett**er** on station**er**y."

Reference Note

For information on **possessive pronouns,** see page 556. For information on **adverbs,** see page 572. For information on **forming contractions,** see page 707.

(continued)

shone	[verb, past tense of *shine*] *emitted light* The sun *shone* brightly this morning.
shown	[verb, past participle of *show*] *revealed, displayed* Li Hua has just *shown* me her scrapbook.
stationary	[adjective] *in a fixed position* These chairs are *stationary*.
stationery	[noun] *writing paper* Use white *stationery* for business letters.
than	[conjunction, used for comparisons] Jimmy enjoys tennis more *than* golfing.
then	[adverb] *at that time; next* Did you know Bianca *then*? I revised my paper, and *then* I proofread it.
their	[possessive of *they*] *belonging to them* The girls gave *their* opinions.
there	[adverb] *at that place;* [also an expletive used to begin a sentence] I'll be *there* on time. *There* isn't any milk left.
they're	[contraction of *they are*] *They're* at the station now.

Exercise 19 **Distinguishing Between Words Often Confused**

Choose the correct word from the pair in parentheses.

EXAMPLE 1. Mrs. Tanaka is our school's (*principal, principle*).

1. *principal*

1. An elephant eats more vegetation (*then,* <u>*than*</u>) any other animal does.
2. One scene of the movie was not (*shone,* <u>*shown*</u>) on TV.
3. The deer was (<u>*stationary*</u>, *stationery*) for a full minute.
4. Gossiping is against his (*principals,* <u>*principles*</u>).
5. Last night many stars (<u>*shone*</u>, *shown*) brightly.
6. I wrote the letter on blue (*stationary,* <u>*stationery*</u>).
7. Rosa learned how to use a (*plain,* <u>*plane*</u>) in industrial arts class.

Learning for Life **Continued on pp. 755–756**

Editing Services. Proofreading for spelling errors is a good way to confront personal spelling problems. Tell the class that they will be offering their proofreading services to another class. The class may be another language arts class at the same grade level.

Obtain from another teacher a set of papers that need proofreading, allowing the students who have written the papers to maintain anonymity by using identifying numbers rather than names on their papers.

8. My (*principal*, *principle*) problem is learning to spell.
9. I hope they remembered (*there*, *their*) homework.
10. Is he (*quite*, *quiet*) sure?

Review D Proofreading for Words Often Confused

Correct each ~~error~~ in word choice in the following sentences.

EXAMPLE 1. Our principle let us out of class early to welcome home our victorious volleyball team.

  1. *principal*

┌HELP─
Some sentences in Review D contain more than one error.

1. King High School won ~~quiet~~ a victory last year—the girls' regional volleyball championship.
2. Everyone wanted to ~~complement~~ the team's abilities.
3. The victory had a positive ~~affect~~ on the whole student body.
4. Hundreds of students went to the airport to meet the team's ~~plain~~.
5. The flight arrived on time, but ~~than~~ it took more ~~then~~ an hour for the aircraft to reach the gate.
6. Finally someone shouted, "~~Their~~ they are!"
7. "~~There~~ coming up the ramp!"
8. Coach Janos asked for ~~quite~~ and introduced each of the girls.
9. ~~They're~~ were loud cheers for each of them, even though quite a few hadn't played in the final game.
10. It was ~~plane~~ that they were quite excited about ~~there~~ success and were looking forward to the official victory rally the next day.

1. quite

2. compliment
3. effect
4. plane
5. then/than

6. There
7. They're
8. quiet
9. There

10. plain/their

threw	[verb] *tossed; pitched* Freddy *threw* three strikes.
through	[preposition] *in one side and out the opposite side* The firetruck raced *through* the heavy traffic.
to	[preposition; also used before the infinitive form of a verb] They've gone *to* the store. She told us *to* wash the windows.
too	[adverb] *also; excessively* I like soccer, and Ted does, *too*. He was *too* tired to think clearly.
two	[adjective or noun] *the sum of one + one* I noticed *two* packages on the sofa.

(continued)

Words Often Confused **755**

Have each student become an "expert" on a particular spelling rule or on a set of words from the **Words Often Confused** list. Each student will read the papers for his or her specialty only (for example, forming plurals of words ending in *y*).

Have students brainstorm to develop a process that the whole class will use, such as learning a particular rule, reading the paper to find words related to that rule, checking a dictionary to be sure the word is not an exception to the rule, and writing

(continued)

waist	[noun] *the middle part of the body* This skirt is too big in the *waist*.
waste	[noun] *unused material;* [verb] *to squander* *Waste* is a major problem in the United States. Don't *waste* your money on that.
weak	[adjective] *feeble, lacking force, not strong* The fawn is still too *weak* to walk.
week	[noun] *seven days* Carol has been gone a *week*.
weather	[noun] *conditions outdoors* The *weather* suddenly changed.
whether	[conjunction indicating alternative or doubt] She wondered *whether* to enter the contest.
who's	[contraction of *who is* or *who has*] I can't imagine *who's* at the door now. *Who's* been marking in my book?
whose	[possessive of *who*] *belonging to whom* *Whose* bicycle is this?
your	[possessive of *you*] *belonging to you* What is *your* idea?
you're	[contraction of *you are*] R.S.V.P. so that I'll know whether *you're* planning to be there.

Exercise 20 Distinguishing Between Words
Often Confused

Choose the correct word from the ones given in parentheses.

EXAMPLE **1.** Lourdes speaks Portuguese, (*to, two, too*).

      1. too

1. Next (*weak, week*) the Bearcats will play the Wolverines.
2. The ball crashed (*threw, through*) the window.
3. (*Your, You're*) up next, Leshe.
4. Giving a speech makes me (*weak, week*) in the knees.
5. (*Your, You're*) sleeve is torn.
6. Each band member wore a gold sash around the (*waist, waste*).
7. (*Whose, Who's*) bat is this?

Exercise 20

ALTERNATIVE LESSON
Have students identify the correct part of speech for each word or contraction below as it is used in the specified sentence.

3. next [*adverb*]

6. around [*preposition*]

9. –n't [*adverb*]

Learning for Life

an appropriate rule designation, such as "27i," on the paper being read.

   Provide a day that students may spend as proofreaders. Ask them each to write brief entries in their writing logs to summarize their experience and to tell what they learned from the activity.

8. (*Whose*, <u>*Who's*</u>) going to be first?
9. No, this isn't a (*waist*, <u>*waste*</u>) of time.
10. (<u>*Whose*</u>, *Who's*) seen my black sweater?

Exercise 21 Proofreading for Words Often Confused

Correct the errors in word choice in the following sentences.

EXAMPLE   **1.** Have you ever had the whether ruin you're plans?

          1. weather, your

1. Last Labor Day weekend, my brother Jorge and I got up early
   Saturday morning and rode our bikes four miles ~~too~~ the beach. **1.** to
2. The two of us were ~~to~~ busy talking ~~too~~ notice that the sky was
   growing darker as we rode along. **2.** too/to
                                3. threw
3. Just as we ~~through~~ our towels on the sand, it started to rain heavily.
4. We ~~waisted~~ the next hour huddled under one of the beach shelters,
   arguing about ~~weather~~ to stay or to go home. **4.** wasted/whether
5. We also got into an argument about ~~who's~~ fault it was. **5.** whose
6. "~~Your~~ the one who had the bright idea," said Jorge. **6.** You're
7. "~~Whose~~ the one who said it would be sunny?" I retorted. **7.** Who's
8. Finally, we pedaled back home ~~threw~~ the driving rain. **8.** through
9. It rained all day Sunday and Monday, ~~to~~. **9.** too
10. We spent the weekend cooped up in the house while ~~whether~~
    forecasters predicted sunny skies for the next ~~weak~~.
                              10. weather/week

Review E Identifying Correctly Spelled Words

Choose the correct word or expression from the pair in parentheses.

EXAMPLE   **1.** a (<u>*stationary*</u>, *stationery*) exercise bicycle

          1. stationary

1. a (<u>*brief*</u>, *breif*) talk
2. (<u>*neither*</u>, *niether*) one
3. (*course*, <u>*coarse*</u>) cloth
4. some good (<u>*advice*</u>, *advise*)
5. fruit for (*desert*, <u>*dessert*</u>)
6. many (*heros*, <u>*heroes*</u>)
7. on the (*cieling*, <u>*ceiling*</u>)
8. two (<u>*copies*</u>, *copys*)
9. looking (*passed*, <u>*past*</u>) him
10. (*weather*, <u>*whether*</u>) to stay
11. the (<u>*altar*</u>, *alter*) boys
12. building (*patioes*, <u>*patios*</u>)
13. recycled (*34*, <u>*thirty-four*</u>) cans
14. we will go (*than*, <u>*then*</u>)
15. a (*mispelled*, <u>*misspelled*</u>) word
16. (*happyly*, <u>*happily*</u>) ever after
17. that's (*awsome*, <u>*awesome*</u>)
18. a (*week*, <u>*weak*</u>) voice
19. this sharp pencil (<u>*led*</u>, *lead*)
20. (*their*, <u>*they're*</u>) his

MECHANICS

Using the Chapter Review

To assess student progress, you may want to compare the types of items missed on the **Diagnostic Preview** to those missed on the **Chapter Review**. If students have not made significant progress, you may want to refer them to **Chapter 28: Correcting Common Errors, Exercises 36–39**, for additional practice.

27

┌HELP───

Some sentences in Part A of the Chapter Review contain more than one error.

4. Occasionally
5. sensible

6. bookshelves

7. O'Daniels
8. awesome / swimmer
9. Extraordinarily
10. fifteenth

11. chief/speeches

12. All right/icy

13. boxes
14. Council

15. C
16. brief

17. precedes

18. daily

Chapter Review

A. Proofreading Sentences to Correct Spelling Errors

Most of the following sentences contain spelling errors. Write the misspelled words correctly. If a sentence is already correct, write *C*.

1. Silas has no doubt that his favorite neice will succede in whatever career she chooses to follow.   **1.** niece/succeed
   2. evenness
2. The winter snow and ice damaged the eveness of the road surface.
3. Some critics' reviews were largely favorable; others said the movie was awful.   **3.** C
4. Occasionaly, we stay home on Saturdays to clean the yard.
5. Cousin Mark bought that car because he thinks it is a senseible compromise between style and economy.
6. I read all the recommended books from cover to cover for the finals, and now that exams are over, the books are safely back on the library bookshelfs where they belong.
7. I asked Patrick O'Daniel how long the O'Daniel's had lived in Texas.
8. In his twenties, Grandpa was an awsome swimer.
9. Extraordinaryly quickly, the snake disappeared into the undergrowth.
10. "As you know," said Ms. Garza, "February 15th—that is, tomorrow—is Colleen's birthday."
11. My cheif objection to attending the ceremony was having to listen to all those speech's.
12. "Alright, then," said Mom. "You can go outside, but be careful on those icey sidewalks."
13. How many boxs were stacked near the door?
14. The members of the United Nations Security Counsel are the United States, Russia, China, France, and the United Kingdom.
15. The engineer accidentally shut down the transmitter.
16. Vivian's account of her experiences in New Guinea was breif but vivid.
17. What do you call the passage that preceeds the main body of our Constitution?
18. The paper is delivered dayly, except on Mondays.

19. The elephant was considerring coming into the clearing.
20. I'm grumpy because I just had an arguement with a friend.

19. considering
20. argument

B. Distinguishing Between Words Often Confused

Choose the correct word from the pair in parentheses.

21. Last night I went (*too, to*) the theater.

22. How did the news (*effect, affect*) him?

23. We need to order some letterhead (*stationary, stationery*) and paper for the photocopier.

24. At the graduation ceremony, Mr. Garcia, the (*principle, principal*), gave a short speech.

25. The (*plain, plane*) finally took off after a two-hour delay.

26. First we sketched the outline, and (*than, then*) we filled in the features of the house.

27. Her duties in her old job were (*quiet, quite*) different from those in the new job.

28. "Son," said Dad, "I'd (*advice, advise*) you to keep at it. Quitters never get anywhere."

29. For (*desert, dessert*) they had frozen yogurt and shredded pineapple.

30. We were all very pleased when we heard that Shawna's dad had been named U.S. (*Counsel, Consul*) in Pretoria, South Africa.

31. Please permit me to introduce (*formerly, formally*) Dr. Villanueva, my sponsor.

32. When parking on an incline, always remember to set the (*break, brake*).

33. I think that tonight's debate is on the subject of (*capital, capitol*) punishment.

34. "(*All together, Altogether*) now," said the choir director.

35. Going to the Christmas concert with the whole family certainly raised my (*morale, moral*).

36. The (*capital, capitol*) of New York State is not New York City, but Albany.

37. 1 wonder (*who's, whose*) parka this is.

38. From Fran's point of view, volunteering to help clean up the city park was as much a question of (*principal, principle*) as goodwill.

39. "Was that really (*you're*, *your*) best effort?" asked Ms. Yokoyama impatiently.

40. He opened his mouth to reply, but Babs had (*all ready*, *already*) gone.

41. Friends never (*dessert*, *desert*) each other.

42. Use a (*led*, *lead*) pencil to sketch the outlines.

43. "How could you (*loose*, *lose*) an entire bag of groceries?" asked Belinda incredulously.

44. The same truck (*past*, *passed*) us three times on the same stretch of highway.

45. Please remember that every journey has (*it's*, *its*) good and bad points.

46. "Improving communication, as many of you will find out, can boost (*moral*, *morale*)," said Ms. Lockheed.

47. The amber harvest moon (*shown*, *shone*) through the rustling branches and onto the badger's burrow.

48. "All the caddies will be paid in full, of (*course*, *coarse*)," said Mr. Glendinning.

49. When the office workers go home, a strange (*quiet*, *quite*) descends on the downtown business district.

50. The tornadoes raced across the barren (*plane*, *plain*).

RESOURCES

Spelling

Review

■ *Grammar, Usage, and Mechanics*, pp. 362, 363, 364, 365, 366

Assessment

■ *Assessment Package*
—*Chapter Tests*, Ch. 27
—*Chapter Tests in Standardized Test Formats*, Ch. 27
■ *Test Generator (One-Stop Planner CD-ROM)*

Writing Application

Using Correct Spelling in a Letter

Spelling Words Correctly   The junior varsity volleyball team is having its best season in several years, but no one else in school seems to know about it. Write a letter to the coach explaining the three best things the team can do to raise awareness and interest throughout the school. Use at least five words from the spelling lists and five words from the lists of words that are often confused.

Prewriting   Begin by making a list of all the ideas you can think of to promote the team. Look at the other successful sports and activities at your school. What do they do to promote themselves? Narrow your list down to the three ideas that are most likely to work.

Writing   Begin your letter by clearly explaining your purpose. Then, list each of your ideas and explain why you think they may help. Include estimates of how much money and time each of the ideas might involve. Conclude by offering to take charge of one part of the effort.

Revising   First, read your letter to make sure all of your ideas are clearly and completely explained. Ask yourself if you have thought about all of your ideas thoroughly. Have you considered all the expenses that each plan may involve? Would anyone be offended or hurt by any of your plans? You may want to have an adult friend or family member look at your ideas to see if they are appropriate. Make sure you have used at least five words from the spelling lists and five words from the lists of words that are often confused.

Publishing   Check your letter carefully for errors in grammar, usage, and punctuation. Then, think about a sport or other activity at school that does not get the recognition and support you think it deserves. Show your letter to the coach or sponsor of the activity, and offer to help carry out some of the ideas to get the activity more recognition.

MECHANICS

Writing Application

(p. 761)

OBJECTIVE

■ **To use correct spelling in a letter to the coach of the volleyball team**

Writing Application

Tip. You may wish to hold a brainstorming session to help students come up with ideas about how to promote the team.

Scoring Rubric. While you will want to pay particular attention to students' use of correct spelling, you will also want to evaluate overall writing performance. You may want to give a split score to indicate development and clarity of the composition as well as spelling skills.

ADVANCED LEARNERS

Some students will not have problems spelling the words in the **75 Commonly Misspelled Words** list. Allow such students to work as a group to compile a list of words that they have encountered in their reading and have had difficulty spelling. Students can then study the words from the list they have compiled instead of spending time studying words they already know how to spell.

TEACHING TIP

Activity. One of the most difficult aspects of English spelling is the prevalence of words with silent letters. For example, *a* is silent in the word *head; b* is silent in the word *numb;* and the first *c* is silent in the word *science.*

Have students work in groups of four or five to locate words with silent letters from the **300 Spelling Words** list. Groups should record all the words with silent letters that they find and circle the silent letter or letters in each word.

75 Commonly Misspelled Words

The following list contains seventy-five words that are often misspelled. To find out which words give you difficulty, ask someone to read you the list in groups of ten. Write down each word, and then check your spelling. In your spelling notebook, make a list of any words you misspelled. Keep reviewing your list until you have mastered the correct spelling.

ache	friend	speak
across		speech
again	grammar	straight
all right	guess	sugar
almost		surely
always	half	
answer	having	tear
	heard	though
belief	hour	through
built		tired
business	instead	together
busy		tomorrow
buy	knew	tonight
	know	tough
can't		trouble
color	laid	truly
coming	likely	Tuesday
cough		
could	making	until
country	meant	
	minute	wear
doctor		Wednesday
doesn't	often	where
don't	once	which
		whole
eager	ready	women
easy	really	won't
every		write
	safety	
February	said	
forty	says	
	shoes	
	since	

300 Spelling Words

Learn to spell the following words this year if you don't already know how.

absence	accommodate	accustomed
absolutely	accompany	achievement
acceptance	accomplish	acquaintance
accidentally	accurate	actually

administration
affectionate
agriculture
amateur
ambassador
analysis
analyze
announcement
anticipate
apology
apparent
appearance
approach
approval
arguing
argument
assurance
attendance
authority
available

basically
beginning
believe
benefit
benefited
boundary

calendar
campaign
capital
category
certificate
characteristic
chief
circuit
circumstance
civilization
column
commissioner
committee
comparison
competent
competition
conceivable

concept
confidential
conscience
conscious
consistency
constitution
continuous
control
cooperate
corporation
correspondence
criticism
criticize
cylinder

debtor
decision
definite
definition
deny
description
despise
diameter
disappearance
disappointment
discipline
disgusted
distinction
distinguished
dominant
duplicate

economic
efficiency
eighth
elaborate
eligible
embarrass
emergency
employee
encouraging
environment
equipped
essential
evidently

exaggerate
exceedingly
excellent
excessive
excitable
exercise
existence
expense
extraordinary

fascinating
fatal
favorably
fictitious
financier
flourish
fraternity
frequent
further

glimpse
glorious
grabbed
gracious
graduating
grammatically
gross
gymnasium

happiness
hasten
heavily
hindrance
humorous
hungrily
hypocrisy
hypocrite

icy
ignorance
incidentally
indicate
imagination
immediately
immense
indispensable

inevitable
innocence
inquiry
insurance
intelligence
interfere
interrupt
interpretation
investigation

jealous

knowledge

leisure
lengthen
lieutenant
likelihood
liveliness
loneliness

magazine
maneuver
marriage
marvelous
mechanical
medieval
merchandise
minimum
mortgage
multitude
muscle
mutual

narrative
naturally
necessary
negligible
niece
noticeable

obligation
obstacle

occasionally
occurrence
offense
official
omit
operation
opportunity
oppose
optimism
orchestra
organization
originally

paid
paradise
parallel
particularly
peasant
peculiar
percentage
performance
personal
personality
perspiration
persuade
petition
philosopher
picnic
planning
pleasant
policies
politician
possess
possibility
practically
precede
precisely
preferred
prejudice
preparation
pressure

primitive
privilege
probably
procedure
proceed
professor
proportion
psychology
publicity
pursuit

qualities
quantities

readily
reasonably
receipt
recognize
recommendation
referring
regretting
reign
relieve
remembrance
removal
renewal
repetition
representative
requirement
residence
resistance
responsibility
restaurant
rhythm
ridiculous

sacrifice
satire
satisfied
scarcely
scheme
scholarship

scissors
senate
sensibility
separate
sergeant
several
shepherd
sheriff
similar
skis
sponsor
solemn
sophomore
source
specific
straighten

substantial
substitute
subtle
succeed
successful
sufficient
summary
superior
suppress
surprise
survey
suspense
suspicion

temperament
tendency

thorough
transferring
tremendous
truly

unanimous
unfortunately
unnecessary
urgent
useful
using

vacancies
vacuum
varies

MECHANICS

Spelling Words   **765**

CHAPTER

28 Correcting Common Errors

Key Language Skills Review

This chapter reviews key skills and concepts that pose special problems for writers.

- **Sentence Fragments and Run-on Sentences**
- **Subject-Verb and Pronoun-Antecedent Agreement**
- **Verb Forms**
- **Clear Pronoun Reference**
- **Comparison of Modifiers**
- **Dangling and Misplaced Modifiers**
- **Standard Usage**
- **Capitalization**
- **Punctuation—End Marks, Commas, Quotation Marks, Apostrophes, Semicolons, and Colons**
- **Spelling**

Most of the exercises in this chapter follow the same format as the exercises found throughout the grammar, usage, and mechanics sections of this textbook. You will notice, however, that two sets of review exercises are presented as standardized tests. These exercises are designed to provide you with practice not only in solving usage and mechanics problems but also in dealing with these kinds of problems on standardized tests.

CHAPTER RESOURCES

Planning

■ *One-Stop Planner CD-ROM*

Practice and Extension

■ *Grammar, Usage, and Mechanics*, pp. 370–403
■ *Developmental Language Skills*, pp. 157–158

Internet

■ go.hrw.com (keyword: EOLang)

Evaluation and Assessment

■ *Chapter Tests*, Ch. 28
■ *Chapter Tests in Standardized Test Formats,* Ch. 28
■ *Test Generator (One-Stop Planner)*

Exercise 1 Revising Sentence Fragments

Each of the following word groups is a sentence fragment. Rewrite each fragment to make it a complete sentence. Add whatever words are necessary to make the meaning of the sentence complete.

EXAMPLE **1.** having already read the book

1. *Having already read the book, I was not surprised by the film's end.*

1. television, radio, newspapers, billboards, magazines, and now the World Wide Web
2. beside the cold, clear spring tumbling down the rocky slopes
3. when we passed through the turnstile
4. to appreciate adequately the complexity of these drum rhythms
5. according to the most recent experiments
6. exercising regularly for thirty minutes at least three times a week
7. trained as a lab assistant at the local junior college
8. who had once actually stood on the Great Wall of China
9. one of the first women of that rank in the Navy
10. where the laundry had been hung on a line in full sunlight

Exercise 2 Identifying Sentences and Revising Sentence Fragments

Identify each numbered word group in the following paragraph as either a sentence fragment (*F*) or a complete sentence (*S*). Then, make each fragment part of a complete sentence either by adding words to it or by combining it with another fragment or sentence in the paragraph. Change the punctuation and capitalization as necessary.

EXAMPLES **[1]** I discovered that the jacket was made of linen.

[2] When I got home.

1. *S*

2. *F—When I got home, I discovered that the jacket was made of linen.*

[1] Before you spend your money on that expensive shirt. [2] Read the label carefully! [3] Because some clothes must be sent to the dry cleaner. [4] They will cost you extra money. [5] A lot of money in the long run. [6] Other clothes must be washed by hand. [7] Requiring extra time and care for their upkeep. [8] If you are looking for quality clothes. [9] That are both attractive and inexpensive to own. [10] It pays to read the label.

Reference Note

For information on **correcting sentence fragments,** see page 326.

1. F	2. S
3. F	4. S
5. F	6. S
7. F	8. F
9. F	10. S

Exercise 1

OBJECTIVE

■ To write complete sentences from sentence fragments

Exercise 1 Revising Sentence Fragments

POSSIBLE ANSWERS

1. Advertisers can promote products through television, radio, newspapers, billboards, magazines, and now the World Wide Web.
2. Mother took Jon's picture beside the cold, clear spring tumbling down the rocky slopes.
3. We showed our admission passes when we passed through the turnstile.
4. Because I lack a strong sense of rhythm, I am not able to appreciate adequately the complexity of these drum rhythms.
5. According to the most recent experiments, that new drug is still not effective in stopping all seizures.
6. My doctor recommends exercising regularly for thirty minutes at least three times a week.
7. I hope to be trained as a lab assistant at the local junior college.
8. My aunt Hatty wrote a historical novel concerning a warrior who had once actually stood on the Great Wall of China.
9. I believe my history textbook has a picture of one of the first women of that rank in the Navy.
10. The children played in the backyard where the laundry had been hung on a line in full sunlight.

Exercise 2

OBJECTIVE

■ To identify and revise sentence fragments

Exercise 2 Identifying Sentences and Revising Sentence Fragments

POSSIBLE ANSWERS

[1–2] Before you spend your money on that expensive shirt, read the label carefully! [3–4] Because some clothes must be sent to the dry cleaner, they will cost you extra money. [5] That can add up to a lot of money in the long run. [6–7] Other clothes must be washed by hand, requiring extra time and care for their upkeep. [8–10] If you are looking for quality clothes that are both attractive and inexpensive to own, it pays to read the label.

Exercise 3

OBJECTIVE

■ To revise run-on sentences

Reference Note

For information on **correcting run-on sentences,** see page 327.

Exercise 3 Revising Run-on Sentences

Each of the following numbered items is a run-on sentence. Revise each run-on, using the method given in brackets after it. Be sure to change punctuation and capitalization as necessary.

EXAMPLE
1. Today's world offers many kinds of popular entertainment earlier Americans relied mainly on music and dancing. [*Use a comma and coordinating conjunction.*]

1. *Today's world offers many kinds of popular entertainment, but earlier Americans relied mainly on music and dancing.* Revisions may vary.

1. Just imagine your life without TV, audio and video recordings, and movies surely you would spend your time quite differently from the way you do now. [*Make two sentences.*]
2. In a world without recorded music, a musician could often attract a crowd even today, good musicians can make a living on the streets of a large city. [*Use a semicolon.*]   3. ∧so
3. Music was important to the early settlers they often made their own instruments. [*Use a comma and a coordinating conjunction.*]
4. Many of the settlers owned fiddles, dulcimers, flutes, and guitars music could be a part of everyday life. [*Use a semicolon, a conjunctive adverb, and a comma*]   4. ∧consequently∧
5. Long before the settlers arrived, there was already plenty of music in North America American Indians prized music and song. [*Use a semicolon.*]
6. The Seneca used rattles similar to the instruments known as maracas Northern Plains Indians used the hand drum. [*Use a comma and a coordinating conjunction.*]   6. ∧and
7. The Maidu played flutes and whistles musicians today often incorporate such American Indian instruments into popular music. [*Make two sentences.*]
8. The banjo is widely regarded as a traditional American musical instrument the banjo originated in Africa. [*Use a semicolon, a conjunctive adverb, and a comma*]   8. ∧however∧
9. West Africans made banjo-like instruments out of gourds for strings, they used dried animal gut. [*Use a semicolon.*]
10. Early banjos had no frets and only four strings frets are the ridges positioned at intervals on the necks of banjos and guitars. [*Make two sentences.*]

Revising Sentence Fragments and Run-on Sentences

Most of the following word groups are either run-on sentences or sentence fragments. Identify and correct each sentence fragment and run-on sentence. If a word group is already a complete sentence, write *C*.

EXAMPLE   **1.** The area where I live used to be a prehistoric sea, sometimes my friends and I find fossilized sharks' teeth.

     1. The area where I live used to be a prehistoric sea, and sometimes my friends and I find fossilized sharks' teeth.

1. Walking slowly over the rocky terrain. **1.** F
2. A strange rock caught our attention Jackie broke it open. **2.** R
3. Inside were rows and rows of brilliant quartz crystals, we gasped at our discovery. **3.** R
4. Gold lies hidden in the West, many people still seek their fortune there. **4.** R
5. Is one of the best places in the world for prospectors. **5.** F
6. When rainfall, a landslide, or some other act of nature alters the landscape. **6.** F
7. Easier to find gold, silver, platinum, and other precious metals. **7.** F
8. Although most commonly used for jewelry, gold has numerous industrial uses. **8.** C
9. You can grow your own crystals, some grow quite quickly. **9.** R
10. With a kit from a hobby shop only two blocks away from my house in Colorado Springs. **10.** F

Choosing Verbs That Agree in Number with Their Subjects

Choose the correct form of the verb in parentheses in each of the following sentences.

EXAMPLE   **1.** One of the customs most readily shared among cultures (*is, are*) games.

     1. is

1. Almost everybody (*has, have*) played games that originated in faraway places.
2. Few of these games (*is, are*) difficult to play.

Reference Note

For information on **subject-verb agreement,** see page 493.

Grammar and Usage   **769**

---

3. Pictures on ancient Greek pottery (*show, shows*) people playing with yo-yos.
4. (*Was, Were*) the first people who ever played the game lacrosse American Indian?
5. Arctic peoples, Africans, the Maori of New Zealand, and others as well (*plays, play*) cat's cradle.
6. Somewhere, somebody in one of the world's cultures probably (*is, are*) spinning a top right now.
7. Not all card games (*uses, use*) a standard deck of cards.
8. Most of these games (*requires, require*) at least two players, and some require four.
9. Several ancient African games still (*enjoys, enjoy*) popularity among children.
10. None of those colorful Chinese tangrams (*turns, turn*) out to be easy to solve.

Exercise 6 Proofreading a Paragraph for Subject-Verb Agreement

Identify the errors in subject-verb agreement in the following paragraph. Then, change each incorrect verb to agree with its subject.

EXAMPLE   **[1]** Many a building design don't meet the needs of people with disabilities.

      1. *don't—doesn't*

1. presents
2. has

3. make
4. pose

5. is
6. seeks

7. are

8. help
9. don't

10. gives

[1] Ordinary houses or a public building sometimes present problems for people with disabilities. [2] For example, a person using a wheelchair or crutches often have difficulty maneuvering in narrow halls. [3] Flights of stairs and a front stoop makes access difficult for anyone using a wheelchair or a walker. [4] Moreover, inadequate shower access or high counters needlessly poses problems for people with wheelchairs. [5] One homebuilder and solver of these problems are Craig Johnson. [6] Johnson, with a team of advisors and decorators, seek to make life easier for people with various disabilities. [7] Johnson recognizes that easy access and freedom from barriers is becoming both an issue for our aging population and a growing business opportunity. [8] Creating designs and making modifications for people with disabilities helps others, too. [9] For instance, doesn't most people find that levers are easier to operate than doorknobs are? [10] Also, neither a handrail nor a ramp give anyone any difficulty; in fact, both can come in handy for everyone.

Exercise 6

OBJECTIVE

■ To identify and correct errors in subject-verb agreement

COMMON ERRORS

Exercise 7 Identifying Antecedents and Writing Pronouns

Each of the following sentences contains a blank where a pronoun should be. Identify the antecedent for each missing pronoun. Then, complete the sentence with a pronoun that agrees with that antecedent.

EXAMPLE   **1.** At about the age of fifteen, Janet Collins followed _____ dream to the Ballet Russe de Monte Carlo.

  1. Janet Collins—her

1. Until Janet Collins, nobody of African heritage had ever made _____ debut on the stage of the Metropolitan Opera House.
2. While waiting to audition, she saw other ballerinas on a winding staircase backstage doing _____ warm-up exercises.
3. All of the people who saw Janet at her audition clapped _____ hands.
4. However, because of Collins's color, Mr. Massine, the choreographer, could not hire her for _____ production.
5. Collins continued practicing, and in the end _____ was rewarded.
6. The Metropolitan Opera opened _____ doors to the prima ballerina.
7. Rudolph Bing admired her adagio dancing so much that _____ gave her many opportunities to leap and jump.
8. Two of her roles were in *Carmen* and *Aida,* and _____ helped to make her famous.
9. To be successful, a ballerina must discipline _____.
10. Either Ms. Lawton or Ms. Vicks will show the class _____ autographed picture of Collins.

Exercise 8 Proofreading for Pronoun-Antecedent Agreement

Proofread the following sentences, and identify pronouns that do not agree with their antecedents. Give the correct form of each incorrect pronoun. If a sentence is already correct, write *C*.

EXAMPLE   **1.** From the earliest times, people all over the world have decorated himself or herself.

  1. himself or herself—themselves

1. Whether for war, religious rituals, or beauty, cosmetics have always had its place in human society.
2. In ancient Egypt, both men and women used various kinds of cosmetics to make himself or herself more attractive.

Reference Note

For information on **pronoun-antecedent agreement,** see page 507.

1. his or her
2. their
3. their
4. his
5. she
6. its
7. he
8. they
9. herself
10. her

1. their
2. themselves

Exercise 7

OBJECTIVE

■ To identify antecedents of missing pronouns and then to supply pronouns that agree with the identified antecedents

Relating to Vocabulary

Ask your students to find *antecedent* in the dictionary and to read its etymology. The word consists of two parts, both from Latin. *Ante–* means "before" and *cedent,* derived from *cedere,* means "going." Ask students how the etymology of the word can help them remember its meaning as applied in grammar. [*An antecedent usually goes before the pronoun that refers to it.*]

Exercise 8

OBJECTIVE

■ To identify and correct errors in pronoun-antecedent agreement

3. C

4. his

5. their

6. they

7. himself or herself

8. her

9. C

10. he

3. In addition, nearly all Egyptians painted their eyelids with green paste to prevent sunburn.

4. One of the Egyptian kings was even buried with rouge and lip color in <u>their</u> tomb.

5. Ancient cosmetics were usually made from natural ingredients, some of which were poisonous to <u>its</u> users.

6. Arsenic and mercury were two of the most dangerous, and <u>it</u> ruined many lives.

7. The Roman man or woman who used cosmetics containing arsenic was slowly killing <u>themselves</u>.

8. Similarly, in Queen Elizabeth I's time, the English girl or woman who used a skin whitener containing mercury risked having <u>their</u> teeth fall out.

9. Since before the time of Cosmis—who sold makeup during the reign of Julius Caesar—to the present, enterprising people have made their fortunes by providing products that help others meet their cultures' standards of beauty.

10. Galen, a man of science in ancient Rome, would be pleased to find that today's cold cream is based on the formula <u>they</u> invented.

Exercise 9

OBJECTIVE

■ **To identify and correct errors in subject-verb and pronoun-antecedent agreement**

COMMON ERRORS

Exercise 9 **Revising Sentences for Agreement**

Each of the following sentences contains either an error in subject-verb agreement or an error in pronoun-antecedent agreement. Revise the sentences to correct each error in agreement.

EXAMPLE   **1.** Either Mr. Baker or Mr. Perez have promised to drive his van on the field trip.

    1. Either Mr. Baker or Mr. Perez has promised to drive his van on the field trip.

1. her
2. are
3. his or her
4. was
5. their
6. was
7. they
8. are

1. Many a girl has taken Shirley Chisholm as ~~their~~ model of success.

2. Here, class, ~~is~~ several classic examples of Aztec art.

3. Each member of the cast knows all of ~~their~~ lines for the play.

4. Beautifully illustrated and written, *Saint George and the Dragon* ~~were~~ awarded the Caldecott Medal.

5. Have Ms. Ivy and Mr. Lee played ~~her and his~~ music for the school?

6. Two dollars ~~were~~ once considered generous pay for an hour's work.

7. All of the travelers were surprised when ~~he or she~~ saw the old purple-and-yellow bus.

8. An international team of archaeological researchers ~~is~~ assembling, one by one, at the site of this exciting discovery.

9. Do Cindy and Brenda practice ~~her~~ dance routine here every day?

10. The two performers ~~has~~ become one of the most popular teams in the history of comedy.

9. their
10. have

Exercise 10 Writing Correct Verb Forms

Complete each sentence with the correct past or past participle form of the verb in italics.

EXAMPLE   **1.** *do*   Have you _____ any research on the Cajun culture?

        1. *done*

1. *blow*   Yesterday, a hurricane _____ through Louisiana, where
1. blew   most Cajuns live.

2. *begin*   The Cajun culture _____ after French immigrants to
2. began   Acadia, Canada, traveled south.

3. *come*   While in Canada, these immigrants _____ to be known as
3. came   Acadians.

4. *take*   In Louisiana, the name Acadian _____ on a different
4. took   pronunciation—"Cajun."

5. *choose*   The Cajuns _____ to befriend the Choctaws, as well as
5. chose   settlers from Germany and Spain.

6. *put*   Cajun cooks _____ to their own use what they learned
6. put   from the Choctaws about native plants and animals.

7. *eat*   They _____ seafood seasoned with the Choctaws' filé,
7. ate   which is powdered sassafras leaves.
8. drank

8. *drink*   They _____ coffee flavored with chicory.

9. *raise*   German settlers in the bayou country _____ the beef and
9. raised   pork that the Cajuns used in their tasty dishes.

10. *bring*   The Cajuns were also delighted with okra, called gumbo
10. brought by the Bantu, who had _____ it with them from Africa.

Exercise 11 Identifying Correct Forms of Irregular Verbs

Choose the <u>correct form of the verb</u> in parentheses in each of the following sentences.

EXAMPLE   **1.** For many years, teams of scientists have (*took, taken*) the opportunity to study the Antarctic Peninsula during the summer.

        1. *taken*

1. The scientists (*went, gone*) there to study the delicate balance of the ecosystem.

Reference Note

For information on **using verbs correctly,** see Chapter 17.

Reference Note

For information on **using irregular verbs,** see page 519.

Exercise 10

OBJECTIVE

- To give the correct past or past participle forms of verbs

Meeting
INDIVIDUAL
NEEDS

LEARNERS HAVING DIFFICULTY
If your students need additional review before attempting **Exercise 10,** you may want to give them some guided practice. Form study groups of two or three students each, and assign the even-numbered items. Go over the answers orally to identify students who are struggling with the material, and reteach concepts as needed. Then, assign the odd-numbered items for students to complete as independent practice.

Exercise 11

OBJECTIVE

- To select the correct forms of irregular verbs

COMMON ERRORS

Meeting
INDIVIDUAL
NEEDS

ENGLISH-LANGUAGE LEARNERS
General Strategies. Some English-language learners who speak languages such as Indonesian, Japanese, Korean, Turkish, and Vietnamese might not understand the idea of irregular verbs because their native languages have few or no irregular verbs. Students might write the present tense forms of these verbs when they should use the past tense. Give students copies of a comprehensive list of the principal parts of irregular verbs with blank spaces left for the past form. Tell students to fill in the past forms of the verbs and to keep the lists in their notebooks.

Exercise 12

O B J E C T I V E

■ **To identify and correct errors in verb forms**

2. These scientists (*knew, knowed*) that worldwide weather patterns are influenced by events in Antarctica.
3. Before the twentieth century, few people (*choosed, chose*) to brave the frigid voyage to the Antarctic.
4. However, new means of transportation have (*brought, brung*) more people, especially scientists, to Antarctica.
5. Such countries as Chile, Britain, and Russia have (*began, begun*) exploring what's beneath Antarctica's ice and snow.
6. No one knows how long Antarctica's waters have (*ran, run*) red with krill, tiny creatures at the bottom of the food chain.
7. Many times, the Ross Ice Shelf has (*shook, shaken*) as a huge iceberg known as B9 has crashed into it.
8. An oil rig could have (*fallen, fell*) if struck by a roving iceberg.
9. If that had happened, a huge oil spill would likely have (*did, done*) major damage to Antarctica's ecosystem.
10. In Antarctica, the nations of the world have been (*gave, given*) an opportunity to work together in peace.

Exercise 12 Proofreading for Correct Verb Forms

Most of the following sentences contain incorrect verb forms. If a form of a verb is wrong, write the correct form. If a sentence already is correct, write *C*.

EXAMPLE **[1]** The brave galleon had rode the waves to an icy grave.
        1. ridden

1. broken
2. driven

3. rang
4. dived

5. raised
6. C
7. sit
8. lies

9. shrunk
10. grown

[1] Over thousands of years of seafaring, many a ship has been broke on the rocks or lost in a storm. **[2]** Thirst for the treasure of these sunken ships has drove opportunists and scholars alike to the dark bottoms of the world's oceans. **[3]** The invention of scuba equipment in 1943 rung in a new era in underwater exploration. **[4]** Since then, treasure hunters and scientists have dove into waters all over the world and surfaced with gold and historical artifacts. **[5]** Expeditions have successfully rose entire ships, such as the *Vasa*, a seventeenth-century Swedish vessel. **[6]** Astonishingly, divers have swum down and inspected the remains of crafts more than forty centuries old! **[7]** Not only ships but also towns set on the ocean floor. **[8]** One such site is the community of Port Royal, which lays near Jamaica. **[9]** Ironically, although many treasures have been found, the search for treasure has not shrinked. **[10]** On the contrary, as technology has improved, the number of underwater expeditions has growed.

Exercise 13 **Proofreading for Correct Verb Forms**

Most of the following sentences contain an incorrect verb form. If the form of a verb is wrong, write the correct form. If a sentence is already correct, write *C*.

EXAMPLE   **1.** His horse weared a braided bridle.

    1. wore

1. Luis Ortega has been ~~describe~~ as history's greatest rawhide braider.
2. For years, collectors and cowhands alike have ~~spoke~~ of him with respectful awe.
3. Ortega was lucky to have had a fine teacher; many braiders do not teach their craft because students have ~~stole~~ their secrets.
4. However, even after a generous American Indian taught Ortega to braid, it ~~taked~~ young Luis many years of practice to perfect his skill.
5. Ortega has never ~~shrinked~~ from hard work.
6. Once a vaquero himself, he ~~throwed~~ many a lasso in his younger days.
7. Since the 1930s, Ortega has ~~wore~~ the title of professional braider.
8. Ortega not only mastered the traditional craft, but also ~~striked~~ out on his own by adding color to braiding.
9. Unlike whips, which have ~~stinged~~ many a runaway steer, a riata is a type of lariat used for roping.
10. Pity the cowhand whose heart must have sunk as a steer ran off with his treasured Ortega riata!

1. described
2. spoken

3. stolen

4. took

5. shrunk
6. threw
7. worn
8. struck

9. stung

10. C

Exercise 14 **Identifying Correct Forms of Pronouns**

Choose the <u>correct pronoun</u> in parentheses in each of the following sentences. Then, tell whether the pronoun is used as a *subject*, a *predicate nominative*, a *direct object*, an *indirect object*, an *object of a preposition*, or an *appositive*.

EXAMPLE   **1.** Mr. Kwan and (*we, us*) members of the recycling club picked up all the litter along the highway last Saturday.

    1. we—subject

1. Do you know (*who, whom*) safely disposes of old batteries?
2. The two Earth Club members who collect items for recycling are James and (*she, her*).
3. (*Who, Whom*) threw these cans in the garbage?
4. Save all recyclable material for (*we, us*) club members.

Reference Note

For information on **using pronouns correctly,** see Chapter 18.

1. sub.
2. p.n.

3. sub.
4. o.p.

Exercise 14

OBJECTIVE

■ To identify correct forms of pronouns and tell how the pronouns are used

Cooperative Learning
General Strategies. You may want to pair students for **Exercise 14.** One student will be responsible for the even-numbered sentences, and the other student will work with the odd-numbered sentences. Tell them to write the sentences in sequence but to answer alternately. Then, they should check each other's work.

COMMON ERRORS

Grammar and Usage   **775**

Exercise 15

OBJECTIVE

■ **To correct inexact pronoun references**

5. app.

5. Give the co-chairpersons, Lisa and (*she, her*), all of the cans that you have collected.

6. d.o.

6. Ask (*whoever, whomever*) you know to save old newspapers for us to collect.

7. p.n.

7. (*Who, Whom*) could the next recycling team leader be?

8. o.p.

8. To (*whom, who*) do we give this cardboard?

9. d.o.

9. The city gave Mr. Kwan, (*who, whom*) everyone in the school respects, an award.

10. i.o.

10. Please give Carl and (*he, him*) the maps you three drew yesterday.

Exercise 15 **Correcting Inexact Pronoun References**

Correct each inexact pronoun reference in the following sentences. If a sentence is already correct, write *C*. Answers will vary.

EXAMPLE   1. When you take medication for your allergies, be sure to read them carefully.

1. *When you take medication for your allergies, be sure to read the directions carefully.*

1. Annie said that she must have sneezed two dozen times today and that it was really bothering her. **1.** the pollen

2. Annie asked Heather several good questions about her new allergy medication. **2.** Heather's

3. Everyone knows that Heather has more problems with pollen allergies than I have. **3.** C

4. Pollen, molds, and animal dander are widespread in our environment; they are three of the most common causes of allergies. **4.** C

5. Different plants release pollen at different times of the year, which is why people have discomfort at various times. **5.** ; consequently

6. Annie asked Sarah about summer allergies because she is especially uncomfortable during July. **6.** Annie

7. To take a pollen count, they place a glass slide coated with oil outside for twenty-four hours. **7.** scientists

8. The slide is then placed under a microscope, and the grains of pollen sticking to it are counted. **8.** the slide

9. When it rains, the pollen count drops because the rain washes the pollen grains from the air. **9.** C

10. In the news reports, they often give the pollen count.

Pollen Grains

Exercise 16 **Proofreading for Clear Pronoun Usage**

Most of the following sentences contain inexact pronoun references. Revise each incorrect sentence. If a sentence is already correct, write *C*.

Reference Note

For information on **using pronouns correctly,** see Chapter 18.

EXAMPLES
1. In India, they belong to laughing clubs.
1. *In India, some people belong to laughing clubs.*

2. These clubs are popular with the people of India because of the conflicts they face every day.
2. *C*

1. Scientists believe that long ago an island slammed into Asia; it created the Himalayas and joined the island to the continent.
2. That landmass is now India, and worlds still collide there, which is seen in the contradictions and conflicts of modern India.
3. India has been independent for more than fifty years, and it has caused many changes in this growing nation.
4. For instance, the famous city of Bombay has been renamed Mumbai, which honors the Hindu goddess Mumba.
5. However, British influences still exist, and that is apparent in English-language street signs.
6. Free-market policies have now been adopted, and many people have taken advantage of that; small, independent businesses are booming.
7. To the refugees who come to Calcutta from Bangladesh, it offers a little hope.
8. There are as many as thirty-seven laughing clubs in Mumbai (members believe it fights stress).
9. At the same time, beside the wall of an alleyway in Calcutta, a woman prepares food for her daughter while she sits in a nearby tree.
10. A country with ample natural resources and millions of highly educated people, India is taking its place on the world stage.

Grammar and Usage   **777**

Exercise 16

OBJECTIVE

■ To identify and correctly revise sentences with unclear pronoun usage

Exercise 16 **Proofreading for Clear Pronoun Usage**

POSSIBLE ANSWERS

1. Scientists believe that long ago an island slammed into Asia; the force of the collision created the Himalayas and joined the island to the continent.
2. That landmass is now India, and worlds still collide there, a situation which is seen in the contradictions and conflicts of modern India.
3. India has been independent for more than fifty years, and independence has caused many changes in this growing nation.
4. For instance, the famous city of Bombay has been renamed Mumbai, a name which honors the Hindu goddess Mumba.
5. However, British influences still exist, and this influence is apparent in English-language street signs.
6. Free-market policies have now been adopted, and many people have taken advantage of this change; small, independent businesses are booming.
7. To the refugees who come to Calcutta from Bangladesh, the city offers a little hope.
8. There are as many as thirty-seven laughing clubs in Mumbai (members believe laughing fights stress).
9. At the same time, beside the wall of an alleyway in Calcutta, a woman prepares food for her daughter who sits in a nearby tree.
10. C

Exercise 17

OBJECTIVE

■ To provide the appropriate comparative or superlative form of a given word

Exercise 18

OBJECTIVE

■ To correct errors in the use of the comparative and superlative forms of modifiers

Reference Note

For information on **using modifers correctly,** see Chapter 19.

1. fewer
2. more
3. worst
4. more
5. better
6. worse
7. best
8. more
9. most
10. best

1. most important
2. C
3. most common
4. more comfortable
5. more likely

Exercise 17 Using Comparative and Superlative Forms

Complete each sentence with the correct comparative or superlative form of the word given in italics.

EXAMPLE   **1.** *well*   Carl can perform CPR _____ than I can.

      1. better

1. *few*   Bicyclists who wear helmets have _____ serious injuries from accidents than bicyclists who do not wear helmets.

2. *many*   Our family follows _____ safety procedures than we used to follow in the past.

3. *bad*   Some of the _____ accidents are more likely to happen in the home than anywhere else.

4. *much*   Is it _____ common to have an accident in the kitchen or in the bathroom?

5. *well*   Emergency crews can spot luminous house numbers _____ than numbers that do not glow in the dark.

6. *bad*   A grease fire will become _____ if you put water on it.

7. *good*   Do you know the _____ way to extinguish an electrical fire?

8. *many*   Smoke detectors are found in _____ homes than ever before.

9. *much*   In many small fires, smoke causes _____ of the damage.

10. *good*   Of course, the _____ safety procedure of all is preventing fires from starting in the first place.

Exercise 18 Proofreading Sentences for Correct Comparative and Superlative Forms

Correct each error in the use of comparative and superlative forms in the following sentences. If no modifiers need to be corrected, write *C*.

EXAMPLE   **1.** Most oftenest, I plan my day in the morning.

      1. Most often

1. One of the importantest skills is the ability to set priorities.

2. You can establish your priorities more easily if you know your goals.

3. Owning a good car, having a rewarding job, and owning a house are three of the most commonest goals people share.

4. You, however, may want a pilot's license, a medical degree, an eighteen-wheeler, or just a comfortabler bed.

5. Whatever your goal, you will be much more likelier to achieve it if you plan your time carefully.

6. Look at even the ~~most small~~ unit of your time.
7. Can you think of ways that you could use your time ~~more better~~ than you do?
8. Try every day to work on your ~~most highest~~ priority.
9. Try ~~more hard~~ to stick to your schedule.
10. With a plan, you can meet your goals ~~quicklier~~ than you could without one.

6. smallest
7. better
8. highest
9. harder
10. more quickly

Exercise 19 **Writing Comparative and Superlative Forms**

Write the comparative and superlative forms of the following modifiers.

EXAMPLE   **1.** kind

1. kinder, kindest; less kind, least kind

1. alone
2. loudly
3. late
4. secretly
5. lucky
6. bad
7. delightful
8. fiercely
9. exact
10. childishly
11. natural
12. wet
13. mysterious
14. gleefully
15. timid
16. contentedly
17. green
18. bravely
19. poor
20. cautiously

Exercise 20 **Correcting Double Negatives**

Revise each of the following sentences to correct the double negative that it contains. Answers may vary.

EXAMPLE   **1.** The jurors couldn't say nothing about the trial.

1. The jurors could say nothing about the trial.

or

The jurors couldn't say anything about the trial.

1. Those machines don't take ~~no~~ dollar bills.
2. My grandfather ~~doesn't~~ hardly ~~let~~ anything bother him. **2.** lets
3. Don't ~~never~~ accept a ride from a stranger! **3.** ever
4. Why didn't ~~no one~~ take a message when Mom called? **4.** anyone
5. Never use ~~none~~ of those microwave oven pans in a regular oven.
6. The movie hadn't scarcely started when the power went off. **5.** any
7. I can't see ~~nothing~~ from here. **7.** anything
8. There aren't ~~none~~ of those tamales left now. **8.** any
9. Don't let ~~nobody~~ tell you that you can't win! **9.** anybody
10. Neither cold nor heat nor ~~nothing~~ else discouraged them.
     10. anything

┌HELP─

Although two possible answers are shown, you need to give only one answer for each item in Exercise 20.

Reference Note
For information on **double negatives,** see page 609.

Grammar and Usage   **779**

Exercise 19

OBJECTIVE

■ **To write the comparative and superlative forms of modifiers**

Exercise 19 **Writing Comparative and Superlative Forms**

ANSWERS
To indicate decreasing comparison, add *less* or *least* to the base form.

1. more, most alone
2. more, most loudly
3. later, latest
4. more, most secretly
5. luckier, luckiest *or* more, most lucky
6. worse, worst
7. more, most delightful
8. more, most fiercely
9. more, most exact
10. more, most childishly
11. more, most natural
12. wetter, wettest
13. more, most mysterious
14. more, most gleefully
15. more, most timid
16. more, most contentedly
17. greener, greenest
18. more, most bravely
19. poorer, poorest
20. more, most cautiously

Exercise 20

OBJECTIVE

■ **To revise sentences to correct double negatives**

COMMON ERRORS

Grammar and Usage   **779**

Exercise 21

OBJECTIVE

- To revise sentences to correct misplaced modifiers

Exercise 22

OBJECTIVE

- To revise sentences with dangling modifiers

Exercise 22 — Correcting Dangling Modifiers

POSSIBLE ANSWERS

1. The coach and the fans in the stands cheered and applauded as the batter rounded third base.

2. Making a schedule will help you manage your time better.

3. C

4. While we were studying for exams, a storm knocked out the electricity.

5. You must select a specific topic or category before beginning your library research.

6. Right in the middle of making a copy of my report, I saw the out-of-paper message flash.

7. Tired from the long hike, we were glad to see our camp.

8. After we hung the new plants, the room appeared larger.

9. To save money, you need a realistic budget.

10. C

Exercise 21 — Correcting Misplaced Modifiers

Revise the following sentences to correct errors in the use of modifiers. You may need to rearrange or add words to make the meaning clear. Answers may vary.

EXAMPLE   1. Cold and overcast, the tour group left the city.

1. *The tour group left the cold and overcast city.*

1. I watched the hawk swoop down and grab its prey with my new pair of binoculars.
2. He is such a hard-working student that he did every bit of his homework when he even got the flu.
3. Running through town, soft moonlight fell on the freight train.
4. You should accept rides from people only you know.
5. A kingfisher sat alertly on the fence post that had been hunting by the creek.
6. I figured out the answer studying the problem.
7. Bulky and dusty, we moved all of the boxes out of the attic.
8. Filled with wildflowers, Amy put that vase on her desk.
9. Suddenly, the bats swarmed out of the cave that we had awakened.
10. A package sat on the doorstep with Michael's name on it.

Exercise 22 — Correcting Dangling Modifiers

Most of the following sentences contain a dangling modifier. If a sentence is incorrect, revise it to correct the dangling modifier. If a sentence is already correct, write *C*.

EXAMPLE   1. Following the path, a tiny cottage came into view.

1. *As we were following the path, a tiny cottage came into view.*

1. Rounding third base, the coach and the fans in the stands cheered and applauded.
2. To manage time better, making a schedule will help.
3. Modified to allow space for an additional bedroom, the floor plan's lack of closets became a problem.
4. While studying for exams, a storm knocked out the electricity.
5. Before beginning your library research, a specific topic or category must be selected.
6. Right in the middle of making a copy of my report, the out-of-paper message flashed.
7. Tired from the long hike, our camp was a welcome sight.

8. After hanging the new plants, the room appeared larger.

9. To save money, a realistic budget is necessary.

10. While we watched the children play, our problems seemed small.

Exercise 23 **Correcting Misplaced and Dangling Modifiers**

The following sentences contain misplaced and dangling modifiers. Revise each sentence to correct the misplaced or dangling modifier.

EXAMPLE   1. Seeing the rescue helicopter, shouts of joy burst out.

    1. *Seeing the rescue helicopter, the crew burst out with shouts of joy.*

1. Customers lined up for copies of the new film about extraterrestrials in the video store.

2. To save a file, a name must be given to it.

3. The spaceship drifted toward the small moon that had lost its engines.

4. Dozens of white daisies decorated the tables, which had been grown in our own garden.

5. Marked by signs saying "Reserved," we couldn't find anywhere to park.

6. Did George Washington ever meet Robert E. Lee, whose face is on our dollar?

7. Following the trail, camp was quickly found.

8. Having advertised all week, all the tickets had been sold.

9. Patient hawks watched for fish soaring over the lake.

10. Mother packed a picnic lunch humming quietly.

Exercise 24 **Correcting Errors in Standard Usage**

Identify and correct each error in the use of formal, standard English in the following sentences. Answers may vary.

EXAMPLE   1. I ain't going to the movies on Saturday.

    1. *ain't—am not*

1. Please bring this note to Ms. Nichols in the gym. 1. take

2. Who else was late to the party beside Ronnie and Ed? 2. besides

3. My science project took alot of time last weekend.

4. Oh, no! I can't find my raincoat anywheres. 4. anywhere

5. Common elements include oxygen, hydrogen, iron, and etc.

6. The weather can effect people's moods. 6. affect

7. Starting next year, each student will wear an uniform. 7. a

Grammar and Usage   **781**

Reference Note

For more on **common usage problems,** see Chapter 20. For information about **formal, standard English,** see page 595.

3. a lot [*or* a great deal]

5. [*or* . . . iron, and others.]

Exercise 23

OBJECTIVE

■ To revise sentences with misplaced and dangling modifiers

Exercise 23 **Correcting Misplaced and Dangling Modifiers**

ANSWERS
Answers will vary. Accept reasonable responses.

1. Customers lined up in the video store for copies of the new film about extraterrestrials.

2. To save a file, one must name it.

3. The spaceship that had lost its engines drifted toward the small moon.

4. Dozens of white daisies, which had been grown in our own garden, decorated the tables.

5. Because of the signs saying "Reserved," we couldn't find anywhere to park.

6. Did George Washington, whose face is on our dollar, ever meet Robert E. Lee?

7. Following the trail, we quickly found the camp.

8. Having been advertised all week, all the tickets had been sold.

9. Patient hawks soaring over the lake watched for fish.

10. Humming quietly, Mother packed a picnic lunch.

Exercise 24

OBJECTIVE

■ To correct errors in the use of standard English

Exercise 25

OBJECTIVE

■ To revise sentences containing errors in standard English usage

TECHNOLOGY **TIP**

Remind students that they can check for proper grammar and usage within their writing by using the grammar-checking function that is common to many popular word-processing programs. Grammar-checking programs will catch a number of mistakes, including double subjects, double negatives, and nonstandard usage such as *anywheres* and *had ought*. However, emphasize that such programs are not foolproof. Sometimes a grammar-checking feature will do little more than highlight a word or phrase and ask the user "Is this word used correctly?" The user of the program must understand the rules of grammar and usage.

---

8. Look out! You almost ~~busted~~ my CD player! **8.** broke
9. Gradually, our dog ~~excepted~~ the new kitten. **9.** accepted
10. The little steam engine pulled ~~all the faster~~ it could. **10.** as fast as

Exercise 25 Correcting Errors in Standard Usage

Revise the following sentences to correct all errors in the use of formal, standard English. Answers may vary.

EXAMPLE   1. Like you would expect, the use of color is very important to artists.

1. *As you would expect, the use of color is very important to artists.*

1. Artists ~~which~~ study color know that color, value, and contrast form the foundation of a good painting. **1.** who [*or* that]
2. Many artists would not even begin ~~no~~ painting ~~without~~ they first planned how they would use these elements. **2.** a/unless
3. One of the basics that nearly all artists learn is ~~where~~ color is divided into warm colors and cool colors. **3.** that
4. ~~Like~~ you might ~~of~~ guessed, red is a warmer color ~~then~~ blue, while green is cooler than orange. **4.** As/have/than
5. The value, or darkness, of a color can indicate that objects differ ~~some~~ in distance from the viewer. **5.** somewhat
6. For example, a dark color may be used to indicate that something is a long ~~ways~~ off. **6.** way
7. ~~Contrast is when~~ two very different colors are placed ~~besides~~ each other. **7.** beside/, they are said to contrast.
8. Contrasting values help to show detail, as does the contrast ~~among~~ this ~~here~~ white page and black type. **8.** between
9. For ~~them~~ artists that work only in black and white, contrast and value are major concerns. **9.** those [*or* artists who]
10. Many people feel that the ~~affect~~ of a painting can depend more on color ~~then~~ on other elements. **10.** effect/than

Grammar and Usage Test: Section 1

DIRECTIONS Either part or all of each of the following sentences is underlined. Using the rules of formal, standard English, choose the answer that correctly expresses the meaning of the underlined word groups. If there is no error, choose A. Indicate your response by shading in the appropriate oval on your answer sheet.

EXAMPLE 1. In 1990, restoration began on the Sphinx, it is an ancient Egyptian statue.

    (A) Sphinx, it is an ancient Egyptian statue

    (B) Sphinx because it is an ancient Egyptian statue

    (C) Sphinx, an ancient Egyptian statue

    (D) Sphinx, being an ancient Egyptian statue

    (E) Sphinx when it was an ancient Egyptian statue

ANSWER 1.   A B C D E

1. The magnificent glass pyramids at the Louvre, which were designed by the American architect I. M. Pei.

    (A) The magnificent glass pyramids at the Louvre, which were designed by the American architect I. M. Pei.

    (B) Being designed by the American architect I. M. Pei, the magnificent glass pyramids at the Louvre.

    (C) The American architect I. M. Pei, who designed the magnificent glass pyramids at the Louvre.

    (D) The American architect I. M. Pei designed the magnificent glass pyramids at the Louvre.

    (E) I. M. Pei, an American architect, designing the magnificent glass pyramids at the Louvre.

2. Have you read about the tornado that damaged so many homes in today's paper?

    (A) about the tornado that damaged so many homes in today's paper

    (B) in today's paper about the tornado that damaged so many homes

    (C) about the tornado in today's paper that damaged so many homes

    (D) about the destructive tornado in today's paper

    (E) today about the destructive tornado in the paper

Grammar and Usage **783**

TEACHING **TIP**

Using the Grammar and Usage Tests. A Correcting Common Errors Standardized Test Answer Sheet that students may use for this **Grammar and Usage Test** is provided in *Chapter Tests in Standardized Test Formats.*

3. Most people believe that the Loch Ness monster is just a <u>myth, sightings of the monster continue to be reported</u>.

   (A) myth, sightings of the monster continue to be reported

   (B) myth, and people report still seeing the monster

   (C) myth. Sightings of the monster continue to be reported

   (D) myth; sightings of the monster continue to be reported

   (E) myth; however, sightings of the monster continue to be reported

4. Tamara told Jenny <u>that she probably made an A.</u>

   (A) that she probably made an A

   (B) that an A was probably what she made

   (C) that Jenny probably made an A

   (D) about her making an A probably

   (E) that her grade was probably an A

5. To fully appreciate many of Gary Soto's stories, <u>some knowledge of Mexican American culture is necessary.</u>

   (A) some knowledge of Mexican American culture is necessary

   (B) the reader needs some knowledge of Mexican American culture

   (C) you must learn all about Mexican American culture

   (D) knowing something about Mexican American culture

   (E) the necessity is to know about Mexican American culture

6. <u>In this article, it says that the Chinese were using paper money by the thirteenth century.</u>

   (A) In this article, it says that the Chinese were using paper money by the thirteenth century.

   (B) According to this article, it says that the Chinese were using paper money by the thirteenth century.

   (C) By the thirteenth century, the Chinese in this article were using paper money.

   (D) In this article, they say that the Chinese were using paper money by the thirteenth century.

   (E) According to this article, the Chinese were using paper money by the thirteenth century.

7. <u>The capital of Liberia, Monrovia, which was named by freed slaves in honor of President James Monroe.</u>

   (A) The capital of Liberia, Monrovia, which was named by freed slaves in honor of President James Monroe.

   (B) Monrovia, the capital of Liberia, named by freed slaves in honor of President James Monroe.

(C) Named by freed slaves, Monrovia, the capital of Liberia, in honor of President James Monroe.

(D) In honor of President James Monroe, freed slaves named the capital of Liberia Monrovia.

(E) In honor of President James Monroe, freed slaves who named Monrovia the capital of Liberia.

8. I bought a collar <u>for my kitten that has a reflective tag and a breakaway buckle</u>.

(A) for my kitten that has a reflective tag and a breakaway buckle

(B) for my kitten with a reflective tag and a breakaway buckle

(C) that has a reflective tag and a breakaway buckle for my kitten

(D) for my kitten having a reflective tag and a breakaway buckle

(E) for my kitten, and it has a reflective tag and a breakaway buckle

9. <u>Henry Ford wanted to make his cars affordable to everyone; that is why he developed an efficient assembly-line method for manufacturing them.</u>

(A) Henry Ford wanted to make his cars affordable to everyone; that is why he developed an efficient assembly-line method for manufacturing them.

(B) Henry Ford wanted to make his cars affordable to everyone so that he could develop an efficient assembly-line method for manufacturing them.

(C) Henry Ford wanted to make his cars affordable to everyone because he developed an efficient assembly-line method for manufacturing them.

(D) Henry Ford developed an efficient assembly-line method for manufacturing his cars because he wanted to make them affordable to everyone.

(E) To develop an efficient assembly-line method for manufacturing his cars, Henry Ford wanted to make them affordable to everyone.

10. <u>Having seen that people in some countries were denied basic civil rights, my uncle's appreciation for the Bill of Rights grew.</u>

(A) Having seen that people in some countries were denied basic civil rights, my uncle's appreciation for the Bill of Rights grew.

(B) My uncle, having seen the Bill of Rights, knew that people in some countries were denied basic civil rights.

(C) When basic civil rights are denied people in some countries, my uncle's appreciation for the Bill of Rights grows.

(D) My uncle's appreciation for people denied basic civil rights in some countries grew as he read the Bill of Rights.

(E) My uncle's appreciation for the Bill of Rights grew after he had seen that people in some countries were denied basic civil rights.

COMMON ERRORS

Grammar and Usage Test: Section 2

DIRECTIONS Read the paragraph below. For each numbered blank, select the word or word group that best completes the sentence. Indicate your response by shading in the appropriate oval on your answer sheet.

EXAMPLE More powerful than optical microscopes, electron microscopes __(1)__ researchers to study extremely small objects.

      1. **(A)** has enabled
            (B) is enabling
            (C) enabling
            (D) enable
            (E) enables

ANSWER   **1.** (A) (B) (C) (**D**) (E)

An electron microscope, using a beam of electrons, __(1)__ a magnified image. Unlike an optical microscope, __(2)__ instrument does not depend on __(3)__ light rays. Instead, an electron lens __(4)__ a system of electromagnetic coils that focus the electron beam. The electrons __(5)__ , of course, aren't visible to the naked eye. Rather, __(6)__ are directed at a specimen to form __(7)__ image on a photographic plate. The wavelength of an electron beam is __(8)__ than the wavelength of light. Therefore, __(9)__ magnification is possible with an electron microscope __(10)__ optical microscope.

---

1. (A) create
    (B) is creating
    (C) creates
    (D) will create
    (E) will have created

2. (A) this here
    (B) this
    (C) these
    (D) these kind of
    (E) that there

3. (A) any
    (B) not one
    (C) no
    (D) hardly any
    (E) barely some

4. (A) use
    (B) has used
    (C) will use
    (D) uses
    (E) had been using

5. (A) themself
   (B) themselves
   (C) theirself
   (D) theirselves
   (E) itself

6. (A) them
   (B) it
   (C) that
   (D) this
   (E) they

7. (A) its
   (B) their
   (C) they're
   (D) its'
   (E) it's

8. (A) short
   (B) shorter
   (C) more short
   (D) more shorter
   (E) shortest

9. (A) good
   (B) gooder
   (C) better
   (D) more better
   (E) more good

10. (A) then with an
    (B) then with a
    (C) than with an
    (D) than with a
    (E) then a

BURE-U OF
MIS-ING
LET-ERS

FRANK & ERNEST reprinted by permission
of Newspaper Enterprise Association, Inc.

COMMON ERRORS

Reference Note

For information on **capital letters,** see Chapter 21.

Exercise 26 Correcting the Capitalization of Words and Phrases

Correct the following words and phrases by either changing lowercase letters to capital letters or changing capital letters to lowercase letters.

EXAMPLE   1. Hank's poem "Waiting for morning in july"

           1. *Hank's poem "Waiting for Morning in July"*

1. geometry I, latin, and civics
2. *national geographic* magazine
3. the god of abraham, isaac, and jacob   3. [*or* God]
4. an Island in the gulf of mexico
5. liberty bell
6. during the great depression
7. readings from "the scarlet ibis"
8. internal revenue service forms
9. mother's day
10. an episode of *party of five*
11. Grandfather Ben and my Cousin
12. Hiroshige's painting *The Moon Beyond The Leaves*
13. an italian custom
14. bill of rights
15. a passage from the koran
16. is that an okidata® printer?
17. dr. and mrs. Dorset
18. a congressional medal of honor recipient
19. chief joseph
20. *King Of The Wind*

Exercise 27 Proofreading for Correct Capitalization

Each of the following sentences contains at least one capitalization error. Correct each error by changing capital letters to lowercase letters or lowercase letters to capital letters.

EXAMPLE   1. In the barn my Dad is building an ultralight plane that we have named the *hummingbird.*

           1. *dad, Hummingbird*

1. The slave knelt at the feet of the statue and said, "Zeus, o, Zeus, Oh please, help me."
2. long ago, Africans shaped tools from stones; we find these stones wherever they lived.

3. My grandma told me that she used to go to Wrigley field with her father and mother.

4. This saturday, instead of going to eagle lake, let's go to the Riverdale High School Festival.

5. A Yale student laid out the plans for a submarine that was used in the American revolution.

6. Fred started sewing kites for himself and his friends and now has a small business known as Fred's fliers.

7. "Have you read *Changes in Latitudes*?" i asked.

8. Because the Panama Canal is too narrow for some supertankers, they sometimes must pass through the waters of the strait of Magellan at the Southern tip of south america.

9. The chess club meets every day after school in the large room East of the auditorium.

10. We think our team, the Kennedy middle school bobcats, is the best in Baker county.

Exercise 28 **Proofreading for Correct Capitalization**

Each of the following sentences contains errors in capitalization. Correct each error by changing capital letters to lowercase letters or lowercase letters to capital letters.

EXAMPLE   1. Often, i feel like a World traveler in my hometown.

         1. *I, world*

1. When I ride the bus down central avenue, I can hear people speaking spanish, hindi, japanese, arabic, and some other languages I don't even recognize.

2. On independence day, my Mother and I drove our old ford thunderbird to Taylor park.

3. Near there we saw mr. Narazaki and Ms. white eagle talking.

4. They were in front of the Lincoln building, where the federal bureau of investigation has offices.

5. On that same Saturday, we also saw several muslim women wearing long robes and veils in front of hill medical center next to the Park.

6. After the band played John philip Sousa's "the Stars And Stripes Forever," people stood beside a statue of the Greek deity Athena and gave readings from the declaration of independence and the bible.

7. Later, mayor Mendoza read a telegram from the president of the united states, gave a speech, and awarded Medals to several people for their public service.

Exercise 28

OBJECTIVE

■ **To proofread for correct capitalization**

8. As soon as the big dipper was clearly visible, the fireworks started, and I thought, "this is definitely the greatest place on Earth!"
9. Next year, I plan to take United States history II at West creek high school.
10. I am going to look in my new history book for a list of all the peoples that make up our country, from the inuits of alaska to the hawaiians of hilo bay.

Reference Note

For information on **using commas correctly,** see page 643.

Exercise 29 Using Commas Correctly

Add and delete commas to punctuate the following sentences correctly.

EXAMPLE
1. A first-aid kit should contain adhesive tape scissors antiseptic and a variety of bandages.

1. *A first-aid kit should contain adhesive tape, scissors, antiseptic, and a variety of bandages.*
Optional commas are underscored.

1. Yes I have a screwdriver and some screws and wood glue.
2. On the balcony of a second-floor apartment a large macaw sat watching us.
3. We moved on October 15; our new address is 5311 East Baker Street, Deerfield Illinois, 60015.
4. All you need to bring are a change of clothes shoes socks a toothbrush and toothpaste.
5. Phobos is I believe one of the moons around Mars Mrs. Farris.
6. Fire damaged a number of houses yet no one was injured not even any pets.
7. Because acrylic a type of water-based paint dries rapidly you must work quickly with it.
8. Birds sang frogs jumped and children played on that hot sunny day.
9. Malfunctioning dangerously the robot moved jerkily toward the table, picked up a dish dropped it on the floor and rolled out the door.
10. Easing up on the throttle she coasted in for a smooth landing.

Exercise 30 Using Commas Correctly

Add and delete commas to punctuate the following sentences correctly.

EXAMPLE
1. They made beads out of small white seashells Ed.

1. *They made beads out of small, white seashells, Ed.*
Optional commas are underscored.

1. Deer thrived sea life flourished and all manner of edible plants grew in the region, that is now California.

Exercise 29

OBJECTIVE

■ To correct sentences with errors in comma usage

Meeting
INDIVIDUAL NEEDS

LEARNING STYLES
Auditory Learners. As a review before assigning **Exercise 29,** write the following sentences on the chalkboard without commas and have students read them aloud, first without pausing for commas, then with the appropriate pauses. Ask students to discuss the differences in meaning they perceive.

1. My brother, Rico, thinks about cars all the time.
2. My brother Rico, who thinks about cars all the time, is out in the garage.
3. My, Rico thinks about cars all the time!

Exercise 30

OBJECTIVE

■ To correct sentences with errors in comma usage

2. Up and down the coastline of California communities of American Indians have lived for centuries.

3. The Karok Pomo Yurok and Modoc are just four of the dozens of peoples living in this area.

4. Skilled in basketwork the Pomo became known for the decoration, variety, and intricate weaving of their baskets.

5. The Yurok developed an elaborate monetary system which they used in fixing a price on every privilege or offense.

6. While many peoples favored dentalium shells as currency they also exchanged other items in trade.

7. Yurok marriages were arranged with care for marriage was an important public and historic alliance.

8. Yes Helen, the Gabrielino hunted with a stick that is similar to the boomerang the famous Australian weapon.

9. Traditionally, the Coast Miwok peoples were each represented by a male chief, and a female chief and a female ceremonial leader called a *maien*.

10. Kintpuash who was also called Captain Jack was the Modoc leader, who escaped capture on November 29 1872.

Exercise 31 **Proofreading for Correct Use of Semicolons and Colons**

Add or delete semicolons and colons to correct the punctuation in the following sentences.

EXAMPLE   **1.** The party starts at 7 30, we will need to leave our house by 7 00.

     1. The party starts at 7:30; we will need to leave our house by 7:00.

1. John is bringing the drinks, ice, and cups and Wanda is bringing the plates, knives, and forks.

2. Compare these three translations of King David's famous song, Psalm 23 1–6.

3. Don't forget to pick up Carlos, Kam, Lisa, and Mary at 7 15 sharp.

4. Twin koalas are rare in captivity consequently, Australia's Yanchep National Park prized Euca and Lyptus, the two born there in 1996.

5. The dance committee still needs to get the following equipment a CD player, outdoor speakers, and a microphone.

6. During our party on the Fourth of July last year, a huge storm forced everyone inside then lightning knocked the power out.

─HELP─

In Exercise 31, you may need to use colons and semicolons to replace incorrectly used commas.

Reference Note

For information on **semicolons and colons,** see Chapter 23.

7. California's seagulls will eat just about anything:clams, chicks, berries, and even the occasional starfish.
8. We have invited exchange students from Dublin, Ireland;Paris, France;and Tokyo, Japan.
9. At 10:30 P.M., he neatly printed the title page, which read "Alfredo in Wonderland:A Tale of an Exchange Student in New York."
10. Bamboo is a versatile and flexible building material;in Indonesia, as in many countries, it has a wide variety of uses.

Exercise 32 Using Punctuation Correctly in Sentences

Add periods, question marks, commas, semicolons, and colons to correct the punctuation in the following sentences.

EXAMPLE

1. In almost every corner of the world dogs do useful work for people

1. *In almost every corner of the world, dogs do useful work for people.*
   Optional commas are underscored.

1. Herding flocks,collies and briards and other varieties of sheepdog are on the job wherever there are sheep.
2. Did you know that German shepherds,which make good guard dogs,can also herd sheep?
3. Dogs guard our homes,assist people with disabilities,herd sheep, and hunt game.
4. Sled dogs include the following breeds:Samoyeds, huskies, Alaskan malamutes, and a few other strong breeds with thick fur.

5. Partners with police the world over,bloodhounds are feared by criminals and praised by the parents of lost children whom these dogs have found.
6. The basenji comes from Africa and is,in fact,called the Congo dog; many people share their homes with these animals,whose ancestors date back to 3000 B.C.
7. Although Mexican Chihuahuas are tiny,they fiercely take on any foe;they don't back down even when facing a larger dog.
8. Brave little Chihuahuas ignore the good advice given in Ecclesiastes 9:4.
9. Those famous lines make an obvious point:"A living dog is better than a dead lion."
10. My favorite neighbor,Edward Nichols,Jr.,bought his Pekingese on Wednesday,January 6,1999.

Exercise 32

OBJECTIVE

■ **To correctly revise sentences containing errors in punctuation**

Exercise 33 Correcting Errors in the Use of Quotation Marks and Other Punctuation

For each of the following sentences, correct any error in the use of quotation marks, commas, and end marks.

Reference Note

For information on **using quotation marks,** see page 686.

EXAMPLE
    1. The troop leader said that we should bring the 'barest essentials': a change of clothes, a toothbrush, and a comb.

    1. The troop leader said that we should bring the "barest essentials": a change of clothes, a toothbrush, and a comb.

1. James seemed excited and said, "Did you see the news last night?"

2. "Sorry, Emma," Becky began, "but I'm late already."

3. When Coach Myers announced the tryouts this morning, she said, "that anyone could try out."

4. Ms. Waters asked us to read "The Tell-Tale Heart" and one other short story of our choice this weekend.

5. They are watching reruns of *The Magic School Bus;* this episode is "Lost in the Solar System."

6. For tomorrow's assignment, read "The Price of Freedom," the next chapter in your textbook.

7. My favorite part of *Reader's Digest* is "Humor in Uniform."

8. "Why don't you title your poem "Words and Music"?" Tom asked.

9. The recent article "Carbon Monoxide: The Silent Killer" details the effects of this deadly gas.

10. "Didn't you hear me yell 'Call 911!'?" asked Erik. 10. 'Call 911!'?"

Exercise 34 Punctuating and Capitalizing Quotations

For each of the following sentences, correct any error in the use of quotation marks, commas, end marks, and capitalization.

EXAMPLE
    1. Larry told me that "you were sitting in the library."

    1. Larry told me that you were sitting in the library.

1. "I can't decide which selection to use for my project" sighed Fran.

2. Mary nodded and said "I haven't made up my mind either." "Are you going to choose a poem or a story"?

3. "I'm going to make a diorama of "Stopping by Woods on a Snowy Evening," interrupted Greg.

4. What if Ms. Hill says 'that you can't'? asked Mary.

5. Didn't she say "anything goes?" Greg answered.

6. "You're right." The instructions say 'write a song, present a play, or draw a picture, added Mary.

Exercise 33

O B J E C T I V E

- **To correct sentences with errors in the use of quotation marks and other punctuation**

Exercise 34

O B J E C T I V E

- **To correct sentences with errors in the use of quotation marks, commas, end marks, and capitalization**

Exercise 34 Punctuating and Capitalizing Quotations

A N S W E R S

1. "I can't decide which selection to use for my project," sighed Fran.

2. Mary nodded and said, "I haven't made up my mind either. Are you going to choose a poem or a story?"

3. "I'm going to make a diorama of 'Stopping by Woods on a Snowy Evening,'" interrupted Greg.

4. "What if Ms. Hill says that you can't?" asked Mary.

5. "Didn't she say, 'Anything goes'?" Greg answered.

6. "You're right. The instructions say, 'Write a song, present a play, or draw a picture,'" added Mary.

COMMON ERRORS

Mechanics   **793**

Exercise 34 Punctuating and Capitalizing Quotations

ANSWERS continued

7. "You play the guitar," Fran pointed out. "Maybe you could write a song."

8. Mary smiled and said, "Great idea!"

9. "What I'd really like to do is write extra verses for Woody Guthrie's song 'This Land Is Your Land,'" Fran said.

10. "Perhaps even," Mary added, "make a video of it!"

Exercise 35

OBJECTIVE

- To correct sentences and groups of words with errors in the use of apostrophes

Exercise 36

OBJECTIVE

- To correct sentences with errors in spelling

Reference Note

For more information on **using apostrophes,** see Chapter 25.

Reference Note

For information on **spelling rules,** see Chapter 27.

1. daily/surely

7. You play the guitar, Fran pointed out. Maybe you could write a song."

8. Mary smiled and said, "great idea!

9. What I'd really like to do is write extra verses for Woody Guthrie's song This Land Is Your Land, Fran said.

10. Perhaps even," Mary added "make a video of it"!

Exercise 35 Using Apostrophes Correctly

Add or delete apostrophes to punctuate the following items correctly. If an item is already correct, write *C*.

EXAMPLE   **1.** Weve got Matts tickets'.

   1. We've got Matt's tickets.

1. Dont use so many sos.
2. Its time for Janes report.
3. Ronnies and Eriks desks
4. Mom and Dads only car
5. PBSs most popular show
6. Who's your brother? **6.** C
7. my sister's-in-laws cars
8. geeses caretaker
9. that baby birds beak
10. Kerrys and your project
11. anyone's guess **11.** C
12. Russs Us look like Ns.
13. Youre right!
14. those foxes dens
15. The blame is theirs'.
16. Lets eat at six oclock.
17. my March of Dimes donation **17.** C
18. She says that shell bring ours.
19. There's still time. **19.** C
20. Bobs dog

Exercise 36 Proofreading for Spelling Errors

Correct each spelling error in the following sentences.

EXAMPLE   **1.** To succede, you must keep triing.

   1. succeed; trying

1. I cannot easily make dayly visits, even though I would surly like to.

2. The judge ~~finaly conceeded~~ that the other driver had been ~~exceding~~ the speed limit.

3. The members of the procession ~~carryed one hundred twenty-five~~ baskets of beautiful flowers.

4. The desert heat and dryness ~~stoped~~ both ~~armys~~.

5. My neighbor's ~~childs~~ are always getting into ~~mischeif~~.

6. A word with two ~~es~~, such as *deer,* has a long vowel sound.

7. The children ~~truely enjoied~~ hearing ~~thier~~ echoes bounce off the canyon walls.

8. The candidate ~~siezed~~ the opportunity to give a ~~breif~~ statement of his ~~beleifs~~.

9. ~~Leafs~~ fluttered off the trees and down the ~~desertted beachs~~ during that ~~1st~~ day of winter.

10. ~~5~~ years ago, each of my ~~brother-in-laws~~ was working two jobs.

2. finally/conceded/ exceeding
3. carried/125
4. stopped/armies
5. children/mischief
6. e's
7. truly/enjoyed/their
8. seized/brief/ beliefs
9. Leaves/deserted/ beaches/first
10. Five/brothers-in-law

Exercise 37 Proofreading for Spelling Errors

For each of the following sentences, write the misspelled word or words correctly.

EXAMPLE   1. Six concrete elfs guarded the doorway to my nieghbor's house.

        1. *elves, neighbor's*

1. Leisure activities may be ~~wholely unecessary~~ for survival, but they make life enjoyable.

2. On the way to Japan, his ~~neice~~ met a Chinese man who spoke perfect English.

3. After the clouds ~~receeded~~, the sun glinted on the wet ~~rooves~~.

4. Three ranch hands were teaching ~~roping~~ to the tourists who had ~~payed~~ for lessons.

5. These attachments are interchangeable, I ~~beleive~~.

6. While my ~~freinds~~ and I were ~~siting~~ on the porch, we saw a white rabbit ~~hoping~~ across the street.

7. Place two heaping ~~spoonsful~~ of flour in a saucepan; then, slice three small ~~tomatos~~.

8. Yes, several ~~attorney-at-laws~~ at our offices are ~~alumnuses~~ of the state university.

9. There must have been over ~~one hundred and fifty~~ people standing in line longer than that.

10. Mr. Brady said that suddenly the ~~terrifing~~ possibility of going to school all year had not seemed so bad to the ~~Bradies~~.

Reference Note
For information on **spelling rules,** see Chapter 27.

1. wholly/unnecessary
2. niece
3. receded/roofs
4. roping/paid
5. believe
6. friends/sitting/ hopping
7. spoonfuls/tomatoes
8. attorneys-at-law/ alumni
9. 150
10. terrifying/Bradys

Exercise 37

OBJECTIVE

■ To correct sentences with errors in spelling

Mechanics   **795**

Mechanics   **795**

Exercise 38

OBJECTIVE

■ To correct sentences with errors in
the use of words often confused

Exercise 39

OBJECTIVE

■ To correct sentences with errors
in the use of words often confused

Reference Note

For information on **words
often confused,** see
page 746.

1. plane's/quiet
2. It's/your
3. dessert/it's
4. their/passed

5. led/their

6. break/pieces
7. chose/through
8. loose/to
9. hear/weak
10. Whose/choose

Exercise 38 **Proofreading for Words Often Confused**

For each of the following sentences, correct any error in word usage.

EXAMPLE   1. A camel caravan in the dessert is a noble sight.

       1. *A camel caravan in the desert is a noble sight.*

1. The roar of the plain's engine broke the quite of the night.
2. Its time to get you're suitcase packed.
3. I put my desert right here on the kitchen table, and now its gone.
4. As the mustangs picked they're way through the canyon, they unknowingly past a cougar hiding in the rocks.
5. Who was the warrior who lead the Zulus in there famous battle against the Boers?
6. Be careful, or you will brake that mirror into a million peaces.
7. Every knight choose his own way threw the forest.
8. First, the pigs got lose; then we spent all day trying too catch them.
9. He couldn't here us; he was too week from the fever.
10. Who's biography did you chose to read?

Exercise 39 **Distinguishing Between Words Often Confused**

Choose the correct word in parentheses in each of the following sentences.

EXAMPLE   1. Is Korean food for dinner (*all right, alright*) with you?

       1. *all right*

1. I believe that Andrew Young began his political career during the 1960s; (*than,* *then*) he became a U.S. representative before being named ambassador to the United Nations.
2. Millie, would you care to explain the first (*principle,* principal) of thermodynamics to the class?
3. A (*stationery,* *stationary*) cold front has been responsible for this week's wonderful weather.
4. Recycling helps cut down on the (*waist,* *waste*) of resources.
5. Did you (*all ready,* *already*) qualify for the race?
6. How would you (*council, consul,* *counsel*) someone in this situation?
7. What (*effects,* affects) will the Internet have on your future career?
8. There's nothing (*plain,* plane) about these stylized medieval reliefs.
9. I think that when it came to scat singing, Sarah Vaughan really was (*all together,* *altogether*) the best.
10. Designing a golf (*coarse,* *course*) must be a challenging task.

Exercise 40   Proofreading a Business Letter

For each numbered item in the following business letter, correct any errors in mechanics. An item may contain more than one error. If an item is already correct, write *C*.

EXAMPLE   **[1]** 813 E Maple St

     1. *813 E. Maple St.*

     813 East Maple Street
[1] Belleville ‚IL⟩ 62223

[2] February 12th, 2001

[3] Customer Service
     Super Sport Shoes
     14 Magenta Road
     Woodinville ‚WA⟩ 98072

[4] Dear Sir or Madam:

[5] Thank you for your prompt response to my
     order (number 51238) for two pairs of   **5.** C
     white jogging shoes. **[6]** These shoe's are
     the most comfortable ones I have ever worn.

[7] However, one of the pairs that I   **7.** received
     recieved is the wrong size. **[8]** This pair
     is to small; consequently, I am returning   **8.** too
     these shoes with this letter. **[9]** Please
     exchange them for one pair of white jog-
     gers two sizes larger. **9.** C

[10] Your's truly,

     Neville Walters

     Neville Walters

Exercise 40

O B J E C T I V E

■ To proofread a business letter to correct errors in mechanics

COMMON ERRORS

TEACHING (**TIP**)

Using the Mechanics Tests. A **Correcting Common Errors Standardized Test Answer Sheet** that students may use for this **Mechanics Test** is provided in *Chapter Tests in Standardized Test Formats.*

Mechanics Test: Section 1

DIRECTIONS   Each of the following sentences contains an underlined word or word group. Choose the answer that shows the correct capitalization, punctuation, and spelling of the underlined part. If there is no error, choose answer E (Correct as is). Indicate your response by shading in the appropriate oval on your answer sheet.

EXAMPLE   1. Marla <u>asked, "did</u> you see the meteor shower last night?"

　　　(**A**) asked, "Did
　　　(**B**) asked "Did
　　　(**C**) asked "did
　　　(**D**) asked did you
　　　(**E**) Correct as is

ANSWER   1. A B C D E

1. We keep a variety of emergency equipment in the trunk of our <u>car, a first-aid</u> kit, jumper cables, a blanket, a flashlight, and road flares.
　　(**A**) car a first-aid　　　　　　(**D**) car: a 1st-aid
　　(**B**) car: a first-aid　　　　　　(**E**) Correct as is
　　(**C**) car; a first-aid

2. Alvin <u>Ailey, who's choreography</u> thrilled audiences for years, formed the dance company that still bears his name.
　　(**A**) Ailey who's choreography　　　(**D**) Ailey, whose choreography
　　(**B**) Ailey whose choreography　　　(**E**) Correct as is
　　(**C**) Ailey who's choreography,

3. Jerome <u>said, "I cant believe</u> that Ben Franklin wanted the turkey to be the symbol for the United States!"
　　(**A**) said, "I can't believe　　　　(**D**) said, 'I can't believe
　　(**B**) said "I can't believe　　　　(**E**) Correct as is
　　(**C**) said, "I can't beleive

4. "Do <u>you," asked Kay 'Know</u> the story of Icarus?"
　　(**A**) you, asked Kay, "know　　　　(**D**) you," asked Kay, 'know
　　(**B**) you?" asked Kay. "Know　　　(**E**) Correct as is
　　(**C**) you," asked Kay, "know

5. I often struggle to open my gym <u>locker; its</u> lock is probably rusty.

(A) locker, its   (D) locker: It's

(B) locker; Its   (E) Correct as is

(C) locker. It's

6. Please <u>bring too tomatos</u>, a head of lettuce, and some feta cheese from the market.

(A) bring: two tomatoes,   (D) bring to tomatoes,

(B) bring 2 tomatoes   (E) Correct as is

(C) bring two tomatoes,

7. "Did Principal Reeves really say, 'We need *less* <u>discipline?</u>" asked Cassandra.

(A) discipline,'"   (D) discipline'"?

(B) discipline'?"   (E) Correct as is

(C) discipline?'

8. Grandfather enjoyed the <u>childrens storys</u> about their visit to the wildlife sanctuary.

(A) childrens story's   (D) children's stories

(B) childrens' stories   (E) Correct as is

(C) childrens stories

9. The Leonards <u>visited: Rome, Italy,</u> Athens, Greece; and Istanbul, Turkey, on their vacation.

(A) visited Rome, Italy;   (D) visited Rome; Italy;

(B) visited: Rome, Italy;   (E) Correct as is

(C) visited, Rome, Italy;

10. Did <u>aunt Susan,</u> bring the coleslaw?

(A) aunt Susan   (D) Aunt, Susan,

(B) aunt, Susan,   (E) Correct as is

(C) Aunt Susan

Mechanics Test: Section 2

DIRECTIONS   Each numbered item below contains an underlined group of words. Choose the answer that shows the correct capitalization, punctuation, and spelling of the underlined part. If there is no error, choose answer E (Correct as is). Indicate your response by shading in the appropriate oval on your answer sheet.

EXAMPLE   **[1]** 200 north Vine Street

     (A) 200 North Vine street

     (B) 200 North Vine Street

     (C) Two-Hundred North Vine Street

     (D) 200, North Vine Street

     (E) Correct as is

ANSWER   1.

---

200 North Vine Street
Austin, TX 78741

[1] May, 5 2001

Athena Wilson
Worldwide Travel, Inc.
4135-A Anderson Avenue
[2] San Antonio, Tex. 78249

[3] Dear Ms. Wilson:

[4] Thank you for you're prompt response to my request for information about traveling to Australia. The color brochures describing the **[5]** different, Australian tours were especially helpful. My family and I are interested in the "Natural Wonders" **[6]** package, that includes day trips to **[7]** the great Barrier reef. **[8]** Well also want to schedule a three-day stay in Sydney. How much will the entire package **[9]** cost, for three adults and one child?

[10] Yours truly

Naomi Baskin
Naomi Baskin

---

1. **(A)** May 5 2001
   (B) May Fifth 2001
   (C) May 5th 2001
   (D) May 5, 2001
   (E) Correct as is

2. **(A)** San Antonio, Tex 78249
   (B) San Antonio Texas 78249
   (C) San Antonio, TX 78249
   (D) San Antonio TX 78249
   (E) Correct as is

3. **(A)** Dear Ms. Wilson,
   (B) Dear ms. Wilson:
   (C) Dear Ms Wilson,
   (D) Dear Ms. Wilson;
   (E) Correct as is

4. **(A)** Thank you for youre
   (B) Thank you for youre'
   (C) Thank you for your
   (D) Thank you for your'
   (E) Correct as is

5. **(A)** different australian
   (B) different Australian
   (C) different, Australian,
   (D) different, australian,
   (E) Correct as is

6. **(A)** package that includes
   (B) package that, includes
   (C) package: that includes
   (D) package that includes:
   (E) Correct as is

7. **(A)** the Great Barrier Reef
   (B) the great Barrier Reef
   (C) the Great Barrier reef
   (D) The great Barrier reef
   (E) Correct as is

8. **(A)** Well, also
   (B) We'll, also,
   (C) We'll also
   (D) We'll, also
   (E) Correct as is

9. **(A)** cost for 3
   (B) cost? For three
   (C) cost: for three
   (D) cost for three
   (E) Correct as is

10. **(A)** Yours' truly,
    (B) Yours truly:
    (C) Your's truly,
    (D) Yours truly,
    (E) Correct as is

Mechanics   **801**

RESOURCES

Correcting Common Errors
Review

- *Grammar, Usage, and Mechanics,* pp. 404, 405, 406, 407

Assessment

- *Assessment Package*
  —*Chapter Tests,* Ch. 28
  —*Chapter Tests in Standardized Test Formats,* Ch. 28
- *Test Generator (One-Stop Planner CD-ROM)*

PART 4

Quick Reference Handbook

The Dictionary

Information About Words

Dictionary Entry A dictionary entry includes the word and information about it. The following items explain the labels in the sample entry.

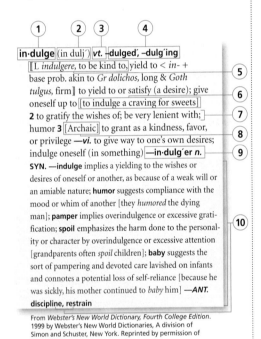

From *Webster's New World Dictionary, Fourth College Edition.* 1999 by Webster's New World Dictionaries, A division of Simon and Schuster, New York. Reprinted by permission of the publisher.

1. **Entry word.** The entry word shows how the word is spelled and how it is divided into syllables. The entry word may also show capitalization and alternate spellings.
2. **Pronunciation.** Pronunciation is shown by the use of phonetic spellings that usually include accent marks and diacritical marks. A pronunciation key explains the meaning of diacritical marks and phonetic symbols.
3. **Part-of-speech labels.** The part-of-speech labels (usually in abbreviated form) indicate how the entry word should be used in a sentence. Some words may be used as more than one part of speech. In this case, a part-of-speech label is given in front of each numbered or lettered series of definitions.
4. **Other forms.** These may show spellings of plural forms of nouns, tenses of verbs, or the comparison forms of adjectives and adverbs.
5. **Etymology.** The etymology is the origin and history of a word. It tells how the word or its parts came into English.
6. **Examples.** Phrases or sentences may demonstrate how the defined word is used.
7. **Definitions.** If a word has more than one meaning, definitions are numbered or lettered.

8. **Special usage labels.** These labels identify words that have special meanings or are used in special ways in certain situations.
9. **Related word forms.** These are various forms of the entry word, usually created by adding suffixes or prefixes.
10. **Synonyms and antonyms.** Synonyms or antonyms appear at the end of some entries.

Other Parts of a Dictionary Most dictionaries also include the following additional information.

- **Abbreviations** Many dictionaries include a chart of common *abbreviations,* including those for governmental agencies, weights, measurements, and the names of states or geographical regions.
- **Biographical and geographical entries** In some dictionaries, a section identifies famous or influential figures in history, listing their professions and birth and death dates. The geographical section lists populated places in the world and includes pronunciations and population size.
- **Colleges and universities** School or college dictionaries list all the colleges and universities in the United States and Canada, indicating each school's location, founding date, and student body size.
- **Copyright** The *copyright* tells you when a dictionary was published. Use the most up-to-date edition; that way, you can be sure that new words and new meanings of old words are included.
- **Guide to the dictionary** Most dictionaries have a few pages that explain how the material is organized and what the abbreviations and typefaces mean.
- **Index** An *index* indicates the location of the dictionary features described previously.

- **Pronunciation key** A *pronunciation key* is provided at the front of any dictionary and also at the bottom of each page or pair of pages within the dictionary.
- **Scholarly essays** Language experts write *scholarly essays* that provide information about the history and growth of English, how a new edition differs from a previous one, and how the dictionary was researched and prepared.

Types of Dictionaries Since dictionaries differ in the types and amount of information they provide, you should choose a dictionary based on the kind of information you need.

- **Abridged** An *abridged* dictionary is the most common type of dictionary. (The word *abridged* means shortened or condensed.) It contains most of the words you are likely to use or encounter in your writing or reading. Abridged dictionaries are arranged in alphabetical order and include basic information such as the spelling, definition, pronunciation, part of speech, and source of a word. If you need more detailed information about a word's history or usage, consult an *unabridged* or *specialized* dictionary instead.
- **Specialized** *Specialized* dictionaries define words or terms that are used in a particular profession, field, or area of interest, such as dictionaries of quotations, synonyms, medical terms, and slang. Specialized dictionaries include information that an abridged dictionary might not have.
- **Unabridged** An *unabridged* dictionary contains nearly all the words in use in a language. For example, the present edition of the twenty-volume *Oxford English Dictionary* contains over 500,000 entries.

Document Design

Manuscript Style

The following chart provides guidelines for preparing handwritten or typed manuscripts. Your teacher may have additional guidelines for you to follow. Remember that these guidelines will help improve the appearance of your papers.

Guidelines for Handwritten or Typed Manuscripts

1. Use only one side of a sheet of paper.

2. Type or write in blue or black ink.

3. If you write by hand, do not skip lines. If you type, double-space the lines.

4. Leave margins of about one inch at the top, sides, and bottom of each page.

5. Indent the first line of each paragraph.

6. Number all the pages except the first page. Place the number in the upper right-hand corner of the page.

7. All pages should be neat and clean. You may make a few corrections with correction fluid, but they should be barely noticeable.

8. Follow your teacher's instructions for placing your name, the date, your class, and the title of your paper on a cover sheet or on the first page of your paper.

Desktop Publishing

Desktop publishing is the production of professional-looking documents, such as reports or newsletters, on a personal computer. Desktop publishers set text (and sometimes visuals) on a page in such a way that they effectively communicate a message.

Page Design or Layout

Before the widespread use of computers changed the printing industry, documents were designed by hand. Page designers worked page by page, cutting, arranging, and pasting strips of text, illustrations, headings, and captions. Now almost anyone with a computer can design an entire document. The following section explains some key concepts for designing pages.

Alignment   *Alignment* refers to how lines of text are arranged on a page. There are several ways text can be aligned.

■ **Left alignment**   Text that is *left aligned* is set so that each line forms a straight edge against the left margin. Most printed documents are set left aligned to aid reading from left to right.

EXAMPLE

This text is left aligned.
Notice how the lines form
a straight edge along the
left margin.

■ **Right alignment**   Text that is *right aligned* is set so that each edge forms a straight line against the right margin. Right-aligned text is not commonly used for large amounts of text because it is difficult to read. Pull-quotes and poetry are occasionally right aligned. (See also **Pull-quote** on page 809.)

EXAMPLE

This text is right aligned.
Notice how the lines
form a straight edge along the
right margin.

■ **Center alignment**   Text that is *center aligned,* or *centered,* is set in the middle of the page. Center-aligned text usually appears in invitations, posters, or advertisements.

EXAMPLE

This text is center aligned.
Each line is evenly spaced
on both sides of an invisible, vertical line
running through the center of this column.

■ **Justified alignment**   *Justified* means the ends of each line of text form a straight edge against the left and right margins. Extra spaces are added between words to make sure that the lines are even.

EXAMPLE

This sample text is justified.
Notice how the lines of text form
neat edges along both margins.

■ **Ragged alignment**   *Ragged* means that the lines of the text do not create a straight edge on both sides. Usually the right side of the text is ragged, as in the example of left alignment in the column at the left.

Bullet   A *bullet* (•) is an icon used to make information in a text stand out. Bullets are often used for lists of parallel items. The bullets attract readers' attention and can make information more accessible to them. Here are some tips for using bullets.

■ Always indent a bulleted list from the main body text.

■ Use plain bullets in formal documents. Other, decorative icons (such as *, # , or +) may be used as bullets only in informal writing, such as brainstormed lists.

■ Make sure that the items in your list are parallel both in the type of information they contain and in construction. For instance, use all nouns or all imperative sentences, as in this bulleted list.

Call out   A *call out* is a line or phrase of text that describes some aspect of a visual, graphic, or illustration. Usually the call out is connected to the visual by an arrow or line. (For examples of call outs, see the labels for **Headings and Subheadings** on page 808.)

Columns and Blocks of Text   Text is easier to read when it is contained in rectangular-shaped areas, such as *columns* or *blocks.* The width of a column or block of text varies, depending on the size of the text and the format of the document. The text in posters, advertisements, and fliers, for example, is usually set in blocks so that it may be read quickly. Text in textbooks, reference books, and newspapers, which contain large quantities of information, usually appears in columns. (See also **Line Length** on page 809.)

Desktop Publishing   **807**

Contrast   *Contrast* refers to the balance of light and dark areas on a page. Dark areas are those that contain blocks of text or visuals. Light areas have little type. A page with high contrast—a balance of light and dark— is easier to read than a page with low contrast—either mostly light or mostly dark. (See also **Contrast** on page 814 and **White Space** on page 810.)

Emphasis   *Emphasis* indicates to a reader which information on a page is most important. For example, the front page of a newspaper uses bold or large headlines and photographs to place emphasis on a particular story. Because readers' eyes are drawn naturally to color, large or bold print, and graphics, these elements are commonly used to create emphasis.

Graphic   A *graphic* is a picture, chart, illustration, or piece of artwork that is used to convey information visually. Short sections of text, such as headings, subheadings, titles, headers, and footers, may also be considered graphics because they serve a visual function. (See also **Visuals** on page 809.)

Gray Page   A *gray page* contains text almost exclusively. It has few or no graphics to indicate visually the organization or structure of the material on the page.

Grid Lines   *Grid lines* are vertical and horizontal intersecting lines that provide structure to a page by dividing it into neat sections. Often grid lines are used to plan the layout or final appearance of a page and do not appear in the printed version of the document.

Gutter   A *gutter* is the margin of space or crevice between two facing pages in a bound book. For example, the gutter on this page runs between this page and the page on the right.

Headers and Footers   *Headers* and *footers* provide information about a printed document. Headers appear in the top margin of a page, and footers appear in the bottom margin. Headers and footers may include

- the name of the author
- the name and date of the publication
- chapter or section titles
- page numbers

Headings and Subheadings   *Headings* and *subheadings* (also called *heads* and *subheads*) are used to give readers clues about the content and organization of a document.

- **Headings**   A *heading* gives readers a general idea what a section of text, such as a chapter, will be about. Headings appear at the beginning of a section of text and are usually set in large, bold letters. Often they appear in a typeface different from that of the body of the text.

- **Subheadings**   A *subheading* is more descriptive than a heading and is used to indicate subsections of the text. Several subheadings usually appear under one heading. Like headings, subheadings are also set in large letters, in bold or italic font, or in a different typeface to distinguish them from the headings and the text.

EXAMPLE

Common Household Pests (heading)
What Makes These Pests Tick? (subheading)

Ants and roaches are common household pests that are difficult to eliminate,   text especially in the warm summer months.

Indentation   *Indentation* is the skipping of a few letter spaces to indicate the beginning of a new paragraph in a text. Whether you are using a computer or writing your work by hand, the indentation should be one-half of an inch from the left margin. If you are working on a computer or typewriter, one-half of an inch is equivalent to five letter spaces. Indentation is also used with bulleted lists.

Line Length   *Line length* is the number of characters (letters, spaces between words, and punctuation marks) a line contains. (Remember, a line is not a sentence; it is a single line of text that may or may not form a complete thought.) The best line length for a document depends on the size of the type and the format of the document. In general, limit line length to sixty-five characters, or about nine or ten words. This makes the text easier to read. (Remember that one goal of desktop publishing is to design texts that are clear and accessible to readers.)

Margins   *Margins* are the spaces that surround the text on a page. Most computer word-processing programs automatically set the side margins at one and one-quarter inches and the top and bottom margins at one inch. Margins are flexible, however. If your teacher recommends different measurements for the margins of your papers, use them instead. (See also **White Space** on page 810 and **Guidelines for Handwritten or Typed Manuscripts** on page 806.)

Pull-quote   A *pull-quote* is a quotation from a text, such as a magazine article or story, that has been turned into an eye-catching graphic and set in the margin. The purpose of the pull-quote is to catch the reader's attention. Consequently, pull-quotes should be short but intriguing "hooks." They should also be quotations that state or suggest an important idea or event in the text.

EXAMPLE

Once upon a time in the middle of winter, when the flakes of snow were falling like feathers from the sky, a Queen sat at a window sewing, and the frame of the window was made of black ebony. And whilst she *"Three drops of blood fell upon the snow."* was sewing and looking out of the window at the snow, she pricked her finger with the needle, and three drops of blood fell upon the snow.

Rule Lines   *Rule lines* are lines used graphically to create visual effects on a page. Rule lines may be thick or thin, vertical or horizontal, and they may separate columns, set text off from a headline or caption, or draw your eye to something on the page. The box around the passage above shows how rule lines may be used.

Title and Subtitle   A *title* is the name of an entire document. *Subtitles* are longer and more descriptive than titles. Often a subtitle is separated from a title by a colon and appears in a smaller typeface. In books, titles and subtitles appear alone on a page (the title page) at the very beginning of the book.

EXAMPLE

The People's Chronology: *A Year-by-Year Record of Human Events from Prehistory to the Present*

Visuals   *Visuals,* like *graphics,* are pictures, charts, illustrations, or artwork that convey information. (See also **Types of Graphics and**

Visuals on page 815 and the "Graphics and Visuals" section on page 813.)

White space   *White space* is any area on a page where there is little or no text, visuals, or graphics. It provides a contrast to the dark ink on a page and helps make the page more readable. Usually, white space is limited to the margins, the gutter, and the spaces between words, lines, and columns. (See also **Contrast** below.)

Type

Type is a particular style of letter and markings used in printing and publishing. When movable type was first introduced, the letters of the type were modeled on handwritten characters or the lettering in manuscript books.

Capital Letters   *Capital* (or *uppercase*) *letters* help readers identify the beginning of a new sentence or idea. Capital letters attract readers' attention and may be used in the following ways to create emphasis in a document.

■ **Dropped or initial cap**   A *dropped* or *initial cap* is an artistic use of a capital letter in the first word of the first paragraph of a text or a section of a text. Dropped caps imitate medieval illuminated manuscripts in which the first letter of a section or chapter was enlarged and transformed into a colorful drawing.

EXAMPLE

O nce upon a time
in the middle of winter . . .

■ **Headings or titles**   Setting a *heading* or *title* in all capital letters helps to create emphasis and contrast in a document such as a newspaper article, especially when the head-

ing or title is in the same typeface as the rest of the text. (See also **Contrast** and **Emphasis** on page 814.)

EXAMPLES

LOCAL STUDENT TO GO TO NATIONAL SPELLING BEE

METAPHORS, SIMILES, AND PERSONIFICATION

■ **Small caps**   *Small caps* are uppercase letters that are reduced in size and used as lowercase letters. Usually they appear in abbreviations of time, such as *9:00 A.M.* and *A.D. 1500*. Small caps may also be combined with true capital letters for an artistic effect.

NOTE   Capital letters can be difficult to read. Use capital letters for contrast or emphasis, not for large bodies of text.

Captions   *Captions* are lines of text that appear under photographs or illustrations. They explain the meaning or importance of a visual and connect it to the text. Because readers tend to look first at the visuals on a page, captions are often the first text they read. Consequently, captions should be concise, accurate, and interesting. Captions may appear in a smaller size type (usually two point sizes smaller) than the main text or in the same type size but italicized. (See also **Font** and **Font, or Point, Size** on page 811.)

Contrast   In terms of typeface, *contrast* refers to the visual effect of using different typefaces in a document. For instance, you might use one typeface for the body of your text and one for the headings and subheadings. Too many different typefaces, however, can create too much contrast, which makes a document difficult to read. (See also **Contrast** on page 814.)

Font A *font* is a complete set of characters of a particular design. In computer software, the word "font" usually stands for a particular typeface which can be manipulated. Size is one of the most common manipulations of font; others are between roman (meaning, in this case, "not slanted") and italic, or between capital letters and lowercase letters. Look at the following examples of fonts. (See also **Fonts, Categories of,** and **Fonts, Styles of** on this page.)

EXAMPLES

ROMAN CAPITALS	*ITALIC CAPITALS*
SMALL CAPITALS	roman lowercase letters
italic lowercase letters	

Font, or Point, Size The size of the type in a document is called the ***font,*** or ***point, size.*** Word-processing software provides many options for sizing text. Many textbooks use type measured at twelve points. Type for headings and headlines may range anywhere from eighteen to forty-eight points. Captions usually appear in nine- to eleven-point type.

Fonts, Categories of The *categories of fonts* refer to a particular style of characters used in print. There are thousands of fonts available, each with its own name and unique appearance. Most typefaces, however, belong to one of the three categories listed below.

■ **Decorative, or script** *Decorative,* or *script,* typefaces have elaborately designed characters that convey a distinct mood or feeling. They can be used to create an artistic effect; however, they should be used sparingly because they are difficult to read.

EXAMPLES

This is an example of Zapf Chancery typeface.

This is an example of Fresh Script typeface.

This is an example of Linoscript typeface.

■ **Sans serif** The characters in *sans-serif* typefaces are formed by neat straight lines, with no small strokes at the ends of the letters. (*Sans serif* means "without serifs, or strokes.") Sans-serif typefaces work well as headings and subheadings, pull-quotes, and captions because they have clean edges and are easy to read in small amounts. (See also **Legibility** on page 812.)

EXAMPLES

Gill Sans is a sans-serif typeface.

Helvetica is a sans-serif typeface.

Futura is a sans-serif typeface.

■ **Serif** The characters in *serif* typefaces have little strokes (*serifs*) attached at each end. Serif typeface was the first style of typeface to be invented and used in printing. The serifs or strokes are believed to be modeled on the connectors between handwritten letters, on which serif type was based. As in handwriting, the little strokes help guide the readers' eyes from letter to letter and word to word. Because of their legibility, serifs are still commonly used to set large bodies of type.

EXAMPLES

Palatino is a serif typeface.

New Century Schoolbook is a serif typeface.

Times is a serif typeface.

NOTE Mixing decorative, sans-serif, and serif typefaces on a page creates high contrast. However, you should generally not use more than two typefaces on a page because too many can confuse readers.

Fonts, Styles of The *styles of fonts* can provide emphasis and contrast to your regular typeface. For example, titles of books or films and captions are often set in *italics.* **Boldface** or *boldface italic* can highlight new or important concepts. In addition, computers and desktop publishing software have made fonts from the printing industry available on computers. Look at the following examples of eye-catching fonts. (See also **Fonts, Categories of** on page 811.)

roman boldface	roman shadow font
roman condensed	***italic boldface***
roman outline font	roman expanded
roman underscored	

NOTE Use care in selecting font styles; avoid using too many styles in any one document. Also be consistent in your use of font styles. For example, if you use italic boldface for one heading, use it for all other headings as well. Remember that your reader may be confused if you change font styles frequently or inconsistently.

Knockout, or Reversed, Type *Knockout,* or *reversed, type* is light type set against a contrasting, dark background for contrast or emphasis. (See also **Contrast** and **Emphasis** on page 814.)

EXAMPLES
Here is dark type set against a light background.
Here is knockout, or reversed, type.

Leading or Line Spacing *Leading* (rhymes with *sledding*), or *line spacing,* is the distance in points between lines of text. Most word processors and typewriters allow you to adjust the amount of line spacing to single-, double-, or even triple-space measurements.

Legibility *Legibility* refers to the ease with which a reader can decipher a short section of text like a headline or cross reference. Clear typefaces and simple fonts in readable sizes make a text more legible.

Lowercase *Lowercase* type consists of lowercase letters, as opposed to capital letters. Lowercase letters are characterized by *ascenders* (rising strokes, as in the letters b and h) and *descenders* (dropping strokes, as in the letters g and y). Most text that you read or write will appear in lowercase type because it is more legible than uppercase type. (See also **Legibility** above.)

Readability *Readability* refers to how easily a text can be read. Unlike legibility, readability refers to the ease of reading long sections of text. Documents with high readability often contain text set in a classic serif typeface (like the Minion typeface you are reading at this moment). (See also **Type** on page 810, **Fonts, Categories of** on page 811, **Font, styles of** on page 811, and **Legibility** above.)

Graphics and Visuals

Graphics and visuals consist of pictures, charts, and other visual representations that are used to

- organize and display data or information
- explain a process or a relationship
- illustrate how something looks, works, or is organized
- show changes over time

It is important to select and develop graphics and visuals carefully. They should convey information clearly and support directly the text that appears on the page. For example, a graph showing the rate of extinction of animal species in the Amazon River Basin would be inappropriate in a text discussing the rate of extinction of animal species in California.

Arrangement and Design

The challenge of designing a document that contains text and graphics or visuals is to arrange all the parts in a way that communicates information and ideas effectively. When you design a document that includes graphics and visuals, consider the following elements.

Accessibility *Accessibility* refers to the ease with which readers can find information in a document. Increase a document's accessibility by labeling any graphics or visuals clearly—their relationship to the text should be immediately clear to readers. (See also **Captions** on page 810 and **Font, Styles of** on page 811.)

Accuracy All graphics or visuals must contain *accurate,* or true, information. Be sure that any data included in a graphic is reliable, up-to-date, and completely accurate. Just as readers must be able to trust the information in the text

of your document, they must also be confident of data in graphics and visuals. Never change data in order to better support your argument.

Color Color naturally attracts a reader's eye, especially when it contrasts with the black and white of text and white space. Color may be used to

- attract the reader's attention
- highlight a piece of information
- indicate that certain items on a page belong together
- show the organization of the parts of a document or page

When choosing colors for your document, remember the following guidelines.

1. **Use colors for emphasis, not for long sections of text.** Some readers might find color text difficult to read. Color should serve a purpose, not just be decorative.
2. **Use two or more colors, but avoid an over-abundance of colors.** Two or more colors provide contrast. A single color, however, will simply look out of place. At the same time, too many colors can confuse your readers. Use a few colors consistently to convey the meaning in a graphic or visual.
3. **Use cool colors, such as blue and green, as background.** These colors have a calming effect.
4. **Use warm colors, such as red and orange, sparingly.** These colors appear to expand or jump off the page.
5. **Choose colors that complement each other.** The colors that appear opposite one another on the color wheel shown on the next page are complementary.

Graphics and Visuals **813**

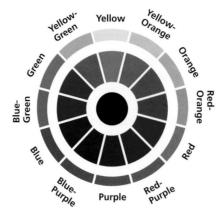

The color wheel above shows how colors relate to one another. The primary colors are yellow, red, and blue; all other colors are the result of combining these colors or mixing them with white or black.

Contrast   *Contrast* is the effect of a striking difference between two things. Contrast can attract attention and make it easier for readers to visualize your text and remember its content. To create contrast within graphics and visuals, use different visual cues for different kinds of information. For example, use different colors for each of the wedges of a pie chart. (See also **Contrast** on page 810 and **Fonts, Styles of** on page 811.)

Emphasis   You can create emphasis by using visual cues—such as color, capital letters, boldface or italic fonts, and large type size—to draw readers' attention to what you want them to see. Visuals and graphics always provide emphasis because they attract a reader's attention before anything else on the page. (See also **Emphasis** on page 808.)

Focus   The content of a visual such as an illustration, photograph, or drawing is its *focus.*

When you choose a visual, always make sure that its focus reinforces the text. Use the following guidelines when choosing visuals to include in your document.

1. Make sure that the subject and its relationship to the text are immediately clear.
2. Crop, or trim, any distracting details.
3. Make sure the subject is shown from an angle that corresponds with the reference to it in the text. For example, if the text refers to an aerial view of Mount Fuji, be sure that the visual shows an aerial view.
4. Make sure the visual includes everything you want to show the reader about the subject. For example, a map of Africa that omits places discussed in the document should be replaced with a map that includes those places.
5. Add any captions or labels that readers will need in order to understand a visual. However, be careful not to add so many labels that the visual becomes cluttered or unclear.
6. Choose visuals that have a tone similar to the tone of the text. For instance, if the text discusses a comical topic, then the visuals and graphics should be equally funny or playful, rather than formal and serious.

Integration   *Integration* refers to the way visuals and text fit together on a page. Visuals and text that are related or cover the same material should be placed close together. In addition, the text should direct the reader's attention to the visual and explain its content.

EXAMPLE

The data in the bar graph below shows that freshmen and juniors are more likely to vote in student elections than sophomores and seniors.

Labels and Captions   To help readers understand them, many graphics and visuals need *labels, captions,* or both. Labels can be used to identify the contents of charts, tables, and diagrams. Usually they appear within the body of the graphic or visual, but sometimes they are linked to the visual or graphic by thin rule lines. As a rule, avoid using more than five labels per visual. Captions are usually full sentences that describe a visual such as a photograph or illustration. They appear directly under, beside, or above the visual. (For examples of labels and captions, see page 817.)

Organization *Organization* refers to the arrangement of text and graphics or visuals on a page. All the elements that deal with a similar subject should be grouped or "chunked" together. Use visual cues such as headings and subheadings, similar typefaces, color, and rule lines to show that certain text and visual elements are related. (See also **Integration** on page 814.)

Type Size and Font Text that appears in visuals and graphics should be obviously different from the main text. The type may appear in the same font as the main text, but should be one to two and one-half points smaller, or in italics. You can also provide a visual contrast by setting all labels and captions in a contrasting typeface. (See also **Labels and Captions** on page 814 and **Fonts, Styles of** on page 811.)

Types of Graphics and Visuals

Graphics and visuals can add to the effectiveness and appeal of a document, but how do you decide which kind to use? Here are some of the different types of graphics and visuals from which you can choose.

Charts *Charts* show relationships among ideas or data. Two types of charts you are likely to use are flowcharts and pie charts.

■ **Flowcharts** A *flowchart* uses geometric shapes linked by arrows to show the sequence of events in a process. Labels are placed inside the shapes, and the direction of the flow is from left to right and from top to bottom.

EXAMPLE

Writing the First Draft of a Research Paper

■ **Pie charts** A *pie chart* is a circle that is divided into wedges. Each wedge represents a certain percentage of the total.

EXAMPLE

Career Goals of Seniors at Felicity High School

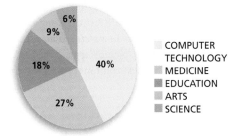

Diagrams *Diagrams* are simple line drawings that can be used to show what something looks like, how something works, or how to do something. Some diagrams are realistic, while others are more abstract, using shapes or symbols to represent things. Diagrams can be drawn by hand or generated by a computer, and they are almost always spare, showing only important details. The diagram below shows how to measure an angle with a protractor.

EXAMPLE

Graphs *Graphs* use numbers to present facts and figures. There are two types of *graphs,* both used to show how one thing changes in relation to another. For instance, a graph might show how the time a person spends watching television changes in relation to the person's age.

■ **Bar graphs** A *bar graph* can be used to compare quantities at a glance, to show trends or changes over time, or to indicate the parts of a whole. Bar graphs are formed along a vertical and horizontal axis. In a *pictograph,* a special kind of bar graph, pictures replace the bars. The example in the next column shows a bar graph.

EXAMPLE

■ **Line graphs** A *line graph* can be used to show changes or trends over time, to compare trends, or to show how two or more variables interact.

EXAMPLE

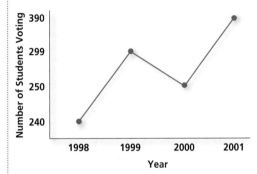

Illustrations *Illustrations,* such as drawings, photographs, and other artwork, may be used to show readers

■ something new, unfamiliar, or indescribable

■ how something works

■ what something or someone looks like

The photograph on the next page illustrates the powerful but graceful swing of baseball player Joe DiMaggio during his record hitting streak in 1941.

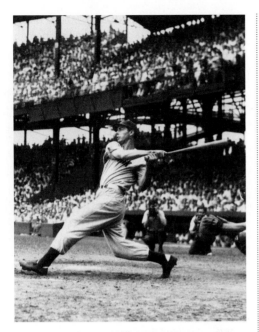

Tables   Using rows and columns, *tables* provide detailed information arranged in an accessible, organized way. In the following examples, notice that information is logically organized and clearly labeled.

EXAMPLES

Two-Column Table

Numbers of Students Voting in School Elections	
Year	Numbers of Students Voting
1998	240
1999	299
2000	250
2001	390

Three-column Table

Numbers of Students Voting in School Elections by Class and Gender		
Class	Numbers of Females Voting	Numbers of Males Voting
Freshmen	60	40
Sophomores	55	50
Juniors	100	97
Seniors	76	85

Storyboards   *Storyboards* depict the scenes of a narrative and can be used to plan a video or to map out the events in a story. They usually consist of boxes containing drawings and text, although sometimes the text appears outside or under the boxes, called *panels*. The following example shows two of the panels that a student created while making a documentary film about school elections.

Allison Gomez giving her campaign speech

Gomez answering students' questions

Graphics and Visuals   **817**

Time Lines *Time lines* identify the events that have taken place over a given period of time. Usually, events are identified or described above the time line and the time demarcations are indicated below it. Some time lines are illustrated.

EXAMPLE

Events in the History of the City of London

Time lines are sometimes used to present the main events in the life of a famous person. In this case, the time line is often arranged vertically in two columns, with the dates in the left column and the corresponding events in the right.

EXAMPLE

Events in the Life of Mark Twain	
1835	Born Samuel Langhorne Clemens in Florida, Missouri.
1853	Began traveling and working as a journeyman printer in St. Louis, Cincinnati, Philadelphia, and New York
1856	Became a river pilot, navigating steamboats on the Mississippi River
1862	Took a job for the *Virginia City Territorial Enterprise* and began writing articles and stories for the paper under the pseudonym Mark Twain
1867	Published *Innocents Abroad*
1870	Married Olivia Langdon
1876	Published *Tom Sawyer*
1883	Published *Life on the Mississippi*
1884	Published *The Adventures of Huckleberry Finn*
1894	Traveled abroad giving lectures to pay for increasing debts
1904	Suffered the death of his wife Livy
1910	Died of angina and heart disease

The History of English: Origins and Uses

History of English

The English language was first written about 1,300 years ago, but was spoken long before that. Over the centuries, English has grown and changed to become the rich, expressive language we use today. The history of this development is a story of people, places, and times.

Beginnings of English   Many of the world's languages come from an early language called *Proto-Indo-European.* We have no records of this parent language, but it was probably spoken by Eastern Europeans six or seven thousand years ago. Tribes of these people slowly migrated across Europe and to India. As they wandered in different directions, each tribe

developed its own *dialect,* or distinct version of the language. The dialects eventually developed into separate languages. The map on this page shows how the Indo-European root word *mater* (mother) developed in some of these languages. The arrows indicate directions of migration.

Old English   Around A.D. 450, tribes known as the Angles and the Saxons invaded Britain. They took over land that had been settled earlier by the Celts. The separate dialects these tribes spoke eventually blended into one language—*Old English,* sometimes called Anglo-Saxon. Modern English still bears traces of its Anglo-Saxon roots. For example, the words *eat, drink,* and *sleep* come from the Old English words *etan, drincan,* and *slæp.* The Anglo-Saxons used an *–s* to form the plurals of many nouns, just as we do. We also have Old English to thank for irregular verb forms such as *swim, swam,* and *swum.*

Middle English   In 1066, the Normans from France seized control of England. For the next 150 years, French was the official language of government, business, and law. Because of this,

The History of English: Origins and Uses   **819**

many English words that are connected with wealth and power come from the French, such as *governor, attorney,* and *fashion.* The common people of England, however, still spoke English—a changing form of the language we call ***Middle English.*** The grammar of English was becoming simpler as many of the complicated word endings disappeared.

The following lines are matching excerpts from the Lord's Prayer (Matthew 6:9–13) in Old English and Middle English. As you can see, Middle English looks much more like the English you know.

> **Old English:** Fæder ure þu þe eart on heofonum, si þin nama gehalgod.

> **Middle English:** Fader oure þat art in hevene, i-halwed bee þi name.

Modern English   Before 1476, speakers and writers in different parts of England used different versions of the language, and therefore they often had trouble understanding each other. When William Caxton set up the first printing press in England around 1476, all of this changed. Early printers standardized spelling, and since London was the center of English trade and culture, they printed all books in London English. London English soon became the standard throughout England. Once standards were set, people wanted to learn the proper way to speak and write their language. Soon, grammar and usage handbooks sprang up, along with the first English dictionaries.

Two other factors influenced Modern English. One factor was its expansion into an international language through the discovery of new lands. From the sixteenth century through the nineteenth century, English merchants, explorers, and settlers spread English to other parts of the globe. They also learned new words from other languages, enriching English with international imports.

EXAMPLES
Japanese: soy   **Dutch:** cruise
Turkish: yogurt   **Spanish:** siesta

The language was also affected by the scientific revolution of this time. Words had to be created to name the new discoveries being made.

EXAMPLES
atmosphere   pneumonia   skeleton

American English   Immigration to the American colonies brought about a new version of the language—***American English.*** Like the United States itself, American English represents a variety of cultures and peoples. Native Americans, Africans, and immigrants from most countries around the world have enriched the language with words from their native tongues. For example, Native Americans gave us *coyote* and *squash; jazz* and *gumbo* came from Africa; and Italian immigrants added *spaghetti* and *ravioli* to the menu.

English in the Twenty-first Century
English has become the most widely used language in the history of the world, with over 750 million users. It is an official language in eighty-seven nations and territories. It is the world language of diplomacy, science, technology, aviation, and international trade. As people around the world contribute to the language, the word count grows. The last count was over 600,000 words. The count grows so quickly that dictionary makers cannot keep up with the growth of English vocabulary.

Varieties of English

English is a rich and flexible language that offers many choices. To speak and write effectively—at home, at school, and on the job—you need to know what the varieties of English are and how to choose among them.

Dialects of American English
Like all languages, American English has many distinct versions, called **dialects.** Everyone uses a dialect, and no dialect is better or worse than another. Each has unique features of grammar, vocabulary, and pronunciation.

■ **Regional dialects** The United States has four major regional dialects: the *Northern,* the *Midland,* the *Southern,* and the *Western.* Pronunciations of words often vary from one dialect region to another. For example, some Southerners pronounce the words *ten* and *tin* the same way—as "tin." Similarly, regions differ in grammar and vocabulary. For example, you may say "sick *to* my stomach" if you come from New York but "sick *at* my stomach" if you come from Georgia. You may drink *soda, tonic,* or *pop* depending on what part of the country you come from.

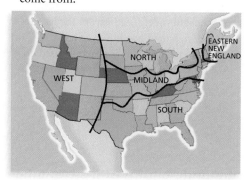

■ **Ethnic dialects** An ethnic dialect is used by people who share the same cultural heritage. Because Americans come from many different cultures, American English includes many different ethnic dialects. The most widely used ethnic dialects are African American Vernacular English and the Hispanic English of many people from Cuba, Mexico, Central America, and Puerto Rico. Many everyday words began as ethnic dialect words but then became part of the general English vocabulary. For example, *tote* and *chigger* came into English through Black dialect, and *avocado* and *taco* were added to English by Hispanic Americans.

Standard American English
Every variety of English has its own set of rules and guidelines. No variety is the best or the most correct. However, ***Standard American English*** (SAE) is the one variety of English that is more widely used and accepted than others in the United States. Because it is commonly understood, SAE allows people from many different regions and cultures to communicate with one another clearly. It is the variety of English you read and hear most often in books and magazines, on radio and television. It is the kind of English that people are expected to use in most school and business situations. This textbook presents many of the rules and guidelines for using standard American English. To identify the differences between standard American English and other varieties of English, this book uses the labels *standard* and *nonstandard.* Nonstandard does not mean wrong language. It means language that is inappropriate in situations where standard English is expected.

Standard English—Formal to Informal

Depending on your audience, purpose, and occasion, the language you use can be formal, informal, or somewhere in between. The following chart shows some of the appropriate uses of very formal and very informal English.

Uses of Formal and Informal English

Formal

Speaking: formal, dignified occasions, such as banquets and dedication ceremonies

Writing: serious papers and reports, tests, business letters

Informal

Speaking: everyday conversation at home, school, work, and recreation

Writing: personal letters, journal entries, and many newspaper and magazine articles

---

You can say the same thing in many different ways. For example, *chow down* and *dine* both mean "eat," but one is much more formal than the other. The main differences between formal and informal English are in sentence structure, word choice, and tone.

Features of Formal and Informal English

Formal

Sentence Structure: longer and more complex

Word Choice: precise, often technical or scientific

Tone: serious and dignified

Informal

Sentence Structure: shorter and simpler

Word Choice: simple and ordinary; often includes contractions, colloquialisms, and slang

Tone: conversational

Uses of Informal English In informal speaking and writing, people constantly make up new words and give new uses to old ones. This makes informal English flexible. Dictionaries help you to see this flexibility by giving labels to different informal uses of words. The two most commonly listed usage labels are **colloquialisms** and **slang.**

- **Colloquialisms** *Colloquialisms* are the informal words and phrases of conversational language. They bring flavor and color to everyday speech and a friendly, conversational tone to writing. Many are figures of speech that aren't meant to be taken literally.

  EXAMPLES

  I may have made a mistake, but you don't have to **fly off the handle** about it.

  Today, many young couples **foot the bill** for their weddings rather than having their parents pay for them.

  My mother told us to quit **making such a racket.**

- **Slang** *Slang* is made up of newly coined words or of old words used in unconventional ways. It is usually clever and colorful. It is often a special language for specific groups of people, such as students and military personnel. Some people use slang to be up-to-date. Sometimes a slang word becomes a lasting and widely used part of the language. More often than not, however, it lives a short and limited life. Slang is generally used only in the most informal speaking situations.

  EXAMPLES

  beat—tired
  bummer—a depressing experience
  cool—pleasing, excellent
  hassle—to annoy, harass
  kooky—strange

The Library/ Media Center

Using Print and Electronic Sources

The library/media center in your school or community provides you with a range of print and electronic sources of information. *Print sources* include books, periodicals (magazines, newspapers, and journals), and specialized forms (such as microforms or vertical files). *Electronic sources* include CD-ROMs, the Internet, DVDs, and online databases. To determine whether a particular source suits your specific purpose, use the features discussed in this section.

> **TIP** Do not limit your searches for information to the library. Real-world documents—schedules, directories, maps, technical directions, user manuals, warranties, product information, and government records—can be excellent sources for specific purposes.

Call Number A *call number* is a unique code assigned to a book in a library. The call number indicates how a book is classified and where it is shelved in the library. The two systems of classification are the Dewey decimal system and the Library of Congress system.

- **Dewey decimal system**   The *Dewey decimal system* assigns numbers to nonfiction books according to ten general subject areas.
- **Library of Congress system**   *The Library of Congress system* uses call numbers that include code letters to identify subject categories. The first code letter identifies a book's general category (such as history) and the second letter identifies the subcategory (such as the Middle Ages). Numbers also identify specific books within a category.

Card Catalog A *card catalog* is a collection of index cards that contains important information about the books in a library. For each book, there are at least two cards, a *title card* and an *author card.* If the book is nonfiction, there is also a third card, a *subject card.* The cards are arranged in alphabetical order and contain the following information:

- The **call number** assigned by the Library of Congress or Dewey decimal system
- The **author's full name,** last name first

- The full **title** and **subtitle** of a book
- The place and date of **publication**
- The general **subject** of a book; a subject card may show specific headings
- A **description** of the book, such as its size and number of pages, and whether it is illustrated
- **Cross-references** to other headings or related topics under which a book is listed

As libraries acquire computer technology, however, card catalogs in drawers are being converted to electronic or online formats. (See also **Online Card Catalog** on this page.)

CD-ROMs A *CD-ROM* (*C*ompact *D*isc-*R*ead *O*nly *M*emory) is a compact disc that is designed to hold visual as well as audio information. The data is encoded digitally and can be accessed only by a computer with a CD-ROM drive. A single CD-ROM may contain the equivalent of 250,000 pages of printed text. Many reference tools, such as encyclopedias, dictionaries, and indexes, are now available on CD-ROMs. CD-ROMs contain the same text as the printed versions but have the added attractions of searching capabilities, interactive graphics, and audio. (See also the **Reference Sources chart** on page 826.)

Internet The *Internet* is a global network of computers. With the Internet, a computer user may access information from another computer or network of computers anywhere in the world. Created in the late 1960s, the Internet was originally used by research scientists to share data electronically with each other. The content exchanged on the Internet has since expanded beyond scientific matters to include almost any topic. The Internet may be used by almost anyone who has a computer equipped with a modem. There are many ways to view material on the Internet, including FTP (File Transfer Protocol), Gopher, and Telnet; as well as *World Wide Web browsers,* which provide access to files and documents, news and discussion groups, bulletin boards, e-mail, and the *World Wide Web* (see page 827). The World Wide Web is the place on the Internet you are most likely to go for your research. (See also the **Evaluating Web Sites chart** on page 831.)

Microforms *Microforms,* photographically reduced articles from newspapers and magazines, can be either *microfilm* or *microfiche.* Special machines are needed to enlarge microfilm and microfiche images and project them onto a screen for viewing or reading.

Online Card Catalog An *online card catalog* is an electronic or computerized version of the card catalog. Instead of searching through individual cards, you may find a book by typing in a book's *title, author,* or *subject.* (If you don't have a specific book in mind, you may type in *key words* that may appear in the title or description of the book.) The computer retrieves information based on your request.

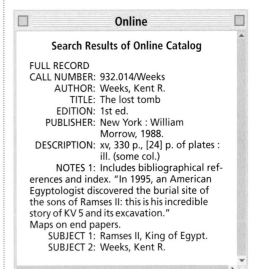

Online

Search Results of Online Catalog

FULL RECORD
CALL NUMBER: 932.014/Weeks
AUTHOR: Weeks, Kent R.
TITLE: The lost tomb
EDITION: 1st ed.
PUBLISHER: New York : William Morrow, 1988.
DESCRIPTION: xv, 330 p., [24] p. of plates : ill. (some col.)
NOTES 1: Includes bibliographical references and index. "In 1995, an American Egyptologist discovered the burial site of the sons of Ramses II: this is his incredible story of KV 5 and its excavation."
Maps on end papers.
SUBJECT 1: Ramses II, King of Egypt.
SUBJECT 2: Weeks, Kent R.

Online Databases An *online database* is a contained system of electronic information that may be accessed only by computer. In most cases, organizations such as universities, libraries, or businesses create or subscribe to databases that are of specific interest to people in the organizations. LEXIS/NEXIS is an example of a subscription-only database. Some databases are public and may be accessed through the World Wide Web.

Online Sources Information that is *online* is information that may be located and accessed by using computers. Computers that are online are able to communicate with each other over telecommunication lines, such as telephone lines and fiber-optic cables, and via satellite. When computers are linked, they form a *network.* Computer networks are what make the Internet and the World Wide Web possible.

Radio, Television, and Film *Radio* and *television* are important sources of news and information. Newscasts, newsmagazines, and documentaries are regular features on radio and television. Documentaries and educational materials are also produced on *film* or *video.* Descriptive listings of radio and television programs appear in newspapers and, in some cases, on the Internet. Indexes of educational films and videos, such as *The Video Source Book* (Gale, 1998) are available at libraries and bookstores. Be sure to check the ratings provided for the films and videos before viewing them.

Readers' Guide to Periodical Literature The *Readers' Guide to Periodical Literature* is an index of articles from more than two hundred fifty magazines and journals (periodicals). As the sample entry on this page shows, the articles are listed alphabetically by author and by subject; the

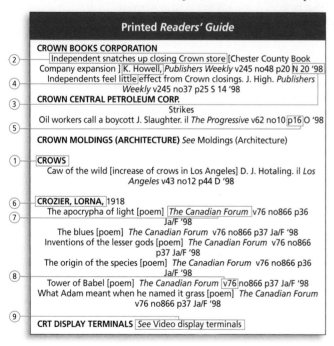

Printed *Readers' Guide*

CROWN BOOKS CORPORATION
(2) Independent snatches up closing Crown store [Chester County Book Company expansion] K. Howell, *Publishers Weekly* v245 no48 p20 N 20 '98
(4) Independents feel little effect from Crown closings. J. High. *Publishers Weekly* v245 no37 p25 S 14 '98
(3) CROWN CENTRAL PETROLEUM CORP.
Strikes
(5) Oil workers call a boycott J. Slaughter. il *The Progressive* v62 no10 p16 O '98

CROWN MOLDINGS (ARCHITECTURE) *See* Moldings (Architecture)

(1) CROWS
Caw of the wild [increase of crows in Los Angeles] D. J. Hotaling. il *Los Angeles* v43 no12 p44 D '98

(6) CROZIER, LORNA, 1918
(7) The apocrypha of light [poem] *The Canadian Forum* v76 no866 p36 Ja/F '98
The blues [poem] *The Canadian Forum* v76 no866 p37 Ja/F '98
Inventions of the lesser gods [poem] *The Canadian Forum* v76 no866 p37 Ja/F '98
The origin of the species [poem] *The Canadian Forum* v76 no866 p36 Ja/F '98
(8) Tower of Babel [poem] *The Canadian Forum* v76 no866 p37 Ja/F '98
What Adam meant when he named it grass [poem] *The Canadian Forum* v76 no866 p37 Ja/F '98

(9) CRT DISPLAY TERMINALS *See* Video display terminals

1. Subject entry
2. Title of article
3. Date of periodical
4. Author of article
5. Page reference
6. Author entry
7. Name of periodical
8. Volume number of periodical
9. Subject cross-reference

headings are set in boldface type. A key located in the front of the *Readers' Guide* explains the meanings of the abbreviations used in the entries.

Reference Books   Reference books are books of specialized information. Examples include encyclopedias, dictionaries, thesauri, indexes, books of quotations, atlases, and almanacs. Reference books focus on one particular topic or kind of information. The information is organized in a logical way, such as alphabetical or chronological order or by category. (See also the **Reference Sources chart** below.)

Reference Sources   There are many different kinds of reference sources that you can use to find specific kinds of information. The chart below identifies and describes common reference sources and provides examples of print and electronic reference sources.

Reference Sources		
Types	**Description**	**Examples**
ALMANACS	Information about current events, facts, statistics, and dates	• *Information Please Almanac* • *The 20th Century Video Almanac* CD-ROM
ATLASES	Maps and geographical information	• *Hammond Atlas of the World* • *Microsoft Encarta World Atlas* CD-ROM
BIOGRAPHICAL REFERENCES (GENERAL)	Information about birth, nationality, and major accomplishments of prominent people	• *Who's Who in America* • *Who's Who 1897–1996: One Hundred Years of Biography* CD-ROM
BIOGRAPHICAL REFERENCES (SPECIALIZED)	Information about people noted for accomplishments in a field or for membership in a group	• *Who's Who Among African Americans* • *Dictionary of Women Artists* • *American Indian: A Multimedia CD-ROM*
BOOKS OF QUOTATIONS	Famous quotations indexed or grouped together by subject	• *The Oxford Dictionary of Quotations* • *Bartlett's Familiar Quotations* CD-ROM
BOOKS OF SYNONYMS	Lists of exact or more interesting words to express ideas	• *Roget's International Thesaurus* • *Oxford Thesaurus on CD-ROM*
ENCYCLOPEDIAS	Articles of general information arranged alphabetically by subject in several volumes	• *The World Book Multimedia Encyclopedia*™ • *Compton's Interactive Encyclopedia* CD-ROM
LITERARY REFERENCES	Information about various works of literature and authors	• *Contemporary Literary Criticism* • *Gale's Literary Index CD-ROM*
STYLE AND WRITING MANUALS	Information about proper writing style and preparation of research papers	• *The Chicago Manual of Style* • *Harbrace College Handbook* CD-ROM • *MLA Style Manual and Guide to Scholarly Publishing*

Vertical File   A *vertical file* is a set of file drawers containing up-to-date materials that are not likely to be cataloged anywhere else, such as pamphlets, newspaper clippings, and photographs. As the use of electronic resources such as the Internet increases, vertical files are less likely to be maintained by libraries in the future.

World Wide Web (*WWW* or the *Web*)
The *World Wide Web* is one part of the Internet. The Web is an enormous system of connected, or linked, documents that contain text, graphics and visuals, sounds, and even video. Documents (*Web sites* or *Web pages*) on the World Wide Web are connected by *hyperlinks.* Clicking on a hyperlink quickly brings up a new site on your screen. To navigate or view the World Wide Web, you must have *browser* software installed on your computer.

World Wide Web, Key Terms   The following terms will help you understand the workings of the World Wide Web.

- **Browser**   A *browser* is a software application that allows you to find and access information on the Web. It allows you to explore, read, save, and download documents, images, sounds, and videos that you may find there. Using a browser to locate and read documents is called *browsing.* (See also **Web Site** on the next page.)

- **Domain**   A *domain* is the name of a computer or server on the Internet from which you may access information. Every Web address specifies a domain, or particular computer. (See also **URL** in the next column.)

- **Home page**   A *home page* is the first screen or page of a Web site. Usually, it identifies the person or organization that sponsored or created the site, provides an index or table of contents for the site, and often includes hyperlinks to related sites on the Web. (See also **Web Site** on the next page.)

- **Hyperlink**   A *hyperlink* is a "button" or code word that allows a user to move from one place or page on the World Wide Web to another. On-screen, hyperlinks usually appear in a contrasting color and are underlined. (See also **HyperText Markup Language** below.)

- **Hypertext**   A *hypertext* program allows a user to find and open related files and documents on the Web without having to quit or close the original file. It allows a user to move to and from one document to another via hyperlinks.

- **Hypertext Markup Language** (HTML)   *Hypertext Markup Language* is the language used to create documents on the World Wide Web.

- **Hypertext Transfer Protocol** (HTTP)   *Hypertext Transfer Protocol* is the language used by browser software to connect to different sites or documents on the World Wide Web.

- **Search engine**   A *search engine* is a tool for finding specific information on the Web. (See also **World Wide Web, Searching** on page 829.)

- **URL** (*U*niform *R*esource *L*ocator)   A *URL* is the address of a specific document on the Web. A typical URL includes words, abbreviations, numbers, and punctuation. The URL shown below would connect you to the listings of science programs that are broadcast on National Public Radio. The parts of the address are explained below.

  1   2   3
  http://www.npr.org/programs/science
  1. The *protocol,* or how the site is formatted.
  2. The *domain name.* Domain names have at least two parts. The part on the left is the name of the company, institution, or other organization. The part on the right is the

general domain. A list of the most common general domain abbreviations follows. (See also *domain* on the previous page.)

Common Domains on the World Wide Web	
com	commercial
edu	educational
gov	governmental
net	administrative
org	nonprofit organization

1. Toolbar The buttons on the toolbar allow you to complete different functions, such as moving to different pages, printing out information, searching, and seeing or hiding images.

2. Location indicator This box shows you the URL, or address, of the site you are seeing before you.

3. Content area This is the area of the screen where the text, images, hyperlinks, and other parts of a Web page appear.

4. Icon By clicking on an icon, you can move to a different page that contains information about the topic listed next to the icon.

5. Hyperlink Hyperlinks are words or phrases that are underlined or are a different color than the rest of the text. Clicking on a hyperlink will take you to another page that contains more information about the word or phrase.

6. Scroll Bar Clicking the arrows at the end of this bar scrolls the page horizontally. There is also a vertical scroll bar on the right side.

3. The **subdirectory name** that shows where the specific piece of information you want is stored. (Each word following a slash requests a more specific search into the site.) Not all addresses will have this part.

- **Web Site (or Web Page)** A *Web site* or *Web page* is a document or location on the Web that is linked to other locations on the Web. Below is a typical example of what you would see if you had located a Web site with a typical browser.

World Wide Web, Plagiarism To take another person's idea or work and present it as your own is called *plagiarism.* Because the World Wide Web is such a vast source of

QUICK REFERENCE HANDBOOK

information and because it is easy to download or copy information, plagiarism of electronic material has become a serious concern. Plagiarism is highly unethical. It is very important, therefore, for you to treat any information you find on the World Wide Web as if it were from a printed or published source. **Make sure that you cite the source of your information.** (See page 227 for examples of **citations of online sources.**)

World Wide Web, Searching   There are three ways to search for information on the World Wide Web: *direct address, search engines,* and *subject catalogs.* Each type of search has benefits and drawbacks, which are described below. In general, unless you know exactly what you are looking for on the Web, a combination of all three types of searches works best. Most search services on the Web allow you to use all three.

- **Direct address**   The most direct way to find a Web site is to type in the Web site's address or URL in the Location box. The address must be typed exactly, using the proper case (upper or lower) and punctuation. This strategy does not work, of course, if you do not have the site's address.

- **Search engines**   *Search engines* allow you to search databases that contain information about the millions of sites on the Web. These databases are compiled automatically by computer programs called robots. *Search engines* are the tools that allow you to search the indexes' databases for specific information. (For more on how to use a search engine, see *World Wide Web, Using Search Engines* in the next column.)

- **Subject catalogs**   A *subject catalog* provides an extensively organized table of contents of the World Wide Web. Information from Web sites is organized in broad categories, such as *Education* and *Entertainment.* (Unlike search engines, subject catalogs are organized by humans, not by machines.) Each category in the catalog contains many specific subcategories, which in turn break down into even more specific sub-subcategories. A subject catalog or Internet guide is searched by starting with a general topic and narrowing down to a specific one.

World Wide Web, Using Search Engines
Unlike subject catalogs, *search engines* allow you to search for Web sites that contain key words or phrases. These search tools also allow you to refine your searches.

- **Key word search**   A *key word search* lets you look for sites that contain specific words or phrases. Type key words in the space provided on the search engine screen and press the Return key or the Search or Find button. The search engine analyzes the Web sites indexed in its database for the words you requested. The results appear in the form of a list. The sites that contain all your key words should appear at the top of the list, and the list continues in descending order of relevant matches. Most search engines assign the items on the list a percentage or rank number to indicate how well the site matched your request. The key word search works best when you have a very clear and specific topic to research.

■ **Refining a Key Word Search** Because search engines may identify hundreds or thousands of Web sites—or none at all—that contain your key words, you should consider *refining,* or focusing, your search. Below are some strategies that may help you. Keep in mind, however, that different search engines may require slightly different commands than those listed here. (The ones here are recommended by the search engine Webcrawler.) Consult the Help section of your search engine for specific commands.

Refining a Key Word Search	
Tip	**How It Works**
Replace general terms with more specific ones.	A key word that is common or used in ways you do not expect can result in irrelevant matches. EXAMPLE If you are interested in long-distance running races, enter *marathon* instead of *race.*
Use quotation marks.	By placing your key words or phrases in quotation marks, you instruct the search engine to find sites that use the words exactly as you have typed them. EXAMPLE Enter "sled dog races" to find sites about the Iditarod. If you enter *sled dog races* without the quotation marks, the search engine may turn up sites about bobsledding or dog grooming.
Use *and* and *not.*	Narrow your search by putting the word *and* between your key words. The search engine will find only Web sites that contain all words connected by *and.* EXAMPLE For sites that mention both the New York and the Boston marathons, enter *New York and Boston and marathon.* Use *not* between key words to make sure that the search engine does not pull up sites that deal with topics that are similar but unrelated. EXAMPLE Enter *marathon not Greece* to avoid Web sites about the Greek city of Marathon.
Use *or.*	To broaden your search, use *or* to let the search engine know that you would accept sites that contain any of your key words. EXAMPLE If you want sites that discuss either the New York or the Boston marathon, enter *New York or Boston marathon.*

World Wide Web, Web Site Evaluation

Because the content of the World Wide Web is not monitored for accuracy in the way most newspapers, books, or television programs are, you must be critical of the information you find there. For questions to help you to *evaluate* a Web site's value as a source of information, see the following chart.

Evaluating Web Sites	
Questions to Ask	**Why You Should Ask**
Who created or sponsored the Web site?	The kind of information on a Web site is determined by the site's creator or sponsor. The Web site's home page should identify who this is. Use only Web sites that are affiliated with reputable organizations, such as government agencies, universities, museums, and national news organizations. The Web sites for these organizations will usually belong in the *edu, gov,* or *org* domains. Reputable Web sites tend to give the names of authors or contributors to the site.
When was the page first posted and is it frequently updated?	This information usually appears at the end of a home page. Most often, it includes a copyright notice, the date of the most recent update, and a link to the creator's e-mail address. As with any reference source, you want the information you obtain from a Web site to be up-to-date.
What other Web pages is the site linked to?	Looking at the links provided in a Web site can help you determine how legitimate it is. If a site is a source of accurate information, it will have links to other reputable Web sites.
Does the Web site present information objectively?	Look for signs of bias, such as strong language or statements of opinion. If the site is trying to be objective, it will present ideas from both sides of an issue or debate.
Is the Web site well designed?	A well-designed Web site has legible type, clear graphics, and working links; it is also easily searched or navigated. The written content of the site should be well organized and well written, with proper spelling, punctuation, and grammar.

Reading and Vocabulary

Reading

Skills and Strategies

You can use the following skills and strategies to become a more effective reader.

Author's Purpose and Point of View, Determining An author's main *purpose* for writing a selection may be to inform, to persuade, to express, or to entertain. To help you identify purpose, look at the form a piece takes. For example, business writing and user manuals are usually written to inform, while policy statements and letters to the editor are often written to persuade. Other forms, such as Web sites, can suit multiple purposes. In addition, authors have opinions or attitudes about their subjects called *point of view.* Determining the author's purpose and point of view will help you to get more meaning from the text and can help you detect bias. If you suspect an author is biased, examine the clarity and accuracy of the information. (See also page 251.)

> EXAMPLE   Volunteering at the hospital is rewarding. Teenage volunteers deliver meals, visit patients, and run errands. Benefit your community and yourself by volunteering today.

> Author's purpose: To persuade teenagers to volunteer at the hospital

> Author's point of view: Volunteering benefits both the individual and the community.

Cause-effect Relationships, Analyzing

A *cause* makes something happen. An *effect* is what happens as a result of that cause. Ask "Why?" and "What are the effects?" as you read to examine causes and effects. (See also page 837.)

> EXAMPLE   Exercising regularly has changed my life! Since I began walking or jogging for thirty minutes four times a week, the results are amazing. Besides feeling better about the way I look, I have more energy and feel happier.

> Analysis: Regular exercise is the *cause* of these *effects*: better appearance, increased energy, and improved mood.

Clue Words, Using Depending on the text structure, writers use certain *clue words* to connect ideas or to show relationships between ideas. You can use these clue words—such as those listed on the next page—to identify the organizational pattern a writer has used. (See also **Text Structures, Analyzing** on page 836.)

Clue Words				
Cause-effect	Chronological Order	Comparison-contrast	Listing	Problem-solution
as a result	after	although	also	as a result
because	as	as well as	finally	consequently
consequently	before	but	for example	furthermore
if . . . then	finally	either . . . or	in fact	indeed
nevertheless	first	however	in the first place	nevertheless
since	not long after	not only . . . but also	most important	otherwise
so that	now	on the other hand	such as	therefore
therefore	second	similarly	to begin with	this led to
this led to	then	unless		thus
thus	when	yet		

Conclusions, Drawing   A *conclusion* is a statement you make by combining information in a text with information you already know. As you read, you gather information, connect it to your experiences, and then draw conclusions that are logical yet specific to the text.

EXAMPLE   Jacob looked around in awe and nervously reached for his mother's hand. The desks looked so big! The water fountain looked so tall! There were so many new faces!

Conclusion: Jacob is a small child experiencing his first day of school.

Fact and Opinion, Distinguishing   A *fact* is something that can be proven true by concrete information. An *opinion* expresses a personal belief or attitude, so it cannot be proven true or false. Facts are often used to support opinions. A reader who can distinguish between a fact and an opinion will not be easily misled. (See also page 287.)

EXAMPLE

Fact: In 1992, Mae C. Jemison became the first African American woman in space. [Reference works support this as a true statement.]

Opinion: The space program needs more female astronauts. [This is what one writer thinks or believes; the statement cannot be proven to be true or false.]

Generalizations, Forming   A reader forms a *generalization* by combining information in a text with personal experience to make a judgment or statement that goes beyond the text to the general world.

EXAMPLE   The city of Davis is taking on a clean, new look. Over the past few months, the streets and sidewalks seem less littered. Residents see almost no drink cans, food wrappers, or plastic containers. City officials report that they have issued no littering citations in the last year. The people of Davis have "cleaned up their act."

Generalization: People are becoming more aware of the need to protect the environment and are taking responsibility for cleaning up after themselves.

Implied Main Idea, Identifying   Some writers do not directly state the main idea; instead, they choose to *imply* or suggest it. In this case, you, the reader, have to analyze the meaning of the details in the text and decide

Reading   **833**

what overall meaning these details combine to express. (See **Conclusions, Drawing** on page 833 and **Stated Main Idea and Supporting Details, Identifying** on page 836.)

EXAMPLE   Training for a marathon should begin at least six months before the actual marathon. Injuries occur when runners add too many miles too quickly, but taking it slow is often hard for enthusiastic runners. The body needs time to adjust to the increased workload, so runners should add only one mile a week to their long weekly run.

Implied main idea: Patience is extremely important in marathon training.

Inferences, Making
An *inference* is an educated guess based on information in the text and on the reader's prior knowledge and experience. As you read, you make decisions about ideas and details that writers do not directly reveal. (See also page 162.)

EXAMPLE   "It's snowing! I can't believe it's snowing!" exclaimed Tara. As she stood with her face pressed to the window, she watched her excited neighbors filter outside. The Smiths were holding hands and dancing around their yard. Little Bart had found a cardboard box and was sliding down the driveway. Tara ran to get her coat.

Inference: Seeing snow was an unusual experience for Tara and her neighbors.

Paraphrasing
A *paraphrase* is a type of summary in which you restate an author's ideas in your own words. Paraphrasing is a good way to check your understanding of the original text. (See also **Paraphrasing** on page 863.)

EXAMPLE   The world's top athletes with disabilities compete at the Paralympic Games, which are held just after the Olympics and at the same location. Competing at the international level requires the same dedication and skill of athletes with disabilities as are required of all athletes. Besides offering the participants

entertainment and social contact, the Paralympic Games help its competing athletes to improve their physical strength, muscular coordination, and self-confidence.

Paraphrase: Top athletes with disabilities from around the world can compete on an international level at the Paralympic Games, which follow the Olympic Games. With the same determination and skill required of all athletes, the disabled athletes gather to compete and socialize. Many find that the experience increases their strength, coordination, and self-esteem.

Persuasive Techniques, Analyzing
An author uses *persuasive techniques* to convince readers to think or act in a certain way. As you read persuasive writing, look for logical reasoning and facts; don't be misled by an overemphasis on emotional appeals or faulty reasoning. (See also page 253.)

EXAMPLE   We need a stoplight at the corner next to the high school. Each school day, 150 vehicles and 350 pedestrians go through the intersection between the hours of 7:00 and 8:00 A.M. and 2:00 and 3:00 P.M. Three students have been hit by cars in the last two years. Every other high school in the state uses stoplights for traffic control. Installing one at our high school will make us an accident-free school.

Analysis: The second and third sentences use facts to support the opinion in the first sentence. The fourth sentence contains an emotional appeal. The final sentence contains faulty reasoning: There is no guarantee that installing a traffic light will make the school accident-free.

Predicting
Predicting is deciding what will happen next. To make predictions, you use information from the text plus your own knowledge and experience.

EXAMPLE   One by one the campers crawled out of their makeshift tents to check the weather. Dark clouds blocked out the sun, and thunder rumbled in the distance. Suddenly, lightning flashed!

Prediction: The campers will be caught in a rainstorm. Because their tents are makeshift, the campers will probably have to break down camp quickly and run for shelter.

Problem-Solution Relationships, Analyzing

A *problem* is an unanswered question. A *solution* is an attempt to answer the question. When authors write about a problem, they usually suggest at least one solution and explain the outcomes and final results of the solution. As a reader, you can analyze a problem by asking three questions: *What is the problem? Who has the problem? Why is it a problem?* Then, you can analyze and evaluate the solution by asking: *What is the outcome of each solution?* (In other words, did the solution work, or did it cause other problems?) *What is the final result of the solution?* (Was the problem solved?)

EXAMPLE Two years ago, Gramercy High School had budgeted enough money to install a computer lab but not enough to hire someone to maintain it. A parent who worked with computers volunteered her time, but she could work only on weekends when students were not in school. Another solution was offered by students—to use student volunteers who could work in the computer lab during lunch or study breaks. The use of student volunteers has been so successful that other schools in the area are trying the idea.

Analysis: *What is the problem?* The problem is that the school did not budget enough money to pay someone to run the computer lab. *Who has the problem?* Students have a problem if the computers in the lab do not work properly. *Why is it a problem?* Without computers, students do not benefit from having the technology available in the school. *What is the outcome of each solution?* One solution, using a parent volunteer, did not work. A second solution, allowing student volunteers to run the lab, did work. *What is the final result?* The final result is that other schools are now using student volunteers.

Reading Log, Using

A *reading log* is simply writing about reading. As you read, write down your honest reactions to the text: Ask questions, make associations, and note especially important passages. You can also use a Reading Log to record any prereading or postreading ideas. Because readers have different experiences, interests, beliefs, and opinions, no two Reading Logs will be alike.

Reading Rate, Adjusting

Reading rate is the speed at which you read a text, as shown in the chart below. How quickly or how slowly you read depends on three factors: why you are

Reading Rates According to Purpose

Reading Rate	Purpose	Example
Scanning	Reading for specific details	Hunting for the name of the town that is used as the setting for a short story
Skimming	Reading for main points	Reviewing chapter headings, subheadings, and time lines in your history textbook the night before a test
Reading for mastery	Reading to understand and remember	Taking notes and outlining a section in your science textbook before you begin your homework
Reading for enjoyment	Reading at the speed you find most comfortable	Reading a magazine article about an interest or hobby

reading—your purpose; the difficulty of the text you are reading; and your background knowledge and experience with the material in the text. Adjusting your reading rate to suit your purpose, the text, and your background knowledge helps you to read more efficiently.

SQ3R   SQ3R is a popular reading-study strategy. SQ3R stands for the five steps in the reading process:

S   *Survey* the entire text. Look briefly at each page—the headings, titles, illustrations, charts, and the material in boldface and italics.

Q   *Question* yourself as you do your survey. What should you know after completing your reading? Make a list of questions to be answered.

R   *Read* the entire selection. Think of answers to your questions as you read.

R   *Recite* in your own words answers to each question.

R   *Review* the material by re-reading quickly, looking over the questions, and recalling the answers.

Remember: By responding actively to what you are reading, you are more likely to recall what you have read.

Stated Main Idea and Supporting Details, Identifying

A *main idea* is the focus or key idea in a piece of writing. Main ideas often appear as topic sentences of paragraphs or in an introductory or concluding paragraph in a longer piece of writing. *Supporting details* support or explain the main idea.

NOTE   A stated main idea is also called an *explicit* main idea. (See also page 91 and **Implied Main Idea, Identifying** on page 833.)

EXAMPLE   Traditional Japanese houses blend with their surroundings. Most are simple, wooden buildings within walled gardens. Rooms are separated by sliding paper screens, which can be removed to allow breezes to blow through the house.

Stated main idea: Traditional Japanese houses blend with their surroundings.

Supporting details: They are usually simple wooden buildings with walled gardens. Paper screens are used to separate rooms.

Summarizing

A *summary* is a short restatement of the main points of a selection. When you *summarize,* you try to present a complete picture of a text by using as few words as possible. (See also **Summarizing** on page 864.)

EXAMPLE   Between December 26 and January 1, African Americans around the world celebrate Kwanzaa. Friends and families gather together to honor the past and to commit to a positive future. The focus of Kwanzaa is centered around seven principles with particular emphasis on family unity. The celebration has many aspects but usually includes rituals, narratives, poetry, singing, dancing, and feasting.

Summary: Kwanzaa is a seven-day African American spiritual holiday celebrating family, community, and culture.

Text Structures, Analyzing

A *text structure* is the pattern a writer uses to organize ideas or events. Writers commonly use five major patterns of organization: *cause-effect, chronological order, comparison-contrast, listing* and *problem-solution.* Being able to recognize how ideas are related will help you to understand a text. Use the guidelines on the next page to analyze a text structure.

1. **Search the text for the main idea.** Look for clue words that signal a specific pattern of organization. (See also the **Clue Words** chart on page 833.)

2. **Study the text for other important ideas.** Think about how the ideas connect, and look for an obvious pattern.

3. **Remember that a writer might use one organizational pattern throughout an entire text or might combine patterns.** (Professional writers often combine patterns.)

4. **Use a graphic organizer to map the relationships among the ideas.** The five common text structures, or organizational patterns, are illustrated below.

■ **Cause-effect pattern** shows the relationship between results and the ideas or events that made the results happen. (See also page 129.) The following example shows how heavy rains (cause) led to damaged crops, lost livestock, lost homes, and casualties (effects).

Causal Chain

■ **Chronological pattern** shows events or ideas happening in sequence. (See also page 359.) The example in the next column shows the sequence for making a smoothie.

Sequence Chain

■ **Comparison-contrast pattern** points out likenesses and/or differences. (See also page 93.) The following example compares baseball and the British sport of cricket.

Venn Diagram

■ **Listing pattern** presents material according to certain criteria such as size, location, or importance. The example on the next page lists details according to their location.

List

1. left: Lake Travis reflecting morning light

2. center: city's skyline in fog

3. right: rolling hills with occasional building

■ **Problem-solution pattern** identifies at least one problem, offers one or more solutions to the problem, and explains the outcomes and the final results of the solutions. The following example shows how a neighborhood dealt with the problem of a vacant lot.

Problem-Solution Analysis

What is the problem?

A vacant neighborhood lot is filled with trash and overgrown with weeds.

Who has the problem?

The people who live in the neighborhood

Why is it a problem?

The lot is a dangerous place for children to play, and it makes people feel bad about the neighborhood.

Attempted solutions

Petition the city to build something new and useful, like a new playground

Organize neighbors to clean up the lot and plant a community garden

Outcomes of attempted solutions

The process was too slow; after six months nothing had been done.

Once enough neighbors were interested, the lot was cleaned up within a few weeks and then divided into garden plots.

Final results

The neighbors eventually turned the lot into a safe, enjoyable place where they could grow flowers and vegetables and meet friends.

Transitional Words and Phrases, Using

Transitions are words and phrases writers use to connect ideas and create coherence. As a reader, your ability to recognize transitions will help you to understand how all the ideas in a selection fit together. (See page 365 for a chart of transitional words and phrases.)

Visuals and Graphics, Interpreting

Visuals and *graphics* convey complex information in a simple, visual format by using pictures or symbols. Well-designed visuals and graphics draw readers to the important information on a page and help them to understand it. Most often, they provide a clear comparison of different but related points of information. As a reader, your task is to interpret the information presented in a visual or graphic and to draw your own conclusions. The most common forms of visuals and graphics are **charts, diagrams, graphs, tables,** and **time lines.**

■ **Diagrams** use symbols (such as circles or arrows) or pictures to compare ideas, show a process, or provide instruction. A **Venn diagram** uses intersecting circles to compare two ideas or things. Keep in mind that diagrams should not be used to present numerical data. The shapes and forms used in diagrams are generally not accurate ways to represent amounts.

Venn Diagram

A   B

Differences   Similarities   Differences

Diagram

Layers of Soil

Topsoil and humus

Subsoil

Rock

Bar Graph

Comparison of Two Students' Study Schedules

- Student 1
- Student 2

Hours Studying (vertical axis: 0, 1, 2, 3, 4, 5)

Day of the Week (Mon, Tues, Wed, Thurs, Fri, Sat, Sun)

Be wary of any graph that switches the vertical and horizontal axes. If the vertical axis indicates time passing, the resulting peaks and valleys shown on the graph may be misleading.

■ **Line and bar graphs** show changes or trends over time. The horizontal axis in a line or bar graph indicates points in time, and the vertical axis shows quantities. In the following examples, notice how the vertical axis on each graph begins at zero. Having a vertical axis start with zero ensures that the data will be plotted accurately. Check for this when reading line or bar graphs.

Reversed Axis Line Graph

Comparison of Two Students' Study Schedules

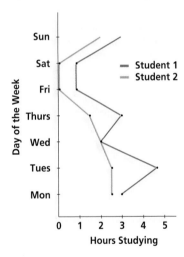

- Student 1
- Student 2

Day of the Week (Sun, Sat, Fri, Thurs, Wed, Tues, Mon)

Hours Studying (0, 1, 2, 3, 4, 5)

Line Graph

Comparison of Two Students' Study Schedules

- Student 1
- Student 2

Hours Studying (vertical axis: 0, 1, 2, 3, 4, 5)

Day of the Week (Mon, Tues, Wed, Thurs, Fri, Sat, Sun)

■ **Pie graphs** show the relationships of the parts of a whole to each other. In the following example, notice how the segments of the pie chart are identified as percentages, not as hours. The emphasis in a pie chart is always on the proportions of the sections, not on the specific amounts of each section nor on the value of the whole pie.

How an Average Student's Day Is Spent

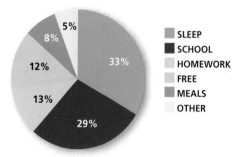

- SLEEP
- SCHOOL
- HOMEWORK
- FREE
- MEALS
- OTHER

- **Tables** provide information in its least processed form. They do not show trends and patterns in data. Readers must draw their own conclusions about any relationships in the data.

Number of hours used for study and grade-point averages of students in Language Arts III		
Student	Study hours per week	GPA at the end of 1st semester
1	15	2.8
2	18	3.6
3	16	3.2

- **Time lines** identify events that take place over the course of time. A time line is basically the horizontal axis of a graph. Events are identified above the time line, and the time periods are indicated below it.

Event 1	Event 2	Event 3	Event 4
Time period	Time period	Time period	Time period

Effective visuals and graphics contain the following elements.

- The **body** presents information in the form of a graph, chart, time line, diagram, or table.
- **Labels** identify and give meaning to the information shown in the graphic.
- A **legend,** or **key,** identifies special symbols, color coding, scales, or other features readers need to know in order to read the graphic; it appears as a small box placed near the body.
- The **source** is where the information contained in the graphic was found.
- A **title** identifies the subject or main idea of the graphic.

As a reader, you should always read graphics or visuals carefully and critically. Keep in mind the following tips:

- **Always read the title, labels, and legend** of any visual or graphic before analyzing the data in a visual or graphic.
- **Draw your own conclusions,** and compare them to those of the writer.
- **Think about the information that is *not* included** in the graphic. Often, important information is left out because it does not match the author's conclusions.
- **Watch out for optical illusions in graphs.** For example, bar graphs and pie charts that are shown in three dimensions are easily misread because some sections look more dense than others.
- **Look for manipulated data** by making sure that the horizontal axis of any graph indicates time, not amount. Also, make sure that the axes of a graph or sections of a pie chart are clearly labeled.

Vocabulary

Context Clues To find clues to the meaning of an unfamiliar word, you can examine its *context,* the group of words or sentences surrounding the unfamiliar word. The following chart shows examples of the common context clues. (See also pages 27, 96, and 132.)

How To Use Context Clues
Type of Clue
Definitions and Restatements: Look for words that define the term or restate it in other words.   *The judge seemed **impartial**, not favoring one side in the case over the other.*
Examples: Look for examples used in context that reveal the meaning of an unfamiliar word.   *Many **sovereigns** attended the exhibit, including the queen of England and the king of Denmark.*
Synonyms: Look for clues that indicate an unfamiliar word is similar in meaning to a familiar word or phrase.   *Rico, like his overjoyed teammates, was **exultant** about the team's victory.*
Antonyms: Look for clues that indicate an unfamiliar word is opposite in meaning to a familiar word or phrase.   *Instead of being stormy, the weather turned **balmy** in the afternoon.*
Cause and Effect: Look for clues that show an unfamiliar word is related to the cause or is the result of an action, feeling, or idea.   *Because his pet lizard was lost, Mark felt **dejected**.*

Word Bank A *word bank* is a list of words that you create from your reading, listening, and viewing. Storing new words in a word bank is a good way to increase your vocabulary. Check your dictionary for the meaning of each new word. You may want to compile your personal word bank in a notebook or on a computer file.

Word Meanings Words have many layers of meanings. Their messages can change depending on the time, the place, and the situation in which they are used. Use the following definitions and examples to help you make sure that your words say what you want them to.

- **Analogies** In an *analogy,* you are asked to analyze the relationship between two words and then identify another pair of words that has the same relationship. Analogy questions often appear on standardized tests because they measure your knowledge of vocabulary as well as your ability to identify relationships and patterns between words.

  EXAMPLE
  1. COOKING : CHEF :: _C_
  A. snow : cold **C.** shaving : barber
  B. drinking : water **D.** running : jumping

- **Clichés** A *cliché* is a tired expression. Its overuse has made its message weak and boring. You can use a thesaurus or a dictionary of synonyms to find livelier, more precise words.

  EXAMPLES busy as a bee, quick as a flash, accidents will happen, last but not least

- **Denotation and connotation** The *denotation* of a word is its direct, plainly expressed meaning—the meaning a dictionary lists. The *connotation* is the meaning suggested by or associated with the word. Because connotations often stir people's feelings, they can have powerful effects on the listener or reader.

EXAMPLE The words *proud* and *arrogant* have similar denotations, but they suggest different ideas. *Proud* can suggest self-respect and a sense of accomplishment. *Arrogant,* on the other hand, has negative connotations of snobbishness or a kind of superior attitude.

- **Euphemisms** A *euphemism* is an agreeable-sounding term that is substituted for a more direct, less pleasant-sounding one. Some euphemisms are used as a courtesy to avoid offending people; however, others are used to mislead people—to hide unpleasant truths or misrepresent the facts.

Euphemism	More Direct Term
passed away	died
underprivileged	poor
sanitation engineer	garbage collector

- **Figurative language** *Figurative language* goes beyond the literal meaning of the words to create a special effect or feeling. The following chart shows the most common types of figurative language.

Type of Figurative Language	Example
A **metaphor** says that something *is* something else.	*The night is a dark cloak.*
Personification gives human characteristics to nonhuman things.	*With open arms, the cozy chair beckoned me.*
A **simile** compares two basically unlike things, using the words *like* or *as.*	*Jumping the hurdle, she looked like a graceful deer.*

- **Idioms** *Idioms* are phrases that mean something different from the literal meanings of the words. Idioms often can't be explained grammatically, and they make no sense if translated word-for-word into another language.

EXAMPLES
I tried to call you, but you were *on the phone.*
We *talked out* the problem.
Suzanne really *gets into* soccer.

- **Jargon** *Jargon* is a special language used by groups of people who share the same profession, occupation, hobby, or field of study. Jargon is effective only if the reader or listener is familiar with its special meaning. Note in the following example how the word *lead* can mean different things to different groups.

EXAMPLE *lead*
Card players—the act of playing first
Electricians—a wire that carries current
Journalists—the opening paragraph of a news story
Musicians—the main melody in a musical composition

- **Loaded words** Words that are intended to provoke strong feeling, either positive or negative, are called **loaded words.** A writer or speaker who wants to prejudice you for or against something may appeal to your emotions with loaded words.

EXAMPLE
After suffering *defeat* in last week's election, Senator Blank addressed a *mere handful of people* last night at the Civic Center.
After suffering a *setback* in last week's election, Senator Blank addressed a *small but spirited audience* last night at the Civic Center.

■ **Multiple meanings** Many English words have more than one meaning. When you use a dictionary to find a word's meaning, look at all the definitions given. Keep in mind the context in which you read or heard the word. Then, try the various definitions in that context until you find the one that fits.

EXAMPLE

My cousin has a *berth* as a summer lifeguard. (The third definition best fits the meaning in context.)
berth (bʉrth) *n.* **1.** the space necessary for safety between a ship and another object **2.** a ship's place at anchor **3.** a position or job **4.** a place to sleep on a ship, train, or airplane

■ **Tired words** A *tired word* is one that has lost its freshness and force. It has been used so often and so carelessly that it has become worn-out and almost meaningless. (See also **Clichés** on page 841.)

EXAMPLES nice, fine, pretty, wonderful, terrific, great

Word Origins The *origin* of a word is its coming into existence. The origin and history of a word—its etymology—often appear in brackets along with its dictionary definition. The following etymology indicates that the word *victory* came to Middle English (ME) from Old French (OFr) and Latin (L).

EXAMPLE: **victory** [ME < OFr *victorie* < L *victoria* < *victor*]

Word Parts Most English words are made up of smaller units called *word parts.* The three types of word parts are *roots, prefixes,* and *suffixes.* Knowing the meanings of these word parts can help you determine the meanings of many unfamiliar words.

■ **Roots** The *root* is the foundation on which a word is built. It carries the word's core meaning, and it is the part to which prefixes and suffixes are added.

Commonly Used Roots		
Roots	**Meanings**	**Examples**
Greek		
–bibli–, –biblio–	book	bibliography, bibliophile
–chron–	time	chronological, synchronize
–dem–	people	democracy, epidemic
–graph–	write, writing	autograph, geography
–log(ue)–, –logy–	study, word	logic, mythology
–micro–	small	microbe, microscope
–phil–	love	audiophile, philharmonic
–phon–	sound	phonograph, euphony
–sym–, –syn–	with, together	symphony, synchronize
Latin		
–aud–, –audit–	hear	audible, auditorium
–bene–	well, good	benefit, benevolent
–cis–	cut	incision, concise
–cogn–	know	recognize, cognition
–duc–, –duct–	lead	educate, conductor
–fid–	belief, faith	fidelity, infidel

(continued)
Vocabulary **843**

Commonly Used Roots *(continued)*		
Roots	**Meanings**	**Examples**
–gen–	birth, kind, origin	generate, generic, generous
–ject–	throw	projectile, reject
–loqu–, –loc–	talk, speech	eloquent, locution
–magn–	large	magnitude, magnify
–mal–	bad	malady, dismal
–mit–, –miss–	send	remit, emissary
–ped–	foot	pedal, quadruped
–pend–, –pens–	hang, weigh	pendant, suspense
–port–	carry, bear	export, important
–tract–	pull, draw	tractor, extract
–vis–, –vid–	see	visible, videotape

■ **Prefixes** A *prefix* is a word part that is added before a root. The word that is created from a prefix and a root combines the meanings of both its parts.

Commonly Used Prefixes		
Prefixes	**Meanings**	**Examples**
Greek		
anti–	against, opposing	antipathy, antithesis
dia–	through, across, between	diagonal, diameter
hemi–	half	hemisphere, hemitrophic
syn–, sym–, syl–, sys–	together, with	synchronize, sympathy, syllable, system
Latin		
bi–	two	bimonthly, bisect
co–, col–, com–, con–, cor–	with, together	coexist, collide, compare, convene, correspond
de–	away, from, off, down	defect, desert, decline
in–, im–	in, into, within	induct, impose
inter–	between, among	intercede, international
non–	not	nonsense, non-cooperative
post–	after, following	postpone, postscript
pre–	before	prevent, predisposed
re–	back, backward, again	revoke, recede, recur
sub–, suf–, sum–, sup–, sus–	under, beneath	subjugate, suffuse, summon, suppose, suspect
trans–	across, beyond	transmission, transfer

Commonly Used Prefixes		
Prefixes	Meanings	Examples
Old English		
mis–	badly, not, wrongly	misfire, misspell
over–	above, excessive	oversee, overdo
un–	not, reverse of	untrue, unfold

■ **Suffixes**   A *suffix* is a word part that is added after a root. Often, adding or changing a suffix will change both a word's meaning and its part of speech, as in *please/pleasure*. *Please* is a verb; *pleasure* is a noun.

Commonly Used Suffixes		
Suffixes	Meanings	Examples
Greek, Latin, and French		
Nouns		
–ance, –ancy	act, quality	acceptance, hesitancy
–ity	state, condition	possibility, ability
–ment	result, action	disappointment
–tion	action, condition	selection, relation
Adjectives		
–able	able, likely	capable, changeable
–ible	able, likely	flexible, possible
–ous	characterized by	religious, furious
Adjectives or Nouns		
–ant, –ent	actor, showing	servant, confident
–ite	formed, showing	composite, favorite
Verbs		
–ate	become, cause	populate, activate
–fy	make, cause	identify, glorify
–ize	make, cause to be	sterilize, idealize
Old English		
Nouns		
–dom	state, condition	freedom, wisdom
–hood	state, condition	childhood, falsehood
–ness	quality, state	softness, shortness
Adjectives		
–en	made of, like	wooden, golden
–ish	suggesting, like	foolish, childish
Verbs		
–en	cause to be	deepen, darken

Words to Learn   The 300 words in the list below may be used as the basis of your vocabulary study this year. Make it a habit to learn unfamiliar words from this list regularly.

abhor
abrasive
acclaim
acknowledge
adage
addicted
adversary
advocate
affected
affirmation
agility
agitation
alleged
allusion
aloof
alteration
amends
amity
animated
annals
apathy
apparition
applicable
arrogance
assess
asterisk
attribute
authenticity
autonomous

belligerent
benefactor
benign
bibliography
bilingual
biographical
bizarre
bland
brochure

buoyant

cadence
carnivorous
cascade
centrifugal
chivalry
chronic
chronological
circumscribe
citadel
clamber
collaborate
collateral
collective
comply
condolence
congeniality
congruent
connive
conspiracy
contaminate
contemptible
convey
cope
credentials
culmination
cumbersome
cynic

deficient
defile
defraud
demoralize
denote
denounce
depict
depreciate
devout
dexterity

diligent
discredit
discreet
discretion
disperse
disrupt
dissuade
docile
drastic
dubious
dupe
dwindle

elapse
elude
emerge
emissary
encore
entice
epic
equation
eradicate
essence
evict
exasperate
expend
exploit
extremely
extrovert

fallacy
fauna
fervent
figurative
flora
fluent
formidable
frenzied
frivolous
functional

galvanize
garb
gaudy
genealogy

genial
granular
grueling

haphazard
havoc
hectic
herald
hereditary
hideous
hindrance
hoax
homage
horde
humanitarian
humanoid
hypothetical

ideally
ideology
immaterial
immunity
impertinent
implement
inaudible
incalculable
incandescent
incessant
incompatible
incomprehensible
inconspicuous
inconvenient
indivisible
induction
infamous
infest
inflammation
influential
ingenuous
initiative
instigate
intact
intensive
intervention
intimate

intimidate
intonation
inventory
inverse
invigorating
irony
irreducible
irretrievable

jaunt
jovial
jurisdiction

kindle

landlocked
larceny
lavish
lax
lethal
liability

maintenance
malicious
manifest
manipulate
meander
medieval
meditate
medley
metamorphosis
metaphor
mimic
misconstrue
moor
morbid
murky

necessitate
negotiate

nimble
nominal
nonchalant

objective
obsession
obtuse
omen
ominous
opaque
oppressive
optimistic
oratory
orthodox
ostracize
ovation

palatial
panorama
paramount
passive
perceptible
perennial
perspective
pessimistic
plaintiff
plaintive
ponderous
potency
potion
precedent
predatory
predominant
premature
preposterous
priority
promenade
prominence

prospective
prowess
pungent

quest
quorum
quota

radical
raucous
ravenous
recede
recession
reconcile
relevant
reluctant
repast
replenish
replica
reprimand
resourceful
retract
retrieve
rostrum

sage
satirical
sector
seethe
simile
sinister
skeptical
smug
soliloquy
solvent
somber
sovereign
sparse

spurn
stagnant
statute
subsequent
superfluous
surmount
surpass
susceptible

tantalizing
tentative
thesis
tolerate
transcribe
transpire
tripod
trivial
turbulent
tycoon

ultimate
uncanny
undergo
unkempt
unscrupulous
upheaval

vanity
veneer
venerable
virtual
volatile

wary
wrangle
wry

yearn

Speaking and Listening

Speaking

Casual conversations with family and friends account for most of the occasions upon which you speak. There are times, however, when you will be required to speak in situations that are not so casual. For every speaking occasion there are certain **conventions of oral language** you should observe. These conventions are the generally agreed upon rules and regulations of oral communication—the proper grammar, vocabulary, and style to use for different audiences, occasions, and purposes. For example, you would not use the same grammar, vocabulary, and style to respond to questions during a job interview that you would to recount an anecdote to a group of friends. No matter what the situation, you can use certain strategies and techniques to become a better speaker.

Debate

A *debate* involves two groups or teams who publicly discuss a controversial topic in a systematic way. The topic under discussion is called the *proposition.* One team, the *affirmative team,* argues that the proposition should be accepted. The other side, the *negative team,* argues that the proposition should be rejected.

Features of a Debate   While there are different formats for debates, some features are common to all of them.

- **Debate proposition**   The issue in a debate is a proposition that is phrased as a resolution and limited to a specific idea. The proposition should be an issue that gives each side an equal chance to build a reasonable case. The proposition should be clearly stated so that debaters and the audience can easily understand it. An example of a clear and debatable proposition is "Resolved: That research on alternatives to fossil fuels should be substantially increased."

- **Debate etiquette**   Proper etiquette, or manners, is required of debaters. Ridicule, sarcasm, and personal attacks are not acceptable. A debate should be won or lost only on the basis of a well-prepared case convincingly delivered. Also, it is customary to refer to debaters with polite terms such as "the first affirmative speaker," "my worthy opponent," "my colleagues," or "my teammates."

- **Debate officials**   A chairperson often rules over a debate. A debater may appeal to the chairperson if he or she believes that any debating rules have been broken by the opposing team. The most common method of determining the winner of a debate is by the decision of three appointed judges. Occasionally, an audience may vote to determine the winning team.

Formats of Debate   Most debates are divided into two parts. In the first part, both sides make constructive speeches, attempting to build their cases by presenting their arguments for or against the proposition and anticipating and attempting to disprove the points of the opposing side. Then, after an intermission, both sides make rebuttal speeches, trying to reply to the other side's best arguments. Specific time limits are assigned for each speech, although these limits vary depending on the type of debate.

- **Traditional, or formal, debate**   This debate format has two speakers on a team. Each member of each team speaks twice within set time limits.

- **Cross-examination debate**   This type of debate also features two affirmative and two negative speakers. In this debate format, participants are allowed to question opponents. During this cross-examination period, a speaker can clarify issues and point out weaknesses in an opponent's position.

- **Lincoln-Douglas debate**   This type of debate commemorates the famous debates between two candidates for senator from Illinois in 1858—Abraham Lincoln and Stephen A. Douglas. This format features one affirmative speaker and one negative speaker debating a proposition.

Preparing for Debate   To be an effective debater, you must prepare carefully by researching the proposition thoroughly, just as you would if you were writing a research paper. You also must identify the *issues,* or main differences, between your position and the position of the opposing team. You must organize support for your arguments in the form of examples, expert testimony, statistics, and logical reasons. You must also organize all your arguments and supporting evidence into a *brief,* an outline of your team's position in the debate. A brief is like a detailed sentence outline of an argumentative essay. Next, you must be prepared to *refute,* or disprove, your opponents' arguments with the same sort of evidence you used to build your own case—logical reasons, facts, statistics, and the like. Last, you must anticipate your opponents' refutations so that you can prepare a *rebuttal,* a rebuilding of your case in which you repair the damage that was done to your arguments when your opponents refuted them.

Formal Speaking Occasions

Formal speaking is done at a specific time and place and for a specific reason. There are steps you can take to prepare for every formal speaking occasion.

Formal Speeches   Formal speeches do not simply happen; like book reports or research papers, they require time and thoughtful preparation. The process of preparing a formal speech is similar to the process of writing a paper. To prepare a formal speech, follow the steps explained below.

1. **Identify your purpose**   Begin the process of preparing a speech by identifying the purpose for your speech. Your general *purpose* is the overall reason you are giving your speech. Most often the purpose of a speech is to inform or to persuade an audience. Common purposes for giving speeches are described in the chart on the next page.

TEACHING **TIP**

Formal Speeches
Have students use the instruction on formal speaking that starts on this page and continues through p. 853 to prepare and deliver a formal speech. This speech can be informative or persuasive. Be sure students follow the steps given. Here are some prompts to help trigger ideas for students' speeches.

- Present a speech on a topic you are studying in another class, such as the discovery of the atom or an important historical event.

- Present a speech in which you convince people to donate money for a plaque honoring a local hero.

- Present a speech to persuade your classmates to vote for your candidate for a position on the student council.

- Present a speech in which you convince people to change a policy that is now in effect at your school.

MULTIPLE INTELLIGENCES

Spatial Intelligence. As students study the **General Types of Speeches** chart on this page, they may benefit from exploring which presentations would require informal, standard, or technical language to meet effectively the purpose, audience, occasion, and task assigned to such a speech. Using the examples bulleted at the right of the chart, create a flashcard game, with each type of presentation written on its own card. Divide the class into three or four teams, and challenge students to think of the circumstances surrounding each flashcard example and to determine whether the appropriate style of speech would be informal, standard, or technical. After a few moments to consult, groups should each perform a quick skit of the speech, complete with the correct style of language. For example, to illustrate "instruction," students might pantomime taking notes as one group member points to the chalkboard and speaks in math jargon. Give extra points to each team for explaining the purpose of the speech, the occasion where the speech might be presented, the audience for the speech, and the task the speech fulfills.

General Types of Speeches		
Type of Speech	**Purpose**	**Examples**
Informative Speech	To present new information to an audience or to provide a new view of old information	• Lecture • News broadcast • Orientation • Instruction
Persuasive Speech	To change an attitude or belief or to move an audience to action	• Campaign speech • Advertisement • Debate
Special Occasion Speech	To entertain or amuse an audience or to acknowledge a special reason for the audience's presence	• After-dinner speech • Anecdote • Oral interpretation of a piece of literature • Speech honoring a retiring teacher

2. **Select a topic** If you may choose the topic of your speech instead of speaking on an assigned topic, be sure to pick a topic in which you are interested. If you are not enthusiastic about your topic, you cannot expect your audience to be enthusiastic. Consider the answers to the following questions in selecting your topic.

   ▪ *What is the occasion of your speech?* What, in other words, prompts you to speak? For example, have you been asked to speak on behalf of your scout troop to a group of veterans on Memorial Day? Your topic should fit the occasion.

   ▪ *How much time will you have to deliver your speech?* You have to limit the scope of your speech to fit the time you are given.

3. **Analyze the audience** Once you select your topic, you must think about how to tailor your speech to your audience's needs or interests. Use the following questions for adapting material to a particular audience.

   ▪ *What does the audience already know about the topic?* Provide enough back-

ground for your audience to understand your speech. Some audiences might need extensive background information. Others might need none.

   ▪ *How interested will the audience be in your topic?* The degree of the audience's interest in your topic should influence the content of your speech. An uninterested audience needs to be convinced that the topic is worthwhile. An interested audience needs to hear information that will justify and maintain their interest.

4. **Gather material and organize content** The next step in preparing a speech is to research the topic you have selected. (For more on the **library or media center,** see "The Library/Media Center" section of the Quick Reference Handbook. For more on **taking notes and preparing outlines,** refer to the "Study Skills" and "Writing" sections of the Quick Reference Handbook.)

5. **Write the speech** In writing your speech, you must think about three things: the structure of your speech, the language you use,

Features of a Formal Speech

Structure

The speech should be composed of three parts:

- an *introduction* with a thesis statement or main idea
- a *body*
- a *conclusion*

Language

The language you use should be appropriate for your audience. Keep in mind the following points.

- Use formal, standard English.
- Use technical terms sparingly and be sure to define them.
- Avoid slang and jargon.

Audience Involvement

It is important to remember that written English sounds different when it is delivered orally. Make your speech more "listener-friendly" by doing the following:

- Use personal pronouns. For example, say "you may think" or "we believe" instead of "one may think" or "people believe."
- Ask questions instead of making statements. For example, instead of telling the audience a fact or statistic, ask them "Did you know that . . . ?" A question like this, which is not meant to be answered but is asked only for effect, is called a *rhetorical question.*

and the way you involve your audience in your material. The chart above shows you the basic features of a formal speech.

6. **Determine method of delivery** Now you need to decide how you will deliver your speech. There are several methods, each of which has advantages and disadvantages.

- The *manuscript speech* is read word-for-word from your written manuscript. This method allows little chance for mistakes, but it does not permit you to respond to audience feedback and often sounds dull and lifeless.

- The *memorized speech* is memorized word-for-word from your written manuscript. This method does give you the freedom to move around and to maintain eye contact with the audience, but it may sound stiff and unnatural. With this method, you also run the risk of forgetting parts of the speech.

- The *extemporaneous speech* is carefully outlined and rehearsed but not memorized. This method sounds natural and allows you to respond to the audience, but requires much rehearsal time. When you organize your materials for an extemporaneous speech, first write out a complete outline. Then, using the guidelines below, prepare note cards that you may refer to as you present your speech.

Guidelines for Extemporaneous Speech Note Cards

1. Put only one key idea, possibly accompanied by a brief example or detail, on each card.

2. Make a special note card for material that you plan to read word-for-word, such as a quotation, a series of dates, or a list of statistics.

3. Make a special note card to indicate when you should pause to show a graphic, such as a chart, diagram, graph, picture, or model.

4. Number your completed cards to keep them in order.

Cooperative Learning

Professional Speeches. Locate recordings of historically significant speeches, such as Abraham Lincoln's Gettysburg Address or Dr. Martin Luther King, Jr.'s "I Have a Dream," and play them in class so that your students can work in pairs to analyze, evaluate, and critique the speakers' use of rhetorical devices. Lead students to identify and critique devices such as repetition, emphasis, and parallelism. Explain to students that the use of these techniques gives power to the speaker's words; they are tools that hook listeners and compel them to stay focused on the speaker's message.

Speaking   **851**

7. **Rehearse the speech** You will give a better and more convincing presentation if you rehearse. One of the ways an audience will judge your presentation is by your use of **nonverbal** and **verbal signals.** You use these signals any time you speak, but they are especially noticeable in a formal speech.

- *Nonverbal Signals* In addition to communicating with words, you can communicate with nonverbal signals, like those described in the following chart.

Communicating with Nonverbal Signals

Nonverbal signals	Tips and Effects
Eye contact	Look directly into the eyes of as many members of the audience as you can. Eye contact communicates honesty and sincerity. It makes the audience feel as if you are speaking *with* them rather than *to* them.
Facial expression	Facial expressions—smiling, frowning, raising an eyebrow, and so on—can reveal your feelings and add to or even take the place of a verbal message.
Gesture	Making relaxed and natural gestures with your head, hands, or arms as you speak emphasizes verbal messages. Nodding the head for "yes" or shaking it for "no" or pointing with the index finger can effectively punctuate your speech.
Posture	Stand up straight and look alert to communicate an air of confidence to your audience.

- *Verbal Signals* Use your voice expressively when you deliver a speech. The following verbal signals will help you communicate your message to an audience.

Communicating with Verbal Signals

Verbal signals	Tips
Diction (the clarity of your pronunciation)	Always speak clearly and carefully so that your listeners can understand you.
Emphasis (the stress put on a word or phrase)	Emphasize key ideas or points in your speech by saying those words with a little more volume than you have been using.
Pause (small silences in your speech)	Use pauses to help listeners catch up or to suggest that what you have said or are about to say is important.
Pitch (the highness or lowness of your voice)	A nervous speaker's pitch tends to be high. Take a deep breath and relax before you speak to keep your pitch natural.
Rate (the speed at which you talk)	Normal speed is about 120 to 160 words per minute. When delivering a speech, speak at a slower-than-normal rate.
Volume (the level of sound you create)	Although you might not be used to speaking loudly, your audience appreciates the extra volume. Be sure to ask listeners if they can hear you before you begin your speech.

8. Deliver the speech Most amateur speakers are nervous before delivering a speech. Here are some suggestions for keeping nervousness from interfering with your speech.

- *Be prepared.* Avoid excessive nervousness by organizing and being familiar with your speech notes and any audiovisual devices you plan to use.
- *Practice your speech.* Rehearse as if you are actually delivering your speech.
- *Focus on your purpose for speaking.* Think about what you want your listeners to do, believe, or feel as a result of your speech.
- *Pay attention to audience feedback.* Different audiences will react differently to your speech. Pay attention to the messages the audience sends you. Are people in the audience alert or are they yawning? Are they shaking their heads in disagreement or nodding in agreement? Depending upon the feedback you receive from the audience, you might need to adjust your pace, use more gestures, or speak more loudly to keep their attention.

9. Use audiovisual devices (if appropriate)
Audiovisual devices are resources that you use to clarify or add to your presentation. Some audiovisual devices that are often used in multimedia presentations are listed below.

- audio recordings (such as cassettes or compact discs)
- images, audio files, and text stored and presented on a computer
- videotapes or videodiscs
- short films
- slides or filmstrips
- graphics such as charts, graphs, illustrations, and diagrams

Use the following questions to determine whether your presentation will benefit from the use of audiovisual devices.

- *Will audiovisual devices help you clarify a point?* Some ideas are easily explained, but others need a visual to help clarify them. Using a chart or a poster will save you time and keep the audience on track.
- *Will the audiovisual devices help the audience remember a point?* Not every point in your speech is equally important. Decide which points will benefit from the emphasis given by the audiovisual.
- *Will the audiovisual devices distract the audience while you are speaking?* Make sure that the audiovisual devices are essential to your talk and can be displayed without distracting the audience.

NOTE Make certain your audience can see or hear the audiovisual device you have chosen. Audio materials should be cued up. Graphics should be large and clear enough to be seen from the back of the audience. (See also **Graphics and Visuals** on page 813.)

Group Discussion A *formal group discussion* occurs when clubs, organizations, and other groups meet to discuss issues of importance. Formal groups often follow an established set of rules known as *parliamentary procedure.* The basic principles of parliamentary procedure, listed below, protect the rights of the individual members of the group while providing a system for dealing with issues that come before the group.

- The majority decides.
- The minority has the right to be heard.
- Decisions are made by voting.
- Only one issue is decided at a time.
- Everyone has the right to be heard and to vote.
- All votes are counted as equal.
- All sides of an issue are debated openly.

Critical Thinking

Evaluation. Have students evaluate a professional speech that is delivered on television. A good source of speeches for this activity is the C-SPAN cable TV network, which routinely presents speeches by government officials and others. If students do not have access to these presentations, you could videotape one or more speeches and show them in class so that students could practice evaluating a speech. In their evaluations, students should address the following points.

- Purpose is clear.
- Main ideas are easily identifiable.
- Speaker considers audience, task, occasion, and purpose.
- Enough information is given to make the key points or claims understandable and believable.
- Language is precise.
- Tone and pitch are appropriate for the audience and occasion.
- Speaker's articulation, enunciation, and pronunciation are correct.
- Speaker keeps eye contact and uses other nonverbal signals to connect with the audience.
- Speaker uses verbal signals such as diction, emphasis, and pauses to communicate the message.

Interviewing

An **interview** is a communication situation in which one person, the *interviewer*, gathers ideas or firsthand information from another person, the *interviewee*.

■ **Conducting an interview**   Successful interviews require careful planning. The following chart provides useful suggestions for planning and conducting an interview.

Conducting an Interview
Preparing for the Interview ■ Make arrangements well in advance. Set up a time that is convenient for the other person to meet with you. ■ Make a list of questions to ask. Make sure the questions are arranged in a logical order and require more than yes or no answers.
Participating in the Interview ■ Arrive on time; be polite and patient. ■ Ask the other person's permission to take notes or use a tape recorder. ■ Avoid argument. Be tactful and courteous. Remember the interview was granted at your request. ■ Listen carefully, and ask follow-up questions if you do not understand an answer or if you think you need more information.
Following up on the Interview ■ Review your notes to refresh your memory, and then make a summary of the material you have gathered. ■ Send a note expressing your appreciation for the interview.

■ **Interviewing for a job**   A job interview can be a nerve-racking situation; being thoroughly prepared to be interviewed can relieve some of the anxiety. The following chart tells you how to be a successful interviewee.

How to Interview for a Position
1. **Arrange an appointment.** Write a business letter of application in which you request an interview for a job. If you are granted an interview, be prompt for your appointment.
2. **Bring a résumé.** If you have not already submitted a résumé, take one to the interview and give it to the interviewer. (See also **Résumés** on page 900.)
3. **Be neat and well groomed.** It is important to look your best when you are interviewing for any type of job.
4. **Answer questions clearly and honestly.** Answer the questions the interviewer asks, adding any additional information that might inform the employer that you are the right person for the job.
5. **Ask questions.** Questions that job applicants usually ask include requests for information about work hours, salary, or chances for advancement. By your questions, show that you know something about the company or business.
6. **Be prepared to be tested.** The employer may require you to take tests that demonstrate your skills, intelligence, or personality.
7. **Follow up the interview.** After the interview, write a short thank-you note. Tell the interviewer that you appreciated the opportunity for the interview and that you look forward to hearing from the company in the near future.

Informal Speaking Occasions

Informal communication involves sharing information in casual situations. Unlike formal speaking situations, in which you are usually at a distance from your audience, informal speaking situations are more personal. The chart below describes some common informal speaking situations and some strategies for dealing with them.

Informal Group Discussion *Informal group discussion* takes place when a small group of people meets for a particular purpose. The following section explains two elements of group discussion.

■ **Identifying a purpose** When the group has a specific purpose or goal, the point of the discussion is how to achieve that purpose or goal. Every group discussion should begin

Informal Speaking Situations		
Situation	**Purpose**	**Preparation and Presentation**
Directions	To explain how to get to a particular place (Informational situation)	• Choose easiest route. • Divide the route into logical steps. • Use terms that are accurate or visual. If necessary, draw a map.
Impromptu speech	To speak on the spur of the moment, without any preparation (Informational or persuasive situation)	• If you choose the topic, think of one that is appropriate for your audience. • Think of a main idea, an interesting beginning, and some supporting ideas. • Speak clearly and in a confident voice. • Use a tone that is appropriate to the topic.
Instructions	To give information on how to do a particular task (Informational situation)	• Divide the information into clear, logical steps. • Give the steps in order. • Make sure your listener understands.

Introductions	To introduce yourself or another person to a person or group (Social situation)	• Take the initiative and introduce yourself if no one else does.
		• When introducing another person, identify the person by name.
		• When introducing another person, it is customary to address first
		  • a person of higher status
		  • an older person before a younger one
		  • the person you know better.

Telephone conversations	To communicate via telephone (Social situation)	• Call people at appropriate times of day. • Identify yourself and state the reason for your call. • Be polite and patient. • Keep your call to an appropriate length.

with the announcement of the purpose of the discussion. Below are typical purposes for group discussion.

Purposes for Discussion

- to brainstorm ideas
- to learn cooperatively
- to make a decision, evaluation, or recommendation
- to make plans
- to negotiate agreements
- to solve a problem
- to resolve conflicts

■ **Participating in Discussion** Each member of a group discussion has certain responsibilities.

All group members: All members of a group discussion are responsible for paying attention to the discussion, respecting all group members' opinions, and offering thoughtful comments.

Chairperson: If a group has chosen a discussion leader or chairperson, he or she is responsible for introducing, guiding, moderating, and closing the discussion. The chairperson helps resolve any conflicts between members and makes sure that the group stays focused on its purpose or goal.

Group Secretary or Recorder: One person from the group usually is asked to take notes on important points or decisions made during a discussion. The group secretary or recorder is responsible for these notes and for reading them aloud at the beginning of the next group discussion.

Oral Interpretation

In an *oral interpretation,* you present your ideas about the meaning of a work of literature by reading the work aloud. You use speaking and acting skills—vocal techniques, facial expression, body language, and gestures—to express your interpretation of the literary work. The following steps help in preparing an oral interpretation.

1. **Find and cut material** When you look for material for an oral interpretation, you usually have a specific purpose, audience, and occasion in mind. As a general rule, no props or costumes are required for oral interpretation. For your oral interpretation, you will need to make an abbreviated version, or ***cutting,*** of a work of fiction or nonfiction, poetry, or drama. Use the following guidelines:
   - Follow the story line of the literary work in time order.
   - Delete tag lines, such as "she replied sadly." Instead, use these clues to tell you how to interpret the character's words as you express them.
   - Delete passages that do not contribute to the overall effect or impression you intend to create with your oral interpretation.

2. **Prepare the reading script** A reading script is usually typed (double-spaced) and can be marked to assist you in your interpretive reading. For example, you might underline words to remind you to use special emphasis or make a slash (/) to indicate where you would like a dramatic pause.

3. **Rehearse your interpretation** Once you have developed a reading script, rehearse different interpretations. Pronounce words carefully. Use body language and gestures to emphasize the meaning or to reveal traits of the major characters in the story as you narrate and act out what they say and do.

4. **Deliver your presentation** To begin your presentation, introduce the piece of literature you are interpreting. Give your audience information that sets the scene, tells something about the author, or gives some necessary details about what has already taken place in the story. Then, deliver your interpretation.

Listening

Active listening involves more than hearing a speaker's words. When you listen actively, you receive verbal and nonverbal messages and construct meanings for and respond to those messages.

Basics of the Listening Process

Listening is an indispensable part of the communication process. The stages in the listening process are explained in the following chart.

The Three Stages of the Listening Process

Before you listen

Be physically and mentally prepared to listen. To be an effective listener, you should be physically comfortable and free of distractions that interfere with your ability to focus.

Determine your reason for listening. Are you listening to be entertained? to be informed? to provide support or understanding? to receive instructions or directions? Identifying a reason for listening sets you up as an active listener.

Decide what you already know about the speaker and the subject. Bringing your prior knowledge of a subject or of a speaker to the surface can make your listening experience more productive.

Add to your prior knowledge of the speaker and the subject. Brainstorming with others or doing individual research to increase your knowledge of the speaker and subject will improve your ability to understand and evaluate both.

Keep an open mind. Set aside any biases, prejudices, or preconceived notions you might have concerning the speaker or the topic of the speech. Make your judgments after listening to what the speaker has to say.

As you listen

Make connections to prior knowledge and experience. Try to relate what the speaker is saying to what you know from other sources—experience, books and magazines, television, school, and so on.

Think of questions you would like to ask the speaker. You may or may not have an opportunity to ask the speaker to clarify a point or expand upon an idea, but making yourself think of questions helps you to focus on the speaker's meaning.

Make educated guesses about what a speaker will say next. If you are wrong, try to determine what misled you.

Find meaning behind what the speaker says directly. Make inferences about a speaker's attitudes or opinions by paying attention to what he or she does not say.

After you listen

Discuss the speaker and his or her message with others. Exchange ideas, agree or disagree with the speaker's opinions, and relate the speaker's words to your experience.

Write a summary and evaluation of the speaker and the presentation. Writing about a presentation clarifies and solidifies your thoughts and opinions.

Critical Thinking

Evaluation. So that students can practice evaluating themselves as listeners, give them a situation in which to apply listening skills. Tell students that as volunteers for a group that matches students with appropriate tutors, it is their job to interview students to determine academic subjects with which they need help. Students should pair up and each make a list of questions to ask to determine the problems the student seeking help has. Partners should take turns playing the role of the student to present a question-and-answer session in class. Finally, all students should evaluate themselves as listeners by using the bulleted items on this page.

Evaluating Yourself as a Listener

For oral communication to be effective, you must be a good listener. In fact, the listener carries as much of the responsibility for clear communication as the speaker does. Therefore, it is important for you to be able to evaluate yourself as a listener. The following chart gives several of the points you should look for when you are evaluating yourself as a listener.

Evaluating Yourself as a Listener

A good listener should

- be mentally and physically prepared to listen
- be able to ignore distracting behavior by the speaker and members of the audience
- focus on the speaker throughout the presentation
- follow the organization of the speaker's presentation
- distinguish between facts and opinions
- think of questions to ask the speaker
- determine the speaker's main idea and primary supporting details
- withhold judgment until the presentation is over
- listen for and detect bias or prejudice on the speaker's part
- reflect upon the presentation after it is over
- ask questions of the speaker if given the opportunity
- discuss the presentation with others
- write a summary or evaluation of the presentation

Four Types of Listening

There are four basic types of listening and a number of purposes associated with each type.

Appreciative (or Aesthetic) Listening

The purpose of this type of listening is enjoyment. When you listen to someone read a story or a poem, you are engaged in appreciative listening. There are certain strategies that can make this type of listening experience more rewarding.

- **Before you listen, activate what you know about the literary work you will hear presented.** What do you know about the work, the author, or other works by the same author? To what literary *genre,* or type, does the work belong? What literary elements—conflict, imagery, character, figurative language, climax, rhyme—are important in this type of literature? Make predictions about what you might hear.

- **While you listen, make connections to other literary works and to your personal experiences.** Does the presentation remind you of something else you have read, seen, or heard? Do any of the descriptions remind you of places you have been, people you have known, or feelings you have had? Try to visualize—see in your mind's eye—what you are hearing.

- **After you listen, discuss the presentation with others and evaluate it.** Were your predictions correct or incorrect? Can you determine the reason for any incorrect predictions? What literary and artistic qualities did you find as you listened? Was the speaker's presentation clear? Did the speaker use the appropriate body language? Did the speaker speak effectively? Write what you liked and did not like about the presentation and why.

Critical Listening In this type of listening, you attempt to understand, analyze, and evaluate the speaker's points and the value of the ideas. Critical listening should be applied to messages heard in school, in the workplace, or in the media. You can use the strategies in the following chart to analyze and evaluate media presentations as well as live presentations.

How to Listen Critically	
What to do	**What to listen for**
Identify the speaker's purpose.	Does the speaker make clear why he or she is giving the speech?
Distinguish between facts and opinions.	Does the speaker make statements with which you agree or disagree? Ask yourself why you disagree. (Such statements are opinions. An opinion is a belief or a judgment about something that cannot be proved. A fact is a statement that can be proved true.)
Identify main ideas.	What are the most important points? (Listen for clue words or phrases, such as *major, main,* and *most important.*)
Identify significant or supporting details.	What dates, names, or facts does the speaker use to support the main points of the speech? What kinds of examples or explanations are used to support the main ideas?
Identify the order of organization.	What kind of order does the speaker use to present the information—time sequence, spatial order, order of importance, logical order?
Listen to detect bias.	Is the speaker biased, or prejudiced, toward one point of view? Does the speaker use extreme or all-inclusive words such as *never* or *always*? Does the speaker acknowledge other points of view?
Evaluate the speaker's credibility.	Does the speaker refer to sources of information? Are the sources respectable or credible, such as newspaper and journal articles or reference materials?
Note comparisons and contrasts.	Are some details compared or contrasted with others?
Predict outcomes and draw conclusions.	What can you reasonably conclude from the facts and evidence presented in the speech?
Look for logic.	Does the speaker build arguments in a logical way? Does the speaker use false logic, such as hasty generalization, false cause and effect, or circular reasoning?
Look for emotional appeals.	Does the speaker use the bandwagon appeal? the glittering generality? snob appeal? plain folks appeal? the veiled threat?
Understand cause and effect.	Do some events described by the speaker relate to or affect others? Does the speaker make the logical connections between cause and effect?

Listening **859**

TEACHING (**TIP**)

Comprehensive Listening
So that students can practice critical and comprehensive listening, have them use the LQ2R Method that is explained on this page. When you plan to lecture on a topic, ask students to practice the LQ2R. You might want to create an LQ2R sheet students can use to help them recall each step. Finally, ask students to reflect on their listening skills by freewriting a short paragraph in response to the following prompts.

From this activity, I learned that listening is _____.

The part of the LQ2R Method that is most beneficial is _____.

Comprehensive Listening When you listen for the content of a message, you are engaged in *comprehensive listening.* Some people call this type of listening *informational listening.* Much of the listening you do in school is of this type. Listening for information and listening to instructions are examples of comprehensive listening.

- **Listening for information** You are often in situations where you listen to acquire information. When a teacher describes a certain chemical reaction, for example, he or she is delivering information you need to understand, not attempting to be persuasive or entertaining. The following strategies are helpful in these situations.

  1. **The LQ2R Method** helps you when you listen for information from a speaker.

     L Listen carefully to material as it is being presented.

     Q Question yourself as you listen. Mentally, or in your notes, make a list of questions as they occur to you.

     R Recite in your own words the information as it is being presented. Summarize the material in your mind.

     R Review the whole presentation. You should restate or reemphasize major points.

  2. **Note Taking** One way to keep track of a speaker's ideas is to take notes. Of course, you cannot possibly write down every word the speaker says. Develop an effective way to jot down the speaker's main points and supporting details as well as your own thoughts, questions, or comments. For example, you could use split-page notes—divide your paper so that forty percent of

the page lies to the left and sixty percent lies to the right. Take brief notes on the left-hand side only, leaving the right-hand side for reorganizing and expanding your notes after listening. (See also **Notes on Reading or Lectures** on page 863.)

- **Listening to instructions** Because instructions are usually made up of a series of steps, you can easily misunderstand them. The following steps can help you make sense of instructions.

  1. **Listen for the order of the steps.** Listen for words such as *first, second, next, then,* and *last* to tell you when one step ends and the next one begins.

  2. **Identify the number of steps in the process.** Take notes if the instructions are long or complicated. Do not hesitate to ask for clarification or for the speaker to slow down as you take notes.

  3. **Visualize each step.** Imagine yourself actually performing each step. Try to get a mental image of what you should be doing at every step in the process.

  4. **Review the steps.** When the speaker is finished, be sure you understand the process from beginning to end. Ask questions if you are unsure.

NOTE When you take a message on the telephone, you are listening for information that answers the basic *5W-How?* questions—*Who? What? When? Where? Why?* and *How?* For example, you should take down details that answer questions such as *Who is calling? What is the message or purpose for the call? Where can the caller be reached? When can the caller be reached?* and *How may you help the caller?*

Empathic (or Reflective) Listening

When you want to help a friend understand a difficult problem or when you want to show someone your understanding and acceptance, you use *empathic listening.* To show empathic listening through your facial expressions and body language and through your responses to the speaker, use the following strategies.

- Do much more listening than talking.

- Show genuine warmth and concern.

- Paraphrase what the speaker says to show your understanding.

- Respond to the speaker's feelings rather than analyze the facts.

- Keep your opinions to yourself.

Special Listening Situations

Some situations—**group discussions** and **interviews,** for example—require that you participate not only as a careful listener, but also as a speaker.

Listening in a Group Discussion

Listening as a member of a group discussion is different from listening as a member of a large audience because you participate as both a listener and a speaker. The following tips should help you participate effectively in a group discussion.

- Sit up, look at each speaker, and nod to show agreement or understanding.

- Demonstrate respect for the other group members by paying attention and not making comments while they are speaking.

- Take notes on each speaker's points and list your questions or comments.

- When you are ready to speak, raise your hand and be recognized.

- Concentrate on what the speaker is saying, not on what you intend to say when it is your turn to speak.

Listening in an Interview
An interview is a unique listening situation that usually takes place between two people: the interviewer and the interviewee. In addition to the strategies recommended in "Conducting an interview" and "Interviewing for a job" on page 854, use the following special listening techniques to make the most of an interview.

- As interviewer

  1. **When you ask a question, listen to the complete answer.** Be courteous and patient; think of related follow-up questions as your interviewee responds.

  2. **Respect the interviewee's opinions, even if you do not agree with him or her.** You may state your disagreement politely only if your comment will serve to prompt the interviewee to clarify, expand, or provide support for a statement or claim. Avoid disagreeing if you are likely to upset your interviewee and disrupt the interview.

  3. **Monitor your nonverbal communication.** Make sure that your nonverbal reactions, such as your facial expressions and gestures, reflect a respectful tone. Maintain good eye contact, nod to show understanding, and smile to indicate your interest.

  4. **Always thank the interviewee at the end of your interview.**

- As interviewee

  1. **Listen to the interviewer's complete question before answering.** If you start answering the question before the interviewer finishes asking it, you might answer the wrong question.

  2. **Answer the question.** Stick to the point the interviewer is addressing. Do not simply ignore the question and respond with something totally off track.

Studying and Test Taking

Study Skills and Strategies

Why Study?

The purpose of studying is not just to do well on tests and get good grades. It is also to help you understand and remember information you may need later. (See also **Test-Taking Skills** on page 865 and **Reading and Vocabulary** on page 832.)

Making a Study Plan   The following suggestions may help you use your study time effectively.

1. **Know what's expected of you before you study.** Record your assignments and the dates they are due on a calendar or planner. Know what your teacher expects you to do or know.
2. **Manage your time.** Divide larger assignments into smaller units. For example, study one section of a chapter, take a break, then study the next section. Schedule time to complete each of the smaller units.
3. **Focus your mind on your studies.** Plan where and when you will study. Have a regular time to study and a place that is strictly for studying. Be realistic about what things distract you. If the television will distract you, turn it off or study where it won't be a problem.

Organizing and Remembering Information

The strategies listed below can help you organize and remember information as you study.

Classifying   *Classification* is a method of organizing items into categories. When you make an outline, for example, you use classification to decide which ideas fit together under a certain heading. When you group things, you identify relationships among them.

EXAMPLE   What do the following cities have in common: London, Paris, Warsaw, Prague, Rome?

Answer   They are all European capitals.

You also classify when you identify patterns. For example, look at the following number sequence.

What is the next number in the series?
8   11   15   20   26   <u>33</u>

Answer   *3* is added to the first number to produce the second number. *4* is added to the second number to produce the third number; *5* is added to the third number; and *6* to the fourth number. Therefore, *7* should be added to the fifth number (26) to produce the answer, which should be *33*.

Graphic Organizers You may find it helpful to reorganize information from a reading passage or from class notes into a chart, map, or diagram. Graphic organizers work by translating information into a visual form. (See also **Graphic Organizers** on page 815.)

Memorization To memorize and remember what you have learned, you should practice in frequent, short, focused sessions. Try playing memory games such as making a word out of the first letters of key terms or ideas.

Notes on Reading or Lectures Taking careful *notes* while reading or listening to a lecture will help you organize and remember information later when you study for tests or write research papers. The steps below explain how to take study notes.

How to Take Notes

1. Recognize and record main points. In a lecture, listen for **key words** and **phrases** used by the speaker, such as *major* or *most important.* Key words like these indicate points that you should remember. In a textbook, pay attention to chapter headings, subheadings, lists, charts, time lines, or illustrations.

2. Summarize what you hear or read. Don't record every detail. Summarize and abbreviate information about key ideas. Indent supporting points to distinguish them from the main points.

3. Note important examples. Make note of important examples that illustrate the main points of the lecture or lesson. Just jotting the phrase *Boston Tea Party* or sketching a divided cell in your notes may jog your memory later.

Look at the following student notes. The student who made these notes arranged details in groups beneath headings (underlined) that indicate the key ideas from the passage.

Jade Snow Wong

Biography
- Chinese American
- born in 1922 in San Francisco
- graduated from Mills College in 1942
- began pottery business in 1946

Early Disappointment
- pottery not accepted at first
- considered too crude, like peasant pots

Perseverance
- received good advice
- continued producing pottery

Success
- pottery sold outside her native community
- people loved simplicity, understated beauty
- business soon thriving, work highly regarded
- awarded regional and national prizes
- pottery placed in museums

Outlines When you write an *outline,* you record important ideas and information, then group them into an organized pattern that shows their order and their relationship to one another. (See also **Formal** and **Informal Outlines** on page 895.)

Paraphrasing A *paraphrase* is a restatement of someone else's ideas in your own words. When you restate an idea in your own words, you are not just switching around words, but actually concentrating on the concept expressed in those words. By considering the concept carefully through paraphrasing, you are often more likely to understand and remember the ideas. A paraphrase is approximately the same length as the original. (See also **Paraphrasing** on page 834.)

SQ3R *SQ3R* stands for *Survey, Question, Read, Recite,* and *Review.* This strategy involves you in actively responding to any text that you are reading. (See also **SQ3R** on page 836.)

Summarizing A *summary* is a restatement in condensed form of the main points of a pas-

sage. When you summarize, you must decide which ideas and details in a passage are important enough to include. Making these decisions helps you remember the information in a passage. (See also **Summarizing** on page 836.)

Writing to Learn Writing is a valuable study tool. By writing, you may focus your thoughts, respond to ideas, record your observations, plan your work, and restate ideas in your own words. Use the different forms of writing described below as you study.

Type of Writing	How It Helps	Guidelines and Examples
Diary	helps you recall your impressions and express your feelings	• Diary writing is often more personal than other writing, so you will want to be sure to keep your diary in a safe place. Try to write in your diary regularly. • Write about your reactions to issues raised during a lecture or in a chapter you read for class.
Freewriting	helps you focus your thoughts	• When freewriting, don't censor your thoughts. Try to get down everything that comes into your mind about your topic. • Write for three minutes after class or after reviewing your notes in order to focus on the most important points.
Journal	helps you record your observations, descriptions, solutions, and questions	• Like diary writing, journal writing is best if you make entries on a regular basis. Remember that you should not worry about making mistakes; you should include observations, reflections, or even inquiries. Also, remember to date all your entries. • Write about problems or successes you had in solving word problems in math.
Learning Log	helps you present a problem, analyze it, and propose a solution	• As you write about your learning process and about the material you are covering in class, make connections between this new information and what you have learned before. You could also create your own vocabulary list of words that are important to remember for a certain unit or class. • Write about the way you will incorporate a source or piece of information into a research paper for your social studies class.

Test-Taking Skills and Strategies

You are likely to take two types of tests in school—**classroom tests** and **standardized tests.** Different kinds of tests will ask different questions; you will need to consider different strategies to approach each.

Classroom Tests

The typical *classroom test* measures how well you use the skills you have learned or whether you have learned certain required information about a subject. You will usually find a combination of many kinds of test questions in a classroom test. For example, a test in a science class might begin with objective multiple-choice questions, and then conclude with an essay question that tests for deeper understanding of a concept. To prepare for a classroom test, familiarize yourself with the material that will be covered, or practice the skill you must demonstrate at the time of testing. Also make sure you are aware of the different kinds of questions that are asked on classroom tests.

Essay Questions In answering an *essay question* you must demonstrate a critical understanding of the material you have learned. More than just knowing details such as dates and definitions, you must often know how these details relate to each other—for example by showing how one event influenced another or by showing how one item compares to another. You will need to be sure to cover all the major points mentioned in the question. Essay questions also test your ability to express your understanding in a well-written, well-organized composition. There is never just one correct answer to any essay question; each student

has different ways of thinking and writing about a topic. Nonetheless, these steps should help you prepare for any essay question:

- Review your textbook and lecture notes carefully.
- Make an outline of your study materials by identifying key ideas and supporting details.
- Create a set of possible questions and practice writing out answers for each.
- Check your answers for accuracy by using your textbook and notes. Revise your answers and use them to spin off new study questions.

How to Answer Essay Questions

1. Preview the test. How many questions does the test ask? Budget your time between preparing and writing each answer.

2. Carefully read all the questions. Note the key terms in each question to be sure what the question is asking. If there are several parts to each question, be sure you cover all parts in your answer.

3. Note key verbs in each question. Every essay question asks you to perform a specific task that is expressed with a verb. Learn to recognize the key verbs that commonly appear on essay tests. (See also the **Key Verbs That Appear in Essay Questions** chart on page 866.)

4. Plan your answer by using prewriting strategies. Make notes or an outline to help you decide what you want to say. Write notes or a rough outline on scratch paper. (See also **Prewriting Techniques** on page 897.)

5. Evaluate and revise as you write. You will rarely have time to redraft your whole essay, so be sure that your main points are strong and well written. Leave time to re-read your answer and to correct any spelling, punctuation, or grammatical errors.

Key Verbs That Appear in Essay Questions		
Key Verb	**Task**	**Sample Question**
Analyze	Look carefully at the parts of something to see how each part works.	**Analyze** the relationship between water quality and aquatic life in local streams.
Argue	Take a stand on an issue and give reasons to support your viewpoint or opinion.	**Argue** whether or not the school year should be twelve months long.
Compare or **Contrast**	Point out the similarities or differences between things, people, or ideas.	**Contrast** the most recent national election with the national election of 1996.
Define	Give specific details that make something or some idea unique.	**Define** the term *federalism* as it applies to the foundations of the United States Constitution.
Demonstrate	Provide examples to support a point.	**Demonstrate** how the use of car seat belts has reduced the number of traffic fatalities across the United States.
Describe	Give a picture in words.	**Describe** the behavior of an Asian elephant when it feels threatened.
Discuss	Examine in detail.	**Discuss** the term *planned obsolescence.*
Explain	Give reasons or make the meaning clear.	**Explain** the development of the American two-party political system.
Summarize	Give a brief overview of the main points.	**Summarize** the *Emancipation Proclamation.*

Each essay question requires you to perform a specific task, expressed with a verb. You can prepare yourself for creating a specific response to these tasks by familiarizing yourself with the key terms and the kinds of information called for in essay questions. Each essay question response is as unique as the person who writes it. Still, a well-written essay meets all of the following guidelines:

- The essay answers the question, including all parts.
- The essay has an introduction, a body, and a conclusion.
- The main ideas and supporting points are clearly presented in the body.
- All the sentences are complete and well written.
- The essay has no errors in spelling, punctuation, or grammar.

Matching Questions   In matching questions, you need to match the items on two lists.

EXAMPLE

Directions: Write the letter of each state (from the right column) next to its capital (in the left column).

_C_   **1.** Trenton   **A.** Montana
_A_   **2.** Helena   **B.** New Hampshire
_B_   **3.** Concord   **C.** New Jersey

How to Answer Matching Questions

1. Read the directions carefully. Sometimes answers may be used more than once.

2. Scan the columns and match items you know first. That way, you can gain some time for evaluating other answers.

3. Complete the matching process. On any remaining items, make an educated guess.

Multiple-Choice Questions   The *multiple-choice question* asks you to select a correct answer from among a number of choices.

EXAMPLE

1. Which of the following items is *not* a characteristic of the manatee, or sea cow?
   A. It can remain underwater for thirty minutes.
   B. It is usually found in small groups.
   C. It is a coldblooded animal.
   D. It prefers water temperatures above 46°C.

How to Answer Multiple-Choice Questions

1. Read the initial statement carefully. Make sure you understand the statement completely before looking at your choices. Always look for qualifiers, such as *not, always,* or *never,* because these words limit or affect the answer. In the example above,

you must choose the quality that a manatee does *not* have.

2. Read all the answers before making a choice. Sometimes the answer includes two or more choices, such as "Both **A** and **B**" or "All of the above." Remember, in the example, you are looking for the quality that a manatee does *not* have, so you must consider the possible answers carefully.

3. Narrow your choices by eliminating the answers you know are incorrect. Some answers are clearly wrong, while others are somewhat related to the correct answer. You may know that manatees can easily stay underwater for thirty minutes. Since you are looking for qualities a manatee does *not* have, you can easily rule out **A**.

4. From the remaining choices, select the answer that makes the most sense. The answer is **C**.

Short-Answer Questions   *Short-answer questions* ask you to explain what you know about a subject in a brief, written reply. In general, short-answer questions require a specific answer of one or two sentences. (Some short-answer questions, such as maps or diagrams that you are supposed to label, or fill-in-the-blank questions, can be answered with one or a few words.)

EXAMPLE

1. Why do insects shed their outer shells?

1. An insect's outer shell does not grow. As the insect grows, it must shed the old shell and grow a new one that fits.

True/False Questions   *True/false questions* ask you to determine whether a given statement is true or false.

EXAMPLE

1. T (F)   All spiders build webs to catch prey for food.

Test-Taking Skills and Strategies   **867**

How to Answer True/False Questions

1. Read the statement carefully.

2. Check for qualifiers. Words such as *always* or *never* qualify or limit a statement's meaning. The example above is false because many spiders hunt their prey without the use of web snares. The word *all* limits the statement and makes it false.

3. Choose an answer based on two following principles: One, if any part of the statement is false, the entire statement is false; and two, a statement is true only if it is entirely and always true.

Standardized Tests

Standardized tests measure the skills you've learned in school. Your scores on these tests are evaluated in comparison to a standard or norm compiled from the scores of other students who have taken the same test. Two tests of this type, the *Scholastic Aptitude Test* (SAT) and the *American College Testing Program* (ACT), are given to students across the entire United States. To help you prepare for standardized tests, keep in mind the three tips in the following chart.

How to Prepare for Standardized Tests

1. Learn what will be tested. Information booklets may be provided. Practice with these or with published study guides.

2. Know what materials you will need. On the day of the test, you may need to bring specific materials, such as your official test registration card, number-two pencils, or lined paper for writing an essay.

3. Determine how the test is evaluated. If there is no penalty for wrong answers, make your best guess on every question. If wrong answers are penalized, however, make guesses only if you are fairly sure of the correct answer.

The following information describes and explains the types of questions and writing prompts you may encounter on standardized tests and provides some strategies for answering them.

Analogy Questions *Analogy questions* ask you to analyze the relationship between a pair of words and to identify a second pair of words that has the same relationship. Analogy questions usually appear on standardized tests in multiple-choice form.

EXAMPLE
Directions: Select the appropriate pair of words to complete the analogy.
TOE : FOOT :: _____
  A. hand : glove   **C.** trumpet : piano
  B. bowl : spoon   **D.** sleeve : jacket

Sometimes, however, analogies are written as fill-in-the-blank questions, and you may need to fill in the missing item.

EXAMPLE
WILD CAT : LION :: tool : ___hammer___

How to Answer Analogy Questions

1. Analyze the first pair of words and identify the relationship between them. In the first example above, the relationship of *toe* to *foot* is that of a part to its whole. (See also **Types of Analogies** chart on page 869.)

2. Express the analogy in sentence or question form. The example would be expressed as, "A *toe* is a part of a *foot,* just as a _____ is a part of a _____." Fill the blanks with the possible answers and see which makes sense. For example, does answer **A** work? Let's check: A *toe* is a part of a *foot,* just as a *hand* is a part of a *glove.*" That answer doesn't make sense.

How to Answer Analogy Questions

Since a spoon is not a part of a bowl and a trumpet is not a part of a piano, **D** must be the correct answer. "A *toe* is a part of a *foot,* just as a *sleeve* is a part of a *jacket.*"

3. Find the best available choice to complete the analogy. If multiple choice answers are provided, select the pair of words that shares the same relationship as the first pair of words. If you must fill in a word, look closely at the first pair and then select a word that has a similar relationship to the single given word.

In addition to these guidelines, remember the following helpful tips for solving analogies.

- **Consider the parts of speech.** Some words may be used as more than one part of speech. If you cannot unlock the relationship in the analogy, it may help to determine if one of the words can be another part of speech.

- **Familiarize yourself with the types of analogy relationships.** Become familiar with the types of analogies typically found on standardized tests. (For more on **identifying analogy relationships,** see the **Types of Analogies** chart below.)

- **Remember: The relationship between the words is important, not the meanings of the individual words.** Look again at the second example on page 868. A *lion* and a *hammer* have nothing in common; but the relationship a *wild cat* has to a *lion* is the same as the one a *tool* has to a *hammer*: classification. A lion is a kind of wild cat and a hammer is a kind of tool.

Although there are many different relationships that can be represented in analogies, a smaller number of specific relationships are fairly common. Examples of these common types are shown in the following chart.

Types of Analogies

Type	Example	Solution
Action to Performer or **Performer to Action**	PLOWING : FARMER : : sewing : tailor	*Plowing* is performed by a *farmer,* just as *sewing* is performed by a *tailor.*
Antonyms	ETHICAL : IMMORAL : : compassionate : cruel	*Ethical* behavior is the opposite of *immoral* behavior, just as *compassionate* is the opposite of *cruel* behavior.
Cause or **Effect**	ACCIDENT : SADNESS : : gift : joy	An *accident* causes *sadness,* just as a *gift* causes *joy.*
Characteristic	LIONS : CARNIVOROUS : : cows : herbivorous	*Lions* are always *carnivorous* (meat eaters), just as *cows* are always *herbivorous* (plant eaters).
Classification	SPIDER : ARACHNID : : frog : amphibian	A *spider* is a kind of *arachnid,* just as a *frog* is a kind of *amphibian.*
Degree	CHUCKLE : LAUGH : : whimper : cry	A *chuckle* is a little *laugh,* just as a *whimper* is a little *cry.*

(continued)

Type	Example	Solution
Measure	THERMOMETER : TEMPERATURE : : clock : time	A *thermometer* is used to measure *temperature,* just as a *clock* is used to measure *time.*
Part to Whole or **Whole to Part**	CHAPTER : BOOK : : act : play	A *chapter* is a part of a *book,* just as an *act* is a part of a *play.*
Place	BATON ROUGE : LOUISIANA : : Paris : France	*Baton Rouge* is the capital of *Louisiana,* just as *Paris* is the capital of *France.*
Synonyms	DRY : ARID : : horrid : ghastly	*Dry* is similar in meaning to *arid,* just as *horrid* is similar in meaning to *ghastly.*
Use	BOW : VIOLIN : : keyboard : computer	A *bow* is used to play the *violin,* just as a *keyboard* is used to operate a *computer.*

Critical-Reading Questions Standardized tests ask questions that test your ability to examine a piece of writing in detail and show your understanding of it. These ***critical-reading questions*** (sometimes called ***on-demand reading questions***) require that you look closely at a particular text to determine its organizational structure, meaning, and purpose. These questions may also require you to decide whether the passage is effective in conveying the writer's intended meaning. Critical-reading questions focus on either a specific element of a passage or on how the writer created his or her work. The following chart shows the usual kind of critical-reading questions and how you should approach answering them. For more information and practice with any of the bulleted items indicated, see the pages referred to in parentheses.

Critical-Reading Test Questions

Rhetorical strategy questions, or **evaluation questions,** ask you to decide how effective a writer's techniques are. These test items have you identify and analyze

- the author's intended audience
- the author's purpose (page 257)
- the author's opinions (page 257)
- the author's tone or point of view (page 257)

Inference questions, or **interpretation questions,** ask you to draw conclusions or make inferences about the information given in a passage. You will often be asked to identify

- unclear information (page 339)
- specific conclusions or inferences that can be drawn about the author or the topic of a passage (page 833)
- conclusions or inferences based on given material (page 158)

(See also **Inference Questions** on page 167.)

Critical-Reading Test Questions

Organization questions, or **main idea** or **detail questions,** ask you to identify how the writer organized the passage. These test items often ask you to find

- the main idea of a passage (page 347)
- arrangement of supporting details (page 359)
- the author's use of particular writing strategies (page 133)
- techniques used to conclude the passage
- transitional devices that make the passage coherent (page 363)

(See also **Main Idea and Detail Questions** on page 28.)

Style questions, or **tone questions,** ask you to look closely at a passage to evaluate the author's use of style. You will often be asked to identify

- the author's intended audience
- the author's voice and tone
- the author's style

Synthesis questions ask you to demonstrate your knowledge of how parts of a passage fit together into a whole. You will be asked to interpret

- the cumulative meaning of details in a passage (page 355)
- techniques used to unify details (page 355)

Vocabulary-in-context questions ask you to infer the meaning of a word from its context in a passage. (page 841)

Here is a typical **reading passage** followed by sample test questions based on this passage.

In our world of microwave ovens and supersonic jets, waiting on a computer seems to be the most tedious of things. Why do these so-called "electronic brains" take so long at times? Probably because they are speaking another language. Computer language is based on the binary number system—that is, all words, images, and sounds are transmitted through an alphabet made up of only two digits: 0 and 1. For example, if we convert our twenty-six-letter alphabet into numbers using only 0 or 1, then A could be 0, B could be 1, C could be 10, D could be 11, and so on. Using this system, the binary code representing the word *dog* could be a long number like 000110111000110.

Can you imagine sending an e-mail message this way, or downloading your favorite song off the Internet? Without a shortcut, one second of a high-definition video would take more than seven hours to reach your home across the average modem.

Mathematics not only helped create this system—a language that machines can understand—but also created means of making it work more efficiently—binary data compression. Systems have been developed that compress data into a form that not only can be transmitted across the Internet in less time, but also can be decompressed without losing any significant amount of the original data. In this way, computer compressors significantly reduce the size of any file for easy transmission across cyberspace.

Sample Critical-Reading Questions

1. What is the main idea of this passage?

   A. Computers use an alphabet of 0's and 1's.

   B. Computers are slower than users expect them to be.

   C. Binary data compression helps speed information exchange over the Internet.

   D. E-mail messages contain huge amounts of information.

[This organization question requires you to identify the paragraph's main idea.]

2. The word *binary* in this passage means

   A. electronic

   B. expressed by two digits

   C. tied together

   D. mechanically complex

[This vocabulary-in-context question requires you to examine the word's context to determine its meaning.]

3. In which of the following sources was the passage most likely originally found?

   A. a computer manual

   B. a Web site introducing readers to the Internet

   C. an introductory mathematics textbook

   D. a scientific journal

[This rhetorical strategy question requires you to identify the author's intended audience.]

4. Microwave ovens and supersonic jets are referred to because

   A. Microwave ovens and supersonic jets both use computers.

   B. The author thinks these two items are more advanced than computers.

   C. Modern people are used to fast technology.

   D. Like the computer, they are twentieth century inventions.

[This inference question requires you to examine the context of these two details to explain their purpose in the passage.]

5. The author of this passage wants to explain

   A. that computers are actually faster than you might think

   B. the binary number system

   C. the mathematical principles behind the Internet

   D. that computers are slow because they use a complex language

[This synthesis question requires you to read the passage as a whole to make a generalization about the passage from the details.]

NOTE Sometimes it helps to compare the wording of the prompt to the wording in the reading passage. Finding the same or similar language may lead you to the place in the passage where the answer can be found. For example, question two in the chart above cites a word (*digit*) that is clearly present in the second paragraph of the reading passage. However, if the same or similar words from the prompt cannot be found within the reading passage, you will have to come up with your own examples or draw your own conclusions.

Multiple-Choice Questions *Multiple-choice questions,* similar to those found on classroom tests, are commonly found in many standardized tests. The multiple-choice questions on standardized tests will generally begin with simpler questions, then become harder the farther you get into the test. Start by answering all the questions you can easily answer before attempting the more difficult ones, because each question, whether easy or difficult, is worth the same amount. Budget your time by not spending too much time on any single question. (See also **Multiple-Choice Questions** on page 866.)

On-Demand Writing Prompts

On-demand writing prompts are the core of many state writing tests. They are similar to essay questions because they require you to write several paragraphs on a broad topic in a limited amount of time. The key difference is that you will not know in advance what the topic of an on-demand writing prompt will be. The compositions that you write will usually be either persuasive, informative, or descriptive.

EXAMPLE

Many states are now requiring all bicyclists under the age of eighteen to wear a helmet when they ride. Write a persuasive essay in which you argue whether or not such helmet laws are a good idea.

Another variation of the on-demand writing prompt is found in proficiency tests that ask a general question that must be answered with specific details pulled from your knowledge of a specific subject area.

EXAMPLE

In many literary works, the setting plays a major part in conveying the author's message. In a well-organized essay, describe how the author manages to strengthen the message of his or her work through the setting. Avoid plot summary.

How to Respond to an On-Demand Writing Prompt

1. Read the prompt and determine what it is telling you to do. Look for key verbs to indicate whether your answer should be persuasive, informative, or descriptive. (See also the **Key Verbs That Appear in Essay Questions** chart on page 866.)

2. Plan your response using prewriting techniques such as freewriting and clustering. (See also **Prewriting Techniques** on page 897.)

3. Evaluate and revise your response as you write. Make sure that your answer has a topic sentence, supporting details, transitions between ideas, and a clear conclusion.

Although you cannot study for the content of an on-demand writing test, you can still prepare yourself by following these steps:

- *Become familiar with the kinds of writing on-demand writing tests often require.* Read and learn to recognize the key qualities of persuasive, informative, and descriptive essays.

- *Practice writing answers to on-demand writing prompts.* If possible, practice with questions that have appeared on standardized tests administered at your school in the past—usually available through your school counselors or library. Use a timer to simulate the time limits of an actual test.

- *Revise and proofread your answers.* If possible, share and discuss your answers with classmates. Talk about the aspects of your answer that show that it is persuasive, informative, or descriptive.

Reasoning or Logic Questions

Some questions may test your reasoning abilities more than your knowledge of a specific subject.

Reasoning or *logic questions* (sometimes called *sentence completion questions*) are multiple-choice questions that measure your ability to recognize certain kinds of relationships. These questions may ask you to analyze a sentence or brief passage and to fill in one or more blanks with the most appropriate word or words given.

EXAMPLE

Considering the vast amounts of information that are _____ through cyberspace, it is a wonder that data compression systems work so _____.

A. exchanged . . . efficiently
B. deciphered . . . technologically
C. busy . . . expensive
D. flying . . . unsuccessfully

How to Answer Reasoning or Logic Questions

1. Be sure that you understand the instructions. Reasoning or logic questions are usually multiple-choice questions.

2. Analyze the relationship implied in the question. Look carefully at the question to gather information about the relationship shared by the items. The example question suggests a cause-and-effect relationship between the amount of information in cyberspace and how data compression systems work.

3. Insert each word or pair of words to see if the sentence makes sense with the insertion. Remember that if a pair of words is asked for, the first word in the suggested pairs may make perfect sense, but the second may not. For example, the first word in answer **D**, *flying,* seems like a possibility but the second word, *unsuccessfully,* makes little sense in the context of the sentence.

Verbal-Expression Questions

Standardized tests often assess how well you understand written expression and grammatical correctness. The following chart shows the four standard types of verbal-expression questions. (For more information and practice on the **grammar, usage, and mechanics elements,** refer to the pages in parentheses.)

Verbal-Expression Questions

Grammar Questions
You identify the correct answer, using standard grammar and usage rules. These test items often cover use of
- principal parts of verbs (page 517)
- pronouns (page 378)
- subject-verb agreement (page 493)

Punctuation Questions
You identify use of correct punctuation. These test items often cover correct use of
- apostrophes and hyphens (pages 698 and 714)
- end marks and commas (page 636)
- parentheses and quotation marks (pages 720 and 793)
- semicolons, colons, and dashes (pages 666 and 714)

Sentence Structure Questions
You show knowledge of what makes a complete sentence. These test items often cover
- combining sentences (page 330)
- fragments and run-ons (pages 320 and 327)
- parallel structure (page 339)
- transitional words (page 364)
- verb usage (page 516)

Revision-in-Context Questions
You show appropriate revision to a composition. These test items often cover
- arranging ideas (page 359)
- composition structure (page 369)
- tone
- unity and coherence (pages 355 and 359)

Standardized tests usually do not ask verbal-expression questions by themselves. Instead, you find them within the context of a reading passage. A sample passage, usually a paragraph, includes several words and phrases that are underlined and numbered. You then choose the answer that best expresses the meaning, is grammatically correct, or is consistent with the style and tone of the passage. Here is a typical verbal-expression test passage followed by sample questions:

> Although the Yamal peninsula of northern Siberia sits atop the world's largest untapped natural gas reserves nearly(1) one third of the Nanet people living there still live as nomadic reindeer herders. Each family of Nanet herders lives(2) in transportable, tepee-like "chooms." The children of the Nanet(3) attend boarding school in Yar Sale, the region's only town. They commute to school by helicopter. They commute by flying in and out of town at the beginning and end of each school year.

There are two basic types of test items used to test verbal expression on national tests.

Most Common Types of Verbal-Expression Test Items

"NO CHANGE" Items

- give a list of suggested revisions of underlined, numbered portions of passage
- always contain one "NO CHANGE" choice if the indicated part is correct as is

Critical Thinking Items

- ask you to analyze and evaluate the passage as a whole
- ask you to make inferences about portions of a passage as related to the whole

Sample Verbal-Expression Questions

1. A. NO CHANGE
   B. reserves; nearly
   C. reserves. Nearly,
   D. reserves, nearly

[This question about punctuation requires that you know appropriate punctuation.]

2. A. NO CHANGE
   B. live
   C. are living
   D. living

[This question about grammar requires that you know correct subject-verb agreement.]

3. Which is the best revision of this portion of the passage?
   A. NO CHANGE
   B. They attend
   C. Their children attend
   D. The children who are Nanet attend

[This revision-in-context question requires that you use revision skills to express best the ideas in the passage.]

4. How should the final two sentences be combined?
   A. The children commute to school by flying in and out of town at the beginning and end of each school year by helicopter.
   B. The children commute to school by helicopter, flying in and out of town at the beginning and end of each school year.
   C. The children commute to school by helicopter; and they commute by flying in and out of town at the beginning and end of each school year.
   D. Because the children commute to school by helicopter, they commute by flying in and out of town at the beginning and end of each school year.

[This question about sentence structure requires you to combine sentences.]

Viewing and Representing

TEACHING TIP

Media Terms

Point out to students that these media terms may be applied to any of the mass media they experience from day to day. Because some forms of media, such as the Internet, are recent developments, the terms in the list continue to evolve. You may want to discuss with students terms of recent coinage they think should be on the lists but are not included. For definitions of many more media terms, please refer to the ancillary *Media Literacy and Communication Skills: A How-to Handbook for High School Students*.

QUICK REFERENCE HANDBOOK

Media Terms

Because media messages, such as advertisements, television programs, music videos, and movies, are a constant part of life, it is important to be able to understand, interpret, analyze, evaluate, and create media messages. The terms defined below refer to many different areas of media communication, including television and film production, advertising, and journalism. The terms are grouped into three lists: **electronic media terms** (below), **general media terms** (page 880), and **print media terms** (page 883). (Terms relating to the Internet and the World Wide Web can be found in the **Library/Media Center** section on page 823; terms relating to use of type and graphics can be found in **Document Design** on page 806.)

Electronic Media Terms

Advertising   (See **Advertising** on page 883.)

Affiliate   An *affiliate* is a privately owned, local television or radio station that presents the programming of a national network. (See also **Network** on page 879.)

Animation   *Animation* is the film art of making drawings appear to move. An animated film may combine drawing, painting, sculpture, or other visual arts. Animators take film or video pictures of a scene at a rate of twenty-four frames per second, making small changes as they go. When viewed, the frames create the illusion of movement. Animation is used in many different types of media messages, including advertising and cartoons. (See also **Advertising** on page 883.)

Broadcasting   *Broadcasting* means using airwaves to send television or radio content over a wide area of potential viewers or listeners. **Commercial broadcasting** is for profit. Advertisers pay broadcasters for airtime in which to persuade the audience to buy their products or services. **Public broadcasting** is not-for-profit. In the United States, the Public Broadcasting Service (PBS) has more than three hundred affiliates, or member stations. The service is funded mostly by the federal government, corporations, and individual viewers and listeners. (See also **Affiliate** on this page.)

Byline   (See **Byline** on page 884.)

Cable Television   *Cable television* is a method of distributing TV signals using cables and wiring instead of airwaves to bring messages into people's homes. There are two principal types of cable TV companies. Some companies *create* original programming in the form of channels or networks, such as all-news networks or all-music channels. Other companies *distribute* packages, or groups, of many different channels into homes.

Camera Angle   The *camera angle* refers to the angle at which a camera is set when it is pointed at its subject. The angle may be low, high, or tilted. The effect of a low angle is to make the subject look tall and powerful. The high angle makes the subject look small. The tilted angle suggests that the subject is not balanced.

Camera Shots   A *camera shot* is what the viewer sees in a movie or video. Just as a story needs many words, a film or video needs many shots in order to create a scene or story. Below are the most common shots used in film production.

- **Close-up shot**   A *close-up shot* is a shot of only the subject, usually a person's face.
- **Extreme close-up shot**   An *extreme close-up shot* is a very close shot, usually of only part of a person's face or part of the subject.
- **Long shot**   A *long shot* is a shot that shows a scene from far away, usually to show a place or setting of a scene.
- **Medium shot**   A *medium shot* is a shot that shows the subject, usually a person from the waist up, and perhaps some of the background.
- **Reverse angle shot**   A *reverse angle shot* is a view of the opposite side of a subject or of another person in the scene.

Channel   In general communication, a *channel* is the means by which a message is communicated. For example, if you are communicating verbally (such as by talking or singing), the channel is sound waves. If you communicate nonverbally (for instance, by gestures, expressions, handshakes, or sounds such as laughter or clapping), the channel is waves of light, sound waves, or the sense of touch. In television and radio, a channel is a fixed band of frequencies used for the transmitting of television or radio broadcasts. (See also **Medium** and **Message** on page 885.)

Copy   (See also **Copy** on page 884.)

Credits   *Credits* refer to the list of names of people who worked to produce a program. This list usually appears at the end of a television program, film, or video or on the back of a compact disc case.

Demographics   (See **Demographics** on page 884.)

Digital Editing   (See **Digital Editing** on page 884.)

Docudrama   *Docudrama* is a type of documentary that blends elements of both documentary and drama to explore an actual historical, political, or social event. For example, docudramas may use actors and scripted dialogue to re-create historical events.

Documentary   *Documentary* is a genre of film and television programming which uses language, sounds, and imagery to provide an interpretation of real-life events. Although documentaries attempt to relate factual information, they may only show one producer's perceptions or point of view. Documentaries often have informative, persuasive, and artistic purposes.

Drama   *Drama* is an art form that tells a story through the speech and actions of the characters in the story. Most dramas use actors who impersonate the characters. Some dramas are performed in a theater, while others are presented on film.

Editor   (See **Editor** on page 884.)

Electronic Media   The term *electronic media* refers to the forms of mass media products that are available to consumers through some type of electronic technology such as a computer or a television. Electronic media products can be found on the Internet, on the radio, and on television.

Feature News   (See **Feature News** on page 884.)

Hard News   (See **Hard News** on page 885.)

In-Camera Editing   *In-camera editing* refers to any editing that is performed through the operation of a video or film camera and not by the cutting and shaping of an editor. The sequence of shots and scenes remains exactly as they were gathered by the camera operator. In-camera editing is an effective method of creating video when editing is time-consuming or equipment is unavailable. To create an effective work using in-camera editing, a great deal of pre-production planning is required, including a complete shot list and storyboards. In most cameras, sound can be added after the images have been shot.

Internet   The *Internet* is a global network of computers. With the Internet, a computer user may access information from another computer or a network of computers anywhere in the world. The Internet may be used by almost anyone who has a computer equipped with a modem.

Lead   (See **Lead** on page 885.)

Marketing   (See **Marketing** on page 885.)

Medium   (See **Medium** on page 885.)

Message   (See **Message** on page 885.)

Multimedia Presentation   A *multimedia presentation* is any presentation that involves two or more forms of media. For example, when you give an oral presentation including visuals (such as slides, transparencies, or posters), you are giving a multimedia presentation, one medium being your voice, the other being the visuals you use to support your presentation. A multimedia presentation that involves the use of presentation software or Web sites is sometimes called a **technology presentation.**

Nielsen Rating   *Nielsen rating* refers to the ratings system invented by the A. C. Nielsen Company, one of the largest marketing research companies in the United States. Nielsen ratings gather information about household television viewing choices from a sample of five thousand households selected to represent the population as a whole. Using a device called a peoplemeter, the firm gathers and later distributes information including the program watched, who was watching it, and the amount of time each viewer spent watching. Nielsen ratings are used to measure a program's popularity and to pinpoint target audiences for shows. Advertisers make decisions about buying airtime for their commercials during specific shows based in part on Nielsen ratings.

Network A *network* is a company that obtains and distributes programming to affiliated local stations or cable systems. Networks are not TV stations, but nearly 85 percent of all TV stations are affiliated with a network. Examples of networks include CBS, ABC, NBC, FOX, and WB. Each local station is responsible for its own programming, but a station that is affiliated with a network receives morning news programs, talk shows, soap operas, national news programs, situation comedies, dramas, and late-night programming. The networks provide the programs free to stations in exchange for the right to sell advertising. (See also **Affiliate** on page 876.)

News (See **News** on page 886.)

Newsmagazine (See **Newsmagazine** on page 885.)

Photography (See **Photography** on page 885.)

Political Advertising (See **Political Advertising** on page 886.)

Producer A *producer* is the person responsible for overseeing the creation of a movie or television or radio program. He or she is responsible for the following tasks.

- developing the overall message
- finding appropriate materials
- organizing a crew or staff
- finding and budgeting funding
- keeping the production on a timetable

Public Access *Public access* refers to the channels on a cable television system that are set aside specifically for use by the public to create a variety of programs. These channels are often controlled by education officials or government leaders.

Ratings *Ratings* are the system of categorizing films, TV programs, or video games by considering whether the content is appropriate for people of different ages. Ratings help adults and children evaluate the content of a message before viewing. (See also **Nielsen Ratings** on page 878.)

Reality TV *Reality television* is the presentation of actual video footage taken by amateurs with police monitors and by surveillance cameras. Usually the footage is highly edited; but because reality TV is presented as an eyewitness account, people tend to find it believable.

Reporter (See **Reporter** on page 886.)

Script A *script* is the text or words of a film, play, or television or radio show. The format for film and TV scripts often includes information about the images to be shown. The script for news broadcasts is called *copy*. (See also **Copy** on page 884.)

Sequencing *Sequencing* is the order in which scenes or images appear in a narrative. In television, film, and video, sequencing is enhanced in the editing process, in which scenes, usually filmed separately and in different locations, are spliced or joined together to create a sense of flow or sequence.

Situation Comedy A *situation comedy* is a television format that involves stories about a regular set of characters in either a home or

Media Terms **879**

work setting. Situation comedies involve humor and focus on life's ordinary problems and solutions. (See also **Genre** on page 882.)

Soft News   (See **Soft News** on page 886.)

Source   (See **Source** on page 886.)

Sponsorship   A *sponsorship* takes place when a business gives money to support a particular TV or radio program in return for commercial airtime. Sponsorship is different from advertising because in sponsorship, a company's name is acknowledged but usually the product is not promoted. Even though public broadcasting does not include commercials, it may include sponsors' names and slogans. (See also **Broadcasting** on page 876.)

Storyboard   A *storyboard* is a visual script, or series of drawings, that indicates the appearance and order of shots and scenes in a script as well as audio and visual cues. (See **Storyboards** on page 817.)

Target Audience   (See also **Target Audience** on page 886.)

Text   (See also **Text** on page 886.)

General Media Terms

Audience   An *audience* is a group of receivers of a media message. Audiences may receive a message by listening, reading, or viewing. The audience is important to understanding the economics of the mass media business, since advertisers pay to reach specific audiences when they place ads in newspapers, magazines, radio, television, or the Internet. Audiences are often identified by specific characteristics, or demographics. (See also **Demographics** on page 884.)

Authority   *Authority* refers to a quality of a message. When a message seems believable because it comes from a trustworthy and knowledgeable individual, the message has authority. For example, we would say a message about the health of a panda would have more authority coming from a zookeeper than from a spectator at the zoo. (See also **Credibility** on this page and **Source** on page 886.)

Bias   A *bias* is a negative connotation or point of view. An editorial writer with a bias may present only one side of an issue or ignore information that does not support his or her position. (See also **Point of View** on page 883.)

Communicator   A *communicator* is a person involved in the act of communicating or sharing messages with another person or persons. The communicator is the person who sends the message to the audience. The receiver takes on the role of communicator when he or she returns the message.

Credibility   *Credibility* is the willingness to believe in a person or to trust what a person says and does. Credibility is not a characteristic of a speaker. It is a perception that exists in the minds of a listener or viewer. (See also **Authority** on this page.)

Critical Viewing   *Critical viewing* is the ability to use critical thinking skills to view, question, analyze, and understand issues presented in visual media, including photography, film, television, and other mass media. Critical viewers use **media literacy** concepts to access, analyze, evaluate, and communicate media messages. On the next page are five key concepts of media literacy and some questions to help you evaluate media messages.

Media Concepts	Evaluation Questions
1. All messages are made by someone. Every media message is written, edited, selected, illustrated, or composed by one or more individuals. Writers, photographers, artists, illustrators, and TV and radio producers all decide which elements (words, images, sounds) to include in a media message, which ones to leave out, and how to arrange and sequence the chosen elements. Knowing how media messages are constructed will help you better interpret the meaning of a message.	Ask yourself: "What words, images, or sounds are used to create the message?" and "What words, images, or sounds may have been left out of the message?"
2. Media messages are not reality, but *representations* of reality that in turn shape people's ideas of the world. Fictional stories in the media can seem realistic if characters act in ways that seem authentic, but, of course, the stories are not real. An eyewitness news account of a fire can seem real, but it usually reflects only one person's point of view, filtered through a TV camera and edited down to a few images and words. Media messages can never match the complexity of the real world. Every media message also affects the way you think about the world. It is important that you judge the accuracy of media messages and whether or not you think the messages reflect reality.	Ask yourself: "What is the point of view or experience of the message maker?" and "How does this message affect the way I think about a particular topic or idea?"
3. Each person interprets media messages differently. Your interpretation of a media message is based on your knowledge and experience. You can use your prior knowledge and experience to examine the many different stylistic features of a message and to evaluate the message within its context.	Ask yourself: "How does the message make me feel?" or "Of what does the message make me think?"
4. People have a wide range of purposes for creating media messages. People create and share messages for many reasons; in modern culture making money is one of the most important. When people have political purposes, they use messages to gain power or authority over others. Understanding how messages operate in terms of their economic, political, social, and aesthetic purposes will help you better understand the context of a work.	Ask yourself: "Who created the message and why?" or "Is the producer's purpose to inform, to influence, to present ideas, to make money, to gain power, or to express ideas?"
5. Each mass medium—from TV to the newspaper to the Internet—has unique characteristics. A media producer makes choices about which forms and techniques are most appropriate to convey a particular message to a particular audience. For example, TV news favors messages that are immediate and visual to appeal to an audience that needs information quickly. Print news stories may provide in-depth analysis for an audience interested in the big picture. Knowing how the medium shapes the message will help you understand why certain techniques were used and what effect the story has on you.	Ask yourself: "Through what medium is the message delivered?" and "How does the form affect the message?" or "How might the techniques used affect various audiences?"

Media Terms **881**

Decoding   *Decoding* is the making of meaning from verbal and nonverbal signals. For example, audiences decode symbols, such as words and pictures, when they watch TV or read a newspaper.

Deconstruction   *Deconstruction* is the process of analyzing, or taking apart, the pieces of a media message to understand its meaning. The process of deconstruction involves looking at both what is stated, such as the words printed on a newspaper page, and what is not directly stated, including elements of the historical, economic, and political context in which the newspaper was created.

Feedback   *Feedback* is a response from an audience to the sender of a message. It can be immediate or delayed. Applause, booing, and asking questions are typical forms of immediate feedback from an audience. Writing a letter to the editor to respond to a newspaper editorial and filling out a questionnaire on a Web page are forms of **delayed feedback.**

Genre   A *genre* is a category of artistic forms or media products that shares **conventions,** or commonly accepted ways of presenting messages. For example, prime-time TV programs usually begin with a short, attention-grabbing segment before the opening credits and commercials. Each genre has a particular audience and conventions. Examples of genres within television include documentary, drama, game show, infomercial, music video, news broadcast, sitcom (situation comedy), soap opera, and talk show.

Interpretation   *Interpretation* is the process of creating meaning from exposure to a message through reading, viewing, or listening.

People's interpretations of messages differ, depending on their life experiences, backgrounds, and points of view.

Media Law   Various government structures, laws, and policies regulate access, content, delivery, and use of the mass media. For example, the *First Amendment* to the Constitution forbids Congress to set up or in any way pass laws limiting speech or the press. *Copyright law* protects the rights of authors and other media owners against the unauthorized publishing, reproduction, and selling of their works. *Censorship* is any governmental attempt to suppress or control people's access to media messages. Some censorship, however, may be used to protect citizens against damage to their reputations (*libel*) or against invasions of their privacy.

News Values   *News values* are the set of criteria journalists use to determine whether information is newsworthy. News values include

- **timeliness**   events or issues that are happening now
- **conflict**   unresolved events or issues that are interesting to the public
- **novelty**   stories that contain unique, interesting elements
- **relevance**   stories that are of interest to local readers
- **human interest**   stories that touch people's emotions
- **prominence**   stories about celebrities, politicians, or other noteworthy people
- **impact**   stories that make a difference in people's lives

If a news event has these features, it is more likely to be covered by the news media.

Newsworthiness *Newsworthiness* is the quality of an event that is worthy of being reported in a newspaper or news broadcast. An event must be of interest or importance to the public in order to be considered newsworthy. (See also **News Values** on page 882.)

Omission An *omission* is what is left out of a media message. All messages are selective and incomplete. For example, some advertisements omit information about the cost or the negative side effects of their products. Some editorials present only one side of an issue, omitting facts and opinions that are contrary to the writer's opinion. Noticing what is not included in a message helps to identify the author's point of view. (See also **Point of View** below.)

Point of View *Point of view* can refer to the position or view of the person reporting a story or telling a tale in the mass media. Point of view is also a literary concept which can be used to interpret mass media texts ranging from docudramas to feature news stories. In the electronic media, point of view can be indicated by the type of narration used or by the type of camera shot used. There are many possible points of view.

Propaganda *Propaganda* is any form of communication that uses persuasive techniques to reach a mass audience. Propaganda was originally defined as the spreading of biased ideas and opinions through lies and deception. This definition gave the concept of propaganda a negative connotation. However, as scholars began to study the topic in the 1940s, they came to realize that propaganda was everywhere. Over time, the concept of propaganda has lost some of its negative connotation. Propaganda is now thought of as the communication of a point of view with the goal of having audience members come to voluntarily accept this position as one of their beliefs. Advertising is one of the major forms of propaganda. (See also **Advertising** below.)

Purpose The *purpose* of a media message is what its sender or creator intends to achieve. Usually, the purpose of a message is to inform, to educate, to persuade, to entertain, to express oneself, or to make money. A message may have a primary and a secondary purpose at the same time.

Sensationalism *Sensationalism* is the media's use or portrayal of material that is intended to generate curiosity, fear, or other strong responses. The material can be exaggerated or shocking in content. Content that refers to romance, death, children, or animals is often sensational. (See also **Reality TV** on page 879 and **Tabloid** on page 886.)

Stereotypes *Stereotypes* are generalized beliefs based on misinformation or insufficient evidence about an entire group of individuals. A stereotype about teenagers, for example, would be that all teenagers sleep late. (See **Stereotypes** on page 153.)

Visual Literacy *Visual literacy* is a person's awareness of how meaning is communicated through visual media, including the use of color, line, shape, and texture.

Print Media Terms

Advertising *Advertising* is the use of images or text to promote or sell a product, service, image, or idea to a wide audience. Advertising is a marketing technique that is designed to persuade an audience. Typical advertising formats include print advertisements in newspapers and magazines, billboards, radio and television commercials, and electronic billboards on the World Wide Web. (See also **Marketing** on page 885 and **Sponsorship** on page 880.)

Byline   A *byline* is the name of the reporter or writer of a report published in a newspaper or magazine or presented on television or radio.

Circulation   *Circulation* is a measurement of the size of the audience for print media. It includes the total number of copies of a publication, such as a newspaper or magazine, that is delivered to subscribers, newsstands, and vendors.

Copy   *Copy* is the text in a media message.

Demographics   *Demographics* are the characteristics that define a particular audience. They include gender, age, educational background, cultural heritage, and income. Advertisers use demographics to target certain audiences. For example, advertisers know that many children watch Saturday morning cartoons, so they will advertise toys during Saturday morning commercial breaks.

Digital Editing   *Digital editing* is the use of computer technology to alter or change an image before it is presented to an audience. Photo editors often edit out distracting elements—such as telephone wires or shadows—from photo illustrations. However, large-scale digital editing of hard-news photographs is thought to be an unethical practice.

Editor   An *editor* supervises reporters. Editors decide what news stories will appear in print media or in broadcasting. They also check facts for accuracy and correct errors. (See also **News Values** on page 882.)

Elements of Design   *Elements of Design* are the parts of an idea's visual representation—such as *color, line, shape* and *texture*—that give meaning to the visual representation. The following list explains how each element communicates meaning. (See also **Document Design** on page 806.)

- *Color* creates mood and adds realism with its visual appeal. Color designates areas of space by separating and emphasizing parts of a visual. Viewers also associate certain items with particular colors. For example, usually oranges and tangerines are associated with the color orange. (See also **Color** on page 813.)
- *Line* determines the direction and speed of the viewer's eye movement. For example, straight lines suggest decisiveness, while curvy lines indicate gracefulness. Lines also communicate factual information in graphic organizers. (See also **Types of Graphics** on page 815).
- *Shape* emphasizes elements in the visual and adds interest. Often, shapes evoke emotional responses. For example, a square represents solidarity, while a circle indicates completeness.
- *Texture* is the manner in which the visual representation appeals to a viewer's sense of touch. Sometimes superficial texture in a visual may be created by cross-hatching, diagonal lines, or stippling.

Feature News   *Feature news,* also called soft news, refers to news stories whose primary purpose is to entertain. Feature stories usually are not timely. Stories about celebrities and ordinary people, places, animals, events, and products are considered feature news because they generate sympathy, curiosity, or amazement in viewers, readers, or listeners. An example of feature news would be a profile of a chef who works in the White House. (See also **Hard News** and **Soft News** on pages 885 and 886.)

Font   A *font* is a style of lettering used for printing text. (See also **Fonts** on page 811.)

Hard News   *Hard news* refers to fact-based reporting of breaking news stories. Hard news answers the basic *5W-How?* questions about timely subjects, such as national and international politics, economics, social issues, the environment, and scientific discoveries. An example of hard news would be a story reporting results the day after a presidential election. (See also **Feature News** on page 884 and **Soft News** on page 886.)

Headline   A *headline* is the title of a newspaper or magazine article, usually set in large or bold type. It has two purposes: to inform the reader of the content of the article and to get the reader's attention.

EXAMPLE

Stock Market Hits Historic High

Lead   A *lead* is the introduction to a newspaper article or a broadcast report. It ranges from one sentence to several paragraphs in length and contains information that motivates a reader or viewer to continue with the story. A lead usually contains the major facts of a story and may also describe a curious or unusual situation to attract reader or viewer attention.

EXAMPLE

CAPE CANAVERAL, July 23—After two postponements this week, space shuttle *Columbia* blasted off early today with the world's most powerful X-ray telescope and Eileen Collins, the first woman to command a U.S. spaceflight.

Marketing   *Marketing* is the process of moving goods or services from the producer to the consumer. It includes identifying consumer wants or needs; designing, packaging, and pricing the product; and arranging for locations where the product will be sold. Marketing also includes promoting the product to a target audience through advertising or other means. (See also **Advertising** on page 883.)

Medium   The *medium* of a message is the form in which it is presented or distributed, including film, video, radio, television, the Internet, and print.

Message   A *message* is a combination of symbols that is communicated to one or more people. Messages are created by people who use symbols, including language, gesture, images, sounds, and electronic forms. Media messages are communicated through various mass media. (See also **Medium** above.)

News   *News* is the presentation of current and interesting information that will interest or affect an audience. Local news is produced by local newspapers and radio and TV stations, which use their own equipment, reporters, and resources. The focus of local news is information that affects a small audience with regional interests. National news is produced by large newspapers and radio and TV stations. Because their resources are greater, national news organizations may cover more national and world issues or events.

Newsmagazine   A *newsmagazine* is a weekly, biweekly, monthly, or bimonthly printed journal that focuses on news issues. On TV, a newsmagazine is a news program divided into several news segments or stories.

Photography   *Photography* is a process of making pictures by using cameras to record patterns of light and images on film or on computer disks. Photography is both an art form and a major component of the mass media; it is used in making still photographs and motion pictures. People sometimes think that "a photograph never lies," but a photograph, like all media messages, is selective and incomplete. Photographers use a wide range of techniques to communicate their points of view, including the framing and composition of an image, the use of filters or digital editing, and the selection of what to include in the frame. (See also **Digital Editing** on page 884 and **Point of View** on page 883.)

Political Advertising   *Political advertising* is the use of the mass media to persuade listeners and viewers about a political candidate's ideas or opinions. Political candidates who use advertising must use techniques similar to those used to sell products. Their messages must be simple and attention-getting. (See also **Advertising** on page 883.)

Print Media   *Print media* refers to the hard copies of mass media products that are printed on paper to be read or looked at by consumers. Examples of print media are newspapers, magazines, pamphlets, and flyers.

Reporter   A *reporter* is a journalist who is responsible for information gathering.

Reporters gather information and work with editors to create TV and print news. (See also **Editor** on page 884.)

Soft News   *Soft news,* or feature news, is the presentation of general interest material, such as celebrities and sports, in a news format. Soft news is designed to entertain readers or viewers. (See also **Feature News** on page 884 and **Hard News** on page 885.)

Source   A *source* is the person who first supplies information or ideas that are then shared with others. Journalists rely on sources for the information they report, and select individuals that they believe are credible and have authority. (See also **Authority** on page 880.)

Tabloid   A *tabloid* is a publication with a newspaper format that provides sensational news items and photographs. Tabloids are highly dependent on stories and photographs of media celebrities. Tabloid producers often admit that the stories they report are either false or exaggerations of the truth.

Target Audience   A *target audience* is a segment of the population for which a product or presentation is designed. (See also **Demographics** on page 884.)

Text   *Text* refers to the symbols used to create a message, such as a book, a magazine article, or a TV show.

Writing

Skills, Structures, and Techniques

You can use the following ideas and information to become a more effective writer.

Business Letters   Use a *business letter* for business-related matters, such as applying for a job or requesting goods or services. A business letter must look and sound professional.

Guidelines for Business Letters
Use plain, unlined $8\frac{1}{2}$" × 11" paper.
Type (single-spaced) or neatly write the letter, using black or blue ink. Avoid typing errors, misspellings, cross-outs, and all smudges.
Use equal margins on all sides.
Use only one side of the paper. Carry over at least two lines onto the second page, if necessary.
Use a polite, respectful, professional tone.
Use formal, standard English. Avoid slang, contractions, and most abbreviations.
Include all necessary information, but get to the point quickly. Be sure your reader knows why you wrote and what you are asking.

■ **Parts**   There are six parts of a business letter, usually arranged on the page in one of two styles. In *block form,* all six parts begin at the left margin. In *modified block form,* the heading, the closing, and your signature are aligned on the right-hand side of the page. All the other parts begin at the left margin, and paragraphs are indented.

1. The *heading* usually has three lines:
   - your street address
   - your city, state, and ZIP Code
   - the date the letter was written
2. The *inside address* gives the name and address of the person to whom you are writing. Use a courtesy title (such as *Mr.* or *Miss*) or a professional title (such as *Dr.* or *Professor*) in front of the person's name. Include the person's business title after the name.
3. The *salutation* is your greeting. Use *Dear,* a courtesy title or professional title, and the person's name. End with a colon. If you don't have the name of a specific person, use a general salutation such as *Dear Sir or Madam:,* or you can use a department or a position title.

4. The *body,* or main part of your letter, contains the message. If you include more than one paragraph, leave a blank line between paragraphs.

5. The *closing* is your ending. Appropriate closings are *Yours truly, Sincerely,* or *Sincerely yours.* End the closing with a comma.

6. Your *signature* should be handwritten in ink, directly below the closing and above your typed or printed name. Always sign your full name with no titles.

Block Style

Modified Block Style

■ **Types**   There are three types of business letters.

1. **Request or order letters** In a *request letter,* you are asking for information about a product or asking for someone's time or

services. Enclose a self-addressed, stamped envelope if you're asking someone to send information. Make requests of individuals well in advance. An *order letter* requests something specific, such as a free brochure. Here is a sample request letter.

```
                    Bethlehem High School
                    700 Delaware Avenue
                    Delmar, NY 12054
                    October 12, 2001

Ms. Ellen Phillips, Staff Writer
The Albany Times Mirror
News Plaza 1000
Albany, NY 12212

Dear Ms. Phillips:

    I would like to invite you
to be one of our speakers at
the Bethlehem High School Career
Day. This year's event will be
December 16, from 9:00 A.M. to
4:00 P.M.

    Please let me know if you
would be interested in speaking
to an audience of about fifty
students for a fifteen-minute
talk about your career in jour-
nalism. We can schedule your talk
at your convenience.

    I look forward to your reply.

                    Yours truly,

                    Jennifer Savage

                    Jennifer Savage,
                    Student Coordinator
                    Career Day 2001
```

2. **Complaint or adjustment letters** The purpose of a *complaint* or *adjustment letter* is to report an error or to state that you have not received services or products that you have reason to expect. In a calm, courteous

TEACHING TIP

■ **Request Letters**
Invite students to write a letter requesting information or inviting someone to speak to students. Remind them to consider as they write that they are asking for a person's time or assistance, so the language of the letter should be respectful.

tone, tell why you are displeased. Tell what solution you want to correct the problem. Here is the body of a sample letter.

```
    On January 2, 2000, I ordered
a plaid shirt from your catalog:
Item # 3121HH, size 38 medium,
described as "a washable
wool/polyester blend." The shirt
cost $27, plus $1.50 shipping and
handling, for a total of $28.50.

    The first time I washed the
shirt, the side seam split apart.
I followed the washing directions
on the label carefully.

    I am returning the shirt.
Please send a replacement shirt
or a refund. Thank you for your
attention to this matter.
```

3. **Appreciation or commendation letters** In an *appreciation* or *commendation letter,* you express your appreciation for a person, a group, an organization, or a product or service. Be specific about why you are pleased. Here is the body of a sample.

```
    I am writing to let you know
how much I enjoyed your museum's
recent exhibition on contemporary
African American artists. My high
school's art class was impressed
and inspired by what we saw. I
particularly enjoyed the paint-
ings by Lawrence and Bearden.
```

Compositions   A *composition* is a longer piece of writing consisting of paragraphs. A composition usually has three main parts: *introduction, body,* and *conclusion.* Each of these has a function, yet they all work together to communicate the writer's main idea.

■ **Introduction**   Your composition's *introduction* should do three things.

1. **Catch readers' attention.** Your introduction should make your readers want to read on.
2. **Set the tone.** Your **tone** can be formal, informal, humorous, or serious. The tone you adopt depends upon the **occasion,** or what prompts you to write on a particular topic, and the makeup of your **audience,** the people who will read your composition.
3. **Present the thesis.** A *thesis statement* is a sentence or two that announces your topic and your main idea about it. A thesis statement works in a composition like a topic sentence works in a paragraph. Your thesis statement can guide you as you plan, write, and revise your paper. Here are some strategies for writing a thesis statement.

Strategy & Example

1. Review the facts and details in your prewriting notes and begin thinking about how they fit together.

Much of the information in my notes on recycling is about the amount of usable and reusable materials we throw away.

2. Ask yourself the following questions: *What is my topic? What do I want to say about my topic?*

Topic: *recycling*

My idea about my topic: *We throw away far too much usable and reusable material.*

3. Sharpen your focus and present a definite, focused idea—a thesis statement.

We would use the earth's limited resources more wisely if we recycled as much as possible.

4. Ask yourself whether your audience will care about your topic. *My audience consists of classmates, most of whom are concerned about the environment. They would be interested in recycling.*

■ **Appreciation Letter**
Ask students to think of a person whom they have needed to thank. Perhaps someone has influenced them positively or offered them a worthy opportunity. Encourage students to write and mail a letter of appreciation.

Cooperative Learning

Technical Document. Students might someday be asked to write a technical document—a type of writing such as a manual or minutes of a meeting. Have pairs of students use the following guidelines to create a technical document.

- Report information and convey ideas logically and correctly.

- Offer detailed and accurate specifications.

- Include scenarios, definitions, and examples to aid comprehension.

- Anticipate readers' problems, mistakes, and misunderstanding.

Have students limit the length of their documents by explaining only one or two procedures or steps, but encourage them to include at least one scenario, one definition, and one example. Students can exchange documents with other pairs of students and discuss their problems, their findings, and their results. You may want to display students' work in the classroom.

Often, an introduction begins with general information and moves to the specific with the thesis as the final statement. The following graphic may help you to visualize the organization.

Introduction

General

Specific
(Thesis)

To write an effective introduction, try one of the following techniques. The examples show how you might introduce a composition about recycling.

- **Body**   The *body* states and develops the composition's main points. Together, all the paragraphs in the body support one main idea—the thesis statement. When writing the body of your composition, keep in mind the following guidelines.

1. Arrange your information in a way that makes sense to your readers. This gives your composition *coherence.*
2. Eliminate any details that do not support your thesis. This gives your paper *unity.*
3. Show how your ideas are connected by using direct references and transitional expressions. (See page 364.)

Technique	Example
Begin with an anecdote or example.	Last weekend when I was baby-sitting a five year-old neighbor, I had an eye-opening experience. I was about to throw away the trash from our snack, when little Ana yelled, "Wait! Aren't you going to recycle that bottle? Don't you care about the earth?" She's right. Recycling is everyone's responsibility.
Begin with a startling fact or by adopting an unusual position.	Our earth is not very pleased with us Americans. Every year we throw away enough office paper to build a twelve-foot-high wall. We dispose of enough diapers to stretch from the earth to the moon seven times. The list goes on.
Use an appropriate quotation.	In her acceptance speech Mayor Cosby said, "Recycling must become the norm—a way of life. With a few minor changes and minimal effort, we can reap great rewards."
Start with background information.	Recycling is the collecting, processing, and reusing of materials. Throughout history people have recycled. For example, metal tools and weapons have been melted and reused for thousands of years.
Begin with a simple statement of your thesis.	With an increase in population and a decrease in natural resources, people around the world are viewing recycling as the way of the future.

■ **Conclusion**   As the final part of your paper, the *conclusion* should do two things:

1. **Leave the reader with a sense of complete-ness.** Most readers don't like to be left hanging or to feel that they have been abruptly dismissed.
2. **Reinforce the main idea.** The conclusion should bring your readers back to the main idea. Often a conclusion begins with a specific statement, such as a restatement of the thesis, and moves to general information.

The following graphic may help you to visualize the organization.

Conclusion

To write an effective conclusion, try one of the techniques in the following chart:

Technique	Example
Restate your main idea.	Our world is changing: The population is increasing and the natural resources are decreasing. To offset this change, many people are committing to recycling.
Summarize your major points.	With an increase in population comes an increase in trash. Landfills are overflowing, so the solution is to produce less trash. Materials ranging from old newspapers to precious metals can be recycled. The recycling process reclaims original materials and uses them in new products.
Close with a final idea or example.	Last year the freshman class initiated a month-long "Recycle Today!" campaign. Throughout the community, the freshmen distributed educational pamphlets. Within the school, they set up recycling containers in the cafeteria and in the courtyard. The response was telling: With a little guidance, people are willing to make recycling a part of their lives.
End with a comment on the topic (a thoughtful reaction or observation, a personal look to the future).	The idea of recycling is catching on. More and more people in my neighborhood are setting out their recycling bins on collection day. The cafeteria's recycling containers are overflowing at lunch. People are showing that they do care about the future of our planet. Maybe it's not too late.
Call on your readers to take action.	Of the 160 million tons of trash we produce each year in the United States, 80 percent is used in landfill, 10 percent is burned, and only 10 percent is recycled. We can change those percentages. Start recycling today.
Refer to your introduction.	The next time you start to throw away a recyclable article, think of Our Earth. Make her smile.

E-mail Electronic mail, or *e-mail,* is correspondence sent via the computer rather than through your local post office. E-mail can be used to write personal, informal letters or to send business messages. Because e-mails are easy to write, send, and receive, many e-mail users ignore the guidelines associated with writing letters. Informal content and format are often acceptable when you write to someone you know well or send comments to a newsgroup or chat group where the discussions are clearly relaxed. However, if you are writing to someone you do not know well for business or research purposes, you should use the following guidelines. Remember: Online etiquette, or "Netiquette," stresses the importance of good manners and common sense in cyberspace, just as etiquette does in the real world.

Envelopes For a letter to arrive promptly at its destination, it must be addressed correctly. Place your complete return address in the top left-hand corner of the envelope. Center on the envelope the name and address of the person to whom you are writing. For a business letter, the addressee's name and address should exactly match the inside address. Use the two-letter state code on the envelope rather than writing out the state name.

E-mail Guidelines

- Keep your message concise and to the point. Limit yourself to one full screen or less of text. Scrolling through long e-mail messages can be tedious.

- Use bulleted lists and indentations to make the document easy for your readers to read on-screen. Bulleted lists are especially helpful if you are raising more than one question or point.

- Always make sure that your spelling, grammar, and punctuation are correct, and use standard English.

- Include salutations, such as "Dear Dr. Brunelli," if you are writing for the first time to someone you do not know. Also, a closing, such as "Sincerely" or "Thank you," followed by your full name is always considered polite.

- Always be polite in your messages—even if you know the person to whom you are writing. Being rude to someone in an e-mail is called *flaming.* Flaming often backfires because there is always the chance that your angry message could be forwarded and read by someone you didn't intend to see it.

- Avoid using capital letters in your messages. CAPITALS CONVEY SHOUTING. No one wants to be shouted at in cyberspace. (If you want to show emphasis, place asterisks [*] on either side of the important word or term instead—for example, "What do you think about the *metaphor* in Chapter 2?"

- Use *emoticons* sparingly and never use them in formal e-mails. *Emoticons* are combinations of symbols that, when you tilt your head to the left, look like faces and suggest feelings. For example, the emoticon :-) suggests laughter or "I'm just kidding." Use them in informal e-mails only.

- Always pay attention to the addresses entered in your address line. Make sure that you are sending appropriate messages to the right people.

- Always fill in the subject line before you send a message. Providing a subject will help your readers prioritize your message, which could be one of many they receive.

- Avoid forwarding e-mail without asking the permission of the original sender. Private e-mails are usually intended for your eyes only.

Forms Printed forms vary, but the following techniques will help you fill out any form—from a job application to a contest entry—accurately and completely.

- Read all of the instructions carefully.

- Type or write neatly. Type, or print your information in either blue or black ink, unless pencil is specified.

- Proofread your completed form and correct errors neatly. Be sure you have given all information requested on the form.

Graphic Organizers A *graphic organizer* is a visual that helps you "see" what you are thinking. You can use graphic organizers to find a subject to write about, to gather information, and to organize your information.

- **Charts** By dividing a subject into its logical parts, you can analyze and organize the details you have gathered. A *chart* helps you to arrange information into categories. The following chart describes scientific research in space with the three branches of science as categories.

Scientific Research in Space	
Branch of Science	**Type of Experiment**
biology	experiments on how zero gravity affects the biological rhythms of living things such as fish and plants
physics	experiments on how zero gravity affects the development or manufacture of crystals
astronomy	studies of the universe, using X-ray astronomy, without the distorting effects of the earth's atmosphere

- **Clustering** (See **Prewriting Techniques** on page 897.)

- **Mapping** (See **Prewriting Techniques** on page 897.)

- **Sequence chain** A *sequence chain* helps you see how one event leads to another. They work well when you are narrating or explaining a process. The following sequence chain organizes notes about tie-dyeing a shirt.

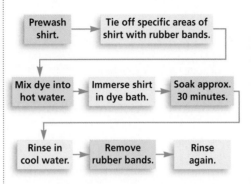

- **Time line** A *time line* organizes information chronologically along a horizontal line from left to right, and from the earliest events to the most recent events. The following example traces civil rights events.

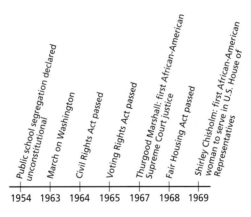

Skills, Structures, and Techniques **893**

- **Venn diagram** A *Venn diagram* uses intersecting circles to show the similarities and differences between two subjects. The area of overlap between the two circles shows how two subjects are similar; the remaining areas show how they are different. In the following Venn diagram, the writer compares and contrasts visiting his two uncles.

Differences   **Similarities**   **Differences**

Uncle in Florida   Uncle in Maine

- can drive to his house
- Uncle Max golfs
- friends in the neighborhood
- weather hot and muggy

- good food
- my own room
- lots of activities
- family dogs

- too far to drive; must fly
- Uncle Ben fishes
- no one my age lives nearby
- weather cool and refreshing

Informal or Personal Letters The content and appearance of a personal letter is less formal than a business letter. Personal letters are usually handwritten rather than typed. Use the modified block form, but do not include an inside address. (See **Business Letters** on page 887.) There are three common types of informal or personal letters.

- **Thank-you letters** A *thank-you letter* tells someone that you appreciate his or her taking time, trouble, or expense on your behalf.

- **Invitations** An informal *invitation* should contain specific information about the occasion, the time and place, and other details your guest might need to know.

- **Letters of regret** Send a *letter of regret* if you have been invited somewhere and are unable to go. A written reply is especially

appropriate if you were sent a written invitation with the letters *R.S.V.P.* (in French, an abbreviation for "please reply").

Manuscript Form When you formally share your composition with others, its appearance is important. These guidelines will help improve the appearance of your paper.

Guidelines for Manuscript Form
Use only one side of a sheet of paper.
Write in blue or black ink, or type.
If you write by hand, don't skip lines. If you type, double-space the lines.
Leave margins of about one inch at the top, sides, and bottom of a page.
Indent the first line of each paragraph.
Number all pages except the first page. Place the number in the upper right-hand corner.
All pages should be neat and clean. You may make a few corrections with correction fluid.
Follow your teacher's instructions for placing your name, the date, your class, and the title of your paper.

Memos A memorandum, or *memo,* is a written message for conducting business within an organization. For example, an individual might send a memo to co-workers to remind them about a meeting, or all employees might receive a memo describing a new policy. An organization or department often has a set format for memos.

Messages Writing a *message* requires listening to information, usually by telephone, and then communicating that information to someone else. Think of the five *W* questions when writing a message.

Who is the message from and for **whom**?
What is the message?
When was the message written (date and time)?
Where can the sender be reached, if necessary?
Why is the message important?

Outlines An *outline* is a plan—a way of grouping and organizing information to show the relationships among ideas. An outline can guide writers to present ideas clearly and can help readers perceive the relationships among ideas.

■ **Formal outlines** A *formal outline* is a highly structured, clearly labeled writing plan. It uses letters and numbers to label main headings and subheadings. An outline can use either words and phrases or complete sentences for each item. Here is an example of a formal outline about preseason athletic training.

```
Title: Is Preseason Training Necessary?
Thesis statement: A preseason training
program that includes lifting weights,
stretching, and living a healthy
lifestyle will greatly improve an
athlete's performance.

   I. Lifting weights
      A. Increased power
      B. Injury prevention
  II. Stretching
      A. Increased flexibility
      B. Injury prevention
 III. Living a healthy lifestyle
      A. Good nutrition
      B. Adequate sleep
      C. Hydration
         1. At least eight glasses of
            water daily
         2. No dehydrating drinks
            a. beverages with caffeine
            b. beverages high in sugar
            c. carbonated beverages
```

■ **Informal outlines or early plans** An *early plan* doesn't have a set form. You simply sort your ideas or facts into groups and arrange the groups in order. To sort your information into groups, ask yourself, *Which items belong together? What do they have in common? Which items don't fit anywhere?* Then, give each group a heading that shows how the items in it are related. Next, order, or arrange, your information in a way that will make sense to your readers: chronological order, spatial order, logical order, or order of importance. Some papers will suggest a natural order; however, more than one order may be possible. Ask yourself, *Is the purpose and the order of each grouping of details understandable?* (See also page 359.)

Paragraphs A *paragraph* is a group of sentences that present and support a main idea; it is also the primary building block in a composition. Although most of the paragraphs in a single composition will often be one of the following major types, many compositions contain more than one type of paragraph. The four types of paragraphs vary by their purpose.

■ **Descriptive paragraphs** A *descriptive paragraph* lets your readers truly see your subject, whether it is a person, an object, or a scene. Descriptive paragraphs often use spatial order and usually contain sensory details.

Sensory
detail 1

The golf bag was enormous. It seemed a dull conservative color when I saw it in the late afternoon gloom of a Florida golf shop. But when I took it out on a practice round the next day, it glowed a rich oxblood color, like a vast sausage. It was very heavy with a metal bottom with brass

(continued)

Skills, Structures, and Techniques **895**

Sensory detail 2

studs around it, and when I first went out, I felt guilty for seeing it on a caddy's back. But the clubs let off a fine chinking sound as the bag was carried, as expensive and exclusive as the sound of a Cadillac door shutting to, and the fact that the porters, caddies, and I myself, whoever carried it, were bent nearly double by its weight only seemed to add to its stature.

Sensory detail 3

George Plimpton, "Golf"

■ **Expository paragraphs** An *expository paragraph* is used to explain and inform. Because explanations are clarified by organizing information into categories, expository paragraphs frequently use logical order. The following paragraph explains what makes the ladies' "long program" in ice-skating unique for both spectators and athletes.

The ladies' "free skate," or long [four-minute] program, is by far the most popular activity in women's sports—the only sports event in which the women's version is more popular than the men's. These four minutes are as pure a dose of live performance as the media offer. For the athletes, they are also among the most pitiless and harrowing four minutes in sports. Although the long program is an endurance event—within a minute and a half the exercise becomes anaerobic—the skater has to continue to look as if she were enjoying herself. The smile at the end of the routine is of the utmost importance: skaters practice many hours in front of the mirror to get it right.

John Seabrook, *The New Yorker*

■ **Narrative paragraphs** A *narrative paragraph* is used to tell a story or to illustrate an event or a series of events, usually in chronological order.

Event 1

Event 2

Event 3

Event 4

Down the stretch, the game belonged to William. With the lead cut to three in the final minutes, William drove, stopped suddenly, pivoted towards the basket, and drew a foul. His knee was aching, but he blocked the pain, as well as the sound of the crowd and Proviso's players telling him not to choke. He allowed himself to see only the basket, as though to make the free throw were as simple as dropping a ball in a bucket that lay at his feet. The ball fluttered from his fingertips and slipped through the net. He hit both free throws and two others to ice the win.

Ben Joravsky, *Hoop Dreams*

■ **Persuasive paragraphs** A *persuasive paragraph* is used to express a writer's opinion about a particular subject, for the purpose of convincing others to share the opinion or to take action. Writers of persuasive paragraphs usually use order of importance or logical order to organize their ideas.

Am I saying that anything goes in sports—as long as you don't get caught? Of course not. Deliberate low blows are wrong in boxing, even when the referee is shielded from the action. Kicking a downed player is wrong on the football field, whether an official sees it or not. Spitballs are wrong in baseball and, while I couldn't swear to it, surely there must be some behavior on a hockey rink that is considered unethical. Dirty play is wrong, and its encouragement—by coaches or fans—can have implications well beyond the playing field.

William Raspberry, *The Washington Post*

Prewriting Techniques You can use the following techniques to find a subject to write about and to gather information about a subject. Although the prewriting techniques are presented separately, you may often use more than one technique at a time. You may also prefer to use some techniques more than others.

■ **Asking the *5W-How?* questions** Ask yourself the reporter's questions—*Who? What? When? Where? Why?* and *How?*—to find ideas to write about.

EXAMPLE

Who are some local people who go fly fishing?
What equipment do you need for fly fishing?
When is the best time of day to fish?
Where are some good local fishing spots?
Why do some people tie their own flies?
How do you tie a fly?

■ **Asking "What if?" questions** To stimulate your creative thinking, ask a variety of "What if?" questions about a subject. Imagine everyday situations that are different, and see where these ideas take you.

EXAMPLE

What if there were no sunlight?
What if everyone spoke the same language?
What if I could travel to another time?
What if our school had no rules?

■ **Brainstorming** Write down a subject, and then list all your ideas about that subject that come into your mind as quickly as you can. Resist the urge to evaluate your ideas; remember that you are trying to come up with as many ideas as possible. Keep going until you run out of ideas. Brainstorming is a good group activity.

EXAMPLE

Movies

expensive to make	ticket prices	movie stars
costumes	popcorn	special effects
cold theaters	soundtracks	bad movies

■ **Clustering** Like brainstorming, clustering (also called *webbing* or *making connections*) is useful for spurring creative ideas. First, write a subject in the middle of your paper. Circle the subject. Then, in the space around the subject, write whatever related ideas occur to you. Circle the new ideas and draw lines to connect the new ideas with the original subject. Continue to branch off as necessary. Let your mind wander, and continue to draw circles and lines to show connections among ideas.

EXAMPLE

■ **Cubing** Investigate a subject by imagining a cube that has one of the following suggestions on each of its six sides: *Describe it. Compare it. Associate it. Analyze it. Apply it. Argue for or against it.* Write for three minutes about each side of the cube.

EXAMPLE

Masks

Apply it. **(Tell how it can be used or what you can do with it.)**

People throughout the ages have worn masks for various reasons. When used in rituals, masks are believed to have great power. In some cultures, masks are used to frighten away evil spirits. Festival and theatrical masks are used for masquerade, entertainment, and storytelling. War masks are worn in battle. Some sports require protective masks.

■ **Freewriting** When you freewrite, you write whatever pops into your head. Think of a word or topic that interests you, and write about it for three to five minutes. Don't worry about complete sentences or proper punctuation. Just write as much as you can. If you cannot think of anything new to write, copy the same word or phrase until something comes to mind.

EXAMPLE

SUMMER: Hot, lazy days. Going to the lake with family and to the community pool with friends.

Television in the mornings. Movies late at night. Lots of good books. Will we visit my cousins? Helping out around the house—mow the grass, baby-sit.

■ **Listening with a focus** You can gather ideas for writing by listening to radio and television programs, audiotapes, and experts in personal or telephone interviews. Write down your topic, and then brainstorm what you already know about it. Make a list of questions that you would like to have answered as you listen. This list of questions should help guide and focus your listening. Listen carefully with your questions in front of you. Take careful notes and pay close attention.

■ **Looping** Looping will help you generate ideas that can be developed into an essay.

1. In this prewriting activity, you start with a topic and freewrite about the topic for a set period of time. The topic may be assigned or may be one of your own choosing. For example, you may be asked to write on the characters in a certain novel.

2. Include anything that comes into your mind on the topic. Even if you cannot think of anything to say, continue writing for the specified period of time. You may write, "I can't think of anything to say," until eventually you do think of something. The important thing is to keep your pen or pencil moving.

3. After the time limit is up, read what you have written and pick out what seems to be most important or "weighty" in the loop. This is the center of gravity for that loop. You may have stated this center of gravity, or you may have to figure it out. For example, you may have written a number of things about a certain character in a novel, and that character would be your center of gravity for the first loop.

4. Finally, write your center of gravity sentence and begin the process again for two more loops. For example, you may turn your attention to other characters in the novel and begin writing. You will discover in the two additional loops two other centers of gravity. These three centers of gravity may then be turned into the three main points of your essay.

- **Mapping** Mapping resembles clustering in form but is used to organize ideas. It is a helpful graphic for determining whether you have enough support for each main idea. Notice how the following map groups main ideas and supporting ideas.

EXAMPLE

creating the treats
original recipe
healthy
tasty
various shapes
natural ingredients
my dogs love them

profit
costs
investment capital

starting my own business—homemade dog treats

market
local sites?
pet stores?
mail order?

packaging
inexpensive
flashy
preserve freshness
recyclable?

- **Pentad** Investigate a subject by imagining a five-pointed star. Each of its points has one of the following questions: *What is happening? Who is causing it to happen? How is it being done? Where and when is it being done? Why is it happening?* After answering each question, determine a focus: Which points did you write the most about, and is there an interaction between those points? This focus will probably be your thesis statement. A pentad is a good prewriting technique to use when you are writing about literature.

EXAMPLE

What is happening?
Roger tries to steal Mrs. Jones's purse. She catches him, drags him home, gives him food and money, and talks to him.

How is it being done?
Roger instigates the attack. Then, Mrs. Jones is in control. At the apartment, Roger does have choices.

When and where is it happening?
Mostly in Mrs. Jones's apartment.

Story: "Thank You, M'am" by Langston Hughes

Who is causing it to happen?
Roger
Mrs. Jones

Why is it happening?
Mrs. Jones wants Roger to see that people can change.

- **Reading with a focus** You can get ideas for writing by reading books, newspapers, or magazines. When you read to find information, don't read everything. Use the index and table of contents to narrow your search. Skim the material, searching only for information about your topic. When you find relevant information, read carefully and take notes.

- **Track Switching** Start by freewriting along a familiar track of thinking, and then switch to another track of thinking about a topic. This technique often leads to fresh ideas. The following steps will help you.

1. Start by creating a statement about your topic, and freewrite about that statement for five minutes. For example, you may begin with a statement such as, "My favorite character in the novel made good choices."

2. Switch tracks by creating a second statement about your topic. Your second statement should be as different as possible from the first statement you made. Write on this track for five minutes. For example, you may write, "Every character in the novel made poor choices."

Résumés

Suggest that students practice writing a résumé for themselves, citing volunteer work and any jobs they have held. At this point, students' jobs may not have been formal employment situations, so remind them to include their accomplishments such as mowing the lawn or babysitting for family members or neighbors. Also, remind them to list special skills, such as computer literacy or proficiency at more than one language.

3. Repeat this back-and-forth writing process for five tracks, letting your words flow along your different tracks of thinking.

■ **Using your five senses** Observe your topic through all five senses: sight, hearing, smell, taste, and touch. If you stop to focus on all the sensory details around you, you will have an endless supply of specific details for your writing.

EXAMPLE Chinese New Year's festival

touch: damp, chilly morning; cool breeze; crisp, crunchy fried wontons

sound: cymbals and drums as parade goes by, cheering of spectators, chatter of street vendors and their customers, gong of passing streetcar

smell: garlic and ginger cooking in hot oil, egg rolls frying, dumplings cooking in bamboo steamers

taste: tangy, hot tea; salty soy sauce on steamed dumpling; spicy hot mustard and sweet plum sauce on egg roll

sight: dazzling light, colorful merchandise, red and gold decorations on dragon in parade, banners with Chinese characters

■ **Visualizing** Visualizing means making mental images of something in your mind's eye. As you "see" your scene, try to use your other senses as well.

EXAMPLE I'm riding down a country road at sunrise on my bicycle. The sunrise's brilliant orange lights up the eastern sky. A few birds chirp noisily and the smell of morning dew and budding blossoms fills the cool, crisp air.

■ **Writer's notebook or journal** Use a special notebook or file folder to record your experiences and observations, feelings and opinions, brilliant ideas and questions. You can also collect print material that has special

meaning to you, such as poems, songs, cartoons, and newspaper articles. Try to write in your notebook daily, and date your entries. Soon your journal will be a sourcebook full of ideas for you to write about.

Résumés A *résumé* is a one-page summary of your skills, education, accomplishments, and experience. When applying for a job or seeking admission to a college, you will probably be asked for a résumé. The following sample résumé is for a summer job applicant. Notice that the work experience supports the job objective.

```
                    Amanda Vinh
                1056 Cape Coral Way
               Wilsonville, NC 54321
                   (555) 328-9087
Objective
    Summer position as a cashier in
    a bookstore
Qualifications
    Familiarity with and a love for
    books
    Excellent people skills
    Experience with cash registers
    and computers
Work Experience
    June, 1998, to present—
    volunteer at local library
    September, 2000—organized
    middle school book fair
    June-August, 2000—cashier at
    Big Brother's Books
Education
    Mountaineer High School,
    Wilsonville, North Carolina
    Presently in ninth grade;
    3.8 grade-point average
Extracurricular
    Math Club, Yearbook Staff
Achievements
    Good Citizen Award—2000
References
    Available on request
```

Revising and Proofreading Symbols

When you are revising and proofreading, indicate any changes by using the symbols shown in the chart below.

Technical Documents   Use the following strategies to help you write technical documents, such as minutes of a meeting, procedures for conducting a meeting, or a manual of rules for conflict resolution.

1. Report information and convey ideas logically and correctly.
2. Offer detailed and accurate specifications.
3. Include scenarios, definitions, and examples to aid comprehension.
4. Anticipate readers' problems, mistakes, and misunderstandings.

Transitions   Transitions, or *transitional expressions,* are words and phrases that show readers how ideas and details fit together. (See page 365 for a chart of transitional expressions.)

Voice   The way a piece of writing "sounds," or its *voice,* is determined by sentence structure, word choice, and tone. Although audience and purpose influence your writing voice, always try to sound honest and natural.

Symbol	Example	Meaning Of Symbol
≡	Fifty-first street	Capitalize a lowercase letter.
/	Jerry's Aunt	Lowercase a capital letter.
∧	differant	Change a letter.
∧	the capital Ohio	Insert a missing word, letter, or punctuation mark.
⌐	beside the river	Replace a word.
ℓ	Where's the the key?	Leave out a word, letter, or punctuation mark.
⌢	an invisibile guest	Leave out and close up.
⌢	a close friend ship	Close up space.
∽	thier	Change the order of letters.
(tr)	Avoid having too many corrections of your paper in the final version.	Transfer the circled words. (Write *tr* in nearby margin.)
¶	¶ "Hi," he smiled.	Begin a new paragraph.
⊙	Stay well	Add a period.
∧	Of course you may be wrong.	Add a comma.
#	icehockey	Add a space.
⊙	one of the following	Add a colon.
∧	Maria Simmons, M.D. Jim Fiorello, Ph.D.	Add a semicolon.
=	a great grandmother	Add a hyphen.
∨	Pauls car	Add an apostrophe.
(stet)	On the fifteenth of July	Keep the crossed-out material. (Write *stet* in nearby margin.)

Grammar at a Glance

─HELP─

Grammar at a Glance is an alphabetical list of special terms and expressions with examples and references to further information. When you encounter a grammar or usage problem in the revising or proofreading stage of your writing, look for help in this section first. You may find all you need to know right here. If you need more information, **Grammar at a Glance** will show you where in the book to turn for a more complete explanation. If you do not find what you are looking for in **Grammar at a Glance,** turn to the index on page 942.

abbreviation An abbreviation is a shortened form of a word or a phrase.

■ **capitalization of**

TITLES USED WITH NAMES	**M**r.	**D**r.	**J**r.	**Ph.D.**
KINDS OF ORGANIZATIONS	**A**ssn.	**I**nc.	**D**ept.	**C**orp.
PARTS OF ADDRESSES	**A**ve.	**S**t.	**B**lvd.	**P.O. B**ox
NAMES OF STATES	[without ZIP Codes]		**K**y.	**T**ex.
			Tenn.	**N. D**ak.
	[with ZIP Codes]		**KY**	**TX**
			TN	**ND**
TIMES	**A.M.**	**P.M.**	**B.C.**	**A.D.**

■ **punctuation of** (See page 639.)

WITH PERIODS	(See preceding examples.)
WITHOUT PERIODS	VCR ESPN NAACP FCC
	DC [D.C. without ZIP Code]
	kg lb tsp km ft
	[Exception: inch = in.]

action verb An action verb expresses physical or mental activity. (See page 387.)

EXAMPLES   Kurt **ran** toward the ledge.

Owen correctly **guessed** the number of jelly beans in the jar.

active voice Active voice is the voice a verb is in when it expresses an action done by its subject. (See page 535. See also **voice.**)

EXAMPLE   Napoleon's armies **conquered** most of western Europe.

adjective An adjective modifies a noun or a pronoun. (See page 382.)

EXAMPLE   **The** peninsula has **high** mountains and **winding** roads.

adjective clause An adjective clause is a subordinate clause that modifies a noun or a pronoun. (See page 473.)

EXAMPLE   The man **who disappeared** was soon found again.

adjective phrase A prepositional phrase that modifies a noun or a pronoun is called an adjective phrase. (See page 443.)

EXAMPLE   We approached the highest peak **in the Alps.**

adverb An adverb modifies a verb, an adjective, or another adverb. (See page 393.)

EXAMPLE   Helen **rarely** loses her temper.

adverb clause An adverb clause is a subordinate clause that modifies a verb, an adjective, or an adverb. (See page 476.)

EXAMPLE   We will try to get indoors **before the storm arrives.**

adverb phrase A prepositional phrase that modifies a verb, an adjective, or an adverb is called an adverb phrase. (See page 445.)

EXAMPLE   Terry cleaned his room **in a few minutes.**

agreement Agreement is the correspondence, or match, between grammatical forms. Grammatical forms agree when they have the same number and gender.

■ **of pronouns and antecedents** (See page 507.)

SINGULAR   **Ethan** politely asked for an increase in **his** allowance.
PLURAL   Ethan's **brothers** politely asked for an increase in **their** allowances.

SINGULAR   **Everyone** in the play made **his or her** own costumes.
PLURAL   **All** of the performers made **their** own costumes.

SINGULAR   Is **Matthew or Terence** looking forward to reciting **his** poem in front of **his** classmates?
PLURAL   **Matthew and Terence** are looking forward to reciting **their** poems in front of **their** classmates.

■ **of subjects and verbs** (See page 493.)

SINGULAR	The art **teacher has painted** a mural on a wall of the cafeteria.
	The art **teacher,** with the help of her students, **has painted** a mural on a wall of the cafeteria.
PLURAL	The art **students have painted** a mural on a wall of the cafeteria.
PLURAL	The art **students,** with the help of their teacher, **have painted** a mural on the wall of the cafeteria.

SINGULAR	**Everyone** in this class **is learning** sign language.
PLURAL	**All** of the students **are learning** sign language.

SINGULAR	**Neither Diego nor I was** ready to compete in the battle of the bands.
PLURAL	**Salsa, reggae, and zydeco were** among the kinds of music played at the band competition.

SINGULAR	Here **is** your book **bag.**
PLURAL	Here **are** your **books.**

SINGULAR	**Ten dollars is** the cost of the ticket.
PLURAL	In this stack of bills, ten **dollars are** torn.

SINGULAR	**Two thirds** of the freshman class **has voted.**
PLURAL	**Two thirds** of the freshmen **have voted.**

SINGULAR	*Symphonies of Wind Instruments* **was composed** by Igor Stravinsky.
PLURAL	Stravinsky's other **symphonies were** also well **received.**

SINGULAR	**Is mathematics** your favorite school subject?
PLURAL	**Are** my **binoculars** in your locker?

ambiguous reference Ambiguous reference occurs when a pronoun incorrectly refers to either of two antecedents. (See page 565.)

AMBIGUOUS	Martina is supposed to meet Jada at the library after she practices her cello lesson.
CLEAR	After **Martina** practices **her** cello lesson, **she** is supposed to meet Jada at the library.
CLEAR	After **Jada** practices **her** cello lesson, **she** is supposed to meet Martina at the library.

antecedent An antecedent is the word or words that a pronoun stands for. (See page 378.)

EXAMPLE **Alfred** sent **Julie** and **Dave** the money **he** owed **them**.
[*Alfred* is the antecedent of *he*. *Julie* and *Dave* are the antecedents of *them*.]

apostrophe

- **to form contractions** (See page 707.)

  EXAMPLES couldn't let's o'clock '99

- **to form plurals of letters, numerals, symbols, and words used as words** (See page 709.)

  EXAMPLES *p*'s and *q*'s *A*'s and *I*'s

  10's and *20*'s *$*'s and *¢*'s

- **to show possession** (See page 699.)

  EXAMPLES gymnast's routine

  gymnasts' routines

  children's toys

  everyone's opinion

  Whitney Houston's and Denzel Washington's performances

  a year's [or twelve months'] leave of absence

appositive An appositive is a noun or a pronoun placed beside another noun or pronoun to identify or describe it. (See page 461.)

EXAMPLE My great-aunt **Rina** was born in Poland.

appositive phrase An appositive phrase consists of an appositive and its modifiers. (See page 461.)

EXAMPLE Kublai Khan, **the first emperor of the Yuan dynasty,** united China under his rule.

article The articles, *a*, *an*, and *the*, are the most frequently used adjectives. (See page 384.)

EXAMPLE On **an** overpass south of **the** city, **an** incident occurred that convinced John that he needed **a** new car.

bad, badly (See page 575.)

NONSTANDARD   Do you think these leftovers smell badly?
STANDARD   Do you think these leftovers smell **bad**?

base form The base form, or infinitive, is one of the four principal parts of a verb. (See page 517.)

EXAMPLE   This computer program has helped me [to] **learn** Spanish.

brackets (See page 726.)

EXAMPLE   The history book points out that "the name Hundred Years' War is a misnomer **[**a wrong name**]**, for the name refers to a series of wars that lasted 116 years **[**1337–1453**]**."

capitalization

■ **of abbreviations and acronyms** (See **abbreviations.**)

■ **of first words** (See page 618.)

EXAMPLES   **M**y sister writes in her journal every night.

               Omar asked, "**W**ould you like to play on my soccer team?"

               Dear Ms. Reuben:

               Sincerely yours,

■ **of proper nouns and proper adjectives** (See page 620.)

Proper Noun	Common Noun
James **L**ovell, **J**r.	astronaut
Alexander the **G**reat	leader
South **A**merica	continent
Appalachian **M**ountains	mountain chain
Minnesota **V**ikings	team
Democratic **P**arty (or **p**arty)	political party
French and **I**ndian **W**ar	historical event
Jurassic **P**eriod	historical period
Mother's **D**ay	holiday
General **M**otors **C**orporation	business

■ **of titles** (See page 629.)

EXAMPLES   **G**overnor Pataki [preceding a name]

Pataki, the **g**overnor of New York [following a name]

Thank you, **G**overnor. [direct address]

Aunt Ramona [*but* our **a**unt Ramona]

***D**ust **T**racks **o**n **a** **R**oad* [novel]

***T**he **L**ion **K**ing* [movie or play]

***N**ova* [TV program]

***M**ona **L**isa* [work of art]

"**T**he **S**tar-**S**pangled **B**anner" [song]

"**A**migo **B**rothers" [short story]

"**N**othing **G**old **C**an **S**tay" [poem]

case of pronouns Case is the form a pronoun takes to show how it is used in a sentence. (See page 549.)

NOMINATIVE   **He** and **I** are making vegetable quesadillas.

Two of the class officers are Eric and **she.**

Either player, Cheryl or **she,** can play shortstop.

We volunteers have worked very hard on the recycling campaign.

Is Ernesto Galarza the author **who** wrote *Barrio Boy*?

Do you know **who** they are?

I helped Ms. Wong as much as **he.** [meaning "as much as he helped Ms. Wong"]

OBJECTIVE   This jacket will not fit Yolanda or **her.**

Aunt Calista brought **him** and **me** souvenirs of her trip to the Philippines.

Were you three cheering for **us** or **them**?

The mayor thanked **us** volunteers for our contributions.

Maya Angelou, **whom** many readers admire, is certainly my favorite author.

One of the candidates for **whom** I will vote is Tamisha.

I helped Ms. Wong as much as **him.** [meaning "as much as I helped him"]

POSSESSIVE   **Your** interpretation of **her** poem was different from **mine.**

clause A clause is a group of words that contains a verb and its subject and is used as part of a sentence. (See page 470.)

INDEPENDENT CLAUSE   Theo installed the blinds

SUBORDINATE CLAUSE   while Dorothy worked on the wiring

colon (See page 675.)

■ **before lists**

EXAMPLES   The recipe calls for the following herbs: thyme, basil, cilantro, and oregano.

       The documentary profiled three women artists of the twentieth century: Audrey Flack, a painter; Louise Nevelson, a sculptor; and Margaret Bourke-White, a photographer.

■ **in conventional situations**

EXAMPLES   6:30 A.M.

       Ecclesiastes 11:7–10

       Computers and You: A Video Guide

       Dear Sir or Madam:

comma (See page 643.)

■ **in a series**

EXAMPLES   Tony, Julian, and Katie helped me make the fruit salad by cutting up the oranges, bananas, grapes, and papayas.

       We rode our bicycles to the park, bought snacks at the juice bar, found a picnic table, and then played chess for an hour.

       The silly cat had run through the living room, over the sofa, between my feet, through the door, across the hall, and up the stairs.

■ **in compound sentences**

EXAMPLES   I like all kinds of music, but jazz is my favorite.

       The students listened to each candidate's speech, and then they left the auditorium to cast their votes.

■ **with nonessential phrases and clauses**

EXAMPLES   Didn't Mount Etna, Europe's largest volcano, erupt a few years ago?

In the mid-1900s, the Inuit, whose ancestors had led nomadic lives of hunting and fishing, began settling in urban areas of the Arctic region.

David will be bringing fresh salsa, which his father makes from tomatoes and herbs that they grow in their garden.

■ **with introductory elements**

EXAMPLES In the first match of the tennis tournament, Pablo competed against the player who was ranked first in the state.

When the exciting game was over, many of the fans raced onto the field to praise and congratulate the winning player.

■ **with interrupters**

EXAMPLES The most memorable part of our vacation, however, was our visit to the Smithsonian Institution.

You might consider making a mobile, for example, or some other simple present.

The most demanding role, I believe, is that of King Lear in Shakespeare's tragedy of the same name.

■ **in conventional situations**

EXAMPLES On Monday, June 5, 2000, the Walkers flew from Detroit, Michigan, to San Juan, Puerto Rico, to attend their family reunion.

I mailed the package to 1620 Palmetto Drive, Tampa, FL 33637, on 15 September 2000.

comma splice A comma splice is a run-on sentence in which two sentences have been joined with only a comma between them. (See page 327. See also **fused sentence** and **run-on sentence**.)

COMMA SPLICE My sister Eileen has a paper route, I help her sometimes, especially when the weather is bad.

REVISED My sister Eileen has a paper route, **and** I help her sometimes, especially when the weather is bad.

REVISED My sister Eileen has a paper route; I help her sometimes, especially when the weather is bad.

REVISED My sister Eileen has a paper route. I help her sometimes, especially when the weather is bad.

comparison of modifiers (See page 577.)

■ **comparison of adjectives and adverbs**

Positive	Comparative	Superlative
strong	strong**er**	strong**est**
happy	happ**ier**	happ**iest**
ambitious	**more** ambitious	**most** ambitious
quietly	**less** quietly	**least** quietly
well/good	**better**	**best**

■ **comparing two**

EXAMPLES   Which is **longer,** the Nile River or the Amazon River?

Of the cheetah and the gazelle, which animal can run **more swiftly**?

Mount Everest is **higher** than **any other** mountain peak in the world.

■ **comparing more than two**

EXAMPLES   Of all of the lakes of the world, the Caspian Sea is the **largest.**

In the school's walkathon, one of the freshmen walked the **farthest.**

complement A complement is a word or word group that completes the meaning of a verb. (See page 427.)

EXAMPLES   I gave **Sally** that **picture.**

This is an old **sofa,** but it's very **comfortable.**

complex sentence A complex sentence has one independent clause and at least one subordinate clause. (See page 482.)

EXAMPLE   Beethoven, who had a hearing impairment most of his adult life, wrote his ninth symphony after he had become deaf.

compound-complex sentence A compound-complex sentence has two or more independent clauses and at least one subordinate clause. (See page 482.)

EXAMPLES   While Arianna was at the shopping mall, she checked both bookstores for Barbara Kingsolver's latest novel, but neither store had a copy in stock.

At the cookout on Saturday, we served yakitori; it is a Japanese dish of bite-sized pieces of meat and vegetables that are placed on skewers and grilled.

compound sentence A compound sentence has two or more independent clauses and no subordinate clauses. (See page 481.)

EXAMPLES   My family and I recently moved into a new house, and now I have a room of my own.

By area, New York City is the largest city in the world; however, by population, Tokyo-Yokohama is the world's largest urban area.

conjunction A conjunction joins words or groups of words. (See page 403.)

EXAMPLES   **Both** Robin **and** Michelle arrived early, **but** all the good seats were taken.

While you were sleeping, I worked out.

contraction A contraction is a shortened form of a word, a numeral, or a group of words. Apostrophes in contractions show where letters or numerals have been omitted. (See page 707. See also **apostrophe.**)

EXAMPLES   you're [you are]   there's [there is or there has]

who's [who is or who has]   they're [they are]

weren't [were not]   it's [it is or it has]

'91–'94 model [1991–1994 model]   o'clock [of the clock]

dangling modifier A dangling modifier is a modifying word, phrase, or clause that does not clearly and sensibly modify a word or a word group in a sentence. (See page 585.)

DANGLING   Riding the Ferris wheel, most of the park's other attractions could be seen.

REVISED   **Riding the Ferris wheel, we** could see most of the park's other attractions.

dash (See page 721.)

EXAMPLE   One of the substitute teachers—Ms. Narazaki, I believe—will accompany us on the field trip.

declarative sentence A declarative sentence makes a statement and is followed by a period. (See page 435.)

EXAMPLE   People still enjoy going to movies, despite the popularity of videos**.**

direct object A direct object is a word or word group that receives the action of the verb or shows the result of the action. A direct object answers the question *Whom?* or *What?* after a transitive verb. (See page 431.)

EXAMPLE   They gave the **oats** to the horse.

double comparison A double comparison is the nonstandard use of two comparative forms (usually *more* and *–er*) or two superlative forms (usually *most* and *–est*) to express comparison. In standard usage, the single comparative form is correct. (See page 582.)

NONSTANDARD	These small boxes are much more heavier than they appear.
STANDARD	These small boxes are much **heavier** than they appear.

double negative A double negative is the nonstandard use of two or more negative words to express a single negative idea. (See page 609.)

NONSTANDARD	The annual sports banquet doesn't cost the athletes nothing.
STANDARD	The annual sports banquet **doesn't** cost the athletes **anything.**
STANDARD	The annual sports banquet costs the athletes **nothing.**
NONSTANDARD	Yesterday, my throat was so sore that I couldn't hardly eat no solid food.
STANDARD	Yesterday, my throat was so sore that I could **hardly** eat **any** solid food.

double subject A double subject occurs when an unnecessary pronoun is used after the subject of a sentence. (See page 603.)

NONSTANDARD	Laura and her sister they have a large aquarium of tropical fish.
STANDARD	**Laura and her sister have** a large aquarium of tropical fish.

end marks (See page 637.)

- **with sentences**

EXAMPLES   Tiger Woods has won the golf tournament. [declarative sentence]

How long has Tiger Woods been playing professional golf? [interrogative sentence]

Oh! [interjection]

What a remarkable golfer Tiger Woods is! [exclamatory sentence]

Imagine how you would feel if you were playing in a tournament with Tiger Woods. [imperative sentence]

Don't talk while someone is hitting the ball! [strong imperative sentence]

- **with abbreviations** (See **abbreviations.**)

EXAMPLES   We are planning to go to Washington, D.C.

When are you going to Washington, D.C.?

essential clause/essential phrase An essential, or restrictive, clause or phrase is necessary to the meaning of a sentence and is not set off by commas. (See page 649.)

EXAMPLES   The man **whose sudden appearance caused the uproar** rose to identify himself. [essential clause]

Students **going on the field trip** should meet in the gym. [essential phrase]

exclamation point (See **end marks.**)

exclamatory sentence An exclamatory sentence expresses strong feeling and is followed by an exclamation point. (See page 436.)

EXAMPLE   That's absolutely incredible!

fragment (See **sentence fragment.**)

fused sentence A fused sentence is a run-on sentence in which sentences have been joined together with no punctuation between them. (See page 327. See also **comma splice** and **run-on sentence.**)

FUSED   According to my research, the Dome of the Rock was built in Jerusalem during the seventh century it is the oldest existing Muslim shrine.

REVISED   According to my research, the Dome of the Rock was built in Jerusalem during the seventh century**.** **It** is the oldest existing Muslim shrine.

REVISED   According to my research, the Dome of the Rock was built in Jerusalem during the seventh century**;** it is the oldest existing Muslim shrine.

general reference A general reference is the incorrect use of a pronoun to refer to a general idea rather than to a specific noun. (See page 565.)

GENERAL   The illusionist escaped from a locked trunk, made various fruits and vegetables dance in the air, and levitated. This thrilled her audience.

REVISED   The illusionist thrilled her audience by escaping from a locked trunk, making various fruits and vegetables dance in the air, and levitating.

REVISED   The illusionist escaped from a locked trunk, made various fruits and vegetables dance in the air, and levitated. These illusions thrilled her audience.

gerund A gerund is a verb form ending in *–ing* that is used as a noun. (See page 453.)

EXAMPLE   **Fishing** for blue crabs is especially popular in the Gulf Coast states.

gerund phrase A gerund phrase consists of a gerund and its modifiers and complements. (See page 455.)

EXAMPLE   **Photographing old stone bridges** is one of Tracy's hobbies.

good, well (See page 575.)

EXAMPLES   Benita is a **good** saxophone player.

Benita played extremely **well** [not *good*] at the tryouts for the school orchestra.

hyphen (See page 716.)

- **to divide words**

  EXAMPLE   In their flower garden, they planted zinnias, marigolds, and dahlias.

- **in compound numbers**

  EXAMPLE   They planted twenty-three varieties of those kinds of
  flowers.

- **with prefixes and suffixes**

  EXAMPLES   All of the flowers were in full bloom by mid-July.

  Our garden is pesticide-free.

imperative mood The imperative mood is used to express a direct
command or request. (See page 543.)

EXAMPLES   **Sit** down! [command]

Please **read** the minutes of our last meeting. [request]

imperative sentence An imperative sentence gives a command or
makes a request and is followed by either a period or an exclamation
point. (See page 435.)

EXAMPLES   Please return this to the display case. [request]

Clean this room now! [command]

incomplete construction An incomplete construction is a clause
or phrase from which words have been omitted. (See page 564.)

EXAMPLE   I like cheddar cheese more **than he [likes cheddar
cheese].**

indefinite reference An indefinite reference is the incorrect use of
the pronoun *you*, *it*, or *they* to refer to no particular person or thing.
(See page 565.)

INDEFINITE   In the first issue of the school newspaper, it shows a calendar
of the school's major events.

REVISED   The first issue of the school newspaper shows a calendar of
the school's major events.

REVISED   In the first issue of the school newspaper is a calendar of the
school's major events.

independent clause An independent clause (also called a *main clause*) expresses a complete thought and can stand by itself as a sentence. (See page 470.)

EXAMPLE **Shawna planted the sunflower seeds and tried to imagine** what the flowers would look like.

indicative mood The indicative mood is used to express a fact, an opinion, or a question. (See page 543.)

EXAMPLES Georgia O'Keeffe **is** famous for her abstract paintings. [fact]

Georgia O'Keeffe, in my opinion, **was** the most talented American artist of the twentieth century. [opinion]

Didn't O'Keeffe **paint** *Cow's Skull: Red, White, and Blue*? [question]

indirect object An indirect object is a noun, pronoun, or word group that often appears in sentences containing direct objects. An indirect object tells *to whom* or *to what* (or *for whom* or *for what*) the action of a transitive verb is done. Indirect objects generally precede direct objects. (See page 432.)

EXAMPLE Sandy gave **Grandma** the watch.

infinitive An infinitive is a verb form, usually preceded by *to,* used as a noun, an adjective, or an adverb. (See page 457.)

EXAMPLE Patty tried **to play** the trumpet but decided she preferred **to learn** the clarinet.

infinitive phrase An infinitive phrase consists of an infinitive and its modifiers and complements. (See page 458.)

EXAMPLE Ms. Snyder tried **to explain the meaning of the phrase,** but we still found it hard to understand.

interjection An interjection expresses emotion and has no grammatical relation to the rest of the sentence. (See page 405.)

EXAMPLE **Oh no!** I completely forgot!

interrogative sentence An interrogative sentence asks a question and is followed by a question mark. (See page 436.)

EXAMPLE Did you visit Las Cruces when you were in New Mexico**?**

intransitive verb An intransitive verb is a verb that does not take an object. (See page 386.)

EXAMPLE   The queen **waved** good-naturedly.

irregular verb An irregular verb is a verb that forms its past and past participle in some way other than by adding *–d* or *–ed* to the base form. (See page 519. See also **regular verb.**)

Base Form	Present Participle	Past	Past Participle
be	[is] being	was, were	[have] been
drive	[is] driving	drove	[have] driven
fall	[is] falling	fell	[have] fallen
go	[is] going	went	[have] gone
run	[is] running	ran	[have] run
sing	[is] singing	sang	[have] sung
speak	[is] speaking	spoke	[have] spoken
think	[is] thinking	thought	[have] thought
write	[is] writing	wrote	[have] written

italics (See page 683.)

■ **for titles**

EXAMPLES   *Their Eyes Were Watching God* [book]

U.S. News & World Report [periodical]

The Ascent of Ethiopia [work of art]

Mozart Portraits [long musical recording]

■ **for words, letters, and symbols used as such and for foreign words**

EXAMPLES   Notice that the word *Tennessee* has four *e*'s, two *n*'s, and two *s*'s.

A *jeu de mots* is a pun or a play on words.

its, it's (See page 751.)

EXAMPLES   **Its** [The coyote's] howling frightened the young campers.

It's [It is] six o'clock.

It's [It has] been raining all day.

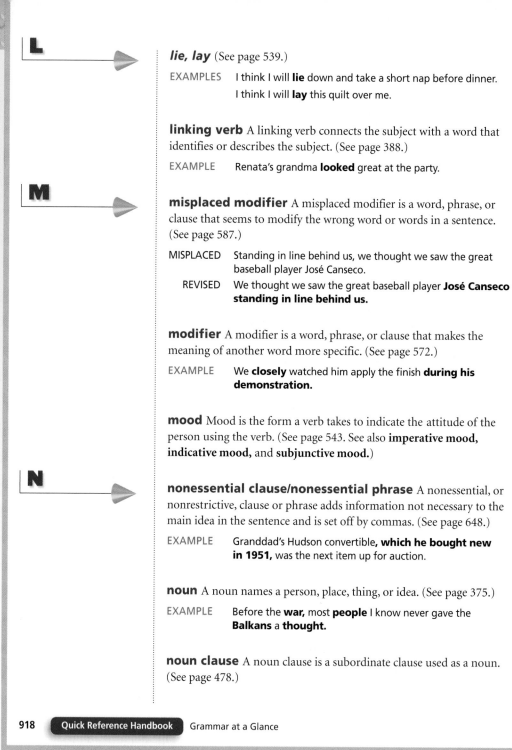

L

lie, lay (See page 539.)

EXAMPLES   I think I will **lie** down and take a short nap before dinner.

I think I will **lay** this quilt over me.

linking verb A linking verb connects the subject with a word that identifies or describes the subject. (See page 388.)

EXAMPLE   Renata's grandma **looked** great at the party.

M

misplaced modifier A misplaced modifier is a word, phrase, or clause that seems to modify the wrong word or words in a sentence. (See page 587.)

MISPLACED   Standing in line behind us, we thought we saw the great baseball player José Canseco.

REVISED   We thought we saw the great baseball player **José Canseco standing in line behind us.**

modifier A modifier is a word, phrase, or clause that makes the meaning of another word more specific. (See page 572.)

EXAMPLE   We **closely** watched him apply the finish **during his demonstration.**

mood Mood is the form a verb takes to indicate the attitude of the person using the verb. (See page 543. See also **imperative mood, indicative mood,** and **subjunctive mood.**)

N

nonessential clause/nonessential phrase A nonessential, or nonrestrictive, clause or phrase adds information not necessary to the main idea in the sentence and is set off by commas. (See page 648.)

EXAMPLE   Granddad's Hudson convertible, **which he bought new in 1951,** was the next item up for auction.

noun A noun names a person, place, thing, or idea. (See page 375.)

EXAMPLE   Before the **war,** most **people** I know never gave the **Balkans** a **thought.**

noun clause A noun clause is a subordinate clause used as a noun. (See page 478.)

EXAMPLE **What's really going to amaze you** is how much I paid for it!

number Number is the form a word takes to indicate whether the word is singular or plural. (See page 492.)

SINGULAR	bird	I	foot	woman
PLURAL	birds	we	feet	women

object of a preposition An object of a preposition is the noun or pronoun that ends a prepositional phrase. (See page 400.)

EXAMPLE   Faced with a huge **pile** of **papers** when she arrived, she took a deep breath and plunged in. [*With a huge pile* and *of papers* are prepositional phrases.]

parallel structure Parallel structure is the use of the same grammatical forms or structures to balance related ideas in a sentence. (See page 339.)

NONPARALLEL   My parents promised to buy a video camera and that they would let me take it on my school trip.

PARALLEL   My parents promised **to buy a video camera** and **to let me take it on my school trip.** [two infinitive phrases]

parentheses (See page 720.)

EXAMPLES   Ganymede **(**see the chart on page 322**)** is our solar system's largest satellite.

Ganymede is our solar system's largest satellite. **(**See the chart on page 322.**)**

participial phrase A participial phrase consists of a participle and its complements and modifiers. (See page 451.)

EXAMPLE   At the wildlife park, we were startled by the gibbons **swinging through the trees.**

participle A participle is a verb form that can be used as an adjective. (See page 449.)

EXAMPLE   The **exhausted** hikers headed for home.

Grammar at a Glance   **919**

passive voice The passive voice is the voice a verb is in when it expresses an action done to its subject. (See page 535. See also **voice.**)

EXAMPLE   The posters on the bulletin board outside the principal's office **were changed** once a week.

period (See **end marks.**)

phrase A phrase is a group of related words that does not contain both a verb and its subject and is used as a single part of speech. (See page 442.)

EXAMPLES   **A man of elegance and style,** Uncle Jesse lives **in Georgia.** [*A man of elegance and style* is an appositive phrase. *Of elegance and style* and *in Georgia* are prepositional phrases.]

Press this lever **to open the cage door.** [*To open the cage door* is an infinitive phrase.]

Smiling at her fans, the actress signed autographs. [*Smiling at her fans* is a participial phrase. *At her fans* is a prepositional phrase.]

Being on time for appointments is courteous. [*Being on time for appointments* is a gerund phrase. *On time* and *for appointments* are prepositional phrases.]

predicate The predicate is the part of a sentence that says something about the subject. (See page 414.)

EXAMPLE   They **had been living in California for twenty years.**

predicate adjective A predicate adjective is an adjective that is in the predicate and that modifies the subject of a sentence or a clause. (See page 429.)

EXAMPLE   Does the garage smell **strange**?

predicate nominative A predicate nominative is a word or word group that is in the predicate and that identifies the subject or refers to it. (See page 429.)

EXAMPLE   Federico Fellini was a famous **filmmaker.**

prefix A prefix is a word part that is added before a base word or root. (See page 735.)

EXAMPLES   un + known = **un**known   il + legible = **il**legible

                re + write = **re**write   pre + school = **pre**school

                self + confidence   trans + Siberian =
                    = **self**-confidence   **trans**-Siberian

                mid + August =   ex + president =
                  mid-August   **ex**-president

preposition A preposition shows the relationship of a noun or a pronoun to some other word in a sentence. (See page 400.)

EXAMPLE   He came **from** Mexico and settled **near** Houston to find jobs **for** his family.

prepositional phrase A prepositional phrase is a group of words that includes a preposition, the object of the preposition (a noun or a pronoun), and any modifiers of that object. (See page 442.)

EXAMPLE   Having breakfast **on the Bar X Ranch** was a real treat **for all of us.**

pronoun A pronoun is used in place of one or more nouns or pronouns. (See page 378.)

EXAMPLES   Colin thinks **he** might be moving upstate.

                Did **you** paint **your** room by **yourself?**

                Some of the puppies look like **their** mother.

question mark (See **end marks.**)

quotation marks (See page 686.)

■ **for direct quotations**

EXAMPLE   "Before the secretary of state returns to Washington, D.C.," said the reporter, "she will visit Dar es Salaam, Tanzania, and Nairobi, Kenya."

■ **with other marks of punctuation** (See also preceding example.)

EXAMPLES   "In which South American country is the Atacama Desert?" asked Geraldo.

Which poem by Edgar Allan Poe begins with the line **""**Once upon a midnight dreary, while I pondered weak and weary**""?**

Carlotta asked, **""**Did Langston Hughes write a poem titled **"**A Dream Deferred**"?""**

■ **for titles**

EXAMPLES   **""**The Rockpile**""** [short story]

""Muddy Kid Comes Home**""** [short poem]

""River Deep, Mountain High**""** [song]

regular verb A regular verb is a verb that forms its past and past participle by adding *–d* or *–ed* to the base form. (See page 518. See also **irregular verb.**)

Base Form	Present Participle	Past	Past Participle
ask	[is] asking	asked	[have] asked
drown	[is] drowning	drowned	[have] drowned
suppose	[is] supposing	supposed	[have] supposed
use	[is] using	used	[have] used

rise, raise (See page 541.)

EXAMPLES   The hot-air balloon is **rising.**

She is **raising** the windows to let in some fresh air.

run-on sentence A run-on sentence is two or more complete sentences run together as one. (See page 327. See also **comma splice** and **fused sentence.**)

RUN-ON   In 1903, Marie Curie and her husband, Pierre, won the Nobel Prize in physics in 1911 she alone won the Nobel Prize in chemistry.

REVISED   In 1903, Marie Curie and her husband, Pierre, won the Nobel Prize in physics**.** In 1911, she alone won the Nobel Prize in chemistry.

REVISED   In 1903, Marie Curie and her husband, Pierre, won the Nobel Prize in physics**;** in 1911, she alone won the Nobel Prize in chemistry.

semicolon (See page 668.)

- **in compound sentences with no conjunction**

  EXAMPLE   Salma decided to read Amy Tan's *The Joy Luck Club*; her English teacher recommended it.

- **in compound sentences with conjunctive adverbs**

  EXAMPLE   Elizabeth went to the library to check out Carson McCullers's *The Member of the Wedding*; **however,** another reader had already checked out the library's only copy.

- **between items in a series when the items contain commas**

  EXAMPLE   This summer I read three great books: *The House on Mango Street,* a collection of short stories by Sandra Cisneros; *Pacific Crossing,* a novel by Gary Soto; and *The Piano Lesson,* a play by August Wilson.

sentence A sentence is a group of words that contains a subject and a verb and expresses a complete thought. (See page 413.)

               S   **V**

EXAMPLE   The leaves scattered on the autumn wind.

sentence fragment A sentence fragment is a group of words that is punctuated as if it were a complete sentence but that does not contain both a subject and a verb or that does not express a complete thought. (See page 320.)

FRAGMENT   The spider monkey, found chiefly in Costa Rica and Nicaragua.

SENTENCE   The spider monkey, found chiefly in Costa Rica and Nicaragua, is an endangered species.

simple sentence A simple sentence has one independent clause and no subordinate clauses. (See page 481.)

EXAMPLES   Dr. Mae C. Jemison is an astronaut.

             Who first walked in space?

sit, set (See page 540.)

EXAMPLES   The music students **sat** quietly, enjoying a sonata by Frédéric Chopin. [past tense of *sit*]

             The music director **set** the sheet music on each student's desk. [past tense of *set*]

slow, slowly (See page 576.)

EXAMPLE   Proceeding **slowly** [not *slow*] through the food court, the mariachi band played festive music to entertain the diners.

stringy sentence A stringy sentence is a sentence that has too many independent clauses. Usually, the clauses are strung together with coordinating conjunctions like *and* or *but*. (See page 340.)

STRINGY   Yesterday afternoon, my friends and I were playing kickball in my backyard, and when Rahm kicked the ball to the fence, we spotted a wren, and it was hobbling on one leg, so I gently picked up the bird and carried it inside to my mother, and she tried hard to make a splint for the injured leg, but she was unsuccessful, so finally she and I decided to take the wren to our veterinarian.

REVISED   Yesterday afternoon, my friends and I were playing kickball in my backyard. When Rahm kicked the ball to the fence, we spotted a wren hobbling on one leg. I gently picked up the bird and carried it inside to my mother. Although she tried hard to make a splint for the injured leg, she was unsuccessful. Finally, she and I decided to take the wren to our veterinarian.

subject The subject tells whom or what a sentence is about. (See page 414.)

EXAMPLE   Isn't the **mayor** going to be there?

subject complement A subject complement is a word or word group that completes the meaning of a linking verb and identifies or modifies the subject. (See page 429.)

EXAMPLE   My grandfather, who is usually **cheerful,** is an **optimist.**

subjunctive mood The subjunctive mood is used to express a suggestion, a necessity, a condition contrary to fact, or a wish. (See page 543.)

EXAMPLES   It is essential that Luisa **attend** the meeting on Monday. [necessity]

If I **were** you, I would apply for the scholarship. [condition contrary to fact]

Ashley wishes she **were** able to go with you to the Juneteenth picnic. [wish]

subordinate clause A subordinate clause (also called a *dependent clause*) has a subject and a verb but does not express a complete thought and cannot stand alone as a sentence. (See page 471. See also **adjective clause, adverb clause,** and **noun clause.**)

EXAMPLE   **After they had dinner,** they sat on the porch and remembered old times.

suffix A suffix is a word part that is added after a base word or root. (See page 735.)

EXAMPLES   brave + ly = brave**ly**   kind + ness = kind**ness**

               happy + ness = happi**ness**   obey + ing = obey**ing**

               drop + ed = dropp**ed**   dream + er = dream**er**

tense of verbs The tense of verbs indicates the time of the action or the state of being expressed by a verb. (See page 528.)

Present Tense

I give	we give
you give	you give
he, she, it gives	they give

Past Tense

I gave	we gave
you gave	you gave
he, she, it gave	they gave

Future Tense

I will (shall) give	we will (shall) give
you will (shall) give	you will (shall) give
he, she, it will (shall) give	they will (shall) give

Present Perfect Tense

I have given	we have given
you have given	you have given
he, she, it has given	they have given

(continued)

(continued)

Past Perfect Tense

I had given	we had given
you had given	you had given
he, she, it had given	they had given

Future Perfect Tense

I will (shall) have given	we will (shall) have given
you will (shall) have given	you will (shall) have given
he, she, it will (shall) have given	they will (shall) have given

transitive verb A transitive verb is an action verb that takes an object. (See page 386.)

EXAMPLE   Ms. Southall **excused** me when I **explained** the situation.

underlining (See **Italics.**)

verb A verb expresses an action or a state of being. (See page 386.)

EXAMPLES   The waters of the Brahmaputra River **flow** from the Himalayan snows.

He **is** happy.

verbal A verbal is a verb form used as an adjective, a noun, or an adverb. (See page 449.)

EXAMPLES   **Chattering** and **screaming,** the monkeys disappeared into the treetops.

I especially enjoyed the **dancing.**

Is that hard **to see?**

verbal phrase A verbal phrase consists of a verbal and its modifiers and complements. (See page 449. See also **participial phrase, gerund phrase,** and **infinitive phrase.**)

EXAMPLES   **Pleased to see his master,** Alf the dachshund wagged his tail vigorously.

Studying together helps me.

He'd like **to give Ella a gift.**

verb phrase A verb phrase consists of a main verb and at least one helping verb. (See page 391.)

EXAMPLE Strange as it **may seem,** I **have** never **eaten** an avocado.

voice Voice is the form a transitive verb takes to indicate whether the subject of the verb performs or receives the action. (See pages 535.)

ACTIVE VOICE Steven Spielberg **directed** the movie.
PASSIVE VOICE The movie **was directed** by Steven Spielberg.

weak reference A weak reference is the incorrect use of a pronoun to refer to an antecedent that has not been expressed. (See page 565.)

WEAK I was surprised to learn that my aunt Frances, who is a programmer for a computer company, does not have one in her home.

REVISED I was surprised to learn that my aunt Frances, who is a programmer for a computer company, does not have a computer in her home.

well (See *good, well.*)

who, whom (See page 559.)

EXAMPLES Enrique, **who** had applied for a part-time job at the animal clinic, asked me to write a letter of recommendation.

Enrique, **whom** I had recommended for a part-time job at the animal clinic, learned today that he will start working this weekend.

wordiness Wordiness is the use of more words than necessary or the use of fancy words where simple ones will do. (See page 341.)

WORDY In spite of the fact that my friend Akira, who is my best friend, is moving to another state, we think that, in our opinion, we will continue to remain good friends due to the fact that we have so much in common.

REVISED Although Akira, my best friend, is moving to another state, we think we will remain good friends because we have so much in common.

Diagramming Appendix

Diagramming Sentences

A *sentence diagram* is a picture of how the parts of a sentence fit together and how the words in a sentence are related.

Reference Note

For more about **subjects** and **verbs,** see page 414.

─HELP─

Notice that a sentence diagram shows the capitalization but not the punctuation of a sentence.

Reference Note

For information about **understood subjects,** see page 423.

Subjects and Verbs

The sentence diagram begins with a horizontal line intersected by a short vertical line that divides the complete subject from the complete predicate.

EXAMPLE   Fish swim.

Fish	swim

Understood Subjects

EXAMPLE   Wait!

(you)	Wait

Nouns of Direct Address

EXAMPLE   Sit, **Fido.**

Reference Note

For information about **nouns of direct address,** see page 656.

Sentences Beginning with *There*

EXAMPLE   **There** is hope.

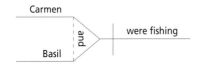

Reference Note

For information about **sentences beginning with *there*,** see page 422.

Compound Subjects

EXAMPLE   **Carmen** and **Basil** were fishing.

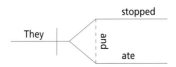

Compound Verbs

EXAMPLE   They **stopped** and **ate.**

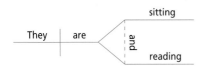

Reference Note

For more about **compound subjects,** see page 424. For more about **compound verbs,** see page 425.

The following diagram shows how a compound verb is diagrammed when the helping verb is not repeated.

EXAMPLE   They are **sitting** and **reading.**

DIAGRAMMING

Compound Subjects and Compound Verbs

EXAMPLE   **Coaches** and **players jumped** and **cheered.**

Sometimes the parts of a compound subject or a compound verb are joined by correlative conjunctions. Correlatives are diagrammed like this:

EXAMPLE   **Both** Bob **and** Teri can **not only** draw **but also** paint.

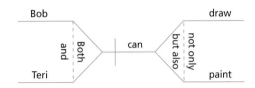

Adjectives and Adverbs

Reference Note

For more about **adjectives,** see page 382. For more about **adverbs,** see page 393.

Both adjectives and adverbs are written on slanted lines connected to the words they modify.

EXAMPLE   **That old** clock has **never** worked.

When an adverb modifies an adjective or an adverb, it is placed on a line connected to the word it modifies.

EXAMPLE   This **very** beautiful glass **almost** never breaks.

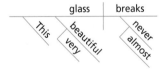

DIAGRAMMING

Notice the position of the modifiers in the following example:

EXAMPLE   **Soon** Anne and **her** sister will graduate and will move.

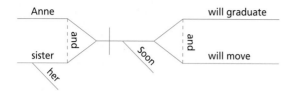

Above, *her* modifies only one part of the compound subject: *sister*. *Soon* modifies both parts of the compound verb: *will graduate* and *will move*.

When a conjunction joins two modifiers, it is diagrammed like this:

EXAMPLE   The **English** and **Australian** athletes worked **long** and **very hard.**

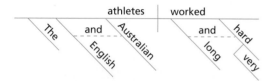

Subject Complements

The subject complement is placed on the horizontal line with the subject and verb. It comes after the verb. A slanted line separates the subject complement from the linking verb.

Predicate Nominatives

EXAMPLE   Cathedrals are large **churches.**

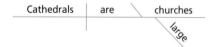

Reference Note

For more about **predicate nominatives,** see page 430.

Predicate Adjectives

Reference Note

For more about **predicate adjectives,** see page 430.

EXAMPLE   Cathedrals are **large.**

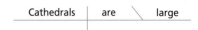

Compound Subject Complements

EXAMPLE   My friend is **small** and **quiet.**

Objects

Direct Objects

Reference Note

For more about **direct objects,** see page 431.

A vertical line separates a direct object from the verb.

EXAMPLE   We like **music.**

Compound Direct Objects

EXAMPLE   We like **plays** and **movies.**

Indirect Objects

Reference Note

For more about **indirect objects,** see page 432.

The indirect object is diagrammed on a horizontal line beneath the verb.

EXAMPLE   Pete bought **Mario** a sandwich.

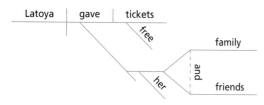

Compound Indirect Objects

EXAMPLE   Latoya gave her **family** and **friends** free tickets.

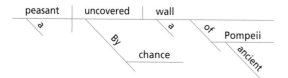

Phrases

Prepositional Phrases

The preposition is placed on a line slanting down from the word
the phrase modifies. The object of the preposition is placed on a
horizontal line connected to the slanting line.

Reference Note

For more information
about **prepositional
phrases,** see page 442.

EXAMPLES   **By chance,** a peasant uncovered a wall **of ancient
Pompeii.** [*By chance* is an adverb phrase modifying the
verb; *of ancient Pompeii* is an adjective phrase modifying the
direct object.]

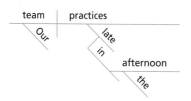

Our team practices late **in the afternoon.** [adverb phrase
modifying an adverb]

They drove **through the Maine woods** and **into southern Canada.** [two phrases modifying the same word]

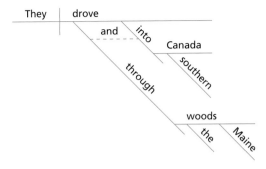

Mom taught the game **to my father, my uncles, and me.** [compound object of preposition]

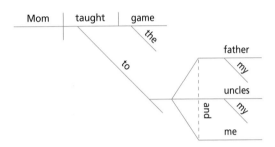

Follow the signs **to Highway 3 in Laconia.** [*In Laconia* is a prepositional phrase modifying the object of another preposition.]

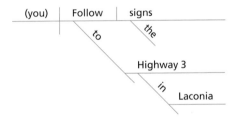

Participles and Participial Phrases

EXAMPLES   I found him **crying.**

Reference Note

For more information about **participles** and **participial phrases,** see page 449.

Wagging its tail, the large dog leaped at me.

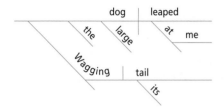

Notice that *tail*, the direct object of the participle *Wagging*, is diagrammed like any other complement.

Gerunds and Gerund Phrases

EXAMPLES   **Walking** is healthful exercise. [gerund used as subject]

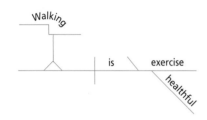

Reference Note

For more about **gerunds** and **gerund phrases,** see page 453.

The constant cold is a good reason for **taking a vacation in the winter.** [gerund phrase used as an object of preposition]

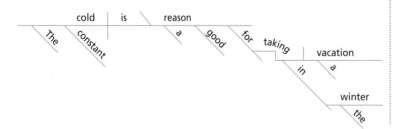

Reference Note

For more information about **infinitives** and **infinitive phrases,** see page 457.

Infinitives and Infinitive Phrases

EXAMPLES   **To leave** would be rude. [infinitive used as subject]

To join the Air Force is her longtime ambition. [infinitive phrase used as subject]

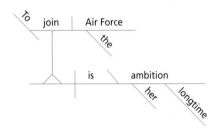

Infinitives and infinitive phrases used as modifiers are diagrammed much as prepositional phrases are.

EXAMPLES   I am happy **to help.**

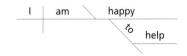

I am leaving early **to get the tickets.** [infinitive phrase used as adverb]

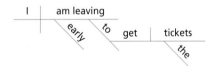

Appositives and Appositive Phrases

Place the appositive in parentheses after the word it identifies or explains.

EXAMPLES   My brother **Josh** is a drummer in the band.

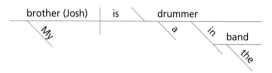

Reference Note

For more information about **appositives** and **appositive phrases,** see page 461.

The next show, **a musical comedy,** was written by Mike Williams, **a talented young playwright.**

Subordinate Clauses

Adjective Clauses

An adjective clause is joined to the word it modifies by a broken line leading from the relative pronoun to the modified word.

Reference Note

For more about **adjective clauses,** see page 473.

EXAMPLES   The restaurant **that we like best** serves excellent seafood.

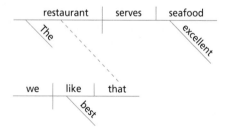

He is the teacher **from whom I take lessons.**

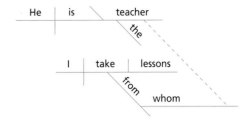

Reference Note

For more about **adverb clauses,** see page 476.

Adverb Clauses

Place the subordinating conjunction that introduces the adverb clause on a broken line leading from the verb in the adverb clause to the word the clause modifies.

EXAMPLE   **If you visit Texas,** you should see the Alamo.

Reference Note

For more about **noun clauses,** see page 478.

Noun Clauses

Noun clauses often begin with introductory words such as *that, what, who,* or *which.* These introductory words may have a function within the subordinate clause, or they may simply connect the clause to the rest of the sentence. How a noun clause is diagrammed depends upon its use in the sentence. It also depends on whether or not the introductory word has a grammatical function in the noun clause.

EXAMPLES   **What you eat** affects your health. [The noun clause is used as the subject of the independent clause. The introductory word *What* functions as the direct object of the noun clause.]

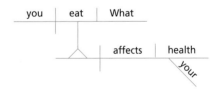

We strongly suspected **that the cat was the thief.** [The noun clause is the direct object of the independent clause. The introductory word *that* does not have a grammatical function within the noun clause.]

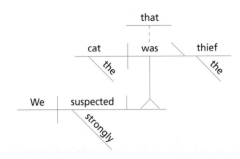

Sometimes the introductory word in a subordinate clause may be omitted. In the example above, the word *that* can be left out: *We strongly suspected the cat was the thief.* To diagram this new sentence, simply omit the word *that* and the solid and broken lines under it from the diagram above. The rest of the diagram stays the same.

Sentences Classified According to Structure

Simple Sentences

EXAMPLES   George Vancouver was exploring the Northwest.

Cities in Washington and British Columbia are named for him.

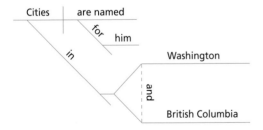

Reference Note

For more about **simple sentences,** see page 481.

Reference Note

For more information about **compound sentences,** see page 481.

Compound Sentences

EXAMPLE   James Baldwin wrote many essays, but he is probably more famous for his novels.

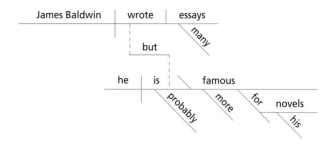

If the compound sentence has a semicolon and no conjunction, place a straight broken line between the two verbs.

EXAMPLE   Baldwin was a distinguished essayist; his nonfiction works include *Notes of a Native Son.*

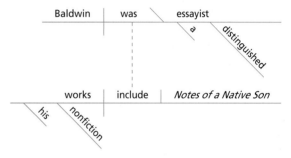

If the clauses of a compound sentence are joined by a semicolon and a conjunctive adverb, place the conjunctive adverb on a slanting line below the verb it modifies.

EXAMPLE   Baldwin was born in New York; however, he lived in France for nearly ten years.

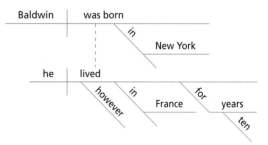

Complex Sentences

EXAMPLE   Jaime Escalante always believed that his students could do well in math.

Reference Note

For more about **complex sentences,** see page 482.

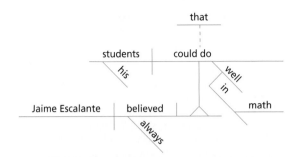

Compound-Complex Sentences

EXAMPLE   Before her plane mysteriously disappeared in 1937, Amelia Earhart had already forged the way for women in aviation, and she was later recognized for her achievements.

Reference Note

For more about **compound-complex sentences,** see page 482.

INDEX

Radio, as information source, 825
Ragged alignment, 807
Raise, rise, 541
Ratings, definition of, 879
"Ray of Hope" (Fretts), 285–86
Read, **principal parts of,** 521
Readability
    in document design, 812
Reader's Guide to Periodical Literature, **purpose of,**
    212, 825–26
Reading
    adjusting reading rate, 835–36
    drawing conclusions and, 163
    for enjoyment, 835
    with focus, 899
    identifying main idea and details, 21–23
    for mastery, 835
    predicting while reading, 56–58
    as process, xxxiv–xxxv, 836
    reading log, 835
Reading skills and focuses
    author's purpose and point of view, 248, 251–52
    cause-and-effect relationships, 124–31
    comparison/contrast article, 88–90
    comparison/contrast structure, 88, 93–95
    critical review, 284–91
    descriptive details, 18, 24–26
    emotional appeals, 248, 253–55
    evaluation criteria for criticism, 284, 289–91
    expressive style, 52, 58–59
    fact and opinions, 284, 287–89
    identifying explicit main idea and supporting
       details, 88, 91–93
    implied cause and effect, 124, 127–28
    implied main idea and supportive details, 18, 21–23
    investigative report, 196–204
    logical appeals, 248, 253–54
    making inferences, 158, 162–63
    opinion piece, 248–55
    organizational pattern of cause-and-effect
       relationships, 124, 129–31
    personal narrative, 52–59
    poetry analysis, 158–65
    predicting outcomes in personal narrative, 52,
       56–57
    primary and secondary sources, 196, 202–204
    summarizing written works, 196, 200–202
    text as support, 158, 164–65
Reality TV, definition of, 879
Real, really, **as modifiers,** 576
Reason, because, 605
Reasons, logical appeal support and, 248, 254
Rebound (Greene), 354

Reference sources. *See also* **Library/media center**
    list of, 212–13, 826
Refining. *See* **Revising**
Reflecting
    cause-and-effect explanation, 148
    comparison/contrast essay, 114
    critical review of sitcom, 312
    I-search paper, 236
    on decisions made in writing, 44
    personal narrative, 77
    persuasive paper, 275
    poetry analysis, 186
    subjective description and, 36
Reflexive pronouns, examples of, 380
"Regarding Fokker Niner-Niner-Easy" (Heat-Moon),
    197–99
Regular comparison of modifiers, 577–78
Regular verbs, definition of, 518, 922
Relative adverbs, 474
Relative pronouns, 380, 473–74
Relevant features, 102
Reporters, definition of, 886
Research. *See also* **I-search paper**
    forming research question, 208–209
    for historical novel, 237
    search journal, 210–11
Resolution, in short stories, 78
Restrictive clauses or phrases. *See* **Essential clauses or**
    phrases
Résumés, 900
Reverse angle shots, as camera shots, 877
Reviewing
    formal reviews, 283
    informal reviews, 283
    informed opinions, 283
    sitcom reviewing, 297–98
Review log, 297, 298
Revising
    cause-and-effect explanation, 143–46
    collaborating, 39
    comparison/contrast essay, 109–11
    conferring, 39
    critical review of sitcom, 306–10
    eliminating irrelevant details, 103
    I-search paper, 231–33
    personal narrative, 72–73
    persuasive paper, 270–72
    poetry analysis, 182–84
    self-evaluation, 39, 72, 109, 143, 182, 231, 270, 306
Rhyme in poetry, 171
Ride, **principal parts of,** 521
Right aligned text, 807
Ring, **principal parts of,** 521
Rise, raise, 541
Roethke, Theodore, 173

ACKNOWLEDGMENTS

For permission to reprint copyrighted material, grateful acknowledgment is made to the following sources:

Ronald Arias: From "El Mago" by Ronald Arias from *El Grito: A Journal of Contemporary Mexican-American Thought*, Spring 1970. Copyright © 1970 by Ronald Arias.

BOA Editions, Ltd., 260 East Avenue, Rochester, NY 14604: From "the thirty eighth year" from *good woman: poems and a memoir 1969–1980* by Lucille Clifton. Copyright © 1987 by Lucille Clifton.

The Boston Globe: From "2028 vision" from *The Boston Globe*, Editorial Page, March 14, 1998, p. A12. Copyright © 1998 by The Boston Globe.

Gwendolyn Brooks: "Maud Martha spares the mouse" from *Maud Martha* by Gwendolyn Brooks. Copyright © 1953, 1993 by Gwendolyn Brooks. Published by First Third World Press, Chicago.

The Estate of Gwendolyn Brooks: From "The Chicago Defender Sends a Man to Little Rock" from *Blacks* by Gwendolyn Brooks. Copyright © 1991 by Gwendolyn Brooks. Published by Third World Press, Chicago.

Daniel Cohen and Henry Morrison, Inc.: From "Jackalope" from *Encyclopedia of Monsters* by Daniel Cohen. Copyright © 1982 by Daniel Cohen.

Estate of Roald Dahl and David Higham Associates: From "Poison" from *Someone Like You* by Roald Dahl. Copyright 1950 by Roald Dahl. Published by Michael Joseph.

Doubleday, a division of Random House, Inc.: From "The Birds" from *Kiss Me Again, Stranger* by Daphne du Maurier. Copyright 1952 by Daphne du Maurier. From "Highway: Michigan" from *The Collected Poems of Theodore Roethke*. Copyright 1940 by Theodore Roethke. From "March 1st" from *Flying Inland* by Kathleen Spivack. Copyright © 1965, 1966, 1967, 1968, 1970, 1971, 1973 by Kathleen Spivack.

Entertainment Weekly: From "Ray of Hope" by Bruce Fretts from *Entertainment Weekly*, April 11, 1997. Copyright © 1997 by Entertainment Weekly.

Florida Classics Library: From *The Everglades: River of Grass* by Marjory Stoneman Douglas. Copyright 1947 by Marjory Stoneman Douglas.

Grove/Atlantic, Inc.: From "Golf" from *The Best of Plimpton* by George Plimpton. Copyright © 1990 by George Plimpton.

HarperCollins Publishers Inc.: From *Imponderables: The Solution to the Mysteries of Everyday Life* by David Feldman. Copyright © 1986 by David Feldman. From *Word Origins and Their Romantic Stories* by Wilfred Funk, Litt.D. Copyright © 1950 by Wilfred Funk, Inc.

Harvard University Press and the Trustees of Amherst College: From "There is no frigate like a book" from *The Poems of Emily Dickinson,* edited by Thomas H. Johnson. Copyright © 1951, 1955, 1979, 1983 by the President and Fellows of Harvard College Press. Published by The Belknap Press of Harvard University Press, Cambridge, MA.

Henry Holt and Company, Inc.: From "Stopping by Woods on a Snowy Evening" from *The Poetry of Robert Frost,* edited by Edward Connery Lathem. Copyright 1951 by Robert Frost; copyright 1923, © 1969 by Henry Holt and Co., Inc. From "Family" (retitled "Paper Airplanes") from *Polite Lies, On Being a Woman Caught Between Cultures* by Kyoko Mori. Copyright © 1997 by Kyoko Mori.

Houghton Mifflin Company: From "Regarding Fokker Niner-Niner-Easy" from *PrairyErth: A Deep Map* by William Least Heat-Moon. Copyright © 1991 by William Least Heat-Moon. All rights reserved.

International Creative Management, Inc.: From "The Portable Phonograph" from *The Watchful Gods and Other Stories* by Walter Van Tilburg Clark. Copyright 1941, © 1969 by Walter Van Tilburg Clark.

Alfred A. Knopf, Inc.: "Dream Deferred" from *Collected Poems* by Langston Hughes. Copyright © 1994 by the Estate of Langston Hughes. From *Martina* by Martina Navratilova with George Vecsey. Copyright © 1985 by Martina Enterprises, Inc

Los Angeles Times Syndicate: From "Time Out! Is Baseball Finnished?" by Bob Secter from *The Miami Herald,* August 3, 1990. Copyright © 1990 by Los Angeles Times Syndicate.

New Directions Publishing Corporation: "Heat, part II of Garden" from *Collected Poems 1912–1944* by H.D. Copyright © 1982 by The Estate of Hilda Doolittle.

NewLine Productions, Inc.: From *Hoop Dreams: A True Story of Hardship and Triumph* by Ben Joravsky. Copyright © 1994 by Fine Line Features. All rights reserved.

The New York Times Company: From "Topics: The Sounds of Manhattan" (retitled "The Sounds of the City") by James Tuite from *The New York Times,* August 6, 1966. Copyright © 1966 by The New York Times Company. From "Bananas for Rent" by Michiko Kakutani from *New York Times Magazine,* November 9, 1997. Copyright © 1997 by The New York Times Company.

Random House, Inc.: From *Extinction: The Causes and Consequences of the Disappearance of Species* by Paul and Anne Ehrlich. Copyright © 1981 by Paul R. Ehrlich and Anne H. Ehrlich.

John Seabrook: From "Born Slippy" by John Seabrook from *The New Yorker,* January 12, 1998. Copyright © 1998 by John Seabrook.

Kathy Svitil: "Hot times in the operating room" by Kathy Svitil from *Discover,* vol. 17, no. 11, November 1996. Copyright © 1996 by Kathy A. Svitil.

University of Connecticut as Executor of the Estate of Edwin Way Teale: From "The Death of a Tree" from *Dune Boy* by Edwin Way Teale. Copyright 1943, © 1971 by Edwin Way Teale.

Viking Penguin, a division of Penguin Putnam Inc.: From *Rebound: The Odyssey of Michael Jordan* by Bob Greene. Copyright © 1995 by John Deadline Enterprises, Inc.

The Washington Post Writers Group: From "Dirty play is wrong, but, hey, let 'em play" by William Raspberry from *The Washington Post,* June 22, 1998, p. A21. Copyright © 1998 by The Washington Post Writers Group.

Nancy Willard: From "Ding-Dong Bell: 'Ariel's Song' from *The Tempest* by William Shakespeare" by Nancy Willard from *Touchstones: American Poets on a Favorite Poem,* edited by Robert Pack and Jay Parini. Copyright © 1996 by Nancy Willard.

The H. W. Wilson Company: Entries from "Crown Books Corporation" to "Crude Oil" from *Readers' Guide to Periodical Literature,* February 1999. Copyright © 1999 by the H. W. Wilson Company.

SOURCES CITED:

From "Peak Flow Meters" and from "85% of Americans Don't Know the Air in Their Homes May Be Hazardous to Their Health" from *The American Lung Association* Web site, accessed March 24, 1999, at http://www/lungusa.org.

From entry "Emoticon" from *New Words in English* by Suzanne Kemmer. Published on *Rice University* Web site, at http://www.owlnet.rice.edu/ling215/NewWords/index.html, 1999.

From "The Granddaddy of the Nation's Trails Began in Mexico" by Douglas Preston from *Smithsonian,* vol. 26, no. 8, November 1995. Published by Smithsonian Institution, Washington, D.C., 1995.

From "What is a mummy?" from *Mummies, Myth and Magic in Ancient Egypt* by Christine El Mahdy. Published by Thames & Hudson Ltd., 1989.

CHAPTER 21: Page 627, Random House, Inc.

CHAPTER 22: Page 651, Gutzon Borglum/Getty Images/FPG; 654, The Newark Museum/Art Resource, NY; 658, Image Copyright ©2001 Photodisc, Inc.

CHAPTER 23: Page 669 (cr), CORBIS/Philip Gould; 669 (br), Library of Congress/HRW; 671, Image Copyright ©2001 Photodisc, Inc.; 673, Doug Perrine/Innerspace Visions Photography; 675, Texas Department of Transportaion.

CHAPTER 24: Page 689, Christie's Images, London, UK/Bridgeman Art Library, London/New York; 694, Image Copyright ©2001 Photodisc, Inc.

CHAPTER 25: Page 702, The Stock Market; 704, 705, Shaker Village of Pleasant Hill, KY; 709, Joe Viesti/Viesti Associates, Inc.

CHAPTER 26: Page 723, One Mile Up, Inc.; 724, HRW Photo Library/courtesy Gibbs Memorial Library, Mexia, Texas.

CHAPTER 27: Page 735, Pat Street; 739, Gutzon Borglum/Getty Images/FPG; 749, Image Copyright ©2001 Photodisc, Inc.

CHAPTER 28: Page 769, 773, Image Copyright ©2001 Photodisc, Inc.; 774, ©1997 Radlund & Associates for Artville; 776, Image Copyright ©2001 Photodisc, Inc.; 777, Mary Miller/HRW Photo; 789, 792, Image Copyright ©2001 Photodisc, Inc.

QUICK REFERENCE HANDBOOK: 817 (tl), CORBIS.

ILLUSTRATION CREDITS

TABLE OF CONTENTS: Page T11 (cl), Franklin Hammond; T12 (tl), HRW.

CHAPTER 1: Page 47 (b), HRW.

CHAPTER 2: Page 57 (br), Leslie Kell.

CHAPTER 4: Page 122 (all), Franklin Hammond.

CHAPTER 5: Page 156 (all), HRW; 162 (b), Leslie Kell.

CHAPTER 6: Page 215 (all), 216 (c), 217 (all), Leslie Kell; 236 (c), HRW.

CHAPTER 11: Page 360 (cl), Ortelius Design.

CHAPTER 12: Page 408 (c), Leslie Kell; 408 (c), Dory Grace.

CHAPTER 13: Page 435 (tr), Joann Daley.

CHAPTER 14: Page 452 (cl), Uhl Studios, Inc.

CHAPTER 15: Page 475 (tr), Keith Bowden.

CHAPTER 22: Page 662 (b), Ortelius Design.

CHAPTER 25: Page 710 (bl), Uhl Studios, Inc.

CHAPTER 27: Page 733 (c), Leslie Kell; 745 (t), Steve Shock.

QRH: Page 832 (cl), David Griffin; 833 (b), HRW; 835 (bl), Keith Bowden; 837 (bl), MapQuest.com, Inc.; 844 (cr), Leslie Kell; 855 (tl), George Kelvin; 914 (cl), HRW.

Grade 9 ATE, Acknowledgments

For permission to reprint copyrighted material, grateful acknowledgment is made to the following sources:

The Boston Globe: From "2028 Vision" from *The Boston Globe,* Editorial Page, March 14, 1998, p. A12. Copyright © 1998 by The Boston Globe.

Liveright Publishing Corporation: From "in Just-" from *Complete Poems, 1904-1962* by E. E. Cummings, edited by George J. Firmage. Copyright © 1923, 1925, 1926, 1931, 1935, 1938, 1939, 1940, 1944, 1945, 1946, 1947, 1948, 1949, 1950, 1951, 1952, 1953, 1954, 1955, 1956, 1957, 1958, 1959, 1960, 1961, 1962 by E. E. Cummings; copyright © 1961, 1963, 1966, 1967, 1968 by Marion Morehouse Cummings; copyright © 1963, 1972, 1973, 1974, 1975, 1976, 1977, 1978, 1979, 1980, 1981, 1982, 1983, 1984, 1985, 1986, 1987, 1988, 1989, 1990, 1991 by the Trustees for the E. E. Cummings Trust.

Los Angeles Times Syndicate: From "Time Out! Is Baseball Finnished?" by Bob Sector from *The Miami Herald,* August 3, 1990. Copyright © 1990 by Los Angeles Times Syndicate.

SOURCES CITED:

From *The Letters of Gustave Flaubert: 1830-1857,* selected, edited and translated by Francis Steegmuller. Published by The Belknap Press of Harvard University Press, Cambridge, MA, 1979.

Quote by D. A. Pennebaker from "Visionaries With Their Eyes on the Truth" from *The New York Times,* May 2, 1999.

Grade 9 Reading Selection Amendments

CHAPTER 1, PAGES 19–20
Excerpted, with internal deletions, as example of a descriptive passage. Changed title of piece, added and changed subheads

CHAPTER 2, PAGES 53–55
Excerpted to focus on short personal reflection

CHAPTER 2, PAGES 79–80
Excerpted to focus on short story techniques

CHAPTER 3, PAGES 89–90
Excerpted, with internal deletions made for space, as an example of a comparison-contrast essay. One paragraph has been split into two. Minor edits for style

CHAPTER 5, PAGES 159–161
Excerpted, with some internal deletions, as an example of a short story analysis

CHAPTER 5, PAGE 165
Excerpted as part of instruction demonstrating the difference between direct quotation and paraphrasing

CHAPTER 5, PAGE 166
Excerpted as part of an example of connotation and denotation. The word *crown* is italicized for emphasis

CHAPTER 5, PAGE 173
Excerpted as parts of a practice set on sound elements in poetry

CHAPTER 5, PAGE 185
Excerpted as examples demonstrating the correct punctuation of quotations

CHAPTER 5, PAGE 185
Excerpted as parts of a practice set on the correct punctuation of quotations

CHAPTER 6, PAGES 197–199
Excerpted, with some internal deletions, as an example of a research article

CHAPTER 8, PAGES 285–286
Excerpted, with some word and mechanics changes and internal deletions, as an example of a critical review

CHAPTER 9, PAGE 321
Excerpted as an example of how an experienced writer may use sentence fragments for creative effect

CHAPTER 11, PAGES 347–348
Excerpted as an example of paragraph main idea

CHAPTER 11, PAGE 349
Excerpted as an example of a paragraph with a topic sentence

CHAPTER 11, PAGE 350
Excerpted as part of an exercise on identifying main idea and topic sentence

CHAPTER 11, PAGE 350
Excerpted as part of an exercise on identifying main idea and topic sentence

CHAPTER 11, PAGE 351
Excerpted as an example of a paragraph using sensory details

Grade 9
Reading Selection Amendments
continued

CHAPTER 11, PAGE 352
Excerpted as an example of a paragraph using facts and statistics to support a main idea
CHAPTER 11, PAGES 352–353
Excerpted as an example of a paragraph using examples to support a main idea
CHAPTER 11, PAGE 353
Excerpted as part of an exercise on supporting details
CHAPTER 11, PAGE 354
Excerpted as an example of a paragraph clincher sentence
CHAPTER 11, PAGES 355–356
Excerpted as an example of paragraph unity
CHAPTER 11, PAGE 356
Excerpted as an example of paragraph unity
CHAPTER 11, PAGE 357
Excerpted as an example of paragraph unity
CHAPTER 11, PAGES 359–360
Excerpted as an example of coherence and chronological order

CHAPTER 11, PAGE 360
Excerpted as an example of coherence and spatial order
CHAPTER 11, PAGE 362
Excerpted as an example of coherence and logical order
CHAPTER 11, PAGE 364
Excerpted as an example of coherence and direct references
CHAPTER 11, PAGES 365–366
Excerpted as an example of coherence and transitional words and phrases
CHAPTER 11, PAGE 370
Excerpted as part of an exercise on dividing a passage into paragraphs
CHAPTER 21, PAGE 618
Excerpted to focus on the concept of capitalization presented in this chapter
CHAPTER 24, PAGE 689
Excerpted to focus on the concept of quotation marks presented in this chapter
CHAPTER 26, PAGES 725–726
Excerpted to focus on the concept of ellipsis points presented in this chapter